Introduction to Algorithms

Third Edition

Thomas H. Cormen
Charles E. Leiserson
Ronald L. Rivest
Clifford Stein

Introduction to Algorithms
Third Edition

The MIT Press
Cambridge, Massachusetts   London, England

© 2009 Massachusetts Institute of Technology

All rights reserved. No part of this book may be reproduced in any form or by any electronic or mechanical means (including photocopying, recording, or information storage and retrieval) without permission in writing from the publisher.

For information about special quantity discounts, please email special_sales@mitpress.mit.edu.

This book was set in Times Roman and Mathtime Pro 2 by the authors.

Printed and bound in the United States of America.

Library of Congress Cataloging-in-Publication Data

Introduction to algorithms / Thomas H. Cormen . . . [et al.].—3rd ed.
   p. cm.
  Includes bibliographical references and index.
  ISBN 978-0-262-03384-8 (hardcover : alk. paper)—ISBN 978-0-262-53305-8 (pbk. : alk. paper)
  1. Computer programming.   2. Computer algorithms.   I. Cormen, Thomas H.

QA76.6.I5858 2009
005.1—dc22
                                                    2009008593

HARDCOVER: 10 9 8 7 6 5
PAPERBACK: 10 9 8 7 6 5 4

Contents

IV *Advanced Design and Analysis Techniques*

VII   *Selected Topics*

VIII *Appendix: Mathematical Background*

Preface

Before there were computers, there were algorithms. But now that there are computers, there are even more algorithms, and algorithms lie at the heart of computing.

This book provides a comprehensive introduction to the modern study of computer algorithms. It presents many algorithms and covers them in considerable depth, yet makes their design and analysis accessible to all levels of readers. We have tried to keep explanations elementary without sacrificing depth of coverage or mathematical rigor.

Each chapter presents an algorithm, a design technique, an application area, or a related topic. Algorithms are described in English and in a pseudocode designed to be readable by anyone who has done a little programming. The book contains 244 figures—many with multiple parts—illustrating how the algorithms work. Since we emphasize *efficiency* as a design criterion, we include careful analyses of the running times of all our algorithms.

The text is intended primarily for use in undergraduate or graduate courses in algorithms or data structures. Because it discusses engineering issues in algorithm design, as well as mathematical aspects, it is equally well suited for self-study by technical professionals.

In this, the third edition, we have once again updated the entire book. The changes cover a broad spectrum, including new chapters, revised pseudocode, and a more active writing style.

To the teacher

We have designed this book to be both versatile and complete. You should find it useful for a variety of courses, from an undergraduate course in data structures up through a graduate course in algorithms. Because we have provided considerably more material than can fit in a typical one-term course, you can consider this book to be a "buffet" or "smorgasbord" from which you can pick and choose the material that best supports the course you wish to teach.

You should find it easy to organize your course around just the chapters you need. We have made chapters relatively self-contained, so that you need not worry about an unexpected and unnecessary dependence of one chapter on another. Each chapter presents the easier material first and the more difficult material later, with section boundaries marking natural stopping points. In an undergraduate course, you might use only the earlier sections from a chapter; in a graduate course, you might cover the entire chapter.

We have included 957 exercises and 158 problems. Each section ends with exercises, and each chapter ends with problems. The exercises are generally short questions that test basic mastery of the material. Some are simple self-check thought exercises, whereas others are more substantial and are suitable as assigned homework. The problems are more elaborate case studies that often introduce new material; they often consist of several questions that lead the student through the steps required to arrive at a solution.

Departing from our practice in previous editions of this book, we have made publicly available solutions to some, but by no means all, of the problems and exercises. Our Web site, http://mitpress.mit.edu/algorithms/, links to these solutions. You will want to check this site to make sure that it does not contain the solution to an exercise or problem that you plan to assign. We expect the set of solutions that we post to grow slowly over time, so you will need to check it each time you teach the course.

We have starred ($\star$) the sections and exercises that are more suitable for graduate students than for undergraduates. A starred section is not necessarily more difficult than an unstarred one, but it may require an understanding of more advanced mathematics. Likewise, starred exercises may require an advanced background or more than average creativity.

To the student

We hope that this textbook provides you with an enjoyable introduction to the field of algorithms. We have attempted to make every algorithm accessible and interesting. To help you when you encounter unfamiliar or difficult algorithms, we describe each one in a step-by-step manner. We also provide careful explanations of the mathematics needed to understand the analysis of the algorithms. If you already have some familiarity with a topic, you will find the chapters organized so that you can skim introductory sections and proceed quickly to the more advanced material.

This is a large book, and your class will probably cover only a portion of its material. We have tried, however, to make this a book that will be useful to you now as a course textbook and also later in your career as a mathematical desk reference or an engineering handbook.

What are the prerequisites for reading this book?

- You should have some programming experience. In particular, you should understand recursive procedures and simple data structures such as arrays and linked lists.

- You should have some facility with mathematical proofs, and especially proofs by mathematical induction. A few portions of the book rely on some knowledge of elementary calculus. Beyond that, Parts I and VIII of this book teach you all the mathematical techniques you will need.

We have heard, loud and clear, the call to supply solutions to problems and exercises. Our Web site, http://mitpress.mit.edu/algorithms/, links to solutions for a few of the problems and exercises. Feel free to check your solutions against ours. We ask, however, that you do not send your solutions to us.

To the professional

The wide range of topics in this book makes it an excellent handbook on algorithms. Because each chapter is relatively self-contained, you can focus on the topics that most interest you.

Most of the algorithms we discuss have great practical utility. We therefore address implementation concerns and other engineering issues. We often provide practical alternatives to the few algorithms that are primarily of theoretical interest.

If you wish to implement any of the algorithms, you should find the translation of our pseudocode into your favorite programming language to be a fairly straightforward task. We have designed the pseudocode to present each algorithm clearly and succinctly. Consequently, we do not address error-handling and other software-engineering issues that require specific assumptions about your programming environment. We attempt to present each algorithm simply and directly without allowing the idiosyncrasies of a particular programming language to obscure its essence.

We understand that if you are using this book outside of a course, then you might be unable to check your solutions to problems and exercises against solutions provided by an instructor. Our Web site, http://mitpress.mit.edu/algorithms/, links to solutions for some of the problems and exercises so that you can check your work. Please do not send your solutions to us.

To our colleagues

We have supplied an extensive bibliography and pointers to the current literature. Each chapter ends with a set of chapter notes that give historical details and references. The chapter notes do not provide a complete reference to the whole field of algorithms, however. Though it may be hard to believe for a book of this size, space constraints prevented us from including many interesting algorithms.

Despite myriad requests from students for solutions to problems and exercises, we have chosen as a matter of policy not to supply references for problems and exercises, to remove the temptation for students to look up a solution rather than to find it themselves.

Changes for the third edition

What has changed between the second and third editions of this book? The magnitude of the changes is on a par with the changes between the first and second editions. As we said about the second-edition changes, depending on how you look at it, the book changed either not much or quite a bit.

A quick look at the table of contents shows that most of the second-edition chapters and sections appear in the third edition. We removed two chapters and one section, but we have added three new chapters and two new sections apart from these new chapters.

We kept the hybrid organization from the first two editions. Rather than organizing chapters by only problem domains or according only to techniques, this book has elements of both. It contains technique-based chapters on divide-and-conquer, dynamic programming, greedy algorithms, amortized analysis, NP-Completeness, and approximation algorithms. But it also has entire parts on sorting, on data structures for dynamic sets, and on algorithms for graph problems. We find that although you need to know how to apply techniques for designing and analyzing algorithms, problems seldom announce to you which techniques are most amenable to solving them.

Here is a summary of the most significant changes for the third edition:

- We added new chapters on van Emde Boas trees and multithreaded algorithms, and we have broken out material on matrix basics into its own appendix chapter.

- We revised the chapter on recurrences to more broadly cover the divide-and-conquer technique, and its first two sections apply divide-and-conquer to solve two problems. The second section of this chapter presents Strassen's algorithm for matrix multiplication, which we have moved from the chapter on matrix operations.

- We removed two chapters that were rarely taught: binomial heaps and sorting networks. One key idea in the sorting networks chapter, the 0-1 principle, appears in this edition within Problem 8-7 as the 0-1 sorting lemma for compare-exchange algorithms. The treatment of Fibonacci heaps no longer relies on binomial heaps as a precursor.

- We revised our treatment of dynamic programming and greedy algorithms. Dynamic programming now leads off with a more interesting problem, rod cutting, than the assembly-line scheduling problem from the second edition. Furthermore, we emphasize memoization a bit more than we did in the second edition, and we introduce the notion of the subproblem graph as a way to understand the running time of a dynamic-programming algorithm. In our opening example of greedy algorithms, the activity-selection problem, we get to the greedy algorithm more directly than we did in the second edition.

- The way we delete a node from binary search trees (which includes red-black trees) now guarantees that the node requested for deletion is the node that is actually deleted. In the first two editions, in certain cases, some other node would be deleted, with its contents moving into the node passed to the deletion procedure. With our new way to delete nodes, if other components of a program maintain pointers to nodes in the tree, they will not mistakenly end up with stale pointers to nodes that have been deleted.

- The material on flow networks now bases flows entirely on edges. This approach is more intuitive than the net flow used in the first two editions.

- With the material on matrix basics and Strassen's algorithm moved to other chapters, the chapter on matrix operations is smaller than in the second edition.

- We have modified our treatment of the Knuth-Morris-Pratt string-matching algorithm.

- We corrected several errors. Most of these errors were posted on our Web site of second-edition errata, but a few were not.

- Based on many requests, we changed the syntax (as it were) of our pseudocode. We now use "$=$" to indicate assignment and "$==$" to test for equality, just as C, C++, Java, and Python do. Likewise, we have eliminated the keywords **do** and **then** and adopted "$//$" as our comment-to-end-of-line symbol. We also now use dot-notation to indicate object attributes. Our pseudocode remains procedural, rather than object-oriented. In other words, rather than running methods on objects, we simply call procedures, passing objects as parameters.

- We added 100 new exercises and 28 new problems. We also updated many bibliography entries and added several new ones.

- Finally, we went through the entire book and rewrote sentences, paragraphs, and sections to make the writing clearer and more active.

Web site

You can use our Web site, http://mitpress.mit.edu/algorithms/, to obtain supplementary information and to communicate with us. The Web site links to a list of known errors, solutions to selected exercises and problems, and (of course) a list explaining the corny professor jokes, as well as other content that we might add. The Web site also tells you how to report errors or make suggestions.

How we produced this book

Like the second edition, the third edition was produced in LaTeX 2_ε. We used the Times font with mathematics typeset using the MathTime Pro 2 fonts. We thank Michael Spivak from Publish or Perish, Inc., Lance Carnes from Personal TeX, Inc., and Tim Tregubov from Dartmouth College for technical support. As in the previous two editions, we compiled the index using Windex, a C program that we wrote, and the bibliography was produced with BibTeX. The PDF files for this book were created on a MacBook running OS 10.5.

We drew the illustrations for the third edition using MacDraw Pro, with some of the mathematical expressions in illustrations laid in with the psfrag package for LaTeX 2_ε. Unfortunately, MacDraw Pro is legacy software, having not been marketed for over a decade now. Happily, we still have a couple of Macintoshes that can run the Classic environment under OS 10.4, and hence they can run MacDraw Pro—mostly. Even under the Classic environment, we find MacDraw Pro to be far easier to use than any other drawing software for the types of illustrations that accompany computer-science text, and it produces beautiful output.[1] Who knows how long our pre-Intel Macs will continue to run, so if anyone from Apple is listening: *Please create an OS X-compatible version of MacDraw Pro!*

Acknowledgments for the third edition

We have been working with the MIT Press for over two decades now, and what a terrific relationship it has been! We thank Ellen Faran, Bob Prior, Ada Brunstein, and Mary Reilly for their help and support.

We were geographically distributed while producing the third edition, working in the Dartmouth College Department of Computer Science, the MIT Computer

---

[1] We investigated several drawing programs that run under Mac OS X, but all had significant shortcomings compared with MacDraw Pro. We briefly attempted to produce the illustrations for this book with a different, well known drawing program. We found that it took at least five times as long to produce each illustration as it took with MacDraw Pro, and the resulting illustrations did not look as good. Hence the decision to revert to MacDraw Pro running on older Macintoshes.

Science and Artificial Intelligence Laboratory, and the Columbia University Department of Industrial Engineering and Operations Research. We thank our respective universities and colleagues for providing such supportive and stimulating environments.

Julie Sussman, P.P.A., once again bailed us out as the technical copyeditor. Time and again, we were amazed at the errors that eluded us, but that Julie caught. She also helped us improve our presentation in several places. If there is a Hall of Fame for technical copyeditors, Julie is a sure-fire, first-ballot inductee. She is nothing short of phenomenal. Thank you, thank you, thank you, Julie! Priya Natarajan also found some errors that we were able to correct before this book went to press. Any errors that remain (and undoubtedly, some do) are the responsibility of the authors (and probably were inserted after Julie read the material).

The treatment for van Emde Boas trees derives from Erik Demaine's notes, which were in turn influenced by Michael Bender. We also incorporated ideas from Javed Aslam, Bradley Kuszmaul, and Hui Zha into this edition.

The chapter on multithreading was based on notes originally written jointly with Harald Prokop. The material was influenced by several others working on the Cilk project at MIT, including Bradley Kuszmaul and Matteo Frigo. The design of the multithreaded pseudocode took its inspiration from the MIT Cilk extensions to C and by Cilk Arts's Cilk++ extensions to C++.

We also thank the many readers of the first and second editions who reported errors or submitted suggestions for how to improve this book. We corrected all the bona fide errors that were reported, and we incorporated as many suggestions as we could. We rejoice that the number of such contributors has grown so great that we must regret that it has become impractical to list them all.

Finally, we thank our wives—Nicole Cormen, Wendy Leiserson, Gail Rivest, and Rebecca Ivry—and our children—Ricky, Will, Debby, and Katie Leiserson; Alex and Christopher Rivest; and Molly, Noah, and Benjamin Stein—for their love and support while we prepared this book. The patience and encouragement of our families made this project possible. We affectionately dedicate this book to them.

THOMAS H. CORMEN   *Lebanon, New Hampshire*
CHARLES E. LEISERSON   *Cambridge, Massachusetts*
RONALD L. RIVEST   *Cambridge, Massachusetts*
CLIFFORD STEIN   *New York, New York*

February 2009

Introduction to Algorithms
Third Edition

I   Foundations

Introduction

This part will start you thinking about designing and analyzing algorithms. It is intended to be a gentle introduction to how we specify algorithms, some of the design strategies we will use throughout this book, and many of the fundamental ideas used in algorithm analysis. Later parts of this book will build upon this base.

Chapter 1 provides an overview of algorithms and their place in modern computing systems. This chapter defines what an algorithm is and lists some examples. It also makes a case that we should consider algorithms as a technology, alongside technologies such as fast hardware, graphical user interfaces, object-oriented systems, and networks.

In Chapter 2, we see our first algorithms, which solve the problem of sorting a sequence of n numbers. They are written in a pseudocode which, although not directly translatable to any conventional programming language, conveys the structure of the algorithm clearly enough that you should be able to implement it in the language of your choice. The sorting algorithms we examine are insertion sort, which uses an incremental approach, and merge sort, which uses a recursive technique known as "divide-and-conquer." Although the time each requires increases with the value of n, the rate of increase differs between the two algorithms. We determine these running times in Chapter 2, and we develop a useful notation to express them.

Chapter 3 precisely defines this notation, which we call asymptotic notation. It starts by defining several asymptotic notations, which we use for bounding algorithm running times from above and/or below. The rest of Chapter 3 is primarily a presentation of mathematical notation, more to ensure that your use of notation matches that in this book than to teach you new mathematical concepts.

Chapter 4 delves further into the divide-and-conquer method introduced in Chapter 2. It provides additional examples of divide-and-conquer algorithms, including Strassen's surprising method for multiplying two square matrices. Chapter 4 contains methods for solving recurrences, which are useful for describing the running times of recursive algorithms. One powerful technique is the "master method," which we often use to solve recurrences that arise from divide-and-conquer algorithms. Although much of Chapter 4 is devoted to proving the correctness of the master method, you may skip this proof yet still employ the master method.

Chapter 5 introduces probabilistic analysis and randomized algorithms. We typically use probabilistic analysis to determine the running time of an algorithm in cases in which, due to the presence of an inherent probability distribution, the running time may differ on different inputs of the same size. In some cases, we assume that the inputs conform to a known probability distribution, so that we are averaging the running time over all possible inputs. In other cases, the probability distribution comes not from the inputs but from random choices made during the course of the algorithm. An algorithm whose behavior is determined not only by its input but by the values produced by a random-number generator is a randomized algorithm. We can use randomized algorithms to enforce a probability distribution on the inputs—thereby ensuring that no particular input always causes poor performance—or even to bound the error rate of algorithms that are allowed to produce incorrect results on a limited basis.

Appendices A–D contain other mathematical material that you will find helpful as you read this book. You are likely to have seen much of the material in the appendix chapters before having read this book (although the specific definitions and notational conventions we use may differ in some cases from what you have seen in the past), and so you should think of the Appendices as reference material. On the other hand, you probably have not already seen most of the material in Part I. All the chapters in Part I and the Appendices are written with a tutorial flavor.

1   The Role of Algorithms in Computing

What are algorithms? Why is the study of algorithms worthwhile? What is the role of algorithms relative to other technologies used in computers? In this chapter, we will answer these questions.

1.1   Algorithms

Informally, an **algorithm** is any well-defined computational procedure that takes some value, or set of values, as **input** and produces some value, or set of values, as **output**. An algorithm is thus a sequence of computational steps that transform the input into the output.

We can also view an algorithm as a tool for solving a well-specified **computational problem**. The statement of the problem specifies in general terms the desired input/output relationship. The algorithm describes a specific computational procedure for achieving that input/output relationship.

For example, we might need to sort a sequence of numbers into nondecreasing order. This problem arises frequently in practice and provides fertile ground for introducing many standard design techniques and analysis tools. Here is how we formally define the **sorting problem**:

Input: A sequence of n numbers $\langle a_1, a_2, \ldots, a_n \rangle$.

Output: A permutation (reordering) $\langle a'_1, a'_2, \ldots, a'_n \rangle$ of the input sequence such that $a'_1 \leq a'_2 \leq \cdots \leq a'_n$.

For example, given the input sequence $\langle 31, 41, 59, 26, 41, 58 \rangle$, a sorting algorithm returns as output the sequence $\langle 26, 31, 41, 41, 58, 59 \rangle$. Such an input sequence is called an **instance** of the sorting problem. In general, an **instance of a problem** consists of the input (satisfying whatever constraints are imposed in the problem statement) needed to compute a solution to the problem.

Because many programs use it as an intermediate step, sorting is a fundamental operation in computer science. As a result, we have a large number of good sorting algorithms at our disposal. Which algorithm is best for a given application depends on—among other factors—the number of items to be sorted, the extent to which the items are already somewhat sorted, possible restrictions on the item values, the architecture of the computer, and the kind of storage devices to be used: main memory, disks, or even tapes.

An algorithm is said to be **correct** if, for every input instance, it halts with the correct output. We say that a correct algorithm **solves** the given computational problem. An incorrect algorithm might not halt at all on some input instances, or it might halt with an incorrect answer. Contrary to what you might expect, incorrect algorithms can sometimes be useful, if we can control their error rate. We shall see an example of an algorithm with a controllable error rate in Chapter 31 when we study algorithms for finding large prime numbers. Ordinarily, however, we shall be concerned only with correct algorithms.

An algorithm can be specified in English, as a computer program, or even as a hardware design. The only requirement is that the specification must provide a precise description of the computational procedure to be followed.

What kinds of problems are solved by algorithms?

Sorting is by no means the only computational problem for which algorithms have been developed. (You probably suspected as much when you saw the size of this book.) Practical applications of algorithms are ubiquitous and include the following examples:

- The Human Genome Project has made great progress toward the goals of identifying all the 100,000 genes in human DNA, determining the sequences of the 3 billion chemical base pairs that make up human DNA, storing this information in databases, and developing tools for data analysis. Each of these steps requires sophisticated algorithms. Although the solutions to the various problems involved are beyond the scope of this book, many methods to solve these biological problems use ideas from several of the chapters in this book, thereby enabling scientists to accomplish tasks while using resources efficiently. The savings are in time, both human and machine, and in money, as more information can be extracted from laboratory techniques.

- The Internet enables people all around the world to quickly access and retrieve large amounts of information. With the aid of clever algorithms, sites on the Internet are able to manage and manipulate this large volume of data. Examples of problems that make essential use of algorithms include finding good routes on which the data will travel (techniques for solving such problems appear in

Chapter 24), and using a search engine to quickly find pages on which particular information resides (related techniques are in Chapters 11 and 32).

- Electronic commerce enables goods and services to be negotiated and exchanged electronically, and it depends on the privacy of personal information such as credit card numbers, passwords, and bank statements. The core technologies used in electronic commerce include public-key cryptography and digital signatures (covered in Chapter 31), which are based on numerical algorithms and number theory.

- Manufacturing and other commercial enterprises often need to allocate scarce resources in the most beneficial way. An oil company may wish to know where to place its wells in order to maximize its expected profit. A political candidate may want to determine where to spend money buying campaign advertising in order to maximize the chances of winning an election. An airline may wish to assign crews to flights in the least expensive way possible, making sure that each flight is covered and that government regulations regarding crew scheduling are met. An Internet service provider may wish to determine where to place additional resources in order to serve its customers more effectively. All of these are examples of problems that can be solved using linear programming, which we shall study in Chapter 29.

Although some of the details of these examples are beyond the scope of this book, we do give underlying techniques that apply to these problems and problem areas. We also show how to solve many specific problems, including the following:

- We are given a road map on which the distance between each pair of adjacent intersections is marked, and we wish to determine the shortest route from one intersection to another. The number of possible routes can be huge, even if we disallow routes that cross over themselves. How do we choose which of all possible routes is the shortest? Here, we model the road map (which is itself a model of the actual roads) as a graph (which we will meet in Part VI and Appendix B), and we wish to find the shortest path from one vertex to another in the graph. We shall see how to solve this problem efficiently in Chapter 24.

- We are given two ordered sequences of symbols, $X = \langle x_1, x_2, \ldots, x_m \rangle$ and $Y = \langle y_1, y_2, \ldots, y_n \rangle$, and we wish to find a longest common subsequence of X and Y. A subsequence of X is just X with some (or possibly all or none) of its elements removed. For example, one subsequence of $\langle A, B, C, D, E, F, G \rangle$ would be $\langle B, C, E, G \rangle$. The length of a longest common subsequence of X and Y gives one measure of how similar these two sequences are. For example, if the two sequences are base pairs in DNA strands, then we might consider them similar if they have a long common subsequence. If X has m symbols and Y has n symbols, then X and Y have 2^m and 2^n possible subsequences, respectively. Selecting all possible subsequences of X and Y and matching them up could take a prohibitively long time unless m and n are very small. We shall see in Chapter 15 how to use a general technique known as dynamic programming to solve this problem much more efficiently.

- We are given a mechanical design in terms of a library of parts, where each part may include instances of other parts, and we need to list the parts in order so that each part appears before any part that uses it. If the design comprises n parts, then there are $n!$ possible orders, where $n!$ denotes the factorial function. Because the factorial function grows faster than even an exponential function, we cannot feasibly generate each possible order and then verify that, within that order, each part appears before the parts using it (unless we have only a few parts). This problem is an instance of topological sorting, and we shall see in Chapter 22 how to solve this problem efficiently.

- We are given n points in the plane, and we wish to find the convex hull of these points. The convex hull is the smallest convex polygon containing the points. Intuitively, we can think of each point as being represented by a nail sticking out from a board. The convex hull would be represented by a tight rubber band that surrounds all the nails. Each nail around which the rubber band makes a turn is a vertex of the convex hull. (See Figure 33.6 on page 1029 for an example.) Any of the 2^n subsets of the points might be the vertices of the convex hull. Knowing which points are vertices of the convex hull is not quite enough, either, since we also need to know the order in which they appear. There are many choices, therefore, for the vertices of the convex hull. Chapter 33 gives two good methods for finding the convex hull.

These lists are far from exhaustive (as you again have probably surmised from this book's heft), but exhibit two characteristics that are common to many interesting algorithmic problems:

1. They have many candidate solutions, the overwhelming majority of which do not solve the problem at hand. Finding one that does, or one that is "best," can present quite a challenge.

2. They have practical applications. Of the problems in the above list, finding the shortest path provides the easiest examples. A transportation firm, such as a trucking or railroad company, has a financial interest in finding shortest paths through a road or rail network because taking shorter paths results in lower labor and fuel costs. Or a routing node on the Internet may need to find the shortest path through the network in order to route a message quickly. Or a person wishing to drive from New York to Boston may want to find driving directions from an appropriate Web site, or she may use her GPS while driving.

Not every problem solved by algorithms has an easily identified set of candidate solutions. For example, suppose we are given a set of numerical values representing samples of a signal, and we want to compute the discrete Fourier transform of these samples. The discrete Fourier transform converts the time domain to the frequency domain, producing a set of numerical coefficients, so that we can determine the strength of various frequencies in the sampled signal. In addition to lying at the heart of signal processing, discrete Fourier transforms have applications in data compression and multiplying large polynomials and integers. Chapter 30 gives an efficient algorithm, the fast Fourier transform (commonly called the FFT), for this problem, and the chapter also sketches out the design of a hardware circuit to compute the FFT.

Data structures

This book also contains several data structures. A ***data structure*** is a way to store and organize data in order to facilitate access and modifications. No single data structure works well for all purposes, and so it is important to know the strengths and limitations of several of them.

Technique

Although you can use this book as a "cookbook" for algorithms, you may someday encounter a problem for which you cannot readily find a published algorithm (many of the exercises and problems in this book, for example). This book will teach you techniques of algorithm design and analysis so that you can develop algorithms on your own, show that they give the correct answer, and understand their efficiency. Different chapters address different aspects of algorithmic problem solving. Some chapters address specific problems, such as finding medians and order statistics in Chapter 9, computing minimum spanning trees in Chapter 23, and determining a maximum flow in a network in Chapter 26. Other chapters address techniques, such as divide-and-conquer in Chapter 4, dynamic programming in Chapter 15, and amortized analysis in Chapter 17.

Hard problems

Most of this book is about efficient algorithms. Our usual measure of efficiency is speed, i.e., how long an algorithm takes to produce its result. There are some problems, however, for which no efficient solution is known. Chapter 34 studies an interesting subset of these problems, which are known as NP-complete.

Why are NP-complete problems interesting? First, although no efficient algorithm for an NP-complete problem has ever been found, nobody has ever proven that an efficient algorithm for one cannot exist. In other words, no one knows whether or not efficient algorithms exist for NP-complete problems. Second, the set of NP-complete problems has the remarkable property that if an efficient algorithm exists for any one of them, then efficient algorithms exist for all of them. This relationship among the NP-complete problems makes the lack of efficient solutions all the more tantalizing. Third, several NP-complete problems are similar, but not identical, to problems for which we do know of efficient algorithms. Computer scientists are intrigued by how a small change to the problem statement can cause a big change to the efficiency of the best known algorithm.

You should know about NP-complete problems because some of them arise surprisingly often in real applications. If you are called upon to produce an efficient algorithm for an NP-complete problem, you are likely to spend a lot of time in a fruitless search. If you can show that the problem is NP-complete, you can instead spend your time developing an efficient algorithm that gives a good, but not the best possible, solution.

As a concrete example, consider a delivery company with a central depot. Each day, it loads up each delivery truck at the depot and sends it around to deliver goods to several addresses. At the end of the day, each truck must end up back at the depot so that it is ready to be loaded for the next day. To reduce costs, the company wants to select an order of delivery stops that yields the lowest overall distance traveled by each truck. This problem is the well-known "traveling-salesman problem," and it is NP-complete. It has no known efficient algorithm. Under certain assumptions, however, we know of efficient algorithms that give an overall distance which is not too far above the smallest possible. Chapter 35 discusses such "approximation algorithms."

Parallelism

For many years, we could count on processor clock speeds increasing at a steady rate. Physical limitations present a fundamental roadblock to ever-increasing clock speeds, however: because power density increases superlinearly with clock speed, chips run the risk of melting once their clock speeds become high enough. In order to perform more computations per second, therefore, chips are being designed to contain not just one but several processing "cores." We can liken these multicore computers to several sequential computers on a single chip; in other words, they are a type of "parallel computer." In order to elicit the best performance from multicore computers, we need to design algorithms with parallelism in mind. Chapter 27 presents a model for "multithreaded" algorithms, which take advantage of multiple cores. This model has advantages from a theoretical standpoint, and it forms the basis of several successful computer programs, including a championship chess program.

Exercises

1.1-1
Give a real-world example that requires sorting or a real-world example that requires computing a convex hull.

1.1-2
Other than speed, what other measures of efficiency might one use in a real-world setting?

1.1-3
Select a data structure that you have seen previously, and discuss its strengths and limitations.

1.1-4
How are the shortest-path and traveling-salesman problems given above similar? How are they different?

1.1-5
Come up with a real-world problem in which only the best solution will do. Then come up with one in which a solution that is "approximately" the best is good enough.

1.2 Algorithms as a technology

Suppose computers were infinitely fast and computer memory was free. Would you have any reason to study algorithms? The answer is yes, if for no other reason than that you would still like to demonstrate that your solution method terminates and does so with the correct answer.

If computers were infinitely fast, any correct method for solving a problem would do. You would probably want your implementation to be within the bounds of good software engineering practice (for example, your implementation should be well designed and documented), but you would most often use whichever method was the easiest to implement.

Of course, computers may be fast, but they are not infinitely fast. And memory may be inexpensive, but it is not free. Computing time is therefore a bounded resource, and so is space in memory. You should use these resources wisely, and algorithms that are efficient in terms of time or space will help you do so.

Efficiency

Different algorithms devised to solve the same problem often differ dramatically in their efficiency. These differences can be much more significant than differences due to hardware and software.

As an example, in Chapter 2, we will see two algorithms for sorting. The first, known as ***insertion sort***, takes time roughly equal to $c_1 n^2$ to sort n items, where c_1 is a constant that does not depend on n. That is, it takes time roughly proportional to n^2. The second, ***merge sort***, takes time roughly equal to $c_2 n \lg n$, where $\lg n$ stands for $\log_2 n$ and c_2 is another constant that also does not depend on n. Insertion sort typically has a smaller constant factor than merge sort, so that $c_1 < c_2$. We shall see that the constant factors can have far less of an impact on the running time than the dependence on the input size n. Let's write insertion sort's running time as $c_1 n \cdot n$ and merge sort's running time as $c_2 n \cdot \lg n$. Then we see that where insertion sort has a factor of n in its running time, merge sort has a factor of $\lg n$, which is much smaller. (For example, when $n = 1000$, $\lg n$ is approximately 10, and when n equals one million, $\lg n$ is approximately only 20.) Although insertion sort usually runs faster than merge sort for small input sizes, once the input size n becomes large enough, merge sort's advantage of $\lg n$ vs. n will more than compensate for the difference in constant factors. No matter how much smaller c_1 is than c_2, there will always be a crossover point beyond which merge sort is faster.

For a concrete example, let us pit a faster computer (computer A) running insertion sort against a slower computer (computer B) running merge sort. They each must sort an array of 10 million numbers. (Although 10 million numbers might seem like a lot, if the numbers are eight-byte integers, then the input occupies about 80 megabytes, which fits in the memory of even an inexpensive laptop computer many times over.) Suppose that computer A executes 10 billion instructions per second (faster than any single sequential computer at the time of this writing) and computer B executes only 10 million instructions per second, so that computer A is 1000 times faster than computer B in raw computing power. To make the difference even more dramatic, suppose that the world's craftiest programmer codes insertion sort in machine language for computer A, and the resulting code requires $2n^2$ instructions to sort n numbers. Suppose further that just an average programmer implements merge sort, using a high-level language with an inefficient compiler, with the resulting code taking $50n \lg n$ instructions. To sort 10 million numbers, computer A takes

$$\frac{2 \cdot (10^7)^2 \text{ instructions}}{10^{10} \text{ instructions/second}} = 20{,}000 \text{ seconds (more than 5.5 hours) },$$

while computer B takes

$$\frac{50 \cdot 10^7 \lg 10^7 \text{ instructions}}{10^7 \text{ instructions/second}} \approx 1163 \text{ seconds (less than 20 minutes)}\ .$$

By using an algorithm whose running time grows more slowly, even with a poor compiler, computer B runs more than 17 times faster than computer A! The advantage of merge sort is even more pronounced when we sort 100 million numbers: where insertion sort takes more than 23 days, merge sort takes under four hours. In general, as the problem size increases, so does the relative advantage of merge sort.

Algorithms and other technologies

The example above shows that we should consider algorithms, like computer hardware, as a ***technology***. Total system performance depends on choosing efficient algorithms as much as on choosing fast hardware. Just as rapid advances are being made in other computer technologies, they are being made in algorithms as well.

You might wonder whether algorithms are truly that important on contemporary computers in light of other advanced technologies, such as

- advanced computer architectures and fabrication technologies,

- easy-to-use, intuitive, graphical user interfaces (GUIs),

- object-oriented systems,

- integrated Web technologies, and

- fast networking, both wired and wireless.

The answer is yes. Although some applications do not explicitly require algorithmic content at the application level (such as some simple, Web-based applications), many do. For example, consider a Web-based service that determines how to travel from one location to another. Its implementation would rely on fast hardware, a graphical user interface, wide-area networking, and also possibly on object orientation. However, it would also require algorithms for certain operations, such as finding routes (probably using a shortest-path algorithm), rendering maps, and interpolating addresses.

Moreover, even an application that does not require algorithmic content at the application level relies heavily upon algorithms. Does the application rely on fast hardware? The hardware design used algorithms. Does the application rely on graphical user interfaces? The design of any GUI relies on algorithms. Does the application rely on networking? Routing in networks relies heavily on algorithms. Was the application written in a language other than machine code? Then it was processed by a compiler, interpreter, or assembler, all of which make extensive use of algorithms. Algorithms are at the core of most technologies used in contemporary computers.

Furthermore, with the ever-increasing capacities of computers, we use them to solve larger problems than ever before. As we saw in the above comparison between insertion sort and merge sort, it is at larger problem sizes that the differences in efficiency between algorithms become particularly prominent.

Having a solid base of algorithmic knowledge and technique is one characteristic that separates the truly skilled programmers from the novices. With modern computing technology, you can accomplish some tasks without knowing much about algorithms, but with a good background in algorithms, you can do much, much more.

Exercises

1.2-1
Give an example of an application that requires algorithmic content at the application level, and discuss the function of the algorithms involved.

1.2-2
Suppose we are comparing implementations of insertion sort and merge sort on the same machine. For inputs of size n, insertion sort runs in $8n^2$ steps, while merge sort runs in $64n \lg n$ steps. For which values of n does insertion sort beat merge sort?

1.2-3
What is the smallest value of n such that an algorithm whose running time is $100n^2$ runs faster than an algorithm whose running time is 2^n on the same machine?

Problems

1-1   Comparison of running times
For each function $f(n)$ and time t in the following table, determine the largest size n of a problem that can be solved in time t, assuming that the algorithm to solve the problem takes $f(n)$ microseconds.

	1 second	1 minute	1 hour	1 day	1 month	1 year	1 century
$\lg n$							
$\sqrt{n}$							
n							
$n \lg n$							
n^2							
n^3							
2^n							
$n!$							

Chapter notes

There are many excellent texts on the general topic of algorithms, including those by Aho, Hopcroft, and Ullman [5, 6]; Baase and Van Gelder [28]; Brassard and Bratley [54]; Dasgupta, Papadimitriou, and Vazirani [82]; Goodrich and Tamassia [148]; Hofri [175]; Horowitz, Sahni, and Rajasekaran [181]; Johnsonbaugh and Schaefer [193]; Kingston [205]; Kleinberg and Tardos [208]; Knuth [209, 210, 211]; Kozen [220]; Levitin [235]; Manber [242]; Mehlhorn [249, 250, 251]; Purdom and Brown [287]; Reingold, Nievergelt, and Deo [293]; Sedgewick [306]; Sedgewick and Flajolet [307]; Skiena [318]; and Wilf [356]. Some of the more practical aspects of algorithm design are discussed by Bentley [42, 43] and Gonnet [145]. Surveys of the field of algorithms can also be found in the *Handbook of Theoretical Computer Science, Volume A* [342] and the CRC *Algorithms and Theory of Computation Handbook* [25]. Overviews of the algorithms used in computational biology can be found in textbooks by Gusfield [156], Pevzner [275], Setubal and Meidanis [310], and Waterman [350].

2 Getting Started

This chapter will familiarize you with the framework we shall use throughout the book to think about the design and analysis of algorithms. It is self-contained, but it does include several references to material that we introduce in Chapters 3 and 4. (It also contains several summations, which Appendix A shows how to solve.)

We begin by examining the insertion sort algorithm to solve the sorting problem introduced in Chapter 1. We define a "pseudocode" that should be familiar to you if you have done computer programming, and we use it to show how we shall specify our algorithms. Having specified the insertion sort algorithm, we then argue that it correctly sorts, and we analyze its running time. The analysis introduces a notation that focuses on how that time increases with the number of items to be sorted. Following our discussion of insertion sort, we introduce the divide-and-conquer approach to the design of algorithms and use it to develop an algorithm called merge sort. We end with an analysis of merge sort's running time.

2.1 Insertion sort

Our first algorithm, insertion sort, solves the **sorting problem** introduced in Chapter 1:

Input: A sequence of n numbers $\langle a_1, a_2, \ldots, a_n \rangle$.

Output: A permutation (reordering) $\langle a'_1, a'_2, \ldots, a'_n \rangle$ of the input sequence such that $a'_1 \leq a'_2 \leq \cdots \leq a'_n$.

The numbers that we wish to sort are also known as the **keys**. Although conceptually we are sorting a sequence, the input comes to us in the form of an array with n elements.

In this book, we shall typically describe algorithms as programs written in a **pseudocode** that is similar in many respects to C, C++, Java, Python, or Pascal. If you have been introduced to any of these languages, you should have little trouble

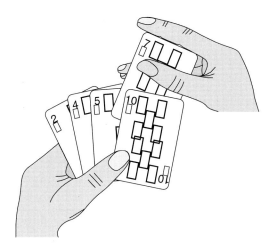

Figure 2.1 Sorting a hand of cards using insertion sort.

reading our algorithms. What separates pseudocode from "real" code is that in pseudocode, we employ whatever expressive method is most clear and concise to specify a given algorithm. Sometimes, the clearest method is English, so do not be surprised if you come across an English phrase or sentence embedded within a section of "real" code. Another difference between pseudocode and real code is that pseudocode is not typically concerned with issues of software engineering. Issues of data abstraction, modularity, and error handling are often ignored in order to convey the essence of the algorithm more concisely.

We start with ***insertion sort***, which is an efficient algorithm for sorting a small number of elements. Insertion sort works the way many people sort a hand of playing cards. We start with an empty left hand and the cards face down on the table. We then remove one card at a time from the table and insert it into the correct position in the left hand. To find the correct position for a card, we compare it with each of the cards already in the hand, from right to left, as illustrated in Figure 2.1. At all times, the cards held in the left hand are sorted, and these cards were originally the top cards of the pile on the table.

We present our pseudocode for insertion sort as a procedure called INSERTION-SORT, which takes as a parameter an array $A[1 . . n]$ containing a sequence of length n that is to be sorted. (In the code, the number n of elements in A is denoted by $A.length$.) The algorithm sorts the input numbers ***in place***: it rearranges the numbers within the array A, with at most a constant number of them stored outside the array at any time. The input array A contains the sorted output sequence when the INSERTION-SORT procedure is finished.

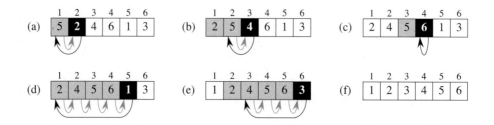

Figure 2.2 The operation of INSERTION-SORT on the array $A = \langle 5, 2, 4, 6, 1, 3 \rangle$. Array indices appear above the rectangles, and values stored in the array positions appear within the rectangles. **(a)–(e)** The iterations of the **for** loop of lines 1–8. In each iteration, the black rectangle holds the key taken from $A[j]$, which is compared with the values in shaded rectangles to its left in the test of line 5. Shaded arrows show array values moved one position to the right in line 6, and black arrows indicate where the key moves to in line 8. **(f)** The final sorted array.

INSERTION-SORT(A)

```
1   for j = 2 to A.length
2       key = A[j]
3       // Insert A[j] into the sorted sequence A[1 .. j − 1].
4       i = j − 1
5       while i > 0 and A[i] > key
6           A[i + 1] = A[i]
7           i = i − 1
8       A[i + 1] = key
```

Loop invariants and the correctness of insertion sort

Figure 2.2 shows how this algorithm works for $A = \langle 5, 2, 4, 6, 1, 3 \rangle$. The index j indicates the "current card" being inserted into the hand. At the beginning of each iteration of the **for** loop, which is indexed by j, the subarray consisting of elements $A[1 .. j − 1]$ constitutes the currently sorted hand, and the remaining subarray $A[j + 1 .. n]$ corresponds to the pile of cards still on the table. In fact, elements $A[1 .. j − 1]$ are the elements *originally* in positions 1 through $j − 1$, but now in sorted order. We state these properties of $A[1 .. j − 1]$ formally as a ***loop invariant***:

> At the start of each iteration of the **for** loop of lines 1–8, the subarray $A[1 .. j − 1]$ consists of the elements originally in $A[1 .. j − 1]$, but in sorted order.

We use loop invariants to help us understand why an algorithm is correct. We must show three things about a loop invariant:

Initialization: It is true prior to the first iteration of the loop.

Maintenance: If it is true before an iteration of the loop, it remains true before the next iteration.

Termination: When the loop terminates, the invariant gives us a useful property that helps show that the algorithm is correct.

When the first two properties hold, the loop invariant is true prior to every iteration of the loop. (Of course, we are free to use established facts other than the loop invariant itself to prove that the loop invariant remains true before each iteration.) Note the similarity to mathematical induction, where to prove that a property holds, you prove a base case and an inductive step. Here, showing that the invariant holds before the first iteration corresponds to the base case, and showing that the invariant holds from iteration to iteration corresponds to the inductive step.

The third property is perhaps the most important one, since we are using the loop invariant to show correctness. Typically, we use the loop invariant along with the condition that caused the loop to terminate. The termination property differs from how we usually use mathematical induction, in which we apply the inductive step infinitely; here, we stop the "induction" when the loop terminates.

Let us see how these properties hold for insertion sort.

Initialization: We start by showing that the loop invariant holds before the first loop iteration, when $j = 2$.[1] The subarray $A[1 .. j - 1]$, therefore, consists of just the single element $A[1]$, which is in fact the original element in $A[1]$. Moreover, this subarray is sorted (trivially, of course), which shows that the loop invariant holds prior to the first iteration of the loop.

Maintenance: Next, we tackle the second property: showing that each iteration maintains the loop invariant. Informally, the body of the **for** loop works by moving $A[j - 1]$, $A[j - 2]$, $A[j - 3]$, and so on by one position to the right until it finds the proper position for $A[j]$ (lines 4–7), at which point it inserts the value of $A[j]$ (line 8). The subarray $A[1 .. j]$ then consists of the elements originally in $A[1 .. j]$, but in sorted order. Incrementing j for the next iteration of the **for** loop then preserves the loop invariant.

A more formal treatment of the second property would require us to state and show a loop invariant for the **while** loop of lines 5–7. At this point, however,

---

[1] When the loop is a **for** loop, the moment at which we check the loop invariant just prior to the first iteration is immediately after the initial assignment to the loop-counter variable and just before the first test in the loop header. In the case of INSERTION-SORT, this time is after assigning 2 to the variable j but before the first test of whether $j \leq A.length$.

we prefer not to get bogged down in such formalism, and so we rely on our informal analysis to show that the second property holds for the outer loop.

Termination: Finally, we examine what happens when the loop terminates. The condition causing the **for** loop to terminate is that $j > A.length = n$. Because each loop iteration increases j by 1, we must have $j = n + 1$ at that time. Substituting $n + 1$ for j in the wording of loop invariant, we have that the subarray $A[1..n]$ consists of the elements originally in $A[1..n]$, but in sorted order. Observing that the subarray $A[1..n]$ is the entire array, we conclude that the entire array is sorted. Hence, the algorithm is correct.

We shall use this method of loop invariants to show correctness later in this chapter and in other chapters as well.

Pseudocode conventions

We use the following conventions in our pseudocode.

- Indentation indicates block structure. For example, the body of the **for** loop that begins on line 1 consists of lines 2–8, and the body of the **while** loop that begins on line 5 contains lines 6–7 but not line 8. Our indentation style applies to **if-else** statements[2] as well. Using indentation instead of conventional indicators of block structure, such as **begin** and **end** statements, greatly reduces clutter while preserving, or even enhancing, clarity.[3]

- The looping constructs **while**, **for**, and **repeat-until** and the **if-else** conditional construct have interpretations similar to those in C, C++, Java, Python, and Pascal.[4] In this book, the loop counter retains its value after exiting the loop, unlike some situations that arise in C++, Java, and Pascal. Thus, immediately after a **for** loop, the loop counter's value is the value that first exceeded the **for** loop bound. We used this property in our correctness argument for insertion sort. The **for** loop header in line 1 is **for** $j = 2$ **to** $A.length$, and so when this loop terminates, $j = A.length + 1$ (or, equivalently, $j = n + 1$, since $n = A.length$). We use the keyword **to** when a **for** loop increments its loop

---

[2]In an **if-else** statement, we indent **else** at the same level as its matching **if**. Although we omit the keyword **then**, we occasionally refer to the portion executed when the test following **if** is true as a *then clause*. For multiway tests, we use **elseif** for tests after the first one.

[3]Each pseudocode procedure in this book appears on one page so that you will not have to discern levels of indentation in code that is split across pages.

[4]Most block-structured languages have equivalent constructs, though the exact syntax may differ. Python lacks **repeat-until** loops, and its **for** loops operate a little differently from the **for** loops in this book.

counter in each iteration, and we use the keyword **downto** when a **for** loop decrements its loop counter. When the loop counter changes by an amount greater than 1, the amount of change follows the optional keyword **by**.

- The symbol "**//**" indicates that the remainder of the line is a comment.

- A multiple assignment of the form $i = j = e$ assigns to both variables i and j the value of expression e; it should be treated as equivalent to the assignment $j = e$ followed by the assignment $i = j$.

- Variables (such as i, j, and *key*) are local to the given procedure. We shall not use global variables without explicit indication.

- We access array elements by specifying the array name followed by the index in square brackets. For example, $A[i]$ indicates the ith element of the array A. The notation ".." is used to indicate a range of values within an array. Thus, $A[1 .. j]$ indicates the subarray of A consisting of the j elements $A[1], A[2], \ldots, A[j]$.

- We typically organize compound data into *objects*, which are composed of *attributes*. We access a particular attribute using the syntax found in many object-oriented programming languages: the object name, followed by a dot, followed by the attribute name. For example, we treat an array as an object with the attribute *length* indicating how many elements it contains. To specify the number of elements in an array A, we write $A.length$.

   We treat a variable representing an array or object as a pointer to the data representing the array or object. For all attributes f of an object x, setting $y = x$ causes $y.f$ to equal $x.f$. Moreover, if we now set $x.f = 3$, then afterward not only does $x.f$ equal 3, but $y.f$ equals 3 as well. In other words, x and y point to the same object after the assignment $y = x$.

   Our attribute notation can "cascade." For example, suppose that the attribute f is itself a pointer to some type of object that has an attribute g. Then the notation $x.f.g$ is implicitly parenthesized as $(x.f).g$. In other words, if we had assigned $y = x.f$, then $x.f.g$ is the same as $y.g$.

   Sometimes, a pointer will refer to no object at all. In this case, we give it the special value NIL.

- We pass parameters to a procedure *by value*: the called procedure receives its own copy of the parameters, and if it assigns a value to a parameter, the change is *not* seen by the calling procedure. When objects are passed, the pointer to the data representing the object is copied, but the object's attributes are not. For example, if x is a parameter of a called procedure, the assignment $x = y$ within the called procedure is not visible to the calling procedure. The assignment $x.f = 3$, however, is visible. Similarly, arrays are passed by pointer, so that a pointer to the array is passed, rather than the entire array, and changes to individual array elements are visible to the calling procedure.

- A **return** statement immediately transfers control back to the point of call in the calling procedure. Most **return** statements also take a value to pass back to the caller. Our pseudocode differs from many programming languages in that we allow multiple values to be returned in a single **return** statement.

- The boolean operators "and" and "or" are **short circuiting**. That is, when we evaluate the expression "x and y" we first evaluate x. If x evaluates to FALSE, then the entire expression cannot evaluate to TRUE, and so we do not evaluate y. If, on the other hand, x evaluates to TRUE, we must evaluate y to determine the value of the entire expression. Similarly, in the expression "x or y" we evaluate the expression y only if x evaluates to FALSE. Short-circuiting operators allow us to write boolean expressions such as "$x \neq$ NIL and $x.f = y$" without worrying about what happens when we try to evaluate $x.f$ when x is NIL.

- The keyword **error** indicates that an error occurred because conditions were wrong for the procedure to have been called. The calling procedure is responsible for handling the error, and so we do not specify what action to take.

Exercises

2.1-1
Using Figure 2.2 as a model, illustrate the operation of INSERTION-SORT on the array $A = \langle 31, 41, 59, 26, 41, 58 \rangle$.

2.1-2
Rewrite the INSERTION-SORT procedure to sort into nonincreasing instead of nondecreasing order.

2.1-3
Consider the **searching problem**:

Input: A sequence of n numbers $A = \langle a_1, a_2, \ldots, a_n \rangle$ and a value v.

Output: An index i such that $v = A[i]$ or the special value NIL if v does not appear in A.

Write pseudocode for **linear search**, which scans through the sequence, looking for v. Using a loop invariant, prove that your algorithm is correct. Make sure that your loop invariant fulfills the three necessary properties.

2.1-4
Consider the problem of adding two n-bit binary integers, stored in two n-element arrays A and B. The sum of the two integers should be stored in binary form in

an $(n + 1)$-element array C. State the problem formally and write pseudocode for adding the two integers.

2.2   Analyzing algorithms

Analyzing an algorithm has come to mean predicting the resources that the algorithm requires. Occasionally, resources such as memory, communication bandwidth, or computer hardware are of primary concern, but most often it is computational time that we want to measure. Generally, by analyzing several candidate algorithms for a problem, we can identify a most efficient one. Such analysis may indicate more than one viable candidate, but we can often discard several inferior algorithms in the process.

Before we can analyze an algorithm, we must have a model of the implementation technology that we will use, including a model for the resources of that technology and their costs. For most of this book, we shall assume a generic one-processor, *random-access machine (RAM)* model of computation as our implementation technology and understand that our algorithms will be implemented as computer programs. In the RAM model, instructions are executed one after another, with no concurrent operations.

Strictly speaking, we should precisely define the instructions of the RAM model and their costs. To do so, however, would be tedious and would yield little insight into algorithm design and analysis. Yet we must be careful not to abuse the RAM model. For example, what if a RAM had an instruction that sorts? Then we could sort in just one instruction. Such a RAM would be unrealistic, since real computers do not have such instructions. Our guide, therefore, is how real computers are designed. The RAM model contains instructions commonly found in real computers: arithmetic (such as add, subtract, multiply, divide, remainder, floor, ceiling), data movement (load, store, copy), and control (conditional and unconditional branch, subroutine call and return). Each such instruction takes a constant amount of time.

The data types in the RAM model are integer and floating point (for storing real numbers). Although we typically do not concern ourselves with precision in this book, in some applications precision is crucial. We also assume a limit on the size of each word of data. For example, when working with inputs of size n, we typically assume that integers are represented by $c \lg n$ bits for some constant $c \geq 1$. We require $c \geq 1$ so that each word can hold the value of n, enabling us to index the individual input elements, and we restrict c to be a constant so that the word size does not grow arbitrarily. (If the word size could grow arbitrarily, we could store huge amounts of data in one word and operate on it all in constant time—clearly an unrealistic scenario.)

Real computers contain instructions not listed above, and such instructions represent a gray area in the RAM model. For example, is exponentiation a constant-time instruction? In the general case, no; it takes several instructions to compute x^y when x and y are real numbers. In restricted situations, however, exponentiation is a constant-time operation. Many computers have a "shift left" instruction, which in constant time shifts the bits of an integer by k positions to the left. In most computers, shifting the bits of an integer by one position to the left is equivalent to multiplication by 2, so that shifting the bits by k positions to the left is equivalent to multiplication by 2^k. Therefore, such computers can compute 2^k in one constant-time instruction by shifting the integer 1 by k positions to the left, as long as k is no more than the number of bits in a computer word. We will endeavor to avoid such gray areas in the RAM model, but we will treat computation of 2^k as a constant-time operation when k is a small enough positive integer.

In the RAM model, we do not attempt to model the memory hierarchy that is common in contemporary computers. That is, we do not model caches or virtual memory. Several computational models attempt to account for memory-hierarchy effects, which are sometimes significant in real programs on real machines. A handful of problems in this book examine memory-hierarchy effects, but for the most part, the analyses in this book will not consider them. Models that include the memory hierarchy are quite a bit more complex than the RAM model, and so they can be difficult to work with. Moreover, RAM-model analyses are usually excellent predictors of performance on actual machines.

Analyzing even a simple algorithm in the RAM model can be a challenge. The mathematical tools required may include combinatorics, probability theory, algebraic dexterity, and the ability to identify the most significant terms in a formula. Because the behavior of an algorithm may be different for each possible input, we need a means for summarizing that behavior in simple, easily understood formulas.

Even though we typically select only one machine model to analyze a given algorithm, we still face many choices in deciding how to express our analysis. We would like a way that is simple to write and manipulate, shows the important characteristics of an algorithm's resource requirements, and suppresses tedious details.

Analysis of insertion sort

The time taken by the INSERTION-SORT procedure depends on the input: sorting a thousand numbers takes longer than sorting three numbers. Moreover, INSERTION-SORT can take different amounts of time to sort two input sequences of the same size depending on how nearly sorted they already are. In general, the time taken by an algorithm grows with the size of the input, so it is traditional to describe the running time of a program as a function of the size of its input. To do so, we need to define the terms "running time" and "size of input" more carefully.

The best notion for ***input size*** depends on the problem being studied. For many problems, such as sorting or computing discrete Fourier transforms, the most natural measure is the *number of items in the input*—for example, the array size n for sorting. For many other problems, such as multiplying two integers, the best measure of input size is the *total number of bits* needed to represent the input in ordinary binary notation. Sometimes, it is more appropriate to describe the size of the input with two numbers rather than one. For instance, if the input to an algorithm is a graph, the input size can be described by the numbers of vertices and edges in the graph. We shall indicate which input size measure is being used with each problem we study.

The ***running time*** of an algorithm on a particular input is the number of primitive operations or "steps" executed. It is convenient to define the notion of step so that it is as machine-independent as possible. For the moment, let us adopt the following view. A constant amount of time is required to execute each line of our pseudocode. One line may take a different amount of time than another line, but we shall assume that each execution of the ith line takes time c_i, where c_i is a constant. This viewpoint is in keeping with the RAM model, and it also reflects how the pseudocode would be implemented on most actual computers.[5]

In the following discussion, our expression for the running time of INSERTION-SORT will evolve from a messy formula that uses all the statement costs c_i to a much simpler notation that is more concise and more easily manipulated. This simpler notation will also make it easy to determine whether one algorithm is more efficient than another.

We start by presenting the INSERTION-SORT procedure with the time "cost" of each statement and the number of times each statement is executed. For each $j = 2, 3, \ldots, n$, where $n = A.length$, we let t_j denote the number of times the **while** loop test in line 5 is executed for that value of j. When a **for** or **while** loop exits in the usual way (i.e., due to the test in the loop header), the test is executed one time more than the loop body. We assume that comments are not executable statements, and so they take no time.

---

[5]There are some subtleties here. Computational steps that we specify in English are often variants of a procedure that requires more than just a constant amount of time. For example, later in this book we might say "sort the points by x-coordinate," which, as we shall see, takes more than a constant amount of time. Also, note that a statement that calls a subroutine takes constant time, though the subroutine, once invoked, may take more. That is, we separate the process of ***calling*** the subroutine—passing parameters to it, etc.—from the process of ***executing*** the subroutine.

INSERTION-SORT(A)	cost	times
1 **for** $j = 2$ **to** $A.length$	c_1	n
2 $key = A[j]$	c_2	$n - 1$
3 // Insert $A[j]$ into the sorted		
sequence $A[1 .. j - 1]$.	0	$n - 1$
4 $i = j - 1$	c_4	$n - 1$
5 **while** $i > 0$ and $A[i] > key$	c_5	$\sum_{j=2}^{n} t_j$
6 $A[i + 1] = A[i]$	c_6	$\sum_{j=2}^{n} (t_j - 1)$
7 $i = i - 1$	c_7	$\sum_{j=2}^{n} (t_j - 1)$
8 $A[i + 1] = key$	c_8	$n - 1$

The running time of the algorithm is the sum of running times for each statement executed; a statement that takes c_i steps to execute and executes n times will contribute $c_i n$ to the total running time.[6] To compute $T(n)$, the running time of INSERTION-SORT on an input of n values, we sum the products of the *cost* and *times* columns, obtaining

$$T(n) = c_1 n + c_2 (n - 1) + c_4 (n - 1) + c_5 \sum_{j=2}^{n} t_j + c_6 \sum_{j=2}^{n} (t_j - 1)$$

$$+ c_7 \sum_{j=2}^{n} (t_j - 1) + c_8 (n - 1) \, .$$

Even for inputs of a given size, an algorithm's running time may depend on *which* input of that size is given. For example, in INSERTION-SORT, the best case occurs if the array is already sorted. For each $j = 2, 3, \ldots, n$, we then find that $A[i] \le key$ in line 5 when i has its initial value of $j - 1$. Thus $t_j = 1$ for $j = 2, 3, \ldots, n$, and the best-case running time is

$$T(n) = c_1 n + c_2 (n - 1) + c_4 (n - 1) + c_5 (n - 1) + c_8 (n - 1)$$
$$= (c_1 + c_2 + c_4 + c_5 + c_8) n - (c_2 + c_4 + c_5 + c_8) \, .$$

We can express this running time as $an + b$ for *constants* a and b that depend on the statement costs c_i; it is thus a ***linear function*** of n.

If the array is in reverse sorted order—that is, in decreasing order—the worst case results. We must compare each element $A[j]$ with each element in the entire sorted subarray $A[1 .. j - 1]$, and so $t_j = j$ for $j = 2, 3, \ldots, n$. Noting that

---

[6]This characteristic does not necessarily hold for a resource such as memory. A statement that references m words of memory and is executed n times does not necessarily reference mn distinct words of memory.

$$\sum_{j=2}^{n} j = \frac{n(n+1)}{2} - 1$$

and

$$\sum_{j=2}^{n} (j-1) = \frac{n(n-1)}{2}$$

(see Appendix A for a review of how to solve these summations), we find that in the worst case, the running time of INSERTION-SORT is

$$
\begin{aligned}
T(n) &= c_1 n + c_2(n-1) + c_4(n-1) + c_5 \left(\frac{n(n+1)}{2} - 1 \right) \\
&\quad + c_6 \left(\frac{n(n-1)}{2} \right) + c_7 \left(\frac{n(n-1)}{2} \right) + c_8(n-1) \\
&= \left(\frac{c_5}{2} + \frac{c_6}{2} + \frac{c_7}{2} \right) n^2 + \left(c_1 + c_2 + c_4 + \frac{c_5}{2} - \frac{c_6}{2} - \frac{c_7}{2} + c_8 \right) n \\
&\quad - (c_2 + c_4 + c_5 + c_8) .
\end{aligned}
$$

We can express this worst-case running time as $an^2 + bn + c$ for constants a, b, and c that again depend on the statement costs c_i; it is thus a *quadratic function* of n.

Typically, as in insertion sort, the running time of an algorithm is fixed for a given input, although in later chapters we shall see some interesting "randomized" algorithms whose behavior can vary even for a fixed input.

Worst-case and average-case analysis

In our analysis of insertion sort, we looked at both the best case, in which the input array was already sorted, and the worst case, in which the input array was reverse sorted. For the remainder of this book, though, we shall usually concentrate on finding only the *worst-case running time*, that is, the longest running time for *any* input of size n. We give three reasons for this orientation.

- The worst-case running time of an algorithm gives us an upper bound on the running time for any input. Knowing it provides a guarantee that the algorithm will never take any longer. We need not make some educated guess about the running time and hope that it never gets much worse.

- For some algorithms, the worst case occurs fairly often. For example, in searching a database for a particular piece of information, the searching algorithm's worst case will often occur when the information is not present in the database. In some applications, searches for absent information may be frequent.

- The "average case" is often roughly as bad as the worst case. Suppose that we randomly choose n numbers and apply insertion sort. How long does it take to determine where in subarray $A[1 .. j - 1]$ to insert element $A[j]$? On average, half the elements in $A[1 .. j - 1]$ are less than $A[j]$, and half the elements are greater. On average, therefore, we check half of the subarray $A[1 .. j - 1]$, and so t_j is about $j/2$. The resulting average-case running time turns out to be a quadratic function of the input size, just like the worst-case running time.

In some particular cases, we shall be interested in the ***average-case*** running time of an algorithm; we shall see the technique of ***probabilistic analysis*** applied to various algorithms throughout this book. The scope of average-case analysis is limited, because it may not be apparent what constitutes an "average" input for a particular problem. Often, we shall assume that all inputs of a given size are equally likely. In practice, this assumption may be violated, but we can sometimes use a ***randomized algorithm***, which makes random choices, to allow a probabilistic analysis and yield an ***expected*** running time. We explore randomized algorithms more in Chapter 5 and in several other subsequent chapters.

Order of growth

We used some simplifying abstractions to ease our analysis of the INSERTION-SORT procedure. First, we ignored the actual cost of each statement, using the constants c_i to represent these costs. Then, we observed that even these constants give us more detail than we really need: we expressed the worst-case running time as $an^2 + bn + c$ for some constants a, b, and c that depend on the statement costs c_i. We thus ignored not only the actual statement costs, but also the abstract costs c_i.

We shall now make one more simplifying abstraction: it is the ***rate of growth***, or ***order of growth***, of the running time that really interests us. We therefore consider only the leading term of a formula (e.g., an^2), since the lower-order terms are relatively insignificant for large values of n. We also ignore the leading term's constant coefficient, since constant factors are less significant than the rate of growth in determining computational efficiency for large inputs. For insertion sort, when we ignore the lower-order terms and the leading term's constant coefficient, we are left with the factor of n^2 from the leading term. We write that insertion sort has a worst-case running time of $\Theta(n^2)$ (pronounced "theta of n-squared"). We shall use Θ-notation informally in this chapter, and we will define it precisely in Chapter 3.

We usually consider one algorithm to be more efficient than another if its worst-case running time has a lower order of growth. Due to constant factors and lower-order terms, an algorithm whose running time has a higher order of growth might take less time for small inputs than an algorithm whose running time has a lower order of growth. But for large enough inputs, a $\Theta(n^2)$ algorithm, for example, will run more quickly in the worst case than a $\Theta(n^3)$ algorithm.

Exercises

2.2-1
Express the function $n^3/1000 - 100n^2 - 100n + 3$ in terms of Θ-notation.

2.2-2
Consider sorting n numbers stored in array A by first finding the smallest element of A and exchanging it with the element in $A[1]$. Then find the second smallest element of A, and exchange it with $A[2]$. Continue in this manner for the first $n - 1$ elements of A. Write pseudocode for this algorithm, which is known as ***selection sort***. What loop invariant does this algorithm maintain? Why does it need to run for only the first $n - 1$ elements, rather than for all n elements? Give the best-case and worst-case running times of selection sort in Θ-notation.

2.2-3
Consider linear search again (see Exercise 2.1-3). How many elements of the input sequence need to be checked on the average, assuming that the element being searched for is equally likely to be any element in the array? How about in the worst case? What are the average-case and worst-case running times of linear search in Θ-notation? Justify your answers.

2.2-4
How can we modify almost any algorithm to have a good best-case running time?

2.3 Designing algorithms

We can choose from a wide range of algorithm design techniques. For insertion sort, we used an ***incremental*** approach: having sorted the subarray $A[1 .. j - 1]$, we inserted the single element $A[j]$ into its proper place, yielding the sorted subarray $A[1 .. j]$.

In this section, we examine an alternative design approach, known as "divide-and-conquer," which we shall explore in more detail in Chapter 4. We'll use divide-and-conquer to design a sorting algorithm whose worst-case running time is much less than that of insertion sort. One advantage of divide-and-conquer algorithms is that their running times are often easily determined using techniques that we will see in Chapter 4.

2.3.1   The divide-and-conquer approach

Many useful algorithms are *recursive* in structure: to solve a given problem, they call themselves recursively one or more times to deal with closely related subproblems. These algorithms typically follow a *divide-and-conquer* approach: they break the problem into several subproblems that are similar to the original problem but smaller in size, solve the subproblems recursively, and then combine these solutions to create a solution to the original problem.

The divide-and-conquer paradigm involves three steps at each level of the recursion:

Divide the problem into a number of subproblems that are smaller instances of the same problem.

Conquer the subproblems by solving them recursively. If the subproblem sizes are small enough, however, just solve the subproblems in a straightforward manner.

Combine the solutions to the subproblems into the solution for the original problem.

The *merge sort* algorithm closely follows the divide-and-conquer paradigm. Intuitively, it operates as follows.

Divide: Divide the n-element sequence to be sorted into two subsequences of $n/2$ elements each.

Conquer: Sort the two subsequences recursively using merge sort.

Combine: Merge the two sorted subsequences to produce the sorted answer.

The recursion "bottoms out" when the sequence to be sorted has length 1, in which case there is no work to be done, since every sequence of length 1 is already in sorted order.

The key operation of the merge sort algorithm is the merging of two sorted sequences in the "combine" step. We merge by calling an auxiliary procedure MERGE(A, p, q, r), where A is an array and p, q, and r are indices into the array such that $p \leq q < r$. The procedure assumes that the subarrays $A[p \mathinner{.\,.} q]$ and $A[q + 1 \mathinner{.\,.} r]$ are in sorted order. It *merges* them to form a single sorted subarray that replaces the current subarray $A[p \mathinner{.\,.} r]$.

Our MERGE procedure takes time $\Theta(n)$, where $n = r - p + 1$ is the total number of elements being merged, and it works as follows. Returning to our card-playing motif, suppose we have two piles of cards face up on a table. Each pile is sorted, with the smallest cards on top. We wish to merge the two piles into a single sorted output pile, which is to be face down on the table. Our basic step consists of choosing the smaller of the two cards on top of the face-up piles, removing it from its pile (which exposes a new top card), and placing this card face down onto the output pile. We repeat this step until one input pile is empty, at which time we just take the remaining input pile and place it face down onto the output pile. Computationally, each basic step takes constant time, since we are comparing just the two top cards. Since we perform at most n basic steps, merging takes $\Theta(n)$ time.

The following pseudocode implements the above idea, but with an additional twist that avoids having to check whether either pile is empty in each basic step. We place on the bottom of each pile a ***sentinel*** card, which contains a special value that we use to simplify our code. Here, we use ∞ as the sentinel value, so that whenever a card with ∞ is exposed, it cannot be the smaller card unless both piles have their sentinel cards exposed. But once that happens, all the nonsentinel cards have already been placed onto the output pile. Since we know in advance that exactly $r - p + 1$ cards will be placed onto the output pile, we can stop once we have performed that many basic steps.

MERGE(A, p, q, r)

```
 1   n₁ = q - p + 1
 2   n₂ = r - q
 3   let L[1 .. n₁ + 1] and R[1 .. n₂ + 1] be new arrays
 4   for i = 1 to n₁
 5       L[i] = A[p + i - 1]
 6   for j = 1 to n₂
 7       R[j] = A[q + j]
 8   L[n₁ + 1] = ∞
 9   R[n₂ + 1] = ∞
10   i = 1
11   j = 1
12   for k = p to r
13       if L[i] ≤ R[j]
14           A[k] = L[i]
15           i = i + 1
16       else A[k] = R[j]
17           j = j + 1
```

In detail, the MERGE procedure works as follows. Line 1 computes the length n_1 of the subarray $A[p \, . . \, q]$, and line 2 computes the length n_2 of the subarray $A[q + 1 \, . . \, r]$. We create arrays L and R ("left" and "right"), of lengths $n_1 + 1$ and $n_2 + 1$, respectively, in line 3; the extra position in each array will hold the sentinel. The **for** loop of lines 4–5 copies the subarray $A[p \, . . \, q]$ into $L[1 \, . . \, n_1]$, and the **for** loop of lines 6–7 copies the subarray $A[q + 1 \, . . \, r]$ into $R[1 \, . . \, n_2]$. Lines 8–9 put the sentinels at the ends of the arrays L and R. Lines 10–17, illus-

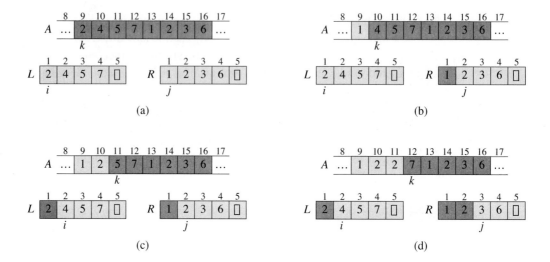

Figure 2.3 The operation of lines 10–17 in the call MERGE($A, 9, 12, 16$), when the subarray $A[9 \mathbin{..} 16]$ contains the sequence $\langle 2, 4, 5, 7, 1, 2, 3, 6 \rangle$. After copying and inserting sentinels, the array L contains $\langle 2, 4, 5, 7, \infty \rangle$, and the array R contains $\langle 1, 2, 3, 6, \infty \rangle$. Lightly shaded positions in A contain their final values, and lightly shaded positions in L and R contain values that have yet to be copied back into A. Taken together, the lightly shaded positions always comprise the values originally in $A[9 \mathbin{..} 16]$, along with the two sentinels. Heavily shaded positions in A contain values that will be copied over, and heavily shaded positions in L and R contain values that have already been copied back into A. **(a)–(h)** The arrays A, L, and R, and their respective indices k, i, and j prior to each iteration of the loop of lines 12–17.

trated in Figure 2.3, perform the $r - p + 1$ basic steps by maintaining the following loop invariant:

> At the start of each iteration of the **for** loop of lines 12–17, the subarray $A[p \mathbin{..} k - 1]$ contains the $k - p$ smallest elements of $L[1 \mathbin{..} n_1 + 1]$ and $R[1 \mathbin{..} n_2 + 1]$, in sorted order. Moreover, $L[i]$ and $R[j]$ are the smallest elements of their arrays that have not been copied back into A.

We must show that this loop invariant holds prior to the first iteration of the **for** loop of lines 12–17, that each iteration of the loop maintains the invariant, and that the invariant provides a useful property to show correctness when the loop terminates.

Initialization: Prior to the first iteration of the loop, we have $k = p$, so that the subarray $A[p \mathbin{..} k - 1]$ is empty. This empty subarray contains the $k - p = 0$ smallest elements of L and R, and since $i = j = 1$, both $L[i]$ and $R[j]$ are the smallest elements of their arrays that have not been copied back into A.

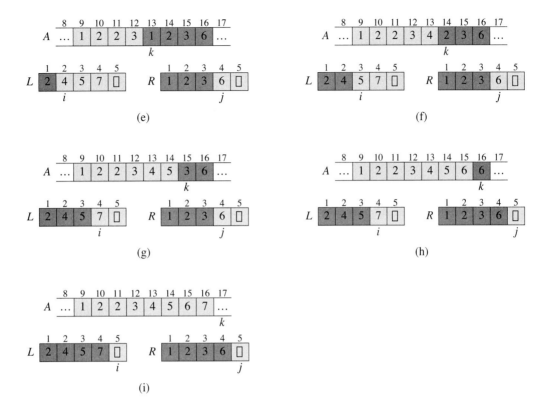

Figure 2.3, continued **(i)** The arrays and indices at termination. At this point, the subarray in $A[9 .. 16]$ is sorted, and the two sentinels in L and R are the only two elements in these arrays that have not been copied into A.

Maintenance: To see that each iteration maintains the loop invariant, let us first suppose that $L[i] \le R[j]$. Then $L[i]$ is the smallest element not yet copied back into A. Because $A[p .. k-1]$ contains the $k - p$ smallest elements, after line 14 copies $L[i]$ into $A[k]$, the subarray $A[p .. k]$ will contain the $k - p + 1$ smallest elements. Incrementing k (in the **for** loop update) and i (in line 15) reestablishes the loop invariant for the next iteration. If instead $L[i] > R[j]$, then lines 16–17 perform the appropriate action to maintain the loop invariant.

Termination: At termination, $k = r + 1$. By the loop invariant, the subarray $A[p .. k-1]$, which is $A[p .. r]$, contains the $k - p = r - p + 1$ smallest elements of $L[1 .. n_1 + 1]$ and $R[1 .. n_2 + 1]$, in sorted order. The arrays L and R together contain $n_1 + n_2 + 2 = r - p + 3$ elements. All but the two largest have been copied back into A, and these two largest elements are the sentinels.

To see that the MERGE procedure runs in $\Theta(n)$ time, where $n = r - p + 1$, observe that each of lines 1–3 and 8–11 takes constant time, the **for** loops of lines 4–7 take $\Theta(n_1 + n_2) = \Theta(n)$ time,[7] and there are n iterations of the **for** loop of lines 12–17, each of which takes constant time.

We can now use the MERGE procedure as a subroutine in the merge sort algorithm. The procedure MERGE-SORT(A, p, r) sorts the elements in the subarray $A[p . . r]$. If $p \geq r$, the subarray has at most one element and is therefore already sorted. Otherwise, the divide step simply computes an index q that partitions $A[p . . r]$ into two subarrays: $A[p . . q]$, containing $\lceil n/2 \rceil$ elements, and $A[q + 1 . . r]$, containing $\lfloor n/2 \rfloor$ elements.[8]

MERGE-SORT(A, p, r)

```
1   if p < r
2        q = ⌊(p + r)/2⌋
3        MERGE-SORT(A, p, q)
4        MERGE-SORT(A, q + 1, r)
5        MERGE(A, p, q, r)
```

To sort the entire sequence $A = \langle A[1], A[2], \ldots, A[n] \rangle$, we make the initial call MERGE-SORT$(A, 1, A.length)$, where once again $A.length = n$. Figure 2.4 illustrates the operation of the procedure bottom-up when n is a power of 2. The algorithm consists of merging pairs of 1-item sequences to form sorted sequences of length 2, merging pairs of sequences of length 2 to form sorted sequences of length 4, and so on, until two sequences of length $n/2$ are merged to form the final sorted sequence of length n.

2.3.2   Analyzing divide-and-conquer algorithms

When an algorithm contains a recursive call to itself, we can often describe its running time by a ***recurrence equation*** or ***recurrence***, which describes the overall running time on a problem of size n in terms of the running time on smaller inputs. We can then use mathematical tools to solve the recurrence and provide bounds on the performance of the algorithm.

---

[7]We shall see in Chapter 3 how to formally interpret equations containing Θ-notation.

[8]The expression $\lceil x \rceil$ denotes the least integer greater than or equal to x, and $\lfloor x \rfloor$ denotes the greatest integer less than or equal to x. These notations are defined in Chapter 3. The easiest way to verify that setting q to $\lfloor (p + r)/2 \rfloor$ yields subarrays $A[p . . q]$ and $A[q + 1 . . r]$ of sizes $\lceil n/2 \rceil$ and $\lfloor n/2 \rfloor$, respectively, is to examine the four cases that arise depending on whether each of p and r is odd or even.

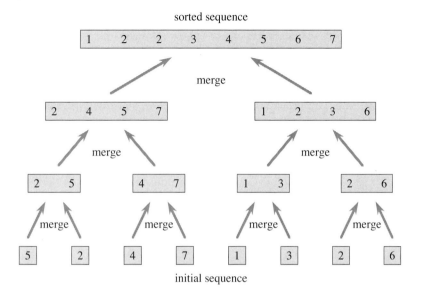

Figure 2.4   The operation of merge sort on the array $A = \langle 5, 2, 4, 7, 1, 3, 2, 6 \rangle$. The lengths of the sorted sequences being merged increase as the algorithm progresses from bottom to top.

A recurrence for the running time of a divide-and-conquer algorithm falls out from the three steps of the basic paradigm. As before, we let $T(n)$ be the running time on a problem of size n. If the problem size is small enough, say $n \leq c$ for some constant c, the straightforward solution takes constant time, which we write as $\Theta(1)$. Suppose that our division of the problem yields a subproblems, each of which is $1/b$ the size of the original. (For merge sort, both a and b are 2, but we shall see many divide-and-conquer algorithms in which $a \neq b$.) It takes time $T(n/b)$ to solve one subproblem of size n/b, and so it takes time $aT(n/b)$ to solve a of them. If we take $D(n)$ time to divide the problem into subproblems and $C(n)$ time to combine the solutions to the subproblems into the solution to the original problem, we get the recurrence

$$T(n) = \begin{cases} \Theta(1) & \text{if } n \leq c\,, \\ aT(n/b) + D(n) + C(n) & \text{otherwise}\,. \end{cases}$$

In Chapter 4, we shall see how to solve common recurrences of this form.

Analysis of merge sort

Although the pseudocode for MERGE-SORT works correctly when the number of elements is not even, our recurrence-based analysis is simplified if we assume that the original problem size is a power of 2. Each divide step then yields two subsequences of size exactly $n/2$. In Chapter 4, we shall see that this assumption does not affect the order of growth of the solution to the recurrence.

We reason as follows to set up the recurrence for $T(n)$, the worst-case running time of merge sort on n numbers. Merge sort on just one element takes constant time. When we have $n > 1$ elements, we break down the running time as follows.

Divide: The divide step just computes the middle of the subarray, which takes constant time. Thus, $D(n) = \Theta(1)$.

Conquer: We recursively solve two subproblems, each of size $n/2$, which contributes $2T(n/2)$ to the running time.

Combine: We have already noted that the MERGE procedure on an n-element subarray takes time $\Theta(n)$, and so $C(n) = \Theta(n)$.

When we add the functions $D(n)$ and $C(n)$ for the merge sort analysis, we are adding a function that is $\Theta(n)$ and a function that is $\Theta(1)$. This sum is a linear function of n, that is, $\Theta(n)$. Adding it to the $2T(n/2)$ term from the "conquer" step gives the recurrence for the worst-case running time $T(n)$ of merge sort:

$$T(n) = \begin{cases} \Theta(1) & \text{if } n = 1 , \\ 2T(n/2) + \Theta(n) & \text{if } n > 1 . \end{cases} \tag{2.1}$$

In Chapter 4, we shall see the "master theorem," which we can use to show that $T(n)$ is $\Theta(n \lg n)$, where $\lg n$ stands for $\log_2 n$. Because the logarithm function grows more slowly than any linear function, for large enough inputs, merge sort, with its $\Theta(n \lg n)$ running time, outperforms insertion sort, whose running time is $\Theta(n^2)$, in the worst case.

We do not need the master theorem to intuitively understand why the solution to the recurrence (2.1) is $T(n) = \Theta(n \lg n)$. Let us rewrite recurrence (2.1) as

$$T(n) = \begin{cases} c & \text{if } n = 1 , \\ 2T(n/2) + cn & \text{if } n > 1 , \end{cases} \tag{2.2}$$

where the constant c represents the time required to solve problems of size 1 as well as the time per array element of the divide and combine steps.[9]

---

[9]It is unlikely that the same constant exactly represents both the time to solve problems of size 1 and the time per array element of the divide and combine steps. We can get around this problem by letting c be the larger of these times and understanding that our recurrence gives an upper bound on the running time, or by letting c be the lesser of these times and understanding that our recurrence gives a lower bound on the running time. Both bounds are on the order of $n \lg n$ and, taken together, give a $\Theta(n \lg n)$ running time.

Figure 2.5 shows how we can solve recurrence (2.2). For convenience, we assume that n is an exact power of 2. Part (a) of the figure shows $T(n)$, which we expand in part (b) into an equivalent tree representing the recurrence. The cn term is the root (the cost incurred at the top level of recursion), and the two subtrees of the root are the two smaller recurrences $T(n/2)$. Part (c) shows this process carried one step further by expanding $T(n/2)$. The cost incurred at each of the two subnodes at the second level of recursion is $cn/2$. We continue expanding each node in the tree by breaking it into its constituent parts as determined by the recurrence, until the problem sizes get down to 1, each with a cost of c. Part (d) shows the resulting ***recursion tree***.

Next, we add the costs across each level of the tree. The top level has total cost cn, the next level down has total cost $c(n/2) + c(n/2) = cn$, the level after that has total cost $c(n/4) + c(n/4) + c(n/4) + c(n/4) = cn$, and so on. In general, the level i below the top has 2^i nodes, each contributing a cost of $c(n/2^i)$, so that the ith level below the top has total cost $2^i c(n/2^i) = cn$. The bottom level has n nodes, each contributing a cost of c, for a total cost of cn.

The total number of levels of the recursion tree in Figure 2.5 is $\lg n + 1$, where n is the number of leaves, corresponding to the input size. An informal inductive argument justifies this claim. The base case occurs when $n = 1$, in which case the tree has only one level. Since $\lg 1 = 0$, we have that $\lg n + 1$ gives the correct number of levels. Now assume as an inductive hypothesis that the number of levels of a recursion tree with 2^i leaves is $\lg 2^i + 1 = i + 1$ (since for any value of i, we have that $\lg 2^i = i$). Because we are assuming that the input size is a power of 2, the next input size to consider is 2^{i+1}. A tree with $n = 2^{i+1}$ leaves has one more level than a tree with 2^i leaves, and so the total number of levels is $(i + 1) + 1 = \lg 2^{i+1} + 1$.

To compute the total cost represented by the recurrence (2.2), we simply add up the costs of all the levels. The recursion tree has $\lg n + 1$ levels, each costing cn, for a total cost of $cn(\lg n + 1) = cn \lg n + cn$. Ignoring the low-order term and the constant c gives the desired result of $\Theta(n \lg n)$.

Exercises

2.3-1
Using Figure 2.4 as a model, illustrate the operation of merge sort on the array $A = \langle 3, 41, 52, 26, 38, 57, 9, 49 \rangle$.

2.3-2
Rewrite the MERGE procedure so that it does not use sentinels, instead stopping once either array L or R has had all its elements copied back to A and then copying the remainder of the other array back into A.

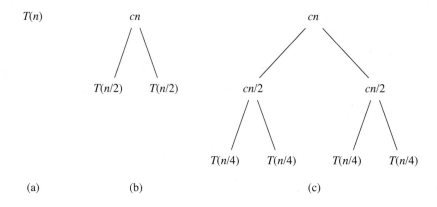

(a)   (b)   (c)

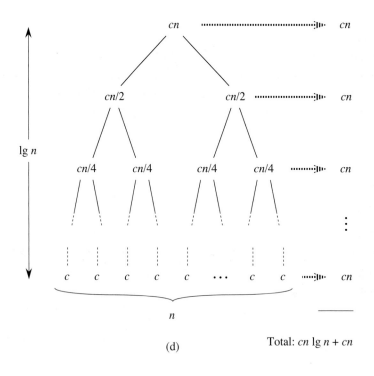

(d)   Total: $cn \lg n + cn$

Figure 2.5 How to construct a recursion tree for the recurrence $T(n) = 2T(n/2) + cn$. Part **(a)** shows $T(n)$, which progressively expands in **(b)–(d)** to form the recursion tree. The fully expanded tree in part (d) has $\lg n + 1$ levels (i.e., it has height $\lg n$, as indicated), and each level contributes a total cost of cn. The total cost, therefore, is $cn \lg n + cn$, which is $\Theta(n \lg n)$.

2.3-3
Use mathematical induction to show that when n is an exact power of 2, the solution of the recurrence

$$T(n) = \begin{cases} 2 & \text{if } n = 2, \\ 2T(n/2) + n & \text{if } n = 2^k, \text{ for } k > 1 \end{cases}$$

is $T(n) = n \lg n$.

2.3-4
We can express insertion sort as a recursive procedure as follows. In order to sort $A[1 .. n]$, we recursively sort $A[1 .. n-1]$ and then insert $A[n]$ into the sorted array $A[1 .. n-1]$. Write a recurrence for the worst-case running time of this recursive version of insertion sort.

2.3-5
Referring back to the searching problem (see Exercise 2.1-3), observe that if the sequence A is sorted, we can check the midpoint of the sequence against v and eliminate half of the sequence from further consideration. The ***binary search*** algorithm repeats this procedure, halving the size of the remaining portion of the sequence each time. Write pseudocode, either iterative or recursive, for binary search. Argue that the worst-case running time of binary search is $\Theta(\lg n)$.

2.3-6
Observe that the **while** loop of lines 5–7 of the INSERTION-SORT procedure in Section 2.1 uses a linear search to scan (backward) through the sorted subarray $A[1 .. j-1]$. Can we use a binary search (see Exercise 2.3-5) instead to improve the overall worst-case running time of insertion sort to $\Theta(n \lg n)$?

2.3-7 ⋆
Describe a $\Theta(n \lg n)$-time algorithm that, given a set S of n integers and another integer x, determines whether or not there exist two elements in S whose sum is exactly x.

Problems

2-1 *Insertion sort on small arrays in merge sort*
Although merge sort runs in $\Theta(n \lg n)$ worst-case time and insertion sort runs in $\Theta(n^2)$ worst-case time, the constant factors in insertion sort can make it faster in practice for small problem sizes on many machines. Thus, it makes sense to ***coarsen*** the leaves of the recursion by using insertion sort within merge sort when

subproblems become sufficiently small. Consider a modification to merge sort in which n/k sublists of length k are sorted using insertion sort and then merged using the standard merging mechanism, where k is a value to be determined.

a. Show that insertion sort can sort the n/k sublists, each of length k, in $\Theta(nk)$ worst-case time.

b. Show how to merge the sublists in $\Theta(n \lg(n/k))$ worst-case time.

c. Given that the modified algorithm runs in $\Theta(nk + n \lg(n/k))$ worst-case time, what is the largest value of k as a function of n for which the modified algorithm has the same running time as standard merge sort, in terms of Θ-notation?

d. How should we choose k in practice?

2-2   *Correctness of bubblesort*

Bubblesort is a popular, but inefficient, sorting algorithm. It works by repeatedly swapping adjacent elements that are out of order.

BUBBLESORT(A)

```
1  for i = 1 to A.length − 1
2      for j = A.length downto i + 1
3          if A[j] < A[j − 1]
4              exchange A[j] with A[j − 1]
```

a. Let A' denote the output of BUBBLESORT(A). To prove that BUBBLESORT is correct, we need to prove that it terminates and that

$$A'[1] \le A'[2] \le \cdots \le A'[n] , \tag{2.3}$$

where $n = A.length$. In order to show that BUBBLESORT actually sorts, what else do we need to prove?

The next two parts will prove inequality (2.3).

b. State precisely a loop invariant for the **for** loop in lines 2–4, and prove that this loop invariant holds. Your proof should use the structure of the loop invariant proof presented in this chapter.

c. Using the termination condition of the loop invariant proved in part (b), state a loop invariant for the **for** loop in lines 1–4 that will allow you to prove inequality (2.3). Your proof should use the structure of the loop invariant proof presented in this chapter.

d. What is the worst-case running time of bubblesort? How does it compare to the running time of insertion sort?

2-3 Correctness of Horner's rule

The following code fragment implements Horner's rule for evaluating a polynomial

$$P(x) = \sum_{k=0}^{n} a_k x^k$$
$$= a_0 + x(a_1 + x(a_2 + \cdots + x(a_{n-1} + x a_n) \cdots)),$$

given the coefficients $a_0, a_1, \ldots, a_n$ and a value for x:

```
1  y = 0
2  for i = n downto 0
3      y = a_i + x · y
```

a. In terms of Θ-notation, what is the running time of this code fragment for Horner's rule?

b. Write pseudocode to implement the naive polynomial-evaluation algorithm that computes each term of the polynomial from scratch. What is the running time of this algorithm? How does it compare to Horner's rule?

c. Consider the following loop invariant:

> At the start of each iteration of the **for** loop of lines 2–3,
> $$y = \sum_{k=0}^{n-(i+1)} a_{k+i+1} x^k .$$

Interpret a summation with no terms as equaling 0. Following the structure of the loop invariant proof presented in this chapter, use this loop invariant to show that, at termination, $y = \sum_{k=0}^{n} a_k x^k$.

d. Conclude by arguing that the given code fragment correctly evaluates a polynomial characterized by the coefficients $a_0, a_1, \ldots, a_n$.

2-4 Inversions

Let $A[1 .. n]$ be an array of n distinct numbers. If $i < j$ and $A[i] > A[j]$, then the pair (i, j) is called an ***inversion*** of A.

a. List the five inversions of the array $\langle 2, 3, 8, 6, 1 \rangle$.

b. What array with elements from the set $\{1, 2, \ldots, n\}$ has the most inversions? How many does it have?

c. What is the relationship between the running time of insertion sort and the number of inversions in the input array? Justify your answer.

d. Give an algorithm that determines the number of inversions in any permutation on n elements in $\Theta(n \lg n)$ worst-case time. (*Hint:* Modify merge sort.)

Chapter notes

In 1968, Knuth published the first of three volumes with the general title *The Art of Computer Programming* [209, 210, 211]. The first volume ushered in the modern study of computer algorithms with a focus on the analysis of running time, and the full series remains an engaging and worthwhile reference for many of the topics presented here. According to Knuth, the word "algorithm" is derived from the name "al-Khowârizmî," a ninth-century Persian mathematician.

Aho, Hopcroft, and Ullman [5] advocated the asymptotic analysis of algorithms—using notations that Chapter 3 introduces, including Θ-notation—as a means of comparing relative performance. They also popularized the use of recurrence relations to describe the running times of recursive algorithms.

Knuth [211] provides an encyclopedic treatment of many sorting algorithms. His comparison of sorting algorithms (page 381) includes exact step-counting analyses, like the one we performed here for insertion sort. Knuth's discussion of insertion sort encompasses several variations of the algorithm. The most important of these is Shell's sort, introduced by D. L. Shell, which uses insertion sort on periodic subsequences of the input to produce a faster sorting algorithm.

Merge sort is also described by Knuth. He mentions that a mechanical collator capable of merging two decks of punched cards in a single pass was invented in 1938. J. von Neumann, one of the pioneers of computer science, apparently wrote a program for merge sort on the EDVAC computer in 1945.

The early history of proving programs correct is described by Gries [153], who credits P. Naur with the first article in this field. Gries attributes loop invariants to R. W. Floyd. The textbook by Mitchell [256] describes more recent progress in proving programs correct.

3 Growth of Functions

The order of growth of the running time of an algorithm, defined in Chapter 2, gives a simple characterization of the algorithm's efficiency and also allows us to compare the relative performance of alternative algorithms. Once the input size n becomes large enough, merge sort, with its $\Theta(n \lg n)$ worst-case running time, beats insertion sort, whose worst-case running time is $\Theta(n^2)$. Although we can sometimes determine the exact running time of an algorithm, as we did for insertion sort in Chapter 2, the extra precision is not usually worth the effort of computing it. For large enough inputs, the multiplicative constants and lower-order terms of an exact running time are dominated by the effects of the input size itself.

When we look at input sizes large enough to make only the order of growth of the running time relevant, we are studying the *asymptotic* efficiency of algorithms. That is, we are concerned with how the running time of an algorithm increases with the size of the input *in the limit*, as the size of the input increases without bound. Usually, an algorithm that is asymptotically more efficient will be the best choice for all but very small inputs.

This chapter gives several standard methods for simplifying the asymptotic analysis of algorithms. The next section begins by defining several types of "asymptotic notation," of which we have already seen an example in Θ-notation. We then present several notational conventions used throughout this book, and finally we review the behavior of functions that commonly arise in the analysis of algorithms.

3.1 Asymptotic notation

The notations we use to describe the asymptotic running time of an algorithm are defined in terms of functions whose domains are the set of natural numbers $\mathbb{N} = \{0, 1, 2, \ldots\}$. Such notations are convenient for describing the worst-case running-time function $T(n)$, which usually is defined only on integer input sizes. We sometimes find it convenient, however, to *abuse* asymptotic notation in a variety of ways. For example, we might extend the notation to the domain of real numbers or, alternatively, restrict it to a subset of the natural numbers. We should make sure, however, to understand the precise meaning of the notation so that when we abuse, we do not *misuse* it. This section defines the basic asymptotic notations and also introduces some common abuses.

Asymptotic notation, functions, and running times

We will use asymptotic notation primarily to describe the running times of algorithms, as when we wrote that insertion sort's worst-case running time is $\Theta(n^2)$. Asymptotic notation actually applies to functions, however. Recall that we characterized insertion sort's worst-case running time as $an^2 + bn + c$, for some constants a, b, and c. By writing that insertion sort's running time is $\Theta(n^2)$, we abstracted away some details of this function. Because asymptotic notation applies to functions, what we were writing as $\Theta(n^2)$ was the function $an^2 + bn + c$, which in that case happened to characterize the worst-case running time of insertion sort.

In this book, the functions to which we apply asymptotic notation will usually characterize the running times of algorithms. But asymptotic notation can apply to functions that characterize some other aspect of algorithms (the amount of space they use, for example), or even to functions that have nothing whatsoever to do with algorithms.

Even when we use asymptotic notation to apply to the running time of an algorithm, we need to understand *which* running time we mean. Sometimes we are interested in the worst-case running time. Often, however, we wish to characterize the running time no matter what the input. In other words, we often wish to make a blanket statement that covers all inputs, not just the worst case. We shall see asymptotic notations that are well suited to characterizing running times no matter what the input.

Θ-notation

In Chapter 2, we found that the worst-case running time of insertion sort is $T(n) = \Theta(n^2)$. Let us define what this notation means. For a given function $g(n)$, we denote by $\Theta(g(n))$ the *set of functions*

$$\Theta(g(n)) = \{f(n) : \text{there exist positive constants } c_1, c_2, \text{ and } n_0 \text{ such that} \\ 0 \le c_1 g(n) \le f(n) \le c_2 g(n) \text{ for all } n \ge n_0\} \text{ .[1]}$$

---

[1] Within set notation, a colon means "such that."

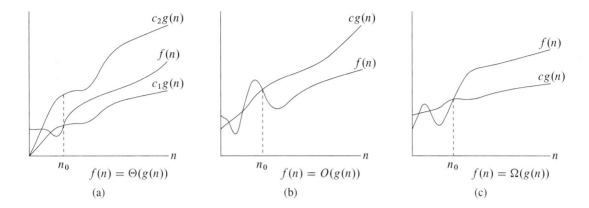

Figure 3.1 Graphic examples of the Θ, O, and Ω notations. In each part, the value of n_0 shown is the minimum possible value; any greater value would also work. **(a)** Θ-notation bounds a function to within constant factors. We write $f(n) = \Theta(g(n))$ if there exist positive constants n_0, c_1, and c_2 such that at and to the right of n_0, the value of $f(n)$ always lies between $c_1 g(n)$ and $c_2 g(n)$ inclusive. **(b)** O-notation gives an upper bound for a function to within a constant factor. We write $f(n) = O(g(n))$ if there are positive constants n_0 and c such that at and to the right of n_0, the value of $f(n)$ always lies on or below $cg(n)$. **(c)** Ω-notation gives a lower bound for a function to within a constant factor. We write $f(n) = \Omega(g(n))$ if there are positive constants n_0 and c such that at and to the right of n_0, the value of $f(n)$ always lies on or above $cg(n)$.

A function $f(n)$ belongs to the set $\Theta(g(n))$ if there exist positive constants c_1 and c_2 such that it can be "sandwiched" between $c_1 g(n)$ and $c_2 g(n)$, for sufficiently large n. Because $\Theta(g(n))$ is a set, we could write "$f(n) \in \Theta(g(n))$" to indicate that $f(n)$ is a member of $\Theta(g(n))$. Instead, we will usually write "$f(n) = \Theta(g(n))$" to express the same notion. You might be confused because we abuse equality in this way, but we shall see later in this section that doing so has its advantages.

Figure 3.1(a) gives an intuitive picture of functions $f(n)$ and $g(n)$, where $f(n) = \Theta(g(n))$. For all values of n at and to the right of n_0, the value of $f(n)$ lies at or above $c_1 g(n)$ and at or below $c_2 g(n)$. In other words, for all $n \geq n_0$, the function $f(n)$ is equal to $g(n)$ to within a constant factor. We say that $g(n)$ is an *asymptotically tight bound* for $f(n)$.

The definition of $\Theta(g(n))$ requires that every member $f(n) \in \Theta(g(n))$ be *asymptotically nonnegative*, that is, that $f(n)$ be nonnegative whenever n is sufficiently large. (An *asymptotically positive* function is one that is positive for all sufficiently large n.) Consequently, the function $g(n)$ itself must be asymptotically nonnegative, or else the set $\Theta(g(n))$ is empty. We shall therefore assume that every function used within Θ-notation is asymptotically nonnegative. This assumption holds for the other asymptotic notations defined in this chapter as well.

In Chapter 2, we introduced an informal notion of Θ-notation that amounted to throwing away lower-order terms and ignoring the leading coefficient of the highest-order term. Let us briefly justify this intuition by using the formal definition to show that $\frac{1}{2}n^2 - 3n = \Theta(n^2)$. To do so, we must determine positive constants c_1, c_2, and n_0 such that

$$c_1 n^2 \le \frac{1}{2}n^2 - 3n \le c_2 n^2$$

for all $n \ge n_0$. Dividing by n^2 yields

$$c_1 \le \frac{1}{2} - \frac{3}{n} \le c_2 \,.$$

We can make the right-hand inequality hold for any value of $n \ge 1$ by choosing any constant $c_2 \ge 1/2$. Likewise, we can make the left-hand inequality hold for any value of $n \ge 7$ by choosing any constant $c_1 \le 1/14$. Thus, by choosing $c_1 = 1/14$, $c_2 = 1/2$, and $n_0 = 7$, we can verify that $\frac{1}{2}n^2 - 3n = \Theta(n^2)$. Certainly, other choices for the constants exist, but the important thing is that *some* choice exists. Note that these constants depend on the function $\frac{1}{2}n^2 - 3n$; a different function belonging to $\Theta(n^2)$ would usually require different constants.

We can also use the formal definition to verify that $6n^3 \ne \Theta(n^2)$. Suppose for the purpose of contradiction that c_2 and n_0 exist such that $6n^3 \le c_2 n^2$ for all $n \ge n_0$. But then dividing by n^2 yields $n \le c_2/6$, which cannot possibly hold for arbitrarily large n, since c_2 is constant.

Intuitively, the lower-order terms of an asymptotically positive function can be ignored in determining asymptotically tight bounds because they are insignificant for large n. When n is large, even a tiny fraction of the highest-order term suffices to dominate the lower-order terms. Thus, setting c_1 to a value that is slightly smaller than the coefficient of the highest-order term and setting c_2 to a value that is slightly larger permits the inequalities in the definition of Θ-notation to be satisfied. The coefficient of the highest-order term can likewise be ignored, since it only changes c_1 and c_2 by a constant factor equal to the coefficient.

As an example, consider any quadratic function $f(n) = an^2 + bn + c$, where a, b, and c are constants and $a > 0$. Throwing away the lower-order terms and ignoring the constant yields $f(n) = \Theta(n^2)$. Formally, to show the same thing, we take the constants $c_1 = a/4$, $c_2 = 7a/4$, and $n_0 = 2 \cdot \max(|b|/a, \sqrt{|c|/a})$. You may verify that $0 \le c_1 n^2 \le an^2 + bn + c \le c_2 n^2$ for all $n \ge n_0$. In general, for any polynomial $p(n) = \sum_{i=0}^{d} a_i n^i$, where the a_i are constants and $a_d > 0$, we have $p(n) = \Theta(n^d)$ (see Problem 3-1).

Since any constant is a degree-0 polynomial, we can express any constant function as $\Theta(n^0)$, or $\Theta(1)$. This latter notation is a minor abuse, however, because the expression does not indicate what variable is tending to infinity.[2] We shall often use the notation $\Theta(1)$ to mean either a constant or a constant function with respect to some variable.

O-notation

The Θ-notation asymptotically bounds a function from above and below. When we have only an ***asymptotic upper bound***, we use O-notation. For a given function $g(n)$, we denote by $O(g(n))$ (pronounced "big-oh of g of n" or sometimes just "oh of g of n") the set of functions

$$O(g(n)) = \{f(n) : \text{there exist positive constants } c \text{ and } n_0 \text{ such that}$$
$$0 \le f(n) \le cg(n) \text{ for all } n \ge n_0\} .$$

We use O-notation to give an upper bound on a function, to within a constant factor. Figure 3.1(b) shows the intuition behind O-notation. For all values n at and to the right of n_0, the value of the function $f(n)$ is on or below $cg(n)$.

We write $f(n) = O(g(n))$ to indicate that a function $f(n)$ is a member of the set $O(g(n))$. Note that $f(n) = \Theta(g(n))$ implies $f(n) = O(g(n))$, since Θ-notation is a stronger notion than O-notation. Written set-theoretically, we have $\Theta(g(n)) \subseteq O(g(n))$. Thus, our proof that any quadratic function $an^2 + bn + c$, where $a > 0$, is in $\Theta(n^2)$ also shows that any such quadratic function is in $O(n^2)$. What may be more surprising is that when $a > 0$, any *linear* function $an + b$ is in $O(n^2)$, which is easily verified by taking $c = a + |b|$ and $n_0 = \max(1, -b/a)$.

If you have seen O-notation before, you might find it strange that we should write, for example, $n = O(n^2)$. In the literature, we sometimes find O-notation informally describing asymptotically tight bounds, that is, what we have defined using Θ-notation. In this book, however, when we write $f(n) = O(g(n))$, we are merely claiming that some constant multiple of $g(n)$ is an asymptotic upper bound on $f(n)$, with no claim about how tight an upper bound it is. Distinguishing asymptotic upper bounds from asymptotically tight bounds is standard in the algorithms literature.

Using O-notation, we can often describe the running time of an algorithm merely by inspecting the algorithm's overall structure. For example, the doubly nested loop structure of the insertion sort algorithm from Chapter 2 immediately yields an $O(n^2)$ upper bound on the worst-case running time: the cost of each iteration of the inner loop is bounded from above by $O(1)$ (constant), the indices i

---

[2]The real problem is that our ordinary notation for functions does not distinguish functions from values. In λ-calculus, the parameters to a function are clearly specified: the function n^2 could be written as $\lambda n.n^2$, or even $\lambda r.r^2$. Adopting a more rigorous notation, however, would complicate algebraic manipulations, and so we choose to tolerate the abuse.

and j are both at most n, and the inner loop is executed at most once for each of the n^2 pairs of values for i and j.

Since O-notation describes an upper bound, when we use it to bound the worst-case running time of an algorithm, we have a bound on the running time of the algorithm on every input—the blanket statement we discussed earlier. Thus, the $O(n^2)$ bound on worst-case running time of insertion sort also applies to its running time on every input. The $\Theta(n^2)$ bound on the worst-case running time of insertion sort, however, does not imply a $\Theta(n^2)$ bound on the running time of insertion sort on *every* input. For example, we saw in Chapter 2 that when the input is already sorted, insertion sort runs in $\Theta(n)$ time.

Technically, it is an abuse to say that the running time of insertion sort is $O(n^2)$, since for a given n, the actual running time varies, depending on the particular input of size n. When we say "the running time is $O(n^2)$," we mean that there is a function $f(n)$ that is $O(n^2)$ such that for any value of n, no matter what particular input of size n is chosen, the running time on that input is bounded from above by the value $f(n)$. Equivalently, we mean that the worst-case running time is $O(n^2)$.

Ω-notation

Just as O-notation provides an asymptotic *upper* bound on a function, Ω-notation provides an ***asymptotic lower bound***. For a given function $g(n)$, we denote by $\Omega(g(n))$ (pronounced "big-omega of g of n" or sometimes just "omega of g of n") the set of functions

$$\Omega(g(n)) = \{f(n) : \text{there exist positive constants } c \text{ and } n_0 \text{ such that}$$
$$0 \leq cg(n) \leq f(n) \text{ for all } n \geq n_0\} .$$

Figure 3.1(c) shows the intuition behind Ω-notation. For all values n at or to the right of n_0, the value of $f(n)$ is on or above $cg(n)$.

From the definitions of the asymptotic notations we have seen thus far, it is easy to prove the following important theorem (see Exercise 3.1-5).

Theorem 3.1
For any two functions $f(n)$ and $g(n)$, we have $f(n) = \Theta(g(n))$ if and only if $f(n) = O(g(n))$ and $f(n) = \Omega(g(n))$.   ∎

As an example of the application of this theorem, our proof that $an^2 + bn + c = \Theta(n^2)$ for any constants a, b, and c, where $a > 0$, immediately implies that $an^2 + bn + c = \Omega(n^2)$ and $an^2 + bn + c = O(n^2)$. In practice, rather than using Theorem 3.1 to obtain asymptotic upper and lower bounds from asymptotically tight bounds, as we did for this example, we usually use it to prove asymptotically tight bounds from asymptotic upper and lower bounds.

When we say that the *running time* (no modifier) of an algorithm is $\Omega(g(n))$, we mean that *no matter what particular input of size n is chosen for each value of n*, the running time on that input is at least a constant times $g(n)$, for sufficiently large n. Equivalently, we are giving a lower bound on the best-case running time of an algorithm. For example, the best-case running time of insertion sort is $\Omega(n)$, which implies that the running time of insertion sort is $\Omega(n)$.

The running time of insertion sort therefore belongs to both $\Omega(n)$ and $O(n^2)$, since it falls anywhere between a linear function of n and a quadratic function of n. Moreover, these bounds are asymptotically as tight as possible: for instance, the running time of insertion sort is not $\Omega(n^2)$, since there exists an input for which insertion sort runs in $\Theta(n)$ time (e.g., when the input is already sorted). It is not contradictory, however, to say that the *worst-case* running time of insertion sort is $\Omega(n^2)$, since there exists an input that causes the algorithm to take $\Omega(n^2)$ time.

Asymptotic notation in equations and inequalities

We have already seen how asymptotic notation can be used within mathematical formulas. For example, in introducing O-notation, we wrote "$n = O(n^2)$." We might also write $2n^2 + 3n + 1 = 2n^2 + \Theta(n)$. How do we interpret such formulas?

When the asymptotic notation stands alone (that is, not within a larger formula) on the right-hand side of an equation (or inequality), as in $n = O(n^2)$, we have already defined the equal sign to mean set membership: $n \in O(n^2)$. In general, however, when asymptotic notation appears in a formula, we interpret it as standing for some anonymous function that we do not care to name. For example, the formula $2n^2 + 3n + 1 = 2n^2 + \Theta(n)$ means that $2n^2 + 3n + 1 = 2n^2 + f(n)$, where $f(n)$ is some function in the set $\Theta(n)$. In this case, we let $f(n) = 3n + 1$, which indeed is in $\Theta(n)$.

Using asymptotic notation in this manner can help eliminate inessential detail and clutter in an equation. For example, in Chapter 2 we expressed the worst-case running time of merge sort as the recurrence

$$T(n) = 2T(n/2) + \Theta(n) \ .$$

If we are interested only in the asymptotic behavior of $T(n)$, there is no point in specifying all the lower-order terms exactly; they are all understood to be included in the anonymous function denoted by the term $\Theta(n)$.

The number of anonymous functions in an expression is understood to be equal to the number of times the asymptotic notation appears. For example, in the expression

$$\sum_{i=1}^{n} O(i) \ ,$$

there is only a single anonymous function (a function of i). This expression is thus *not* the same as $O(1) + O(2) + \cdots + O(n)$, which doesn't really have a clean interpretation.

In some cases, asymptotic notation appears on the left-hand side of an equation, as in

$$2n^2 + \Theta(n) = \Theta(n^2) \, .$$

We interpret such equations using the following rule: *No matter how the anonymous functions are chosen on the left of the equal sign, there is a way to choose the anonymous functions on the right of the equal sign to make the equation valid.* Thus, our example means that for *any* function $f(n) \in \Theta(n)$, there is *some* function $g(n) \in \Theta(n^2)$ such that $2n^2 + f(n) = g(n)$ for all n. In other words, the right-hand side of an equation provides a coarser level of detail than the left-hand side.

We can chain together a number of such relationships, as in

$$\begin{aligned} 2n^2 + 3n + 1 &= 2n^2 + \Theta(n) \\ &= \Theta(n^2) \, . \end{aligned}$$

We can interpret each equation separately by the rules above. The first equation says that there is *some* function $f(n) \in \Theta(n)$ such that $2n^2 + 3n + 1 = 2n^2 + f(n)$ for all n. The second equation says that for *any* function $g(n) \in \Theta(n)$ (such as the $f(n)$ just mentioned), there is *some* function $h(n) \in \Theta(n^2)$ such that $2n^2 + g(n) = h(n)$ for all n. Note that this interpretation implies that $2n^2 + 3n + 1 = \Theta(n^2)$, which is what the chaining of equations intuitively gives us.

o-notation

The asymptotic upper bound provided by O-notation may or may not be asymptotically tight. The bound $2n^2 = O(n^2)$ is asymptotically tight, but the bound $2n = O(n^2)$ is not. We use o-notation to denote an upper bound that is not asymptotically tight. We formally define $o(g(n))$ ("little-oh of g of n") as the set

$$o(g(n)) = \{f(n) : \text{ for any positive constant } c > 0, \text{ there exists a constant} \\ n_0 > 0 \text{ such that } 0 \le f(n) < cg(n) \text{ for all } n \ge n_0\} \, .$$

For example, $2n = o(n^2)$, but $2n^2 \ne o(n^2)$.

The definitions of O-notation and o-notation are similar. The main difference is that in $f(n) = O(g(n))$, the bound $0 \le f(n) \le cg(n)$ holds for *some* constant $c > 0$, but in $f(n) = o(g(n))$, the bound $0 \le f(n) < cg(n)$ holds for *all* constants $c > 0$. Intuitively, in o-notation, the function $f(n)$ becomes insignificant relative to $g(n)$ as n approaches infinity; that is,

$$\lim_{n \to \infty} \frac{f(n)}{g(n)} = 0 \,. \tag{3.1}$$

Some authors use this limit as a definition of the o-notation; the definition in this book also restricts the anonymous functions to be asymptotically nonnegative.

ω-notation

By analogy, ω-notation is to Ω-notation as o-notation is to O-notation. We use ω-notation to denote a lower bound that is not asymptotically tight. One way to define it is by

$f(n) \in \omega(g(n))$ if and only if $g(n) \in o(f(n))$.

Formally, however, we define $\omega(g(n))$ ("little-omega of g of n") as the set

$\omega(g(n)) = \{f(n) :$ for any positive constant $c > 0$, there exists a constant $n_0 > 0$ such that $0 \le cg(n) < f(n)$ for all $n \ge n_0\}$.

For example, $n^2/2 = \omega(n)$, but $n^2/2 \ne \omega(n^2)$. The relation $f(n) = \omega(g(n))$ implies that

$$\lim_{n \to \infty} \frac{f(n)}{g(n)} = \infty \,,$$

if the limit exists. That is, $f(n)$ becomes arbitrarily large relative to $g(n)$ as n approaches infinity.

Comparing functions

Many of the relational properties of real numbers apply to asymptotic comparisons as well. For the following, assume that $f(n)$ and $g(n)$ are asymptotically positive.

Transitivity:

$$f(n) = \Theta(g(n)) \text{ and } g(n) = \Theta(h(n)) \quad \text{imply} \quad f(n) = \Theta(h(n)) \,,$$
$$f(n) = O(g(n)) \text{ and } g(n) = O(h(n)) \quad \text{imply} \quad f(n) = O(h(n)) \,,$$
$$f(n) = \Omega(g(n)) \text{ and } g(n) = \Omega(h(n)) \quad \text{imply} \quad f(n) = \Omega(h(n)) \,,$$
$$f(n) = o(g(n)) \text{ and } g(n) = o(h(n)) \quad \text{imply} \quad f(n) = o(h(n)) \,,$$
$$f(n) = \omega(g(n)) \text{ and } g(n) = \omega(h(n)) \quad \text{imply} \quad f(n) = \omega(h(n)) \,.$$

Reflexivity:

$$f(n) = \Theta(f(n)) \,,$$
$$f(n) = O(f(n)) \,,$$
$$f(n) = \Omega(f(n)) \,.$$

Symmetry:

$$f(n) = \Theta(g(n)) \text{ if and only if } g(n) = \Theta(f(n)) .$$

Transpose symmetry:

$$f(n) = O(g(n)) \text{ if and only if } g(n) = \Omega(f(n)) ,$$
$$f(n) = o(g(n)) \text{ if and only if } g(n) = \omega(f(n)) .$$

Because these properties hold for asymptotic notations, we can draw an analogy between the asymptotic comparison of two functions f and g and the comparison of two real numbers a and b:

$$
\begin{array}{lll}
f(n) = O(g(n)) & \text{is like} & a \le b , \\
f(n) = \Omega(g(n)) & \text{is like} & a \ge b , \\
f(n) = \Theta(g(n)) & \text{is like} & a = b , \\
f(n) = o(g(n)) & \text{is like} & a < b , \\
f(n) = \omega(g(n)) & \text{is like} & a > b .
\end{array}
$$

We say that $f(n)$ is **asymptotically smaller** than $g(n)$ if $f(n) = o(g(n))$, and $f(n)$ is **asymptotically larger** than $g(n)$ if $f(n) = \omega(g(n))$.

One property of real numbers, however, does not carry over to asymptotic notation:

Trichotomy: For any two real numbers a and b, exactly one of the following must hold: $a < b$, $a = b$, or $a > b$.

Although any two real numbers can be compared, not all functions are asymptotically comparable. That is, for two functions $f(n)$ and $g(n)$, it may be the case that neither $f(n) = O(g(n))$ nor $f(n) = \Omega(g(n))$ holds. For example, we cannot compare the functions n and $n^{1+\sin n}$ using asymptotic notation, since the value of the exponent in $n^{1+\sin n}$ oscillates between 0 and 2, taking on all values in between.

Exercises

3.1-1
Let $f(n)$ and $g(n)$ be asymptotically nonnegative functions. Using the basic definition of Θ-notation, prove that $\max(f(n), g(n)) = \Theta(f(n) + g(n))$.

3.1-2
Show that for any real constants a and b, where $b > 0$,

$$(n + a)^b = \Theta(n^b) . \tag{3.2}$$

3.1-3
Explain why the statement, "The running time of algorithm A is at least $O(n^2)$," is meaningless.

3.1-4
Is $2^{n+1} = O(2^n)$? Is $2^{2n} = O(2^n)$?

3.1-5
Prove Theorem 3.1.

3.1-6
Prove that the running time of an algorithm is $\Theta(g(n))$ if and only if its worst-case running time is $O(g(n))$ and its best-case running time is $\Omega(g(n))$.

3.1-7
Prove that $o(g(n)) \cap \omega(g(n))$ is the empty set.

3.1-8
We can extend our notation to the case of two parameters n and m that can go to infinity independently at different rates. For a given function $g(n, m)$, we denote by $O(g(n, m))$ the set of functions

$$O(g(n, m)) = \{f(n, m) : \text{there exist positive constants } c, n_0, \text{ and } m_0$$
$$\text{such that } 0 \le f(n, m) \le cg(n, m)$$
$$\text{for all } n \ge n_0 \text{ or } m \ge m_0\} .$$

Give corresponding definitions for $\Omega(g(n, m))$ and $\Theta(g(n, m))$.

3.2   Standard notations and common functions

This section reviews some standard mathematical functions and notations and explores the relationships among them. It also illustrates the use of the asymptotic notations.

Monotonicity

A function $f(n)$ is ***monotonically increasing*** if $m \le n$ implies $f(m) \le f(n)$. Similarly, it is ***monotonically decreasing*** if $m \le n$ implies $f(m) \ge f(n)$. A function $f(n)$ is ***strictly increasing*** if $m < n$ implies $f(m) < f(n)$ and ***strictly decreasing*** if $m < n$ implies $f(m) > f(n)$.

Floors and ceilings

For any real number x, we denote the greatest integer less than or equal to x by $\lfloor x \rfloor$ (read "the floor of x") and the least integer greater than or equal to x by $\lceil x \rceil$ (read "the ceiling of x"). For all real x,

$$x - 1 < \lfloor x \rfloor \le x \le \lceil x \rceil < x + 1 . \tag{3.3}$$

For any integer n,

$$\lceil n/2 \rceil + \lfloor n/2 \rfloor = n ,$$

and for any real number $x \ge 0$ and integers $a, b > 0$,

$$\left\lceil \frac{\lceil x/a \rceil}{b} \right\rceil = \left\lceil \frac{x}{ab} \right\rceil , \tag{3.4}$$

$$\left\lfloor \frac{\lfloor x/a \rfloor}{b} \right\rfloor = \left\lfloor \frac{x}{ab} \right\rfloor , \tag{3.5}$$

$$\left\lceil \frac{a}{b} \right\rceil \le \frac{a + (b - 1)}{b} , \tag{3.6}$$

$$\left\lfloor \frac{a}{b} \right\rfloor \ge \frac{a - (b - 1)}{b} . \tag{3.7}$$

The floor function $f(x) = \lfloor x \rfloor$ is monotonically increasing, as is the ceiling function $f(x) = \lceil x \rceil$.

Modular arithmetic

For any integer a and any positive integer n, the value $a \bmod n$ is the **remainder** (or **residue**) of the quotient a/n:

$$a \bmod n = a - n \lfloor a/n \rfloor . \tag{3.8}$$

It follows that

$$0 \le a \bmod n < n . \tag{3.9}$$

Given a well-defined notion of the remainder of one integer when divided by another, it is convenient to provide special notation to indicate equality of remainders. If $(a \bmod n) = (b \bmod n)$, we write $a \equiv b \pmod{n}$ and say that a is **equivalent** to b, modulo n. In other words, $a \equiv b \pmod{n}$ if a and b have the same remainder when divided by n. Equivalently, $a \equiv b \pmod{n}$ if and only if n is a divisor of $b - a$. We write $a \not\equiv b \pmod{n}$ if a is not equivalent to b, modulo n.

Polynomials

Given a nonnegative integer d, a ***polynomial in n of degree d*** is a function $p(n)$ of the form

$$p(n) = \sum_{i=0}^{d} a_i n^i ,$$

where the constants $a_0, a_1, \ldots, a_d$ are the ***coefficients*** of the polynomial and $a_d \neq 0$. A polynomial is asymptotically positive if and only if $a_d > 0$. For an asymptotically positive polynomial $p(n)$ of degree d, we have $p(n) = \Theta(n^d)$. For any real constant $a \geq 0$, the function n^a is monotonically increasing, and for any real constant $a \leq 0$, the function n^a is monotonically decreasing. We say that a function $f(n)$ is ***polynomially bounded*** if $f(n) = O(n^k)$ for some constant k.

Exponentials

For all real $a > 0$, m, and n, we have the following identities:

$$
\begin{aligned}
a^0 &= 1, \\
a^1 &= a, \\
a^{-1} &= 1/a, \\
(a^m)^n &= a^{mn}, \\
(a^m)^n &= (a^n)^m, \\
a^m a^n &= a^{m+n}.
\end{aligned}
$$

For all n and $a \geq 1$, the function a^n is monotonically increasing in n. When convenient, we shall assume $0^0 = 1$.

We can relate the rates of growth of polynomials and exponentials by the following fact. For all real constants a and b such that $a > 1$,

$$\lim_{n \to \infty} \frac{n^b}{a^n} = 0 , \tag{3.10}$$

from which we can conclude that

$$n^b = o(a^n) .$$

Thus, any exponential function with a base strictly greater than 1 grows faster than any polynomial function.

Using e to denote $2.71828\ldots$, the base of the natural logarithm function, we have for all real x,

$$e^x = 1 + x + \frac{x^2}{2!} + \frac{x^3}{3!} + \cdots = \sum_{i=0}^{\infty} \frac{x^i}{i!} , \tag{3.11}$$

where "!" denotes the factorial function defined later in this section. For all real x, we have the inequality

$$e^x \geq 1 + x ,\tag{3.12}$$

where equality holds only when $x = 0$. When $|x| \leq 1$, we have the approximation

$$1 + x \leq e^x \leq 1 + x + x^2 .\tag{3.13}$$

When $x \to 0$, the approximation of e^x by $1 + x$ is quite good:

$$e^x = 1 + x + \Theta(x^2) .$$

(In this equation, the asymptotic notation is used to describe the limiting behavior as $x \to 0$ rather than as $x \to \infty$.) We have for all x,

$$\lim_{n \to \infty} \left(1 + \frac{x}{n}\right)^n = e^x .\tag{3.14}$$

Logarithms

We shall use the following notations:

$$
\begin{aligned}
\lg n &= \log_2 n && \text{(binary logarithm)} , \\
\ln n &= \log_e n && \text{(natural logarithm)} , \\
\lg^k n &= (\lg n)^k && \text{(exponentiation)} , \\
\lg \lg n &= \lg(\lg n) && \text{(composition)} .
\end{aligned}
$$

An important notational convention we shall adopt is that *logarithm functions will apply only to the next term in the formula*, so that $\lg n + k$ will mean $(\lg n) + k$ and not $\lg(n + k)$. If we hold $b > 1$ constant, then for $n > 0$, the function $\log_b n$ is strictly increasing.

For all real $a > 0$, $b > 0$, $c > 0$, and n,

$$
\begin{aligned}
a &= b^{\log_b a} , \\
\log_c(ab) &= \log_c a + \log_c b , \\
\log_b a^n &= n \log_b a , \\
\log_b a &= \frac{\log_c a}{\log_c b} , \tag{3.15}\\
\log_b(1/a) &= -\log_b a , \\
\log_b a &= \frac{1}{\log_a b} , \\
a^{\log_b c} &= c^{\log_b a} , \tag{3.16}
\end{aligned}
$$

where, in each equation above, logarithm bases are not 1.

By equation (3.15), changing the base of a logarithm from one constant to another changes the value of the logarithm by only a constant factor, and so we shall often use the notation "$\lg n$" when we don't care about constant factors, such as in O-notation. Computer scientists find 2 to be the most natural base for logarithms because so many algorithms and data structures involve splitting a problem into two parts.

There is a simple series expansion for $\ln(1 + x)$ when $|x| < 1$:

$$\ln(1 + x) = x - \frac{x^2}{2} + \frac{x^3}{3} - \frac{x^4}{4} + \frac{x^5}{5} - \cdots .$$

We also have the following inequalities for $x > -1$:

$$\frac{x}{1 + x} \leq \ln(1 + x) \leq x , \tag{3.17}$$

where equality holds only for $x = 0$.

We say that a function $f(n)$ is **polylogarithmically bounded** if $f(n) = O(\lg^k n)$ for some constant k. We can relate the growth of polynomials and polylogarithms by substituting $\lg n$ for n and 2^a for a in equation (3.10), yielding

$$\lim_{n \to \infty} \frac{\lg^b n}{(2^a)^{\lg n}} = \lim_{n \to \infty} \frac{\lg^b n}{n^a} = 0 .$$

From this limit, we can conclude that

$$\lg^b n = o(n^a)$$

for any constant $a > 0$. Thus, any positive polynomial function grows faster than any polylogarithmic function.

Factorials

The notation $n!$ (read "n factorial") is defined for integers $n \geq 0$ as

$$n! = \begin{cases} 1 & \text{if } n = 0 , \\ n \cdot (n - 1)! & \text{if } n > 0 . \end{cases}$$

Thus, $n! = 1 \cdot 2 \cdot 3 \cdots n$.

A weak upper bound on the factorial function is $n! \leq n^n$, since each of the n terms in the factorial product is at most n. **Stirling's approximation**,

$$n! = \sqrt{2\pi n} \left(\frac{n}{e}\right)^n \left(1 + \Theta\left(\frac{1}{n}\right)\right) , \tag{3.18}$$

where e is the base of the natural logarithm, gives us a tighter upper bound, and a lower bound as well. As Exercise 3.2-3 asks you to prove,

$$n! = o(n^n) \,,$$
$$n! = \omega(2^n) \,,$$
$$\lg(n!) = \Theta(n \lg n) \,, \tag{3.19}$$

where Stirling's approximation is helpful in proving equation (3.19). The following equation also holds for all $n \geq 1$:

$$n! = \sqrt{2\pi n} \left(\frac{n}{e}\right)^n e^{\alpha_n} \tag{3.20}$$

where

$$\frac{1}{12n + 1} < \alpha_n < \frac{1}{12n} \,. \tag{3.21}$$

Functional iteration

We use the notation $f^{(i)}(n)$ to denote the function $f(n)$ iteratively applied i times to an initial value of n. Formally, let $f(n)$ be a function over the reals. For non-negative integers i, we recursively define

$$f^{(i)}(n) = \begin{cases} n & \text{if } i = 0 \,, \\ f(f^{(i-1)}(n)) & \text{if } i > 0 \,. \end{cases}$$

For example, if $f(n) = 2n$, then $f^{(i)}(n) = 2^i n$.

The iterated logarithm function

We use the notation $\lg^* n$ (read "log star of n") to denote the iterated logarithm, defined as follows. Let $\lg^{(i)} n$ be as defined above, with $f(n) = \lg n$. Because the logarithm of a nonpositive number is undefined, $\lg^{(i)} n$ is defined only if $\lg^{(i-1)} n > 0$. Be sure to distinguish $\lg^{(i)} n$ (the logarithm function applied i times in succession, starting with argument n) from $\lg^i n$ (the logarithm of n raised to the ith power). Then we define the iterated logarithm function as

$$\lg^* n = \min \left\{ i \geq 0 : \lg^{(i)} n \leq 1 \right\} \,.$$

The iterated logarithm is a *very* slowly growing function:

$$
\begin{aligned}
\lg^* 2 &= 1 \,, \\
\lg^* 4 &= 2 \,, \\
\lg^* 16 &= 3 \,, \\
\lg^* 65536 &= 4 \,, \\
\lg^* (2^{65536}) &= 5 \,.
\end{aligned}
$$

Since the number of atoms in the observable universe is estimated to be about 10^{80}, which is much less than 2^{65536}, we rarely encounter an input size n such that $\lg^* n > 5$.

Fibonacci numbers

We define the **Fibonacci numbers** by the following recurrence:

$$
\begin{aligned}
F_0 &= 0, \\
F_1 &= 1, \\
F_i &= F_{i-1} + F_{i-2} \qquad \text{for } i \geq 2.
\end{aligned}
\tag{3.22}
$$

Thus, each Fibonacci number is the sum of the two previous ones, yielding the sequence

$$0, 1, 1, 2, 3, 5, 8, 13, 21, 34, 55, \ldots .$$

Fibonacci numbers are related to the **golden ratio** ϕ and to its conjugate $\widehat{\phi}$, which are the two roots of the equation

$$x^2 = x + 1 \tag{3.23}$$

and are given by the following formulas (see Exercise 3.2-6):

$$
\begin{aligned}
\phi &= \frac{1 + \sqrt{5}}{2} \\
&= 1.61803\ldots, \\
\widehat{\phi} &= \frac{1 - \sqrt{5}}{2} \\
&= -.61803\ldots .
\end{aligned}
\tag{3.24}
$$

Specifically, we have

$$F_i = \frac{\phi^i - \widehat{\phi}^i}{\sqrt{5}},$$

which we can prove by induction (Exercise 3.2-7). Since $\left|\widehat{\phi}\right| < 1$, we have

$$
\begin{aligned}
\frac{\left|\widehat{\phi}^i\right|}{\sqrt{5}} &< \frac{1}{\sqrt{5}} \\
&< \frac{1}{2},
\end{aligned}
$$

which implies that

$$F_i = \left\lfloor \frac{\phi^i}{\sqrt{5}} + \frac{1}{2} \right\rfloor , \tag{3.25}$$

which is to say that the ith Fibonacci number F_i is equal to $\phi^i / \sqrt{5}$ rounded to the nearest integer. Thus, Fibonacci numbers grow exponentially.

Exercises

3.2-1
Show that if $f(n)$ and $g(n)$ are monotonically increasing functions, then so are the functions $f(n) + g(n)$ and $f(g(n))$, and if $f(n)$ and $g(n)$ are in addition nonnegative, then $f(n) \cdot g(n)$ is monotonically increasing.

3.2-2
Prove equation (3.16).

3.2-3
Prove equation (3.19). Also prove that $n! = \omega(2^n)$ and $n! = o(n^n)$.

3.2-4 ★
Is the function $\lceil \lg n \rceil !$ polynomially bounded? Is the function $\lceil \lg \lg n \rceil !$ polynomially bounded?

3.2-5 ★
Which is asymptotically larger: $\lg(\lg^* n)$ or $\lg^*(\lg n)$?

3.2-6
Show that the golden ratio ϕ and its conjugate $\widehat{\phi}$ both satisfy the equation $x^2 = x + 1$.

3.2-7
Prove by induction that the ith Fibonacci number satisfies the equality

$$F_i = \frac{\phi^i - \widehat{\phi}^i}{\sqrt{5}} ,$$

where ϕ is the golden ratio and $\widehat{\phi}$ is its conjugate.

3.2-8
Show that $k \ln k = \Theta(n)$ implies $k = \Theta(n/\ln n)$.

Problems

3-1 Asymptotic behavior of polynomials
Let

$$p(n) = \sum_{i=0}^{d} a_i n^i \,,$$

where $a_d > 0$, be a degree-d polynomial in n, and let k be a constant. Use the definitions of the asymptotic notations to prove the following properties.

a. If $k \geq d$, then $p(n) = O(n^k)$.

b. If $k \leq d$, then $p(n) = \Omega(n^k)$.

c. If $k = d$, then $p(n) = \Theta(n^k)$.

d. If $k > d$, then $p(n) = o(n^k)$.

e. If $k < d$, then $p(n) = \omega(n^k)$.

3-2 Relative asymptotic growths
Indicate, for each pair of expressions (A, B) in the table below, whether A is O, o, Ω, ω, or Θ of B. Assume that $k \geq 1$, $\epsilon > 0$, and $c > 1$ are constants. Your answer should be in the form of the table with "yes" or "no" written in each box.

	A	B	O	o	Ω	ω	Θ
a.	$\lg^k n$	n^ϵ					
b.	n^k	c^n					
c.	$\sqrt{n}$	$n^{\sin n}$					
d.	2^n	$2^{n/2}$					
e.	$n^{\lg c}$	$c^{\lg n}$					
f.	$\lg(n!)$	$\lg(n^n)$					

3-3 Ordering by asymptotic growth rates
a. Rank the following functions by order of growth; that is, find an arrangement $g_1, g_2, \ldots, g_{30}$ of the functions satisfying $g_1 = \Omega(g_2)$, $g_2 = \Omega(g_3)$, $\ldots$, $g_{29} = \Omega(g_{30})$. Partition your list into equivalence classes such that functions $f(n)$ and $g(n)$ are in the same class if and only if $f(n) = \Theta(g(n))$.

$$\lg(\lg^* n) \quad 2^{\lg^* n} \quad (\sqrt{2})^{\lg n} \quad n^2 \quad n! \quad (\lg n)!$$

$$(\tfrac{3}{2})^n \quad n^3 \quad \lg^2 n \quad \lg(n!) \quad 2^{2^n} \quad n^{1/\lg n}$$

$$\ln \ln n \quad \lg^* n \quad n \cdot 2^n \quad n^{\lg \lg n} \quad \ln n \quad 1$$

$$2^{\lg n} \quad (\lg n)^{\lg n} \quad e^n \quad 4^{\lg n} \quad (n+1)! \quad \sqrt{\lg n}$$

$$\lg^*(\lg n) \quad 2^{\sqrt{2 \lg n}} \quad n \quad 2^n \quad n \lg n \quad 2^{2^{n+1}}$$

b. Give an example of a single nonnegative function $f(n)$ such that for all functions $g_i(n)$ in part (a), $f(n)$ is neither $O(g_i(n))$ nor $\Omega(g_i(n))$.

3-4   *Asymptotic notation properties*

Let $f(n)$ and $g(n)$ be asymptotically positive functions. Prove or disprove each of the following conjectures.

a. $f(n) = O(g(n))$ implies $g(n) = O(f(n))$.

b. $f(n) + g(n) = \Theta(\min(f(n), g(n)))$.

c. $f(n) = O(g(n))$ implies $\lg(f(n)) = O(\lg(g(n)))$, where $\lg(g(n)) \geq 1$ and $f(n) \geq 1$ for all sufficiently large n.

d. $f(n) = O(g(n))$ implies $2^{f(n)} = O\left(2^{g(n)}\right)$.

e. $f(n) = O\left((f(n))^2\right)$.

f. $f(n) = O(g(n))$ implies $g(n) = \Omega(f(n))$.

g. $f(n) = \Theta(f(n/2))$.

h. $f(n) + o(f(n)) = \Theta(f(n))$.

3-5   *Variations on O and Ω*

Some authors define Ω in a slightly different way than we do; let's use $\overset{\infty}{\Omega}$ (read "omega infinity") for this alternative definition. We say that $f(n) = \overset{\infty}{\Omega}(g(n))$ if there exists a positive constant c such that $f(n) \geq cg(n) \geq 0$ for infinitely many integers n.

a. Show that for any two functions $f(n)$ and $g(n)$ that are asymptotically nonnegative, either $f(n) = O(g(n))$ or $f(n) = \overset{\infty}{\Omega}(g(n))$ or both, whereas this is not true if we use Ω in place of $\overset{\infty}{\Omega}$.

b. Describe the potential advantages and disadvantages of using $\overset{\infty}{\Omega}$ instead of Ω to characterize the running times of programs.

Some authors also define O in a slightly different manner; let's use O' for the alternative definition. We say that $f(n) = O'(g(n))$ if and only if $|f(n)| = O(g(n))$.

c. What happens to each direction of the "if and only if" in Theorem 3.1 if we substitute O' for O but still use Ω?

Some authors define $\widetilde{O}$ (read "soft-oh") to mean O with logarithmic factors ignored:

$$\widetilde{O}(g(n)) = \{f(n) : \text{ there exist positive constants } c, k, \text{ and } n_0 \text{ such that}$$
$$0 \leq f(n) \leq cg(n)\lg^k(n) \text{ for all } n \geq n_0\} .$$

d. Define $\widetilde{\Omega}$ and $\widetilde{\Theta}$ in a similar manner. Prove the corresponding analog to Theorem 3.1.

3-6 *Iterated functions*

We can apply the iteration operator $*$ used in the $\lg^*$ function to any monotonically increasing function $f(n)$ over the reals. For a given constant $c \in \mathbb{R}$, we define the iterated function f_c^* by

$$f_c^*(n) = \min\{i \geq 0 : f^{(i)}(n) \leq c\} ,$$

which need not be well defined in all cases. In other words, the quantity $f_c^*(n)$ is the number of iterated applications of the function f required to reduce its argument down to c or less.

For each of the following functions $f(n)$ and constants c, give as tight a bound as possible on $f_c^*(n)$.

	$f(n)$	c	$f_c^*(n)$
a.	$n - 1$	0	
b.	$\lg n$	1	
c.	$n/2$	1	
d.	$n/2$	2	
e.	$\sqrt{n}$	2	
f.	$\sqrt{n}$	1	
g.	$n^{1/3}$	2	
h.	$n/\lg n$	2	

Chapter notes

Knuth [209] traces the origin of the O-notation to a number-theory text by P. Bach-mann in 1892. The o-notation was invented by E. Landau in 1909 for his discussion of the distribution of prime numbers. The Ω and Θ notations were advocated by Knuth [213] to correct the popular, but technically sloppy, practice in the literature of using O-notation for both upper and lower bounds. Many people continue to use the O-notation where the Θ-notation is more technically precise. Further dis-cussion of the history and development of asymptotic notations appears in works by Knuth [209, 213] and Brassard and Bratley [54].

Not all authors define the asymptotic notations in the same way, although the various definitions agree in most common situations. Some of the alternative def-initions encompass functions that are not asymptotically nonnegative, as long as their absolute values are appropriately bounded.

Equation (3.20) is due to Robbins [297]. Other properties of elementary math-ematical functions can be found in any good mathematical reference, such as Abramowitz and Stegun [1] or Zwillinger [362], or in a calculus book, such as Apostol [18] or Thomas et al. [334]. Knuth [209] and Graham, Knuth, and Patash-nik [152] contain a wealth of material on discrete mathematics as used in computer science.

4 Divide-and-Conquer

In Section 2.3.1, we saw how merge sort serves as an example of the divide-and-conquer paradigm. Recall that in divide-and-conquer, we solve a problem recursively, applying three steps at each level of the recursion:

Divide the problem into a number of subproblems that are smaller instances of the same problem.

Conquer the subproblems by solving them recursively. If the subproblem sizes are small enough, however, just solve the subproblems in a straightforward manner.

Combine the solutions to the subproblems into the solution for the original problem.

When the subproblems are large enough to solve recursively, we call that the ***recursive case***. Once the subproblems become small enough that we no longer recurse, we say that the recursion "bottoms out" and that we have gotten down to the ***base case***. Sometimes, in addition to subproblems that are smaller instances of the same problem, we have to solve subproblems that are not quite the same as the original problem. We consider solving such subproblems as part of the combine step.

In this chapter, we shall see more algorithms based on divide-and-conquer. The first one solves the maximum-subarray problem: it takes as input an array of numbers, and it determines the contiguous subarray whose values have the greatest sum. Then we shall see two divide-and-conquer algorithms for multiplying $n \times n$ matrices. One runs in $\Theta(n^3)$ time, which is no better than the straightforward method of multiplying square matrices. But the other, Strassen's algorithm, runs in $O(n^{2.81})$ time, which beats the straightforward method asymptotically.

Recurrences

Recurrences go hand in hand with the divide-and-conquer paradigm, because they give us a natural way to characterize the running times of divide-and-conquer algorithms. A ***recurrence*** is an equation or inequality that describes a function in terms of its value on smaller inputs. For example, in Section 2.3.2 we described the worst-case running time $T(n)$ of the MERGE-SORT procedure by the recurrence

$$T(n) = \begin{cases} \Theta(1) & \text{if } n = 1, \\ 2T(n/2) + \Theta(n) & \text{if } n > 1, \end{cases} \tag{4.1}$$

whose solution we claimed to be $T(n) = \Theta(n \lg n)$.

Recurrences can take many forms. For example, a recursive algorithm might divide subproblems into unequal sizes, such as a 2/3-to-1/3 split. If the divide and combine steps take linear time, such an algorithm would give rise to the recurrence $T(n) = T(2n/3) + T(n/3) + \Theta(n)$.

Subproblems are not necessarily constrained to being a constant fraction of the original problem size. For example, a recursive version of linear search (see Exercise 2.1-3) would create just one subproblem containing only one element fewer than the original problem. Each recursive call would take constant time plus the time for the recursive calls it makes, yielding the recurrence $T(n) = T(n - 1) + \Theta(1)$.

This chapter offers three methods for solving recurrences—that is, for obtaining asymptotic "Θ" or "O" bounds on the solution:

- In the **substitution method**, we guess a bound and then use mathematical induction to prove our guess correct.

- The **recursion-tree method** converts the recurrence into a tree whose nodes represent the costs incurred at various levels of the recursion. We use techniques for bounding summations to solve the recurrence.

- The **master method** provides bounds for recurrences of the form

  $$T(n) = aT(n/b) + f(n), \tag{4.2}$$

  where $a \geq 1$, $b > 1$, and $f(n)$ is a given function. Such recurrences arise frequently. A recurrence of the form in equation (4.2) characterizes a divide-and-conquer algorithm that creates a subproblems, each of which is $1/b$ the size of the original problem, and in which the divide and combine steps together take $f(n)$ time.

  To use the master method, you will need to memorize three cases, but once you do that, you will easily be able to determine asymptotic bounds for many simple recurrences. We will use the master method to determine the running times of the divide-and-conquer algorithms for the maximum-subarray problem and for matrix multiplication, as well as for other algorithms based on divide-and-conquer elsewhere in this book.

Occasionally, we shall see recurrences that are not equalities but rather inequalities, such as $T(n) \leq 2T(n/2) + \Theta(n)$. Because such a recurrence states only an upper bound on $T(n)$, we will couch its solution using O-notation rather than Θ-notation. Similarly, if the inequality were reversed to $T(n) \geq 2T(n/2) + \Theta(n)$, then because the recurrence gives only a lower bound on $T(n)$, we would use Ω-notation in its solution.

Technicalities in recurrences

In practice, we neglect certain technical details when we state and solve recurrences. For example, if we call MERGE-SORT on n elements when n is odd, we end up with subproblems of size $\lfloor n/2 \rfloor$ and $\lceil n/2 \rceil$. Neither size is actually $n/2$, because $n/2$ is not an integer when n is odd. Technically, the recurrence describing the worst-case running time of MERGE-SORT is really

$$T(n) = \begin{cases} \Theta(1) & \text{if } n = 1, \\ T(\lceil n/2 \rceil) + T(\lfloor n/2 \rfloor) + \Theta(n) & \text{if } n > 1. \end{cases} \tag{4.3}$$

Boundary conditions represent another class of details that we typically ignore. Since the running time of an algorithm on a constant-sized input is a constant, the recurrences that arise from the running times of algorithms generally have $T(n) = \Theta(1)$ for sufficiently small n. Consequently, for convenience, we shall generally omit statements of the boundary conditions of recurrences and assume that $T(n)$ is constant for small n. For example, we normally state recurrence (4.1) as

$$T(n) = 2T(n/2) + \Theta(n), \tag{4.4}$$

without explicitly giving values for small n. The reason is that although changing the value of $T(1)$ changes the exact solution to the recurrence, the solution typically doesn't change by more than a constant factor, and so the order of growth is unchanged.

When we state and solve recurrences, we often omit floors, ceilings, and boundary conditions. We forge ahead without these details and later determine whether or not they matter. They usually do not, but you should know when they do. Experience helps, and so do some theorems stating that these details do not affect the asymptotic bounds of many recurrences characterizing divide-and-conquer algorithms (see Theorem 4.1). In this chapter, however, we shall address some of these details and illustrate the fine points of recurrence solution methods.

4.1   The maximum-subarray problem

Suppose that you have been offered the opportunity to invest in the Volatile Chemical Corporation. Like the chemicals the company produces, the stock price of the Volatile Chemical Corporation is rather volatile. You are allowed to buy one unit of stock only one time and then sell it at a later date, buying and selling after the close of trading for the day. To compensate for this restriction, you are allowed to learn what the price of the stock will be in the future. Your goal is to maximize your profit. Figure 4.1 shows the price of the stock over a 17-day period. You may buy the stock at any one time, starting after day 0, when the price is \$100 per share. Of course, you would want to "buy low, sell high"—buy at the lowest possible price and later on sell at the highest possible price—to maximize your profit. Unfortunately, you might not be able to buy at the lowest price and then sell at the highest price within a given period. In Figure 4.1, the lowest price occurs after day 7, which occurs after the highest price, after day 1.

You might think that you can always maximize profit by either buying at the lowest price or selling at the highest price. For example, in Figure 4.1, we would maximize profit by buying at the lowest price, after day 7. If this strategy always worked, then it would be easy to determine how to maximize profit: find the highest and lowest prices, and then work left from the highest price to find the lowest prior price, work right from the lowest price to find the highest later price, and take the pair with the greater difference. Figure 4.2 shows a simple counterexample,

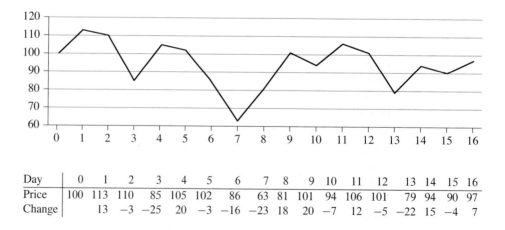

Day	0	1	2	3	4	5	6	7	8	9	10	11	12	13	14	15	16
Price	100	113	110	85	105	102	86	63	81	101	94	106	101	79	94	90	97
Change		13	−3	−25	20	−3	−16	−23	18	20	−7	12	−5	−22	15	−4	7

Figure 4.1   Information about the price of stock in the Volatile Chemical Corporation after the close of trading over a period of 17 days. The horizontal axis of the chart indicates the day, and the vertical axis shows the price. The bottom row of the table gives the change in price from the previous day.

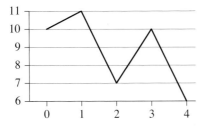

Day	0	1	2	3	4
Price	10	11	7	10	6
Change		1	−4	3	−4

Figure 4.2   An example showing that the maximum profit does not always start at the lowest price or end at the highest price. Again, the horizontal axis indicates the day, and the vertical axis shows the price. Here, the maximum profit of $3 per share would be earned by buying after day 2 and selling after day 3. The price of $7 after day 2 is not the lowest price overall, and the price of $10 after day 3 is not the highest price overall.

demonstrating that the maximum profit sometimes comes neither by buying at the lowest price nor by selling at the highest price.

A brute-force solution

We can easily devise a brute-force solution to this problem: just try every possible pair of buy and sell dates in which the buy date precedes the sell date. A period of n days has $\binom{n}{2}$ such pairs of dates. Since $\binom{n}{2}$ is $\Theta(n^2)$, and the best we can hope for is to evaluate each pair of dates in constant time, this approach would take $\Omega(n^2)$ time. Can we do better?

A transformation

In order to design an algorithm with an $o(n^2)$ running time, we will look at the input in a slightly different way. We want to find a sequence of days over which the net change from the first day to the last is maximum. Instead of looking at the daily prices, let us instead consider the daily change in price, where the change on day i is the difference between the prices after day $i - 1$ and after day i. The table in Figure 4.1 shows these daily changes in the bottom row. If we treat this row as an array A, shown in Figure 4.3, we now want to find the nonempty, contiguous subarray of A whose values have the largest sum. We call this contiguous subarray the **maximum subarray**. For example, in the array of Figure 4.3, the maximum subarray of $A[1 .. 16]$ is $A[8 .. 11]$, with the sum 43. Thus, you would want to buy the stock just before day 8 (that is, after day 7) and sell it after day 11, earning a profit of $43 per share.

   At first glance, this transformation does not help. We still need to check $\binom{n-1}{2} = \Theta(n^2)$ subarrays for a period of n days. Exercise 4.1-2 asks you to show

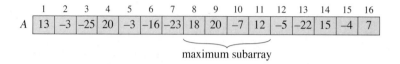

maximum subarray

Figure 4.3   The change in stock prices as a maximum-subarray problem.   Here, the subarray $A[8 .. 11]$, with sum 43, has the greatest sum of any contiguous subarray of array A.

that although computing the cost of one subarray might take time proportional to the length of the subarray, when computing all $\Theta(n^2)$ subarray sums, we can organize the computation so that each subarray sum takes $O(1)$ time, given the values of previously computed subarray sums, so that the brute-force solution takes $\Theta(n^2)$ time.

So let us seek a more efficient solution to the maximum-subarray problem. When doing so, we will usually speak of "a" maximum subarray rather than "the" maximum subarray, since there could be more than one subarray that achieves the maximum sum.

The maximum-subarray problem is interesting only when the array contains some negative numbers. If all the array entries were nonnegative, then the maximum-subarray problem would present no challenge, since the entire array would give the greatest sum.

A solution using divide-and-conquer

Let's think about how we might solve the maximum-subarray problem using the divide-and-conquer technique. Suppose we want to find a maximum subarray of the subarray $A[low .. high]$. Divide-and-conquer suggests that we divide the subarray into two subarrays of as equal size as possible. That is, we find the midpoint, say mid, of the subarray, and consider the subarrays $A[low .. mid]$ and $A[mid + 1 .. high]$. As Figure 4.4(a) shows, any contiguous subarray $A[i .. j]$ of $A[low .. high]$ must lie in exactly one of the following places:

- entirely in the subarray $A[low .. mid]$, so that $low \leq i \leq j \leq mid$,

- entirely in the subarray $A[mid + 1 .. high]$, so that $mid < i \leq j \leq high$, or

- crossing the midpoint, so that $low \leq i \leq mid < j \leq high$.

Therefore, a maximum subarray of $A[low .. high]$ must lie in exactly one of these places. In fact, a maximum subarray of $A[low .. high]$ must have the greatest sum over all subarrays entirely in $A[low .. mid]$, entirely in $A[mid + 1 .. high]$, or crossing the midpoint. We can find maximum subarrays of $A[low .. mid]$ and $A[mid+1 .. high]$ recursively, because these two subproblems are smaller instances of the problem of finding a maximum subarray. Thus, all that is left to do is find a

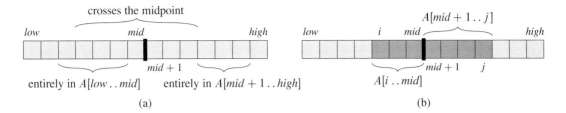

Figure 4.4   **(a)** Possible locations of subarrays of $A[low .. high]$: entirely in $A[low .. mid]$, entirely in $A[mid + 1 .. high]$, or crossing the midpoint *mid*. **(b)** Any subarray of $A[low .. high]$ crossing the midpoint comprises two subarrays $A[i .. mid]$ and $A[mid + 1 .. j]$, where $low \leq i \leq mid$ and $mid < j \leq high$.

maximum subarray that crosses the midpoint, and take a subarray with the largest sum of the three.

We can easily find a maximum subarray crossing the midpoint in time linear in the size of the subarray $A[low .. high]$. This problem is *not* a smaller instance of our original problem, because it has the added restriction that the subarray it chooses must cross the midpoint. As Figure 4.4(b) shows, any subarray crossing the midpoint is itself made of two subarrays $A[i .. mid]$ and $A[mid + 1 .. j]$, where $low \leq i \leq mid$ and $mid < j \leq high$. Therefore, we just need to find maximum subarrays of the form $A[i .. mid]$ and $A[mid + 1 .. j]$ and then combine them. The procedure FIND-MAX-CROSSING-SUBARRAY takes as input the array A and the indices *low*, *mid*, and *high*, and it returns a tuple containing the indices demarcating a maximum subarray that crosses the midpoint, along with the sum of the values in a maximum subarray.

FIND-MAX-CROSSING-SUBARRAY$(A, low, mid, high)$

```
 1   left-sum = −∞
 2   sum = 0
 3   for i = mid downto low
 4       sum = sum + A[i]
 5       if sum > left-sum
 6           left-sum = sum
 7           max-left = i
 8   right-sum = −∞
 9   sum = 0
10   for j = mid + 1 to high
11       sum = sum + A[j]
12       if sum > right-sum
13           right-sum = sum
14           max-right = j
15   return (max-left, max-right, left-sum + right-sum)
```

This procedure works as follows. Lines 1–7 find a maximum subarray of the left half, $A[low..mid]$. Since this subarray must contain $A[mid]$, the **for** loop of lines 3–7 starts the index i at mid and works down to low, so that every subarray it considers is of the form $A[i..mid]$. Lines 1–2 initialize the variables *left-sum*, which holds the greatest sum found so far, and *sum*, holding the sum of the entries in $A[i..mid]$. Whenever we find, in line 5, a subarray $A[i..mid]$ with a sum of values greater than *left-sum*, we update *left-sum* to this subarray's sum in line 6, and in line 7 we update the variable *max-left* to record this index i. Lines 8–14 work analogously for the right half, $A[mid+1..high]$. Here, the **for** loop of lines 10–14 starts the index j at $mid+1$ and works up to $high$, so that every subarray it considers is of the form $A[mid+1..j]$. Finally, line 15 returns the indices *max-left* and *max-right* that demarcate a maximum subarray crossing the midpoint, along with the sum *left-sum* + *right-sum* of the values in the subarray $A[max\text{-}left..max\text{-}right]$.

If the subarray $A[low..high]$ contains n entries (so that $n = high - low + 1$), we claim that the call FIND-MAX-CROSSING-SUBARRAY$(A, low, mid, high)$ takes $\Theta(n)$ time. Since each iteration of each of the two **for** loops takes $\Theta(1)$ time, we just need to count up how many iterations there are altogether. The **for** loop of lines 3–7 makes $mid - low + 1$ iterations, and the **for** loop of lines 10–14 makes $high - mid$ iterations, and so the total number of iterations is

$$
\begin{aligned}
(mid - low + 1) + (high - mid) \quad &= \quad high - low + 1 \\
&= \quad n \; .
\end{aligned}
$$

With a linear-time FIND-MAX-CROSSING-SUBARRAY procedure in hand, we can write pseudocode for a divide-and-conquer algorithm to solve the maximum-subarray problem:

FIND-MAXIMUM-SUBARRAY$(A, low, high)$

```
1   if high == low
2       return (low, high, A[low])              // base case: only one element
3   else mid = ⌊(low + high)/2⌋
4       (left-low, left-high, left-sum) =
                FIND-MAXIMUM-SUBARRAY(A, low, mid)
5       (right-low, right-high, right-sum) =
                FIND-MAXIMUM-SUBARRAY(A, mid + 1, high)
6       (cross-low, cross-high, cross-sum) =
                FIND-MAX-CROSSING-SUBARRAY(A, low, mid, high)
7       if left-sum ≥ right-sum and left-sum ≥ cross-sum
8           return (left-low, left-high, left-sum)
9       elseif right-sum ≥ left-sum and right-sum ≥ cross-sum
10          return (right-low, right-high, right-sum)
11      else return (cross-low, cross-high, cross-sum)
```

The initial call FIND-MAXIMUM-SUBARRAY($A, 1, A.length$) will find a maximum subarray of $A[1 .. n]$.

Similar to FIND-MAX-CROSSING-SUBARRAY, the recursive procedure FIND-MAXIMUM-SUBARRAY returns a tuple containing the indices that demarcate a maximum subarray, along with the sum of the values in a maximum subarray. Line 1 tests for the base case, where the subarray has just one element. A subarray with just one element has only one subarray—itself—and so line 2 returns a tuple with the starting and ending indices of just the one element, along with its value. Lines 3–11 handle the recursive case. Line 3 does the divide part, computing the index *mid* of the midpoint. Let's refer to the subarray $A[low .. mid]$ as the **left subarray** and to $A[mid + 1 .. high]$ as the **right subarray**. Because we know that the subarray $A[low .. high]$ contains at least two elements, each of the left and right subarrays must have at least one element. Lines 4 and 5 conquer by recursively finding maximum subarrays within the left and right subarrays, respectively. Lines 6–11 form the combine part. Line 6 finds a maximum subarray that crosses the midpoint. (Recall that because line 6 solves a subproblem that is not a smaller instance of the original problem, we consider it to be in the combine part.) Line 7 tests whether the left subarray contains a subarray with the maximum sum, and line 8 returns that maximum subarray. Otherwise, line 9 tests whether the right subarray contains a subarray with the maximum sum, and line 10 returns that maximum subarray. If neither the left nor right subarrays contain a subarray achieving the maximum sum, then a maximum subarray must cross the midpoint, and line 11 returns it.

Analyzing the divide-and-conquer algorithm

Next we set up a recurrence that describes the running time of the recursive FIND-MAXIMUM-SUBARRAY procedure. As we did when we analyzed merge sort in Section 2.3.2, we make the simplifying assumption that the original problem size is a power of 2, so that all subproblem sizes are integers. We denote by $T(n)$ the running time of FIND-MAXIMUM-SUBARRAY on a subarray of n elements. For starters, line 1 takes constant time. The base case, when $n = 1$, is easy: line 2 takes constant time, and so

$$T(1) = \Theta(1) . \tag{4.5}$$

The recursive case occurs when $n > 1$. Lines 1 and 3 take constant time. Each of the subproblems solved in lines 4 and 5 is on a subarray of $n/2$ elements (our assumption that the original problem size is a power of 2 ensures that $n/2$ is an integer), and so we spend $T(n/2)$ time solving each of them. Because we have to solve two subproblems—for the left subarray and for the right subarray—the contribution to the running time from lines 4 and 5 comes to $2T(n/2)$. As we have already seen, the call to FIND-MAX-CROSSING-SUBARRAY in line 6 takes $\Theta(n)$ time. Lines 7–11 take only $\Theta(1)$ time. For the recursive case, therefore, we have

$$
\begin{aligned}
T(n) &= \Theta(1) + 2T(n/2) + \Theta(n) + \Theta(1) \\
&= 2T(n/2) + \Theta(n) \,.
\end{aligned}
\tag{4.6}
$$

Combining equations (4.5) and (4.6) gives us a recurrence for the running time $T(n)$ of FIND-MAXIMUM-SUBARRAY:

$$
T(n) = \begin{cases} \Theta(1) & \text{if } n = 1 \,, \\ 2T(n/2) + \Theta(n) & \text{if } n > 1 \,. \end{cases}
\tag{4.7}
$$

This recurrence is the same as recurrence (4.1) for merge sort. As we shall see from the master method in Section 4.5, this recurrence has the solution $T(n) = \Theta(n \lg n)$. You might also revisit the recursion tree in Figure 2.5 to understand why the solution should be $T(n) = \Theta(n \lg n)$.

Thus, we see that the divide-and-conquer method yields an algorithm that is asymptotically faster than the brute-force method. With merge sort and now the maximum-subarray problem, we begin to get an idea of how powerful the divide-and-conquer method can be. Sometimes it will yield the asymptotically fastest algorithm for a problem, and other times we can do even better. As Exercise 4.1-5 shows, there is in fact a linear-time algorithm for the maximum-subarray problem, and it does not use divide-and-conquer.

Exercises

4.1-1
What does FIND-MAXIMUM-SUBARRAY return when all elements of A are negative?

4.1-2
Write pseudocode for the brute-force method of solving the maximum-subarray problem. Your procedure should run in $\Theta(n^2)$ time.

4.1-3
Implement both the brute-force and recursive algorithms for the maximum-subarray problem on your own computer. What problem size n_0 gives the crossover point at which the recursive algorithm beats the brute-force algorithm? Then, change the base case of the recursive algorithm to use the brute-force algorithm whenever the problem size is less than n_0. Does that change the crossover point?

4.1-4
Suppose we change the definition of the maximum-subarray problem to allow the result to be an empty subarray, where the sum of the values of an empty subar-

ray is 0. How would you change any of the algorithms that do not allow empty subarrays to permit an empty subarray to be the result?

4.1-5
Use the following ideas to develop a nonrecursive, linear-time algorithm for the maximum-subarray problem. Start at the left end of the array, and progress toward the right, keeping track of the maximum subarray seen so far. Knowing a maximum subarray of $A[1 .. j]$, extend the answer to find a maximum subarray ending at index $j + 1$ by using the following observation: a maximum subarray of $A[1 .. j + 1]$ is either a maximum subarray of $A[1 .. j]$ or a subarray $A[i .. j + 1]$, for some $1 \leq i \leq j + 1$. Determine a maximum subarray of the form $A[i .. j + 1]$ in constant time based on knowing a maximum subarray ending at index j.

4.2   Strassen's algorithm for matrix multiplication

If you have seen matrices before, then you probably know how to multiply them. (Otherwise, you should read Section D.1 in Appendix D.) If $A = (a_{ij})$ and $B = (b_{ij})$ are square $n \times n$ matrices, then in the product $C = A \cdot B$, we define the entry c_{ij}, for $i, j = 1, 2, \ldots, n$, by

$$c_{ij} = \sum_{k=1}^{n} a_{ik} \cdot b_{kj} \, . \tag{4.8}$$

We must compute n^2 matrix entries, and each is the sum of n values. The following procedure takes $n \times n$ matrices A and B and multiplies them, returning their $n \times n$ product C. We assume that each matrix has an attribute *rows*, giving the number of rows in the matrix.

SQUARE-MATRIX-MULTIPLY(A, B)

```
1   n = A.rows
2   let C be a new n × n matrix
3   for i = 1 to n
4       for j = 1 to n
5           cᵢⱼ = 0
6           for k = 1 to n
7               cᵢⱼ = cᵢⱼ + aᵢₖ · bₖⱼ
8   return C
```

The SQUARE-MATRIX-MULTIPLY procedure works as follows. The **for** loop of lines 3–7 computes the entries of each row i, and within a given row i, the

for loop of lines 4–7 computes each of the entries c_{ij}, for each column j. Line 5 initializes c_{ij} to 0 as we start computing the sum given in equation (4.8), and each iteration of the **for** loop of lines 6–7 adds in one more term of equation (4.8).

Because each of the triply-nested **for** loops runs exactly n iterations, and each execution of line 7 takes constant time, the SQUARE-MATRIX-MULTIPLY procedure takes $\Theta(n^3)$ time.

You might at first think that any matrix multiplication algorithm must take $\Omega(n^3)$ time, since the natural definition of matrix multiplication requires that many multiplications. You would be incorrect, however: we have a way to multiply matrices in $o(n^3)$ time. In this section, we shall see Strassen's remarkable recursive algorithm for multiplying $n \times n$ matrices. It runs in $\Theta(n^{\lg 7})$ time, which we shall show in Section 4.5. Since $\lg 7$ lies between 2.80 and 2.81, Strassen's algorithm runs in $O(n^{2.81})$ time, which is asymptotically better than the simple SQUARE-MATRIX-MULTIPLY procedure.

A simple divide-and-conquer algorithm

To keep things simple, when we use a divide-and-conquer algorithm to compute the matrix product $C = A \cdot B$, we assume that n is an exact power of 2 in each of the $n \times n$ matrices. We make this assumption because in each divide step, we will divide $n \times n$ matrices into four $n/2 \times n/2$ matrices, and by assuming that n is an exact power of 2, we are guaranteed that as long as $n \geq 2$, the dimension $n/2$ is an integer.

Suppose that we partition each of A, B, and C into four $n/2 \times n/2$ matrices

$$A = \begin{pmatrix} A_{11} & A_{12} \\ A_{21} & A_{22} \end{pmatrix}, \quad B = \begin{pmatrix} B_{11} & B_{12} \\ B_{21} & B_{22} \end{pmatrix}, \quad C = \begin{pmatrix} C_{11} & C_{12} \\ C_{21} & C_{22} \end{pmatrix}, \tag{4.9}$$

so that we rewrite the equation $C = A \cdot B$ as

$$\begin{pmatrix} C_{11} & C_{12} \\ C_{21} & C_{22} \end{pmatrix} = \begin{pmatrix} A_{11} & A_{12} \\ A_{21} & A_{22} \end{pmatrix} \cdot \begin{pmatrix} B_{11} & B_{12} \\ B_{21} & B_{22} \end{pmatrix}. \tag{4.10}$$

Equation (4.10) corresponds to the four equations

$$C_{11} = A_{11} \cdot B_{11} + A_{12} \cdot B_{21}, \tag{4.11}$$
$$C_{12} = A_{11} \cdot B_{12} + A_{12} \cdot B_{22}, \tag{4.12}$$
$$C_{21} = A_{21} \cdot B_{11} + A_{22} \cdot B_{21}, \tag{4.13}$$
$$C_{22} = A_{21} \cdot B_{12} + A_{22} \cdot B_{22}. \tag{4.14}$$

Each of these four equations specifies two multiplications of $n/2 \times n/2$ matrices and the addition of their $n/2 \times n/2$ products. We can use these equations to create a straightforward, recursive, divide-and-conquer algorithm:

SQUARE-MATRIX-MULTIPLY-RECURSIVE(A, B)

1   $n = A.rows$
2   let C be a new $n \times n$ matrix
3   **if** $n == 1$
4       $c_{11} = a_{11} \cdot b_{11}$
5   **else** partition A, B, and C as in equations (4.9)
6       $C_{11} =$ SQUARE-MATRIX-MULTIPLY-RECURSIVE(A_{11}, B_{11})
          $+$ SQUARE-MATRIX-MULTIPLY-RECURSIVE(A_{12}, B_{21})
7       $C_{12} =$ SQUARE-MATRIX-MULTIPLY-RECURSIVE(A_{11}, B_{12})
          $+$ SQUARE-MATRIX-MULTIPLY-RECURSIVE(A_{12}, B_{22})
8       $C_{21} =$ SQUARE-MATRIX-MULTIPLY-RECURSIVE(A_{21}, B_{11})
          $+$ SQUARE-MATRIX-MULTIPLY-RECURSIVE(A_{22}, B_{21})
9       $C_{22} =$ SQUARE-MATRIX-MULTIPLY-RECURSIVE(A_{21}, B_{12})
          $+$ SQUARE-MATRIX-MULTIPLY-RECURSIVE(A_{22}, B_{22})
10 **return** C

This pseudocode glosses over one subtle but important implementation detail. How do we partition the matrices in line 5? If we were to create 12 new $n/2 \times n/2$ matrices, we would spend $\Theta(n^2)$ time copying entries. In fact, we can partition the matrices without copying entries. The trick is to use index calculations. We identify a submatrix by a range of row indices and a range of column indices of the original matrix. We end up representing a submatrix a little differently from how we represent the original matrix, which is the subtlety we are glossing over. The advantage is that, since we can specify submatrices by index calculations, executing line 5 takes only $\Theta(1)$ time (although we shall see that it makes no difference asymptotically to the overall running time whether we copy or partition in place).

Now, we derive a recurrence to characterize the running time of SQUARE-MATRIX-MULTIPLY-RECURSIVE. Let $T(n)$ be the time to multiply two $n \times n$ matrices using this procedure. In the base case, when $n = 1$, we perform just the one scalar multiplication in line 4, and so

$$T(1) = \Theta(1) . \tag{4.15}$$

The recursive case occurs when $n > 1$. As discussed, partitioning the matrices in line 5 takes $\Theta(1)$ time, using index calculations. In lines 6–9, we recursively call SQUARE-MATRIX-MULTIPLY-RECURSIVE a total of eight times. Because each recursive call multiplies two $n/2 \times n/2$ matrices, thereby contributing $T(n/2)$ to the overall running time, the time taken by all eight recursive calls is $8T(n/2)$. We also must account for the four matrix additions in lines 6–9. Each of these matrices contains $n^2/4$ entries, and so each of the four matrix additions takes $\Theta(n^2)$ time. Since the number of matrix additions is a constant, the total time spent adding matrices in lines 6–9 is $\Theta(n^2)$. (Again, we use index calculations to place the results of the matrix additions into the correct positions of matrix C, with an overhead of $\Theta(1)$ time per entry.) The total time for the recursive case, therefore, is the sum of the partitioning time, the time for all the recursive calls, and the time to add the matrices resulting from the recursive calls:

$$
\begin{aligned}
T(n) &= \Theta(1) + 8T(n/2) + \Theta(n^2) \\
&= 8T(n/2) + \Theta(n^2) .
\end{aligned}
\tag{4.16}
$$

Notice that if we implemented partitioning by copying matrices, which would cost $\Theta(n^2)$ time, the recurrence would not change, and hence the overall running time would increase by only a constant factor.

Combining equations (4.15) and (4.16) gives us the recurrence for the running time of SQUARE-MATRIX-MULTIPLY-RECURSIVE:

$$
T(n) = \begin{cases} \Theta(1) & \text{if } n = 1 , \\ 8T(n/2) + \Theta(n^2) & \text{if } n > 1 . \end{cases}
\tag{4.17}
$$

As we shall see from the master method in Section 4.5, recurrence (4.17) has the solution $T(n) = \Theta(n^3)$. Thus, this simple divide-and-conquer approach is no faster than the straightforward SQUARE-MATRIX-MULTIPLY procedure.

Before we continue on to examining Strassen's algorithm, let us review where the components of equation (4.16) came from. Partitioning each $n \times n$ matrix by index calculation takes $\Theta(1)$ time, but we have two matrices to partition. Although you could say that partitioning the two matrices takes $\Theta(2)$ time, the constant of 2 is subsumed by the Θ-notation. Adding two matrices, each with, say, k entries, takes $\Theta(k)$ time. Since the matrices we add each have $n^2/4$ entries, you could say that adding each pair takes $\Theta(n^2/4)$ time. Again, however, the Θ-notation subsumes the constant factor of $1/4$, and we say that adding two $n/2 \times n/2$ matrices takes $\Theta(n^2)$ time. We have four such matrix additions, and once again, instead of saying that they take $\Theta(4n^2)$ time, we say that they take $\Theta(n^2)$ time. (Of course, you might observe that we could say that the four matrix additions take $\Theta(4n^2/4)$ time, and that $4n^2/4 = n^2$, but the point here is that Θ-notation subsumes constant factors, whatever they are.) Thus, we end up with two terms of $\Theta(n^2)$, which we can combine into one.

When we account for the eight recursive calls, however, we cannot just subsume the constant factor of 8. In other words, we must say that together they take $8T(n/2)$ time, rather than just $T(n/2)$ time. You can get a feel for why by looking back at the recursion tree in Figure 2.5, for recurrence (2.1) (which is identical to recurrence (4.7)), with the recursive case $T(n) = 2T(n/2) + \Theta(n)$. The factor of 2 determined how many children each tree node had, which in turn determined how many terms contributed to the sum at each level of the tree. If we were to ignore the factor of 8 in equation (4.16) or the factor of 2 in recurrence (4.1), the recursion tree would just be linear, rather than "bushy," and each level would contribute only one term to the sum.

Bear in mind, therefore, that although asymptotic notation subsumes constant multiplicative factors, recursive notation such as $T(n/2)$ does not.

Strassen's method

The key to Strassen's method is to make the recursion tree slightly less bushy. That is, instead of performing eight recursive multiplications of $n/2 \times n/2$ matrices, it performs only seven. The cost of eliminating one matrix multiplication will be several new additions of $n/2 \times n/2$ matrices, but still only a constant number of additions. As before, the constant number of matrix additions will be subsumed by Θ-notation when we set up the recurrence equation to characterize the running time.

Strassen's method is not at all obvious. (This might be the biggest understatement in this book.) It has four steps:

1. Divide the input matrices A and B and output matrix C into $n/2 \times n/2$ submatrices, as in equation (4.9). This step takes $\Theta(1)$ time by index calculation, just as in SQUARE-MATRIX-MULTIPLY-RECURSIVE.

2. Create 10 matrices $S_1, S_2, \ldots, S_{10}$, each of which is $n/2 \times n/2$ and is the sum or difference of two matrices created in step 1. We can create all 10 matrices in $\Theta(n^2)$ time.

3. Using the submatrices created in step 1 and the 10 matrices created in step 2, recursively compute seven matrix products $P_1, P_2, \ldots, P_7$. Each matrix P_i is $n/2 \times n/2$.

4. Compute the desired submatrices $C_{11}, C_{12}, C_{21}, C_{22}$ of the result matrix C by adding and subtracting various combinations of the P_i matrices. We can compute all four submatrices in $\Theta(n^2)$ time.

We shall see the details of steps 2–4 in a moment, but we already have enough information to set up a recurrence for the running time of Strassen's method. Let us assume that once the matrix size n gets down to 1, we perform a simple scalar multiplication, just as in line 4 of SQUARE-MATRIX-MULTIPLY-RECURSIVE. When $n > 1$, steps 1, 2, and 4 take a total of $\Theta(n^2)$ time, and step 3 requires us to perform seven multiplications of $n/2 \times n/2$ matrices. Hence, we obtain the following recurrence for the running time $T(n)$ of Strassen's algorithm:

$$T(n) = \begin{cases} \Theta(1) & \text{if } n = 1 , \\ 7T(n/2) + \Theta(n^2) & \text{if } n > 1 . \end{cases} \qquad (4.18)$$

We have traded off one matrix multiplication for a constant number of matrix additions. Once we understand recurrences and their solutions, we shall see that this tradeoff actually leads to a lower asymptotic running time. By the master method in Section 4.5, recurrence (4.18) has the solution $T(n) = \Theta(n^{\lg 7})$.

We now proceed to describe the details. In step 2, we create the following 10 matrices:

$$
\begin{aligned}
S_1 &= B_{12} - B_{22} \,, \\
S_2 &= A_{11} + A_{12} \,, \\
S_3 &= A_{21} + A_{22} \,, \\
S_4 &= B_{21} - B_{11} \,, \\
S_5 &= A_{11} + A_{22} \,, \\
S_6 &= B_{11} + B_{22} \,, \\
S_7 &= A_{12} - A_{22} \,, \\
S_8 &= B_{21} + B_{22} \,, \\
S_9 &= A_{11} - A_{21} \,, \\
S_{10} &= B_{11} + B_{12} \,.
\end{aligned}
$$

Since we must add or subtract $n/2 \times n/2$ matrices 10 times, this step does indeed take $\Theta(n^2)$ time.

In step 3, we recursively multiply $n/2 \times n/2$ matrices seven times to compute the following $n/2 \times n/2$ matrices, each of which is the sum or difference of products of A and B submatrices:

$$
\begin{aligned}
P_1 &= A_{11} \cdot S_1 &&= A_{11} \cdot B_{12} - A_{11} \cdot B_{22} \,, \\
P_2 &= S_2 \cdot B_{22} &&= A_{11} \cdot B_{22} + A_{12} \cdot B_{22} \,, \\
P_3 &= S_3 \cdot B_{11} &&= A_{21} \cdot B_{11} + A_{22} \cdot B_{11} \,, \\
P_4 &= A_{22} \cdot S_4 &&= A_{22} \cdot B_{21} - A_{22} \cdot B_{11} \,, \\
P_5 &= S_5 \cdot S_6 &&= A_{11} \cdot B_{11} + A_{11} \cdot B_{22} + A_{22} \cdot B_{11} + A_{22} \cdot B_{22} \,, \\
P_6 &= S_7 \cdot S_8 &&= A_{12} \cdot B_{21} + A_{12} \cdot B_{22} - A_{22} \cdot B_{21} - A_{22} \cdot B_{22} \,, \\
P_7 &= S_9 \cdot S_{10} &&= A_{11} \cdot B_{11} + A_{11} \cdot B_{12} - A_{21} \cdot B_{11} - A_{21} \cdot B_{12} \,.
\end{aligned}
$$

Note that the only multiplications we need to perform are those in the middle column of the above equations. The right-hand column just shows what these products equal in terms of the original submatrices created in step 1.

Step 4 adds and subtracts the P_i matrices created in step 3 to construct the four $n/2 \times n/2$ submatrices of the product C. We start with

$$
C_{11} = P_5 + P_4 - P_2 + P_6 \,.
$$

Expanding out the right-hand side, with the expansion of each P_i on its own line and vertically aligning terms that cancel out, we see that C_{11} equals

$$
\begin{array}{llll}
A_{11} \cdot B_{11} + A_{11} \cdot B_{22} + A_{22} \cdot B_{11} + A_{22} \cdot B_{22} & & & \\
\quad - A_{22} \cdot B_{11} & & + A_{22} \cdot B_{21} & \\
\quad - A_{11} \cdot B_{22} & & & - A_{12} \cdot B_{22} \\
& - A_{22} \cdot B_{22} - A_{22} \cdot B_{21} + A_{12} \cdot B_{22} + A_{12} \cdot B_{21} & \\
\hline
A_{11} \cdot B_{11} & & & + A_{12} \cdot B_{21} \, ,
\end{array}
$$

which corresponds to equation (4.11).

Similarly, we set

$$C_{12} = P_1 + P_2 \, ,$$

and so C_{12} equals

$$
\begin{array}{ll}
A_{11} \cdot B_{12} - A_{11} \cdot B_{22} & \\
\quad + A_{11} \cdot B_{22} + A_{12} \cdot B_{22} & \\
\hline
A_{11} \cdot B_{12} \quad\quad\quad + A_{12} \cdot B_{22} \, , &
\end{array}
$$

corresponding to equation (4.12).

Setting

$$C_{21} = P_3 + P_4$$

makes C_{21} equal

$$
\begin{array}{ll}
A_{21} \cdot B_{11} + A_{22} \cdot B_{11} & \\
\quad - A_{22} \cdot B_{11} + A_{22} \cdot B_{21} & \\
\hline
A_{21} \cdot B_{11} \quad\quad\quad + A_{22} \cdot B_{21} \, , &
\end{array}
$$

corresponding to equation (4.13).

Finally, we set

$$C_{22} = P_5 + P_1 - P_3 - P_7 \, ,$$

so that C_{22} equals

$$
\begin{array}{lll}
A_{11} \cdot B_{11} + A_{11} \cdot B_{22} + A_{22} \cdot B_{11} + A_{22} \cdot B_{22} & & \\
\quad - A_{11} \cdot B_{22} & + A_{11} \cdot B_{12} & \\
\quad\quad - A_{22} \cdot B_{11} & & \\
- A_{11} \cdot B_{11} & - A_{11} \cdot B_{12} + A_{21} \cdot B_{11} + A_{21} \cdot B_{12} & - A_{21} \cdot B_{11} \\
\hline
A_{22} \cdot B_{22} & & + A_{21} \cdot B_{12} \, ,
\end{array}
$$

which corresponds to equation (4.14). Altogether, we add or subtract $n/2 \times n/2$ matrices eight times in step 4, and so this step indeed takes $\Theta(n^2)$ time.

Thus, we see that Strassen's algorithm, comprising steps 1–4, produces the correct matrix product and that recurrence (4.18) characterizes its running time. Since we shall see in Section 4.5 that this recurrence has the solution $T(n) = \Theta(n^{\lg 7})$, Strassen's method is asymptotically faster than the straightforward SQUARE-MATRIX-MULTIPLY procedure. The notes at the end of this chapter discuss some of the practical aspects of Strassen's algorithm.

Exercises

Note: Although Exercises 4.2-3, 4.2-4, and 4.2-5 are about variants on Strassen's algorithm, you should read Section 4.5 before trying to solve them.

4.2-1
Use Strassen's algorithm to compute the matrix product

$$\begin{pmatrix} 1 & 3 \\ 7 & 5 \end{pmatrix} \begin{pmatrix} 6 & 8 \\ 4 & 2 \end{pmatrix} .$$

Show your work.

4.2-2
Write pseudocode for Strassen's algorithm.

4.2-3
How would you modify Strassen's algorithm to multiply $n \times n$ matrices in which n is not an exact power of 2? Show that the resulting algorithm runs in time $\Theta(n^{\lg 7})$.

4.2-4
What is the largest k such that if you can multiply 3×3 matrices using k multiplications (not assuming commutativity of multiplication), then you can multiply $n \times n$ matrices in time $o(n^{\lg 7})$? What would the running time of this algorithm be?

4.2-5
V. Pan has discovered a way of multiplying 68×68 matrices using 132,464 multiplications, a way of multiplying 70×70 matrices using 143,640 multiplications, and a way of multiplying 72×72 matrices using 155,424 multiplications. Which method yields the best asymptotic running time when used in a divide-and-conquer matrix-multiplication algorithm? How does it compare to Strassen's algorithm?

4.2-6

How quickly can you multiply a $kn \times n$ matrix by an $n \times kn$ matrix, using Strassen's algorithm as a subroutine? Answer the same question with the order of the input matrices reversed.

4.2-7

Show how to multiply the complex numbers $a + bi$ and $c + di$ using only three multiplications of real numbers. The algorithm should take a, b, c, and d as input and produce the real component $ac - bd$ and the imaginary component $ad + bc$ separately.

4.3 The substitution method for solving recurrences

Now that we have seen how recurrences characterize the running times of divide-and-conquer algorithms, we will learn how to solve recurrences. We start in this section with the "substitution" method.

The **substitution method** for solving recurrences comprises two steps:

1. Guess the form of the solution.

2. Use mathematical induction to find the constants and show that the solution works.

We substitute the guessed solution for the function when applying the inductive hypothesis to smaller values; hence the name "substitution method." This method is powerful, but we must be able to guess the form of the answer in order to apply it.

We can use the substitution method to establish either upper or lower bounds on a recurrence. As an example, let us determine an upper bound on the recurrence

$$T(n) = 2T(\lfloor n/2 \rfloor) + n , \tag{4.19}$$

which is similar to recurrences (4.3) and (4.4). We guess that the solution is $T(n) = O(n \lg n)$. The substitution method requires us to prove that $T(n) \leq cn \lg n$ for an appropriate choice of the constant $c > 0$. We start by assuming that this bound holds for all positive $m < n$, in particular for $m = \lfloor n/2 \rfloor$, yielding $T(\lfloor n/2 \rfloor) \leq c \lfloor n/2 \rfloor \lg(\lfloor n/2 \rfloor)$. Substituting into the recurrence yields

$$
\begin{aligned}
T(n) &\leq 2(c \lfloor n/2 \rfloor \lg(\lfloor n/2 \rfloor)) + n \\
&\leq cn \lg(n/2) + n \\
&= cn \lg n - cn \lg 2 + n \\
&= cn \lg n - cn + n \\
&\leq cn \lg n ,
\end{aligned}
$$

where the last step holds as long as $c \geq 1$.

Mathematical induction now requires us to show that our solution holds for the boundary conditions. Typically, we do so by showing that the boundary conditions are suitable as base cases for the inductive proof. For the recurrence (4.19), we must show that we can choose the constant c large enough so that the bound $T(n) \leq cn \lg n$ works for the boundary conditions as well. This requirement can sometimes lead to problems. Let us assume, for the sake of argument, that $T(1) = 1$ is the sole boundary condition of the recurrence. Then for $n = 1$, the bound $T(n) \leq cn \lg n$ yields $T(1) \leq c1 \lg 1 = 0$, which is at odds with $T(1) = 1$. Consequently, the base case of our inductive proof fails to hold.

We can overcome this obstacle in proving an inductive hypothesis for a specific boundary condition with only a little more effort. In the recurrence (4.19), for example, we take advantage of asymptotic notation requiring us only to prove $T(n) \leq cn \lg n$ for $n \geq n_0$, where n_0 is a constant *that we get to choose*. We keep the troublesome boundary condition $T(1) = 1$, but remove it from consideration in the inductive proof. We do so by first observing that for $n > 3$, the recurrence does not depend directly on $T(1)$. Thus, we can replace $T(1)$ by $T(2)$ and $T(3)$ as the base cases in the inductive proof, letting $n_0 = 2$. Note that we make a distinction between the base case of the recurrence ($n = 1$) and the base cases of the inductive proof ($n = 2$ and $n = 3$). With $T(1) = 1$, we derive from the recurrence that $T(2) = 4$ and $T(3) = 5$. Now we can complete the inductive proof that $T(n) \leq cn \lg n$ for some constant $c \geq 1$ by choosing c large enough so that $T(2) \leq c2 \lg 2$ and $T(3) \leq c3 \lg 3$. As it turns out, any choice of $c \geq 2$ suffices for the base cases of $n = 2$ and $n = 3$ to hold. For most of the recurrences we shall examine, it is straightforward to extend boundary conditions to make the inductive assumption work for small n, and we shall not always explicitly work out the details.

Making a good guess

Unfortunately, there is no general way to guess the correct solutions to recurrences. Guessing a solution takes experience and, occasionally, creativity. Fortunately, though, you can use some heuristics to help you become a good guesser. You can also use recursion trees, which we shall see in Section 4.4, to generate good guesses.

If a recurrence is similar to one you have seen before, then guessing a similar solution is reasonable. As an example, consider the recurrence

$$T(n) = 2T(\lfloor n/2 \rfloor + 17) + n \; ,$$

which looks difficult because of the added "17" in the argument to T on the right-hand side. Intuitively, however, this additional term cannot substantially affect the solution to the recurrence. When n is large, the difference between $\lfloor n/2 \rfloor$ and $\lfloor n/2 \rfloor + 17$ is not that large: both cut n nearly evenly in half. Consequently, we make the guess that $T(n) = O(n \lg n)$, which you can verify as correct by using the substitution method (see Exercise 4.3-6).

Another way to make a good guess is to prove loose upper and lower bounds on the recurrence and then reduce the range of uncertainty. For example, we might start with a lower bound of $T(n) = \Omega(n)$ for the recurrence (4.19), since we have the term n in the recurrence, and we can prove an initial upper bound of $T(n) = O(n^2)$. Then, we can gradually lower the upper bound and raise the lower bound until we converge on the correct, asymptotically tight solution of $T(n) = \Theta(n \lg n)$.

Subtleties

Sometimes you might correctly guess an asymptotic bound on the solution of a recurrence, but somehow the math fails to work out in the induction. The problem frequently turns out to be that the inductive assumption is not strong enough to prove the detailed bound. If you revise the guess by subtracting a lower-order term when you hit such a snag, the math often goes through.

Consider the recurrence

$$T(n) = T(\lfloor n/2 \rfloor) + T(\lceil n/2 \rceil) + 1 .$$

We guess that the solution is $T(n) = O(n)$, and we try to show that $T(n) \leq cn$ for an appropriate choice of the constant c. Substituting our guess in the recurrence, we obtain

$$
\begin{aligned}
T(n) &\leq c \lfloor n/2 \rfloor + c \lceil n/2 \rceil + 1 \\
&= cn + 1 ,
\end{aligned}
$$

which does not imply $T(n) \leq cn$ for any choice of c. We might be tempted to try a larger guess, say $T(n) = O(n^2)$. Although we can make this larger guess work, our original guess of $T(n) = O(n)$ is correct. In order to show that it is correct, however, we must make a stronger inductive hypothesis.

Intuitively, our guess is nearly right: we are off only by the constant 1, a lower-order term. Nevertheless, mathematical induction does not work unless we prove the exact form of the inductive hypothesis. We overcome our difficulty by *subtracting* a lower-order term from our previous guess. Our new guess is $T(n) \leq cn - d$, where $d \geq 0$ is a constant. We now have

$$
\begin{aligned}
T(n) &\leq (c \lfloor n/2 \rfloor - d) + (c \lceil n/2 \rceil - d) + 1 \\
&= cn - 2d + 1 \\
&\leq cn - d ,
\end{aligned}
$$

as long as $d \geq 1$. As before, we must choose the constant c large enough to handle the boundary conditions.

You might find the idea of subtracting a lower-order term counterintuitive. After all, if the math does not work out, we should increase our guess, right? Not necessarily! When proving an upper bound by induction, it may actually be more difficult to prove that a weaker upper bound holds, because in order to prove the weaker bound, we must use the same weaker bound inductively in the proof. In our current example, when the recurrence has more than one recursive term, we get to subtract out the lower-order term of the proposed bound once per recursive term. In the above example, we subtracted out the constant d twice, once for the $T(\lfloor n/2 \rfloor)$ term and once for the $T(\lceil n/2 \rceil)$ term. We ended up with the inequality $T(n) \leq cn - 2d + 1$, and it was easy to find values of d to make $cn - 2d + 1$ be less than or equal to $cn - d$.

Avoiding pitfalls

It is easy to err in the use of asymptotic notation. For example, in the recurrence (4.19) we can falsely "prove" $T(n) = O(n)$ by guessing $T(n) \leq cn$ and then arguing

$$
\begin{aligned}
T(n) &\leq 2(c \lfloor n/2 \rfloor) + n \\
&\leq cn + n \\
&= O(n) , \qquad \Longleftarrow \textit{wrong!!}
\end{aligned}
$$

since c is a constant. The error is that we have not proved the *exact form* of the inductive hypothesis, that is, that $T(n) \leq cn$. We therefore will explicitly prove that $T(n) \leq cn$ when we want to show that $T(n) = O(n)$.

Changing variables

Sometimes, a little algebraic manipulation can make an unknown recurrence similar to one you have seen before. As an example, consider the recurrence

$$
T(n) = 2T\left(\lfloor \sqrt{n} \rfloor\right) + \lg n ,
$$

which looks difficult. We can simplify this recurrence, though, with a change of variables. For convenience, we shall not worry about rounding off values, such as $\sqrt{n}$, to be integers. Renaming $m = \lg n$ yields

$$
T(2^m) = 2T(2^{m/2}) + m .
$$

We can now rename $S(m) = T(2^m)$ to produce the new recurrence

$$
S(m) = 2S(m/2) + m ,
$$

which is very much like recurrence (4.19). Indeed, this new recurrence has the same solution: $S(m) = O(m \lg m)$. Changing back from $S(m)$ to $T(n)$, we obtain

$$T(n) = T(2^m) = S(m) = O(m \lg m) = O(\lg n \lg \lg n).$$

Exercises

4.3-1
Show that the solution of $T(n) = T(n - 1) + n$ is $O(n^2)$.

4.3-2
Show that the solution of $T(n) = T(\lceil n/2 \rceil) + 1$ is $O(\lg n)$.

4.3-3
We saw that the solution of $T(n) = 2T(\lfloor n/2 \rfloor) + n$ is $O(n \lg n)$. Show that the solution of this recurrence is also $\Omega(n \lg n)$. Conclude that the solution is $\Theta(n \lg n)$.

4.3-4
Show that by making a different inductive hypothesis, we can overcome the difficulty with the boundary condition $T(1) = 1$ for recurrence (4.19) without adjusting the boundary conditions for the inductive proof.

4.3-5
Show that $\Theta(n \lg n)$ is the solution to the "exact" recurrence (4.3) for merge sort.

4.3-6
Show that the solution to $T(n) = 2T(\lfloor n/2 \rfloor + 17) + n$ is $O(n \lg n)$.

4.3-7
Using the master method in Section 4.5, you can show that the solution to the recurrence $T(n) = 4T(n/3) + n$ is $T(n) = \Theta(n^{\log_3 4})$. Show that a substitution proof with the assumption $T(n) \le cn^{\log_3 4}$ fails. Then show how to subtract off a lower-order term to make a substitution proof work.

4.3-8
Using the master method in Section 4.5, you can show that the solution to the recurrence $T(n) = 4T(n/2) + n$ is $T(n) = \Theta(n^2)$. Show that a substitution proof with the assumption $T(n) \le cn^2$ fails. Then show how to subtract off a lower-order term to make a substitution proof work.

4.3-9

Solve the recurrence $T(n) = 3T(\sqrt{n}) + \log n$ by making a change of variables. Your solution should be asymptotically tight. Do not worry about whether values are integral.

4.4   The recursion-tree method for solving recurrences

Although you can use the substitution method to provide a succinct proof that a solution to a recurrence is correct, you might have trouble coming up with a good guess. Drawing out a recursion tree, as we did in our analysis of the merge sort recurrence in Section 2.3.2, serves as a straightforward way to devise a good guess. In a ***recursion tree***, each node represents the cost of a single subproblem somewhere in the set of recursive function invocations. We sum the costs within each level of the tree to obtain a set of per-level costs, and then we sum all the per-level costs to determine the total cost of all levels of the recursion.

A recursion tree is best used to generate a good guess, which you can then verify by the substitution method. When using a recursion tree to generate a good guess, you can often tolerate a small amount of "sloppiness," since you will be verifying your guess later on. If you are very careful when drawing out a recursion tree and summing the costs, however, you can use a recursion tree as a direct proof of a solution to a recurrence. In this section, we will use recursion trees to generate good guesses, and in Section 4.6, we will use recursion trees directly to prove the theorem that forms the basis of the master method.

For example, let us see how a recursion tree would provide a good guess for the recurrence $T(n) = 3T(\lfloor n/4 \rfloor) + \Theta(n^2)$. We start by focusing on finding an upper bound for the solution. Because we know that floors and ceilings usually do not matter when solving recurrences (here's an example of sloppiness that we can tolerate), we create a recursion tree for the recurrence $T(n) = 3T(n/4) + cn^2$, having written out the implied constant coefficient $c > 0$.

Figure 4.5 shows how we derive the recursion tree for $T(n) = 3T(n/4) + cn^2$. For convenience, we assume that n is an exact power of 4 (another example of tolerable sloppiness) so that all subproblem sizes are integers. Part (a) of the figure shows $T(n)$, which we expand in part (b) into an equivalent tree representing the recurrence. The cn^2 term at the root represents the cost at the top level of recursion, and the three subtrees of the root represent the costs incurred by the subproblems of size $n/4$. Part (c) shows this process carried one step further by expanding each node with cost $T(n/4)$ from part (b). The cost for each of the three children of the root is $c(n/4)^2$. We continue expanding each node in the tree by breaking it into its constituent parts as determined by the recurrence.

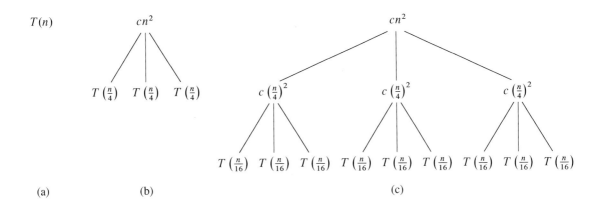

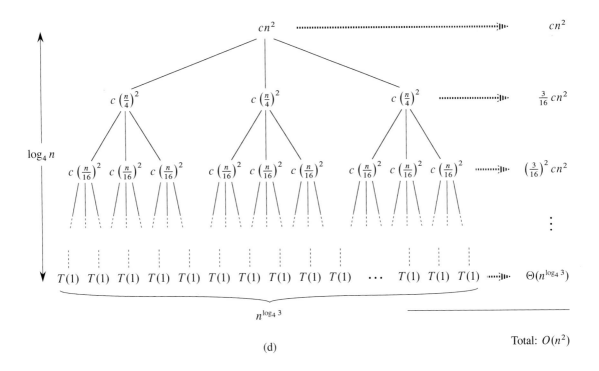

Figure 4.5 Constructing a recursion tree for the recurrence $T(n) = 3T(n/4) + cn^2$. Part **(a)** shows $T(n)$, which progressively expands in **(b)–(d)** to form the recursion tree. The fully expanded tree in part (d) has height $\log_4 n$ (it has $\log_4 n + 1$ levels).

Because subproblem sizes decrease by a factor of 4 each time we go down one level, we eventually must reach a boundary condition. How far from the root do we reach one? The subproblem size for a node at depth i is $n/4^i$. Thus, the subproblem size hits $n = 1$ when $n/4^i = 1$ or, equivalently, when $i = \log_4 n$. Thus, the tree has $\log_4 n + 1$ levels (at depths $0, 1, 2, \ldots, \log_4 n$).

Next we determine the cost at each level of the tree. Each level has three times more nodes than the level above, and so the number of nodes at depth i is 3^i. Because subproblem sizes reduce by a factor of 4 for each level we go down from the root, each node at depth i, for $i = 0, 1, 2, \ldots, \log_4 n - 1$, has a cost of $c(n/4^i)^2$. Multiplying, we see that the total cost over all nodes at depth i, for $i = 0, 1, 2, \ldots, \log_4 n - 1$, is $3^i c(n/4^i)^2 = (3/16)^i cn^2$. The bottom level, at depth $\log_4 n$, has $3^{\log_4 n} = n^{\log_4 3}$ nodes, each contributing cost $T(1)$, for a total cost of $n^{\log_4 3} T(1)$, which is $\Theta(n^{\log_4 3})$, since we assume that $T(1)$ is a constant.

Now we add up the costs over all levels to determine the cost for the entire tree:

$$T(n) = cn^2 + \frac{3}{16} cn^2 + \left(\frac{3}{16}\right)^2 cn^2 + \cdots + \left(\frac{3}{16}\right)^{\log_4 n - 1} cn^2 + \Theta(n^{\log_4 3})$$

$$= \sum_{i=0}^{\log_4 n - 1} \left(\frac{3}{16}\right)^i cn^2 + \Theta(n^{\log_4 3})$$

$$= \frac{(3/16)^{\log_4 n} - 1}{(3/16) - 1} cn^2 + \Theta(n^{\log_4 3}) \qquad \text{(by equation (A.5))}.$$

This last formula looks somewhat messy until we realize that we can again take advantage of small amounts of sloppiness and use an infinite decreasing geometric series as an upper bound. Backing up one step and applying equation (A.6), we have

$$T(n) = \sum_{i=0}^{\log_4 n - 1} \left(\frac{3}{16}\right)^i cn^2 + \Theta(n^{\log_4 3})$$

$$< \sum_{i=0}^{\infty} \left(\frac{3}{16}\right)^i cn^2 + \Theta(n^{\log_4 3})$$

$$= \frac{1}{1 - (3/16)} cn^2 + \Theta(n^{\log_4 3})$$

$$= \frac{16}{13} cn^2 + \Theta(n^{\log_4 3})$$

$$= O(n^2).$$

Thus, we have derived a guess of $T(n) = O(n^2)$ for our original recurrence $T(n) = 3T(\lfloor n/4 \rfloor) + \Theta(n^2)$. In this example, the coefficients of cn^2 form a decreasing geometric series and, by equation (A.6), the sum of these coefficients

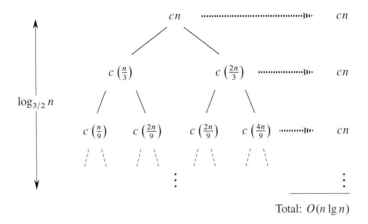

Total: $O(n \lg n)$

Figure 4.6   A recursion tree for the recurrence $T(n) = T(n/3) + T(2n/3) + cn$.

is bounded from above by the constant $16/13$. Since the root's contribution to the total cost is cn^2, the root contributes a constant fraction of the total cost. In other words, the cost of the root dominates the total cost of the tree.

In fact, if $O(n^2)$ is indeed an upper bound for the recurrence (as we shall verify in a moment), then it must be a tight bound. Why? The first recursive call contributes a cost of $\Theta(n^2)$, and so $\Omega(n^2)$ must be a lower bound for the recurrence.

Now we can use the substitution method to verify that our guess was correct, that is, $T(n) = O(n^2)$ is an upper bound for the recurrence $T(n) = 3T(\lfloor n/4 \rfloor) + \Theta(n^2)$. We want to show that $T(n) \le dn^2$ for some constant $d > 0$. Using the same constant $c > 0$ as before, we have

$$
\begin{aligned}
T(n) &\le 3T(\lfloor n/4 \rfloor) + cn^2 \\
&\le 3d \lfloor n/4 \rfloor^2 + cn^2 \\
&\le 3d(n/4)^2 + cn^2 \\
&= \frac{3}{16} dn^2 + cn^2 \\
&\le dn^2 ,
\end{aligned}
$$

where the last step holds as long as $d \ge (16/13)c$.

In another, more intricate, example, Figure 4.6 shows the recursion tree for

$$T(n) = T(n/3) + T(2n/3) + O(n) .$$

(Again, we omit floor and ceiling functions for simplicity.) As before, we let c represent the constant factor in the $O(n)$ term. When we add the values across the levels of the recursion tree shown in the figure, we get a value of cn for every level.

The longest simple path from the root to a leaf is $n \rightarrow (2/3)n \rightarrow (2/3)^2 n \rightarrow \cdots \rightarrow 1$. Since $(2/3)^k n = 1$ when $k = \log_{3/2} n$, the height of the tree is $\log_{3/2} n$.

Intuitively, we expect the solution to the recurrence to be at most the number of levels times the cost of each level, or $O(cn \log_{3/2} n) = O(n \lg n)$. Figure 4.6 shows only the top levels of the recursion tree, however, and not every level in the tree contributes a cost of cn. Consider the cost of the leaves. If this recursion tree were a complete binary tree of height $\log_{3/2} n$, there would be $2^{\log_{3/2} n} = n^{\log_{3/2} 2}$ leaves. Since the cost of each leaf is a constant, the total cost of all leaves would then be $\Theta(n^{\log_{3/2} 2})$ which, since $\log_{3/2} 2$ is a constant strictly greater than 1, is $\omega(n \lg n)$. This recursion tree is not a complete binary tree, however, and so it has fewer than $n^{\log_{3/2} 2}$ leaves. Moreover, as we go down from the root, more and more internal nodes are absent. Consequently, levels toward the bottom of the recursion tree contribute less than cn to the total cost. We could work out an accurate accounting of all costs, but remember that we are just trying to come up with a guess to use in the substitution method. Let us tolerate the sloppiness and attempt to show that a guess of $O(n \lg n)$ for the upper bound is correct.

Indeed, we can use the substitution method to verify that $O(n \lg n)$ is an upper bound for the solution to the recurrence. We show that $T(n) \leq dn \lg n$, where d is a suitable positive constant. We have

$$
\begin{aligned}
T(n) \quad &\leq \quad T(n/3) + T(2n/3) + cn \\
&\leq \quad d(n/3)\lg(n/3) + d(2n/3)\lg(2n/3) + cn \\
&= \quad (d(n/3)\lg n - d(n/3)\lg 3) \\
&\qquad\qquad + (d(2n/3)\lg n - d(2n/3)\lg(3/2)) + cn \\
&= \quad dn \lg n - d((n/3)\lg 3 + (2n/3)\lg(3/2)) + cn \\
&= \quad dn \lg n - d((n/3)\lg 3 + (2n/3)\lg 3 - (2n/3)\lg 2) + cn \\
&= \quad dn \lg n - dn(\lg 3 - 2/3) + cn \\
&\leq \quad dn \lg n \,,
\end{aligned}
$$

as long as $d \geq c/(\lg 3 - (2/3))$. Thus, we did not need to perform a more accurate accounting of costs in the recursion tree.

Exercises

4.4-1
Use a recursion tree to determine a good asymptotic upper bound on the recurrence $T(n) = 3T(\lfloor n/2 \rfloor) + n$. Use the substitution method to verify your answer.

4.4-2
Use a recursion tree to determine a good asymptotic upper bound on the recurrence $T(n) = T(n/2) + n^2$. Use the substitution method to verify your answer.

4.4-3

Use a recursion tree to determine a good asymptotic upper bound on the recurrence $T(n) = 4T(n/2 + 2) + n$. Use the substitution method to verify your answer.

4.4-4

Use a recursion tree to determine a good asymptotic upper bound on the recurrence $T(n) = 2T(n - 1) + 1$. Use the substitution method to verify your answer.

4.4-5

Use a recursion tree to determine a good asymptotic upper bound on the recurrence $T(n) = T(n-1) + T(n/2) + n$. Use the substitution method to verify your answer.

4.4-6

Argue that the solution to the recurrence $T(n) = T(n/3) + T(2n/3) + cn$, where c is a constant, is $\Omega(n \lg n)$ by appealing to a recursion tree.

4.4-7

Draw the recursion tree for $T(n) = 4T(\lfloor n/2 \rfloor) + cn$, where c is a constant, and provide a tight asymptotic bound on its solution. Verify your bound by the substitution method.

4.4-8

Use a recursion tree to give an asymptotically tight solution to the recurrence $T(n) = T(n - a) + T(a) + cn$, where $a \geq 1$ and $c > 0$ are constants.

4.4-9

Use a recursion tree to give an asymptotically tight solution to the recurrence $T(n) = T(\alpha n) + T((1 - \alpha)n) + cn$, where α is a constant in the range $0 < \alpha < 1$ and $c > 0$ is also a constant.

4.5   The master method for solving recurrences

The master method provides a "cookbook" method for solving recurrences of the form

$$T(n) = aT(n/b) + f(n) , \tag{4.20}$$

where $a \geq 1$ and $b > 1$ are constants and $f(n)$ is an asymptotically positive function. To use the master method, you will need to memorize three cases, but then you will be able to solve many recurrences quite easily, often without pencil and paper.

The recurrence (4.20) describes the running time of an algorithm that divides a problem of size n into a subproblems, each of size n/b, where a and b are positive constants. The a subproblems are solved recursively, each in time $T(n/b)$. The function $f(n)$ encompasses the cost of dividing the problem and combining the results of the subproblems. For example, the recurrence arising from Strassen's algorithm has $a = 7$, $b = 2$, and $f(n) = \Theta(n^2)$.

As a matter of technical correctness, the recurrence is not actually well defined, because n/b might not be an integer. Replacing each of the a terms $T(n/b)$ with either $T(\lfloor n/b \rfloor)$ or $T(\lceil n/b \rceil)$ will not affect the asymptotic behavior of the recurrence, however. (We will prove this assertion in the next section.) We normally find it convenient, therefore, to omit the floor and ceiling functions when writing divide-and-conquer recurrences of this form.

The master theorem

The master method depends on the following theorem.

Theorem 4.1 (Master theorem)
Let $a \geq 1$ and $b > 1$ be constants, let $f(n)$ be a function, and let $T(n)$ be defined on the nonnegative integers by the recurrence

$$T(n) = aT(n/b) + f(n) \,,$$

where we interpret n/b to mean either $\lfloor n/b \rfloor$ or $\lceil n/b \rceil$. Then $T(n)$ has the following asymptotic bounds:

1. If $f(n) = O(n^{\log_b a - \epsilon})$ for some constant $\epsilon > 0$, then $T(n) = \Theta(n^{\log_b a})$.

2. If $f(n) = \Theta(n^{\log_b a})$, then $T(n) = \Theta(n^{\log_b a} \lg n)$.

3. If $f(n) = \Omega(n^{\log_b a + \epsilon})$ for some constant $\epsilon > 0$, and if $af(n/b) \leq cf(n)$ for some constant $c < 1$ and all sufficiently large n, then $T(n) = \Theta(f(n))$.   ∎

Before applying the master theorem to some examples, let's spend a moment trying to understand what it says. In each of the three cases, we compare the function $f(n)$ with the function $n^{\log_b a}$. Intuitively, the larger of the two functions determines the solution to the recurrence. If, as in case 1, the function $n^{\log_b a}$ is the larger, then the solution is $T(n) = \Theta(n^{\log_b a})$. If, as in case 3, the function $f(n)$ is the larger, then the solution is $T(n) = \Theta(f(n))$. If, as in case 2, the two functions are the same size, we multiply by a logarithmic factor, and the solution is $T(n) = \Theta(n^{\log_b a} \lg n) = \Theta(f(n) \lg n)$.

Beyond this intuition, you need to be aware of some technicalities. In the first case, not only must $f(n)$ be smaller than $n^{\log_b a}$, it must be *polynomially* smaller.

That is, $f(n)$ must be asymptotically smaller than $n^{\log_b a}$ by a factor of n^ϵ for some constant $\epsilon > 0$. In the third case, not only must $f(n)$ be larger than $n^{\log_b a}$, it also must be polynomially larger and in addition satisfy the "regularity" condition that $af(n/b) \le cf(n)$. This condition is satisfied by most of the polynomially bounded functions that we shall encounter.

Note that the three cases do not cover all the possibilities for $f(n)$. There is a gap between cases 1 and 2 when $f(n)$ is smaller than $n^{\log_b a}$ but not polynomially smaller. Similarly, there is a gap between cases 2 and 3 when $f(n)$ is larger than $n^{\log_b a}$ but not polynomially larger. If the function $f(n)$ falls into one of these gaps, or if the regularity condition in case 3 fails to hold, you cannot use the master method to solve the recurrence.

Using the master method

To use the master method, we simply determine which case (if any) of the master theorem applies and write down the answer.

As a first example, consider

$$T(n) = 9T(n/3) + n .$$

For this recurrence, we have $a = 9$, $b = 3$, $f(n) = n$, and thus we have that $n^{\log_b a} = n^{\log_3 9} = \Theta(n^2)$. Since $f(n) = O(n^{\log_3 9 - \epsilon})$, where $\epsilon = 1$, we can apply case 1 of the master theorem and conclude that the solution is $T(n) = \Theta(n^2)$.

Now consider

$$T(n) = T(2n/3) + 1,$$

in which $a = 1$, $b = 3/2$, $f(n) = 1$, and $n^{\log_b a} = n^{\log_{3/2} 1} = n^0 = 1$. Case 2 applies, since $f(n) = \Theta(n^{\log_b a}) = \Theta(1)$, and thus the solution to the recurrence is $T(n) = \Theta(\lg n)$.

For the recurrence

$$T(n) = 3T(n/4) + n \lg n ,$$

we have $a = 3$, $b = 4$, $f(n) = n \lg n$, and $n^{\log_b a} = n^{\log_4 3} = O(n^{0.793})$. Since $f(n) = \Omega(n^{\log_4 3 + \epsilon})$, where $\epsilon \approx 0.2$, case 3 applies if we can show that the regularity condition holds for $f(n)$. For sufficiently large n, we have that $af(n/b) = 3(n/4) \lg(n/4) \le (3/4)n \lg n = cf(n)$ for $c = 3/4$. Consequently, by case 3, the solution to the recurrence is $T(n) = \Theta(n \lg n)$.

The master method does not apply to the recurrence

$$T(n) = 2T(n/2) + n \lg n ,$$

even though it appears to have the proper form: $a = 2$, $b = 2$, $f(n) = n \lg n$, and $n^{\log_b a} = n$. You might mistakenly think that case 3 should apply, since

$f(n) = n \lg n$ is asymptotically larger than $n^{\log_b a} = n$. The problem is that it is not *polynomially* larger. The ratio $f(n)/n^{\log_b a} = (n \lg n)/n = \lg n$ is asymptotically less than n^ϵ for any positive constant ϵ. Consequently, the recurrence falls into the gap between case 2 and case 3. (See Exercise 4.6-2 for a solution.)

Let's use the master method to solve the recurrences we saw in Sections 4.1 and 4.2. Recurrence (4.7),

$$T(n) = 2T(n/2) + \Theta(n),$$

characterizes the running times of the divide-and-conquer algorithm for both the maximum-subarray problem and merge sort. (As is our practice, we omit stating the base case in the recurrence.) Here, we have $a = 2$, $b = 2$, $f(n) = \Theta(n)$, and thus we have that $n^{\log_b a} = n^{\log_2 2} = n$. Case 2 applies, since $f(n) = \Theta(n)$, and so we have the solution $T(n) = \Theta(n \lg n)$.

Recurrence (4.17),

$$T(n) = 8T(n/2) + \Theta(n^2),$$

describes the running time of the first divide-and-conquer algorithm that we saw for matrix multiplication. Now we have $a = 8$, $b = 2$, and $f(n) = \Theta(n^2)$, and so $n^{\log_b a} = n^{\log_2 8} = n^3$. Since n^3 is polynomially larger than $f(n)$ (that is, $f(n) = O(n^{3-\epsilon})$ for $\epsilon = 1$), case 1 applies, and $T(n) = \Theta(n^3)$.

Finally, consider recurrence (4.18),

$$T(n) = 7T(n/2) + \Theta(n^2),$$

which describes the running time of Strassen's algorithm. Here, we have $a = 7$, $b = 2$, $f(n) = \Theta(n^2)$, and thus $n^{\log_b a} = n^{\log_2 7}$. Rewriting $\log_2 7$ as $\lg 7$ and recalling that $2.80 < \lg 7 < 2.81$, we see that $f(n) = O(n^{\lg 7 - \epsilon})$ for $\epsilon = 0.8$. Again, case 1 applies, and we have the solution $T(n) = \Theta(n^{\lg 7})$.

Exercises

4.5-1
Use the master method to give tight asymptotic bounds for the following recurrences.

a. $T(n) = 2T(n/4) + 1$.

b. $T(n) = 2T(n/4) + \sqrt{n}$.

c. $T(n) = 2T(n/4) + n$.

d. $T(n) = 2T(n/4) + n^2$.

4.5-2

Professor Caesar wishes to develop a matrix-multiplication algorithm that is asymptotically faster than Strassen's algorithm. His algorithm will use the divide-and-conquer method, dividing each matrix into pieces of size $n/4 \times n/4$, and the divide and combine steps together will take $\Theta(n^2)$ time. He needs to determine how many subproblems his algorithm has to create in order to beat Strassen's algorithm. If his algorithm creates a subproblems, then the recurrence for the running time $T(n)$ becomes $T(n) = aT(n/4) + \Theta(n^2)$. What is the largest integer value of a for which Professor Caesar's algorithm would be asymptotically faster than Strassen's algorithm?

4.5-3

Use the master method to show that the solution to the binary-search recurrence $T(n) = T(n/2) + \Theta(1)$ is $T(n) = \Theta(\lg n)$. (See Exercise 2.3-5 for a description of binary search.)

4.5-4

Can the master method be applied to the recurrence $T(n) = 4T(n/2) + n^2 \lg n$? Why or why not? Give an asymptotic upper bound for this recurrence.

4.5-5   ★

Consider the regularity condition $af(n/b) \leq cf(n)$ for some constant $c < 1$, which is part of case 3 of the master theorem. Give an example of constants $a \geq 1$ and $b > 1$ and a function $f(n)$ that satisfies all the conditions in case 3 of the master theorem except the regularity condition.

★   4.6   Proof of the master theorem

This section contains a proof of the master theorem (Theorem 4.1). You do not need to understand the proof in order to apply the master theorem.

The proof appears in two parts. The first part analyzes the master recurrence (4.20), under the simplifying assumption that $T(n)$ is defined only on exact powers of $b > 1$, that is, for $n = 1, b, b^2, \ldots$. This part gives all the intuition needed to understand why the master theorem is true. The second part shows how to extend the analysis to all positive integers n; it applies mathematical technique to the problem of handling floors and ceilings.

In this section, we shall sometimes abuse our asymptotic notation slightly by using it to describe the behavior of functions that are defined only over exact powers of b. Recall that the definitions of asymptotic notations require that bounds be proved for all sufficiently large numbers, not just those that are powers of b. Since we could make new asymptotic notations that apply only to the set $\{b^i : i = 0, 1, 2, \ldots\}$, instead of to the nonnegative numbers, this abuse is minor.

Nevertheless, we must always be on guard when we use asymptotic notation over a limited domain lest we draw improper conclusions. For example, proving that $T(n) = O(n)$ when n is an exact power of 2 does not guarantee that $T(n) = O(n)$. The function $T(n)$ could be defined as

$$T(n) = \begin{cases} n & \text{if } n = 1, 2, 4, 8, \ldots, \\ n^2 & \text{otherwise}, \end{cases}$$

in which case the best upper bound that applies to all values of n is $T(n) = O(n^2)$. Because of this sort of drastic consequence, we shall never use asymptotic notation over a limited domain without making it absolutely clear from the context that we are doing so.

4.6.1   The proof for exact powers

The first part of the proof of the master theorem analyzes the recurrence (4.20)

$$T(n) = aT(n/b) + f(n),$$

for the master method, under the assumption that n is an exact power of $b > 1$, where b need not be an integer. We break the analysis into three lemmas. The first reduces the problem of solving the master recurrence to the problem of evaluating an expression that contains a summation. The second determines bounds on this summation. The third lemma puts the first two together to prove a version of the master theorem for the case in which n is an exact power of b.

Lemma 4.2
Let $a \geq 1$ and $b > 1$ be constants, and let $f(n)$ be a nonnegative function defined on exact powers of b. Define $T(n)$ on exact powers of b by the recurrence

$$T(n) = \begin{cases} \Theta(1) & \text{if } n = 1, \\ aT(n/b) + f(n) & \text{if } n = b^i, \end{cases}$$

where i is a positive integer. Then

$$T(n) = \Theta(n^{\log_b a}) + \sum_{j=0}^{\log_b n - 1} a^j f(n/b^j). \qquad (4.21)$$

Proof   We use the recursion tree in Figure 4.7. The root of the tree has cost $f(n)$, and it has a children, each with cost $f(n/b)$. (It is convenient to think of a as being

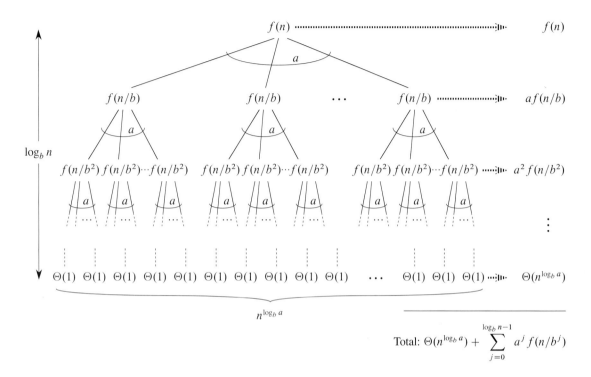

Figure 4.7 The recursion tree generated by $T(n) = aT(n/b) + f(n)$. The tree is a complete a-ary tree with $n^{\log_b a}$ leaves and height $\log_b n$. The cost of the nodes at each depth is shown at the right, and their sum is given in equation (4.21).

an integer, especially when visualizing the recursion tree, but the mathematics does not require it.) Each of these children has a children, making a^2 nodes at depth 2, and each of the a children has cost $f(n/b^2)$. In general, there are a^j nodes at depth j, and each has cost $f(n/b^j)$. The cost of each leaf is $T(1) = \Theta(1)$, and each leaf is at depth $\log_b n$, since $n/b^{\log_b n} = 1$. There are $a^{\log_b n} = n^{\log_b a}$ leaves in the tree.

We can obtain equation (4.21) by summing the costs of the nodes at each depth in the tree, as shown in the figure. The cost for all internal nodes at depth j is $a^j f(n/b^j)$, and so the total cost of all internal nodes is

$$\sum_{j=0}^{\log_b n - 1} a^j f(n/b^j) \, .$$

In the underlying divide-and-conquer algorithm, this sum represents the costs of dividing problems into subproblems and then recombining the subproblems. The cost of all the leaves, which is the cost of doing all $n^{\log_b a}$ subproblems of size 1, is $\Theta(n^{\log_b a})$. ∎

In terms of the recursion tree, the three cases of the master theorem correspond to cases in which the total cost of the tree is (1) dominated by the costs in the leaves, (2) evenly distributed among the levels of the tree, or (3) dominated by the cost of the root.

The summation in equation (4.21) describes the cost of the dividing and combining steps in the underlying divide-and-conquer algorithm. The next lemma provides asymptotic bounds on the summation's growth.

Lemma 4.3
Let $a \geq 1$ and $b > 1$ be constants, and let $f(n)$ be a nonnegative function defined on exact powers of b. A function $g(n)$ defined over exact powers of b by

$$g(n) = \sum_{j=0}^{\log_b n - 1} a^j f(n/b^j) \qquad (4.22)$$

has the following asymptotic bounds for exact powers of b:

1. If $f(n) = O(n^{\log_b a - \epsilon})$ for some constant $\epsilon > 0$, then $g(n) = O(n^{\log_b a})$.

2. If $f(n) = \Theta(n^{\log_b a})$, then $g(n) = \Theta(n^{\log_b a} \lg n)$.

3. If $af(n/b) \leq cf(n)$ for some constant $c < 1$ and for all sufficiently large n, then $g(n) = \Theta(f(n))$.

Proof   For case 1, we have $f(n) = O(n^{\log_b a - \epsilon})$, which implies that $f(n/b^j) = O((n/b^j)^{\log_b a - \epsilon})$. Substituting into equation (4.22) yields

$$g(n) = O\left(\sum_{j=0}^{\log_b n - 1} a^j \left(\frac{n}{b^j}\right)^{\log_b a - \epsilon} \right). \qquad (4.23)$$

We bound the summation within the O-notation by factoring out terms and simplifying, which leaves an increasing geometric series:

$$\sum_{j=0}^{\log_b n - 1} a^j \left(\frac{n}{b^j}\right)^{\log_b a - \epsilon} = n^{\log_b a - \epsilon} \sum_{j=0}^{\log_b n - 1} \left(\frac{ab^\epsilon}{b^{\log_b a}}\right)^j$$

$$= n^{\log_b a - \epsilon} \sum_{j=0}^{\log_b n - 1} (b^\epsilon)^j$$

$$= n^{\log_b a - \epsilon} \left(\frac{b^{\epsilon \log_b n} - 1}{b^\epsilon - 1}\right)$$

$$= n^{\log_b a - \epsilon} \left(\frac{n^\epsilon - 1}{b^\epsilon - 1} \right) .$$

Since b and ϵ are constants, we can rewrite the last expression as $n^{\log_b a - \epsilon} O(n^\epsilon) = O(n^{\log_b a})$. Substituting this expression for the summation in equation (4.23) yields

$$g(n) = O(n^{\log_b a}) ,$$

thereby proving case 1.

Because case 2 assumes that $f(n) = \Theta(n^{\log_b a})$, we have that $f(n/b^j) = \Theta((n/b^j)^{\log_b a})$. Substituting into equation (4.22) yields

$$g(n) = \Theta \left(\sum_{j=0}^{\log_b n - 1} a^j \left(\frac{n}{b^j} \right)^{\log_b a} \right) . \tag{4.24}$$

We bound the summation within the Θ-notation as in case 1, but this time we do not obtain a geometric series. Instead, we discover that every term of the summation is the same:

$$\sum_{j=0}^{\log_b n - 1} a^j \left(\frac{n}{b^j} \right)^{\log_b a} = n^{\log_b a} \sum_{j=0}^{\log_b n - 1} \left(\frac{a}{b^{\log_b a}} \right)^j$$

$$= n^{\log_b a} \sum_{j=0}^{\log_b n - 1} 1$$

$$= n^{\log_b a} \log_b n .$$

Substituting this expression for the summation in equation (4.24) yields

$$g(n) = \Theta(n^{\log_b a} \log_b n)$$
$$= \Theta(n^{\log_b a} \lg n) ,$$

proving case 2.

We prove case 3 similarly. Since $f(n)$ appears in the definition (4.22) of $g(n)$ and all terms of $g(n)$ are nonnegative, we can conclude that $g(n) = \Omega(f(n))$ for exact powers of b. We assume in the statement of the lemma that $af(n/b) \le cf(n)$ for some constant $c < 1$ and all sufficiently large n. We rewrite this assumption as $f(n/b) \le (c/a)f(n)$ and iterate j times, yielding $f(n/b^j) \le (c/a)^j f(n)$ or, equivalently, $a^j f(n/b^j) \le c^j f(n)$, where we assume that the values we iterate on are sufficiently large. This inequality holds for all but at most a constant number of terms with the smallest such values n/b^j, for which $a^j f(n/b^j) = O(1)$.

Substituting into equation (4.22) and simplifying yields a geometric series, but unlike the series in case 1, this one has decreasing terms. We use an $O(1)$ term to capture the terms that are not covered by our assumption that n is sufficiently large:

$$
\begin{aligned}
g(n) &= \sum_{j=0}^{\log_b n - 1} a^j f(n/b^j) \\
&\leq \sum_{j=0}^{\log_b n - 1} c^j f(n) + O(1) \\
&\leq f(n) \sum_{j=0}^{\infty} c^j + O(1) \\
&= f(n) \left(\frac{1}{1-c} \right) + O(1) \\
&= O(f(n)),
\end{aligned}
$$

since c is a constant. Thus, we can conclude that $g(n) = \Theta(f(n))$ for exact powers of b. With case 3 proved, the proof of the lemma is complete. ∎

We can now prove a version of the master theorem for the case in which n is an exact power of b.

Lemma 4.4

Let $a \geq 1$ and $b > 1$ be constants, and let $f(n)$ be a nonnegative function defined on exact powers of b. Define $T(n)$ on exact powers of b by the recurrence

$$
T(n) = \begin{cases} \Theta(1) & \text{if } n = 1, \\ aT(n/b) + f(n) & \text{if } n = b^i, \end{cases}
$$

where i is a positive integer. Then $T(n)$ has the following asymptotic bounds for exact powers of b:

1. If $f(n) = O(n^{\log_b a - \epsilon})$ for some constant $\epsilon > 0$, then $T(n) = \Theta(n^{\log_b a})$.

2. If $f(n) = \Theta(n^{\log_b a})$, then $T(n) = \Theta(n^{\log_b a} \lg n)$.

3. If $f(n) = \Omega(n^{\log_b a + \epsilon})$ for some constant $\epsilon > 0$, and if $af(n/b) \leq cf(n)$ for some constant $c < 1$ and all sufficiently large n, then $T(n) = \Theta(f(n))$.

Proof We use the bounds in Lemma 4.3 to evaluate the summation (4.21) from Lemma 4.2. For case 1, we have

$$
\begin{aligned}
T(n) &= \Theta(n^{\log_b a}) + O(n^{\log_b a}) \\
&= \Theta(n^{\log_b a}),
\end{aligned}
$$

and for case 2,

$$
\begin{aligned}
T(n) &= \Theta(n^{\log_b a}) + \Theta(n^{\log_b a} \lg n) \\
&= \Theta(n^{\log_b a} \lg n) .
\end{aligned}
$$

For case 3,

$$
\begin{aligned}
T(n) &= \Theta(n^{\log_b a}) + \Theta(f(n)) \\
&= \Theta(f(n)) ,
\end{aligned}
$$

because $f(n) = \Omega(n^{\log_b a + \epsilon})$. ∎

4.6.2 Floors and ceilings

To complete the proof of the master theorem, we must now extend our analysis to the situation in which floors and ceilings appear in the master recurrence, so that the recurrence is defined for all integers, not for just exact powers of b. Obtaining a lower bound on

$$
T(n) = aT(\lceil n/b \rceil) + f(n) \tag{4.25}
$$

and an upper bound on

$$
T(n) = aT(\lfloor n/b \rfloor) + f(n) \tag{4.26}
$$

is routine, since we can push through the bound $\lceil n/b \rceil \geq n/b$ in the first case to yield the desired result, and we can push through the bound $\lfloor n/b \rfloor \leq n/b$ in the second case. We use much the same technique to lower-bound the recurrence (4.26) as to upper-bound the recurrence (4.25), and so we shall present only this latter bound.

We modify the recursion tree of Figure 4.7 to produce the recursion tree in Figure 4.8. As we go down in the recursion tree, we obtain a sequence of recursive invocations on the arguments

n ,

$\lceil n/b \rceil$,

$\lceil \lceil n/b \rceil /b \rceil$,

$\lceil \lceil \lceil n/b \rceil /b \rceil /b \rceil$,

$\vdots$

Let us denote the jth element in the sequence by n_j, where

$$
n_j = \begin{cases} n & \text{if } j = 0 , \\ \lceil n_{j-1}/b \rceil & \text{if } j > 0 . \end{cases} \tag{4.27}
$$

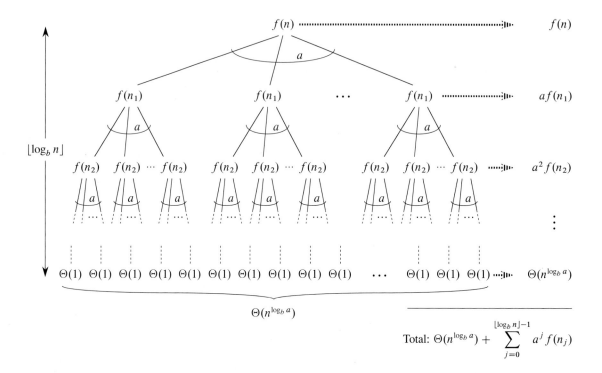

Figure 4.8   The recursion tree generated by $T(n) = aT(\lceil n/b \rceil) + f(n)$. The recursive argument n_j is given by equation (4.27).

Our first goal is to determine the depth k such that n_k is a constant. Using the inequality $\lceil x \rceil \leq x + 1$, we obtain

$$
\begin{aligned}
n_0 &\leq n, \\
n_1 &\leq \frac{n}{b} + 1, \\
n_2 &\leq \frac{n}{b^2} + \frac{1}{b} + 1, \\
n_3 &\leq \frac{n}{b^3} + \frac{1}{b^2} + \frac{1}{b} + 1, \\
&\vdots
\end{aligned}
$$

In general, we have

$$
\begin{aligned}
n_j &\le \frac{n}{b^j} + \sum_{i=0}^{j-1} \frac{1}{b^i} \\
&< \frac{n}{b^j} + \sum_{i=0}^{\infty} \frac{1}{b^i} \\
&= \frac{n}{b^j} + \frac{b}{b-1} \; .
\end{aligned}
$$

Letting $j = \lfloor \log_b n \rfloor$, we obtain

$$
\begin{aligned}
n_{\lfloor \log_b n \rfloor} &< \frac{n}{b^{\lfloor \log_b n \rfloor}} + \frac{b}{b-1} \\
&< \frac{n}{b^{\log_b n - 1}} + \frac{b}{b-1} \\
&= \frac{n}{n/b} + \frac{b}{b-1} \\
&= b + \frac{b}{b-1} \\
&= O(1) \, ,
\end{aligned}
$$

and thus we see that at depth $\lfloor \log_b n \rfloor$, the problem size is at most a constant.

From Figure 4.8, we see that

$$
T(n) = \Theta(n^{\log_b a}) + \sum_{j=0}^{\lfloor \log_b n \rfloor - 1} a^j f(n_j) \, ,
\tag{4.28}
$$

which is much the same as equation (4.21), except that n is an arbitrary integer and not restricted to be an exact power of b.

We can now evaluate the summation

$$
g(n) = \sum_{j=0}^{\lfloor \log_b n \rfloor - 1} a^j f(n_j)
\tag{4.29}
$$

from equation (4.28) in a manner analogous to the proof of Lemma 4.3. Beginning with case 3, if $af(\lceil n/b \rceil) \le cf(n)$ for $n > b + b/(b-1)$, where $c < 1$ is a constant, then it follows that $a^j f(n_j) \le c^j f(n)$. Therefore, we can evaluate the sum in equation (4.29) just as in Lemma 4.3. For case 2, we have $f(n) = \Theta(n^{\log_b a})$. If we can show that $f(n_j) = O(n^{\log_b a}/a^j) = O((n/b^j)^{\log_b a})$, then the proof for case 2 of Lemma 4.3 will go through. Observe that $j \le \lfloor \log_b n \rfloor$ implies $b^j/n \le 1$. The bound $f(n) = O(n^{\log_b a})$ implies that there exists a constant $c > 0$ such that for all sufficiently large n_j,

$$f(n_j) \leq c \left(\frac{n}{b^j} + \frac{b}{b-1} \right)^{\log_b a}$$

$$- c \left(\frac{n}{b^j} \left(1 + \frac{b^j}{n} \cdot \frac{b}{b-1} \right) \right)^{\log_b a}$$

$$= c \left(\frac{n^{\log_b a}}{a^j} \right) \left(1 + \left(\frac{b^j}{n} \cdot \frac{b}{b-1} \right) \right)^{\log_b a}$$

$$\leq c \left(\frac{n^{\log_b a}}{a^j} \right) \left(1 + \frac{b}{b-1} \right)^{\log_b a}$$

$$= O \left(\frac{n^{\log_b a}}{a^j} \right) ,$$

since $c(1 + b/(b-1))^{\log_b a}$ is a constant. Thus, we have proved case 2. The proof of case 1 is almost identical. The key is to prove the bound $f(n_j) = O((n/b^j)^{\log_b a - \epsilon})$, which is similar to the corresponding proof of case 2, though the algebra is more intricate.

We have now proved the upper bounds in the master theorem for all integers n. The proof of the lower bounds is similar.

Exercises

4.6-1 ★
Give a simple and exact expression for n_j in equation (4.27) for the case in which b is a positive integer instead of an arbitrary real number.

4.6-2 ★
Show that if $f(n) = \Theta(n^{\log_b a} \lg^k n)$, where $k \geq 0$, then the master recurrence has solution $T(n) = \Theta(n^{\log_b a} \lg^{k+1} n)$. For simplicity, confine your analysis to exact powers of b.

4.6-3 ★
Show that case 3 of the master theorem is overstated, in the sense that the regularity condition $af(n/b) \leq cf(n)$ for some constant $c < 1$ implies that there exists a constant $\epsilon > 0$ such that $f(n) = \Omega(n^{\log_b a + \epsilon})$.

Problems

4-1   Recurrence examples

Give asymptotic upper and lower bounds for $T(n)$ in each of the following recurrences. Assume that $T(n)$ is constant for $n \leq 2$. Make your bounds as tight as possible, and justify your answers.

a. $T(n) = 2T(n/2) + n^4$.

b. $T(n) = T(7n/10) + n$.

c. $T(n) = 16T(n/4) + n^2$.

d. $T(n) = 7T(n/3) + n^2$.

e. $T(n) = 7T(n/2) + n^2$.

f. $T(n) = 2T(n/4) + \sqrt{n}$.

g. $T(n) = T(n - 2) + n^2$.

4-2   Parameter-passing costs

Throughout this book, we assume that parameter passing during procedure calls takes constant time, even if an N-element array is being passed. This assumption is valid in most systems because a pointer to the array is passed, not the array itself. This problem examines the implications of three parameter-passing strategies:

1. An array is passed by pointer. Time $= \Theta(1)$.

2. An array is passed by copying. Time $= \Theta(N)$, where N is the size of the array.

3. An array is passed by copying only the subrange that might be accessed by the called procedure. Time $= \Theta(q - p + 1)$ if the subarray $A[p \mathinner{.\,.} q]$ is passed.

a. Consider the recursive binary search algorithm for finding a number in a sorted array (see Exercise 2.3-5). Give recurrences for the worst-case running times of binary search when arrays are passed using each of the three methods above, and give good upper bounds on the solutions of the recurrences. Let N be the size of the original problem and n be the size of a subproblem.

b. Redo part (a) for the MERGE-SORT algorithm from Section 2.3.1.

4-3   More recurrence examples

Give asymptotic upper and lower bounds for $T(n)$ in each of the following recurrences. Assume that $T(n)$ is constant for sufficiently small n. Make your bounds as tight as possible, and justify your answers.

a. $T(n) = 4T(n/3) + n \lg n$.

b. $T(n) = 3T(n/3) + n/\lg n$.

c. $T(n) = 4T(n/2) + n^2 \sqrt{n}$.

d. $T(n) = 3T(n/3 - 2) + n/2$.

e. $T(n) = 2T(n/2) + n/\lg n$.

f. $T(n) = T(n/2) + T(n/4) + T(n/8) + n$.

g. $T(n) = T(n-1) + 1/n$.

h. $T(n) = T(n-1) + \lg n$.

i. $T(n) = T(n-2) + 1/\lg n$.

j. $T(n) = \sqrt{n}T(\sqrt{n}) + n$.

4-4   Fibonacci numbers

This problem develops properties of the Fibonacci numbers, which are defined by recurrence (3.22). We shall use the technique of generating functions to solve the Fibonacci recurrence. Define the **generating function** (or **formal power series**) $\mathcal{F}$ as

$$\mathcal{F}(z) \; = \; \sum_{i=0}^{\infty} F_i z^i$$
$$= \; 0 + z + z^2 + 2z^3 + 3z^4 + 5z^5 + 8z^6 + 13z^7 + 21z^8 + \cdots,$$

where F_i is the ith Fibonacci number.

a. Show that $\mathcal{F}(z) = z + z\mathcal{F}(z) + z^2\mathcal{F}(z)$.

b. Show that

$$
\begin{aligned}
\mathcal{F}(z) &= \frac{z}{1 - z - z^2} \\
&= \frac{z}{(1 - \phi z)(1 - \hat{\phi} z)} \\
&= \frac{1}{\sqrt{5}} \left(\frac{1}{1 - \phi z} - \frac{1}{1 - \hat{\phi} z} \right) ,
\end{aligned}
$$

where

$$
\phi = \frac{1 + \sqrt{5}}{2} = 1.61803\ldots
$$

and

$$
\hat{\phi} = \frac{1 - \sqrt{5}}{2} = -0.61803\ldots .
$$

c. Show that

$$
\mathcal{F}(z) = \sum_{i=0}^{\infty} \frac{1}{\sqrt{5}} (\phi^i - \hat{\phi}^i) z^i .
$$

d. Use part (c) to prove that $F_i = \phi^i / \sqrt{5}$ for $i > 0$, rounded to the nearest integer. (*Hint:* Observe that $\left| \hat{\phi} \right| < 1$.)

4-5 *Chip testing*

Professor Diogenes has n supposedly identical integrated-circuit chips that in principle are capable of testing each other. The professor's test jig accommodates two chips at a time. When the jig is loaded, each chip tests the other and reports whether it is good or bad. A good chip always reports accurately whether the other chip is good or bad, but the professor cannot trust the answer of a bad chip. Thus, the four possible outcomes of a test are as follows:

Chip A says	Chip B says	Conclusion
B is good	A is good	both are good, or both are bad
B is good	A is bad	at least one is bad
B is bad	A is good	at least one is bad
B is bad	A is bad	at least one is bad

a. Show that if at least $n/2$ chips are bad, the professor cannot necessarily determine which chips are good using any strategy based on this kind of pairwise test. Assume that the bad chips can conspire to fool the professor.

b. Consider the problem of finding a single good chip from among n chips, assuming that more than $n/2$ of the chips are good. Show that $\lfloor n/2 \rfloor$ pairwise tests are sufficient to reduce the problem to one of nearly half the size.

c. Show that the good chips can be identified with $\Theta(n)$ pairwise tests, assuming that more than $n/2$ of the chips are good. Give and solve the recurrence that describes the number of tests.

4-6 *Monge arrays*

An $m \times n$ array A of real numbers is a **Monge array** if for all i, j, k, and l such that $1 \le i < k \le m$ and $1 \le j < l \le n$, we have

$$A[i, j] + A[k, l] \le A[i, l] + A[k, j] .$$

In other words, whenever we pick two rows and two columns of a Monge array and consider the four elements at the intersections of the rows and the columns, the sum of the upper-left and lower-right elements is less than or equal to the sum of the lower-left and upper-right elements. For example, the following array is Monge:

```
10   17   13   28   23
17   22   16   29   23
24   28   22   34   24
11   13    6   17    7
45   44   32   37   23
36   33   19   21    6
75   66   51   53   34
```

a. Prove that an array is Monge if and only if for all $i = 1, 2, ..., m - 1$ and $j = 1, 2, ..., n - 1$, we have

$$A[i, j] + A[i + 1, j + 1] \le A[i, j + 1] + A[i + 1, j] .$$

(*Hint:* For the "if" part, use induction separately on rows and columns.)

b. The following array is not Monge. Change one element in order to make it Monge. (*Hint:* Use part (a).)

```
37   23   22   32
21    6    7   10
53   34   30   31
32   13    9    6
43   21   15    8
```

c. Let $f(i)$ be the index of the column containing the leftmost minimum element of row i. Prove that $f(1) \leq f(2) \leq \cdots \leq f(m)$ for any $m \times n$ Monge array.

d. Here is a description of a divide-and-conquer algorithm that computes the leftmost minimum element in each row of an $m \times n$ Monge array A:

> Construct a submatrix A' of A consisting of the even-numbered rows of A. Recursively determine the leftmost minimum for each row of A'. Then compute the leftmost minimum in the odd-numbered rows of A.

Explain how to compute the leftmost minimum in the odd-numbered rows of A (given that the leftmost minimum of the even-numbered rows is known) in $O(m + n)$ time.

e. Write the recurrence describing the running time of the algorithm described in part (d). Show that its solution is $O(m + n \log m)$.

Chapter notes

Divide-and-conquer as a technique for designing algorithms dates back to at least 1962 in an article by Karatsuba and Ofman [194]. It might have been used well before then, however; according to Heideman, Johnson, and Burrus [163], C. F. Gauss devised the first fast Fourier transform algorithm in 1805, and Gauss's formulation breaks the problem into smaller subproblems whose solutions are combined.

The maximum-subarray problem in Section 4.1 is a minor variation on a problem studied by Bentley [43, Chapter 7].

Strassen's algorithm [325] caused much excitement when it was published in 1969. Before then, few imagined the possibility of an algorithm asymptotically faster than the basic SQUARE-MATRIX-MULTIPLY procedure. The asymptotic upper bound for matrix multiplication has been improved since then. The most asymptotically efficient algorithm for multiplying $n \times n$ matrices to date, due to Coppersmith and Winograd [78], has a running time of $O(n^{2.376})$. The best lower bound known is just the obvious $\Omega(n^2)$ bound (obvious because we must fill in n^2 elements of the product matrix).

From a practical point of view, Strassen's algorithm is often not the method of choice for matrix multiplication, for four reasons:

1. The constant factor hidden in the $\Theta(n^{\lg 7})$ running time of Strassen's algorithm is larger than the constant factor in the $\Theta(n^3)$-time SQUARE-MATRIX-MULTIPLY procedure.

2. When the matrices are sparse, methods tailored for sparse matrices are faster.

3. Strassen's algorithm is not quite as numerically stable as SQUARE-MATRIX-MULTIPLY. In other words, because of the limited precision of computer arithmetic on noninteger values, larger errors accumulate in Strassen's algorithm than in SQUARE-MATRIX-MULTIPLY.

4. The submatrices formed at the levels of recursion consume space.

The latter two reasons were mitigated around 1990. Higham [167] demonstrated that the difference in numerical stability had been overemphasized; although Strassen's algorithm is too numerically unstable for some applications, it is within acceptable limits for others. Bailey, Lee, and Simon [32] discuss techniques for reducing the memory requirements for Strassen's algorithm.

In practice, fast matrix-multiplication implementations for dense matrices use Strassen's algorithm for matrix sizes above a "crossover point," and they switch to a simpler method once the subproblem size reduces to below the crossover point. The exact value of the crossover point is highly system dependent. Analyses that count operations but ignore effects from caches and pipelining have produced crossover points as low as $n = 8$ (by Higham [167]) or $n = 12$ (by Huss-Lederman et al. [186]). D'Alberto and Nicolau [81] developed an adaptive scheme, which determines the crossover point by benchmarking when their software package is installed. They found crossover points on various systems ranging from $n = 400$ to $n = 2150$, and they could not find a crossover point on a couple of systems.

Recurrences were studied as early as 1202 by L. Fibonacci, for whom the Fibonacci numbers are named. A. De Moivre introduced the method of generating functions (see Problem 4-4) for solving recurrences. The master method is adapted from Bentley, Haken, and Saxe [44], which provides the extended method justified by Exercise 4.6-2. Knuth [209] and Liu [237] show how to solve linear recurrences using the method of generating functions. Purdom and Brown [287] and Graham, Knuth, and Patashnik [152] contain extended discussions of recurrence solving.

Several researchers, including Akra and Bazzi [13], Roura [299], Verma [346], and Yap [360], have given methods for solving more general divide-and-conquer recurrences than are solved by the master method. We describe the result of Akra and Bazzi here, as modified by Leighton [228]. The Akra-Bazzi method works for recurrences of the form

$$T(x) = \begin{cases} \Theta(1) & \text{if } 1 \le x \le x_0, \\ \sum_{i=1}^{k} a_i T(b_i x) + f(x) & \text{if } x > x_0, \end{cases} \qquad (4.30)$$

where

- $x \ge 1$ is a real number,

- x_0 is a constant such that $x_0 \ge 1/b_i$ and $x_0 \ge 1/(1 - b_i)$ for $i = 1, 2, \ldots, k$,

- a_i is a positive constant for $i = 1, 2, \ldots, k$ and $\sum_{i=1}^{k} a_i \ge 1$,

- b_i is a constant in the range $0 < b_i < 1$ for $i = 1, 2, \ldots, k$,

- $k \geq 1$ is an integer constant, and

- $f(x)$ is a nonnegative function that satisfies the **polynomial-growth condition**: there exist positive constants c_1 and c_2 such that for all $x \geq 1$, for $i = 1, 2, \ldots, k$, and for all u such that $b_i x \leq u \leq x$, we have $c_1 f(x) \leq f(u) \leq c_2 f(x)$. (If $|f'(x)|$ is upper-bounded by some polynomial in x, then $f(x)$ satisfies the polynomial-growth condition. For example, $f(x) = x^\alpha \lg^\beta x$ satisfies this condition for any real constants α and β.)

Although the master method does not apply to a recurrence such as $T(n) = T(\lfloor n/3 \rfloor) + T(\lfloor 2n/3 \rfloor) + O(n)$, the Akra-Bazzi method does. To solve the recurrence (4.30), we first find the unique real number p such that $\sum_{i=1}^{k} a_i b_i^p = 1$. (Such a p always exists.) The solution to the recurrence is then

$$T(x) = \Theta \left(x^p \left(1 + \int_1^x \frac{f(u)}{u^{p+1}} \, du \right) \right) .$$

The Akra-Bazzi method can be somewhat difficult to use, but it serves in solving recurrences that model division of the problem into substantially unequally sized subproblems. The master method is simpler to use, but it applies only when subproblem sizes are equal.

5 Probabilistic Analysis and Randomized Algorithms

This chapter introduces probabilistic analysis and randomized algorithms. If you are unfamiliar with the basics of probability theory, you should read Appendix C, which reviews this material. We shall revisit probabilistic analysis and randomized algorithms several times throughout this book.

5.1 The hiring problem

Suppose that you need to hire a new office assistant. Your previous attempts at hiring have been unsuccessful, and you decide to use an employment agency. The employment agency sends you one candidate each day. You interview that person and then decide either to hire that person or not. You must pay the employment agency a small fee to interview an applicant. To actually hire an applicant is more costly, however, since you must fire your current office assistant and pay a substantial hiring fee to the employment agency. You are committed to having, at all times, the best possible person for the job. Therefore, you decide that, after interviewing each applicant, if that applicant is better qualified than the current office assistant, you will fire the current office assistant and hire the new applicant. You are willing to pay the resulting price of this strategy, but you wish to estimate what that price will be.

The procedure HIRE-ASSISTANT, given below, expresses this strategy for hiring in pseudocode. It assumes that the candidates for the office assistant job are numbered 1 through n. The procedure assumes that you are able to, after interviewing candidate i, determine whether candidate i is the best candidate you have seen so far. To initialize, the procedure creates a dummy candidate, numbered 0, who is less qualified than each of the other candidates.

Hire-Assistant(n)

```
1  best = 0          // candidate 0 is a least-qualified dummy candidate
2  for i = 1 to n
3      interview candidate i
4      if candidate i is better than candidate best
5          best = i
6          hire candidate i
```

The cost model for this problem differs from the model described in Chapter 2. We focus not on the running time of Hire-Assistant, but instead on the costs incurred by interviewing and hiring. On the surface, analyzing the cost of this algorithm may seem very different from analyzing the running time of, say, merge sort. The analytical techniques used, however, are identical whether we are analyzing cost or running time. In either case, we are counting the number of times certain basic operations are executed.

Interviewing has a low cost, say c_i, whereas hiring is expensive, costing c_h. Letting m be the number of people hired, the total cost associated with this algorithm is $O(c_i n + c_h m)$. No matter how many people we hire, we always interview n candidates and thus always incur the cost $c_i n$ associated with interviewing. We therefore concentrate on analyzing $c_h m$, the hiring cost. This quantity varies with each run of the algorithm.

This scenario serves as a model for a common computational paradigm. We often need to find the maximum or minimum value in a sequence by examining each element of the sequence and maintaining a current "winner." The hiring problem models how often we update our notion of which element is currently winning.

Worst-case analysis

In the worst case, we actually hire every candidate that we interview. This situation occurs if the candidates come in strictly increasing order of quality, in which case we hire n times, for a total hiring cost of $O(c_h n)$.

Of course, the candidates do not always come in increasing order of quality. In fact, we have no idea about the order in which they arrive, nor do we have any control over this order. Therefore, it is natural to ask what we expect to happen in a typical or average case.

Probabilistic analysis

Probabilistic analysis is the use of probability in the analysis of problems. Most commonly, we use probabilistic analysis to analyze the running time of an algorithm. Sometimes we use it to analyze other quantities, such as the hiring cost in procedure HIRE-ASSISTANT. In order to perform a probabilistic analysis, we must use knowledge of, or make assumptions about, the distribution of the inputs. Then we analyze our algorithm, computing an average-case running time, where we take the average over the distribution of the possible inputs. Thus we are, in effect, averaging the running time over all possible inputs. When reporting such a running time, we will refer to it as the ***average-case running time***.

We must be very careful in deciding on the distribution of inputs. For some problems, we may reasonably assume something about the set of all possible inputs, and then we can use probabilistic analysis as a technique for designing an efficient algorithm and as a means for gaining insight into a problem. For other problems, we cannot describe a reasonable input distribution, and in these cases we cannot use probabilistic analysis.

For the hiring problem, we can assume that the applicants come in a random order. What does that mean for this problem? We assume that we can compare any two candidates and decide which one is better qualified; that is, there is a total order on the candidates. (See Appendix B for the definition of a total order.) Thus, we can rank each candidate with a unique number from 1 through n, using $rank(i)$ to denote the rank of applicant i, and adopt the convention that a higher rank corresponds to a better qualified applicant. The ordered list $\langle rank(1), rank(2), \ldots, rank(n) \rangle$ is a permutation of the list $\langle 1, 2, \ldots, n \rangle$. Saying that the applicants come in a random order is equivalent to saying that this list of ranks is equally likely to be any one of the $n!$ permutations of the numbers 1 through n. Alternatively, we say that the ranks form a ***uniform random permutation***; that is, each of the possible $n!$ permutations appears with equal probability.

Section 5.2 contains a probabilistic analysis of the hiring problem.

Randomized algorithms

In order to use probabilistic analysis, we need to know something about the distribution of the inputs. In many cases, we know very little about the input distribution. Even if we do know something about the distribution, we may not be able to model this knowledge computationally. Yet we often can use probability and randomness as a tool for algorithm design and analysis, by making the behavior of part of the algorithm random.

In the hiring problem, it may seem as if the candidates are being presented to us in a random order, but we have no way of knowing whether or not they really are. Thus, in order to develop a randomized algorithm for the hiring problem, we must have greater control over the order in which we interview the candidates. We will, therefore, change the model slightly. We say that the employment agency has n candidates, and they send us a list of the candidates in advance. On each day, we choose, randomly, which candidate to interview. Although we know nothing about the candidates (besides their names), we have made a significant change. Instead of relying on a guess that the candidates come to us in a random order, we have instead gained control of the process and enforced a random order.

More generally, we call an algorithm *randomized* if its behavior is determined not only by its input but also by values produced by a *random-number generator*. We shall assume that we have at our disposal a random-number generator RANDOM. A call to RANDOM(a, b) returns an integer between a and b, inclusive, with each such integer being equally likely. For example, RANDOM($0, 1$) produces 0 with probability $1/2$, and it produces 1 with probability $1/2$. A call to RANDOM($3, 7$) returns either 3, 4, 5, 6, or 7, each with probability $1/5$. Each integer returned by RANDOM is independent of the integers returned on previous calls. You may imagine RANDOM as rolling a $(b - a + 1)$-sided die to obtain its output. (In practice, most programming environments offer a *pseudorandom-number generator*: a deterministic algorithm returning numbers that "look" statistically random.)

When analyzing the running time of a randomized algorithm, we take the expectation of the running time over the distribution of values returned by the random number generator. We distinguish these algorithms from those in which the input is random by referring to the running time of a randomized algorithm as an *expected running time*. In general, we discuss the average-case running time when the probability distribution is over the inputs to the algorithm, and we discuss the expected running time when the algorithm itself makes random choices.

Exercises

5.1-1
Show that the assumption that we are always able to determine which candidate is best, in line 4 of procedure HIRE-ASSISTANT, implies that we know a total order on the ranks of the candidates.

5.1-2 ⋆
Describe an implementation of the procedure RANDOM(a, b) that only makes calls to RANDOM($0, 1$). What is the expected running time of your procedure, as a function of a and b?

5.1-3 ⋆
Suppose that you want to output 0 with probability $1/2$ and 1 with probability $1/2$. At your disposal is a procedure BIASED-RANDOM, that outputs either 0 or 1. It outputs 1 with some probability p and 0 with probability $1 - p$, where $0 < p < 1$, but you do not know what p is. Give an algorithm that uses BIASED-RANDOM as a subroutine, and returns an unbiased answer, returning 0 with probability $1/2$

and 1 with probability $1/2$. What is the expected running time of your algorithm as a function of p?

5.2   Indicator random variables

In order to analyze many algorithms, including the hiring problem, we use indicator random variables. Indicator random variables provide a convenient method for converting between probabilities and expectations. Suppose we are given a sample space S and an event A. Then the ***indicator random variable*** $I\{A\}$ associated with event A is defined as

$$I\{A\} = \begin{cases} 1 & \text{if } A \text{ occurs ,} \\ 0 & \text{if } A \text{ does not occur .} \end{cases} \qquad (5.1)$$

As a simple example, let us determine the expected number of heads that we obtain when flipping a fair coin. Our sample space is $S = \{H, T\}$, with $\Pr\{H\} = \Pr\{T\} = 1/2$. We can then define an indicator random variable X_H, associated with the coin coming up heads, which is the event H. This variable counts the number of heads obtained in this flip, and it is 1 if the coin comes up heads and 0 otherwise. We write

$$\begin{aligned} X_H &= I\{H\} \\ &= \begin{cases} 1 & \text{if } H \text{ occurs ,} \\ 0 & \text{if } T \text{ occurs .} \end{cases} \end{aligned}$$

The expected number of heads obtained in one flip of the coin is simply the expected value of our indicator variable X_H:

$$\begin{aligned} E[X_H] &= E[I\{H\}] \\ &= 1 \cdot \Pr\{H\} + 0 \cdot \Pr\{T\} \\ &= 1 \cdot (1/2) + 0 \cdot (1/2) \\ &= 1/2 . \end{aligned}$$

Thus the expected number of heads obtained by one flip of a fair coin is $1/2$. As the following lemma shows, the expected value of an indicator random variable associated with an event A is equal to the probability that A occurs.

Lemma 5.1
Given a sample space S and an event A in the sample space S, let $X_A = I\{A\}$. Then $E[X_A] = \Pr\{A\}$.

Proof By the definition of an indicator random variable from equation (5.1) and the definition of expected value, we have

$$
\begin{aligned}
\mathrm{E}[X_A] &= \mathrm{E}[\mathrm{I}\{A\}] \\
&= 1 \cdot \mathrm{Pr}\{A\} + 0 \cdot \mathrm{Pr}\{\overline{A}\} \\
&= \mathrm{Pr}\{A\} \ ,
\end{aligned}
$$

where $\overline{A}$ denotes $S - A$, the complement of A. ∎

Although indicator random variables may seem cumbersome for an application such as counting the expected number of heads on a flip of a single coin, they are useful for analyzing situations in which we perform repeated random trials. For example, indicator random variables give us a simple way to arrive at the result of equation (C.37). In this equation, we compute the number of heads in n coin flips by considering separately the probability of obtaining 0 heads, 1 head, 2 heads, etc. The simpler method proposed in equation (C.38) instead uses indicator random variables implicitly. Making this argument more explicit, we let X_i be the indicator random variable associated with the event in which the ith flip comes up heads: $X_i = \mathrm{I}\{\text{the } i\text{th flip results in the event } H\}$. Let X be the random variable denoting the total number of heads in the n coin flips, so that

$$
X = \sum_{i=1}^{n} X_i \ .
$$

We wish to compute the expected number of heads, and so we take the expectation of both sides of the above equation to obtain

$$
\mathrm{E}[X] = \mathrm{E}\left[\sum_{i=1}^{n} X_i\right] \ .
$$

The above equation gives the expectation of the sum of n indicator random variables. By Lemma 5.1, we can easily compute the expectation of each of the random variables. By equation (C.21)—linearity of expectation—it is easy to compute the expectation of the sum: it equals the sum of the expectations of the n random variables. Linearity of expectation makes the use of indicator random variables a powerful analytical technique; it applies even when there is dependence among the random variables. We now can easily compute the expected number of heads:

$$
\begin{aligned}
\mathrm{E}[X] &= \mathrm{E}\left[\sum_{i=1}^{n} X_i\right] \\
&= \sum_{i=1}^{n} \mathrm{E}[X_i] \\
&= \sum_{i=1}^{n} 1/2 \\
&= n/2 \,.
\end{aligned}
$$

Thus, compared to the method used in equation (C.37), indicator random variables greatly simplify the calculation. We shall use indicator random variables throughout this book.

Analysis of the hiring problem using indicator random variables

Returning to the hiring problem, we now wish to compute the expected number of times that we hire a new office assistant. In order to use a probabilistic analysis, we assume that the candidates arrive in a random order, as discussed in the previous section. (We shall see in Section 5.3 how to remove this assumption.) Let X be the random variable whose value equals the number of times we hire a new office assistant. We could then apply the definition of expected value from equation (C.20) to obtain

$$
\mathrm{E}[X] = \sum_{x=1}^{n} x \, \Pr\{X = x\} \,,
$$

but this calculation would be cumbersome. We shall instead use indicator random variables to greatly simplify the calculation.

To use indicator random variables, instead of computing $\mathrm{E}[X]$ by defining one variable associated with the number of times we hire a new office assistant, we define n variables related to whether or not each particular candidate is hired. In particular, we let X_i be the indicator random variable associated with the event in which the ith candidate is hired. Thus,

$$
\begin{aligned}
X_i &= \mathrm{I}\{\text{candidate } i \text{ is hired}\} \\
&= \begin{cases} 1 & \text{if candidate } i \text{ is hired}, \\ 0 & \text{if candidate } i \text{ is not hired}, \end{cases}
\end{aligned}
$$

and

$$
X = X_1 + X_2 + \cdots + X_n \,. \tag{5.2}
$$

By Lemma 5.1, we have that

$$E[X_i] = \Pr\{\text{candidate } i \text{ is hired}\} \;,$$

and we must therefore compute the probability that lines 5–6 of HIRE-ASSISTANT are executed.

Candidate i is hired, in line 6, exactly when candidate i is better than each of candidates 1 through $i - 1$. Because we have assumed that the candidates arrive in a random order, the first i candidates have appeared in a random order. Any one of these first i candidates is equally likely to be the best-qualified so far. Candidate i has a probability of $1/i$ of being better qualified than candidates 1 through $i - 1$ and thus a probability of $1/i$ of being hired. By Lemma 5.1, we conclude that

$$E[X_i] = 1/i \;. \tag{5.3}$$

Now we can compute $E[X]$:

$$
\begin{aligned}
E[X] &= E\left[\sum_{i=1}^{n} X_i\right] && \text{(by equation (5.2))} && (5.4)\\
&= \sum_{i=1}^{n} E[X_i] && \text{(by linearity of expectation)} \\
&= \sum_{i=1}^{n} 1/i && \text{(by equation (5.3))} \\
&= \ln n + O(1) && \text{(by equation (A.7))} \;. && (5.5)
\end{aligned}
$$

Even though we interview n people, we actually hire only approximately $\ln n$ of them, on average. We summarize this result in the following lemma.

Lemma 5.2

Assuming that the candidates are presented in a random order, algorithm HIRE-ASSISTANT has an average-case total hiring cost of $O(c_h \ln n)$.

Proof The bound follows immediately from our definition of the hiring cost and equation (5.5), which shows that the expected number of hires is approximately $\ln n$.   ∎

The average-case hiring cost is a significant improvement over the worst-case hiring cost of $O(c_h n)$.

Exercises

5.2-1

In HIRE-ASSISTANT, assuming that the candidates are presented in a random order, what is the probability that you hire exactly one time? What is the probability that you hire exactly n times?

5.2-2

In HIRE-ASSISTANT, assuming that the candidates are presented in a random order, what is the probability that you hire exactly twice?

5.2-3

Use indicator random variables to compute the expected value of the sum of n dice.

5.2-4

Use indicator random variables to solve the following problem, which is known as the ***hat-check problem***. Each of n customers gives a hat to a hat-check person at a restaurant. The hat-check person gives the hats back to the customers in a random order. What is the expected number of customers who get back their own hat?

5.2-5

Let $A[1 .. n]$ be an array of n distinct numbers. If $i < j$ and $A[i] > A[j]$, then the pair (i, j) is called an ***inversion*** of A. (See Problem 2-4 for more on inversions.) Suppose that the elements of A form a uniform random permutation of $\langle 1, 2, \ldots, n \rangle$. Use indicator random variables to compute the expected number of inversions.

5.3   Randomized algorithms

In the previous section, we showed how knowing a distribution on the inputs can help us to analyze the average-case behavior of an algorithm. Many times, we do not have such knowledge, thus precluding an average-case analysis. As mentioned in Section 5.1, we may be able to use a randomized algorithm.

For a problem such as the hiring problem, in which it is helpful to assume that all permutations of the input are equally likely, a probabilistic analysis can guide the development of a randomized algorithm. Instead of assuming a distribution of inputs, we impose a distribution. In particular, before running the algorithm, we randomly permute the candidates in order to enforce the property that every permutation is equally likely. Although we have modified the algorithm, we still expect to hire a new office assistant approximately $\ln n$ times. But now we expect this to be the case for *any* input, rather than for inputs drawn from a particular distribution.

Let us further explore the distinction between probabilistic analysis and randomized algorithms. In Section 5.2, we claimed that, assuming that the candidates arrive in a random order, the expected number of times we hire a new office assistant is about $\ln n$. Note that the algorithm here is deterministic; for any particular input, the number of times a new office assistant is hired is always the same. Furthermore, the number of times we hire a new office assistant differs for different inputs, and it depends on the ranks of the various candidates. Since this number depends only on the ranks of the candidates, we can represent a particular input by listing, in order, the ranks of the candidates, i.e., $\langle rank(1), rank(2), \ldots, rank(n) \rangle$. Given the rank list $A_1 = \langle 1, 2, 3, 4, 5, 6, 7, 8, 9, 10 \rangle$, a new office assistant is always hired 10 times, since each successive candidate is better than the previous one, and lines 5–6 are executed in each iteration. Given the list of ranks $A_2 = \langle 10, 9, 8, 7, 6, 5, 4, 3, 2, 1 \rangle$, a new office assistant is hired only once, in the first iteration. Given a list of ranks $A_3 = \langle 5, 2, 1, 8, 4, 7, 10, 9, 3, 6 \rangle$, a new office assistant is hired three times, upon interviewing the candidates with ranks 5, 8, and 10. Recalling that the cost of our algorithm depends on how many times we hire a new office assistant, we see that there are expensive inputs such as A_1, inexpensive inputs such as A_2, and moderately expensive inputs such as A_3.

Consider, on the other hand, the randomized algorithm that first permutes the candidates and then determines the best candidate. In this case, we randomize in the algorithm, not in the input distribution. Given a particular input, say A_3 above, we cannot say how many times the maximum is updated, because this quantity differs with each run of the algorithm. The first time we run the algorithm on A_3, it may produce the permutation A_1 and perform 10 updates; but the second time we run the algorithm, we may produce the permutation A_2 and perform only one update. The third time we run it, we may perform some other number of updates. Each time we run the algorithm, the execution depends on the random choices made and is likely to differ from the previous execution of the algorithm. For this algorithm and many other randomized algorithms, *no particular input elicits its worst-case behavior*. Even your worst enemy cannot produce a bad input array, since the random permutation makes the input order irrelevant. The randomized algorithm performs badly only if the random-number generator produces an "unlucky" permutation.

For the hiring problem, the only change needed in the code is to randomly permute the array.

RANDOMIZED-HIRE-ASSISTANT(n)

```
1   randomly permute the list of candidates
2   best = 0          // candidate 0 is a least-qualified dummy candidate
3   for i = 1 to n
4       interview candidate i
5       if candidate i is better than candidate best
6           best = i
7           hire candidate i
```

With this simple change, we have created a randomized algorithm whose performance matches that obtained by assuming that the candidates were presented in a random order.

Lemma 5.3
The expected hiring cost of the procedure RANDOMIZED-HIRE-ASSISTANT is $O(c_h \ln n)$.

Proof   After permuting the input array, we have achieved a situation identical to that of the probabilistic analysis of HIRE-ASSISTANT.   ■

Comparing Lemmas 5.2 and 5.3 highlights the difference between probabilistic analysis and randomized algorithms. In Lemma 5.2, we make an assumption about the input. In Lemma 5.3, we make no such assumption, although randomizing the input takes some additional time. To remain consistent with our terminology, we couched Lemma 5.2 in terms of the average-case hiring cost and Lemma 5.3 in terms of the expected hiring cost. In the remainder of this section, we discuss some issues involved in randomly permuting inputs.

Randomly permuting arrays

Many randomized algorithms randomize the input by permuting the given input array. (There are other ways to use randomization.) Here, we shall discuss two methods for doing so. We assume that we are given an array A which, without loss of generality, contains the elements 1 through n. Our goal is to produce a random permutation of the array.

One common method is to assign each element $A[i]$ of the array a random priority $P[i]$, and then sort the elements of A according to these priorities. For example, if our initial array is $A = \langle 1, 2, 3, 4 \rangle$ and we choose random priorities $P = \langle 36, 3, 62, 19 \rangle$, we would produce an array $B = \langle 2, 4, 1, 3 \rangle$, since the second priority is the smallest, followed by the fourth, then the first, and finally the third. We call this procedure PERMUTE-BY-SORTING:

PERMUTE-BY-SORTING(A)

```
1  n = A.length
2  let P[1..n] be a new array
3  for i = 1 to n
4      P[i] = RANDOM(1, n³)
5  sort A, using P as sort keys
```

Line 4 chooses a random number between 1 and n^3. We use a range of 1 to n^3 to make it likely that all the priorities in P are unique. (Exercise 5.3-5 asks you to prove that the probability that all entries are unique is at least $1 - 1/n$, and Exercise 5.3-6 asks how to implement the algorithm even if two or more priorities are identical.) Let us assume that all the priorities are unique.

The time-consuming step in this procedure is the sorting in line 5. As we shall see in Chapter 8, if we use a comparison sort, sorting takes $\Omega(n \lg n)$ time. We can achieve this lower bound, since we have seen that merge sort takes $\Theta(n \lg n)$ time. (We shall see other comparison sorts that take $\Theta(n \lg n)$ time in Part II. Exercise 8.3-4 asks you to solve the very similar problem of sorting numbers in the range 0 to $n^3 - 1$ in $O(n)$ time.) After sorting, if $P[i]$ is the jth smallest priority, then $A[i]$ lies in position j of the output. In this manner we obtain a permutation. It remains to prove that the procedure produces a ***uniform random permutation***, that is, that the procedure is equally likely to produce every permutation of the numbers 1 through n.

Lemma 5.4

Procedure PERMUTE-BY-SORTING produces a uniform random permutation of the input, assuming that all priorities are distinct.

Proof We start by considering the particular permutation in which each element $A[i]$ receives the ith smallest priority. We shall show that this permutation occurs with probability exactly $1/n!$. For $i = 1, 2, \ldots, n$, let E_i be the event that element $A[i]$ receives the ith smallest priority. Then we wish to compute the probability that for all i, event E_i occurs, which is

$$\Pr\{E_1 \cap E_2 \cap E_3 \cap \cdots \cap E_{n-1} \cap E_n\} \ .$$

Using Exercise C.2-5, this probability is equal to

$$\Pr\{E_1\} \cdot \Pr\{E_2 \mid E_1\} \cdot \Pr\{E_3 \mid E_2 \cap E_1\} \cdot \Pr\{E_4 \mid E_3 \cap E_2 \cap E_1\}$$
$$\cdots \Pr\{E_i \mid E_{i-1} \cap E_{i-2} \cap \cdots \cap E_1\} \cdots \Pr\{E_n \mid E_{n-1} \cap \cdots \cap E_1\} \ .$$

We have that $\Pr\{E_1\} = 1/n$ because it is the probability that one priority chosen randomly out of a set of n is the smallest priority. Next, we observe that $\Pr\{E_2 \mid E_1\} = 1/(n-1)$ because given that element $A[1]$ has the small-est priority, each of the remaining $n-1$ elements has an equal chance of having the second smallest priority. In general, for $i = 2, 3, \ldots, n$, we have that $\Pr\{E_i \mid E_{i-1} \cap E_{i-2} \cap \cdots \cap E_1\} = 1/(n-i+1)$, since, given that elements $A[1]$ through $A[i-1]$ have the $i-1$ smallest priorities (in order), each of the remaining $n-(i-1)$ elements has an equal chance of having the ith smallest priority. Thus, we have

$$\Pr\{E_1 \cap E_2 \cap E_3 \cap \cdots \cap E_{n-1} \cap E_n\} = \left(\frac{1}{n}\right)\left(\frac{1}{n-1}\right)\cdots\left(\frac{1}{2}\right)\left(\frac{1}{1}\right)$$
$$= \frac{1}{n!},$$

and we have shown that the probability of obtaining the identity permutation is $1/n!$.

We can extend this proof to work for any permutation of priorities. Consider any fixed permutation $\sigma = \langle \sigma(1), \sigma(2), \ldots, \sigma(n) \rangle$ of the set $\{1, 2, \ldots, n\}$. Let us denote by r_i the rank of the priority assigned to element $A[i]$, where the element with the jth smallest priority has rank j. If we define E_i as the event in which element $A[i]$ receives the $\sigma(i)$th smallest priority, or $r_i = \sigma(i)$, the same proof still applies. Therefore, if we calculate the probability of obtaining any particular permutation, the calculation is identical to the one above, so that the probability of obtaining this permutation is also $1/n!$.   ∎

You might think that to prove that a permutation is a uniform random permuta-tion, it suffices to show that, for each element $A[i]$, the probability that the element winds up in position j is $1/n$. Exercise 5.3-4 shows that this weaker condition is, in fact, insufficient.

A better method for generating a random permutation is to permute the given array in place. The procedure RANDOMIZE-IN-PLACE does so in $O(n)$ time. In its ith iteration, it chooses the element $A[i]$ randomly from among elements $A[i]$ through $A[n]$. Subsequent to the ith iteration, $A[i]$ is never altered.

RANDOMIZE-IN-PLACE(A)

```
1   n = A.length
2   for i = 1 to n
3       swap A[i] with A[RANDOM(i, n)]
```

We shall use a loop invariant to show that procedure RANDOMIZE-IN-PLACE produces a uniform random permutation. A ***k-permutation*** on a set of n ele-ments is a sequence containing k of the n elements, with no repetitions. (See Appendix C.) There are $n!/(n-k)!$ such possible k-permutations.

Lemma 5.5
Procedure RANDOMIZE-IN-PLACE computes a uniform random permutation.

Proof   We use the following loop invariant:

> Just prior to the ith iteration of the **for** loop of lines 2–3, for each possible $(i - 1)$-permutation of the n elements, the subarray $A[1 .. i - 1]$ contains this $(i - 1)$-permutation with probability $(n - i + 1)!/n!$.

We need to show that this invariant is true prior to the first loop iteration, that each iteration of the loop maintains the invariant, and that the invariant provides a useful property to show correctness when the loop terminates.

Initialization: Consider the situation just before the first loop iteration, so that $i = 1$. The loop invariant says that for each possible 0-permutation, the subarray $A[1 .. 0]$ contains this 0-permutation with probability $(n - i + 1)!/n! = n!/n! = 1$. The subarray $A[1 .. 0]$ is an empty subarray, and a 0-permutation has no elements. Thus, $A[1 .. 0]$ contains any 0-permutation with probability 1, and the loop invariant holds prior to the first iteration.

Maintenance: We assume that just before the ith iteration, each possible $(i - 1)$-permutation appears in the subarray $A[1 .. i - 1]$ with probability $(n - i + 1)!/n!$, and we shall show that after the ith iteration, each possible i-permutation appears in the subarray $A[1 .. i]$ with probability $(n - i)!/n!$. Incrementing i for the next iteration then maintains the loop invariant.

Let us examine the ith iteration. Consider a particular i-permutation, and denote the elements in it by $\langle x_1, x_2, \ldots, x_i \rangle$. This permutation consists of an $(i - 1)$-permutation $\langle x_1, \ldots, x_{i-1} \rangle$ followed by the value x_i that the algorithm places in $A[i]$. Let E_1 denote the event in which the first $i - 1$ iterations have created the particular $(i - 1)$-permutation $\langle x_1, \ldots, x_{i-1} \rangle$ in $A[1 .. i - 1]$. By the loop invariant, $\Pr\{E_1\} = (n - i + 1)!/n!$. Let E_2 be the event that ith iteration puts x_i in position $A[i]$. The i-permutation $\langle x_1, \ldots, x_i \rangle$ appears in $A[1 .. i]$ precisely when both E_1 and E_2 occur, and so we wish to compute $\Pr\{E_2 \cap E_1\}$. Using equation (C.14), we have

$$\Pr\{E_2 \cap E_1\} = \Pr\{E_2 \mid E_1\} \Pr\{E_1\} \ .$$

The probability $\Pr\{E_2 \mid E_1\}$ equals $1/(n-i+1)$ because in line 3 the algorithm chooses x_i randomly from the $n - i + 1$ values in positions $A[i .. n]$. Thus, we have

$$
\begin{aligned}
\Pr\{E_2 \cap E_1\} &= \Pr\{E_2 \mid E_1\} \Pr\{E_1\} \\
&= \frac{1}{n-i+1} \cdot \frac{(n-i+1)!}{n!} \\
&= \frac{(n-i)!}{n!} \; .
\end{aligned}
$$

Termination: At termination, $i = n+1$, and we have that the subarray $A[1 \ldots n]$ is a given n-permutation with probability $(n-(n+1)+1)!/n! = 0!/n! = 1/n!$.

Thus, RANDOMIZE-IN-PLACE produces a uniform random permutation. ∎

A randomized algorithm is often the simplest and most efficient way to solve a problem. We shall use randomized algorithms occasionally throughout this book.

Exercises

5.3-1

Professor Marceau objects to the loop invariant used in the proof of Lemma 5.5. He questions whether it is true prior to the first iteration. He reasons that we could just as easily declare that an empty subarray contains no 0-permutations. Therefore, the probability that an empty subarray contains a 0-permutation should be 0, thus invalidating the loop invariant prior to the first iteration. Rewrite the procedure RANDOMIZE-IN-PLACE so that its associated loop invariant applies to a nonempty subarray prior to the first iteration, and modify the proof of Lemma 5.5 for your procedure.

5.3-2

Professor Kelp decides to write a procedure that produces at random any permutation besides the identity permutation. He proposes the following procedure:

PERMUTE-WITHOUT-IDENTITY(A)

```
1   n = A.length
2   for i = 1 to n − 1
3       swap A[i] with A[RANDOM(i + 1, n)]
```

Does this code do what Professor Kelp intends?

5.3-3

Suppose that instead of swapping element $A[i]$ with a random element from the subarray $A[i \ldots n]$, we swapped it with a random element from anywhere in the array:

PERMUTE-WITH-ALL(*A*)

```
1  n = A.length
2  for i = 1 to n
3      swap A[i] with A[RANDOM(1, n)]
```

Does this code produce a uniform random permutation? Why or why not?

5.3-4

Professor Armstrong suggests the following procedure for generating a uniform random permutation:

PERMUTE-BY-CYCLIC(*A*)

```
1  n = A.length
2  let B[1 .. n] be a new array
3  offset = RANDOM(1, n)
4  for i = 1 to n
5      dest = i + offset
6      if dest > n
7          dest = dest - n
8      B[dest] = A[i]
9  return B
```

Show that each element $A[i]$ has a $1/n$ probability of winding up in any particular position in B. Then show that Professor Armstrong is mistaken by showing that the resulting permutation is not uniformly random.

5.3-5 ★

Prove that in the array P in procedure PERMUTE-BY-SORTING, the probability that all elements are unique is at least $1 - 1/n$.

5.3-6

Explain how to implement the algorithm PERMUTE-BY-SORTING to handle the case in which two or more priorities are identical. That is, your algorithm should produce a uniform random permutation, even if two or more priorities are identical.

5.3-7

Suppose we want to create a ***random sample*** of the set $\{1, 2, 3, \ldots, n\}$, that is, an m-element subset S, where $0 \leq m \leq n$, such that each m-subset is equally likely to be created. One way would be to set $A[i] = i$ for $i = 1, 2, 3, \ldots, n$, call RANDOMIZE-IN-PLACE(*A*), and then take just the first m array elements. This method would make n calls to the RANDOM procedure. If n is much larger than m, we can create a random sample with fewer calls to RANDOM. Show that the following recursive procedure returns a random m-subset S of $\{1, 2, 3, \ldots, n\}$, in which each m-subset is equally likely, while making only m calls to RANDOM:

RANDOM-SAMPLE(m, n)

```
1   if m == 0
2       return ∅
3   else S = RANDOM-SAMPLE(m − 1, n − 1)
4       i = RANDOM(1, n)
5       if i ∈ S
6           S = S ∪ {n}
7       else S = S ∪ {i}
8       return S
```

★ 5.4   Probabilistic analysis and further uses of indicator random variables

This advanced section further illustrates probabilistic analysis by way of four examples. The first determines the probability that in a room of k people, two of them share the same birthday. The second example examines what happens when we randomly toss balls into bins. The third investigates "streaks" of consecutive heads when we flip coins. The final example analyzes a variant of the hiring problem in which you have to make decisions without actually interviewing all the candidates.

5.4.1   The birthday paradox

Our first example is the **birthday paradox**. How many people must there be in a room before there is a 50% chance that two of them were born on the same day of the year? The answer is surprisingly few. The paradox is that it is in fact far fewer than the number of days in a year, or even half the number of days in a year, as we shall see.

To answer this question, we index the people in the room with the integers $1, 2, \ldots, k$, where k is the number of people in the room. We ignore the issue of leap years and assume that all years have $n = 365$ days. For $i = 1, 2, \ldots, k$, let b_i be the day of the year on which person i's birthday falls, where $1 \le b_i \le n$. We also assume that birthdays are uniformly distributed across the n days of the year, so that $\Pr\{b_i = r\} = 1/n$ for $i = 1, 2, \ldots, k$ and $r = 1, 2, \ldots, n$.

The probability that two given people, say i and j, have matching birthdays depends on whether the random selection of birthdays is independent. We assume from now on that birthdays are independent, so that the probability that i's birthday and j's birthday both fall on day r is

$$
\begin{aligned}
\Pr\{b_i = r \text{ and } b_j = r\} &= \Pr\{b_i = r\}\Pr\{b_j = r\} \\
&= 1/n^2 .
\end{aligned}
$$

Thus, the probability that they both fall on the same day is

$$
\begin{aligned}
\Pr\{b_i = b_j\} &= \sum_{r=1}^{n} \Pr\{b_i = r \text{ and } b_j = r\} \\
&= \sum_{r=1}^{n}(1/n^2) \\
&= 1/n .
\end{aligned}
\tag{5.6}
$$

More intuitively, once b_i is chosen, the probability that b_j is chosen to be the same day is $1/n$. Thus, the probability that i and j have the same birthday is the same as the probability that the birthday of one of them falls on a given day. Notice, however, that this coincidence depends on the assumption that the birthdays are independent.

We can analyze the probability of at least 2 out of k people having matching birthdays by looking at the complementary event. The probability that at least two of the birthdays match is 1 minus the probability that all the birthdays are different. The event that k people have distinct birthdays is

$$
B_k = \bigcap_{i=1}^{k} A_i ,
$$

where A_i is the event that person i's birthday is different from person j's for all $j < i$. Since we can write $B_k = A_k \cap B_{k-1}$, we obtain from equation (C.16) the recurrence

$$
\Pr\{B_k\} = \Pr\{B_{k-1}\}\Pr\{A_k \mid B_{k-1}\} ,
\tag{5.7}
$$

where we take $\Pr\{B_1\} = \Pr\{A_1\} = 1$ as an initial condition. In other words, the probability that $b_1, b_2, \ldots, b_k$ are distinct birthdays is the probability that $b_1, b_2, \ldots, b_{k-1}$ are distinct birthdays times the probability that $b_k \neq b_i$ for $i = 1, 2, \ldots, k - 1$, given that $b_1, b_2, \ldots, b_{k-1}$ are distinct.

If $b_1, b_2, \ldots, b_{k-1}$ are distinct, the conditional probability that $b_k \neq b_i$ for $i = 1, 2, \ldots, k - 1$ is $\Pr\{A_k \mid B_{k-1}\} = (n - k + 1)/n$, since out of the n days, $n - (k - 1)$ days are not taken. We iteratively apply the recurrence (5.7) to obtain

$$
\begin{aligned}
\Pr\{B_k\} &= \Pr\{B_{k-1}\}\Pr\{A_k \mid B_{k-1}\} \\
&= \Pr\{B_{k-2}\}\Pr\{A_{k-1} \mid B_{k-2}\}\Pr\{A_k \mid B_{k-1}\} \\
&\;\;\vdots \\
&= \Pr\{B_1\}\Pr\{A_2 \mid B_1\}\Pr\{A_3 \mid B_2\}\cdots\Pr\{A_k \mid B_{k-1}\} \\
&= 1\cdot\left(\frac{n-1}{n}\right)\left(\frac{n-2}{n}\right)\cdots\left(\frac{n-k+1}{n}\right) \\
&= 1\cdot\left(1-\frac{1}{n}\right)\left(1-\frac{2}{n}\right)\cdots\left(1-\frac{k-1}{n}\right).
\end{aligned}
$$

Inequality (3.12), $1 + x \le e^x$, gives us

$$
\begin{aligned}
\Pr\{B_k\} &\le e^{-1/n}e^{-2/n}\cdots e^{-(k-1)/n} \\
&= e^{-\sum_{i=1}^{k-1} i/n} \\
&= e^{-k(k-1)/2n} \\
&\le 1/2
\end{aligned}
$$

when $-k(k-1)/2n \le \ln(1/2)$. The probability that all k birthdays are distinct is at most $1/2$ when $k(k-1) \ge 2n\ln 2$ or, solving the quadratic equation, when $k \ge (1 + \sqrt{1 + (8\ln 2)n})/2$. For $n = 365$, we must have $k \ge 23$. Thus, if at least 23 people are in a room, the probability is at least $1/2$ that at least two people have the same birthday. On Mars, a year is 669 Martian days long; it therefore takes 31 Martians to get the same effect.

An analysis using indicator random variables

We can use indicator random variables to provide a simpler but approximate analysis of the birthday paradox. For each pair (i, j) of the k people in the room, we define the indicator random variable X_{ij}, for $1 \le i < j \le k$, by

$$
\begin{aligned}
X_{ij} &= \mathrm{I}\{\text{person } i \text{ and person } j \text{ have the same birthday}\} \\
&= \begin{cases} 1 & \text{if person } i \text{ and person } j \text{ have the same birthday},\\ 0 & \text{otherwise}. \end{cases}
\end{aligned}
$$

By equation (5.6), the probability that two people have matching birthdays is $1/n$, and thus by Lemma 5.1, we have

$$
\begin{aligned}
\mathrm{E}[X_{ij}] &= \Pr\{\text{person } i \text{ and person } j \text{ have the same birthday}\} \\
&= 1/n .
\end{aligned}
$$

Letting X be the random variable that counts the number of pairs of individuals having the same birthday, we have

$$X = \sum_{i=1}^{k-1} \sum_{j=i+1}^{k} X_{ij} \,.$$

Taking expectations of both sides and applying linearity of expectation, we obtain

$$
\begin{aligned}
E[X] &= E\left[\sum_{i=1}^{k-1} \sum_{j=i+1}^{k} X_{ij} \right] \\
&= \sum_{i=1}^{k-1} \sum_{j=i+1}^{k} E[X_{ij}] \\
&= \binom{k}{2} \frac{1}{n} \\
&= \frac{k(k-1)}{2n} \,.
\end{aligned}
$$

When $k(k-1) \geq 2n$, therefore, the expected number of pairs of people with the same birthday is at least 1. Thus, if we have at least $\sqrt{2n}+1$ individuals in a room, we can expect at least two to have the same birthday. For $n = 365$, if $k = 28$, the expected number of pairs with the same birthday is $(28 \cdot 27)/(2 \cdot 365) \approx 1.0356$. Thus, with at least 28 people, we expect to find at least one matching pair of birthdays. On Mars, where a year is 669 Martian days long, we need at least 38 Martians.

The first analysis, which used only probabilities, determined the number of people required for the probability to exceed $1/2$ that a matching pair of birthdays exists, and the second analysis, which used indicator random variables, determined the number such that the expected number of matching birthdays is 1. Although the exact numbers of people differ for the two situations, they are the same asymptotically: $\Theta(\sqrt{n})$.

5.4.2 Balls and bins

Consider a process in which we randomly toss identical balls into b bins, numbered $1, 2, \ldots, b$. The tosses are independent, and on each toss the ball is equally likely to end up in any bin. The probability that a tossed ball lands in any given bin is $1/b$. Thus, the ball-tossing process is a sequence of Bernoulli trials (see Appendix C.4) with a probability $1/b$ of success, where success means that the ball falls in the given bin. This model is particularly useful for analyzing hashing (see Chapter 11), and we can answer a variety of interesting questions about the ball-tossing process. (Problem C-1 asks additional questions about balls and bins.)

How many balls fall in a given bin? The number of balls that fall in a given bin follows the binomial distribution $b(k; n, 1/b)$. If we toss n balls, equation (C.37) tells us that the expected number of balls that fall in the given bin is n/b.

How many balls must we toss, on the average, until a given bin contains a ball? The number of tosses until the given bin receives a ball follows the geometric distribution with probability $1/b$ and, by equation (C.32), the expected number of tosses until success is $1/(1/b) = b$.

How many balls must we toss until every bin contains at least one ball? Let us call a toss in which a ball falls into an empty bin a "hit." We want to know the expected number n of tosses required to get b hits.

Using the hits, we can partition the n tosses into stages. The ith stage consists of the tosses after the $(i-1)$st hit until the ith hit. The first stage consists of the first toss, since we are guaranteed to have a hit when all bins are empty. For each toss during the ith stage, $i-1$ bins contain balls and $b-i+1$ bins are empty. Thus, for each toss in the ith stage, the probability of obtaining a hit is $(b-i+1)/b$.

Let n_i denote the number of tosses in the ith stage. Thus, the number of tosses required to get b hits is $n = \sum_{i=1}^{b} n_i$. Each random variable n_i has a geometric distribution with probability of success $(b-i+1)/b$ and thus, by equation (C.32), we have

$$E[n_i] = \frac{b}{b-i+1} .$$

By linearity of expectation, we have

$$
\begin{aligned}
E[n] &= E\left[\sum_{i=1}^{b} n_i\right] \\
&= \sum_{i=1}^{b} E[n_i] \\
&= \sum_{i=1}^{b} \frac{b}{b-i+1} \\
&= b\sum_{i=1}^{b} \frac{1}{i} \\
&= b(\ln b + O(1)) \quad \text{(by equation (A.7))} .
\end{aligned}
$$

It therefore takes approximately $b \ln b$ tosses before we can expect that every bin has a ball. This problem is also known as the ***coupon collector's problem***, which says that a person trying to collect each of b different coupons expects to acquire approximately $b \ln b$ randomly obtained coupons in order to succeed.

5.4.3   Streaks

Suppose you flip a fair coin n times. What is the longest streak of consecutive heads that you expect to see? The answer is $\Theta(\lg n)$, as the following analysis shows.

We first prove that the expected length of the longest streak of heads is $O(\lg n)$. The probability that each coin flip is a head is $1/2$. Let A_{ik} be the event that a streak of heads of length at least k begins with the ith coin flip or, more precisely, the event that the k consecutive coin flips $i, i + 1, \ldots, i + k - 1$ yield only heads, where $1 \le k \le n$ and $1 \le i \le n - k + 1$. Since coin flips are mutually independent, for any given event A_{ik}, the probability that all k flips are heads is

$$\Pr\{A_{ik}\} = 1/2^k \, . \tag{5.8}$$

For $k = 2\lceil \lg n \rceil$,

$$
\begin{aligned}
\Pr\{A_{i,2\lceil \lg n \rceil}\} &= 1/2^{2\lceil \lg n \rceil} \\
&\le 1/2^{2\lg n} \\
&= 1/n^2 \, ,
\end{aligned}
$$

and thus the probability that a streak of heads of length at least $2\lceil \lg n \rceil$ begins in position i is quite small. There are at most $n - 2\lceil \lg n \rceil + 1$ positions where such a streak can begin. The probability that a streak of heads of length at least $2\lceil \lg n \rceil$ begins anywhere is therefore

$$
\begin{aligned}
\Pr\left\{ \bigcup_{i=1}^{n-2\lceil \lg n \rceil+1} A_{i,2\lceil \lg n \rceil} \right\} &\le \sum_{i=1}^{n-2\lceil \lg n \rceil+1} 1/n^2 \\
&< \sum_{i=1}^{n} 1/n^2 \\
&= 1/n \, ,
\end{aligned}
\tag{5.9}
$$

since by Boole's inequality (C.19), the probability of a union of events is at most the sum of the probabilities of the individual events. (Note that Boole's inequality holds even for events such as these that are not independent.)

We now use inequality (5.9) to bound the length of the longest streak. For $j = 0, 1, 2, \ldots, n$, let L_j be the event that the longest streak of heads has length exactly j, and let L be the length of the longest streak. By the definition of expected value, we have

$$\mathrm{E}[L] = \sum_{j=0}^{n} j \Pr\{L_j\} \, . \tag{5.10}$$

We could try to evaluate this sum using upper bounds on each $\Pr\{L_j\}$ similar to those computed in inequality (5.9). Unfortunately, this method would yield weak bounds. We can use some intuition gained by the above analysis to obtain a good bound, however. Informally, we observe that for no individual term in the summation in equation (5.10) are both the factors j and $\Pr\{L_j\}$ large. Why? When $j \geq 2\lceil \lg n \rceil$, then $\Pr\{L_j\}$ is very small, and when $j < 2\lceil \lg n \rceil$, then j is fairly small. More formally, we note that the events L_j for $j = 0, 1, \ldots, n$ are disjoint, and so the probability that a streak of heads of length at least $2\lceil \lg n \rceil$ begins anywhere is $\sum_{j=2\lceil \lg n \rceil}^{n} \Pr\{L_j\}$. By inequality (5.9), we have $\sum_{j=2\lceil \lg n \rceil}^{n} \Pr\{L_j\} < 1/n$. Also, noting that $\sum_{j=0}^{n} \Pr\{L_j\} = 1$, we have that $\sum_{j=0}^{2\lceil \lg n \rceil-1} \Pr\{L_j\} \leq 1$. Thus, we obtain

$$
\begin{aligned}
\mathrm{E}\,[L] \;&=\; \sum_{j=0}^{n} j \Pr\{L_j\} \\[2mm]
&=\; \sum_{j=0}^{2\lceil \lg n \rceil-1} j \Pr\{L_j\} + \sum_{j=2\lceil \lg n \rceil}^{n} j \Pr\{L_j\} \\[2mm]
&<\; \sum_{j=0}^{2\lceil \lg n \rceil-1} (2\lceil \lg n \rceil) \Pr\{L_j\} + \sum_{j=2\lceil \lg n \rceil}^{n} n \Pr\{L_j\} \\[2mm]
&=\; 2\lceil \lg n \rceil \sum_{j=0}^{2\lceil \lg n \rceil-1} \Pr\{L_j\} + n \sum_{j=2\lceil \lg n \rceil}^{n} \Pr\{L_j\} \\[2mm]
&<\; 2\lceil \lg n \rceil \cdot 1 + n \cdot (1/n) \\[2mm]
&=\; O(\lg n)\,.
\end{aligned}
$$

The probability that a streak of heads exceeds $r\lceil \lg n \rceil$ flips diminishes quickly with r. For $r \geq 1$, the probability that a streak of at least $r\lceil \lg n \rceil$ heads starts in position i is

$$
\begin{aligned}
\Pr\{A_{i,r\lceil \lg n \rceil}\} \;&=\; 1/2^{r\lceil \lg n \rceil} \\[1mm]
&\leq\; 1/n^r\,.
\end{aligned}
$$

Thus, the probability is at most $n/n^r = 1/n^{r-1}$ that the longest streak is at least $r\lceil \lg n \rceil$, or equivalently, the probability is at least $1 - 1/n^{r-1}$ that the longest streak has length less than $r\lceil \lg n \rceil$.

As an example, for $n = 1000$ coin flips, the probability of having a streak of at least $2\lceil \lg n \rceil = 20$ heads is at most $1/n = 1/1000$. The chance of having a streak longer than $3\lceil \lg n \rceil = 30$ heads is at most $1/n^2 = 1/1{,}000{,}000$.

We now prove a complementary lower bound: the expected length of the longest streak of heads in n coin flips is $\Omega(\lg n)$. To prove this bound, we look for streaks of length s by partitioning the n flips into approximately n/s groups of s flips each. If we choose $s = \lfloor (\lg n)/2 \rfloor$, we can show that it is likely that at least one of these groups comes up all heads, and hence it is likely that the longest streak has length at least $s = \Omega(\lg n)$. We then show that the longest streak has expected length $\Omega(\lg n)$.

We partition the n coin flips into at least $\lfloor n/ \lfloor (\lg n)/2 \rfloor \rfloor$ groups of $\lfloor (\lg n)/2 \rfloor$ consecutive flips, and we bound the probability that no group comes up all heads. By equation (5.8), the probability that the group starting in position i comes up all heads is

$$
\begin{aligned}
\Pr\{A_{i,\lfloor(\lg n)/2\rfloor}\} &= 1/2^{\lfloor(\lg n)/2\rfloor} \\
&\geq 1/\sqrt{n} \ .
\end{aligned}
$$

The probability that a streak of heads of length at least $\lfloor (\lg n)/2 \rfloor$ does not begin in position i is therefore at most $1 - 1/\sqrt{n}$. Since the $\lfloor n/ \lfloor (\lg n)/2 \rfloor \rfloor$ groups are formed from mutually exclusive, independent coin flips, the probability that every one of these groups *fails* to be a streak of length $\lfloor (\lg n)/2 \rfloor$ is at most

$$
\begin{aligned}
\left(1 - 1/\sqrt{n}\right)^{\lfloor n/\lfloor(\lg n)/2\rfloor\rfloor} &\leq \left(1 - 1/\sqrt{n}\right)^{n/\lfloor(\lg n)/2\rfloor-1} \\
&\leq \left(1 - 1/\sqrt{n}\right)^{2n/\lg n-1} \\
&\leq e^{-(2n/\lg n-1)/\sqrt{n}} \\
&= O(e^{-\lg n}) \\
&= O(1/n) \ .
\end{aligned}
$$

For this argument, we used inequality (3.12), $1 + x \leq e^x$, and the fact, which you might want to verify, that $(2n/ \lg n - 1)/\sqrt{n} \geq \lg n$ for sufficiently large n.

Thus, the probability that the longest streak equals or exceeds $\lfloor (\lg n)/2 \rfloor$ is

$$
\sum_{j=\lfloor(\lg n)/2\rfloor}^{n} \Pr\{L_j\} \geq 1 - O(1/n) \ . \tag{5.11}
$$

We can now calculate a lower bound on the expected length of the longest streak, beginning with equation (5.10) and proceeding in a manner similar to our analysis of the upper bound:

$$
\begin{aligned}
\mathrm{E}[L] \;&=\; \sum_{j=0}^{n} j \Pr\{L_j\} \\[2mm]
&=\; \sum_{j=0}^{\lfloor (\lg n)/2 \rfloor - 1} j \Pr\{L_j\} + \sum_{j=\lfloor (\lg n)/2 \rfloor}^{n} j \Pr\{L_j\} \\[2mm]
&\geq\; \sum_{j=0}^{\lfloor (\lg n)/2 \rfloor - 1} 0 \cdot \Pr\{L_j\} + \sum_{j=\lfloor (\lg n)/2 \rfloor}^{n} \lfloor (\lg n)/2 \rfloor \Pr\{L_j\} \\[2mm]
&=\; 0 \cdot \sum_{j=0}^{\lfloor (\lg n)/2 \rfloor - 1} \Pr\{L_j\} + \lfloor (\lg n)/2 \rfloor \sum_{j=\lfloor (\lg n)/2 \rfloor}^{n} \Pr\{L_j\} \\[2mm]
&\geq\; 0 + \lfloor (\lg n)/2 \rfloor \left(1 - O(1/n)\right) \qquad \text{(by inequality (5.11))} \\[2mm]
&=\; \Omega(\lg n) \,.
\end{aligned}
$$

As with the birthday paradox, we can obtain a simpler but approximate analysis using indicator random variables. We let $X_{ik} = \mathrm{I}\{A_{ik}\}$ be the indicator random variable associated with a streak of heads of length at least k beginning with the ith coin flip. To count the total number of such streaks, we define

$$
X = \sum_{i=1}^{n-k+1} X_{ik} \,.
$$

Taking expectations and using linearity of expectation, we have

$$
\begin{aligned}
\mathrm{E}[X] \;&=\; \mathrm{E}\left[\sum_{i=1}^{n-k+1} X_{ik} \right] \\[2mm]
&=\; \sum_{i=1}^{n-k+1} \mathrm{E}[X_{ik}] \\[2mm]
&=\; \sum_{i=1}^{n-k+1} \Pr\{A_{ik}\} \\[2mm]
&=\; \sum_{i=1}^{n-k+1} 1/2^k \\[2mm]
&=\; \frac{n - k + 1}{2^k} \,.
\end{aligned}
$$

By plugging in various values for k, we can calculate the expected number of streaks of length k. If this number is large (much greater than 1), then we expect many streaks of length k to occur and the probability that one occurs is high. If this number is small (much less than 1), then we expect few streaks of length k to occur and the probability that one occurs is low. If $k = c \lg n$, for some positive constant c, we obtain

$$
\begin{aligned}
\mathrm{E}\,[X] \;&=\; \frac{n - c \lg n + 1}{2^{c \lg n}} \\[4pt]
&=\; \frac{n - c \lg n + 1}{n^c} \\[4pt]
&=\; \frac{1}{n^{c-1}} - \frac{(c \lg n - 1)/n}{n^{c-1}} \\[4pt]
&=\; \Theta(1/n^{c-1}) \,.
\end{aligned}
$$

If c is large, the expected number of streaks of length $c \lg n$ is small, and we conclude that they are unlikely to occur. On the other hand, if $c = 1/2$, then we obtain $\mathrm{E}\,[X] = \Theta(1/n^{1/2-1}) = \Theta(n^{1/2})$, and we expect that there are a large number of streaks of length $(1/2) \lg n$. Therefore, one streak of such a length is likely to occur. From these rough estimates alone, we can conclude that the expected length of the longest streak is $\Theta(\lg n)$.

5.4.4   The on-line hiring problem

As a final example, we consider a variant of the hiring problem. Suppose now that we do not wish to interview all the candidates in order to find the best one. We also do not wish to hire and fire as we find better and better applicants. Instead, we are willing to settle for a candidate who is close to the best, in exchange for hiring exactly once. We must obey one company requirement: after each interview we must either immediately offer the position to the applicant or immediately reject the applicant. What is the trade-off between minimizing the amount of interviewing and maximizing the quality of the candidate hired?

We can model this problem in the following way. After meeting an applicant, we are able to give each one a score; let *score(i)* denote the score we give to the ith applicant, and assume that no two applicants receive the same score. After we have seen j applicants, we know which of the j has the highest score, but we do not know whether any of the remaining $n - j$ applicants will receive a higher score. We decide to adopt the strategy of selecting a positive integer $k < n$, interviewing and then rejecting the first k applicants, and hiring the first applicant thereafter who has a higher score than all preceding applicants. If it turns out that the best-qualified applicant was among the first k interviewed, then we hire the nth applicant. We formalize this strategy in the procedure On-Line-Maximum(k, n), which returns the index of the candidate we wish to hire.

ON-LINE-MAXIMUM(k, n)

```
1   bestscore = −∞
2   for i = 1 to k
3       if score(i) > bestscore
4           bestscore = score(i)
5   for i = k + 1 to n
6       if score(i) > bestscore
7           return i
8   return n
```

We wish to determine, for each possible value of k, the probability that we hire the most qualified applicant. We then choose the best possible k, and implement the strategy with that value. For the moment, assume that k is fixed. Let $M(j) = \max_{1 \le i \le j} \{score(i)\}$ denote the maximum score among applicants 1 through j. Let S be the event that we succeed in choosing the best-qualified applicant, and let S_i be the event that we succeed when the best-qualified applicant is the ith one interviewed. Since the various S_i are disjoint, we have that $\Pr\{S\} = \sum_{i=1}^{n} \Pr\{S_i\}$. Noting that we never succeed when the best-qualified applicant is one of the first k, we have that $\Pr\{S_i\} = 0$ for $i = 1, 2, \ldots, k$. Thus, we obtain

$$\Pr\{S\} = \sum_{i=k+1}^{n} \Pr\{S_i\} \ . \tag{5.12}$$

We now compute $\Pr\{S_i\}$. In order to succeed when the best-qualified applicant is the ith one, two things must happen. First, the best-qualified applicant must be in position i, an event which we denote by B_i. Second, the algorithm must not select any of the applicants in positions $k + 1$ through $i - 1$, which happens only if, for each j such that $k + 1 \le j \le i - 1$, we find that $score(j) < bestscore$ in line 6. (Because scores are unique, we can ignore the possibility of $score(j) = bestscore$.) In other words, all of the values $score(k + 1)$ through $score(i - 1)$ must be less than $M(k)$; if any are greater than $M(k)$, we instead return the index of the first one that is greater. We use O_i to denote the event that none of the applicants in position $k + 1$ through $i - 1$ are chosen. Fortunately, the two events B_i and O_i are independent. The event O_i depends only on the relative ordering of the values in positions 1 through $i - 1$, whereas B_i depends only on whether the value in position i is greater than the values in all other positions. The ordering of the values in positions 1 through $i - 1$ does not affect whether the value in position i is greater than all of them, and the value in position i does not affect the ordering of the values in positions 1 through $i - 1$. Thus we can apply equation (C.15) to obtain

$$\Pr\{S_i\} = \Pr\{B_i \cap O_i\} = \Pr\{B_i\}\Pr\{O_i\} .$$

The probability $\Pr\{B_i\}$ is clearly $1/n$, since the maximum is equally likely to be in any one of the n positions. For event O_i to occur, the maximum value in positions 1 through $i-1$, which is equally likely to be in any of these $i-1$ positions, must be in one of the first k positions. Consequently, $\Pr\{O_i\} = k/(i-1)$ and $\Pr\{S_i\} = k/(n(i-1))$. Using equation (5.12), we have

$$
\begin{aligned}
\Pr\{S\} &= \sum_{i=k+1}^{n} \Pr\{S_i\} \\
&= \sum_{i=k+1}^{n} \frac{k}{n(i-1)} \\
&= \frac{k}{n} \sum_{i=k+1}^{n} \frac{1}{i-1} \\
&= \frac{k}{n} \sum_{i=k}^{n-1} \frac{1}{i} .
\end{aligned}
$$

We approximate by integrals to bound this summation from above and below. By the inequalities (A.12), we have

$$\int_{k}^{n} \frac{1}{x}\, dx \leq \sum_{i=k}^{n-1} \frac{1}{i} \leq \int_{k-1}^{n-1} \frac{1}{x}\, dx .$$

Evaluating these definite integrals gives us the bounds

$$\frac{k}{n}(\ln n - \ln k) \leq \Pr\{S\} \leq \frac{k}{n}(\ln(n-1) - \ln(k-1)) ,$$

which provide a rather tight bound for $\Pr\{S\}$. Because we wish to maximize our probability of success, let us focus on choosing the value of k that maximizes the lower bound on $\Pr\{S\}$. (Besides, the lower-bound expression is easier to maximize than the upper-bound expression.) Differentiating the expression $(k/n)(\ln n - \ln k)$ with respect to k, we obtain

$$\frac{1}{n}(\ln n - \ln k - 1) .$$

Setting this derivative equal to 0, we see that we maximize the lower bound on the probability when $\ln k = \ln n - 1 = \ln(n/e)$ or, equivalently, when $k = n/e$. Thus, if we implement our strategy with $k = n/e$, we succeed in hiring our best-qualified applicant with probability at least $1/e$.

Exercises

5.4-1
How many people must there be in a room before the probability that someone has the same birthday as you do is at least $1/2$? How many people must there be before the probability that at least two people have a birthday on July 4 is greater than $1/2$?

5.4-2
Suppose that we toss balls into b bins until some bin contains two balls. Each toss is independent, and each ball is equally likely to end up in any bin. What is the expected number of ball tosses?

5.4-3 ★
For the analysis of the birthday paradox, is it important that the birthdays be mutually independent, or is pairwise independence sufficient? Justify your answer.

5.4-4 ★
How many people should be invited to a party in order to make it likely that there are *three* people with the same birthday?

5.4-5 ★
What is the probability that a k-string over a set of size n forms a k-permutation? How does this question relate to the birthday paradox?

5.4-6 ★
Suppose that n balls are tossed into n bins, where each toss is independent and the ball is equally likely to end up in any bin. What is the expected number of empty bins? What is the expected number of bins with exactly one ball?

5.4-7 ★
Sharpen the lower bound on streak length by showing that in n flips of a fair coin, the probability is less than $1/n$ that no streak longer than $\lg n - 2 \lg \lg n$ consecutive heads occurs.

Problems

5-1 *Probabilistic counting*

With a b-bit counter, we can ordinarily only count up to $2^b - 1$. With R. Morris's *probabilistic counting*, we can count up to a much larger value at the expense of some loss of precision.

We let a counter value of i represent a count of n_i for $i = 0, 1, \ldots, 2^b - 1$, where the n_i form an increasing sequence of nonnegative values. We assume that the initial value of the counter is 0, representing a count of $n_0 = 0$. The INCREMENT operation works on a counter containing the value i in a probabilistic manner. If $i = 2^b - 1$, then the operation reports an overflow error. Otherwise, the INCREMENT operation increases the counter by 1 with probability $1/(n_{i+1} - n_i)$, and it leaves the counter unchanged with probability $1 - 1/(n_{i+1} - n_i)$.

If we select $n_i = i$ for all $i \geq 0$, then the counter is an ordinary one. More interesting situations arise if we select, say, $n_i = 2^{i-1}$ for $i > 0$ or $n_i = F_i$ (the ith Fibonacci number—see Section 3.2).

For this problem, assume that n_{2^b-1} is large enough that the probability of an overflow error is negligible.

a. Show that the expected value represented by the counter after n INCREMENT operations have been performed is exactly n.

b. The analysis of the variance of the count represented by the counter depends on the sequence of the n_i. Let us consider a simple case: $n_i = 100i$ for all $i \geq 0$. Estimate the variance in the value represented by the register after n INCREMENT operations have been performed.

5-2 *Searching an unsorted array*

This problem examines three algorithms for searching for a value x in an unsorted array A consisting of n elements.

Consider the following randomized strategy: pick a random index i into A. If $A[i] = x$, then we terminate; otherwise, we continue the search by picking a new random index into A. We continue picking random indices into A until we find an index j such that $A[j] = x$ or until we have checked every element of A. Note that we pick from the whole set of indices each time, so that we may examine a given element more than once.

a. Write pseudocode for a procedure RANDOM-SEARCH to implement the strategy above. Be sure that your algorithm terminates when all indices into A have been picked.

b. Suppose that there is exactly one index i such that $A[i] = x$. What is the expected number of indices into A that we must pick before we find x and RANDOM-SEARCH terminates?

c. Generalizing your solution to part (b), suppose that there are $k \geq 1$ indices i such that $A[i] = x$. What is the expected number of indices into A that we must pick before we find x and RANDOM-SEARCH terminates? Your answer should be a function of n and k.

d. Suppose that there are no indices i such that $A[i] = x$. What is the expected number of indices into A that we must pick before we have checked all elements of A and RANDOM-SEARCH terminates?

Now consider a deterministic linear search algorithm, which we refer to as DETERMINISTIC-SEARCH. Specifically, the algorithm searches A for x in order, considering $A[1], A[2], A[3], \ldots, A[n]$ until either it finds $A[i] = x$ or it reaches the end of the array. Assume that all possible permutations of the input array are equally likely.

e. Suppose that there is exactly one index i such that $A[i] = x$. What is the average-case running time of DETERMINISTIC-SEARCH? What is the worst-case running time of DETERMINISTIC-SEARCH?

f. Generalizing your solution to part (e), suppose that there are $k \geq 1$ indices i such that $A[i] = x$. What is the average-case running time of DETERMINISTIC-SEARCH? What is the worst-case running time of DETERMINISTIC-SEARCH? Your answer should be a function of n and k.

g. Suppose that there are no indices i such that $A[i] = x$. What is the average-case running time of DETERMINISTIC-SEARCH? What is the worst-case running time of DETERMINISTIC-SEARCH?

Finally, consider a randomized algorithm SCRAMBLE-SEARCH that works by first randomly permuting the input array and then running the deterministic linear search given above on the resulting permuted array.

h. Letting k be the number of indices i such that $A[i] = x$, give the worst-case and expected running times of SCRAMBLE-SEARCH for the cases in which $k = 0$ and $k = 1$. Generalize your solution to handle the case in which $k \geq 1$.

i. Which of the three searching algorithms would you use? Explain your answer.

Chapter notes

Bollobás [53], Hofri [174], and Spencer [321] contain a wealth of advanced probabilistic techniques. The advantages of randomized algorithms are discussed and surveyed by Karp [200] and Rabin [288]. The textbook by Motwani and Raghavan [262] gives an extensive treatment of randomized algorithms.

Several variants of the hiring problem have been widely studied. These problems are more commonly referred to as "secretary problems." An example of work in this area is the paper by Ajtai, Meggido, and Waarts [11].

II Sorting and Order Statistics

Introduction

This part presents several algorithms that solve the following *sorting problem*:

Input: A sequence of n numbers $\langle a_1, a_2, \ldots, a_n \rangle$.

Output: A permutation (reordering) $\langle a_1', a_2', \ldots, a_n' \rangle$ of the input sequence such that $a_1' \leq a_2' \leq \cdots \leq a_n'$.

The input sequence is usually an n-element array, although it may be represented in some other fashion, such as a linked list.

The structure of the data

In practice, the numbers to be sorted are rarely isolated values. Each is usually part of a collection of data called a *record*. Each record contains a *key*, which is the value to be sorted. The remainder of the record consists of *satellite data*, which are usually carried around with the key. In practice, when a sorting algorithm permutes the keys, it must permute the satellite data as well. If each record includes a large amount of satellite data, we often permute an array of pointers to the records rather than the records themselves in order to minimize data movement.

In a sense, it is these implementation details that distinguish an algorithm from a full-blown program. A sorting algorithm describes the *method* by which we determine the sorted order, regardless of whether we are sorting individual numbers or large records containing many bytes of satellite data. Thus, when focusing on the problem of sorting, we typically assume that the input consists only of numbers. Translating an algorithm for sorting numbers into a program for sorting records is conceptually straightforward, although in a given engineering situation other subtleties may make the actual programming task a challenge.

Why sorting?

Many computer scientists consider sorting to be the most fundamental problem in the study of algorithms. There are several reasons:

- Sometimes an application inherently needs to sort information. For example, in order to prepare customer statements, banks need to sort checks by check number.

- Algorithms often use sorting as a key subroutine. For example, a program that renders graphical objects which are layered on top of each other might have to sort the objects according to an "above" relation so that it can draw these objects from bottom to top. We shall see numerous algorithms in this text that use sorting as a subroutine.

- We can draw from among a wide variety of sorting algorithms, and they employ a rich set of techniques. In fact, many important techniques used throughout algorithm design appear in the body of sorting algorithms that have been developed over the years. In this way, sorting is also a problem of historical interest.

- We can prove a nontrivial lower bound for sorting (as we shall do in Chapter 8). Our best upper bounds match the lower bound asymptotically, and so we know that our sorting algorithms are asymptotically optimal. Moreover, we can use the lower bound for sorting to prove lower bounds for certain other problems.

- Many engineering issues come to the fore when implementing sorting algorithms. The fastest sorting program for a particular situation may depend on many factors, such as prior knowledge about the keys and satellite data, the memory hierarchy (caches and virtual memory) of the host computer, and the software environment. Many of these issues are best dealt with at the algorithmic level, rather than by "tweaking" the code.

Sorting algorithms

We introduced two algorithms that sort n real numbers in Chapter 2. Insertion sort takes $\Theta(n^2)$ time in the worst case. Because its inner loops are tight, however, it is a fast in-place sorting algorithm for small input sizes. (Recall that a sorting algorithm sorts *in place* if only a constant number of elements of the input array are ever stored outside the array.) Merge sort has a better asymptotic running time, $\Theta(n \lg n)$, but the MERGE procedure it uses does not operate in place.

In this part, we shall introduce two more algorithms that sort arbitrary real numbers. Heapsort, presented in Chapter 6, sorts n numbers in place in $O(n \lg n)$ time. It uses an important data structure, called a heap, with which we can also implement a priority queue.

Quicksort, in Chapter 7, also sorts n numbers in place, but its worst-case running time is $\Theta(n^2)$. Its expected running time is $\Theta(n \lg n)$, however, and it generally outperforms heapsort in practice. Like insertion sort, quicksort has tight code, and so the hidden constant factor in its running time is small. It is a popular algorithm for sorting large input arrays.

Insertion sort, merge sort, heapsort, and quicksort are all comparison sorts: they determine the sorted order of an input array by comparing elements. Chapter 8 begins by introducing the decision-tree model in order to study the performance limitations of comparison sorts. Using this model, we prove a lower bound of $\Omega(n \lg n)$ on the worst-case running time of any comparison sort on n inputs, thus showing that heapsort and merge sort are asymptotically optimal comparison sorts.

Chapter 8 then goes on to show that we can beat this lower bound of $\Omega(n \lg n)$ if we can gather information about the sorted order of the input by means other than comparing elements. The counting sort algorithm, for example, assumes that the input numbers are in the set $\{0, 1, \ldots, k\}$. By using array indexing as a tool for determining relative order, counting sort can sort n numbers in $\Theta(k + n)$ time. Thus, when $k = O(n)$, counting sort runs in time that is linear in the size of the input array. A related algorithm, radix sort, can be used to extend the range of counting sort. If there are n integers to sort, each integer has d digits, and each digit can take on up to k possible values, then radix sort can sort the numbers in $\Theta(d(n + k))$ time. When d is a constant and k is $O(n)$, radix sort runs in linear time. A third algorithm, bucket sort, requires knowledge of the probabilistic distribution of numbers in the input array. It can sort n real numbers uniformly distributed in the half-open interval $[0, 1)$ in average-case $O(n)$ time.

The following table summarizes the running times of the sorting algorithms from Chapters 2 and 6–8. As usual, n denotes the number of items to sort. For counting sort, the items to sort are integers in the set $\{0, 1, \ldots, k\}$. For radix sort, each item is a d-digit number, where each digit takes on k possible values. For bucket sort, we assume that the keys are real numbers uniformly distributed in the half-open interval $[0, 1)$. The rightmost column gives the average-case or expected running time, indicating which it gives when it differs from the worst-case running time. We omit the average-case running time of heapsort because we do not analyze it in this book.

Algorithm	Worst-case running time	Average-case/expected running time
Insertion sort	$\Theta(n^2)$	$\Theta(n^2)$
Merge sort	$\Theta(n \lg n)$	$\Theta(n \lg n)$
Heapsort	$O(n \lg n)$	—
Quicksort	$\Theta(n^2)$	$\Theta(n \lg n)$ (expected)
Counting sort	$\Theta(k + n)$	$\Theta(k + n)$
Radix sort	$\Theta(d(n + k))$	$\Theta(d(n + k))$
Bucket sort	$\Theta(n^2)$	$\Theta(n)$ (average-case)

Order statistics

The ith order statistic of a set of n numbers is the ith smallest number in the set. We can, of course, select the ith order statistic by sorting the input and indexing the ith element of the output. With no assumptions about the input distribution, this method runs in $\Omega(n \lg n)$ time, as the lower bound proved in Chapter 8 shows.

In Chapter 9, we show that we can find the ith smallest element in $O(n)$ time, even when the elements are arbitrary real numbers. We present a randomized algorithm with tight pseudocode that runs in $\Theta(n^2)$ time in the worst case, but whose expected running time is $O(n)$. We also give a more complicated algorithm that runs in $O(n)$ worst-case time.

Background

Although most of this part does not rely on difficult mathematics, some sections do require mathematical sophistication. In particular, analyses of quicksort, bucket sort, and the order-statistic algorithm use probability, which is reviewed in Appendix C, and the material on probabilistic analysis and randomized algorithms in Chapter 5. The analysis of the worst-case linear-time algorithm for order statistics involves somewhat more sophisticated mathematics than the other worst-case analyses in this part.

6   Heapsort

In this chapter, we introduce another sorting algorithm: heapsort. Like merge sort, but unlike insertion sort, heapsort's running time is $O(n \lg n)$. Like insertion sort, but unlike merge sort, heapsort sorts in place: only a constant number of array elements are stored outside the input array at any time. Thus, heapsort combines the better attributes of the two sorting algorithms we have already discussed.

Heapsort also introduces another algorithm design technique: using a data structure, in this case one we call a "heap," to manage information. Not only is the heap data structure useful for heapsort, but it also makes an efficient priority queue. The heap data structure will reappear in algorithms in later chapters.

The term "heap" was originally coined in the context of heapsort, but it has since come to refer to "garbage-collected storage," such as the programming languages Java and Lisp provide. Our heap data structure is *not* garbage-collected storage, and whenever we refer to heaps in this book, we shall mean a data structure rather than an aspect of garbage collection.

6.1   Heaps

The *(binary) heap* data structure is an array object that we can view as a nearly complete binary tree (see Section B.5.3), as shown in Figure 6.1. Each node of the tree corresponds to an element of the array. The tree is completely filled on all levels except possibly the lowest, which is filled from the left up to a point. An array A that represents a heap is an object with two attributes: $A.length$, which (as usual) gives the number of elements in the array, and $A.heap\text{-}size$, which represents how many elements in the heap are stored within array A. That is, although $A[1 \mathrel{..} A.length]$ may contain numbers, only the elements in $A[1 \mathrel{..} A.heap\text{-}size]$, where $0 \le A.heap\text{-}size \le A.length$, are valid elements of the heap. The root of the tree is $A[1]$, and given the index i of a node, we can easily compute the indices of its parent, left child, and right child:

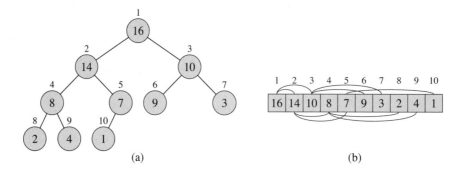

Figure 6.1 A max-heap viewed as **(a)** a binary tree and **(b)** an array. The number within the circle at each node in the tree is the value stored at that node. The number above a node is the corresponding index in the array. Above and below the array are lines showing parent-child relationships; parents are always to the left of their children. The tree has height three; the node at index 4 (with value 8) has height one.

PARENT(i)

1   **return** $\lfloor i/2 \rfloor$

LEFT(i)

1   **return** $2i$

RIGHT(i)

1   **return** $2i + 1$

On most computers, the LEFT procedure can compute $2i$ in one instruction by simply shifting the binary representation of i left by one bit position. Similarly, the RIGHT procedure can quickly compute $2i + 1$ by shifting the binary representation of i left by one bit position and then adding in a 1 as the low-order bit. The PARENT procedure can compute $\lfloor i/2 \rfloor$ by shifting i right one bit position. Good implementations of heapsort often implement these procedures as "macros" or "in-line" procedures.

There are two kinds of binary heaps: max-heaps and min-heaps. In both kinds, the values in the nodes satisfy a **heap property**, the specifics of which depend on the kind of heap. In a **max-heap**, the **max-heap property** is that for every node i other than the root,

$$A[\text{PARENT}(i)] \geq A[i] \,,$$

that is, the value of a node is at most the value of its parent. Thus, the largest element in a max-heap is stored at the root, and the subtree rooted at a node contains values no larger than that contained at the node itself. A ***min-heap*** is organized in the opposite way; the ***min-heap property*** is that for every node i other than the root,

$$A[\text{PARENT}(i)] \le A[i] .$$

The smallest element in a min-heap is at the root.

For the heapsort algorithm, we use max-heaps. Min-heaps commonly implement priority queues, which we discuss in Section 6.5. We shall be precise in specifying whether we need a max-heap or a min-heap for any particular application, and when properties apply to either max-heaps or min-heaps, we just use the term "heap."

Viewing a heap as a tree, we define the ***height*** of a node in a heap to be the number of edges on the longest simple downward path from the node to a leaf, and we define the height of the heap to be the height of its root. Since a heap of n elements is based on a complete binary tree, its height is $\Theta(\lg n)$ (see Exercise 6.1-2). We shall see that the basic operations on heaps run in time at most proportional to the height of the tree and thus take $O(\lg n)$ time. The remainder of this chapter presents some basic procedures and shows how they are used in a sorting algorithm and a priority-queue data structure.

- The MAX-HEAPIFY procedure, which runs in $O(\lg n)$ time, is the key to maintaining the max-heap property.

- The BUILD-MAX-HEAP procedure, which runs in linear time, produces a max-heap from an unordered input array.

- The HEAPSORT procedure, which runs in $O(n \lg n)$ time, sorts an array in place.

- The MAX-HEAP-INSERT, HEAP-EXTRACT-MAX, HEAP-INCREASE-KEY, and HEAP-MAXIMUM procedures, which run in $O(\lg n)$ time, allow the heap data structure to implement a priority queue.

Exercises

6.1-1
What are the minimum and maximum numbers of elements in a heap of height h?

6.1-2
Show that an n-element heap has height $\lfloor \lg n \rfloor$.

6.1-3
Show that in any subtree of a max-heap, the root of the subtree contains the largest value occurring anywhere in that subtree.

6.1-4

Where in a max-heap might the smallest element reside, assuming that all elements are distinct?

6.1-5

Is an array that is in sorted order a min-heap?

6.1-6

Is the array with values $\langle 23, 17, 14, 6, 13, 10, 1, 5, 7, 12 \rangle$ a max-heap?

6.1-7

Show that, with the array representation for storing an n-element heap, the leaves are the nodes indexed by $\lfloor n/2 \rfloor + 1, \lfloor n/2 \rfloor + 2, \ldots, n$.

6.2   Maintaining the heap property

In order to maintain the max-heap property, we call the procedure MAX-HEAPIFY. Its inputs are an array A and an index i into the array. When it is called, MAX-HEAPIFY assumes that the binary trees rooted at LEFT(i) and RIGHT(i) are max-heaps, but that $A[i]$ might be smaller than its children, thus violating the max-heap property. MAX-HEAPIFY lets the value at $A[i]$ "float down" in the max-heap so that the subtree rooted at index i obeys the max-heap property.

MAX-HEAPIFY(A, i)

```
 1   l = LEFT(i)
 2   r = RIGHT(i)
 3   if l ≤ A.heap-size and A[l] > A[i]
 4       largest = l
 5   else largest = i
 6   if r ≤ A.heap-size and A[r] > A[largest]
 7       largest = r
 8   if largest ≠ i
 9       exchange A[i] with A[largest]
10       MAX-HEAPIFY(A, largest)
```

Figure 6.2 illustrates the action of MAX-HEAPIFY. At each step, the largest of the elements $A[i]$, $A[\text{LEFT}(i)]$, and $A[\text{RIGHT}(i)]$ is determined, and its index is stored in *largest*. If $A[i]$ is largest, then the subtree rooted at node i is already a max-heap and the procedure terminates. Otherwise, one of the two children has the largest element, and $A[i]$ is swapped with $A[largest]$, which causes node i and its

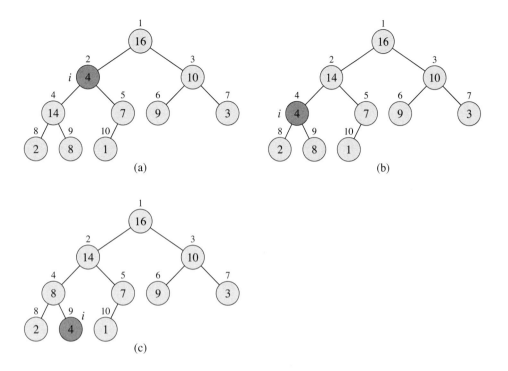

Figure 6.2 The action of MAX-HEAPIFY($A, 2$), where $A.heap\text{-}size = 10$. **(a)** The initial configuration, with $A[2]$ at node $i = 2$ violating the max-heap property since it is not larger than both children. The max-heap property is restored for node 2 in **(b)** by exchanging $A[2]$ with $A[4]$, which destroys the max-heap property for node 4. The recursive call MAX-HEAPIFY($A, 4$) now has $i = 4$. After swapping $A[4]$ with $A[9]$, as shown in **(c)**, node 4 is fixed up, and the recursive call MAX-HEAPIFY($A, 9$) yields no further change to the data structure.

children to satisfy the max-heap property. The node indexed by *largest*, however, now has the original value $A[i]$, and thus the subtree rooted at *largest* might violate the max-heap property. Consequently, we call MAX-HEAPIFY recursively on that subtree.

The running time of MAX-HEAPIFY on a subtree of size n rooted at a given node i is the $\Theta(1)$ time to fix up the relationships among the elements $A[i]$, $A[\text{LEFT}(i)]$, and $A[\text{RIGHT}(i)]$, plus the time to run MAX-HEAPIFY on a subtree rooted at one of the children of node i (assuming that the recursive call occurs). The children's subtrees each have size at most $2n/3$—the worst case occurs when the bottom level of the tree is exactly half full—and therefore we can describe the running time of MAX-HEAPIFY by the recurrence

$$T(n) \le T(2n/3) + \Theta(1) \ .$$

The solution to this recurrence, by case 2 of the master theorem (Theorem 4.1), is $T(n) = O(\lg n)$. Alternatively, we can characterize the running time of MAX-HEAPIFY on a node of height h as $O(h)$.

Exercises

6.2-1
Using Figure 6.2 as a model, illustrate the operation of MAX-HEAPIFY$(A, 3)$ on the array $A = \langle 27, 17, 3, 16, 13, 10, 1, 5, 7, 12, 4, 8, 9, 0 \rangle$.

6.2-2
Starting with the procedure MAX-HEAPIFY, write pseudocode for the procedure MIN-HEAPIFY(A, i), which performs the corresponding manipulation on a min-heap. How does the running time of MIN-HEAPIFY compare to that of MAX-HEAPIFY?

6.2-3
What is the effect of calling MAX-HEAPIFY(A, i) when the element $A[i]$ is larger than its children?

6.2-4
What is the effect of calling MAX-HEAPIFY(A, i) for $i > A.heap\text{-}size/2$?

6.2-5
The code for MAX-HEAPIFY is quite efficient in terms of constant factors, except possibly for the recursive call in line 10, which might cause some compilers to produce inefficient code. Write an efficient MAX-HEAPIFY that uses an iterative control construct (a loop) instead of recursion.

6.2-6
Show that the worst-case running time of MAX-HEAPIFY on a heap of size n is $\Omega(\lg n)$. (*Hint:* For a heap with n nodes, give node values that cause MAX-HEAPIFY to be called recursively at every node on a simple path from the root down to a leaf.)

6.3   Building a heap

We can use the procedure MAX-HEAPIFY in a bottom-up manner to convert an array $A[1..n]$, where $n = A.length$, into a max-heap. By Exercise 6.1-7, the elements in the subarray $A[(\lfloor n/2 \rfloor + 1)..n]$ are all leaves of the tree, and so each is a 1-element heap to begin with. The procedure BUILD-MAX-HEAP goes through the remaining nodes of the tree and runs MAX-HEAPIFY on each one.

BUILD-MAX-HEAP(A)

```
1   A.heap-size = A.length
2   for i = ⌊A.length/2⌋ downto 1
3       MAX-HEAPIFY(A, i)
```

Figure 6.3 shows an example of the action of BUILD-MAX-HEAP.

To show why BUILD-MAX-HEAP works correctly, we use the following loop invariant:

> At the start of each iteration of the **for** loop of lines 2–3, each node $i + 1$, $i + 2, \ldots, n$ is the root of a max-heap.

We need to show that this invariant is true prior to the first loop iteration, that each iteration of the loop maintains the invariant, and that the invariant provides a useful property to show correctness when the loop terminates.

Initialization: Prior to the first iteration of the loop, $i = \lfloor n/2 \rfloor$. Each node $\lfloor n/2 \rfloor + 1, \lfloor n/2 \rfloor + 2, \ldots, n$ is a leaf and is thus the root of a trivial max-heap.

Maintenance: To see that each iteration maintains the loop invariant, observe that the children of node i are numbered higher than i. By the loop invariant, therefore, they are both roots of max-heaps. This is precisely the condition required for the call MAX-HEAPIFY(A, i) to make node i a max-heap root. Moreover, the MAX-HEAPIFY call preserves the property that nodes $i + 1, i + 2, \ldots, n$ are all roots of max-heaps. Decrementing i in the **for** loop update reestablishes the loop invariant for the next iteration.

Termination: At termination, $i = 0$. By the loop invariant, each node $1, 2, \ldots, n$ is the root of a max-heap. In particular, node 1 is.

We can compute a simple upper bound on the running time of BUILD-MAX-HEAP as follows. Each call to MAX-HEAPIFY costs $O(\lg n)$ time, and BUILD-MAX-HEAP makes $O(n)$ such calls. Thus, the running time is $O(n \lg n)$. This upper bound, though correct, is not asymptotically tight.

We can derive a tighter bound by observing that the time for MAX-HEAPIFY to run at a node varies with the height of the node in the tree, and the heights of most nodes are small. Our tighter analysis relies on the properties that an n-element heap has height $\lfloor \lg n \rfloor$ (see Exercise 6.1-2) and at most $\lceil n/2^{h+1} \rceil$ nodes of any height h (see Exercise 6.3-3).

The time required by MAX-HEAPIFY when called on a node of height h is $O(h)$, and so we can express the total cost of BUILD-MAX-HEAP as being bounded from above by

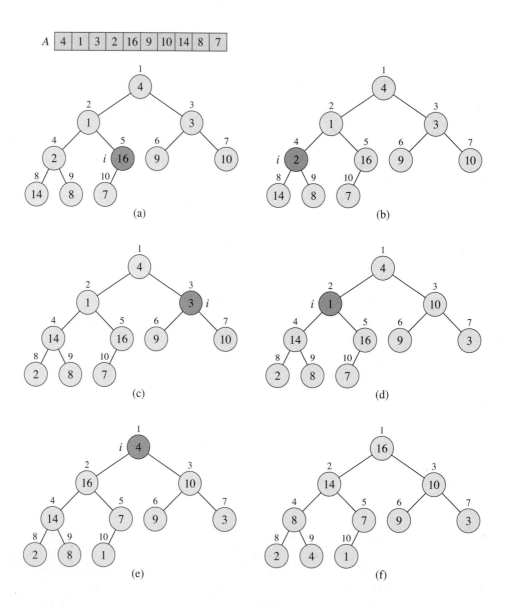

Figure 6.3 The operation of BUILD-MAX-HEAP, showing the data structure before the call to MAX-HEAPIFY in line 3 of BUILD-MAX-HEAP. **(a)** A 10-element input array A and the binary tree it represents. The figure shows that the loop index i refers to node 5 before the call MAX-HEAPIFY(A, i). **(b)** The data structure that results. The loop index i for the next iteration refers to node 4. **(c)–(e)** Subsequent iterations of the **for** loop in BUILD-MAX-HEAP. Observe that whenever MAX-HEAPIFY is called on a node, the two subtrees of that node are both max-heaps. **(f)** The max-heap after BUILD-MAX-HEAP finishes.

$$\sum_{h=0}^{\lfloor \lg n \rfloor} \left\lceil \frac{n}{2^{h+1}} \right\rceil O(h) = O\left(n \sum_{h=0}^{\lfloor \lg n \rfloor} \frac{h}{2^h} \right) .$$

We evaluate the last summation by substituting $x = 1/2$ in the formula (A.8), yielding

$$\sum_{h=0}^{\infty} \frac{h}{2^h} = \frac{1/2}{(1 - 1/2)^2}$$

$$= 2 .$$

Thus, we can bound the running time of BUILD-MAX-HEAP as

$$O\left(n \sum_{h=0}^{\lfloor \lg n \rfloor} \frac{h}{2^h} \right) = O\left(n \sum_{h=0}^{\infty} \frac{h}{2^h} \right)$$

$$= O(n) .$$

Hence, we can build a max-heap from an unordered array in linear time.

We can build a min-heap by the procedure BUILD-MIN-HEAP, which is the same as BUILD-MAX-HEAP but with the call to MAX-HEAPIFY in line 3 replaced by a call to MIN-HEAPIFY (see Exercise 6.2-2). BUILD-MIN-HEAP produces a min-heap from an unordered linear array in linear time.

Exercises

6.3-1
Using Figure 6.3 as a model, illustrate the operation of BUILD-MAX-HEAP on the array $A = \langle 5, 3, 17, 10, 84, 19, 6, 22, 9 \rangle$.

6.3-2
Why do we want the loop index i in line 2 of BUILD-MAX-HEAP to decrease from $\lfloor A.length/2 \rfloor$ to 1 rather than increase from 1 to $\lfloor A.length/2 \rfloor$?

6.3-3
Show that there are at most $\lceil n/2^{h+1} \rceil$ nodes of height h in any n-element heap.

6.4   The heapsort algorithm

The heapsort algorithm starts by using BUILD-MAX-HEAP to build a max-heap on the input array $A[1 .. n]$, where $n = A.length$. Since the maximum element of the array is stored at the root $A[1]$, we can put it into its correct final position by exchanging it with $A[n]$. If we now discard node n from the heap—and we can do so by simply decrementing $A.heap\text{-}size$—we observe that the children of the root remain max-heaps, but the new root element might violate the max-heap property. All we need to do to restore the max-heap property, however, is call MAX-HEAPIFY$(A, 1)$, which leaves a max-heap in $A[1 .. n - 1]$. The heapsort algorithm then repeats this process for the max-heap of size $n - 1$ down to a heap of size 2. (See Exercise 6.4-2 for a precise loop invariant.)

HEAPSORT(A)

```
1   BUILD-MAX-HEAP(A)
2   for i = A.length downto 2
3       exchange A[1] with A[i]
4       A.heap-size = A.heap-size - 1
5       MAX-HEAPIFY(A, 1)
```

Figure 6.4 shows an example of the operation of HEAPSORT after line 1 has built the initial max-heap. The figure shows the max-heap before the first iteration of the **for** loop of lines 2–5 and after each iteration.

The HEAPSORT procedure takes time $O(n \lg n)$, since the call to BUILD-MAX-HEAP takes time $O(n)$ and each of the $n - 1$ calls to MAX-HEAPIFY takes time $O(\lg n)$.

Exercises

6.4-1
Using Figure 6.4 as a model, illustrate the operation of HEAPSORT on the array $A = \langle 5, 13, 2, 25, 7, 17, 20, 8, 4 \rangle$.

6.4-2
Argue the correctness of HEAPSORT using the following loop invariant:

> At the start of each iteration of the **for** loop of lines 2–5, the subarray $A[1 .. i]$ is a max-heap containing the i smallest elements of $A[1 .. n]$, and the subarray $A[i + 1 .. n]$ contains the $n - i$ largest elements of $A[1 .. n]$, sorted.

6.4-3
What is the running time of HEAPSORT on an array A of length n that is already sorted in increasing order? What about decreasing order?

6.4-4
Show that the worst-case running time of HEAPSORT is $\Omega(n \lg n)$.

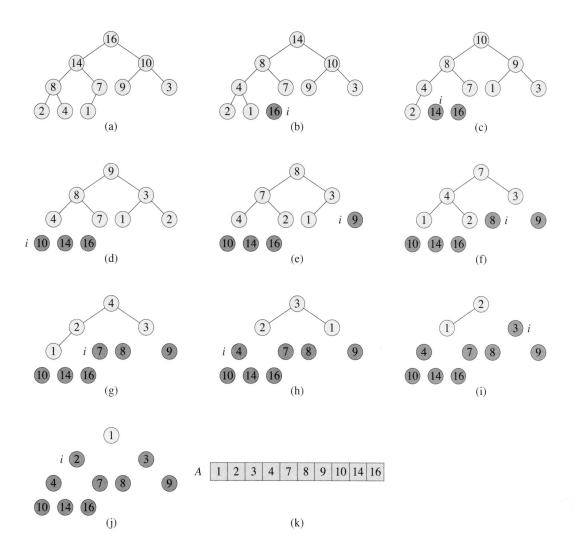

Figure 6.4 The operation of HEAPSORT. **(a)** The max-heap data structure just after BUILD-MAX-HEAP has built it in line 1. **(b)–(j)** The max-heap just after each call of MAX-HEAPIFY in line 5, showing the value of *i* at that time. Only lightly shaded nodes remain in the heap. **(k)** The resulting sorted array *A*.

6.4-5 ★

Show that when all elements are distinct, the best-case running time of HEAPSORT is $\Omega(n \lg n)$.

6.5 Priority queues

Heapsort is an excellent algorithm, but a good implementation of quicksort, presented in Chapter 7, usually beats it in practice. Nevertheless, the heap data structure itself has many uses. In this section, we present one of the most popular applications of a heap: as an efficient priority queue. As with heaps, priority queues come in two forms: max-priority queues and min-priority queues. We will focus here on how to implement max-priority queues, which are in turn based on max-heaps; Exercise 6.5-3 asks you to write the procedures for min-priority queues.

A *priority queue* is a data structure for maintaining a set S of elements, each with an associated value called a *key*. A *max-priority queue* supports the following operations:

INSERT(S, x) inserts the element x into the set S, which is equivalent to the operation $S = S \cup \{x\}$.

MAXIMUM(S) returns the element of S with the largest key.

EXTRACT-MAX(S) removes and returns the element of S with the largest key.

INCREASE-KEY(S, x, k) increases the value of element x's key to the new value k, which is assumed to be at least as large as x's current key value.

Among their other applications, we can use max-priority queues to schedule jobs on a shared computer. The max-priority queue keeps track of the jobs to be performed and their relative priorities. When a job is finished or interrupted, the scheduler selects the highest-priority job from among those pending by calling EXTRACT-MAX. The scheduler can add a new job to the queue at any time by calling INSERT.

Alternatively, a *min-priority queue* supports the operations INSERT, MINIMUM, EXTRACT-MIN, and DECREASE-KEY. A min-priority queue can be used in an event-driven simulator. The items in the queue are events to be simulated, each with an associated time of occurrence that serves as its key. The events must be simulated in order of their time of occurrence, because the simulation of an event can cause other events to be simulated in the future. The simulation program calls EXTRACT-MIN at each step to choose the next event to simulate. As new events are produced, the simulator inserts them into the min-priority queue by calling INSERT.

We shall see other uses for min-priority queues, highlighting the DECREASE-KEY operation, in Chapters 23 and 24.

Not surprisingly, we can use a heap to implement a priority queue. In a given application, such as job scheduling or event-driven simulation, elements of a priority queue correspond to objects in the application. We often need to determine which application object corresponds to a given priority-queue element, and vice versa. When we use a heap to implement a priority queue, therefore, we often need to store a *handle* to the corresponding application object in each heap element. The exact makeup of the handle (such as a pointer or an integer) depends on the application. Similarly, we need to store a handle to the corresponding heap element in each application object. Here, the handle would typically be an array index. Because heap elements change locations within the array during heap operations, an actual implementation, upon relocating a heap element, would also have to update the array index in the corresponding application object. Because the details of accessing application objects depend heavily on the application and its implementation, we shall not pursue them here, other than noting that in practice, these handles do need to be correctly maintained.

Now we discuss how to implement the operations of a max-priority queue. The procedure HEAP-MAXIMUM implements the MAXIMUM operation in $\Theta(1)$ time.

HEAP-MAXIMUM(A)
1   **return** $A[1]$

The procedure HEAP-EXTRACT-MAX implements the EXTRACT-MAX operation. It is similar to the **for** loop body (lines 3–5) of the HEAPSORT procedure.

HEAP-EXTRACT-MAX(A)
1   **if** $A.heap\text{-}size < 1$
2   **error** "heap underflow"
3    $max = A[1]$
4    $A[1] = A[A.heap\text{-}size]$
5    $A.heap\text{-}size = A.heap\text{-}size - 1$
6   MAX-HEAPIFY($A, 1$)
7   **return** max

The running time of HEAP-EXTRACT-MAX is $O(\lg n)$, since it performs only a constant amount of work on top of the $O(\lg n)$ time for MAX-HEAPIFY.

The procedure HEAP-INCREASE-KEY implements the INCREASE-KEY operation. An index i into the array identifies the priority-queue element whose key we wish to increase. The procedure first updates the key of element $A[i]$ to its new value. Because increasing the key of $A[i]$ might violate the max-heap property, the procedure then, in a manner reminiscent of the insertion loop (lines 5–7) of INSERTION-SORT from Section 2.1, traverses a simple path from this node toward the root to find a proper place for the newly increased key. As HEAP-INCREASE-KEY traverses this path, it repeatedly compares an element to its parent, exchanging their keys and continuing if the element's key is larger, and terminating if the element's key is smaller, since the max-heap property now holds. (See Exercise 6.5-5 for a precise loop invariant.)

HEAP-INCREASE-KEY (A, i, key)

```
1   if key < A[i]
2       error "new key is smaller than current key"
3   A[i] = key
4   while i > 1 and A[PARENT(i)] < A[i]
5       exchange A[i] with A[PARENT(i)]
6       i = PARENT(i)
```

Figure 6.5 shows an example of a HEAP-INCREASE-KEY operation. The running time of HEAP-INCREASE-KEY on an n-element heap is $O(\lg n)$, since the path traced from the node updated in line 3 to the root has length $O(\lg n)$.

The procedure MAX-HEAP-INSERT implements the INSERT operation. It takes as an input the key of the new element to be inserted into max-heap A. The procedure first expands the max-heap by adding to the tree a new leaf whose key is $-\infty$. Then it calls HEAP-INCREASE-KEY to set the key of this new node to its correct value and maintain the max-heap property.

MAX-HEAP-INSERT (A, key)

```
1   A.heap-size = A.heap-size + 1
2   A[A.heap-size] = -∞
3   HEAP-INCREASE-KEY(A, A.heap-size, key)
```

The running time of MAX-HEAP-INSERT on an n-element heap is $O(\lg n)$.

In summary, a heap can support any priority-queue operation on a set of size n in $O(\lg n)$ time.

Exercises

6.5-1
Illustrate the operation of HEAP-EXTRACT-MAX on the heap $A = \langle 15, 13, 9, 5, 12, 8, 7, 4, 0, 6, 2, 1 \rangle$.

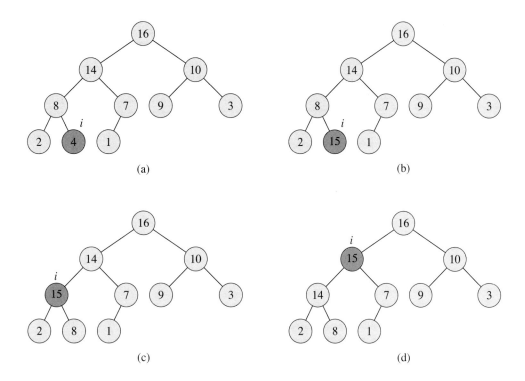

Figure 6.5   The operation of HEAP-INCREASE-KEY. **(a)** The max-heap of Figure 6.4(a) with a node whose index is i heavily shaded. **(b)** This node has its key increased to 15. **(c)** After one iteration of the **while** loop of lines 4–6, the node and its parent have exchanged keys, and the index i moves up to the parent. **(d)** The max-heap after one more iteration of the **while** loop. At this point, $A[\text{PARENT}(i)] \geq A[i]$. The max-heap property now holds and the procedure terminates.

6.5-2
Illustrate the operation of MAX-HEAP-INSERT$(A, 10)$ on the heap $A = \langle 15, 13, 9, 5, 12, 8, 7, 4, 0, 6, 2, 1 \rangle$.

6.5-3
Write pseudocode for the procedures HEAP-MINIMUM, HEAP-EXTRACT-MIN, HEAP-DECREASE-KEY, and MIN-HEAP-INSERT that implement a min-priority queue with a min-heap.

6.5-4
Why do we bother setting the key of the inserted node to $-\infty$ in line 2 of MAX-HEAP-INSERT when the next thing we do is increase its key to the desired value?

6.5-5

Argue the correctness of HEAP-INCREASE-KEY using the following loop invariant:

> At the start of each iteration of the **while** loop of lines 4–6, $A[\text{PARENT}(i)] \geq A[\text{LEFT}(i)]$ and $A[\text{PARENT}(i)] \geq A[\text{RIGHT}(i)]$, if these nodes exist, and the subarray $A[1 .. A.\textit{heap-size}]$ satisfies the max-heap property, except that there may be one violation: $A[i]$ may be larger than $A[\text{PARENT}(i)]$.

You may assume that the subarray $A[1 .. A.\textit{heap-size}]$ satisfies the max-heap property at the time HEAP-INCREASE-KEY is called.

6.5-6

Each exchange operation on line 5 of HEAP-INCREASE-KEY typically requires three assignments. Show how to use the idea of the inner loop of INSERTION-SORT to reduce the three assignments down to just one assignment.

6.5-7

Show how to implement a first-in, first-out queue with a priority queue. Show how to implement a stack with a priority queue. (Queues and stacks are defined in Section 10.1.)

6.5-8

The operation HEAP-DELETE(A, i) deletes the item in node i from heap A. Give an implementation of HEAP-DELETE that runs in $O(\lg n)$ time for an n-element max-heap.

6.5-9

Give an $O(n \lg k)$-time algorithm to merge k sorted lists into one sorted list, where n is the total number of elements in all the input lists. (*Hint:* Use a min-heap for k-way merging.)

Problems

6-1   *Building a heap using insertion*

We can build a heap by repeatedly calling MAX-HEAP-INSERT to insert the elements into the heap. Consider the following variation on the BUILD-MAX-HEAP procedure:

BUILD-MAX-HEAP$'(A)$

```
1   A.heap-size = 1
2   for i = 2 to A.length
3       MAX-HEAP-INSERT(A, A[i])
```

a. Do the procedures BUILD-MAX-HEAP and BUILD-MAX-HEAP$'$ always create the same heap when run on the same input array? Prove that they do, or provide a counterexample.

b. Show that in the worst case, BUILD-MAX-HEAP$'$ requires $\Theta(n \lg n)$ time to build an n-element heap.

6-2 *Analysis of d-ary heaps*

A ***d-ary heap*** is like a binary heap, but (with one possible exception) non-leaf nodes have d children instead of 2 children.

a. How would you represent a d-ary heap in an array?

b. What is the height of a d-ary heap of n elements in terms of n and d?

c. Give an efficient implementation of EXTRACT-MAX in a d-ary max-heap. Analyze its running time in terms of d and n.

d. Give an efficient implementation of INSERT in a d-ary max-heap. Analyze its running time in terms of d and n.

e. Give an efficient implementation of INCREASE-KEY(A, i, k), which flags an error if $k < A[i]$, but otherwise sets $A[i] = k$ and then updates the d-ary max-heap structure appropriately. Analyze its running time in terms of d and n.

6-3 *Young tableaus*

An $m \times n$ ***Young tableau*** is an $m \times n$ matrix such that the entries of each row are in sorted order from left to right and the entries of each column are in sorted order from top to bottom. Some of the entries of a Young tableau may be ∞, which we treat as nonexistent elements. Thus, a Young tableau can be used to hold $r \le mn$ finite numbers.

a. Draw a 4×4 Young tableau containing the elements $\{9, 16, 3, 2, 4, 8, 5, 14, 12\}$.

b. Argue that an $m \times n$ Young tableau Y is empty if $Y[1, 1] = \infty$. Argue that Y is full (contains mn elements) if $Y[m, n] < \infty$.

c. Give an algorithm to implement EXTRACT-MIN on a nonempty $m \times n$ Young tableau that runs in $O(m + n)$ time. Your algorithm should use a recursive subroutine that solves an $m \times n$ problem by recursively solving either an $(m - 1) \times n$ or an $m \times (n - 1)$ subproblem. (*Hint:* Think about MAX-HEAPIFY.) Define $T(p)$, where $p = m + n$, to be the maximum running time of EXTRACT-MIN on any $m \times n$ Young tableau. Give and solve a recurrence for $T(p)$ that yields the $O(m + n)$ time bound.

d. Show how to insert a new element into a nonfull $m \times n$ Young tableau in $O(m + n)$ time.

e. Using no other sorting method as a subroutine, show how to use an $n \times n$ Young tableau to sort n^2 numbers in $O(n^3)$ time.

f. Give an $O(m + n)$-time algorithm to determine whether a given number is stored in a given $m \times n$ Young tableau.

Chapter notes

The heapsort algorithm was invented by Williams [357], who also described how to implement a priority queue with a heap. The BUILD-MAX-HEAP procedure was suggested by Floyd [106].

We use min-heaps to implement min-priority queues in Chapters 16, 23, and 24. We also give an implementation with improved time bounds for certain operations in Chapter 19 and, assuming that the keys are drawn from a bounded set of non-negative integers, Chapter 20.

If the data are b-bit integers, and the computer memory consists of addressable b-bit words, Fredman and Willard [115] showed how to implement MINIMUM in $O(1)$ time and INSERT and EXTRACT-MIN in $O(\sqrt{\lg n})$ time. Thorup [337] has improved the $O(\sqrt{\lg n})$ bound to $O(\lg \lg n)$ time. This bound uses an amount of space unbounded in n, but it can be implemented in linear space by using randomized hashing.

An important special case of priority queues occurs when the sequence of EXTRACT-MIN operations is ***monotone***, that is, the values returned by successive EXTRACT-MIN operations are monotonically increasing over time. This case arises in several important applications, such as Dijkstra's single-source shortest-paths algorithm, which we discuss in Chapter 24, and in discrete-event simulation. For Dijkstra's algorithm it is particularly important that the DECREASE-KEY operation be implemented efficiently. For the monotone case, if the data are integers in the range $1, 2, \ldots, C$, Ahuja, Mehlhorn, Orlin, and Tarjan [8] describe how to implement EXTRACT-MIN and INSERT in $O(\lg C)$ amortized time (see Chapter 17 for more on amortized analysis) and DECREASE-KEY in $O(1)$ time, using a data structure called a radix heap. The $O(\lg C)$ bound can be improved to $O(\sqrt{\lg C})$ using Fibonacci heaps (see Chapter 19) in conjunction with radix heaps. Cherkassky, Goldberg, and Silverstein [65] further improved the bound to $O(\lg^{1/3+\epsilon} C)$ expected time by combining the multilevel bucketing structure of Denardo and Fox [85] with the heap of Thorup mentioned earlier. Raman [291] further improved these results to obtain a bound of $O(\min(\lg^{1/4+\epsilon} C, \lg^{1/3+\epsilon} n))$, for any fixed $\epsilon > 0$.

7   Quicksort

The quicksort algorithm has a worst-case running time of $\Theta(n^2)$ on an input array of n numbers. Despite this slow worst-case running time, quicksort is often the best practical choice for sorting because it is remarkably efficient on the average: its expected running time is $\Theta(n \lg n)$, and the constant factors hidden in the $\Theta(n \lg n)$ notation are quite small. It also has the advantage of sorting in place (see page 17), and it works well even in virtual-memory environments.

Section 7.1 describes the algorithm and an important subroutine used by quicksort for partitioning. Because the behavior of quicksort is complex, we start with an intuitive discussion of its performance in Section 7.2 and postpone its precise analysis to the end of the chapter. Section 7.3 presents a version of quicksort that uses random sampling. This algorithm has a good expected running time and, when all elements are distinct, no particular input elicits its worst-case behavior. (See Problem 7-2 for the case in which elements may be equal.) Section 7.4 analyzes the randomized algorithm, showing that it runs in $\Theta(n^2)$ time in the worst case and, assuming distinct elements, in expected $O(n \lg n)$ time.

7.1   Description of quicksort

Quicksort, like merge sort, applies the divide-and-conquer paradigm introduced in Section 2.3.1. Here is the three-step divide-and-conquer process for sorting a typical subarray $A[p \mathinner{.\,.} r]$:

Divide: Partition (rearrange) the array $A[p \mathinner{.\,.} r]$ into two (possibly empty) subarrays $A[p \mathinner{.\,.} q-1]$ and $A[q+1 \mathinner{.\,.} r]$ such that each element of $A[p \mathinner{.\,.} q-1]$ is less than or equal to $A[q]$, which is, in turn, less than or equal to each element of $A[q+1 \mathinner{.\,.} r]$. Compute the index q as part of this partitioning procedure.

Conquer: Sort the two subarrays $A[p \mathinner{.\,.} q-1]$ and $A[q+1 \mathinner{.\,.} r]$ by recursive calls to quicksort.

Combine: Because the subarrays are already sorted, no work is needed to combine them: the entire array $A[p \mathinner{\ldotp\ldotp} r]$ is now sorted.

The following procedure implements quicksort:

QUICKSORT(A, p, r)

1   **if** $p < r$
2       $q =$ PARTITION(A, p, r)
3   QUICKSORT$(A, p, q - 1)$
4   QUICKSORT$(A, q + 1, r)$

To sort an entire array A, the initial call is QUICKSORT$(A, 1, A.length)$.

Partitioning the array

The key to the algorithm is the PARTITION procedure, which rearranges the subarray $A[p \mathinner{\ldotp\ldotp} r]$ in place.

PARTITION(A, p, r)

1   $x = A[r]$
2   $i = p - 1$
3   **for** $j = p$ **to** $r - 1$
4   **if** $A[j] \leq x$
5           $i = i + 1$
6   exchange $A[i]$ with $A[j]$
7   exchange $A[i + 1]$ with $A[r]$
8   **return** $i + 1$

Figure 7.1 shows how PARTITION works on an 8-element array. PARTITION always selects an element $x = A[r]$ as a ***pivot*** element around which to partition the subarray $A[p \mathinner{\ldotp\ldotp} r]$. As the procedure runs, it partitions the array into four (possibly empty) regions. At the start of each iteration of the **for** loop in lines 3–6, the regions satisfy certain properties, shown in Figure 7.2. We state these properties as a loop invariant:

> At the beginning of each iteration of the loop of lines 3–6, for any array index k,
>
> 1. If $p \leq k \leq i$, then $A[k] \leq x$.
> 2. If $i + 1 \leq k \leq j - 1$, then $A[k] > x$.
> 3. If $k = r$, then $A[k] = x$.

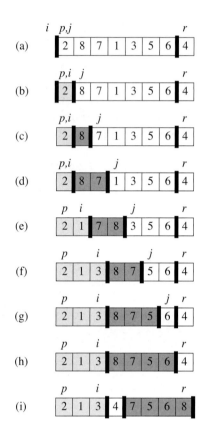

Figure 7.1 The operation of PARTITION on a sample array. Array entry $A[r]$ becomes the pivot element x. Lightly shaded array elements are all in the first partition with values no greater than x. Heavily shaded elements are in the second partition with values greater than x. The unshaded elements have not yet been put in one of the first two partitions, and the final white element is the pivot x. **(a)** The initial array and variable settings. None of the elements have been placed in either of the first two partitions. **(b)** The value 2 is "swapped with itself" and put in the partition of smaller values. **(c)–(d)** The values 8 and 7 are added to the partition of larger values. **(e)** The values 1 and 8 are swapped, and the smaller partition grows. **(f)** The values 3 and 7 are swapped, and the smaller partition grows. **(g)–(h)** The larger partition grows to include 5 and 6, and the loop terminates. **(i)** In lines 7–8, the pivot element is swapped so that it lies between the two partitions.

The indices between j and $r - 1$ are not covered by any of the three cases, and the values in these entries have no particular relationship to the pivot x.

We need to show that this loop invariant is true prior to the first iteration, that each iteration of the loop maintains the invariant, and that the invariant provides a useful property to show correctness when the loop terminates.

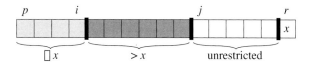

Figure 7.2 The four regions maintained by the procedure PARTITION on a subarray $A[p \, . \, . \, r]$. The values in $A[p \, . \, . \, i]$ are all less than or equal to x, the values in $A[i + 1 \, . \, . \, j - 1]$ are all greater than x, and $A[r] = x$. The subarray $A[j \, . \, . \, r - 1]$ can take on any values.

Initialization: Prior to the first iteration of the loop, $i = p - 1$ and $j = p$. Because no values lie between p and i and no values lie between $i + 1$ and $j - 1$, the first two conditions of the loop invariant are trivially satisfied. The assignment in line 1 satisfies the third condition.

Maintenance: As Figure 7.3 shows, we consider two cases, depending on the outcome of the test in line 4. Figure 7.3(a) shows what happens when $A[j] > x$; the only action in the loop is to increment j. After j is incremented, condition 2 holds for $A[j - 1]$ and all other entries remain unchanged. Figure 7.3(b) shows what happens when $A[j] \leq x$; the loop increments i, swaps $A[i]$ and $A[j]$, and then increments j. Because of the swap, we now have that $A[i] \leq x$, and condition 1 is satisfied. Similarly, we also have that $A[j - 1] > x$, since the item that was swapped into $A[j - 1]$ is, by the loop invariant, greater than x.

Termination: At termination, $j = r$. Therefore, every entry in the array is in one of the three sets described by the invariant, and we have partitioned the values in the array into three sets: those less than or equal to x, those greater than x, and a singleton set containing x.

The final two lines of PARTITION finish up by swapping the pivot element with the leftmost element greater than x, thereby moving the pivot into its correct place in the partitioned array, and then returning the pivot's new index. The output of PARTITION now satisfies the specifications given for the divide step. In fact, it satisfies a slightly stronger condition: after line 2 of QUICKSORT, $A[q]$ is strictly less than every element of $A[q + 1 \, . \, . \, r]$.

The running time of PARTITION on the subarray $A[p \, . \, . \, r]$ is $\Theta(n)$, where $n = r - p + 1$ (see Exercise 7.1-3).

Exercises

7.1-1
Using Figure 7.1 as a model, illustrate the operation of PARTITION on the array $A = \langle 13, 19, 9, 5, 12, 8, 7, 4, 21, 2, 6, 11 \rangle$.

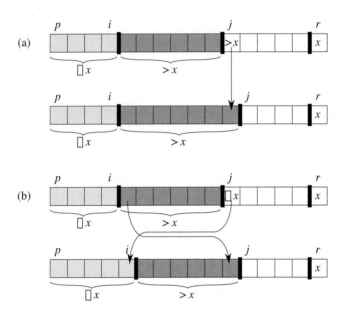

Figure 7.3   The two cases for one iteration of procedure PARTITION. **(a)** If $A[j] > x$, the only action is to increment j, which maintains the loop invariant. **(b)** If $A[j] \leq x$, index i is incremented, $A[i]$ and $A[j]$ are swapped, and then j is incremented. Again, the loop invariant is maintained.

7.1-2

What value of q does PARTITION return when all elements in the array $A[p \mathinner{.\,.} r]$ have the same value? Modify PARTITION so that $q = \lfloor (p + r)/2 \rfloor$ when all elements in the array $A[p \mathinner{.\,.} r]$ have the same value.

7.1-3

Give a brief argument that the running time of PARTITION on a subarray of size n is $\Theta(n)$.

7.1-4

How would you modify QUICKSORT to sort into nonincreasing order?

7.2   Performance of quicksort

The running time of quicksort depends on whether the partitioning is balanced or unbalanced, which in turn depends on which elements are used for partitioning. If the partitioning is balanced, the algorithm runs asymptotically as fast as merge sort. If the partitioning is unbalanced, however, it can run asymptotically as slowly as insertion sort. In this section, we shall informally investigate how quicksort performs under the assumptions of balanced versus unbalanced partitioning.

Worst-case partitioning

The worst-case behavior for quicksort occurs when the partitioning routine produces one subproblem with $n - 1$ elements and one with 0 elements. (We prove this claim in Section 7.4.1.) Let us assume that this unbalanced partitioning arises in each recursive call. The partitioning costs $\Theta(n)$ time. Since the recursive call on an array of size 0 just returns, $T(0) = \Theta(1)$, and the recurrence for the running time is

$$
\begin{aligned}
T(n) &= T(n-1) + T(0) + \Theta(n) \\
&= T(n-1) + \Theta(n) \ .
\end{aligned}
$$

Intuitively, if we sum the costs incurred at each level of the recursion, we get an arithmetic series (equation (A.2)), which evaluates to $\Theta(n^2)$. Indeed, it is straightforward to use the substitution method to prove that the recurrence $T(n) = T(n-1) + \Theta(n)$ has the solution $T(n) = \Theta(n^2)$. (See Exercise 7.2-1.)

Thus, if the partitioning is maximally unbalanced at every recursive level of the algorithm, the running time is $\Theta(n^2)$. Therefore the worst-case running time of quicksort is no better than that of insertion sort. Moreover, the $\Theta(n^2)$ running time occurs when the input array is already completely sorted—a common situation in which insertion sort runs in $O(n)$ time.

Best-case partitioning

In the most even possible split, PARTITION produces two subproblems, each of size no more than $n/2$, since one is of size $\lfloor n/2 \rfloor$ and one of size $\lceil n/2 \rceil - 1$. In this case, quicksort runs much faster. The recurrence for the running time is then

$$
T(n) = 2T(n/2) + \Theta(n) \ ,
$$

where we tolerate the sloppiness from ignoring the floor and ceiling and from subtracting 1. By case 2 of the master theorem (Theorem 4.1), this recurrence has the solution $T(n) = \Theta(n \lg n)$. By equally balancing the two sides of the partition at every level of the recursion, we get an asymptotically faster algorithm.

Balanced partitioning

The average-case running time of quicksort is much closer to the best case than to the worst case, as the analyses in Section 7.4 will show. The key to understand-

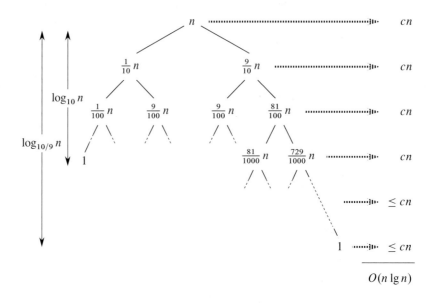

Figure 7.4   A recursion tree for QUICKSORT in which PARTITION always produces a 9-to-1 split, yielding a running time of $O(n \lg n)$. Nodes show subproblem sizes, with per-level costs on the right. The per-level costs include the constant c implicit in the $\Theta(n)$ term.

ing why is to understand how the balance of the partitioning is reflected in the recurrence that describes the running time.

Suppose, for example, that the partitioning algorithm always produces a 9-to-1 proportional split, which at first blush seems quite unbalanced. We then obtain the recurrence

$$T(n) = T(9n/10) + T(n/10) + cn \;,$$

on the running time of quicksort, where we have explicitly included the constant c hidden in the $\Theta(n)$ term. Figure 7.4 shows the recursion tree for this recurrence. Notice that every level of the tree has cost cn, until the recursion reaches a boundary condition at depth $\log_{10} n = \Theta(\lg n)$, and then the levels have cost at most cn. The recursion terminates at depth $\log_{10/9} n = \Theta(\lg n)$. The total cost of quicksort is therefore $O(n \lg n)$. Thus, with a 9-to-1 proportional split at every level of recursion, which intuitively seems quite unbalanced, quicksort runs in $O(n \lg n)$ time—asymptotically the same as if the split were right down the middle. Indeed, even a 99-to-1 split yields an $O(n \lg n)$ running time. In fact, any split of *constant* proportionality yields a recursion tree of depth $\Theta(\lg n)$, where the cost at each level is $O(n)$. The running time is therefore $O(n \lg n)$ whenever the split has constant proportionality.

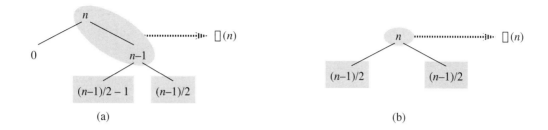

Figure 7.5 **(a)** Two levels of a recursion tree for quicksort. The partitioning at the root costs n and produces a "bad" split: two subarrays of sizes 0 and $n - 1$. The partitioning of the subarray of size $n - 1$ costs $n - 1$ and produces a "good" split: subarrays of size $(n - 1)/2 - 1$ and $(n - 1)/2$. **(b)** A single level of a recursion tree that is very well balanced. In both parts, the partitioning cost for the subproblems shown with elliptical shading is $\Theta(n)$. Yet the subproblems remaining to be solved in (a), shown with square shading, are no larger than the corresponding subproblems remaining to be solved in (b).

Intuition for the average case

To develop a clear notion of the randomized behavior of quicksort, we must make an assumption about how frequently we expect to encounter the various inputs. The behavior of quicksort depends on the relative ordering of the values in the array elements given as the input, and not by the particular values in the array. As in our probabilistic analysis of the hiring problem in Section 5.2, we will assume for now that all permutations of the input numbers are equally likely.

When we run quicksort on a random input array, the partitioning is highly unlikely to happen in the same way at every level, as our informal analysis has assumed. We expect that some of the splits will be reasonably well balanced and that some will be fairly unbalanced. For example, Exercise 7.2-6 asks you to show that about 80 percent of the time PARTITION produces a split that is more balanced than 9 to 1, and about 20 percent of the time it produces a split that is less balanced than 9 to 1.

In the average case, PARTITION produces a mix of "good" and "bad" splits. In a recursion tree for an average-case execution of PARTITION, the good and bad splits are distributed randomly throughout the tree. Suppose, for the sake of intuition, that the good and bad splits alternate levels in the tree, and that the good splits are best-case splits and the bad splits are worst-case splits. Figure 7.5(a) shows the splits at two consecutive levels in the recursion tree. At the root of the tree, the cost is n for partitioning, and the subarrays produced have sizes $n - 1$ and 0: the worst case. At the next level, the subarray of size $n - 1$ undergoes best-case partitioning into subarrays of size $(n - 1)/2 - 1$ and $(n - 1)/2$. Let's assume that the boundary-condition cost is 1 for the subarray of size 0.

The combination of the bad split followed by the good split produces three sub-arrays of sizes 0, $(n - 1)/2 - 1$, and $(n - 1)/2$ at a combined partitioning cost of $\Theta(n) + \Theta(n - 1) = \Theta(n)$. Certainly, this situation is no worse than that in Figure 7.5(b), namely a single level of partitioning that produces two subarrays of size $(n - 1)/2$, at a cost of $\Theta(n)$. Yet this latter situation is balanced! Intuitively, the $\Theta(n - 1)$ cost of the bad split can be absorbed into the $\Theta(n)$ cost of the good split, and the resulting split is good. Thus, the running time of quicksort, when levels alternate between good and bad splits, is like the running time for good splits alone: still $O(n \lg n)$, but with a slightly larger constant hidden by the O-notation. We shall give a rigorous analysis of the expected running time of a randomized version of quicksort in Section 7.4.2.

Exercises

7.2-1
Use the substitution method to prove that the recurrence $T(n) = T(n - 1) + \Theta(n)$ has the solution $T(n) = \Theta(n^2)$, as claimed at the beginning of Section 7.2.

7.2-2
What is the running time of QUICKSORT when all elements of array A have the same value?

7.2-3
Show that the running time of QUICKSORT is $\Theta(n^2)$ when the array A contains distinct elements and is sorted in decreasing order.

7.2-4
Banks often record transactions on an account in order of the times of the transactions, but many people like to receive their bank statements with checks listed in order by check number. People usually write checks in order by check number, and merchants usually cash them with reasonable dispatch. The problem of converting time-of-transaction ordering to check-number ordering is therefore the problem of sorting almost-sorted input. Argue that the procedure INSERTION-SORT would tend to beat the procedure QUICKSORT on this problem.

7.2-5
Suppose that the splits at every level of quicksort are in the proportion $1 - \alpha$ to α, where $0 < \alpha \leq 1/2$ is a constant. Show that the minimum depth of a leaf in the recursion tree is approximately $-\lg n / \lg \alpha$ and the maximum depth is approximately $-\lg n / \lg(1 - \alpha)$. (Don't worry about integer round-off.)

7.2-6 ★

Argue that for any constant $0 < \alpha \le 1/2$, the probability is approximately $1 - 2\alpha$ that on a random input array, PARTITION produces a split more balanced than $1 - \alpha$ to α.

7.3 A randomized version of quicksort

In exploring the average-case behavior of quicksort, we have made an assumption that all permutations of the input numbers are equally likely. In an engineering situation, however, we cannot always expect this assumption to hold. (See Exercise 7.2-4.) As we saw in Section 5.3, we can sometimes add randomization to an algorithm in order to obtain good expected performance over all inputs. Many people regard the resulting randomized version of quicksort as the sorting algorithm of choice for large enough inputs.

In Section 5.3, we randomized our algorithm by explicitly permuting the input. We could do so for quicksort also, but a different randomization technique, called *random sampling*, yields a simpler analysis. Instead of always using $A[r]$ as the pivot, we will select a randomly chosen element from the subarray $A[p \mathinner{.\,.} r]$. We do so by first exchanging element $A[r]$ with an element chosen at random from $A[p \mathinner{.\,.} r]$. By randomly sampling the range $p, \ldots, r$, we ensure that the pivot element $x = A[r]$ is equally likely to be any of the $r - p + 1$ elements in the subarray. Because we randomly choose the pivot element, we expect the split of the input array to be reasonably well balanced on average.

The changes to PARTITION and QUICKSORT are small. In the new partition procedure, we simply implement the swap before actually partitioning:

RANDOMIZED-PARTITION(A, p, r)

1 $i = $ RANDOM(p, r)
2 exchange $A[r]$ with $A[i]$
3 **return** PARTITION(A, p, r)

The new quicksort calls RANDOMIZED-PARTITION in place of PARTITION:

RANDOMIZED-QUICKSORT(A, p, r)

1 **if** $p < r$
2      $q = $ RANDOMIZED-PARTITION(A, p, r)
3   RANDOMIZED-QUICKSORT$(A, p, q - 1)$
4   RANDOMIZED-QUICKSORT$(A, q + 1, r)$

We analyze this algorithm in the next section.

Exercises

7.3-1
Why do we analyze the expected running time of a randomized algorithm and not its worst-case running time?

7.3-2
When RANDOMIZED-QUICKSORT runs, how many calls are made to the random-number generator RANDOM in the worst case? How about in the best case? Give your answer in terms of Θ-notation.

7.4   Analysis of quicksort

Section 7.2 gave some intuition for the worst-case behavior of quicksort and for why we expect it to run quickly. In this section, we analyze the behavior of quicksort more rigorously. We begin with a worst-case analysis, which applies to either QUICKSORT or RANDOMIZED-QUICKSORT, and conclude with an analysis of the expected running time of RANDOMIZED-QUICKSORT.

7.4.1   Worst-case analysis

We saw in Section 7.2 that a worst-case split at every level of recursion in quicksort produces a $\Theta(n^2)$ running time, which, intuitively, is the worst-case running time of the algorithm. We now prove this assertion.

Using the substitution method (see Section 4.3), we can show that the running time of quicksort is $O(n^2)$. Let $T(n)$ be the worst-case time for the procedure QUICKSORT on an input of size n. We have the recurrence

$$T(n) = \max_{0 \le q \le n-1} (T(q) + T(n - q - 1)) + \Theta(n) , \tag{7.1}$$

where the parameter q ranges from 0 to $n - 1$ because the procedure PARTITION produces two subproblems with total size $n - 1$. We guess that $T(n) \le cn^2$ for some constant c. Substituting this guess into recurrence (7.1), we obtain

$$
\begin{aligned}
T(n) &\le \max_{0 \le q \le n-1} (cq^2 + c(n - q - 1)^2) + \Theta(n) \\
&= c \cdot \max_{0 \le q \le n-1} (q^2 + (n - q - 1)^2) + \Theta(n) .
\end{aligned}
$$

The expression $q^2 + (n - q - 1)^2$ achieves a maximum over the parameter's range $0 \le q \le n - 1$ at either endpoint. To verify this claim, note that the second derivative of the expression with respect to q is positive (see Exercise 7.4-3). This observation gives us the bound $\max_{0 \leq q \leq n-1}(q^2 + (n - q - 1)^2) \leq (n - 1)^2 = n^2 - 2n + 1$. Continuing with our bounding of $T(n)$, we obtain

$$
\begin{aligned}
T(n) &\leq cn^2 - c(2n - 1) + \Theta(n) \\
&\leq cn^2,
\end{aligned}
$$

since we can pick the constant c large enough so that the $c(2n - 1)$ term dominates the $\Theta(n)$ term. Thus, $T(n) = O(n^2)$. We saw in Section 7.2 a specific case in which quicksort takes $\Omega(n^2)$ time: when partitioning is unbalanced. Alternatively, Exercise 7.4-1 asks you to show that recurrence (7.1) has a solution of $T(n) = \Omega(n^2)$. Thus, the (worst-case) running time of quicksort is $\Theta(n^2)$.

7.4.2 Expected running time

We have already seen the intuition behind why the expected running time of RANDOMIZED-QUICKSORT is $O(n \lg n)$: if, in each level of recursion, the split induced by RANDOMIZED-PARTITION puts any constant fraction of the elements on one side of the partition, then the recursion tree has depth $\Theta(\lg n)$, and $O(n)$ work is performed at each level. Even if we add a few new levels with the most unbalanced split possible between these levels, the total time remains $O(n \lg n)$. We can analyze the expected running time of RANDOMIZED-QUICKSORT precisely by first understanding how the partitioning procedure operates and then using this understanding to derive an $O(n \lg n)$ bound on the expected running time. This upper bound on the expected running time, combined with the $\Theta(n \lg n)$ best-case bound we saw in Section 7.2, yields a $\Theta(n \lg n)$ expected running time. We assume throughout that the values of the elements being sorted are distinct.

Running time and comparisons

The QUICKSORT and RANDOMIZED-QUICKSORT procedures differ only in how they select pivot elements; they are the same in all other respects. We can therefore couch our analysis of RANDOMIZED-QUICKSORT by discussing the QUICKSORT and PARTITION procedures, but with the assumption that pivot elements are selected randomly from the subarray passed to RANDOMIZED-PARTITION.

The running time of QUICKSORT is dominated by the time spent in the PARTITION procedure. Each time the PARTITION procedure is called, it selects a pivot element, and this element is never included in any future recursive calls to QUICKSORT and PARTITION. Thus, there can be at most n calls to PARTITION over the entire execution of the quicksort algorithm. One call to PARTITION takes $O(1)$ time plus an amount of time that is proportional to the number of iterations of the **for** loop in lines 3–6. Each iteration of this **for** loop performs a comparison in line 4, comparing the pivot element to another element of the array A. Therefore, if we can count the total number of times that line 4 is executed, we can bound the total time spent in the **for** loop during the entire execution of QUICKSORT.

Lemma 7.1
Let X be the number of comparisons performed in line 4 of PARTITION over the entire execution of QUICKSORT on an n-element array. Then the running time of QUICKSORT is $O(n + X)$.

Proof   By the discussion above, the algorithm makes at most n calls to PARTITION, each of which does a constant amount of work and then executes the **for** loop some number of times. Each iteration of the **for** loop executes line 4.   ■

Our goal, therefore, is to compute X, the total number of comparisons performed in all calls to PARTITION. We will not attempt to analyze how many comparisons are made in *each* call to PARTITION. Rather, we will derive an overall bound on the total number of comparisons. To do so, we must understand when the algorithm compares two elements of the array and when it does not. For ease of analysis, we rename the elements of the array A as $z_1, z_2, \ldots, z_n$, with z_i being the ith smallest element. We also define the set $Z_{ij} = \{z_i, z_{i+1}, \ldots, z_j\}$ to be the set of elements between z_i and z_j, inclusive.

When does the algorithm compare z_i and z_j? To answer this question, we first observe that each pair of elements is compared at most once. Why? Elements are compared only to the pivot element and, after a particular call of PARTITION finishes, the pivot element used in that call is never again compared to any other elements.

Our analysis uses indicator random variables (see Section 5.2). We define

$$X_{ij} = \mathrm{I}\{z_i \text{ is compared to } z_j\} \, ,$$

where we are considering whether the comparison takes place at any time during the execution of the algorithm, not just during one iteration or one call of PARTITION. Since each pair is compared at most once, we can easily characterize the total number of comparisons performed by the algorithm:

$$X = \sum_{i=1}^{n-1} \sum_{j=i+1}^{n} X_{ij} \, .$$

Taking expectations of both sides, and then using linearity of expectation and Lemma 5.1, we obtain

$$\mathrm{E}[X] = \mathrm{E}\left[\sum_{i=1}^{n-1} \sum_{j=i+1}^{n} X_{ij}\right]$$

$$= \sum_{i=1}^{n-1} \sum_{j=i+1}^{n} \mathrm{E}[X_{ij}]$$

$$= \sum_{i=1}^{n-1} \sum_{j=i+1}^{n} \Pr\{z_i \text{ is compared to } z_j\} \ . \tag{7.2}$$

It remains to compute $\Pr\{z_i \text{ is compared to } z_j\}$. Our analysis assumes that the RANDOMIZED-PARTITION procedure chooses each pivot randomly and independently.

Let us think about when two items are *not* compared. Consider an input to quicksort of the numbers 1 through 10 (in any order), and suppose that the first pivot element is 7. Then the first call to PARTITION separates the numbers into two sets: $\{1, 2, 3, 4, 5, 6\}$ and $\{8, 9, 10\}$. In doing so, the pivot element 7 is compared to all other elements, but no number from the first set (e.g., 2) is or ever will be compared to any number from the second set (e.g., 9).

In general, because we assume that element values are distinct, once a pivot x is chosen with $z_i < x < z_j$, we know that z_i and z_j cannot be compared at any subsequent time. If, on the other hand, z_i is chosen as a pivot before any other item in Z_{ij}, then z_i will be compared to each item in Z_{ij}, except for itself. Similarly, if z_j is chosen as a pivot before any other item in Z_{ij}, then z_j will be compared to each item in Z_{ij}, except for itself. In our example, the values 7 and 9 are compared because 7 is the first item from $Z_{7,9}$ to be chosen as a pivot. In contrast, 2 and 9 will never be compared because the first pivot element chosen from $Z_{2,9}$ is 7. Thus, z_i and z_j are compared if and only if the first element to be chosen as a pivot from Z_{ij} is either z_i or z_j.

We now compute the probability that this event occurs. Prior to the point at which an element from Z_{ij} has been chosen as a pivot, the whole set Z_{ij} is together in the same partition. Therefore, any element of Z_{ij} is equally likely to be the first one chosen as a pivot. Because the set Z_{ij} has $j - i + 1$ elements, and because pivots are chosen randomly and independently, the probability that any given element is the first one chosen as a pivot is $1/(j - i + 1)$. Thus, we have

$$\begin{aligned}
\Pr\{z_i \text{ is compared to } z_j\} &= \Pr\{z_i \text{ or } z_j \text{ is first pivot chosen from } Z_{ij}\} \\
&= \Pr\{z_i \text{ is first pivot chosen from } Z_{ij}\} \\
&\quad + \Pr\{z_j \text{ is first pivot chosen from } Z_{ij}\} \\
&= \frac{1}{j - i + 1} + \frac{1}{j - i + 1} \\
&= \frac{2}{j - i + 1} \ . \tag{7.3}
\end{aligned}$$

The second line follows because the two events are mutually exclusive. Combining equations (7.2) and (7.3), we get that

$$E[X] = \sum_{i=1}^{n-1} \sum_{j=i+1}^{n} \frac{2}{j-i+1}.$$

We can evaluate this sum using a change of variables ($k = j - i$) and the bound on the harmonic series in equation (A.7):

$$
\begin{aligned}
E[X] &= \sum_{i=1}^{n-1} \sum_{j=i+1}^{n} \frac{2}{j-i+1} \\
&= \sum_{i=1}^{n-1} \sum_{k=1}^{n-i} \frac{2}{k+1} \\
&< \sum_{i=1}^{n-1} \sum_{k=1}^{n} \frac{2}{k} \\
&= \sum_{i=1}^{n-1} O(\lg n) \\
&= O(n \lg n).
\end{aligned}
\tag{7.4}
$$

Thus we conclude that, using RANDOMIZED-PARTITION, the expected running time of quicksort is $O(n \lg n)$ when element values are distinct.

Exercises

7.4-1
Show that in the recurrence

$$T(n) = \max_{0 \le q \le n-1} (T(q) + T(n-q-1)) + \Theta(n),$$

$T(n) = \Omega(n^2)$.

7.4-2
Show that quicksort's best-case running time is $\Omega(n \lg n)$.

7.4-3
Show that the expression $q^2 + (n-q-1)^2$ achieves a maximum over $q = 0, 1, \ldots, n-1$ when $q = 0$ or $q = n - 1$.

7.4-4
Show that RANDOMIZED-QUICKSORT's expected running time is $\Omega(n \lg n)$.

7.4-5

We can improve the running time of quicksort in practice by taking advantage of the fast running time of insertion sort when its input is "nearly" sorted. Upon calling quicksort on a subarray with fewer than k elements, let it simply return without sorting the subarray. After the top-level call to quicksort returns, run insertion sort on the entire array to finish the sorting process. Argue that this sorting algorithm runs in $O(nk + n \lg(n/k))$ expected time. How should we pick k, both in theory and in practice?

7.4-6 ★

Consider modifying the PARTITION procedure by randomly picking three elements from array A and partitioning about their median (the middle value of the three elements). Approximate the probability of getting at worst an α-to-$(1 - \alpha)$ split, as a function of α in the range $0 < \alpha < 1$.

Problems

7-1 *Hoare partition correctness*

The version of PARTITION given in this chapter is not the original partitioning algorithm. Here is the original partition algorithm, which is due to C. A. R. Hoare:

HOARE-PARTITION(A, p, r)

```
1   x = A[p]
2   i = p − 1
3   j = r + 1
4   while TRUE
5       repeat
6           j = j − 1
7       until A[j] ≤ x
8       repeat
9           i = i + 1
10      until A[i] ≥ x
11      if i < j
12          exchange A[i] with A[j]
13      else return j
```

    a. Demonstrate the operation of HOARE-PARTITION on the array $A = \langle 13, 19, 9, 5, 12, 8, 7, 4, 11, 2, 6, 21 \rangle$, showing the values of the array and auxiliary values after each iteration of the **while** loop in lines 4–13.

The next three questions ask you to give a careful argument that the procedure HOARE-PARTITION is correct. Assuming that the subarray $A[p \mathinner{.\,.} r]$ contains at least two elements, prove the following:

b. The indices i and j are such that we never access an element of A outside the subarray $A[p \mathinner{.\,.} r]$.

c. When HOARE-PARTITION terminates, it returns a value j such that $p \leq j < r$.

d. Every element of $A[p \mathinner{.\,.} j]$ is less than or equal to every element of $A[j + 1 \mathinner{.\,.} r]$ when HOARE-PARTITION terminates.

The PARTITION procedure in Section 7.1 separates the pivot value (originally in $A[r]$) from the two partitions it forms. The HOARE-PARTITION procedure, on the other hand, always places the pivot value (originally in $A[p]$) into one of the two partitions $A[p \mathinner{.\,.} j]$ and $A[j + 1 \mathinner{.\,.} r]$. Since $p \leq j < r$, this split is always nontrivial.

e. Rewrite the QUICKSORT procedure to use HOARE-PARTITION.

7-2 Quicksort with equal element values

The analysis of the expected running time of randomized quicksort in Section 7.4.2 assumes that all element values are distinct. In this problem, we examine what happens when they are not.

a. Suppose that all element values are equal. What would be randomized quicksort's running time in this case?

b. The PARTITION procedure returns an index q such that each element of $A[p \mathinner{.\,.} q - 1]$ is less than or equal to $A[q]$ and each element of $A[q + 1 \mathinner{.\,.} r]$ is greater than $A[q]$. Modify the PARTITION procedure to produce a procedure PARTITION$'(A, p, r)$, which permutes the elements of $A[p \mathinner{.\,.} r]$ and returns two indices q and t, where $p \leq q \leq t \leq r$, such that

- all elements of $A[q \mathinner{.\,.} t]$ are equal,
- each element of $A[p \mathinner{.\,.} q - 1]$ is less than $A[q]$, and
- each element of $A[t + 1 \mathinner{.\,.} r]$ is greater than $A[q]$.

Like PARTITION, your PARTITION$'$ procedure should take $\Theta(r - p)$ time.

c. Modify the RANDOMIZED-PARTITION procedure to call PARTITION$'$, and name the new procedure RANDOMIZED-PARTITION$'$. Then modify the QUICKSORT procedure to produce a procedure QUICKSORT$'(A, p, r)$ that calls

RANDOMIZED-PARTITION' and recurses only on partitions of elements not known to be equal to each other.

d. Using QUICKSORT', how would you adjust the analysis in Section 7.4.2 to avoid the assumption that all elements are distinct?

7-3 *Alternative quicksort analysis*

An alternative analysis of the running time of randomized quicksort focuses on the expected running time of each individual recursive call to RANDOMIZED-QUICKSORT, rather than on the number of comparisons performed.

a. Argue that, given an array of size n, the probability that any particular element is chosen as the pivot is $1/n$. Use this to define indicator random variables $X_i = \mathrm{I}\{i\text{th smallest element is chosen as the pivot}\}$. What is $\mathrm{E}[X_i]$?

b. Let $T(n)$ be a random variable denoting the running time of quicksort on an array of size n. Argue that

$$\mathrm{E}[T(n)] = \mathrm{E}\left[\sum_{q=1}^{n} X_q \left(T(q-1) + T(n-q) + \Theta(n)\right)\right]. \qquad (7.5)$$

c. Show that we can rewrite equation (7.5) as

$$\mathrm{E}[T(n)] = \frac{2}{n} \sum_{q=2}^{n-1} \mathrm{E}[T(q)] + \Theta(n). \qquad (7.6)$$

d. Show that

$$\sum_{k=2}^{n-1} k \lg k \le \frac{1}{2}n^2 \lg n - \frac{1}{8}n^2. \qquad (7.7)$$

(*Hint:* Split the summation into two parts, one for $k = 2, 3, \ldots, \lceil n/2 \rceil - 1$ and one for $k = \lceil n/2 \rceil, \ldots, n - 1$.)

e. Using the bound from equation (7.7), show that the recurrence in equation (7.6) has the solution $\mathrm{E}[T(n)] = \Theta(n \lg n)$. (*Hint:* Show, by substitution, that $\mathrm{E}[T(n)] \le an \lg n$ for sufficiently large n and for some positive constant a.)

7-4   *Stack depth for quicksort*

The QUICKSORT algorithm of Section 7.1 contains two recursive calls to itself. After QUICKSORT calls PARTITION, it recursively sorts the left subarray and then it recursively sorts the right subarray. The second recursive call in QUICKSORT is not really necessary; we can avoid it by using an iterative control structure. This technique, called ***tail recursion***, is provided automatically by good compilers. Consider the following version of quicksort, which simulates tail recursion:

TAIL-RECURSIVE-QUICKSORT(A, p, r)

```
1  while p < r
2      // Partition and sort left subarray.
3      q = PARTITION(A, p, r)
4      TAIL-RECURSIVE-QUICKSORT(A, p, q − 1)
5      p = q + 1
```

a. Argue that TAIL-RECURSIVE-QUICKSORT$(A, 1, A.length)$ correctly sorts the array A.

Compilers usually execute recursive procedures by using a ***stack*** that contains pertinent information, including the parameter values, for each recursive call. The information for the most recent call is at the top of the stack, and the information for the initial call is at the bottom. Upon calling a procedure, its information is ***pushed*** onto the stack; when it terminates, its information is ***popped***. Since we assume that array parameters are represented by pointers, the information for each procedure call on the stack requires $O(1)$ stack space. The ***stack depth*** is the maximum amount of stack space used at any time during a computation.

b. Describe a scenario in which TAIL-RECURSIVE-QUICKSORT's stack depth is $\Theta(n)$ on an n-element input array.

c. Modify the code for TAIL-RECURSIVE-QUICKSORT so that the worst-case stack depth is $\Theta(\lg n)$. Maintain the $O(n \lg n)$ expected running time of the algorithm.

7-5   *Median-of-3 partition*

One way to improve the RANDOMIZED-QUICKSORT procedure is to partition around a pivot that is chosen more carefully than by picking a random element from the subarray. One common approach is the ***median-of-3*** method: choose the pivot as the median (middle element) of a set of 3 elements randomly selected from the subarray. (See Exercise 7.4-6.) For this problem, let us assume that the elements in the input array $A[1 . . n]$ are distinct and that $n \geq 3$. We denote the sorted output array by $A'[1 \mathbin{..} n]$. Using the median-of-3 method to choose the pivot element x, define $p_i = \Pr\{x = A'[i]\}$.

a. Give an exact formula for p_i as a function of n and i for $i = 2, 3, \ldots, n-1$. (Note that $p_1 = p_n = 0$.)

b. By what amount have we increased the likelihood of choosing the pivot as $x = A'[\lfloor (n+1)/2 \rfloor]$, the median of $A[1 \mathbin{..} n]$, compared with the ordinary implementation? Assume that $n \to \infty$, and give the limiting ratio of these probabilities.

c. If we define a "good" split to mean choosing the pivot as $x = A'[i]$, where $n/3 \le i \le 2n/3$, by what amount have we increased the likelihood of getting a good split compared with the ordinary implementation? (*Hint:* Approximate the sum by an integral.)

d. Argue that in the $\Omega(n \lg n)$ running time of quicksort, the median-of-3 method affects only the constant factor.

7-6   *Fuzzy sorting of intervals*

Consider a sorting problem in which we do not know the numbers exactly. Instead, for each number, we know an interval on the real line to which it belongs. That is, we are given n closed intervals of the form $[a_i, b_i]$, where $a_i \le b_i$. We wish to *fuzzy-sort* these intervals, i.e., to produce a permutation $\langle i_1, i_2, \ldots, i_n \rangle$ of the intervals such that for $j = 1, 2, \ldots, n$, there exist $c_j \in [a_{i_j}, b_{i_j}]$ satisfying $c_1 \le c_2 \le \cdots \le c_n$.

a. Design a randomized algorithm for fuzzy-sorting n intervals. Your algorithm should have the general structure of an algorithm that quicksorts the left endpoints (the a_i values), but it should take advantage of overlapping intervals to improve the running time. (As the intervals overlap more and more, the problem of fuzzy-sorting the intervals becomes progressively easier. Your algorithm should take advantage of such overlapping, to the extent that it exists.)

b. Argue that your algorithm runs in expected time $\Theta(n \lg n)$ in general, but runs in expected time $\Theta(n)$ when all of the intervals overlap (i.e., when there exists a value x such that $x \in [a_i, b_i]$ for all i). Your algorithm should not be checking for this case explicitly; rather, its performance should naturally improve as the amount of overlap increases.

Chapter notes

The quicksort procedure was invented by Hoare [170]; Hoare's version appears in Problem 7-1. The PARTITION procedure given in Section 7.1 is due to N. Lomuto. The analysis in Section 7.4 is due to Avrim Blum. Sedgewick [305] and Bentley [43] provide a good reference on the details of implementation and how they matter.

McIlroy [248] showed how to engineer a "killer adversary" that produces an array on which virtually any implementation of quicksort takes $\Theta(n^2)$ time. If the implementation is randomized, the adversary produces the array after seeing the random choices of the quicksort algorithm.

8 Sorting in Linear Time

We have now introduced several algorithms that can sort n numbers in $O(n \lg n)$ time. Merge sort and heapsort achieve this upper bound in the worst case; quicksort achieves it on average. Moreover, for each of these algorithms, we can produce a sequence of n input numbers that causes the algorithm to run in $\Omega(n \lg n)$ time.

These algorithms share an interesting property: *the sorted order they determine is based only on comparisons between the input elements.* We call such sorting algorithms **comparison sorts**. All the sorting algorithms introduced thus far are comparison sorts.

In Section 8.1, we shall prove that any comparison sort must make $\Omega(n \lg n)$ comparisons in the worst case to sort n elements. Thus, merge sort and heapsort are asymptotically optimal, and no comparison sort exists that is faster by more than a constant factor.

Sections 8.2, 8.3, and 8.4 examine three sorting algorithms—counting sort, radix sort, and bucket sort—that run in linear time. Of course, these algorithms use operations other than comparisons to determine the sorted order. Consequently, the $\Omega(n \lg n)$ lower bound does not apply to them.

8.1 Lower bounds for sorting

In a comparison sort, we use only comparisons between elements to gain order information about an input sequence $\langle a_1, a_2, \ldots, a_n \rangle$. That is, given two elements a_i and a_j, we perform one of the tests $a_i < a_j$, $a_i \leq a_j$, $a_i = a_j$, $a_i \geq a_j$, or $a_i > a_j$ to determine their relative order. We may not inspect the values of the elements or gain order information about them in any other way.

In this section, we assume without loss of generality that all the input elements are distinct. Given this assumption, comparisons of the form $a_i = a_j$ are useless, so we can assume that no comparisons of this form are made. We also note that the comparisons $a_i \leq a_j$, $a_i \geq a_j$, $a_i > a_j$, and $a_i < a_j$ are all equivalent in that

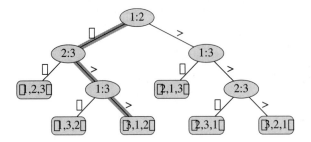

Figure 8.1 The decision tree for insertion sort operating on three elements. An internal node annotated by $i:j$ indicates a comparison between a_i and a_j. A leaf annotated by the permutation $\langle \pi(1), \pi(2), \ldots, \pi(n) \rangle$ indicates the ordering $a_{\pi(1)} \leq a_{\pi(2)} \leq \cdots \leq a_{\pi(n)}$. The shaded path indicates the decisions made when sorting the input sequence $\langle a_1 = 6, a_2 = 8, a_3 = 5 \rangle$; the permutation $\langle 3, 1, 2 \rangle$ at the leaf indicates that the sorted ordering is $a_3 = 5 \leq a_1 = 6 \leq a_2 = 8$. There are $3! = 6$ possible permutations of the input elements, and so the decision tree must have at least 6 leaves.

they yield identical information about the relative order of a_i and a_j. We therefore assume that all comparisons have the form $a_i \leq a_j$.

The decision-tree model

We can view comparison sorts abstractly in terms of decision trees. A ***decision tree*** is a full binary tree that represents the comparisons between elements that are performed by a particular sorting algorithm operating on an input of a given size. Control, data movement, and all other aspects of the algorithm are ignored. Figure 8.1 shows the decision tree corresponding to the insertion sort algorithm from Section 2.1 operating on an input sequence of three elements.

In a decision tree, we annotate each internal node by $i:j$ for some i and j in the range $1 \leq i, j \leq n$, where n is the number of elements in the input sequence. We also annotate each leaf by a permutation $\langle \pi(1), \pi(2), \ldots, \pi(n) \rangle$. (See Section C.1 for background on permutations.) The execution of the sorting algorithm corresponds to tracing a simple path from the root of the decision tree down to a leaf. Each internal node indicates a comparison $a_i \leq a_j$. The left subtree then dictates subsequent comparisons once we know that $a_i \leq a_j$, and the right subtree dictates subsequent comparisons knowing that $a_i > a_j$. When we come to a leaf, the sorting algorithm has established the ordering $a_{\pi(1)} \leq a_{\pi(2)} \leq \cdots \leq a_{\pi(n)}$. Because any correct sorting algorithm must be able to produce each permutation of its input, each of the $n!$ permutations on n elements must appear as one of the leaves of the decision tree for a comparison sort to be correct. Furthermore, each of these leaves must be reachable from the root by a downward path corresponding to an actual execution of the comparison sort. (We shall refer to such leaves as "reachable.") Thus, we shall consider only decision trees in which each permutation appears as a reachable leaf.

A lower bound for the worst case

The length of the longest simple path from the root of a decision tree to any of its reachable leaves represents the worst-case number of comparisons that the corresponding sorting algorithm performs. Consequently, the worst-case number of comparisons for a given comparison sort algorithm equals the height of its decision tree. A lower bound on the heights of all decision trees in which each permutation appears as a reachable leaf is therefore a lower bound on the running time of any comparison sort algorithm. The following theorem establishes such a lower bound.

Theorem 8.1
Any comparison sort algorithm requires $\Omega(n \lg n)$ comparisons in the worst case.

Proof   From the preceding discussion, it suffices to determine the height of a decision tree in which each permutation appears as a reachable leaf. Consider a decision tree of height h with l reachable leaves corresponding to a comparison sort on n elements. Because each of the $n!$ permutations of the input appears as some leaf, we have $n! \leq l$. Since a binary tree of height h has no more than 2^h leaves, we have

$$n! \leq l \leq 2^h \, ,$$

which, by taking logarithms, implies

$$
\begin{aligned}
h \;\; &\geq \;\; \lg(n!) \quad\;\; \text{(since the lg function is monotonically increasing)} \\
&= \;\; \Omega(n \lg n) \quad \text{(by equation (3.19))} \;\; .
\end{aligned}
$$
  ∎

Corollary 8.2
Heapsort and merge sort are asymptotically optimal comparison sorts.

Proof   The $O(n \lg n)$ upper bounds on the running times for heapsort and merge sort match the $\Omega(n \lg n)$ worst-case lower bound from Theorem 8.1.
  ∎

Exercises

8.1-1
What is the smallest possible depth of a leaf in a decision tree for a comparison sort?

8.1-2

Obtain asymptotically tight bounds on $\lg(n!)$ without using Stirling's approximation. Instead, evaluate the summation $\sum_{k=1}^{n} \lg k$ using techniques from Section A.2.

8.1-3

Show that there is no comparison sort whose running time is linear for at least half of the $n!$ inputs of length n. What about a fraction of $1/n$ of the inputs of length n? What about a fraction $1/2^n$?

8.1-4

Suppose that you are given a sequence of n elements to sort. The input sequence consists of n/k subsequences, each containing k elements. The elements in a given subsequence are all smaller than the elements in the succeeding subsequence and larger than the elements in the preceding subsequence. Thus, all that is needed to sort the whole sequence of length n is to sort the k elements in each of the n/k subsequences. Show an $\Omega(n \lg k)$ lower bound on the number of comparisons needed to solve this variant of the sorting problem. (*Hint:* It is not rigorous to simply combine the lower bounds for the individual subsequences.)

8.2   Counting sort

Counting sort assumes that each of the n input elements is an integer in the range 0 to k, for some integer k. When $k = O(n)$, the sort runs in $\Theta(n)$ time.

Counting sort determines, for each input element x, the number of elements less than x. It uses this information to place element x directly into its position in the output array. For example, if 17 elements are less than x, then x belongs in output position 18. We must modify this scheme slightly to handle the situation in which several elements have the same value, since we do not want to put them all in the same position.

In the code for counting sort, we assume that the input is an array $A[1 \mathinner{\ldotp\ldotp} n]$, and thus $A.length = n$. We require two other arrays: the array $B[1 \mathinner{\ldotp\ldotp} n]$ holds the sorted output, and the array $C[0 \mathinner{\ldotp\ldotp} k]$ provides temporary working storage.

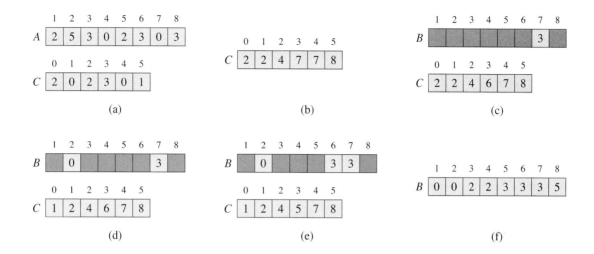

Figure 8.2 The operation of COUNTING-SORT on an input array $A[1 \mathinner{\ldotp\ldotp} 8]$, where each element of A is a nonnegative integer no larger than $k = 5$. **(a)** The array A and the auxiliary array C after line 5. **(b)** The array C after line 8. **(c)–(e)** The output array B and the auxiliary array C after one, two, and three iterations of the loop in lines 10–12, respectively. Only the lightly shaded elements of array B have been filled in. **(f)** The final sorted output array B.

COUNTING-SORT(A, B, k)

```
 1   let C[0 .. k] be a new array
 2   for i = 0 to k
 3       C[i] = 0
 4   for j = 1 to A.length
 5       C[A[j]] = C[A[j]] + 1
 6   // C[i] now contains the number of elements equal to i.
 7   for i = 1 to k
 8       C[i] = C[i] + C[i − 1]
 9   // C[i] now contains the number of elements less than or equal to i.
10   for j = A.length downto 1
11       B[C[A[j]]] = A[j]
12       C[A[j]] = C[A[j]] − 1
```

Figure 8.2 illustrates counting sort. After the **for** loop of lines 2–3 initializes the array C to all zeros, the **for** loop of lines 4–5 inspects each input element. If the value of an input element is i, we increment $C[i]$. Thus, after line 5, $C[i]$ holds the number of input elements equal to i for each integer $i = 0, 1, \ldots, k$. Lines 7–8 determine for each $i = 0, 1, \ldots, k$ how many input elements are less than or equal to i by keeping a running sum of the array C.

Finally, the **for** loop of lines 10–12 places each element $A[j]$ into its correct sorted position in the output array B. If all n elements are distinct, then when we first enter line 10, for each $A[j]$, the value $C[A[j]]$ is the correct final position of $A[j]$ in the output array, since there are $C[A[j]]$ elements less than or equal to $A[j]$. Because the elements might not be distinct, we decrement $C[A[j]]$ each time we place a value $A[j]$ into the B array. Decrementing $C[A[j]]$ causes the next input element with a value equal to $A[j]$, if one exists, to go to the position immediately before $A[j]$ in the output array.

How much time does counting sort require? The **for** loop of lines 2–3 takes time $\Theta(k)$, the **for** loop of lines 4–5 takes time $\Theta(n)$, the **for** loop of lines 7–8 takes time $\Theta(k)$, and the **for** loop of lines 10–12 takes time $\Theta(n)$. Thus, the overall time is $\Theta(k + n)$. In practice, we usually use counting sort when we have $k = O(n)$, in which case the running time is $\Theta(n)$.

Counting sort beats the lower bound of $\Omega(n \lg n)$ proved in Section 8.1 because it is not a comparison sort. In fact, no comparisons between input elements occur anywhere in the code. Instead, counting sort uses the actual values of the elements to index into an array. The $\Omega(n \lg n)$ lower bound for sorting does not apply when we depart from the comparison sort model.

An important property of counting sort is that it is *stable*: numbers with the same value appear in the output array in the same order as they do in the input array. That is, it breaks ties between two numbers by the rule that whichever number appears first in the input array appears first in the output array. Normally, the property of stability is important only when satellite data are carried around with the element being sorted. Counting sort's stability is important for another reason: counting sort is often used as a subroutine in radix sort. As we shall see in the next section, in order for radix sort to work correctly, counting sort must be stable.

Exercises

8.2-1
Using Figure 8.2 as a model, illustrate the operation of Counting-Sort on the array $A = \langle 6, 0, 2, 0, 1, 3, 4, 6, 1, 3, 2 \rangle$.

8.2-2
Prove that Counting-Sort is stable.

8.2-3
Suppose that we were to rewrite the **for** loop header in line 10 of the Counting-Sort as

10   **for** $j = 1$ **to** $A.length$

Show that the algorithm still works properly. Is the modified algorithm stable?

8.2-4

Describe an algorithm that, given n integers in the range 0 to k, preprocesses its input and then answers any query about how many of the n integers fall into a range $[a \mathinner{.\,.} b]$ in $O(1)$ time. Your algorithm should use $\Theta(n + k)$ preprocessing time.

8.3 Radix sort

Radix sort is the algorithm used by the card-sorting machines you now find only in computer museums. The cards have 80 columns, and in each column a machine can punch a hole in one of 12 places. The sorter can be mechanically "programmed" to examine a given column of each card in a deck and distribute the card into one of 12 bins depending on which place has been punched. An operator can then gather the cards bin by bin, so that cards with the first place punched are on top of cards with the second place punched, and so on.

For decimal digits, each column uses only 10 places. (The other two places are reserved for encoding nonnumeric characters.) A d-digit number would then occupy a field of d columns. Since the card sorter can look at only one column at a time, the problem of sorting n cards on a d-digit number requires a sorting algorithm.

Intuitively, you might sort numbers on their *most significant* digit, sort each of the resulting bins recursively, and then combine the decks in order. Unfortunately, since the cards in 9 of the 10 bins must be put aside to sort each of the bins, this procedure generates many intermediate piles of cards that you would have to keep track of. (See Exercise 8.3-5.)

Radix sort solves the problem of card sorting—counterintuitively—by sorting on the *least significant* digit first. The algorithm then combines the cards into a single deck, with the cards in the 0 bin preceding the cards in the 1 bin preceding the cards in the 2 bin, and so on. Then it sorts the entire deck again on the second-least significant digit and recombines the deck in a like manner. The process continues until the cards have been sorted on all d digits. Remarkably, at that point the cards are fully sorted on the d-digit number. Thus, only d passes through the deck are required to sort. Figure 8.3 shows how radix sort operates on a "deck" of seven 3-digit numbers.

In order for radix sort to work correctly, the digit sorts must be stable. The sort performed by a card sorter is stable, but the operator has to be wary about not changing the order of the cards as they come out of a bin, even though all the cards in a bin have the same digit in the chosen column.

```
329      720      720      329
457      355      329      355
657      436      436      436
839 ···⫶⊪· 457 ···⫶⊪· 839 ···⫶⊪· 457
436      657      355      657
720      329      457      720
355      839      657      839
```

Figure 8.3 The operation of radix sort on a list of seven 3-digit numbers. The leftmost column is the input. The remaining columns show the list after successive sorts on increasingly significant digit positions. Shading indicates the digit position sorted on to produce each list from the previous one.

In a typical computer, which is a sequential random-access machine, we sometimes use radix sort to sort records of information that are keyed by multiple fields. For example, we might wish to sort dates by three keys: year, month, and day. We could run a sorting algorithm with a comparison function that, given two dates, compares years, and if there is a tie, compares months, and if another tie occurs, compares days. Alternatively, we could sort the information three times with a stable sort: first on day, next on month, and finally on year.

The code for radix sort is straightforward. The following procedure assumes that each element in the n-element array A has d digits, where digit 1 is the lowest-order digit and digit d is the highest-order digit.

RADIX-SORT(A, d)

1 **for** $i = 1$ **to** d
2   use a stable sort to sort array A on digit i

Lemma 8.3
Given n d-digit numbers in which each digit can take on up to k possible values, RADIX-SORT correctly sorts these numbers in $\Theta(d(n + k))$ time if the stable sort it uses takes $\Theta(n + k)$ time.

Proof   The correctness of radix sort follows by induction on the column being sorted (see Exercise 8.3-3). The analysis of the running time depends on the stable sort used as the intermediate sorting algorithm. When each digit is in the range 0 to $k-1$ (so that it can take on k possible values), and k is not too large, counting sort is the obvious choice. Each pass over n d-digit numbers then takes time $\Theta(n + k)$. There are d passes, and so the total time for radix sort is $\Theta(d(n + k))$.   ∎

When d is constant and $k = O(n)$, we can make radix sort run in linear time. More generally, we have some flexibility in how to break each key into digits.

Lemma 8.4

Given n b-bit numbers and any positive integer $r \leq b$, RADIX-SORT correctly sorts these numbers in $\Theta((b/r)(n + 2^r))$ time if the stable sort it uses takes $\Theta(n + k)$ time for inputs in the range 0 to k.

Proof   For a value $r \leq b$, we view each key as having $d = \lceil b/r \rceil$ digits of r bits each. Each digit is an integer in the range 0 to $2^r - 1$, so that we can use counting sort with $k = 2^r$. (For example, we can view a 32-bit word as having four 8-bit digits, so that $b = 32$, $r = 8$, $k = 2^r = 256$, and $d = b/r = 4$.) Each pass of counting sort takes time $\Theta(n + k) = \Theta(n + 2^r)$ and there are d passes, for a total running time of $\Theta(d(n + 2^r)) = \Theta((b/r)(n + 2^r))$.   ∎

For given values of n and b, we wish to choose the value of r, with $r \leq b$, that minimizes the expression $(b/r)(n + 2^r)$. If $b < \lfloor \lg n \rfloor$, then for any value of $r \leq b$, we have that $(n + 2^r) = \Theta(n)$. Thus, choosing $r = b$ yields a running time of $(b/b)(n + 2^b) = \Theta(n)$, which is asymptotically optimal. If $b \geq \lfloor \lg n \rfloor$, then choosing $r = \lfloor \lg n \rfloor$ gives the best time to within a constant factor, which we can see as follows. Choosing $r = \lfloor \lg n \rfloor$ yields a running time of $\Theta(bn/\lg n)$. As we increase r above $\lfloor \lg n \rfloor$, the 2^r term in the numerator increases faster than the r term in the denominator, and so increasing r above $\lfloor \lg n \rfloor$ yields a running time of $\Omega(bn/\lg n)$. If instead we were to decrease r below $\lfloor \lg n \rfloor$, then the b/r term increases and the $n + 2^r$ term remains at $\Theta(n)$.

Is radix sort preferable to a comparison-based sorting algorithm, such as quicksort? If $b = O(\lg n)$, as is often the case, and we choose $r \approx \lg n$, then radix sort's running time is $\Theta(n)$, which appears to be better than quicksort's expected running time of $\Theta(n \lg n)$. The constant factors hidden in the Θ-notation differ, however. Although radix sort may make fewer passes than quicksort over the n keys, each pass of radix sort may take significantly longer. Which sorting algorithm we prefer depends on the characteristics of the implementations, of the underlying machine (e.g., quicksort often uses hardware caches more effectively than radix sort), and of the input data. Moreover, the version of radix sort that uses counting sort as the intermediate stable sort does not sort in place, which many of the $\Theta(n \lg n)$-time comparison sorts do. Thus, when primary memory storage is at a premium, we might prefer an in-place algorithm such as quicksort.

Exercises

8.3-1
Using Figure 8.3 as a model, illustrate the operation of RADIX-SORT on the following list of English words: COW, DOG, SEA, RUG, ROW, MOB, BOX, TAB, BAR, EAR, TAR, DIG, BIG, TEA, NOW, FOX.

8.3-2

Which of the following sorting algorithms are stable: insertion sort, merge sort, heapsort, and quicksort? Give a simple scheme that makes any comparison sort stable. How much additional time and space does your scheme entail?

8.3-3

Use induction to prove that radix sort works. Where does your proof need the assumption that the intermediate sort is stable?

8.3-4

Show how to sort n integers in the range 0 to $n^3 - 1$ in $O(n)$ time.

8.3-5 ★

In the first card-sorting algorithm in this section, exactly how many sorting passes are needed to sort d-digit decimal numbers in the worst case? How many piles of cards would an operator need to keep track of in the worst case?

8.4   Bucket sort

Bucket sort assumes that the input is drawn from a uniform distribution and has an average-case running time of $O(n)$. Like counting sort, bucket sort is fast because it assumes something about the input. Whereas counting sort assumes that the input consists of integers in a small range, bucket sort assumes that the input is generated by a random process that distributes elements uniformly and independently over the interval $[0, 1)$. (See Section C.2 for a definition of uniform distribution.)

Bucket sort divides the interval $[0, 1)$ into n equal-sized subintervals, or *buckets*, and then distributes the n input numbers into the buckets. Since the inputs are uniformly and independently distributed over $[0, 1)$, we do not expect many numbers to fall into each bucket. To produce the output, we simply sort the numbers in each bucket and then go through the buckets in order, listing the elements in each.

Our code for bucket sort assumes that the input is an n-element array A and that each element $A[i]$ in the array satisfies $0 \le A[i] < 1$. The code requires an auxiliary array $B[0 .. n - 1]$ of linked lists (buckets) and assumes that there is a mechanism for maintaining such lists. (Section 10.2 describes how to implement basic operations on linked lists.)

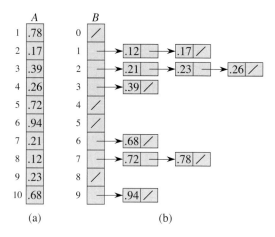

Figure 8.4   The operation of BUCKET-SORT for $n = 10$. **(a)** The input array $A[1 .. 10]$. **(b)** The array $B[0 .. 9]$ of sorted lists (buckets) after line 8 of the algorithm. Bucket i holds values in the half-open interval $[i/10, (i + 1)/10)$. The sorted output consists of a concatenation in order of the lists $B[0], B[1], \ldots, B[9]$.

BUCKET-SORT(A)

```
1   n = A.length
2   let B[0 .. n − 1] be a new array
3   for i = 0 to n − 1
4       make B[i] an empty list
5   for i = 1 to n
6       insert A[i] into list B[⌊n A[i]⌋]
7   for i = 0 to n − 1
8       sort list B[i] with insertion sort
9   concatenate the lists B[0], B[1], . . . , B[n − 1] together in order
```

Figure 8.4 shows the operation of bucket sort on an input array of 10 numbers.

To see that this algorithm works, consider two elements $A[i]$ and $A[j]$. Assume without loss of generality that $A[i] \leq A[j]$. Since $\lfloor n A[i] \rfloor \leq \lfloor n A[j] \rfloor$, either element $A[i]$ goes into the same bucket as $A[j]$ or it goes into a bucket with a lower index. If $A[i]$ and $A[j]$ go into the same bucket, then the **for** loop of lines 7–8 puts them into the proper order. If $A[i]$ and $A[j]$ go into different buckets, then line 9 puts them into the proper order. Therefore, bucket sort works correctly.

To analyze the running time, observe that all lines except line 8 take $O(n)$ time in the worst case. We need to analyze the total time taken by the n calls to insertion sort in line 8.

To analyze the cost of the calls to insertion sort, let n_i be the random variable denoting the number of elements placed in bucket $B[i]$. Since insertion sort runs in quadratic time (see Section 2.2), the running time of bucket sort is

$$T(n) = \Theta(n) + \sum_{i=0}^{n-1} O(n_i^2) \ .$$

We now analyze the average-case running time of bucket sort, by computing the expected value of the running time, where we take the expectation over the input distribution. Taking expectations of both sides and using linearity of expectation, we have

$$
\begin{aligned}
\mathrm{E}\left[T(n)\right] & = \mathrm{E}\left[\Theta(n) + \sum_{i=0}^{n-1} O(n_i^2)\right] \\
& = \Theta(n) + \sum_{i=0}^{n-1} \mathrm{E}\left[O(n_i^2)\right] \quad \text{(by linearity of expectation)} \\
& = \Theta(n) + \sum_{i=0}^{n-1} O\left(\mathrm{E}\left[n_i^2\right]\right) \quad \text{(by equation (C.22))} \ .
\end{aligned}
\tag{8.1}
$$

We claim that

$$\mathrm{E}\left[n_i^2\right] = 2 - 1/n \tag{8.2}$$

for $i = 0, 1, \ldots, n-1$. It is no surprise that each bucket i has the same value of $\mathrm{E}\left[n_i^2\right]$, since each value in the input array A is equally likely to fall in any bucket. To prove equation (8.2), we define indicator random variables

$$X_{ij} = \mathrm{I}\{A[j] \text{ falls in bucket } i\}$$

for $i = 0, 1, \ldots, n-1$ and $j = 1, 2, \ldots, n$. Thus,

$$n_i = \sum_{j=1}^{n} X_{ij} \ .$$

To compute $\mathrm{E}\left[n_i^2\right]$, we expand the square and regroup terms:

$$E\left[n_i^2\right] = E\left[\left(\sum_{j=1}^{n} X_{ij}\right)^2\right]$$

$$= E\left[\sum_{j=1}^{n}\sum_{k=1}^{n} X_{ij}X_{ik}\right]$$

$$= E\left[\sum_{j=1}^{n} X_{ij}^2 + \sum_{1\le j\le n}\sum_{\substack{1\le k\le n\\ k\ne j}} X_{ij}X_{ik}\right]$$

$$= \sum_{j=1}^{n} E\left[X_{ij}^2\right] + \sum_{1\le j\le n}\sum_{\substack{1\le k\le n\\ k\ne j}} E\left[X_{ij}X_{ik}\right]\ , \qquad (8.3)$$

where the last line follows by linearity of expectation. We evaluate the two summations separately. Indicator random variable X_{ij} is 1 with probability $1/n$ and 0 otherwise, and therefore

$$E\left[X_{ij}^2\right] = 1^2 \cdot \frac{1}{n} + 0^2 \cdot \left(1 - \frac{1}{n}\right)$$

$$= \frac{1}{n}\ .$$

When $k \ne j$, the variables X_{ij} and X_{ik} are independent, and hence

$$E\left[X_{ij}X_{ik}\right] = E\left[X_{ij}\right]E\left[X_{ik}\right]$$

$$= \frac{1}{n}\cdot\frac{1}{n}$$

$$= \frac{1}{n^2}\ .$$

Substituting these two expected values in equation (8.3), we obtain

$$E\left[n_i^2\right] = \sum_{j=1}^{n}\frac{1}{n} + \sum_{1\le j\le n}\sum_{\substack{1\le k\le n\\ k\ne j}}\frac{1}{n^2}$$

$$= n\cdot\frac{1}{n} + n(n-1)\cdot\frac{1}{n^2}$$

$$= 1 + \frac{n-1}{n}$$

$$= 2 - \frac{1}{n}\ ,$$

which proves equation (8.2).

Using this expected value in equation (8.1), we conclude that the average-case running time for bucket sort is $\Theta(n) + n \cdot O(2 - 1/n) = \Theta(n)$.

Even if the input is not drawn from a uniform distribution, bucket sort may still run in linear time. As long as the input has the property that the sum of the squares of the bucket sizes is linear in the total number of elements, equation (8.1) tells us that bucket sort will run in linear time.

Exercises

8.4-1
Using Figure 8.4 as a model, illustrate the operation of BUCKET-SORT on the array $A = \langle.79, .13, .16, .64, .39, .20, .89, .53, .71, .42\rangle$.

8.4-2
Explain why the worst-case running time for bucket sort is $\Theta(n^2)$. What simple change to the algorithm preserves its linear average-case running time and makes its worst-case running time $O(n \lg n)$?

8.4-3
Let X be a random variable that is equal to the number of heads in two flips of a fair coin. What is $\mathrm{E}[X^2]$? What is $\mathrm{E}^2[X]$?

8.4-4 ★
We are given n points in the unit circle, $p_i = (x_i, y_i)$, such that $0 < x_i^2 + y_i^2 \leq 1$ for $i = 1, 2, \ldots, n$. Suppose that the points are uniformly distributed; that is, the probability of finding a point in any region of the circle is proportional to the area of that region. Design an algorithm with an average-case running time of $\Theta(n)$ to sort the n points by their distances $d_i = \sqrt{x_i^2 + y_i^2}$ from the origin. (*Hint:* Design the bucket sizes in BUCKET-SORT to reflect the uniform distribution of the points in the unit circle.)

8.4-5 ★
A ***probability distribution function*** $P(x)$ for a random variable X is defined by $P(x) = \mathrm{Pr}\{X \leq x\}$. Suppose that we draw a list of n random variables $X_1, X_2, \ldots, X_n$ from a continuous probability distribution function P that is computable in $O(1)$ time. Give an algorithm that sorts these numbers in linear average-case time.

Problems

8-1   *Probabilistic lower bounds on comparison sorting*

In this problem, we prove a probabilistic $\Omega(n \lg n)$ lower bound on the running time of any deterministic or randomized comparison sort on n distinct input elements. We begin by examining a deterministic comparison sort A with decision tree T_A. We assume that every permutation of A's inputs is equally likely.

a. Suppose that each leaf of T_A is labeled with the probability that it is reached given a random input. Prove that exactly $n!$ leaves are labeled $1/n!$ and that the rest are labeled 0.

b. Let $D(T)$ denote the external path length of a decision tree T; that is, $D(T)$ is the sum of the depths of all the leaves of T. Let T be a decision tree with $k > 1$ leaves, and let LT and RT be the left and right subtrees of T. Show that $D(T) = D(LT) + D(RT) + k$.

c. Let $d(k)$ be the minimum value of $D(T)$ over all decision trees T with $k > 1$ leaves. Show that $d(k) = \min_{1 \le i \le k-1} \{d(i) + d(k - i) + k\}$. (*Hint:* Consider a decision tree T with k leaves that achieves the minimum. Let i_0 be the number of leaves in LT and $k - i_0$ the number of leaves in RT.)

d. Prove that for a given value of $k > 1$ and i in the range $1 \le i \le k - 1$, the function $i \lg i + (k - i) \lg(k - i)$ is minimized at $i = k/2$. Conclude that $d(k) = \Omega(k \lg k)$.

e. Prove that $D(T_A) = \Omega(n! \lg(n!))$, and conclude that the average-case time to sort n elements is $\Omega(n \lg n)$.

Now, consider a *randomized* comparison sort B. We can extend the decision-tree model to handle randomization by incorporating two kinds of nodes: ordinary comparison nodes and "randomization" nodes. A randomization node models a random choice of the form RANDOM$(1, r)$ made by algorithm B; the node has r children, each of which is equally likely to be chosen during an execution of the algorithm.

f. Show that for any randomized comparison sort B, there exists a deterministic comparison sort A whose expected number of comparisons is no more than those made by B.

8-2   *Sorting in place in linear time*

Suppose that we have an array of n data records to sort and that the key of each record has the value 0 or 1. An algorithm for sorting such a set of records might possess some subset of the following three desirable characteristics:

1. The algorithm runs in $O(n)$ time.

2. The algorithm is stable.

3. The algorithm sorts in place, using no more than a constant amount of storage space in addition to the original array.

a. Give an algorithm that satisfies criteria 1 and 2 above.

b. Give an algorithm that satisfies criteria 1 and 3 above.

c. Give an algorithm that satisfies criteria 2 and 3 above.

d. Can you use any of your sorting algorithms from parts (a)–(c) as the sorting method used in line 2 of RADIX-SORT, so that RADIX-SORT sorts n records with b-bit keys in $O(bn)$ time? Explain how or why not.

e. Suppose that the n records have keys in the range from 1 to k. Show how to modify counting sort so that it sorts the records in place in $O(n + k)$ time. You may use $O(k)$ storage outside the input array. Is your algorithm stable? (*Hint:* How would you do it for $k = 3$?)

8-3   *Sorting variable-length items*

a. You are given an array of integers, where different integers may have different numbers of digits, but the total number of digits over *all* the integers in the array is n. Show how to sort the array in $O(n)$ time.

b. You are given an array of strings, where different strings may have different numbers of characters, but the total number of characters over all the strings is n. Show how to sort the strings in $O(n)$ time.

   (Note that the desired order here is the standard alphabetical order; for example, a < ab < b.)

8-4   *Water jugs*

Suppose that you are given n red and n blue water jugs, all of different shapes and sizes. All red jugs hold different amounts of water, as do the blue ones. Moreover, for every red jug, there is a blue jug that holds the same amount of water, and vice versa.

Your task is to find a grouping of the jugs into pairs of red and blue jugs that hold the same amount of water. To do so, you may perform the following operation: pick a pair of jugs in which one is red and one is blue, fill the red jug with water, and then pour the water into the blue jug. This operation will tell you whether the red or the blue jug can hold more water, or that they have the same volume. Assume that such a comparison takes one time unit. Your goal is to find an algorithm that makes a minimum number of comparisons to determine the grouping. Remember that you may not directly compare two red jugs or two blue jugs.

a. Describe a deterministic algorithm that uses $\Theta(n^2)$ comparisons to group the jugs into pairs.

b. Prove a lower bound of $\Omega(n \lg n)$ for the number of comparisons that an algorithm solving this problem must make.

c. Give a randomized algorithm whose expected number of comparisons is $O(n \lg n)$, and prove that this bound is correct. What is the worst-case number of comparisons for your algorithm?

8-5   *Average sorting*

Suppose that, instead of sorting an array, we just require that the elements increase on average. More precisely, we call an n-element array A **k-sorted** if, for all $i = 1, 2, \ldots, n - k$, the following holds:

$$\frac{\sum_{j=i}^{i+k-1} A[j]}{k} \le \frac{\sum_{j=i+1}^{i+k} A[j]}{k} .$$

a. What does it mean for an array to be 1-sorted?

b. Give a permutation of the numbers $1, 2, \ldots, 10$ that is 2-sorted, but not sorted.

c. Prove that an n-element array is k-sorted if and only if $A[i] \le A[i + k]$ for all $i = 1, 2, \ldots, n - k$.

d. Give an algorithm that k-sorts an n-element array in $O(n \lg(n/k))$ time.

We can also show a lower bound on the time to produce a k-sorted array, when k is a constant.

e. Show that we can sort a k-sorted array of length n in $O(n \lg k)$ time. (*Hint:* Use the solution to Exercise 6.5-9.)

f. Show that when k is a constant, k-sorting an n-element array requires $\Omega(n \lg n)$ time. (*Hint:* Use the solution to the previous part along with the lower bound on comparison sorts.)

8-6   *Lower bound on merging sorted lists*

The problem of merging two sorted lists arises frequently. We have seen a procedure for it as the subroutine MERGE in Section 2.3.1. In this problem, we will prove a lower bound of $2n - 1$ on the worst-case number of comparisons required to merge two sorted lists, each containing n items.

First we will show a lower bound of $2n - o(n)$ comparisons by using a decision tree.

a. Given $2n$ numbers, compute the number of possible ways to divide them into two sorted lists, each with n numbers.

b. Using a decision tree and your answer to part (a), show that any algorithm that correctly merges two sorted lists must perform at least $2n - o(n)$ comparisons.

Now we will show a slightly tighter $2n - 1$ bound.

c. Show that if two elements are consecutive in the sorted order and from different lists, then they must be compared.

d. Use your answer to the previous part to show a lower bound of $2n - 1$ comparisons for merging two sorted lists.

8-7   *The 0-1 sorting lemma and columnsort*

A *compare-exchange* operation on two array elements $A[i]$ and $A[j]$, where $i < j$, has the form

COMPARE-EXCHANGE(A, i, j)

```
1   if A[i] > A[j]
2       exchange A[i] with A[j]
```

After the compare-exchange operation, we know that $A[i] \le A[j]$.

An *oblivious compare-exchange algorithm* operates solely by a sequence of prespecified compare-exchange operations. The indices of the positions compared in the sequence must be determined in advance, and although they can depend on the number of elements being sorted, they cannot depend on the values being sorted, nor can they depend on the result of any prior compare-exchange operation. For example, here is insertion sort expressed as an oblivious compare-exchange algorithm:

INSERTION-SORT(A)

```
1   for j = 2 to A.length
2       for i = j - 1 downto 1
3           COMPARE-EXCHANGE(A, i, i + 1)
```

The **0-1 sorting lemma** provides a powerful way to prove that an oblivious compare-exchange algorithm produces a sorted result. It states that if an oblivious compare-exchange algorithm correctly sorts all input sequences consisting of only 0s and 1s, then it correctly sorts all inputs containing arbitrary values.

You will prove the 0-1 sorting lemma by proving its contrapositive: if an oblivious compare-exchange algorithm fails to sort an input containing arbitrary values, then it fails to sort some 0-1 input. Assume that an oblivious compare-exchange algorithm X fails to correctly sort the array $A[1 . . n]$. Let $A[p]$ be the smallest value in A that algorithm X puts into the wrong location, and let $A[q]$ be the value that algorithm X moves to the location into which $A[p]$ should have gone. Define an array $B[1 . . n]$ of 0s and 1s as follows:

$$B[i] = \begin{cases} 0 & \text{if } A[i] \leq A[p] , \\ 1 & \text{if } A[i] > A[p] . \end{cases}$$

a. Argue that $A[q] > A[p]$, so that $B[p] = 0$ and $B[q] = 1$.

b. To complete the proof of the 0-1 sorting lemma, prove that algorithm X fails to sort array B correctly.

Now you will use the 0-1 sorting lemma to prove that a particular sorting algorithm works correctly. The algorithm, **columnsort**, works on a rectangular array of n elements. The array has r rows and s columns (so that $n = rs$), subject to three restrictions:

- r must be even,

- s must be a divisor of r, and

- $r \geq 2s^2$.

When columnsort completes, the array is sorted in **column-major order**: reading down the columns, from left to right, the elements monotonically increase.

Columnsort operates in eight steps, regardless of the value of n. The odd steps are all the same: sort each column individually. Each even step is a fixed permutation. Here are the steps:

1. Sort each column.

2. Transpose the array, but reshape it back to r rows and s columns. In other words, turn the leftmost column into the top r/s rows, in order; turn the next column into the next r/s rows, in order; and so on.

3. Sort each column.

4. Perform the inverse of the permutation performed in step 2.

(a)

10	14	5
8	7	17
12	1	6
16	9	11
4	15	2
18	3	13

(b)

4	1	2
8	3	5
10	7	6
12	9	11
16	14	13
18	15	17

(c)

4	8	10
12	16	18
1	3	7
9	14	15
2	5	6
11	13	17

(d)

1	3	6
2	5	7
4	8	10
9	13	15
11	14	17
12	16	18

(e)

1	4	11
3	8	14
6	10	17
2	9	12
5	13	16
7	15	18

(f)

1	4	11
2	8	12
3	9	14
5	10	16
6	13	17
7	15	18

(g)

	5	10	16
	6	13	17
	7	15	18
1	4	11	
2	8	12	
3	9	14	

(h)

	4	10	16
	5	11	17
	6	12	18
1	7	13	
2	8	14	
3	9	15	

(i)

1	7	13
2	8	14
3	9	15
4	10	16
5	11	17
6	12	18

Figure 8.5   The steps of columnsort. **(a)** The input array with 6 rows and 3 columns. **(b)** After sorting each column in step 1. **(c)** After transposing and reshaping in step 2. **(d)** After sorting each column in step 3. **(e)** After performing step 4, which inverts the permutation from step 2. **(f)** After sorting each column in step 5. **(g)** After shifting by half a column in step 6. **(h)** After sorting each column in step 7. **(i)** After performing step 8, which inverts the permutation from step 6. The array is now sorted in column-major order.

5. Sort each column.

6. Shift the top half of each column into the bottom half of the same column, and shift the bottom half of each column into the top half of the next column to the right. Leave the top half of the leftmost column empty. Shift the bottom half of the last column into the top half of a new rightmost column, and leave the bottom half of this new column empty.

7. Sort each column.

8. Perform the inverse of the permutation performed in step 6.

Figure 8.5 shows an example of the steps of columnsort with $r = 6$ and $s = 3$. (Even though this example violates the requirement that $r \geq 2s^2$, it happens to work.)

   c. Argue that we can treat columnsort as an oblivious compare-exchange algorithm, even if we do not know what sorting method the odd steps use.

   Although it might seem hard to believe that columnsort actually sorts, you will use the 0-1 sorting lemma to prove that it does. The 0-1 sorting lemma applies because we can treat columnsort as an oblivious compare-exchange algorithm. A couple of definitions will help you apply the 0-1 sorting lemma. We say that an area of an array is **clean** if we know that it contains either all 0s or all 1s. Otherwise, the area might contain mixed 0s and 1s, and it is **dirty**. From here on, assume that the input array contains only 0s and 1s, and that we can treat it as an array with r rows and s columns.

d. Prove that after steps 1–3, the array consists of some clean rows of 0s at the top, some clean rows of 1s at the bottom, and at most s dirty rows between them.

e. Prove that after step 4, the array, read in column-major order, starts with a clean area of 0s, ends with a clean area of 1s, and has a dirty area of at most s^2 elements in the middle.

f. Prove that steps 5–8 produce a fully sorted 0-1 output. Conclude that column-sort correctly sorts all inputs containing arbitrary values.

g. Now suppose that s does not divide r. Prove that after steps 1–3, the array consists of some clean rows of 0s at the top, some clean rows of 1s at the bottom, and at most $2s - 1$ dirty rows between them. How large must r be, compared with s, for columnsort to correctly sort when s does not divide r?

h. Suggest a simple change to step 1 that allows us to maintain the requirement that $r \geq 2s^2$ even when s does not divide r, and prove that with your change, columnsort correctly sorts.

Chapter notes

The decision-tree model for studying comparison sorts was introduced by Ford and Johnson [110]. Knuth's comprehensive treatise on sorting [211] covers many variations on the sorting problem, including the information-theoretic lower bound on the complexity of sorting given here. Ben-Or [39] studied lower bounds for sorting using generalizations of the decision-tree model.

Knuth credits H. H. Seward with inventing counting sort in 1954, as well as with the idea of combining counting sort with radix sort. Radix sorting starting with the least significant digit appears to be a folk algorithm widely used by operators of mechanical card-sorting machines. According to Knuth, the first published reference to the method is a 1929 document by L. J. Comrie describing punched-card equipment. Bucket sorting has been in use since 1956, when the basic idea was proposed by E. J. Isaac and R. C. Singleton [188].

Munro and Raman [263] give a stable sorting algorithm that performs $O(n^{1+\epsilon})$ comparisons in the worst case, where $0 < \epsilon \leq 1$ is any fixed constant. Although any of the $O(n \lg n)$-time algorithms make fewer comparisons, the algorithm by Munro and Raman moves data only $O(n)$ times and operates in place.

The case of sorting n b-bit integers in $o(n \lg n)$ time has been considered by many researchers. Several positive results have been obtained, each under slightly different assumptions about the model of computation and the restrictions placed on the algorithm. All the results assume that the computer memory is divided into addressable b-bit words. Fredman and Willard [115] introduced the fusion tree data structure and used it to sort n integers in $O(n \lg n / \lg \lg n)$ time. This bound was later improved to $O(n \sqrt{\lg n})$ time by Andersson [16]. These algorithms require the use of multiplication and several precomputed constants. Andersson, Hagerup, Nilsson, and Raman [17] have shown how to sort n integers in $O(n \lg \lg n)$ time without using multiplication, but their method requires storage that can be un-bounded in terms of n. Using multiplicative hashing, we can reduce the storage needed to $O(n)$, but then the $O(n \lg \lg n)$ worst-case bound on the running time becomes an expected-time bound. Generalizing the exponential search trees of Andersson [16], Thorup [335] gave an $O(n(\lg \lg n)^2)$-time sorting algorithm that does not use multiplication or randomization, and it uses linear space. Combining these techniques with some new ideas, Han [158] improved the bound for sorting to $O(n \lg \lg n \lg \lg \lg n)$ time. Although these algorithms are important theoretical breakthroughs, they are all fairly complicated and at the present time seem unlikely to compete with existing sorting algorithms in practice.

The columnsort algorithm in Problem 8-7 is by Leighton [227].

9 Medians and Order Statistics

The ith **order statistic** of a set of n elements is the ith smallest element. For example, the **minimum** of a set of elements is the first order statistic ($i = 1$), and the **maximum** is the nth order statistic ($i = n$). A **median**, informally, is the "halfway point" of the set. When n is odd, the median is unique, occurring at $i = (n + 1)/2$. When n is even, there are two medians, occurring at $i = n/2$ and $i = n/2 + 1$. Thus, regardless of the parity of n, medians occur at $i = \lfloor (n + 1)/2 \rfloor$ (the **lower median**) and $i = \lceil (n + 1)/2 \rceil$ (the **upper median**). For simplicity in this text, however, we consistently use the phrase "the median" to refer to the lower median.

This chapter addresses the problem of selecting the ith order statistic from a set of n distinct numbers. We assume for convenience that the set contains distinct numbers, although virtually everything that we do extends to the situation in which a set contains repeated values. We formally specify the **selection problem** as follows:

Input: A set A of n (distinct) numbers and an integer i, with $1 \le i \le n$.

Output: The element $x \in A$ that is larger than exactly $i - 1$ other elements of A.

We can solve the selection problem in $O(n \lg n)$ time, since we can sort the numbers using heapsort or merge sort and then simply index the ith element in the output array. This chapter presents faster algorithms.

In Section 9.1, we examine the problem of selecting the minimum and maximum of a set of elements. More interesting is the general selection problem, which we investigate in the subsequent two sections. Section 9.2 analyzes a practical randomized algorithm that achieves an $O(n)$ expected running time, assuming distinct elements. Section 9.3 contains an algorithm of more theoretical interest that achieves the $O(n)$ running time in the worst case.

9.1   Minimum and maximum

How many comparisons are necessary to determine the minimum of a set of n elements? We can easily obtain an upper bound of $n - 1$ comparisons: examine each element of the set in turn and keep track of the smallest element seen so far. In the following procedure, we assume that the set resides in array A, where $A.length = n$.

MINIMUM(A)

```
1   min = A[1]
2   for i = 2 to A.length
3       if min > A[i]
4           min = A[i]
5   return min
```

We can, of course, find the maximum with $n - 1$ comparisons as well.

Is this the best we can do? Yes, since we can obtain a lower bound of $n - 1$ comparisons for the problem of determining the minimum. Think of any algorithm that determines the minimum as a tournament among the elements. Each comparison is a match in the tournament in which the smaller of the two elements wins. Observing that every element except the winner must lose at least one match, we conclude that $n - 1$ comparisons are necessary to determine the minimum. Hence, the algorithm MINIMUM is optimal with respect to the number of comparisons performed.

Simultaneous minimum and maximum

In some applications, we must find both the minimum and the maximum of a set of n elements. For example, a graphics program may need to scale a set of (x, y) data to fit onto a rectangular display screen or other graphical output device. To do so, the program must first determine the minimum and maximum value of each coordinate.

At this point, it should be obvious how to determine both the minimum and the maximum of n elements using $\Theta(n)$ comparisons, which is asymptotically optimal: simply find the minimum and maximum independently, using $n - 1$ comparisons for each, for a total of $2n - 2$ comparisons.

In fact, we can find both the minimum and the maximum using at most $3 \lfloor n/2 \rfloor$ comparisons. We do so by maintaining both the minimum and maximum elements seen thus far. Rather than processing each element of the input by comparing it against the current minimum and maximum, at a cost of 2 comparisons per element, we process elements in pairs. We compare pairs of elements from the input first *with each other*, and then we compare the smaller with the current minimum and the larger to the current maximum, at a cost of 3 comparisons for every 2 elements.

How we set up initial values for the current minimum and maximum depends on whether n is odd or even. If n is odd, we set both the minimum and maximum to the value of the first element, and then we process the rest of the elements in pairs. If n is even, we perform 1 comparison on the first 2 elements to determine the initial values of the minimum and maximum, and then process the rest of the elements in pairs as in the case for odd n.

Let us analyze the total number of comparisons. If n is odd, then we perform $3 \lfloor n/2 \rfloor$ comparisons. If n is even, we perform 1 initial comparison followed by $3(n-2)/2$ comparisons, for a total of $3n/2 - 2$. Thus, in either case, the total number of comparisons is at most $3 \lfloor n/2 \rfloor$.

Exercises

9.1-1
Show that the second smallest of n elements can be found with $n + \lceil \lg n \rceil - 2$ comparisons in the worst case. (*Hint:* Also find the smallest element.)

9.1-2 ★
Prove the lower bound of $\lceil 3n/2 \rceil - 2$ comparisons in the worst case to find both the maximum and minimum of n numbers. (*Hint:* Consider how many numbers are potentially either the maximum or minimum, and investigate how a comparison affects these counts.)

9.2 Selection in expected linear time

The general selection problem appears more difficult than the simple problem of finding a minimum. Yet, surprisingly, the asymptotic running time for both problems is the same: $\Theta(n)$. In this section, we present a divide-and-conquer algorithm for the selection problem. The algorithm RANDOMIZED-SELECT is modeled after the quicksort algorithm of Chapter 7. As in quicksort, we partition the input array recursively. But unlike quicksort, which recursively processes both sides of the partition, RANDOMIZED-SELECT works on only one side of the partition. This difference shows up in the analysis: whereas quicksort has an expected running time of $\Theta(n \lg n)$, the expected running time of RANDOMIZED-SELECT is $\Theta(n)$, assuming that the elements are distinct.

RANDOMIZED-SELECT uses the procedure RANDOMIZED-PARTITION introduced in Section 7.3. Thus, like RANDOMIZED-QUICKSORT, it is a randomized algorithm, since its behavior is determined in part by the output of a random-number
generator. The following code for RANDOMIZED-SELECT returns the ith smallest
element of the array $A[p \dots r]$.

RANDOMIZED-SELECT(A, p, r, i)

```
1   if p == r
2       return A[p]
3   q = RANDOMIZED-PARTITION(A, p, r)
4   k = q − p + 1
5   if i == k          // the pivot value is the answer
6       return A[q]
7   elseif i < k
8       return RANDOMIZED-SELECT(A, p, q − 1, i)
9   else return RANDOMIZED-SELECT(A, q + 1, r, i − k)
```

The RANDOMIZED-SELECT procedure works as follows. Line 1 checks for the
base case of the recursion, in which the subarray $A[p \dots r]$ consists of just one
element. In this case, i must equal 1, and we simply return $A[p]$ in line 2 as the
ith smallest element. Otherwise, the call to RANDOMIZED-PARTITION in line 3
partitions the array $A[p \dots r]$ into two (possibly empty) subarrays $A[p \dots q − 1]$
and $A[q + 1 \dots r]$ such that each element of $A[p \dots q − 1]$ is less than or equal
to $A[q]$, which in turn is less than each element of $A[q + 1 \dots r]$. As in quicksort,
we will refer to $A[q]$ as the ***pivot*** element. Line 4 computes the number k of
elements in the subarray $A[p \dots q]$, that is, the number of elements in the low side
of the partition, plus one for the pivot element. Line 5 then checks whether $A[q]$ is
the ith smallest element. If it is, then line 6 returns $A[q]$. Otherwise, the algorithm
determines in which of the two subarrays $A[p \dots q − 1]$ and $A[q + 1 \dots r]$ the ith
smallest element lies. If $i < k$, then the desired element lies on the low side of
the partition, and line 8 recursively selects it from the subarray. If $i > k$, however,
then the desired element lies on the high side of the partition. Since we already
know k values that are smaller than the ith smallest element of $A[p \dots r]$—namely,
the elements of $A[p \dots q]$—the desired element is the $(i − k)$th smallest element
of $A[q + 1 \dots r]$, which line 9 finds recursively. The code appears to allow recursive
calls to subarrays with 0 elements, but Exercise 9.2-1 asks you to show that this
situation cannot happen.

The worst-case running time for RANDOMIZED-SELECT is $\Theta(n^2)$, even to find
the minimum, because we could be extremely unlucky and always partition around
the largest remaining element, and partitioning takes $\Theta(n)$ time. We will see that

the algorithm has a linear expected running time, though, and because it is random-ized, no particular input elicits the worst-case behavior.

To analyze the expected running time of RANDOMIZED-SELECT, we let the run-ning time on an input array $A[p \mathrel{.\,.} r]$ of n elements be a random variable that we denote by $T(n)$, and we obtain an upper bound on $\mathrm{E}[T(n)]$ as follows. The pro-cedure RANDOMIZED-PARTITION is equally likely to return any element as the pivot. Therefore, for each k such that $1 \leq k \leq n$, the subarray $A[p \mathrel{.\,.} q]$ has k ele-ments (all less than or equal to the pivot) with probability $1/n$. For $k = 1, 2, \ldots, n$, we define indicator random variables X_k where

$$X_k = \mathrm{I}\{\text{the subarray } A[p \mathrel{.\,.} q] \text{ has exactly } k \text{ elements}\} \;,$$

and so, assuming that the elements are distinct, we have

$$\mathrm{E}[X_k] = 1/n \;. \tag{9.1}$$

When we call RANDOMIZED-SELECT and choose $A[q]$ as the pivot element, we do not know, a priori, if we will terminate immediately with the correct answer, recurse on the subarray $A[p \mathrel{.\,.} q - 1]$, or recurse on the subarray $A[q + 1 \mathrel{.\,.} r]$. This decision depends on where the ith smallest element falls relative to $A[q]$. Assuming that $T(n)$ is monotonically increasing, we can upper-bound the time needed for the recursive call by the time needed for the recursive call on the largest possible input. In other words, to obtain an upper bound, we assume that the ith element is always on the side of the partition with the greater number of elements. For a given call of RANDOMIZED-SELECT, the indicator random variable X_k has the value 1 for exactly one value of k, and it is 0 for all other k. When $X_k = 1$, the two subarrays on which we might recurse have sizes $k - 1$ and $n - k$. Hence, we have the recurrence

$$\begin{aligned}
T(n) &\leq \sum_{k=1}^{n} X_k \cdot (T(\max(k - 1, n - k)) + O(n)) \\
&= \sum_{k=1}^{n} X_k \cdot T(\max(k - 1, n - k)) + O(n) \;.
\end{aligned}$$

Taking expected values, we have

$$\text{E}[T(n)]$$

$$\leq \text{E}\left[\sum_{k=1}^{n} X_k \cdot T(\max(k-1, n-k)) + O(n)\right]$$

$$= \sum_{k=1}^{n} \text{E}[X_k \cdot T(\max(k-1, n-k))] + O(n) \qquad \text{(by linearity of expectation)}$$

$$= \sum_{k=1}^{n} \text{E}[X_k] \cdot \text{E}[T(\max(k-1, n-k))] + O(n) \quad \text{(by equation (C.24))}$$

$$= \sum_{k=1}^{n} \frac{1}{n} \cdot \text{E}[T(\max(k-1, n-k))] + O(n) \qquad \text{(by equation (9.1))} \ .$$

In order to apply equation (C.24), we rely on X_k and $T(\max(k-1, n-k))$ being independent random variables. Exercise 9.2-2 asks you to justify this assertion.

Let us consider the expression $\max(k-1, n-k)$. We have

$$\max(k-1, n-k) = \begin{cases} k-1 & \text{if } k > \lceil n/2 \rceil \ , \\ n-k & \text{if } k \leq \lceil n/2 \rceil \ . \end{cases}$$

If n is even, each term from $T(\lceil n/2 \rceil)$ up to $T(n-1)$ appears exactly twice in the summation, and if n is odd, all these terms appear twice and $T(\lfloor n/2 \rfloor)$ appears once. Thus, we have

$$\text{E}[T(n)] \leq \frac{2}{n} \sum_{k=\lfloor n/2 \rfloor}^{n-1} \text{E}[T(k)] + O(n) \ .$$

We show that $\text{E}[T(n)] = O(n)$ by substitution. Assume that $\text{E}[T(n)] \leq cn$ for some constant c that satisfies the initial conditions of the recurrence. We assume that $T(n) = O(1)$ for n less than some constant; we shall pick this constant later. We also pick a constant a such that the function described by the $O(n)$ term above (which describes the non-recursive component of the running time of the algorithm) is bounded from above by an for all $n > 0$. Using this inductive hypothesis, we have

$$\text{E}[T(n)] \ \leq \ \frac{2}{n} \sum_{k=\lfloor n/2 \rfloor}^{n-1} ck + an$$

$$= \ \frac{2c}{n}\left(\sum_{k=1}^{n-1} k - \sum_{k=1}^{\lfloor n/2 \rfloor - 1} k\right) + an$$

$$\begin{aligned}
&= \frac{2c}{n}\left(\frac{(n-1)n}{2} - \frac{(\lfloor n/2\rfloor - 1)\lfloor n/2\rfloor}{2}\right) + an \\
&\leq \frac{2c}{n}\left(\frac{(n-1)n}{2} - \frac{(n/2-2)(n/2-1)}{2}\right) + an \\
&= \frac{2c}{n}\left(\frac{n^2 - n}{2} - \frac{n^2/4 - 3n/2 + 2}{2}\right) + an \\
&= \frac{c}{n}\left(\frac{3n^2}{4} + \frac{n}{2} - 2\right) + an \\
&= c\left(\frac{3n}{4} + \frac{1}{2} - \frac{2}{n}\right) + an \\
&\leq \frac{3cn}{4} + \frac{c}{2} + an \\
&= cn - \left(\frac{cn}{4} - \frac{c}{2} - an\right) .
\end{aligned}$$

In order to complete the proof, we need to show that for sufficiently large n, this last expression is at most cn or, equivalently, that $cn/4 - c/2 - an \geq 0$. If we add $c/2$ to both sides and factor out n, we get $n(c/4 - a) \geq c/2$. As long as we choose the constant c so that $c/4 - a > 0$, i.e., $c > 4a$, we can divide both sides by $c/4 - a$, giving

$$n \geq \frac{c/2}{c/4 - a} = \frac{2c}{c - 4a} .$$

Thus, if we assume that $T(n) = O(1)$ for $n < 2c/(c-4a)$, then $\mathrm{E}\,[T(n)] = O(n)$. We conclude that we can find any order statistic, and in particular the median, in expected linear time, assuming that the elements are distinct.

Exercises

9.2-1
Show that RANDOMIZED-SELECT never makes a recursive call to a 0-length array.

9.2-2
Argue that the indicator random variable X_k and the value $T(\max(k - 1, n - k))$ are independent.

9.2-3
Write an iterative version of RANDOMIZED-SELECT.

9.2-4

Suppose we use RANDOMIZED-SELECT to select the minimum element of the array $A = \langle 3, 2, 9, 0, 7, 5, 4, 8, 6, 1 \rangle$. Describe a sequence of partitions that results in a worst-case performance of RANDOMIZED-SELECT.

9.3   Selection in worst-case linear time

We now examine a selection algorithm whose running time is $O(n)$ in the worst case. Like RANDOMIZED-SELECT, the algorithm SELECT finds the desired element by recursively partitioning the input array. Here, however, we *guarantee* a good split upon partitioning the array. SELECT uses the deterministic partitioning algorithm PARTITION from quicksort (see Section 7.1), but modified to take the element to partition around as an input parameter.

The SELECT algorithm determines the ith smallest of an input array of $n > 1$ distinct elements by executing the following steps. (If $n = 1$, then SELECT merely returns its only input value as the ith smallest.)

1. Divide the n elements of the input array into $\lfloor n/5 \rfloor$ groups of 5 elements each and at most one group made up of the remaining n mod 5 elements.

2. Find the median of each of the $\lceil n/5 \rceil$ groups by first insertion-sorting the elements of each group (of which there are at most 5) and then picking the median from the sorted list of group elements.

3. Use SELECT recursively to find the median x of the $\lceil n/5 \rceil$ medians found in step 2. (If there are an even number of medians, then by our convention, x is the lower median.)

4. Partition the input array around the median-of-medians x using the modified version of PARTITION. Let k be one more than the number of elements on the low side of the partition, so that x is the kth smallest element and there are $n - k$ elements on the high side of the partition.

5. If $i = k$, then return x. Otherwise, use SELECT recursively to find the ith smallest element on the low side if $i < k$, or the $(i - k)$th smallest element on the high side if $i > k$.

To analyze the running time of SELECT, we first determine a lower bound on the number of elements that are greater than the partitioning element x. Figure 9.1 helps us to visualize this bookkeeping. At least half of the medians found in

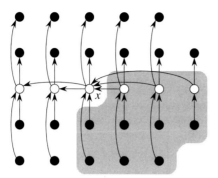

Figure 9.1 Analysis of the algorithm SELECT. The n elements are represented by small circles, and each group of 5 elements occupies a column. The medians of the groups are whitened, and the median-of-medians x is labeled. (When finding the median of an even number of elements, we use the lower median.) Arrows go from larger elements to smaller, from which we can see that 3 out of every full group of 5 elements to the right of x are greater than x, and 3 out of every group of 5 elements to the left of x are less than x. The elements known to be greater than x appear on a shaded background.

step 2 are greater than or equal to the median-of-medians x.[1] Thus, at least half of the $\lceil n/5 \rceil$ groups contribute at least 3 elements that are greater than x, except for the one group that has fewer than 5 elements if 5 does not divide n exactly, and the one group containing x itself. Discounting these two groups, it follows that the number of elements greater than x is at least

$$3 \left(\left\lceil \frac{1}{2} \left\lceil \frac{n}{5} \right\rceil \right\rceil - 2 \right) \geq \frac{3n}{10} - 6 \,.$$

Similarly, at least $3n/10 - 6$ elements are less than x. Thus, in the worst case, step 5 calls SELECT recursively on at most $7n/10 + 6$ elements.

We can now develop a recurrence for the worst-case running time $T(n)$ of the algorithm SELECT. Steps 1, 2, and 4 take $O(n)$ time. (Step 2 consists of $O(n)$ calls of insertion sort on sets of size $O(1)$.) Step 3 takes time $T(\lceil n/5 \rceil)$, and step 5 takes time at most $T(7n/10 + 6)$, assuming that T is monotonically increasing. We make the assumption, which seems unmotivated at first, that any input of fewer than 140 elements requires $O(1)$ time; the origin of the magic constant 140 will be clear shortly. We can therefore obtain the recurrence

---

[1] Because of our assumption that the numbers are distinct, all medians except x are either greater than or less than x.

$$T(n) \leq \begin{cases} O(1) & \text{if } n < 140 , \\ T(\lceil n/5 \rceil) + T(7n/10 + 6) + O(n) & \text{if } n \geq 140 . \end{cases}$$

We show that the running time is linear by substitution. More specifically, we will show that $T(n) \leq cn$ for some suitably large constant c and all $n > 0$. We begin by assuming that $T(n) \leq cn$ for some suitably large constant c and all $n < 140$; this assumption holds if c is large enough. We also pick a constant a such that the function described by the $O(n)$ term above (which describes the non-recursive component of the running time of the algorithm) is bounded above by an for all $n > 0$. Substituting this inductive hypothesis into the right-hand side of the recurrence yields

$$\begin{aligned} T(n) &\leq c \lceil n/5 \rceil + c(7n/10 + 6) + an \\ &\leq cn/5 + c + 7cn/10 + 6c + an \\ &= 9cn/10 + 7c + an \\ &= cn + (-cn/10 + 7c + an) , \end{aligned}$$

which is at most cn if

$$-cn/10 + 7c + an \leq 0 . \tag{9.2}$$

Inequality (9.2) is equivalent to the inequality $c \geq 10a(n/(n - 70))$ when $n > 70$. Because we assume that $n \geq 140$, we have $n/(n - 70) \leq 2$, and so choosing $c \geq 20a$ will satisfy inequality (9.2). (Note that there is nothing special about the constant 140; we could replace it by any integer strictly greater than 70 and then choose c accordingly.) The worst-case running time of SELECT is therefore linear.

As in a comparison sort (see Section 8.1), SELECT and RANDOMIZED-SELECT determine information about the relative order of elements only by comparing elements. Recall from Chapter 8 that sorting requires $\Omega(n \lg n)$ time in the comparison model, even on average (see Problem 8-1). The linear-time sorting algorithms in Chapter 8 make assumptions about the input. In contrast, the linear-time selection algorithms in this chapter do not require any assumptions about the input. They are not subject to the $\Omega(n \lg n)$ lower bound because they manage to solve the selection problem without sorting. Thus, solving the selection problem by sorting and indexing, as presented in the introduction to this chapter, is asymptotically inefficient.

Exercises

9.3-1
In the algorithm SELECT, the input elements are divided into groups of 5. Will the algorithm work in linear time if they are divided into groups of 7? Argue that SELECT does not run in linear time if groups of 3 are used.

9.3-2
Analyze SELECT to show that if $n \geq 140$, then at least $\lceil n/4 \rceil$ elements are greater than the median-of-medians x and at least $\lceil n/4 \rceil$ elements are less than x.

9.3-3
Show how quicksort can be made to run in $O(n \lg n)$ time in the worst case, assuming that all elements are distinct.

9.3-4 ★
Suppose that an algorithm uses only comparisons to find the ith smallest element in a set of n elements. Show that it can also find the $i - 1$ smaller elements and the $n - i$ larger elements without performing any additional comparisons.

9.3-5
Suppose that you have a "black-box" worst-case linear-time median subroutine. Give a simple, linear-time algorithm that solves the selection problem for an arbitrary order statistic.

9.3-6
The kth *quantiles* of an n-element set are the $k - 1$ order statistics that divide the sorted set into k equal-sized sets (to within 1). Give an $O(n \lg k)$-time algorithm to list the kth quantiles of a set.

9.3-7
Describe an $O(n)$-time algorithm that, given a set S of n distinct numbers and a positive integer $k \leq n$, determines the k numbers in S that are closest to the median of S.

9.3-8
Let $X[1 \mathinner{.\,.} n]$ and $Y[1 \mathinner{.\,.} n]$ be two arrays, each containing n numbers already in sorted order. Give an $O(\lg n)$-time algorithm to find the median of all $2n$ elements in arrays X and Y.

9.3-9
Professor Olay is consulting for an oil company, which is planning a large pipeline running east to west through an oil field of n wells. The company wants to connect

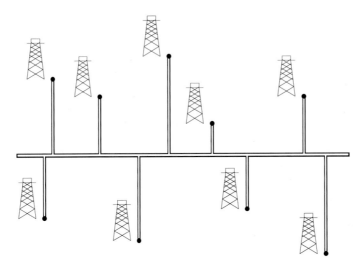

Figure 9.2   Professor Olay needs to determine the position of the east-west oil pipeline that minimizes the total length of the north-south spurs.

a spur pipeline from each well directly to the main pipeline along a shortest route (either north or south), as shown in Figure 9.2. Given the x- and y-coordinates of the wells, how should the professor pick the optimal location of the main pipeline, which would be the one that minimizes the total length of the spurs? Show how to determine the optimal location in linear time.

Problems

9-1   Largest i numbers in sorted order

Given a set of n numbers, we wish to find the i largest in sorted order using a comparison-based algorithm. Find the algorithm that implements each of the following methods with the best asymptotic worst-case running time, and analyze the running times of the algorithms in terms of n and i.

a. Sort the numbers, and list the i largest.

b. Build a max-priority queue from the numbers, and call EXTRACT-MAX i times.

c. Use an order-statistic algorithm to find the ith largest number, partition around that number, and sort the i largest numbers.

9-2 Weighted median

For n distinct elements $x_1, x_2, \ldots, x_n$ with positive weights $w_1, w_2, \ldots, w_n$ such that $\sum_{i=1}^{n} w_i = 1$, the **weighted (lower) median** is the element x_k satisfying

$$\sum_{x_i < x_k} w_i < \frac{1}{2}$$

and

$$\sum_{x_i > x_k} w_i \leq \frac{1}{2} .$$

For example, if the elements are $0.1, 0.35, 0.05, 0.1, 0.15, 0.05, 0.2$ and each element equals its weight (that is, $w_i = x_i$ for $i = 1, 2, \ldots, 7$), then the median is 0.1, but the weighted median is 0.2.

a. Argue that the median of $x_1, x_2, \ldots, x_n$ is the weighted median of the x_i with weights $w_i = 1/n$ for $i = 1, 2, \ldots, n$.

b. Show how to compute the weighted median of n elements in $O(n \lg n)$ worst-case time using sorting.

c. Show how to compute the weighted median in $\Theta(n)$ worst-case time using a linear-time median algorithm such as SELECT from Section 9.3.

The **post-office location problem** is defined as follows. We are given n points $p_1, p_2, \ldots, p_n$ with associated weights $w_1, w_2, \ldots, w_n$. We wish to find a point p (not necessarily one of the input points) that minimizes the sum $\sum_{i=1}^{n} w_i \, d(p, p_i)$, where $d(a, b)$ is the distance between points a and b.

d. Argue that the weighted median is a best solution for the 1-dimensional post-office location problem, in which points are simply real numbers and the distance between points a and b is $d(a, b) = |a - b|$.

e. Find the best solution for the 2-dimensional post-office location problem, in which the points are (x, y) coordinate pairs and the distance between points $a = (x_1, y_1)$ and $b = (x_2, y_2)$ is the **Manhattan distance** given by $d(a, b) = |x_1 - x_2| + |y_1 - y_2|$.

9-3 Small order statistics

We showed that the worst-case number $T(n)$ of comparisons used by SELECT to select the ith order statistic from n numbers satisfies $T(n) = \Theta(n)$, but the constant hidden by the Θ-notation is rather large. When i is small relative to n, we can implement a different procedure that uses SELECT as a subroutine but makes fewer comparisons in the worst case.

a. Describe an algorithm that uses $U_i(n)$ comparisons to find the ith smallest of n elements, where

$$U_i(n) = \begin{cases} T(n) & \text{if } i \geq n/2, \\ \lfloor n/2 \rfloor + U_i(\lceil n/2 \rceil) + T(2i) & \text{otherwise .} \end{cases}$$

(*Hint:* Begin with $\lfloor n/2 \rfloor$ disjoint pairwise comparisons, and recurse on the set containing the smaller element from each pair.)

b. Show that, if $i < n/2$, then $U_i(n) = n + O(T(2i)\lg(n/i))$.

c. Show that if i is a constant less than $n/2$, then $U_i(n) = n + O(\lg n)$.

d. Show that if $i = n/k$ for $k \geq 2$, then $U_i(n) = n + O(T(2n/k)\lg k)$.

9-4   *Alternative analysis of randomized selection*

In this problem, we use indicator random variables to analyze the RANDOMIZED-SELECT procedure in a manner akin to our analysis of RANDOMIZED-QUICKSORT in Section 7.4.2.

As in the quicksort analysis, we assume that all elements are distinct, and we rename the elements of the input array A as $z_1, z_2, \ldots, z_n$, where z_i is the ith smallest element. Thus, the call RANDOMIZED-SELECT$(A, 1, n, k)$ returns z_k.

For $1 \leq i < j \leq n$, let

$X_{ijk} = \text{I}\{z_i \text{ is compared with } z_j \text{ sometime during the execution of the algorithm to find } z_k\}$.

a. Give an exact expression for $\text{E}[X_{ijk}]$. (*Hint:* Your expression may have different values, depending on the values of i, j, and k.)

b. Let X_k denote the total number of comparisons between elements of array A when finding z_k. Show that

$$\text{E}[X_k] \leq 2\left(\sum_{i=1}^{k}\sum_{j=k}^{n}\frac{1}{j-i+1} + \sum_{j=k+1}^{n}\frac{j-k-1}{j-k+1} + \sum_{i=1}^{k-2}\frac{k-i-1}{k-i+1}\right) .$$

c. Show that $\text{E}[X_k] \leq 4n$.

d. Conclude that, assuming all elements of array A are distinct, RANDOMIZED-SELECT runs in expected time $O(n)$.

Chapter notes

The worst-case linear-time median-finding algorithm was devised by Blum, Floyd, Pratt, Rivest, and Tarjan [50]. The fast randomized version is due to Hoare [169]. Floyd and Rivest [108] have developed an improved randomized version that partitions around an element recursively selected from a small sample of the elements.

It is still unknown exactly how many comparisons are needed to determine the median. Bent and John [41] gave a lower bound of $2n$ comparisons for median finding, and Schönhage, Paterson, and Pippenger [302] gave an upper bound of $3n$. Dor and Zwick have improved on both of these bounds. Their upper bound [93] is slightly less than $2.95n$, and their lower bound [94] is $(2 + \epsilon)n$, for a small positive constant ϵ, thereby improving slightly on related work by Dor et al. [92]. Paterson [272] describes some of these results along with other related work.

III Data Structures

Introduction

Sets are as fundamental to computer science as they are to mathematics. Whereas mathematical sets are unchanging, the sets manipulated by algorithms can grow, shrink, or otherwise change over time. We call such sets *dynamic*. The next five chapters present some basic techniques for representing finite dynamic sets and manipulating them on a computer.

Algorithms may require several different types of operations to be performed on sets. For example, many algorithms need only the ability to insert elements into, delete elements from, and test membership in a set. We call a dynamic set that supports these operations a *dictionary*. Other algorithms require more complicated operations. For example, min-priority queues, which Chapter 6 introduced in the context of the heap data structure, support the operations of inserting an element into and extracting the smallest element from a set. The best way to implement a dynamic set depends upon the operations that must be supported.

Elements of a dynamic set

In a typical implementation of a dynamic set, each element is represented by an object whose attributes can be examined and manipulated if we have a pointer to the object. (Section 10.3 discusses the implementation of objects and pointers in programming environments that do not contain them as basic data types.) Some kinds of dynamic sets assume that one of the object's attributes is an identifying *key*. If the keys are all different, we can think of the dynamic set as being a set of key values. The object may contain *satellite data*, which are carried around in other object attributes but are otherwise unused by the set implementation. It may also have attributes that are manipulated by the set operations; these attributes may contain data or pointers to other objects in the set.

Some dynamic sets presuppose that the keys are drawn from a totally ordered set, such as the real numbers, or the set of all words under the usual alphabetic ordering. A total ordering allows us to define the minimum element of the set, for example, or to speak of the next element larger than a given element in a set.

Operations on dynamic sets

Operations on a dynamic set can be grouped into two categories: *queries*, which simply return information about the set, and *modifying operations*, which change the set. Here is a list of typical operations. Any specific application will usually require only a few of these to be implemented.

SEARCH(S, k)

A query that, given a set S and a key value k, returns a pointer x to an element in S such that $x.key = k$, or NIL if no such element belongs to S.

INSERT(S, x)

A modifying operation that augments the set S with the element pointed to by x. We usually assume that any attributes in element x needed by the set implementation have already been initialized.

DELETE(S, x)

A modifying operation that, given a pointer x to an element in the set S, removes x from S. (Note that this operation takes a pointer to an element x, not a key value.)

MINIMUM(S)

A query on a totally ordered set S that returns a pointer to the element of S with the smallest key.

MAXIMUM(S)

A query on a totally ordered set S that returns a pointer to the element of S with the largest key.

SUCCESSOR(S, x)

A query that, given an element x whose key is from a totally ordered set S, returns a pointer to the next larger element in S, or NIL if x is the maximum element.

PREDECESSOR(S, x)

A query that, given an element x whose key is from a totally ordered set S, returns a pointer to the next smaller element in S, or NIL if x is the minimum element.

In some situations, we can extend the queries SUCCESSOR and PREDECESSOR so that they apply to sets with nondistinct keys. For a set on n keys, the normal presumption is that a call to MINIMUM followed by $n - 1$ calls to SUCCESSOR enumerates the elements in the set in sorted order.

We usually measure the time taken to execute a set operation in terms of the size of the set. For example, Chapter 13 describes a data structure that can support any of the operations listed above on a set of size n in time $O(\lg n)$.

Overview of Part III

Chapters 10–14 describe several data structures that we can use to implement dynamic sets; we shall use many of these later to construct efficient algorithms for a variety of problems. We already saw another important data structure—the heap—in Chapter 6.

Chapter 10 presents the essentials of working with simple data structures such as stacks, queues, linked lists, and rooted trees. It also shows how to implement objects and pointers in programming environments that do not support them as primitives. If you have taken an introductory programming course, then much of this material should be familiar to you.

Chapter 11 introduces hash tables, which support the dictionary operations IN-SERT, DELETE, and SEARCH. In the worst case, hashing requires $\Theta(n)$ time to perform a SEARCH operation, but the expected time for hash-table operations is $O(1)$. The analysis of hashing relies on probability, but most of the chapter requires no background in the subject.

Binary search trees, which are covered in Chapter 12, support all the dynamic-set operations listed above. In the worst case, each operation takes $\Theta(n)$ time on a tree with n elements, but on a randomly built binary search tree, the expected time for each operation is $O(\lg n)$. Binary search trees serve as the basis for many other data structures.

Chapter 13 introduces red-black trees, which are a variant of binary search trees. Unlike ordinary binary search trees, red-black trees are guaranteed to perform well: operations take $O(\lg n)$ time in the worst case. A red-black tree is a balanced search tree; Chapter 18 in Part V presents another kind of balanced search tree, called a B-tree. Although the mechanics of red-black trees are somewhat intricate, you can glean most of their properties from the chapter without studying the mechanics in detail. Nevertheless, you probably will find walking through the code to be quite instructive.

In Chapter 14, we show how to augment red-black trees to support operations other than the basic ones listed above. First, we augment them so that we can dynamically maintain order statistics for a set of keys. Then, we augment them in a different way to maintain intervals of real numbers.

10   Elementary Data Structures

In this chapter, we examine the representation of dynamic sets by simple data structures that use pointers. Although we can construct many complex data structures using pointers, we present only the rudimentary ones: stacks, queues, linked lists, and rooted trees. We also show ways to synthesize objects and pointers from arrays.

10.1   Stacks and queues

Stacks and queues are dynamic sets in which the element removed from the set by the DELETE operation is prespecified. In a *stack*, the element deleted from the set is the one most recently inserted: the stack implements a *last-in, first-out*, or *LIFO*, policy. Similarly, in a *queue*, the element deleted is always the one that has been in the set for the longest time: the queue implements a *first-in, first-out*, or *FIFO*, policy. There are several efficient ways to implement stacks and queues on a computer. In this section we show how to use a simple array to implement each.

Stacks

The INSERT operation on a stack is often called PUSH, and the DELETE operation, which does not take an element argument, is often called POP. These names are allusions to physical stacks, such as the spring-loaded stacks of plates used in cafeterias. The order in which plates are popped from the stack is the reverse of the order in which they were pushed onto the stack, since only the top plate is accessible.

As Figure 10.1 shows, we can implement a stack of at most n elements with an array $S[1 \mathbin{..} n]$. The array has an attribute $S.top$ that indexes the most recently

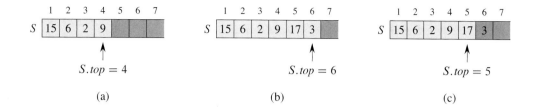

Figure 10.1   An array implementation of a stack *S*. Stack elements appear only in the lightly shaded positions. **(a)** Stack *S* has 4 elements. The top element is 9. **(b)** Stack *S* after the calls PUSH(*S*, 17) and PUSH(*S*, 3). **(c)** Stack *S* after the call POP(*S*) has returned the element 3, which is the one most recently pushed. Although element 3 still appears in the array, it is no longer in the stack; the top is element 17.

inserted element. The stack consists of elements $S[1 .. S.top]$, where $S[1]$ is the element at the bottom of the stack and $S[S.top]$ is the element at the top.

When $S.top = 0$, the stack contains no elements and is ***empty***. We can test to see whether the stack is empty by query operation STACK-EMPTY. If we attempt to pop an empty stack, we say the stack ***underflows***, which is normally an error. If $S.top$ exceeds n, the stack ***overflows***. (In our pseudocode implementation, we don't worry about stack overflow.)

We can implement each of the stack operations with just a few lines of code:

STACK-EMPTY(*S*)

1   **if** $S.top == 0$
2   **return** TRUE
3   **else return** FALSE

PUSH(*S*, *x*)

1   $S.top = S.top + 1$
2   $S[S.top] = x$

POP(*S*)

1   **if** STACK-EMPTY(*S*)
2   **error** "underflow"
3   **else** $S.top = S.top - 1$
4   **return** $S[S.top + 1]$

Figure 10.1 shows the effects of the modifying operations PUSH and POP. Each of the three stack operations takes $O(1)$ time.

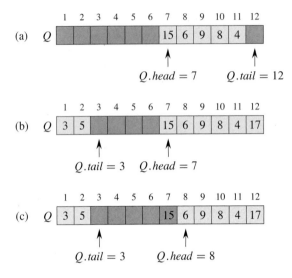

Figure 10.2 A queue implemented using an array $Q[1..12]$. Queue elements appear only in the lightly shaded positions. **(a)** The queue has 5 elements, in locations $Q[7..11]$. **(b)** The configuration of the queue after the calls $\text{ENQUEUE}(Q, 17)$, $\text{ENQUEUE}(Q, 3)$, and $\text{ENQUEUE}(Q, 5)$. **(c)** The configuration of the queue after the call $\text{DEQUEUE}(Q)$ returns the key value 15 formerly at the head of the queue. The new head has key 6.

Queues

We call the INSERT operation on a queue ENQUEUE, and we call the DELETE operation DEQUEUE; like the stack operation POP, DEQUEUE takes no element argument. The FIFO property of a queue causes it to operate like a line of customers waiting to pay a cashier. The queue has a ***head*** and a ***tail***. When an element is enqueued, it takes its place at the tail of the queue, just as a newly arriving customer takes a place at the end of the line. The element dequeued is always the one at the head of the queue, like the customer at the head of the line who has waited the longest.

Figure 10.2 shows one way to implement a queue of at most $n-1$ elements using an array $Q[1..n]$. The queue has an attribute $Q.head$ that indexes, or points to, its head. The attribute $Q.tail$ indexes the next location at which a newly arriving element will be inserted into the queue. The elements in the queue reside in locations $Q.head, Q.head + 1, \ldots, Q.tail - 1$, where we "wrap around" in the sense that location 1 immediately follows location n in a circular order. When $Q.head = Q.tail$, the queue is empty. Initially, we have $Q.head = Q.tail = 1$. If we attempt to dequeue an element from an empty queue, the queue underflows.

When $Q.head = Q.tail + 1$ or both $Q.head = 1$ and $Q.tail = Q.length$, the queue is full, and if we attempt to enqueue an element, then the queue overflows.

In our procedures ENQUEUE and DEQUEUE, we have omitted the error checking for underflow and overflow. (Exercise 10.1-4 asks you to supply code that checks for these two error conditions.) The pseudocode assumes that $n = Q.length$.

ENQUEUE(Q, x)

```
1   Q[Q.tail] = x
2   if Q.tail == Q.length
3       Q.tail = 1
4   else Q.tail = Q.tail + 1
```

DEQUEUE(Q)

```
1   x = Q[Q.head]
2   if Q.head == Q.length
3       Q.head = 1
4   else Q.head = Q.head + 1
5   return x
```

Figure 10.2 shows the effects of the ENQUEUE and DEQUEUE operations. Each operation takes $O(1)$ time.

Exercises

10.1-1
Using Figure 10.1 as a model, illustrate the result of each operation in the sequence PUSH($S, 4$), PUSH($S, 1$), PUSH($S, 3$), POP(S), PUSH($S, 8$), and POP(S) on an initially empty stack S stored in array $S[1 .. 6]$.

10.1-2
Explain how to implement two stacks in one array $A[1 .. n]$ in such a way that neither stack overflows unless the total number of elements in both stacks together is n. The PUSH and POP operations should run in $O(1)$ time.

10.1-3
Using Figure 10.2 as a model, illustrate the result of each operation in the sequence ENQUEUE($Q, 4$), ENQUEUE($Q, 1$), ENQUEUE($Q, 3$), DEQUEUE(Q), ENQUEUE($Q, 8$), and DEQUEUE(Q) on an initially empty queue Q stored in array $Q[1 .. 6]$.

10.1-4
Rewrite ENQUEUE and DEQUEUE to detect underflow and overflow of a queue.

10.1-5
Whereas a stack allows insertion and deletion of elements at only one end, and a queue allows insertion at one end and deletion at the other end, a **deque** (double-ended queue) allows insertion and deletion at both ends. Write four $O(1)$-time procedures to insert elements into and delete elements from both ends of a deque implemented by an array.

10.1-6
Show how to implement a queue using two stacks. Analyze the running time of the queue operations.

10.1-7
Show how to implement a stack using two queues. Analyze the running time of the stack operations.

10.2   Linked lists

A **linked list** is a data structure in which the objects are arranged in a linear order. Unlike an array, however, in which the linear order is determined by the array indices, the order in a linked list is determined by a pointer in each object. Linked lists provide a simple, flexible representation for dynamic sets, supporting (though not necessarily efficiently) all the operations listed on page 230.

As shown in Figure 10.3, each element of a **doubly linked list** L is an object with an attribute *key* and two other pointer attributes: *next* and *prev*. The object may also contain other satellite data. Given an element x in the list, $x.next$ points to its successor in the linked list, and $x.prev$ points to its predecessor. If $x.prev = $ NIL, the element x has no predecessor and is therefore the first element, or **head**, of the list. If $x.next = $ NIL, the element x has no successor and is therefore the last element, or **tail**, of the list. An attribute $L.head$ points to the first element of the list. If $L.head = $ NIL, the list is empty.

A list may have one of several forms. It may be either singly linked or doubly linked, it may be sorted or not, and it may be circular or not. If a list is **singly linked**, we omit the *prev* pointer in each element. If a list is **sorted**, the linear order of the list corresponds to the linear order of keys stored in elements of the list; the minimum element is then the head of the list, and the maximum element is the tail. If the list is **unsorted**, the elements can appear in any order. In a **circular list**, the *prev* pointer of the head of the list points to the tail, and the *next* pointer of the tail of the list points to the head. We can think of a circular list as a ring of

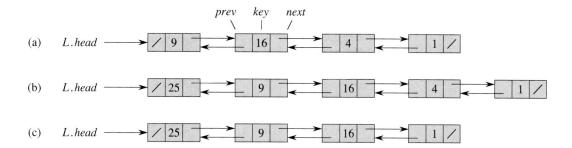

Figure 10.3   **(a)** A doubly linked list L representing the dynamic set $\{1, 4, 9, 16\}$. Each element in the list is an object with attributes for the key and pointers (shown by arrows) to the next and previous objects. The *next* attribute of the tail and the *prev* attribute of the head are NIL, indicated by a diagonal slash. The attribute $L.head$ points to the head. **(b)** Following the execution of LIST-INSERT(L, x), where $x.key = 25$, the linked list has a new object with key 25 as the new head. This new object points to the old head with key 9. **(c)** The result of the subsequent call LIST-DELETE(L, x), where x points to the object with key 4.

elements. In the remainder of this section, we assume that the lists with which we are working are unsorted and doubly linked.

Searching a linked list

The procedure LIST-SEARCH(L, k) finds the first element with key k in list L by a simple linear search, returning a pointer to this element. If no object with key k appears in the list, then the procedure returns NIL. For the linked list in Figure 10.3(a), the call LIST-SEARCH($L, 4$) returns a pointer to the third element, and the call LIST-SEARCH($L, 7$) returns NIL.

LIST-SEARCH(L, k)

1   $x = L.head$
2   **while** $x \neq$ NIL and $x.key \neq k$
3       $x = x.next$
4   **return** x

To search a list of n objects, the LIST-SEARCH procedure takes $\Theta(n)$ time in the worst case, since it may have to search the entire list.

Inserting into a linked list

Given an element x whose *key* attribute has already been set, the LIST-INSERT procedure "splices" x onto the front of the linked list, as shown in Figure 10.3(b).

LIST-INSERT(L, x)

```
1   x.next = L.head
2   if L.head ≠ NIL
3       L.head.prev = x
4   L.head = x
5   x.prev = NIL
```

(Recall that our attribute notation can cascade, so that $L.head.prev$ denotes the *prev* attribute of the object that $L.head$ points to.) The running time for LIST-INSERT on a list of n elements is $O(1)$.

Deleting from a linked list

The procedure LIST-DELETE removes an element x from a linked list L. It must be given a pointer to x, and it then "splices" x out of the list by updating pointers. If we wish to delete an element with a given key, we must first call LIST-SEARCH to retrieve a pointer to the element.

LIST-DELETE(L, x)

```
1   if x.prev ≠ NIL
2       x.prev.next = x.next
3   else L.head = x.next
4   if x.next ≠ NIL
5       x.next.prev = x.prev
```

Figure 10.3(c) shows how an element is deleted from a linked list. LIST-DELETE runs in $O(1)$ time, but if we wish to delete an element with a given key, $\Theta(n)$ time is required in the worst case because we must first call LIST-SEARCH to find the element.

Sentinels

The code for LIST-DELETE would be simpler if we could ignore the boundary conditions at the head and tail of the list:

LIST-DELETE'(L, x)

```
1   x.prev.next = x.next
2   x.next.prev = x.prev
```

A *sentinel* is a dummy object that allows us to simplify boundary conditions. For example, suppose that we provide with list L an object $L.nil$ that represents NIL

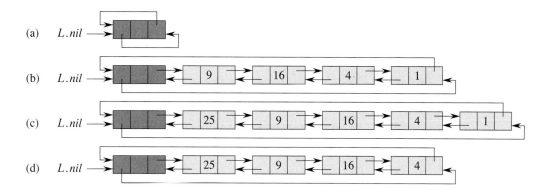

Figure 10.4   A circular, doubly linked list with a sentinel. The sentinel $L.nil$ appears between the head and tail. The attribute $L.head$ is no longer needed, since we can access the head of the list by $L.nil.next$. **(a)** An empty list. **(b)** The linked list from Figure 10.3(a), with key 9 at the head and key 1 at the tail. **(c)** The list after executing LIST-INSERT$'(L, x)$, where $x.key = 25$. The new object becomes the head of the list. **(d)** The list after deleting the object with key 1. The new tail is the object with key 4.

but has all the attributes of the other objects in the list. Wherever we have a reference to NIL in list code, we replace it by a reference to the sentinel $L.nil$. As shown in Figure 10.4, this change turns a regular doubly linked list into a ***circular, doubly linked list with a sentinel***, in which the sentinel $L.nil$ lies between the head and tail. The attribute $L.nil.next$ points to the head of the list, and $L.nil.prev$ points to the tail. Similarly, both the *next* attribute of the tail and the *prev* attribute of the head point to $L.nil$. Since $L.nil.next$ points to the head, we can eliminate the attribute $L.head$ altogether, replacing references to it by references to $L.nil.next$. Figure 10.4(a) shows that an empty list consists of just the sentinel, and both $L.nil.next$ and $L.nil.prev$ point to $L.nil$.

The code for LIST-SEARCH remains the same as before, but with the references to NIL and $L.head$ changed as specified above:

LIST-SEARCH$'(L, k)$

1   $x = L.nil.next$
2   **while** $x \neq L.nil$ and $x.key \neq k$
3       $x = x.next$
4   **return** x

We use the two-line procedure LIST-DELETE$'$ from before to delete an element from the list. The following procedure inserts an element into the list:

LIST-INSERT$'(L, x)$

1   $x.next = L.nil.next$
2   $L.nil.next.prev = x$
3   $L.nil.next = x$
4   $x.prev = L.nil$

Figure 10.4 shows the effects of LIST-INSERT$'$ and LIST-DELETE$'$ on a sample list.

Sentinels rarely reduce the asymptotic time bounds of data structure operations, but they can reduce constant factors. The gain from using sentinels within loops is usually a matter of clarity of code rather than speed; the linked list code, for example, becomes simpler when we use sentinels, but we save only $O(1)$ time in the LIST-INSERT$'$ and LIST-DELETE$'$ procedures. In other situations, however, the use of sentinels helps to tighten the code in a loop, thus reducing the coefficient of, say, n or n^2 in the running time.

We should use sentinels judiciously. When there are many small lists, the extra storage used by their sentinels can represent significant wasted memory. In this book, we use sentinels only when they truly simplify the code.

Exercises

10.2-1
Can you implement the dynamic-set operation INSERT on a singly linked list in $O(1)$ time? How about DELETE?

10.2-2
Implement a stack using a singly linked list L. The operations PUSH and POP should still take $O(1)$ time.

10.2-3
Implement a queue by a singly linked list L. The operations ENQUEUE and DE-QUEUE should still take $O(1)$ time.

10.2-4
As written, each loop iteration in the LIST-SEARCH$'$ procedure requires two tests: one for $x \neq L.nil$ and one for $x.key \neq k$. Show how to eliminate the test for $x \neq L.nil$ in each iteration.

10.2-5
Implement the dictionary operations INSERT, DELETE, and SEARCH using singly linked, circular lists. What are the running times of your procedures?

10.2-6
The dynamic-set operation UNION takes two disjoint sets S_1 and S_2 as input, and
it returns a set $S = S_1 \cup S_2$ consisting of all the elements of S_1 and S_2. The
sets S_1 and S_2 are usually destroyed by the operation. Show how to support UNION
in $O(1)$ time using a suitable list data structure.

10.2-7
Give a $\Theta(n)$-time nonrecursive procedure that reverses a singly linked list of n
elements. The procedure should use no more than constant storage beyond that
needed for the list itself.

10.2-8   ★
Explain how to implement doubly linked lists using only one pointer value $x.np$ per
item instead of the usual two (*next* and *prev*). Assume that all pointer values can be
interpreted as k-bit integers, and define $x.np$ to be $x.np = x.next$ XOR $x.prev$,
the k-bit "exclusive-or" of $x.next$ and $x.prev$. (The value NIL is represented by 0.)
Be sure to describe what information you need to access the head of the list. Show
how to implement the SEARCH, INSERT, and DELETE operations on such a list.
Also show how to reverse such a list in $O(1)$ time.

10.3   Implementing pointers and objects

How do we implement pointers and objects in languages that do not provide them?
In this section, we shall see two ways of implementing linked data structures without an explicit pointer data type. We shall synthesize objects and pointers from
arrays and array indices.

A multiple-array representation of objects

We can represent a collection of objects that have the same attributes by using an
array for each attribute. As an example, Figure 10.5 shows how we can implement
the linked list of Figure 10.3(a) with three arrays. The array *key* holds the values
of the keys currently in the dynamic set, and the pointers reside in the arrays *next*
and *prev*. For a given array index x, the array entries $key[x]$, $next[x]$, and $prev[x]$
represent an object in the linked list. Under this interpretation, a pointer x is simply
a common index into the *key*, *next*, and *prev* arrays.

In Figure 10.3(a), the object with key 4 follows the object with key 16 in the
linked list. In Figure 10.5, key 4 appears in $key[2]$, and key 16 appears in $key[5]$,
and so $next[5] = 2$ and $prev[2] = 5$. Although the constant NIL appears in the *next*

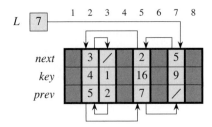

Figure 10.5 The linked list of Figure 10.3(a) represented by the arrays *key*, *next*, and *prev*. Each vertical slice of the arrays represents a single object. Stored pointers correspond to the array indices shown at the top; the arrows show how to interpret them. Lightly shaded object positions contain list elements. The variable L keeps the index of the head.

attribute of the tail and the *prev* attribute of the head, we usually use an integer (such as 0 or -1) that cannot possibly represent an actual index into the arrays. A variable L holds the index of the head of the list.

A single-array representation of objects

The words in a computer memory are typically addressed by integers from 0 to $M - 1$, where M is a suitably large integer. In many programming languages, an object occupies a contiguous set of locations in the computer memory. A pointer is simply the address of the first memory location of the object, and we can address other memory locations within the object by adding an offset to the pointer.

We can use the same strategy for implementing objects in programming environments that do not provide explicit pointer data types. For example, Figure 10.6 shows how to use a single array A to store the linked list from Figures 10.3(a) and 10.5. An object occupies a contiguous subarray $A[j .. k]$. Each attribute of the object corresponds to an offset in the range from 0 to $k - j$, and a pointer to the object is the index j. In Figure 10.6, the offsets corresponding to *key*, *next*, and *prev* are 0, 1, and 2, respectively. To read the value of $i.prev$, given a pointer i, we add the value i of the pointer to the offset 2, thus reading $A[i + 2]$.

The single-array representation is flexible in that it permits objects of different lengths to be stored in the same array. The problem of managing such a heterogeneous collection of objects is more difficult than the problem of managing a homogeneous collection, where all objects have the same attributes. Since most of the data structures we shall consider are composed of homogeneous elements, it will be sufficient for our purposes to use the multiple-array representation of objects.

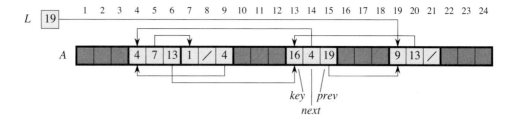

Figure 10.6   The linked list of Figures 10.3(a) and 10.5 represented in a single array A. Each list element is an object that occupies a contiguous subarray of length 3 within the array. The three attributes *key*, *next*, and *prev* correspond to the offsets 0, 1, and 2, respectively, within each object. A pointer to an object is the index of the first element of the object. Objects containing list elements are lightly shaded, and arrows show the list ordering.

Allocating and freeing objects

To insert a key into a dynamic set represented by a doubly linked list, we must allocate a pointer to a currently unused object in the linked-list representation. Thus, it is useful to manage the storage of objects not currently used in the linked-list representation so that one can be allocated. In some systems, a ***garbage collector*** is responsible for determining which objects are unused. Many applications, however, are simple enough that they can bear responsibility for returning an unused object to a storage manager. We shall now explore the problem of allocating and freeing (or deallocating) homogeneous objects using the example of a doubly linked list represented by multiple arrays.

Suppose that the arrays in the multiple-array representation have length m and that at some moment the dynamic set contains $n \leq m$ elements. Then n objects represent elements currently in the dynamic set, and the remaining $m-n$ objects are ***free***; the free objects are available to represent elements inserted into the dynamic set in the future.

We keep the free objects in a singly linked list, which we call the ***free list***. The free list uses only the *next* array, which stores the *next* pointers within the list. The head of the free list is held in the global variable *free*. When the dynamic set represented by linked list L is nonempty, the free list may be intertwined with list L, as shown in Figure 10.7. Note that each object in the representation is either in list L or in the free list, but not in both.

The free list acts like a stack: the next object allocated is the last one freed. We can use a list implementation of the stack operations PUSH and POP to implement the procedures for freeing and allocating objects, respectively. We assume that the global variable *free* used in the following procedures points to the first element of the free list.

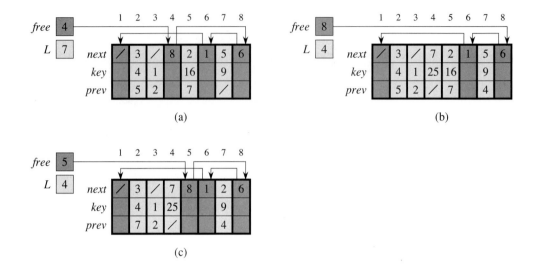

Figure 10.7 The effect of the ALLOCATE-OBJECT and FREE-OBJECT procedures. **(a)** The list of Figure 10.5 (lightly shaded) and a free list (heavily shaded). Arrows show the free-list structure. **(b)** The result of calling ALLOCATE-OBJECT() (which returns index 4), setting *key*[4] to 25, and calling LIST-INSERT(L, 4). The new free-list head is object 8, which had been *next*[4] on the free list. **(c)** After executing LIST-DELETE(L, 5), we call FREE-OBJECT(5). Object 5 becomes the new free-list head, with object 8 following it on the free list.

ALLOCATE-OBJECT()

```
1  if free == NIL
2      error "out of space"
3  else x = free
4      free = x.next
5      return x
```

FREE-OBJECT(x)

```
1  x.next = free
2  free = x
```

The free list initially contains all n unallocated objects. Once the free list has been exhausted, running the ALLOCATE-OBJECT procedure signals an error. We can even service several linked lists with just a single free list. Figure 10.8 shows two linked lists and a free list intertwined through *key*, *next*, and *prev* arrays.

The two procedures run in $O(1)$ time, which makes them quite practical. We can modify them to work for any homogeneous collection of objects by letting any one of the attributes in the object act like a *next* attribute in the free list.

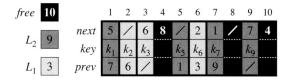

Figure 10.8 Two linked lists, L_1 (lightly shaded) and L_2 (heavily shaded), and a free list (darkened) intertwined.

Exercises

10.3-1
Draw a picture of the sequence $\langle 13, 4, 8, 19, 5, 11 \rangle$ stored as a doubly linked list using the multiple-array representation. Do the same for the single-array representation.

10.3-2
Write the procedures ALLOCATE-OBJECT and FREE-OBJECT for a homogeneous collection of objects implemented by the single-array representation.

10.3-3
Why don't we need to set or reset the *prev* attributes of objects in the implementation of the ALLOCATE-OBJECT and FREE-OBJECT procedures?

10.3-4
It is often desirable to keep all elements of a doubly linked list compact in storage, using, for example, the first m index locations in the multiple-array representation. (This is the case in a paged, virtual-memory computing environment.) Explain how to implement the procedures ALLOCATE-OBJECT and FREE-OBJECT so that the representation is compact. Assume that there are no pointers to elements of the linked list outside the list itself. (*Hint:* Use the array implementation of a stack.)

10.3-5
Let L be a doubly linked list of length n stored in arrays *key*, *prev*, and *next* of length m. Suppose that these arrays are managed by ALLOCATE-OBJECT and FREE-OBJECT procedures that keep a doubly linked free list F. Suppose further that of the m items, exactly n are on list L and $m - n$ are on the free list. Write a procedure COMPACTIFY-LIST(L, F) that, given the list L and the free list F, moves the items in L so that they occupy array positions $1, 2, \ldots, n$ and adjusts the free list F so that it remains correct, occupying array positions $n + 1, n + 2, \ldots, m$. The running time of your procedure should be $\Theta(n)$, and it should use only a constant amount of extra space. Argue that your procedure is correct.

10.4   Representing rooted trees

The methods for representing lists given in the previous section extend to any homogeneous data structure. In this section, we look specifically at the problem of representing rooted trees by linked data structures. We first look at binary trees, and then we present a method for rooted trees in which nodes can have an arbitrary number of children.

We represent each node of a tree by an object. As with linked lists, we assume that each node contains a *key* attribute. The remaining attributes of interest are pointers to other nodes, and they vary according to the type of tree.

Binary trees

Figure 10.9 shows how we use the attributes p, *left*, and *right* to store pointers to the parent, left child, and right child of each node in a binary tree T. If $x.p = \text{NIL}$, then x is the root. If node x has no left child, then $x.left = \text{NIL}$, and similarly for the right child. The root of the entire tree T is pointed to by the attribute $T.root$. If $T.root = \text{NIL}$, then the tree is empty.

Rooted trees with unbounded branching

We can extend the scheme for representing a binary tree to any class of trees in which the number of children of each node is at most some constant k: we replace the *left* and *right* attributes by $child_1, child_2, \ldots, child_k$. This scheme no longer works when the number of children of a node is unbounded, since we do not know how many attributes (arrays in the multiple-array representation) to allocate in advance. Moreover, even if the number of children k is bounded by a large constant but most nodes have a small number of children, we may waste a lot of memory.

Fortunately, there is a clever scheme to represent trees with arbitrary numbers of children. It has the advantage of using only $O(n)$ space for any n-node rooted tree. The **left-child, right-sibling representation** appears in Figure 10.10. As before, each node contains a parent pointer p, and $T.root$ points to the root of tree T. Instead of having a pointer to each of its children, however, each node x has only two pointers:

1. $x.left\text{-}child$ points to the leftmost child of node x, and

2. $x.right\text{-}sibling$ points to the sibling of x immediately to its right.

If node x has no children, then $x.left\text{-}child = \text{NIL}$, and if node x is the rightmost child of its parent, then $x.right\text{-}sibling = \text{NIL}$.

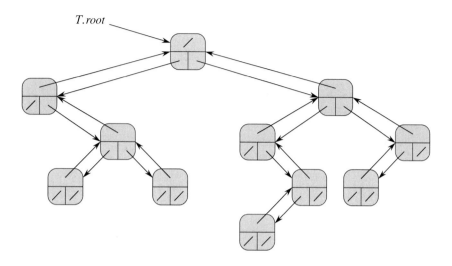

Figure 10.9   The representation of a binary tree T. Each node x has the attributes $x.p$ (top), $x.left$ (lower left), and $x.right$ (lower right). The *key* attributes are not shown.

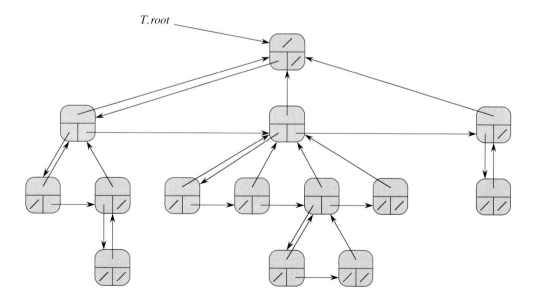

Figure 10.10   The left-child, right-sibling representation of a tree T. Each node x has attributes $x.p$ (top), $x.left$-$child$ (lower left), and $x.right$-$sibling$ (lower right). The *key* attributes are not shown.

Other tree representations

We sometimes represent rooted trees in other ways. In Chapter 6, for example, we represented a heap, which is based on a complete binary tree, by a single array plus the index of the last node in the heap. The trees that appear in Chapter 21 are traversed only toward the root, and so only the parent pointers are present; there are no pointers to children. Many other schemes are possible. Which scheme is best depends on the application.

Exercises

10.4-1
Draw the binary tree rooted at index 6 that is represented by the following attributes:

index	key	left	right
1	12	7	3
2	15	8	NIL
3	4	10	NIL
4	10	5	9
5	2	NIL	NIL
6	18	1	4
7	7	NIL	NIL
8	14	6	2
9	21	NIL	NIL
10	5	NIL	NIL

10.4-2
Write an $O(n)$-time recursive procedure that, given an n-node binary tree, prints out the key of each node in the tree.

10.4-3
Write an $O(n)$-time nonrecursive procedure that, given an n-node binary tree, prints out the key of each node in the tree. Use a stack as an auxiliary data structure.

10.4-4
Write an $O(n)$-time procedure that prints all the keys of an arbitrary rooted tree with n nodes, where the tree is stored using the left-child, right-sibling representation.

10.4-5 ★
Write an $O(n)$-time nonrecursive procedure that, given an n-node binary tree, prints out the key of each node. Use no more than constant extra space outside

of the tree itself and do not modify the tree, even temporarily, during the procedure.

10.4-6 ★

The left-child, right-sibling representation of an arbitrary rooted tree uses three pointers in each node: *left-child*, *right-sibling*, and *parent*. From any node, its parent can be reached and identified in constant time and all its children can be reached and identified in time linear in the number of children. Show how to use only two pointers and one boolean value in each node so that the parent of a node or all of its children can be reached and identified in time linear in the number of children.

Problems

10-1 *Comparisons among lists*

For each of the four types of lists in the following table, what is the asymptotic worst-case running time for each dynamic-set operation listed?

	unsorted, singly linked	sorted, singly linked	unsorted, doubly linked	sorted, doubly linked
SEARCH(L, k)				
INSERT(L, x)				
DELETE(L, x)				
SUCCESSOR(L, x)				
PREDECESSOR(L, x)				
MINIMUM(L)				
MAXIMUM(L)				

10-2   *Mergeable heaps using linked lists*

A ***mergeable heap*** supports the following operations: MAKE-HEAP (which creates an empty mergeable heap), INSERT, MINIMUM, EXTRACT-MIN, and UNION.[1] Show how to implement mergeable heaps using linked lists in each of the following cases. Try to make each operation as efficient as possible. Analyze the running time of each operation in terms of the size of the dynamic set(s) being operated on.

a. Lists are sorted.

b. Lists are unsorted.

c. Lists are unsorted, and dynamic sets to be merged are disjoint.

10-3   *Searching a sorted compact list*

Exercise 10.3-4 asked how we might maintain an n-element list compactly in the first n positions of an array. We shall assume that all keys are distinct and that the compact list is also sorted, that is, $key[i] < key[next[i]]$ for all $i = 1, 2, \ldots, n$ such that $next[i] \neq$ NIL. We will also assume that we have a variable L that contains the index of the first element on the list. Under these assumptions, you will show that we can use the following randomized algorithm to search the list in $O(\sqrt{n})$ expected time.

COMPACT-LIST-SEARCH(L, n, k)

```
1   i = L
2   while i ≠ NIL and key[i] < k
3        j = RANDOM(1, n)
4        if key[i] < key[j] and key[j] ≤ k
5             i = j
6             if key[i] == k
7                  return i
8        i = next[i]
9   if i == NIL or key[i] > k
10       return NIL
11  else return i
```

If we ignore lines 3–7 of the procedure, we have an ordinary algorithm for searching a sorted linked list, in which index i points to each position of the list in

---

[1]Because we have defined a mergeable heap to support MINIMUM and EXTRACT-MIN, we can also refer to it as a ***mergeable min-heap***. Alternatively, if it supported MAXIMUM and EXTRACT-MAX, it would be a ***mergeable max-heap***.

turn. The search terminates once the index i "falls off" the end of the list or once $key[i] \geq k$. In the latter case, if $key[i] = k$, clearly we have found a key with the value k. If, however, $key[i] > k$, then we will never find a key with the value k, and so terminating the search was the right thing to do.

Lines 3–7 attempt to skip ahead to a randomly chosen position j. Such a skip benefits us if $key[j]$ is larger than $key[i]$ and no larger than k; in such a case, j marks a position in the list that i would have to reach during an ordinary list search. Because the list is compact, we know that any choice of j between 1 and n indexes some object in the list rather than a slot on the free list.

Instead of analyzing the performance of COMPACT-LIST-SEARCH directly, we shall analyze a related algorithm, COMPACT-LIST-SEARCH', which executes two separate loops. This algorithm takes an additional parameter t which determines an upper bound on the number of iterations of the first loop.

COMPACT-LIST-SEARCH'(L, n, k, t)

```
 1  i = L
 2  for q = 1 to t
 3      j = RANDOM(1, n)
 4      if key[i] < key[j] and key[j] ≤ k
 5          i = j
 6          if key[i] == k
 7              return i
 8  while i ≠ NIL and key[i] < k
 9      i = next[i]
10  if i == NIL or key[i] > k
11      return NIL
12  else return i
```

To compare the execution of the algorithms COMPACT-LIST-SEARCH(L, n, k) and COMPACT-LIST-SEARCH'(L, n, k, t), assume that the sequence of integers returned by the calls of RANDOM$(1, n)$ is the same for both algorithms.

a. Suppose that COMPACT-LIST-SEARCH(L, n, k) takes t iterations of the **while** loop of lines 2–8. Argue that COMPACT-LIST-SEARCH'(L, n, k, t) returns the same answer and that the total number of iterations of both the **for** and **while** loops within COMPACT-LIST-SEARCH' is at least t.

In the call COMPACT-LIST-SEARCH'(L, n, k, t), let X_t be the random variable that describes the distance in the linked list (that is, through the chain of *next* pointers) from position i to the desired key k after t iterations of the **for** loop of lines 2–7 have occurred.

b. Argue that the expected running time of COMPACT-LIST-SEARCH$'(L, n, k, t)$ is $O(t + \mathrm{E}[X_t])$.

c. Show that $\mathrm{E}[X_t] \leq \sum_{r=1}^{n}(1 - r/n)^t$. (*Hint:* Use equation (C.25).)

d. Show that $\sum_{r=0}^{n-1} r^t \leq n^{t+1}/(t + 1)$.

e. Prove that $\mathrm{E}[X_t] \leq n/(t + 1)$.

f. Show that COMPACT-LIST-SEARCH$'(L, n, k, t)$ runs in $O(t + n/t)$ expected time.

g. Conclude that COMPACT-LIST-SEARCH runs in $O(\sqrt{n})$ expected time.

h. Why do we assume that all keys are distinct in COMPACT-LIST-SEARCH? Argue that random skips do not necessarily help asymptotically when the list contains repeated key values.

Chapter notes

Aho, Hopcroft, and Ullman [6] and Knuth [209] are excellent references for elementary data structures. Many other texts cover both basic data structures and their implementation in a particular programming language. Examples of these types of textbooks include Goodrich and Tamassia [147], Main [241], Shaffer [311], and Weiss [352, 353, 354]. Gonnet [145] provides experimental data on the performance of many data-structure operations.

The origin of stacks and queues as data structures in computer science is unclear, since corresponding notions already existed in mathematics and paper-based business practices before the introduction of digital computers. Knuth [209] cites A. M. Turing for the development of stacks for subroutine linkage in 1947.

Pointer-based data structures also seem to be a folk invention. According to Knuth, pointers were apparently used in early computers with drum memories. The A-1 language developed by G. M. Hopper in 1951 represented algebraic formulas as binary trees. Knuth credits the IPL-II language, developed in 1956 by A. Newell, J. C. Shaw, and H. A. Simon, for recognizing the importance and promoting the use of pointers. Their IPL-III language, developed in 1957, included explicit stack operations.

11 Hash Tables

Many applications require a dynamic set that supports only the dictionary operations INSERT, SEARCH, and DELETE. For example, a compiler that translates a programming language maintains a symbol table, in which the keys of elements are arbitrary character strings corresponding to identifiers in the language. A hash table is an effective data structure for implementing dictionaries. Although searching for an element in a hash table can take as long as searching for an element in a linked list— $\Theta(n)$ time in the worst case—in practice, hashing performs extremely well. Under reasonable assumptions, the average time to search for an element in a hash table is $O(1)$.

A hash table generalizes the simpler notion of an ordinary array. Directly addressing into an ordinary array makes effective use of our ability to examine an arbitrary position in an array in $O(1)$ time. Section 11.1 discusses direct addressing in more detail. We can take advantage of direct addressing when we can afford to allocate an array that has one position for every possible key.

When the number of keys actually stored is small relative to the total number of possible keys, hash tables become an effective alternative to directly addressing an array, since a hash table typically uses an array of size proportional to the number of keys actually stored. Instead of using the key as an array index directly, the array index is *computed* from the key. Section 11.2 presents the main ideas, focusing on "chaining" as a way to handle "collisions," in which more than one key maps to the same array index. Section 11.3 describes how we can compute array indices from keys using hash functions. We present and analyze several variations on the basic theme. Section 11.4 looks at "open addressing," which is another way to deal with collisions. The bottom line is that hashing is an extremely effective and practical technique: the basic dictionary operations require only $O(1)$ time on the average. Section 11.5 explains how "perfect hashing" can support searches in $O(1)$ *worst-case* time, when the set of keys being stored is static (that is, when the set of keys never changes once stored).

11.1   Direct-address tables

Direct addressing is a simple technique that works well when the universe U of keys is reasonably small. Suppose that an application needs a dynamic set in which each element has a key drawn from the universe $U = \{0, 1, \ldots, m - 1\}$, where m is not too large. We shall assume that no two elements have the same key.

To represent the dynamic set, we use an array, or ***direct-address table***, denoted by $T[0 \mathinner{\ldotp\ldotp} m - 1]$, in which each position, or ***slot***, corresponds to a key in the universe U. Figure 11.1 illustrates the approach; slot k points to an element in the set with key k. If the set contains no element with key k, then $T[k] = \text{NIL}$.

The dictionary operations are trivial to implement:

DIRECT-ADDRESS-SEARCH(T, k)

1   **return** $T[k]$

DIRECT-ADDRESS-INSERT(T, x)

1   $T[x.key] = x$

DIRECT-ADDRESS-DELETE(T, x)

1   $T[x.key] = \text{NIL}$

Each of these operations takes only $O(1)$ time.

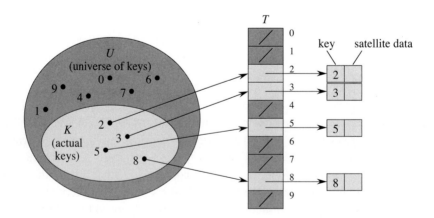

Figure 11.1   How to implement a dynamic set by a direct-address table T. Each key in the universe $U = \{0, 1, \ldots, 9\}$ corresponds to an index in the table. The set $K = \{2, 3, 5, 8\}$ of actual keys determines the slots in the table that contain pointers to elements. The other slots, heavily shaded, contain NIL.

For some applications, the direct-address table itself can hold the elements in the dynamic set. That is, rather than storing an element's key and satellite data in an object external to the direct-address table, with a pointer from a slot in the table to the object, we can store the object in the slot itself, thus saving space. We would use a special key within an object to indicate an empty slot. Moreover, it is often unnecessary to store the key of the object, since if we have the index of an object in the table, we have its key. If keys are not stored, however, we must have some way to tell whether the slot is empty.

Exercises

11.1-1
Suppose that a dynamic set S is represented by a direct-address table T of length m. Describe a procedure that finds the maximum element of S. What is the worst-case performance of your procedure?

11.1-2
A ***bit vector*** is simply an array of bits (0s and 1s). A bit vector of length m takes much less space than an array of m pointers. Describe how to use a bit vector to represent a dynamic set of distinct elements with no satellite data. Dictionary operations should run in $O(1)$ time.

11.1-3
Suggest how to implement a direct-address table in which the keys of stored elements do not need to be distinct and the elements can have satellite data. All three dictionary operations (INSERT, DELETE, and SEARCH) should run in $O(1)$ time. (Don't forget that DELETE takes as an argument a pointer to an object to be deleted, not a key.)

11.1-4   ★
We wish to implement a dictionary by using direct addressing on a *huge* array. At the start, the array entries may contain garbage, and initializing the entire array is impractical because of its size. Describe a scheme for implementing a direct-address dictionary on a huge array. Each stored object should use $O(1)$ space; the operations SEARCH, INSERT, and DELETE should take $O(1)$ time each; and initializing the data structure should take $O(1)$ time. (*Hint:* Use an additional array, treated somewhat like a stack whose size is the number of keys actually stored in the dictionary, to help determine whether a given entry in the huge array is valid or not.)

11.2   Hash tables

The downside of direct addressing is obvious: if the universe U is large, storing a table T of size $|U|$ may be impractical, or even impossible, given the memory available on a typical computer. Furthermore, the set K of keys *actually stored* may be so small relative to U that most of the space allocated for T would be wasted.

When the set K of keys stored in a dictionary is much smaller than the universe U of all possible keys, a hash table requires much less storage than a direct-address table. Specifically, we can reduce the storage requirement to $\Theta(|K|)$ while we maintain the benefit that searching for an element in the hash table still requires only $O(1)$ time. The catch is that this bound is for the *average-case time*, whereas for direct addressing it holds for the *worst-case time*.

With direct addressing, an element with key k is stored in slot k. With hashing, this element is stored in slot $h(k)$; that is, we use a **hash function** h to compute the slot from the key k. Here, h maps the universe U of keys into the slots of a **hash table** $T[0 \,.\,.\, m-1]$:

$$h : U \to \{0, 1, \ldots, m-1\} \;,$$

where the size m of the hash table is typically much less than $|U|$. We say that an element with key k **hashes** to slot $h(k)$; we also say that $h(k)$ is the **hash value** of key k. Figure 11.2 illustrates the basic idea. The hash function reduces the range of array indices and hence the size of the array. Instead of a size of $|U|$, the array can have size m.

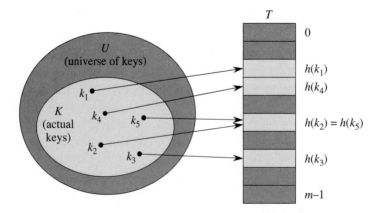

Figure 11.2   Using a hash function h to map keys to hash-table slots. Because keys k_2 and k_5 map to the same slot, they collide.

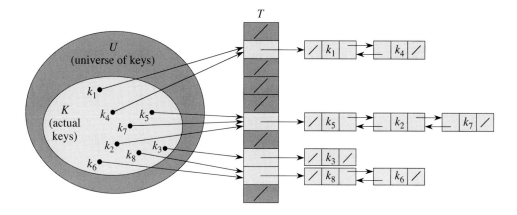

Figure 11.3 Collision resolution by chaining. Each hash-table slot $T[j]$ contains a linked list of all the keys whose hash value is j. For example, $h(k_1) = h(k_4)$ and $h(k_5) = h(k_7) = h(k_2)$. The linked list can be either singly or doubly linked; we show it as doubly linked because deletion is faster that way.

There is one hitch: two keys may hash to the same slot. We call this situation a ***collision***. Fortunately, we have effective techniques for resolving the conflict created by collisions.

Of course, the ideal solution would be to avoid collisions altogether. We might try to achieve this goal by choosing a suitable hash function h. One idea is to make h appear to be "random," thus avoiding collisions or at least minimizing their number. The very term "to hash," evoking images of random mixing and chopping, captures the spirit of this approach. (Of course, a hash function h must be deterministic in that a given input k should always produce the same output $h(k)$.) Because $|U| > m$, however, there must be at least two keys that have the same hash value; avoiding collisions altogether is therefore impossible. Thus, while a well-designed, "random"-looking hash function can minimize the number of collisions, we still need a method for resolving the collisions that do occur.

The remainder of this section presents the simplest collision resolution technique, called chaining. Section 11.4 introduces an alternative method for resolving collisions, called open addressing.

Collision resolution by chaining

In ***chaining***, we place all the elements that hash to the same slot into the same linked list, as Figure 11.3 shows. Slot j contains a pointer to the head of the list of all stored elements that hash to j; if there are no such elements, slot j contains NIL.

The dictionary operations on a hash table T are easy to implement when collisions are resolved by chaining:

CHAINED-HASH-INSERT(T, x)

1   insert x at the head of list $T[h(x.key)]$

CHAINED-HASH-SEARCH(T, k)

1   search for an element with key k in list $T[h(k)]$

CHAINED-HASH-DELETE(T, x)

1   delete x from the list $T[h(x.key)]$

The worst-case running time for insertion is $O(1)$. The insertion procedure is fast in part because it assumes that the element x being inserted is not already present in the table; if necessary, we can check this assumption (at additional cost) by searching for an element whose key is $x.key$ before we insert. For searching, the worst-case running time is proportional to the length of the list; we shall analyze this operation more closely below. We can delete an element in $O(1)$ time if the lists are doubly linked, as Figure 11.3 depicts. (Note that CHAINED-HASH-DELETE takes as input an element x and not its key k, so that we don't have to search for x first. If the hash table supports deletion, then its linked lists should be doubly linked so that we can delete an item quickly. If the lists were only singly linked, then to delete element x, we would first have to find x in the list $T[h(x.key)]$ so that we could update the *next* attribute of x's predecessor. With singly linked lists, both deletion and searching would have the same asymptotic running times.)

Analysis of hashing with chaining

How well does hashing with chaining perform? In particular, how long does it take to search for an element with a given key?

Given a hash table T with m slots that stores n elements, we define the **load factor** α for T as n/m, that is, the average number of elements stored in a chain. Our analysis will be in terms of α, which can be less than, equal to, or greater than 1.

The worst-case behavior of hashing with chaining is terrible: all n keys hash to the same slot, creating a list of length n. The worst-case time for searching is thus $\Theta(n)$ plus the time to compute the hash function—no better than if we used one linked list for all the elements. Clearly, we do not use hash tables for their worst-case performance. (Perfect hashing, described in Section 11.5, does provide good worst-case performance when the set of keys is static, however.)

The average-case performance of hashing depends on how well the hash function h distributes the set of keys to be stored among the m slots, on the average.

Section 11.3 discusses these issues, but for now we shall assume that any given element is equally likely to hash into any of the m slots, independently of where any other element has hashed to. We call this the assumption of ***simple uniform hashing***.

For $j = 0, 1, \ldots, m - 1$, let us denote the length of the list $T[j]$ by n_j, so that

$$n = n_0 + n_1 + \cdots + n_{m-1} \,, \tag{11.1}$$

and the expected value of n_j is $\mathrm{E}[n_j] = \alpha = n/m$.

We assume that $O(1)$ time suffices to compute the hash value $h(k)$, so that the time required to search for an element with key k depends linearly on the length $n_{h(k)}$ of the list $T[h(k)]$. Setting aside the $O(1)$ time required to compute the hash function and to access slot $h(k)$, let us consider the expected number of elements examined by the search algorithm, that is, the number of elements in the list $T[h(k)]$ that the algorithm checks to see whether any have a key equal to k. We shall consider two cases. In the first, the search is unsuccessful: no element in the table has key k. In the second, the search successfully finds an element with key k.

Theorem 11.1
In a hash table in which collisions are resolved by chaining, an unsuccessful search takes average-case time $\Theta(1+\alpha)$, under the assumption of simple uniform hashing.

Proof   Under the assumption of simple uniform hashing, any key k not already stored in the table is equally likely to hash to any of the m slots. The expected time to search unsuccessfully for a key k is the expected time to search to the end of list $T[h(k)]$, which has expected length $\mathrm{E}[n_{h(k)}] = \alpha$. Thus, the expected number of elements examined in an unsuccessful search is α, and the total time required (including the time for computing $h(k)$) is $\Theta(1 + \alpha)$.   ∎

The situation for a successful search is slightly different, since each list is not equally likely to be searched. Instead, the probability that a list is searched is proportional to the number of elements it contains. Nonetheless, the expected search time still turns out to be $\Theta(1 + \alpha)$.

Theorem 11.2
In a hash table in which collisions are resolved by chaining, a successful search takes average-case time $\Theta(1+\alpha)$, under the assumption of simple uniform hashing.

Proof   We assume that the element being searched for is equally likely to be any of the n elements stored in the table. The number of elements examined during a successful search for an element x is one more than the number of elements that appear before x in x's list. Because new elements are placed at the front of the list, elements before x in the list were all inserted after x was inserted. To find the expected number of elements examined, we take the average, over the n elements x in the table, of 1 plus the expected number of elements added to x's list after x was added to the list. Let x_i denote the ith element inserted into the table, for $i = 1, 2, \ldots, n$, and let $k_i = x_i.key$. For keys k_i and k_j, we define the indicator random variable $X_{ij} = I\{h(k_i) = h(k_j)\}$. Under the assumption of simple uniform hashing, we have $\Pr\{h(k_i) = h(k_j)\} = 1/m$, and so by Lemma 5.1, $E[X_{ij}] = 1/m$. Thus, the expected number of elements examined in a successful search is

$$
\begin{aligned}
E\left[\frac{1}{n}\sum_{i=1}^{n}\left(1 + \sum_{j=i+1}^{n} X_{ij}\right)\right] & \\
&= \frac{1}{n}\sum_{i=1}^{n}\left(1 + \sum_{j=i+1}^{n} E[X_{ij}]\right) \quad \text{(by linearity of expectation)} \\
&= \frac{1}{n}\sum_{i=1}^{n}\left(1 + \sum_{j=i+1}^{n} \frac{1}{m}\right) \\
&= 1 + \frac{1}{nm}\sum_{i=1}^{n}(n - i) \\
&= 1 + \frac{1}{nm}\left(\sum_{i=1}^{n} n - \sum_{i=1}^{n} i\right) \\
&= 1 + \frac{1}{nm}\left(n^2 - \frac{n(n+1)}{2}\right) \quad \text{(by equation (A.1))} \\
&= 1 + \frac{n - 1}{2m} \\
&= 1 + \frac{\alpha}{2} - \frac{\alpha}{2n} \; .
\end{aligned}
$$

Thus, the total time required for a successful search (including the time for computing the hash function) is $\Theta(2 + \alpha/2 - \alpha/2n) = \Theta(1 + \alpha)$. ∎

What does this analysis mean? If the number of hash-table slots is at least proportional to the number of elements in the table, we have $n = O(m)$ and, consequently, $\alpha = n/m = O(m)/m = O(1)$. Thus, searching takes constant time on average. Since insertion takes $O(1)$ worst-case time and deletion takes $O(1)$ worst-case time when the lists are doubly linked, we can support all dictionary operations in $O(1)$ time on average.

Exercises

11.2-1
Suppose we use a hash function h to hash n distinct keys into an array T of length m. Assuming simple uniform hashing, what is the expected number of collisions? More precisely, what is the expected cardinality of $\{\{k,l\} : k \neq l$ and $h(k) = h(l)\}$?

11.2-2
Demonstrate what happens when we insert the keys $5, 28, 19, 15, 20, 33, 12, 17, 10$ into a hash table with collisions resolved by chaining. Let the table have 9 slots, and let the hash function be $h(k) = k \bmod 9$.

11.2-3
Professor Marley hypothesizes that he can obtain substantial performance gains by modifying the chaining scheme to keep each list in sorted order. How does the professor's modification affect the running time for successful searches, unsuccessful searches, insertions, and deletions?

11.2-4
Suggest how to allocate and deallocate storage for elements within the hash table itself by linking all unused slots into a free list. Assume that one slot can store a flag and either one element plus a pointer or two pointers. All dictionary and free-list operations should run in $O(1)$ expected time. Does the free list need to be doubly linked, or does a singly linked free list suffice?

11.2-5
Suppose that we are storing a set of n keys into a hash table of size m. Show that if the keys are drawn from a universe U with $|U| > nm$, then U has a subset of size n consisting of keys that all hash to the same slot, so that the worst-case searching time for hashing with chaining is $\Theta(n)$.

11.2-6
Suppose we have stored n keys in a hash table of size m, with collisions resolved by chaining, and that we know the length of each chain, including the length L of the longest chain. Describe a procedure that selects a key uniformly at random from among the keys in the hash table and returns it in expected time $O(L \cdot (1 + 1/\alpha))$.

11.3   Hash functions

In this section, we discuss some issues regarding the design of good hash functions and then present three schemes for their creation. Two of the schemes, hashing by division and hashing by multiplication, are heuristic in nature, whereas the third scheme, universal hashing, uses randomization to provide provably good performance.

What makes a good hash function?

A good hash function satisfies (approximately) the assumption of simple uniform hashing: each key is equally likely to hash to any of the m slots, independently of where any other key has hashed to. Unfortunately, we typically have no way to check this condition, since we rarely know the probability distribution from which the keys are drawn. Moreover, the keys might not be drawn independently.

Occasionally we do know the distribution. For example, if we know that the keys are random real numbers k independently and uniformly distributed in the range $0 \le k < 1$, then the hash function

$$h(k) = \lfloor km \rfloor$$

satisfies the condition of simple uniform hashing.

In practice, we can often employ heuristic techniques to create a hash function that performs well. Qualitative information about the distribution of keys may be useful in this design process. For example, consider a compiler's symbol table, in which the keys are character strings representing identifiers in a program. Closely related symbols, such as `pt` and `pts`, often occur in the same program. A good hash function would minimize the chance that such variants hash to the same slot.

A good approach derives the hash value in a way that we expect to be independent of any patterns that might exist in the data. For example, the "division method" (discussed in Section 11.3.1) computes the hash value as the remainder when the key is divided by a specified prime number. This method frequently gives good results, assuming that we choose a prime number that is unrelated to any patterns in the distribution of keys.

Finally, we note that some applications of hash functions might require stronger properties than are provided by simple uniform hashing. For example, we might want keys that are "close" in some sense to yield hash values that are far apart. (This property is especially desirable when we are using linear probing, defined in Section 11.4.) Universal hashing, described in Section 11.3.3, often provides the desired properties.

Interpreting keys as natural numbers

Most hash functions assume that the universe of keys is the set $\mathbb{N} = \{0, 1, 2, \ldots\}$ of natural numbers. Thus, if the keys are not natural numbers, we find a way to interpret them as natural numbers. For example, we can interpret a character string as an integer expressed in suitable radix notation. Thus, we might interpret the identifier pt as the pair of decimal integers $(112, 116)$, since $\mathtt{p} = 112$ and $\mathtt{t} = 116$ in the ASCII character set; then, expressed as a radix-128 integer, pt becomes $(112 \cdot 128) + 116 = 14452$. In the context of a given application, we can usually devise some such method for interpreting each key as a (possibly large) natural number. In what follows, we assume that the keys are natural numbers.

11.3.1 The division method

In the ***division method*** for creating hash functions, we map a key k into one of m slots by taking the remainder of k divided by m. That is, the hash function is

$$h(k) = k \bmod m \ .$$

For example, if the hash table has size $m = 12$ and the key is $k = 100$, then $h(k) = 4$. Since it requires only a single division operation, hashing by division is quite fast.

When using the division method, we usually avoid certain values of m. For example, m should not be a power of 2, since if $m = 2^p$, then $h(k)$ is just the p lowest-order bits of k. Unless we know that all low-order p-bit patterns are equally likely, we are better off designing the hash function to depend on all the bits of the key. As Exercise 11.3-3 asks you to show, choosing $m = 2^p - 1$ when k is a character string interpreted in radix 2^p may be a poor choice, because permuting the characters of k does not change its hash value.

A prime not too close to an exact power of 2 is often a good choice for m. For example, suppose we wish to allocate a hash table, with collisions resolved by chaining, to hold roughly $n = 2000$ character strings, where a character has 8 bits. We don't mind examining an average of 3 elements in an unsuccessful search, and so we allocate a hash table of size $m = 701$. We could choose $m = 701$ because it is a prime near $2000/3$ but not near any power of 2. Treating each key k as an integer, our hash function would be

$$h(k) = k \bmod 701 \ .$$

11.3.2 The multiplication method

The ***multiplication method*** for creating hash functions operates in two steps. First, we multiply the key k by a constant A in the range $0 < A < 1$ and extract the

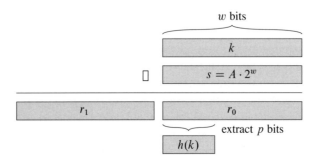

Figure 11.4 The multiplication method of hashing. The w-bit representation of the key k is multiplied by the w-bit value $s = A \cdot 2^w$. The p highest-order bits of the lower w-bit half of the product form the desired hash value $h(k)$.

fractional part of kA. Then, we multiply this value by m and take the floor of the result. In short, the hash function is

$$h(k) = \lfloor m \, (kA \bmod 1) \rfloor \ ,$$

where "$kA \bmod 1$" means the fractional part of kA, that is, $kA - \lfloor kA \rfloor$.

An advantage of the multiplication method is that the value of m is not critical. We typically choose it to be a power of 2 ($m = 2^p$ for some integer p), since we can then easily implement the function on most computers as follows. Suppose that the word size of the machine is w bits and that k fits into a single word. We restrict A to be a fraction of the form $s/2^w$, where s is an integer in the range $0 < s < 2^w$. Referring to Figure 11.4, we first multiply k by the w-bit integer $s = A \cdot 2^w$. The result is a $2w$-bit value $r_1 2^w + r_0$, where r_1 is the high-order word of the product and r_0 is the low-order word of the product. The desired p-bit hash value consists of the p most significant bits of r_0.

Although this method works with any value of the constant A, it works better with some values than with others. The optimal choice depends on the characteristics of the data being hashed. Knuth [211] suggests that

$$A \approx (\sqrt{5} - 1)/2 = 0.6180339887\ldots \tag{11.2}$$

is likely to work reasonably well.

As an example, suppose we have $k = 123456$, $p = 14$, $m = 2^{14} = 16384$, and $w = 32$. Adapting Knuth's suggestion, we choose A to be the fraction of the form $s/2^{32}$ that is closest to $(\sqrt{5} - 1)/2$, so that $A = 2654435769/2^{32}$. Then $k \cdot s = 327706022297664 = (76300 \cdot 2^{32}) + 17612864$, and so $r_1 = 76300$ and $r_0 = 17612864$. The 14 most significant bits of r_0 yield the value $h(k) = 67$.

★   **11.3.3   Universal hashing**

If a malicious adversary chooses the keys to be hashed by some fixed hash function, then the adversary can choose n keys that all hash to the same slot, yielding an average retrieval time of $\Theta(n)$. Any fixed hash function is vulnerable to such terrible worst-case behavior; the only effective way to improve the situation is to choose the hash function *randomly* in a way that is *independent* of the keys that are actually going to be stored. This approach, called ***universal hashing***, can yield provably good performance on average, no matter which keys the adversary chooses.

In universal hashing, at the beginning of execution we select the hash function at random from a carefully designed class of functions. As in the case of quicksort, randomization guarantees that no single input will always evoke worst-case behavior. Because we randomly select the hash function, the algorithm can behave differently on each execution, even for the same input, guaranteeing good average-case performance for any input. Returning to the example of a compiler's symbol table, we find that the programmer's choice of identifiers cannot now cause consistently poor hashing performance. Poor performance occurs only when the compiler chooses a random hash function that causes the set of identifiers to hash poorly, but the probability of this situation occurring is small and is the same for any set of identifiers of the same size.

Let $\mathcal{H}$ be a finite collection of hash functions that map a given universe U of keys into the range $\{0, 1, \ldots, m - 1\}$. Such a collection is said to be ***universal*** if for each pair of distinct keys $k, l \in U$, the number of hash functions $h \in \mathcal{H}$ for which $h(k) = h(l)$ is at most $|\mathcal{H}|/m$. In other words, with a hash function randomly chosen from $\mathcal{H}$, the chance of a collision between distinct keys k and l is no more than the chance $1/m$ of a collision if $h(k)$ and $h(l)$ were randomly and independently chosen from the set $\{0, 1, \ldots, m - 1\}$.

The following theorem shows that a universal class of hash functions gives good average-case behavior. Recall that n_i denotes the length of list $T[i]$.

Theorem 11.3
Suppose that a hash function h is chosen randomly from a universal collection of hash functions and has been used to hash n keys into a table T of size m, using chaining to resolve collisions. If key k is not in the table, then the expected length $\mathrm{E}\left[n_{h(k)}\right]$ of the list that key k hashes to is at most the load factor $\alpha = n/m$. If key k is in the table, then the expected length $\mathrm{E}\left[n_{h(k)}\right]$ of the list containing key k is at most $1 + \alpha$.

Proof   We note that the expectations here are over the choice of the hash function and do not depend on any assumptions about the distribution of the keys. For each pair k and l of distinct keys, define the indicator random variable

$X_{kl} = I\{h(k) = h(l)\}$. Since by the definition of a universal collection of hash functions, a single pair of keys collides with probability at most $1/m$, we have $\Pr\{h(k) = h(l)\} \leq 1/m$. By Lemma 5.1, therefore, we have $E[X_{kl}] \leq 1/m$.

Next we define, for each key k, the random variable Y_k that equals the number of keys other than k that hash to the same slot as k, so that

$$Y_k = \sum_{\substack{l \in T \\ l \neq k}} X_{kl} .$$

Thus we have

$$
\begin{aligned}
E[Y_k] &= E\left[\sum_{\substack{l \in T \\ l \neq k}} X_{kl}\right] \\
&= \sum_{\substack{l \in T \\ l \neq k}} E[X_{kl}] \quad \text{(by linearity of expectation)} \\
&\leq \sum_{\substack{l \in T \\ l \neq k}} \frac{1}{m} .
\end{aligned}
$$

The remainder of the proof depends on whether key k is in table T.

- If $k \notin T$, then $n_{h(k)} = Y_k$ and $|\{l : l \in T \text{ and } l \neq k\}| = n$. Thus $E[n_{h(k)}] = E[Y_k] \leq n/m = \alpha$.

- If $k \in T$, then because key k appears in list $T[h(k)]$ and the count Y_k does not include key k, we have $n_{h(k)} = Y_k + 1$ and $|\{l : l \in T \text{ and } l \neq k\}| = n - 1$. Thus $E[n_{h(k)}] = E[Y_k] + 1 \leq (n-1)/m + 1 = 1 + \alpha - 1/m < 1 + \alpha$. ∎

The following corollary says universal hashing provides the desired payoff: it has now become impossible for an adversary to pick a sequence of operations that forces the worst-case running time. By cleverly randomizing the choice of hash function at run time, we guarantee that we can process every sequence of operations with a good average-case running time.

Corollary 11.4
Using universal hashing and collision resolution by chaining in an initially empty table with m slots, it takes expected time $\Theta(n)$ to handle any sequence of n INSERT, SEARCH, and DELETE operations containing $O(m)$ INSERT operations.

Proof Since the number of insertions is $O(m)$, we have $n = O(m)$ and so $\alpha = O(1)$. The INSERT and DELETE operations take constant time and, by Theorem 11.3, the expected time for each SEARCH operation is $O(1)$. By linearity of expectation, therefore, the expected time for the entire sequence of n operations is $O(n)$. Since each operation takes $\Omega(1)$ time, the $\Theta(n)$ bound follows.   ∎

Designing a universal class of hash functions

It is quite easy to design a universal class of hash functions, as a little number theory will help us prove. You may wish to consult Chapter 31 first if you are unfamiliar with number theory.

We begin by choosing a prime number p large enough so that every possible key k is in the range 0 to $p - 1$, inclusive. Let $\mathbb{Z}_p$ denote the set $\{0, 1, \ldots, p - 1\}$, and let $\mathbb{Z}_p^*$ denote the set $\{1, 2, \ldots, p - 1\}$. Since p is prime, we can solve equations modulo p with the methods given in Chapter 31. Because we assume that the size of the universe of keys is greater than the number of slots in the hash table, we have $p > m$.

We now define the hash function h_{ab} for any $a \in \mathbb{Z}_p^*$ and any $b \in \mathbb{Z}_p$ using a linear transformation followed by reductions modulo p and then modulo m:

$$h_{ab}(k) = ((ak + b) \bmod p) \bmod m . \tag{11.3}$$

For example, with $p = 17$ and $m = 6$, we have $h_{3,4}(8) = 5$. The family of all such hash functions is

$$\mathcal{H}_{pm} = \{h_{ab} : a \in \mathbb{Z}_p^* \text{ and } b \in \mathbb{Z}_p\} . \tag{11.4}$$

Each hash function h_{ab} maps $\mathbb{Z}_p$ to $\mathbb{Z}_m$. This class of hash functions has the nice property that the size m of the output range is arbitrary—not necessarily prime—a feature which we shall use in Section 11.5. Since we have $p - 1$ choices for a and p choices for b, the collection $\mathcal{H}_{pm}$ contains $p(p - 1)$ hash functions.

Theorem 11.5
The class $\mathcal{H}_{pm}$ of hash functions defined by equations (11.3) and (11.4) is universal.

Proof   Consider two distinct keys k and l from $\mathbb{Z}_p$, so that $k \neq l$. For a given hash function h_{ab} we let

$$r = (ak + b) \bmod p ,$$
$$s = (al + b) \bmod p .$$

We first note that $r \neq s$. Why? Observe that

$$r - s \equiv a(k - l) \pmod{p} .$$

It follows that $r \neq s$ because p is prime and both a and $(k - l)$ are nonzero modulo p, and so their product must also be nonzero modulo p by Theorem 31.6. Therefore, when computing any $h_{ab} \in \mathcal{H}_{pm}$, distinct inputs k and l map to distinct values r and s modulo p; there are no collisions yet at the "mod p level." Moreover, each of the possible $p(p-1)$ choices for the pair (a,b) with $a \neq 0$ yields a *different* resulting pair (r,s) with $r \neq s$, since we can solve for a and b given r and s:

$$a = \left((r-s)((k-l)^{-1} \bmod p)\right) \bmod p\ ,$$
$$b = (r-ak) \bmod p\ ,$$

where $((k-l)^{-1} \bmod p)$ denotes the unique multiplicative inverse, modulo p, of $k-l$. Since there are only $p(p-1)$ possible pairs (r,s) with $r \neq s$, there is a one-to-one correspondence between pairs (a,b) with $a \neq 0$ and pairs (r,s) with $r \neq s$. Thus, for any given pair of inputs k and l, if we pick (a,b) uniformly at random from $\mathbb{Z}_p^* \times \mathbb{Z}_p$, the resulting pair (r,s) is equally likely to be any pair of distinct values modulo p.

Therefore, the probability that distinct keys k and l collide is equal to the probability that $r \equiv s \pmod{m}$ when r and s are randomly chosen as distinct values modulo p. For a given value of r, of the $p-1$ possible remaining values for s, the number of values s such that $s \neq r$ and $s \equiv r \pmod{m}$ is at most

$$\lceil p/m \rceil - 1 \leq ((p+m-1)/m) - 1 \quad \text{(by inequality (3.6))}$$
$$= (p-1)/m\ .$$

The probability that s collides with r when reduced modulo m is at most $((p-1)/m)/(p-1) = 1/m$.

Therefore, for any pair of distinct values $k, l \in \mathbb{Z}_p$,

$$\Pr\{h_{ab}(k) = h_{ab}(l)\} \leq 1/m\ ,$$

so that $\mathcal{H}_{pm}$ is indeed universal. ∎

Exercises

11.3-1
Suppose we wish to search a linked list of length n, where each element contains a key k along with a hash value $h(k)$. Each key is a long character string. How might we take advantage of the hash values when searching the list for an element with a given key?

11.3-2
Suppose that we hash a string of r characters into m slots by treating it as a radix-128 number and then using the division method. We can easily represent the number m as a 32-bit computer word, but the string of r characters, treated as a radix-128 number, takes many words. How can we apply the division method to compute the hash value of the character string without using more than a constant number of words of storage outside the string itself?

11.3-3

Consider a version of the division method in which $h(k) = k \bmod m$, where $m = 2^p - 1$ and k is a character string interpreted in radix 2^p. Show that if we can derive string x from string y by permuting its characters, then x and y hash to the same value. Give an example of an application in which this property would be undesirable in a hash function.

11.3-4

Consider a hash table of size $m = 1000$ and a corresponding hash function $h(k) = \lfloor m (kA \bmod 1) \rfloor$ for $A = (\sqrt{5} - 1)/2$. Compute the locations to which the keys 61, 62, 63, 64, and 65 are mapped.

11.3-5 ★

Define a family $\mathcal{H}$ of hash functions from a finite set U to a finite set B to be **ϵ-universal** if for all pairs of distinct elements k and l in U,

$$\Pr\{h(k) = h(l)\} \leq \epsilon ,$$

where the probability is over the choice of the hash function h drawn at random from the family $\mathcal{H}$. Show that an ϵ-universal family of hash functions must have

$$\epsilon \geq \frac{1}{|B|} - \frac{1}{|U|} .$$

11.3-6 ★

Let U be the set of n-tuples of values drawn from $\mathbb{Z}_p$, and let $B = \mathbb{Z}_p$, where p is prime. Define the hash function $h_b : U \rightarrow B$ for $b \in \mathbb{Z}_p$ on an input n-tuple $\langle a_0, a_1, \ldots, a_{n-1} \rangle$ from U as

$$h_b(\langle a_0, a_1, \ldots, a_{n-1} \rangle) = \left(\sum_{j=0}^{n-1} a_j b^j \right) \bmod p ,$$

and let $\mathcal{H} = \{h_b : b \in \mathbb{Z}_p\}$. Argue that $\mathcal{H}$ is $((n-1)/p)$-universal according to the definition of ϵ-universal in Exercise 11.3-5. (*Hint:* See Exercise 31.4-4.)

11.4   Open addressing

In **open addressing**, all elements occupy the hash table itself. That is, each table entry contains either an element of the dynamic set or NIL. When searching for an element, we systematically examine table slots until either we find the desired element or we have ascertained that the element is not in the table. No lists and no elements are stored outside the table, unlike in chaining. Thus, in open addressing, the hash table can "fill up" so that no further insertions can be made; one consequence is that the load factor α can never exceed 1.

Of course, we could store the linked lists for chaining inside the hash table, in the otherwise unused hash-table slots (see Exercise 11.2-4), but the advantage of open addressing is that it avoids pointers altogether. Instead of following pointers, we *compute* the sequence of slots to be examined. The extra memory freed by not storing pointers provides the hash table with a larger number of slots for the same amount of memory, potentially yielding fewer collisions and faster retrieval.

To perform insertion using open addressing, we successively examine, or *probe*, the hash table until we find an empty slot in which to put the key. Instead of being fixed in the order $0, 1, \ldots, m - 1$ (which requires $\Theta(n)$ search time), the sequence of positions probed *depends upon the key being inserted*. To determine which slots to probe, we extend the hash function to include the probe number (starting from 0) as a second input. Thus, the hash function becomes

$$h : U \times \{0, 1, \ldots, m - 1\} \to \{0, 1, \ldots, m - 1\} \ .$$

With open addressing, we require that for every key k, the *probe sequence*

$$\langle h(k, 0), h(k, 1), \ldots, h(k, m - 1) \rangle$$

be a permutation of $\langle 0, 1, \ldots, m - 1 \rangle$, so that every hash-table position is eventually considered as a slot for a new key as the table fills up. In the following pseudocode, we assume that the elements in the hash table T are keys with no satellite information; the key k is identical to the element containing key k. Each slot contains either a key or NIL (if the slot is empty). The HASH-INSERT procedure takes as input a hash table T and a key k. It either returns the slot number where it stores key k or flags an error because the hash table is already full.

HASH-INSERT(T, k)

```
1  i = 0
2  repeat
3      j = h(k, i)
4      if T[j] == NIL
5          T[j] = k
6          return j
7      else i = i + 1
8  until i == m
9  error "hash table overflow"
```

The algorithm for searching for key k probes the same sequence of slots that the insertion algorithm examined when key k was inserted. Therefore, the search can terminate (unsuccessfully) when it finds an empty slot, since k would have been inserted there and not later in its probe sequence. (This argument assumes that keys are not deleted from the hash table.) The procedure HASH-SEARCH takes as input a hash table T and a key k, returning j if it finds that slot j contains key k, or NIL if key k is not present in table T.

HASH-SEARCH(T, k)

```
1  i = 0
2  repeat
3      j = h(k, i)
4      if T[j] == k
5          return j
6      i = i + 1
7  until T[j] == NIL or i == m
8  return NIL
```

Deletion from an open-address hash table is difficult. When we delete a key from slot i, we cannot simply mark that slot as empty by storing NIL in it. If we did, we might be unable to retrieve any key k during whose insertion we had probed slot i and found it occupied. We can solve this problem by marking the slot, storing in it the special value DELETED instead of NIL. We would then modify the procedure HASH-INSERT to treat such a slot as if it were empty so that we can insert a new key there. We do not need to modify HASH-SEARCH, since it will pass over DELETED values while searching. When we use the special value DELETED, however, search times no longer depend on the load factor α, and for this reason chaining is more commonly selected as a collision resolution technique when keys must be deleted.

In our analysis, we assume ***uniform hashing***: the probe sequence of each key is equally likely to be any of the $m!$ permutations of $\langle 0, 1, \ldots, m-1 \rangle$. Uniform hashing generalizes the notion of simple uniform hashing defined earlier to a hash function that produces not just a single number, but a whole probe sequence. True uniform hashing is difficult to implement, however, and in practice suitable approximations (such as double hashing, defined below) are used.

We will examine three commonly used techniques to compute the probe sequences required for open addressing: linear probing, quadratic probing, and double hashing. These techniques all guarantee that $\langle h(k, 0), h(k, 1), \ldots, h(k, m-1) \rangle$ is a permutation of $\langle 0, 1, \ldots, m-1 \rangle$ for each key k. None of these techniques fulfills the assumption of uniform hashing, however, since none of them is capable of generating more than m^2 different probe sequences (instead of the $m!$ that uniform hashing requires). Double hashing has the greatest number of probe sequences and, as one might expect, seems to give the best results.

Linear probing

Given an ordinary hash function $h' : U \rightarrow \{0, 1, \ldots, m-1\}$, which we refer to as an **auxiliary hash function**, the method of **linear probing** uses the hash function

$$h(k, i) = (h'(k) + i) \bmod m$$

for $i = 0, 1, \ldots, m-1$. Given key k, we first probe $T[h'(k)]$, i.e., the slot given by the auxiliary hash function. We next probe slot $T[h'(k) + 1]$, and so on up to slot $T[m-1]$. Then we wrap around to slots $T[0], T[1], \ldots$ until we finally probe slot $T[h'(k) - 1]$. Because the initial probe determines the entire probe sequence, there are only m distinct probe sequences.

Linear probing is easy to implement, but it suffers from a problem known as **primary clustering**. Long runs of occupied slots build up, increasing the average search time. Clusters arise because an empty slot preceded by i full slots gets filled next with probability $(i+1)/m$. Long runs of occupied slots tend to get longer, and the average search time increases.

Quadratic probing

Quadratic probing uses a hash function of the form

$$h(k, i) = (h'(k) + c_1 i + c_2 i^2) \bmod m \;, \tag{11.5}$$

where h' is an auxiliary hash function, c_1 and c_2 are positive auxiliary constants, and $i = 0, 1, \ldots, m-1$. The initial position probed is $T[h'(k)]$; later positions probed are offset by amounts that depend in a quadratic manner on the probe number i. This method works much better than linear probing, but to make full use of the hash table, the values of c_1, c_2, and m are constrained. Problem 11-3 shows one way to select these parameters. Also, if two keys have the same initial probe position, then their probe sequences are the same, since $h(k_1, 0) = h(k_2, 0)$ implies $h(k_1, i) = h(k_2, i)$. This property leads to a milder form of clustering, called **secondary clustering**. As in linear probing, the initial probe determines the entire sequence, and so only m distinct probe sequences are used.

Double hashing

Double hashing offers one of the best methods available for open addressing because the permutations produced have many of the characteristics of randomly chosen permutations. **Double hashing** uses a hash function of the form

$$h(k, i) = (h_1(k) + i h_2(k)) \bmod m \;,$$

where both h_1 and h_2 are auxiliary hash functions. The initial probe goes to position $T[h_1(k)]$; successive probe positions are offset from previous positions by the

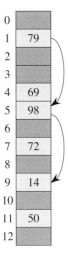

Figure 11.5 Insertion by double hashing. Here we have a hash table of size 13 with $h_1(k) = k \bmod 13$ and $h_2(k) = 1 + (k \bmod 11)$. Since $14 \equiv 1 \pmod{13}$ and $14 \equiv 3 \pmod{11}$, we insert the key 14 into empty slot 9, after examining slots 1 and 5 and finding them to be occupied.

amount $h_2(k)$, modulo m. Thus, unlike the case of linear or quadratic probing, the probe sequence here depends in two ways upon the key k, since the initial probe position, the offset, or both, may vary. Figure 11.5 gives an example of insertion by double hashing.

The value $h_2(k)$ must be relatively prime to the hash-table size m for the entire hash table to be searched. (See Exercise 11.4-4.) A convenient way to ensure this condition is to let m be a power of 2 and to design h_2 so that it always produces an odd number. Another way is to let m be prime and to design h_2 so that it always returns a positive integer less than m. For example, we could choose m prime and let

$$h_1(k) = k \bmod m ,$$
$$h_2(k) = 1 + (k \bmod m') ,$$

where m' is chosen to be slightly less than m (say, $m - 1$). For example, if $k = 123456$, $m = 701$, and $m' = 700$, we have $h_1(k) = 80$ and $h_2(k) = 257$, so that we first probe position 80, and then we examine every 257th slot (modulo m) until we find the key or have examined every slot.

When m is prime or a power of 2, double hashing improves over linear or quadratic probing in that $\Theta(m^2)$ probe sequences are used, rather than $\Theta(m)$, since each possible $(h_1(k), h_2(k))$ pair yields a distinct probe sequence. As a result, for such values of m, the performance of double hashing appears to be very close to the performance of the "ideal" scheme of uniform hashing.

Although values of m other than primes or powers of 2 could in principle be used with double hashing, in practice it becomes more difficult to efficiently generate $h_2(k)$ in a way that ensures that it is relatively prime to m, in part because the relative density $\phi(m)/m$ of such numbers may be small (see equation (31.24)).

Analysis of open-address hashing

As in our analysis of chaining, we express our analysis of open addressing in terms of the load factor $\alpha = n/m$ of the hash table. Of course, with open addressing, at most one element occupies each slot, and thus $n \leq m$, which implies $\alpha \leq 1$.

We assume that we are using uniform hashing. In this idealized scheme, the probe sequence $\langle h(k, 0), h(k, 1), \ldots, h(k, m - 1)\rangle$ used to insert or search for each key k is equally likely to be any permutation of $\langle 0, 1, \ldots, m - 1\rangle$. Of course, a given key has a unique fixed probe sequence associated with it; what we mean here is that, considering the probability distribution on the space of keys and the operation of the hash function on the keys, each possible probe sequence is equally likely.

We now analyze the expected number of probes for hashing with open addressing under the assumption of uniform hashing, beginning with an analysis of the number of probes made in an unsuccessful search.

Theorem 11.6
Given an open-address hash table with load factor $\alpha = n/m < 1$, the expected number of probes in an unsuccessful search is at most $1/(1-\alpha)$, assuming uniform hashing.

Proof   In an unsuccessful search, every probe but the last accesses an occupied slot that does not contain the desired key, and the last slot probed is empty. Let us define the random variable X to be the number of probes made in an unsuccessful search, and let us also define the event A_i, for $i = 1, 2, \ldots$, to be the event that an ith probe occurs and it is to an occupied slot. Then the event $\{X \geq i\}$ is the intersection of events $A_1 \cap A_2 \cap \cdots \cap A_{i-1}$. We will bound $\Pr\{X \geq i\}$ by bounding $\Pr\{A_1 \cap A_2 \cap \cdots \cap A_{i-1}\}$. By Exercise C.2-5,

$$\Pr\{A_1 \cap A_2 \cap \cdots \cap A_{i-1}\} = \Pr\{A_1\} \cdot \Pr\{A_2 \mid A_1\} \cdot \Pr\{A_3 \mid A_1 \cap A_2\} \cdots$$
$$\Pr\{A_{i-1} \mid A_1 \cap A_2 \cap \cdots \cap A_{i-2}\} \ .$$

Since there are n elements and m slots, $\Pr\{A_1\} = n/m$. For $j > 1$, the probability that there is a jth probe and it is to an occupied slot, given that the first $j - 1$ probes were to occupied slots, is $(n - j + 1)/(m - j + 1)$. This probability follows because we would be finding one of the remaining $(n - (j - 1))$ elements in one of the $(m - (j - 1))$ unexamined slots, and by the assumption of uniform hashing, the probability is the ratio of these quantities. Observing that $n < m$ implies that $(n - j)/(m - j) \leq n/m$ for all j such that $0 \leq j < m$, we have for all i such that $1 \leq i \leq m$,

$$
\begin{aligned}
\Pr\{X \geq i\} &= \frac{n}{m} \cdot \frac{n-1}{m-1} \cdot \frac{n-2}{m-2} \cdots \frac{n-i+2}{m-i+2} \\
&\leq \left(\frac{n}{m}\right)^{i-1} \\
&= \alpha^{i-1} .
\end{aligned}
$$

Of course, $\Pr\{X \geq i\} = 0$ for $i > m$. Now, we use equation (C.25) to bound the expected number of probes:

$$
\begin{aligned}
\mathrm{E}[X] &= \sum_{i=1}^{\infty} \Pr\{X \geq i\} \\
&= \sum_{i=1}^{m} \Pr\{X \geq i\} + \sum_{i>m} \Pr\{X \geq i\} \\
&\leq \sum_{i=1}^{\infty} \alpha^{i-1} + 0 \\
&= \sum_{i=0}^{\infty} \alpha^{i} \\
&= \frac{1}{1-\alpha} .
\end{aligned}
$$
∎

This bound of $1/(1-\alpha) = 1 + \alpha + \alpha^2 + \alpha^3 + \cdots$ has an intuitive interpretation. We always make the first probe. With probability approximately α, the first probe finds an occupied slot, so that we need to probe a second time. With probability approximately α^2, the first two slots are occupied so that we make a third probe, and so on.

If α is a constant, Theorem 11.6 predicts that an unsuccessful search runs in $O(1)$ time. For example, if the hash table is half full, the average number of probes in an unsuccessful search is at most $1/(1 - .5) = 2$. If it is 90 percent full, the average number of probes is at most $1/(1 - .9) = 10$.

Theorem 11.6 gives us the performance of the HASH-INSERT procedure almost immediately.

Corollary 11.7
Inserting an element into an open-address hash table with load factor α requires at most $1/(1 - \alpha)$ probes on average, assuming uniform hashing.

Proof An element is inserted only if there is room in the table, and thus $\alpha < 1$. Inserting a key requires an unsuccessful search followed by placing the key into the first empty slot found. Thus, the expected number of probes is at most $1/(1-\alpha)$. ∎

We have to do a little more work to compute the expected number of probes for a successful search.

Theorem 11.8
Given an open-address hash table with load factor $\alpha < 1$, the expected number of probes in a successful search is at most

$$\frac{1}{\alpha} \ln \frac{1}{1 - \alpha} ,$$

assuming uniform hashing and assuming that each key in the table is equally likely to be searched for.

Proof A search for a key k reproduces the same probe sequence as when the element with key k was inserted. By Corollary 11.7, if k was the $(i + 1)$st key inserted into the hash table, the expected number of probes made in a search for k is at most $1/(1 - i/m) = m/(m - i)$. Averaging over all n keys in the hash table gives us the expected number of probes in a successful search:

$$
\begin{aligned}
\frac{1}{n} \sum_{i=0}^{n-1} \frac{m}{m - i} &= \frac{m}{n} \sum_{i=0}^{n-1} \frac{1}{m - i} \\
&= \frac{1}{\alpha} \sum_{k=m-n+1}^{m} \frac{1}{k} \\
&\leq \frac{1}{\alpha} \int_{m-n}^{m} (1/x)\, dx \quad \text{(by inequality (A.12))} \\
&= \frac{1}{\alpha} \ln \frac{m}{m - n} \\
&= \frac{1}{\alpha} \ln \frac{1}{1 - \alpha} .
\end{aligned}
$$

∎

If the hash table is half full, the expected number of probes in a successful search is less than 1.387. If the hash table is 90 percent full, the expected number of probes is less than 2.559.

Exercises

11.4-1
Consider inserting the keys $10, 22, 31, 4, 15, 28, 17, 88, 59$ into a hash table of
length $m = 11$ using open addressing with the auxiliary hash function $h'(k) = k$.
Illustrate the result of inserting these keys using linear probing, using quadratic
probing with $c_1 = 1$ and $c_2 = 3$, and using double hashing with $h_1(k) = k$ and
$h_2(k) = 1 + (k \bmod (m - 1))$.

11.4-2
Write pseudocode for HASH-DELETE as outlined in the text, and modify HASH-
INSERT to handle the special value DELETED.

11.4-3
Consider an open-address hash table with uniform hashing. Give upper bounds
on the expected number of probes in an unsuccessful search and on the expected
number of probes in a successful search when the load factor is $3/4$ and when it
is $7/8$.

11.4-4 ★
Suppose that we use double hashing to resolve collisions—that is, we use the hash
function $h(k, i) = (h_1(k) + ih_2(k)) \bmod m$. Show that if m and $h_2(k)$ have
greatest common divisor $d \geq 1$ for some key k, then an unsuccessful search for
key k examines $(1/d)$th of the hash table before returning to slot $h_1(k)$. Thus,
when $d = 1$, so that m and $h_2(k)$ are relatively prime, the search may examine the
entire hash table. (*Hint:* See Chapter 31.)

11.4-5 ★
Consider an open-address hash table with a load factor α. Find the nonzero value α
for which the expected number of probes in an unsuccessful search equals twice
the expected number of probes in a successful search. Use the upper bounds given
by Theorems 11.6 and 11.8 for these expected numbers of probes.

★ **11.5   Perfect hashing**

Although hashing is often a good choice for its excellent average-case performance, hashing can also provide excellent *worst-case* performance when the set of
keys is ***static***: once the keys are stored in the table, the set of keys never changes.
Some applications naturally have static sets of keys: consider the set of reserved
words in a programming language, or the set of file names on a CD-ROM. We

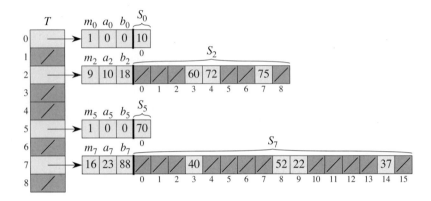

Figure 11.6 Using perfect hashing to store the set $K = \{10, 22, 37, 40, 52, 60, 70, 72, 75\}$. The outer hash function is $h(k) = ((ak + b) \bmod p) \bmod m$, where $a = 3$, $b = 42$, $p = 101$, and $m = 9$. For example, $h(75) = 2$, and so key 75 hashes to slot 2 of table T. A secondary hash table S_j stores all keys hashing to slot j. The size of hash table S_j is $m_j = n_j^2$, and the associated hash function is $h_j(k) = ((a_j k + b_j) \bmod p) \bmod m_j$. Since $h_2(75) = 7$, key 75 is stored in slot 7 of secondary hash table S_2. No collisions occur in any of the secondary hash tables, and so searching takes constant time in the worst case.

call a hashing technique ***perfect hashing*** if $O(1)$ memory accesses are required to perform a search in the worst case.

To create a perfect hashing scheme, we use two levels of hashing, with universal hashing at each level. Figure 11.6 illustrates the approach.

The first level is essentially the same as for hashing with chaining: we hash the n keys into m slots using a hash function h carefully selected from a family of universal hash functions.

Instead of making a linked list of the keys hashing to slot j, however, we use a small ***secondary hash table*** S_j with an associated hash function h_j. By choosing the hash functions h_j carefully, we can guarantee that there are no collisions at the secondary level.

In order to guarantee that there are no collisions at the secondary level, however, we will need to let the size m_j of hash table S_j be the square of the number n_j of keys hashing to slot j. Although you might think that the quadratic dependence of m_j on n_j may seem likely to cause the overall storage requirement to be excessive, we shall show that by choosing the first-level hash function well, we can limit the expected total amount of space used to $O(n)$.

We use hash functions chosen from the universal classes of hash functions of Section 11.3.3. The first-level hash function comes from the class $\mathcal{H}_{pm}$, where as in Section 11.3.3, p is a prime number greater than any key value. Those keys hashing to slot j are re-hashed into a secondary hash table S_j of size m_j using a hash function h_j chosen from the class $\mathcal{H}_{p,m_j}$.[1]

We shall proceed in two steps. First, we shall determine how to ensure that the secondary tables have no collisions. Second, we shall show that the expected amount of memory used overall—for the primary hash table and all the secondary hash tables—is $O(n)$.

Theorem 11.9
Suppose that we store n keys in a hash table of size $m = n^2$ using a hash function h randomly chosen from a universal class of hash functions. Then, the probability is less than $1/2$ that there are any collisions.

Proof   There are $\binom{n}{2}$ pairs of keys that may collide; each pair collides with probability $1/m$ if h is chosen at random from a universal family $\mathcal{H}$ of hash functions. Let X be a random variable that counts the number of collisions. When $m = n^2$, the expected number of collisions is

$$
\begin{aligned}
\mathrm{E}\left[X\right] &= \binom{n}{2} \cdot \frac{1}{n^2} \\
&= \frac{n^2 - n}{2} \cdot \frac{1}{n^2} \\
&< 1/2 .
\end{aligned}
$$

(This analysis is similar to the analysis of the birthday paradox in Section 5.4.1.) Applying Markov's inequality (C.30), $\Pr\{X \geq t\} \leq \mathrm{E}\left[X\right]/t$, with $t = 1$, completes the proof.   ∎

In the situation described in Theorem 11.9, where $m = n^2$, it follows that a hash function h chosen at random from $\mathcal{H}$ is more likely than not to have *no* collisions. Given the set K of n keys to be hashed (remember that K is static), it is thus easy to find a collision-free hash function h with a few random trials.

When n is large, however, a hash table of size $m = n^2$ is excessive. Therefore, we adopt the two-level hashing approach, and we use the approach of Theorem 11.9 only to hash the entries within each slot. We use an outer, or first-level, hash function h to hash the keys into $m = n$ slots. Then, if n_j keys hash to slot j, we use a secondary hash table S_j of size $m_j = n_j^2$ to provide collision-free constant-time lookup.

---

[1]When $n_j = m_j = 1$, we don't really need a hash function for slot j; when we choose a hash function $h_{ab}(k) = ((ak + b) \bmod p) \bmod m_j$ for such a slot, we just use $a = b = 0$.

We now turn to the issue of ensuring that the overall memory used is $O(n)$. Since the size m_j of the jth secondary hash table grows quadratically with the number n_j of keys stored, we run the risk that the overall amount of storage could be excessive.

If the first-level table size is $m = n$, then the amount of memory used is $O(n)$ for the primary hash table, for the storage of the sizes m_j of the secondary hash tables, and for the storage of the parameters a_j and b_j defining the secondary hash functions h_j drawn from the class $\mathcal{H}_{p,m_j}$ of Section 11.3.3 (except when $n_j = 1$ and we use $a = b = 0$). The following theorem and a corollary provide a bound on the expected combined sizes of all the secondary hash tables. A second corollary bounds the probability that the combined size of all the secondary hash tables is superlinear (actually, that it equals or exceeds $4n$).

Theorem 11.10

Suppose that we store n keys in a hash table of size $m = n$ using a hash function h randomly chosen from a universal class of hash functions. Then, we have

$$\mathrm{E}\left[\sum_{j=0}^{m-1} n_j^2\right] < 2n \ ,$$

where n_j is the number of keys hashing to slot j.

Proof   We start with the following identity, which holds for any nonnegative integer a:

$$a^2 = a + 2\binom{a}{2} \ . \tag{11.6}$$

We have

$$\mathrm{E}\left[\sum_{j=0}^{m-1} n_j^2\right]$$

$$= \ \mathrm{E}\left[\sum_{j=0}^{m-1}\left(n_j + 2\binom{n_j}{2}\right)\right] \qquad \text{(by equation (11.6))}$$

$$= \ \mathrm{E}\left[\sum_{j=0}^{m-1} n_j\right] + 2\,\mathrm{E}\left[\sum_{j=0}^{m-1}\binom{n_j}{2}\right] \qquad \text{(by linearity of expectation)}$$

$$= \ \mathrm{E}\left[n\right] + 2\,\mathrm{E}\left[\sum_{j=0}^{m-1}\binom{n_j}{2}\right] \qquad \text{(by equation (11.1))}$$

$$= n + 2\,\mathrm{E}\left[\sum_{j=0}^{m-1}\binom{n_j}{2}\right] \qquad \text{(since } n \text{ is not a random variable) .}$$

To evaluate the summation $\sum_{j=0}^{m-1}\binom{n_j}{2}$, we observe that it is just the total number of pairs of keys in the hash table that collide. By the properties of universal hashing, the expected value of this summation is at most

$$\binom{n}{2}\frac{1}{m} = \frac{n(n-1)}{2m}$$

$$= \frac{n-1}{2},$$

since $m = n$. Thus,

$$\mathrm{E}\left[\sum_{j=0}^{m-1}n_j^2\right] \leq n + 2\frac{n-1}{2}$$

$$= 2n - 1$$

$$< 2n .$$

∎

Corollary 11.11
Suppose that we store n keys in a hash table of size $m = n$ using a hash function h randomly chosen from a universal class of hash functions, and we set the size of each secondary hash table to $m_j = n_j^2$ for $j = 0, 1, \ldots, m-1$. Then, the expected amount of storage required for all secondary hash tables in a perfect hashing scheme is less than $2n$.

Proof   Since $m_j = n_j^2$ for $j = 0, 1, \ldots, m-1$, Theorem 11.10 gives

$$\mathrm{E}\left[\sum_{j=0}^{m-1}m_j\right] = \mathrm{E}\left[\sum_{j=0}^{m-1}n_j^2\right]$$

$$< 2n , \tag{11.7}$$

which completes the proof.

∎

Corollary 11.12
Suppose that we store n keys in a hash table of size $m = n$ using a hash function h randomly chosen from a universal class of hash functions, and we set the size of each secondary hash table to $m_j = n_j^2$ for $j = 0, 1, \ldots, m-1$. Then, the probability is less than $1/2$ that the total storage used for secondary hash tables equals or exceeds $4n$.

Proof   Again we apply Markov's inequality (C.30), $\Pr\{X \geq t\} \leq \mathrm{E}[X]/t$, this time to inequality (11.7), with $X = \sum_{j=0}^{m-1} m_j$ and $t = 4n$:

$$
\begin{aligned}
\Pr\left\{\sum_{j=0}^{m-1} m_j \geq 4n\right\} &\leq \frac{\mathrm{E}\left[\sum_{j=0}^{m-1} m_j\right]}{4n} \\
&< \frac{2n}{4n} \\
&= 1/2 \ .
\end{aligned}
$$
∎

From Corollary 11.12, we see that if we test a few randomly chosen hash functions from the universal family, we will quickly find one that uses a reasonable amount of storage.

Exercises

11.5-1   ★
Suppose that we insert n keys into a hash table of size m using open addressing and uniform hashing. Let $p(n, m)$ be the probability that no collisions occur. Show that $p(n, m) \leq e^{-n(n-1)/2m}$. (*Hint:* See equation (3.12).) Argue that when n exceeds $\sqrt{m}$, the probability of avoiding collisions goes rapidly to zero.

Problems

11-1   Longest-probe bound for hashing
Suppose that we use an open-addressed hash table of size m to store $n \leq m/2$ items.

a. Assuming uniform hashing, show that for $i = 1, 2, \ldots, n$, the probability is at most 2^{-k} that the ith insertion requires strictly more than k probes.

b. Show that for $i = 1, 2, \ldots, n$, the probability is $O(1/n^2)$ that the ith insertion requires more than $2 \lg n$ probes.

Let the random variable X_i denote the number of probes required by the ith insertion. You have shown in part (b) that $\Pr\{X_i > 2 \lg n\} = O(1/n^2)$. Let the random variable $X = \max_{1 \leq i \leq n} X_i$ denote the maximum number of probes required by any of the n insertions.

c. Show that $\Pr\{X > 2 \lg n\} = O(1/n)$.

d. Show that the expected length $\mathrm{E}[X]$ of the longest probe sequence is $O(\lg n)$.

11-2   *Slot-size bound for chaining*

Suppose that we have a hash table with n slots, with collisions resolved by chaining, and suppose that n keys are inserted into the table. Each key is equally likely to be hashed to each slot. Let M be the maximum number of keys in any slot after all the keys have been inserted. Your mission is to prove an $O(\lg n / \lg \lg n)$ upper bound on $\mathrm{E}[M]$, the expected value of M.

a. Argue that the probability Q_k that exactly k keys hash to a particular slot is given by

$$Q_k = \left(\frac{1}{n}\right)^k \left(1 - \frac{1}{n}\right)^{n-k} \binom{n}{k}.$$

b. Let P_k be the probability that $M = k$, that is, the probability that the slot containing the most keys contains k keys. Show that $P_k \leq n Q_k$.

c. Use Stirling's approximation, equation (3.18), to show that $Q_k < e^k / k^k$.

d. Show that there exists a constant $c > 1$ such that $Q_{k_0} < 1/n^3$ for $k_0 = c \lg n / \lg \lg n$. Conclude that $P_k < 1/n^2$ for $k \geq k_0 = c \lg n / \lg \lg n$.

e. Argue that

$$\mathrm{E}[M] \leq \Pr\left\{M > \frac{c \lg n}{\lg \lg n}\right\} \cdot n + \Pr\left\{M \leq \frac{c \lg n}{\lg \lg n}\right\} \cdot \frac{c \lg n}{\lg \lg n}.$$

Conclude that $\mathrm{E}[M] = O(\lg n / \lg \lg n)$.

11-3   *Quadratic probing*

Suppose that we are given a key k to search for in a hash table with positions $0, 1, \ldots, m - 1$, and suppose that we have a hash function h mapping the key space into the set $\{0, 1, \ldots, m - 1\}$. The search scheme is as follows:

1. Compute the value $j = h(k)$, and set $i = 0$.

2. Probe in position j for the desired key k. If you find it, or if this position is empty, terminate the search.

3. Set $i = i + 1$. If i now equals m, the table is full, so terminate the search. Otherwise, set $j = (i + j) \bmod m$, and return to step 2.

Assume that m is a power of 2.

a. Show that this scheme is an instance of the general "quadratic probing" scheme by exhibiting the appropriate constants c_1 and c_2 for equation (11.5).

b. Prove that this algorithm examines every table position in the worst case.

11-4   *Hashing and authentication*

Let $\mathcal{H}$ be a class of hash functions in which each hash function $h \in \mathcal{H}$ maps the universe U of keys to $\{0, 1, \ldots, m - 1\}$. We say that $\mathcal{H}$ is **k-universal** if, for every fixed sequence of k distinct keys $\langle x^{(1)}, x^{(2)}, \ldots, x^{(k)} \rangle$ and for any h chosen at random from $\mathcal{H}$, the sequence $\langle h(x^{(1)}), h(x^{(2)}), \ldots, h(x^{(k)}) \rangle$ is equally likely to be any of the m^k sequences of length k with elements drawn from $\{0, 1, \ldots, m - 1\}$.

a. Show that if the family $\mathcal{H}$ of hash functions is 2-universal, then it is universal.

b. Suppose that the universe U is the set of n-tuples of values drawn from $\mathbb{Z}_p = \{0, 1, \ldots, p - 1\}$, where p is prime. Consider an element $x = \langle x_0, x_1, \ldots, x_{n-1} \rangle \in U$. For any n-tuple $a = \langle a_0, a_1, \ldots, a_{n-1} \rangle \in U$, define the hash function h_a by

$$h_a(x) = \left(\sum_{j=0}^{n-1} a_j x_j \right) \bmod p \, .$$

Let $\mathcal{H} = \{h_a\}$. Show that $\mathcal{H}$ is universal, but not 2-universal. (*Hint:* Find a key for which all hash functions in $\mathcal{H}$ produce the same value.)

c. Suppose that we modify $\mathcal{H}$ slightly from part (b): for any $a \in U$ and for any $b \in \mathbb{Z}_p$, define

$$h'_{ab}(x) = \left(\sum_{j=0}^{n-1} a_j x_j + b \right) \bmod p$$

and $\mathcal{H}' = \{h'_{ab}\}$. Argue that $\mathcal{H}'$ is 2-universal. (*Hint:* Consider fixed n-tuples $x \in U$ and $y \in U$, with $x_i \neq y_i$ for some i. What happens to $h'_{ab}(x)$ and $h'_{ab}(y)$ as a_i and b range over $\mathbb{Z}_p$?)

d. Suppose that Alice and Bob secretly agree on a hash function h from a 2-universal family $\mathcal{H}$ of hash functions. Each $h \in \mathcal{H}$ maps from a universe of keys U to $\mathbb{Z}_p$, where p is prime. Later, Alice sends a message m to Bob over the Internet, where $m \in U$. She authenticates this message to Bob by also sending an authentication tag $t = h(m)$, and Bob checks that the pair (m, t) he receives indeed satisfies $t = h(m)$. Suppose that an adversary intercepts (m, t) en route and tries to fool Bob by replacing the pair (m, t) with a different pair (m', t'). Argue that the probability that the adversary succeeds in fooling Bob into accepting (m', t') is at most $1/p$, no matter how much computing power the adversary has, and even if the adversary knows the family $\mathcal{H}$ of hash functions used.

Chapter notes

Knuth [211] and Gonnet [145] are excellent references for the analysis of hashing algorithms. Knuth credits H. P. Luhn (1953) for inventing hash tables, along with the chaining method for resolving collisions. At about the same time, G. M. Amdahl originated the idea of open addressing.

Carter and Wegman introduced the notion of universal classes of hash functions in 1979 [58].

Fredman, Komlós, and Szemerédi [112] developed the perfect hashing scheme for static sets presented in Section 11.5. An extension of their method to dynamic sets, handling insertions and deletions in amortized expected time $O(1)$, has been given by Dietzfelbinger et al. [86].

12   Binary Search Trees

The search tree data structure supports many dynamic-set operations, including SEARCH, MINIMUM, MAXIMUM, PREDECESSOR, SUCCESSOR, INSERT, and DELETE. Thus, we can use a search tree both as a dictionary and as a priority queue.

Basic operations on a binary search tree take time proportional to the height of the tree. For a complete binary tree with n nodes, such operations run in $\Theta(\lg n)$ worst-case time. If the tree is a linear chain of n nodes, however, the same operations take $\Theta(n)$ worst-case time. We shall see in Section 12.4 that the expected height of a randomly built binary search tree is $O(\lg n)$, so that basic dynamic-set operations on such a tree take $\Theta(\lg n)$ time on average.

In practice, we can't always guarantee that binary search trees are built randomly, but we can design variations of binary search trees with good guaranteed worst-case performance on basic operations. Chapter 13 presents one such variation, red-black trees, which have height $O(\lg n)$. Chapter 18 introduces B-trees, which are particularly good for maintaining databases on secondary (disk) storage.

After presenting the basic properties of binary search trees, the following sections show how to walk a binary search tree to print its values in sorted order, how to search for a value in a binary search tree, how to find the minimum or maximum element, how to find the predecessor or successor of an element, and how to insert into or delete from a binary search tree. The basic mathematical properties of trees appear in Appendix B.

12.1   What is a binary search tree?

A binary search tree is organized, as the name suggests, in a binary tree, as shown in Figure 12.1. We can represent such a tree by a linked data structure in which each node is an object. In addition to a *key* and satellite data, each node contains attributes *left*, *right*, and *p* that point to the nodes corresponding to its left child,

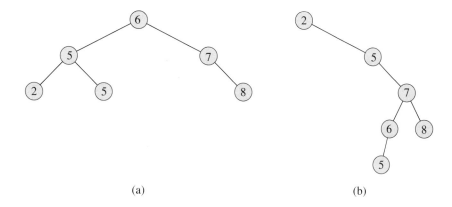

(a)   (b)

Figure 12.1   Binary search trees. For any node x, the keys in the left subtree of x are at most $x.key$, and the keys in the right subtree of x are at least $x.key$. Different binary search trees can represent the same set of values. The worst-case running time for most search-tree operations is proportional to the height of the tree. **(a)** A binary search tree on 6 nodes with height 2. **(b)** A less efficient binary search tree with height 4 that contains the same keys.

its right child, and its parent, respectively. If a child or the parent is missing, the appropriate attribute contains the value NIL. The root node is the only node in the tree whose parent is NIL.

The keys in a binary search tree are always stored in such a way as to satisfy the ***binary-search-tree property***:

> Let x be a node in a binary search tree. If y is a node in the left subtree of x, then $y.key \leq x.key$. If y is a node in the right subtree of x, then $y.key \geq x.key$.

Thus, in Figure 12.1(a), the key of the root is 6, the keys 2, 5, and 5 in its left subtree are no larger than 6, and the keys 7 and 8 in its right subtree are no smaller than 6. The same property holds for every node in the tree. For example, the key 5 in the root's left child is no smaller than the key 2 in that node's left subtree and no larger than the key 5 in the right subtree.

The binary-search-tree property allows us to print out all the keys in a binary search tree in sorted order by a simple recursive algorithm, called an ***inorder tree walk***. This algorithm is so named because it prints the key of the root of a subtree between printing the values in its left subtree and printing those in its right subtree. (Similarly, a ***preorder tree walk*** prints the root before the values in either subtree, and a ***postorder tree walk*** prints the root after the values in its subtrees.) To use the following procedure to print all the elements in a binary search tree T, we call INORDER-TREE-WALK($T.root$).

INORDER-TREE-WALK(x)

1   **if** $x \neq$ NIL
2   INORDER-TREE-WALK$(x.left)$
3   print $x.key$
4   INORDER-TREE-WALK$(x.right)$

As an example, the inorder tree walk prints the keys in each of the two binary search trees from Figure 12.1 in the order $2, 5, 5, 6, 7, 8$. The correctness of the algorithm follows by induction directly from the binary-search-tree property.

It takes $\Theta(n)$ time to walk an n-node binary search tree, since after the initial call, the procedure calls itself recursively exactly twice for each node in the tree—once for its left child and once for its right child. The following theorem gives a formal proof that it takes linear time to perform an inorder tree walk.

Theorem 12.1
If x is the root of an n-node subtree, then the call INORDER-TREE-WALK(x) takes $\Theta(n)$ time.

Proof   Let $T(n)$ denote the time taken by INORDER-TREE-WALK when it is called on the root of an n-node subtree. Since INORDER-TREE-WALK visits all n nodes of the subtree, we have $T(n) = \Omega(n)$. It remains to show that $T(n) = O(n)$.

Since INORDER-TREE-WALK takes a small, constant amount of time on an empty subtree (for the test $x \neq$ NIL), we have $T(0) = c$ for some constant $c > 0$.

For $n > 0$, suppose that INORDER-TREE-WALK is called on a node x whose left subtree has k nodes and whose right subtree has $n - k - 1$ nodes. The time to perform INORDER-TREE-WALK(x) is bounded by $T(n) \leq T(k) + T(n-k-1) + d$ for some constant $d > 0$ that reflects an upper bound on the time to execute the body of INORDER-TREE-WALK(x), exclusive of the time spent in recursive calls.

We use the substitution method to show that $T(n) = O(n)$ by proving that $T(n) \leq (c + d)n + c$. For $n = 0$, we have $(c + d) \cdot 0 + c = c = T(0)$. For $n > 0$, we have

$$
\begin{aligned}
T(n) &\leq T(k) + T(n - k - 1) + d \\
&= ((c + d)k + c) + ((c + d)(n - k - 1) + c) + d \\
&= (c + d)n + c - (c + d) + c + d \\
&= (c + d)n + c,
\end{aligned}
$$

which completes the proof.   ∎

Exercises

12.1-1
For the set of $\{1, 4, 5, 10, 16, 17, 21\}$ of keys, draw binary search trees of heights 2, 3, 4, 5, and 6.

12.1-2
What is the difference between the binary-search-tree property and the min-heap property (see page 153)? Can the min-heap property be used to print out the keys of an n-node tree in sorted order in $O(n)$ time? Show how, or explain why not.

12.1-3
Give a nonrecursive algorithm that performs an inorder tree walk. (*Hint:* An easy solution uses a stack as an auxiliary data structure. A more complicated, but elegant, solution uses no stack but assumes that we can test two pointers for equality.)

12.1-4
Give recursive algorithms that perform preorder and postorder tree walks in $\Theta(n)$ time on a tree of n nodes.

12.1-5
Argue that since sorting n elements takes $\Omega(n \lg n)$ time in the worst case in the comparison model, any comparison-based algorithm for constructing a binary search tree from an arbitrary list of n elements takes $\Omega(n \lg n)$ time in the worst case.

12.2   Querying a binary search tree

We often need to search for a key stored in a binary search tree. Besides the SEARCH operation, binary search trees can support such queries as MINIMUM, MAXIMUM, SUCCESSOR, and PREDECESSOR. In this section, we shall examine these operations and show how to support each one in time $O(h)$ on any binary search tree of height h.

Searching

We use the following procedure to search for a node with a given key in a binary search tree. Given a pointer to the root of the tree and a key k, TREE-SEARCH returns a pointer to a node with key k if one exists; otherwise, it returns NIL.

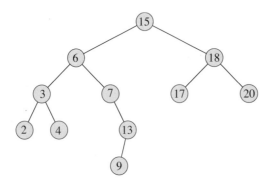

Figure 12.2   Queries on a binary search tree. To search for the key 13 in the tree, we follow the path $15 \to 6 \to 7 \to 13$ from the root. The minimum key in the tree is 2, which is found by following *left* pointers from the root. The maximum key 20 is found by following *right* pointers from the root. The successor of the node with key 15 is the node with key 17, since it is the minimum key in the right subtree of 15. The node with key 13 has no right subtree, and thus its successor is its lowest ancestor whose left child is also an ancestor. In this case, the node with key 15 is its successor.

TREE-SEARCH(x, k)

1   **if** $x ==$ NIL or $k == x.key$
2   **return** x
3   **if** $k < x.key$
4   **return** TREE-SEARCH$(x.left, k)$
5   **else return** TREE-SEARCH$(x.right, k)$

The procedure begins its search at the root and traces a simple path downward in the tree, as shown in Figure 12.2. For each node x it encounters, it compares the key k with $x.key$. If the two keys are equal, the search terminates. If k is smaller than $x.key$, the search continues in the left subtree of x, since the binary-search-tree property implies that k could not be stored in the right subtree. Symmetrically, if k is larger than $x.key$, the search continues in the right subtree. The nodes encountered during the recursion form a simple path downward from the root of the tree, and thus the running time of TREE-SEARCH is $O(h)$, where h is the height of the tree.

We can rewrite this procedure in an iterative fashion by "unrolling" the recursion into a **while** loop. On most computers, the iterative version is more efficient.

ITERATIVE-TREE-SEARCH(x, k)

1   **while** $x \neq$ NIL and $k \neq x.key$
2   **if** $k < x.key$
3           $x = x.left$
4   **else** $x = x.right$
5   **return** x

Minimum and maximum

We can always find an element in a binary search tree whose key is a minimum by following *left* child pointers from the root until we encounter a NIL, as shown in Figure 12.2. The following procedure returns a pointer to the minimum element in the subtree rooted at a given node x, which we assume to be non-NIL:

TREE-MINIMUM(x)

1   **while** $x.left \neq$ NIL
2       $x = x.left$
3   **return** x

The binary-search-tree property guarantees that TREE-MINIMUM is correct. If a node x has no left subtree, then since every key in the right subtree of x is at least as large as $x.key$, the minimum key in the subtree rooted at x is $x.key$. If node x has a left subtree, then since no key in the right subtree is smaller than $x.key$ and every key in the left subtree is not larger than $x.key$, the minimum key in the subtree rooted at x resides in the subtree rooted at $x.left$.

The pseudocode for TREE-MAXIMUM is symmetric:

TREE-MAXIMUM(x)

1   **while** $x.right \neq$ NIL
2       $x = x.right$
3   **return** x

Both of these procedures run in $O(h)$ time on a tree of height h since, as in TREE-SEARCH, the sequence of nodes encountered forms a simple path downward from the root.

Successor and predecessor

Given a node in a binary search tree, sometimes we need to find its successor in the sorted order determined by an inorder tree walk. If all keys are distinct, the successor of a node x is the node with the smallest key greater than $x.key$. The structure of a binary search tree allows us to determine the successor of a node without ever comparing keys. The following procedure returns the successor of a node x in a binary search tree if it exists, and NIL if x has the largest key in the tree:

TREE-SUCCESSOR(x)

```
1  if x.right ≠ NIL
2      return TREE-MINIMUM(x.right)
3  y = x.p
4  while y ≠ NIL and x == y.right
5      x = y
6      y = y.p
7  return y
```

We break the code for TREE-SUCCESSOR into two cases. If the right subtree of node x is nonempty, then the successor of x is just the leftmost node in x's right subtree, which we find in line 2 by calling TREE-MINIMUM($x.right$). For example, the successor of the node with key 15 in Figure 12.2 is the node with key 17.

On the other hand, as Exercise 12.2-6 asks you to show, if the right subtree of node x is empty and x has a successor y, then y is the lowest ancestor of x whose left child is also an ancestor of x. In Figure 12.2, the successor of the node with key 13 is the node with key 15. To find y, we simply go up the tree from x until we encounter a node that is the left child of its parent; lines 3–7 of TREE-SUCCESSOR handle this case.

The running time of TREE-SUCCESSOR on a tree of height h is $O(h)$, since we either follow a simple path up the tree or follow a simple path down the tree. The procedure TREE-PREDECESSOR, which is symmetric to TREE-SUCCESSOR, also runs in time $O(h)$.

Even if keys are not distinct, we define the successor and predecessor of any node x as the node returned by calls made to TREE-SUCCESSOR(x) and TREE-PREDECESSOR(x), respectively.

In summary, we have proved the following theorem.

Theorem 12.2
We can implement the dynamic-set operations SEARCH, MINIMUM, MAXIMUM, SUCCESSOR, and PREDECESSOR so that each one runs in $O(h)$ time on a binary search tree of height h.   ∎

Exercises

12.2-1

Suppose that we have numbers between 1 and 1000 in a binary search tree, and we want to search for the number 363. Which of the following sequences could *not* be the sequence of nodes examined?

a. 2, 252, 401, 398, 330, 344, 397, 363.

b. 924, 220, 911, 244, 898, 258, 362, 363.

c. 925, 202, 911, 240, 912, 245, 363.

d. 2, 399, 387, 219, 266, 382, 381, 278, 363.

e. 935, 278, 347, 621, 299, 392, 358, 363.

12.2-2

Write recursive versions of TREE-MINIMUM and TREE-MAXIMUM.

12.2-3

Write the TREE-PREDECESSOR procedure.

12.2-4

Professor Bunyan thinks he has discovered a remarkable property of binary search trees. Suppose that the search for key k in a binary search tree ends up in a leaf. Consider three sets: A, the keys to the left of the search path; B, the keys on the search path; and C, the keys to the right of the search path. Professor Bunyan claims that any three keys $a \in A$, $b \in B$, and $c \in C$ must satisfy $a \leq b \leq c$. Give a smallest possible counterexample to the professor's claim.

12.2-5

Show that if a node in a binary search tree has two children, then its successor has no left child and its predecessor has no right child.

12.2-6

Consider a binary search tree T whose keys are distinct. Show that if the right subtree of a node x in T is empty and x has a successor y, then y is the lowest ancestor of x whose left child is also an ancestor of x. (Recall that every node is its own ancestor.)

12.2-7

An alternative method of performing an inorder tree walk of an n-node binary search tree finds the minimum element in the tree by calling TREE-MINIMUM and then making $n - 1$ calls to TREE-SUCCESSOR. Prove that this algorithm runs in $\Theta(n)$ time.

12.2-8

Prove that no matter what node we start at in a height-h binary search tree, k successive calls to TREE-SUCCESSOR take $O(k + h)$ time.

12.2-9

Let T be a binary search tree whose keys are distinct, let x be a leaf node, and let y be its parent. Show that $y.key$ is either the smallest key in T larger than $x.key$ or the largest key in T smaller than $x.key$.

12.3   Insertion and deletion

The operations of insertion and deletion cause the dynamic set represented by a binary search tree to change. The data structure must be modified to reflect this change, but in such a way that the binary-search-tree property continues to hold. As we shall see, modifying the tree to insert a new element is relatively straightforward, but handling deletion is somewhat more intricate.

Insertion

To insert a new value v into a binary search tree T, we use the procedure TREE-INSERT. The procedure takes a node z for which $z.key = v$, $z.left = $ NIL, and $z.right = $ NIL. It modifies T and some of the attributes of z in such a way that it inserts z into an appropriate position in the tree.

TREE-INSERT(T, z)

```
 1   y = NIL
 2   x = T.root
 3   while x ≠ NIL
 4       y = x
 5       if z.key < x.key
 6           x = x.left
 7       else x = x.right
 8   z.p = y
 9   if y == NIL
10       T.root = z        // tree T was empty
11   elseif z.key < y.key
12       y.left = z
13   else y.right = z
```

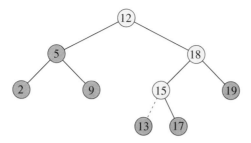

Figure 12.3   Inserting an item with key 13 into a binary search tree. Lightly shaded nodes indicate the simple path from the root down to the position where the item is inserted. The dashed line indicates the link in the tree that is added to insert the item.

Figure 12.3 shows how TREE-INSERT works. Just like the procedures TREE-SEARCH and ITERATIVE-TREE-SEARCH, TREE-INSERT begins at the root of the tree and the pointer x traces a simple path downward looking for a NIL to replace with the input item z. The procedure maintains the ***trailing pointer*** y as the parent of x. After initialization, the **while** loop in lines 3–7 causes these two pointers to move down the tree, going left or right depending on the comparison of $z.key$ with $x.key$, until x becomes NIL. This NIL occupies the position where we wish to place the input item z. We need the trailing pointer y, because by the time we find the NIL where z belongs, the search has proceeded one step beyond the node that needs to be changed. Lines 8–13 set the pointers that cause z to be inserted.

Like the other primitive operations on search trees, the procedure TREE-INSERT runs in $O(h)$ time on a tree of height h.

Deletion

The overall strategy for deleting a node z from a binary search tree T has three basic cases but, as we shall see, one of the cases is a bit tricky.

- If z has no children, then we simply remove it by modifying its parent to replace z with NIL as its child.

- If z has just one child, then we elevate that child to take z's position in the tree by modifying z's parent to replace z by z's child.

- If z has two children, then we find z's successor y—which must be in z's right subtree—and have y take z's position in the tree. The rest of z's original right subtree becomes y's new right subtree, and z's left subtree becomes y's new left subtree. This case is the tricky one because, as we shall see, it matters whether y is z's right child.

The procedure for deleting a given node z from a binary search tree T takes as arguments pointers to T and z. It organizes its cases a bit differently from the three cases outlined previously by considering the four cases shown in Figure 12.4.

- If z has no left child (part (a) of the figure), then we replace z by its right child, which may or may not be NIL. When z's right child is NIL, this case deals with the situation in which z has no children. When z's right child is non-NIL, this case handles the situation in which z has just one child, which is its right child.

- If z has just one child, which is its left child (part (b) of the figure), then we replace z by its left child.

- Otherwise, z has both a left and a right child. We find z's successor y, which lies in z's right subtree and has no left child (see Exercise 12.2-5). We want to splice y out of its current location and have it replace z in the tree.

  - If y is z's right child (part (c)), then we replace z by y, leaving y's right child alone.

  - Otherwise, y lies within z's right subtree but is not z's right child (part (d)). In this case, we first replace y by its own right child, and then we replace z by y.

In order to move subtrees around within the binary search tree, we define a subroutine TRANSPLANT, which replaces one subtree as a child of its parent with another subtree. When TRANSPLANT replaces the subtree rooted at node u with the subtree rooted at node v, node u's parent becomes node v's parent, and u's parent ends up having v as its appropriate child.

TRANSPLANT(T, u, v)

```
1   if u.p == NIL
2       T.root = v
3   elseif u == u.p.left
4       u.p.left = v
5   else u.p.right = v
6   if v ≠ NIL
7       v.p = u.p
```

Lines 1–2 handle the case in which u is the root of T. Otherwise, u is either a left child or a right child of its parent. Lines 3–4 take care of updating $u.p.left$ if u is a left child, and line 5 updates $u.p.right$ if u is a right child. We allow v to be NIL, and lines 6–7 update $v.p$ if v is non-NIL. Note that TRANSPLANT does not attempt to update $v.left$ and $v.right$; doing so, or not doing so, is the responsibility of TRANSPLANT's caller.

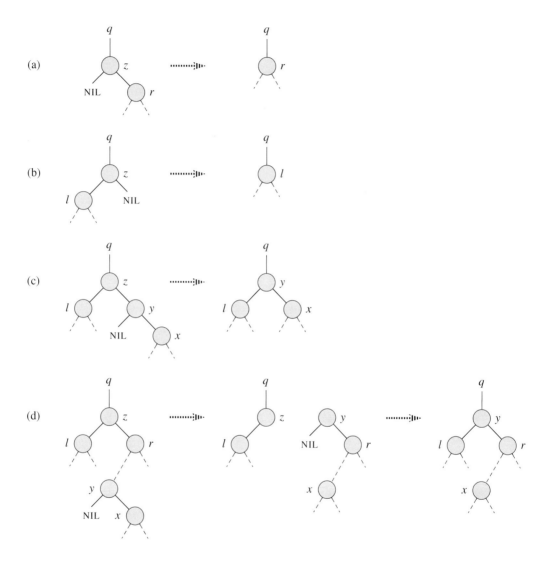

Figure 12.4   Deleting a node z from a binary search tree. Node z may be the root, a left child of node q, or a right child of q. **(a)** Node z has no left child. We replace z by its right child r, which may or may not be NIL. **(b)** Node z has a left child l but no right child. We replace z by l. **(c)** Node z has two children; its left child is node l, its right child is its successor y, and y's right child is node x. We replace z by y, updating y's left child to become l, but leaving x as y's right child. **(d)** Node z has two children (left child l and right child r), and its successor $y \neq r$ lies within the subtree rooted at r. We replace y by its own right child x, and we set y to be r's parent. Then, we set y to be q's child and the parent of l.

With the TRANSPLANT procedure in hand, here is the procedure that deletes node z from binary search tree T:

TREE-DELETE(T, z)

```
 1   if z.left == NIL
 2        TRANSPLANT(T, z, z.right)
 3   elseif z.right == NIL
 4        TRANSPLANT(T, z, z.left)
 5   else y = TREE-MINIMUM(z.right)
 6        if y.p ≠ z
 7             TRANSPLANT(T, y, y.right)
 8             y.right = z.right
 9             y.right.p = y
10        TRANSPLANT(T, z, y)
11        y.left = z.left
12        y.left.p = y
```

The TREE-DELETE procedure executes the four cases as follows. Lines 1–2 handle the case in which node z has no left child, and lines 3–4 handle the case in which z has a left child but no right child. Lines 5–12 deal with the remaining two cases, in which z has two children. Line 5 finds node y, which is the successor of z. Because z has a nonempty right subtree, its successor must be the node in that subtree with the smallest key; hence the call to TREE-MINIMUM$(z.right)$. As we noted before, y has no left child. We want to splice y out of its current location, and it should replace z in the tree. If y is z's right child, then lines 10–12 replace z as a child of its parent by y and replace y's left child by z's left child. If y is not z's right child, lines 7–9 replace y as a child of its parent by y's right child and turn z's right child into y's right child, and then lines 10–12 replace z as a child of its parent by y and replace y's left child by z's left child.

Each line of TREE-DELETE, including the calls to TRANSPLANT, takes constant time, except for the call to TREE-MINIMUM in line 5. Thus, TREE-DELETE runs in $O(h)$ time on a tree of height h.

In summary, we have proved the following theorem.

Theorem 12.3
We can implement the dynamic-set operations INSERT and DELETE so that each one runs in $O(h)$ time on a binary search tree of height h. ∎

Exercises

12.3-1
Give a recursive version of the TREE-INSERT procedure.

12.3-2
Suppose that we construct a binary search tree by repeatedly inserting distinct values into the tree. Argue that the number of nodes examined in searching for a value in the tree is one plus the number of nodes examined when the value was first inserted into the tree.

12.3-3
We can sort a given set of n numbers by first building a binary search tree containing these numbers (using TREE-INSERT repeatedly to insert the numbers one by one) and then printing the numbers by an inorder tree walk. What are the worst-case and best-case running times for this sorting algorithm?

12.3-4
Is the operation of deletion "commutative" in the sense that deleting x and then y from a binary search tree leaves the same tree as deleting y and then x? Argue why it is or give a counterexample.

12.3-5
Suppose that instead of each node x keeping the attribute $x.p$, pointing to x's parent, it keeps $x.succ$, pointing to x's successor. Give pseudocode for SEARCH, INSERT, and DELETE on a binary search tree T using this representation. These procedures should operate in time $O(h)$, where h is the height of the tree T. (*Hint:* You may wish to implement a subroutine that returns the parent of a node.)

12.3-6
When node z in TREE-DELETE has two children, we could choose node y as its predecessor rather than its successor. What other changes to TREE-DELETE would be necessary if we did so? Some have argued that a fair strategy, giving equal priority to predecessor and successor, yields better empirical performance. How might TREE-DELETE be changed to implement such a fair strategy?

★   **12.4   Randomly built binary search trees**

We have shown that each of the basic operations on a binary search tree runs in $O(h)$ time, where h is the height of the tree. The height of a binary search tree varies, however, as items are inserted and deleted. If, for example, the n items are inserted in strictly increasing order, the tree will be a chain with height $n - 1$. On the other hand, Exercise B.5-4 shows that $h \geq \lfloor \lg n \rfloor$. As with quicksort, we can show that the behavior of the average case is much closer to the best case than to the worst case.

Unfortunately, little is known about the average height of a binary search tree when both insertion and deletion are used to create it. When the tree is created by insertion alone, the analysis becomes more tractable. Let us therefore define a ***randomly built binary search tree*** on n keys as one that arises from inserting the keys in random order into an initially empty tree, where each of the $n!$ permutations of the input keys is equally likely. (Exercise 12.4-3 asks you to show that this notion is different from assuming that every binary search tree on n keys is equally likely.) In this section, we shall prove the following theorem.

Theorem 12.4
The expected height of a randomly built binary search tree on n distinct keys is $O(\lg n)$.

Proof   We start by defining three random variables that help measure the height of a randomly built binary search tree. We denote the height of a randomly built binary search tree on n keys by X_n, and we define the ***exponential height*** $Y_n = 2^{X_n}$. When we build a binary search tree on n keys, we choose one key as that of the root, and we let R_n denote the random variable that holds this key's ***rank*** within the set of n keys; that is, R_n holds the position that this key would occupy if the set of keys were sorted. The value of R_n is equally likely to be any element of the set $\{1, 2, \ldots, n\}$. If $R_n = i$, then the left subtree of the root is a randomly built binary search tree on $i - 1$ keys, and the right subtree is a randomly built binary search tree on $n - i$ keys. Because the height of a binary tree is 1 more than the larger of the heights of the two subtrees of the root, the exponential height of a binary tree is twice the larger of the exponential heights of the two subtrees of the root. If we know that $R_n = i$, it follows that

$$Y_n = 2 \cdot \max(Y_{i-1}, Y_{n-i}) \ .$$

As base cases, we have that $Y_1 = 1$, because the exponential height of a tree with 1 node is $2^0 = 1$ and, for convenience, we define $Y_0 = 0$.

Next, define indicator random variables $Z_{n,1}, Z_{n,2}, \ldots, Z_{n,n}$, where

$$Z_{n,i} = I\{R_n = i\} \ .$$

Because R_n is equally likely to be any element of $\{1, 2, \ldots, n\}$, it follows that $\Pr\{R_n = i\} = 1/n$ for $i = 1, 2, \ldots, n$, and hence, by Lemma 5.1, we have

$$E[Z_{n,i}] = 1/n \ , \tag{12.1}$$

for $i = 1, 2, \ldots, n$. Because exactly one value of $Z_{n,i}$ is 1 and all others are 0, we also have

$$Y_n = \sum_{i=1}^{n} Z_{n,i} \left(2 \cdot \max(Y_{i-1}, Y_{n-i}) \right) .$$

We shall show that $\mathrm{E}[Y_n]$ is polynomial in n, which will ultimately imply that $\mathrm{E}[X_n] = O(\lg n)$.

We claim that the indicator random variable $Z_{n,i} = \mathrm{I}\{R_n = i\}$ is independent of the values of Y_{i-1} and Y_{n-i}. Having chosen $R_n = i$, the left subtree (whose exponential height is Y_{i-1}) is randomly built on the $i - 1$ keys whose ranks are less than i. This subtree is just like any other randomly built binary search tree on $i - 1$ keys. Other than the number of keys it contains, this subtree's structure is not affected at all by the choice of $R_n = i$, and hence the random variables Y_{i-1} and $Z_{n,i}$ are independent. Likewise, the right subtree, whose exponential height is Y_{n-i}, is randomly built on the $n - i$ keys whose ranks are greater than i. Its structure is independent of the value of R_n, and so the random variables Y_{n-i} and $Z_{n,i}$ are independent. Hence, we have

$$
\begin{aligned}
\mathrm{E}[Y_n] &= \mathrm{E}\left[\sum_{i=1}^{n} Z_{n,i} \left(2 \cdot \max(Y_{i-1}, Y_{n-i}) \right) \right] \\
&= \sum_{i=1}^{n} \mathrm{E}\left[Z_{n,i} \left(2 \cdot \max(Y_{i-1}, Y_{n-i}) \right) \right] && \text{(by linearity of expectation)} \\
&= \sum_{i=1}^{n} \mathrm{E}[Z_{n,i}] \, \mathrm{E}\left[2 \cdot \max(Y_{i-1}, Y_{n-i}) \right] && \text{(by independence)} \\
&= \sum_{i=1}^{n} \frac{1}{n} \cdot \mathrm{E}\left[2 \cdot \max(Y_{i-1}, Y_{n-i}) \right] && \text{(by equation (12.1))} \\
&= \frac{2}{n} \sum_{i=1}^{n} \mathrm{E}\left[\max(Y_{i-1}, Y_{n-i}) \right] && \text{(by equation (C.22))} \\
&\le \frac{2}{n} \sum_{i=1}^{n} \left(\mathrm{E}[Y_{i-1}] + \mathrm{E}[Y_{n-i}] \right) && \text{(by Exercise C.3-4) .}
\end{aligned}
$$

Since each term $\mathrm{E}[Y_0], \mathrm{E}[Y_1], \ldots, \mathrm{E}[Y_{n-1}]$ appears twice in the last summation, once as $\mathrm{E}[Y_{i-1}]$ and once as $\mathrm{E}[Y_{n-i}]$, we have the recurrence

$$\mathrm{E}[Y_n] \le \frac{4}{n} \sum_{i=0}^{n-1} \mathrm{E}[Y_i] . \tag{12.2}$$

Using the substitution method, we shall show that for all positive integers n, the recurrence (12.2) has the solution

$$E[Y_n] \le \frac{1}{4}\binom{n+3}{3}.$$

In doing so, we shall use the identity

$$\sum_{i=0}^{n-1}\binom{i+3}{3} = \binom{n+3}{4}.\qquad\qquad(12.3)$$

(Exercise 12.4-1 asks you to prove this identity.)

For the base cases, we note that the bounds $0 = Y_0 = E[Y_0] \le (1/4)\binom{3}{3} = 1/4$ and $1 = Y_1 = E[Y_1] \le (1/4)\binom{1+3}{3} = 1$ hold. For the inductive case, we have that

$$
\begin{aligned}
E[Y_n] \;&\le\; \frac{4}{n}\sum_{i=0}^{n-1} E[Y_i] \\[4pt]
&\le\; \frac{4}{n}\sum_{i=0}^{n-1}\frac{1}{4}\binom{i+3}{3} \qquad\text{(by the inductive hypothesis)} \\[4pt]
&=\; \frac{1}{n}\sum_{i=0}^{n-1}\binom{i+3}{3} \\[4pt]
&=\; \frac{1}{n}\binom{n+3}{4} \qquad\qquad\text{(by equation (12.3))} \\[4pt]
&=\; \frac{1}{n}\cdot\frac{(n+3)!}{4!\,(n-1)!} \\[4pt]
&=\; \frac{1}{4}\cdot\frac{(n+3)!}{3!\,n!} \\[4pt]
&=\; \frac{1}{4}\binom{n+3}{3}.
\end{aligned}
$$

We have bounded $E[Y_n]$, but our ultimate goal is to bound $E[X_n]$. As Exercise 12.4-4 asks you to show, the function $f(x) = 2^x$ is convex (see page 1199). Therefore, we can employ Jensen's inequality (C.26), which says that

$$
\begin{aligned}
2^{E[X_n]} \;&\le\; E\left[2^{X_n}\right] \\
&=\; E[Y_n]\,,
\end{aligned}
$$

as follows:

$$2^{E[X_n]} \;\le\; \frac{1}{4}\binom{n+3}{3}$$

$$= \frac{1}{4} \cdot \frac{(n+3)(n+2)(n+1)}{6}$$

$$= \frac{n^3 + 6n^2 + 11n + 6}{24}.$$

Taking logarithms of both sides gives $\mathrm{E}\,[X_n] = O(\lg n)$. ∎

Exercises

12.4-1
Prove equation (12.3).

12.4-2
Describe a binary search tree on n nodes such that the average depth of a node in the tree is $\Theta(\lg n)$ but the height of the tree is $\omega(\lg n)$. Give an asymptotic upper bound on the height of an n-node binary search tree in which the average depth of a node is $\Theta(\lg n)$.

12.4-3
Show that the notion of a randomly chosen binary search tree on n keys, where each binary search tree of n keys is equally likely to be chosen, is different from the notion of a randomly built binary search tree given in this section. (*Hint:* List the possibilities when $n = 3$.)

12.4-4
Show that the function $f(x) = 2^x$ is convex.

12.4-5 ★
Consider RANDOMIZED-QUICKSORT operating on a sequence of n distinct input numbers. Prove that for any constant $k > 0$, all but $O(1/n^k)$ of the $n!$ input permutations yield an $O(n \lg n)$ running time.

Problems

12-1 Binary search trees with equal keys
Equal keys pose a problem for the implementation of binary search trees.

a. What is the asymptotic performance of TREE-INSERT when used to insert n items with identical keys into an initially empty binary search tree?

We propose to improve TREE-INSERT by testing before line 5 to determine whether $z.key = x.key$ and by testing before line 11 to determine whether $z.key = y.key$.

If equality holds, we implement one of the following strategies. For each strategy, find the asymptotic performance of inserting n items with identical keys into an initially empty binary search tree. (The strategies are described for line 5, in which we compare the keys of z and x. Substitute y for x to arrive at the strategies for line 11.)

b. Keep a boolean flag $x.b$ at node x, and set x to either $x.left$ or $x.right$ based on the value of $x.b$, which alternates between FALSE and TRUE each time we visit x while inserting a node with the same key as x.

c. Keep a list of nodes with equal keys at x, and insert z into the list.

d. Randomly set x to either $x.left$ or $x.right$. (Give the worst-case performance and informally derive the expected running time.)

12-2   *Radix trees*

Given two strings $a = a_0 a_1 \ldots a_p$ and $b = b_0 b_1 \ldots b_q$, where each a_i and each b_j is in some ordered set of characters, we say that string a is ***lexicographically less than*** string b if either

1. there exists an integer j, where $0 \le j \le \min(p, q)$, such that $a_i = b_i$ for all $i = 0, 1, \ldots, j - 1$ and $a_j < b_j$, or

2. $p < q$ and $a_i = b_i$ for all $i = 0, 1, \ldots, p$.

For example, if a and b are bit strings, then $10100 < 10110$ by rule 1 (letting $j = 3$) and $10100 < 101000$ by rule 2. This ordering is similar to that used in English-language dictionaries.

The ***radix tree*** data structure shown in Figure 12.5 stores the bit strings 1011, 10, 011, 100, and 0. When searching for a key $a = a_0 a_1 \ldots a_p$, we go left at a node of depth i if $a_i = 0$ and right if $a_i = 1$. Let S be a set of distinct bit strings whose lengths sum to n. Show how to use a radix tree to sort S lexicographically in $\Theta(n)$ time. For the example in Figure 12.5, the output of the sort should be the sequence 0, 011, 10, 100, 1011.

12-3   *Average node depth in a randomly built binary search tree*

In this problem, we prove that the average depth of a node in a randomly built binary search tree with n nodes is $O(\lg n)$. Although this result is weaker than that of Theorem 12.4, the technique we shall use reveals a surprising similarity between the building of a binary search tree and the execution of RANDOMIZED-QUICKSORT from Section 7.3.

We define the ***total path length*** $P(T)$ of a binary tree T as the sum, over all nodes x in T, of the depth of node x, which we denote by $d(x, T)$.

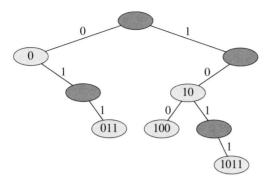

Figure 12.5 A radix tree storing the bit strings 1011, 10, 011, 100, and 0. We can determine each node's key by traversing the simple path from the root to that node. There is no need, therefore, to store the keys in the nodes; the keys appear here for illustrative purposes only. Nodes are heavily shaded if the keys corresponding to them are not in the tree; such nodes are present only to establish a path to other nodes.

a. Argue that the average depth of a node in T is

$$\frac{1}{n} \sum_{x \in T} d(x, T) = \frac{1}{n} P(T) \,.$$

Thus, we wish to show that the expected value of $P(T)$ is $O(n \lg n)$.

b. Let T_L and T_R denote the left and right subtrees of tree T, respectively. Argue that if T has n nodes, then

$$P(T) = P(T_L) + P(T_R) + n - 1 \,.$$

c. Let $P(n)$ denote the average total path length of a randomly built binary search tree with n nodes. Show that

$$P(n) = \frac{1}{n} \sum_{i=0}^{n-1} (P(i) + P(n - i - 1) + n - 1) \,.$$

d. Show how to rewrite $P(n)$ as

$$P(n) = \frac{2}{n} \sum_{k=1}^{n-1} P(k) + \Theta(n) \,.$$

e. Recalling the alternative analysis of the randomized version of quicksort given in Problem 7-3, conclude that $P(n) = O(n \lg n)$.

At each recursive invocation of quicksort, we choose a random pivot element to partition the set of elements being sorted. Each node of a binary search tree partitions the set of elements that fall into the subtree rooted at that node.

f. Describe an implementation of quicksort in which the comparisons to sort a set of elements are exactly the same as the comparisons to insert the elements into a binary search tree. (The order in which comparisons are made may differ, but the same comparisons must occur.)

12-4   *Number of different binary trees*

Let b_n denote the number of different binary trees with n nodes. In this problem, you will find a formula for b_n, as well as an asymptotic estimate.

a. Show that $b_0 = 1$ and that, for $n \geq 1$,

$$b_n = \sum_{k=0}^{n-1} b_k b_{n-1-k} \ .$$

b. Referring to Problem 4-4 for the definition of a generating function, let $B(x)$ be the generating function

$$B(x) = \sum_{n=0}^{\infty} b_n x^n \ .$$

Show that $B(x) = xB(x)^2 + 1$, and hence one way to express $B(x)$ in closed form is

$$B(x) = \frac{1}{2x} \left(1 - \sqrt{1 - 4x} \right) \ .$$

The **Taylor expansion** of $f(x)$ around the point $x = a$ is given by

$$f(x) = \sum_{k=0}^{\infty} \frac{f^{(k)}(a)}{k!} (x - a)^k \ ,$$

where $f^{(k)}(x)$ is the kth derivative of f evaluated at x.

c. Show that

$$b_n = \frac{1}{n+1} \binom{2n}{n}$$

(the nth **Catalan number**) by using the Taylor expansion of $\sqrt{1-4x}$ around $x = 0$. (If you wish, instead of using the Taylor expansion, you may use the generalization of the binomial expansion (C.4) to nonintegral exponents n, where for any real number n and for any integer k, we interpret $\binom{n}{k}$ to be $n(n-1)\cdots(n-k+1)/k!$ if $k \geq 0$, and 0 otherwise.)

d. Show that

$$b_n = \frac{4^n}{\sqrt{\pi}n^{3/2}}\left(1 + O(1/n)\right) .$$

Chapter notes

Knuth [211] contains a good discussion of simple binary search trees as well as many variations. Binary search trees seem to have been independently discovered by a number of people in the late 1950s. Radix trees are often called "tries," which comes from the middle letters in the word *retrieval*. Knuth [211] also discusses them.

Many texts, including the first two editions of this book, have a somewhat simpler method of deleting a node from a binary search tree when both of its children are present. Instead of replacing node z by its successor y, we delete node y but copy its key and satellite data into node z. The downside of this approach is that the node actually deleted might not be the node passed to the delete procedure. If other components of a program maintain pointers to nodes in the tree, they could mistakenly end up with "stale" pointers to nodes that have been deleted. Although the deletion method presented in this edition of this book is a bit more complicated, it guarantees that a call to delete node z deletes node z and only node z.

Section 15.5 will show how to construct an optimal binary search tree when we know the search frequencies before constructing the tree. That is, given the frequencies of searching for each key and the frequencies of searching for values that fall between keys in the tree, we construct a binary search tree for which a set of searches that follows these frequencies examines the minimum number of nodes.

The proof in Section 12.4 that bounds the expected height of a randomly built binary search tree is due to Aslam [24]. Martínez and Roura [243] give randomized algorithms for insertion into and deletion from binary search trees in which the result of either operation is a random binary search tree. Their definition of a random binary search tree differs—only slightly—from that of a randomly built binary search tree in this chapter, however.

13   Red-Black Trees

Chapter 12 showed that a binary search tree of height h can support any of the basic dynamic-set operations—such as SEARCH, PREDECESSOR, SUCCESSOR, MINIMUM, MAXIMUM, INSERT, and DELETE—in $O(h)$ time. Thus, the set operations are fast if the height of the search tree is small. If its height is large, however, the set operations may run no faster than with a linked list. Red-black trees are one of many search-tree schemes that are "balanced" in order to guarantee that basic dynamic-set operations take $O(\lg n)$ time in the worst case.

13.1   Properties of red-black trees

A *red-black tree* is a binary search tree with one extra bit of storage per node: its *color*, which can be either RED or BLACK. By constraining the node colors on any simple path from the root to a leaf, red-black trees ensure that no such path is more than twice as long as any other, so that the tree is approximately *balanced*.

Each node of the tree now contains the attributes *color*, *key*, *left*, *right*, and *p*. If a child or the parent of a node does not exist, the corresponding pointer attribute of the node contains the value NIL. We shall regard these NILs as being pointers to leaves (external nodes) of the binary search tree and the normal, key-bearing nodes as being internal nodes of the tree.

A red-black tree is a binary tree that satisfies the following *red-black properties*:

1. Every node is either red or black.

2. The root is black.

3. Every leaf (NIL) is black.

4. If a node is red, then both its children are black.

5. For each node, all simple paths from the node to descendant leaves contain the same number of black nodes.

Figure 13.1(a) shows an example of a red-black tree.

As a matter of convenience in dealing with boundary conditions in red-black tree code, we use a single sentinel to represent NIL (see page 238). For a red-black tree T, the sentinel $T.nil$ is an object with the same attributes as an ordinary node in the tree. Its *color* attribute is BLACK, and its other attributes—p, *left*, *right*, and *key*—can take on arbitrary values. As Figure 13.1(b) shows, all pointers to NIL are replaced by pointers to the sentinel $T.nil$.

We use the sentinel so that we can treat a NIL child of a node x as an ordinary node whose parent is x. Although we instead could add a distinct sentinel node for each NIL in the tree, so that the parent of each NIL is well defined, that approach would waste space. Instead, we use the one sentinel $T.nil$ to represent all the NILs—all leaves and the root's parent. The values of the attributes p, *left*, *right*, and *key* of the sentinel are immaterial, although we may set them during the course of a procedure for our convenience.

We generally confine our interest to the internal nodes of a red-black tree, since they hold the key values. In the remainder of this chapter, we omit the leaves when we draw red-black trees, as shown in Figure 13.1(c).

We call the number of black nodes on any simple path from, but not including, a node x down to a leaf the ***black-height*** of the node, denoted bh(x). By property 5, the notion of black-height is well defined, since all descending simple paths from the node have the same number of black nodes. We define the black-height of a red-black tree to be the black-height of its root.

The following lemma shows why red-black trees make good search trees.

Lemma 13.1
A red-black tree with n internal nodes has height at most $2 \lg(n + 1)$.

Proof We start by showing that the subtree rooted at any node x contains at least $2^{\text{bh}(x)} - 1$ internal nodes. We prove this claim by induction on the height of x. If the height of x is 0, then x must be a leaf ($T.nil$), and the subtree rooted at x indeed contains at least $2^{\text{bh}(x)} - 1 = 2^0 - 1 = 0$ internal nodes. For the inductive step, consider a node x that has positive height and is an internal node with two children. Each child has a black-height of either bh(x) or bh(x) − 1, depending on whether its color is red or black, respectively. Since the height of a child of x is less than the height of x itself, we can apply the inductive hypothesis to conclude that each child has at least $2^{\text{bh}(x)-1} - 1$ internal nodes. Thus, the subtree rooted at x contains at least $(2^{\text{bh}(x)-1} - 1) + (2^{\text{bh}(x)-1} - 1) + 1 = 2^{\text{bh}(x)} - 1$ internal nodes, which proves the claim.

To complete the proof of the lemma, let h be the height of the tree. According to property 4, at least half the nodes on any simple path from the root to a leaf, not

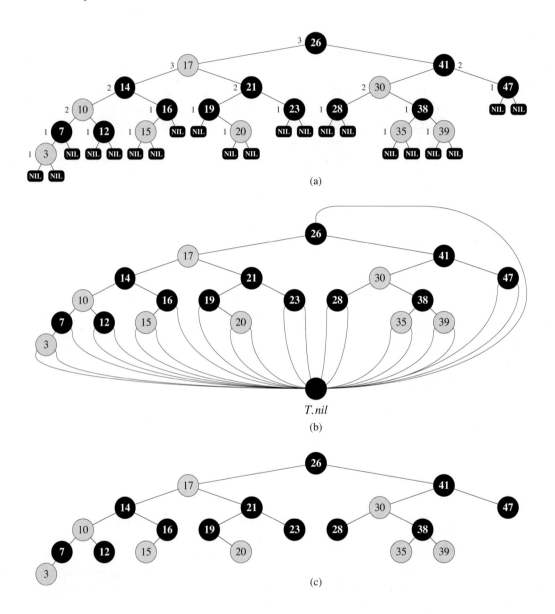

Figure 13.1 A red-black tree with black nodes darkened and red nodes shaded. Every node in a red-black tree is either red or black, the children of a red node are both black, and every simple path from a node to a descendant leaf contains the same number of black nodes. **(a)** Every leaf, shown as a NIL, is black. Each non-NIL node is marked with its black-height; NILs have black-height 0. **(b)** The same red-black tree but with each NIL replaced by the single sentinel $T.nil$, which is always black, and with black-heights omitted. The root's parent is also the sentinel. **(c)** The same red-black tree but with leaves and the root's parent omitted entirely. We shall use this drawing style in the remainder of this chapter.

including the root, must be black. Consequently, the black-height of the root must be at least $h/2$; thus,

$$n \geq 2^{h/2} - 1 \,.$$

Moving the 1 to the left-hand side and taking logarithms on both sides yields $\lg(n + 1) \geq h/2$, or $h \leq 2\lg(n + 1)$. ■

As an immediate consequence of this lemma, we can implement the dynamic-set operations SEARCH, MINIMUM, MAXIMUM, SUCCESSOR, and PREDECESSOR in $O(\lg n)$ time on red-black trees, since each can run in $O(h)$ time on a binary search tree of height h (as shown in Chapter 12) and any red-black tree on n nodes is a binary search tree with height $O(\lg n)$. (Of course, references to NIL in the algorithms of Chapter 12 would have to be replaced by $T.nil$.) Although the algorithms TREE-INSERT and TREE-DELETE from Chapter 12 run in $O(\lg n)$ time when given a red-black tree as input, they do not directly support the dynamic-set operations INSERT and DELETE, since they do not guarantee that the modified binary search tree will be a red-black tree. We shall see in Sections 13.3 and 13.4, however, how to support these two operations in $O(\lg n)$ time.

Exercises

13.1-1
In the style of Figure 13.1(a), draw the complete binary search tree of height 3 on the keys $\{1, 2, \ldots, 15\}$. Add the NIL leaves and color the nodes in three different ways such that the black-heights of the resulting red-black trees are 2, 3, and 4.

13.1-2
Draw the red-black tree that results after TREE-INSERT is called on the tree in Figure 13.1 with key 36. If the inserted node is colored red, is the resulting tree a red-black tree? What if it is colored black?

13.1-3
Let us define a ***relaxed red-black tree*** as a binary search tree that satisfies red-black properties 1, 3, 4, and 5. In other words, the root may be either red or black. Consider a relaxed red-black tree T whose root is red. If we color the root of T black but make no other changes to T, is the resulting tree a red-black tree?

13.1-4
Suppose that we "absorb" every red node in a red-black tree into its black parent, so that the children of the red node become children of the black parent. (Ignore what happens to the keys.) What are the possible degrees of a black node after all

its red children are absorbed? What can you say about the depths of the leaves of the resulting tree?

13.1-5

Show that the longest simple path from a node x in a red-black tree to a descendant leaf has length at most twice that of the shortest simple path from node x to a descendant leaf.

13.1-6

What is the largest possible number of internal nodes in a red-black tree with black-height k? What is the smallest possible number?

13.1-7

Describe a red-black tree on n keys that realizes the largest possible ratio of red internal nodes to black internal nodes. What is this ratio? What tree has the smallest possible ratio, and what is the ratio?

13.2   Rotations

The search-tree operations TREE-INSERT and TREE-DELETE, when run on a red-black tree with n keys, take $O(\lg n)$ time. Because they modify the tree, the result may violate the red-black properties enumerated in Section 13.1. To restore these properties, we must change the colors of some of the nodes in the tree and also change the pointer structure.

We change the pointer structure through ***rotation***, which is a local operation in a search tree that preserves the binary-search-tree property. Figure 13.2 shows the two kinds of rotations: left rotations and right rotations. When we do a left rotation on a node x, we assume that its right child y is not $T.nil$; x may be any node in the tree whose right child is not $T.nil$. The left rotation "pivots" around the link from x to y. It makes y the new root of the subtree, with x as y's left child and y's left child as x's right child.

The pseudocode for LEFT-ROTATE assumes that $x.right \neq T.nil$ and that the root's parent is $T.nil$.

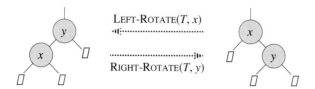

Figure 13.2 The rotation operations on a binary search tree. The operation LEFT-ROTATE(T, x) transforms the configuration of the two nodes on the right into the configuration on the left by changing a constant number of pointers. The inverse operation RIGHT-ROTATE(T, y) transforms the configuration on the left into the configuration on the right. The letters α, β, and γ represent arbitrary subtrees. A rotation operation preserves the binary-search-tree property: the keys in α precede $x.key$, which precedes the keys in β, which precede $y.key$, which precedes the keys in γ.

LEFT-ROTATE(T, x)

```
 1  y = x.right            // set y
 2  x.right = y.left       // turn y's left subtree into x's right subtree
 3  if y.left ≠ T.nil
 4      y.left.p = x
 5  y.p = x.p              // link x's parent to y
 6  if x.p == T.nil
 7      T.root = y
 8  elseif x == x.p.left
 9      x.p.left = y
10  else x.p.right = y
11  y.left = x             // put x on y's left
12  x.p = y
```

Figure 13.3 shows an example of how LEFT-ROTATE modifies a binary search tree. The code for RIGHT-ROTATE is symmetric. Both LEFT-ROTATE and RIGHT-ROTATE run in $O(1)$ time. Only pointers are changed by a rotation; all other attributes in a node remain the same.

Exercises

13.2-1
Write pseudocode for RIGHT-ROTATE.

13.2-2
Argue that in every n-node binary search tree, there are exactly $n - 1$ possible rotations.

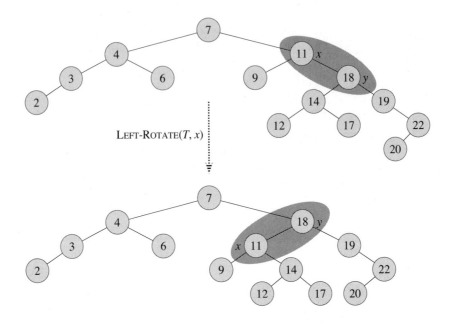

Figure 13.3 An example of how the procedure LEFT-ROTATE(T, x) modifies a binary search tree. Inorder tree walks of the input tree and the modified tree produce the same listing of key values.

13.2-3
Let a, b, and c be arbitrary nodes in subtrees α, β, and γ, respectively, in the right tree of Figure 13.2. How do the depths of a, b, and c change when a left rotation is performed on node x in the figure?

13.2-4
Show that any arbitrary n-node binary search tree can be transformed into any other arbitrary n-node binary search tree using $O(n)$ rotations. (*Hint:* First show that at most $n - 1$ right rotations suffice to transform the tree into a right-going chain.)

13.2-5   ★
We say that a binary search tree T_1 can be ***right-converted*** to binary search tree T_2 if it is possible to obtain T_2 from T_1 via a series of calls to RIGHT-ROTATE. Give an example of two trees T_1 and T_2 such that T_1 cannot be right-converted to T_2. Then, show that if a tree T_1 can be right-converted to T_2, it can be right-converted using $O(n^2)$ calls to RIGHT-ROTATE.

13.3 Insertion

We can insert a node into an n-node red-black tree in $O(\lg n)$ time. To do so, we use a slightly modified version of the TREE-INSERT procedure (Section 12.3) to insert node z into the tree T as if it were an ordinary binary search tree, and then we color z red. (Exercise 13.3-1 asks you to explain why we choose to make node z red rather than black.) To guarantee that the red-black properties are preserved, we then call an auxiliary procedure RB-INSERT-FIXUP to recolor nodes and perform rotations. The call RB-INSERT(T, z) inserts node z, whose *key* is assumed to have already been filled in, into the red-black tree T.

RB-INSERT(T, z)

```
 1   y = T.nil
 2   x = T.root
 3   while x ≠ T.nil
 4        y = x
 5        if z.key < x.key
 6             x = x.left
 7        else x = x.right
 8   z.p = y
 9   if y == T.nil
10        T.root = z
11   elseif z.key < y.key
12        y.left = z
13   else y.right = z
14   z.left = T.nil
15   z.right = T.nil
16   z.color = RED
17   RB-INSERT-FIXUP(T, z)
```

The procedures TREE-INSERT and RB-INSERT differ in four ways. First, all instances of NIL in TREE-INSERT are replaced by $T.nil$. Second, we set $z.left$ and $z.right$ to $T.nil$ in lines 14–15 of RB-INSERT, in order to maintain the proper tree structure. Third, we color z red in line 16. Fourth, because coloring z red may cause a violation of one of the red-black properties, we call RB-INSERT-FIXUP(T, z) in line 17 of RB-INSERT to restore the red-black properties.

RB-INSERT-FIXUP(T, z)

```
1   while z.p.color == RED
2       if z.p == z.p.p.left
3           y = z.p.p.right
4           if y.color == RED
5               z.p.color = BLACK              // case 1
6               y.color = BLACK                // case 1
7               z.p.p.color = RED              // case 1
8               z = z.p.p                      // case 1
9           else if z == z.p.right
10              z = z.p                        // case 2
11              LEFT-ROTATE(T, z)              // case 2
12              z.p.color = BLACK              // case 3
13              z.p.p.color = RED              // case 3
14              RIGHT-ROTATE(T, z.p.p)         // case 3
15      else (same as then clause
                 with "right" and "left" exchanged)
16  T.root.color = BLACK
```

To understand how RB-INSERT-FIXUP works, we shall break our examination of the code into three major steps. First, we shall determine what violations of the red-black properties are introduced in RB-INSERT when node z is inserted and colored red. Second, we shall examine the overall goal of the **while** loop in lines 1–15. Finally, we shall explore each of the three cases[1] within the **while** loop's body and see how they accomplish the goal. Figure 13.4 shows how RB-INSERT-FIXUP operates on a sample red-black tree.

Which of the red-black properties might be violated upon the call to RB-INSERT-FIXUP? Property 1 certainly continues to hold, as does property 3, since both children of the newly inserted red node are the sentinel $T.nil$. Property 5, which says that the number of black nodes is the same on every simple path from a given node, is satisfied as well, because node z replaces the (black) sentinel, and node z is red with sentinel children. Thus, the only properties that might be violated are property 2, which requires the root to be black, and property 4, which says that a red node cannot have a red child. Both possible violations are due to z being colored red. Property 2 is violated if z is the root, and property 4 is violated if z's parent is red. Figure 13.4(a) shows a violation of property 4 after the node z has been inserted.

---

[1]Case 2 falls through into case 3, and so these two cases are not mutually exclusive.

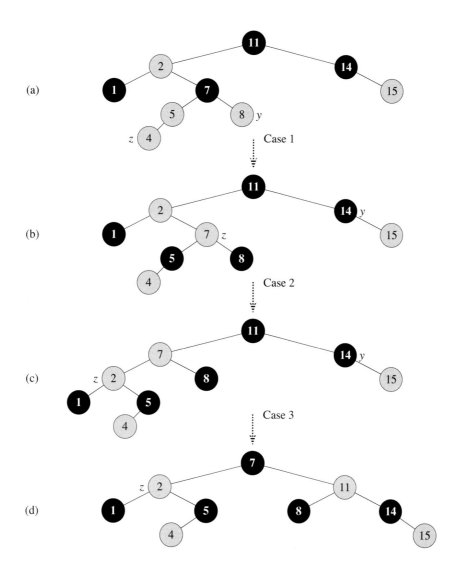

Figure 13.4 The operation of RB-INSERT-FIXUP. **(a)** A node z after insertion. Because both z and its parent $z.p$ are red, a violation of property 4 occurs. Since z's uncle y is red, case 1 in the code applies. We recolor nodes and move the pointer z up the tree, resulting in the tree shown in **(b)**. Once again, z and its parent are both red, but z's uncle y is black. Since z is the right child of $z.p$, case 2 applies. We perform a left rotation, and the tree that results is shown in **(c)**. Now, z is the left child of its parent, and case 3 applies. Recoloring and right rotation yield the tree in **(d)**, which is a legal red-black tree.

The **while** loop in lines 1–15 maintains the following three-part invariant at the start of each iteration of the loop:

  a. Node z is red.

  b. If $z.p$ is the root, then $z.p$ is black.

  c. If the tree violates any of the red-black properties, then it violates at most one of them, and the violation is of either property 2 or property 4. If the tree violates property 2, it is because z is the root and is red. If the tree violates property 4, it is because both z and $z.p$ are red.

Part (c), which deals with violations of red-black properties, is more central to showing that RB-INSERT-FIXUP restores the red-black properties than parts (a) and (b), which we use along the way to understand situations in the code. Because we'll be focusing on node z and nodes near it in the tree, it helps to know from part (a) that z is red. We shall use part (b) to show that the node $z.p.p$ exists when we reference it in lines 2, 3, 7, 8, 13, and 14.

Recall that we need to show that a loop invariant is true prior to the first iteration of the loop, that each iteration maintains the loop invariant, and that the loop invariant gives us a useful property at loop termination.

We start with the initialization and termination arguments. Then, as we examine how the body of the loop works in more detail, we shall argue that the loop maintains the invariant upon each iteration. Along the way, we shall also demonstrate that each iteration of the loop has two possible outcomes: either the pointer z moves up the tree, or we perform some rotations and then the loop terminates.

Initialization: Prior to the first iteration of the loop, we started with a red-black tree with no violations, and we added a red node z. We show that each part of the invariant holds at the time RB-INSERT-FIXUP is called:

  a. When RB-INSERT-FIXUP is called, z is the red node that was added.

  b. If $z.p$ is the root, then $z.p$ started out black and did not change prior to the call of RB-INSERT-FIXUP.

  c. We have already seen that properties 1, 3, and 5 hold when RB-INSERT-FIXUP is called.

  If the tree violates property 2, then the red root must be the newly added node z, which is the only internal node in the tree. Because the parent and both children of z are the sentinel, which is black, the tree does not also violate property 4. Thus, this violation of property 2 is the only violation of red-black properties in the entire tree.

  If the tree violates property 4, then, because the children of node z are black sentinels and the tree had no other violations prior to z being added, the violation must be because both z and $z.p$ are red. Moreover, the tree violates no other red-black properties.

Termination: When the loop terminates, it does so because $z.p$ is black. (If z is the root, then $z.p$ is the sentinel *T.nil*, which is black.) Thus, the tree does not violate property 4 at loop termination. By the loop invariant, the only property that might fail to hold is property 2. Line 16 restores this property, too, so that when RB-INSERT-FIXUP terminates, all the red-black properties hold.

Maintenance: We actually need to consider six cases in the **while** loop, but three of them are symmetric to the other three, depending on whether line 2 determines z's parent $z.p$ to be a left child or a right child of z's grandparent $z.p.p$. We have given the code only for the situation in which $z.p$ is a left child. The node $z.p.p$ exists, since by part (b) of the loop invariant, if $z.p$ is the root, then $z.p$ is black. Since we enter a loop iteration only if $z.p$ is red, we know that $z.p$ cannot be the root. Hence, $z.p.p$ exists.

We distinguish case 1 from cases 2 and 3 by the color of z's parent's sibling, or "uncle." Line 3 makes y point to z's uncle $z.p.p.right$, and line 4 tests y's color. If y is red, then we execute case 1. Otherwise, control passes to cases 2 and 3. In all three cases, z's grandparent $z.p.p$ is black, since its parent $z.p$ is red, and property 4 is violated only between z and $z.p$.

Case 1: z's uncle y is red

Figure 13.5 shows the situation for case 1 (lines 5–8), which occurs when both $z.p$ and y are red. Because $z.p.p$ is black, we can color both $z.p$ and y black, thereby fixing the problem of z and $z.p$ both being red, and we can color $z.p.p$ red, thereby maintaining property 5. We then repeat the **while** loop with $z.p.p$ as the new node z. The pointer z moves up two levels in the tree.

Now, we show that case 1 maintains the loop invariant at the start of the next iteration. We use z to denote node z in the current iteration, and $z' = z.p.p$ to denote the node that will be called node z at the test in line 1 upon the next iteration.

a. Because this iteration colors $z.p.p$ red, node z' is red at the start of the next iteration.

b. The node $z'.p$ is $z.p.p.p$ in this iteration, and the color of this node does not change. If this node is the root, it was black prior to this iteration, and it remains black at the start of the next iteration.

c. We have already argued that case 1 maintains property 5, and it does not introduce a violation of properties 1 or 3.

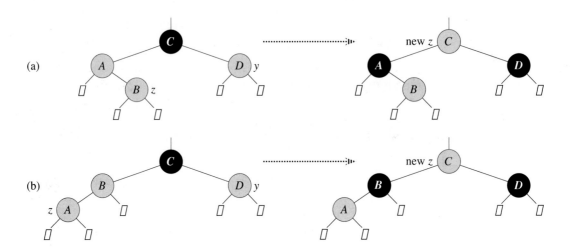

Figure 13.5   Case 1 of the procedure RB-INSERT-FIXUP. Property 4 is violated, since z and its parent $z.p$ are both red. We take the same action whether **(a)** z is a right child or **(b)** z is a left child. Each of the subtrees α, β, γ, δ, and ε has a black root, and each has the same black-height. The code for case 1 changes the colors of some nodes, preserving property 5: all downward simple paths from a node to a leaf have the same number of blacks. The **while** loop continues with node z's grandparent $z.p.p$ as the new z. Any violation of property 4 can now occur only between the new z, which is red, and its parent, if it is red as well.

If node z' is the root at the start of the next iteration, then case 1 corrected the lone violation of property 4 in this iteration. Since z' is red and it is the root, property 2 becomes the only one that is violated, and this violation is due to z'.

If node z' is not the root at the start of the next iteration, then case 1 has not created a violation of property 2. Case 1 corrected the lone violation of property 4 that existed at the start of this iteration. It then made z' red and left $z'.p$ alone. If $z'.p$ was black, there is no violation of property 4. If $z'.p$ was red, coloring z' red created one violation of property 4 between z' and $z'.p$.

Case 2: *z's uncle y is black and z is a right child*
Case 3: *z's uncle y is black and z is a left child*

In cases 2 and 3, the color of z's uncle y is black. We distinguish the two cases according to whether z is a right or left child of $z.p$. Lines 10–11 constitute case 2, which is shown in Figure 13.6 together with case 3. In case 2, node z is a right child of its parent. We immediately use a left rotation to transform the situation into case 3 (lines 12–14), in which node z is a left child. Because

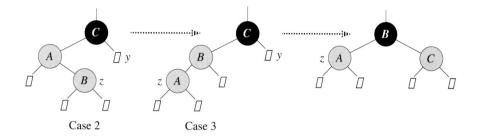

Figure 13.6 Cases 2 and 3 of the procedure RB-INSERT-FIXUP. As in case 1, property 4 is violated in either case 2 or case 3 because z and its parent $z.p$ are both red. Each of the subtrees α, β, γ, and δ has a black root (α, β, and γ from property 4, and δ because otherwise we would be in case 1), and each has the same black-height. We transform case 2 into case 3 by a left rotation, which preserves property 5: all downward simple paths from a node to a leaf have the same number of blacks. Case 3 causes some color changes and a right rotation, which also preserve property 5. The **while** loop then terminates, because property 4 is satisfied: there are no longer two red nodes in a row.

both z and $z.p$ are red, the rotation affects neither the black-height of nodes nor property 5. Whether we enter case 3 directly or through case 2, z's uncle y is black, since otherwise we would have executed case 1. Additionally, the node $z.p.p$ exists, since we have argued that this node existed at the time that lines 2 and 3 were executed, and after moving z up one level in line 10 and then down one level in line 11, the identity of $z.p.p$ remains unchanged. In case 3, we execute some color changes and a right rotation, which preserve property 5, and then, since we no longer have two red nodes in a row, we are done. The **while** loop does not iterate another time, since $z.p$ is now black.

We now show that cases 2 and 3 maintain the loop invariant. (As we have just argued, $z.p$ will be black upon the next test in line 1, and the loop body will not execute again.)

a. Case 2 makes z point to $z.p$, which is red. No further change to z or its color occurs in cases 2 and 3.

b. Case 3 makes $z.p$ black, so that if $z.p$ is the root at the start of the next iteration, it is black.

c. As in case 1, properties 1, 3, and 5 are maintained in cases 2 and 3.

  Since node z is not the root in cases 2 and 3, we know that there is no violation of property 2. Cases 2 and 3 do not introduce a violation of property 2, since the only node that is made red becomes a child of a black node by the rotation in case 3.

  Cases 2 and 3 correct the lone violation of property 4, and they do not introduce another violation.

Having shown that each iteration of the loop maintains the invariant, we have shown that RB-INSERT-FIXUP correctly restores the red-black properties.

Analysis

What is the running time of RB-INSERT? Since the height of a red-black tree on n nodes is $O(\lg n)$, lines 1–16 of RB-INSERT take $O(\lg n)$ time. In RB-INSERT-FIXUP, the **while** loop repeats only if case 1 occurs, and then the pointer z moves two levels up the tree. The total number of times the **while** loop can be executed is therefore $O(\lg n)$. Thus, RB-INSERT takes a total of $O(\lg n)$ time. Moreover, it never performs more than two rotations, since the **while** loop terminates if case 2 or case 3 is executed.

Exercises

13.3-1
In line 16 of RB-INSERT, we set the color of the newly inserted node z to red. Observe that if we had chosen to set z's color to black, then property 4 of a red-black tree would not be violated. Why didn't we choose to set z's color to black?

13.3-2
Show the red-black trees that result after successively inserting the keys $41, 38, 31, 12, 19, 8$ into an initially empty red-black tree.

13.3-3
Suppose that the black-height of each of the subtrees $\alpha, \beta, \gamma, \delta, \varepsilon$ in Figures 13.5 and 13.6 is k. Label each node in each figure with its black-height to verify that the indicated transformation preserves property 5.

13.3-4
Professor Teach is concerned that RB-INSERT-FIXUP might set $T.nil.color$ to RED, in which case the test in line 1 would not cause the loop to terminate when z is the root. Show that the professor's concern is unfounded by arguing that RB-INSERT-FIXUP never sets $T.nil.color$ to RED.

13.3-5
Consider a red-black tree formed by inserting n nodes with RB-INSERT. Argue that if $n > 1$, the tree has at least one red node.

13.3-6
Suggest how to implement RB-INSERT efficiently if the representation for red-black trees includes no storage for parent pointers.

13.4   Deletion

Like the other basic operations on an n-node red-black tree, deletion of a node takes time $O(\lg n)$. Deleting a node from a red-black tree is a bit more complicated than inserting a node.

The procedure for deleting a node from a red-black tree is based on the TREE-DELETE procedure (Section 12.3). First, we need to customize the TRANSPLANT subroutine that TREE-DELETE calls so that it applies to a red-black tree:

RB-TRANSPLANT(T, u, v)

```
1   if u.p == T.nil
2       T.root = v
3   elseif u == u.p.left
4       u.p.left = v
5   else u.p.right = v
6   v.p = u.p
```

The procedure RB-TRANSPLANT differs from TRANSPLANT in two ways. First, line 1 references the sentinel $T.nil$ instead of NIL. Second, the assignment to $v.p$ in line 6 occurs unconditionally: we can assign to $v.p$ even if v points to the sentinel. In fact, we shall exploit the ability to assign to $v.p$ when $v = T.nil$.

The procedure RB-DELETE is like the TREE-DELETE procedure, but with additional lines of pseudocode. Some of the additional lines keep track of a node y that might cause violations of the red-black properties. When we want to delete node z and z has fewer than two children, then z is removed from the tree, and we want y to be z. When z has two children, then y should be z's successor, and y moves into z's position in the tree. We also remember y's color before it is removed from or moved within the tree, and we keep track of the node x that moves into y's original position in the tree, because node x might also cause violations of the red-black properties. After deleting node z, RB-DELETE calls an auxiliary procedure RB-DELETE-FIXUP, which changes colors and performs rotations to restore the red-black properties.

RB-DELETE(T, z)

```
 1  y = z
 2  y-original-color = y.color
 3  if z.left == T.nil
 4      x = z.right
 5      RB-TRANSPLANT(T, z, z.right)
 6  elseif z.right == T.nil
 7      x = z.left
 8      RB-TRANSPLANT(T, z, z.left)
 9  else y = TREE-MINIMUM(z.right)
10      y-original-color = y.color
11      x = y.right
12      if y.p == z
13          x.p = y
14      else RB-TRANSPLANT(T, y, y.right)
15          y.right = z.right
16          y.right.p = y
17      RB-TRANSPLANT(T, z, y)
18      y.left = z.left
19      y.left.p = y
20      y.color = z.color
21  if y-original-color == BLACK
22      RB-DELETE-FIXUP(T, x)
```

Although RB-DELETE contains almost twice as many lines of pseudocode as TREE-DELETE, the two procedures have the same basic structure. You can find each line of TREE-DELETE within RB-DELETE (with the changes of replacing NIL by $T.nil$ and replacing calls to TRANSPLANT by calls to RB-TRANSPLANT), executed under the same conditions.

Here are the other differences between the two procedures:

- We maintain node y as the node either removed from the tree or moved within the tree. Line 1 sets y to point to node z when z has fewer than two children and is therefore removed. When z has two children, line 9 sets y to point to z's successor, just as in TREE-DELETE, and y will move into z's position in the tree.

- Because node y's color might change, the variable y-original-color stores y's color before any changes occur. Lines 2 and 10 set this variable immediately after assignments to y. When z has two children, then $y \neq z$ and node y moves into node z's original position in the red-black tree; line 20 gives y the same color as z. We need to save y's original color in order to test it at the end of RB-DELETE; if it was black, then removing or moving y could cause violations of the red-black properties.

- As discussed, we keep track of the node x that moves into node y's original position. The assignments in lines 4, 7, and 11 set x to point to either y's only child or, if y has no children, the sentinel $T.nil$. (Recall from Section 12.3 that y has no left child.)

- Since node x moves into node y's original position, the attribute $x.p$ is always set to point to the original position in the tree of y's parent, even if x is, in fact, the sentinel $T.nil$. Unless z is y's original parent (which occurs only when z has two children and its successor y is z's right child), the assignment to $x.p$ takes place in line 6 of RB-TRANSPLANT. (Observe that when RB-TRANSPLANT is called in lines 5, 8, or 14, the third parameter passed is the same as x.)

  When y's original parent is z, however, we do not want $x.p$ to point to y's original parent, since we are removing that node from the tree. Because node y will move up to take z's position in the tree, setting $x.p$ to y in line 13 causes $x.p$ to point to the original position of y's parent, even if $x = T.nil$.

- Finally, if node y was black, we might have introduced one or more violations of the red-black properties, and so we call RB-DELETE-FIXUP in line 22 to restore the red-black properties. If y was red, the red-black properties still hold when y is removed or moved, for the following reasons:

  1. No black-heights in the tree have changed.
  2. No red nodes have been made adjacent. Because y takes z's place in the tree, along with z's color, we cannot have two adjacent red nodes at y's new position in the tree. In addition, if y was not z's right child, then y's original right child x replaces y in the tree. If y is red, then x must be black, and so replacing y by x cannot cause two red nodes to become adjacent.
  3. Since y could not have been the root if it was red, the root remains black.

If node y was black, three problems may arise, which the call of RB-DELETE-FIXUP will remedy. First, if y had been the root and a red child of y becomes the new root, we have violated property 2. Second, if both x and $x.p$ are red, then we have violated property 4. Third, moving y within the tree causes any simple path that previously contained y to have one fewer black node. Thus, property 5 is now violated by any ancestor of y in the tree. We can correct the violation of property 5 by saying that node x, now occupying y's original position, has an "extra" black. That is, if we add 1 to the count of black nodes on any simple path that contains x, then under this interpretation, property 5 holds. When we remove or move the black node y, we "push" its blackness onto node x. The problem is that now node x is neither red nor black, thereby violating property 1. Instead, node x is either "doubly black" or "red-and-black," and it contributes either 2 or 1, respectively, to the count of black nodes on simple paths containing x. The *color* attribute of x will still be either RED (if x is red-and-black) or BLACK (if x is doubly black). In other words, the extra black on a node is reflected in x's pointing to the node rather than in the *color* attribute.

We can now see the procedure RB-DELETE-FIXUP and examine how it restores the red-black properties to the search tree.

RB-DELETE-FIXUP(T, x)

```
 1   while x ≠ T.root and x.color == BLACK
 2       if x == x.p.left
 3           w = x.p.right
 4           if w.color == RED
 5               w.color = BLACK                                    // case 1
 6               x.p.color = RED                                    // case 1
 7               LEFT-ROTATE(T, x.p)                                // case 1
 8               w = x.p.right                                      // case 1
 9           if w.left.color == BLACK and w.right.color == BLACK
10               w.color = RED                                      // case 2
11               x = x.p                                            // case 2
12           else if w.right.color == BLACK
13                   w.left.color = BLACK                           // case 3
14                   w.color = RED                                  // case 3
15                   RIGHT-ROTATE(T, w)                             // case 3
16                   w = x.p.right                                  // case 3
17               w.color = x.p.color                                // case 4
18               x.p.color = BLACK                                  // case 4
19               w.right.color = BLACK                              // case 4
20               LEFT-ROTATE(T, x.p)                                // case 4
21               x = T.root                                         // case 4
22       else (same as then clause with "right" and "left" exchanged)
23   x.color = BLACK
```

The procedure RB-DELETE-FIXUP restores properties 1, 2, and 4. Exercises 13.4-1 and 13.4-2 ask you to show that the procedure restores properties 2 and 4, and so in the remainder of this section, we shall focus on property 1. The goal of the **while** loop in lines 1–22 is to move the extra black up the tree until

1. x points to a red-and-black node, in which case we color x (singly) black in line 23;

2. x points to the root, in which case we simply "remove" the extra black; or

3. having performed suitable rotations and recolorings, we exit the loop.

Within the **while** loop, x always points to a nonroot doubly black node. We determine in line 2 whether x is a left child or a right child of its parent $x.p$. (We have given the code for the situation in which x is a left child; the situation in which x is a right child—line 22—is symmetric.) We maintain a pointer w to the sibling of x. Since node x is doubly black, node w cannot be $T.nil$, because otherwise, the number of blacks on the simple path from $x.p$ to the (singly black) leaf w would be smaller than the number on the simple path from $x.p$ to x.

The four cases[2] in the code appear in Figure 13.7. Before examining each case in detail, let's look more generally at how we can verify that the transformation in each of the cases preserves property 5. The key idea is that in each case, the transformation applied preserves the number of black nodes (including x's extra black) from (and including) the root of the subtree shown to each of the subtrees $\alpha, \beta, \dots, \zeta$. Thus, if property 5 holds prior to the transformation, it continues to hold afterward. For example, in Figure 13.7(a), which illustrates case 1, the number of black nodes from the root to either subtree α or β is 3, both before and after the transformation. (Again, remember that node x adds an extra black.) Similarly, the number of black nodes from the root to any of γ, δ, ε, and ζ is 2, both before and after the transformation. In Figure 13.7(b), the counting must involve the value c of the *color* attribute of the root of the subtree shown, which can be either RED or BLACK. If we define count(RED) = 0 and count(BLACK) = 1, then the number of black nodes from the root to α is $2 + \text{count}(c)$, both before and after the transformation. In this case, after the transformation, the new node x has *color* attribute c, but this node is really either red-and-black (if $c = $ RED) or doubly black (if $c = $ BLACK). You can verify the other cases similarly (see Exercise 13.4-5).

Case 1: x's sibling w is red

Case 1 (lines 5–8 of RB-DELETE-FIXUP and Figure 13.7(a)) occurs when node w, the sibling of node x, is red. Since w must have black children, we can switch the colors of w and $x.p$ and then perform a left-rotation on $x.p$ without violating any of the red-black properties. The new sibling of x, which is one of w's children prior to the rotation, is now black, and thus we have converted case 1 into case 2, 3, or 4.

Cases 2, 3, and 4 occur when node w is black; they are distinguished by the colors of w's children.

---

[2]As in RB-INSERT-FIXUP, the cases in RB-DELETE-FIXUP are not mutually exclusive.

Case 2: x's sibling w is black, and both of w's children are black

In case 2 (lines 10–11 of RB-DELETE-FIXUP and Figure 13.7(b)), both of w's children are black. Since w is also black, we take one black off both x and w, leaving x with only one black and leaving w red. To compensate for removing one black from x and w, we would like to add an extra black to $x.p$, which was originally either red or black. We do so by repeating the **while** loop with $x.p$ as the new node x. Observe that if we enter case 2 through case 1, the new node x is red-and-black, since the original $x.p$ was red. Hence, the value c of the *color* attribute of the new node x is RED, and the loop terminates when it tests the loop condition. We then color the new node x (singly) black in line 23.

Case 3: x's sibling w is black, w's left child is red, and w's right child is black

Case 3 (lines 13–16 and Figure 13.7(c)) occurs when w is black, its left child is red, and its right child is black. We can switch the colors of w and its left child $w.left$ and then perform a right rotation on w without violating any of the red-black properties. The new sibling w of x is now a black node with a red right child, and thus we have transformed case 3 into case 4.

Case 4: x's sibling w is black, and w's right child is red

Case 4 (lines 17–21 and Figure 13.7(d)) occurs when node x's sibling w is black and w's right child is red. By making some color changes and performing a left rotation on $x.p$, we can remove the extra black on x, making it singly black, without violating any of the red-black properties. Setting x to be the root causes the **while** loop to terminate when it tests the loop condition.

Analysis

What is the running time of RB-DELETE? Since the height of a red-black tree of n nodes is $O(\lg n)$, the total cost of the procedure without the call to RB-DELETE-FIXUP takes $O(\lg n)$ time. Within RB-DELETE-FIXUP, each of cases 1, 3, and 4 lead to termination after performing a constant number of color changes and at most three rotations. Case 2 is the only case in which the **while** loop can be repeated, and then the pointer x moves up the tree at most $O(\lg n)$ times, performing no rotations. Thus, the procedure RB-DELETE-FIXUP takes $O(\lg n)$ time and performs at most three rotations, and the overall time for RB-DELETE is therefore also $O(\lg n)$.

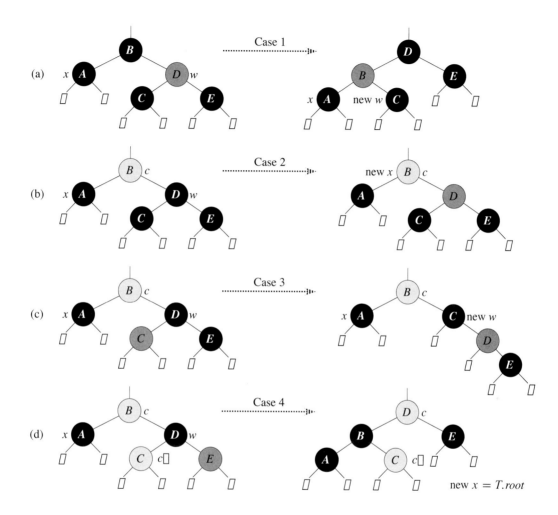

Figure 13.7 The cases in the **while** loop of the procedure RB-DELETE-FIXUP. Darkened nodes have *color* attributes BLACK, heavily shaded nodes have *color* attributes RED, and lightly shaded nodes have *color* attributes represented by c and c′, which may be either RED or BLACK. The letters $\alpha, \beta, \ldots, \zeta$ represent arbitrary subtrees. Each case transforms the configuration on the left into the configuration on the right by changing some colors and/or performing a rotation. Any node pointed to by x has an extra black and is either doubly black or red-and-black. Only case 2 causes the loop to repeat. **(a)** Case 1 is transformed to case 2, 3, or 4 by exchanging the colors of nodes B and D and performing a left rotation. **(b)** In case 2, the extra black represented by the pointer x moves up the tree by coloring node D red and setting x to point to node B. If we enter case 2 through case 1, the **while** loop terminates because the new node x is red-and-black, and therefore the value c of its *color* attribute is RED. **(c)** Case 3 is transformed to case 4 by exchanging the colors of nodes C and D and performing a right rotation. **(d)** Case 4 removes the extra black represented by x by changing some colors and performing a left rotation (without violating the red-black properties), and then the loop terminates.

Exercises

13.4-1
Argue that after executing RB-DELETE-FIXUP, the root of the tree must be black.

13.4-2
Argue that if in RB-DELETE both x and $x.p$ are red, then property 4 is restored by the call to RB-DELETE-FIXUP(T, x).

13.4-3
In Exercise 13.3-2, you found the red-black tree that results from successively inserting the keys $41, 38, 31, 12, 19, 8$ into an initially empty tree. Now show the red-black trees that result from the successive deletion of the keys in the order $8, 12, 19, 31, 38, 41$.

13.4-4
In which lines of the code for RB-DELETE-FIXUP might we examine or modify the sentinel $T.nil$?

13.4-5
In each of the cases of Figure 13.7, give the count of black nodes from the root of the subtree shown to each of the subtrees $\alpha, \beta, \ldots, \zeta$, and verify that each count remains the same after the transformation. When a node has a *color* attribute c or c', use the notation count(c) or count(c') symbolically in your count.

13.4-6
Professors Skelton and Baron are concerned that at the start of case 1 of RB-DELETE-FIXUP, the node $x.p$ might not be black. If the professors are correct, then lines 5–6 are wrong. Show that $x.p$ must be black at the start of case 1, so that the professors have nothing to worry about.

13.4-7
Suppose that a node x is inserted into a red-black tree with RB-INSERT and then is immediately deleted with RB-DELETE. Is the resulting red-black tree the same as the initial red-black tree? Justify your answer.

Problems

13-1   Persistent dynamic sets

During the course of an algorithm, we sometimes find that we need to maintain past versions of a dynamic set as it is updated. We call such a set *persistent*. One way to implement a persistent set is to copy the entire set whenever it is modified, but this approach can slow down a program and also consume much space. Sometimes, we can do much better.

Consider a persistent set S with the operations INSERT, DELETE, and SEARCH, which we implement using binary search trees as shown in Figure 13.8(a). We maintain a separate root for every version of the set. In order to insert the key 5 into the set, we create a new node with key 5. This node becomes the left child of a new node with key 7, since we cannot modify the existing node with key 7. Similarly, the new node with key 7 becomes the left child of a new node with key 8 whose right child is the existing node with key 10. The new node with key 8 becomes, in turn, the right child of a new root r' with key 4 whose left child is the existing node with key 3. We thus copy only part of the tree and share some of the nodes with the original tree, as shown in Figure 13.8(b).

Assume that each tree node has the attributes *key*, *left*, and *right* but no parent. (See also Exercise 13.3-6.)

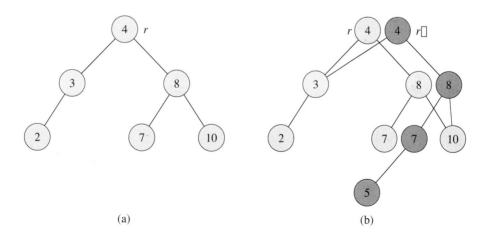

(a)   (b)

Figure 13.8   **(a)** A binary search tree with keys $2, 3, 4, 7, 8, 10$. **(b)** The persistent binary search tree that results from the insertion of key 5. The most recent version of the set consists of the nodes reachable from the root r', and the previous version consists of the nodes reachable from r. Heavily shaded nodes are added when key 5 is inserted.

a. For a general persistent binary search tree, identify the nodes that we need to change to insert a key k or delete a node y.

b. Write a procedure PERSISTENT-TREE-INSERT that, given a persistent tree T and a key k to insert, returns a new persistent tree T' that is the result of inserting k into T.

c. If the height of the persistent binary search tree T is h, what are the time and space requirements of your implementation of PERSISTENT-TREE-INSERT? (The space requirement is proportional to the number of new nodes allocated.)

d. Suppose that we had included the parent attribute in each node. In this case, PERSISTENT-TREE-INSERT would need to perform additional copying. Prove that PERSISTENT-TREE-INSERT would then require $\Omega(n)$ time and space, where n is the number of nodes in the tree.

e. Show how to use red-black trees to guarantee that the worst-case running time and space are $O(\lg n)$ per insertion or deletion.

13-2   *Join operation on red-black trees*

The *join* operation takes two dynamic sets S_1 and S_2 and an element x such that for any $x_1 \in S_1$ and $x_2 \in S_2$, we have $x_1.key \le x.key \le x_2.key$. It returns a set $S = S_1 \cup \{x\} \cup S_2$. In this problem, we investigate how to implement the join operation on red-black trees.

a. Given a red-black tree T, let us store its black-height as the new attribute $T.bh$. Argue that RB-INSERT and RB-DELETE can maintain the bh attribute without requiring extra storage in the nodes of the tree and without increasing the asymptotic running times. Show that while descending through T, we can determine the black-height of each node we visit in $O(1)$ time per node visited.

We wish to implement the operation RB-JOIN(T_1, x, T_2), which destroys T_1 and T_2 and returns a red-black tree $T = T_1 \cup \{x\} \cup T_2$. Let n be the total number of nodes in T_1 and T_2.

b. Assume that $T_1.bh \ge T_2.bh$. Describe an $O(\lg n)$-time algorithm that finds a black node y in T_1 with the largest key from among those nodes whose black-height is $T_2.bh$.

c. Let T_y be the subtree rooted at y. Describe how $T_y \cup \{x\} \cup T_2$ can replace T_y in $O(1)$ time without destroying the binary-search-tree property.

d. What color should we make x so that red-black properties 1, 3, and 5 are maintained? Describe how to enforce properties 2 and 4 in $O(\lg n)$ time.

e. Argue that no generality is lost by making the assumption in part (b). Describe the symmetric situation that arises when $T_1.bh \leq T_2.bh$.

f. Argue that the running time of RB-JOIN is $O(\lg n)$.

13-3 AVL trees

An **AVL tree** is a binary search tree that is **height balanced**: for each node x, the heights of the left and right subtrees of x differ by at most 1. To implement an AVL tree, we maintain an extra attribute in each node: $x.h$ is the height of node x. As for any other binary search tree T, we assume that $T.root$ points to the root node.

a. Prove that an AVL tree with n nodes has height $O(\lg n)$. (*Hint:* Prove that an AVL tree of height h has at least F_h nodes, where F_h is the hth Fibonacci number.)

b. To insert into an AVL tree, we first place a node into the appropriate place in binary search tree order. Afterward, the tree might no longer be height balanced. Specifically, the heights of the left and right children of some node might differ by 2. Describe a procedure BALANCE(x), which takes a subtree rooted at x whose left and right children are height balanced and have heights that differ by at most 2, i.e., $|x.right.h - x.left.h| \leq 2$, and alters the subtree rooted at x to be height balanced. (*Hint:* Use rotations.)

c. Using part (b), describe a recursive procedure AVL-INSERT(x, z) that takes a node x within an AVL tree and a newly created node z (whose key has already been filled in), and adds z to the subtree rooted at x, maintaining the property that x is the root of an AVL tree. As in TREE-INSERT from Section 12.3, assume that $z.key$ has already been filled in and that $z.left = $ NIL and $z.right = $ NIL; also assume that $z.h = 0$. Thus, to insert the node z into the AVL tree T, we call AVL-INSERT$(T.root, z)$.

d. Show that AVL-INSERT, run on an n-node AVL tree, takes $O(\lg n)$ time and performs $O(1)$ rotations.

13-4 Treaps

If we insert a set of n items into a binary search tree, the resulting tree may be horribly unbalanced, leading to long search times. As we saw in Section 12.4, however, randomly built binary search trees tend to be balanced. Therefore, one strategy that, on average, builds a balanced tree for a fixed set of items would be to randomly permute the items and then insert them in that order into the tree.

What if we do not have all the items at once? If we receive the items one at a time, can we still randomly build a binary search tree out of them?

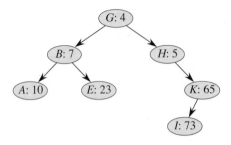

Figure 13.9   A treap. Each node x is labeled with $x.key: x.priority$. For example, the root has key G and priority 4.

We will examine a data structure that answers this question in the affirmative. A **treap** is a binary search tree with a modified way of ordering the nodes. Figure 13.9 shows an example. As usual, each node x in the tree has a key value $x.key$. In addition, we assign $x.priority$, which is a random number chosen independently for each node. We assume that all priorities are distinct and also that all keys are distinct. The nodes of the treap are ordered so that the keys obey the binary-search-tree property and the priorities obey the min-heap order property:

- If v is a left child of u, then $v.key < u.key$.

- If v is a right child of u, then $v.key > u.key$.

- If v is a child of u, then $v.priority > u.priority$.

(This combination of properties is why the tree is called a "treap": it has features of both a binary search tree and a heap.)

It helps to think of treaps in the following way. Suppose that we insert nodes $x_1, x_2, \ldots, x_n$, with associated keys, into a treap. Then the resulting treap is the tree that would have been formed if the nodes had been inserted into a normal binary search tree in the order given by their (randomly chosen) priorities, i.e., $x_i.priority < x_j.priority$ means that we had inserted x_i before x_j.

a. Show that given a set of nodes $x_1, x_2, \ldots, x_n$, with associated keys and priorities, all distinct, the treap associated with these nodes is unique.

b. Show that the expected height of a treap is $\Theta(\lg n)$, and hence the expected time to search for a value in the treap is $\Theta(\lg n)$.

Let us see how to insert a new node into an existing treap. The first thing we do is assign to the new node a random priority. Then we call the insertion algorithm, which we call TREAP-INSERT, whose operation is illustrated in Figure 13.10.

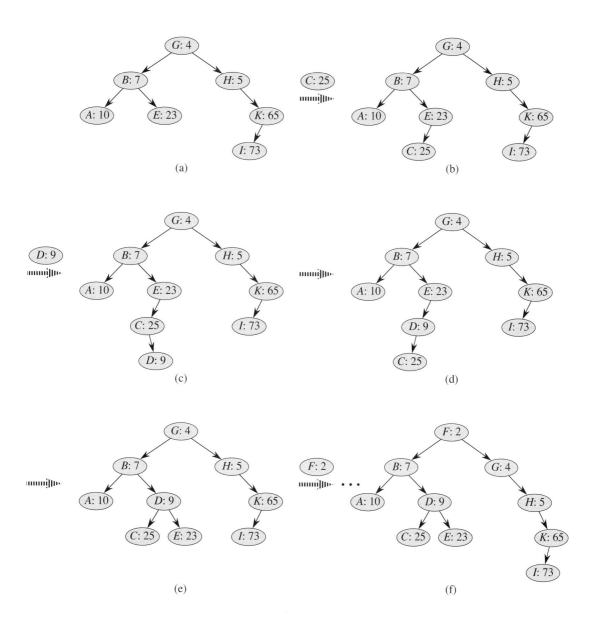

Figure 13.10 The operation of TREAP-INSERT. **(a)** The original treap, prior to insertion. **(b)** The treap after inserting a node with key C and priority 25. **(c)–(d)** Intermediate stages when inserting a node with key D and priority 9. **(e)** The treap after the insertion of parts (c) and (d) is done. **(f)** The treap after inserting a node with key F and priority 2.

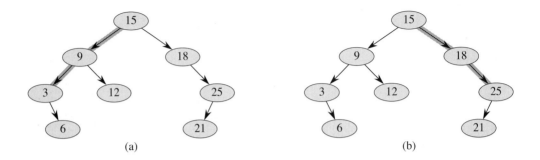

Figure 13.11   Spines of a binary search tree. The left spine is shaded in **(a)**, and the right spine is shaded in **(b)**.

c. Explain how TREAP-INSERT works. Explain the idea in English and give pseudocode. (*Hint:* Execute the usual binary-search-tree insertion procedure and then perform rotations to restore the min-heap order property.)

d. Show that the expected running time of TREAP-INSERT is $\Theta(\lg n)$.

TREAP-INSERT performs a search and then a sequence of rotations. Although these two operations have the same expected running time, they have different costs in practice. A search reads information from the treap without modifying it. In contrast, a rotation changes parent and child pointers within the treap. On most computers, read operations are much faster than write operations. Thus we would like TREAP-INSERT to perform few rotations. We will show that the expected number of rotations performed is bounded by a constant.

In order to do so, we will need some definitions, which Figure 13.11 depicts. The *left spine* of a binary search tree T is the simple path from the root to the node with the smallest key. In other words, the left spine is the simple path from the root that consists of only left edges. Symmetrically, the *right spine* of T is the simple path from the root consisting of only right edges. The *length* of a spine is the number of nodes it contains.

e. Consider the treap T immediately after TREAP-INSERT has inserted node x. Let C be the length of the right spine of the left subtree of x. Let D be the length of the left spine of the right subtree of x. Prove that the total number of rotations that were performed during the insertion of x is equal to $C + D$.

We will now calculate the expected values of C and D. Without loss of generality, we assume that the keys are $1, 2, \ldots, n$, since we are comparing them only to one another.

For nodes x and y in treap T, where $y \neq x$, let $k = x.key$ and $i = y.key$. We define indicator random variables

$X_{ik} = \text{I}\{y$ is in the right spine of the left subtree of $x\}$.

f. Show that $X_{ik} = 1$ if and only if $y.priority > x.priority$, $y.key < x.key$, and, for every z such that $y.key < z.key < x.key$, we have $y.priority < z.priority$.

g. Show that

$$\Pr\{X_{ik} = 1\} = \frac{(k - i - 1)!}{(k - i + 1)!}$$

$$= \frac{1}{(k - i + 1)(k - i)} .$$

h. Show that

$$\text{E}[C] = \sum_{j=1}^{k-1} \frac{1}{j(j + 1)}$$

$$= 1 - \frac{1}{k} .$$

i. Use a symmetry argument to show that

$$\text{E}[D] = 1 - \frac{1}{n - k + 1} .$$

j. Conclude that the expected number of rotations performed when inserting a node into a treap is less than 2.

Chapter notes

The idea of balancing a search tree is due to Adel'son-Vel'skiĭ and Landis [2], who introduced a class of balanced search trees called "AVL trees" in 1962, described in Problem 13-3. Another class of search trees, called "2-3 trees," was introduced by J. E. Hopcroft (unpublished) in 1970. A 2-3 tree maintains balance by manipulating the degrees of nodes in the tree. Chapter 18 covers a generalization of 2-3 trees introduced by Bayer and McCreight [35], called "B-trees."

Red-black trees were invented by Bayer [34] under the name "symmetric binary B-trees." Guibas and Sedgewick [155] studied their properties at length and introduced the red/black color convention. Andersson [15] gives a simpler-to-code variant of red-black trees. Weiss [351] calls this variant AA-trees. An AA-tree is similar to a red-black tree except that left children may never be red.

Treaps, the subject of Problem 13-4, were proposed by Seidel and Aragon [309]. They are the default implementation of a dictionary in LEDA [253], which is a well-implemented collection of data structures and algorithms.

There are many other variations on balanced binary trees, including weight-balanced trees [264], k-neighbor trees [245], and scapegoat trees [127]. Perhaps the most intriguing are the "splay trees" introduced by Sleator and Tarjan [320], which are "self-adjusting." (See Tarjan [330] for a good description of splay trees.) Splay trees maintain balance without any explicit balance condition such as color. Instead, "splay operations" (which involve rotations) are performed within the tree every time an access is made. The amortized cost (see Chapter 17) of each operation on an n-node tree is $O(\lg n)$.

Skip lists [286] provide an alternative to balanced binary trees. A skip list is a linked list that is augmented with a number of additional pointers. Each dictionary operation runs in expected time $O(\lg n)$ on a skip list of n items.

14 Augmenting Data Structures

Some engineering situations require no more than a "textbook" data structure—such as a doubly linked list, a hash table, or a binary search tree—but many others require a dash of creativity. Only in rare situations will you need to create an entirely new type of data structure, though. More often, it will suffice to augment a textbook data structure by storing additional information in it. You can then program new operations for the data structure to support the desired application. Augmenting a data structure is not always straightforward, however, since the added information must be updated and maintained by the ordinary operations on the data structure.

This chapter discusses two data structures that we construct by augmenting red-black trees. Section 14.1 describes a data structure that supports general order-statistic operations on a dynamic set. We can then quickly find the ith smallest number in a set or the rank of a given element in the total ordering of the set. Section 14.2 abstracts the process of augmenting a data structure and provides a theorem that can simplify the process of augmenting red-black trees. Section 14.3 uses this theorem to help design a data structure for maintaining a dynamic set of intervals, such as time intervals. Given a query interval, we can then quickly find an interval in the set that overlaps it.

14.1 Dynamic order statistics

Chapter 9 introduced the notion of an order statistic. Specifically, the ith order statistic of a set of n elements, where $i \in \{1, 2, \ldots, n\}$, is simply the element in the set with the ith smallest key. We saw how to determine any order statistic in $O(n)$ time from an unordered set. In this section, we shall see how to modify red-black trees so that we can determine any order statistic for a dynamic set in $O(\lg n)$ time. We shall also see how to compute the *rank* of an element—its position in the linear order of the set—in $O(\lg n)$ time.

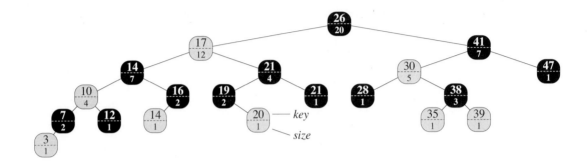

Figure 14.1 An order-statistic tree, which is an augmented red-black tree. Shaded nodes are red, and darkened nodes are black. In addition to its usual attributes, each node x has an attribute $x.size$, which is the number of nodes, other than the sentinel, in the subtree rooted at x.

Figure 14.1 shows a data structure that can support fast order-statistic operations. An ***order-statistic tree*** T is simply a red-black tree with additional information stored in each node. Besides the usual red-black tree attributes $x.key$, $x.color$, $x.p$, $x.left$, and $x.right$ in a node x, we have another attribute, $x.size$. This attribute contains the number of (internal) nodes in the subtree rooted at x (including x itself), that is, the size of the subtree. If we define the sentinel's size to be 0—that is, we set $T.nil.size$ to be 0—then we have the identity

$$x.size = x.left.size + x.right.size + 1 \ .$$

We do not require keys to be distinct in an order-statistic tree. (For example, the tree in Figure 14.1 has two keys with value 14 and two keys with value 21.) In the presence of equal keys, the above notion of rank is not well defined. We remove this ambiguity for an order-statistic tree by defining the rank of an element as the position at which it would be printed in an inorder walk of the tree. In Figure 14.1, for example, the key 14 stored in a black node has rank 5, and the key 14 stored in a red node has rank 6.

Retrieving an element with a given rank

Before we show how to maintain this size information during insertion and deletion, let us examine the implementation of two order-statistic queries that use this additional information. We begin with an operation that retrieves an element with a given rank. The procedure OS-SELECT(x, i) returns a pointer to the node containing the ith smallest key in the subtree rooted at x. To find the node with the ith smallest key in an order-statistic tree T, we call OS-SELECT$(T.root, i)$.

OS-SELECT(x, i)

```
1  r = x.left.size + 1
2  if i == r
3      return x
4  elseif i < r
5      return OS-SELECT(x.left, i)
6  else return OS-SELECT(x.right, i − r)
```

In line 1 of OS-SELECT, we compute r, the rank of node x within the subtree rooted at x. The value of $x.left.size$ is the number of nodes that come before x in an inorder tree walk of the subtree rooted at x. Thus, $x.left.size + 1$ is the rank of x within the subtree rooted at x. If $i = r$, then node x is the ith smallest element, and so we return x in line 3. If $i < r$, then the ith smallest element resides in x's left subtree, and so we recurse on $x.left$ in line 5. If $i > r$, then the ith smallest element resides in x's right subtree. Since the subtree rooted at x contains r elements that come before x's right subtree in an inorder tree walk, the ith smallest element in the subtree rooted at x is the $(i − r)$th smallest element in the subtree rooted at $x.right$. Line 6 determines this element recursively.

To see how OS-SELECT operates, consider a search for the 17th smallest element in the order-statistic tree of Figure 14.1. We begin with x as the root, whose key is 26, and with $i = 17$. Since the size of 26's left subtree is 12, its rank is 13. Thus, we know that the node with rank 17 is the $17 − 13 = 4$th smallest element in 26's right subtree. After the recursive call, x is the node with key 41, and $i = 4$. Since the size of 41's left subtree is 5, its rank within its subtree is 6. Thus, we know that the node with rank 4 is the 4th smallest element in 41's left subtree. After the recursive call, x is the node with key 30, and its rank within its subtree is 2. Thus, we recurse once again to find the $4 − 2 = 2$nd smallest element in the subtree rooted at the node with key 38. We now find that its left subtree has size 1, which means it is the second smallest element. Thus, the procedure returns a pointer to the node with key 38.

Because each recursive call goes down one level in the order-statistic tree, the total time for OS-SELECT is at worst proportional to the height of the tree. Since the tree is a red-black tree, its height is $O(\lg n)$, where n is the number of nodes. Thus, the running time of OS-SELECT is $O(\lg n)$ for a dynamic set of n elements.

Determining the rank of an element

Given a pointer to a node x in an order-statistic tree T, the procedure OS-RANK returns the position of x in the linear order determined by an inorder tree walk of T.

OS-RANK(T, x)

```
1   r = x.left.size + 1
2   y = x
3   while y ≠ T.root
4       if y == y.p.right
5           r = r + y.p.left.size + 1
6       y = y.p
7   return r
```

The procedure works as follows. We can think of node x's rank as the number of nodes preceding x in an inorder tree walk, plus 1 for x itself. OS-RANK maintains the following loop invariant:

> At the start of each iteration of the **while** loop of lines 3–6, r is the rank of $x.key$ in the subtree rooted at node y.

We use this loop invariant to show that OS-RANK works correctly as follows:

Initialization: Prior to the first iteration, line 1 sets r to be the rank of $x.key$ within the subtree rooted at x. Setting $y = x$ in line 2 makes the invariant true the first time the test in line 3 executes.

Maintenance: At the end of each iteration of the **while** loop, we set $y = y.p$. Thus we must show that if r is the rank of $x.key$ in the subtree rooted at y at the start of the loop body, then r is the rank of $x.key$ in the subtree rooted at $y.p$ at the end of the loop body. In each iteration of the **while** loop, we consider the subtree rooted at $y.p$. We have already counted the number of nodes in the subtree rooted at node y that precede x in an inorder walk, and so we must add the nodes in the subtree rooted at y's sibling that precede x in an inorder walk, plus 1 for $y.p$ if it, too, precedes x. If y is a left child, then neither $y.p$ nor any node in $y.p$'s right subtree precedes x, and so we leave r alone. Otherwise, y is a right child and all the nodes in $y.p$'s left subtree precede x, as does $y.p$ itself. Thus, in line 5, we add $y.p.left.size + 1$ to the current value of r.

Termination: The loop terminates when $y = T.root$, so that the subtree rooted at y is the entire tree. Thus, the value of r is the rank of $x.key$ in the entire tree.

As an example, when we run OS-RANK on the order-statistic tree of Figure 14.1 to find the rank of the node with key 38, we get the following sequence of values of $y.key$ and r at the top of the **while** loop:

iteration	$y.key$	r
1	38	2
2	30	4
3	41	4
4	26	17

The procedure returns the rank 17.

Since each iteration of the **while** loop takes $O(1)$ time, and y goes up one level in the tree with each iteration, the running time of OS-RANK is at worst proportional to the height of the tree: $O(\lg n)$ on an n-node order-statistic tree.

Maintaining subtree sizes

Given the *size* attribute in each node, OS-SELECT and OS-RANK can quickly compute order-statistic information. But unless we can efficiently maintain these attributes within the basic modifying operations on red-black trees, our work will have been for naught. We shall now show how to maintain subtree sizes for both insertion and deletion without affecting the asymptotic running time of either operation.

We noted in Section 13.3 that insertion into a red-black tree consists of two phases. The first phase goes down the tree from the root, inserting the new node as a child of an existing node. The second phase goes up the tree, changing colors and performing rotations to maintain the red-black properties.

To maintain the subtree sizes in the first phase, we simply increment $x.size$ for each node x on the simple path traversed from the root down toward the leaves. The new node added gets a *size* of 1. Since there are $O(\lg n)$ nodes on the traversed path, the additional cost of maintaining the *size* attributes is $O(\lg n)$.

In the second phase, the only structural changes to the underlying red-black tree are caused by rotations, of which there are at most two. Moreover, a rotation is a local operation: only two nodes have their *size* attributes invalidated. The link around which the rotation is performed is incident on these two nodes. Referring to the code for LEFT-ROTATE(T, x) in Section 13.2, we add the following lines:

```
13   y.size = x.size
14   x.size = x.left.size + x.right.size + 1
```

Figure 14.2 illustrates how the attributes are updated. The change to RIGHT-ROTATE is symmetric.

Since at most two rotations are performed during insertion into a red-black tree, we spend only $O(1)$ additional time updating *size* attributes in the second phase. Thus, the total time for insertion into an n-node order-statistic tree is $O(\lg n)$, which is asymptotically the same as for an ordinary red-black tree.

Deletion from a red-black tree also consists of two phases: the first operates on the underlying search tree, and the second causes at most three rotations and otherwise performs no structural changes. (See Section 13.4.) The first phase removes one node z from the tree and could move up to two other nodes within the tree (nodes y and x in Figure 12.4). To update the subtree sizes, we simply traverse a simple path from the lowest node that moves (starting from its original

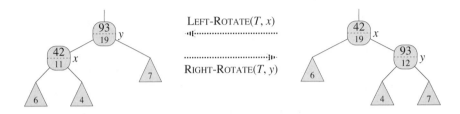

Figure 14.2   Updating subtree sizes during rotations. The link around which we rotate is incident on the two nodes whose *size* attributes need to be updated. The updates are local, requiring only the *size* information stored in x, y, and the roots of the subtrees shown as triangles.

position within the tree) up to the root, decrementing the *size* attribute of each node on the path. Since this path has length $O(\lg n)$ in an n-node red-black tree, the additional time spent maintaining *size* attributes in the first phase is $O(\lg n)$. We handle the $O(1)$ rotations in the second phase of deletion in the same manner as for insertion. Thus, both insertion and deletion, including maintaining the *size* attributes, take $O(\lg n)$ time for an n-node order-statistic tree.

Exercises

14.1-1
Show how OS-SELECT($T.root$, 10) operates on the red-black tree T of Figure 14.1.

14.1-2
Show how OS-RANK(T, x) operates on the red-black tree T of Figure 14.1 and the node x with $x.key = 35$.

14.1-3
Write a nonrecursive version of OS-SELECT.

14.1-4
Write a recursive procedure OS-KEY-RANK(T, k) that takes as input an order-statistic tree T and a key k and returns the rank of k in the dynamic set represented by T. Assume that the keys of T are distinct.

14.1-5
Given an element x in an n-node order-statistic tree and a natural number i, how can we determine the ith successor of x in the linear order of the tree in $O(\lg n)$ time?

14.1-6

Observe that whenever we reference the *size* attribute of a node in either OS-SELECT or OS-RANK, we use it only to compute a rank. Accordingly, suppose we store in each node its rank in the subtree of which it is the root. Show how to maintain this information during insertion and deletion. (Remember that these two operations can cause rotations.)

14.1-7

Show how to use an order-statistic tree to count the number of inversions (see Problem 2-4) in an array of size n in time $O(n \lg n)$.

14.1-8 ★

Consider n chords on a circle, each defined by its endpoints. Describe an $O(n \lg n)$-time algorithm to determine the number of pairs of chords that intersect inside the circle. (For example, if the n chords are all diameters that meet at the center, then the correct answer is $\binom{n}{2}$.) Assume that no two chords share an endpoint.

14.2   How to augment a data structure

The process of augmenting a basic data structure to support additional functionality occurs quite frequently in algorithm design. We shall use it again in the next section to design a data structure that supports operations on intervals. In this section, we examine the steps involved in such augmentation. We shall also prove a theorem that allows us to augment red-black trees easily in many cases.

We can break the process of augmenting a data structure into four steps:

1. Choose an underlying data structure.

2. Determine additional information to maintain in the underlying data structure.

3. Verify that we can maintain the additional information for the basic modifying operations on the underlying data structure.

4. Develop new operations.

As with any prescriptive design method, you should not blindly follow the steps in the order given. Most design work contains an element of trial and error, and progress on all steps usually proceeds in parallel. There is no point, for example, in determining additional information and developing new operations (steps 2 and 4) if we will not be able to maintain the additional information efficiently. Nevertheless, this four-step method provides a good focus for your efforts in augmenting a data structure, and it is also a good way to organize the documentation of an augmented data structure.

We followed these steps in Section 14.1 to design our order-statistic trees. For step 1, we chose red-black trees as the underlying data structure. A clue to the suitability of red-black trees comes from their efficient support of other dynamic-set operations on a total order, such as MINIMUM, MAXIMUM, SUCCESSOR, and PREDECESSOR.

For step 2, we added the *size* attribute, in which each node x stores the size of the subtree rooted at x. Generally, the additional information makes operations more efficient. For example, we could have implemented OS-SELECT and OS-RANK using just the keys stored in the tree, but they would not have run in $O(\lg n)$ time. Sometimes, the additional information is pointer information rather than data, as in Exercise 14.2-1.

For step 3, we ensured that insertion and deletion could maintain the *size* attributes while still running in $O(\lg n)$ time. Ideally, we should need to update only a few elements of the data structure in order to maintain the additional information. For example, if we simply stored in each node its rank in the tree, the OS-SELECT and OS-RANK procedures would run quickly, but inserting a new minimum element would cause a change to this information in every node of the tree. When we store subtree sizes instead, inserting a new element causes information to change in only $O(\lg n)$ nodes.

For step 4, we developed the operations OS-SELECT and OS-RANK. After all, the need for new operations is why we bother to augment a data structure in the first place. Occasionally, rather than developing new operations, we use the additional information to expedite existing ones, as in Exercise 14.2-1.

Augmenting red-black trees

When red-black trees underlie an augmented data structure, we can prove that insertion and deletion can always efficiently maintain certain kinds of additional information, thereby making step 3 very easy. The proof of the following theorem is similar to the argument from Section 14.1 that we can maintain the *size* attribute for order-statistic trees.

Theorem 14.1 (Augmenting a red-black tree)
Let f be an attribute that augments a red-black tree T of n nodes, and suppose that the value of f for each node x depends on only the information in nodes x, $x.left$, and $x.right$, possibly including $x.left.f$ and $x.right.f$. Then, we can maintain the values of f in all nodes of T during insertion and deletion without asymptotically affecting the $O(\lg n)$ performance of these operations.

Proof   The main idea of the proof is that a change to an f attribute in a node x propagates only to ancestors of x in the tree. That is, changing $x.f$ may require $x.p.f$ to be updated, but nothing else; updating $x.p.f$ may require $x.p.p.f$ to be updated, but nothing else; and so on up the tree. Once we have updated $T.root.f$, no other node will depend on the new value, and so the process terminates. Since the height of a red-black tree is $O(\lg n)$, changing an f attribute in a node costs $O(\lg n)$ time in updating all nodes that depend on the change.

Insertion of a node x into T consists of two phases. (See Section 13.3.) The first phase inserts x as a child of an existing node $x.p$. We can compute the value of $x.f$ in $O(1)$ time since, by supposition, it depends only on information in the other attributes of x itself and the information in x's children, but x's children are both the sentinel $T.nil$. Once we have computed $x.f$, the change propagates up the tree. Thus, the total time for the first phase of insertion is $O(\lg n)$. During the second phase, the only structural changes to the tree come from rotations. Since only two nodes change in a rotation, the total time for updating the f attributes is $O(\lg n)$ per rotation. Since the number of rotations during insertion is at most two, the total time for insertion is $O(\lg n)$.

Like insertion, deletion has two phases. (See Section 13.4.) In the first phase, changes to the tree occur when a node is deleted, and at most two other nodes could move within the tree. Propagating the updates to f caused by these changes costs at most $O(\lg n)$, since the changes modify the tree locally along a simple path from the lowest changed node to the root. Fixing up the red-black tree during the second phase requires at most three rotations, and each rotation requires at most $O(\lg n)$ time to propagate the updates to f. Thus, like insertion, the total time for deletion is $O(\lg n)$.   ∎

In many cases, such as maintaining the *size* attributes in order-statistic trees, the cost of updating after a rotation is $O(1)$, rather than the $O(\lg n)$ derived in the proof of Theorem 14.1. Exercise 14.2-3 gives an example.

Exercises

14.2-1
Show, by adding pointers to the nodes, how to support each of the dynamic-set queries MINIMUM, MAXIMUM, SUCCESSOR, and PREDECESSOR in $O(1)$ worst-case time on an augmented order-statistic tree. The asymptotic performance of other operations on order-statistic trees should not be affected.

14.2-2
Can we maintain the black-heights of nodes in a red-black tree as attributes in the nodes of the tree without affecting the asymptotic performance of any of the red-black tree operations? Show how, or argue why not. How about maintaining the depths of nodes?

14.2-3 ★

Let $\otimes$ be an associative binary operator, and let a be an attribute maintained in each node of a red-black tree. Suppose that we want to include in each node x an additional attribute f such that $x.f = x_1.a \otimes x_2.a \otimes \cdots \otimes x_m.a$, where $x_1, x_2, \ldots, x_m$ is the inorder listing of nodes in the subtree rooted at x. Show how to update the f attributes in $O(1)$ time after a rotation. Modify your argument slightly to apply it to the *size* attributes in order-statistic trees.

14.2-4 ★

We wish to augment red-black trees with an operation RB-ENUMERATE(x, a, b) that outputs all the keys k such that $a \le k \le b$ in a red-black tree rooted at x. Describe how to implement RB-ENUMERATE in $\Theta(m + \lg n)$ time, where m is the number of keys that are output and n is the number of internal nodes in the tree. (*Hint:* You do not need to add new attributes to the red-black tree.)

14.3   Interval trees

In this section, we shall augment red-black trees to support operations on dynamic sets of intervals. A **closed interval** is an ordered pair of real numbers $[t_1, t_2]$, with $t_1 \le t_2$. The interval $[t_1, t_2]$ represents the set $\{t \in \mathbb{R} : t_1 \le t \le t_2\}$. **Open** and **half-open** intervals omit both or one of the endpoints from the set, respectively. In this section, we·shall assume that intervals are closed; extending the results to open and half-open intervals is conceptually straightforward.

Intervals are convenient for representing events that each occupy a continuous period of time. We might, for example, wish to query a database of time intervals to find out what events occurred during a given interval. The data structure in this section provides an efficient means for maintaining such an interval database.

We can represent an interval $[t_1, t_2]$ as an object i, with attributes $i.low = t_1$ (the **low endpoint**) and $i.high = t_2$ (the **high endpoint**). We say that intervals i and i' **overlap** if $i \cap i' \ne \emptyset$, that is, if $i.low \le i'.high$ and $i'.low \le i.high$. As Figure 14.3 shows, any two intervals i and i' satisfy the **interval trichotomy**; that is, exactly one of the following three properties holds:

a. i and i' overlap,

b. i is to the left of i' (i.e., $i.high < i'.low$),

c. i is to the right of i' (i.e., $i'.high < i.low$).

An **interval tree** is a red-black tree that maintains a dynamic set of elements, with each element x containing an interval $x.int$. Interval trees support the following operations:

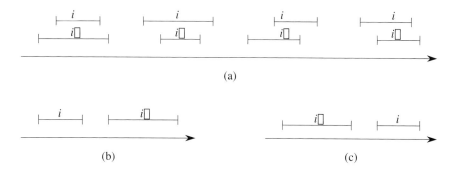

(a)

(b)   (c)

Figure 14.3   The interval trichotomy for two closed intervals i and i'. **(a)** If i and i' overlap, there are four situations; in each, $i.low \leq i'.high$ and $i'.low \leq i.high$. **(b)** The intervals do not overlap, and $i.high < i'.low$. **(c)** The intervals do not overlap, and $i'.high < i.low$.

INTERVAL-INSERT(T, x) adds the element x, whose *int* attribute is assumed to contain an interval, to the interval tree T.

INTERVAL-DELETE(T, x) removes the element x from the interval tree T.

INTERVAL-SEARCH(T, i) returns a pointer to an element x in the interval tree T such that $x.int$ overlaps interval i, or a pointer to the sentinel $T.nil$ if no such element is in the set.

Figure 14.4 shows how an interval tree represents a set of intervals. We shall track the four-step method from Section 14.2 as we review the design of an interval tree and the operations that run on it.

Step 1: Underlying data structure

We choose a red-black tree in which each node x contains an interval $x.int$ and the key of x is the low endpoint, $x.int.low$, of the interval. Thus, an inorder tree walk of the data structure lists the intervals in sorted order by low endpoint.

Step 2: Additional information

In addition to the intervals themselves, each node x contains a value $x.max$, which is the maximum value of any interval endpoint stored in the subtree rooted at x.

Step 3: Maintaining the information

We must verify that insertion and deletion take $O(\lg n)$ time on an interval tree of n nodes. We can determine $x.max$ given interval $x.int$ and the *max* values of node x's children:

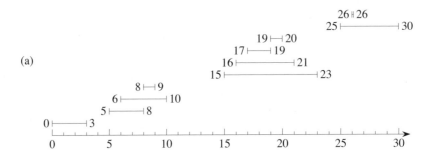

(a)

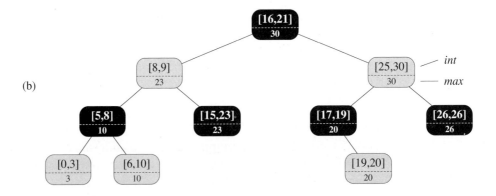

(b)

Figure 14.4   An interval tree. **(a)** A set of 10 intervals, shown sorted bottom to top by left endpoint. **(b)** The interval tree that represents them. Each node x contains an interval, shown above the dashed line, and the maximum value of any interval endpoint in the subtree rooted at x, shown below the dashed line. An inorder tree walk of the tree lists the nodes in sorted order by left endpoint.

$$x.max = \max(x.int.high, x.left.max, x.right.max) \,.$$

Thus, by Theorem 14.1, insertion and deletion run in $O(\lg n)$ time. In fact, we can update the *max* attributes after a rotation in $O(1)$ time, as Exercises 14.2-3 and 14.3-1 show.

Step 4: Developing new operations

The only new operation we need is INTERVAL-SEARCH(T, i), which finds a node in tree T whose interval overlaps interval i. If there is no interval that overlaps i in the tree, the procedure returns a pointer to the sentinel $T.nil$.

INTERVAL-SEARCH(T, i)

```
1   x = T.root
2   while x ≠ T.nil and i does not overlap x.int
3       if x.left ≠ T.nil and x.left.max ≥ i.low
4           x = x.left
5       else x = x.right
6   return x
```

The search for an interval that overlaps i starts with x at the root of the tree and proceeds downward. It terminates when either it finds an overlapping interval or x points to the sentinel $T.nil$. Since each iteration of the basic loop takes $O(1)$ time, and since the height of an n-node red-black tree is $O(\lg n)$, the INTERVAL-SEARCH procedure takes $O(\lg n)$ time.

Before we see why INTERVAL-SEARCH is correct, let's examine how it works on the interval tree in Figure 14.4. Suppose we wish to find an interval that overlaps the interval $i = [22, 25]$. We begin with x as the root, which contains $[16, 21]$ and does not overlap i. Since $x.left.max = 23$ is greater than $i.low = 22$, the loop continues with x as the left child of the root—the node containing $[8, 9]$, which also does not overlap i. This time, $x.left.max = 10$ is less than $i.low = 22$, and so the loop continues with the right child of x as the new x. Because the interval $[15, 23]$ stored in this node overlaps i, the procedure returns this node.

As an example of an unsuccessful search, suppose we wish to find an interval that overlaps $i = [11, 14]$ in the interval tree of Figure 14.4. We once again begin with x as the root. Since the root's interval $[16, 21]$ does not overlap i, and since $x.left.max = 23$ is greater than $i.low = 11$, we go left to the node containing $[8, 9]$. Interval $[8, 9]$ does not overlap i, and $x.left.max = 10$ is less than $i.low = 11$, and so we go right. (Note that no interval in the left subtree overlaps i.) Interval $[15, 23]$ does not overlap i, and its left child is $T.nil$, so again we go right, the loop terminates, and we return the sentinel $T.nil$.

To see why INTERVAL-SEARCH is correct, we must understand why it suffices to examine a single path from the root. The basic idea is that at any node x, if $x.int$ does not overlap i, the search always proceeds in a safe direction: the search will definitely find an overlapping interval if the tree contains one. The following theorem states this property more precisely.

Theorem 14.2

Any execution of INTERVAL-SEARCH(T, i) either returns a node whose interval overlaps i, or it returns $T.nil$ and the tree T contains no node whose interval overlaps i.

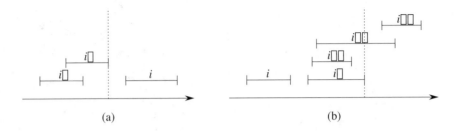

Figure 14.5   Intervals in the proof of Theorem 14.2. The value of $x.left.max$ is shown in each case as a dashed line. **(a)** The search goes right. No interval i' in x's left subtree can overlap i. **(b)** The search goes left. The left subtree of x contains an interval that overlaps i (situation not shown), or x's left subtree contains an interval i' such that $i'.high = x.left.max$. Since i does not overlap i', neither does it overlap any interval i'' in x's right subtree, since $i'.low \le i''.low$.

Proof   The **while** loop of lines 2–5 terminates either when $x = T.nil$ or i overlaps $x.int$. In the latter case, it is certainly correct to return x. Therefore, we focus on the former case, in which the **while** loop terminates because $x = T.nil$.

  We use the following invariant for the **while** loop of lines 2–5:

> If tree T contains an interval that overlaps i, then the subtree rooted at x contains such an interval.

We use this loop invariant as follows:

Initialization: Prior to the first iteration, line 1 sets x to be the root of T, so that the invariant holds.

Maintenance: Each iteration of the **while** loop executes either line 4 or line 5. We shall show that both cases maintain the loop invariant.

  If line 5 is executed, then because of the branch condition in line 3, we have $x.left = T.nil$, or $x.left.max < i.low$. If $x.left = T.nil$, the subtree rooted at $x.left$ clearly contains no interval that overlaps i, and so setting x to $x.right$ maintains the invariant. Suppose, therefore, that $x.left \ne T.nil$ and $x.left.max < i.low$. As Figure 14.5(a) shows, for each interval i' in x's left subtree, we have

$$\begin{aligned} i'.high \;&\le\; x.left.max \\ &<\; i.low \,. \end{aligned}$$

By the interval trichotomy, therefore, i' and i do not overlap. Thus, the left subtree of x contains no intervals that overlap i, so that setting x to $x.right$ maintains the invariant.

If, on the other hand, line 4 is executed, then we will show that the contrapositive of the loop invariant holds. That is, if the subtree rooted at $x.left$ contains no interval overlapping i, then no interval anywhere in the tree overlaps i. Since line 4 is executed, then because of the branch condition in line 3, we have $x.left.max \geq i.low$. Moreover, by definition of the *max* attribute, x's left subtree must contain some interval i' such that

$$
\begin{aligned}
i'.high &= x.left.max \\
&\geq i.low .
\end{aligned}
$$

(Figure 14.5(b) illustrates the situation.) Since i and i' do not overlap, and since it is not true that $i'.high < i.low$, it follows by the interval trichotomy that $i.high < i'.low$. Interval trees are keyed on the low endpoints of intervals, and thus the search-tree property implies that for any interval i'' in x's right subtree,

$$
\begin{aligned}
i.high &< i'.low \\
&\leq i''.low .
\end{aligned}
$$

By the interval trichotomy, i and i'' do not overlap. We conclude that whether or not any interval in x's left subtree overlaps i, setting x to $x.left$ maintains the invariant.

Termination: If the loop terminates when $x = T.nil$, then the subtree rooted at x contains no interval overlapping i. The contrapositive of the loop invariant implies that T contains no interval that overlaps i. Hence it is correct to return $x = T.nil$. ∎

Thus, the INTERVAL-SEARCH procedure works correctly.

Exercises

14.3-1
Write pseudocode for LEFT-ROTATE that operates on nodes in an interval tree and updates the *max* attributes in $O(1)$ time.

14.3-2
Rewrite the code for INTERVAL-SEARCH so that it works properly when all intervals are open.

14.3-3
Describe an efficient algorithm that, given an interval i, returns an interval overlapping i that has the minimum low endpoint, or $T.nil$ if no such interval exists.

14.3-4

Given an interval tree T and an interval i, describe how to list all intervals in T that overlap i in $O(\min(n, k \lg n))$ time, where k is the number of intervals in the output list. (*Hint:* One simple method makes several queries, modifying the tree between queries. A slightly more complicated method does not modify the tree.)

14.3-5

Suggest modifications to the interval-tree procedures to support the new operation INTERVAL-SEARCH-EXACTLY(T, i), where T is an interval tree and i is an interval. The operation should return a pointer to a node x in T such that $x.int.low = i.low$ and $x.int.high = i.high$, or $T.nil$ if T contains no such node. All operations, including INTERVAL-SEARCH-EXACTLY, should run in $O(\lg n)$ time on an n-node interval tree.

14.3-6

Show how to maintain a dynamic set Q of numbers that supports the operation MIN-GAP, which gives the magnitude of the difference of the two closest numbers in Q. For example, if $Q = \{1, 5, 9, 15, 18, 22\}$, then MIN-GAP$(Q)$ returns $18 - 15 = 3$, since 15 and 18 are the two closest numbers in Q. Make the operations INSERT, DELETE, SEARCH, and MIN-GAP as efficient as possible, and analyze their running times.

14.3-7   ★

VLSI databases commonly represent an integrated circuit as a list of rectangles. Assume that each rectangle is rectilinearly oriented (sides parallel to the x- and y-axes), so that we represent a rectangle by its minimum and maximum x- and y-coordinates. Give an $O(n \lg n)$-time algorithm to decide whether or not a set of n rectangles so represented contains two rectangles that overlap. Your algorithm need not report all intersecting pairs, but it must report that an overlap exists if one rectangle entirely covers another, even if the boundary lines do not intersect. (*Hint:* Move a "sweep" line across the set of rectangles.)

Problems

14-1   *Point of maximum overlap*

Suppose that we wish to keep track of a ***point of maximum overlap*** in a set of intervals—a point with the largest number of intervals in the set that overlap it.

a. Show that there will always be a point of maximum overlap that is an endpoint of one of the segments.

b. Design a data structure that efficiently supports the operations INTERVAL-INSERT, INTERVAL-DELETE, and FIND-POM, which returns a point of maximum overlap. (*Hint:* Keep a red-black tree of all the endpoints. Associate a value of $+1$ with each left endpoint, and associate a value of -1 with each right endpoint. Augment each node of the tree with some extra information to maintain the point of maximum overlap.)

14-2   *Josephus permutation*

We define the ***Josephus problem*** as follows. Suppose that n people form a circle and that we are given a positive integer $m \leq n$. Beginning with a designated first person, we proceed around the circle, removing every mth person. After each person is removed, counting continues around the circle that remains. This process continues until we have removed all n people. The order in which the people are removed from the circle defines the ***(n, m)-Josephus permutation*** of the integers $1, 2, \ldots, n$. For example, the $(7, 3)$-Josephus permutation is $\langle 3, 6, 2, 7, 5, 1, 4 \rangle$.

a. Suppose that m is a constant. Describe an $O(n)$-time algorithm that, given an integer n, outputs the (n, m)-Josephus permutation.

b. Suppose that m is not a constant. Describe an $O(n \lg n)$-time algorithm that, given integers n and m, outputs the (n, m)-Josephus permutation.

Chapter notes

In their book, Preparata and Shamos [282] describe several of the interval trees that appear in the literature, citing work by H. Edelsbrunner (1980) and E. M. McCreight (1981). The book details an interval tree that, given a static database of n intervals, allows us to enumerate all k intervals that overlap a given query interval in $O(k + \lg n)$ time.

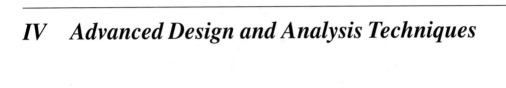

IV Advanced Design and Analysis Techniques

Introduction

This part covers three important techniques used in designing and analyzing efficient algorithms: dynamic programming (Chapter 15), greedy algorithms (Chapter 16), and amortized analysis (Chapter 17). Earlier parts have presented other widely applicable techniques, such as divide-and-conquer, randomization, and how to solve recurrences. The techniques in this part are somewhat more sophisticated, but they help us to attack many computational problems. The themes introduced in this part will recur later in this book.

Dynamic programming typically applies to optimization problems in which we make a set of choices in order to arrive at an optimal solution. As we make each choice, subproblems of the same form often arise. Dynamic programming is effective when a given subproblem may arise from more than one partial set of choices; the key technique is to store the solution to each such subproblem in case it should reappear. Chapter 15 shows how this simple idea can sometimes transform exponential-time algorithms into polynomial-time algorithms.

Like dynamic-programming algorithms, greedy algorithms typically apply to optimization problems in which we make a set of choices in order to arrive at an optimal solution. The idea of a greedy algorithm is to make each choice in a locally optimal manner. A simple example is coin-changing: to minimize the number of U.S. coins needed to make change for a given amount, we can repeatedly select the largest-denomination coin that is not larger than the amount that remains. A greedy approach provides an optimal solution for many such problems much more quickly than would a dynamic-programming approach. We cannot always easily tell whether a greedy approach will be effective, however. Chapter 16 introduces matroid theory, which provides a mathematical basis that can help us to show that a greedy algorithm yields an optimal solution.

We use amortized analysis to analyze certain algorithms that perform a sequence of similar operations. Instead of bounding the cost of the sequence of operations by bounding the actual cost of each operation separately, an amortized analysis provides a bound on the actual cost of the entire sequence. One advantage of this approach is that although some operations might be expensive, many others might be cheap. In other words, many of the operations might run in well under the worst-case time. Amortized analysis is not just an analysis tool, however; it is also a way of thinking about the design of algorithms, since the design of an algorithm and the analysis of its running time are often closely intertwined. Chapter 17 introduces three ways to perform an amortized analysis of an algorithm.

15   Dynamic Programming

Dynamic programming, like the divide-and-conquer method, solves problems by combining the solutions to subproblems. ("Programming" in this context refers to a tabular method, not to writing computer code.) As we saw in Chapters 2 and 4, divide-and-conquer algorithms partition the problem into disjoint subproblems, solve the subproblems recursively, and then combine their solutions to solve the original problem. In contrast, dynamic programming applies when the subproblems overlap—that is, when subproblems share subsubproblems. In this context, a divide-and-conquer algorithm does more work than necessary, repeatedly solving the common subsubproblems. A dynamic-programming algorithm solves each subsubproblem just once and then saves its answer in a table, thereby avoiding the work of recomputing the answer every time it solves each subsubproblem.

We typically apply dynamic programming to *optimization problems*. Such problems can have many possible solutions. Each solution has a value, and we wish to find a solution with the optimal (minimum or maximum) value. We call such a solution *an* optimal solution to the problem, as opposed to *the* optimal solution, since there may be several solutions that achieve the optimal value.

When developing a dynamic-programming algorithm, we follow a sequence of four steps:

1. Characterize the structure of an optimal solution.

2. Recursively define the value of an optimal solution.

3. Compute the value of an optimal solution, typically in a bottom-up fashion.

4. Construct an optimal solution from computed information.

Steps 1–3 form the basis of a dynamic-programming solution to a problem. If we need only the value of an optimal solution, and not the solution itself, then we can omit step 4. When we do perform step 4, we sometimes maintain additional information during step 3 so that we can easily construct an optimal solution.

The sections that follow use the dynamic-programming method to solve some optimization problems. Section 15.1 examines the problem of cutting a rod into rods of smaller length in a way that maximizes their total value. Section 15.2 asks how we can multiply a chain of matrices while performing the fewest total scalar multiplications. Given these examples of dynamic programming, Section 15.3 discusses two key characteristics that a problem must have for dynamic programming to be a viable solution technique. Section 15.4 then shows how to find the longest common subsequence of two sequences via dynamic programming. Finally, Section 15.5 uses dynamic programming to construct binary search trees that are optimal, given a known distribution of keys to be looked up.

15.1   Rod cutting

Our first example uses dynamic programming to solve a simple problem in deciding where to cut steel rods. Serling Enterprises buys long steel rods and cuts them into shorter rods, which it then sells. Each cut is free. The management of Serling Enterprises wants to know the best way to cut up the rods.

We assume that we know, for $i = 1, 2, \ldots$, the price p_i in dollars that Serling Enterprises charges for a rod of length i inches. Rod lengths are always an integral number of inches. Figure 15.1 gives a sample price table.

The *rod-cutting problem* is the following. Given a rod of length n inches and a table of prices p_i for $i = 1, 2, \ldots, n$, determine the maximum revenue r_n obtainable by cutting up the rod and selling the pieces. Note that if the price p_n for a rod of length n is large enough, an optimal solution may require no cutting at all.

Consider the case when $n = 4$. Figure 15.2 shows all the ways to cut up a rod of 4 inches in length, including the way with no cuts at all. We see that cutting a 4-inch rod into two 2-inch pieces produces revenue $p_2 + p_2 = 5 + 5 = 10$, which is optimal.

We can cut up a rod of length n in 2^{n-1} different ways, since we have an independent option of cutting, or not cutting, at distance i inches from the left end,

length i	1	2	3	4	5	6	7	8	9	10
price p_i	1	5	8	9	10	17	17	20	24	30

Figure 15.1   A sample price table for rods. Each rod of length i inches earns the company p_i dollars of revenue.

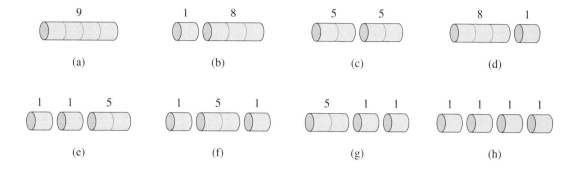

(a)   (b)   (c)   (d)

(e)   (f)   (g)   (h)

Figure 15.2   The 8 possible ways of cutting up a rod of length 4.   Above each piece is the value of that piece, according to the sample price chart of Figure 15.1.   The optimal strategy is part (c)—cutting the rod into two pieces of length 2—which has total value 10.

for $i = 1, 2, \ldots, n - 1$.[1]   We denote a decomposition into pieces using ordinary additive notation, so that $7 = 2 + 2 + 3$ indicates that a rod of length 7 is cut into three pieces—two of length 2 and one of length 3.   If an optimal solution cuts the rod into k pieces, for some $1 \le k \le n$, then an optimal decomposition

$$n = i_1 + i_2 + \cdots + i_k$$

of the rod into pieces of lengths i_1, i_2, ..., i_k provides maximum corresponding revenue

$$r_n = p_{i_1} + p_{i_2} + \cdots + p_{i_k} \, .$$

For our sample problem, we can determine the optimal revenue figures r_i, for $i = 1, 2, \ldots, 10$, by inspection, with the corresponding optimal decompositions

---

[1]If we required the pieces to be cut in order of nondecreasing size, there would be fewer ways to consider.   For $n = 4$, we would consider only 5 such ways: parts (a), (b), (c), (e), and (h) in Figure 15.2.   The number of ways is called the **partition function**; it is approximately equal to $e^{\pi \sqrt{2n/3}}/4n\sqrt{3}$.   This quantity is less than 2^{n-1}, but still much greater than any polynomial in n. We shall not pursue this line of inquiry further, however.

$$
\begin{aligned}
r_1 &= 1 && \text{from solution } 1 = 1 \quad \text{(no cuts)}, \\
r_2 &= 5 && \text{from solution } 2 = 2 \quad \text{(no cuts)}, \\
r_3 &= 8 && \text{from solution } 3 = 3 \quad \text{(no cuts)}, \\
r_4 &= 10 && \text{from solution } 4 = 2 + 2, \\
r_5 &= 13 && \text{from solution } 5 = 2 + 3, \\
r_6 &= 17 && \text{from solution } 6 = 6 \quad \text{(no cuts)}, \\
r_7 &= 18 && \text{from solution } 7 = 1 + 6 \text{ or } 7 = 2 + 2 + 3, \\
r_8 &= 22 && \text{from solution } 8 = 2 + 6, \\
r_9 &= 25 && \text{from solution } 9 = 3 + 6, \\
r_{10} &= 30 && \text{from solution } 10 = 10 \quad \text{(no cuts)}.
\end{aligned}
$$

More generally, we can frame the values r_n for $n \geq 1$ in terms of optimal revenues from shorter rods:

$$
r_n = \max\left(p_n, r_1 + r_{n-1}, r_2 + r_{n-2}, \ldots, r_{n-1} + r_1\right) . \tag{15.1}
$$

The first argument, p_n, corresponds to making no cuts at all and selling the rod of length n as is. The other $n - 1$ arguments to max correspond to the maximum revenue obtained by making an initial cut of the rod into two pieces of size i and $n - i$, for each $i = 1, 2, \ldots, n - 1$, and then optimally cutting up those pieces further, obtaining revenues r_i and r_{n-i} from those two pieces. Since we don't know ahead of time which value of i optimizes revenue, we have to consider all possible values for i and pick the one that maximizes revenue. We also have the option of picking no i at all if we can obtain more revenue by selling the rod uncut.

Note that to solve the original problem of size n, we solve smaller problems of the same type, but of smaller sizes. Once we make the first cut, we may consider the two pieces as independent instances of the rod-cutting problem. The overall optimal solution incorporates optimal solutions to the two related subproblems, maximizing revenue from each of those two pieces. We say that the rod-cutting problem exhibits *optimal substructure*: optimal solutions to a problem incorporate optimal solutions to related subproblems, which we may solve independently.

In a related, but slightly simpler, way to arrange a recursive structure for the rod-cutting problem, we view a decomposition as consisting of a first piece of length i cut off the left-hand end, and then a right-hand remainder of length $n - i$. Only the remainder, and not the first piece, may be further divided. We may view every decomposition of a length-n rod in this way: as a first piece followed by some decomposition of the remainder. When doing so, we can couch the solution with no cuts at all as saying that the first piece has size $i = n$ and revenue p_n and that the remainder has size 0 with corresponding revenue $r_0 = 0$. We thus obtain the following simpler version of equation (15.1):

$$
r_n = \max_{1 \leq i \leq n}\left(p_i + r_{n-i}\right) . \tag{15.2}
$$

In this formulation, an optimal solution embodies the solution to only *one* related subproblem—the remainder—rather than two.

Recursive top-down implementation

The following procedure implements the computation implicit in equation (15.2) in a straightforward, top-down, recursive manner.

CUT-ROD(p, n)

1   **if** $n == 0$
2   **return** 0
3   $q = -\infty$
4   **for** $i = 1$ **to** n
5        $q = \max(q, p[i] + \text{CUT-ROD}(p, n - i))$
6   **return** q

Procedure CUT-ROD takes as input an array $p[1 .. n]$ of prices and an integer n, and it returns the maximum revenue possible for a rod of length n. If $n = 0$, no revenue is possible, and so CUT-ROD returns 0 in line 2. Line 3 initializes the maximum revenue q to $-\infty$, so that the **for** loop in lines 4–5 correctly computes $q = \max_{1 \le i \le n}(p_i + \text{CUT-ROD}(p, n - i))$; line 6 then returns this value. A simple induction on n proves that this answer is equal to the desired answer r_n, using equation (15.2).

If you were to code up CUT-ROD in your favorite programming language and run it on your computer, you would find that once the input size becomes moderately large, your program would take a long time to run. For $n = 40$, you would find that your program takes at least several minutes, and most likely more than an hour. In fact, you would find that each time you increase n by 1, your program's running time would approximately double.

Why is CUT-ROD so inefficient? The problem is that CUT-ROD calls itself recursively over and over again with the same parameter values; it solves the same subproblems repeatedly. Figure 15.3 illustrates what happens for $n = 4$: CUT-ROD(p, n) calls CUT-ROD($p, n - i$) for $i = 1, 2, \ldots, n$. Equivalently, CUT-ROD(p, n) calls CUT-ROD(p, j) for each $j = 0, 1, \ldots, n - 1$. When this process unfolds recursively, the amount of work done, as a function of n, grows explosively.

To analyze the running time of CUT-ROD, let $T(n)$ denote the total number of calls made to CUT-ROD when called with its second parameter equal to n. This expression equals the number of nodes in a subtree whose root is labeled n in the recursion tree. The count includes the initial call at its root. Thus, $T(0) = 1$ and

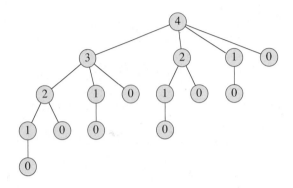

Figure 15.3 The recursion tree showing recursive calls resulting from a call CUT-ROD(p, n) for $n = 4$. Each node label gives the size n of the corresponding subproblem, so that an edge from a parent with label s to a child with label t corresponds to cutting off an initial piece of size $s - t$ and leaving a remaining subproblem of size t. A path from the root to a leaf corresponds to one of the 2^{n-1} ways of cutting up a rod of length n. In general, this recursion tree has 2^n nodes and 2^{n-1} leaves.

$$T(n) = 1 + \sum_{j=0}^{n-1} T(j) \,. \tag{15.3}$$

The initial 1 is for the call at the root, and the term $T(j)$ counts the number of calls (including recursive calls) due to the call CUT-ROD$(p, n - i)$, where $j = n - i$. As Exercise 15.1-1 asks you to show,

$$T(n) = 2^n \,, \tag{15.4}$$

and so the running time of CUT-ROD is exponential in n.

In retrospect, this exponential running time is not so surprising. CUT-ROD explicitly considers all the 2^{n-1} possible ways of cutting up a rod of length n. The tree of recursive calls has 2^{n-1} leaves, one for each possible way of cutting up the rod. The labels on the simple path from the root to a leaf give the sizes of each remaining right-hand piece before making each cut. That is, the labels give the corresponding cut points, measured from the right-hand end of the rod.

Using dynamic programming for optimal rod cutting

We now show how to convert CUT-ROD into an efficient algorithm, using dynamic programming.

The dynamic-programming method works as follows. Having observed that a naive recursive solution is inefficient because it solves the same subproblems repeatedly, we arrange for each subproblem to be solved only once, saving its solution. If we need to refer to this subproblem's solution again later, we can just look it up, rather than recompute it. Dynamic programming thus uses additional memory to save computation time; it serves an example of a ***time-memory trade-off***. The savings may be dramatic: an exponential-time solution may be transformed into a polynomial-time solution. A dynamic-programming approach runs in polynomial time when the number of *distinct* subproblems involved is polynomial in the input size and we can solve each such subproblem in polynomial time.

There are usually two equivalent ways to implement a dynamic-programming approach. We shall illustrate both of them with our rod-cutting example.

The first approach is ***top-down with memoization***.[2] In this approach, we write the procedure recursively in a natural manner, but modified to save the result of each subproblem (usually in an array or hash table). The procedure now first checks to see whether it has previously solved this subproblem. If so, it returns the saved value, saving further computation at this level; if not, the procedure computes the value in the usual manner. We say that the recursive procedure has been ***memoized***; it "remembers" what results it has computed previously.

The second approach is the ***bottom-up method***. This approach typically depends on some natural notion of the "size" of a subproblem, such that solving any particular subproblem depends only on solving "smaller" subproblems. We sort the subproblems by size and solve them in size order, smallest first. When solving a particular subproblem, we have already solved all of the smaller subproblems its solution depends upon, and we have saved their solutions. We solve each subproblem only once, and when we first see it, we have already solved all of its prerequisite subproblems.

These two approaches yield algorithms with the same asymptotic running time, except in unusual circumstances where the top-down approach does not actually recurse to examine all possible subproblems. The bottom-up approach often has much better constant factors, since it has less overhead for procedure calls.

Here is the pseudocode for the top-down CUT-ROD procedure, with memoization added:

MEMOIZED-CUT-ROD(p, n)

1   let $r[0 .. n]$ be a new array
2   **for** $i = 0$ **to** n
3       $r[i] = -\infty$
4   **return** MEMOIZED-CUT-ROD-AUX(p, n, r)

---

[2]This is not a misspelling. The word really is *memoization*, not *memorization*. *Memoization* comes from *memo*, since the technique consists of recording a value so that we can look it up later.

MEMOIZED-CUT-ROD-AUX(p, n, r)

```
1  if r[n] ≥ 0
2      return r[n]
3  if n == 0
4      q = 0
5  else q = -∞
6      for i = 1 to n
7          q = max(q, p[i] + MEMOIZED-CUT-ROD-AUX(p, n - i, r))
8  r[n] = q
9  return q
```

Here, the main procedure MEMOIZED-CUT-ROD initializes a new auxiliary array $r[0..n]$ with the value $-\infty$, a convenient choice with which to denote "unknown." (Known revenue values are always nonnegative.) It then calls its helper routine, MEMOIZED-CUT-ROD-AUX.

The procedure MEMOIZED-CUT-ROD-AUX is just the memoized version of our previous procedure, CUT-ROD. It first checks in line 1 to see whether the desired value is already known and, if it is, then line 2 returns it. Otherwise, lines 3–7 compute the desired value q in the usual manner, line 8 saves it in $r[n]$, and line 9 returns it.

The bottom-up version is even simpler:

BOTTOM-UP-CUT-ROD(p, n)

```
1  let r[0..n] be a new array
2  r[0] = 0
3  for j = 1 to n
4      q = -∞
5      for i = 1 to j
6          q = max(q, p[i] + r[j - i])
7      r[j] = q
8  return r[n]
```

For the bottom-up dynamic-programming approach, BOTTOM-UP-CUT-ROD uses the natural ordering of the subproblems: a subproblem of size i is "smaller" than a subproblem of size j if $i < j$. Thus, the procedure solves subproblems of sizes $j = 0, 1, \ldots, n$, in that order.

Line 1 of procedure BOTTOM-UP-CUT-ROD creates a new array $r[0..n]$ in which to save the results of the subproblems, and line 2 initializes $r[0]$ to 0, since a rod of length 0 earns no revenue. Lines 3–6 solve each subproblem of size j, for $j = 1, 2, \ldots, n$, in order of increasing size. The approach used to solve a problem of a particular size j is the same as that used by CUT-ROD, except that line 6 now

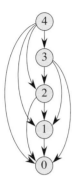

Figure 15.4 The subproblem graph for the rod-cutting problem with $n = 4$. The vertex labels give the sizes of the corresponding subproblems. A directed edge (x, y) indicates that we need a solution to subproblem y when solving subproblem x. This graph is a reduced version of the tree of Figure 15.3, in which all nodes with the same label are collapsed into a single vertex and all edges go from parent to child.

directly references array entry $r[j - i]$ instead of making a recursive call to solve the subproblem of size $j - i$. Line 7 saves in $r[j]$ the solution to the subproblem of size j. Finally, line 8 returns $r[n]$, which equals the optimal value r_n.

The bottom-up and top-down versions have the same asymptotic running time. The running time of procedure BOTTOM-UP-CUT-ROD is $\Theta(n^2)$, due to its doubly-nested loop structure. The number of iterations of its inner **for** loop, in lines 5–6, forms an arithmetic series. The running time of its top-down counterpart, MEMOIZED-CUT-ROD, is also $\Theta(n^2)$, although this running time may be a little harder to see. Because a recursive call to solve a previously solved subproblem returns immediately, MEMOIZED-CUT-ROD solves each subproblem just once. It solves subproblems for sizes $0, 1, \ldots, n$. To solve a subproblem of size n, the **for** loop of lines 6–7 iterates n times. Thus, the total number of iterations of this **for** loop, over all recursive calls of MEMOIZED-CUT-ROD, forms an arithmetic series, giving a total of $\Theta(n^2)$ iterations, just like the inner **for** loop of BOTTOM-UP-CUT-ROD. (We actually are using a form of aggregate analysis here. We shall see aggregate analysis in detail in Section 17.1.)

Subproblem graphs

When we think about a dynamic-programming problem, we should understand the set of subproblems involved and how subproblems depend on one another.

The ***subproblem graph*** for the problem embodies exactly this information. Figure 15.4 shows the subproblem graph for the rod-cutting problem with $n = 4$. It is a directed graph, containing one vertex for each distinct subproblem. The subproblem graph has a directed edge from the vertex for subproblem x to the vertex for subproblem y if determining an optimal solution for subproblem x involves directly considering an optimal solution for subproblem y. For example, the subproblem graph contains an edge from x to y if a top-down recursive procedure for solving x directly calls itself to solve y. We can think of the subproblem graph as a "reduced" or "collapsed" version of the recursion tree for the top-down recursive method, in which we coalesce all nodes for the same subproblem into a single vertex and direct all edges from parent to child.

The bottom-up method for dynamic programming considers the vertices of the subproblem graph in such an order that we solve the subproblems y adjacent to a given subproblem x before we solve subproblem x. (Recall from Section B.4 that the adjacency relation is not necessarily symmetric.) Using the terminology from Chapter 22, in a bottom-up dynamic-programming algorithm, we consider the vertices of the subproblem graph in an order that is a "reverse topological sort," or a "topological sort of the transpose" (see Section 22.4) of the subproblem graph. In other words, no subproblem is considered until all of the subproblems it depends upon have been solved. Similarly, using notions from the same chapter, we can view the top-down method (with memoization) for dynamic programming as a "depth-first search" of the subproblem graph (see Section 22.3).

The size of the subproblem graph $G = (V, E)$ can help us determine the running time of the dynamic programming algorithm. Since we solve each subproblem just once, the running time is the sum of the times needed to solve each subproblem. Typically, the time to compute the solution to a subproblem is proportional to the degree (number of outgoing edges) of the corresponding vertex in the subproblem graph, and the number of subproblems is equal to the number of vertices in the subproblem graph. In this common case, the running time of dynamic programming is linear in the number of vertices and edges.

Reconstructing a solution

Our dynamic-programming solutions to the rod-cutting problem return the value of an optimal solution, but they do not return an actual solution: a list of piece sizes. We can extend the dynamic-programming approach to record not only the optimal *value* computed for each subproblem, but also a *choice* that led to the optimal value. With this information, we can readily print an optimal solution.

Here is an extended version of BOTTOM-UP-CUT-ROD that computes, for each rod size j, not only the maximum revenue r_j, but also s_j, the optimal size of the first piece to cut off:

EXTENDED-BOTTOM-UP-CUT-ROD(p, n)

```
1   let r[0 . . n] and s[1 . . n] be new arrays
2   r[0] = 0
3   for j = 1 to n
4       q = -∞
5       for i = 1 to j
6           if q < p[i] + r[j - i]
7               q = p[i] + r[j - i]
8               s[j] = i
9       r[j] = q
10  return r and s
```

This procedure is similar to BOTTOM-UP-CUT-ROD, except that it creates the array s in line 1, and it updates $s[j]$ in line 8 to hold the optimal size i of the first piece to cut off when solving a subproblem of size j.

The following procedure takes a price table p and a rod size n, and it calls EXTENDED-BOTTOM-UP-CUT-ROD to compute the array $s[1 . . n]$ of optimal first-piece sizes and then prints out the complete list of piece sizes in an optimal decomposition of a rod of length n:

PRINT-CUT-ROD-SOLUTION(p, n)

```
1   (r, s) = EXTENDED-BOTTOM-UP-CUT-ROD(p, n)
2   while n > 0
3       print s[n]
4       n = n - s[n]
```

In our rod-cutting example, the call EXTENDED-BOTTOM-UP-CUT-ROD($p, 10$) would return the following arrays:

i	0	1	2	3	4	5	6	7	8	9	10
$r[i]$	0	1	5	8	10	13	17	18	22	25	30
$s[i]$		1	2	3	2	2	6	1	2	3	10

A call to PRINT-CUT-ROD-SOLUTION($p, 10$) would print just 10, but a call with $n = 7$ would print the cuts 1 and 6, corresponding to the first optimal decomposition for r_7 given earlier.

Exercises

15.1-1

Show that equation (15.4) follows from equation (15.3) and the initial condition $T(0) = 1$.

15.1-2

Show, by means of a counterexample, that the following "greedy" strategy does not always determine an optimal way to cut rods. Define the *density* of a rod of length i to be p_i/i, that is, its value per inch. The greedy strategy for a rod of length n cuts off a first piece of length i, where $1 \le i \le n$, having maximum density. It then continues by applying the greedy strategy to the remaining piece of length $n - i$.

15.1-3

Consider a modification of the rod-cutting problem in which, in addition to a price p_i for each rod, each cut incurs a fixed cost of c. The revenue associated with a solution is now the sum of the prices of the pieces minus the costs of making the cuts. Give a dynamic-programming algorithm to solve this modified problem.

15.1-4

Modify MEMOIZED-CUT-ROD to return not only the value but the actual solution, too.

15.1-5

The Fibonacci numbers are defined by recurrence (3.22). Give an $O(n)$-time dynamic-programming algorithm to compute the nth Fibonacci number. Draw the subproblem graph. How many vertices and edges are in the graph?

15.2   Matrix-chain multiplication

Our next example of dynamic programming is an algorithm that solves the problem of matrix-chain multiplication. We are given a sequence (chain) $\langle A_1, A_2, \ldots, A_n \rangle$ of n matrices to be multiplied, and we wish to compute the product

$$A_1 A_2 \cdots A_n \, . \tag{15.5}$$

We can evaluate the expression (15.5) using the standard algorithm for multiplying pairs of matrices as a subroutine once we have parenthesized it to resolve all ambiguities in how the matrices are multiplied together. Matrix multiplication is associative, and so all parenthesizations yield the same product. A product of matrices is *fully parenthesized* if it is either a single matrix or the product of two fully parenthesized matrix products, surrounded by parentheses. For example, if the chain of matrices is $\langle A_1, A_2, A_3, A_4 \rangle$, then we can fully parenthesize the product $A_1 A_2 A_3 A_4$ in five distinct ways:

$(A_1(A_2(A_3 A_4)))$,
$(A_1((A_2 A_3)A_4))$,
$((A_1 A_2)(A_3 A_4))$,
$((A_1(A_2 A_3))A_4)$,
$(((A_1 A_2)A_3)A_4)$.

How we parenthesize a chain of matrices can have a dramatic impact on the cost of evaluating the product. Consider first the cost of multiplying two matrices. The standard algorithm is given by the following pseudocode, which generalizes the SQUARE-MATRIX-MULTIPLY procedure from Section 4.2. The attributes *rows* and *columns* are the numbers of rows and columns in a matrix.

MATRIX-MULTIPLY(A, B)

```
1   if A.columns ≠ B.rows
2       error "incompatible dimensions"
3   else let C be a new A.rows × B.columns matrix
4       for i = 1 to A.rows
5           for j = 1 to B.columns
6               c_ij = 0
7               for k = 1 to A.columns
8                   c_ij = c_ij + a_ik · b_kj
9   return C
```

We can multiply two matrices A and B only if they are **compatible**: the number of columns of A must equal the number of rows of B. If A is a $p \times q$ matrix and B is a $q \times r$ matrix, the resulting matrix C is a $p \times r$ matrix. The time to compute C is dominated by the number of scalar multiplications in line 8, which is pqr. In what follows, we shall express costs in terms of the number of scalar multiplications.

To illustrate the different costs incurred by different parenthesizations of a matrix product, consider the problem of a chain $\langle A_1, A_2, A_3 \rangle$ of three matrices. Suppose that the dimensions of the matrices are 10×100, 100×5, and 5×50, respectively. If we multiply according to the parenthesization $((A_1 A_2)A_3)$, we perform $10 \cdot 100 \cdot 5 = 5000$ scalar multiplications to compute the 10×5 matrix product $A_1 A_2$, plus another $10 \cdot 5 \cdot 50 = 2500$ scalar multiplications to multiply this matrix by A_3, for a total of 7500 scalar multiplications. If instead we multiply according to the parenthesization $(A_1(A_2 A_3))$, we perform $100 \cdot 5 \cdot 50 = 25,000$ scalar multiplications to compute the 100×50 matrix product $A_2 A_3$, plus another $10 \cdot 100 \cdot 50 = 50,000$ scalar multiplications to multiply A_1 by this matrix, for a total of 75,000 scalar multiplications. Thus, computing the product according to the first parenthesization is 10 times faster.

We state the **matrix-chain multiplication problem** as follows: given a chain $\langle A_1, A_2, \ldots, A_n \rangle$ of n matrices, where for $i = 1, 2, \ldots, n$, matrix A_i has dimension

$p_{i-1} \times p_i$, fully parenthesize the product $A_1 A_2 \cdots A_n$ in a way that minimizes the number of scalar multiplications.

Note that in the matrix-chain multiplication problem, we are not actually multiplying matrices. Our goal is only to determine an order for multiplying matrices that has the lowest cost. Typically, the time invested in determining this optimal order is more than paid for by the time saved later on when actually performing the matrix multiplications (such as performing only 7500 scalar multiplications instead of 75,000).

Counting the number of parenthesizations

Before solving the matrix-chain multiplication problem by dynamic programming, let us convince ourselves that exhaustively checking all possible parenthesizations does not yield an efficient algorithm. Denote the number of alternative parenthesizations of a sequence of n matrices by $P(n)$. When $n = 1$, we have just one matrix and therefore only one way to fully parenthesize the matrix product. When $n \geq 2$, a fully parenthesized matrix product is the product of two fully parenthesized matrix subproducts, and the split between the two subproducts may occur between the kth and $(k + 1)$st matrices for any $k = 1, 2, \ldots, n - 1$. Thus, we obtain the recurrence

$$P(n) = \begin{cases} 1 & \text{if } n = 1, \\ \displaystyle\sum_{k=1}^{n-1} P(k)P(n - k) & \text{if } n \geq 2. \end{cases} \quad (15.6)$$

Problem 12-4 asked you to show that the solution to a similar recurrence is the sequence of *Catalan numbers*, which grows as $\Omega(4^n / n^{3/2})$. A simpler exercise (see Exercise 15.2-3) is to show that the solution to the recurrence (15.6) is $\Omega(2^n)$. The number of solutions is thus exponential in n, and the brute-force method of exhaustive search makes for a poor strategy when determining how to optimally parenthesize a matrix chain.

Applying dynamic programming

We shall use the dynamic-programming method to determine how to optimally parenthesize a matrix chain. In so doing, we shall follow the four-step sequence that we stated at the beginning of this chapter:

1. Characterize the structure of an optimal solution.

2. Recursively define the value of an optimal solution.

3. Compute the value of an optimal solution.

4. Construct an optimal solution from computed information.

We shall go through these steps in order, demonstrating clearly how we apply each step to the problem.

Step 1: The structure of an optimal parenthesization

For our first step in the dynamic-programming paradigm, we find the optimal substructure and then use it to construct an optimal solution to the problem from optimal solutions to subproblems. In the matrix-chain multiplication problem, we can perform this step as follows. For convenience, let us adopt the notation $A_{i..j}$, where $i \leq j$, for the matrix that results from evaluating the product $A_i A_{i+1} \cdots A_j$. Observe that if the problem is nontrivial, i.e., $i < j$, then to parenthesize the product $A_i A_{i+1} \cdots A_j$, we must split the product between A_k and A_{k+1} for some integer k in the range $i \leq k < j$. That is, for some value of k, we first compute the matrices $A_{i..k}$ and $A_{k+1..j}$ and then multiply them together to produce the final product $A_{i..j}$. The cost of parenthesizing this way is the cost of computing the matrix $A_{i..k}$, plus the cost of computing $A_{k+1..j}$, plus the cost of multiplying them together.

The optimal substructure of this problem is as follows. Suppose that to optimally parenthesize $A_i A_{i+1} \cdots A_j$, we split the product between A_k and A_{k+1}. Then the way we parenthesize the "prefix" subchain $A_i A_{i+1} \cdots A_k$ within this optimal parenthesization of $A_i A_{i+1} \cdots A_j$ must be an optimal parenthesization of $A_i A_{i+1} \cdots A_k$. Why? If there were a less costly way to parenthesize $A_i A_{i+1} \cdots A_k$, then we could substitute that parenthesization in the optimal parenthesization of $A_i A_{i+1} \cdots A_j$ to produce another way to parenthesize $A_i A_{i+1} \cdots A_j$ whose cost was lower than the optimum: a contradiction. A similar observation holds for how we parenthesize the subchain $A_{k+1} A_{k+2} \cdots A_j$ in the optimal parenthesization of $A_i A_{i+1} \cdots A_j$: it must be an optimal parenthesization of $A_{k+1} A_{k+2} \cdots A_j$.

Now we use our optimal substructure to show that we can construct an optimal solution to the problem from optimal solutions to subproblems. We have seen that any solution to a nontrivial instance of the matrix-chain multiplication problem requires us to split the product, and that any optimal solution contains within it optimal solutions to subproblem instances. Thus, we can build an optimal solution to an instance of the matrix-chain multiplication problem by splitting the problem into two subproblems (optimally parenthesizing $A_i A_{i+1} \cdots A_k$ and $A_{k+1} A_{k+2} \cdots A_j$), finding optimal solutions to subproblem instances, and then combining these optimal subproblem solutions. We must ensure that when we search for the correct place to split the product, we have considered all possible places, so that we are sure of having examined the optimal one.

Step 2: A recursive solution

Next, we define the cost of an optimal solution recursively in terms of the optimal solutions to subproblems. For the matrix-chain multiplication problem, we pick as our subproblems the problems of determining the minimum cost of parenthesizing $A_i A_{i+1} \cdots A_j$ for $1 \leq i \leq j \leq n$. Let $m[i, j]$ be the minimum number of scalar multiplications needed to compute the matrix $A_{i..j}$; for the full problem, the lowest-cost way to compute $A_{1..n}$ would thus be $m[1, n]$.

We can define $m[i, j]$ recursively as follows. If $i = j$, the problem is trivial; the chain consists of just one matrix $A_{i..i} = A_i$, so that no scalar multiplications are necessary to compute the product. Thus, $m[i, i] = 0$ for $i = 1, 2, \ldots, n$. To compute $m[i, j]$ when $i < j$, we take advantage of the structure of an optimal solution from step 1. Let us assume that to optimally parenthesize, we split the product $A_i A_{i+1} \cdots A_j$ between A_k and A_{k+1}, where $i \leq k < j$. Then, $m[i, j]$ equals the minimum cost for computing the subproducts $A_{i..k}$ and $A_{k+1..j}$, plus the cost of multiplying these two matrices together. Recalling that each matrix A_i is $p_{i-1} \times p_i$, we see that computing the matrix product $A_{i..k} A_{k+1..j}$ takes $p_{i-1} p_k p_j$ scalar multiplications. Thus, we obtain

$$m[i, j] = m[i, k] + m[k + 1, j] + p_{i-1} p_k p_j \ .$$

This recursive equation assumes that we know the value of k, which we do not. There are only $j - i$ possible values for k, however, namely $k = i, i+1, \ldots, j-1$. Since the optimal parenthesization must use one of these values for k, we need only check them all to find the best. Thus, our recursive definition for the minimum cost of parenthesizing the product $A_i A_{i+1} \cdots A_j$ becomes

$$m[i, j] = \begin{cases} 0 & \text{if } i = j \ , \\ \min_{i \leq k < j} \{m[i, k] + m[k + 1, j] + p_{i-1} p_k p_j\} & \text{if } i < j \ . \end{cases} \qquad (15.7)$$

The $m[i, j]$ values give the costs of optimal solutions to subproblems, but they do not provide all the information we need to construct an optimal solution. To help us do so, we define $s[i, j]$ to be a value of k at which we split the product $A_i A_{i+1} \cdots A_j$ in an optimal parenthesization. That is, $s[i, j]$ equals a value k such that $m[i, j] = m[i, k] + m[k + 1, j] + p_{i-1} p_k p_j$.

Step 3: Computing the optimal costs

At this point, we could easily write a recursive algorithm based on recurrence (15.7) to compute the minimum cost $m[1, n]$ for multiplying $A_1 A_2 \cdots A_n$. As we saw for the rod-cutting problem, and as we shall see in Section 15.3, this recursive algorithm takes exponential time, which is no better than the brute-force method of checking each way of parenthesizing the product.

Observe that we have relatively few distinct subproblems: one subproblem for each choice of i and j satisfying $1 \le i \le j \le n$, or $\binom{n}{2} + n = \Theta(n^2)$ in all. A recursive algorithm may encounter each subproblem many times in different branches of its recursion tree. This property of overlapping subproblems is the second hallmark of when dynamic programming applies (the first hallmark being optimal substructure).

Instead of computing the solution to recurrence (15.7) recursively, we compute the optimal cost by using a tabular, bottom-up approach. (We present the corresponding top-down approach using memoization in Section 15.3.)

We shall implement the tabular, bottom-up method in the procedure MATRIX-CHAIN-ORDER, which appears below. This procedure assumes that matrix A_i has dimensions $p_{i-1} \times p_i$ for $i = 1, 2, \ldots, n$. Its input is a sequence $p = \langle p_0, p_1, \ldots, p_n \rangle$, where $p.length = n + 1$. The procedure uses an auxiliary table $m[1 \ldots n, 1 \ldots n]$ for storing the $m[i, j]$ costs and another auxiliary table $s[1 \ldots n - 1, 2 \ldots n]$ that records which index of k achieved the optimal cost in computing $m[i, j]$. We shall use the table s to construct an optimal solution.

In order to implement the bottom-up approach, we must determine which entries of the table we refer to when computing $m[i, j]$. Equation (15.7) shows that the cost $m[i, j]$ of computing a matrix-chain product of $j - i + 1$ matrices depends only on the costs of computing matrix-chain products of fewer than $j - i + 1$ matrices. That is, for $k = i, i + 1, \ldots, j - 1$, the matrix $A_{i..k}$ is a product of $k - i + 1 < j - i + 1$ matrices and the matrix $A_{k+1..j}$ is a product of $j - k < j - i + 1$ matrices. Thus, the algorithm should fill in the table m in a manner that corresponds to solving the parenthesization problem on matrix chains of increasing length. For the subproblem of optimally parenthesizing the chain $A_i A_{i+1} \cdots A_j$, we consider the subproblem size to be the length $j - i + 1$ of the chain.

MATRIX-CHAIN-ORDER(p)

```
 1  n = p.length − 1
 2  let m[1..n, 1..n] and s[1..n − 1, 2..n] be new tables
 3  for i = 1 to n
 4      m[i, i] = 0
 5  for l = 2 to n              // l is the chain length
 6      for i = 1 to n − l + 1
 7          j = i + l − 1
 8          m[i, j] = ∞
 9          for k = i to j − 1
10              q = m[i, k] + m[k + 1, j] + p_{i−1} p_k p_j
11              if q < m[i, j]
12                  m[i, j] = q
13                  s[i, j] = k
14  return m and s
```

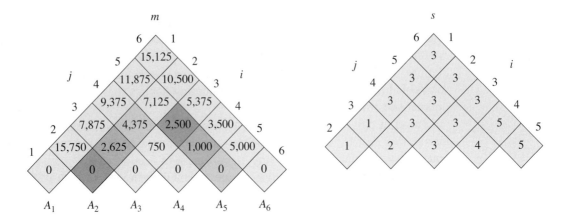

Figure 15.5 The m and s tables computed by MATRIX-CHAIN-ORDER for $n = 6$ and the following matrix dimensions:

matrix	A_1	A_2	A_3	A_4	A_5	A_6
dimension	30×35	35×15	15×5	5×10	10×20	20×25

The tables are rotated so that the main diagonal runs horizontally. The m table uses only the main diagonal and upper triangle, and the s table uses only the upper triangle. The minimum number of scalar multiplications to multiply the 6 matrices is $m[1, 6] = 15{,}125$. Of the darker entries, the pairs that have the same shading are taken together in line 10 when computing

$$m[2, 5] = \min \begin{cases} m[2, 2] + m[3, 5] + p_1 p_2 p_5 = 0 + 2500 + 35 \cdot 15 \cdot 20 = 13{,}000 \,, \\ m[2, 3] + m[4, 5] + p_1 p_3 p_5 = 2625 + 1000 + 35 \cdot 5 \cdot 20 = 7125 \,, \\ m[2, 4] + m[5, 5] + p_1 p_4 p_5 = 4375 + 0 + 35 \cdot 10 \cdot 20 = 11{,}375 \end{cases}$$
$$= 7125 \,.$$

The algorithm first computes $m[i, i] = 0$ for $i = 1, 2, \ldots, n$ (the minimum costs for chains of length 1) in lines 3–4. It then uses recurrence (15.7) to compute $m[i, i + 1]$ for $i = 1, 2, \ldots, n - 1$ (the minimum costs for chains of length $l = 2$) during the first execution of the **for** loop in lines 5–13. The second time through the loop, it computes $m[i, i+2]$ for $i = 1, 2, \ldots, n-2$ (the minimum costs for chains of length $l = 3$), and so forth. At each step, the $m[i, j]$ cost computed in lines 10–13 depends only on table entries $m[i, k]$ and $m[k + 1, j]$ already computed.

Figure 15.5 illustrates this procedure on a chain of $n = 6$ matrices. Since we have defined $m[i, j]$ only for $i \le j$, only the portion of the table m on or above the main diagonal is used. The figure shows the table rotated to make the main diagonal run horizontally. The matrix chain is listed along the bottom. Using this layout, we can find the minimum cost $m[i, j]$ for multiplying a subchain $A_i A_{i+1} \cdots A_j$ of matrices at the intersection of lines running northeast from A_i and northwest from A_j. Each horizontal row in the table contains the entries for matrix chains of the same length. MATRIX-CHAIN-ORDER computes the rows from bottom to top and from left to right within each row. It computes each entry $m[i, j]$ using the products $p_{i-1}p_k p_j$ for $k = i, i + 1, \ldots, j - 1$ and all entries southwest and southeast from $m[i, j]$.

A simple inspection of the nested loop structure of MATRIX-CHAIN-ORDER yields a running time of $O(n^3)$ for the algorithm. The loops are nested three deep, and each loop index (l, i, and k) takes on at most $n - 1$ values. Exercise 15.2-5 asks you to show that the running time of this algorithm is in fact also $\Omega(n^3)$. The algorithm requires $\Theta(n^2)$ space to store the m and s tables. Thus, MATRIX-CHAIN-ORDER is much more efficient than the exponential-time method of enumerating all possible parenthesizations and checking each one.

Step 4: Constructing an optimal solution

Although MATRIX-CHAIN-ORDER determines the optimal number of scalar multiplications needed to compute a matrix-chain product, it does not directly show how to multiply the matrices. The table $s[1 \mathinner{.\,.} n - 1, 2 \mathinner{.\,.} n]$ gives us the information we need to do so. Each entry $s[i, j]$ records a value of k such that an optimal parenthesization of $A_i A_{i+1} \cdots A_j$ splits the product between A_k and A_{k+1}. Thus, we know that the final matrix multiplication in computing $A_{1 \mathinner{.\,.} n}$ optimally is $A_{1 \mathinner{.\,.} s[1,n]} A_{s[1,n]+1 \mathinner{.\,.} n}$. We can determine the earlier matrix multiplications recursively, since $s[1, s[1, n]]$ determines the last matrix multiplication when computing $A_{1 \mathinner{.\,.} s[1,n]}$ and $s[s[1, n] + 1, n]$ determines the last matrix multiplication when computing $A_{s[1,n]+1 \mathinner{.\,.} n}$. The following recursive procedure prints an optimal parenthesization of $\langle A_i, A_{i+1}, \ldots, A_j \rangle$, given the s table computed by MATRIX-CHAIN-ORDER and the indices i and j. The initial call PRINT-OPTIMAL-PARENS$(s, 1, n)$ prints an optimal parenthesization of $\langle A_1, A_2, \ldots, A_n \rangle$.

PRINT-OPTIMAL-PARENS(s, i, j)

```
1  if i == j
2      print "A"ᵢ
3  else print "("
4      PRINT-OPTIMAL-PARENS(s, i, s[i, j])
5      PRINT-OPTIMAL-PARENS(s, s[i, j] + 1, j)
6      print ")"
```

In the example of Figure 15.5, the call PRINT-OPTIMAL-PARENS$(s, 1, 6)$ prints the parenthesization $((A_1(A_2 A_3))((A_4 A_5)A_6))$.

Exercises

15.2-1
Find an optimal parenthesization of a matrix-chain product whose sequence of dimensions is $\langle 5, 10, 3, 12, 5, 50, 6 \rangle$.

15.2-2
Give a recursive algorithm MATRIX-CHAIN-MULTIPLY(A, s, i, j) that actually performs the optimal matrix-chain multiplication, given the sequence of matrices $\langle A_1, A_2, \ldots, A_n \rangle$, the s table computed by MATRIX-CHAIN-ORDER, and the indices i and j. (The initial call would be MATRIX-CHAIN-MULTIPLY$(A, s, 1, n)$.)

15.2-3
Use the substitution method to show that the solution to the recurrence (15.6) is $\Omega(2^n)$.

15.2-4
Describe the subproblem graph for matrix-chain multiplication with an input chain of length n. How many vertices does it have? How many edges does it have, and which edges are they?

15.2-5
Let $R(i, j)$ be the number of times that table entry $m[i, j]$ is referenced while computing other table entries in a call of MATRIX-CHAIN-ORDER. Show that the total number of references for the entire table is

$$\sum_{i=1}^{n} \sum_{j=i}^{n} R(i, j) = \frac{n^3 - n}{3} .$$

(*Hint:* You may find equation (A.3) useful.)

15.2-6
Show that a full parenthesization of an n-element expression has exactly $n - 1$ pairs of parentheses.

15.3   Elements of dynamic programming

Although we have just worked through two examples of the dynamic-programming method, you might still be wondering just when the method applies. From an engineering perspective, when should we look for a dynamic-programming solution to a problem? In this section, we examine the two key ingredients that an optimization problem must have in order for dynamic programming to apply: optimal substructure and overlapping subproblems. We also revisit and discuss more fully how memoization might help us take advantage of the overlapping-subproblems property in a top-down recursive approach.

Optimal substructure

The first step in solving an optimization problem by dynamic programming is to characterize the structure of an optimal solution. Recall that a problem exhibits *optimal substructure* if an optimal solution to the problem contains within it optimal solutions to subproblems. Whenever a problem exhibits optimal substructure, we have a good clue that dynamic programming might apply. (As Chapter 16 discusses, it also might mean that a greedy strategy applies, however.) In dynamic programming, we build an optimal solution to the problem from optimal solutions to subproblems. Consequently, we must take care to ensure that the range of subproblems we consider includes those used in an optimal solution.

We discovered optimal substructure in both of the problems we have examined in this chapter so far. In Section 15.1, we observed that the optimal way of cutting up a rod of length n (if we make any cuts at all) involves optimally cutting up the two pieces resulting from the first cut. In Section 15.2, we observed that an optimal parenthesization of $A_i A_{i+1} \cdots A_j$ that splits the product between A_k and A_{k+1} contains within it optimal solutions to the problems of parenthesizing $A_i A_{i+1} \cdots A_k$ and $A_{k+1} A_{k+2} \cdots A_j$.

You will find yourself following a common pattern in discovering optimal substructure:

1. You show that a solution to the problem consists of making a choice, such as choosing an initial cut in a rod or choosing an index at which to split the matrix chain. Making this choice leaves one or more subproblems to be solved.

2. You suppose that for a given problem, you are given the choice that leads to an optimal solution. You do not concern yourself yet with how to determine this choice. You just assume that it has been given to you.

3. Given this choice, you determine which subproblems ensue and how to best characterize the resulting space of subproblems.

4. You show that the solutions to the subproblems used within an optimal solution to the problem must themselves be optimal by using a "cut-and-paste" technique. You do so by supposing that each of the subproblem solutions is not optimal and then deriving a contradiction. In particular, by "cutting out" the nonoptimal solution to each subproblem and "pasting in" the optimal one, you show that you can get a better solution to the original problem, thus contradicting your supposition that you already had an optimal solution. If an optimal

solution gives rise to more than one subproblem, they are typically so similar that you can modify the cut-and-paste argument for one to apply to the others with little effort.

To characterize the space of subproblems, a good rule of thumb says to try to keep the space as simple as possible and then expand it as necessary. For example, the space of subproblems that we considered for the rod-cutting problem contained the problems of optimally cutting up a rod of length i for each size i. This subproblem space worked well, and we had no need to try a more general space of subproblems.

Conversely, suppose that we had tried to constrain our subproblem space for matrix-chain multiplication to matrix products of the form $A_1 A_2 \cdots A_j$. As before, an optimal parenthesization must split this product between A_k and A_{k+1} for some $1 \le k < j$. Unless we could guarantee that k always equals $j - 1$, we would find that we had subproblems of the form $A_1 A_2 \cdots A_k$ and $A_{k+1} A_{k+2} \cdots A_j$, and that the latter subproblem is not of the form $A_1 A_2 \cdots A_j$. For this problem, we needed to allow our subproblems to vary at "both ends," that is, to allow both i and j to vary in the subproblem $A_i A_{i+1} \cdots A_j$.

Optimal substructure varies across problem domains in two ways:

1. how many subproblems an optimal solution to the original problem uses, and

2. how many choices we have in determining which subproblem(s) to use in an optimal solution.

In the rod-cutting problem, an optimal solution for cutting up a rod of size n uses just one subproblem (of size $n - i$), but we must consider n choices for i in order to determine which one yields an optimal solution. Matrix-chain multiplication for the subchain $A_i A_{i+1} \cdots A_j$ serves as an example with two subproblems and $j - i$ choices. For a given matrix A_k at which we split the product, we have two subproblems—parenthesizing $A_i A_{i+1} \cdots A_k$ and parenthesizing $A_{k+1} A_{k+2} \cdots A_j$—and we must solve *both* of them optimally. Once we determine the optimal solutions to subproblems, we choose from among $j - i$ candidates for the index k.

Informally, the running time of a dynamic-programming algorithm depends on the product of two factors: the number of subproblems overall and how many choices we look at for each subproblem. In rod cutting, we had $\Theta(n)$ subproblems overall, and at most n choices to examine for each, yielding an $O(n^2)$ running time. Matrix-chain multiplication had $\Theta(n^2)$ subproblems overall, and in each we had at most $n - 1$ choices, giving an $O(n^3)$ running time (actually, a $\Theta(n^3)$ running time, by Exercise 15.2-5).

Usually, the subproblem graph gives an alternative way to perform the same analysis. Each vertex corresponds to a subproblem, and the choices for a subproblem are the edges incident from that subproblem. Recall that in rod cutting, the subproblem graph had n vertices and at most n edges per vertex, yielding an $O(n^2)$ running time. For matrix-chain multiplication, if we were to draw the subproblem graph, it would have $\Theta(n^2)$ vertices and each vertex would have degree at most $n - 1$, giving a total of $O(n^3)$ vertices and edges.

Dynamic programming often uses optimal substructure in a bottom-up fashion. That is, we first find optimal solutions to subproblems and, having solved the subproblems, we find an optimal solution to the problem. Finding an optimal solution to the problem entails making a choice among subproblems as to which we will use in solving the problem. The cost of the problem solution is usually the subproblem costs plus a cost that is directly attributable to the choice itself. In rod cutting, for example, first we solved the subproblems of determining optimal ways to cut up rods of length i for $i = 0, 1, \ldots, n - 1$, and then we determined which such subproblem yielded an optimal solution for a rod of length n, using equation (15.2). The cost attributable to the choice itself is the term p_i in equation (15.2). In matrix-chain multiplication, we determined optimal parenthesizations of subchains of $A_i A_{i+1} \cdots A_j$, and then we chose the matrix A_k at which to split the product. The cost attributable to the choice itself is the term $p_{i-1} p_k p_j$.

In Chapter 16, we shall examine "greedy algorithms," which have many similarities to dynamic programming. In particular, problems to which greedy algorithms apply have optimal substructure. One major difference between greedy algorithms and dynamic programming is that instead of first finding optimal solutions to subproblems and then making an informed choice, greedy algorithms first make a "greedy" choice—the choice that looks best at the time—and then solve a resulting subproblem, without bothering to solve all possible related smaller subproblems. Surprisingly, in some cases this strategy works!

Subtleties

You should be careful not to assume that optimal substructure applies when it does not. Consider the following two problems in which we are given a directed graph $G = (V, E)$ and vertices $u, v \in V$.

Unweighted shortest path:[3] Find a path from u to v consisting of the fewest edges. Such a path must be simple, since removing a cycle from a path produces a path with fewer edges.

---

[3] We use the term "unweighted" to distinguish this problem from that of finding shortest paths with weighted edges, which we shall see in Chapters 24 and 25. We can use the breadth-first search technique of Chapter 22 to solve the unweighted problem.

Figure 15.6 A directed graph showing that the problem of finding a longest simple path in an unweighted directed graph does not have optimal substructure. The path $q \rightarrow r \rightarrow t$ is a longest simple path from q to t, but the subpath $q \rightarrow r$ is not a longest simple path from q to r, nor is the subpath $r \rightarrow t$ a longest simple path from r to t.

Unweighted longest simple path: Find a simple path from u to v consisting of the most edges. We need to include the requirement of simplicity because otherwise we can traverse a cycle as many times as we like to create paths with an arbitrarily large number of edges.

The unweighted shortest-path problem exhibits optimal substructure, as follows. Suppose that $u \neq v$, so that the problem is nontrivial. Then, any path p from u to v must contain an intermediate vertex, say w. (Note that w may be u or v.) Thus, we can decompose the path $u \overset{p}{\leadsto} v$ into subpaths $u \overset{p_1}{\leadsto} w \overset{p_2}{\leadsto} v$. Clearly, the number of edges in p equals the number of edges in p_1 plus the number of edges in p_2. We claim that if p is an optimal (i.e., shortest) path from u to v, then p_1 must be a shortest path from u to w. Why? We use a "cut-and-paste" argument: if there were another path, say p'_1, from u to w with fewer edges than p_1, then we could cut out p_1 and paste in p'_1 to produce a path $u \overset{p'_1}{\leadsto} w \overset{p_2}{\leadsto} v$ with fewer edges than p, thus contradicting p's optimality. Symmetrically, p_2 must be a shortest path from w to v. Thus, we can find a shortest path from u to v by considering all intermediate vertices w, finding a shortest path from u to w and a shortest path from w to v, and choosing an intermediate vertex w that yields the overall shortest path. In Section 25.2, we use a variant of this observation of optimal substructure to find a shortest path between every pair of vertices on a weighted, directed graph.

You might be tempted to assume that the problem of finding an unweighted longest simple path exhibits optimal substructure as well. After all, if we decompose a longest simple path $u \overset{p}{\leadsto} v$ into subpaths $u \overset{p_1}{\leadsto} w \overset{p_2}{\leadsto} v$, then mustn't p_1 be a longest simple path from u to w, and mustn't p_2 be a longest simple path from w to v? The answer is no! Figure 15.6 supplies an example. Consider the path $q \rightarrow r \rightarrow t$, which is a longest simple path from q to t. Is $q \rightarrow r$ a longest simple path from q to r? No, for the path $q \rightarrow s \rightarrow t \rightarrow r$ is a simple path that is longer. Is $r \rightarrow t$ a longest simple path from r to t? No again, for the path $r \rightarrow q \rightarrow s \rightarrow t$ is a simple path that is longer.

This example shows that for longest simple paths, not only does the problem lack optimal substructure, but we cannot necessarily assemble a "legal" solution to the problem from solutions to subproblems. If we combine the longest simple paths $q \rightarrow s \rightarrow t \rightarrow r$ and $r \rightarrow q \rightarrow s \rightarrow t$, we get the path $q \rightarrow s \rightarrow t \rightarrow r \rightarrow q \rightarrow s \rightarrow t$, which is not simple. Indeed, the problem of finding an unweighted longest simple path does not appear to have any sort of optimal substructure. No efficient dynamic-programming algorithm for this problem has ever been found. In fact, this problem is NP-complete, which—as we shall see in Chapter 34—means that we are unlikely to find a way to solve it in polynomial time.

Why is the substructure of a longest simple path so different from that of a shortest path? Although a solution to a problem for both longest and shortest paths uses two subproblems, the subproblems in finding the longest simple path are not *independent*, whereas for shortest paths they are. What do we mean by subproblems being independent? We mean that the solution to one subproblem does not affect the solution to another subproblem of the same problem. For the example of Figure 15.6, we have the problem of finding a longest simple path from q to t with two subproblems: finding longest simple paths from q to r and from r to t. For the first of these subproblems, we choose the path $q \rightarrow s \rightarrow t \rightarrow r$, and so we have also used the vertices s and t. We can no longer use these vertices in the second subproblem, since the combination of the two solutions to subproblems would yield a path that is not simple. If we cannot use vertex t in the second problem, then we cannot solve it at all, since t is required to be on the path that we find, and it is not the vertex at which we are "splicing" together the subproblem solutions (that vertex being r). Because we use vertices s and t in one subproblem solution, we cannot use them in the other subproblem solution. We must use at least one of them to solve the other subproblem, however, and we must use both of them to solve it optimally. Thus, we say that these subproblems are not independent. Looked at another way, using resources in solving one subproblem (those resources being vertices) renders them unavailable for the other subproblem.

Why, then, are the subproblems independent for finding a shortest path? The answer is that by nature, the subproblems do not share resources. We claim that if a vertex w is on a shortest path p from u to v, then we can splice together *any* shortest path $u \overset{p_1}{\rightsquigarrow} w$ and *any* shortest path $w \overset{p_2}{\rightsquigarrow} v$ to produce a shortest path from u to v. We are assured that, other than w, no vertex can appear in both paths p_1 and p_2. Why? Suppose that some vertex $x \neq w$ appears in both p_1 and p_2, so that we can decompose p_1 as $u \overset{p_{ux}}{\rightsquigarrow} x \rightsquigarrow w$ and p_2 as $w \rightsquigarrow x \overset{p_{xv}}{\rightsquigarrow} v$. By the optimal substructure of this problem, path p has as many edges as p_1 and p_2 together; let's say that p has e edges. Now let us construct a path $p' = u \overset{p_{ux}}{\rightsquigarrow} x \overset{p_{xv}}{\rightsquigarrow} v$ from u to v. Because we have excised the paths from x to w and from w to x, each of which contains at least one edge, path p' contains at most $e - 2$ edges, which contradicts the assumption that p is a shortest path. Thus, we are assured that the subproblems for the shortest-path problem are independent.

Both problems examined in Sections 15.1 and 15.2 have independent subproblems. In matrix-chain multiplication, the subproblems are multiplying subchains $A_i A_{i+1} \cdots A_k$ and $A_{k+1} A_{k+2} \cdots A_j$. These subchains are disjoint, so that no matrix could possibly be included in both of them. In rod cutting, to determine the best way to cut up a rod of length n, we look at the best ways of cutting up rods of length i for $i = 0, 1, \ldots, n-1$. Because an optimal solution to the length-n problem includes just one of these subproblem solutions (after we have cut off the first piece), independence of subproblems is not an issue.

Overlapping subproblems

The second ingredient that an optimization problem must have for dynamic programming to apply is that the space of subproblems must be "small" in the sense that a recursive algorithm for the problem solves the same subproblems over and over, rather than always generating new subproblems. Typically, the total number of distinct subproblems is a polynomial in the input size. When a recursive algorithm revisits the same problem repeatedly, we say that the optimization problem has *overlapping subproblems*.[4] In contrast, a problem for which a divide-and-conquer approach is suitable usually generates brand-new problems at each step of the recursion. Dynamic-programming algorithms typically take advantage of overlapping subproblems by solving each subproblem once and then storing the solution in a table where it can be looked up when needed, using constant time per lookup.

In Section 15.1, we briefly examined how a recursive solution to rod cutting makes exponentially many calls to find solutions of smaller subproblems. Our dynamic-programming solution takes an exponential-time recursive algorithm down to quadratic time.

To illustrate the overlapping-subproblems property in greater detail, let us reexamine the matrix-chain multiplication problem. Referring back to Figure 15.5, observe that MATRIX-CHAIN-ORDER repeatedly looks up the solution to subproblems in lower rows when solving subproblems in higher rows. For example, it references entry $m[3, 4]$ four times: during the computations of $m[2, 4]$, $m[1, 4]$,

---

[4]It may seem strange that dynamic programming relies on subproblems being both independent and overlapping. Although these requirements may sound contradictory, they describe two different notions, rather than two points on the same axis. Two subproblems of the same problem are independent if they do not share resources. Two subproblems are overlapping if they are really the same subproblem that occurs as a subproblem of different problems.

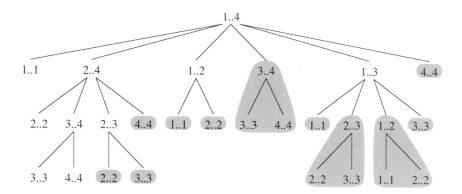

Figure 15.7 The recursion tree for the computation of RECURSIVE-MATRIX-CHAIN(p, 1, 4). Each node contains the parameters i and j. The computations performed in a shaded subtree are replaced by a single table lookup in MEMOIZED-MATRIX-CHAIN.

$m[3, 5]$, and $m[3, 6]$. If we were to recompute $m[3, 4]$ each time, rather than just looking it up, the running time would increase dramatically. To see how, consider the following (inefficient) recursive procedure that determines $m[i, j]$, the minimum number of scalar multiplications needed to compute the matrix-chain product $A_{i..j} = A_i A_{i+1} \cdots A_j$. The procedure is based directly on the recurrence (15.7).

RECURSIVE-MATRIX-CHAIN(p, i, j)

1   **if** $i == j$
2   **return** 0
3   $m[i, j] = \infty$
4   **for** $k = i$ **to** $j - 1$
5       $q = $ RECURSIVE-MATRIX-CHAIN(p, i, k)
                $+ $ RECURSIVE-MATRIX-CHAIN($p, k + 1, j$)
                $+ p_{i-1} p_k p_j$
6   **if** $q < m[i, j]$
7           $m[i, j] = q$
8   **return** $m[i, j]$

Figure 15.7 shows the recursion tree produced by the call RECURSIVE-MATRIX-CHAIN($p, 1, 4$). Each node is labeled by the values of the parameters i and j. Observe that some pairs of values occur many times.

In fact, we can show that the time to compute $m[1, n]$ by this recursive procedure is at least exponential in n. Let $T(n)$ denote the time taken by RECURSIVE-MATRIX-CHAIN to compute an optimal parenthesization of a chain of n matrices. Because the execution of lines 1–2 and of lines 6–7 each take at least unit time, as does the multiplication in line 5, inspection of the procedure yields the recurrence

$$T(1) \geq 1,$$

$$T(n) \geq 1 + \sum_{k=1}^{n-1}(T(k) + T(n-k) + 1) \qquad \text{for } n > 1.$$

Noting that for $i = 1, 2, \ldots, n-1$, each term $T(i)$ appears once as $T(k)$ and once as $T(n-k)$, and collecting the $n-1$ 1s in the summation together with the 1 out front, we can rewrite the recurrence as

$$T(n) \geq 2\sum_{i=1}^{n-1} T(i) + n. \tag{15.8}$$

We shall prove that $T(n) = \Omega(2^n)$ using the substitution method. Specifically, we shall show that $T(n) \geq 2^{n-1}$ for all $n \geq 1$. The basis is easy, since $T(1) \geq 1 = 2^0$. Inductively, for $n \geq 2$ we have

$$
\begin{aligned}
T(n) &\geq 2\sum_{i=1}^{n-1} 2^{i-1} + n \\
&= 2\sum_{i=0}^{n-2} 2^i + n \\
&= 2(2^{n-1} - 1) + n \quad \text{(by equation (A.5))} \\
&= 2^n - 2 + n \\
&\geq 2^{n-1},
\end{aligned}
$$

which completes the proof. Thus, the total amount of work performed by the call RECURSIVE-MATRIX-CHAIN$(p, 1, n)$ is at least exponential in n.

Compare this top-down, recursive algorithm (without memoization) with the bottom-up dynamic-programming algorithm. The latter is more efficient because it takes advantage of the overlapping-subproblems property. Matrix-chain multiplication has only $\Theta(n^2)$ distinct subproblems, and the dynamic-programming algorithm solves each exactly once. The recursive algorithm, on the other hand, must again solve each subproblem every time it reappears in the recursion tree. Whenever a recursion tree for the natural recursive solution to a problem contains the same subproblem repeatedly, and the total number of distinct subproblems is small, dynamic programming can improve efficiency, sometimes dramatically.

Reconstructing an optimal solution

As a practical matter, we often store which choice we made in each subproblem in a table so that we do not have to reconstruct this information from the costs that we stored.

For matrix-chain multiplication, the table $s[i, j]$ saves us a significant amount of work when reconstructing an optimal solution. Suppose that we did not maintain the $s[i, j]$ table, having filled in only the table $m[i, j]$ containing optimal subproblem costs. We choose from among $j - i$ possibilities when we determine which subproblems to use in an optimal solution to parenthesizing $A_i A_{i+1} \cdots A_j$, and $j - i$ is not a constant. Therefore, it would take $\Theta(j - i) = \omega(1)$ time to reconstruct which subproblems we chose for a solution to a given problem. By storing in $s[i, j]$ the index of the matrix at which we split the product $A_i A_{i+1} \cdots A_j$, we can reconstruct each choice in $O(1)$ time.

Memoization

As we saw for the rod-cutting problem, there is an alternative approach to dynamic programming that often offers the efficiency of the bottom-up dynamic-programming approach while maintaining a top-down strategy. The idea is to *memoize* the natural, but inefficient, recursive algorithm. As in the bottom-up approach, we maintain a table with subproblem solutions, but the control structure for filling in the table is more like the recursive algorithm.

A memoized recursive algorithm maintains an entry in a table for the solution to each subproblem. Each table entry initially contains a special value to indicate that the entry has yet to be filled in. When the subproblem is first encountered as the recursive algorithm unfolds, its solution is computed and then stored in the table. Each subsequent time that we encounter this subproblem, we simply look up the value stored in the table and return it.[5]

Here is a memoized version of RECURSIVE-MATRIX-CHAIN. Note where it resembles the memoized top-down method for the rod-cutting problem.

---

[5]This approach presupposes that we know the set of all possible subproblem parameters and that we have established the relationship between table positions and subproblems. Another, more general, approach is to memoize by using hashing with the subproblem parameters as keys.

MEMOIZED-MATRIX-CHAIN(p)

```
1   n = p.length − 1
2   let m[1 .. n, 1 .. n] be a new table
3   for i = 1 to n
4       for j = i to n
5           m[i, j] = ∞
6   return LOOKUP-CHAIN(m, p, 1, n)
```

LOOKUP-CHAIN(m, p, i, j)

```
1   if m[i, j] < ∞
2       return m[i, j]
3   if i == j
4       m[i, j] = 0
5   else for k = i to j − 1
6           q = LOOKUP-CHAIN(m, p, i, k)
                + LOOKUP-CHAIN(m, p, k + 1, j) + p_{i−1} p_k p_j
7           if q < m[i, j]
8               m[i, j] = q
9   return m[i, j]
```

The MEMOIZED-MATRIX-CHAIN procedure, like MATRIX-CHAIN-ORDER, maintains a table $m[1 .. n, 1 .. n]$ of computed values of $m[i, j]$, the minimum number of scalar multiplications needed to compute the matrix $A_{i..j}$. Each table entry initially contains the value ∞ to indicate that the entry has yet to be filled in. Upon calling LOOKUP-CHAIN(m, p, i, j), if line 1 finds that $m[i, j] < \infty$, then the procedure simply returns the previously computed cost $m[i, j]$ in line 2. Otherwise, the cost is computed as in RECURSIVE-MATRIX-CHAIN, stored in $m[i, j]$, and returned. Thus, LOOKUP-CHAIN(m, p, i, j) always returns the value of $m[i, j]$, but it computes it only upon the first call of LOOKUP-CHAIN with these specific values of i and j.

Figure 15.7 illustrates how MEMOIZED-MATRIX-CHAIN saves time compared with RECURSIVE-MATRIX-CHAIN. Shaded subtrees represent values that it looks up rather than recomputes.

Like the bottom-up dynamic-programming algorithm MATRIX-CHAIN-ORDER, the procedure MEMOIZED-MATRIX-CHAIN runs in $O(n^3)$ time. Line 5 of MEMOIZED-MATRIX-CHAIN executes $\Theta(n^2)$ times. We can categorize the calls of LOOKUP-CHAIN into two types:

1. calls in which $m[i, j] = \infty$, so that lines 3–9 execute, and

2. calls in which $m[i, j] < \infty$, so that LOOKUP-CHAIN simply returns in line 2.

There are $\Theta(n^2)$ calls of the first type, one per table entry. All calls of the second type are made as recursive calls by calls of the first type. Whenever a given call of LOOKUP-CHAIN makes recursive calls, it makes $O(n)$ of them. Therefore, there are $O(n^3)$ calls of the second type in all. Each call of the second type takes $O(1)$ time, and each call of the first type takes $O(n)$ time plus the time spent in its recursive calls. The total time, therefore, is $O(n^3)$. Memoization thus turns an $\Omega(2^n)$-time algorithm into an $O(n^3)$-time algorithm.

In summary, we can solve the matrix-chain multiplication problem by either a top-down, memoized dynamic-programming algorithm or a bottom-up dynamic-programming algorithm in $O(n^3)$ time. Both methods take advantage of the overlapping-subproblems property. There are only $\Theta(n^2)$ distinct subproblems in total, and either of these methods computes the solution to each subproblem only once. Without memoization, the natural recursive algorithm runs in exponential time, since solved subproblems are repeatedly solved.

In general practice, if all subproblems must be solved at least once, a bottom-up dynamic-programming algorithm usually outperforms the corresponding top-down memoized algorithm by a constant factor, because the bottom-up algorithm has no overhead for recursion and less overhead for maintaining the table. Moreover, for some problems we can exploit the regular pattern of table accesses in the dynamic-programming algorithm to reduce time or space requirements even further. Alternatively, if some subproblems in the subproblem space need not be solved at all, the memoized solution has the advantage of solving only those subproblems that are definitely required.

Exercises

15.3-1
Which is a more efficient way to determine the optimal number of multiplications in a matrix-chain multiplication problem: enumerating all the ways of parenthesizing the product and computing the number of multiplications for each, or running RECURSIVE-MATRIX-CHAIN? Justify your answer.

15.3-2
Draw the recursion tree for the MERGE-SORT procedure from Section 2.3.1 on an array of 16 elements. Explain why memoization fails to speed up a good divide-and-conquer algorithm such as MERGE-SORT.

15.3-3
Consider a variant of the matrix-chain multiplication problem in which the goal is to parenthesize the sequence of matrices so as to maximize, rather than minimize,

the number of scalar multiplications. Does this problem exhibit optimal substructure?

15.3-4

As stated, in dynamic programming we first solve the subproblems and then choose which of them to use in an optimal solution to the problem. Professor Capulet claims that we do not always need to solve all the subproblems in order to find an optimal solution. She suggests that we can find an optimal solution to the matrix-chain multiplication problem by always choosing the matrix A_k at which to split the subproduct $A_i A_{i+1} \cdots A_j$ (by selecting k to minimize the quantity $p_{i-1} p_k p_j$) *before* solving the subproblems. Find an instance of the matrix-chain multiplication problem for which this greedy approach yields a suboptimal solution.

15.3-5

Suppose that in the rod-cutting problem of Section 15.1, we also had limit l_i on the number of pieces of length i that we are allowed to produce, for $i = 1, 2, \ldots, n$. Show that the optimal-substructure property described in Section 15.1 no longer holds.

15.3-6

Imagine that you wish to exchange one currency for another. You realize that instead of directly exchanging one currency for another, you might be better off making a series of trades through other currencies, winding up with the currency you want. Suppose that you can trade n different currencies, numbered $1, 2, \ldots, n$, where you start with currency 1 and wish to wind up with currency n. You are given, for each pair of currencies i and j, an exchange rate r_{ij}, meaning that if you start with d units of currency i, you can trade for dr_{ij} units of currency j. A sequence of trades may entail a commission, which depends on the number of trades you make. Let c_k be the commission that you are charged when you make k trades. Show that, if $c_k = 0$ for all $k = 1, 2, \ldots, n$, then the problem of finding the best sequence of exchanges from currency 1 to currency n exhibits optimal substructure. Then show that if commissions c_k are arbitrary values, then the problem of finding the best sequence of exchanges from currency 1 to currency n does not necessarily exhibit optimal substructure.

15.4   Longest common subsequence

Biological applications often need to compare the DNA of two (or more) different organisms. A strand of DNA consists of a string of molecules called

bases, where the possible bases are adenine, guanine, cytosine, and thymine. Representing each of these bases by its initial letter, we can express a strand of DNA as a string over the finite set $\{A, C, G, T\}$. (See Appendix C for the definition of a string.) For example, the DNA of one organism may be $S_1 = ACCGGTCGAGTGCGCGGAAGCCGGCCGAA$, and the DNA of another organism may be $S_2 = GTCGTTCGGAATGCCGTTGCTCTGTAAA$. One reason to compare two strands of DNA is to determine how "similar" the two strands are, as some measure of how closely related the two organisms are. We can, and do, define similarity in many different ways. For example, we can say that two DNA strands are similar if one is a substring of the other. (Chapter 32 explores algorithms to solve this problem.) In our example, neither S_1 nor S_2 is a substring of the other. Alternatively, we could say that two strands are similar if the number of changes needed to turn one into the other is small. (Problem 15-5 looks at this notion.) Yet another way to measure the similarity of strands S_1 and S_2 is by finding a third strand S_3 in which the bases in S_3 appear in each of S_1 and S_2; these bases must appear in the same order, but not necessarily consecutively. The longer the strand S_3 we can find, the more similar S_1 and S_2 are. In our example, the longest strand S_3 is $GTCGTCGGAAGCCGGCCGAA$.

We formalize this last notion of similarity as the longest-common-subsequence problem. A subsequence of a given sequence is just the given sequence with zero or more elements left out. Formally, given a sequence $X = \langle x_1, x_2, \ldots, x_m \rangle$, another sequence $Z = \langle z_1, z_2, \ldots, z_k \rangle$ is a ***subsequence*** of X if there exists a strictly increasing sequence $\langle i_1, i_2, \ldots, i_k \rangle$ of indices of X such that for all $j = 1, 2, \ldots, k$, we have $x_{i_j} = z_j$. For example, $Z = \langle B, C, D, B \rangle$ is a subsequence of $X = \langle A, B, C, B, D, A, B \rangle$ with corresponding index sequence $\langle 2, 3, 5, 7 \rangle$.

Given two sequences X and Y, we say that a sequence Z is a ***common subsequence*** of X and Y if Z is a subsequence of both X and Y. For example, if $X = \langle A, B, C, B, D, A, B \rangle$ and $Y = \langle B, D, C, A, B, A \rangle$, the sequence $\langle B, C, A \rangle$ is a common subsequence of both X and Y. The sequence $\langle B, C, A \rangle$ is not a *longest* common subsequence (LCS) of X and Y, however, since it has length 3 and the sequence $\langle B, C, B, A \rangle$, which is also common to both X and Y, has length 4. The sequence $\langle B, C, B, A \rangle$ is an LCS of X and Y, as is the sequence $\langle B, D, A, B \rangle$, since X and Y have no common subsequence of length 5 or greater.

In the ***longest-common-subsequence problem***, we are given two sequences $X = \langle x_1, x_2, \ldots, x_m \rangle$ and $Y = \langle y_1, y_2, \ldots, y_n \rangle$ and wish to find a maximum-length common subsequence of X and Y. This section shows how to efficiently solve the LCS problem using dynamic programming.

Step 1: Characterizing a longest common subsequence

In a brute-force approach to solving the LCS problem, we would enumerate all subsequences of X and check each subsequence to see whether it is also a subsequence of Y, keeping track of the longest subsequence we find. Each subsequence of X corresponds to a subset of the indices $\{1, 2, \ldots, m\}$ of X. Because X has 2^m subsequences, this approach requires exponential time, making it impractical for long sequences.

The LCS problem has an optimal-substructure property, however, as the following theorem shows. As we shall see, the natural classes of subproblems correspond to pairs of "prefixes" of the two input sequences. To be precise, given a sequence $X = \langle x_1, x_2, \ldots, x_m \rangle$, we define the ith **prefix** of X, for $i = 0, 1, \ldots, m$, as $X_i = \langle x_1, x_2, \ldots, x_i \rangle$. For example, if $X = \langle A, B, C, B, D, A, B \rangle$, then $X_4 = \langle A, B, C, B \rangle$ and X_0 is the empty sequence.

Theorem 15.1 (Optimal substructure of an LCS)
Let $X = \langle x_1, x_2, \ldots, x_m \rangle$ and $Y = \langle y_1, y_2, \ldots, y_n \rangle$ be sequences, and let $Z = \langle z_1, z_2, \ldots, z_k \rangle$ be any LCS of X and Y.

1. If $x_m = y_n$, then $z_k = x_m = y_n$ and Z_{k-1} is an LCS of X_{m-1} and Y_{n-1}.

2. If $x_m \neq y_n$, then $z_k \neq x_m$ implies that Z is an LCS of X_{m-1} and Y.

3. If $x_m \neq y_n$, then $z_k \neq y_n$ implies that Z is an LCS of X and Y_{n-1}.

Proof   (1) If $z_k \neq x_m$, then we could append $x_m = y_n$ to Z to obtain a common subsequence of X and Y of length $k + 1$, contradicting the supposition that Z is a *longest* common subsequence of X and Y. Thus, we must have $z_k = x_m = y_n$. Now, the prefix Z_{k-1} is a length-$(k - 1)$ common subsequence of X_{m-1} and Y_{n-1}. We wish to show that it is an LCS. Suppose for the purpose of contradiction that there exists a common subsequence W of X_{m-1} and Y_{n-1} with length greater than $k - 1$. Then, appending $x_m = y_n$ to W produces a common subsequence of X and Y whose length is greater than k, which is a contradiction.

(2) If $z_k \neq x_m$, then Z is a common subsequence of X_{m-1} and Y. If there were a common subsequence W of X_{m-1} and Y with length greater than k, then W would also be a common subsequence of X_m and Y, contradicting the assumption that Z is an LCS of X and Y.

(3) The proof is symmetric to (2).   ∎

The way that Theorem 15.1 characterizes longest common subsequences tells us that an LCS of two sequences contains within it an LCS of prefixes of the two sequences. Thus, the LCS problem has an optimal-substructure property. A recursive solution also has the overlapping-subproblems property, as we shall see in a moment.

Step 2: A recursive solution

Theorem 15.1 implies that we should examine either one or two subproblems when finding an LCS of $X = \langle x_1, x_2, \ldots, x_m \rangle$ and $Y = \langle y_1, y_2, \ldots, y_n \rangle$. If $x_m = y_n$, we must find an LCS of X_{m-1} and Y_{n-1}. Appending $x_m = y_n$ to this LCS yields an LCS of X and Y. If $x_m \neq y_n$, then we must solve two subproblems: finding an LCS of X_{m-1} and Y and finding an LCS of X and Y_{n-1}. Whichever of these two LCSs is longer is an LCS of X and Y. Because these cases exhaust all possibilities, we know that one of the optimal subproblem solutions must appear within an LCS of X and Y.

We can readily see the overlapping-subproblems property in the LCS problem. To find an LCS of X and Y, we may need to find the LCSs of X and Y_{n-1} and of X_{m-1} and Y. But each of these subproblems has the subsubproblem of finding an LCS of X_{m-1} and Y_{n-1}. Many other subproblems share subsubproblems.

As in the matrix-chain multiplication problem, our recursive solution to the LCS problem involves establishing a recurrence for the value of an optimal solution. Let us define $c[i, j]$ to be the length of an LCS of the sequences X_i and Y_j. If either $i = 0$ or $j = 0$, one of the sequences has length 0, and so the LCS has length 0. The optimal substructure of the LCS problem gives the recursive formula

$$c[i, j] = \begin{cases} 0 & \text{if } i = 0 \text{ or } j = 0, \\ c[i-1, j-1] + 1 & \text{if } i, j > 0 \text{ and } x_i = y_j, \\ \max(c[i, j-1], c[i-1, j]) & \text{if } i, j > 0 \text{ and } x_i \neq y_j. \end{cases} \tag{15.9}$$

Observe that in this recursive formulation, a condition in the problem restricts which subproblems we may consider. When $x_i = y_j$, we can and should consider the subproblem of finding an LCS of X_{i-1} and Y_{j-1}. Otherwise, we instead consider the two subproblems of finding an LCS of X_i and Y_{j-1} and of X_{i-1} and Y_j. In the previous dynamic-programming algorithms we have examined—for rod cutting and matrix-chain multiplication—we ruled out no subproblems due to conditions in the problem. Finding an LCS is not the only dynamic-programming algorithm that rules out subproblems based on conditions in the problem. For example, the edit-distance problem (see Problem 15-5) has this characteristic.

Step 3: Computing the length of an LCS

Based on equation (15.9), we could easily write an exponential-time recursive algorithm to compute the length of an LCS of two sequences. Since the LCS problem has only $\Theta(mn)$ distinct subproblems, however, we can use dynamic programming to compute the solutions bottom up.

Procedure LCS-LENGTH takes two sequences $X = \langle x_1, x_2, \ldots, x_m \rangle$ and $Y = \langle y_1, y_2, \ldots, y_n \rangle$ as inputs. It stores the $c[i, j]$ values in a table $c[0 \ldots m, 0 \ldots n]$, and it computes the entries in ***row-major*** order. (That is, the procedure fills in the first row of c from left to right, then the second row, and so on.) The procedure also maintains the table $b[1 \ldots m, 1 \ldots n]$ to help us construct an optimal solution. Intuitively, $b[i, j]$ points to the table entry corresponding to the optimal subproblem solution chosen when computing $c[i, j]$. The procedure returns the b and c tables; $c[m, n]$ contains the length of an LCS of X and Y.

LCS-LENGTH(X, Y)

```
 1   m = X.length
 2   n = Y.length
 3   let b[1..m, 1..n] and c[0..m, 0..n] be new tables
 4   for i = 1 to m
 5       c[i, 0] = 0
 6   for j = 0 to n
 7       c[0, j] = 0
 8   for i = 1 to m
 9       for j = 1 to n
10           if xᵢ == yⱼ
11               c[i, j] = c[i − 1, j − 1] + 1
12               b[i, j] = "↖"
13           elseif c[i − 1, j] ≥ c[i, j − 1]
14               c[i, j] = c[i − 1, j]
15               b[i, j] = "↑"
16           else c[i, j] = c[i, j − 1]
17               b[i, j] = "←"
18   return c and b
```

Figure 15.8 shows the tables produced by LCS-LENGTH on the sequences $X = \langle A, B, C, B, D, A, B \rangle$ and $Y = \langle B, D, C, A, B, A \rangle$. The running time of the procedure is $\Theta(mn)$, since each table entry takes $\Theta(1)$ time to compute.

Step 4: Constructing an LCS

The b table returned by LCS-LENGTH enables us to quickly construct an LCS of $X = \langle x_1, x_2, \ldots, x_m \rangle$ and $Y = \langle y_1, y_2, \ldots, y_n \rangle$. We simply begin at $b[m, n]$ and trace through the table by following the arrows. Whenever we encounter a "↖" in entry $b[i, j]$, it implies that $x_i = y_j$ is an element of the LCS that LCS-LENGTH

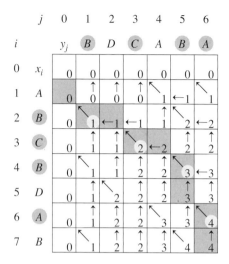

Figure 15.8 The c and b tables computed by LCS-LENGTH on the sequences $X = \langle A, B, C, B,$ $D, A, B \rangle$ and $Y = \langle B, D, C, A, B, A \rangle$. The square in row i and column j contains the value of $c[i, j]$ and the appropriate arrow for the value of $b[i, j]$. The entry 4 in $c[7, 6]$—the lower right-hand corner of the table—is the length of an LCS $\langle B, C, B, A \rangle$ of X and Y. For $i, j > 0$, entry $c[i, j]$ depends only on whether $x_i = y_j$ and the values in entries $c[i - 1, j]$, $c[i, j - 1]$, and $c[i - 1, j - 1]$, which are computed before $c[i, j]$. To reconstruct the elements of an LCS, follow the $b[i, j]$ arrows from the lower right-hand corner; the sequence is shaded. Each "↖" on the shaded sequence corresponds to an entry (highlighted) for which $x_i = y_j$ is a member of an LCS.

found. With this method, we encounter the elements of this LCS in reverse order. The following recursive procedure prints out an LCS of X and Y in the proper, forward order. The initial call is PRINT-LCS($b, X, X.length, Y.length$).

PRINT-LCS(b, X, i, j)

1   **if** $i == 0$ or $j == 0$
2   **return**
3   **if** $b[i, j] ==$ "↖"
4   PRINT-LCS($b, X, i - 1, j - 1$)
5   print x_i
6   **elseif** $b[i, j] ==$ "↑"
7   PRINT-LCS($b, X, i - 1, j$)
8   **else** PRINT-LCS($b, X, i, j - 1$)

For the b table in Figure 15.8, this procedure prints $BCBA$. The procedure takes time $O(m + n)$, since it decrements at least one of i and j in each recursive call.

Improving the code

Once you have developed an algorithm, you will often find that you can improve on the time or space it uses. Some changes can simplify the code and improve constant factors but otherwise yield no asymptotic improvement in performance. Others can yield substantial asymptotic savings in time and space.

In the LCS algorithm, for example, we can eliminate the b table altogether. Each $c[i, j]$ entry depends on only three other c table entries: $c[i-1, j-1]$, $c[i-1, j]$, and $c[i, j-1]$. Given the value of $c[i, j]$, we can determine in $O(1)$ time which of these three values was used to compute $c[i, j]$, without inspecting table b. Thus, we can reconstruct an LCS in $O(m+n)$ time using a procedure similar to PRINT-LCS. (Exercise 15.4-2 asks you to give the pseudocode.) Although we save $\Theta(mn)$ space by this method, the auxiliary space requirement for computing an LCS does not asymptotically decrease, since we need $\Theta(mn)$ space for the c table anyway.

We can, however, reduce the asymptotic space requirements for LCS-LENGTH, since it needs only two rows of table c at a time: the row being computed and the previous row. (In fact, as Exercise 15.4-4 asks you to show, we can use only slightly more than the space for one row of c to compute the length of an LCS.) This improvement works if we need only the length of an LCS; if we need to reconstruct the elements of an LCS, the smaller table does not keep enough information to retrace our steps in $O(m + n)$ time.

Exercises

15.4-1
Determine an LCS of $\langle 1, 0, 0, 1, 0, 1, 0, 1 \rangle$ and $\langle 0, 1, 0, 1, 1, 0, 1, 1, 0 \rangle$.

15.4-2
Give pseudocode to reconstruct an LCS from the completed c table and the original sequences $X = \langle x_1, x_2, \ldots, x_m \rangle$ and $Y = \langle y_1, y_2, \ldots, y_n \rangle$ in $O(m + n)$ time, without using the b table.

15.4-3
Give a memoized version of LCS-LENGTH that runs in $O(mn)$ time.

15.4-4
Show how to compute the length of an LCS using only $2 \cdot \min(m, n)$ entries in the c table plus $O(1)$ additional space. Then show how to do the same thing, but using $\min(m, n)$ entries plus $O(1)$ additional space.

15.4-5
Give an $O(n^2)$-time algorithm to find the longest monotonically increasing subsequence of a sequence of n numbers.

15.4-6   ★
Give an $O(n \lg n)$-time algorithm to find the longest monotonically increasing subsequence of a sequence of n numbers. (*Hint:* Observe that the last element of a candidate subsequence of length i is at least as large as the last element of a candidate subsequence of length $i - 1$. Maintain candidate subsequences by linking them through the input sequence.)

15.5   Optimal binary search trees

Suppose that we are designing a program to translate text from English to French. For each occurrence of each English word in the text, we need to look up its French equivalent. We could perform these lookup operations by building a binary search tree with n English words as keys and their French equivalents as satellite data. Because we will search the tree for each individual word in the text, we want the total time spent searching to be as low as possible. We could ensure an $O(\lg n)$ search time per occurrence by using a red-black tree or any other balanced binary search tree. Words appear with different frequencies, however, and a frequently used word such as *the* may appear far from the root while a rarely used word such as *machicolation* appears near the root. Such an organization would slow down the translation, since the number of nodes visited when searching for a key in a binary search tree equals one plus the depth of the node containing the key. We want words that occur frequently in the text to be placed nearer the root.[6] Moreover, some words in the text might have no French translation,[7] and such words would not appear in the binary search tree at all. How do we organize a binary search tree so as to minimize the number of nodes visited in all searches, given that we know how often each word occurs?

What we need is known as an ***optimal binary search tree***. Formally, we are given a sequence $K = \langle k_1, k_2, \ldots, k_n \rangle$ of n distinct keys in sorted order (so that $k_1 < k_2 < \cdots < k_n$), and we wish to build a binary search tree from these keys. For each key k_i, we have a probability p_i that a search will be for k_i. Some searches may be for values not in K, and so we also have $n + 1$ "dummy keys"

---

[6]If the subject of the text is castle architecture, we might want *machicolation* to appear near the root.

[7]Yes, *machicolation* has a French counterpart: *mâchicoulis*.

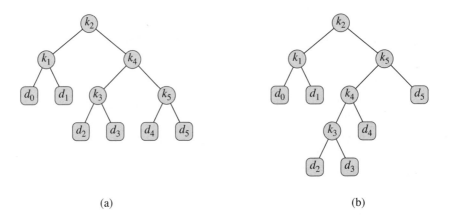

(a)   (b)

Figure 15.9   Two binary search trees for a set of $n = 5$ keys with the following probabilities:

i	0	1	2	3	4	5
p_i		0.15	0.10	0.05	0.10	0.20
q_i	0.05	0.10	0.05	0.05	0.05	0.10

(a) A binary search tree with expected search cost 2.80. **(b)** A binary search tree with expected search cost 2.75. This tree is optimal.

$d_0, d_1, d_2, \ldots, d_n$ representing values not in K. In particular, d_0 represents all values less than k_1, d_n represents all values greater than k_n, and for $i = 1, 2, \ldots, n-1$, the dummy key d_i represents all values between k_i and k_{i+1}. For each dummy key d_i, we have a probability q_i that a search will correspond to d_i. Figure 15.9 shows two binary search trees for a set of $n = 5$ keys. Each key k_i is an internal node, and each dummy key d_i is a leaf. Every search is either successful (finding some key k_i) or unsuccessful (finding some dummy key d_i), and so we have

$$\sum_{i=1}^{n} p_i + \sum_{i=0}^{n} q_i = 1 . \tag{15.10}$$

Because we have probabilities of searches for each key and each dummy key, we can determine the expected cost of a search in a given binary search tree T. Let us assume that the actual cost of a search equals the number of nodes examined, i.e., the depth of the node found by the search in T, plus 1. Then the expected cost of a search in T is

$$\mathrm{E}\,[\text{search cost in } T] = \sum_{i=1}^{n}(\mathrm{depth}_T(k_i) + 1) \cdot p_i + \sum_{i=0}^{n}(\mathrm{depth}_T(d_i) + 1) \cdot q_i$$

$$= 1 + \sum_{i=1}^{n}\mathrm{depth}_T(k_i) \cdot p_i + \sum_{i=0}^{n}\mathrm{depth}_T(d_i) \cdot q_i , \tag{15.11}$$

where depth_T denotes a node's depth in the tree T. The last equality follows from equation (15.10). In Figure 15.9(a), we can calculate the expected search cost node by node:

node	depth	probability	contribution
k_1	1	0.15	0.30
k_2	0	0.10	0.10
k_3	2	0.05	0.15
k_4	1	0.10	0.20
k_5	2	0.20	0.60
d_0	2	0.05	0.15
d_1	2	0.10	0.30
d_2	3	0.05	0.20
d_3	3	0.05	0.20
d_4	3	0.05	0.20
d_5	3	0.10	0.40
Total			2.80

For a given set of probabilities, we wish to construct a binary search tree whose expected search cost is smallest. We call such a tree an ***optimal binary search tree***. Figure 15.9(b) shows an optimal binary search tree for the probabilities given in the figure caption; its expected cost is 2.75. This example shows that an optimal binary search tree is not necessarily a tree whose overall height is smallest. Nor can we necessarily construct an optimal binary search tree by always putting the key with the greatest probability at the root. Here, key k_5 has the greatest search probability of any key, yet the root of the optimal binary search tree shown is k_2. (The lowest expected cost of any binary search tree with k_5 at the root is 2.85.)

As with matrix-chain multiplication, exhaustive checking of all possibilities fails to yield an efficient algorithm. We can label the nodes of any n-node binary tree with the keys $k_1, k_2, \ldots, k_n$ to construct a binary search tree, and then add in the dummy keys as leaves. In Problem 12-4, we saw that the number of binary trees with n nodes is $\Omega(4^n/n^{3/2})$, and so we would have to examine an exponential number of binary search trees in an exhaustive search. Not surprisingly, we shall solve this problem with dynamic programming.

Step 1: The structure of an optimal binary search tree

To characterize the optimal substructure of optimal binary search trees, we start with an observation about subtrees. Consider any subtree of a binary search tree. It must contain keys in a contiguous range $k_i, \ldots, k_j$, for some $1 \leq i \leq j \leq n$. In addition, a subtree that contains keys $k_i, \ldots, k_j$ must also have as its leaves the dummy keys $d_{i-1}, \ldots, d_j$.

Now we can state the optimal substructure: if an optimal binary search tree T has a subtree T' containing keys $k_i, \ldots, k_j$, then this subtree T' must be optimal as well for the subproblem with keys $k_i, \ldots, k_j$ and dummy keys $d_{i-1}, \ldots, d_j$. The usual cut-and-paste argument applies. If there were a subtree T'' whose expected cost is lower than that of T', then we could cut T' out of T and paste in T'', resulting in a binary search tree of lower expected cost than T, thus contradicting the optimality of T.

We need to use the optimal substructure to show that we can construct an optimal solution to the problem from optimal solutions to subproblems. Given keys $k_i, \ldots, k_j$, one of these keys, say k_r ($i \leq r \leq j$), is the root of an optimal subtree containing these keys. The left subtree of the root k_r contains the keys $k_i, \ldots, k_{r-1}$ (and dummy keys $d_{i-1}, \ldots, d_{r-1}$), and the right subtree contains the keys $k_{r+1}, \ldots, k_j$ (and dummy keys $d_r, \ldots, d_j$). As long as we examine all candidate roots k_r, where $i \leq r \leq j$, and we determine all optimal binary search trees containing $k_i, \ldots, k_{r-1}$ and those containing $k_{r+1}, \ldots, k_j$, we are guaranteed that we will find an optimal binary search tree.

There is one detail worth noting about "empty" subtrees. Suppose that in a subtree with keys $k_i, \ldots, k_j$, we select k_i as the root. By the above argument, k_i's left subtree contains the keys $k_i, \ldots, k_{i-1}$. We interpret this sequence as containing no keys. Bear in mind, however, that subtrees also contain dummy keys. We adopt the convention that a subtree containing keys $k_i, \ldots, k_{i-1}$ has no actual keys but does contain the single dummy key d_{i-1}. Symmetrically, if we select k_j as the root, then k_j's right subtree contains the keys $k_{j+1}, \ldots, k_j$; this right subtree contains no actual keys, but it does contain the dummy key d_j.

Step 2: A recursive solution

We are ready to define the value of an optimal solution recursively. We pick our subproblem domain as finding an optimal binary search tree containing the keys $k_i, \ldots, k_j$, where $i \geq 1$, $j \leq n$, and $j \geq i - 1$. (When $j = i - 1$, there are no actual keys; we have just the dummy key d_{i-1}.) Let us define $e[i, j]$ as the expected cost of searching an optimal binary search tree containing the keys $k_i, \ldots, k_j$. Ultimately, we wish to compute $e[1, n]$.

The easy case occurs when $j = i - 1$. Then we have just the dummy key d_{i-1}. The expected search cost is $e[i, i - 1] = q_{i-1}$.

When $j \geq i$, we need to select a root k_r from among $k_i, \ldots, k_j$ and then make an optimal binary search tree with keys $k_i, \ldots, k_{r-1}$ as its left subtree and an optimal binary search tree with keys $k_{r+1}, \ldots, k_j$ as its right subtree. What happens to the expected search cost of a subtree when it becomes a subtree of a node? The depth of each node in the subtree increases by 1. By equation (15.11), the expected search cost of this subtree increases by the sum of all the probabilities in the subtree. For a subtree with keys $k_i, \ldots, k_j$, let us denote this sum of probabilities as

$$w(i, j) = \sum_{l=i}^{j} p_l + \sum_{l=i-1}^{j} q_l \, . \tag{15.12}$$

Thus, if k_r is the root of an optimal subtree containing keys $k_i, \ldots, k_j$, we have

$$e[i, j] = p_r + (e[i, r-1] + w(i, r-1)) + (e[r+1, j] + w(r+1, j)) \, .$$

Noting that

$$w(i, j) = w(i, r-1) + p_r + w(r+1, j) \, ,$$

we rewrite $e[i, j]$ as

$$e[i, j] = e[i, r-1] + e[r+1, j] + w(i, j) \, . \tag{15.13}$$

The recursive equation (15.13) assumes that we know which node k_r to use as the root. We choose the root that gives the lowest expected search cost, giving us our final recursive formulation:

$$e[i, j] = \begin{cases} q_{i-1} & \text{if } j = i - 1 \, , \\ \min_{i \le r \le j} \{e[i, r-1] + e[r+1, j] + w(i, j)\} & \text{if } i \le j \, . \end{cases} \tag{15.14}$$

The $e[i, j]$ values give the expected search costs in optimal binary search trees. To help us keep track of the structure of optimal binary search trees, we define *root*$[i, j]$, for $1 \le i \le j \le n$, to be the index r for which k_r is the root of an optimal binary search tree containing keys $k_i, \ldots, k_j$. Although we will see how to compute the values of *root*$[i, j]$, we leave the construction of an optimal binary search tree from these values as Exercise 15.5-1.

Step 3: Computing the expected search cost of an optimal binary search tree

At this point, you may have noticed some similarities between our characterizations of optimal binary search trees and matrix-chain multiplication. For both problem domains, our subproblems consist of contiguous index subranges. A direct, recursive implementation of equation (15.14) would be as inefficient as a direct, recursive matrix-chain multiplication algorithm. Instead, we store the $e[i, j]$ values in a table $e[1 \mathinner{.\,.} n+1, 0 \mathinner{.\,.} n]$. The first index needs to run to $n + 1$ rather than n because in order to have a subtree containing only the dummy key d_n, we need to compute and store $e[n + 1, n]$. The second index needs to start from 0 because in order to have a subtree containing only the dummy key d_0, we need to compute and store $e[1, 0]$. We use only the entries $e[i, j]$ for which $j \ge i - 1$. We also use a table *root*$[i, j]$, for recording the root of the subtree containing keys $k_i, \ldots, k_j$. This table uses only the entries for which $1 \le i \le j \le n$.

We will need one other table for efficiency. Rather than compute the value of $w(i, j)$ from scratch every time we are computing $e[i, j]$—which would take

$\Theta(j - i)$ additions—we store these values in a table $w[1 . . n + 1, 0 . . n]$. For the base case, we compute $w[i, i - 1] = q_{i-1}$ for $1 \le i \le n + 1$. For $j \ge i$, we compute

$$w[i, j] = w[i, j - 1] + p_j + q_j . \tag{15.15}$$

Thus, we can compute the $\Theta(n^2)$ values of $w[i, j]$ in $\Theta(1)$ time each.

The pseudocode that follows takes as inputs the probabilities $p_1, \ldots, p_n$ and $q_0, \ldots, q_n$ and the size n, and it returns the tables e and *root*.

OPTIMAL-BST(p, q, n)

```
 1   let e[1 . . n + 1, 0 . . n], w[1 . . n + 1, 0 . . n],
           and root[1 . . n, 1 . . n] be new tables
 2   for i = 1 to n + 1
 3       e[i, i − 1] = q_{i−1}
 4       w[i, i − 1] = q_{i−1}
 5   for l = 1 to n
 6       for i = 1 to n − l + 1
 7           j = i + l − 1
 8           e[i, j] = ∞
 9           w[i, j] = w[i, j − 1] + p_j + q_j
10           for r = i to j
11               t = e[i, r − 1] + e[r + 1, j] + w[i, j]
12               if t < e[i, j]
13                   e[i, j] = t
14                   root[i, j] = r
15   return e and root
```

From the description above and the similarity to the MATRIX-CHAIN-ORDER procedure in Section 15.2, you should find the operation of this procedure to be fairly straightforward. The **for** loop of lines 2–4 initializes the values of $e[i, i - 1]$ and $w[i, i - 1]$. The **for** loop of lines 5–14 then uses the recurrences (15.14) and (15.15) to compute $e[i, j]$ and $w[i, j]$ for all $1 \le i \le j \le n$. In the first iteration, when $l = 1$, the loop computes $e[i, i]$ and $w[i, i]$ for $i = 1, 2, \ldots, n$. The second iteration, with $l = 2$, computes $e[i, i+1]$ and $w[i, i+1]$ for $i = 1, 2, \ldots, n-1$, and so forth. The innermost **for** loop, in lines 10–14, tries each candidate index r to determine which key k_r to use as the root of an optimal binary search tree containing keys $k_i, \ldots, k_j$. This **for** loop saves the current value of the index r in $root[i, j]$ whenever it finds a better key to use as the root.

Figure 15.10 shows the tables $e[i, j]$, $w[i, j]$, and $root[i, j]$ computed by the procedure OPTIMAL-BST on the key distribution shown in Figure 15.9. As in the matrix-chain multiplication example of Figure 15.5, the tables are rotated to make

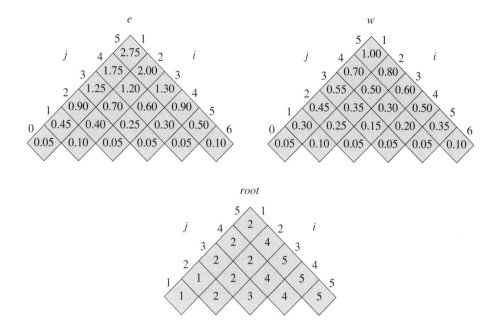

Figure 15.10 The tables $e[i, j]$, $w[i, j]$, and $root[i, j]$ computed by OPTIMAL-BST on the key distribution shown in Figure 15.9. The tables are rotated so that the diagonals run horizontally.

the diagonals run horizontally. OPTIMAL-BST computes the rows from bottom to top and from left to right within each row.

The OPTIMAL-BST procedure takes $\Theta(n^3)$ time, just like MATRIX-CHAIN-ORDER. We can easily see that its running time is $O(n^3)$, since its **for** loops are nested three deep and each loop index takes on at most n values. The loop indices in OPTIMAL-BST do not have exactly the same bounds as those in MATRIX-CHAIN-ORDER, but they are within at most 1 in all directions. Thus, like MATRIX-CHAIN-ORDER, the OPTIMAL-BST procedure takes $\Omega(n^3)$ time.

Exercises

15.5-1
Write pseudocode for the procedure CONSTRUCT-OPTIMAL-BST(*root*) which, given the table *root*, outputs the structure of an optimal binary search tree. For the example in Figure 15.10, your procedure should print out the structure

k_2 is the root
k_1 is the left child of k_2
d_0 is the left child of k_1
d_1 is the right child of k_1
k_5 is the right child of k_2
k_4 is the left child of k_5
k_3 is the left child of k_4
d_2 is the left child of k_3
d_3 is the right child of k_3
d_4 is the right child of k_4
d_5 is the right child of k_5

corresponding to the optimal binary search tree shown in Figure 15.9(b).

15.5-2
Determine the cost and structure of an optimal binary search tree for a set of $n = 7$ keys with the following probabilities:

i	0	1	2	3	4	5	6	7
p_i		0.04	0.06	0.08	0.02	0.10	0.12	0.14
q_i	0.06	0.06	0.06	0.06	0.05	0.05	0.05	0.05

15.5-3
Suppose that instead of maintaining the table $w[i, j]$, we computed the value of $w(i, j)$ directly from equation (15.12) in line 9 of OPTIMAL-BST and used this computed value in line 11. How would this change affect the asymptotic running time of OPTIMAL-BST?

15.5-4 ★
Knuth [212] has shown that there are always roots of optimal subtrees such that $root[i, j - 1] \leq root[i, j] \leq root[i + 1, j]$ for all $1 \leq i < j \leq n$. Use this fact to modify the OPTIMAL-BST procedure to run in $\Theta(n^2)$ time.

Problems

15-1   *Longest simple path in a directed acyclic graph*
Suppose that we are given a directed acyclic graph $G = (V, E)$ with real-valued edge weights and two distinguished vertices s and t. Describe a dynamic-programming approach for finding a longest weighted simple path from s to t. What does the subproblem graph look like? What is the efficiency of your algorithm?

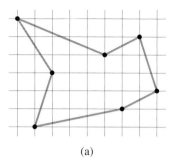 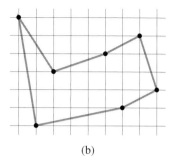

(a)   (b)

Figure 15.11 Seven points in the plane, shown on a unit grid. **(a)** The shortest closed tour, with length approximately 24.89. This tour is not bitonic. **(b)** The shortest bitonic tour for the same set of points. Its length is approximately 25.58.

15-2   Longest palindrome subsequence

A *palindrome* is a nonempty string over some alphabet that reads the same forward and backward. Examples of palindromes are all strings of length 1, `civic`, `racecar`, and `aibohphobia` (fear of palindromes).

Give an efficient algorithm to find the longest palindrome that is a subsequence of a given input string. For example, given the input `character`, your algorithm should return `carac`. What is the running time of your algorithm?

15-3   Bitonic euclidean traveling-salesman problem

In the *euclidean traveling-salesman problem*, we are given a set of n points in the plane, and we wish to find the shortest closed tour that connects all n points. Figure 15.11(a) shows the solution to a 7-point problem. The general problem is NP-hard, and its solution is therefore believed to require more than polynomial time (see Chapter 34).

J. L. Bentley has suggested that we simplify the problem by restricting our attention to *bitonic tours*, that is, tours that start at the leftmost point, go strictly rightward to the rightmost point, and then go strictly leftward back to the starting point. Figure 15.11(b) shows the shortest bitonic tour of the same 7 points. In this case, a polynomial-time algorithm is possible.

Describe an $O(n^2)$-time algorithm for determining an optimal bitonic tour. You may assume that no two points have the same x-coordinate and that all operations on real numbers take unit time. (*Hint:* Scan left to right, maintaining optimal possibilities for the two parts of the tour.)

15-4   Printing neatly

Consider the problem of neatly printing a paragraph with a monospaced font (all characters having the same width) on a printer. The input text is a sequence of n

words of lengths $l_1, l_2, \ldots, l_n$, measured in characters. We want to print this paragraph neatly on a number of lines that hold a maximum of M characters each. Our criterion of "neatness" is as follows. If a given line contains words i through j, where $i \leq j$, and we leave exactly one space between words, the number of extra space characters at the end of the line is $M - j + i - \sum_{k=i}^{j} l_k$, which must be nonnegative so that the words fit on the line. We wish to minimize the sum, over all lines except the last, of the cubes of the numbers of extra space characters at the ends of lines. Give a dynamic-programming algorithm to print a paragraph of n words neatly on a printer. Analyze the running time and space requirements of your algorithm.

15-5   *Edit distance*

In order to transform one source string of text $x[1 \mathinner{.\,.} m]$ to a target string $y[1 \mathinner{.\,.} n]$, we can perform various transformation operations. Our goal is, given x and y, to produce a series of transformations that change x to y. We use an array z—assumed to be large enough to hold all the characters it will need—to hold the intermediate results. Initially, z is empty, and at termination, we should have $z[j] = y[j]$ for $j = 1, 2, \ldots, n$. We maintain current indices i into x and j into z, and the operations are allowed to alter z and these indices. Initially, $i = j = 1$. We are required to examine every character in x during the transformation, which means that at the end of the sequence of transformation operations, we must have $i = m + 1$.

We may choose from among six transformation operations:

Copy a character from x to z by setting $z[j] = x[i]$ and then incrementing both i and j. This operation examines $x[i]$.

Replace a character from x by another character c, by setting $z[j] = c$, and then incrementing both i and j. This operation examines $x[i]$.

Delete a character from x by incrementing i but leaving j alone. This operation examines $x[i]$.

Insert the character c into z by setting $z[j] = c$ and then incrementing j, but leaving i alone. This operation examines no characters of x.

Twiddle (i.e., exchange) the next two characters by copying them from x to z but in the opposite order; we do so by setting $z[j] = x[i + 1]$ and $z[j + 1] = x[i]$ and then setting $i = i + 2$ and $j = j + 2$. This operation examines $x[i]$ and $x[i + 1]$.

Kill the remainder of x by setting $i = m + 1$. This operation examines all characters in x that have not yet been examined. This operation, if performed, must be the final operation.

As an example, one way to transform the source string `algorithm` to the target string `altruistic` is to use the following sequence of operations, where the underlined characters are $x[i]$ and $z[j]$ after the operation:

Operation	x	z
initial strings	algorithm	_
copy	algorithm	a_
copy	algorithm	al_
replace by t	algorithm	alt_
delete	algorithm	alt_
copy	algorithm	altr_
insert u	algorithm	altru_
insert i	algorithm	altrui_
insert s	algorithm	altruis_
twiddle	algorithm	altruisti_
insert c	algorithm	altruistic_
kill	algorithm_	altruistic_

Note that there are several other sequences of transformation operations that transform `algorithm` to `altruistic`.

Each of the transformation operations has an associated cost. The cost of an operation depends on the specific application, but we assume that each operation's cost is a constant that is known to us. We also assume that the individual costs of the copy and replace operations are less than the combined costs of the delete and insert operations; otherwise, the copy and replace operations would not be used. The cost of a given sequence of transformation operations is the sum of the costs of the individual operations in the sequence. For the sequence above, the cost of transforming `algorithm` to `altruistic` is

$$(3 \cdot \text{cost(copy)}) + \text{cost(replace)} + \text{cost(delete)} + (4 \cdot \text{cost(insert)})$$
$$+ \text{cost(twiddle)} + \text{cost(kill)} .$$

a. Given two sequences $x[1 .. m]$ and $y[1 .. n]$ and set of transformation-operation costs, the ***edit distance*** from x to y is the cost of the least expensive operation sequence that transforms x to y. Describe a dynamic-programming algorithm that finds the edit distance from $x[1 .. m]$ to $y[1 .. n]$ and prints an optimal operation sequence. Analyze the running time and space requirements of your algorithm.

The edit-distance problem generalizes the problem of aligning two DNA sequences (see, for example, Setubal and Meidanis [310, Section 3.2]). There are several methods for measuring the similarity of two DNA sequences by aligning them. One such method to align two sequences x and y consists of inserting spaces at arbitrary locations in the two sequences (including at either end) so that the resulting sequences x' and y' have the same length but do not have a space in the same position (i.e., for no position j are both $x'[j]$ and $y'[j]$ a space). Then we assign a "score" to each position. Position j receives a score as follows:

- +1 if $x'[j] = y'[j]$ and neither is a space,
- −1 if $x'[j] \neq y'[j]$ and neither is a space,
- −2 if either $x'[j]$ or $y'[j]$ is a space.

The score for the alignment is the sum of the scores of the individual positions. For example, given the sequences $x = $ GATCGGCAT and $y = $ CAATGTGAATC, one alignment is

```
G ATCG GCAT
CAAT GTGAATC
-*++*+*+-++*
```

A + under a position indicates a score of +1 for that position, a − indicates a score of −1, and a ∗ indicates a score of −2, so that this alignment has a total score of $6 \cdot 1 - 2 \cdot 1 - 4 \cdot 2 = -4$.

b. Explain how to cast the problem of finding an optimal alignment as an edit distance problem using a subset of the transformation operations copy, replace, delete, insert, twiddle, and kill.

15-6 *Planning a company party*

Professor Stewart is consulting for the president of a corporation that is planning a company party. The company has a hierarchical structure; that is, the supervisor relation forms a tree rooted at the president. The personnel office has ranked each employee with a conviviality rating, which is a real number. In order to make the party fun for all attendees, the president does not want both an employee and his or her immediate supervisor to attend.

Professor Stewart is given the tree that describes the structure of the corporation, using the left-child, right-sibling representation described in Section 10.4. Each node of the tree holds, in addition to the pointers, the name of an employee and that employee's conviviality ranking. Describe an algorithm to make up a guest list that maximizes the sum of the conviviality ratings of the guests. Analyze the running time of your algorithm.

15-7 *Viterbi algorithm*

We can use dynamic programming on a directed graph $G = (V, E)$ for speech recognition. Each edge $(u, v) \in E$ is labeled with a sound $\sigma(u, v)$ from a finite set Σ of sounds. The labeled graph is a formal model of a person speaking a restricted language. Each path in the graph starting from a distinguished vertex $v_0 \in V$ corresponds to a possible sequence of sounds produced by the model. We define the label of a directed path to be the concatenation of the labels of the edges on that path.

a. Describe an efficient algorithm that, given an edge-labeled graph G with distinguished vertex v_0 and a sequence $s = \langle \sigma_1, \sigma_2, \ldots, \sigma_k \rangle$ of sounds from Σ, returns a path in G that begins at v_0 and has s as its label, if any such path exists. Otherwise, the algorithm should return NO-SUCH-PATH. Analyze the running time of your algorithm. (*Hint:* You may find concepts from Chapter 22 useful.)

Now, suppose that every edge $(u, v) \in E$ has an associated nonnegative probability $p(u, v)$ of traversing the edge (u, v) from vertex u and thus producing the corresponding sound. The sum of the probabilities of the edges leaving any vertex equals 1. The probability of a path is defined to be the product of the probabilities of its edges. We can view the probability of a path beginning at v_0 as the probability that a "random walk" beginning at v_0 will follow the specified path, where we randomly choose which edge to take leaving a vertex u according to the probabilities of the available edges leaving u.

b. Extend your answer to part (a) so that if a path is returned, it is a *most probable path* starting at v_0 and having label s. Analyze the running time of your algorithm.

15-8 *Image compression by seam carving*

We are given a color picture consisting of an $m \times n$ array $A[1 \mathinner{.\,.} m, 1 \mathinner{.\,.} n]$ of pixels, where each pixel specifies a triple of red, green, and blue (RGB) intensities. Suppose that we wish to compress this picture slightly. Specifically, we wish to remove one pixel from each of the m rows, so that the whole picture becomes one pixel narrower. To avoid disturbing visual effects, however, we require that the pixels removed in two adjacent rows be in the same or adjacent columns; the pixels removed form a "seam" from the top row to the bottom row where successive pixels in the seam are adjacent vertically or diagonally.

a. Show that the number of such possible seams grows at least exponentially in m, assuming that $n > 1$.

b. Suppose now that along with each pixel $A[i, j]$, we have calculated a real-valued disruption measure $d[i, j]$, indicating how disruptive it would be to remove pixel $A[i, j]$. Intuitively, the lower a pixel's disruption measure, the more similar the pixel is to its neighbors. Suppose further that we define the disruption measure of a seam to be the sum of the disruption measures of its pixels.

Give an algorithm to find a seam with the lowest disruption measure. How efficient is your algorithm?

15-9   *Breaking a string*

A certain string-processing language allows a programmer to break a string into two pieces. Because this operation copies the string, it costs n time units to break a string of n characters into two pieces. Suppose a programmer wants to break a string into many pieces. The order in which the breaks occur can affect the total amount of time used. For example, suppose that the programmer wants to break a 20-character string after characters 2, 8, and 10 (numbering the characters in ascending order from the left-hand end, starting from 1). If she programs the breaks to occur in left-to-right order, then the first break costs 20 time units, the second break costs 18 time units (breaking the string from characters 3 to 20 at character 8), and the third break costs 12 time units, totaling 50 time units. If she programs the breaks to occur in right-to-left order, however, then the first break costs 20 time units, the second break costs 10 time units, and the third break costs 8 time units, totaling 38 time units. In yet another order, she could break first at 8 (costing 20), then break the left piece at 2 (costing 8), and finally the right piece at 10 (costing 12), for a total cost of 40.

Design an algorithm that, given the numbers of characters after which to break, determines a least-cost way to sequence those breaks. More formally, given a string S with n characters and an array $L[1 . . m]$ containing the break points, compute the lowest cost for a sequence of breaks, along with a sequence of breaks that achieves this cost.

15-10   *Planning an investment strategy*

Your knowledge of algorithms helps you obtain an exciting job with the Acme Computer Company, along with a \$10,000 signing bonus. You decide to invest this money with the goal of maximizing your return at the end of 10 years. You decide to use the Amalgamated Investment Company to manage your investments. Amalgamated Investments requires you to observe the following rules. It offers n different investments, numbered 1 through n. In each year j, investment i provides a return rate of r_{ij}. In other words, if you invest d dollars in investment i in year j, then at the end of year j, you have dr_{ij} dollars. The return rates are guaranteed, that is, you are given all the return rates for the next 10 years for each investment. You make investment decisions only once per year. At the end of each year, you can leave the money made in the previous year in the same investments, or you can shift money to other investments, by either shifting money between existing investments or moving money to a new investment. If you do not move your money between two consecutive years, you pay a fee of f_1 dollars, whereas if you switch your money, you pay a fee of f_2 dollars, where $f_2 > f_1$.

a. The problem, as stated, allows you to invest your money in multiple investments in each year. Prove that there exists an optimal investment strategy that, in each year, puts all the money into a single investment. (Recall that an optimal investment strategy maximizes the amount of money after 10 years and is not concerned with any other objectives, such as minimizing risk.)

b. Prove that the problem of planning your optimal investment strategy exhibits optimal substructure.

c. Design an algorithm that plans your optimal investment strategy. What is the running time of your algorithm?

d. Suppose that Amalgamated Investments imposed the additional restriction that, at any point, you can have no more than \$15,000 in any one investment. Show that the problem of maximizing your income at the end of 10 years no longer exhibits optimal substructure.

15-11   *Inventory planning*

The Rinky Dink Company makes machines that resurface ice rinks. The demand for such products varies from month to month, and so the company needs to develop a strategy to plan its manufacturing given the fluctuating, but predictable, demand. The company wishes to design a plan for the next n months. For each month i, the company knows the demand d_i, that is, the number of machines that it will sell. Let $D = \sum_{i=1}^{n} d_i$ be the total demand over the next n months. The company keeps a full-time staff who provide labor to manufacture up to m machines per month. If the company needs to make more than m machines in a given month, it can hire additional, part-time labor, at a cost that works out to c dollars per machine. Furthermore, if, at the end of a month, the company is holding any unsold machines, it must pay inventory costs. The cost for holding j machines is given as a function $h(j)$ for $j = 1, 2, \ldots, D$, where $h(j) \geq 0$ for $1 \leq j \leq D$ and $h(j) \leq h(j + 1)$ for $1 \leq j \leq D - 1$.

Give an algorithm that calculates a plan for the company that minimizes its costs while fulfilling all the demand. The running time should be polynomial in n and D.

15-12   *Signing free-agent baseball players*

Suppose that you are the general manager for a major-league baseball team. During the off-season, you need to sign some free-agent players for your team. The team owner has given you a budget of \$X$ to spend on free agents. You are allowed to spend less than \$X$ altogether, but the owner will fire you if you spend any more than \$X$.

You are considering N different positions, and for each position, P free-agent players who play that position are available.[8] Because you do not want to overload your roster with too many players at any position, for each position you may sign at most one free agent who plays that position. (If you do not sign any players at a particular position, then you plan to stick with the players you already have at that position.)

To determine how valuable a player is going to be, you decide to use a sabermetric statistic[9] known as "VORP," or "value over replacement player." A player with a higher VORP is more valuable than a player with a lower VORP. A player with a higher VORP is not necessarily more expensive to sign than a player with a lower VORP, because factors other than a player's value determine how much it costs to sign him.

For each available free-agent player, you have three pieces of information:

- the player's position,

- the amount of money it will cost to sign the player, and

- the player's VORP.

Devise an algorithm that maximizes the total VORP of the players you sign while spending no more than $\$X$ altogether. You may assume that each player signs for a multiple of $\$100,000$. Your algorithm should output the total VORP of the players you sign, the total amount of money you spend, and a list of which players you sign. Analyze the running time and space requirement of your algorithm.

Chapter notes

R. Bellman began the systematic study of dynamic programming in 1955. The word "programming," both here and in linear programming, refers to using a tabular solution method. Although optimization techniques incorporating elements of dynamic programming were known earlier, Bellman provided the area with a solid mathematical basis [37].

---

[8] Although there are nine positions on a baseball team, N is not necessarily equal to 9 because some general managers have particular ways of thinking about positions. For example, a general manager might consider right-handed pitchers and left-handed pitchers to be separate "positions," as well as starting pitchers, long relief pitchers (relief pitchers who can pitch several innings), and short relief pitchers (relief pitchers who normally pitch at most only one inning).

[9] *Sabermetrics* is the application of statistical analysis to baseball records. It provides several ways to compare the relative values of individual players.

Galil and Park [125] classify dynamic-programming algorithms according to the size of the table and the number of other table entries each entry depends on. They call a dynamic-programming algorithm tD/eD if its table size is $O(n^t)$ and each entry depends on $O(n^e)$ other entries. For example, the matrix-chain multiplication algorithm in Section 15.2 would be $2D/1D$, and the longest-common-subsequence algorithm in Section 15.4 would be $2D/0D$.

Hu and Shing [182, 183] give an $O(n \lg n)$-time algorithm for the matrix-chain multiplication problem.

The $O(mn)$-time algorithm for the longest-common-subsequence problem appears to be a folk algorithm. Knuth [70] posed the question of whether subquadratic algorithms for the LCS problem exist. Masek and Paterson [244] answered this question in the affirmative by giving an algorithm that runs in $O(mn/\lg n)$ time, where $n \leq m$ and the sequences are drawn from a set of bounded size. For the special case in which no element appears more than once in an input sequence, Szymanski [326] shows how to solve the problem in $O((n + m) \lg(n + m))$ time. Many of these results extend to the problem of computing string edit distances (Problem 15-5).

An early paper on variable-length binary encodings by Gilbert and Moore [133] had applications to constructing optimal binary search trees for the case in which all probabilities p_i are 0; this paper contains an $O(n^3)$-time algorithm. Aho, Hopcroft, and Ullman [5] present the algorithm from Section 15.5. Exercise 15.5-4 is due to Knuth [212]. Hu and Tucker [184] devised an algorithm for the case in which all probabilities p_i are 0 that uses $O(n^2)$ time and $O(n)$ space; subsequently, Knuth [211] reduced the time to $O(n \lg n)$.

Problem 15-8 is due to Avidan and Shamir [27], who have posted on the Web a wonderful video illustrating this image-compression technique.

16 Greedy Algorithms

Algorithms for optimization problems typically go through a sequence of steps, with a set of choices at each step. For many optimization problems, using dynamic programming to determine the best choices is overkill; simpler, more efficient algorithms will do. A **_greedy algorithm_** always makes the choice that looks best at the moment. That is, it makes a locally optimal choice in the hope that this choice will lead to a globally optimal solution. This chapter explores optimization problems for which greedy algorithms provide optimal solutions. Before reading this chapter, you should read about dynamic programming in Chapter 15, particularly Section 15.3.

Greedy algorithms do not always yield optimal solutions, but for many problems they do. We shall first examine, in Section 16.1, a simple but nontrivial problem, the activity-selection problem, for which a greedy algorithm efficiently computes an optimal solution. We shall arrive at the greedy algorithm by first considering a dynamic-programming approach and then showing that we can always make greedy choices to arrive at an optimal solution. Section 16.2 reviews the basic elements of the greedy approach, giving a direct approach for proving greedy algorithms correct. Section 16.3 presents an important application of greedy techniques: designing data-compression (Huffman) codes. In Section 16.4, we investigate some of the theory underlying combinatorial structures called "matroids," for which a greedy algorithm always produces an optimal solution. Finally, Section 16.5 applies matroids to solve a problem of scheduling unit-time tasks with deadlines and penalties.

The greedy method is quite powerful and works well for a wide range of problems. Later chapters will present many algorithms that we can view as applications of the greedy method, including minimum-spanning-tree algorithms (Chapter 23), Dijkstra's algorithm for shortest paths from a single source (Chapter 24), and Chvátal's greedy set-covering heuristic (Chapter 35). Minimum-spanning-tree algorithms furnish a classic example of the greedy method. Although you can read this chapter and Chapter 23 independently of each other, you might find it useful to read them together.

16.1 An activity-selection problem

Our first example is the problem of scheduling several competing activities that require exclusive use of a common resource, with a goal of selecting a maximum-size set of mutually compatible activities. Suppose we have a set $S = \{a_1, a_2, \ldots, a_n\}$ of n proposed *activities* that wish to use a resource, such as a lecture hall, which can serve only one activity at a time. Each activity a_i has a *start time* s_i and a *finish time* f_i, where $0 \le s_i < f_i < \infty$. If selected, activity a_i takes place during the half-open time interval $[s_i, f_i)$. Activities a_i and a_j are *compatible* if the intervals $[s_i, f_i)$ and $[s_j, f_j)$ do not overlap. That is, a_i and a_j are compatible if $s_i \ge f_j$ or $s_j \ge f_i$. In the *activity-selection problem*, we wish to select a maximum-size subset of mutually compatible activities. We assume that the activities are sorted in monotonically increasing order of finish time:

$$f_1 \le f_2 \le f_3 \le \cdots \le f_{n-1} \le f_n . \tag{16.1}$$

(We shall see later the advantage that this assumption provides.) For example, consider the following set S of activities:

i	1	2	3	4	5	6	7	8	9	10	11
s_i	1	3	0	5	3	5	6	8	8	2	12
f_i	4	5	6	7	9	9	10	11	12	14	16

For this example, the subset $\{a_3, a_9, a_{11}\}$ consists of mutually compatible activities. It is not a maximum subset, however, since the subset $\{a_1, a_4, a_8, a_{11}\}$ is larger. In fact, $\{a_1, a_4, a_8, a_{11}\}$ is a largest subset of mutually compatible activities; another largest subset is $\{a_2, a_4, a_9, a_{11}\}$.

We shall solve this problem in several steps. We start by thinking about a dynamic-programming solution, in which we consider several choices when determining which subproblems to use in an optimal solution. We shall then observe that we need to consider only one choice—the greedy choice—and that when we make the greedy choice, only one subproblem remains. Based on these observations, we shall develop a recursive greedy algorithm to solve the activity-scheduling problem. We shall complete the process of developing a greedy solution by converting the recursive algorithm to an iterative one. Although the steps we shall go through in this section are slightly more involved than is typical when developing a greedy algorithm, they illustrate the relationship between greedy algorithms and dynamic programming.

The optimal substructure of the activity-selection problem

We can easily verify that the activity-selection problem exhibits optimal substructure. Let us denote by S_{ij} the set of activities that start after activity a_i finishes and that finish before activity a_j starts. Suppose that we wish to find a maximum set of mutually compatible activities in S_{ij}, and suppose further that such a maximum set is A_{ij}, which includes some activity a_k. By including a_k in an optimal solution, we are left with two subproblems: finding mutually compatible activities in the set S_{ik} (activities that start after activity a_i finishes and that finish before activity a_k starts) and finding mutually compatible activities in the set S_{kj} (activities that start after activity a_k finishes and that finish before activity a_j starts). Let $A_{ik} = A_{ij} \cap S_{ik}$ and $A_{kj} = A_{ij} \cap S_{kj}$, so that A_{ik} contains the activities in A_{ij} that finish before a_k starts and A_{kj} contains the activities in A_{ij} that start after a_k finishes. Thus, we have $A_{ij} = A_{ik} \cup \{a_k\} \cup A_{kj}$, and so the maximum-size set A_{ij} of mutually compatible activities in S_{ij} consists of $|A_{ij}| = |A_{ik}| + |A_{kj}| + 1$ activities.

The usual cut-and-paste argument shows that the optimal solution A_{ij} must also include optimal solutions to the two subproblems for S_{ik} and S_{kj}. If we could find a set A'_{kj} of mutually compatible activities in S_{kj} where $|A'_{kj}| > |A_{kj}|$, then we could use A'_{kj}, rather than A_{kj}, in a solution to the subproblem for S_{ij}. We would have constructed a set of $|A_{ik}| + |A'_{kj}| + 1 > |A_{ik}| + |A_{kj}| + 1 = |A_{ij}|$ mutually compatible activities, which contradicts the assumption that A_{ij} is an optimal solution. A symmetric argument applies to the activities in S_{ik}.

This way of characterizing optimal substructure suggests that we might solve the activity-selection problem by dynamic programming. If we denote the size of an optimal solution for the set S_{ij} by $c[i, j]$, then we would have the recurrence

$$c[i, j] = c[i, k] + c[k, j] + 1 .$$

Of course, if we did not know that an optimal solution for the set S_{ij} includes activity a_k, we would have to examine all activities in S_{ij} to find which one to choose, so that

$$c[i, j] = \begin{cases} 0 & \text{if } S_{ij} = \emptyset , \\ \max_{a_k \in S_{ij}} \{c[i, k] + c[k, j] + 1\} & \text{if } S_{ij} \neq \emptyset . \end{cases} \tag{16.2}$$

We could then develop a recursive algorithm and memoize it, or we could work bottom-up and fill in table entries as we go along. But we would be overlooking another important characteristic of the activity-selection problem that we can use to great advantage.

Making the greedy choice

What if we could choose an activity to add to our optimal solution without having to first solve all the subproblems? That could save us from having to consider all the choices inherent in recurrence (16.2). In fact, for the activity-selection problem, we need consider only one choice: the greedy choice.

What do we mean by the greedy choice for the activity-selection problem? Intuition suggests that we should choose an activity that leaves the resource available for as many other activities as possible. Now, of the activities we end up choosing, one of them must be the first one to finish. Our intuition tells us, therefore, to choose the activity in S with the earliest finish time, since that would leave the resource available for as many of the activities that follow it as possible. (If more than one activity in S has the earliest finish time, then we can choose any such activity.) In other words, since the activities are sorted in monotonically increasing order by finish time, the greedy choice is activity a_1. Choosing the first activity to finish is not the only way to think of making a greedy choice for this problem; Exercise 16.1-3 asks you to explore other possibilities.

If we make the greedy choice, we have only one remaining subproblem to solve: finding activities that start after a_1 finishes. Why don't we have to consider activities that finish before a_1 starts? We have that $s_1 < f_1$, and f_1 is the earliest finish time of any activity, and therefore no activity can have a finish time less than or equal to s_1. Thus, all activities that are compatible with activity a_1 must start after a_1 finishes.

Furthermore, we have already established that the activity-selection problem exhibits optimal substructure. Let $S_k = \{a_i \in S : s_i \geq f_k\}$ be the set of activities that start after activity a_k finishes. If we make the greedy choice of activity a_1, then S_1 remains as the only subproblem to solve.[1] Optimal substructure tells us that if a_1 is in the optimal solution, then an optimal solution to the original problem consists of activity a_1 and all the activities in an optimal solution to the subproblem S_1.

One big question remains: is our intuition correct? Is the greedy choice—in which we choose the first activity to finish—always part of some optimal solution? The following theorem shows that it is.

---

[1] We sometimes refer to the sets S_k as subproblems rather than as just sets of activities. It will always be clear from the context whether we are referring to S_k as a set of activities or as a subproblem whose input is that set.

Theorem 16.1

Consider any nonempty subproblem S_k, and let a_m be an activity in S_k with the earliest finish time. Then a_m is included in some maximum-size subset of mutually compatible activities of S_k.

Proof   Let A_k be a maximum-size subset of mutually compatible activities in S_k, and let a_j be the activity in A_k with the earliest finish time. If $a_j = a_m$, we are done, since we have shown that a_m is in some maximum-size subset of mutually compatible activities of S_k. If $a_j \neq a_m$, let the set $A'_k = A_k - \{a_j\} \cup \{a_m\}$ be A_k but substituting a_m for a_j. The activities in A'_k are disjoint, which follows because the activities in A_k are disjoint, a_j is the first activity in A_k to finish, and $f_m \leq f_j$. Since $|A'_k| = |A_k|$, we conclude that A'_k is a maximum-size subset of mutually compatible activities of S_k, and it includes a_m.   ∎

Thus, we see that although we might be able to solve the activity-selection problem with dynamic programming, we don't need to. (Besides, we have not yet examined whether the activity-selection problem even has overlapping subproblems.) Instead, we can repeatedly choose the activity that finishes first, keep only the activities compatible with this activity, and repeat until no activities remain. Moreover, because we always choose the activity with the earliest finish time, the finish times of the activities we choose must strictly increase. We can consider each activity just once overall, in monotonically increasing order of finish times.

An algorithm to solve the activity-selection problem does not need to work bottom-up, like a table-based dynamic-programming algorithm. Instead, it can work top-down, choosing an activity to put into the optimal solution and then solving the subproblem of choosing activities from those that are compatible with those already chosen. Greedy algorithms typically have this top-down design: make a choice and then solve a subproblem, rather than the bottom-up technique of solving subproblems before making a choice.

A recursive greedy algorithm

Now that we have seen how to bypass the dynamic-programming approach and instead use a top-down, greedy algorithm, we can write a straightforward, recursive procedure to solve the activity-selection problem. The procedure RECURSIVE-ACTIVITY-SELECTOR takes the start and finish times of the activities, represented as arrays s and f,[2] the index k that defines the subproblem S_k it is to solve, and

---

[2]Because the pseudocode takes s and f as arrays, it indexes into them with square brackets rather than subscripts.

the size n of the original problem. It returns a maximum-size set of mutually compatible activities in S_k. We assume that the n input activities are already ordered by monotonically increasing finish time, according to equation (16.1). If not, we can sort them into this order in $O(n \lg n)$ time, breaking ties arbitrarily. In order to start, we add the fictitious activity a_0 with $f_0 = 0$, so that subproblem S_0 is the entire set of activities S. The initial call, which solves the entire problem, is RECURSIVE-ACTIVITY-SELECTOR$(s, f, 0, n)$.

RECURSIVE-ACTIVITY-SELECTOR(s, f, k, n)
1   $m = k + 1$
2   **while** $m \leq n$ and $s[m] < f[k]$ // find the first activity in S_k to finish
3       $m = m + 1$
4   **if** $m \leq n$
5   **return** $\{a_m\} \cup$ RECURSIVE-ACTIVITY-SELECTOR(s, f, m, n)
6   **else return** $\emptyset$

Figure 16.1 shows the operation of the algorithm. In a given recursive call RECURSIVE-ACTIVITY-SELECTOR(s, f, k, n), the **while** loop of lines 2–3 looks for the first activity in S_k to finish. The loop examines $a_{k+1}, a_{k+2}, \ldots, a_n$, until it finds the first activity a_m that is compatible with a_k; such an activity has $s_m \geq f_k$. If the loop terminates because it finds such an activity, line 5 returns the union of $\{a_m\}$ and the maximum-size subset of S_m returned by the recursive call RECURSIVE-ACTIVITY-SELECTOR(s, f, m, n). Alternatively, the loop may terminate because $m > n$, in which case we have examined all activities in S_k without finding one that is compatible with a_k. In this case, $S_k = \emptyset$, and so the procedure returns $\emptyset$ in line 6.

Assuming that the activities have already been sorted by finish times, the running time of the call RECURSIVE-ACTIVITY-SELECTOR$(s, f, 0, n)$ is $\Theta(n)$, which we can see as follows. Over all recursive calls, each activity is examined exactly once in the **while** loop test of line 2. In particular, activity a_i is examined in the last call made in which $k < i$.

An iterative greedy algorithm

We easily can convert our recursive procedure to an iterative one. The procedure RECURSIVE-ACTIVITY-SELECTOR is almost "tail recursive" (see Problem 7-4): it ends with a recursive call to itself followed by a union operation. It is usually a straightforward task to transform a tail-recursive procedure to an iterative form; in fact, some compilers for certain programming languages perform this task automatically. As written, RECURSIVE-ACTIVITY-SELECTOR works for subproblems S_k, i.e., subproblems that consist of the last activities to finish.

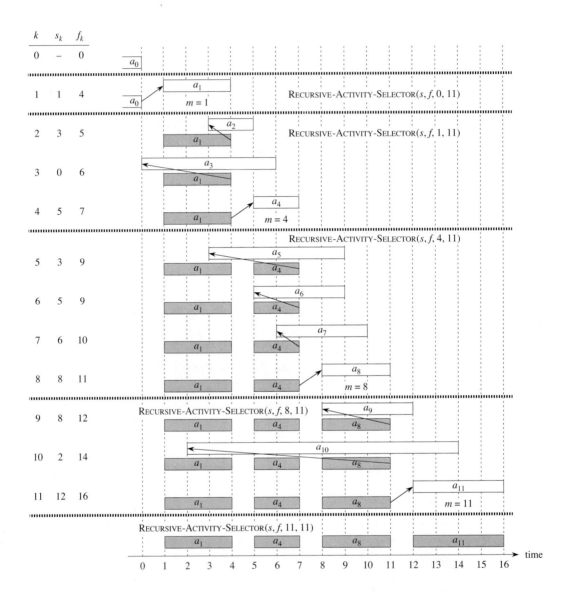

Figure 16.1 The operation of RECURSIVE-ACTIVITY-SELECTOR on the 11 activities given earlier. Activities considered in each recursive call appear between horizontal lines. The fictitious activity a_0 finishes at time 0, and the initial call RECURSIVE-ACTIVITY-SELECTOR($s, f, 0, 11$), selects activity a_1. In each recursive call, the activities that have already been selected are shaded, and the activity shown in white is being considered. If the starting time of an activity occurs before the finish time of the most recently added activity (the arrow between them points left), it is rejected. Otherwise (the arrow points directly up or to the right), it is selected. The last recursive call, RECURSIVE-ACTIVITY-SELECTOR($s, f, 11, 11$), returns ∅. The resulting set of selected activities is $\{a_1, a_4, a_8, a_{11}\}$.

The procedure GREEDY-ACTIVITY-SELECTOR is an iterative version of the procedure RECURSIVE-ACTIVITY-SELECTOR. It also assumes that the input activities are ordered by monotonically increasing finish time. It collects selected activities into a set A and returns this set when it is done.

GREEDY-ACTIVITY-SELECTOR(s, f)

```
1   n = s.length
2   A = {a₁}
3   k = 1
4   for m = 2 to n
5        if s[m] ≥ f[k]
6             A = A ∪ {aₘ}
7             k = m
8   return A
```

The procedure works as follows. The variable k indexes the most recent addition
to A, corresponding to the activity a_k in the recursive version. Since we consider
the activities in order of monotonically increasing finish time, f_k is always the
maximum finish time of any activity in A. That is,

$$f_k = \max \{ f_i : a_i \in A \} .$$ (16.3)

Lines 2–3 select activity a_1, initialize A to contain just this activity, and initialize k
to index this activity. The **for** loop of lines 4–7 finds the earliest activity in S_k to
finish. The loop considers each activity a_m in turn and adds a_m to A if it is compatible with all previously selected activities; such an activity is the earliest in S_k to
finish. To see whether activity a_m is compatible with every activity currently in A,
it suffices by equation (16.3) to check (in line 5) that its start time s_m is not earlier
than the finish time f_k of the activity most recently added to A. If activity a_m is
compatible, then lines 6–7 add activity a_m to A and set k to m. The set A returned
by the call GREEDY-ACTIVITY-SELECTOR(s, f) is precisely the set returned by
the call RECURSIVE-ACTIVITY-SELECTOR$(s, f, 0, n)$.

Like the recursive version, GREEDY-ACTIVITY-SELECTOR schedules a set of n
activities in $\Theta(n)$ time, assuming that the activities were already sorted initially by
their finish times.

Exercises

16.1-1
Give a dynamic-programming algorithm for the activity-selection problem, based
on recurrence (16.2). Have your algorithm compute the sizes $c[i, j]$ as defined
above and also produce the maximum-size subset of mutually compatible activities.

Assume that the inputs have been sorted as in equation (16.1). Compare the running time of your solution to the running time of GREEDY-ACTIVITY-SELECTOR.

16.1-2

Suppose that instead of always selecting the first activity to finish, we instead select the last activity to start that is compatible with all previously selected activities. Describe how this approach is a greedy algorithm, and prove that it yields an optimal solution.

16.1-3

Not just any greedy approach to the activity-selection problem produces a maximum-size set of mutually compatible activities. Give an example to show that the approach of selecting the activity of least duration from among those that are compatible with previously selected activities does not work. Do the same for the approaches of always selecting the compatible activity that overlaps the fewest other remaining activities and always selecting the compatible remaining activity with the earliest start time.

16.1-4

Suppose that we have a set of activities to schedule among a large number of lecture halls, where any activity can take place in any lecture hall. We wish to schedule all the activities using as few lecture halls as possible. Give an efficient greedy algorithm to determine which activity should use which lecture hall.

   (This problem is also known as the ***interval-graph coloring problem***. We can create an interval graph whose vertices are the given activities and whose edges connect incompatible activities. The smallest number of colors required to color every vertex so that no two adjacent vertices have the same color corresponds to finding the fewest lecture halls needed to schedule all of the given activities.)

16.1-5

Consider a modification to the activity-selection problem in which each activity a_i has, in addition to a start and finish time, a value v_i. The objective is no longer to maximize the number of activities scheduled, but instead to maximize the total value of the activities scheduled. That is, we wish to choose a set A of compatible activities such that $\sum_{a_k \in A} v_k$ is maximized. Give a polynomial-time algorithm for this problem.

16.2   Elements of the greedy strategy

A greedy algorithm obtains an optimal solution to a problem by making a sequence of choices. At each decision point, the algorithm makes the choice that seems best at the moment. This heuristic strategy does not always produce an optimal solution, but as we saw in the activity-selection problem, sometimes it does. This section discusses some of the general properties of greedy methods.

The process that we followed in Section 16.1 to develop a greedy algorithm was a bit more involved than is typical. We went through the following steps:

1. Determine the optimal substructure of the problem.

2. Develop a recursive solution. (For the activity-selection problem, we formulated recurrence (16.2), but we bypassed developing a recursive algorithm based on this recurrence.)

3. Show that if we make the greedy choice, then only one subproblem remains.

4. Prove that it is always safe to make the greedy choice. (Steps 3 and 4 can occur in either order.)

5. Develop a recursive algorithm that implements the greedy strategy.

6. Convert the recursive algorithm to an iterative algorithm.

In going through these steps, we saw in great detail the dynamic-programming underpinnings of a greedy algorithm. For example, in the activity-selection problem, we first defined the subproblems S_{ij}, where both i and j varied. We then found that if we always made the greedy choice, we could restrict the subproblems to be of the form S_k.

Alternatively, we could have fashioned our optimal substructure with a greedy choice in mind, so that the choice leaves just one subproblem to solve. In the activity-selection problem, we could have started by dropping the second subscript and defining subproblems of the form S_k. Then, we could have proven that a greedy choice (the first activity a_m to finish in S_k), combined with an optimal solution to the remaining set S_m of compatible activities, yields an optimal solution to S_k. More generally, we design greedy algorithms according to the following sequence of steps:

1. Cast the optimization problem as one in which we make a choice and are left with one subproblem to solve.

2. Prove that there is always an optimal solution to the original problem that makes the greedy choice, so that the greedy choice is always safe.

3. Demonstrate optimal substructure by showing that, having made the greedy choice, what remains is a subproblem with the property that if we combine an optimal solution to the subproblem with the greedy choice we have made, we arrive at an optimal solution to the original problem.

We shall use this more direct process in later sections of this chapter. Nevertheless, beneath every greedy algorithm, there is almost always a more cumbersome dynamic-programming solution.

How can we tell whether a greedy algorithm will solve a particular optimization problem? No way works all the time, but the greedy-choice property and optimal substructure are the two key ingredients. If we can demonstrate that the problem has these properties, then we are well on the way to developing a greedy algorithm for it.

Greedy-choice property

The first key ingredient is the ***greedy-choice property***: we can assemble a globally optimal solution by making locally optimal (greedy) choices. In other words, when we are considering which choice to make, we make the choice that looks best in the current problem, without considering results from subproblems.

Here is where greedy algorithms differ from dynamic programming. In dynamic programming, we make a choice at each step, but the choice usually depends on the solutions to subproblems. Consequently, we typically solve dynamic-programming problems in a bottom-up manner, progressing from smaller subproblems to larger subproblems. (Alternatively, we can solve them top down, but memoizing. Of course, even though the code works top down, we still must solve the subproblems before making a choice.) In a greedy algorithm, we make whatever choice seems best at the moment and then solve the subproblem that remains. The choice made by a greedy algorithm may depend on choices so far, but it cannot depend on any future choices or on the solutions to subproblems. Thus, unlike dynamic programming, which solves the subproblems before making the first choice, a greedy algorithm makes its first choice before solving any subproblems. A dynamic-programming algorithm proceeds bottom up, whereas a greedy strategy usually progresses in a top-down fashion, making one greedy choice after another, reducing each given problem instance to a smaller one.

Of course, we must prove that a greedy choice at each step yields a globally optimal solution. Typically, as in the case of Theorem 16.1, the proof examines a globally optimal solution to some subproblem. It then shows how to modify the solution to substitute the greedy choice for some other choice, resulting in one similar, but smaller, subproblem.

We can usually make the greedy choice more efficiently than when we have to consider a wider set of choices. For example, in the activity-selection problem, assuming that we had already sorted the activities in monotonically increasing order of finish times, we needed to examine each activity just once. By preprocessing the input or by using an appropriate data structure (often a priority queue), we often can make greedy choices quickly, thus yielding an efficient algorithm.

Optimal substructure

A problem exhibits *optimal substructure* if an optimal solution to the problem contains within it optimal solutions to subproblems. This property is a key ingredient of assessing the applicability of dynamic programming as well as greedy algorithms. As an example of optimal substructure, recall how we demonstrated in Section 16.1 that if an optimal solution to subproblem S_{ij} includes an activity a_k, then it must also contain optimal solutions to the subproblems S_{ik} and S_{kj}. Given this optimal substructure, we argued that if we knew which activity to use as a_k, we could construct an optimal solution to S_{ij} by selecting a_k along with all activities in optimal solutions to the subproblems S_{ik} and S_{kj}. Based on this observation of optimal substructure, we were able to devise the recurrence (16.2) that described the value of an optimal solution.

We usually use a more direct approach regarding optimal substructure when applying it to greedy algorithms. As mentioned above, we have the luxury of assuming that we arrived at a subproblem by having made the greedy choice in the original problem. All we really need to do is argue that an optimal solution to the subproblem, combined with the greedy choice already made, yields an optimal solution to the original problem. This scheme implicitly uses induction on the subproblems to prove that making the greedy choice at every step produces an optimal solution.

Greedy versus dynamic programming

Because both the greedy and dynamic-programming strategies exploit optimal substructure, you might be tempted to generate a dynamic-programming solution to a problem when a greedy solution suffices or, conversely, you might mistakenly think that a greedy solution works when in fact a dynamic-programming solution is required. To illustrate the subtleties between the two techniques, let us investigate two variants of a classical optimization problem.

The *0-1 knapsack problem* is the following. A thief robbing a store finds n items. The ith item is worth v_i dollars and weighs w_i pounds, where v_i and w_i are integers. The thief wants to take as valuable a load as possible, but he can carry at most W pounds in his knapsack, for some integer W. Which items should he take? (We call this the 0-1 knapsack problem because for each item, the thief must either take it or leave it behind; he cannot take a fractional amount of an item or take an item more than once.)

In the ***fractional knapsack problem***, the setup is the same, but the thief can take fractions of items, rather than having to make a binary (0-1) choice for each item. You can think of an item in the 0-1 knapsack problem as being like a gold ingot and an item in the fractional knapsack problem as more like gold dust.

Both knapsack problems exhibit the optimal-substructure property. For the 0-1 problem, consider the most valuable load that weighs at most W pounds. If we remove item j from this load, the remaining load must be the most valuable load weighing at most $W - w_j$ that the thief can take from the $n - 1$ original items excluding j. For the comparable fractional problem, consider that if we remove a weight w of one item j from the optimal load, the remaining load must be the most valuable load weighing at most $W - w$ that the thief can take from the $n - 1$ original items plus $w_j - w$ pounds of item j.

Although the problems are similar, we can solve the fractional knapsack problem by a greedy strategy, but we cannot solve the 0-1 problem by such a strategy. To solve the fractional problem, we first compute the value per pound v_i / w_i for each item. Obeying a greedy strategy, the thief begins by taking as much as possible of the item with the greatest value per pound. If the supply of that item is exhausted and he can still carry more, he takes as much as possible of the item with the next greatest value per pound, and so forth, until he reaches his weight limit W. Thus, by sorting the items by value per pound, the greedy algorithm runs in $O(n \lg n)$ time. We leave the proof that the fractional knapsack problem has the greedy-choice property as Exercise 16.2-1.

To see that this greedy strategy does not work for the 0-1 knapsack problem, consider the problem instance illustrated in Figure 16.2(a). This example has 3 items and a knapsack that can hold 50 pounds. Item 1 weighs 10 pounds and is worth 60 dollars. Item 2 weighs 20 pounds and is worth 100 dollars. Item 3 weighs 30 pounds and is worth 120 dollars. Thus, the value per pound of item 1 is 6 dollars per pound, which is greater than the value per pound of either item 2 (5 dollars per pound) or item 3 (4 dollars per pound). The greedy strategy, therefore, would take item 1 first. As you can see from the case analysis in Figure 16.2(b), however, the optimal solution takes items 2 and 3, leaving item 1 behind. The two possible solutions that take item 1 are both suboptimal.

For the comparable fractional problem, however, the greedy strategy, which takes item 1 first, does yield an optimal solution, as shown in Figure 16.2(c). Taking item 1 doesn't work in the 0-1 problem because the thief is unable to fill his knapsack to capacity, and the empty space lowers the effective value per pound of his load. In the 0-1 problem, when we consider whether to include an item in the knapsack, we must compare the solution to the subproblem that includes the item with the solution to the subproblem that excludes the item before we can make the

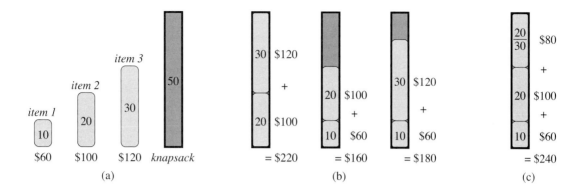

Figure 16.2   An example showing that the greedy strategy does not work for the 0-1 knapsack problem. **(a)** The thief must select a subset of the three items shown whose weight must not exceed 50 pounds. **(b)** The optimal subset includes items 2 and 3. Any solution with item 1 is suboptimal, even though item 1 has the greatest value per pound. **(c)** For the fractional knapsack problem, taking the items in order of greatest value per pound yields an optimal solution.

choice. The problem formulated in this way gives rise to many overlapping sub-problems—a hallmark of dynamic programming, and indeed, as Exercise 16.2-2 asks you to show, we can use dynamic programming to solve the 0-1 problem.

Exercises

16.2-1
Prove that the fractional knapsack problem has the greedy-choice property.

16.2-2
Give a dynamic-programming solution to the 0-1 knapsack problem that runs in $O(n\,W)$ time, where n is the number of items and W is the maximum weight of items that the thief can put in his knapsack.

16.2-3
Suppose that in a 0-1 knapsack problem, the order of the items when sorted by increasing weight is the same as their order when sorted by decreasing value. Give an efficient algorithm to find an optimal solution to this variant of the knapsack problem, and argue that your algorithm is correct.

16.2-4
Professor Gekko has always dreamed of inline skating across North Dakota. He plans to cross the state on highway U.S. 2, which runs from Grand Forks, on the eastern border with Minnesota, to Williston, near the western border with Montana.

The professor can carry two liters of water, and he can skate m miles before running out of water. (Because North Dakota is relatively flat, the professor does not have to worry about drinking water at a greater rate on uphill sections than on flat or downhill sections.) The professor will start in Grand Forks with two full liters of water. His official North Dakota state map shows all the places along U.S. 2 at which he can refill his water and the distances between these locations.

The professor's goal is to minimize the number of water stops along his route across the state. Give an efficient method by which he can determine which water stops he should make. Prove that your strategy yields an optimal solution, and give its running time.

16.2-5

Describe an efficient algorithm that, given a set $\{x_1, x_2, \ldots, x_n\}$ of points on the real line, determines the smallest set of unit-length closed intervals that contains all of the given points. Argue that your algorithm is correct.

16.2-6 ★

Show how to solve the fractional knapsack problem in $O(n)$ time.

16.2-7

Suppose you are given two sets A and B, each containing n positive integers. You can choose to reorder each set however you like. After reordering, let a_i be the ith element of set A, and let b_i be the ith element of set B. You then receive a payoff of $\prod_{i=1}^{n} a_i^{b_i}$. Give an algorithm that will maximize your payoff. Prove that your algorithm maximizes the payoff, and state its running time.

16.3   Huffman codes

Huffman codes compress data very effectively: savings of 20% to 90% are typical, depending on the characteristics of the data being compressed. We consider the data to be a sequence of characters. Huffman's greedy algorithm uses a table giving how often each character occurs (i.e., its frequency) to build up an optimal way of representing each character as a binary string.

Suppose we have a 100,000-character data file that we wish to store compactly. We observe that the characters in the file occur with the frequencies given by Figure 16.3. That is, only 6 different characters appear, and the character a occurs 45,000 times.

We have many options for how to represent such a file of information. Here, we consider the problem of designing a *binary character code* (or *code* for short)

	a	b	c	d	e	f
Frequency (in thousands)	45	13	12	16	9	5
Fixed-length codeword	000	001	010	011	100	101
Variable-length codeword	0	101	100	111	1101	1100

Figure 16.3   A character-coding problem. A data file of 100,000 characters contains only the characters a–f, with the frequencies indicated. If we assign each character a 3-bit codeword, we can encode the file in 300,000 bits. Using the variable-length code shown, we can encode the file in only 224,000 bits.

in which each character is represented by a unique binary string, which we call a **codeword**. If we use a **fixed-length code**, we need 3 bits to represent 6 characters: a = 000, b = 001, ..., f = 101. This method requires 300,000 bits to code the entire file. Can we do better?

A **variable-length code** can do considerably better than a fixed-length code, by giving frequent characters short codewords and infrequent characters long codewords. Figure 16.3 shows such a code; here the 1-bit string 0 represents a, and the 4-bit string 1100 represents f. This code requires

$$(45 \cdot 1 \; + \; 13 \cdot 3 \; + \; 12 \cdot 3 \; + \; 16 \cdot 3 \; + \; 9 \cdot 4 \; + \; 5 \cdot 4) \cdot 1,000 = 224,000 \text{ bits}$$

to represent the file, a savings of approximately 25%. In fact, this is an optimal character code for this file, as we shall see.

Prefix codes

We consider here only codes in which no codeword is also a prefix of some other codeword. Such codes are called **prefix codes**.[3] Although we won't prove it here, a prefix code can always achieve the optimal data compression among any character code, and so we suffer no loss of generality by restricting our attention to prefix codes.

Encoding is always simple for any binary character code; we just concatenate the codewords representing each character of the file. For example, with the variable-length prefix code of Figure 16.3, we code the 3-character file abc as $0 \cdot 101 \cdot 100 = 0101100$, where "·" denotes concatenation.

Prefix codes are desirable because they simplify decoding. Since no codeword is a prefix of any other, the codeword that begins an encoded file is unambiguous. We can simply identify the initial codeword, translate it back to the original char-

---

[3]Perhaps "prefix-free codes" would be a better name, but the term "prefix codes" is standard in the literature.

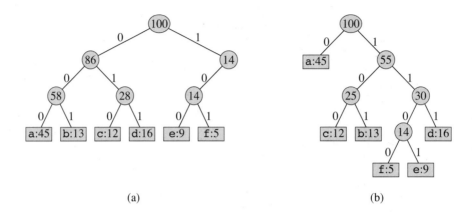

Figure 16.4 Trees corresponding to the coding schemes in Figure 16.3. Each leaf is labeled with a character and its frequency of occurrence. Each internal node is labeled with the sum of the frequencies of the leaves in its subtree. **(a)** The tree corresponding to the fixed-length code $a = 000, \ldots,$ $f = 101$. **(b)** The tree corresponding to the optimal prefix code $a = 0, b = 101, \ldots, f = 1100$.

acter, and repeat the decoding process on the remainder of the encoded file. In our example, the string 001011101 parses uniquely as $0 \cdot 0 \cdot 101 \cdot 1101$, which decodes to `aabe`.

The decoding process needs a convenient representation for the prefix code so that we can easily pick off the initial codeword. A binary tree whose leaves are the given characters provides one such representation. We interpret the binary codeword for a character as the simple path from the root to that character, where 0 means "go to the left child" and 1 means "go to the right child." Figure 16.4 shows the trees for the two codes of our example. Note that these are not binary search trees, since the leaves need not appear in sorted order and internal nodes do not contain character keys.

An optimal code for a file is always represented by a *full* binary tree, in which every nonleaf node has two children (see Exercise 16.3-2). The fixed-length code in our example is not optimal since its tree, shown in Figure 16.4(a), is not a full binary tree: it contains codewords beginning $10\ldots$, but none beginning $11\ldots$. Since we can now restrict our attention to full binary trees, we can say that if C is the alphabet from which the characters are drawn and all character frequencies are positive, then the tree for an optimal prefix code has exactly $|C|$ leaves, one for each letter of the alphabet, and exactly $|C| - 1$ internal nodes (see Exercise B.5-3).

Given a tree T corresponding to a prefix code, we can easily compute the number of bits required to encode a file. For each character c in the alphabet C, let the attribute $c.freq$ denote the frequency of c in the file and let $d_T(c)$ denote the depth of c's leaf in the tree. Note that $d_T(c)$ is also the length of the codeword for character c. The number of bits required to encode a file is thus

$$B(T) = \sum_{c \in C} c.freq \cdot d_T(c) \,, \tag{16.4}$$

which we define as the **cost** of the tree T.

Constructing a Huffman code

Huffman invented a greedy algorithm that constructs an optimal prefix code called a **Huffman code**. In line with our observations in Section 16.2, its proof of correctness relies on the greedy-choice property and optimal substructure. Rather than demonstrating that these properties hold and then developing pseudocode, we present the pseudocode first. Doing so will help clarify how the algorithm makes greedy choices.

In the pseudocode that follows, we assume that C is a set of n characters and that each character $c \in C$ is an object with an attribute $c.freq$ giving its frequency. The algorithm builds the tree T corresponding to the optimal code in a bottom-up manner. It begins with a set of $|C|$ leaves and performs a sequence of $|C| - 1$ "merging" operations to create the final tree. The algorithm uses a min-priority queue Q, keyed on the *freq* attribute, to identify the two least-frequent objects to merge together. When we merge two objects, the result is a new object whose frequency is the sum of the frequencies of the two objects that were merged.

HUFFMAN(C)

```
1   n = |C|
2   Q = C
3   for i = 1 to n - 1
4       allocate a new node z
5       z.left = x = EXTRACT-MIN(Q)
6       z.right = y = EXTRACT-MIN(Q)
7       z.freq = x.freq + y.freq
8       INSERT(Q, z)
9   return EXTRACT-MIN(Q)      // return the root of the tree
```

For our example, Huffman's algorithm proceeds as shown in Figure 16.5. Since the alphabet contains 6 letters, the initial queue size is $n = 6$, and 5 merge steps build the tree. The final tree represents the optimal prefix code. The codeword for a letter is the sequence of edge labels on the simple path from the root to the letter.

Line 2 initializes the min-priority queue Q with the characters in C. The **for** loop in lines 3–8 repeatedly extracts the two nodes x and y of lowest frequency

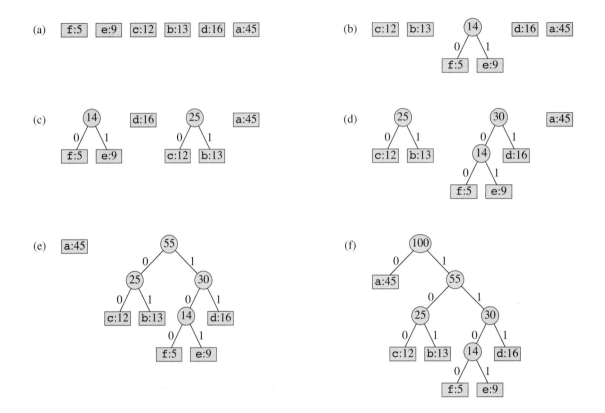

Figure 16.5 The steps of Huffman's algorithm for the frequencies given in Figure 16.3. Each part shows the contents of the queue sorted into increasing order by frequency. At each step, the two trees with lowest frequencies are merged. Leaves are shown as rectangles containing a character and its frequency. Internal nodes are shown as circles containing the sum of the frequencies of their children. An edge connecting an internal node with its children is labeled 0 if it is an edge to a left child and 1 if it is an edge to a right child. The codeword for a letter is the sequence of labels on the edges connecting the root to the leaf for that letter. **(a)** The initial set of $n = 6$ nodes, one for each letter. **(b)**–**(e)** Intermediate stages. **(f)** The final tree.

from the queue, replacing them in the queue with a new node z representing their merger. The frequency of z is computed as the sum of the frequencies of x and y in line 7. The node z has x as its left child and y as its right child. (This order is arbitrary; switching the left and right child of any node yields a different code of the same cost.) After $n - 1$ mergers, line 9 returns the one node left in the queue, which is the root of the code tree.

Although the algorithm would produce the same result if we were to excise the variables x and y—assigning directly to $z.left$ and $z.right$ in lines 5 and 6, and changing line 7 to $z.freq = z.left.freq + z.right.freq$—we shall use the node names x and y in the proof of correctness. Therefore, we find it convenient to leave them in.

To analyze the running time of Huffman's algorithm, we assume that Q is implemented as a binary min-heap (see Chapter 6). For a set C of n characters, we can initialize Q in line 2 in $O(n)$ time using the BUILD-MIN-HEAP procedure discussed in Section 6.3. The **for** loop in lines 3–8 executes exactly $n - 1$ times, and since each heap operation requires time $O(\lg n)$, the loop contributes $O(n \lg n)$ to the running time. Thus, the total running time of HUFFMAN on a set of n characters is $O(n \lg n)$. We can reduce the running time to $O(n \lg \lg n)$ by replacing the binary min-heap with a van Emde Boas tree (see Chapter 20).

Correctness of Huffman's algorithm

To prove that the greedy algorithm HUFFMAN is correct, we show that the problem of determining an optimal prefix code exhibits the greedy-choice and optimal-substructure properties. The next lemma shows that the greedy-choice property holds.

Lemma 16.2
Let C be an alphabet in which each character $c \in C$ has frequency $c.freq$. Let x and y be two characters in C having the lowest frequencies. Then there exists an optimal prefix code for C in which the codewords for x and y have the same length and differ only in the last bit.

Proof   The idea of the proof is to take the tree T representing an arbitrary optimal prefix code and modify it to make a tree representing another optimal prefix code such that the characters x and y appear as sibling leaves of maximum depth in the new tree. If we can construct such a tree, then the codewords for x and y will have the same length and differ only in the last bit.

Let a and b be two characters that are sibling leaves of maximum depth in T. Without loss of generality, we assume that $a.freq \le b.freq$ and $x.freq \le y.freq$. Since $x.freq$ and $y.freq$ are the two lowest leaf frequencies, in order, and $a.freq$ and $b.freq$ are two arbitrary frequencies, in order, we have $x.freq \le a.freq$ and $y.freq \le b.freq$.

In the remainder of the proof, it is possible that we could have $x.freq = a.freq$ or $y.freq = b.freq$. However, if we had $x.freq = b.freq$, then we would also have $a.freq = b.freq = x.freq = y.freq$ (see Exercise 16.3-1), and the lemma would be trivially true. Thus, we will assume that $x.freq \ne b.freq$, which means that $x \ne b$.

As Figure 16.6 shows, we exchange the positions in T of a and x to produce a tree T', and then we exchange the positions in T' of b and y to produce a tree T''

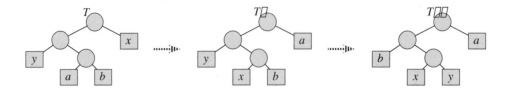

Figure 16.6 An illustration of the key step in the proof of Lemma 16.2. In the optimal tree T, leaves a and b are two siblings of maximum depth. Leaves x and y are the two characters with the lowest frequencies; they appear in arbitrary positions in T. Assuming that $x \neq b$, swapping leaves a and x produces tree T', and then swapping leaves b and y produces tree T''. Since each swap does not increase the cost, the resulting tree T'' is also an optimal tree.

in which x and y are sibling leaves of maximum depth. (Note that if $x = b$ but $y \neq a$, then tree T'' does not have x and y as sibling leaves of maximum depth. Because we assume that $x \neq b$, this situation cannot occur.) By equation (16.4), the difference in cost between T and T' is

$$
\begin{aligned}
B(T) - B(T') \\
&= \sum_{c \in C} c.freq \cdot d_T(c) - \sum_{c \in C} c.freq \cdot d_{T'}(c) \\
&= x.freq \cdot d_T(x) + a.freq \cdot d_T(a) - x.freq \cdot d_{T'}(x) - a.freq \cdot d_{T'}(a) \\
&= x.freq \cdot d_T(x) + a.freq \cdot d_T(a) - x.freq \cdot d_T(a) - a.freq \cdot d_T(x) \\
&= (a.freq - x.freq)(d_T(a) - d_T(x)) \\
&\geq 0 ,
\end{aligned}
$$

because both $a.freq - x.freq$ and $d_T(a) - d_T(x)$ are nonnegative. More specifically, $a.freq - x.freq$ is nonnegative because x is a minimum-frequency leaf, and $d_T(a) - d_T(x)$ is nonnegative because a is a leaf of maximum depth in T. Similarly, exchanging y and b does not increase the cost, and so $B(T') - B(T'')$ is nonnegative. Therefore, $B(T'') \leq B(T)$, and since T is optimal, we have $B(T) \leq B(T'')$, which implies $B(T'') = B(T)$. Thus, T'' is an optimal tree in which x and y appear as sibling leaves of maximum depth, from which the lemma follows. ∎

Lemma 16.2 implies that the process of building up an optimal tree by mergers can, without loss of generality, begin with the greedy choice of merging together those two characters of lowest frequency. Why is this a greedy choice? We can view the cost of a single merger as being the sum of the frequencies of the two items being merged. Exercise 16.3-4 shows that the total cost of the tree constructed equals the sum of the costs of its mergers. Of all possible mergers at each step, HUFFMAN chooses the one that incurs the least cost.

The next lemma shows that the problem of constructing optimal prefix codes has the optimal-substructure property.

Lemma 16.3
Let C be a given alphabet with frequency $c.freq$ defined for each character $c \in C$. Let x and y be two characters in C with minimum frequency. Let C' be the alphabet C with the characters x and y removed and a new character z added, so that $C' = C - \{x, y\} \cup \{z\}$. Define *freq* for C' as for C, except that $z.freq = x.freq + y.freq$. Let T' be any tree representing an optimal prefix code for the alphabet C'. Then the tree T, obtained from T' by replacing the leaf node for z with an internal node having x and y as children, represents an optimal prefix code for the alphabet C.

Proof   We first show how to express the cost $B(T)$ of tree T in terms of the cost $B(T')$ of tree T', by considering the component costs in equation (16.4). For each character $c \in C - \{x, y\}$, we have that $d_T(c) = d_{T'}(c)$, and hence $c.freq \cdot d_T(c) = c.freq \cdot d_{T'}(c)$. Since $d_T(x) = d_T(y) = d_{T'}(z) + 1$, we have

$$
\begin{aligned}
x.freq \cdot d_T(x) + y.freq \cdot d_T(y) &= (x.freq + y.freq)(d_{T'}(z) + 1) \\
&= z.freq \cdot d_{T'}(z) + (x.freq + y.freq) \, ,
\end{aligned}
$$

from which we conclude that

$$B(T) = B(T') + x.freq + y.freq$$

or, equivalently,

$$B(T') = B(T) - x.freq - y.freq \, .$$

We now prove the lemma by contradiction. Suppose that T does not represent an optimal prefix code for C. Then there exists an optimal tree T'' such that $B(T'') < B(T)$. Without loss of generality (by Lemma 16.2), T'' has x and y as siblings. Let T''' be the tree T'' with the common parent of x and y replaced by a leaf z with frequency $z.freq = x.freq + y.freq$. Then

$$
\begin{aligned}
B(T''') &= B(T'') - x.freq - y.freq \\
&< B(T) - x.freq - y.freq \\
&= B(T') \, ,
\end{aligned}
$$

yielding a contradiction to the assumption that T' represents an optimal prefix code for C'. Thus, T must represent an optimal prefix code for the alphabet C.   ∎

Theorem 16.4
Procedure HUFFMAN produces an optimal prefix code.

Proof   Immediate from Lemmas 16.2 and 16.3.   ∎

Exercises

16.3-1
Explain why, in the proof of Lemma 16.2, if $x.freq = b.freq$, then we must have $a.freq = b.freq = x.freq = y.freq$.

16.3-2
Prove that a binary tree that is not full cannot correspond to an optimal prefix code.

16.3-3
What is an optimal Huffman code for the following set of frequencies, based on the first 8 Fibonacci numbers?

a:1 b:1 c:2 d:3 e:5 f:8 g:13 h:21

Can you generalize your answer to find the optimal code when the frequencies are the first n Fibonacci numbers?

16.3-4
Prove that we can also express the total cost of a tree for a code as the sum, over all internal nodes, of the combined frequencies of the two children of the node.

16.3-5
Prove that if we order the characters in an alphabet so that their frequencies are monotonically decreasing, then there exists an optimal code whose codeword lengths are monotonically increasing.

16.3-6
Suppose we have an optimal prefix code on a set $C = \{0, 1, \ldots, n-1\}$ of characters and we wish to transmit this code using as few bits as possible. Show how to represent any optimal prefix code on C using only $2n - 1 + n \lceil \lg n \rceil$ bits. (*Hint:* Use $2n - 1$ bits to specify the structure of the tree, as discovered by a walk of the tree.)

16.3-7
Generalize Huffman's algorithm to ternary codewords (i.e., codewords using the symbols 0, 1, and 2), and prove that it yields optimal ternary codes.

16.3-8
Suppose that a data file contains a sequence of 8-bit characters such that all 256 characters are about equally common: the maximum character frequency is less than twice the minimum character frequency. Prove that Huffman coding in this case is no more efficient than using an ordinary 8-bit fixed-length code.

16.3-9
Show that no compression scheme can expect to compress a file of randomly chosen 8-bit characters by even a single bit. (*Hint:* Compare the number of possible files with the number of possible encoded files.)

★ 16.4   Matroids and greedy methods

In this section, we sketch a beautiful theory about greedy algorithms. This theory describes many situations in which the greedy method yields optimal solutions. It involves combinatorial structures known as "matroids." Although this theory does not cover all cases for which a greedy method applies (for example, it does not cover the activity-selection problem of Section 16.1 or the Huffman-coding problem of Section 16.3), it does cover many cases of practical interest. Furthermore, this theory has been extended to cover many applications; see the notes at the end of this chapter for references.

Matroids

A *matroid* is an ordered pair $M = (S, I)$ satisfying the following conditions.

1. S is a finite set.

2. I is a nonempty family of subsets of S, called the *independent* subsets of S, such that if $B \in I$ and $A \subseteq B$, then $A \in I$. We say that I is *hereditary* if it satisfies this property. Note that the empty set $\emptyset$ is necessarily a member of I.

3. If $A \in I$, $B \in I$, and $|A| < |B|$, then there exists some element $x \in B - A$ such that $A \cup \{x\} \in I$. We say that M satisfies the *exchange property*.

The word "matroid" is due to Hassler Whitney. He was studying *matric matroids*, in which the elements of S are the rows of a given matrix and a set of rows is independent if they are linearly independent in the usual sense. As Exercise 16.4-2 asks you to show, this structure defines a matroid.

As another example of matroids, consider the *graphic matroid* $M_G = (S_G, I_G)$ defined in terms of a given undirected graph $G = (V, E)$ as follows:

- The set S_G is defined to be E, the set of edges of G.

- If A is a subset of E, then $A \in I_G$ if and only if A is acyclic. That is, a set of edges A is independent if and only if the subgraph $G_A = (V, A)$ forms a forest.

The graphic matroid M_G is closely related to the minimum-spanning-tree problem, which Chapter 23 covers in detail.

Theorem 16.5

If $G = (V, E)$ is an undirected graph, then $M_G = (S_G, \mathcal{I}_G)$ is a matroid.

Proof   Clearly, $S_G = E$ is a finite set. Furthermore, $\mathcal{I}_G$ is hereditary, since a subset of a forest is a forest. Putting it another way, removing edges from an acyclic set of edges cannot create cycles.

Thus, it remains to show that M_G satisfies the exchange property. Suppose that $G_A = (V, A)$ and $G_B = (V, B)$ are forests of G and that $|B| > |A|$. That is, A and B are acyclic sets of edges, and B contains more edges than A does.

We claim that a forest $F = (V_F, E_F)$ contains exactly $|V_F| - |E_F|$ trees. To see why, suppose that F consists of t trees, where the ith tree contains v_i vertices and e_i edges. Then, we have

$$
\begin{aligned}
|E_F| &= \sum_{i=1}^{t} e_i \\
&= \sum_{i=1}^{t} (v_i - 1) \quad \text{(by Theorem B.2)} \\
&= \sum_{i=1}^{t} v_i - t \\
&= |V_F| - t \, ,
\end{aligned}
$$

which implies that $t = |V_F| - |E_F|$. Thus, forest G_A contains $|V| - |A|$ trees, and forest G_B contains $|V| - |B|$ trees.

Since forest G_B has fewer trees than forest G_A does, forest G_B must contain some tree T whose vertices are in two different trees in forest G_A. Moreover, since T is connected, it must contain an edge (u, v) such that vertices u and v are in different trees in forest G_A. Since the edge (u, v) connects vertices in two different trees in forest G_A, we can add the edge (u, v) to forest G_A without creating a cycle. Therefore, M_G satisfies the exchange property, completing the proof that M_G is a matroid.   ∎

Given a matroid $M = (S, \mathcal{I})$, we call an element $x \notin A$ an ***extension*** of $A \in \mathcal{I}$ if we can add x to A while preserving independence; that is, x is an extension of A if $A \cup \{x\} \in \mathcal{I}$. As an example, consider a graphic matroid M_G. If A is an independent set of edges, then edge e is an extension of A if and only if e is not in A and the addition of e to A does not create a cycle.

If A is an independent subset in a matroid M, we say that A is ***maximal*** if it has no extensions. That is, A is maximal if it is not contained in any larger independent subset of M. The following property is often useful.

Theorem 16.6
All maximal independent subsets in a matroid have the same size.

Proof Suppose to the contrary that A is a maximal independent subset of M and there exists another larger maximal independent subset B of M. Then, the exchange property implies that for some $x \in B - A$, we can extend A to a larger independent set $A \cup \{x\}$, contradicting the assumption that A is maximal. ∎

As an illustration of this theorem, consider a graphic matroid M_G for a connected, undirected graph G. Every maximal independent subset of M_G must be a free tree with exactly $|V| - 1$ edges that connects all the vertices of G. Such a tree is called a ***spanning tree*** of G.

We say that a matroid $M = (S, \mathcal{I})$ is ***weighted*** if it is associated with a weight function w that assigns a strictly positive weight $w(x)$ to each element $x \in S$. The weight function w extends to subsets of S by summation:

$$w(A) = \sum_{x \in A} w(x)$$

for any $A \subseteq S$. For example, if we let $w(e)$ denote the weight of an edge e in a graphic matroid M_G, then $w(A)$ is the total weight of the edges in edge set A.

Greedy algorithms on a weighted matroid

Many problems for which a greedy approach provides optimal solutions can be formulated in terms of finding a maximum-weight independent subset in a weighted matroid. That is, we are given a weighted matroid $M = (S, \mathcal{I})$, and we wish to find an independent set $A \in \mathcal{I}$ such that $w(A)$ is maximized. We call such a subset that is independent and has maximum possible weight an ***optimal*** subset of the matroid. Because the weight $w(x)$ of any element $x \in S$ is positive, an optimal subset is always a maximal independent subset—it always helps to make A as large as possible.

For example, in the ***minimum-spanning-tree problem***, we are given a connected undirected graph $G = (V, E)$ and a length function w such that $w(e)$ is the (positive) length of edge e. (We use the term "length" here to refer to the original edge weights for the graph, reserving the term "weight" to refer to the weights in the associated matroid.) We wish to find a subset of the edges that connects all of the vertices together and has minimum total length. To view this as a problem of finding an optimal subset of a matroid, consider the weighted matroid M_G with weight function w', where $w'(e) = w_0 - w(e)$ and w_0 is larger than the maximum length of any edge. In this weighted matroid, all weights are positive and an optimal subset is a spanning tree of minimum total length in the original graph. More specifically, each maximal independent subset A corresponds to a spanning tree with $|V| - 1$ edges, and since

$$
\begin{aligned}
w'(A) &= \sum_{e \in A} w'(e) \\
&= \sum_{e \in A} (w_0 - w(e)) \\
&= (|V| - 1)w_0 - \sum_{e \in A} w(e) \\
&= (|V| - 1)w_0 - w(A)
\end{aligned}
$$

for any maximal independent subset A, an independent subset that maximizes the quantity $w'(A)$ must minimize $w(A)$. Thus, any algorithm that can find an optimal subset A in an arbitrary matroid can solve the minimum-spanning-tree problem.

Chapter 23 gives algorithms for the minimum-spanning-tree problem, but here we give a greedy algorithm that works for any weighted matroid. The algorithm takes as input a weighted matroid $M = (S, I)$ with an associated positive weight function w, and it returns an optimal subset A. In our pseudocode, we denote the components of M by $M.S$ and $M.I$ and the weight function by w. The algorithm is greedy because it considers in turn each element $x \in S$, in order of monotonically decreasing weight, and immediately adds it to the set A being accumulated if $A \cup \{x\}$ is independent.

GREEDY(M, w)

```
1   A = ∅
2   sort M.S into monotonically decreasing order by weight w
3   for each x ∈ M.S, taken in monotonically decreasing order by weight w(x)
4       if A ∪ {x} ∈ M.I
5           A = A ∪ {x}
6   return A
```

Line 4 checks whether adding each element x to A would maintain A as an independent set. If A would remain independent, then line 5 adds x to A. Otherwise, x is discarded. Since the empty set is independent, and since each iteration of the **for** loop maintains A's independence, the subset A is always independent, by induction. Therefore, GREEDY always returns an independent subset A. We shall see in a moment that A is a subset of maximum possible weight, so that A is an optimal subset.

The running time of GREEDY is easy to analyze. Let n denote $|S|$. The sorting phase of GREEDY takes time $O(n \lg n)$. Line 4 executes exactly n times, once for each element of S. Each execution of line 4 requires a check on whether or not the set $A \cup \{x\}$ is independent. If each such check takes time $O(f(n))$, the entire algorithm runs in time $O(n \lg n + n f(n))$.

We now prove that GREEDY returns an optimal subset.

Lemma 16.7 (Matroids exhibit the greedy-choice property)

Suppose that $M = (S, I)$ is a weighted matroid with weight function w and that S is sorted into monotonically decreasing order by weight. Let x be the first element of S such that $\{x\}$ is independent, if any such x exists. If x exists, then there exists an optimal subset A of S that contains x.

Proof If no such x exists, then the only independent subset is the empty set and the lemma is vacuously true. Otherwise, let B be any nonempty optimal subset. Assume that $x \notin B$; otherwise, letting $A = B$ gives an optimal subset of S that contains x.

No element of B has weight greater than $w(x)$. To see why, observe that $y \in B$ implies that $\{y\}$ is independent, since $B \in I$ and I is hereditary. Our choice of x therefore ensures that $w(x) \geq w(y)$ for any $y \in B$.

Construct the set A as follows. Begin with $A = \{x\}$. By the choice of x, set A is independent. Using the exchange property, repeatedly find a new element of B that we can add to A until $|A| = |B|$, while preserving the independence of A. At that point, A and B are the same except that A has x and B has some other element y. That is, $A = B - \{y\} \cup \{x\}$ for some $y \in B$, and so

$$
\begin{aligned}
w(A) &= w(B) - w(y) + w(x) \\
&\geq w(B) .
\end{aligned}
$$

Because set B is optimal, set A, which contains x, must also be optimal. ∎

We next show that if an element is not an option initially, then it cannot be an option later.

Lemma 16.8

Let $M = (S, I)$ be any matroid. If x is an element of S that is an extension of some independent subset A of S, then x is also an extension of $\emptyset$.

Proof Since x is an extension of A, we have that $A \cup \{x\}$ is independent. Since I is hereditary, $\{x\}$ must be independent. Thus, x is an extension of $\emptyset$. ∎

Corollary 16.9

Let $M = (S, I)$ be any matroid. If x is an element of S such that x is not an extension of $\emptyset$, then x is not an extension of any independent subset A of S.

Proof This corollary is simply the contrapositive of Lemma 16.8. ∎

Corollary 16.9 says that any element that cannot be used immediately can never be used. Therefore, GREEDY cannot make an error by passing over any initial elements in S that are not an extension of $\emptyset$, since they can never be used.

Lemma 16.10 (Matroids exhibit the optimal-substructure property)

Let x be the first element of S chosen by GREEDY for the weighted matroid $M = (S, \mathcal{I})$. The remaining problem of finding a maximum-weight independent subset containing x reduces to finding a maximum-weight independent subset of the weighted matroid $M' = (S', \mathcal{I}')$, where

$$
\begin{aligned}
S' &= \{y \in S : \{x, y\} \in \mathcal{I}\} \, , \\
\mathcal{I}' &= \{B \subseteq S - \{x\} : B \cup \{x\} \in \mathcal{I}\} \, ,
\end{aligned}
$$

and the weight function for M' is the weight function for M, restricted to S'. (We call M' the **contraction** of M by the element x.)

Proof If A is any maximum-weight independent subset of M containing x, then $A' = A - \{x\}$ is an independent subset of M'. Conversely, any independent subset A' of M' yields an independent subset $A = A' \cup \{x\}$ of M. Since we have in both cases that $w(A) = w(A') + w(x)$, a maximum-weight solution in M containing x yields a maximum-weight solution in M', and vice versa. ∎

Theorem 16.11 (Correctness of the greedy algorithm on matroids)

If $M = (S, \mathcal{I})$ is a weighted matroid with weight function w, then GREEDY(M, w) returns an optimal subset.

Proof By Corollary 16.9, any elements that GREEDY passes over initially because they are not extensions of $\emptyset$ can be forgotten about, since they can never be useful. Once GREEDY selects the first element x, Lemma 16.7 implies that the algorithm does not err by adding x to A, since there exists an optimal subset containing x. Finally, Lemma 16.10 implies that the remaining problem is one of finding an optimal subset in the matroid M' that is the contraction of M by x. After the procedure GREEDY sets A to $\{x\}$, we can interpret all of its remaining steps as acting in the matroid $M' = (S', \mathcal{I}')$, because B is independent in M' if and only if $B \cup \{x\}$ is independent in M, for all sets $B \in \mathcal{I}'$. Thus, the subsequent operation of GREEDY will find a maximum-weight independent subset for M', and the overall operation of GREEDY will find a maximum-weight independent subset for M. ∎

Exercises

16.4-1
Show that $(S, \mathcal{I}_k)$ is a matroid, where S is any finite set and $\mathcal{I}_k$ is the set of all subsets of S of size at most k, where $k \leq |S|$.

16.4-2   ★
Given an $m \times n$ matrix T over some field (such as the reals), show that $(S, \mathcal{I})$ is a matroid, where S is the set of columns of T and $A \in \mathcal{I}$ if and only if the columns in A are linearly independent.

16.4-3   ★
Show that if $(S, \mathcal{I})$ is a matroid, then $(S, \mathcal{I}')$ is a matroid, where

$$\mathcal{I}' = \{A' : S - A' \text{ contains some maximal } A \in \mathcal{I}\} \ .$$

That is, the maximal independent sets of $(S, \mathcal{I}')$ are just the complements of the maximal independent sets of $(S, \mathcal{I})$.

16.4-4   ★
Let S be a finite set and let $S_1, S_2, \ldots, S_k$ be a partition of S into nonempty disjoint subsets. Define the structure $(S, \mathcal{I})$ by the condition that $\mathcal{I} = \{A : |A \cap S_i| \leq 1$ for $i = 1, 2, \ldots, k\}$. Show that $(S, \mathcal{I})$ is a matroid. That is, the set of all sets A that contain at most one member of each subset in the partition determines the independent sets of a matroid.

16.4-5
Show how to transform the weight function of a weighted matroid problem, where the desired optimal solution is a *minimum-weight* maximal independent subset, to make it a standard weighted-matroid problem. Argue carefully that your transformation is correct.

★   16.5   A task-scheduling problem as a matroid

An interesting problem that we can solve using matroids is the problem of optimally scheduling unit-time tasks on a single processor, where each task has a deadline, along with a penalty paid if the task misses its deadline. The problem looks complicated, but we can solve it in a surprisingly simple manner by casting it as a matroid and using a greedy algorithm.

A ***unit-time task*** is a job, such as a program to be run on a computer, that requires exactly one unit of time to complete. Given a finite set S of unit-time tasks, a *schedule* for S is a permutation of S specifying the order in which to perform these tasks. The first task in the schedule begins at time 0 and finishes at time 1, the second task begins at time 1 and finishes at time 2, and so on.

The problem of ***scheduling unit-time tasks with deadlines and penalties for a single processor*** has the following inputs:

- a set $S = \{a_1, a_2, \ldots, a_n\}$ of n unit-time tasks;

- a set of n integer ***deadlines*** $d_1, d_2, \ldots, d_n$, such that each d_i satisfies $1 \le d_i \le n$ and task a_i is supposed to finish by time d_i; and

- a set of n nonnegative weights or ***penalties*** $w_1, w_2, \ldots, w_n$, such that we incur a penalty of w_i if task a_i is not finished by time d_i, and we incur no penalty if a task finishes by its deadline.

We wish to find a schedule for S that minimizes the total penalty incurred for missed deadlines.

Consider a given schedule. We say that a task is ***late*** in this schedule if it finishes after its deadline. Otherwise, the task is ***early*** in the schedule. We can always transform an arbitrary schedule into ***early-first form***, in which the early tasks precede the late tasks. To see why, note that if some early task a_i follows some late task a_j, then we can switch the positions of a_i and a_j, and a_i will still be early and a_j will still be late.

Furthermore, we claim that we can always transform an arbitrary schedule into ***canonical form***, in which the early tasks precede the late tasks and we schedule the early tasks in order of monotonically increasing deadlines. To do so, we put the schedule into early-first form. Then, as long as there exist two early tasks a_i and a_j finishing at respective times k and $k+1$ in the schedule such that $d_j < d_i$, we swap the positions of a_i and a_j. Since a_j is early before the swap, $k+1 \le d_j$. Therefore, $k+1 < d_i$, and so a_i is still early after the swap. Because task a_j is moved earlier in the schedule, it remains early after the swap.

The search for an optimal schedule thus reduces to finding a set A of tasks that we assign to be early in the optimal schedule. Having determined A, we can create the actual schedule by listing the elements of A in order of monotonically increasing deadlines, then listing the late tasks (i.e., $S - A$) in any order, producing a canonical ordering of the optimal schedule.

We say that a set A of tasks is ***independent*** if there exists a schedule for these tasks such that no tasks are late. Clearly, the set of early tasks for a schedule forms an independent set of tasks. Let $\mathcal{I}$ denote the set of all independent sets of tasks.

Consider the problem of determining whether a given set A of tasks is independent. For $t = 0, 1, 2, \ldots, n$, let $N_t(A)$ denote the number of tasks in A whose deadline is t or earlier. Note that $N_0(A) = 0$ for any set A.

Lemma 16.12
For any set of tasks A, the following statements are equivalent.

1. The set A is independent.

2. For $t = 0, 1, 2, \ldots, n$, we have $N_t(A) \leq t$.

3. If the tasks in A are scheduled in order of monotonically increasing deadlines, then no task is late.

Proof To show that (1) implies (2), we prove the contrapositive: if $N_t(A) > t$ for some t, then there is no way to make a schedule with no late tasks for set A, because more than t tasks must finish before time t. Therefore, (1) implies (2). If (2) holds, then (3) must follow: there is no way to "get stuck" when scheduling the tasks in order of monotonically increasing deadlines, since (2) implies that the ith largest deadline is at least i. Finally, (3) trivially implies (1). ∎

Using property 2 of Lemma 16.12, we can easily compute whether or not a given set of tasks is independent (see Exercise 16.5-2).

The problem of minimizing the sum of the penalties of the late tasks is the same as the problem of maximizing the sum of the penalties of the early tasks. The following theorem thus ensures that we can use the greedy algorithm to find an independent set A of tasks with the maximum total penalty.

Theorem 16.13
If S is a set of unit-time tasks with deadlines, and $\mathcal{I}$ is the set of all independent sets of tasks, then the corresponding system $(S, \mathcal{I})$ is a matroid.

Proof Every subset of an independent set of tasks is certainly independent. To prove the exchange property, suppose that B and A are independent sets of tasks and that $|B| > |A|$. Let k be the largest t such that $N_t(B) \leq N_t(A)$. (Such a value of t exists, since $N_0(A) = N_0(B) = 0$.) Since $N_n(B) = |B|$ and $N_n(A) = |A|$, but $|B| > |A|$, we must have that $k < n$ and that $N_j(B) > N_j(A)$ for all j in the range $k + 1 \leq j \leq n$. Therefore, B contains more tasks with deadline $k + 1$ than A does. Let a_i be a task in $B - A$ with deadline $k + 1$. Let $A' = A \cup \{a_i\}$.

We now show that A' must be independent by using property 2 of Lemma 16.12. For $0 \leq t \leq k$, we have $N_t(A') = N_t(A) \leq t$, since A is independent. For $k < t \leq n$, we have $N_t(A') \leq N_t(B) \leq t$, since B is independent. Therefore, A' is independent, completing our proof that $(S, \mathcal{I})$ is a matroid. ∎

By Theorem 16.11, we can use a greedy algorithm to find a maximum-weight independent set of tasks A. We can then create an optimal schedule having the tasks in A as its early tasks. This method is an efficient algorithm for scheduling

				Task			
a_i	1	2	3	4	5	6	7
d_i	4	2	4	3	1	4	6
w_i	70	60	50	40	30	20	10

Figure 16.7 An instance of the problem of scheduling unit-time tasks with deadlines and penalties for a single processor.

unit-time tasks with deadlines and penalties for a single processor. The running time is $O(n^2)$ using GREEDY, since each of the $O(n)$ independence checks made by that algorithm takes time $O(n)$ (see Exercise 16.5-2). Problem 16-4 gives a faster implementation.

Figure 16.7 demonstrates an example of the problem of scheduling unit-time tasks with deadlines and penalties for a single processor. In this example, the greedy algorithm selects, in order, tasks a_1, a_2, a_3, and a_4, then rejects a_5 (because $N_4(\{a_1, a_2, a_3, a_4, a_5\}) = 5$) and a_6 (because $N_4(\{a_1, a_2, a_3, a_4, a_6\}) = 5$), and finally accepts a_7. The final optimal schedule is

$$\langle a_2, a_4, a_1, a_3, a_7, a_5, a_6 \rangle ,$$

which has a total penalty incurred of $w_5 + w_6 = 50$.

Exercises

16.5-1
Solve the instance of the scheduling problem given in Figure 16.7, but with each penalty w_i replaced by $80 - w_i$.

16.5-2
Show how to use property 2 of Lemma 16.12 to determine in time $O(|A|)$ whether or not a given set A of tasks is independent.

Problems

16-1   Coin changing
Consider the problem of making change for n cents using the fewest number of coins. Assume that each coin's value is an integer.

a. Describe a greedy algorithm to make change consisting of quarters, dimes, nickels, and pennies. Prove that your algorithm yields an optimal solution.

b. Suppose that the available coins are in the denominations that are powers of c, i.e., the denominations are $c^0, c^1, \ldots, c^k$ for some integers $c > 1$ and $k \geq 1$. Show that the greedy algorithm always yields an optimal solution.

c. Give a set of coin denominations for which the greedy algorithm does not yield an optimal solution. Your set should include a penny so that there is a solution for every value of n.

d. Give an $O(nk)$-time algorithm that makes change for any set of k different coin denominations, assuming that one of the coins is a penny.

16-2 *Scheduling to minimize average completion time*

Suppose you are given a set $S = \{a_1, a_2, \ldots, a_n\}$ of tasks, where task a_i requires p_i units of processing time to complete, once it has started. You have one computer on which to run these tasks, and the computer can run only one task at a time. Let c_i be the ***completion time*** of task a_i, that is, the time at which task a_i completes processing. Your goal is to minimize the average completion time, that is, to minimize $(1/n) \sum_{i=1}^{n} c_i$. For example, suppose there are two tasks, a_1 and a_2, with $p_1 = 3$ and $p_2 = 5$, and consider the schedule in which a_2 runs first, followed by a_1. Then $c_2 = 5$, $c_1 = 8$, and the average completion time is $(5 + 8)/2 = 6.5$. If task a_1 runs first, however, then $c_1 = 3$, $c_2 = 8$, and the average completion time is $(3 + 8)/2 = 5.5$.

a. Give an algorithm that schedules the tasks so as to minimize the average completion time. Each task must run non-preemptively, that is, once task a_i starts, it must run continuously for p_i units of time. Prove that your algorithm minimizes the average completion time, and state the running time of your algorithm.

b. Suppose now that the tasks are not all available at once. That is, each task cannot start until its ***release time*** r_i. Suppose also that we allow ***preemption***, so that a task can be suspended and restarted at a later time. For example, a task a_i with processing time $p_i = 6$ and release time $r_i = 1$ might start running at time 1 and be preempted at time 4. It might then resume at time 10 but be preempted at time 11, and it might finally resume at time 13 and complete at time 15. Task a_i has run for a total of 6 time units, but its running time has been divided into three pieces. In this scenario, a_i's completion time is 15. Give an algorithm that schedules the tasks so as to minimize the average completion time in this new scenario. Prove that your algorithm minimizes the average completion time, and state the running time of your algorithm.

16-3 *Acyclic subgraphs*

a. The *incidence matrix* for an undirected graph $G = (V, E)$ is a $|V| \times |E|$ matrix M such that $M_{ve} = 1$ if edge e is incident on vertex v, and $M_{ve} = 0$ otherwise. Argue that a set of columns of M is linearly independent over the field of integers modulo 2 if and only if the corresponding set of edges is acyclic.

b. Suppose that we associate a nonnegative weight $w(e)$ with each edge in an undirected graph $G = (V, E)$. Give an efficient algorithm to find an acyclic subset of E of maximum total weight.

c. Let $G(V, E)$ be an arbitrary directed graph, and let $(E, \mathcal{I})$ be defined so that $A \in \mathcal{I}$ if and only if A does not contain any directed cycles. Give an example of a directed graph G such that the associated system $(E, \mathcal{I})$ is not a matroid. Specify which defining condition for a matroid fails to hold.

d. The *incidence matrix* for a directed graph $G = (V, E)$ with no self-loops is a $|V| \times |E|$ matrix M such that $M_{ve} = -1$ if edge e leaves vertex v, $M_{ve} = 1$ if edge e enters vertex v, and $M_{ve} = 0$ otherwise. Argue that if a set of columns of M is linearly independent, then the corresponding set of edges does not contain a directed cycle.

e. Exercise 16.4-2 tells us that the set of linearly independent sets of columns of any matrix M forms a matroid. Explain carefully why the results of parts (c) and (d) are not contradictory. How can there fail to be a perfect correspondence between the notion of a set of edges being acyclic and the notion of the associated set of columns of the incidence matrix being linearly independent?

16-4 *Scheduling variations*

Consider the following algorithm for the problem from Section 16.5 of scheduling unit-time tasks with deadlines and penalties. Let all n time slots be initially empty, where time slot i is the unit-length slot of time that finishes at time i. We consider the tasks in order of monotonically decreasing penalty. When considering task a_j, if there exists a time slot at or before a_j's deadline d_j that is still empty, assign a_j to the latest such slot, filling it. If there is no such slot, assign task a_j to the latest of the as yet unfilled slots.

a. Argue that this algorithm always gives an optimal answer.

b. Use the fast disjoint-set forest presented in Section 21.3 to implement the algorithm efficiently. Assume that the set of input tasks has already been sorted into monotonically decreasing order by penalty. Analyze the running time of your implementation.

16-5   Off-line caching

Modern computers use a cache to store a small amount of data in a fast memory. Even though a program may access large amounts of data, by storing a small subset of the main memory in the *cache*—a small but faster memory—overall access time can greatly decrease. When a computer program executes, it makes a sequence $\langle r_1, r_2, \ldots, r_n \rangle$ of n memory requests, where each request is for a particular data element. For example, a program that accesses 4 distinct elements $\{a, b, c, d\}$ might make the sequence of requests $\langle d, b, d, b, d, a, c, d, b, a, c, b \rangle$. Let k be the size of the cache. When the cache contains k elements and the program requests the $(k + 1)$st element, the system must decide, for this and each subsequent request, which k elements to keep in the cache. More precisely, for each request r_i, the cache-management algorithm checks whether element r_i is already in the cache. If it is, then we have a *cache hit*; otherwise, we have a *cache miss*. Upon a cache miss, the system retrieves r_i from the main memory, and the cache-management algorithm must decide whether to keep r_i in the cache. If it decides to keep r_i and the cache already holds k elements, then it must evict one element to make room for r_i. The cache-management algorithm evicts data with the goal of minimizing the number of cache misses over the entire sequence of requests.

Typically, caching is an on-line problem. That is, we have to make decisions about which data to keep in the cache without knowing the future requests. Here, however, we consider the off-line version of this problem, in which we are given in advance the entire sequence of n requests and the cache size k, and we wish to minimize the total number of cache misses.

We can solve this off-line problem by a greedy strategy called *furthest-in-future*, which chooses to evict the item in the cache whose next access in the request sequence comes furthest in the future.

a. Write pseudocode for a cache manager that uses the furthest-in-future strategy. The input should be a sequence $\langle r_1, r_2, \ldots, r_n \rangle$ of requests and a cache size k, and the output should be a sequence of decisions about which data element (if any) to evict upon each request. What is the running time of your algorithm?

b. Show that the off-line caching problem exhibits optimal substructure.

c. Prove that furthest-in-future produces the minimum possible number of cache misses.

Chapter notes

Much more material on greedy algorithms and matroids can be found in Lawler [224] and Papadimitriou and Steiglitz [271].

The greedy algorithm first appeared in the combinatorial optimization literature in a 1971 article by Edmonds [101], though the theory of matroids dates back to a 1935 article by Whitney [355].

Our proof of the correctness of the greedy algorithm for the activity-selection problem is based on that of Gavril [131]. The task-scheduling problem is studied in Lawler [224]; Horowitz, Sahni, and Rajasekaran [181]; and Brassard and Bratley [54].

Huffman codes were invented in 1952 [185]; Lelewer and Hirschberg [231] surveys data-compression techniques known as of 1987.

An extension of matroid theory to greedoid theory was pioneered by Korte and Lovász [216, 217, 218, 219], who greatly generalize the theory presented here.

17   Amortized Analysis

In an **amortized analysis**, we average the time required to perform a sequence of data-structure operations over all the operations performed. With amortized analysis, we can show that the average cost of an operation is small, if we average over a sequence of operations, even though a single operation within the sequence might be expensive. Amortized analysis differs from average-case analysis in that probability is not involved; an amortized analysis guarantees the *average performance of each operation in the worst case*.

The first three sections of this chapter cover the three most common techniques used in amortized analysis. Section 17.1 starts with aggregate analysis, in which we determine an upper bound $T(n)$ on the total cost of a sequence of n operations. The average cost per operation is then $T(n)/n$. We take the average cost as the amortized cost of each operation, so that all operations have the same amortized cost.

Section 17.2 covers the accounting method, in which we determine an amortized cost of each operation. When there is more than one type of operation, each type of operation may have a different amortized cost. The accounting method overcharges some operations early in the sequence, storing the overcharge as "prepaid credit" on specific objects in the data structure. Later in the sequence, the credit pays for operations that are charged less than they actually cost.

Section 17.3 discusses the potential method, which is like the accounting method in that we determine the amortized cost of each operation and may overcharge operations early on to compensate for undercharges later. The potential method maintains the credit as the "potential energy" of the data structure as a whole instead of associating the credit with individual objects within the data structure.

We shall use two examples to examine these three methods. One is a stack with the additional operation MULTIPOP, which pops several objects at once. The other is a binary counter that counts up from 0 by means of the single operation INCREMENT.

While reading this chapter, bear in mind that the charges assigned during an amortized analysis are for analysis purposes only. They need not—and should not—appear in the code. If, for example, we assign a credit to an object x when using the accounting method, we have no need to assign an appropriate amount to some attribute, such as $x.credit$, in the code.

When we perform an amortized analysis, we often gain insight into a particular data structure, and this insight can help us optimize the design. In Section 17.4, for example, we shall use the potential method to analyze a dynamically expanding and contracting table.

17.1   Aggregate analysis

In **aggregate analysis**, we show that for all n, a sequence of n operations takes *worst-case* time $T(n)$ in total. In the worst case, the average cost, or **amortized cost**, per operation is therefore $T(n)/n$. Note that this amortized cost applies to each operation, even when there are several types of operations in the sequence. The other two methods we shall study in this chapter, the accounting method and the potential method, may assign different amortized costs to different types of operations.

Stack operations

In our first example of aggregate analysis, we analyze stacks that have been augmented with a new operation. Section 10.1 presented the two fundamental stack operations, each of which takes $O(1)$ time:

PUSH(S, x) pushes object x onto stack S.

POP(S) pops the top of stack S and returns the popped object. Calling POP on an empty stack generates an error.

Since each of these operations runs in $O(1)$ time, let us consider the cost of each to be 1. The total cost of a sequence of n PUSH and POP operations is therefore n, and the actual running time for n operations is therefore $\Theta(n)$.

Now we add the stack operation MULTIPOP(S, k), which removes the k top objects of stack S, popping the entire stack if the stack contains fewer than k objects. Of course, we assume that k is positive; otherwise the MULTIPOP operation leaves the stack unchanged. In the following pseudocode, the operation STACK-EMPTY returns TRUE if there are no objects currently on the stack, and FALSE otherwise.

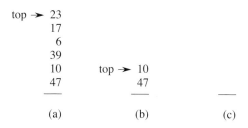

Figure 17.1   The action of MULTIPOP on a stack S, shown initially in **(a)**. The top 4 objects are popped by MULTIPOP$(S, 4)$, whose result is shown in **(b)**. The next operation is MULTIPOP$(S, 7)$, which empties the stack—shown in **(c)**—since there were fewer than 7 objects remaining.

MULTIPOP(S, k)

1   **while** not STACK-EMPTY(S) and $k > 0$
2   POP(S)
3       $k = k - 1$

Figure 17.1 shows an example of MULTIPOP.

What is the running time of MULTIPOP(S, k) on a stack of s objects? The actual running time is linear in the number of POP operations actually executed, and thus we can analyze MULTIPOP in terms of the abstract costs of 1 each for PUSH and POP. The number of iterations of the **while** loop is the number $\min(s, k)$ of objects popped off the stack. Each iteration of the loop makes one call to POP in line 2. Thus, the total cost of MULTIPOP is $\min(s, k)$, and the actual running time is a linear function of this cost.

Let us analyze a sequence of n PUSH, POP, and MULTIPOP operations on an initially empty stack. The worst-case cost of a MULTIPOP operation in the sequence is $O(n)$, since the stack size is at most n. The worst-case time of any stack operation is therefore $O(n)$, and hence a sequence of n operations costs $O(n^2)$, since we may have $O(n)$ MULTIPOP operations costing $O(n)$ each. Although this analysis is correct, the $O(n^2)$ result, which we obtained by considering the worst-case cost of each operation individually, is not tight.

Using aggregate analysis, we can obtain a better upper bound that considers the entire sequence of n operations. In fact, although a single MULTIPOP operation can be expensive, any sequence of n PUSH, POP, and MULTIPOP operations on an initially empty stack can cost at most $O(n)$. Why? We can pop each object from the stack at most once for each time we have pushed it onto the stack. Therefore, the number of times that POP can be called on a nonempty stack, including calls within MULTIPOP, is at most the number of PUSH operations, which is at most n. For any value of n, any sequence of n PUSH, POP, and MULTIPOP operations takes a total of $O(n)$ time. The average cost of an operation is $O(n)/n = O(1)$. In aggregate analysis, we assign the amortized cost of each operation to be the average cost. In this example, therefore, all three stack operations have an amortized cost of $O(1)$.

We emphasize again that although we have just shown that the average cost, and hence the running time, of a stack operation is $O(1)$, we did not use probabilistic reasoning. We actually showed a *worst-case* bound of $O(n)$ on a sequence of n operations. Dividing this total cost by n yielded the average cost per operation, or the amortized cost.

Incrementing a binary counter

As another example of aggregate analysis, consider the problem of implementing a k-bit binary counter that counts upward from 0. We use an array $A[0 \mathinner{.\,.} k-1]$ of bits, where $A.length = k$, as the counter. A binary number x that is stored in the counter has its lowest-order bit in $A[0]$ and its highest-order bit in $A[k-1]$, so that $x = \sum_{i=0}^{k-1} A[i] \cdot 2^i$. Initially, $x = 0$, and thus $A[i] = 0$ for $i = 0, 1, \ldots, k-1$. To add 1 (modulo 2^k) to the value in the counter, we use the following procedure.

INCREMENT(A)

```
1   i = 0
2   while i < A.length and A[i] == 1
3       A[i] = 0
4       i = i + 1
5   if i < A.length
6       A[i] = 1
```

Figure 17.2 shows what happens to a binary counter as we increment it 16 times, starting with the initial value 0 and ending with the value 16. At the start of each iteration of the **while** loop in lines 2–4, we wish to add a 1 into position i. If $A[i] = 1$, then adding 1 flips the bit to 0 in position i and yields a carry of 1, to be added into position $i + 1$ on the next iteration of the loop. Otherwise, the loop ends, and then, if $i < k$, we know that $A[i] = 0$, so that line 6 adds a 1 into position i, flipping the 0 to a 1. The cost of each INCREMENT operation is linear in the number of bits flipped.

As with the stack example, a cursory analysis yields a bound that is correct but not tight. A single execution of INCREMENT takes time $\Theta(k)$ in the worst case, in which array A contains all 1s. Thus, a sequence of n INCREMENT operations on an initially zero counter takes time $O(nk)$ in the worst case.

We can tighten our analysis to yield a worst-case cost of $O(n)$ for a sequence of n INCREMENT operations by observing that not all bits flip each time INCREMENT is called. As Figure 17.2 shows, $A[0]$ does flip each time INCREMENT is called. The next bit up, $A[1]$, flips only every other time: a sequence of n INCREMENT

Counter value	A[7]	A[6]	A[5]	A[4]	A[3]	A[2]	A[1]	A[0]	Total cost
0	0	0	0	0	0	0	0	0	0
1	0	0	0	0	0	0	0	1	1
2	0	0	0	0	0	0	1	0	3
3	0	0	0	0	0	0	1	1	4
4	0	0	0	0	0	1	0	0	7
5	0	0	0	0	0	1	0	1	8
6	0	0	0	0	0	1	1	0	10
7	0	0	0	0	0	1	1	1	11
8	0	0	0	0	1	0	0	0	15
9	0	0	0	0	1	0	0	1	16
10	0	0	0	0	1	0	1	0	18
11	0	0	0	0	1	0	1	1	19
12	0	0	0	0	1	1	0	0	22
13	0	0	0	0	1	1	0	1	23
14	0	0	0	0	1	1	1	0	25
15	0	0	0	0	1	1	1	1	26
16	0	0	0	1	0	0	0	0	31

Figure 17.2   An 8-bit binary counter as its value goes from 0 to 16 by a sequence of 16 INCREMENT operations. Bits that flip to achieve the next value are shaded. The running cost for flipping bits is shown at the right. Notice that the total cost is always less than twice the total number of INCREMENT operations.

operations on an initially zero counter causes $A[1]$ to flip $\lfloor n/2 \rfloor$ times. Similarly, bit $A[2]$ flips only every fourth time, or $\lfloor n/4 \rfloor$ times in a sequence of n INCREMENT operations. In general, for $i = 0, 1, \ldots, k - 1$, bit $A[i]$ flips $\lfloor n/2^i \rfloor$ times in a sequence of n INCREMENT operations on an initially zero counter. For $i \geq k$, bit $A[i]$ does not exist, and so it cannot flip. The total number of flips in the sequence is thus

$$\sum_{i=0}^{k-1} \left\lfloor \frac{n}{2^i} \right\rfloor \; < \; n \sum_{i=0}^{\infty} \frac{1}{2^i}$$
$$= \; 2n \, ,$$

by equation (A.6). The worst-case time for a sequence of n INCREMENT operations on an initially zero counter is therefore $O(n)$. The average cost of each operation, and therefore the amortized cost per operation, is $O(n)/n = O(1)$.

Exercises

17.1-1
If the set of stack operations included a MULTIPUSH operation, which pushes k items onto the stack, would the $O(1)$ bound on the amortized cost of stack operations continue to hold?

17.1-2
Show that if a DECREMENT operation were included in the k-bit counter example, n operations could cost as much as $\Theta(nk)$ time.

17.1-3
Suppose we perform a sequence of n operations on a data structure in which the ith operation costs i if i is an exact power of 2, and 1 otherwise. Use aggregate analysis to determine the amortized cost per operation.

17.2   The accounting method

In the ***accounting method*** of amortized analysis, we assign differing charges to different operations, with some operations charged more or less than they actually cost. We call the amount we charge an operation its ***amortized cost***. When an operation's amortized cost exceeds its actual cost, we assign the difference to specific objects in the data structure as ***credit***. Credit can help pay for later operations whose amortized cost is less than their actual cost. Thus, we can view the amortized cost of an operation as being split between its actual cost and credit that is either deposited or used up. Different operations may have different amortized costs. This method differs from aggregate analysis, in which all operations have the same amortized cost.

We must choose the amortized costs of operations carefully. If we want to show that in the worst case the average cost per operation is small by analyzing with amortized costs, we must ensure that the total amortized cost of a sequence of operations provides an upper bound on the total actual cost of the sequence. Moreover, as in aggregate analysis, this relationship must hold for all sequences of operations. If we denote the actual cost of the ith operation by c_i and the amortized cost of the ith operation by $\hat{c}_i$, we require

$$\sum_{i=1}^{n} \hat{c}_i \geq \sum_{i=1}^{n} c_i \tag{17.1}$$

for all sequences of n operations. The total credit stored in the data structure is the difference between the total amortized cost and the total actual cost, or

$\sum_{i=1}^{n} \hat{c}_i - \sum_{i=1}^{n} c_i$. By inequality (17.1), the total credit associated with the data structure must be nonnegative at all times. If we ever were to allow the total credit to become negative (the result of undercharging early operations with the promise of repaying the account later on), then the total amortized costs incurred at that time would be below the total actual costs incurred; for the sequence of operations up to that time, the total amortized cost would not be an upper bound on the total actual cost. Thus, we must take care that the total credit in the data structure never becomes negative.

Stack operations

To illustrate the accounting method of amortized analysis, let us return to the stack example. Recall that the actual costs of the operations were

PUSH   1 ,
POP   1 ,
MULTIPOP $\min(k, s)$,

where k is the argument supplied to MULTIPOP and s is the stack size when it is called. Let us assign the following amortized costs:

PUSH   2 ,
POP   0 ,
MULTIPOP   0 .

Note that the amortized cost of MULTIPOP is a constant (0), whereas the actual cost is variable. Here, all three amortized costs are constant. In general, the amortized costs of the operations under consideration may differ from each other, and they may even differ asymptotically.

We shall now show that we can pay for any sequence of stack operations by charging the amortized costs. Suppose we use a dollar bill to represent each unit of cost. We start with an empty stack. Recall the analogy of Section 10.1 between the stack data structure and a stack of plates in a cafeteria. When we push a plate on the stack, we use 1 dollar to pay the actual cost of the push and are left with a credit of 1 dollar (out of the 2 dollars charged), which we leave on top of the plate. At any point in time, every plate on the stack has a dollar of credit on it.

The dollar stored on the plate serves as prepayment for the cost of popping it from the stack. When we execute a POP operation, we charge the operation nothing and pay its actual cost using the credit stored in the stack. To pop a plate, we take the dollar of credit off the plate and use it to pay the actual cost of the operation. Thus, by charging the PUSH operation a little bit more, we can charge the POP operation nothing.

Moreover, we can also charge MULTIPOP operations nothing. To pop the first plate, we take the dollar of credit off the plate and use it to pay the actual cost of a POP operation. To pop a second plate, we again have a dollar of credit on the plate to pay for the POP operation, and so on. Thus, we have always charged enough up front to pay for MULTIPOP operations. In other words, since each plate on the stack has 1 dollar of credit on it, and the stack always has a nonnegative number of plates, we have ensured that the amount of credit is always nonnegative. Thus, for *any* sequence of n PUSH, POP, and MULTIPOP operations, the total amortized cost is an upper bound on the total actual cost. Since the total amortized cost is $O(n)$, so is the total actual cost.

Incrementing a binary counter

As another illustration of the accounting method, we analyze the INCREMENT operation on a binary counter that starts at zero. As we observed earlier, the running time of this operation is proportional to the number of bits flipped, which we shall use as our cost for this example. Let us once again use a dollar bill to represent each unit of cost (the flipping of a bit in this example).

For the amortized analysis, let us charge an amortized cost of 2 dollars to set a bit to 1. When a bit is set, we use 1 dollar (out of the 2 dollars charged) to pay for the actual setting of the bit, and we place the other dollar on the bit as credit to be used later when we flip the bit back to 0. At any point in time, every 1 in the counter has a dollar of credit on it, and thus we can charge nothing to reset a bit to 0; we just pay for the reset with the dollar bill on the bit.

Now we can determine the amortized cost of INCREMENT. The cost of resetting the bits within the **while** loop is paid for by the dollars on the bits that are reset. The INCREMENT procedure sets at most one bit, in line 6, and therefore the amortized cost of an INCREMENT operation is at most 2 dollars. The number of 1s in the counter never becomes negative, and thus the amount of credit stays nonnegative at all times. Thus, for n INCREMENT operations, the total amortized cost is $O(n)$, which bounds the total actual cost.

Exercises

17.2-1
Suppose we perform a sequence of stack operations on a stack whose size never exceeds k. After every k operations, we make a copy of the entire stack for backup purposes. Show that the cost of n stack operations, including copying the stack, is $O(n)$ by assigning suitable amortized costs to the various stack operations.

17.2-2
Redo Exercise 17.1-3 using an accounting method of analysis.

17.2-3
Suppose we wish not only to increment a counter but also to reset it to zero (i.e., make all bits in it 0). Counting the time to examine or modify a bit as $\Theta(1)$, show how to implement a counter as an array of bits so that any sequence of n INCREMENT and RESET operations takes time $O(n)$ on an initially zero counter. (*Hint:* Keep a pointer to the high-order 1.)

17.3   The potential method

Instead of representing prepaid work as credit stored with specific objects in the data structure, the **potential method** of amortized analysis represents the prepaid work as "potential energy," or just "potential," which can be released to pay for future operations. We associate the potential with the data structure as a whole rather than with specific objects within the data structure.

The potential method works as follows. We will perform n operations, starting with an initial data structure D_0. For each $i = 1, 2, \ldots, n$, we let c_i be the actual cost of the ith operation and D_i be the data structure that results after applying the ith operation to data structure D_{i-1}. A **potential function** Φ maps each data structure D_i to a real number $\Phi(D_i)$, which is the **potential** associated with data structure D_i. The **amortized cost** $\hat{c}_i$ of the ith operation with respect to potential function Φ is defined by

$$\hat{c}_i = c_i + \Phi(D_i) - \Phi(D_{i-1}) \; . \tag{17.2}$$

The amortized cost of each operation is therefore its actual cost plus the change in potential due to the operation. By equation (17.2), the total amortized cost of the n operations is

$$
\begin{aligned}
\sum_{i=1}^{n} \hat{c}_i &= \sum_{i=1}^{n} (c_i + \Phi(D_i) - \Phi(D_{i-1})) \\
&= \sum_{i=1}^{n} c_i + \Phi(D_n) - \Phi(D_0) \; .
\end{aligned} \tag{17.3}
$$

The second equality follows from equation (A.9) because the $\Phi(D_i)$ terms telescope.

If we can define a potential function Φ so that $\Phi(D_n) \geq \Phi(D_0)$, then the total amortized cost $\sum_{i=1}^{n} \hat{c}_i$ gives an upper bound on the total actual cost $\sum_{i=1}^{n} c_i$.

In practice, we do not always know how many operations might be performed. Therefore, if we require that $\Phi(D_i) \geq \Phi(D_0)$ for all i, then we guarantee, as in the accounting method, that we pay in advance. We usually just define $\Phi(D_0)$ to be 0 and then show that $\Phi(D_i) \geq 0$ for all i. (See Exercise 17.3-1 for an easy way to handle cases in which $\Phi(D_0) \neq 0$.)

Intuitively, if the potential difference $\Phi(D_i) - \Phi(D_{i-1})$ of the ith operation is positive, then the amortized cost $\hat{c}_i$ represents an overcharge to the ith operation, and the potential of the data structure increases. If the potential difference is negative, then the amortized cost represents an undercharge to the ith operation, and the decrease in the potential pays for the actual cost of the operation.

The amortized costs defined by equations (17.2) and (17.3) depend on the choice of the potential function Φ. Different potential functions may yield different amortized costs yet still be upper bounds on the actual costs. We often find trade-offs that we can make in choosing a potential function; the best potential function to use depends on the desired time bounds.

Stack operations

To illustrate the potential method, we return once again to the example of the stack operations PUSH, POP, and MULTIPOP. We define the potential function Φ on a stack to be the number of objects in the stack. For the empty stack D_0 with which we start, we have $\Phi(D_0) = 0$. Since the number of objects in the stack is never negative, the stack D_i that results after the ith operation has nonnegative potential, and thus

$$
\begin{aligned}
\Phi(D_i) &\geq 0 \\
&= \Phi(D_0) \, .
\end{aligned}
$$

The total amortized cost of n operations with respect to Φ therefore represents an upper bound on the actual cost.

Let us now compute the amortized costs of the various stack operations. If the ith operation on a stack containing s objects is a PUSH operation, then the potential difference is

$$
\begin{aligned}
\Phi(D_i) - \Phi(D_{i-1}) &= (s+1) - s \\
&= 1 \, .
\end{aligned}
$$

By equation (17.2), the amortized cost of this PUSH operation is

$$
\begin{aligned}
\hat{c}_i &= c_i + \Phi(D_i) - \Phi(D_{i-1}) \\
&= 1 + 1 \\
&= 2 \, .
\end{aligned}
$$

Suppose that the ith operation on the stack is MULTIPOP(S, k), which causes $k' = \min(k, s)$ objects to be popped off the stack. The actual cost of the operation is k', and the potential difference is

$$\Phi(D_i) - \Phi(D_{i-1}) = -k' \, .$$

Thus, the amortized cost of the MULTIPOP operation is

$$
\begin{aligned}
\hat{c}_i &= c_i + \Phi(D_i) - \Phi(D_{i-1}) \\
&= k' - k' \\
&= 0 \, .
\end{aligned}
$$

Similarly, the amortized cost of an ordinary POP operation is 0.

The amortized cost of each of the three operations is $O(1)$, and thus the total amortized cost of a sequence of n operations is $O(n)$. Since we have already argued that $\Phi(D_i) \geq \Phi(D_0)$, the total amortized cost of n operations is an upper bound on the total actual cost. The worst-case cost of n operations is therefore $O(n)$.

Incrementing a binary counter

As another example of the potential method, we again look at incrementing a binary counter. This time, we define the potential of the counter after the ith INCREMENT operation to be b_i, the number of 1s in the counter after the ith operation.

Let us compute the amortized cost of an INCREMENT operation. Suppose that the ith INCREMENT operation resets t_i bits. The actual cost of the operation is therefore at most $t_i + 1$, since in addition to resetting t_i bits, it sets at most one bit to 1. If $b_i = 0$, then the ith operation resets all k bits, and so $b_{i-1} = t_i = k$. If $b_i > 0$, then $b_i = b_{i-1} - t_i + 1$. In either case, $b_i \leq b_{i-1} - t_i + 1$, and the potential difference is

$$
\begin{aligned}
\Phi(D_i) - \Phi(D_{i-1}) &\leq (b_{i-1} - t_i + 1) - b_{i-1} \\
&= 1 - t_i \, .
\end{aligned}
$$

The amortized cost is therefore

$$
\begin{aligned}
\hat{c}_i &= c_i + \Phi(D_i) - \Phi(D_{i-1}) \\
&\leq (t_i + 1) + (1 - t_i) \\
&= 2 \, .
\end{aligned}
$$

If the counter starts at zero, then $\Phi(D_0) = 0$. Since $\Phi(D_i) \geq 0$ for all i, the total amortized cost of a sequence of n INCREMENT operations is an upper bound on the total actual cost, and so the worst-case cost of n INCREMENT operations is $O(n)$.

The potential method gives us an easy way to analyze the counter even when it does not start at zero. The counter starts with b_0 1s, and after n INCREMENT operations it has b_n 1s, where $0 \leq b_0, b_n \leq k$. (Recall that k is the number of bits in the counter.) We can rewrite equation (17.3) as

$$\sum_{i=1}^{n} c_i = \sum_{i=1}^{n} \hat{c}_i - \Phi(D_n) + \Phi(D_0) \, . \tag{17.4}$$

We have $\hat{c}_i \leq 2$ for all $1 \leq i \leq n$. Since $\Phi(D_0) = b_0$ and $\Phi(D_n) = b_n$, the total actual cost of n INCREMENT operations is

$$\begin{aligned}
\sum_{i=1}^{n} c_i &\leq \sum_{i=1}^{n} 2 - b_n + b_0 \\
&= 2n - b_n + b_0 \, .
\end{aligned}$$

Note in particular that since $b_0 \leq k$, as long as $k = O(n)$, the total actual cost is $O(n)$. In other words, if we execute at least $n = \Omega(k)$ INCREMENT operations, the total actual cost is $O(n)$, no matter what initial value the counter contains.

Exercises

17.3-1
Suppose we have a potential function Φ such that $\Phi(D_i) \geq \Phi(D_0)$ for all i, but $\Phi(D_0) \neq 0$. Show that there exists a potential function Φ' such that $\Phi'(D_0) = 0$, $\Phi'(D_i) \geq 0$ for all $i \geq 1$, and the amortized costs using Φ' are the same as the amortized costs using Φ.

17.3-2
Redo Exercise 17.1-3 using a potential method of analysis.

17.3-3
Consider an ordinary binary min-heap data structure with n elements supporting the instructions INSERT and EXTRACT-MIN in $O(\lg n)$ worst-case time. Give a potential function Φ such that the amortized cost of INSERT is $O(\lg n)$ and the amortized cost of EXTRACT-MIN is $O(1)$, and show that it works.

17.3-4
What is the total cost of executing n of the stack operations PUSH, POP, and MULTIPOP, assuming that the stack begins with s_0 objects and finishes with s_n objects?

17.3-5
Suppose that a counter begins at a number with b 1s in its binary representation, rather than at 0. Show that the cost of performing n INCREMENT operations is $O(n)$ if $n = \Omega(b)$. (Do not assume that b is constant.)

17.3-6

Show how to implement a queue with two ordinary stacks (Exercise 10.1-6) so that the amortized cost of each ENQUEUE and each DEQUEUE operation is $O(1)$.

17.3-7

Design a data structure to support the following two operations for a dynamic multiset S of integers, which allows duplicate values:

INSERT(S, x) inserts x into S.

DELETE-LARGER-HALF(S) deletes the largest $\lceil |S| /2 \rceil$ elements from S.

Explain how to implement this data structure so that any sequence of m INSERT and DELETE-LARGER-HALF operations runs in $O(m)$ time. Your implementation should also include a way to output the elements of S in $O(|S|)$ time.

17.4 Dynamic tables

We do not always know in advance how many objects some applications will store in a table. We might allocate space for a table, only to find out later that it is not enough. We must then reallocate the table with a larger size and copy all objects stored in the original table over into the new, larger table. Similarly, if many objects have been deleted from the table, it may be worthwhile to reallocate the table with a smaller size. In this section, we study this problem of dynamically expanding and contracting a table. Using amortized analysis, we shall show that the amortized cost of insertion and deletion is only $O(1)$, even though the actual cost of an operation is large when it triggers an expansion or a contraction. Moreover, we shall see how to guarantee that the unused space in a dynamic table never exceeds a constant fraction of the total space.

We assume that the dynamic table supports the operations TABLE-INSERT and TABLE-DELETE. TABLE-INSERT inserts into the table an item that occupies a single *slot*, that is, a space for one item. Likewise, TABLE-DELETE removes an item from the table, thereby freeing a slot. The details of the data-structuring method used to organize the table are unimportant; we might use a stack (Section 10.1), a heap (Chapter 6), or a hash table (Chapter 11). We might also use an array or collection of arrays to implement object storage, as we did in Section 10.3.

We shall find it convenient to use a concept introduced in our analysis of hashing (Chapter 11). We define the *load factor* $\alpha(T)$ of a nonempty table T to be the number of items stored in the table divided by the size (number of slots) of the table. We assign an empty table (one with no slots) size 0, and we define its load factor to be 1. If the load factor of a dynamic table is bounded below by a constant, the unused space in the table is never more than a constant fraction of the total amount of space.

We start by analyzing a dynamic table in which we only insert items. We then consider the more general case in which we both insert and delete items.

17.4.1   Table expansion

Let us assume that storage for a table is allocated as an array of slots. A table fills up when all slots have been used or, equivalently, when its load factor is 1.[1] In some software environments, upon attempting to insert an item into a full table, the only alternative is to abort with an error. We shall assume, however, that our software environment, like many modern ones, provides a memory-management system that can allocate and free blocks of storage on request. Thus, upon inserting an item into a full table, we can ***expand*** the table by allocating a new table with more slots than the old table had. Because we always need the table to reside in contiguous memory, we must allocate a new array for the larger table and then copy items from the old table into the new table.

A common heuristic allocates a new table with twice as many slots as the old one. If the only table operations are insertions, then the load factor of the table is always at least $1/2$, and thus the amount of wasted space never exceeds half the total space in the table.

In the following pseudocode, we assume that T is an object representing the table. The attribute $T.table$ contains a pointer to the block of storage representing the table, $T.num$ contains the number of items in the table, and $T.size$ gives the total number of slots in the table. Initially, the table is empty: $T.num = T.size = 0$.

TABLE-INSERT(T, x)

```
 1  if T.size == 0
 2      allocate T.table with 1 slot
 3      T.size = 1
 4  if T.num == T.size
 5      allocate new-table with 2 · T.size slots
 6      insert all items in T.table into new-table
 7      free T.table
 8      T.table = new-table
 9      T.size = 2 · T.size
10  insert x into T.table
11  T.num = T.num + 1
```

---

[1]In some situations, such as an open-address hash table, we may wish to consider a table to be full if its load factor equals some constant strictly less than 1. (See Exercise 17.4-1.)

Notice that we have two "insertion" procedures here: the TABLE-INSERT procedure itself and the ***elementary insertion*** into a table in lines 6 and 10. We can analyze the running time of TABLE-INSERT in terms of the number of elementary insertions by assigning a cost of 1 to each elementary insertion. We assume that the actual running time of TABLE-INSERT is linear in the time to insert individual items, so that the overhead for allocating an initial table in line 2 is constant and the overhead for allocating and freeing storage in lines 5 and 7 is dominated by the cost of transferring items in line 6. We call the event in which lines 5–9 are executed an ***expansion***.

Let us analyze a sequence of n TABLE-INSERT operations on an initially empty table. What is the cost c_i of the ith operation? If the current table has room for the new item (or if this is the first operation), then $c_i = 1$, since we need only perform the one elementary insertion in line 10. If the current table is full, however, and an expansion occurs, then $c_i = i$: the cost is 1 for the elementary insertion in line 10 plus $i - 1$ for the items that we must copy from the old table to the new table in line 6. If we perform n operations, the worst-case cost of an operation is $O(n)$, which leads to an upper bound of $O(n^2)$ on the total running time for n operations.

This bound is not tight, because we rarely expand the table in the course of n TABLE-INSERT operations. Specifically, the ith operation causes an expansion only when $i - 1$ is an exact power of 2. The amortized cost of an operation is in fact $O(1)$, as we can show using aggregate analysis. The cost of the ith operation is

$$c_i = \begin{cases} i & \text{if } i - 1 \text{ is an exact power of 2 ,} \\ 1 & \text{otherwise .} \end{cases}$$

The total cost of n TABLE-INSERT operations is therefore

$$\begin{aligned} \sum_{i=1}^{n} c_i & \le n + \sum_{j=0}^{\lfloor \lg n \rfloor} 2^j \\ & < n + 2n \\ & = 3n , \end{aligned}$$

because at most n operations cost 1 and the costs of the remaining operations form a geometric series. Since the total cost of n TABLE-INSERT operations is bounded by $3n$, the amortized cost of a single operation is at most 3.

By using the accounting method, we can gain some feeling for why the amortized cost of a TABLE-INSERT operation should be 3. Intuitively, each item pays for 3 elementary insertions: inserting itself into the current table, moving itself when the table expands, and moving another item that has already been moved once when the table expands. For example, suppose that the size of the table is m immediately after an expansion. Then the table holds $m/2$ items, and it contains no credit. We charge 3 dollars for each insertion. The elementary insertion that occurs immediately costs 1 dollar. We place another dollar as credit on the item inserted. We place the third dollar as credit on one of the $m/2$ items already in the table. The table will not fill again until we have inserted another $m/2 - 1$ items, and thus, by the time the table contains m items and is full, we will have placed a dollar on each item to pay to reinsert it during the expansion.

We can use the potential method to analyze a sequence of n TABLE-INSERT operations, and we shall use it in Section 17.4.2 to design a TABLE-DELETE operation that has an $O(1)$ amortized cost as well. We start by defining a potential function Φ that is 0 immediately after an expansion but builds to the table size by the time the table is full, so that we can pay for the next expansion by the potential. The function

$$\Phi(T) = 2 \cdot T.num - T.size \qquad (17.5)$$

is one possibility. Immediately after an expansion, we have $T.num = T.size/2$, and thus $\Phi(T) = 0$, as desired. Immediately before an expansion, we have $T.num = T.size$, and thus $\Phi(T) = T.num$, as desired. The initial value of the potential is 0, and since the table is always at least half full, $T.num \geq T.size/2$, which implies that $\Phi(T)$ is always nonnegative. Thus, the sum of the amortized costs of n TABLE-INSERT operations gives an upper bound on the sum of the actual costs.

To analyze the amortized cost of the ith TABLE-INSERT operation, we let num_i denote the number of items stored in the table after the ith operation, $size_i$ denote the total size of the table after the ith operation, and Φ_i denote the potential after the ith operation. Initially, we have $num_0 = 0$, $size_0 = 0$, and $\Phi_0 = 0$.

If the ith TABLE-INSERT operation does not trigger an expansion, then we have $size_i = size_{i-1}$ and the amortized cost of the operation is

$$
\begin{aligned}
\hat{c}_i &= c_i + \Phi_i - \Phi_{i-1} \\
&= 1 + (2 \cdot num_i - size_i) - (2 \cdot num_{i-1} - size_{i-1}) \\
&= 1 + (2 \cdot num_i - size_i) - (2(num_i - 1) - size_i) \\
&= 3 .
\end{aligned}
$$

If the ith operation does trigger an expansion, then we have $size_i = 2 \cdot size_{i-1}$ and $size_{i-1} = num_{i-1} = num_i - 1$, which implies that $size_i = 2 \cdot (num_i - 1)$. Thus, the amortized cost of the operation is

$$
\begin{aligned}
\hat{c}_i &= c_i + \Phi_i - \Phi_{i-1} \\
&= num_i + (2 \cdot num_i - size_i) - (2 \cdot num_{i-1} - size_{i-1}) \\
&= num_i + (2 \cdot num_i - 2 \cdot (num_i - 1)) - (2(num_i - 1) - (num_i - 1)) \\
&= num_i + 2 - (num_i - 1) \\
&= 3 .
\end{aligned}
$$

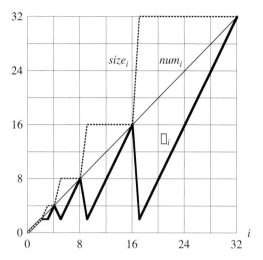

Figure 17.3   The effect of a sequence of n TABLE-INSERT operations on the number num_i of items in the table, the number $size_i$ of slots in the table, and the potential $\Phi_i = 2 \cdot num_i - size_i$, each being measured after the ith operation. The thin line shows num_i, the dashed line shows $size_i$, and the thick line shows Φ_i. Notice that immediately before an expansion, the potential has built up to the number of items in the table, and therefore it can pay for moving all the items to the new table. Afterwards, the potential drops to 0, but it is immediately increased by 2 upon inserting the item that caused the expansion.

Figure 17.3 plots the values of num_i, $size_i$, and Φ_i against i. Notice how the potential builds to pay for expanding the table.

17.4.2   Table expansion and contraction

To implement a TABLE-DELETE operation, it is simple enough to remove the specified item from the table. In order to limit the amount of wasted space, however, we might wish to **contract** the table when the load factor becomes too small. Table contraction is analogous to table expansion: when the number of items in the table drops too low, we allocate a new, smaller table and then copy the items from the old table into the new one. We can then free the storage for the old table by returning it to the memory-management system. Ideally, we would like to preserve two properties:

- the load factor of the dynamic table is bounded below by a positive constant, and

- the amortized cost of a table operation is bounded above by a constant.

We assume that we measure the cost in terms of elementary insertions and deletions.

You might think that we should double the table size upon inserting an item into a full table and halve the size when a deleting an item would cause the table to become less than half full. This strategy would guarantee that the load factor of the table never drops below $1/2$, but unfortunately, it can cause the amortized cost of an operation to be quite large. Consider the following scenario. We perform n operations on a table T, where n is an exact power of 2. The first $n/2$ operations are insertions, which by our previous analysis cost a total of $\Theta(n)$. At the end of this sequence of insertions, $T.num = T.size = n/2$. For the second $n/2$ operations, we perform the following sequence:

insert, delete, delete, insert, insert, delete, delete, insert, insert, ...

The first insertion causes the table to expand to size n. The two following deletions cause the table to contract back to size $n/2$. Two further insertions cause another expansion, and so forth. The cost of each expansion and contraction is $\Theta(n)$, and there are $\Theta(n)$ of them. Thus, the total cost of the n operations is $\Theta(n^2)$, making the amortized cost of an operation $\Theta(n)$.

The downside of this strategy is obvious: after expanding the table, we do not delete enough items to pay for a contraction. Likewise, after contracting the table, we do not insert enough items to pay for an expansion.

We can improve upon this strategy by allowing the load factor of the table to drop below $1/2$. Specifically, we continue to double the table size upon inserting an item into a full table, but we halve the table size when deleting an item causes the table to become less than $1/4$ full, rather than $1/2$ full as before. The load factor of the table is therefore bounded below by the constant $1/4$.

Intuitively, we would consider a load factor of $1/2$ to be ideal, and the table's potential would then be 0. As the load factor deviates from $1/2$, the potential increases so that by the time we expand or contract the table, the table has garnered sufficient potential to pay for copying all the items into the newly allocated table. Thus, we will need a potential function that has grown to $T.num$ by the time that the load factor has either increased to 1 or decreased to $1/4$. After either expanding or contracting the table, the load factor goes back to $1/2$ and the table's potential reduces back to 0.

We omit the code for TABLE-DELETE, since it is analogous to TABLE-INSERT. For our analysis, we shall assume that whenever the number of items in the table drops to 0, we free the storage for the table. That is, if $T.num = 0$, then $T.size = 0$.

We can now use the potential method to analyze the cost of a sequence of n TABLE-INSERT and TABLE-DELETE operations. We start by defining a potential function Φ that is 0 immediately after an expansion or contraction and builds as the load factor increases to 1 or decreases to $1/4$. Let us denote the load fac-

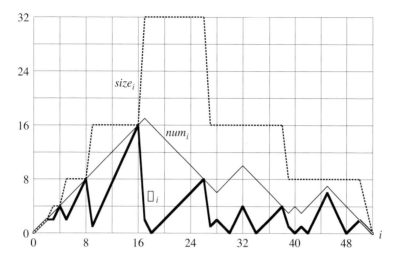

Figure 17.4 The effect of a sequence of n TABLE-INSERT and TABLE-DELETE operations on the number num_i of items in the table, the number $size_i$ of slots in the table, and the potential

$$\Phi_i = \begin{cases} 2 \cdot num_i - size_i & \text{if } \alpha_i \geq 1/2 \,, \\ size_i/2 - num_i & \text{if } \alpha_i < 1/2 \,, \end{cases}$$

each measured after the ith operation. The thin line shows num_i, the dashed line shows $size_i$, and the thick line shows Φ_i. Notice that immediately before an expansion, the potential has built up to the number of items in the table, and therefore it can pay for moving all the items to the new table. Likewise, immediately before a contraction, the potential has built up to the number of items in the table.

tor of a nonempty table T by $\alpha(T) = T.num/T.size$. Since for an empty table, $T.num = T.size = 0$ and $\alpha(T) = 1$, we always have $T.num = \alpha(T) \cdot T.size$, whether the table is empty or not. We shall use as our potential function

$$\Phi(T) = \begin{cases} 2 \cdot T.num - T.size & \text{if } \alpha(T) \geq 1/2 \,, \\ T.size/2 - T.num & \text{if } \alpha(T) < 1/2 \,. \end{cases} \tag{17.6}$$

Observe that the potential of an empty table is 0 and that the potential is never negative. Thus, the total amortized cost of a sequence of operations with respect to Φ provides an upper bound on the actual cost of the sequence.

Before proceeding with a precise analysis, we pause to observe some properties of the potential function, as illustrated in Figure 17.4. Notice that when the load factor is $1/2$, the potential is 0. When the load factor is 1, we have $T.size = T.num$, which implies $\Phi(T) = T.num$, and thus the potential can pay for an expansion if an item is inserted. When the load factor is $1/4$, we have $T.size = 4 \cdot T.num$, which implies $\Phi(T) = T.num$, and thus the potential can pay for a contraction if an item is deleted.

To analyze a sequence of n TABLE-INSERT and TABLE-DELETE operations, we let c_i denote the actual cost of the ith operation, $\hat{c}_i$ denote its amortized cost with respect to Φ, num_i denote the number of items stored in the table after the ith operation, $size_i$ denote the total size of the table after the ith operation, α_i denote the load factor of the table after the ith operation, and Φ_i denote the potential after the ith operation. Initially, $num_0 = 0$, $size_0 = 0$, $\alpha_0 = 1$, and $\Phi_0 = 0$.

We start with the case in which the ith operation is TABLE-INSERT. The analysis is identical to that for table expansion in Section 17.4.1 if $\alpha_{i-1} \geq 1/2$. Whether the table expands or not, the amortized cost $\hat{c}_i$ of the operation is at most 3. If $\alpha_{i-1} < 1/2$, the table cannot expand as a result of the operation, since the table expands only when $\alpha_{i-1} = 1$. If $\alpha_i < 1/2$ as well, then the amortized cost of the ith operation is

$$
\begin{aligned}
\hat{c}_i &= c_i + \Phi_i - \Phi_{i-1} \\
&= 1 + (size_i/2 - num_i) - (size_{i-1}/2 - num_{i-1}) \\
&= 1 + (size_i/2 - num_i) - (size_i/2 - (num_i - 1)) \\
&= 0 .
\end{aligned}
$$

If $\alpha_{i-1} < 1/2$ but $\alpha_i \geq 1/2$, then

$$
\begin{aligned}
\hat{c}_i &= c_i + \Phi_i - \Phi_{i-1} \\
&= 1 + (2 \cdot num_i - size_i) - (size_{i-1}/2 - num_{i-1}) \\
&= 1 + (2(num_{i-1} + 1) - size_{i-1}) - (size_{i-1}/2 - num_{i-1}) \\
&= 3 \cdot num_{i-1} - \frac{3}{2} size_{i-1} + 3 \\
&= 3\alpha_{i-1} size_{i-1} - \frac{3}{2} size_{i-1} + 3 \\
&< \frac{3}{2} size_{i-1} - \frac{3}{2} size_{i-1} + 3 \\
&= 3 .
\end{aligned}
$$

Thus, the amortized cost of a TABLE-INSERT operation is at most 3.

We now turn to the case in which the ith operation is TABLE-DELETE. In this case, $num_i = num_{i-1} - 1$. If $\alpha_{i-1} < 1/2$, then we must consider whether the operation causes the table to contract. If it does not, then $size_i = size_{i-1}$ and the amortized cost of the operation is

$$
\begin{aligned}
\hat{c}_i &= c_i + \Phi_i - \Phi_{i-1} \\
&= 1 + (size_i/2 - num_i) - (size_{i-1}/2 - num_{i-1}) \\
&= 1 + (size_i/2 - num_i) - (size_i/2 - (num_i + 1)) \\
&= 2 .
\end{aligned}
$$

If $\alpha_{i-1} < 1/2$ and the ith operation does trigger a contraction, then the actual cost of the operation is $c_i = num_i + 1$, since we delete one item and move num_i items. We have $size_i/2 = size_{i-1}/4 = num_{i-1} = num_i + 1$, and the amortized cost of the operation is

$$
\begin{aligned}
\hat{c}_i &= c_i + \Phi_i - \Phi_{i-1} \\
&= (num_i + 1) + (size_i/2 - num_i) - (size_{i-1}/2 - num_{i-1}) \\
&= (num_i + 1) + ((num_i + 1) - num_i) - ((2 \cdot num_i + 2) - (num_i + 1)) \\
&= 1 .
\end{aligned}
$$

When the ith operation is a TABLE-DELETE and $\alpha_{i-1} \geq 1/2$, the amortized cost is also bounded above by a constant. We leave the analysis as Exercise 17.4-2.

In summary, since the amortized cost of each operation is bounded above by a constant, the actual time for any sequence of n operations on a dynamic table is $O(n)$.

Exercises

17.4-1
Suppose that we wish to implement a dynamic, open-address hash table. Why might we consider the table to be full when its load factor reaches some value α that is strictly less than 1? Describe briefly how to make insertion into a dynamic, open-address hash table run in such a way that the expected value of the amortized cost per insertion is $O(1)$. Why is the expected value of the actual cost per insertion not necessarily $O(1)$ for all insertions?

17.4-2
Show that if $\alpha_{i-1} \geq 1/2$ and the ith operation on a dynamic table is TABLE-DELETE, then the amortized cost of the operation with respect to the potential function (17.6) is bounded above by a constant.

17.4-3
Suppose that instead of contracting a table by halving its size when its load factor drops below $1/4$, we contract it by multiplying its size by $2/3$ when its load factor drops below $1/3$. Using the potential function

$$\Phi(T) = |2 \cdot T.num - T.size| ,$$

show that the amortized cost of a TABLE-DELETE that uses this strategy is bounded above by a constant.

Problems

17-1 *Bit-reversed binary counter*

Chapter 30 examines an important algorithm called the fast Fourier transform, or FFT. The first step of the FFT algorithm performs a ***bit-reversal permutation*** on an input array $A[0 .. n-1]$ whose length is $n = 2^k$ for some nonnegative integer k. This permutation swaps elements whose indices have binary representations that are the reverse of each other.

We can express each index a as a k-bit sequence $\langle a_{k-1}, a_{k-2}, \ldots, a_0 \rangle$, where $a = \sum_{i=0}^{k-1} a_i \, 2^i$. We define

$$\mathrm{rev}_k(\langle a_{k-1}, a_{k-2}, \ldots, a_0 \rangle) = \langle a_0, a_1, \ldots, a_{k-1} \rangle \, ;$$

thus,

$$\mathrm{rev}_k(a) = \sum_{i=0}^{k-1} a_{k-i-1} 2^i \, .$$

For example, if $n = 16$ (or, equivalently, $k = 4$), then $\mathrm{rev}_k(3) = 12$, since the 4-bit representation of 3 is 0011, which when reversed gives 1100, the 4-bit representation of 12.

a. Given a function rev_k that runs in $\Theta(k)$ time, write an algorithm to perform the bit-reversal permutation on an array of length $n = 2^k$ in $O(nk)$ time.

We can use an algorithm based on an amortized analysis to improve the running time of the bit-reversal permutation. We maintain a "bit-reversed counter" and a procedure BIT-REVERSED-INCREMENT that, when given a bit-reversed-counter value a, produces $\mathrm{rev}_k(\mathrm{rev}_k(a) + 1)$. If $k = 4$, for example, and the bit-reversed counter starts at 0, then successive calls to BIT-REVERSED-INCREMENT produce the sequence

$$0000, 1000, 0100, 1100, 0010, 1010, \ldots = 0, 8, 4, 12, 2, 10, \ldots \, .$$

b. Assume that the words in your computer store k-bit values and that in unit time, your computer can manipulate the binary values with operations such as shifting left or right by arbitrary amounts, bitwise-AND, bitwise-OR, etc. Describe an implementation of the BIT-REVERSED-INCREMENT procedure that allows the bit-reversal permutation on an n-element array to be performed in a total of $O(n)$ time.

c. Suppose that you can shift a word left or right by only one bit in unit time. Is it still possible to implement an $O(n)$-time bit-reversal permutation?

17-2 *Making binary search dynamic*

Binary search of a sorted array takes logarithmic search time, but the time to insert a new element is linear in the size of the array. We can improve the time for insertion by keeping several sorted arrays.

Specifically, suppose that we wish to support SEARCH and INSERT on a set of n elements. Let $k = \lceil \lg(n + 1) \rceil$, and let the binary representation of n be $\langle n_{k-1}, n_{k-2}, \ldots, n_0 \rangle$. We have k sorted arrays $A_0, A_1, \ldots, A_{k-1}$, where for $i = 0, 1, \ldots, k - 1$, the length of array A_i is 2^i. Each array is either full or empty, depending on whether $n_i = 1$ or $n_i = 0$, respectively. The total number of elements held in all k arrays is therefore $\sum_{i=0}^{k-1} n_i 2^i = n$. Although each individual array is sorted, elements in different arrays bear no particular relationship to each other.

a. Describe how to perform the SEARCH operation for this data structure. Analyze its worst-case running time.

b. Describe how to perform the INSERT operation. Analyze its worst-case and amortized running times.

c. Discuss how to implement DELETE.

17-3 *Amortized weight-balanced trees*

Consider an ordinary binary search tree augmented by adding to each node x the attribute $x.size$ giving the number of keys stored in the subtree rooted at x. Let α be a constant in the range $1/2 \le \alpha < 1$. We say that a given node x is $\boldsymbol{\alpha}$-*balanced* if $x.left.size \le \alpha \cdot x.size$ and $x.right.size \le \alpha \cdot x.size$. The tree as a whole is $\boldsymbol{\alpha}$-*balanced* if every node in the tree is α-balanced. The following amortized approach to maintaining weight-balanced trees was suggested by G. Varghese.

a. A $1/2$-balanced tree is, in a sense, as balanced as it can be. Given a node x in an arbitrary binary search tree, show how to rebuild the subtree rooted at x so that it becomes $1/2$-balanced. Your algorithm should run in time $\Theta(x.size)$, and it can use $O(x.size)$ auxiliary storage.

b. Show that performing a search in an n-node α-balanced binary search tree takes $O(\lg n)$ worst-case time.

For the remainder of this problem, assume that the constant α is strictly greater than $1/2$. Suppose that we implement INSERT and DELETE as usual for an n-node binary search tree, except that after every such operation, if any node in the tree is no longer α-balanced, then we "rebuild" the subtree rooted at the highest such node in the tree so that it becomes $1/2$-balanced.

We shall analyze this rebuilding scheme using the potential method. For a node x in a binary search tree T, we define

$$\Delta(x) = |x.left.size - x.right.size| \; ,$$

and we define the potential of T as

$$\Phi(T) = c \sum_{x \in T : \Delta(x) \geq 2} \Delta(x) \, ,$$

where c is a sufficiently large constant that depends on α.

c. Argue that any binary search tree has nonnegative potential and that a $1/2$-balanced tree has potential 0.

d. Suppose that m units of potential can pay for rebuilding an m-node subtree. How large must c be in terms of α in order for it to take $O(1)$ amortized time to rebuild a subtree that is not α-balanced?

e. Show that inserting a node into or deleting a node from an n-node α-balanced tree costs $O(\lg n)$ amortized time.

17-4   *The cost of restructuring red-black trees*

There are four basic operations on red-black trees that perform ***structural modifications***: node insertions, node deletions, rotations, and color changes. We have seen that RB-INSERT and RB-DELETE use only $O(1)$ rotations, node insertions, and node deletions to maintain the red-black properties, but they may make many more color changes.

a. Describe a legal red-black tree with n nodes such that calling RB-INSERT to add the $(n+1)$st node causes $\Omega(\lg n)$ color changes. Then describe a legal red-black tree with n nodes for which calling RB-DELETE on a particular node causes $\Omega(\lg n)$ color changes.

Although the worst-case number of color changes per operation can be logarithmic, we shall prove that any sequence of m RB-INSERT and RB-DELETE operations on an initially empty red-black tree causes $O(m)$ structural modifications in the worst case. Note that we count each color change as a structural modification.

b. Some of the cases handled by the main loop of the code of both RB-INSERT-FIXUP and RB-DELETE-FIXUP are ***terminating***: once encountered, they cause the loop to terminate after a constant number of additional operations. For each of the cases of RB-INSERT-FIXUP and RB-DELETE-FIXUP, specify which are terminating and which are not. (*Hint:* Look at Figures 13.5, 13.6, and 13.7.)

We shall first analyze the structural modifications when only insertions are performed. Let T be a red-black tree, and define $\Phi(T)$ to be the number of red nodes in T. Assume that 1 unit of potential can pay for the structural modifications performed by any of the three cases of RB-INSERT-FIXUP.

c. Let T' be the result of applying Case 1 of RB-INSERT-FIXUP to T. Argue that $\Phi(T') = \Phi(T) - 1$.

d. When we insert a node into a red-black tree using RB-INSERT, we can break the operation into three parts. List the structural modifications and potential changes resulting from lines 1–16 of RB-INSERT, from nonterminating cases of RB-INSERT-FIXUP, and from terminating cases of RB-INSERT-FIXUP.

e. Using part (d), argue that the amortized number of structural modifications performed by any call of RB-INSERT is $O(1)$.

We now wish to prove that there are $O(m)$ structural modifications when there are both insertions and deletions. Let us define, for each node x,

$$
w(x) = \begin{cases}
0 & \text{if } x \text{ is red ,} \\
1 & \text{if } x \text{ is black and has no red children ,} \\
0 & \text{if } x \text{ is black and has one red child ,} \\
2 & \text{if } x \text{ is black and has two red children .}
\end{cases}
$$

Now we redefine the potential of a red-black tree T as

$$
\Phi(T) = \sum_{x \in T} w(x) ,
$$

and let T' be the tree that results from applying any nonterminating case of RB-INSERT-FIXUP or RB-DELETE-FIXUP to T.

f. Show that $\Phi(T') \le \Phi(T) - 1$ for all nonterminating cases of RB-INSERT-FIXUP. Argue that the amortized number of structural modifications performed by any call of RB-INSERT-FIXUP is $O(1)$.

g. Show that $\Phi(T') \le \Phi(T) - 1$ for all nonterminating cases of RB-DELETE-FIXUP. Argue that the amortized number of structural modifications performed by any call of RB-DELETE-FIXUP is $O(1)$.

h. Complete the proof that in the worst case, any sequence of m RB-INSERT and RB-DELETE operations performs $O(m)$ structural modifications.

17-5   *Competitive analysis of self-organizing lists with move-to-front*

A *self-organizing list* is a linked list of n elements, in which each element has a unique key. When we search for an element in the list, we are given a key, and we want to find an element with that key.

A self-organizing list has two important properties:

1. To find an element in the list, given its key, we must traverse the list from the beginning until we encounter the element with the given key. If that element is the kth element from the start of the list, then the cost to find the element is k.

2. We may reorder the list elements after any operation, according to a given rule with a given cost. We may choose any heuristic we like to decide how to reorder the list.

Assume that we start with a given list of n elements, and we are given an access sequence $\sigma = \langle \sigma_1, \sigma_2, \ldots, \sigma_m \rangle$ of keys to find, in order. The cost of the sequence is the sum of the costs of the individual accesses in the sequence.

Out of the various possible ways to reorder the list after an operation, this problem focuses on transposing adjacent list elements—switching their positions in the list—with a unit cost for each transpose operation. You will show, by means of a potential function, that a particular heuristic for reordering the list, move-to-front, entails a total cost no worse than 4 times that of any other heuristic for maintaining the list order—even if the other heuristic knows the access sequence in advance! We call this type of analysis a *competitive analysis*.

For a heuristic H and a given initial ordering of the list, denote the access cost of sequence σ by $C_H(\sigma)$. Let m be the number of accesses in σ.

a. Argue that if heuristic H does not know the access sequence in advance, then the worst-case cost for H on an access sequence σ is $C_H(\sigma) = \Omega(mn)$.

With the ***move-to-front*** heuristic, immediately after searching for an element x, we move x to the first position on the list (i.e., the front of the list).

Let $\mathrm{rank}_L(x)$ denote the rank of element x in list L, that is, the position of x in list L. For example, if x is the fourth element in L, then $\mathrm{rank}_L(x) = 4$. Let c_i denote the cost of access σ_i using the move-to-front heuristic, which includes the cost of finding the element in the list and the cost of moving it to the front of the list by a series of transpositions of adjacent list elements.

b. Show that if σ_i accesses element x in list L using the move-to-front heuristic, then $c_i = 2 \cdot \mathrm{rank}_L(x) - 1$.

Now we compare move-to-front with any other heuristic H that processes an access sequence according to the two properties above. Heuristic H may transpose elements in the list in any way it wants, and it might even know the entire access sequence in advance.

Let L_i be the list after access σ_i using move-to-front, and let L_i^* be the list after access σ_i using heuristic H. We denote the cost of access σ_i by c_i for move-to-front and by c_i^* for heuristic H. Suppose that heuristic H performs t_i^* transpositions during access σ_i.

c. In part (b), you showed that $c_i = 2 \cdot \mathrm{rank}_{L_{i-1}}(x) - 1$. Now show that $c_i^* = \mathrm{rank}_{L_{i-1}^*}(x) + t_i^*$.

We define an **inversion** in list L_i as a pair of elements y and z such that y precedes z in L_i and z precedes y in list L_i^*. Suppose that list L_i has q_i inversions after processing the access sequence $\langle \sigma_1, \sigma_2, \ldots, \sigma_i \rangle$. Then, we define a potential function Φ that maps L_i to a real number by $\Phi(L_i) = 2q_i$. For example, if L_i has the elements $\langle e, c, a, d, b \rangle$ and L_i^* has the elements $\langle c, a, b, d, e \rangle$, then L_i has 5 inversions $((e, c), (e, a), (e, d), (e, b), (d, b))$, and so $\Phi(L_i) = 10$. Observe that $\Phi(L_i) \geq 0$ for all i and that, if move-to-front and heuristic H start with the same list L_0, then $\Phi(L_0) = 0$.

d. Argue that a transposition either increases the potential by 2 or decreases the potential by 2.

Suppose that access σ_i finds the element x. To understand how the potential changes due to σ_i, let us partition the elements other than x into four sets, depending on where they are in the lists just before the ith access:

- Set A consists of elements that precede x in both L_{i-1} and L_{i-1}^*.
- Set B consists of elements that precede x in L_{i-1} and follow x in L_{i-1}^*.
- Set C consists of elements that follow x in L_{i-1} and precede x in L_{i-1}^*.
- Set D consists of elements that follow x in both L_{i-1} and L_{i-1}^*.

e. Argue that $\mathrm{rank}_{L_{i-1}}(x) = |A| + |B| + 1$ and $\mathrm{rank}_{L_{i-1}^*}(x) = |A| + |C| + 1$.

f. Show that access σ_i causes a change in potential of

$$\Phi(L_i) - \Phi(L_{i-1}) \leq 2(|A| - |B| + t_i^*) \, ,$$

where, as before, heuristic H performs t_i^* transpositions during access σ_i.

Define the amortized cost $\hat{c}_i$ of access σ_i by $\hat{c}_i = c_i + \Phi(L_i) - \Phi(L_{i-1})$.

g. Show that the amortized cost $\hat{c}_i$ of access σ_i is bounded from above by $4c_i^*$.

h. Conclude that the cost $C_{\mathrm{MTF}}(\sigma)$ of access sequence σ with move-to-front is at most 4 times the cost $C_H(\sigma)$ of σ with any other heuristic H, assuming that both heuristics start with the same list.

Chapter notes

Aho, Hopcroft, and Ullman [5] used aggregate analysis to determine the running time of operations on a disjoint-set forest; we shall analyze this data structure using the potential method in Chapter 21. Tarjan [331] surveys the accounting and potential methods of amortized analysis and presents several applications. He attributes the accounting method to several authors, including M. R. Brown, R. E. Tarjan, S. Huddleston, and K. Mehlhorn. He attributes the potential method to D. D. Sleator. The term "amortized" is due to D. D. Sleator and R. E. Tarjan.

Potential functions are also useful for proving lower bounds for certain types of problems. For each configuration of the problem, we define a potential function that maps the configuration to a real number. Then we determine the potential Φ_{init} of the initial configuration, the potential Φ_{final} of the final configuration, and the maximum change in potential $\Delta\Phi_{max}$ due to any step. The number of steps must therefore be at least $|\Phi_{final} - \Phi_{init}| / |\Delta\Phi_{max}|$. Examples of potential functions to prove lower bounds in I/O complexity appear in works by Cormen, Sundquist, and Wisniewski [79]; Floyd [107]; and Aggarwal and Vitter [3]. Krumme, Cybenko, and Venkataraman [221] applied potential functions to prove lower bounds on ***gossiping***: communicating a unique item from each vertex in a graph to every other vertex.

The move-to-front heuristic from Problem 17-5 works quite well in practice. Moreover, if we recognize that when we find an element, we can splice it out of its position in the list and relocate it to the front of the list in constant time, we can show that the cost of move-to-front is at most twice the cost of any other heuristic including, again, one that knows the entire access sequence in advance.

V   Advanced Data Structures

Introduction

This part returns to studying data structures that support operations on dynamic sets, but at a more advanced level than Part III. Two of the chapters, for example, make extensive use of the amortized analysis techniques we saw in Chapter 17.

Chapter 18 presents B-trees, which are balanced search trees specifically designed to be stored on disks. Because disks operate much more slowly than random-access memory, we measure the performance of B-trees not only by how much computing time the dynamic-set operations consume but also by how many disk accesses they perform. For each B-tree operation, the number of disk accesses increases with the height of the B-tree, but B-tree operations keep the height low.

Chapter 19 gives an implementation of a mergeable heap, which supports the operations INSERT, MINIMUM, EXTRACT-MIN, and UNION.[1] The UNION operation unites, or merges, two heaps. Fibonacci heaps—the data structure in Chapter 19—also support the operations DELETE and DECREASE-KEY. We use amortized time bounds to measure the performance of Fibonacci heaps. The operations INSERT, MINIMUM, and UNION take only $O(1)$ actual and amortized time on Fibonacci heaps, and the operations EXTRACT-MIN and DELETE take $O(\lg n)$ amortized time. The most significant advantage of Fibonacci heaps, however, is that DECREASE-KEY takes only $O(1)$ amortized time. Because the DECREASE-

---

[1] As in Problem 10-2, we have defined a mergeable heap to support MINIMUM and EXTRACT-MIN, and so we can also refer to it as a *mergeable min-heap*. Alternatively, if it supported MAXIMUM and EXTRACT-MAX, it would be a *mergeable max-heap*. Unless we specify otherwise, mergeable heaps will be by default mergeable min-heaps.

KEY operation takes constant amortized time, Fibonacci heaps are key components of some of the asymptotically fastest algorithms to date for graph problems.

Noting that we can beat the $\Omega(n \lg n)$ lower bound for sorting when the keys are integers in a restricted range, Chapter 20 asks whether we can design a data structure that supports the dynamic-set operations SEARCH, INSERT, DELETE, MINIMUM, MAXIMUM, SUCCESSOR, and PREDECESSOR in $o(\lg n)$ time when the keys are integers in a restricted range. The answer turns out to be that we can, by using a recursive data structure known as a van Emde Boas tree. If the keys are unique integers drawn from the set $\{0, 1, 2, \ldots, u - 1\}$, where u is an exact power of 2, then van Emde Boas trees support each of the above operations in $O(\lg \lg u)$ time.

Finally, Chapter 21 presents data structures for disjoint sets. We have a universe of n elements that are partitioned into dynamic sets. Initially, each element belongs to its own singleton set. The operation UNION unites two sets, and the query FIND-SET identifies the unique set that contains a given element at the moment. By representing each set as a simple rooted tree, we obtain surprisingly fast operations: a sequence of m operations runs in $O(m \, \alpha(n))$ time, where $\alpha(n)$ is an incredibly slowly growing function—$\alpha(n)$ is at most 4 in any conceivable application. The amortized analysis that proves this time bound is as complex as the data structure is simple.

The topics covered in this part are by no means the only examples of "advanced" data structures. Other advanced data structures include the following:

- **Dynamic trees**, introduced by Sleator and Tarjan [319] and discussed by Tarjan [330], maintain a forest of disjoint rooted trees. Each edge in each tree has a real-valued cost. Dynamic trees support queries to find parents, roots, edge costs, and the minimum edge cost on a simple path from a node up to a root. Trees may be manipulated by cutting edges, updating all edge costs on a simple path from a node up to a root, linking a root into another tree, and making a node the root of the tree it appears in. One implementation of dynamic trees gives an $O(\lg n)$ amortized time bound for each operation; a more complicated implementation yields $O(\lg n)$ worst-case time bounds. Dynamic trees are used in some of the asymptotically fastest network-flow algorithms.

- **Splay trees**, developed by Sleator and Tarjan [320] and, again, discussed by Tarjan [330], are a form of binary search tree on which the standard search-tree operations run in $O(\lg n)$ amortized time. One application of splay trees simplifies dynamic trees.

- **Persistent** data structures allow queries, and sometimes updates as well, on past versions of a data structure. Driscoll, Sarnak, Sleator, and Tarjan [97] present techniques for making linked data structures persistent with only a small time and space cost. Problem 13-1 gives a simple example of a persistent dynamic set.

- As in Chapter 20, several data structures allow a faster implementation of dictionary operations (INSERT, DELETE, and SEARCH) for a restricted universe of keys. By taking advantage of these restrictions, they are able to achieve better worst-case asymptotic running times than comparison-based data structures. Fredman and Willard introduced *fusion trees* [115], which were the first data structure to allow faster dictionary operations when the universe is restricted to integers. They showed how to implement these operations in $O(\lg n / \lg \lg n)$ time. Several subsequent data structures, including *exponential search trees* [16], have also given improved bounds on some or all of the dictionary operations and are mentioned in the chapter notes throughout this book.

- *Dynamic graph data structures* support various queries while allowing the structure of a graph to change through operations that insert or delete vertices or edges. Examples of the queries that they support include vertex connectivity [166], edge connectivity, minimum spanning trees [165], biconnectivity, and transitive closure [164].

Chapter notes throughout this book mention additional data structures.

18   B-Trees

B-trees are balanced search trees designed to work well on disks or other direct-access secondary storage devices. B-trees are similar to red-black trees (Chapter 13), but they are better at minimizing disk I/O operations. Many database systems use B-trees, or variants of B-trees, to store information.

B-trees differ from red-black trees in that B-tree nodes may have many children, from a few to thousands. That is, the "branching factor" of a B-tree can be quite large, although it usually depends on characteristics of the disk unit used. B-trees are similar to red-black trees in that every n-node B-tree has height $O(\lg n)$. The exact height of a B-tree can be considerably less than that of a red-black tree, however, because its branching factor, and hence the base of the logarithm that expresses its height, can be much larger. Therefore, we can also use B-trees to implement many dynamic-set operations in time $O(\lg n)$.

B-trees generalize binary search trees in a natural manner. Figure 18.1 shows a simple B-tree. If an internal B-tree node x contains $x.n$ keys, then x has $x.n + 1$ children. The keys in node x serve as dividing points separating the range of keys handled by x into $x.n + 1$ subranges, each handled by one child of x. When searching for a key in a B-tree, we make an $(x.n + 1)$-way decision based on comparisons with the $x.n$ keys stored at node x. The structure of leaf nodes differs from that of internal nodes; we will examine these differences in Section 18.1.

Section 18.1 gives a precise definition of B-trees and proves that the height of a B-tree grows only logarithmically with the number of nodes it contains. Section 18.2 describes how to search for a key and insert a key into a B-tree, and Section 18.3 discusses deletion. Before proceeding, however, we need to ask why we evaluate data structures designed to work on a disk differently from data structures designed to work in main random-access memory.

Data structures on secondary storage

Computer systems take advantage of various technologies that provide memory capacity. The **primary memory** (or **main memory**) of a computer system normally

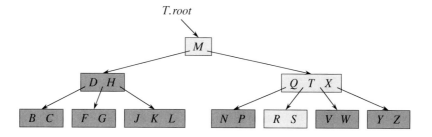

Figure 18.1 A B-tree whose keys are the consonants of English. An internal node x containing $x.n$ keys has $x.n + 1$ children. All leaves are at the same depth in the tree. The lightly shaded nodes are examined in a search for the letter R.

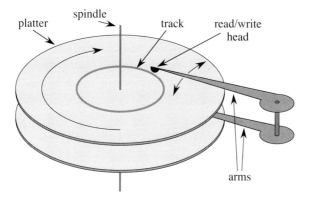

Figure 18.2 A typical disk drive. It comprises one or more platters (two platters are shown here) that rotate around a spindle. Each platter is read and written with a head at the end of an arm. Arms rotate around a common pivot axis. A track is the surface that passes beneath the read/write head when the head is stationary.

consists of silicon memory chips. This technology is typically more than an order of magnitude more expensive per bit stored than magnetic storage technology, such as tapes or disks. Most computer systems also have **secondary storage** based on magnetic disks; the amount of such secondary storage often exceeds the amount of primary memory by at least two orders of magnitude.

Figure 18.2 shows a typical disk drive. The drive consists of one or more **platters**, which rotate at a constant speed around a common **spindle**. A magnetizable material covers the surface of each platter. The drive reads and writes each platter by a **head** at the end of an **arm**. The arms can move their heads toward or away from the spindle. When a given head is stationary, the surface that passes underneath it is called a ***track***. Multiple platters increase only the disk drive's capacity and not its performance.

Although disks are cheaper and have higher capacity than main memory, they are much, much slower because they have moving mechanical parts.[1] The mechanical motion has two components: platter rotation and arm movement. As of this writing, commodity disks rotate at speeds of 5400–15,000 revolutions per minute (RPM). We typically see 15,000 RPM speeds in server-grade drives, 7200 RPM speeds in drives for desktops, and 5400 RPM speeds in drives for laptops. Although 7200 RPM may seem fast, one rotation takes 8.33 milliseconds, which is over 5 orders of magnitude longer than the 50 nanosecond access times (more or less) commonly found for silicon memory. In other words, if we have to wait a full rotation for a particular item to come under the read/write head, we could access main memory more than 100,000 times during that span. On average we have to wait for only half a rotation, but still, the difference in access times for silicon memory compared with disks is enormous. Moving the arms also takes some time. As of this writing, average access times for commodity disks are in the range of 8 to 11 milliseconds.

In order to amortize the time spent waiting for mechanical movements, disks access not just one item but several at a time. Information is divided into a number of equal-sized ***pages*** of bits that appear consecutively within tracks, and each disk read or write is of one or more entire pages. For a typical disk, a page might be 2^{11} to 2^{14} bytes in length. Once the read/write head is positioned correctly and the disk has rotated to the beginning of the desired page, reading or writing a magnetic disk is entirely electronic (aside from the rotation of the disk), and the disk can quickly read or write large amounts of data.

Often, accessing a page of information and reading it from a disk takes longer than examining all the information read. For this reason, in this chapter we shall look separately at the two principal components of the running time:

- the number of disk accesses, and

- the CPU (computing) time.

We measure the number of disk accesses in terms of the number of pages of information that need to be read from or written to the disk. We note that disk-access time is not constant—it depends on the distance between the current track and the desired track and also on the initial rotational position of the disk. We shall

---

[1] As of this writing, solid-state drives have recently come onto the consumer market. Although they are faster than mechanical disk drives, they cost more per gigabyte and have lower capacities than mechanical disk drives.

nonetheless use the number of pages read or written as a first-order approximation of the total time spent accessing the disk.

In a typical B-tree application, the amount of data handled is so large that all the data do not fit into main memory at once. The B-tree algorithms copy selected pages from disk into main memory as needed and write back onto disk the pages that have changed. B-tree algorithms keep only a constant number of pages in main memory at any time; thus, the size of main memory does not limit the size of B-trees that can be handled.

We model disk operations in our pseudocode as follows. Let x be a pointer to an object. If the object is currently in the computer's main memory, then we can refer to the attributes of the object as usual: $x.key$, for example. If the object referred to by x resides on disk, however, then we must perform the operation DISK-READ(x) to read object x into main memory before we can refer to its attributes. (We assume that if x is already in main memory, then DISK-READ(x) requires no disk accesses; it is a "no-op.") Similarly, the operation DISK-WRITE(x) is used to save any changes that have been made to the attributes of object x. That is, the typical pattern for working with an object is as follows:

> x = a pointer to some object
> DISK-READ(x)
> operations that access and/or modify the attributes of x
> DISK-WRITE(x)   **//** omitted if no attributes of x were changed
> other operations that access but do not modify attributes of x

The system can keep only a limited number of pages in main memory at any one time. We shall assume that the system flushes from main memory pages no longer in use; our B-tree algorithms will ignore this issue.

Since in most systems the running time of a B-tree algorithm depends primarily on the number of DISK-READ and DISK-WRITE operations it performs, we typically want each of these operations to read or write as much information as possible. Thus, a B-tree node is usually as large as a whole disk page, and this size limits the number of children a B-tree node can have.

For a large B-tree stored on a disk, we often see branching factors between 50 and 2000, depending on the size of a key relative to the size of a page. A large branching factor dramatically reduces both the height of the tree and the number of disk accesses required to find any key. Figure 18.3 shows a B-tree with a branching factor of 1001 and height 2 that can store over one billion keys; nevertheless, since we can keep the root node permanently in main memory, we can find any key in this tree by making at most only two disk accesses.

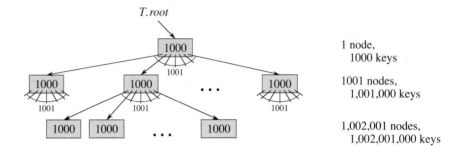

Figure 18.3 A B-tree of height 2 containing over one billion keys. Shown inside each node x is $x.n$, the number of keys in x. Each internal node and leaf contains 1000 keys. This B-tree has 1001 nodes at depth 1 and over one million leaves at depth 2.

18.1   Definition of B-trees

To keep things simple, we assume, as we have for binary search trees and red-black trees, that any "satellite information" associated with a key resides in the same node as the key. In practice, one might actually store with each key just a pointer to another disk page containing the satellite information for that key. The pseudocode in this chapter implicitly assumes that the satellite information associated with a key, or the pointer to such satellite information, travels with the key whenever the key is moved from node to node. A common variant on a B-tree, known as a **B^+-tree**, stores all the satellite information in the leaves and stores only keys and child pointers in the internal nodes, thus maximizing the branching factor of the internal nodes.

A **B-tree** T is a rooted tree (whose root is $T.root$) having the following properties:

1. Every node x has the following attributes:

    a. $x.n$, the number of keys currently stored in node x,

    b. the $x.n$ keys themselves, $x.key_1, x.key_2, \ldots, x.key_{x.n}$, stored in nondecreasing order, so that $x.key_1 \leq x.key_2 \leq \cdots \leq x.key_{x.n}$,

    c. $x.leaf$, a boolean value that is TRUE if x is a leaf and FALSE if x is an internal node.

2. Each internal node x also contains $x.n + 1$ pointers $x.c_1, x.c_2, \ldots, x.c_{x.n+1}$ to its children. Leaf nodes have no children, and so their c_i attributes are undefined.

3. The keys $x.key_i$ separate the ranges of keys stored in each subtree: if k_i is any key stored in the subtree with root $x.c_i$, then

$$k_1 \leq x.key_1 \leq k_2 \leq x.key_2 \leq \cdots \leq x.key_{x.n} \leq k_{x.n+1} \, .$$

4. All leaves have the same depth, which is the tree's height h.

5. Nodes have lower and upper bounds on the number of keys they can contain. We express these bounds in terms of a fixed integer $t \geq 2$ called the ***minimum degree*** of the B-tree:

   a. Every node other than the root must have at least $t - 1$ keys. Every internal node other than the root thus has at least t children. If the tree is nonempty, the root must have at least one key.

   b. Every node may contain at most $2t - 1$ keys. Therefore, an internal node may have at most $2t$ children. We say that a node is ***full*** if it contains exactly $2t - 1$ keys.[2]

The simplest B-tree occurs when $t = 2$. Every internal node then has either 2, 3, or 4 children, and we have a ***2-3-4 tree***. In practice, however, much larger values of t yield B-trees with smaller height.

The height of a B-tree

The number of disk accesses required for most operations on a B-tree is proportional to the height of the B-tree. We now analyze the worst-case height of a B-tree.

Theorem 18.1
If $n \geq 1$, then for any n-key B-tree T of height h and minimum degree $t \geq 2$,

$$h \leq \log_t \frac{n + 1}{2} \, .$$

Proof   The root of a B-tree T contains at least one key, and all other nodes contain at least $t - 1$ keys. Thus, T, whose height is h, has at least 2 nodes at depth 1, at least $2t$ nodes at depth 2, at least $2t^2$ nodes at depth 3, and so on, until at depth h it has at least $2t^{h-1}$ nodes. Figure 18.4 illustrates such a tree for $h = 3$. Thus, the

---

[2]Another common variant on a B-tree, known as a ***B*-tree***, requires each internal node to be at least $2/3$ full, rather than at least half full, as a B-tree requires.

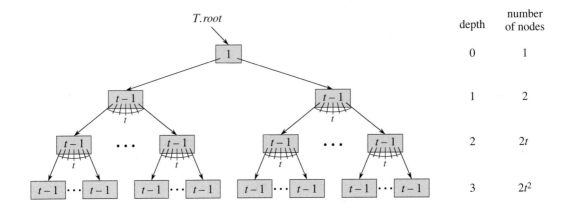

Figure 18.4 A B-tree of height 3 containing a minimum possible number of keys. Shown inside each node x is $x.n$.

number n of keys satisfies the inequality

$$n \;\geq\; 1 + (t-1)\sum_{i=1}^{h} 2t^{i-1}$$

$$= \; 1 + 2(t-1)\left(\frac{t^h - 1}{t-1}\right)$$

$$= \; 2t^h - 1 \,.$$

By simple algebra, we get $t^h \leq (n+1)/2$. Taking base-t logarithms of both sides proves the theorem.   ∎

Here we see the power of B-trees, as compared with red-black trees. Although the height of the tree grows as $O(\lg n)$ in both cases (recall that t is a constant), for B-trees the base of the logarithm can be many times larger. Thus, B-trees save a factor of about $\lg t$ over red-black trees in the number of nodes examined for most tree operations. Because we usually have to access the disk to examine an arbitrary node in a tree, B-trees avoid a substantial number of disk accesses.

Exercises

18.1-1
Why don't we allow a minimum degree of $t = 1$?

18.1-2
For what values of t is the tree of Figure 18.1 a legal B-tree?

18.1-3
Show all legal B-trees of minimum degree 2 that represent $\{1, 2, 3, 4, 5\}$.

18.1-4
As a function of the minimum degree t, what is the maximum number of keys that can be stored in a B-tree of height h?

18.1-5
Describe the data structure that would result if each black node in a red-black tree were to absorb its red children, incorporating their children with its own.

18.2   Basic operations on B-trees

In this section, we present the details of the operations B-TREE-SEARCH, B-TREE-CREATE, and B-TREE-INSERT. In these procedures, we adopt two conventions:

- The root of the B-tree is always in main memory, so that we never need to perform a DISK-READ on the root; we do have to perform a DISK-WRITE of the root, however, whenever the root node is changed.

- Any nodes that are passed as parameters must already have had a DISK-READ operation performed on them.

The procedures we present are all "one-pass" algorithms that proceed downward from the root of the tree, without having to back up.

Searching a B-tree

Searching a B-tree is much like searching a binary search tree, except that instead of making a binary, or "two-way," branching decision at each node, we make a multiway branching decision according to the number of the node's children. More precisely, at each internal node x, we make an $(x.n + 1)$-way branching decision.

B-TREE-SEARCH is a straightforward generalization of the TREE-SEARCH procedure defined for binary search trees. B-TREE-SEARCH takes as input a pointer to the root node x of a subtree and a key k to be searched for in that subtree. The top-level call is thus of the form B-TREE-SEARCH($T.root, k$). If k is in the B-tree, B-TREE-SEARCH returns the ordered pair (y, i) consisting of a node y and an index i such that $y.key_i = k$. Otherwise, the procedure returns NIL.

B-TREE-SEARCH(x, k)

```
1  i = 1
2  while i ≤ x.n and k > x.key_i
3      i = i + 1
4  if i ≤ x.n and k == x.key_i
5      return (x, i)
6  elseif x.leaf
7      return NIL
8  else DISK-READ(x.c_i)
9      return B-TREE-SEARCH(x.c_i, k)
```

Using a linear-search procedure, lines 1–3 find the smallest index i such that $k \le x.key_i$, or else they set i to $x.n + 1$. Lines 4–5 check to see whether we have now discovered the key, returning if we have. Otherwise, lines 6–9 either terminate the search unsuccessfully (if x is a leaf) or recurse to search the appropriate subtree of x, after performing the necessary DISK-READ on that child.

Figure 18.1 illustrates the operation of B-TREE-SEARCH. The procedure examines the lightly shaded nodes during a search for the key R.

As in the TREE-SEARCH procedure for binary search trees, the nodes encountered during the recursion form a simple path downward from the root of the tree. The B-TREE-SEARCH procedure therefore accesses $O(h) = O(\log_t n)$ disk pages, where h is the height of the B-tree and n is the number of keys in the B-tree. Since $x.n < 2t$, the **while** loop of lines 2–3 takes $O(t)$ time within each node, and the total CPU time is $O(th) = O(t \log_t n)$.

Creating an empty B-tree

To build a B-tree T, we first use B-TREE-CREATE to create an empty root node and then call B-TREE-INSERT to add new keys. Both of these procedures use an auxiliary procedure ALLOCATE-NODE, which allocates one disk page to be used as a new node in $O(1)$ time. We can assume that a node created by ALLOCATE-NODE requires no DISK-READ, since there is as yet no useful information stored on the disk for that node.

B-TREE-CREATE(T)

```
1  x = ALLOCATE-NODE()
2  x.leaf = TRUE
3  x.n = 0
4  DISK-WRITE(x)
5  T.root = x
```

B-TREE-CREATE requires $O(1)$ disk operations and $O(1)$ CPU time.

Inserting a key into a B-tree

Inserting a key into a B-tree is significantly more complicated than inserting a key into a binary search tree. As with binary search trees, we search for the leaf position at which to insert the new key. With a B-tree, however, we cannot simply create a new leaf node and insert it, as the resulting tree would fail to be a valid B-tree. Instead, we insert the new key into an existing leaf node. Since we cannot insert a key into a leaf node that is full, we introduce an operation that *splits* a full node y (having $2t - 1$ keys) around its *median key* $y.key_t$ into two nodes having only $t - 1$ keys each. The median key moves up into y's parent to identify the dividing point between the two new trees. But if y's parent is also full, we must split it before we can insert the new key, and thus we could end up splitting full nodes all the way up the tree.

As with a binary search tree, we can insert a key into a B-tree in a single pass down the tree from the root to a leaf. To do so, we do not wait to find out whether we will actually need to split a full node in order to do the insertion. Instead, as we travel down the tree searching for the position where the new key belongs, we split each full node we come to along the way (including the leaf itself). Thus whenever we want to split a full node y, we are assured that its parent is not full.

Splitting a node in a B-tree

The procedure B-TREE-SPLIT-CHILD takes as input a *nonfull* internal node x (assumed to be in main memory) and an index i such that $x.c_i$ (also assumed to be in main memory) is a *full* child of x. The procedure then splits this child in two and adjusts x so that it has an additional child. To split a full root, we will first make the root a child of a new empty root node, so that we can use B-TREE-SPLIT-CHILD. The tree thus grows in height by one; splitting is the only means by which the tree grows.

Figure 18.5 illustrates this process. We split the full node $y = x.c_i$ about its median key S, which moves up into y's parent node x. Those keys in y that are greater than the median key move into a new node z, which becomes a new child of x.

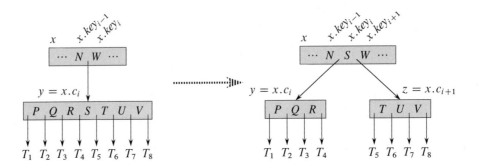

Figure 18.5   Splitting a node with $t = 4$. Node $y = x.c_i$ splits into two nodes, y and z, and the median key S of y moves up into y's parent.

B-TREE-SPLIT-CHILD(x, i)

```
 1   z = ALLOCATE-NODE()
 2   y = x.cᵢ
 3   z.leaf = y.leaf
 4   z.n = t − 1
 5   for j = 1 to t − 1
 6       z.keyⱼ = y.keyⱼ₊ₜ
 7   if not y.leaf
 8       for j = 1 to t
 9           z.cⱼ = y.cⱼ₊ₜ
10   y.n = t − 1
11   for j = x.n + 1 downto i + 1
12       x.cⱼ₊₁ = x.cⱼ
13   x.cᵢ₊₁ = z
14   for j = x.n downto i
15       x.keyⱼ₊₁ = x.keyⱼ
16   x.keyᵢ = y.keyₜ
17   x.n = x.n + 1
18   DISK-WRITE(y)
19   DISK-WRITE(z)
20   DISK-WRITE(x)
```

B-TREE-SPLIT-CHILD works by straightforward "cutting and pasting." Here, x is the parent of the node being split, and y is x's ith child (set in line 2). Node y originally has $2t$ children ($2t - 1$ keys) but is reduced to t children ($t - 1$ keys) by this operation. Node z takes the t largest children ($t - 1$ keys) from y, and

z becomes a new child of x, positioned just after y in x's table of children. The median key of y moves up to become the key in x that separates y and z.

Lines 1–9 create node z and give it the largest $t - 1$ keys and corresponding t children of y. Line 10 adjusts the key count for y. Finally, lines 11–17 insert z as a child of x, move the median key from y up to x in order to separate y from z, and adjust x's key count. Lines 18–20 write out all modified disk pages. The CPU time used by B-TREE-SPLIT-CHILD is $\Theta(t)$, due to the loops on lines 5–6 and 8–9. (The other loops run for $O(t)$ iterations.) The procedure performs $O(1)$ disk operations.

Inserting a key into a B-tree in a single pass down the tree

We insert a key k into a B-tree T of height h in a single pass down the tree, requiring $O(h)$ disk accesses. The CPU time required is $O(th) = O(t \log_t n)$. The B-TREE-INSERT procedure uses B-TREE-SPLIT-CHILD to guarantee that the recursion never descends to a full node.

B-TREE-INSERT(T, k)

```
 1  r = T.root
 2  if r.n == 2t − 1
 3      s = ALLOCATE-NODE()
 4      T.root = s
 5      s.leaf = FALSE
 6      s.n = 0
 7      s.c₁ = r
 8      B-TREE-SPLIT-CHILD(s, 1)
 9      B-TREE-INSERT-NONFULL(s, k)
10  else B-TREE-INSERT-NONFULL(r, k)
```

Lines 3–9 handle the case in which the root node r is full: the root splits and a new node s (having two children) becomes the root. Splitting the root is the only way to increase the height of a B-tree. Figure 18.6 illustrates this case. Unlike a binary search tree, a B-tree increases in height at the top instead of at the bottom. The procedure finishes by calling B-TREE-INSERT-NONFULL to insert key k into the tree rooted at the nonfull root node. B-TREE-INSERT-NONFULL recurses as necessary down the tree, at all times guaranteeing that the node to which it recurses is not full by calling B-TREE-SPLIT-CHILD as necessary.

The auxiliary recursive procedure B-TREE-INSERT-NONFULL inserts key k into node x, which is assumed to be nonfull when the procedure is called. The operation of B-TREE-INSERT and the recursive operation of B-TREE-INSERT-NONFULL guarantee that this assumption is true.

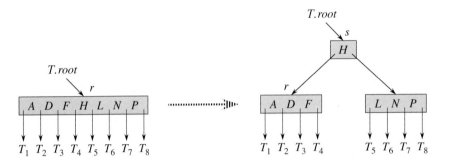

Figure 18.6 Splitting the root with $t = 4$. Root node r splits in two, and a new root node s is created. The new root contains the median key of r and has the two halves of r as children. The B-tree grows in height by one when the root is split.

B-TREE-INSERT-NONFULL(x, k)

```
 1   i = x.n
 2   if x.leaf
 3       while i ≥ 1 and k < x.key_i
 4           x.key_{i+1} = x.key_i
 5           i = i − 1
 6       x.key_{i+1} = k
 7       x.n = x.n + 1
 8       DISK-WRITE(x)
 9   else while i ≥ 1 and k < x.key_i
10           i = i − 1
11       i = i + 1
12       DISK-READ(x.c_i)
13       if x.c_i.n == 2t − 1
14           B-TREE-SPLIT-CHILD(x, i)
15           if k > x.key_i
16               i = i + 1
17       B-TREE-INSERT-NONFULL(x.c_i, k)
```

The B-TREE-INSERT-NONFULL procedure works as follows. Lines 3–8 handle the case in which x is a leaf node by inserting key k into x. If x is not a leaf node, then we must insert k into the appropriate leaf node in the subtree rooted at internal node x. In this case, lines 9–11 determine the child of x to which the recursion descends. Line 13 detects whether the recursion would descend to a full child, in which case line 14 uses B-TREE-SPLIT-CHILD to split that child into two nonfull children, and lines 15–16 determine which of the two children is now the correct one to descend to. (Note that there is no need for a DISK-READ$(x.c_i)$ after line 16 increments i, since the recursion will descend in this case to a child that was just created by B-TREE-SPLIT-CHILD.) The net effect of lines 13–16 is thus to guarantee that the procedure never recurses to a full node. Line 17 then recurses to insert k into the appropriate subtree. Figure 18.7 illustrates the various cases of inserting into a B-tree.

For a B-tree of height h, B-TREE-INSERT performs $O(h)$ disk accesses, since only $O(1)$ DISK-READ and DISK-WRITE operations occur between calls to B-TREE-INSERT-NONFULL. The total CPU time used is $O(th) = O(t \log_t n)$. Since B-TREE-INSERT-NONFULL is tail-recursive, we can alternatively implement it as a **while** loop, thereby demonstrating that the number of pages that need to be in main memory at any time is $O(1)$.

Exercises

18.2-1
Show the results of inserting the keys

$$F, S, Q, K, C, L, H, T, V, W, M, R, N, P, A, B, X, Y, D, Z, E$$

in order into an empty B-tree with minimum degree 2. Draw only the configurations of the tree just before some node must split, and also draw the final configuration.

18.2-2
Explain under what circumstances, if any, redundant DISK-READ or DISK-WRITE operations occur during the course of executing a call to B-TREE-INSERT. (A redundant DISK-READ is a DISK-READ for a page that is already in memory. A redundant DISK-WRITE writes to disk a page of information that is identical to what is already stored there.)

18.2-3
Explain how to find the minimum key stored in a B-tree and how to find the predecessor of a given key stored in a B-tree.

18.2-4 ⋆
Suppose that we insert the keys $\{1, 2, \ldots, n\}$ into an empty B-tree with minimum degree 2. How many nodes does the final B-tree have?

18.2-5
Since leaf nodes require no pointers to children, they could conceivably use a different (larger) t value than internal nodes for the same disk page size. Show how to modify the procedures for creating and inserting into a B-tree to handle this variation.

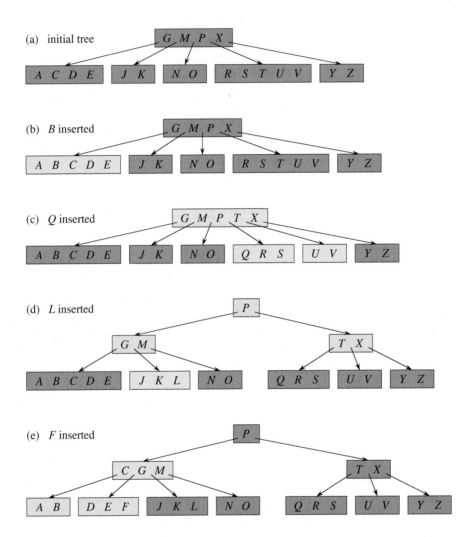

Figure 18.7 Inserting keys into a B-tree. The minimum degree t for this B-tree is 3, so a node can hold at most 5 keys. Nodes that are modified by the insertion process are lightly shaded. **(a)** The initial tree for this example. **(b)** The result of inserting B into the initial tree; this is a simple insertion into a leaf node. **(c)** The result of inserting Q into the previous tree. The node $RSTUV$ splits into two nodes containing RS and UV, the key T moves up to the root, and Q is inserted in the leftmost of the two halves (the RS node). **(d)** The result of inserting L into the previous tree. The root splits right away, since it is full, and the B-tree grows in height by one. Then L is inserted into the leaf containing JK. **(e)** The result of inserting F into the previous tree. The node $ABCDE$ splits before F is inserted into the rightmost of the two halves (the DE node).

18.2-6
Suppose that we were to implement B-TREE-SEARCH to use binary search rather than linear search within each node. Show that this change makes the CPU time required $O(\lg n)$, independently of how t might be chosen as a function of n.

18.2-7
Suppose that disk hardware allows us to choose the size of a disk page arbitrarily, but that the time it takes to read the disk page is $a + bt$, where a and b are specified constants and t is the minimum degree for a B-tree using pages of the selected size. Describe how to choose t so as to minimize (approximately) the B-tree search time. Suggest an optimal value of t for the case in which $a = 5$ milliseconds and $b = 10$ microseconds.

18.3 Deleting a key from a B-tree

Deletion from a B-tree is analogous to insertion but a little more complicated, because we can delete a key from any node—not just a leaf—and when we delete a key from an internal node, we will have to rearrange the node's children. As in insertion, we must guard against deletion producing a tree whose structure violates the B-tree properties. Just as we had to ensure that a node didn't get too big due to insertion, we must ensure that a node doesn't get too small during deletion (except that the root is allowed to have fewer than the minimum number $t - 1$ of keys). Just as a simple insertion algorithm might have to back up if a node on the path to where the key was to be inserted was full, a simple approach to deletion might have to back up if a node (other than the root) along the path to where the key is to be deleted has the minimum number of keys.

The procedure B-TREE-DELETE deletes the key k from the subtree rooted at x. We design this procedure to guarantee that whenever it calls itself recursively on a node x, the number of keys in x is at least the minimum degree t. Note that this condition requires one more key than the minimum required by the usual B-tree conditions, so that sometimes a key may have to be moved into a child node before recursion descends to that child. This strengthened condition allows us to delete a key from the tree in one downward pass without having to "back up" (with one exception, which we'll explain). You should interpret the following specification for deletion from a B-tree with the understanding that if the root node x ever becomes an internal node having no keys (this situation can occur in cases 2c and 3b on pages 501–502), then we delete x, and x's only child $x.c_1$ becomes the new root of the tree, decreasing the height of the tree by one and preserving the property that the root of the tree contains at least one key (unless the tree is empty).

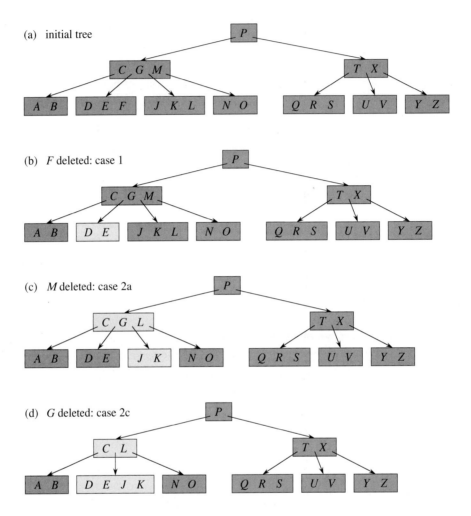

Figure 18.8   Deleting keys from a B-tree. The minimum degree for this B-tree is $t = 3$, so a node (other than the root) cannot have fewer than 2 keys. Nodes that are modified are lightly shaded. **(a)** The B-tree of Figure 18.7(e). **(b)** Deletion of F. This is case 1: simple deletion from a leaf. **(c)** Deletion of M. This is case 2a: the predecessor L of M moves up to take M's position. **(d)** Deletion of G. This is case 2c: we push G down to make node $DEGJK$ and then delete G from this leaf (case 1).

We sketch how deletion works instead of presenting the pseudocode. Figure 18.8 illustrates the various cases of deleting keys from a B-tree.

1. If the key k is in node x and x is a leaf, delete the key k from x.

2. If the key k is in node x and x is an internal node, do the following:

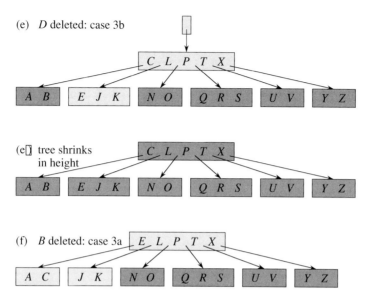

(e)   *D* deleted: case 3b

(e′)   tree shrinks
    in height

(f)   *B* deleted: case 3a

Figure 18.8, continued   **(e)** Deletion of D. This is case 3b: the recursion cannot descend to node CL because it has only 2 keys, so we push P down and merge it with CL and TX to form $CLPTX$; then we delete D from a leaf (case 1). **(e′)** After (e), we delete the root and the tree shrinks in height by one. **(f)** Deletion of B. This is case 3a: C moves to fill B's position and E moves to fill C's position.

    a. If the child y that precedes k in node x has at least t keys, then find the predecessor k' of k in the subtree rooted at y. Recursively delete k', and replace k by k' in x. (We can find k' and delete it in a single downward pass.)

    b. If y has fewer than t keys, then, symmetrically, examine the child z that follows k in node x. If z has at least t keys, then find the successor k' of k in the subtree rooted at z. Recursively delete k', and replace k by k' in x. (We can find k' and delete it in a single downward pass.)

    c. Otherwise, if both y and z have only $t-1$ keys, merge k and all of z into y, so that x loses both k and the pointer to z, and y now contains $2t-1$ keys. Then free z and recursively delete k from y.

3. If the key k is not present in internal node x, determine the root $x.c_i$ of the appropriate subtree that must contain k, if k is in the tree at all. If $x.c_i$ has only $t-1$ keys, execute step 3a or 3b as necessary to guarantee that we descend to a node containing at least t keys. Then finish by recursing on the appropriate child of x.

a. If $x.c_i$ has only $t - 1$ keys but has an immediate sibling with at least t keys, give $x.c_i$ an extra key by moving a key from x down into $x.c_i$, moving a key from $x.c_i$'s immediate left or right sibling up into x, and moving the appropriate child pointer from the sibling into $x.c_i$.

b. If $x.c_i$ and both of $x.c_i$'s immediate siblings have $t - 1$ keys, merge $x.c_i$ with one sibling, which involves moving a key from x down into the new merged node to become the median key for that node.

Since most of the keys in a B-tree are in the leaves, we may expect that in practice, deletion operations are most often used to delete keys from leaves. The B-TREE-DELETE procedure then acts in one downward pass through the tree, without having to back up. When deleting a key in an internal node, however, the procedure makes a downward pass through the tree but may have to return to the node from which the key was deleted to replace the key with its predecessor or successor (cases 2a and 2b).

Although this procedure seems complicated, it involves only $O(h)$ disk operations for a B-tree of height h, since only $O(1)$ calls to DISK-READ and DISK-WRITE are made between recursive invocations of the procedure. The CPU time required is $O(th) = O(t \log_t n)$.

Exercises

18.3-1
Show the results of deleting C, P, and V, in order, from the tree of Figure 18.8(f).

18.3-2
Write pseudocode for B-TREE-DELETE.

Problems

18-1   Stacks on secondary storage
Consider implementing a stack in a computer that has a relatively small amount of fast primary memory and a relatively large amount of slower disk storage. The operations PUSH and POP work on single-word values. The stack we wish to support can grow to be much larger than can fit in memory, and thus most of it must be stored on disk.

A simple, but inefficient, stack implementation keeps the entire stack on disk. We maintain in memory a stack pointer, which is the disk address of the top element on the stack. If the pointer has value p, the top element is the $(p \bmod m)$th word on page $\lfloor p/m \rfloor$ of the disk, where m is the number of words per page.

To implement the PUSH operation, we increment the stack pointer, read the appropriate page into memory from disk, copy the element to be pushed to the appropriate word on the page, and write the page back to disk. A POP operation is similar. We save the top of the stack, decrement the stack pointer, read in the appropriate page from disk, and return the saved value. We need not write back the page, since it was not modified.

Because disk operations are relatively expensive, we count two costs for any implementation: the total number of disk accesses and the total CPU time. Any disk access to a page of m words incurs charges of one disk access and $\Theta(m)$ CPU time.

a. Asymptotically, what is the worst-case number of disk accesses for n stack operations using this simple implementation? What is the CPU time for n stack operations? (Express your answer in terms of m and n for this and subsequent parts.)

Now consider a stack implementation in which we keep one page of the stack in memory. (We also maintain a small amount of memory to keep track of which page is currently in memory.) We can perform a stack operation only if the relevant disk page resides in memory. If necessary, we can write the page currently in memory to the disk and read in the new page from the disk to memory. If the relevant disk page is already in memory, then no disk accesses are required.

b. What is the worst-case number of disk accesses required for n PUSH operations? What is the CPU time?

c. What is the worst-case number of disk accesses required for n stack operations? What is the CPU time?

Suppose that we now implement the stack by keeping two pages in memory (in addition to a small number of words for bookkeeping).

d. Describe how to manage the stack pages so that the amortized number of disk accesses for any stack operation is $O(1/m)$ and the amortized CPU time for any stack operation is $O(1)$.

18-2 *Joining and splitting 2-3-4 trees*

The *join* operation takes two dynamic sets S' and S'' and an element x such that for any $x' \in S'$ and $x'' \in S''$, we have $x'.key < x.key < x''.key$. It returns a set $S = S' \cup \{x\} \cup S''$. The *split* operation is like an "inverse" join: given a dynamic set S and an element $x \in S$, it creates a set S' that consists of all elements in $S - \{x\}$ whose keys are less than $x.key$ and a set S'' that consists of all elements in $S - \{x\}$ whose keys are greater than $x.key$. In this problem, we investigate how to implement these operations on 2-3-4 trees. We assume for convenience that elements consist only of keys and that all key values are distinct.

   a. Show how to maintain, for every node x of a 2-3-4 tree, the height of the subtree rooted at x as an attribute $x.height$. Make sure that your implementation does not affect the asymptotic running times of searching, insertion, and deletion.

   b. Show how to implement the join operation. Given two 2-3-4 trees T' and T'' and a key k, the join operation should run in $O(1 + |h' - h''|)$ time, where h' and h'' are the heights of T' and T'', respectively.

   c. Consider the simple path p from the root of a 2-3-4 tree T to a given key k, the set S' of keys in T that are less than k, and the set S'' of keys in T that are greater than k. Show that p breaks S' into a set of trees $\{T_0', T_1', \ldots, T_m'\}$ and a set of keys $\{k_1', k_2', \ldots, k_m'\}$, where, for $i = 1, 2, \ldots, m$, we have $y < k_i' < z$ for any keys $y \in T_{i-1}'$ and $z \in T_i'$. What is the relationship between the heights of T_{i-1}' and T_i'? Describe how p breaks S'' into sets of trees and keys.

   d. Show how to implement the split operation on T. Use the join operation to assemble the keys in S' into a single 2-3-4 tree T' and the keys in S'' into a single 2-3-4 tree T''. The running time of the split operation should be $O(\lg n)$, where n is the number of keys in T. (*Hint:* The costs for joining should telescope.)

Chapter notes

Knuth [211], Aho, Hopcroft, and Ullman [5], and Sedgewick [306] give further discussions of balanced-tree schemes and B-trees. Comer [74] provides a comprehensive survey of B-trees. Guibas and Sedgewick [155] discuss the relationships among various kinds of balanced-tree schemes, including red-black trees and 2-3-4 trees.

In 1970, J. E. Hopcroft invented 2-3 trees, a precursor to B-trees and 2-3-4 trees, in which every internal node has either two or three children. Bayer and McCreight [35] introduced B-trees in 1972; they did not explain their choice of name.

Bender, Demaine, and Farach-Colton [40] studied how to make B-trees perform well in the presence of memory-hierarchy effects. Their ***cache-oblivious*** algorithms work efficiently without explicitly knowing the data transfer sizes within the memory hierarchy.

19 Fibonacci Heaps

The Fibonacci heap data structure serves a dual purpose. First, it supports a set of operations that constitutes what is known as a "mergeable heap." Second, several Fibonacci-heap operations run in constant amortized time, which makes this data structure well suited for applications that invoke these operations frequently.

Mergeable heaps

A *mergeable heap* is any data structure that supports the following five operations, in which each element has a *key*:

MAKE-HEAP() creates and returns a new heap containing no elements.

INSERT(H, x) inserts element x, whose *key* has already been filled in, into heap H.

MINIMUM(H) returns a pointer to the element in heap H whose key is minimum.

EXTRACT-MIN(H) deletes the element from heap H whose key is minimum, returning a pointer to the element.

UNION(H_1, H_2) creates and returns a new heap that contains all the elements of heaps H_1 and H_2. Heaps H_1 and H_2 are "destroyed" by this operation.

In addition to the mergeable-heap operations above, Fibonacci heaps also support the following two operations:

DECREASE-KEY(H, x, k) assigns to element x within heap H the new key value k, which we assume to be no greater than its current key value.[1]

DELETE(H, x) deletes element x from heap H.

---

[1] As mentioned in the introduction to Part V, our default mergeable heaps are mergeable min-heaps, and so the operations MINIMUM, EXTRACT-MIN, and DECREASE-KEY apply. Alternatively, we could define a *mergeable max-heap* with the operations MAXIMUM, EXTRACT-MAX, and INCREASE-KEY.

Procedure	Binary heap (worst-case)	Fibonacci heap (amortized)
MAKE-HEAP	$\Theta(1)$	$\Theta(1)$
INSERT	$\Theta(\lg n)$	$\Theta(1)$
MINIMUM	$\Theta(1)$	$\Theta(1)$
EXTRACT-MIN	$\Theta(\lg n)$	$O(\lg n)$
UNION	$\Theta(n)$	$\Theta(1)$
DECREASE-KEY	$\Theta(\lg n)$	$\Theta(1)$
DELETE	$\Theta(\lg n)$	$O(\lg n)$

Figure 19.1   Running times for operations on two implementations of mergeable heaps. The number of items in the heap(s) at the time of an operation is denoted by n.

As the table in Figure 19.1 shows, if we don't need the UNION operation, ordinary binary heaps, as used in heapsort (Chapter 6), work fairly well. Operations other than UNION run in worst-case time $O(\lg n)$ on a binary heap. If we need to support the UNION operation, however, binary heaps perform poorly. By concatenating the two arrays that hold the binary heaps to be merged and then running BUILD-MIN-HEAP (see Section 6.3), the UNION operation takes $\Theta(n)$ time in the worst case.

Fibonacci heaps, on the other hand, have better asymptotic time bounds than binary heaps for the INSERT, UNION, and DECREASE-KEY operations, and they have the same asymptotic running times for the remaining operations. Note, however, that the running times for Fibonacci heaps in Figure 19.1 are amortized time bounds, not worst-case per-operation time bounds. The UNION operation takes only constant amortized time in a Fibonacci heap, which is significantly better than the linear worst-case time required in a binary heap (assuming, of course, that an amortized time bound suffices).

Fibonacci heaps in theory and practice

From a theoretical standpoint, Fibonacci heaps are especially desirable when the number of EXTRACT-MIN and DELETE operations is small relative to the number of other operations performed. This situation arises in many applications. For example, some algorithms for graph problems may call DECREASE-KEY once per edge. For dense graphs, which have many edges, the $\Theta(1)$ amortized time of each call of DECREASE-KEY adds up to a big improvement over the $\Theta(\lg n)$ worst-case time of binary heaps. Fast algorithms for problems such as computing minimum spanning trees (Chapter 23) and finding single-source shortest paths (Chapter 24) make essential use of Fibonacci heaps.

From a practical point of view, however, the constant factors and programming complexity of Fibonacci heaps make them less desirable than ordinary binary (or k-ary) heaps for most applications, except for certain applications that manage large amounts of data. Thus, Fibonacci heaps are predominantly of theoretical interest. If a much simpler data structure with the same amortized time bounds as Fibonacci heaps were developed, it would be of practical use as well.

Both binary heaps and Fibonacci heaps are inefficient in how they support the operation SEARCH; it can take a while to find an element with a given key. For this reason, operations such as DECREASE-KEY and DELETE that refer to a given element require a pointer to that element as part of their input. As in our discussion of priority queues in Section 6.5, when we use a mergeable heap in an application, we often store a handle to the corresponding application object in each mergeable-heap element, as well as a handle to the corresponding mergeable-heap element in each application object. The exact nature of these handles depends on the application and its implementation.

Like several other data structures that we have seen, Fibonacci heaps are based on rooted trees. We represent each element by a node within a tree, and each node has a *key* attribute. For the remainder of this chapter, we shall use the term "node" instead of "element." We shall also ignore issues of allocating nodes prior to insertion and freeing nodes following deletion, assuming instead that the code calling the heap procedures deals with these details.

Section 19.1 defines Fibonacci heaps, discusses how we represent them, and presents the potential function used for their amortized analysis. Section 19.2 shows how to implement the mergeable-heap operations and achieve the amortized time bounds shown in Figure 19.1. The remaining two operations, DECREASE-KEY and DELETE, form the focus of Section 19.3. Finally, Section 19.4 finishes a key part of the analysis and also explains the curious name of the data structure.

19.1   Structure of Fibonacci heaps

A *Fibonacci heap* is a collection of rooted trees that are *min-heap ordered*. That is, each tree obeys the *min-heap property*: the key of a node is greater than or equal to the key of its parent. Figure 19.2(a) shows an example of a Fibonacci heap.

As Figure 19.2(b) shows, each node x contains a pointer $x.p$ to its parent and a pointer $x.child$ to any one of its children. The children of x are linked together in a circular, doubly linked list, which we call the *child list* of x. Each child y in a child list has pointers $y.left$ and $y.right$ that point to y's left and right siblings, respectively. If node y is an only child, then $y.left = y.right = y$. Siblings may appear in a child list in any order.

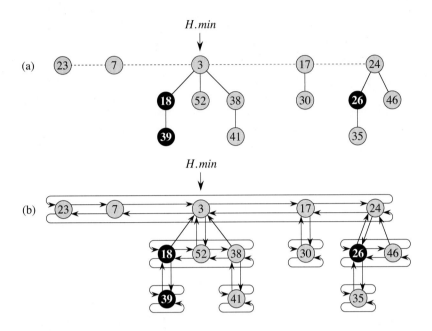

Figure 19.2 **(a)** A Fibonacci heap consisting of five min-heap-ordered trees and 14 nodes. The dashed line indicates the root list. The minimum node of the heap is the node containing the key 3. Black nodes are marked. The potential of this particular Fibonacci heap is $5 + 2 \cdot 3 = 11$. **(b)** A more complete representation showing pointers p (up arrows), *child* (down arrows), and *left* and *right* (sideways arrows). The remaining figures in this chapter omit these details, since all the information shown here can be determined from what appears in part (a).

Circular, doubly linked lists (see Section 10.2) have two advantages for use in Fibonacci heaps. First, we can insert a node into any location or remove a node from anywhere in a circular, doubly linked list in $O(1)$ time. Second, given two such lists, we can concatenate them (or "splice" them together) into one circular, doubly linked list in $O(1)$ time. In the descriptions of Fibonacci heap operations, we shall refer to these operations informally, letting you fill in the details of their implementations if you wish.

Each node has two other attributes. We store the number of children in the child list of node x in $x.degree$. The boolean-valued attribute $x.mark$ indicates whether node x has lost a child since the last time x was made the child of another node. Newly created nodes are unmarked, and a node x becomes unmarked whenever it is made the child of another node. Until we look at the DECREASE-KEY operation in Section 19.3, we will just set all *mark* attributes to FALSE.

We access a given Fibonacci heap H by a pointer $H.min$ to the root of a tree containing the minimum key; we call this node the ***minimum node*** of the Fibonacci heap. If more than one root has a key with the minimum value, then any such root may serve as the minimum node. When a Fibonacci heap H is empty, $H.min$ is NIL.

The roots of all the trees in a Fibonacci heap are linked together using their *left* and *right* pointers into a circular, doubly linked list called the ***root list*** of the Fibonacci heap. The pointer $H.min$ thus points to the node in the root list whose key is minimum. Trees may appear in any order within a root list.

We rely on one other attribute for a Fibonacci heap H: $H.n$, the number of nodes currently in H.

Potential function

As mentioned, we shall use the potential method of Section 17.3 to analyze the performance of Fibonacci heap operations. For a given Fibonacci heap H, we indicate by $t(H)$ the number of trees in the root list of H and by $m(H)$ the number of marked nodes in H. We then define the potential $\Phi(H)$ of Fibonacci heap H by

$$\Phi(H) = t(H) + 2m(H) \,. \tag{19.1}$$

(We will gain some intuition for this potential function in Section 19.3.) For example, the potential of the Fibonacci heap shown in Figure 19.2 is $5 + 2 \cdot 3 = 11$. The potential of a set of Fibonacci heaps is the sum of the potentials of its constituent Fibonacci heaps. We shall assume that a unit of potential can pay for a constant amount of work, where the constant is sufficiently large to cover the cost of any of the specific constant-time pieces of work that we might encounter.

We assume that a Fibonacci heap application begins with no heaps. The initial potential, therefore, is 0, and by equation (19.1), the potential is nonnegative at all subsequent times. From equation (17.3), an upper bound on the total amortized cost provides an upper bound on the total actual cost for the sequence of operations.

Maximum degree

The amortized analyses we shall perform in the remaining sections of this chapter assume that we know an upper bound $D(n)$ on the maximum degree of any node in an n-node Fibonacci heap. We won't prove it, but when only the mergeable-heap operations are supported, $D(n) \le \lfloor \lg n \rfloor$. (Problem 19-2(d) asks you to prove this property.) In Sections 19.3 and 19.4, we shall show that when we support DECREASE-KEY and DELETE as well, $D(n) = O(\lg n)$.

19.2   Mergeable-heap operations

The mergeable-heap operations on Fibonacci heaps delay work as long as possible. The various operations have performance trade-offs. For example, we insert a node by adding it to the root list, which takes just constant time. If we were to start with an empty Fibonacci heap and then insert k nodes, the Fibonacci heap would consist of just a root list of k nodes. The trade-off is that if we then perform an EXTRACT-MIN operation on Fibonacci heap H, after removing the node that $H.min$ points to, we would have to look through each of the remaining $k - 1$ nodes in the root list to find the new minimum node. As long as we have to go through the entire root list during the EXTRACT-MIN operation, we also consolidate nodes into min-heap-ordered trees to reduce the size of the root list. We shall see that, no matter what the root list looks like before an EXTRACT-MIN operation, afterward each node in the root list has a degree that is unique within the root list, which leads to a root list of size at most $D(n) + 1$.

Creating a new Fibonacci heap

To make an empty Fibonacci heap, the MAKE-FIB-HEAP procedure allocates and returns the Fibonacci heap object H, where $H.n = 0$ and $H.min = $ NIL; there are no trees in H. Because $t(H) = 0$ and $m(H) = 0$, the potential of the empty Fibonacci heap is $\Phi(H) = 0$. The amortized cost of MAKE-FIB-HEAP is thus equal to its $O(1)$ actual cost.

Inserting a node

The following procedure inserts node x into Fibonacci heap H, assuming that the node has already been allocated and that $x.key$ has already been filled in.

FIB-HEAP-INSERT(H, x)

```
 1   x.degree = 0
 2   x.p = NIL
 3   x.child = NIL
 4   x.mark = FALSE
 5   if H.min == NIL
 6       create a root list for H containing just x
 7       H.min = x
 8   else insert x into H's root list
 9       if x.key < H.min.key
10           H.min = x
11   H.n = H.n + 1
```

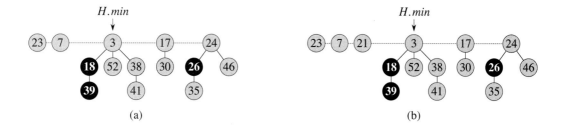

Figure 19.3 Inserting a node into a Fibonacci heap. **(a)** A Fibonacci heap H. **(b)** Fibonacci heap H after inserting the node with key 21. The node becomes its own min-heap-ordered tree and is then added to the root list, becoming the left sibling of the root.

Lines 1–4 initialize some of the structural attributes of node x. Line 5 tests to see whether Fibonacci heap H is empty. If it is, then lines 6–7 make x be the only node in H's root list and set $H.min$ to point to x. Otherwise, lines 8–10 insert x into H's root list and update $H.min$ if necessary. Finally, line 11 increments $H.n$ to reflect the addition of the new node. Figure 19.3 shows a node with key 21 inserted into the Fibonacci heap of Figure 19.2.

To determine the amortized cost of FIB-HEAP-INSERT, let H be the input Fibonacci heap and H' be the resulting Fibonacci heap. Then, $t(H') = t(H) + 1$ and $m(H') = m(H)$, and the increase in potential is

$$((t(H) + 1) + 2 m(H)) - (t(H) + 2 m(H)) = 1 .$$

Since the actual cost is $O(1)$, the amortized cost is $O(1) + 1 = O(1)$.

Finding the minimum node

The minimum node of a Fibonacci heap H is given by the pointer $H.min$, so we can find the minimum node in $O(1)$ actual time. Because the potential of H does not change, the amortized cost of this operation is equal to its $O(1)$ actual cost.

Uniting two Fibonacci heaps

The following procedure unites Fibonacci heaps H_1 and H_2, destroying H_1 and H_2 in the process. It simply concatenates the root lists of H_1 and H_2 and then determines the new minimum node. Afterward, the objects representing H_1 and H_2 will never be used again.

FIB-HEAP-UNION(H_1, H_2)

```
1   H = MAKE-FIB-HEAP()
2   H.min = H₁.min
3   concatenate the root list of H₂ with the root list of H
4   if (H₁.min == NIL) or (H₂.min ≠ NIL and H₂.min.key < H₁.min.key)
5       H.min = H₂.min
6   H.n = H₁.n + H₂.n
7   return H
```

Lines 1–3 concatenate the root lists of H_1 and H_2 into a new root list H. Lines 2, 4, and 5 set the minimum node of H, and line 6 sets $H.n$ to the total number of nodes. Line 7 returns the resulting Fibonacci heap H. As in the FIB-HEAP-INSERT procedure, all roots remain roots.

The change in potential is

$$\Phi(H) - (\Phi(H_1) + \Phi(H_2))$$
$$= (t(H) + 2m(H)) - ((t(H_1) + 2m(H_1)) + (t(H_2) + 2m(H_2)))$$
$$= 0,$$

because $t(H) = t(H_1) + t(H_2)$ and $m(H) = m(H_1) + m(H_2)$. The amortized cost of FIB-HEAP-UNION is therefore equal to its $O(1)$ actual cost.

Extracting the minimum node

The process of extracting the minimum node is the most complicated of the operations presented in this section. It is also where the delayed work of consolidating trees in the root list finally occurs. The following pseudocode extracts the minimum node. The code assumes for convenience that when a node is removed from a linked list, pointers remaining in the list are updated, but pointers in the extracted node are left unchanged. It also calls the auxiliary procedure CONSOLIDATE, which we shall see shortly.

FIB-HEAP-EXTRACT-MIN(H)

```
1   z = H.min
2   if z ≠ NIL
3       for each child x of z
4           add x to the root list of H
5           x.p = NIL
6       remove z from the root list of H
7       if z == z.right
8           H.min = NIL
9       else H.min = z.right
10          CONSOLIDATE(H)
11      H.n = H.n − 1
12  return z
```

As Figure 19.4 illustrates, FIB-HEAP-EXTRACT-MIN works by first making a root out of each of the minimum node's children and removing the minimum node from the root list. It then consolidates the root list by linking roots of equal degree until at most one root remains of each degree.

We start in line 1 by saving a pointer z to the minimum node; the procedure returns this pointer at the end. If z is NIL, then Fibonacci heap H is already empty and we are done. Otherwise, we delete node z from H by making all of z's children roots of H in lines 3–5 (putting them into the root list) and removing z from the root list in line 6. If z is its own right sibling after line 6, then z was the only node on the root list and it had no children, so all that remains is to make the Fibonacci heap empty in line 8 before returning z. Otherwise, we set the pointer $H.min$ into the root list to point to a root other than z (in this case, z's right sibling), which is not necessarily going to be the new minimum node when FIB-HEAP-EXTRACT-MIN is done. Figure 19.4(b) shows the Fibonacci heap of Figure 19.4(a) after executing line 9.

The next step, in which we reduce the number of trees in the Fibonacci heap, is *consolidating* the root list of H, which the call CONSOLIDATE(H) accomplishes. Consolidating the root list consists of repeatedly executing the following steps until every root in the root list has a distinct *degree* value:

1. Find two roots x and y in the root list with the same degree. Without loss of generality, let $x.key \le y.key$.

2. **Link** y to x: remove y from the root list, and make y a child of x by calling the FIB-HEAP-LINK procedure. This procedure increments the attribute $x.degree$ and clears the mark on y.

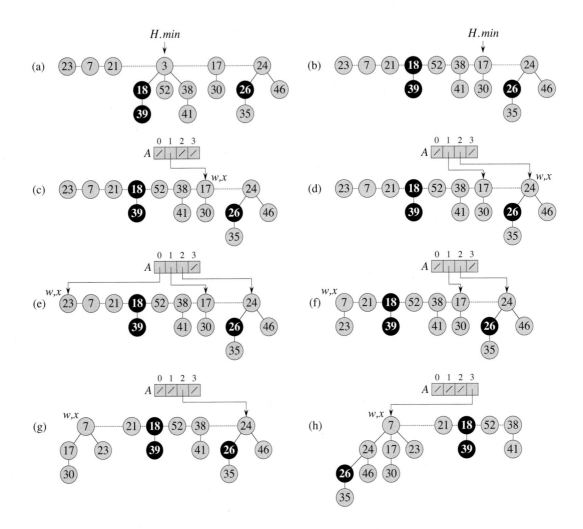

Figure 19.4 The action of FIB-HEAP-EXTRACT-MIN. **(a)** A Fibonacci heap H. **(b)** The situation after removing the minimum node z from the root list and adding its children to the root list. **(c)–(e)** The array A and the trees after each of the first three iterations of the **for** loop of lines 4–14 of the procedure CONSOLIDATE. The procedure processes the root list by starting at the node pointed to by $H.min$ and following *right* pointers. Each part shows the values of w and x at the end of an iteration. **(f)–(h)** The next iteration of the **for** loop, with the values of w and x shown at the end of each iteration of the **while** loop of lines 7–13. Part (f) shows the situation after the first time through the **while** loop. The node with key 23 has been linked to the node with key 7, which x now points to. In part (g), the node with key 17 has been linked to the node with key 7, which x still points to. In part (h), the node with key 24 has been linked to the node with key 7. Since no node was previously pointed to by $A[3]$, at the end of the **for** loop iteration, $A[3]$ is set to point to the root of the resulting tree.

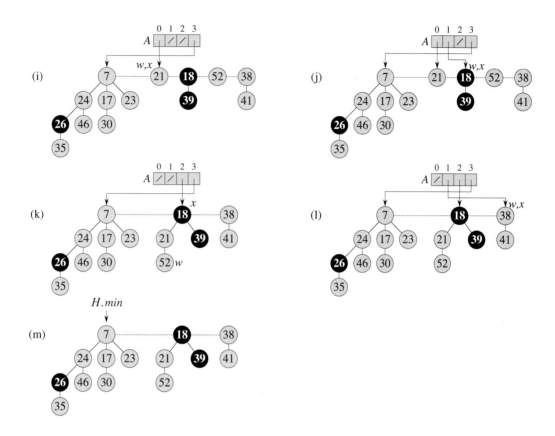

Figure 19.4, continued (i)–(l) The situation after each of the next four iterations of the **for** loop. (m) Fibonacci heap H after reconstructing the root list from the array A and determining the new $H.min$ pointer.

The procedure CONSOLIDATE uses an auxiliary array $A[0 \mathinner{\ldotp\ldotp} D(H.n)]$ to keep track of roots according to their degrees. If $A[i] = y$, then y is currently a root with $y.degree = i$. Of course, in order to allocate the array we have to know how to calculate the upper bound $D(H.n)$ on the maximum degree, but we will see how to do so in Section 19.4.

CONSOLIDATE(H)

```
 1   let A[0 .. D(H.n)] be a new array
 2   for i = 0 to D(H.n)
 3       A[i] = NIL
 4   for each node w in the root list of H
 5       x = w
 6       d = x.degree
 7       while A[d] ≠ NIL
 8           y = A[d]           // another node with the same degree as x
 9           if x.key > y.key
10               exchange x with y
11           FIB-HEAP-LINK(H, y, x)
12           A[d] = NIL
13           d = d + 1
14       A[d] = x
15   H.min = NIL
16   for i = 0 to D(H.n)
17       if A[i] ≠ NIL
18           if H.min == NIL
19               create a root list for H containing just A[i]
20               H.min = A[i]
21           else insert A[i] into H's root list
22               if A[i].key < H.min.key
23                   H.min = A[i]
```

FIB-HEAP-LINK(H, y, x)

```
1   remove y from the root list of H
2   make y a child of x, incrementing x.degree
3   y.mark = FALSE
```

In detail, the CONSOLIDATE procedure works as follows. Lines 1–3 allocate and initialize the array A by making each entry NIL. The **for** loop of lines 4–14 processes each root w in the root list. As we link roots together, w may be linked to some other node and no longer be a root. Nevertheless, w is always in a tree rooted at some node x, which may or may not be w itself. Because we want at most one root with each degree, we look in the array A to see whether it contains a root y with the same degree as x. If it does, then we link the roots x and y but guaranteeing that x remains a root after linking. That is, we link y to x after first exchanging the pointers to the two roots if y's key is smaller than x's key. After we link y to x, the degree of x has increased by 1, and so we continue this process, linking x and another root whose degree equals x's new degree, until no other root that we have processed has the same degree as x. We then set the appropriate entry of A to point to x, so that as we process roots later on, we have recorded that x is the unique root of its degree that we have already processed. When this **for** loop terminates, at most one root of each degree will remain, and the array A will point to each remaining root.

The **while** loop of lines 7–13 repeatedly links the root x of the tree containing node w to another tree whose root has the same degree as x, until no other root has the same degree. This **while** loop maintains the following invariant:

> At the start of each iteration of the **while** loop, $d = x.degree$.

We use this loop invariant as follows:

Initialization: Line 6 ensures that the loop invariant holds the first time we enter the loop.

Maintenance: In each iteration of the **while** loop, $A[d]$ points to some root y. Because $d = x.degree = y.degree$, we want to link x and y. Whichever of x and y has the smaller key becomes the parent of the other as a result of the link operation, and so lines 9–10 exchange the pointers to x and y if necessary. Next, we link y to x by the call FIB-HEAP-LINK(H, y, x) in line 11. This call increments $x.degree$ but leaves $y.degree$ as d. Node y is no longer a root, and so line 12 removes the pointer to it in array A. Because the call of FIB-HEAP-LINK increments the value of $x.degree$, line 13 restores the invariant that $d = x.degree$.

Termination: We repeat the **while** loop until $A[d] = $ NIL, in which case there is no other root with the same degree as x.

After the **while** loop terminates, we set $A[d]$ to x in line 14 and perform the next iteration of the **for** loop.

Figures 19.4(c)–(e) show the array A and the resulting trees after the first three iterations of the **for** loop of lines 4–14. In the next iteration of the **for** loop, three links occur; their results are shown in Figures 19.4(f)–(h). Figures 19.4(i)–(l) show the result of the next four iterations of the **for** loop.

All that remains is to clean up. Once the **for** loop of lines 4–14 completes, line 15 empties the root list, and lines 16–23 reconstruct it from the array A. The resulting Fibonacci heap appears in Figure 19.4(m). After consolidating the root list, FIB-HEAP-EXTRACT-MIN finishes up by decrementing $H.n$ in line 11 and returning a pointer to the deleted node z in line 12.

We are now ready to show that the amortized cost of extracting the minimum node of an n-node Fibonacci heap is $O(D(n))$. Let H denote the Fibonacci heap just prior to the FIB-HEAP-EXTRACT-MIN operation.

We start by accounting for the actual cost of extracting the minimum node. An $O(D(n))$ contribution comes from FIB-HEAP-EXTRACT-MIN processing at most $D(n)$ children of the minimum node and from the work in lines 2–3 and 16–23 of CONSOLIDATE. It remains to analyze the contribution from the **for** loop of lines 4–14 in CONSOLIDATE, for which we use an aggregate analysis. The size of the root list upon calling CONSOLIDATE is at most $D(n) + t(H) - 1$, since it consists of the original $t(H)$ root-list nodes, minus the extracted root node, plus the children of the extracted node, which number at most $D(n)$. Within a given iteration of the **for** loop of lines 4–14, the number of iterations of the **while** loop of lines 7–13 depends on the root list. But we know that every time through the **while** loop, one of the roots is linked to another, and thus the total number of iterations of the **while** loop over all iterations of the **for** loop is at most the number of roots in the root list. Hence, the total amount of work performed in the **for** loop is at most proportional to $D(n) + t(H)$. Thus, the total actual work in extracting the minimum node is $O(D(n) + t(H))$.

The potential before extracting the minimum node is $t(H) + 2m(H)$, and the potential afterward is at most $(D(n) + 1) + 2m(H)$, since at most $D(n) + 1$ roots remain and no nodes become marked during the operation. The amortized cost is thus at most

$$
\begin{aligned}
O(D(n) + t(H)) &+ ((D(n) + 1) + 2m(H)) - (t(H) + 2m(H)) \\
&= O(D(n)) + O(t(H)) - t(H) \\
&= O(D(n)) ,
\end{aligned}
$$

since we can scale up the units of potential to dominate the constant hidden in $O(t(H))$. Intuitively, the cost of performing each link is paid for by the reduction in potential due to the link's reducing the number of roots by one. We shall see in Section 19.4 that $D(n) = O(\lg n)$, so that the amortized cost of extracting the minimum node is $O(\lg n)$.

Exercises

19.2-1
Show the Fibonacci heap that results from calling FIB-HEAP-EXTRACT-MIN on the Fibonacci heap shown in Figure 19.4(m).

19.3   Decreasing a key and deleting a node

In this section, we show how to decrease the key of a node in a Fibonacci heap in $O(1)$ amortized time and how to delete any node from an n-node Fibonacci heap in $O(D(n))$ amortized time. In Section 19.4, we will show that the maximum degree $D(n)$ is $O(\lg n)$, which will imply that FIB-HEAP-EXTRACT-MIN and FIB-HEAP-DELETE run in $O(\lg n)$ amortized time.

Decreasing a key

In the following pseudocode for the operation FIB-HEAP-DECREASE-KEY, we assume as before that removing a node from a linked list does not change any of the structural attributes in the removed node.

FIB-HEAP-DECREASE-KEY(H, x, k)

```
1   if k > x.key
2       error "new key is greater than current key"
3   x.key = k
4   y = x.p
5   if y ≠ NIL and x.key < y.key
6       CUT(H, x, y)
7       CASCADING-CUT(H, y)
8   if x.key < H.min.key
9       H.min = x
```

CUT(H, x, y)

```
1   remove x from the child list of y, decrementing y.degree
2   add x to the root list of H
3   x.p = NIL
4   x.mark = FALSE
```

CASCADING-CUT(H, y)

```
1   z = y.p
2   if z ≠ NIL
3       if y.mark == FALSE
4           y.mark = TRUE
5       else CUT(H, y, z)
6           CASCADING-CUT(H, z)
```

The FIB-HEAP-DECREASE-KEY procedure works as follows. Lines 1–3 ensure that the new key is no greater than the current key of x and then assign the new key to x. If x is a root or if $x.key \geq y.key$, where y is x's parent, then no structural changes need occur, since min-heap order has not been violated. Lines 4–5 test for this condition.

If min-heap order has been violated, many changes may occur. We start by *cutting* x in line 6. The CUT procedure "cuts" the link between x and its parent y, making x a root.

We use the *mark* attributes to obtain the desired time bounds. They record a little piece of the history of each node. Suppose that the following events have happened to node x:

1. at some time, x was a root,

2. then x was linked to (made the child of) another node,

3. then two children of x were removed by cuts.

As soon as the second child has been lost, we cut x from its parent, making it a new root. The attribute $x.mark$ is TRUE if steps 1 and 2 have occurred and one child of x has been cut. The CUT procedure, therefore, clears $x.mark$ in line 4, since it performs step 1. (We can now see why line 3 of FIB-HEAP-LINK clears $y.mark$: node y is being linked to another node, and so step 2 is being performed. The next time a child of y is cut, $y.mark$ will be set to TRUE.)

We are not yet done, because x might be the second child cut from its parent y since the time that y was linked to another node. Therefore, line 7 of FIB-HEAP-DECREASE-KEY attempts to perform a ***cascading-cut*** operation on y. If y is a root, then the test in line 2 of CASCADING-CUT causes the procedure to just return. If y is unmarked, the procedure marks it in line 4, since its first child has just been cut, and returns. If y is marked, however, it has just lost its second child; y is cut in line 5, and CASCADING-CUT calls itself recursively in line 6 on y's parent z. The CASCADING-CUT procedure recurses its way up the tree until it finds either a root or an unmarked node.

Once all the cascading cuts have occurred, lines 8–9 of FIB-HEAP-DECREASE-KEY finish up by updating $H.min$ if necessary. The only node whose key changed was the node x whose key decreased. Thus, the new minimum node is either the original minimum node or node x.

Figure 19.5 shows the execution of two calls of FIB-HEAP-DECREASE-KEY, starting with the Fibonacci heap shown in Figure 19.5(a). The first call, shown in Figure 19.5(b), involves no cascading cuts. The second call, shown in Figures 19.5(c)–(e), invokes two cascading cuts.

We shall now show that the amortized cost of FIB-HEAP-DECREASE-KEY is only $O(1)$. We start by determining its actual cost. The FIB-HEAP-DECREASE-KEY procedure takes $O(1)$ time, plus the time to perform the cascading cuts. Suppose that a given invocation of FIB-HEAP-DECREASE-KEY results in c calls of CASCADING-CUT (the call made from line 7 of FIB-HEAP-DECREASE-KEY followed by $c - 1$ recursive calls of CASCADING-CUT). Each call of CASCADING-CUT takes $O(1)$ time exclusive of recursive calls. Thus, the actual cost of FIB-HEAP-DECREASE-KEY, including all recursive calls, is $O(c)$.

We next compute the change in potential. Let H denote the Fibonacci heap just prior to the FIB-HEAP-DECREASE-KEY operation. The call to CUT in line 6 of

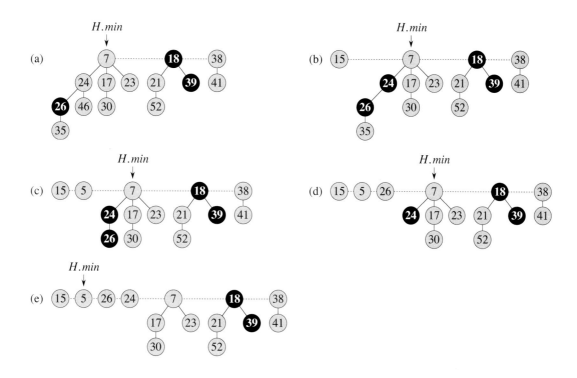

Figure 19.5 Two calls of FIB-HEAP-DECREASE-KEY. **(a)** The initial Fibonacci heap. **(b)** The node with key 46 has its key decreased to 15. The node becomes a root, and its parent (with key 24), which had previously been unmarked, becomes marked. **(c)–(e)** The node with key 35 has its key decreased to 5. In part (c), the node, now with key 5, becomes a root. Its parent, with key 26, is marked, so a cascading cut occurs. The node with key 26 is cut from its parent and made an unmarked root in (d). Another cascading cut occurs, since the node with key 24 is marked as well. This node is cut from its parent and made an unmarked root in part (e). The cascading cuts stop at this point, since the node with key 7 is a root. (Even if this node were not a root, the cascading cuts would stop, since it is unmarked.) Part (e) shows the result of the FIB-HEAP-DECREASE-KEY operation, with *H.min* pointing to the new minimum node.

FIB-HEAP-DECREASE-KEY creates a new tree rooted at node x and clears x's mark bit (which may have already been FALSE). Each call of CASCADING-CUT, except for the last one, cuts a marked node and clears the mark bit. Afterward, the Fibonacci heap contains $t(H) + c$ trees (the original $t(H)$ trees, $c-1$ trees produced by cascading cuts, and the tree rooted at x) and at most $m(H) - c + 2$ marked nodes ($c-1$ were unmarked by cascading cuts and the last call of CASCADING-CUT may have marked a node). The change in potential is therefore at most

$$((t(H) + c) + 2(m(H) - c + 2)) - (t(H) + 2m(H)) = 4 - c .$$

Thus, the amortized cost of FIB-HEAP-DECREASE-KEY is at most

$$O(c) + 4 - c = O(1) \, ,$$

since we can scale up the units of potential to dominate the constant hidden in $O(c)$.

You can now see why we defined the potential function to include a term that is twice the number of marked nodes. When a marked node y is cut by a cascading cut, its mark bit is cleared, which reduces the potential by 2. One unit of potential pays for the cut and the clearing of the mark bit, and the other unit compensates for the unit increase in potential due to node y becoming a root.

Deleting a node

The following pseudocode deletes a node from an n-node Fibonacci heap in $O(D(n))$ amortized time. We assume that there is no key value of $-\infty$ currently in the Fibonacci heap.

FIB-HEAP-DELETE(H, x)

1   FIB-HEAP-DECREASE-KEY$(H, x, -\infty)$
2   FIB-HEAP-EXTRACT-MIN(H)

FIB-HEAP-DELETE makes x become the minimum node in the Fibonacci heap by giving it a uniquely small key of $-\infty$. The FIB-HEAP-EXTRACT-MIN procedure then removes node x from the Fibonacci heap. The amortized time of FIB-HEAP-DELETE is the sum of the $O(1)$ amortized time of FIB-HEAP-DECREASE-KEY and the $O(D(n))$ amortized time of FIB-HEAP-EXTRACT-MIN. Since we shall see in Section 19.4 that $D(n) = O(\lg n)$, the amortized time of FIB-HEAP-DELETE is $O(\lg n)$.

Exercises

19.3-1
Suppose that a root x in a Fibonacci heap is marked. Explain how x came to be a marked root. Argue that it doesn't matter to the analysis that x is marked, even though it is not a root that was first linked to another node and then lost one child.

19.3-2
Justify the $O(1)$ amortized time of FIB-HEAP-DECREASE-KEY as an average cost per operation by using aggregate analysis.

19.4   Bounding the maximum degree

To prove that the amortized time of FIB-HEAP-EXTRACT-MIN and FIB-HEAP-DELETE is $O(\lg n)$, we must show that the upper bound $D(n)$ on the degree of any node of an n-node Fibonacci heap is $O(\lg n)$. In particular, we shall show that $D(n) \leq \lfloor \log_\phi n \rfloor$, where ϕ is the golden ratio, defined in equation (3.24) as

$$\phi = (1 + \sqrt{5})/2 = 1.61803\ldots .$$

The key to the analysis is as follows. For each node x within a Fibonacci heap, define $\text{size}(x)$ to be the number of nodes, including x itself, in the subtree rooted at x. (Note that x need not be in the root list—it can be any node at all.) We shall show that $\text{size}(x)$ is exponential in $x.degree$. Bear in mind that $x.degree$ is always maintained as an accurate count of the degree of x.

Lemma 19.1
Let x be any node in a Fibonacci heap, and suppose that $x.degree = k$. Let $y_1, y_2, \ldots, y_k$ denote the children of x in the order in which they were linked to x, from the earliest to the latest. Then, $y_1.degree \geq 0$ and $y_i.degree \geq i - 2$ for $i = 2, 3, \ldots, k$.

Proof   Obviously, $y_1.degree \geq 0$.

For $i \geq 2$, we note that when y_i was linked to x, all of $y_1, y_2, \ldots, y_{i-1}$ were children of x, and so we must have had $x.degree \geq i - 1$. Because node y_i is linked to x (by CONSOLIDATE) only if $x.degree = y_i.degree$, we must have also had $y_i.degree \geq i - 1$ at that time. Since then, node y_i has lost at most one child, since it would have been cut from x (by CASCADING-CUT) if it had lost two children. We conclude that $y_i.degree \geq i - 2$.   ∎

We finally come to the part of the analysis that explains the name "Fibonacci heaps." Recall from Section 3.2 that for $k = 0, 1, 2, \ldots$, the kth Fibonacci number is defined by the recurrence

$$F_k = \begin{cases} 0 & \text{if } k = 0, \\ 1 & \text{if } k = 1, \\ F_{k-1} + F_{k-2} & \text{if } k \geq 2. \end{cases}$$

The following lemma gives another way to express F_k.

Lemma 19.2
For all integers $k \geq 0$,

$$F_{k+2} = 1 + \sum_{i=0}^{k} F_i \,.$$

Proof   The proof is by induction on k. When $k = 0$,

$$
\begin{aligned}
1 + \sum_{i=0}^{0} F_i &= 1 + F_0 \\
&= 1 + 0 \\
&= F_2 \,.
\end{aligned}
$$

We now assume the inductive hypothesis that $F_{k+1} = 1 + \sum_{i=0}^{k-1} F_i$, and we have

$$
\begin{aligned}
F_{k+2} &= F_k + F_{k+1} \\
&= F_k + \left(1 + \sum_{i=0}^{k-1} F_i\right) \\
&= 1 + \sum_{i=0}^{k} F_i \,.
\end{aligned}
$$

$\blacksquare$

Lemma 19.3
For all integers $k \geq 0$, the $(k + 2)$nd Fibonacci number satisfies $F_{k+2} \geq \phi^k$.

Proof   The proof is by induction on k. The base cases are for $k = 0$ and $k = 1$. When $k = 0$ we have $F_2 = 1 = \phi^0$, and when $k = 1$ we have $F_3 = 2 > 1.619 > \phi^1$. The inductive step is for $k \geq 2$, and we assume that $F_{i+2} > \phi^i$ for $i = 0, 1, \ldots, k-1$. Recall that ϕ is the positive root of equation (3.23), $x^2 = x+1$. Thus, we have

$$
\begin{aligned}
F_{k+2} &= F_{k+1} + F_k \\
&\geq \phi^{k-1} + \phi^{k-2} \quad \text{(by the inductive hypothesis)} \\
&= \phi^{k-2}(\phi + 1) \\
&= \phi^{k-2} \cdot \phi^2 \quad\quad \text{(by equation (3.23))} \\
&= \phi^k \,.
\end{aligned}
$$

$\blacksquare$

The following lemma and its corollary complete the analysis.

Lemma 19.4
Let x be any node in a Fibonacci heap, and let $k = x.degree$. Then $size(x) \geq F_{k+2} \geq \phi^k$, where $\phi = (1 + \sqrt{5})/2$.

Proof Let s_k denote the minimum possible size of any node of degree k in any Fibonacci heap. Trivially, $s_0 = 1$ and $s_1 = 2$. The number s_k is at most $size(x)$ and, because adding children to a node cannot decrease the node's size, the value of s_k increases monotonically with k. Consider some node z, in any Fibonacci heap, such that $z.degree = k$ and $size(z) = s_k$. Because $s_k \leq size(x)$, we compute a lower bound on $size(x)$ by computing a lower bound on s_k. As in Lemma 19.1, let $y_1, y_2, \ldots, y_k$ denote the children of z in the order in which they were linked to z. To bound s_k, we count one for z itself and one for the first child y_1 (for which $size(y_1) \geq 1$), giving

$$
\begin{aligned}
size(x) \;\geq\; & s_k \\
\geq\; & 2 + \sum_{i=2}^{k} s_{y_i.degree} \\
\geq\; & 2 + \sum_{i=2}^{k} s_{i-2} \;,
\end{aligned}
$$

where the last line follows from Lemma 19.1 (so that $y_i.degree \geq i - 2$) and the monotonicity of s_k (so that $s_{y_i.degree} \geq s_{i-2}$).

We now show by induction on k that $s_k \geq F_{k+2}$ for all nonnegative integers k. The bases, for $k = 0$ and $k = 1$, are trivial. For the inductive step, we assume that $k \geq 2$ and that $s_i \geq F_{i+2}$ for $i = 0, 1, \ldots, k - 1$. We have

$$
\begin{aligned}
s_k \;\geq\; & 2 + \sum_{i=2}^{k} s_{i-2} \\
\geq\; & 2 + \sum_{i=2}^{k} F_i \\
=\; & 1 + \sum_{i=0}^{k} F_i \\
=\; & F_{k+2} & \text{(by Lemma 19.2)} \\
\geq\; & \phi^k & \text{(by Lemma 19.3) .}
\end{aligned}
$$

Thus, we have shown that $size(x) \geq s_k \geq F_{k+2} \geq \phi^k$. ∎

Corollary 19.5

The maximum degree $D(n)$ of any node in an n-node Fibonacci heap is $O(\lg n)$.

Proof Let x be any node in an n-node Fibonacci heap, and let $k = x.degree$. By Lemma 19.4, we have $n \geq \text{size}(x) \geq \phi^k$. Taking base-$\phi$ logarithms gives us $k \leq \log_\phi n$. (In fact, because k is an integer, $k \leq \lfloor \log_\phi n \rfloor$.) The maximum degree $D(n)$ of any node is thus $O(\lg n)$. ∎

Exercises

19.4-1

Professor Pinocchio claims that the height of an n-node Fibonacci heap is $O(\lg n)$. Show that the professor is mistaken by exhibiting, for any positive integer n, a sequence of Fibonacci-heap operations that creates a Fibonacci heap consisting of just one tree that is a linear chain of n nodes.

19.4-2

Suppose we generalize the cascading-cut rule to cut a node x from its parent as soon as it loses its kth child, for some integer constant k. (The rule in Section 19.3 uses $k = 2$.) For what values of k is $D(n) = O(\lg n)$ and the asymptotic amortized operation costs remain unchanged?

Problems

19-1 *Alternative implementation of deletion*

Professor Pisano has proposed the following variant of the FIB-HEAP-DELETE procedure, claiming that it runs faster when the node being deleted is not the node pointed to by $H.min$.

PISANO-DELETE(H, x)

```
1   if x == H.min
2       FIB-HEAP-EXTRACT-MIN(H)
3   else y = x.p
4       if y ≠ NIL
5           CUT(H, x, y)
6           CASCADING-CUT(H, y)
7       add x's child list to the root list of H
8       remove x from the root list of H
```

a. The professor's claim that this procedure runs faster is based partly on the assumption that line 7 can be performed in $O(1)$ actual time. What is wrong with this assumption?

b. Give a good upper bound on the actual time of PISANO-DELETE when x is not $H.min$. Your bound should be in terms of $x.degree$ and the number c of calls to the CASCADING-CUT procedure.

c. Suppose that we call PISANO-DELETE(H, x), and let H' be the Fibonacci heap that results. Assuming that node x is not a root, bound the potential of H' in terms of $x.degree$, c, $t(H)$, and $m(H)$.

d. Conclude that the amortized time for PISANO-DELETE is asymptotically no better than for FIB-HEAP-DELETE, even when $x \neq H.min$.

19-2 Binomial trees and binomial heaps

The **binomial tree** B_k is an ordered tree (see Section B.5.2) defined recursively. As shown in Figure 19.6(a), the binomial tree B_0 consists of a single node. The binomial tree B_k consists of two binomial trees B_{k-1} that are linked together so that the root of one is the leftmost child of the root of the other. Figure 19.6(b) shows the binomial trees B_0 through B_4.

a. Show that for the binomial tree B_k,

1. there are 2^k nodes,
2. the height of the tree is k,
3. there are exactly $\binom{k}{i}$ nodes at depth i for $i = 0, 1, \ldots, k$, and
4. the root has degree k, which is greater than that of any other node; moreover, as Figure 19.6(c) shows, if we number the children of the root from left to right by $k - 1, k - 2, \ldots, 0$, then child i is the root of a subtree B_i.

A **binomial heap** H is a set of binomial trees that satisfies the following properties:

1. Each node has a *key* (like a Fibonacci heap).
2. Each binomial tree in H obeys the min-heap property.
3. For any nonnegative integer k, there is at most one binomial tree in H whose root has degree k.

b. Suppose that a binomial heap H has a total of n nodes. Discuss the relationship between the binomial trees that H contains and the binary representation of n. Conclude that H consists of at most $\lfloor \lg n \rfloor + 1$ binomial trees.

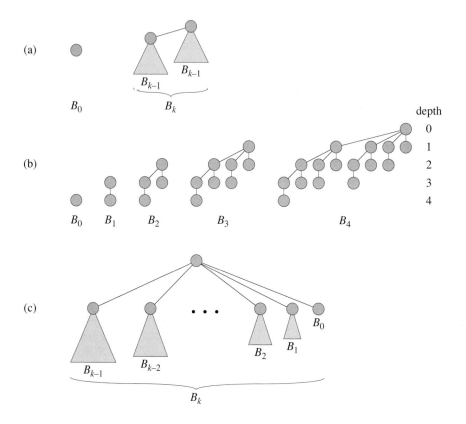

Figure 19.6   **(a)** The recursive definition of the binomial tree B_k. Triangles represent rooted subtrees. **(b)** The binomial trees B_0 through B_4. Node depths in B_4 are shown. **(c)** Another way of looking at the binomial tree B_k.

Suppose that we represent a binomial heap as follows. The left-child, right-sibling scheme of Section 10.4 represents each binomial tree within a binomial heap. Each node contains its key; pointers to its parent, to its leftmost child, and to the sibling immediately to its right (these pointers are NIL when appropriate); and its degree (as in Fibonacci heaps, how many children it has). The roots form a singly linked root list, ordered by the degrees of the roots (from low to high), and we access the binomial heap by a pointer to the first node on the root list.

c. Complete the description of how to represent a binomial heap (i.e., name the attributes, describe when attributes have the value NIL, and define how the root list is organized), and show how to implement the same seven operations on binomial heaps as this chapter implemented on Fibonacci heaps. Each operation should run in $O(\lg n)$ worst-case time, where n is the number of nodes in the binomial heap (or in the case of the UNION operation, in the two binomial heaps that are being united). The MAKE-HEAP operation should take constant time.

d. Suppose that we were to implement only the mergeable-heap operations on a Fibonacci heap (i.e., we do not implement the DECREASE-KEY or DELETE operations). How would the trees in a Fibonacci heap resemble those in a binomial heap? How would they differ? Show that the maximum degree in an n-node Fibonacci heap would be at most $\lfloor \lg n \rfloor$.

e. Professor McGee has devised a new data structure based on Fibonacci heaps. A McGee heap has the same structure as a Fibonacci heap and supports just the mergeable-heap operations. The implementations of the operations are the same as for Fibonacci heaps, except that insertion and union consolidate the root list as their last step. What are the worst-case running times of operations on McGee heaps?

19-3 *More Fibonacci-heap operations*

We wish to augment a Fibonacci heap H to support two new operations without changing the amortized running time of any other Fibonacci-heap operations.

a. The operation FIB-HEAP-CHANGE-KEY(H, x, k) changes the key of node x to the value k. Give an efficient implementation of FIB-HEAP-CHANGE-KEY, and analyze the amortized running time of your implementation for the cases in which k is greater than, less than, or equal to $x.key$.

b. Give an efficient implementation of FIB-HEAP-PRUNE(H, r), which deletes $q = \min(r, H.n)$ nodes from H. You may choose any q nodes to delete. Analyze the amortized running time of your implementation. (*Hint:* You may need to modify the data structure and potential function.)

19-4 *2-3-4 heaps*

Chapter 18 introduced the 2-3-4 tree, in which every internal node (other than possibly the root) has two, three, or four children and all leaves have the same depth. In this problem, we shall implement **2-3-4 heaps**, which support the mergeable-heap operations.

The 2-3-4 heaps differ from 2-3-4 trees in the following ways. In 2-3-4 heaps, only leaves store keys, and each leaf x stores exactly one key in the attribute $x.key$. The keys in the leaves may appear in any order. Each internal node x contains a value $x.small$ that is equal to the smallest key stored in any leaf in the subtree rooted at x. The root r contains an attribute $r.height$ that gives the height of the tree. Finally, 2-3-4 heaps are designed to be kept in main memory, so that disk reads and writes are not needed.

Implement the following 2-3-4 heap operations. In parts (a)–(e), each operation should run in $O(\lg n)$ time on a 2-3-4 heap with n elements. The UNION operation in part (f) should run in $O(\lg n)$ time, where n is the number of elements in the two input heaps.

a. MINIMUM, which returns a pointer to the leaf with the smallest key.

b. DECREASE-KEY, which decreases the key of a given leaf x to a given value $k \leq x.key$.

c. INSERT, which inserts leaf x with key k.

d. DELETE, which deletes a given leaf x.

e. EXTRACT-MIN, which extracts the leaf with the smallest key.

f. UNION, which unites two 2-3-4 heaps, returning a single 2-3-4 heap and destroying the input heaps.

Chapter notes

Fredman and Tarjan [114] introduced Fibonacci heaps. Their paper also describes the application of Fibonacci heaps to the problems of single-source shortest paths, all-pairs shortest paths, weighted bipartite matching, and the minimum-spanning-tree problem.

Subsequently, Driscoll, Gabow, Shrairman, and Tarjan [96] developed "relaxed heaps" as an alternative to Fibonacci heaps. They devised two varieties of relaxed heaps. One gives the same amortized time bounds as Fibonacci heaps. The other allows DECREASE-KEY to run in $O(1)$ worst-case (not amortized) time and EXTRACT-MIN and DELETE to run in $O(\lg n)$ worst-case time. Relaxed heaps also have some advantages over Fibonacci heaps in parallel algorithms.

See also the chapter notes for Chapter 6 for other data structures that support fast DECREASE-KEY operations when the sequence of values returned by EXTRACT-MIN calls are monotonically increasing over time and the data are integers in a specific range.

20 van Emde Boas Trees

In previous chapters, we saw data structures that support the operations of a priority queue—binary heaps in Chapter 6, red-black trees in Chapter 13,[1] and Fibonacci heaps in Chapter 19. In each of these data structures, at least one important operation took $O(\lg n)$ time, either worst case or amortized. In fact, because each of these data structures bases its decisions on comparing keys, the $\Omega(n \lg n)$ lower bound for sorting in Section 8.1 tells us that at least one operation will have to take $\Omega(\lg n)$ time. Why? If we could perform both the INSERT and EXTRACT-MIN operations in $o(\lg n)$ time, then we could sort n keys in $o(n \lg n)$ time by first performing n INSERT operations, followed by n EXTRACT-MIN operations.

We saw in Chapter 8, however, that sometimes we can exploit additional information about the keys to sort in $o(n \lg n)$ time. In particular, with counting sort we can sort n keys, each an integer in the range 0 to k, in time $\Theta(n + k)$, which is $\Theta(n)$ when $k = O(n)$.

Since we can circumvent the $\Omega(n \lg n)$ lower bound for sorting when the keys are integers in a bounded range, you might wonder whether we can perform each of the priority-queue operations in $o(\lg n)$ time in a similar scenario. In this chapter, we shall see that we can: van Emde Boas trees support the priority-queue operations, and a few others, each in $O(\lg \lg n)$ worst-case time. The hitch is that the keys must be integers in the range 0 to $n - 1$, with no duplicates allowed.

Specifically, van Emde Boas trees support each of the dynamic set operations listed on page 230—SEARCH, INSERT, DELETE, MINIMUM, MAXIMUM, SUCCESSOR, and PREDECESSOR—in $O(\lg \lg n)$ time. In this chapter, we will omit discussion of satellite data and focus only on storing keys. Because we concentrate on keys and disallow duplicate keys to be stored, instead of describing the SEARCH

---

[1] Chapter 13 does not explicitly discuss how to implement EXTRACT-MIN and DECREASE-KEY, but we can easily build these operations for any data structure that supports MINIMUM, DELETE, and INSERT.

operation, we will implement the simpler operation $\text{MEMBER}(S, x)$, which returns a boolean indicating whether the value x is currently in dynamic set S.

So far, we have used the parameter n for two distinct purposes: the number of elements in the dynamic set, and the range of the possible values. To avoid any further confusion, from here on we will use n to denote the number of elements currently in the set and u as the range of possible values, so that each van Emde Boas tree operation runs in $O(\lg \lg u)$ time. We call the set $\{0, 1, 2, \ldots, u - 1\}$ the ***universe*** of values that can be stored and u the ***universe size***. We assume throughout this chapter that u is an exact power of 2, i.e., $u = 2^k$ for some integer $k \geq 1$.

Section 20.1 starts us out by examining some simple approaches that will get us going in the right direction. We enhance these approaches in Section 20.2, introducing proto van Emde Boas structures, which are recursive but do not achieve our goal of $O(\lg \lg u)$-time operations. Section 20.3 modifies proto van Emde Boas structures to develop van Emde Boas trees, and it shows how to implement each operation in $O(\lg \lg u)$ time.

20.1   Preliminary approaches

In this section, we shall examine various approaches for storing a dynamic set. Although none will achieve the $O(\lg \lg u)$ time bounds that we desire, we will gain insights that will help us understand van Emde Boas trees when we see them later in this chapter.

Direct addressing

Direct addressing, as we saw in Section 11.1, provides the simplest approach to storing a dynamic set. Since in this chapter we are concerned only with storing keys, we can simplify the direct-addressing approach to store the dynamic set as a bit vector, as discussed in Exercise 11.1-2. To store a dynamic set of values from the universe $\{0, 1, 2, \ldots, u - 1\}$, we maintain an array $A[0 \mathinner{.\,.} u - 1]$ of u bits. The entry $A[x]$ holds a 1 if the value x is in the dynamic set, and it holds a 0 otherwise. Although we can perform each of the INSERT, DELETE, and MEMBER operations in $O(1)$ time with a bit vector, the remaining operations—MINIMUM, MAXIMUM, SUCCESSOR, and PREDECESSOR—each take $\Theta(u)$ time in the worst case because

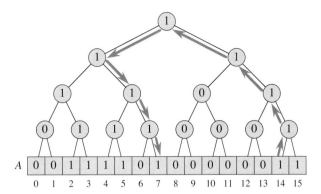

Figure 20.1   A binary tree of bits superimposed on top of a bit vector representing the set $\{2, 3, 4, 5, 7, 14, 15\}$ when $u = 16$. Each internal node contains a 1 if and only if some leaf in its subtree contains a 1. The arrows show the path followed to determine the predecessor of 14 in the set.

we might have to scan through $\Theta(u)$ elements.[2] For example, if a set contains only the values 0 and $u - 1$, then to find the successor of 0, we would have to scan entries 1 through $u - 2$ before finding a 1 in $A[u - 1]$.

Superimposing a binary tree structure

We can short-cut long scans in the bit vector by superimposing a binary tree of bits on top of it. Figure 20.1 shows an example. The entries of the bit vector form the leaves of the binary tree, and each internal node contains a 1 if and only if any leaf in its subtree contains a 1. In other words, the bit stored in an internal node is the logical-or of its two children.

The operations that took $\Theta(u)$ worst-case time with an unadorned bit vector now use the tree structure:

- To find the minimum value in the set, start at the root and head down toward the leaves, always taking the leftmost node containing a 1.

- To find the maximum value in the set, start at the root and head down toward the leaves, always taking the rightmost node containing a 1.

---

[2]We assume throughout this chapter that MINIMUM and MAXIMUM return NIL if the dynamic set is empty and that SUCCESSOR and PREDECESSOR return NIL if the element they are given has no successor or predecessor, respectively.

- To find the successor of x, start at the leaf indexed by x, and head up toward the root until we enter a node from the left and this node has a 1 in its right child z. Then head down through node z, always taking the leftmost node containing a 1 (i.e., find the minimum value in the subtree rooted at the right child z).

- To find the predecessor of x, start at the leaf indexed by x, and head up toward the root until we enter a node from the right and this node has a 1 in its left child z. Then head down through node z, always taking the rightmost node containing a 1 (i.e., find the maximum value in the subtree rooted at the left child z).

Figure 20.1 shows the path taken to find the predecessor, 7, of the value 14.

We also augment the INSERT and DELETE operations appropriately. When inserting a value, we store a 1 in each node on the simple path from the appropriate leaf up to the root. When deleting a value, we go from the appropriate leaf up to the root, recomputing the bit in each internal node on the path as the logical-or of its two children.

Since the height of the tree is $\lg u$ and each of the above operations makes at most one pass up the tree and at most one pass down, each operation takes $O(\lg u)$ time in the worst case.

This approach is only marginally better than just using a red-black tree. We can still perform the MEMBER operation in $O(1)$ time, whereas searching a red-black tree takes $O(\lg n)$ time. Then again, if the number n of elements stored is much smaller than the size u of the universe, a red-black tree would be faster for all the other operations.

Superimposing a tree of constant height

What happens if we superimpose a tree with greater degree? Let us assume that the size of the universe is $u = 2^{2k}$ for some integer k, so that $\sqrt{u}$ is an integer. Instead of superimposing a binary tree on top of the bit vector, we superimpose a tree of degree $\sqrt{u}$. Figure 20.2(a) shows such a tree for the same bit vector as in Figure 20.1. The height of the resulting tree is always 2.

As before, each internal node stores the logical-or of the bits within its subtree, so that the $\sqrt{u}$ internal nodes at depth 1 summarize each group of $\sqrt{u}$ values. As Figure 20.2(b) demonstrates, we can think of these nodes as an array $summary[0 \mathrel{..} \sqrt{u} - 1]$, where $summary[i]$ contains a 1 if and only if the subarray $A[i\sqrt{u} \mathrel{..} (i + 1)\sqrt{u} - 1]$ contains a 1. We call this $\sqrt{u}$-bit subarray of A the ith **cluster**. For a given value of x, the bit $A[x]$ appears in cluster number $\lfloor x/\sqrt{u} \rfloor$. Now INSERT becomes an $O(1)$-time operation: to insert x, set both $A[x]$ and $summary[\lfloor x/\sqrt{u} \rfloor]$ to 1. We can use the $summary$ array to perform

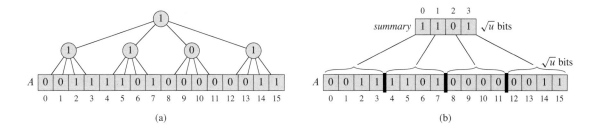

Figure 20.2   **(a)** A tree of degree $\sqrt{u}$ superimposed on top of the same bit vector as in Figure 20.1. Each internal node stores the logical-or of the bits in its subtree. **(b)** A view of the same structure, but with the internal nodes at depth 1 treated as an array *summary*$[0 \mathbin{.\,.} \sqrt{u} - 1]$, where *summary*$[i]$ is the logical-or of the subarray $A[i\sqrt{u} \mathbin{.\,.} (i+1)\sqrt{u} - 1]$.

each of the operations MINIMUM, MAXIMUM, SUCCESSOR, PREDECESSOR, and DELETE in $O(\sqrt{u})$ time:

- To find the minimum (maximum) value, find the leftmost (rightmost) entry in *summary* that contains a 1, say *summary*$[i]$, and then do a linear search within the ith cluster for the leftmost (rightmost) 1.

- To find the successor (predecessor) of x, first search to the right (left) within its cluster. If we find a 1, that position gives the result. Otherwise, let $i = \lfloor x/\sqrt{u} \rfloor$ and search to the right (left) within the *summary* array from index i. The first position that holds a 1 gives the index of a cluster. Search within that cluster for the leftmost (rightmost) 1. That position holds the successor (predecessor).

- To delete the value x, let $i = \lfloor x/\sqrt{u} \rfloor$. Set $A[x]$ to 0 and then set *summary*$[i]$ to the logical-or of the bits in the ith cluster.

In each of the above operations, we search through at most two clusters of $\sqrt{u}$ bits plus the *summary* array, and so each operation takes $O(\sqrt{u})$ time.

At first glance, it seems as though we have made negative progress. Superimposing a binary tree gave us $O(\lg u)$-time operations, which are asymptotically faster than $O(\sqrt{u})$ time. Using a tree of degree $\sqrt{u}$ will turn out to be a key idea of van Emde Boas trees, however. We continue down this path in the next section.

Exercises

20.1-1
Modify the data structures in this section to support duplicate keys.

20.1-2
Modify the data structures in this section to support keys that have associated satellite data.

20.1-3
Observe that, using the structures in this section, the way we find the successor and predecessor of a value x does not depend on whether x is in the set at the time. Show how to find the successor of x in a binary search tree when x is not stored in the tree.

20.1-4
Suppose that instead of superimposing a tree of degree $\sqrt{u}$, we were to superimpose a tree of degree $u^{1/k}$, where $k > 1$ is a constant. What would be the height of such a tree, and how long would each of the operations take?

20.2   A recursive structure

In this section, we modify the idea of superimposing a tree of degree $\sqrt{u}$ on top of a bit vector. In the previous section, we used a summary structure of size $\sqrt{u}$, with each entry pointing to another structure of size $\sqrt{u}$. Now, we make the structure recursive, shrinking the universe size by the square root at each level of recursion. Starting with a universe of size u, we make structures holding $\sqrt{u} = u^{1/2}$ items, which themselves hold structures of $u^{1/4}$ items, which hold structures of $u^{1/8}$ items, and so on, down to a base size of 2.

For simplicity, in this section, we assume that $u = 2^{2^k}$ for some integer k, so that $u, u^{1/2}, u^{1/4}, \dots$ are integers. This restriction would be quite severe in practice, allowing only values of u in the sequence $2, 4, 16, 256, 65536, \dots$. We shall see in the next section how to relax this assumption and assume only that $u = 2^k$ for some integer k. Since the structure we examine in this section is only a precursor to the true van Emde Boas tree structure, we tolerate this restriction in favor of aiding our understanding.

Recalling that our goal is to achieve running times of $O(\lg \lg u)$ for the operations, let's think about how we might obtain such running times. At the end of Section 4.3, we saw that by changing variables, we could show that the recurrence

$$T(n) = 2T\left(\lfloor \sqrt{n} \rfloor\right) + \lg n \tag{20.1}$$

has the solution $T(n) = O(\lg n \lg \lg n)$. Let's consider a similar, but simpler, recurrence:

$$T(u) = T(\sqrt{u}) + O(1) . \tag{20.2}$$

If we use the same technique, changing variables, we can show that recurrence (20.2) has the solution $T(u) = O(\lg \lg u)$. Let $m = \lg u$, so that $u = 2^m$ and we have

$$T(2^m) = T(2^{m/2}) + O(1) .$$

Now we rename $S(m) = T(2^m)$, giving the new recurrence

$$S(m) = S(m/2) + O(1) .$$

By case 2 of the master method, this recurrence has the solution $S(m) = O(\lg m)$. We change back from $S(m)$ to $T(u)$, giving $T(u) = T(2^m) = S(m) = O(\lg m) = O(\lg \lg u)$.

Recurrence (20.2) will guide our search for a data structure. We will design a recursive data structure that shrinks by a factor of $\sqrt{u}$ in each level of its recursion. When an operation traverses this data structure, it will spend a constant amount of time at each level before recursing to the level below. Recurrence (20.2) will then characterize the running time of the operation.

Here is another way to think of how the term $\lg \lg u$ ends up in the solution to recurrence (20.2). As we look at the universe size in each level of the recursive data structure, we see the sequence $u, u^{1/2}, u^{1/4}, u^{1/8}, \ldots$. If we consider how many bits we need to store the universe size at each level, we need $\lg u$ at the top level, and each level needs half the bits of the previous level. In general, if we start with b bits and halve the number of bits at each level, then after $\lg b$ levels, we get down to just one bit. Since $b = \lg u$, we see that after $\lg \lg u$ levels, we have a universe size of 2.

Looking back at the data structure in Figure 20.2, a given value x resides in cluster number $\lfloor x/\sqrt{u} \rfloor$. If we view x as a $\lg u$-bit binary integer, that cluster number, $\lfloor x/\sqrt{u} \rfloor$, is given by the most significant $(\lg u)/2$ bits of x. Within its cluster, x appears in position $x \bmod \sqrt{u}$, which is given by the least significant $(\lg u)/2$ bits of x. We will need to index in this way, and so let us define some functions that will help us do so:

$$
\begin{aligned}
\text{high}(x) &= \lfloor x/\sqrt{u} \rfloor , \\
\text{low}(x) &= x \bmod \sqrt{u} , \\
\text{index}(x, y) &= x\sqrt{u} + y .
\end{aligned}
$$

The function $\text{high}(x)$ gives the most significant $(\lg u)/2$ bits of x, producing the number of x's cluster. The function $\text{low}(x)$ gives the least significant $(\lg u)/2$ bits of x and provides x's position within its cluster. The function $\text{index}(x, y)$ builds an element number from x and y, treating x as the most significant $(\lg u)/2$ bits of the element number and y as the least significant $(\lg u)/2$ bits. We have the identity $x = \text{index}(\text{high}(x), \text{low}(x))$. The value of u used by each of these functions will

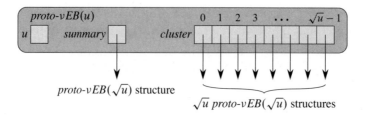

proto-vEB(√u̅) structure

√u̅ proto-vEB(√u̅) structures

Figure 20.3 The information in a *proto-vEB(u)* structure when $u \geq 4$. The structure contains the universe size u, a pointer *summary* to a *proto-vEB($\sqrt{u}$)* structure, and an array *cluster*$[0 \dots \sqrt{u} - 1]$ of $\sqrt{u}$ pointers to *proto-vEB($\sqrt{u}$)* structures.

always be the universe size of the data structure in which we call the function, which changes as we descend into the recursive structure.

20.2.1   Proto van Emde Boas structures

Taking our cue from recurrence (20.2), let us design a recursive data structure to support the operations. Although this data structure will fail to achieve our goal of $O(\lg \lg u)$ time for some operations, it serves as a basis for the van Emde Boas tree structure that we will see in Section 20.3.

For the universe $\{0, 1, 2, \dots, u - 1\}$, we define a ***proto van Emde Boas structure***, or ***proto-vEB structure***, which we denote as *proto-vEB(u)*, recursively as follows. Each *proto-vEB(u)* structure contains an attribute u giving its universe size. In addition, it contains the following:

- If $u = 2$, then it is the base size, and it contains an array $A[0 \dots 1]$ of two bits.

- Otherwise, $u = 2^{2^k}$ for some integer $k \geq 1$, so that $u \geq 4$. In addition to the universe size u, the data structure *proto-vEB(u)* contains the following attributes, illustrated in Figure 20.3:

  - a pointer named *summary* to a *proto-vEB($\sqrt{u}$)* structure and
  - an array *cluster*$[0 \dots \sqrt{u} - 1]$ of $\sqrt{u}$ pointers, each to a *proto-vEB($\sqrt{u}$)* structure.

The element x, where $0 \leq x < u$, is recursively stored in the cluster numbered $high(x)$ as element $low(x)$ within that cluster.

In the two-level structure of the previous section, the root stores a summary array of size $\sqrt{u}$, in which each entry contains a bit. From the index of each entry, we can compute the starting index of the subarray of size $\sqrt{u}$ that the bit summarizes. In the proto-vEB structure, we use explicit pointers rather than index calculations.

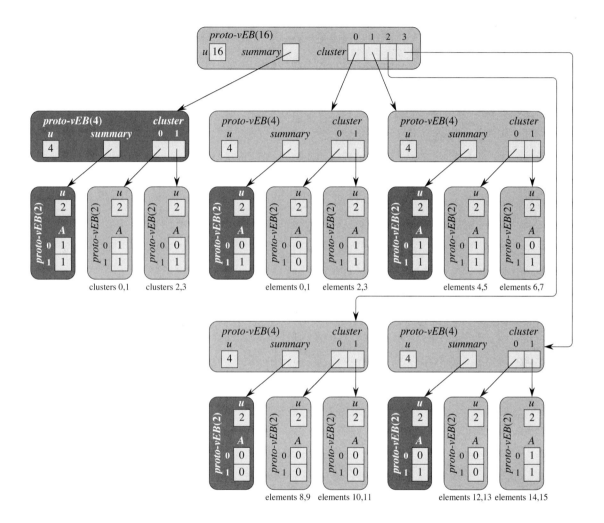

Figure 20.4 A *proto-vEB*(16) structure representing the set {2, 3, 4, 5, 7, 14, 15}. It points to four *proto-vEB*(4) structures in *cluster*[0 . . 3], and to a summary structure, which is also a *proto-vEB*(4). Each *proto-vEB*(4) structure points to two *proto-vEB*(2) structures in *cluster*[0 . . 1], and to a *proto-vEB*(2) summary. Each *proto-vEB*(2) structure contains just an array *A*[0 . . 1] of two bits. The *proto-vEB*(2) structures above "elements *i, j*" store bits *i* and *j* of the actual dynamic set, and the *proto-vEB*(2) structures above "clusters *i, j*" store the summary bits for clusters *i* and *j* in the top-level *proto-vEB*(16) structure. For clarity, heavy shading indicates the top level of a proto-vEB structure that stores summary information for its parent structure; such a proto-vEB structure is otherwise identical to any other proto-vEB structure with the same universe size.

The array *summary* contains the summary bits stored recursively in a proto-vEB structure, and the array *cluster* contains $\sqrt{u}$ pointers.

Figure 20.4 shows a fully expanded *proto-vEB*(16) structure representing the set $\{2, 3, 4, 5, 7, 14, 15\}$. If the value i is in the proto-vEB structure pointed to by *summary*, then the ith cluster contains some value in the set being represented. As in the tree of constant height, *cluster*[i] represents the values $i\sqrt{u}$ through $(i + 1)\sqrt{u} - 1$, which form the ith cluster.

At the base level, the elements of the actual dynamic sets are stored in some of the *proto-vEB*(2) structures, and the remaining *proto-vEB*(2) structures store summary bits. Beneath each of the non-summary base structures, the figure indicates which bits it stores. For example, the *proto-vEB*(2) structure labeled "elements 6,7" stores bit 6 (0, since element 6 is not in the set) in its $A[0]$ and bit 7 (1, since element 7 is in the set) in its $A[1]$.

Like the clusters, each summary is just a dynamic set with universe size $\sqrt{u}$, and so we represent each summary as a *proto-vEB*($\sqrt{u}$) structure. The four summary bits for the main *proto-vEB*(16) structure are in the leftmost *proto-vEB*(4) structure, and they ultimately appear in two *proto-vEB*(2) structures. For example, the *proto-vEB*(2) structure labeled "clusters 2,3" has $A[0] = 0$, indicating that cluster 2 of the *proto-vEB*(16) structure (containing elements 8, 9, 10, 11) is all 0, and $A[1] = 1$, telling us that cluster 3 (containing elements 12, 13, 14, 15) has at least one 1. Each *proto-vEB*(4) structure points to its own summary, which is itself stored as a *proto-vEB*(2) structure. For example, look at the *proto-vEB*(2) structure just to the left of the one labeled "elements 0,1." Because its $A[0]$ is 0, it tells us that the "elements 0,1" structure is all 0, and because its $A[1]$ is 1, we know that the "elements 2,3" structure contains at least one 1.

20.2.2   Operations on a proto van Emde Boas structure

We shall now describe how to perform operations on a proto-vEB structure. We first examine the query operations—MEMBER, MINIMUM, and SUCCESSOR—which do not change the proto-vEB structure. We then discuss INSERT and DELETE. We leave MAXIMUM and PREDECESSOR, which are symmetric to MINIMUM and SUCCESSOR, respectively, as Exercise 20.2-1.

Each of the MEMBER, SUCCESSOR, PREDECESSOR, INSERT, and DELETE operations takes a parameter x, along with a proto-vEB structure V. Each of these operations assumes that $0 \leq x < V.u$.

Determining whether a value is in the set

To perform MEMBER(x), we need to find the bit corresponding to x within the appropriate *proto-vEB*(2) structure. We can do so in $O(\lg\lg u)$ time, bypassing the *summary* structures altogether. The following procedure takes a *proto-vEB* structure V and a value x, and it returns a bit indicating whether x is in the dynamic set held by V.

PROTO-VEB-MEMBER(V, x)

1 **if** $V.u == 2$
2   **return** $V.A[x]$
3 **else return** PROTO-VEB-MEMBER$(V.cluster[\text{high}(x)], \text{low}(x))$

The PROTO-VEB-MEMBER procedure works as follows. Line 1 tests whether we are in a base case, where V is a *proto-vEB(2)* structure. Line 2 handles the base case, simply returning the appropriate bit of array A. Line 3 deals with the recursive case, "drilling down" into the appropriate smaller proto-vEB structure. The value high(x) says which *proto-vEB($\sqrt{u}$)* structure we visit, and low(x) determines which element within that *proto-vEB($\sqrt{u}$)* structure we are querying.

Let's see what happens when we call PROTO-VEB-MEMBER$(V, 6)$ on the *proto-vEB(16)* structure in Figure 20.4. Since high$(6) = 1$ when $u = 16$, we recurse into the *proto-vEB(4)* structure in the upper right, and we ask about element low$(6) = 2$ of that structure. In this recursive call, $u = 4$, and so we recurse again. With $u = 4$, we have high$(2) = 1$ and low$(2) = 0$, and so we ask about element 0 of the *proto-vEB(2)* structure in the upper right. This recursive call turns out to be a base case, and so it returns $A[0] = 0$ back up through the chain of recursive calls. Thus, we get the result that PROTO-VEB-MEMBER$(V, 6)$ returns 0, indicating that 6 is not in the set.

To determine the running time of PROTO-VEB-MEMBER, let $T(u)$ denote its running time on a *proto-vEB(u)* structure. Each recursive call takes constant time, not including the time taken by the recursive calls that it makes. When PROTO-VEB-MEMBER makes a recursive call, it makes a call on a *proto-vEB($\sqrt{u}$)* structure. Thus, we can characterize the running time by the recurrence $T(u) = T(\sqrt{u}) + O(1)$, which we have already seen as recurrence (20.2). Its solution is $T(u) = O(\lg \lg u)$, and so we conclude that PROTO-VEB-MEMBER runs in time $O(\lg \lg u)$.

Finding the minimum element

Now we examine how to perform the MINIMUM operation. The procedure PROTO-VEB-MINIMUM(V) returns the minimum element in the proto-vEB structure V, or NIL if V represents an empty set.

PROTO-VEB-MINIMUM(V)

```
 1  if V.u == 2
 2      if V.A[0] == 1
 3          return 0
 4      elseif V.A[1] == 1
 5          return 1
 6      else return NIL
 7  else min-cluster = PROTO-VEB-MINIMUM(V.summary)
 8      if min-cluster == NIL
 9          return NIL
10      else offset = PROTO-VEB-MINIMUM(V.cluster[min-cluster])
11          return index(min-cluster, offset)
```

This procedure works as follows. Line 1 tests for the base case, which lines 2–6 handle by brute force. Lines 7–11 handle the recursive case. First, line 7 finds the number of the first cluster that contains an element of the set. It does so by recursively calling PROTO-VEB-MINIMUM on $V.summary$, which is a *proto-vEB*$(\sqrt{u})$ structure. Line 7 assigns this cluster number to the variable *min-cluster*. If the set is empty, then the recursive call returned NIL, and line 9 returns NIL. Otherwise, the minimum element of the set is somewhere in cluster number *min-cluster*. The recursive call in line 10 finds the offset within the cluster of the minimum element in this cluster. Finally, line 11 constructs the value of the minimum element from the cluster number and offset, and it returns this value.

Although querying the summary information allows us to quickly find the cluster containing the minimum element, because this procedure makes two recursive calls on *proto-vEB*$(\sqrt{u})$ structures, it does not run in $O(\lg\lg u)$ time in the worst case. Letting $T(u)$ denote the worst-case time for PROTO-VEB-MINIMUM on a *proto-vEB*(u) structure, we have the recurrence

$$T(u) = 2T(\sqrt{u}) + O(1) \,. \tag{20.3}$$

Again, we use a change of variables to solve this recurrence, letting $m = \lg u$, which gives

$$T(2^m) = 2T(2^{m/2}) + O(1) \,.$$

Renaming $S(m) = T(2^m)$ gives

$$S(m) = 2S(m/2) + O(1) \,,$$

which, by case 1 of the master method, has the solution $S(m) = \Theta(m)$. By changing back from $S(m)$ to $T(u)$, we have that $T(u) = T(2^m) = S(m) = \Theta(m) = \Theta(\lg u)$. Thus, we see that because of the second recursive call, PROTO-VEB-MINIMUM runs in $\Theta(\lg u)$ time rather than the desired $O(\lg\lg u)$ time.

Finding the successor

The SUCCESSOR operation is even worse. In the worst case, it makes two recursive calls, along with a call to PROTO-VEB-MINIMUM. The procedure PROTO-VEB-SUCCESSOR(V, x) returns the smallest element in the proto-vEB structure V that is greater than x, or NIL if no element in V is greater than x. It does not require x to be a member of the set, but it does assume that $0 \leq x < V.u$.

PROTO-VEB-SUCCESSOR(V, x)

```
 1  if V.u == 2
 2      if x == 0 and V.A[1] == 1
 3          return 1
 4      else return NIL
 5  else offset = PROTO-VEB-SUCCESSOR(V.cluster[high(x)], low(x))
 6      if offset ≠ NIL
 7          return index(high(x), offset)
 8      else succ-cluster = PROTO-VEB-SUCCESSOR(V.summary, high(x))
 9          if succ-cluster == NIL
10              return NIL
11          else offset = PROTO-VEB-MINIMUM(V.cluster[succ-cluster])
12              return index(succ-cluster, offset)
```

The PROTO-VEB-SUCCESSOR procedure works as follows. As usual, line 1 tests for the base case, which lines 2–4 handle by brute force: the only way that x can have a successor within a *proto-vEB(2)* structure is when $x = 0$ and $A[1]$ is 1. Lines 5–12 handle the recursive case. Line 5 searches for a successor to x within x's cluster, assigning the result to *offset*. Line 6 determines whether x has a successor within its cluster; if it does, then line 7 computes and returns the value of this successor. Otherwise, we have to search in other clusters. Line 8 assigns to *succ-cluster* the number of the next nonempty cluster, using the summary information to find it. Line 9 tests whether *succ-cluster* is NIL, with line 10 returning NIL if all succeeding clusters are empty. If *succ-cluster* is non-NIL, line 11 assigns the first element within that cluster to *offset*, and line 12 computes and returns the minimum element in that cluster.

In the worst case, PROTO-VEB-SUCCESSOR calls itself recursively twice on *proto-vEB($\sqrt{u}$)* structures, and it makes one call to PROTO-VEB-MINIMUM on a *proto-vEB($\sqrt{u}$)* structure. Thus, the recurrence for the worst-case running time $T(u)$ of PROTO-VEB-SUCCESSOR is

$$
\begin{aligned}
T(u) &= 2T(\sqrt{u}) + \Theta(\lg \sqrt{u}) \\
&= 2T(\sqrt{u}) + \Theta(\lg u) \, .
\end{aligned}
$$

We can employ the same technique that we used for recurrence (20.1) to show that this recurrence has the solution $T(u) = \Theta(\lg u \lg \lg u)$. Thus, PROTO-VEB-SUCCESSOR is asymptotically slower than PROTO-VEB-MINIMUM.

Inserting an element

To insert an element, we need to insert it into the appropriate cluster and also set the summary bit for that cluster to 1. The procedure PROTO-VEB-INSERT(V, x) inserts the value x into the proto-vEB structure V.

PROTO-VEB-INSERT(V, x)

```
1  if V.u == 2
2      V.A[x] = 1
3  else PROTO-VEB-INSERT(V.cluster[high(x)], low(x))
4      PROTO-VEB-INSERT(V.summary, high(x))
```

In the base case, line 2 sets the appropriate bit in the array A to 1. In the recursive case, the recursive call in line 3 inserts x into the appropriate cluster, and line 4 sets the summary bit for that cluster to 1.

Because PROTO-VEB-INSERT makes two recursive calls in the worst case, recurrence (20.3) characterizes its running time. Hence, PROTO-VEB-INSERT runs in $\Theta(\lg u)$ time.

Deleting an element

The DELETE operation is more complicated than insertion. Whereas we can always set a summary bit to 1 when inserting, we cannot always reset the same summary bit to 0 when deleting. We need to determine whether any bit in the appropriate cluster is 1. As we have defined proto-vEB structures, we would have to examine all $\sqrt{u}$ bits within a cluster to determine whether any of them are 1. Alternatively, we could add an attribute n to the proto-vEB structure, counting how many elements it has. We leave implementation of PROTO-VEB-DELETE as Exercises 20.2-2 and 20.2-3.

Clearly, we need to modify the proto-vEB structure to get each operation down to making at most one recursive call. We will see in the next section how to do so.

Exercises

20.2-1
Write pseudocode for the procedures PROTO-VEB-MAXIMUM and PROTO-VEB-PREDECESSOR.

20.2-2
Write pseudocode for PROTO-VEB-DELETE. It should update the appropriate summary bit by scanning the related bits within the cluster. What is the worst-case running time of your procedure?

20.2-3
Add the attribute n to each proto-vEB structure, giving the number of elements currently in the set it represents, and write pseudocode for PROTO-VEB-DELETE that uses the attribute n to decide when to reset summary bits to 0. What is the worst-case running time of your procedure? What other procedures need to change because of the new attribute? Do these changes affect their running times?

20.2-4
Modify the proto-vEB structure to support duplicate keys.

20.2-5
Modify the proto-vEB structure to support keys that have associated satellite data.

20.2-6
Write pseudocode for a procedure that creates a *proto-vEB(u)* structure.

20.2-7
Argue that if line 9 of PROTO-VEB-MINIMUM is executed, then the proto-vEB structure is empty.

20.2-8
Suppose that we designed a proto-vEB structure in which each *cluster* array had only $u^{1/4}$ elements. What would the running times of each operation be?

20.3   The van Emde Boas tree

The proto-vEB structure of the previous section is close to what we need to achieve $O(\lg \lg u)$ running times. It falls short because we have to recurse too many times in most of the operations. In this section, we shall design a data structure that is similar to the proto-vEB structure but stores a little more information, thereby removing the need for some of the recursion.

In Section 20.2, we observed that the assumption that we made about the universe size—that $u = 2^{2^k}$ for some integer k—is unduly restrictive, confining the possible values of u to an overly sparse set. From this point on, therefore, we will allow the universe size u to be any exact power of 2, and when $\sqrt{u}$ is not an inte-

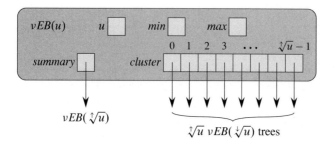

Figure 20.5   The information in a $vEB(u)$ tree when $u > 2$. The structure contains the universe size u, elements *min* and *max*, a pointer *summary* to a $vEB(\sqrt[\uparrow]{u})$ tree, and an array $cluster[0 .. \sqrt[\uparrow]{u} - 1]$ of $\sqrt[\uparrow]{u}$ pointers to $vEB(\sqrt[\downarrow]{u})$ trees.

ger—that is, if u is an odd power of 2 ($u = 2^{2k+1}$ for some integer $k \geq 0$)—then we will divide the $\lg u$ bits of a number into the most significant $\lceil (\lg u)/2 \rceil$ bits and the least significant $\lfloor (\lg u)/2 \rfloor$ bits. For convenience, we denote $2^{\lceil (\lg u)/2 \rceil}$ (the "upper square root" of u) by $\sqrt[\uparrow]{u}$ and $2^{\lfloor (\lg u)/2 \rfloor}$ (the "lower square root" of u) by $\sqrt[\downarrow]{u}$, so that $u = \sqrt[\uparrow]{u} \cdot \sqrt[\downarrow]{u}$ and, when u is an even power of 2 ($u = 2^{2k}$ for some integer k), $\sqrt[\uparrow]{u} = \sqrt[\downarrow]{u} = \sqrt{u}$. Because we now allow u to be an odd power of 2, we must redefine our helpful functions from Section 20.2:

$$\text{high}(x) = \left\lfloor x / \sqrt[\downarrow]{u} \right\rfloor ,$$
$$\text{low}(x) = x \bmod \sqrt[\downarrow]{u} ,$$
$$\text{index}(x, y) = x \sqrt[\downarrow]{u} + y .$$

20.3.1   van Emde Boas trees

The **van Emde Boas tree**, or **vEB tree**, modifies the proto-vEB structure. We denote a vEB tree with a universe size of u as $vEB(u)$ and, unless u equals the base size of 2, the attribute *summary* points to a $vEB(\sqrt[\uparrow]{u})$ tree and the array $cluster[0 .. \sqrt[\uparrow]{u} - 1]$ points to $\sqrt[\uparrow]{u}$ $vEB(\sqrt[\downarrow]{u})$ trees. As Figure 20.5 illustrates, a vEB tree contains two attributes not found in a proto-vEB structure:

- *min* stores the minimum element in the vEB tree, and

- *max* stores the maximum element in the vEB tree.

Furthermore, the element stored in *min* does not appear in any of the recursive $vEB(\sqrt[\downarrow]{u})$ trees that the *cluster* array points to. The elements stored in a $vEB(u)$ tree V, therefore, are $V.min$ plus all the elements recursively stored in the $vEB(\sqrt[\downarrow]{u})$ trees pointed to by $V.cluster[0 .. \sqrt[\uparrow]{u} - 1]$. Note that when a vEB tree contains two or more elements, we treat *min* and *max* differently: the element stored in *min* does not appear in any of the clusters, but unless the vEB tree contains just one element (so that the minimum and maximum elements are the same), the element stored in *max* does.

Since the base size is 2, a $vEB(2)$ tree does not need the array A that the corresponding *proto-vEB(2)* structure has. Instead, we can determine its elements from its *min* and *max* attributes. In a vEB tree with no elements, regardless of its universe size u, both *min* and *max* are NIL.

Figure 20.6 shows a $vEB(16)$ tree V holding the set $\{2, 3, 4, 5, 7, 14, 15\}$. Because the smallest element is 2, $V.min$ equals 2, and even though $\text{high}(2) = 0$, the element 2 does not appear in the $vEB(4)$ tree pointed to by $V.cluster[0]$: notice that $V.cluster[0].min$ equals 3, and so 2 is not in this vEB tree. Similarly, since $V.cluster[0].min$ equals 3, and 2 and 3 are the only elements in $V.cluster[0]$, the $vEB(2)$ clusters within $V.cluster[0]$ are empty.

The *min* and *max* attributes will turn out to be key to reducing the number of recursive calls within the operations on vEB trees. These attributes will help us in four ways:

1. The MINIMUM and MAXIMUM operations do not even need to recurse, for they can just return the values of *min* or *max*.

2. The SUCCESSOR operation can avoid making a recursive call to determine whether the successor of a value x lies within $\text{high}(x)$. That is because x's successor lies within its cluster if and only if x is strictly less than the *max* attribute of its cluster. A symmetric argument holds for PREDECESSOR and *min*.

3. We can tell whether a vEB tree has no elements, exactly one element, or at least two elements in constant time from its *min* and *max* values. This ability will help in the INSERT and DELETE operations. If *min* and *max* are both NIL, then the vEB tree has no elements. If *min* and *max* are non-NIL but are equal to each other, then the vEB tree has exactly one element. Otherwise, both *min* and *max* are non-NIL but are unequal, and the vEB tree has two or more elements.

4. If we know that a vEB tree is empty, we can insert an element into it by updating only its *min* and *max* attributes. Hence, we can insert into an empty vEB tree in constant time. Similarly, if we know that a vEB tree has only one element, we can delete that element in constant time by updating only *min* and *max*. These properties will allow us to cut short the chain of recursive calls.

Even if the universe size u is an odd power of 2, the difference in the sizes of the summary vEB tree and the clusters will not turn out to affect the asymptotic running times of the vEB-tree operations. The recursive procedures that implement the vEB-tree operations will all have running times characterized by the recurrence

$$T(u) \leq T(\sqrt[\uparrow]{u}) + O(1) \,. \tag{20.4}$$

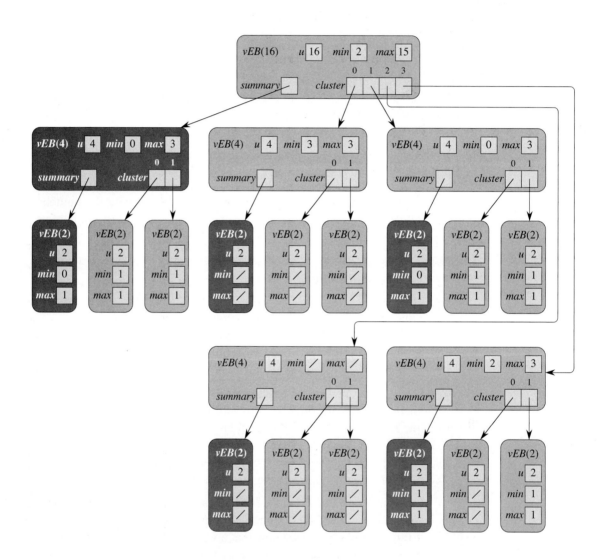

Figure 20.6   A $vEB(16)$ tree corresponding to the proto-vEB tree in Figure 20.4. It stores the set $\{2, 3, 4, 5, 7, 14, 15\}$. Slashes indicate NIL values. The value stored in the *min* attribute of a vEB tree does not appear in any of its clusters. Heavy shading serves the same purpose here as in Figure 20.4.

This recurrence looks similar to recurrence (20.2), and we will solve it in a similar fashion. Letting $m = \lg u$, we rewrite it as

$$T(2^m) \leq T(2^{\lceil m/2 \rceil}) + O(1) \ .$$

Noting that $\lceil m/2 \rceil \leq 2m/3$ for all $m \geq 2$, we have

$$T(2^m) \leq T(2^{2m/3}) + O(1) \ .$$

Letting $S(m) = T(2^m)$, we rewrite this last recurrence as

$$S(m) \leq S(2m/3) + O(1) \ ,$$

which, by case 2 of the master method, has the solution $S(m) = O(\lg m)$. (In terms of the asymptotic solution, the fraction $2/3$ does not make any difference compared with the fraction $1/2$, because when we apply the master method, we find that $\log_{3/2} 1 = \log_2 1 = 0$.) Thus, we have $T(u) = T(2^m) = S(m) = O(\lg m) = O(\lg \lg u)$.

Before using a van Emde Boas tree, we must know the universe size u, so that we can create a van Emde Boas tree of the appropriate size that initially represents an empty set. As Problem 20-1 asks you to show, the total space requirement of a van Emde Boas tree is $O(u)$, and it is straightforward to create an empty tree in $\Theta(u)$ time. In contrast, we can create an empty red-black tree in constant time. Therefore, we might not want to use a van Emde Boas tree when we perform only a small number of operations, since the time to create the data structure would exceed the time saved in the individual operations. This drawback is usually not significant, since we typically use a simple data structure, such as an array or linked list, to represent a set with only a few elements.

20.3.2   Operations on a van Emde Boas tree

We are now ready to see how to perform operations on a van Emde Boas tree. As we did for the proto van Emde Boas structure, we will consider the querying operations first, and then INSERT and DELETE. Due to the slight asymmetry between the minimum and maximum elements in a vEB tree—when a vEB tree contains at least two elements, the minimum element does not appear within a cluster but the maximum element does—we will provide pseudocode for all five querying operations. As in the operations on proto van Emde Boas structures, the operations here that take parameters V and x, where V is a van Emde Boas tree and x is an element, assume that $0 \leq x < V.u$.

Finding the minimum and maximum elements

Because we store the minimum and maximum in the attributes *min* and *max*, two of the operations are one-liners, taking constant time:

VEB-TREE-MINIMUM(V)

1 **return** $V.min$

VEB-TREE-MAXIMUM(V)

1 **return** $V.max$

Determining whether a value is in the set

The procedure VEB-TREE-MEMBER(V, x) has a recursive case like that of PROTO-VEB-MEMBER, but the base case is a little different. We also check directly whether x equals the minimum or maximum element. Since a vEB tree doesn't store bits as a proto-vEB structure does, we design VEB-TREE-MEMBER to return TRUE or FALSE rather than 1 or 0.

VEB-TREE-MEMBER(V, x)

1 **if** $x == V.min$ or $x == V.max$
2   **return** TRUE
3 **elseif** $V.u == 2$
4   **return** FALSE
5 **else return** VEB-TREE-MEMBER$(V.cluster[\text{high}(x)], \text{low}(x))$

Line 1 checks to see whether x equals either the minimum or maximum element. If it does, line 2 returns TRUE. Otherwise, line 3 tests for the base case. Since a $vEB(2)$ tree has no elements other than those in min and max, if it is the base case, line 4 returns FALSE. The other possibility—it is not a base case and x equals neither min nor max—is handled by the recursive call in line 5.

Recurrence (20.4) characterizes the running time of the VEB-TREE-MEMBER procedure, and so this procedure takes $O(\lg \lg u)$ time.

Finding the successor and predecessor

Next we see how to implement the SUCCESSOR operation. Recall that the procedure PROTO-VEB-SUCCESSOR(V, x) could make two recursive calls: one to determine whether x's successor resides in the same cluster as x and, if it does not, one to find the cluster containing x's successor. Because we can access the maximum value in a vEB tree quickly, we can avoid making two recursive calls, and instead make one recursive call on either a cluster or on the summary, but not on both.

VEB-TREE-SUCCESSOR(*V*, *x*)

```
 1  if V.u == 2
 2      if x == 0 and V.max == 1
 3          return 1
 4      else return NIL
 5  elseif V.min ≠ NIL and x < V.min
 6      return V.min
 7  else max-low = VEB-TREE-MAXIMUM(V.cluster[high(x)])
 8      if max-low ≠ NIL and low(x) < max-low
 9          offset = VEB-TREE-SUCCESSOR(V.cluster[high(x)], low(x))
10          return index(high(x), offset)
11      else succ-cluster = VEB-TREE-SUCCESSOR(V.summary, high(x))
12          if succ-cluster == NIL
13              return NIL
14          else offset = VEB-TREE-MINIMUM(V.cluster[succ-cluster])
15              return index(succ-cluster, offset)
```

This procedure has six **return** statements and several cases. We start with the base case in lines 2–4, which returns 1 in line 3 if we are trying to find the successor of 0 and 1 is in the 2-element set; otherwise, the base case returns NIL in line 4.

If we are not in the base case, we next check in line 5 whether x is strictly less than the minimum element. If so, then we simply return the minimum element in line 6.

If we get to line 7, then we know that we are not in a base case and that x is greater than or equal to the minimum value in the vEB tree V. Line 7 assigns to *max-low* the maximum element in x's cluster. If x's cluster contains some element that is greater than x, then we know that x's successor lies somewhere within x's cluster. Line 8 tests for this condition. If x's successor is within x's cluster, then line 9 determines where in the cluster it is, and line 10 returns the successor in the same way as line 7 of PROTO-VEB-SUCCESSOR.

We get to line 11 if x is greater than or equal to the greatest element in its cluster. In this case, lines 11–15 find x's successor in the same way as lines 8–12 of PROTO-VEB-SUCCESSOR.

It is easy to see how recurrence (20.4) characterizes the running time of VEB-TREE-SUCCESSOR. Depending on the result of the test in line 8, the procedure calls itself recursively in either line 9 (on a vEB tree with universe size $\sqrt[\downarrow]{u}$) or line 11 (on a vEB tree with universe size $\sqrt[\uparrow]{u}$). In either case, the one recursive call is on a vEB tree with universe size at most $\sqrt[\uparrow]{u}$. The remainder of the procedure, including the calls to VEB-TREE-MINIMUM and VEB-TREE-MAXIMUM, takes $O(1)$ time. Hence, VEB-TREE-SUCCESSOR runs in $O(\lg \lg u)$ worst-case time.

The VEB-TREE-PREDECESSOR procedure is symmetric to the VEB-TREE-SUCCESSOR procedure, but with one additional case:

VEB-TREE-PREDECESSOR(V, x)

```
 1  if V.u == 2
 2      if x == 1 and V.min == 0
 3          return 0
 4      else return NIL
 5  elseif V.max ≠ NIL and x > V.max
 6      return V.max
 7  else min-low = VEB-TREE-MINIMUM(V.cluster[high(x)])
 8      if min-low ≠ NIL and low(x) > min-low
 9          offset = VEB-TREE-PREDECESSOR(V.cluster[high(x)], low(x))
10          return index(high(x), offset)
11      else pred-cluster = VEB-TREE-PREDECESSOR(V.summary, high(x))
12          if pred-cluster == NIL
13              if V.min ≠ NIL and x > V.min
14                  return V.min
15              else return NIL
16          else offset = VEB-TREE-MAXIMUM(V.cluster[pred-cluster])
17              return index(pred-cluster, offset)
```

Lines 13–14 form the additional case. This case occurs when x's predecessor, if it exists, does not reside in x's cluster. In VEB-TREE-SUCCESSOR, we were assured that if x's successor resides outside of x's cluster, then it must reside in a higher-numbered cluster. But if x's predecessor is the minimum value in vEB tree V, then the predecessor resides in no cluster at all. Line 13 checks for this condition, and line 14 returns the minimum value as appropriate.

This extra case does not affect the asymptotic running time of VEB-TREE-PREDECESSOR when compared with VEB-TREE-SUCCESSOR, and so VEB-TREE-PREDECESSOR runs in $O(\lg \lg u)$ worst-case time.

Inserting an element

Now we examine how to insert an element into a vEB tree. Recall that PROTO-VEB-INSERT made two recursive calls: one to insert the element and one to insert the element's cluster number into the summary. The VEB-TREE-INSERT procedure will make only one recursive call. How can we get away with just one? When we insert an element, either the cluster that it goes into already has another element or it does not. If the cluster already has another element, then the cluster number is already in the summary, and so we do not need to make that recursive call. If the cluster does not already have another element, then the element being inserted becomes the only element in the cluster, and we do not need to recurse to insert an element into an empty vEB tree:

VEB-EMPTY-TREE-INSERT(V, x)

1 $V.min = x$
2 $V.max = x$

With this procedure in hand, here is the pseudocode for VEB-TREE-INSERT(V, x), which assumes that x is not already an element in the set represented by vEB tree V:

VEB-TREE-INSERT(V, x)

 1 **if** $V.min ==$ NIL
 2   VEB-EMPTY-TREE-INSERT(V, x)
 3 **else if** $x < V.min$
 4   exchange x with $V.min$
 5   **if** $V.u > 2$
 6   **if** VEB-TREE-MINIMUM($V.cluster$[high(x)]) $==$ NIL
 7   VEB-TREE-INSERT($V.summary$, high(x))
 8   VEB-EMPTY-TREE-INSERT($V.cluster$[high(x)], low(x))
 9   **else** VEB-TREE-INSERT($V.cluster$[high(x)], low(x))
10   **if** $x > V.max$
11          $V.max = x$

   This procedure works as follows. Line 1 tests whether V is an empty vEB tree and, if it is, then line 2 handles this easy case. Lines 3–11 assume that V is not empty, and therefore some element will be inserted into one of V's clusters. But that element might not necessarily be the element x passed to VEB-TREE-INSERT. If $x < min$, as tested in line 3, then x needs to become the new min. We don't want to lose the original min, however, and so we need to insert it into one of V's clusters. In this case, line 4 exchanges x with min, so that we insert the original min into one of V's clusters.

   We execute lines 6–9 only if V is not a base-case vEB tree. Line 6 determines whether the cluster that x will go into is currently empty. If so, then line 7 inserts x's cluster number into the summary and line 8 handles the easy case of inserting x into an empty cluster. If x's cluster is not currently empty, then line 9 inserts x into its cluster. In this case, we do not need to update the summary, since x's cluster number is already a member of the summary.

   Finally, lines 10–11 take care of updating max if $x > max$. Note that if V is a base-case vEB tree that is not empty, then lines 3–4 and 10–11 update min and max properly.

Once again, we can easily see how recurrence (20.4) characterizes the running time. Depending on the result of the test in line 6, either the recursive call in line 7 (run on a vEB tree with universe size $\sqrt[\uparrow]{u}$) or the recursive call in line 9 (run on a vEB with universe size $\sqrt[\downarrow]{u}$) executes. In either case, the one recursive call is on a vEB tree with universe size at most $\sqrt[\uparrow]{u}$. Because the remainder of VEB-TREE-INSERT takes $O(1)$ time, recurrence (20.4) applies, and so the running time is $O(\lg \lg u)$.

Deleting an element

Finally, we look at how to delete an element from a vEB tree. The procedure VEB-TREE-DELETE(V, x) assumes that x is currently an element in the set represented by the vEB tree V.

VEB-TREE-DELETE(V, x)

```
 1   if V.min == V.max
 2        V.min = NIL
 3        V.max = NIL
 4   elseif V.u == 2
 5        if x == 0
 6            V.min = 1
 7        else V.min = 0
 8        V.max = V.min
 9   else if x == V.min
10            first-cluster = VEB-TREE-MINIMUM(V.summary)
11            x = index(first-cluster,
                    VEB-TREE-MINIMUM(V.cluster[first-cluster]))
12            V.min = x
13        VEB-TREE-DELETE(V.cluster[high(x)], low(x))
14        if VEB-TREE-MINIMUM(V.cluster[high(x)]) == NIL
15            VEB-TREE-DELETE(V.summary, high(x))
16            if x == V.max
17                summary-max = VEB-TREE-MAXIMUM(V.summary)
18                if summary-max == NIL
19                    V.max = V.min
20                else V.max = index(summary-max,
                            VEB-TREE-MAXIMUM(V.cluster[summary-max]))
21        elseif x == V.max
22            V.max = index(high(x),
                    VEB-TREE-MAXIMUM(V.cluster[high(x)]))
```

The VEB-TREE-DELETE procedure works as follows. If the vEB tree V contains only one element, then it's just as easy to delete it as it was to insert an element into an empty vEB tree: just set *min* and *max* to NIL. Lines 1–3 handle this case. Otherwise, V has at least two elements. Line 4 tests whether V is a base-case vEB tree and, if so, lines 5–8 set *min* and *max* to the one remaining element.

Lines 9–22 assume that V has two or more elements and that $u \geq 4$. In this case, we will have to delete an element from a cluster. The element we delete from a cluster might not be x, however, because if x equals *min*, then once we have deleted x, some other element within one of V's clusters becomes the new *min*, and we have to delete that other element from its cluster. If the test in line 9 reveals that we are in this case, then line 10 sets *first-cluster* to the number of the cluster that contains the lowest element other than *min*, and line 11 sets x to the value of the lowest element in that cluster. This element becomes the new *min* in line 12 and, because we set x to its value, it is the element that will be deleted from its cluster.

When we reach line 13, we know that we need to delete element x from its cluster, whether x was the value originally passed to VEB-TREE-DELETE or x is the element becoming the new minimum. Line 13 deletes x from its cluster. That cluster might now become empty, which line 14 tests, and if it does, then we need to remove x's cluster number from the summary, which line 15 handles. After updating the summary, we might need to update *max*. Line 16 checks to see whether we are deleting the maximum element in V and, if we are, then line 17 sets *summary-max* to the number of the highest-numbered nonempty cluster. (The call VEB-TREE-MAXIMUM($V.summary$) works because we have already recursively called VEB-TREE-DELETE on $V.summary$, and therefore $V.summary.max$ has already been updated as necessary.) If all of V's clusters are empty, then the only remaining element in V is *min*; line 18 checks for this case, and line 19 updates *max* appropriately. Otherwise, line 20 sets *max* to the maximum element in the highest-numbered nonempty cluster. (If this cluster is where the element has been deleted, we again rely on the recursive call in line 13 having already corrected that cluster's *max* attribute.)

Finally, we have to handle the case in which x's cluster did not become empty due to x being deleted. Although we do not have to update the summary in this case, we might have to update *max*. Line 21 tests for this case, and if we have to update *max*, line 22 does so (again relying on the recursive call to have corrected *max* in the cluster).

Now we show that VEB-TREE-DELETE runs in $O(\lg \lg u)$ time in the worst case. At first glance, you might think that recurrence (20.4) does not always apply, because a single call of VEB-TREE-DELETE can make two recursive calls: one on line 13 and one on line 15. Although the procedure can make both recursive calls, let's think about what happens when it does. In order for the recursive call on line 15 to occur, the test on line 14 must show that x's cluster is empty. The only way that x's cluster can be empty is if x was the only element in its cluster when we made the recursive call on line 13. But if x was the only element in its cluster, then that recursive call took $O(1)$ time, because it executed only lines 1–3. Thus, we have two mutually exclusive possibilities:

- The recursive call on line 13 took constant time.

- The recursive call on line 15 did not occur.

In either case, recurrence (20.4) characterizes the running time of VEB-TREE-DELETE, and hence its worst-case running time is $O(\lg \lg u)$.

Exercises

20.3-1
Modify vEB trees to support duplicate keys.

20.3-2
Modify vEB trees to support keys that have associated satellite data.

20.3-3
Write pseudocode for a procedure that creates an empty van Emde Boas tree.

20.3-4
What happens if you call VEB-TREE-INSERT with an element that is already in the vEB tree? What happens if you call VEB-TREE-DELETE with an element that is not in the vEB tree? Explain why the procedures exhibit the behavior that they do. Show how to modify vEB trees and their operations so that we can check in constant time whether an element is present.

20.3-5
Suppose that instead of $\sqrt[\uparrow]{u}$ clusters, each with universe size $\sqrt[\downarrow]{u}$, we constructed vEB trees to have $u^{1/k}$ clusters, each with universe size $u^{1-1/k}$, where $k > 1$ is a constant. If we were to modify the operations appropriately, what would be their running times? For the purpose of analysis, assume that $u^{1/k}$ and $u^{1-1/k}$ are always integers.

20.3-6
Creating a vEB tree with universe size u requires $\Theta(u)$ time. Suppose we wish to explicitly account for that time. What is the smallest number of operations n for which the amortized time of each operation in a vEB tree is $O(\lg \lg u)$?

Problems

20-1 *Space requirements for van Emde Boas trees*

This problem explores the space requirements for van Emde Boas trees and suggests a way to modify the data structure to make its space requirement depend on the number n of elements actually stored in the tree, rather than on the universe size u. For simplicity, assume that $\sqrt{u}$ is always an integer.

a. Explain why the following recurrence characterizes the space requirement $P(u)$ of a van Emde Boas tree with universe size u:

$$P(u) = (\sqrt{u} + 1)P(\sqrt{u}) + \Theta(\sqrt{u}) . \tag{20.5}$$

b. Prove that recurrence (20.5) has the solution $P(u) = O(u)$.

In order to reduce the space requirements, let us define a ***reduced-space van Emde Boas tree***, or ***RS-vEB tree***, as a vEB tree V but with the following changes:

- The attribute $V.cluster$, rather than being stored as a simple array of pointers to vEB trees with universe size $\sqrt{u}$, is a hash table (see Chapter 11) stored as a dynamic table (see Section 17.4). Corresponding to the array version of $V.cluster$, the hash table stores pointers to RS-vEB trees with universe size $\sqrt{u}$. To find the ith cluster, we look up the key i in the hash table, so that we can find the ith cluster by a single search in the hash table.

- The hash table stores only pointers to nonempty clusters. A search in the hash table for an empty cluster returns NIL, indicating that the cluster is empty.

- The attribute $V.summary$ is NIL if all clusters are empty. Otherwise, $V.summary$ points to an RS-vEB tree with universe size $\sqrt{u}$.

Because the hash table is implemented with a dynamic table, the space it requires is proportional to the number of nonempty clusters.

When we need to insert an element into an empty RS-vEB tree, we create the RS-vEB tree by calling the following procedure, where the parameter u is the universe size of the RS-vEB tree:

CREATE-NEW-RS-VEB-TREE(u)

```
1  allocate a new vEB tree V
2  V.u = u
3  V.min = NIL
4  V.max = NIL
5  V.summary = NIL
6  create V.cluster as an empty dynamic hash table
7  return V
```

c. Modify the VEB-TREE-INSERT procedure to produce pseudocode for the procedure RS-VEB-TREE-INSERT(V, x), which inserts x into the RS-vEB tree V, calling CREATE-NEW-RS-VEB-TREE as appropriate.

d. Modify the VEB-TREE-SUCCESSOR procedure to produce pseudocode for the procedure RS-VEB-TREE-SUCCESSOR(V, x), which returns the successor of x in RS-vEB tree V, or NIL if x has no successor in V.

e. Prove that, under the assumption of simple uniform hashing, your RS-VEB-TREE-INSERT and RS-VEB-TREE-SUCCESSOR procedures run in $O(\lg \lg u)$ expected amortized time.

f. Assuming that elements are never deleted from a vEB tree, prove that the space requirement for the RS-vEB tree structure is $O(n)$, where n is the number of elements actually stored in the RS-vEB tree.

g. RS-vEB trees have another advantage over vEB trees: they require less time to create. How long does it take to create an empty RS-vEB tree?

20-2 *y-fast tries*

This problem investigates D. Willard's "y-fast tries" which, like van Emde Boas trees, perform each of the operations MEMBER, MINIMUM, MAXIMUM, PREDECESSOR, and SUCCESSOR on elements drawn from a universe with size u in $O(\lg \lg u)$ worst-case time. The INSERT and DELETE operations take $O(\lg \lg u)$ amortized time. Like reduced-space van Emde Boas trees (see Problem 20-1), y-fast tries use only $O(n)$ space to store n elements. The design of y-fast tries relies on perfect hashing (see Section 11.5).

As a preliminary structure, suppose that we create a perfect hash table containing not only every element in the dynamic set, but every prefix of the binary representation of every element in the set. For example, if $u = 16$, so that $\lg u = 4$, and $x = 13$ is in the set, then because the binary representation of 13 is 1101, the perfect hash table would contain the strings 1, 11, 110, and 1101. In addition to the hash table, we create a doubly linked list of the elements currently in the set, in increasing order.

a. How much space does this structure require?

b. Show how to perform the MINIMUM and MAXIMUM operations in $O(1)$ time; the MEMBER, PREDECESSOR, and SUCCESSOR operations in $O(\lg \lg u)$ time; and the INSERT and DELETE operations in $O(\lg u)$ time.

To reduce the space requirement to $O(n)$, we make the following changes to the data structure:

- We cluster the n elements into $n/\lg u$ groups of size $\lg u$. (Assume for now that $\lg u$ divides n.) The first group consists of the $\lg u$ smallest elements in the set, the second group consists of the next $\lg u$ smallest elements, and so on.

- We designate a "representative" value for each group. The representative of the ith group is at least as large as the largest element in the ith group, and it is smaller than every element of the $(i+1)$st group. (The representative of the last group can be the maximum possible element $u - 1$.) Note that a representative might be a value not currently in the set.

- We store the $\lg u$ elements of each group in a balanced binary search tree, such as a red-black tree. Each representative points to the balanced binary search tree for its group, and each balanced binary search tree points to its group's representative.

- The perfect hash table stores only the representatives, which are also stored in a doubly linked list in increasing order.

We call this structure a **y-fast trie**.

c. Show that a y-fast trie requires only $O(n)$ space to store n elements.

d. Show how to perform the MINIMUM and MAXIMUM operations in $O(\lg \lg u)$ time with a y-fast trie.

e. Show how to perform the MEMBER operation in $O(\lg \lg u)$ time.

f. Show how to perform the PREDECESSOR and SUCCESSOR operations in $O(\lg \lg u)$ time.

g. Explain why the INSERT and DELETE operations take $\Omega(\lg \lg u)$ time.

h. Show how to relax the requirement that each group in a y-fast trie has exactly $\lg u$ elements to allow INSERT and DELETE to run in $O(\lg \lg u)$ amortized time without affecting the asymptotic running times of the other operations.

Chapter notes

The data structure in this chapter is named after P. van Emde Boas, who described an early form of the idea in 1975 [339]. Later papers by van Emde Boas [340] and van Emde Boas, Kaas, and Zijlstra [341] refined the idea and the exposition. Mehlhorn and Näher [252] subsequently extended the ideas to apply to universe sizes that are prime. Mehlhorn's book [249] contains a slightly different treatment of van Emde Boas trees than the one in this chapter.

Using the ideas behind van Emde Boas trees, Dementiev et al. [83] developed a nonrecursive, three-level search tree that ran faster than van Emde Boas trees in their own experiments.

Wang and Lin [347] designed a hardware-pipelined version of van Emde Boas trees, which achieves constant amortized time per operation and uses $O(\lg \lg u)$ stages in the pipeline.

A lower bound by Pătraşcu and Thorup [273, 274] for finding the predecessor shows that van Emde Boas trees are optimal for this operation, even if randomization is allowed.

21   Data Structures for Disjoint Sets

Some applications involve grouping n distinct elements into a collection of disjoint sets. These applications often need to perform two operations in particular: finding the unique set that contains a given element and uniting two sets. This chapter explores methods for maintaining a data structure that supports these operations.

Section 21.1 describes the operations supported by a disjoint-set data structure and presents a simple application. In Section 21.2, we look at a simple linked-list implementation for disjoint sets. Section 21.3 presents a more efficient representation using rooted trees. The running time using the tree representation is theoretically superlinear, but for all practical purposes it is linear. Section 21.4 defines and discusses a very quickly growing function and its very slowly growing inverse, which appears in the running time of operations on the tree-based implementation, and then, by a complex amortized analysis, proves an upper bound on the running time that is just barely superlinear.

21.1   Disjoint-set operations

A *disjoint-set data structure* maintains a collection $\mathcal{S} = \{S_1, S_2, \ldots, S_k\}$ of disjoint dynamic sets. We identify each set by a *representative*, which is some member of the set. In some applications, it doesn't matter which member is used as the representative; we care only that if we ask for the representative of a dynamic set twice without modifying the set between the requests, we get the same answer both times. Other applications may require a prespecified rule for choosing the representative, such as choosing the smallest member in the set (assuming, of course, that the elements can be ordered).

As in the other dynamic-set implementations we have studied, we represent each element of a set by an object. Letting x denote an object, we wish to support the following operations:

MAKE-SET(x) creates a new set whose only member (and thus representative) is x. Since the sets are disjoint, we require that x not already be in some other set.

UNION(x, y) unites the dynamic sets that contain x and y, say S_x and S_y, into a new set that is the union of these two sets. We assume that the two sets are disjoint prior to the operation. The representative of the resulting set is any member of $S_x \cup S_y$, although many implementations of UNION specifically choose the representative of either S_x or S_y as the new representative. Since we require the sets in the collection to be disjoint, conceptually we destroy sets S_x and S_y, removing them from the collection $\mathcal{S}$. In practice, we often absorb the elements of one of the sets into the other set.

FIND-SET(x) returns a pointer to the representative of the (unique) set containing x.

Throughout this chapter, we shall analyze the running times of disjoint-set data structures in terms of two parameters: n, the number of MAKE-SET operations, and m, the total number of MAKE-SET, UNION, and FIND-SET operations. Since the sets are disjoint, each UNION operation reduces the number of sets by one. After $n - 1$ UNION operations, therefore, only one set remains. The number of UNION operations is thus at most $n - 1$. Note also that since the MAKE-SET operations are included in the total number of operations m, we have $m \geq n$. We assume that the n MAKE-SET operations are the first n operations performed.

An application of disjoint-set data structures

One of the many applications of disjoint-set data structures arises in determining the connected components of an undirected graph (see Section B.4). Figure 21.1(a), for example, shows a graph with four connected components.

The procedure CONNECTED-COMPONENTS that follows uses the disjoint-set operations to compute the connected components of a graph. Once CONNECTED-COMPONENTS has preprocessed the graph, the procedure SAME-COMPONENT answers queries about whether two vertices are in the same connected component.[1] (In pseudocode, we denote the set of vertices of a graph G by $G.V$ and the set of edges by $G.E$.)

---

[1] When the edges of the graph are static — not changing over time — we can compute the connected components faster by using depth-first search (Exercise 22.3-12). Sometimes, however, the edges are added dynamically and we need to maintain the connected components as each edge is added. In this case, the implementation given here can be more efficient than running a new depth-first search for each new edge.

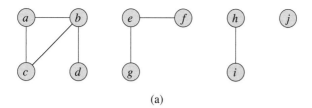

(a)

Edge processed	Collection of disjoint sets									
initial sets	{a}	{b}	{c}	{d}	{e}	{f}	{g}	{h}	{i}	{j}
(b,d)	{a}	{b,d}	{c}		{e}	{f}	{g}	{h}	{i}	{j}
(e,g)	{a}	{b,d}	{c}		{e,g}	{f}		{h}	{i}	{j}
(a,c)	{a,c}	{b,d}			{e,g}	{f}		{h}	{i}	{j}
(h,i)	{a,c}	{b,d}			{e,g}	{f}		{h,i}		{j}
(a,b)	{a,b,c,d}				{e,g}	{f}		{h,i}		{j}
(e,f)	{a,b,c,d}				{e,f,g}			{h,i}		{j}
(b,c)	{a,b,c,d}				{e,f,g}			{h,i}		{j}

(b)

Figure 21.1   **(a)** A graph with four connected components: $\{a, b, c, d\}$, $\{e, f, g\}$, $\{h, i\}$, and $\{j\}$. **(b)** The collection of disjoint sets after processing each edge.

CONNECTED-COMPONENTS(G)

1   **for** each vertex $v \in G.V$
2   MAKE-SET(v)
3   **for** each edge $(u, v) \in G.E$
4   **if** FIND-SET(u) $\neq$ FIND-SET(v)
5   UNION(u, v)

SAME-COMPONENT(u, v)

1   **if** FIND-SET(u) $==$ FIND-SET(v)
2   **return** TRUE
3   **else return** FALSE

The procedure CONNECTED-COMPONENTS initially places each vertex v in its own set. Then, for each edge (u, v), it unites the sets containing u and v. By Exercise 21.1-2, after processing all the edges, two vertices are in the same connected component if and only if the corresponding objects are in the same set. Thus, CONNECTED-COMPONENTS computes sets in such a way that the procedure SAME-COMPONENT can determine whether two vertices are in the same connected component. Figure 21.1(b) illustrates how Connected-Components computes the disjoint sets.

In an actual implementation of this connected-components algorithm, the representations of the graph and the disjoint-set data structure would need to reference each other. That is, an object representing a vertex would contain a pointer to the corresponding disjoint-set object, and vice versa. These programming details depend on the implementation language, and we do not address them further here.

Exercises

21.1-1
Suppose that Connected-Components is run on the undirected graph $G = (V, E)$, where $V = \{a, b, c, d, e, f, g, h, i, j, k\}$ and the edges of E are processed in the order $(d, i), (f, k), (g, i), (b, g), (a, h), (i, j), (d, k), (b, j), (d, f), (g, j), (a, e)$. List the vertices in each connected component after each iteration of lines 3–5.

21.1-2
Show that after all edges are processed by Connected-Components, two vertices are in the same connected component if and only if they are in the same set.

21.1-3
During the execution of Connected-Components on an undirected graph $G = (V, E)$ with k connected components, how many times is Find-Set called? How many times is Union called? Express your answers in terms of $|V|$, $|E|$, and k.

21.2   Linked-list representation of disjoint sets

Figure 21.2(a) shows a simple way to implement a disjoint-set data structure: each set is represented by its own linked list. The object for each set has attributes *head*, pointing to the first object in the list, and *tail*, pointing to the last object. Each object in the list contains a set member, a pointer to the next object in the list, and a pointer back to the set object. Within each linked list, the objects may appear in any order. The representative is the set member in the first object in the list.

With this linked-list representation, both Make-Set and Find-Set are easy, requiring $O(1)$ time. To carry out Make-Set(x), we create a new linked list whose only object is x. For Find-Set(x), we just follow the pointer from x back to its set object and then return the member in the object that *head* points to. For example, in Figure 21.2(a), the call Find-Set(g) would return f.

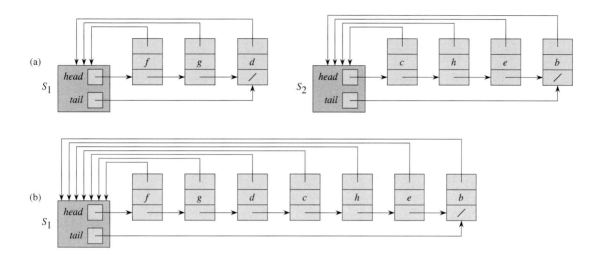

Figure 21.2   **(a)** Linked-list representations of two sets. Set S_1 contains members d, f, and g, with representative f, and set S_2 contains members b, c, e, and h, with representative c. Each object in the list contains a set member, a pointer to the next object in the list, and a pointer back to the set object. Each set object has pointers *head* and *tail* to the first and last objects, respectively. **(b)** The result of UNION(g, e), which appends the linked list containing e to the linked list containing g. The representative of the resulting set is f. The set object for e's list, S_2, is destroyed.

A simple implementation of union

The simplest implementation of the UNION operation using the linked-list set representation takes significantly more time than MAKE-SET or FIND-SET. As Figure 21.2(b) shows, we perform UNION(x, y) by appending y's list onto the end of x's list. The representative of x's list becomes the representative of the resulting set. We use the *tail* pointer for x's list to quickly find where to append y's list. Because all members of y's list join x's list, we can destroy the set object for y's list. Unfortunately, we must update the pointer to the set object for each object originally on y's list, which takes time linear in the length of y's list. In Figure 21.2, for example, the operation UNION(g, e) causes pointers to be updated in the objects for b, c, e, and h.

In fact, we can easily construct a sequence of m operations on n objects that requires $\Theta(n^2)$ time. Suppose that we have objects $x_1, x_2, \ldots, x_n$. We execute the sequence of n MAKE-SET operations followed by $n - 1$ UNION operations shown in Figure 21.3, so that $m = 2n - 1$. We spend $\Theta(n)$ time performing the n MAKE-SET operations. Because the ith UNION operation updates i objects, the total number of objects updated by all $n - 1$ UNION operations is

Operation	Number of objects updated
MAKE-SET(x_1)	1
MAKE-SET(x_2)	1
$\vdots$	$\vdots$
MAKE-SET(x_n)	1
UNION(x_2, x_1)	1
UNION(x_3, x_2)	2
UNION(x_4, x_3)	3
$\vdots$	$\vdots$
UNION(x_n, x_{n-1})	$n-1$

Figure 21.3   A sequence of $2n - 1$ operations on n objects that takes $\Theta(n^2)$ time, or $\Theta(n)$ time per operation on average, using the linked-list set representation and the simple implementation of UNION.

$$\sum_{i=1}^{n-1} i = \Theta(n^2)\,.$$

The total number of operations is $2n - 1$, and so each operation on average requires $\Theta(n)$ time. That is, the amortized time of an operation is $\Theta(n)$.

A weighted-union heuristic

In the worst case, the above implementation of the UNION procedure requires an average of $\Theta(n)$ time per call because we may be appending a longer list onto a shorter list; we must update the pointer to the set object for each member of the longer list. Suppose instead that each list also includes the length of the list (which we can easily maintain) and that we always append the shorter list onto the longer, breaking ties arbitrarily. With this simple *weighted-union heuristic*, a single UNION operation can still take $\Omega(n)$ time if both sets have $\Omega(n)$ members. As the following theorem shows, however, a sequence of m MAKE-SET, UNION, and FIND-SET operations, n of which are MAKE-SET operations, takes $O(m + n \lg n)$ time.

Theorem 21.1
Using the linked-list representation of disjoint sets and the weighted-union heuristic, a sequence of m MAKE-SET, UNION, and FIND-SET operations, n of which are MAKE-SET operations, takes $O(m + n \lg n)$ time.

Proof   Because each UNION operation unites two disjoint sets, we perform at most $n - 1$ UNION operations over all. We now bound the total time taken by these UNION operations. We start by determining, for each object, an upper bound on the number of times the object's pointer back to its set object is updated. Consider a particular object x. We know that each time x's pointer was updated, x must have started in the smaller set. The first time x's pointer was updated, therefore, the resulting set must have had at least 2 members. Similarly, the next time x's pointer was updated, the resulting set must have had at least 4 members. Continuing on, we observe that for any $k \leq n$, after x's pointer has been updated $\lceil \lg k \rceil$ times, the resulting set must have at least k members. Since the largest set has at most n members, each object's pointer is updated at most $\lceil \lg n \rceil$ times over all the UNION operations. Thus the total time spent updating object pointers over all UNION operations is $O(n \lg n)$. We must also account for updating the *tail* pointers and the list lengths, which take only $\Theta(1)$ time per UNION operation. The total time spent in all UNION operations is thus $O(n \lg n)$.

The time for the entire sequence of m operations follows easily. Each MAKE-SET and FIND-SET operation takes $O(1)$ time, and there are $O(m)$ of them. The total time for the entire sequence is thus $O(m + n \lg n)$.   ■

Exercises

21.2-1
Write pseudocode for MAKE-SET, FIND-SET, and UNION using the linked-list representation and the weighted-union heuristic. Make sure to specify the attributes that you assume for set objects and list objects.

21.2-2
Show the data structure that results and the answers returned by the FIND-SET operations in the following program. Use the linked-list representation with the weighted-union heuristic.

```
 1   for i = 1 to 16
 2       MAKE-SET(x_i)
 3   for i = 1 to 15 by 2
 4       UNION(x_i, x_{i+1})
 5   for i = 1 to 13 by 4
 6       UNION(x_i, x_{i+2})
 7   UNION(x_1, x_5)
 8   UNION(x_11, x_13)
 9   UNION(x_1, x_10)
10   FIND-SET(x_2)
11   FIND-SET(x_9)
```

Assume that if the sets containing x_i and x_j have the same size, then the operation UNION(x_i, x_j) appends x_j's list onto x_i's list.

21.2-3
Adapt the aggregate proof of Theorem 21.1 to obtain amortized time bounds of $O(1)$ for MAKE-SET and FIND-SET and $O(\lg n)$ for UNION using the linked-list representation and the weighted-union heuristic.

21.2-4
Give a tight asymptotic bound on the running time of the sequence of operations in Figure 21.3 assuming the linked-list representation and the weighted-union heuristic.

21.2-5
Professor Gompers suspects that it might be possible to keep just one pointer in each set object, rather than two (*head* and *tail*), while keeping the number of pointers in each list element at two. Show that the professor's suspicion is well founded by describing how to represent each set by a linked list such that each operation has the same running time as the operations described in this section. Describe also how the operations work. Your scheme should allow for the weighted-union heuristic, with the same effect as described in this section. (*Hint:* Use the tail of a linked list as its set's representative.)

21.2-6
Suggest a simple change to the UNION procedure for the linked-list representation that removes the need to keep the *tail* pointer to the last object in each list. Whether or not the weighted-union heuristic is used, your change should not change the asymptotic running time of the UNION procedure. (*Hint:* Rather than appending one list to another, splice them together.)

21.3   Disjoint-set forests

In a faster implementation of disjoint sets, we represent sets by rooted trees, with each node containing one member and each tree representing one set. In a ***disjoint-set forest***, illustrated in Figure 21.4(a), each member points only to its parent. The root of each tree contains the representative and is its own parent. As we shall see, although the straightforward algorithms that use this representation are no faster than ones that use the linked-list representation, by introducing two heuristics—"union by rank" and "path compression"—we can achieve an asymptotically optimal disjoint-set data structure.

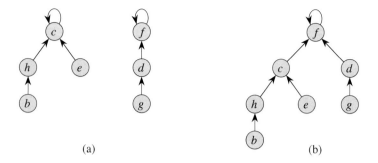

Figure 21.4   A disjoint-set forest. **(a)** Two trees representing the two sets of Figure 21.2. The tree on the left represents the set $\{b, c, e, h\}$, with c as the representative, and the tree on the right represents the set $\{d, f, g\}$, with f as the representative. **(b)** The result of UNION(e, g).

We perform the three disjoint-set operations as follows. A MAKE-SET operation simply creates a tree with just one node. We perform a FIND-SET operation by following parent pointers until we find the root of the tree. The nodes visited on this simple path toward the root constitute the *find path*. A UNION operation, shown in Figure 21.4(b), causes the root of one tree to point to the root of the other.

Heuristics to improve the running time

So far, we have not improved on the linked-list implementation. A sequence of $n - 1$ UNION operations may create a tree that is just a linear chain of n nodes. By using two heuristics, however, we can achieve a running time that is almost linear in the total number of operations m.

The first heuristic, **union by rank**, is similar to the weighted-union heuristic we used with the linked-list representation. The obvious approach would be to make the root of the tree with fewer nodes point to the root of the tree with more nodes. Rather than explicitly keeping track of the size of the subtree rooted at each node, we shall use an approach that eases the analysis. For each node, we maintain a **rank**, which is an upper bound on the height of the node. In union by rank, we make the root with smaller rank point to the root with larger rank during a UNION operation.

The second heuristic, **path compression**, is also quite simple and highly effective. As shown in Figure 21.5, we use it during FIND-SET operations to make each node on the find path point directly to the root. Path compression does not change any ranks.

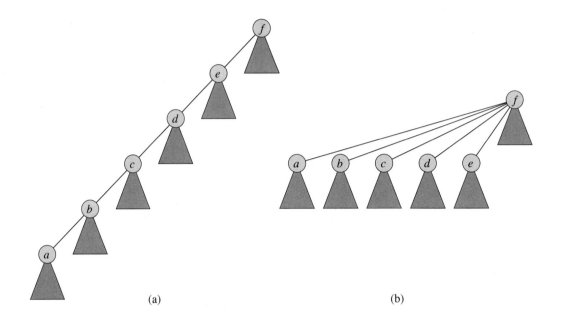

(a)   (b)

Figure 21.5   Path compression during the operation FIND-SET. Arrows and self-loops at roots are omitted. **(a)** A tree representing a set prior to executing FIND-SET(a). Triangles represent subtrees whose roots are the nodes shown. Each node has a pointer to its parent. **(b)** The same set after executing FIND-SET(a). Each node on the find path now points directly to the root.

Pseudocode for disjoint-set forests

To implement a disjoint-set forest with the union-by-rank heuristic, we must keep track of ranks. With each node x, we maintain the integer value $x.rank$, which is an upper bound on the height of x (the number of edges in the longest simple path from a descendant leaf to x). When MAKE-SET creates a singleton set, the single node in the corresponding tree has an initial rank of 0. Each FIND-SET operation leaves all ranks unchanged. The UNION operation has two cases, depending on whether the roots of the trees have equal rank. If the roots have unequal rank, we make the root with higher rank the parent of the root with lower rank, but the ranks themselves remain unchanged. If, instead, the roots have equal ranks, we arbitrarily choose one of the roots as the parent and increment its rank.

Let us put this method into pseudocode. We designate the parent of node x by $x.p$. The LINK procedure, a subroutine called by UNION, takes pointers to two roots as inputs.

MAKE-SET(x)

1   $x.p = x$
2   $x.rank = 0$

UNION(x, y)

1   LINK(FIND-SET(x), FIND-SET(y))

LINK(x, y)

1   **if** $x.rank > y.rank$
2       $y.p = x$
3   **else** $x.p = y$
4   **if** $x.rank == y.rank$
5           $y.rank = y.rank + 1$

The FIND-SET procedure with path compression is quite simple:

FIND-SET(x)

1   **if** $x \neq x.p$
2       $x.p =$ FIND-SET($x.p$)
3   **return** $x.p$

The FIND-SET procedure is a *two-pass method*: as it recurses, it makes one pass up the find path to find the root, and as the recursion unwinds, it makes a second pass back down the find path to update each node to point directly to the root. Each call of FIND-SET(x) returns $x.p$ in line 3. If x is the root, then FIND-SET skips line 2 and instead returns $x.p$, which is x; this is the case in which the recursion bottoms out. Otherwise, line 2 executes, and the recursive call with parameter $x.p$ returns a pointer to the root. Line 2 updates node x to point directly to the root, and line 3 returns this pointer.

Effect of the heuristics on the running time

Separately, either union by rank or path compression improves the running time of the operations on disjoint-set forests, and the improvement is even greater when we use the two heuristics together. Alone, union by rank yields a running time of $O(m \lg n)$ (see Exercise 21.4-4), and this bound is tight (see Exercise 21.3-3). Although we shall not prove it here, for a sequence of n MAKE-SET operations (and hence at most $n - 1$ UNION operations) and f FIND-SET operations, the path-compression heuristic alone gives a worst-case running time of $\Theta(n + f \cdot (1 + \log_{2 + f/n} n))$.

When we use both union by rank and path compression, the worst-case running time is $O(m\,\alpha(n))$, where $\alpha(n)$ is a *very* slowly growing function, which we define in Section 21.4. In any conceivable application of a disjoint-set data structure, $\alpha(n) \leq 4$; thus, we can view the running time as linear in m in all practical situations. Strictly speaking, however, it is superlinear. In Section 21.4, we prove this upper bound.

Exercises

21.3-1
Redo Exercise 21.2-2 using a disjoint-set forest with union by rank and path compression.

21.3-2
Write a nonrecursive version of FIND-SET with path compression.

21.3-3
Give a sequence of m MAKE-SET, UNION, and FIND-SET operations, n of which are MAKE-SET operations, that takes $\Omega(m \lg n)$ time when we use union by rank only.

21.3-4
Suppose that we wish to add the operation PRINT-SET(x), which is given a node x and prints all the members of x's set, in any order. Show how we can add just a single attribute to each node in a disjoint-set forest so that PRINT-SET(x) takes time linear in the number of members of x's set and the asymptotic running times of the other operations are unchanged. Assume that we can print each member of the set in $O(1)$ time.

21.3-5   ★
Show that any sequence of m MAKE-SET, FIND-SET, and LINK operations, where all the LINK operations appear before any of the FIND-SET operations, takes only $O(m)$ time if we use both path compression and union by rank. What happens in the same situation if we use only the path-compression heuristic?

★ 21.4 Analysis of union by rank with path compression

As noted in Section 21.3, the combined union-by-rank and path-compression heuristic runs in time $O(m \, \alpha(n))$ for m disjoint-set operations on n elements. In this section, we shall examine the function α to see just how slowly it grows. Then we prove this running time using the potential method of amortized analysis.

A very quickly growing function and its very slowly growing inverse

For integers $k \geq 0$ and $j \geq 1$, we define the function $A_k(j)$ as

$$A_k(j) = \begin{cases} j + 1 & \text{if } k = 0, \\ A_{k-1}^{(j+1)}(j) & \text{if } k \geq 1, \end{cases}$$

where the expression $A_{k-1}^{(j+1)}(j)$ uses the functional-iteration notation given in Section 3.2. Specifically, $A_{k-1}^{(0)}(j) = j$ and $A_{k-1}^{(i)}(j) = A_{k-1}(A_{k-1}^{(i-1)}(j))$ for $i \geq 1$. We will refer to the parameter k as the *level* of the function A.

The function $A_k(j)$ strictly increases with both j and k. To see just how quickly this function grows, we first obtain closed-form expressions for $A_1(j)$ and $A_2(j)$.

Lemma 21.2
For any integer $j \geq 1$, we have $A_1(j) = 2j + 1$.

Proof We first use induction on i to show that $A_0^{(i)}(j) = j + i$. For the base case, we have $A_0^{(0)}(j) = j = j + 0$. For the inductive step, assume that $A_0^{(i-1)}(j) = j + (i - 1)$. Then $A_0^{(i)}(j) = A_0(A_0^{(i-1)}(j)) = (j + (i - 1)) + 1 = j + i$. Finally, we note that $A_1(j) = A_0^{(j+1)}(j) = j + (j + 1) = 2j + 1$. ∎

Lemma 21.3
For any integer $j \geq 1$, we have $A_2(j) = 2^{j+1}(j + 1) - 1$.

Proof We first use induction on i to show that $A_1^{(i)}(j) = 2^i(j + 1) - 1$. For the base case, we have $A_1^{(0)}(j) = j = 2^0(j + 1) - 1$. For the inductive step, assume that $A_1^{(i-1)}(j) = 2^{i-1}(j + 1) - 1$. Then $A_1^{(i)}(j) = A_1(A_1^{(i-1)}(j)) = A_1(2^{i-1}(j + 1) - 1) = 2 \cdot (2^{i-1}(j+1)-1)+1 = 2^i(j+1)-2+1 = 2^i(j+1)-1$. Finally, we note that $A_2(j) = A_1^{(j+1)}(j) = 2^{j+1}(j + 1) - 1$. ∎

Now we can see how quickly $A_k(j)$ grows by simply examining $A_k(1)$ for levels $k = 0, 1, 2, 3, 4$. From the definition of $A_0(j)$ and the above lemmas, we have $A_0(1) = 1 + 1 = 2$, $A_1(1) = 2 \cdot 1 + 1 = 3$, and $A_2(1) = 2^{1+1} \cdot (1 + 1) - 1 = 7$.

We also have

$$
\begin{aligned}
A_3(1) &= A_2^{(2)}(1) \\
&= A_2(A_2(1)) \\
&= A_2(7) \\
&= 2^8 \cdot 8 - 1 \\
&= 2^{11} - 1 \\
&= 2047
\end{aligned}
$$

and

$$
\begin{aligned}
A_4(1) &= A_3^{(2)}(1) \\
&= A_3(A_3(1)) \\
&= A_3(2047) \\
&= A_2^{(2048)}(2047) \\
&\gg A_2(2047) \\
&= 2^{2048} \cdot 2048 - 1 \\
&> 2^{2048} \\
&= (2^4)^{512} \\
&= 16^{512} \\
&\gg 10^{80} \,,
\end{aligned}
$$

which is the estimated number of atoms in the observable universe. (The symbol "$\gg$" denotes the "much-greater-than" relation.)

We define the inverse of the function $A_k(n)$, for integer $n \geq 0$, by

$$
\alpha(n) = \min \{ k : A_k(1) \geq n \} \,.
$$

In words, $\alpha(n)$ is the lowest level k for which $A_k(1)$ is at least n. From the above values of $A_k(1)$, we see that

$$
\alpha(n) = \begin{cases}
0 & \text{for } 0 \leq n \leq 2 \,, \\
1 & \text{for } n = 3 \,, \\
2 & \text{for } 4 \leq n \leq 7 \,, \\
3 & \text{for } 8 \leq n \leq 2047 \,, \\
4 & \text{for } 2048 \leq n \leq A_4(1) \,.
\end{cases}
$$

It is only for values of n so large that the term "astronomical" understates them (greater than $A_4(1)$, a huge number) that $\alpha(n) > 4$, and so $\alpha(n) \leq 4$ for all practical purposes.

Properties of ranks

In the remainder of this section, we prove an $O(m\,\alpha(n))$ bound on the running time of the disjoint-set operations with union by rank and path compression. In order to prove this bound, we first prove some simple properties of ranks.

Lemma 21.4
For all nodes x, we have $x.rank \leq x.p.rank$, with strict inequality if $x \neq x.p$. The value of $x.rank$ is initially 0 and increases through time until $x \neq x.p$; from then on, $x.rank$ does not change. The value of $x.p.rank$ monotonically increases over time.

Proof   The proof is a straightforward induction on the number of operations, using the implementations of MAKE-SET, UNION, and FIND-SET that appear in Section 21.3. We leave it as Exercise 21.4-1.   ∎

Corollary 21.5
As we follow the simple path from any node toward a root, the node ranks strictly increase.   ∎

Lemma 21.6
Every node has rank at most $n - 1$.

Proof   Each node's rank starts at 0, and it increases only upon LINK operations. Because there are at most $n - 1$ UNION operations, there are also at most $n - 1$ LINK operations. Because each LINK operation either leaves all ranks alone or increases some node's rank by 1, all ranks are at most $n - 1$.   ∎

Lemma 21.6 provides a weak bound on ranks. In fact, every node has rank at most $\lfloor \lg n \rfloor$ (see Exercise 21.4-2). The looser bound of Lemma 21.6 will suffice for our purposes, however.

Proving the time bound

We shall use the potential method of amortized analysis (see Section 17.3) to prove the $O(m\,\alpha(n))$ time bound. In performing the amortized analysis, we will find it convenient to assume that we invoke the LINK operation rather than the UNION operation. That is, since the parameters of the LINK procedure are pointers to two roots, we act as though we perform the appropriate FIND-SET operations separately. The following lemma shows that even if we count the extra FIND-SET operations induced by UNION calls, the asymptotic running time remains unchanged.

Lemma 21.7

Suppose we convert a sequence S' of m' MAKE-SET, UNION, and FIND-SET operations into a sequence S of m MAKE-SET, LINK, and FIND-SET operations by turning each UNION into two FIND-SET operations followed by a LINK. Then, if sequence S runs in $O(m\,\alpha(n))$ time, sequence S' runs in $O(m'\,\alpha(n))$ time.

Proof   Since each UNION operation in sequence S' is converted into three operations in S, we have $m' \leq m \leq 3m'$. Since $m = O(m')$, an $O(m\,\alpha(n))$ time bound for the converted sequence S implies an $O(m'\,\alpha(n))$ time bound for the original sequence S'.   ∎

In the remainder of this section, we shall assume that the initial sequence of m' MAKE-SET, UNION, and FIND-SET operations has been converted to a sequence of m MAKE-SET, LINK, and FIND-SET operations. We now prove an $O(m\,\alpha(n))$ time bound for the converted sequence and appeal to Lemma 21.7 to prove the $O(m'\,\alpha(n))$ running time of the original sequence of m' operations.

Potential function

The potential function we use assigns a potential $\phi_q(x)$ to each node x in the disjoint-set forest after q operations. We sum the node potentials for the potential of the entire forest: $\Phi_q = \sum_x \phi_q(x)$, where Φ_q denotes the potential of the forest after q operations. The forest is empty prior to the first operation, and we arbitrarily set $\Phi_0 = 0$. No potential Φ_q will ever be negative.

The value of $\phi_q(x)$ depends on whether x is a tree root after the qth operation. If it is, or if $x.rank = 0$, then $\phi_q(x) = \alpha(n) \cdot x.rank$.

Now suppose that after the qth operation, x is not a root and that $x.rank \geq 1$. We need to define two auxiliary functions on x before we can define $\phi_q(x)$. First we define

$$\text{level}(x) = \max \{k : x.p.rank \geq A_k(x.rank)\} \ .$$

That is, $\text{level}(x)$ is the greatest level k for which A_k, applied to x's rank, is no greater than x's parent's rank.

We claim that

$$0 \leq \text{level}(x) < \alpha(n) \ , \tag{21.1}$$

which we see as follows. We have

$$
\begin{aligned}
x.p.rank \ &\geq \ x.rank + 1 \quad \text{(by Lemma 21.4)} \\
&= \ A_0(x.rank) \quad \text{(by definition of } A_0(j)) \ ,
\end{aligned}
$$

which implies that $\text{level}(x) \geq 0$, and we have

$$A_{\alpha(n)}(x.rank) \quad \geq \quad A_{\alpha(n)}(1) \quad \text{(because } A_k(j) \text{ is strictly increasing)}$$
$$\geq \quad n \qquad\quad \text{(by the definition of } \alpha(n))$$
$$> \quad x.p.rank \quad \text{(by Lemma 21.6)} ,$$

which implies that $\text{level}(x) < \alpha(n)$. Note that because $x.p.rank$ monotonically increases over time, so does $\text{level}(x)$.

The second auxiliary function applies when $x.rank \geq 1$:

$$\text{iter}(x) = \max \left\{ i : x.p.rank \geq A^{(i)}_{\text{level}(x)}(x.rank) \right\} .$$

That is, $\text{iter}(x)$ is the largest number of times we can iteratively apply $A_{\text{level}(x)}$, applied initially to x's rank, before we get a value greater than x's parent's rank.

We claim that when $x.rank \geq 1$, we have

$$1 \leq \text{iter}(x) \leq x.rank , \tag{21.2}$$

which we see as follows. We have

$$x.p.rank \quad \geq \quad A_{\text{level}(x)}(x.rank) \quad \text{(by definition of level}(x))$$
$$= \quad A^{(1)}_{\text{level}(x)}(x.rank) \quad \text{(by definition of functional iteration)} ,$$

which implies that $\text{iter}(x) \geq 1$, and we have

$$A^{(x.rank+1)}_{\text{level}(x)}(x.rank) \quad = \quad A_{\text{level}(x)+1}(x.rank) \quad \text{(by definition of } A_k(j))$$
$$> \quad x.p.rank \qquad\quad \text{(by definition of level}(x)) ,$$

which implies that $\text{iter}(x) \leq x.rank$. Note that because $x.p.rank$ monotonically increases over time, in order for $\text{iter}(x)$ to decrease, $\text{level}(x)$ must increase. As long as $\text{level}(x)$ remains unchanged, $\text{iter}(x)$ must either increase or remain unchanged.

With these auxiliary functions in place, we are ready to define the potential of node x after q operations:

$$\phi_q(x) = \begin{cases} \alpha(n) \cdot x.rank & \text{if } x \text{ is a root or } x.rank = 0 , \\ (\alpha(n) - \text{level}(x)) \cdot x.rank - \text{iter}(x) & \text{if } x \text{ is not a root and } x.rank \geq 1 . \end{cases}$$

We next investigate some useful properties of node potentials.

Lemma 21.8
For every node x, and for all operation counts q, we have

$$0 \leq \phi_q(x) \leq \alpha(n) \cdot x.rank .$$

Proof   If x is a root or $x.rank = 0$, then $\phi_q(x) = \alpha(n) \cdot x.rank$ by definition. Now suppose that x is not a root and that $x.rank \geq 1$. We obtain a lower bound on $\phi_q(x)$ by maximizing level(x) and iter(x). By the bound (21.1), level$(x) \leq \alpha(n) - 1$, and by the bound (21.2), iter$(x) \leq x.rank$. Thus,

$$
\begin{aligned}
\phi_q(x) &= (\alpha(n) - \text{level}(x)) \cdot x.rank - \text{iter}(x) \\
&\geq (\alpha(n) - (\alpha(n) - 1)) \cdot x.rank - x.rank \\
&= x.rank - x.rank \\
&= 0 \; .
\end{aligned}
$$

Similarly, we obtain an upper bound on $\phi_q(x)$ by minimizing level(x) and iter(x). By the bound (21.1), level$(x) \geq 0$, and by the bound (21.2), iter$(x) \geq 1$. Thus,

$$
\begin{aligned}
\phi_q(x) &\leq (\alpha(n) - 0) \cdot x.rank - 1 \\
&= \alpha(n) \cdot x.rank - 1 \\
&< \alpha(n) \cdot x.rank \; .
\end{aligned}
$$

■

Corollary 21.9
If node x is not a root and $x.rank > 0$, then $\phi_q(x) < \alpha(n) \cdot x.rank$. ■

Potential changes and amortized costs of operations

We are now ready to examine how the disjoint-set operations affect node potentials. With an understanding of the change in potential due to each operation, we can determine each operation's amortized cost.

Lemma 21.10
Let x be a node that is not a root, and suppose that the qth operation is either a LINK or FIND-SET. Then after the qth operation, $\phi_q(x) \leq \phi_{q-1}(x)$. Moreover, if $x.rank \geq 1$ and either level(x) or iter(x) changes due to the qth operation, then $\phi_q(x) \leq \phi_{q-1}(x) - 1$. That is, x's potential cannot increase, and if it has positive rank and either level(x) or iter(x) changes, then x's potential drops by at least 1.

Proof   Because x is not a root, the qth operation does not change $x.rank$, and because n does not change after the initial n MAKE-SET operations, $\alpha(n)$ remains unchanged as well. Hence, these components of the formula for x's potential remain the same after the qth operation. If $x.rank = 0$, then $\phi_q(x) = \phi_{q-1}(x) = 0$. Now assume that $x.rank \geq 1$.

Recall that level(x) monotonically increases over time. If the qth operation leaves level(x) unchanged, then iter(x) either increases or remains unchanged. If both level(x) and iter(x) are unchanged, then $\phi_q(x) = \phi_{q-1}(x)$. If level$(x)$

is unchanged and iter(x) increases, then it increases by at least 1, and so $\phi_q(x) \le \phi_{q-1}(x) - 1$.

Finally, if the qth operation increases level(x), it increases by at least 1, so that the value of the term $(\alpha(n) - \text{level}(x)) \cdot x.rank$ drops by at least $x.rank$. Because level(x) increased, the value of iter(x) might drop, but according to the bound (21.2), the drop is by at most $x.rank - 1$. Thus, the increase in potential due to the change in iter(x) is less than the decrease in potential due to the change in level(x), and we conclude that $\phi_q(x) \le \phi_{q-1}(x) - 1$. ∎

Our final three lemmas show that the amortized cost of each MAKE-SET, LINK, and FIND-SET operation is $O(\alpha(n))$. Recall from equation (17.2) that the amortized cost of each operation is its actual cost plus the change in potential due to the operation.

Lemma 21.11
The amortized cost of each MAKE-SET operation is $O(1)$.

Proof Suppose that the qth operation is MAKE-SET(x). This operation creates node x with rank 0, so that $\phi_q(x) = 0$. No other ranks or potentials change, and so $\Phi_q = \Phi_{q-1}$. Noting that the actual cost of the MAKE-SET operation is $O(1)$ completes the proof. ∎

Lemma 21.12
The amortized cost of each LINK operation is $O(\alpha(n))$.

Proof Suppose that the qth operation is LINK(x, y). The actual cost of the LINK operation is $O(1)$. Without loss of generality, suppose that the LINK makes y the parent of x.

To determine the change in potential due to the LINK, we note that the only nodes whose potentials may change are x, y, and the children of y just prior to the operation. We shall show that the only node whose potential can increase due to the LINK is y, and that its increase is at most $\alpha(n)$:

- By Lemma 21.10, any node that is y's child just before the LINK cannot have its potential increase due to the LINK.

- From the definition of $\phi_q(x)$, we see that, since x was a root just before the qth operation, $\phi_{q-1}(x) = \alpha(n) \cdot x.rank$. If $x.rank = 0$, then $\phi_q(x) = \phi_{q-1}(x) = 0$. Otherwise,

$$\phi_q(x) \; < \; \alpha(n) \cdot x.rank \quad \text{(by Corollary 21.9)}$$
$$= \; \phi_{q-1}(x) \,,$$

and so x's potential decreases.

- Because y is a root prior to the LINK, $\phi_{q-1}(y) = \alpha(n) \cdot y.rank$. The LINK operation leaves y as a root, and it either leaves y's rank alone or it increases y's rank by 1. Therefore, either $\phi_q(y) = \phi_{q-1}(y)$ or $\phi_q(y) = \phi_{q-1}(y) + \alpha(n)$.

The increase in potential due to the LINK operation, therefore, is at most $\alpha(n)$. The amortized cost of the LINK operation is $O(1) + \alpha(n) = O(\alpha(n))$.   ∎

Lemma 21.13
The amortized cost of each FIND-SET operation is $O(\alpha(n))$.

Proof   Suppose that the qth operation is a FIND-SET and that the find path contains s nodes. The actual cost of the FIND-SET operation is $O(s)$. We shall show that no node's potential increases due to the FIND-SET and that at least $\max(0, s - (\alpha(n) + 2))$ nodes on the find path have their potential decrease by at least 1.

To see that no node's potential increases, we first appeal to Lemma 21.10 for all nodes other than the root. If x is the root, then its potential is $\alpha(n) \cdot x.rank$, which does not change.

Now we show that at least $\max(0, s - (\alpha(n) + 2))$ nodes have their potential decrease by at least 1. Let x be a node on the find path such that $x.rank > 0$ and x is followed somewhere on the find path by another node y that is not a root, where $\text{level}(y) = \text{level}(x)$ just before the FIND-SET operation. (Node y need not *immediately* follow x on the find path.) All but at most $\alpha(n) + 2$ nodes on the find path satisfy these constraints on x. Those that do not satisfy them are the first node on the find path (if it has rank 0), the last node on the path (i.e., the root), and the last node w on the path for which $\text{level}(w) = k$, for each $k = 0, 1, 2, \ldots, \alpha(n) - 1$.

Let us fix such a node x, and we shall show that x's potential decreases by at least 1. Let $k = \text{level}(x) = \text{level}(y)$. Just prior to the path compression caused by the FIND-SET, we have

$$
\begin{aligned}
x.p.rank &\geq A_k^{(\text{iter}(x))}(x.rank) &&\text{(by definition of iter}(x)) \; , \\
y.p.rank &\geq A_k(y.rank) &&\text{(by definition of level}(y)) \; , \\
y.rank &\geq x.p.rank &&\text{(by Corollary 21.5 and because} \\
&&&\quad y \text{ follows } x \text{ on the find path)} \; .
\end{aligned}
$$

Putting these inequalities together and letting i be the value of iter(x) before path compression, we have

$$
\begin{aligned}
y.p.rank &\geq A_k(y.rank) \\
&\geq A_k(x.p.rank) &&\text{(because } A_k(j) \text{ is strictly increasing)} \\
&\geq A_k(A_k^{(\text{iter}(x))}(x.rank)) \\
&= A_k^{(i+1)}(x.rank) \; .
\end{aligned}
$$

Because path compression will make x and y have the same parent, we know that after path compression, $x.p.rank = y.p.rank$ and that the path compression does not decrease $y.p.rank$. Since $x.rank$ does not change, after path compression we have that $x.p.rank \geq A_k^{(i+1)}(x.rank)$. Thus, path compression will cause either iter(x) to increase (to at least $i + 1$) or level(x) to increase (which occurs if iter(x) increases to at least $x.rank + 1$). In either case, by Lemma 21.10, we have $\phi_q(x) \leq \phi_{q-1}(x) - 1$. Hence, x's potential decreases by at least 1.

The amortized cost of the FIND-SET operation is the actual cost plus the change in potential. The actual cost is $O(s)$, and we have shown that the total potential decreases by at least $\max(0, s - (\alpha(n) + 2))$. The amortized cost, therefore, is at most $O(s) - (s - (\alpha(n) + 2)) = O(s) - s + O(\alpha(n)) = O(\alpha(n))$, since we can scale up the units of potential to dominate the constant hidden in $O(s)$. ∎

Putting the preceding lemmas together yields the following theorem.

Theorem 21.14
A sequence of m MAKE-SET, UNION, and FIND-SET operations, n of which are MAKE-SET operations, can be performed on a disjoint-set forest with union by rank and path compression in worst-case time $O(m \, \alpha(n))$.

Proof   Immediate from Lemmas 21.7, 21.11, 21.12, and 21.13. ∎

Exercises

21.4-1
Prove Lemma 21.4.

21.4-2
Prove that every node has rank at most $\lfloor \lg n \rfloor$.

21.4-3
In light of Exercise 21.4-2, how many bits are necessary to store $x.rank$ for each node x?

21.4-4
Using Exercise 21.4-2, give a simple proof that operations on a disjoint-set forest with union by rank but without path compression run in $O(m \lg n)$ time.

21.4-5
Professor Dante reasons that because node ranks increase strictly along a simple path to the root, node levels must monotonically increase along the path. In other

words, if $x.rank > 0$ and $x.p$ is not a root, then $\text{level}(x) \leq \text{level}(x.p)$. Is the professor correct?

21.4-6 ★

Consider the function $\alpha'(n) = \min \{k : A_k(1) \geq \lg(n + 1)\}$. Show that $\alpha'(n) \leq 3$ for all practical values of n and, using Exercise 21.4-2, show how to modify the potential-function argument to prove that we can perform a sequence of m MAKE-SET, UNION, and FIND-SET operations, n of which are MAKE-SET operations, on a disjoint-set forest with union by rank and path compression in worst-case time $O(m \, \alpha'(n))$.

Problems

21-1 *Off-line minimum*

The ***off-line minimum problem*** asks us to maintain a dynamic set T of elements from the domain $\{1, 2, \ldots, n\}$ under the operations INSERT and EXTRACT-MIN. We are given a sequence S of n INSERT and m EXTRACT-MIN calls, where each key in $\{1, 2, \ldots, n\}$ is inserted exactly once. We wish to determine which key is returned by each EXTRACT-MIN call. Specifically, we wish to fill in an array *extracted*$[1 .. m]$, where for $i = 1, 2, \ldots, m$, *extracted*$[i]$ is the key returned by the ith EXTRACT-MIN call. The problem is "off-line" in the sense that we are allowed to process the entire sequence S before determining any of the returned keys.

a. In the following instance of the off-line minimum problem, each operation INSERT(i) is represented by the value of i and each EXTRACT-MIN is represented by the letter E:

   $4, 8, E, 3, E, 9, 2, 6, E, E, E, 1, 7, E, 5$.

   Fill in the correct values in the *extracted* array.

To develop an algorithm for this problem, we break the sequence S into homogeneous subsequences. That is, we represent S by

$$I_1, E, I_2, E, I_3, \ldots, I_m, E, I_{m+1} ,$$

where each E represents a single EXTRACT-MIN call and each I_j represents a (possibly empty) sequence of INSERT calls. For each subsequence I_j, we initially place the keys inserted by these operations into a set K_j, which is empty if I_j is empty. We then do the following:

OFF-LINE-MINIMUM(m, n)

```
1   for i = 1 to n
2       determine j such that i ∈ Kⱼ
3       if j ≠ m + 1
4           extracted[j] = i
5           let l be the smallest value greater than j
                   for which set Kₗ exists
6               Kₗ = Kⱼ ∪ Kₗ, destroying Kⱼ
7   return extracted
```

b. Argue that the array *extracted* returned by OFF-LINE-MINIMUM is correct.

c. Describe how to implement OFF-LINE-MINIMUM efficiently with a disjoint-set data structure. Give a tight bound on the worst-case running time of your implementation.

21-2 Depth determination

In the **depth-determination problem**, we maintain a forest $\mathcal{F} = \{T_i\}$ of rooted trees under three operations:

MAKE-TREE(v) creates a tree whose only node is v.

FIND-DEPTH(v) returns the depth of node v within its tree.

GRAFT(r, v) makes node r, which is assumed to be the root of a tree, become the child of node v, which is assumed to be in a different tree than r but may or may not itself be a root.

a. Suppose that we use a tree representation similar to a disjoint-set forest: $v.p$ is the parent of node v, except that $v.p = v$ if v is a root. Suppose further that we implement GRAFT(r, v) by setting $r.p = v$ and FIND-DEPTH(v) by following the find path up to the root, returning a count of all nodes other than v encountered. Show that the worst-case running time of a sequence of m MAKE-TREE, FIND-DEPTH, and GRAFT operations is $\Theta(m^2)$.

By using the union-by-rank and path-compression heuristics, we can reduce the worst-case running time. We use the disjoint-set forest $\mathcal{S} = \{S_i\}$, where each set S_i (which is itself a tree) corresponds to a tree T_i in the forest $\mathcal{F}$. The tree structure within a set S_i, however, does not necessarily correspond to that of T_i. In fact, the implementation of S_i does not record the exact parent-child relationships but nevertheless allows us to determine any node's depth in T_i.

The key idea is to maintain in each node v a "pseudodistance" $v.d$, which is defined so that the sum of the pseudodistances along the simple path from v to the root of its set S_i equals the depth of v in T_i. That is, if the simple path from v to its root in S_i is $v_0, v_1, \ldots, v_k$, where $v_0 = v$ and v_k is S_i's root, then the depth of v in T_i is $\sum_{j=0}^{k} v_j.d$.

b. Give an implementation of MAKE-TREE.

c. Show how to modify FIND-SET to implement FIND-DEPTH. Your implementation should perform path compression, and its running time should be linear in the length of the find path. Make sure that your implementation updates pseudodistances correctly.

d. Show how to implement GRAFT(r, v), which combines the sets containing r and v, by modifying the UNION and LINK procedures. Make sure that your implementation updates pseudodistances correctly. Note that the root of a set S_i is not necessarily the root of the corresponding tree T_i.

e. Give a tight bound on the worst-case running time of a sequence of m MAKE-TREE, FIND-DEPTH, and GRAFT operations, n of which are MAKE-TREE operations.

21-3   *Tarjan's off-line least-common-ancestors algorithm*

The ***least common ancestor*** of two nodes u and v in a rooted tree T is the node w that is an ancestor of both u and v and that has the greatest depth in T. In the ***off-line least-common-ancestors problem***, we are given a rooted tree T and an arbitrary set $P = \{\{u, v\}\}$ of unordered pairs of nodes in T, and we wish to determine the least common ancestor of each pair in P.

To solve the off-line least-common-ancestors problem, the following procedure performs a tree walk of T with the initial call LCA$(T.root)$. We assume that each node is colored WHITE prior to the walk.

LCA(u)

```
 1   MAKE-SET(u)
 2   FIND-SET(u).ancestor = u
 3   for each child v of u in T
 4       LCA(v)
 5       UNION(u, v)
 6       FIND-SET(u).ancestor = u
 7   u.color = BLACK
 8   for each node v such that {u, v} ∈ P
 9       if v.color == BLACK
10           print "The least common ancestor of"
                 u "and" v "is" FIND-SET(v).ancestor
```

a. Argue that line 10 executes exactly once for each pair $\{u, v\} \in P$.

b. Argue that at the time of the call $\text{LCA}(u)$, the number of sets in the disjoint-set data structure equals the depth of u in T.

c. Prove that LCA correctly prints the least common ancestor of u and v for each pair $\{u, v\} \in P$.

d. Analyze the running time of LCA, assuming that we use the implementation of the disjoint-set data structure in Section 21.3.

Chapter notes

Many of the important results for disjoint-set data structures are due at least in part to R. E. Tarjan. Using aggregate analysis, Tarjan [328, 330] gave the first tight upper bound in terms of the very slowly growing inverse $\widehat{\alpha}(m, n)$ of Ackermann's function. (The function $A_k(j)$ given in Section 21.4 is similar to Ackermann's function, and the function $\alpha(n)$ is similar to the inverse. Both $\alpha(n)$ and $\widehat{\alpha}(m, n)$ are at most 4 for all conceivable values of m and n.) An $O(m \lg^* n)$ upper bound was proven earlier by Hopcroft and Ullman [5, 179]. The treatment in Section 21.4 is adapted from a later analysis by Tarjan [332], which is in turn based on an analysis by Kozen [220]. Harfst and Reingold [161] give a potential-based version of Tarjan's earlier bound.

Tarjan and van Leeuwen [333] discuss variants on the path-compression heuristic, including "one-pass methods," which sometimes offer better constant factors in their performance than do two-pass methods. As with Tarjan's earlier analyses of the basic path-compression heuristic, the analyses by Tarjan and van Leeuwen are aggregate. Harfst and Reingold [161] later showed how to make a small change to the potential function to adapt their path-compression analysis to these one-pass variants. Gabow and Tarjan [121] show that in certain applications, the disjoint-set operations can be made to run in $O(m)$ time.

Tarjan [329] showed that a lower bound of $\Omega(m \, \widehat{\alpha}(m, n))$ time is required for operations on any disjoint-set data structure satisfying certain technical conditions. This lower bound was later generalized by Fredman and Saks [113], who showed that in the worst case, $\Omega(m \, \widehat{\alpha}(m, n))$ ($\lg n$)-bit words of memory must be accessed.

VI   Graph Algorithms

Introduction

Graph problems pervade computer science, and algorithms for working with them are fundamental to the field. Hundreds of interesting computational problems are couched in terms of graphs. In this part, we touch on a few of the more significant ones.

Chapter 22 shows how we can represent a graph in a computer and then discusses algorithms based on searching a graph using either breadth-first search or depth-first search. The chapter gives two applications of depth-first search: topologically sorting a directed acyclic graph and decomposing a directed graph into its strongly connected components.

Chapter 23 describes how to compute a minimum-weight spanning tree of a graph: the least-weight way of connecting all of the vertices together when each edge has an associated weight. The algorithms for computing minimum spanning trees serve as good examples of greedy algorithms (see Chapter 16).

Chapters 24 and 25 consider how to compute shortest paths between vertices when each edge has an associated length or "weight." Chapter 24 shows how to find shortest paths from a given source vertex to all other vertices, and Chapter 25 examines methods to compute shortest paths between every pair of vertices.

Finally, Chapter 26 shows how to compute a maximum flow of material in a flow network, which is a directed graph having a specified source vertex of material, a specified sink vertex, and specified capacities for the amount of material that can traverse each directed edge. This general problem arises in many forms, and a good algorithm for computing maximum flows can help solve a variety of related problems efficiently.

When we characterize the running time of a graph algorithm on a given graph $G = (V, E)$, we usually measure the size of the input in terms of the number of vertices $|V|$ and the number of edges $|E|$ of the graph. That is, we describe the size of the input with two parameters, not just one. We adopt a common notational convention for these parameters. Inside asymptotic notation (such as O-notation or Θ-notation), and *only* inside such notation, the symbol V denotes $|V|$ and the symbol E denotes $|E|$. For example, we might say, "the algorithm runs in time $O(VE)$," meaning that the algorithm runs in time $O(|V| |E|)$. This convention makes the running-time formulas easier to read, without risk of ambiguity.

Another convention we adopt appears in pseudocode. We denote the vertex set of a graph G by $G.V$ and its edge set by $G.E$. That is, the pseudocode views vertex and edge sets as attributes of a graph.

22   Elementary Graph Algorithms

This chapter presents methods for representing a graph and for searching a graph. Searching a graph means systematically following the edges of the graph so as to visit the vertices of the graph. A graph-searching algorithm can discover much about the structure of a graph. Many algorithms begin by searching their input graph to obtain this structural information. Several other graph algorithms elaborate on basic graph searching. Techniques for searching a graph lie at the heart of the field of graph algorithms.

Section 22.1 discusses the two most common computational representations of graphs: as adjacency lists and as adjacency matrices. Section 22.2 presents a simple graph-searching algorithm called breadth-first search and shows how to create a breadth-first tree. Section 22.3 presents depth-first search and proves some standard results about the order in which depth-first search visits vertices. Section 22.4 provides our first real application of depth-first search: topologically sorting a directed acyclic graph. A second application of depth-first search, finding the strongly connected components of a directed graph, is the topic of Section 22.5.

22.1   Representations of graphs

We can choose between two standard ways to represent a graph $G = (V, E)$: as a collection of adjacency lists or as an adjacency matrix. Either way applies to both directed and undirected graphs. Because the adjacency-list representation provides a compact way to represent *sparse* graphs—those for which $|E|$ is much less than $|V|^2$—it is usually the method of choice. Most of the graph algorithms presented in this book assume that an input graph is represented in adjacency-list form. We may prefer an adjacency-matrix representation, however, when the graph is *dense*—$|E|$ is close to $|V|^2$—or when we need to be able to tell quickly if there is an edge connecting two given vertices. For example, two of the all-pairs

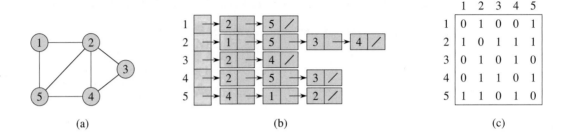

Figure 22.1 Two representations of an undirected graph. **(a)** An undirected graph G with 5 vertices and 7 edges. **(b)** An adjacency-list representation of G. **(c)** The adjacency-matrix representation of G.

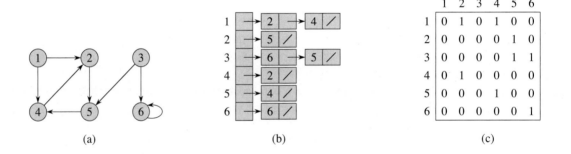

Figure 22.2 Two representations of a directed graph. **(a)** A directed graph G with 6 vertices and 8 edges. **(b)** An adjacency-list representation of G. **(c)** The adjacency-matrix representation of G.

shortest-paths algorithms presented in Chapter 25 assume that their input graphs are represented by adjacency matrices.

The ***adjacency-list representation*** of a graph $G = (V, E)$ consists of an array *Adj* of $|V|$ lists, one for each vertex in V. For each $u \in V$, the adjacency list *Adj*[u] contains all the vertices v such that there is an edge $(u, v) \in E$. That is, *Adj*[u] consists of all the vertices adjacent to u in G. (Alternatively, it may contain pointers to these vertices.) Since the adjacency lists represent the edges of a graph, in pseudocode we treat the array *Adj* as an attribute of the graph, just as we treat the edge set E. In pseudocode, therefore, we will see notation such as $G.Adj[u]$. Figure 22.1(b) is an adjacency-list representation of the undirected graph in Figure 22.1(a). Similarly, Figure 22.2(b) is an adjacency-list representation of the directed graph in Figure 22.2(a).

If G is a directed graph, the sum of the lengths of all the adjacency lists is $|E|$, since an edge of the form (u, v) is represented by having v appear in *Adj*[u]. If G is

an undirected graph, the sum of the lengths of all the adjacency lists is $2\,|E|$, since
if (u, v) is an undirected edge, then u appears in v's adjacency list and vice versa.
For both directed and undirected graphs, the adjacency-list representation has the
desirable property that the amount of memory it requires is $\Theta(V + E)$.

We can readily adapt adjacency lists to represent **weighted graphs**, that is, graphs
for which each edge has an associated **weight**, typically given by a **weight function**
$w : E \rightarrow \mathbb{R}$. For example, let $G = (V, E)$ be a weighted graph with weight
function w. We simply store the weight $w(u, v)$ of the edge $(u, v) \in E$ with
vertex v in u's adjacency list. The adjacency-list representation is quite robust in
that we can modify it to support many other graph variants.

A potential disadvantage of the adjacency-list representation is that it provides
no quicker way to determine whether a given edge (u, v) is present in the graph
than to search for v in the adjacency list $Adj[u]$. An adjacency-matrix representation of the graph remedies this disadvantage, but at the cost of using asymptotically
more memory. (See Exercise 22.1-8 for suggestions of variations on adjacency lists
that permit faster edge lookup.)

For the **adjacency-matrix representation** of a graph $G = (V, E)$, we assume
that the vertices are numbered $1, 2, \ldots, |V|$ in some arbitrary manner. Then the
adjacency-matrix representation of a graph G consists of a $|V| \times |V|$ matrix
$A = (a_{ij})$ such that

$$a_{ij} = \begin{cases} 1 & \text{if } (i, j) \in E , \\ 0 & \text{otherwise} . \end{cases}$$

Figures 22.1(c) and 22.2(c) are the adjacency matrices of the undirected and directed graphs in Figures 22.1(a) and 22.2(a), respectively. The adjacency matrix of
a graph requires $\Theta(V^2)$ memory, independent of the number of edges in the graph.

Observe the symmetry along the main diagonal of the adjacency matrix in Figure 22.1(c). Since in an undirected graph, (u, v) and (v, u) represent the same
edge, the adjacency matrix A of an undirected graph is its own transpose: $A = A^{\mathrm{T}}$.
In some applications, it pays to store only the entries on and above the diagonal of
the adjacency matrix, thereby cutting the memory needed to store the graph almost
in half.

Like the adjacency-list representation of a graph, an adjacency matrix can represent a weighted graph. For example, if $G = (V, E)$ is a weighted graph with edge-
weight function w, we can simply store the weight $w(u, v)$ of the edge $(u, v) \in E$
as the entry in row u and column v of the adjacency matrix. If an edge does not
exist, we can store a NIL value as its corresponding matrix entry, though for many
problems it is convenient to use a value such as 0 or ∞.

Although the adjacency-list representation is asymptotically at least as space-
efficient as the adjacency-matrix representation, adjacency matrices are simpler,
and so we may prefer them when graphs are reasonably small. Moreover, adja-

cency matrices carry a further advantage for unweighted graphs: they require only one bit per entry.

Representing attributes

Most algorithms that operate on graphs need to maintain attributes for vertices and/or edges. We indicate these attributes using our usual notation, such as $v.d$ for an attribute d of a vertex v. When we indicate edges as pairs of vertices, we use the same style of notation. For example, if edges have an attribute f, then we denote this attribute for edge (u, v) by $(u, v).f$. For the purpose of presenting and understanding algorithms, our attribute notation suffices.

   Implementing vertex and edge attributes in real programs can be another story entirely. There is no one best way to store and access vertex and edge attributes. For a given situation, your decision will likely depend on the programming language you are using, the algorithm you are implementing, and how the rest of your program uses the graph. If you represent a graph using adjacency lists, one design represents vertex attributes in additional arrays, such as an array $d[1 .. |V|]$ that parallels the *Adj* array. If the vertices adjacent to u are in $Adj[u]$, then what we call the attribute $u.d$ would actually be stored in the array entry $d[u]$. Many other ways of implementing attributes are possible. For example, in an object-oriented programming language, vertex attributes might be represented as instance variables within a subclass of a `Vertex` class.

Exercises

22.1-1
Given an adjacency-list representation of a directed graph, how long does it take to compute the out-degree of every vertex? How long does it take to compute the in-degrees?

22.1-2
Give an adjacency-list representation for a complete binary tree on 7 vertices. Give an equivalent adjacency-matrix representation. Assume that vertices are numbered from 1 to 7 as in a binary heap.

22.1-3
The ***transpose*** of a directed graph $G = (V, E)$ is the graph $G^{\mathrm{T}} = (V, E^{\mathrm{T}})$, where $E^{\mathrm{T}} = \{(v, u) \in V \times V : (u, v) \in E\}$. Thus, G^{T} is G with all its edges reversed. Describe efficient algorithms for computing G^{T} from G, for both the adjacency-list and adjacency-matrix representations of G. Analyze the running times of your algorithms.

22.1-4

Given an adjacency-list representation of a multigraph $G = (V, E)$, describe an $O(V + E)$-time algorithm to compute the adjacency-list representation of the "equivalent" undirected graph $G' = (V, E')$, where E' consists of the edges in E with all multiple edges between two vertices replaced by a single edge and with all self-loops removed.

22.1-5

The *square* of a directed graph $G = (V, E)$ is the graph $G^2 = (V, E^2)$ such that $(u, v) \in E^2$ if and only if G contains a path with at most two edges between u and v. Describe efficient algorithms for computing G^2 from G for both the adjacency-list and adjacency-matrix representations of G. Analyze the running times of your algorithms.

22.1-6

Most graph algorithms that take an adjacency-matrix representation as input require time $\Omega(V^2)$, but there are some exceptions. Show how to determine whether a directed graph G contains a *universal sink*—a vertex with in-degree $|V| - 1$ and out-degree 0—in time $O(V)$, given an adjacency matrix for G.

22.1-7

The *incidence matrix* of a directed graph $G = (V, E)$ with no self-loops is a $|V| \times |E|$ matrix $B = (b_{ij})$ such that

$$b_{ij} = \begin{cases} -1 & \text{if edge } j \text{ leaves vertex } i \text{ ,} \\ 1 & \text{if edge } j \text{ enters vertex } i \text{ ,} \\ 0 & \text{otherwise .} \end{cases}$$

Describe what the entries of the matrix product BB^T represent, where B^T is the transpose of B.

22.1-8

Suppose that instead of a linked list, each array entry $Adj[u]$ is a hash table containing the vertices v for which $(u, v) \in E$. If all edge lookups are equally likely, what is the expected time to determine whether an edge is in the graph? What disadvantages does this scheme have? Suggest an alternate data structure for each edge list that solves these problems. Does your alternative have disadvantages compared to the hash table?

22.2   Breadth-first search

Breadth-first search is one of the simplest algorithms for searching a graph and the archetype for many important graph algorithms. Prim's minimum-spanning-tree algorithm (Section 23.2) and Dijkstra's single-source shortest-paths algorithm (Section 24.3) use ideas similar to those in breadth-first search.

Given a graph $G = (V, E)$ and a distinguished ***source*** vertex s, breadth-first search systematically explores the edges of G to "discover" every vertex that is reachable from s. It computes the distance (smallest number of edges) from s to each reachable vertex. It also produces a "breadth-first tree" with root s that contains all reachable vertices. For any vertex v reachable from s, the simple path in the breadth-first tree from s to v corresponds to a "shortest path" from s to v in G, that is, a path containing the smallest number of edges. The algorithm works on both directed and undirected graphs.

Breadth-first search is so named because it expands the frontier between discovered and undiscovered vertices uniformly across the breadth of the frontier. That is, the algorithm discovers all vertices at distance k from s before discovering any vertices at distance $k + 1$.

To keep track of progress, breadth-first search colors each vertex white, gray, or black. All vertices start out white and may later become gray and then black. A vertex is ***discovered*** the first time it is encountered during the search, at which time it becomes nonwhite. Gray and black vertices, therefore, have been discovered, but breadth-first search distinguishes between them to ensure that the search proceeds in a breadth-first manner.[1] If $(u, v) \in E$ and vertex u is black, then vertex v is either gray or black; that is, all vertices adjacent to black vertices have been discovered. Gray vertices may have some adjacent white vertices; they represent the frontier between discovered and undiscovered vertices.

Breadth-first search constructs a breadth-first tree, initially containing only its root, which is the source vertex s. Whenever the search discovers a white vertex v in the course of scanning the adjacency list of an already discovered vertex u, the vertex v and the edge (u, v) are added to the tree. We say that u is the ***predecessor*** or ***parent*** of v in the breadth-first tree. Since a vertex is discovered at most once, it has at most one parent. Ancestor and descendant relationships in the breadth-first tree are defined relative to the root s as usual: if u is on the simple path in the tree from the root s to vertex v, then u is an ancestor of v and v is a descendant of u.

---

[1] We distinguish between gray and black vertices to help us understand how breadth-first search operates. In fact, as Exercise 22.2-3 shows, we would get the same result even if we did not distinguish between gray and black vertices.

The breadth-first-search procedure BFS below assumes that the input graph $G = (V, E)$ is represented using adjacency lists. It attaches several additional attributes to each vertex in the graph. We store the color of each vertex $u \in V$ in the attribute $u.color$ and the predecessor of u in the attribute $u.\pi$. If u has no predecessor (for example, if $u = s$ or u has not been discovered), then $u.\pi = \text{NIL}$. The attribute $u.d$ holds the distance from the source s to vertex u computed by the algorithm. The algorithm also uses a first-in, first-out queue Q (see Section 10.1) to manage the set of gray vertices.

BFS(G, s)

```
 1   for each vertex u ∈ G.V − {s}
 2        u.color = WHITE
 3        u.d = ∞
 4        u.π = NIL
 5   s.color = GRAY
 6   s.d = 0
 7   s.π = NIL
 8   Q = ∅
 9   ENQUEUE(Q, s)
10   while Q ≠ ∅
11        u = DEQUEUE(Q)
12        for each v ∈ G.Adj[u]
13             if v.color == WHITE
14                  v.color = GRAY
15                  v.d = u.d + 1
16                  v.π = u
17                  ENQUEUE(Q, v)
18        u.color = BLACK
```

Figure 22.3 illustrates the progress of BFS on a sample graph.

The procedure BFS works as follows. With the exception of the source vertex s, lines 1–4 paint every vertex white, set $u.d$ to be infinity for each vertex u, and set the parent of every vertex to be NIL. Line 5 paints s gray, since we consider it to be discovered as the procedure begins. Line 6 initializes $s.d$ to 0, and line 7 sets the predecessor of the source to be NIL. Lines 8–9 initialize Q to the queue containing just the vertex s.

The **while** loop of lines 10–18 iterates as long as there remain gray vertices, which are discovered vertices that have not yet had their adjacency lists fully examined. This **while** loop maintains the following invariant:

At the test in line 10, the queue Q consists of the set of gray vertices.

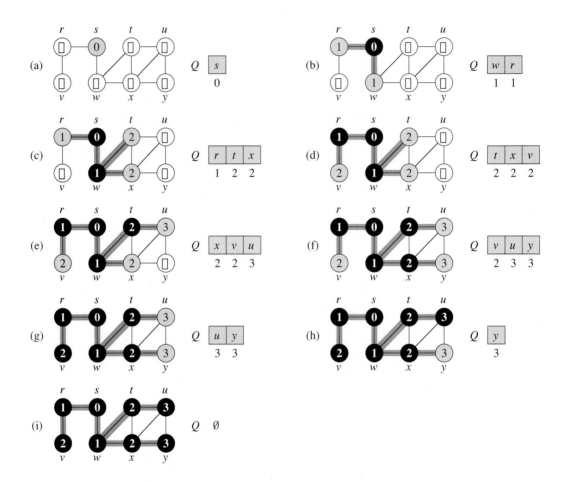

Figure 22.3 The operation of BFS on an undirected graph. Tree edges are shown shaded as they are produced by BFS. The value of $u.d$ appears within each vertex u. The queue Q is shown at the beginning of each iteration of the **while** loop of lines 10–18. Vertex distances appear below vertices in the queue.

Although we won't use this loop invariant to prove correctness, it is easy to see that it holds prior to the first iteration and that each iteration of the loop maintains the invariant. Prior to the first iteration, the only gray vertex, and the only vertex in Q, is the source vertex s. Line 11 determines the gray vertex u at the head of the queue Q and removes it from Q. The **for** loop of lines 12–17 considers each vertex v in the adjacency list of u. If v is white, then it has not yet been discovered, and the procedure discovers it by executing lines 14–17. The procedure paints vertex v gray, sets its distance $v.d$ to $u.d+1$, records u as its parent $v.\pi$, and places it at the tail of the queue Q. Once the procedure has examined all the vertices on u's adjacency list, it blackens u in line 18. The loop invariant is maintained because whenever a vertex is painted gray (in line 14) it is also enqueued (in line 17), and whenever a vertex is dequeued (in line 11) it is also painted black (in line 18).

The results of breadth-first search may depend upon the order in which the neighbors of a given vertex are visited in line 12: the breadth-first tree may vary, but the distances d computed by the algorithm will not. (See Exercise 22.2-5.)

Analysis

Before proving the various properties of breadth-first search, we take on the somewhat easier job of analyzing its running time on an input graph $G = (V, E)$. We use aggregate analysis, as we saw in Section 17.1. After initialization, breadth-first search never whitens a vertex, and thus the test in line 13 ensures that each vertex is enqueued at most once, and hence dequeued at most once. The operations of enqueuing and dequeuing take $O(1)$ time, and so the total time devoted to queue operations is $O(V)$. Because the procedure scans the adjacency list of each vertex only when the vertex is dequeued, it scans each adjacency list at most once. Since the sum of the lengths of all the adjacency lists is $\Theta(E)$, the total time spent in scanning adjacency lists is $O(E)$. The overhead for initialization is $O(V)$, and thus the total running time of the BFS procedure is $O(V + E)$. Thus, breadth-first search runs in time linear in the size of the adjacency-list representation of G.

Shortest paths

At the beginning of this section, we claimed that breadth-first search finds the distance to each reachable vertex in a graph $G = (V, E)$ from a given source vertex $s \in V$. Define the ***shortest-path distance*** $\delta(s, v)$ from s to v as the minimum number of edges in any path from vertex s to vertex v; if there is no path from s to v, then $\delta(s, v) = \infty$. We call a path of length $\delta(s, v)$ from s to v a ***shortest path***[2] from s to v. Before showing that breadth-first search correctly computes shortest-path distances, we investigate an important property of shortest-path distances.

---

[2]In Chapters 24 and 25, we shall generalize our study of shortest paths to weighted graphs, in which every edge has a real-valued weight and the weight of a path is the sum of the weights of its constituent edges. The graphs considered in the present chapter are unweighted or, equivalently, all edges have unit weight.

Lemma 22.1
Let $G = (V, E)$ be a directed or undirected graph, and let $s \in V$ be an arbitrary vertex. Then, for any edge $(u, v) \in E$,

$$\delta(s, v) \leq \delta(s, u) + 1 .$$

Proof   If u is reachable from s, then so is v. In this case, the shortest path from s to v cannot be longer than the shortest path from s to u followed by the edge (u, v), and thus the inequality holds. If u is not reachable from s, then $\delta(s, u) = \infty$, and the inequality holds.   ∎

We want to show that BFS properly computes $v.d = \delta(s, v)$ for each vertex $v \in V$. We first show that $v.d$ bounds $\delta(s, v)$ from above.

Lemma 22.2
Let $G = (V, E)$ be a directed or undirected graph, and suppose that BFS is run on G from a given source vertex $s \in V$. Then upon termination, for each vertex $v \in V$, the value $v.d$ computed by BFS satisfies $v.d \geq \delta(s, v)$.

Proof   We use induction on the number of ENQUEUE operations. Our inductive hypothesis is that $v.d \geq \delta(s, v)$ for all $v \in V$.

The basis of the induction is the situation immediately after enqueuing s in line 9 of BFS. The inductive hypothesis holds here, because $s.d = 0 = \delta(s, s)$ and $v.d = \infty \geq \delta(s, v)$ for all $v \in V - \{s\}$.

For the inductive step, consider a white vertex v that is discovered during the search from a vertex u. The inductive hypothesis implies that $u.d \geq \delta(s, u)$. From the assignment performed by line 15 and from Lemma 22.1, we obtain

$$
\begin{aligned}
v.d &= u.d + 1 \\
&\geq \delta(s, u) + 1 \\
&\geq \delta(s, v) .
\end{aligned}
$$

Vertex v is then enqueued, and it is never enqueued again because it is also grayed and the **then** clause of lines 14–17 is executed only for white vertices. Thus, the value of $v.d$ never changes again, and the inductive hypothesis is maintained.   ∎

To prove that $v.d = \delta(s, v)$, we must first show more precisely how the queue Q operates during the course of BFS. The next lemma shows that at all times, the queue holds at most two distinct d values.

Lemma 22.3

Suppose that during the execution of BFS on a graph $G = (V, E)$, the queue Q contains the vertices $\langle v_1, v_2, \ldots, v_r \rangle$, where v_1 is the head of Q and v_r is the tail. Then, $v_r.d \leq v_1.d + 1$ and $v_i.d \leq v_{i+1}.d$ for $i = 1, 2, \ldots, r - 1$.

Proof The proof is by induction on the number of queue operations. Initially, when the queue contains only s, the lemma certainly holds.

For the inductive step, we must prove that the lemma holds after both dequeuing and enqueuing a vertex. If the head v_1 of the queue is dequeued, v_2 becomes the new head. (If the queue becomes empty, then the lemma holds vacuously.) By the inductive hypothesis, $v_1.d \leq v_2.d$. But then we have $v_r.d \leq v_1.d + 1 \leq v_2.d + 1$, and the remaining inequalities are unaffected. Thus, the lemma follows with v_2 as the head.

In order to understand what happens upon enqueuing a vertex, we need to examine the code more closely. When we enqueue a vertex v in line 17 of BFS, it becomes v_{r+1}. At that time, we have already removed vertex u, whose adjacency list is currently being scanned, from the queue Q, and by the inductive hypothesis, the new head v_1 has $v_1.d \geq u.d$. Thus, $v_{r+1}.d = v.d = u.d + 1 \leq v_1.d + 1$. From the inductive hypothesis, we also have $v_r.d \leq u.d + 1$, and so $v_r.d \leq u.d + 1 = v.d = v_{r+1}.d$, and the remaining inequalities are unaffected. Thus, the lemma follows when v is enqueued. ∎

The following corollary shows that the d values at the time that vertices are enqueued are monotonically increasing over time.

Corollary 22.4

Suppose that vertices v_i and v_j are enqueued during the execution of BFS, and that v_i is enqueued before v_j. Then $v_i.d \leq v_j.d$ at the time that v_j is enqueued.

Proof Immediate from Lemma 22.3 and the property that each vertex receives a finite d value at most once during the course of BFS. ∎

We can now prove that breadth-first search correctly finds shortest-path distances.

Theorem 22.5 (Correctness of breadth-first search)

Let $G = (V, E)$ be a directed or undirected graph, and suppose that BFS is run on G from a given source vertex $s \in V$. Then, during its execution, BFS discovers every vertex $v \in V$ that is reachable from the source s, and upon termination, $v.d = \delta(s, v)$ for all $v \in V$. Moreover, for any vertex $v \neq s$ that is reachable from s, one of the shortest paths from s to v is a shortest path from s to $v.\pi$ followed by the edge $(v.\pi, v)$.

Proof Assume, for the purpose of contradiction, that some vertex receives a d value not equal to its shortest-path distance. Let v be the vertex with minimum $\delta(s, v)$ that receives such an incorrect d value; clearly $v \neq s$. By Lemma 22.2, $v.d \geq \delta(s, v)$, and thus we have that $v.d > \delta(s, v)$. Vertex v must be reachable from s, for if it is not, then $\delta(s, v) = \infty \geq v.d$. Let u be the vertex immediately preceding v on a shortest path from s to v, so that $\delta(s, v) = \delta(s, u) + 1$. Because $\delta(s, u) < \delta(s, v)$, and because of how we chose v, we have $u.d = \delta(s, u)$. Putting these properties together, we have

$$v.d > \delta(s, v) = \delta(s, u) + 1 = u.d + 1 . \tag{22.1}$$

Now consider the time when BFS chooses to dequeue vertex u from Q in line 11. At this time, vertex v is either white, gray, or black. We shall show that in each of these cases, we derive a contradiction to inequality (22.1). If v is white, then line 15 sets $v.d = u.d + 1$, contradicting inequality (22.1). If v is black, then it was already removed from the queue and, by Corollary 22.4, we have $v.d \leq u.d$, again contradicting inequality (22.1). If v is gray, then it was painted gray upon dequeuing some vertex w, which was removed from Q earlier than u and for which $v.d = w.d + 1$. By Corollary 22.4, however, $w.d \leq u.d$, and so we have $v.d = w.d + 1 \leq u.d + 1$, once again contradicting inequality (22.1).

Thus we conclude that $v.d = \delta(s, v)$ for all $v \in V$. All vertices v reachable from s must be discovered, for otherwise they would have $\infty = v.d > \delta(s, v)$. To conclude the proof of the theorem, observe that if $v.\pi = u$, then $v.d = u.d + 1$. Thus, we can obtain a shortest path from s to v by taking a shortest path from s to $v.\pi$ and then traversing the edge $(v.\pi, v)$.   ∎

Breadth-first trees

The procedure BFS builds a breadth-first tree as it searches the graph, as Figure 22.3 illustrates. The tree corresponds to the π attributes. More formally, for a graph $G = (V, E)$ with source s, we define the ***predecessor subgraph*** of G as $G_\pi = (V_\pi, E_\pi)$, where

$$V_\pi = \{v \in V : v.\pi \neq \text{NIL}\} \cup \{s\}$$

and

$$E_\pi = \{(v.\pi, v) : v \in V_\pi - \{s\}\} .$$

The predecessor subgraph G_π is a ***breadth-first tree*** if V_π consists of the vertices reachable from s and, for all $v \in V_\pi$, the subgraph G_π contains a unique simple path from s to v that is also a shortest path from s to v in G. A breadth-first tree is in fact a tree, since it is connected and $|E_\pi| = |V_\pi| - 1$ (see Theorem B.2). We call the edges in E_π **tree edges**.

The following lemma shows that the predecessor subgraph produced by the BFS procedure is a breadth-first tree.

Lemma 22.6

When applied to a directed or undirected graph $G = (V, E)$, procedure BFS constructs π so that the predecessor subgraph $G_\pi = (V_\pi, E_\pi)$ is a breadth-first tree.

Proof Line 16 of BFS sets $v.\pi = u$ if and only if $(u, v) \in E$ and $\delta(s, v) < \infty$ — that is, if v is reachable from s — and thus V_π consists of the vertices in V reachable from s. Since G_π forms a tree, by Theorem B.2, it contains a unique simple path from s to each vertex in V_π. By applying Theorem 22.5 inductively, we conclude that every such path is a shortest path in G. ∎

The following procedure prints out the vertices on a shortest path from s to v, assuming that BFS has already computed a breadth-first tree:

PRINT-PATH(G, s, v)

```
1  if v == s
2      print s
3  elseif v.π == NIL
4      print "no path from" s "to" v "exists"
5  else PRINT-PATH(G, s, v.π)
6      print v
```

This procedure runs in time linear in the number of vertices in the path printed, since each recursive call is for a path one vertex shorter.

Exercises

22.2-1
Show the d and π values that result from running breadth-first search on the directed graph of Figure 22.2(a), using vertex 3 as the source.

22.2-2
Show the d and π values that result from running breadth-first search on the undirected graph of Figure 22.3, using vertex u as the source.

22.2-3

Show that using a single bit to store each vertex color suffices by arguing that the BFS procedure would produce the same result if line 18 were removed.

22.2-4

What is the running time of BFS if we represent its input graph by an adjacency matrix and modify the algorithm to handle this form of input?

22.2-5

Argue that in a breadth-first search, the value $u.d$ assigned to a vertex u is independent of the order in which the vertices appear in each adjacency list. Using Figure 22.3 as an example, show that the breadth-first tree computed by BFS can depend on the ordering within adjacency lists.

22.2-6

Give an example of a directed graph $G = (V, E)$, a source vertex $s \in V$, and a set of tree edges $E_\pi \subseteq E$ such that for each vertex $v \in V$, the unique simple path in the graph (V, E_π) from s to v is a shortest path in G, yet the set of edges E_π cannot be produced by running BFS on G, no matter how the vertices are ordered in each adjacency list.

22.2-7

There are two types of professional wrestlers: "babyfaces" ("good guys") and "heels" ("bad guys"). Between any pair of professional wrestlers, there may or may not be a rivalry. Suppose we have n professional wrestlers and we have a list of r pairs of wrestlers for which there are rivalries. Give an $O(n + r)$-time algorithm that determines whether it is possible to designate some of the wrestlers as babyfaces and the remainder as heels such that each rivalry is between a babyface and a heel. If it is possible to perform such a designation, your algorithm should produce it.

22.2-8 ★

The ***diameter*** of a tree $T = (V, E)$ is defined as $\max_{u,v \in V} \delta(u, v)$, that is, the largest of all shortest-path distances in the tree. Give an efficient algorithm to compute the diameter of a tree, and analyze the running time of your algorithm.

22.2-9

Let $G = (V, E)$ be a connected, undirected graph. Give an $O(V + E)$-time algorithm to compute a path in G that traverses each edge in E exactly once in each direction. Describe how you can find your way out of a maze if you are given a large supply of pennies.

22.3   Depth-first search

The strategy followed by depth-first search is, as its name implies, to search "deeper" in the graph whenever possible. Depth-first search explores edges out of the most recently discovered vertex v that still has unexplored edges leaving it. Once all of v's edges have been explored, the search "backtracks" to explore edges leaving the vertex from which v was discovered. This process continues until we have discovered all the vertices that are reachable from the original source vertex. If any undiscovered vertices remain, then depth-first search selects one of them as a new source, and it repeats the search from that source. The algorithm repeats this entire process until it has discovered every vertex.[3]

As in breadth-first search, whenever depth-first search discovers a vertex v during a scan of the adjacency list of an already discovered vertex u, it records this event by setting v's predecessor attribute $v.\pi$ to u. Unlike breadth-first search, whose predecessor subgraph forms a tree, the predecessor subgraph produced by a depth-first search may be composed of several trees, because the search may repeat from multiple sources. Therefore, we define the ***predecessor subgraph*** of a depth-first search slightly differently from that of a breadth-first search: we let $G_\pi = (V, E_\pi)$, where

$$E_\pi = \{(v.\pi, v) : v \in V \text{ and } v.\pi \neq \text{NIL}\} \ .$$

The predecessor subgraph of a depth-first search forms a ***depth-first forest*** comprising several ***depth-first trees***. The edges in E_π are ***tree edges***.

As in breadth-first search, depth-first search colors vertices during the search to indicate their state. Each vertex is initially white, is grayed when it is ***discovered*** in the search, and is blackened when it is ***finished***, that is, when its adjacency list has been examined completely. This technique guarantees that each vertex ends up in exactly one depth-first tree, so that these trees are disjoint.

Besides creating a depth-first forest, depth-first search also ***timestamps*** each vertex. Each vertex v has two timestamps: the first timestamp $v.d$ records when v is first discovered (and grayed), and the second timestamp $v.f$ records when the search finishes examining v's adjacency list (and blackens v). These timestamps

---

[3]It may seem arbitrary that breadth-first search is limited to only one source whereas depth-first search may search from multiple sources. Although conceptually, breadth-first search could proceed from multiple sources and depth-first search could be limited to one source, our approach reflects how the results of these searches are typically used. Breadth-first search usually serves to find shortest-path distances (and the associated predecessor subgraph) from a given source. Depth-first search is often a subroutine in another algorithm, as we shall see later in this chapter.

provide important information about the structure of the graph and are generally helpful in reasoning about the behavior of depth-first search.

The procedure DFS below records when it discovers vertex u in the attribute $u.d$ and when it finishes vertex u in the attribute $u.f$. These timestamps are integers between 1 and $2|V|$, since there is one discovery event and one finishing event for each of the $|V|$ vertices. For every vertex u,

$$u.d < u.f\,. \tag{22.2}$$

Vertex u is WHITE before time $u.d$, GRAY between time $u.d$ and time $u.f$, and BLACK thereafter.

The following pseudocode is the basic depth-first-search algorithm. The input graph G may be undirected or directed. The variable *time* is a global variable that we use for timestamping.

DFS(G)

```
1   for each vertex u ∈ G.V
2       u.color = WHITE
3       u.π = NIL
4   time = 0
5   for each vertex u ∈ G.V
6       if u.color == WHITE
7           DFS-VISIT(G, u)
```

DFS-VISIT(G, u)

```
 1   time = time + 1         // white vertex u has just been discovered
 2   u.d = time
 3   u.color = GRAY
 4   for each v ∈ G.Adj[u]   // explore edge (u, v)
 5       if v.color == WHITE
 6           v.π = u
 7           DFS-VISIT(G, v)
 8   u.color = BLACK         // blacken u; it is finished
 9   time = time + 1
10   u.f = time
```

Figure 22.4 illustrates the progress of DFS on the graph shown in Figure 22.2.

Procedure DFS works as follows. Lines 1–3 paint all vertices white and initialize their π attributes to NIL. Line 4 resets the global time counter. Lines 5–7 check each vertex in V in turn and, when a white vertex is found, visit it using DFS-VISIT. Every time DFS-VISIT(G, u) is called in line 7, vertex u becomes

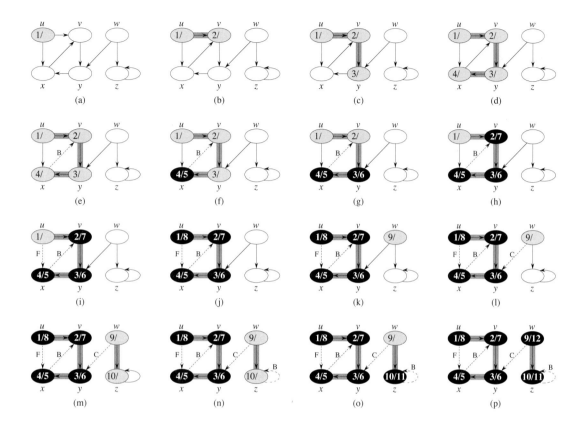

Figure 22.4   The progress of the depth-first-search algorithm DFS on a directed graph. As edges are explored by the algorithm, they are shown as either shaded (if they are tree edges) or dashed (otherwise). Nontree edges are labeled B, C, or F according to whether they are back, cross, or forward edges. Timestamps within vertices indicate discovery time/finishing times.

the root of a new tree in the depth-first forest. When DFS returns, every vertex u has been assigned a ***discovery time*** $u.d$ and a ***finishing time*** $u.f$.

In each call DFS-V$_{\text{ISIT}}$(G, u), vertex u is initially white. Line 1 increments the global variable *time*, line 2 records the new value of *time* as the discovery time $u.d$, and line 3 paints u gray. Lines 4–7 examine each vertex v adjacent to u and recursively visit v if it is white. As each vertex $v \in Adj[u]$ is considered in line 4, we say that edge (u, v) is ***explored*** by the depth-first search. Finally, after every edge leaving u has been explored, lines 8–10 paint u black, increment *time*, and record the finishing time in $u.f$.

Note that the results of depth-first search may depend upon the order in which line 5 of DFS examines the vertices and upon the order in which line 4 of DFS-V$_{\text{ISIT}}$ visits the neighbors of a vertex. These different visitation orders tend not to cause problems in practice, as we can usually use *any* depth-first search result effectively, with essentially equivalent results.

What is the running time of DFS? The loops on lines 1–3 and lines 5–7 of DFS take time $\Theta(V)$, exclusive of the time to execute the calls to DFS-VISIT. As we did for breadth-first search, we use aggregate analysis. The procedure DFS-VISIT is called exactly once for each vertex $v \in V$, since the vertex u on which DFS-VISIT is invoked must be white and the first thing DFS-VISIT does is paint vertex u gray. During an execution of DFS-VISIT(G, v), the loop on lines 4–7 executes $|Adj[v]|$ times. Since

$$\sum_{v \in V} |Adj[v]| = \Theta(E) \,,$$

the total cost of executing lines 4–7 of DFS-VISIT is $\Theta(E)$. The running time of DFS is therefore $\Theta(V + E)$.

Properties of depth-first search

Depth-first search yields valuable information about the structure of a graph. Perhaps the most basic property of depth-first search is that the predecessor subgraph G_π does indeed form a forest of trees, since the structure of the depth-first trees exactly mirrors the structure of recursive calls of DFS-VISIT. That is, $u = v.\pi$ if and only if DFS-VISIT(G, v) was called during a search of u's adjacency list. Additionally, vertex v is a descendant of vertex u in the depth-first forest if and only if v is discovered during the time in which u is gray.

Another important property of depth-first search is that discovery and finishing times have ***parenthesis structure***. If we represent the discovery of vertex u with a left parenthesis "$(u$" and represent its finishing by a right parenthesis "$u)$", then the history of discoveries and finishings makes a well-formed expression in the sense that the parentheses are properly nested. For example, the depth-first search of Figure 22.5(a) corresponds to the parenthesization shown in Figure 22.5(b). The following theorem provides another way to characterize the parenthesis structure.

Theorem 22.7 (Parenthesis theorem)
In any depth-first search of a (directed or undirected) graph $G = (V, E)$, for any two vertices u and v, exactly one of the following three conditions holds:

- the intervals $[u.d, u.f]$ and $[v.d, v.f]$ are entirely disjoint, and neither u nor v is a descendant of the other in the depth-first forest,

- the interval $[u.d, u.f]$ is contained entirely within the interval $[v.d, v.f]$, and u is a descendant of v in a depth-first tree, or

- the interval $[v.d, v.f]$ is contained entirely within the interval $[u.d, u.f]$, and v is a descendant of u in a depth-first tree.

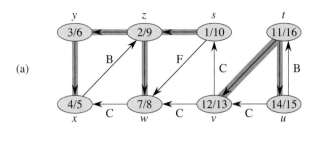

(a)

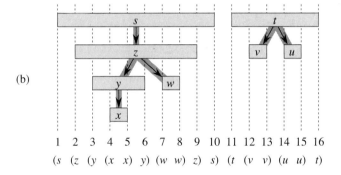

(b)

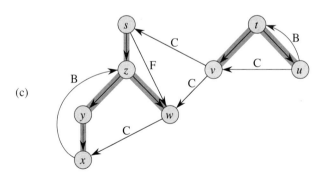

(c)

Figure 22.5   Properties of depth-first search. **(a)** The result of a depth-first search of a directed graph. Vertices are timestamped and edge types are indicated as in Figure 22.4. **(b)** Intervals for the discovery time and finishing time of each vertex correspond to the parenthesization shown. Each rectangle spans the interval given by the discovery and finishing times of the corresponding vertex. Only tree edges are shown. If two intervals overlap, then one is nested within the other, and the vertex corresponding to the smaller interval is a descendant of the vertex corresponding to the larger. **(c)** The graph of part (a) redrawn with all tree and forward edges going down within a depth-first tree and all back edges going up from a descendant to an ancestor.

Proof   We begin with the case in which $u.d < v.d$. We consider two subcases, according to whether $v.d < u.f$ or not. The first subcase occurs when $v.d < u.f$, so v was discovered while u was still gray, which implies that v is a descendant of u. Moreover, since v was discovered more recently than u, all of its outgoing edges are explored, and v is finished, before the search returns to and finishes u. In this case, therefore, the interval $[v.d, v.f]$ is entirely contained within the interval $[u.d, u.f]$. In the other subcase, $u.f < v.d$, and by inequality (22.2), $u.d < u.f < v.d < v.f$; thus the intervals $[u.d, u.f]$ and $[v.d, v.f]$ are disjoint. Because the intervals are disjoint, neither vertex was discovered while the other was gray, and so neither vertex is a descendant of the other.

The case in which $v.d < u.d$ is similar, with the roles of u and v reversed in the above argument.   ■

Corollary 22.8 (Nesting of descendants' intervals)
Vertex v is a proper descendant of vertex u in the depth-first forest for a (directed or undirected) graph G if and only if $u.d < v.d < v.f < u.f$.

Proof   Immediate from Theorem 22.7.   ■

The next theorem gives another important characterization of when one vertex is a descendant of another in the depth-first forest.

Theorem 22.9 (White-path theorem)
In a depth-first forest of a (directed or undirected) graph $G = (V, E)$, vertex v is a descendant of vertex u if and only if at the time $u.d$ that the search discovers u, there is a path from u to v consisting entirely of white vertices.

Proof $\Rightarrow$: If $v = u$, then the path from u to v contains just vertex u, which is still white when we set the value of $u.d$. Now, suppose that v is a proper descendant of u in the depth-first forest. By Corollary 22.8, $u.d < v.d$, and so v is white at time $u.d$. Since v can be any descendant of u, all vertices on the unique simple path from u to v in the depth-first forest are white at time $u.d$.

$\Leftarrow$: Suppose that there is a path of white vertices from u to v at time $u.d$, but v does not become a descendant of u in the depth-first tree. Without loss of generality, assume that every vertex other than v along the path becomes a descendant of u. (Otherwise, let v be the closest vertex to u along the path that doesn't become a descendant of u.) Let w be the predecessor of v in the path, so that w is a descendant of u (w and u may in fact be the same vertex). By Corollary 22.8, $w.f \leq u.f$. Because v must be discovered after u is discovered, but before w is finished, we have $u.d < v.d < w.f \leq u.f$. Theorem 22.7 then implies that the interval $[v.d, v.f]$

is contained entirely within the interval $[u.d, u.f]$. By Corollary 22.8, v must after all be a descendant of u. ∎

Classification of edges

Another interesting property of depth-first search is that the search can be used to classify the edges of the input graph $G = (V, E)$. The type of each edge can provide important information about a graph. For example, in the next section, we shall see that a directed graph is acyclic if and only if a depth-first search yields no "back" edges (Lemma 22.11).

We can define four edge types in terms of the depth-first forest G_π produced by a depth-first search on G:

1. ***Tree edges*** are edges in the depth-first forest G_π. Edge (u, v) is a tree edge if v was first discovered by exploring edge (u, v).

2. ***Back edges*** are those edges (u, v) connecting a vertex u to an ancestor v in a depth-first tree. We consider self-loops, which may occur in directed graphs, to be back edges.

3. ***Forward edges*** are those nontree edges (u, v) connecting a vertex u to a descendant v in a depth-first tree.

4. ***Cross edges*** are all other edges. They can go between vertices in the same depth-first tree, as long as one vertex is not an ancestor of the other, or they can go between vertices in different depth-first trees.

In Figures 22.4 and 22.5, edge labels indicate edge types. Figure 22.5(c) also shows how to redraw the graph of Figure 22.5(a) so that all tree and forward edges head downward in a depth-first tree and all back edges go up. We can redraw any graph in this fashion.

The DFS algorithm has enough information to classify some edges as it encounters them. The key idea is that when we first explore an edge (u, v), the color of vertex v tells us something about the edge:

1. WHITE indicates a tree edge,

2. GRAY indicates a back edge, and

3. BLACK indicates a forward or cross edge.

The first case is immediate from the specification of the algorithm. For the second case, observe that the gray vertices always form a linear chain of descendants corresponding to the stack of active DFS-VISIT invocations; the number of gray vertices is one more than the depth in the depth-first forest of the vertex most recently discovered. Exploration always proceeds from the deepest gray vertex, so an edge that reaches another gray vertex has reached an ancestor. The third case handles the remaining possibility; Exercise 22.3-5 asks you to show that such an edge (u, v) is a forward edge if $u.d < v.d$ and a cross edge if $u.d > v.d$.

An undirected graph may entail some ambiguity in how we classify edges, since (u, v) and (v, u) are really the same edge. In such a case, we classify the edge as the *first* type in the classification list that applies. Equivalently (see Exercise 22.3-6), we classify the edge according to whichever of (u, v) or (v, u) the search encounters first.

We now show that forward and cross edges never occur in a depth-first search of an undirected graph.

Theorem 22.10
In a depth-first search of an undirected graph G, every edge of G is either a tree edge or a back edge.

Proof Let (u, v) be an arbitrary edge of G, and suppose without loss of generality that $u.d < v.d$. Then the search must discover and finish v before it finishes u (while u is gray), since v is on u's adjacency list. If the first time that the search explores edge (u, v), it is in the direction from u to v, then v is undiscovered (white) until that time, for otherwise the search would have explored this edge already in the direction from v to u. Thus, (u, v) becomes a tree edge. If the search explores (u, v) first in the direction from v to u, then (u, v) is a back edge, since u is still gray at the time the edge is first explored.   ■

We shall see several applications of these theorems in the following sections.

Exercises

22.3-1
Make a 3-by-3 chart with row and column labels WHITE, GRAY, and BLACK. In each cell (i, j), indicate whether, at any point during a depth-first search of a directed graph, there can be an edge from a vertex of color i to a vertex of color j. For each possible edge, indicate what edge types it can be. Make a second such chart for depth-first search of an undirected graph.

22.3-2
Show how depth-first search works on the graph of Figure 22.6. Assume that the **for** loop of lines 5–7 of the DFS procedure considers the vertices in alphabetical order, and assume that each adjacency list is ordered alphabetically. Show the discovery and finishing times for each vertex, and show the classification of each edge.

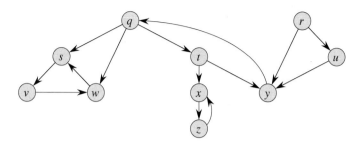

Figure 22.6   A directed graph for use in Exercises 22.3-2 and 22.5-2.

22.3-3
Show the parenthesis structure of the depth-first search of Figure 22.4.

22.3-4
Show that using a single bit to store each vertex color suffices by arguing that the DFS procedure would produce the same result if line 8 of DFS-VISIT was removed.

22.3-5
Show that edge (u, v) is

a. a tree edge or forward edge if and only if $u.d < v.d < v.f < u.f$,

b. a back edge if and only if $v.d \leq u.d < u.f \leq v.f$, and

c. a cross edge if and only if $v.d < v.f < u.d < u.f$.

22.3-6
Show that in an undirected graph, classifying an edge (u, v) as a tree edge or a back edge according to whether (u, v) or (v, u) is encountered first during the depth-first search is equivalent to classifying it according to the ordering of the four types in the classification scheme.

22.3-7
Rewrite the procedure DFS, using a stack to eliminate recursion.

22.3-8
Give a counterexample to the conjecture that if a directed graph G contains a path from u to v, and if $u.d < v.d$ in a depth-first search of G, then v is a descendant of u in the depth-first forest produced.

22.3-9
Give a counterexample to the conjecture that if a directed graph G contains a path from u to v, then any depth-first search must result in $v.d \leq u.f$.

22.3-10
Modify the pseudocode for depth-first search so that it prints out every edge in the directed graph G, together with its type. Show what modifications, if any, you need to make if G is undirected.

22.3-11
Explain how a vertex u of a directed graph can end up in a depth-first tree containing only u, even though u has both incoming and outgoing edges in G.

22.3-12
Show that we can use a depth-first search of an undirected graph G to identify the connected components of G, and that the depth-first forest contains as many trees as G has connected components. More precisely, show how to modify depth-first search so that it assigns to each vertex v an integer label $v.cc$ between 1 and k, where k is the number of connected components of G, such that $u.cc = v.cc$ if and only if u and v are in the same connected component.

22.3-13   ★
A directed graph $G = (V, E)$ is ***singly connected*** if $u \rightsquigarrow v$ implies that G contains at most one simple path from u to v for all vertices $u, v \in V$. Give an efficient algorithm to determine whether or not a directed graph is singly connected.

22.4   Topological sort

This section shows how we can use depth-first search to perform a topological sort of a directed acyclic graph, or a "dag" as it is sometimes called. A ***topological sort*** of a dag $G = (V, E)$ is a linear ordering of all its vertices such that if G contains an edge (u, v), then u appears before v in the ordering. (If the graph contains a cycle, then no linear ordering is possible.) We can view a topological sort of a graph as an ordering of its vertices along a horizontal line so that all directed edges go from left to right. Topological sorting is thus different from the usual kind of "sorting" studied in Part II.

Many applications use directed acyclic graphs to indicate precedences among events. Figure 22.7 gives an example that arises when Professor Bumstead gets dressed in the morning. The professor must don certain garments before others (e.g., socks before shoes). Other items may be put on in any order (e.g., socks and

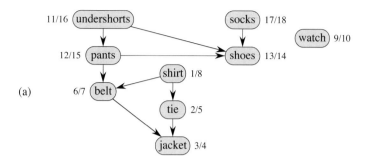

(a)

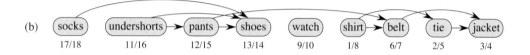

(b)

Figure 22.7   **(a)** Professor Bumstead topologically sorts his clothing when getting dressed. Each directed edge (u, v) means that garment u must be put on before garment v. The discovery and finishing times from a depth-first search are shown next to each vertex. **(b)** The same graph shown topologically sorted, with its vertices arranged from left to right in order of decreasing finishing time. All directed edges go from left to right.

pants). A directed edge (u, v) in the dag of Figure 22.7(a) indicates that garment u must be donned before garment v. A topological sort of this dag therefore gives an order for getting dressed. Figure 22.7(b) shows the topologically sorted dag as an ordering of vertices along a horizontal line such that all directed edges go from left to right.

The following simple algorithm topologically sorts a dag:

TOPOLOGICAL-SORT(G)

1   call DFS(G) to compute finishing times $v.f$ for each vertex v
2   as each vertex is finished, insert it onto the front of a linked list
3   **return** the linked list of vertices

Figure 22.7(b) shows how the topologically sorted vertices appear in reverse order of their finishing times.

We can perform a topological sort in time $\Theta(V + E)$, since depth-first search takes $\Theta(V + E)$ time and it takes $O(1)$ time to insert each of the $|V|$ vertices onto the front of the linked list.

We prove the correctness of this algorithm using the following key lemma characterizing directed acyclic graphs.

Lemma 22.11
A directed graph G is acyclic if and only if a depth-first search of G yields no back edges.

Proof $\Rightarrow$: Suppose that a depth-first search produces a back edge (u, v). Then vertex v is an ancestor of vertex u in the depth-first forest. Thus, G contains a path from v to u, and the back edge (u, v) completes a cycle.

  $\Leftarrow$: Suppose that G contains a cycle c. We show that a depth-first search of G yields a back edge. Let v be the first vertex to be discovered in c, and let (u, v) be the preceding edge in c. At time $v.d$, the vertices of c form a path of white vertices from v to u. By the white-path theorem, vertex u becomes a descendant of v in the depth-first forest. Therefore, (u, v) is a back edge. ∎

Theorem 22.12
TOPOLOGICAL-SORT produces a topological sort of the directed acyclic graph provided as its input.

Proof Suppose that DFS is run on a given dag $G = (V, E)$ to determine finishing times for its vertices. It suffices to show that for any pair of distinct vertices $u, v \in V$, if G contains an edge from u to v, then $v.f < u.f$. Consider any edge (u, v) explored by $\text{DFS}(G)$. When this edge is explored, v cannot be gray, since then v would be an ancestor of u and (u, v) would be a back edge, contradicting Lemma 22.11. Therefore, v must be either white or black. If v is white, it becomes a descendant of u, and so $v.f < u.f$. If v is black, it has already been finished, so that $v.f$ has already been set. Because we are still exploring from u, we have yet to assign a timestamp to $u.f$, and so once we do, we will have $v.f < u.f$ as well. Thus, for any edge (u, v) in the dag, we have $v.f < u.f$, proving the theorem. ∎

Exercises

22.4-1
Show the ordering of vertices produced by TOPOLOGICAL-SORT when it is run on the dag of Figure 22.8, under the assumption of Exercise 22.3-2.

22.4-2
Give a linear-time algorithm that takes as input a directed acyclic graph $G = (V, E)$ and two vertices s and t, and returns the number of simple paths from s to t in G. For example, the directed acyclic graph of Figure 22.8 contains exactly four simple paths from vertex p to vertex v: *pov*, *poryv*, *posryv*, and *psryv*. (Your algorithm needs only to count the simple paths, not list them.)

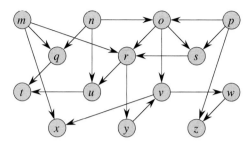

Figure 22.8   A dag for topological sorting.

22.4-3
Give an algorithm that determines whether or not a given undirected graph $G = (V, E)$ contains a simple cycle. Your algorithm should run in $O(V)$ time, independent of $|E|$.

22.4-4
Prove or disprove: If a directed graph G contains cycles, then TOPOLOGICAL-SORT(G) produces a vertex ordering that minimizes the number of "bad" edges that are inconsistent with the ordering produced.

22.4-5
Another way to perform topological sorting on a directed acyclic graph $G = (V, E)$ is to repeatedly find a vertex of in-degree 0, output it, and remove it and all of its outgoing edges from the graph. Explain how to implement this idea so that it runs in time $O(V + E)$. What happens to this algorithm if G has cycles?

22.5   Strongly connected components

We now consider a classic application of depth-first search: decomposing a directed graph into its strongly connected components. This section shows how to do so using two depth-first searches. Many algorithms that work with directed graphs begin with such a decomposition. After decomposing the graph into strongly connected components, such algorithms run separately on each one and then combine the solutions according to the structure of connections among components.

Recall from Appendix B that a strongly connected component of a directed graph $G = (V, E)$ is a maximal set of vertices $C \subseteq V$ such that for every pair of vertices u and v in C, we have both $u \leadsto v$ and $v \leadsto u$; that is, vertices u and v are reachable from each other. Figure 22.9 shows an example.

(a)

(b)

(c)

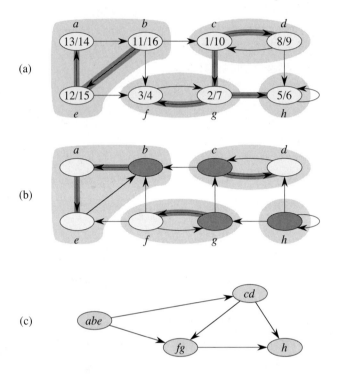

Figure 22.9   **(a)** A directed graph G. Each shaded region is a strongly connected component of G. Each vertex is labeled with its discovery and finishing times in a depth-first search, and tree edges are shaded. **(b)** The graph G^T, the transpose of G, with the depth-first forest computed in line 3 of STRONGLY-CONNECTED-COMPONENTS shown and tree edges shaded. Each strongly connected component corresponds to one depth-first tree. Vertices b, c, g, and h, which are heavily shaded, are the roots of the depth-first trees produced by the depth-first search of G^T. **(c)** The acyclic component graph G^{SCC} obtained by contracting all edges within each strongly connected component of G so that only a single vertex remains in each component.

Our algorithm for finding strongly connected components of a graph $G = (V, E)$ uses the transpose of G, which we defined in Exercise 22.1-3 to be the graph $G^T = (V, E^T)$, where $E^T = \{(u, v) : (v, u) \in E\}$. That is, E^T consists of the edges of G with their directions reversed. Given an adjacency-list representation of G, the time to create G^T is $O(V + E)$. It is interesting to observe that G and G^T have exactly the same strongly connected components: u and v are reachable from each other in G if and only if they are reachable from each other in G^T. Figure 22.9(b) shows the transpose of the graph in Figure 22.9(a), with the strongly connected components shaded.

The following linear-time (i.e., $\Theta(V+E)$-time) algorithm computes the strongly connected components of a directed graph $G = (V, E)$ using two depth-first searches, one on G and one on G^{T}.

STRONGLY-CONNECTED-COMPONENTS(G)

1   call DFS(G) to compute finishing times $u.f$ for each vertex u
2   compute G^{T}
3   call DFS(G^{T}), but in the main loop of DFS, consider the vertices
        in order of decreasing $u.f$ (as computed in line 1)
4   output the vertices of each tree in the depth-first forest formed in line 3 as a
        separate strongly connected component

The idea behind this algorithm comes from a key property of the ***component graph*** $G^{\mathrm{SCC}} = (V^{\mathrm{SCC}}, E^{\mathrm{SCC}})$, which we define as follows. Suppose that G has strongly connected components $C_1, C_2, \ldots, C_k$. The vertex set V^{SCC} is $\{v_1, v_2, \ldots, v_k\}$, and it contains a vertex v_i for each strongly connected component C_i of G. There is an edge $(v_i, v_j) \in E^{\mathrm{SCC}}$ if G contains a directed edge (x, y) for some $x \in C_i$ and some $y \in C_j$. Looked at another way, by contracting all edges whose incident vertices are within the same strongly connected component of G, the resulting graph is G^{SCC}. Figure 22.9(c) shows the component graph of the graph in Figure 22.9(a).

The key property is that the component graph is a dag, which the following lemma implies.

Lemma 22.13

Let C and C' be distinct strongly connected components in directed graph $G = (V, E)$, let $u, v \in C$, let $u', v' \in C'$, and suppose that G contains a path $u \rightsquigarrow u'$. Then G cannot also contain a path $v' \rightsquigarrow v$.

Proof   If G contains a path $v' \rightsquigarrow v$, then it contains paths $u \rightsquigarrow u' \rightsquigarrow v'$ and $v' \rightsquigarrow v \rightsquigarrow u$. Thus, u and v' are reachable from each other, thereby contradicting the assumption that C and C' are distinct strongly connected components.   ■

We shall see that by considering vertices in the second depth-first search in decreasing order of the finishing times that were computed in the first depth-first search, we are, in essence, visiting the vertices of the component graph (each of which corresponds to a strongly connected component of G) in topologically sorted order.

Because the STRONGLY-CONNECTED-COMPONENTS procedure performs two depth-first searches, there is the potential for ambiguity when we discuss $u.d$ or $u.f$. In this section, these values always refer to the discovery and finishing times as computed by the first call of DFS, in line 1.

We extend the notation for discovery and finishing times to sets of vertices. If $U \subseteq V$, then we define $d(U) = \min_{u \in U} \{u.d\}$ and $f(U) = \max_{u \in U} \{u.f\}$. That is, $d(U)$ and $f(U)$ are the earliest discovery time and latest finishing time, respectively, of any vertex in U.

The following lemma and its corollary give a key property relating strongly connected components and finishing times in the first depth-first search.

Lemma 22.14

Let C and C' be distinct strongly connected components in directed graph $G = (V, E)$. Suppose that there is an edge $(u, v) \in E$, where $u \in C$ and $v \in C'$. Then $f(C) > f(C')$.

Proof We consider two cases, depending on which strongly connected component, C or C', had the first discovered vertex during the depth-first search.

If $d(C) < d(C')$, let x be the first vertex discovered in C. At time $x.d$, all vertices in C and C' are white. At that time, G contains a path from x to each vertex in C consisting only of white vertices. Because $(u, v) \in E$, for any vertex $w \in C'$, there is also a path in G at time $x.d$ from x to w consisting only of white vertices: $x \rightsquigarrow u \rightarrow v \rightsquigarrow w$. By the white-path theorem, all vertices in C and C' become descendants of x in the depth-first tree. By Corollary 22.8, x has the latest finishing time of any of its descendants, and so $x.f = f(C) > f(C')$.

If instead we have $d(C) > d(C')$, let y be the first vertex discovered in C'. At time $y.d$, all vertices in C' are white and G contains a path from y to each vertex in C' consisting only of white vertices. By the white-path theorem, all vertices in C' become descendants of y in the depth-first tree, and by Corollary 22.8, $y.f = f(C')$. At time $y.d$, all vertices in C are white. Since there is an edge (u, v) from C to C', Lemma 22.13 implies that there cannot be a path from C' to C. Hence, no vertex in C is reachable from y. At time $y.f$, therefore, all vertices in C are still white. Thus, for any vertex $w \in C$, we have $w.f > y.f$, which implies that $f(C) > f(C')$.   ∎

The following corollary tells us that each edge in G^T that goes between different strongly connected components goes from a component with an earlier finishing time (in the first depth-first search) to a component with a later finishing time.

Corollary 22.15

Let C and C' be distinct strongly connected components in directed graph $G = (V, E)$. Suppose that there is an edge $(u, v) \in E^\mathrm{T}$, where $u \in C$ and $v \in C'$. Then $f(C) < f(C')$.

Proof   Since $(u, v) \in E^{\mathrm{T}}$, we have $(v, u) \in E$. Because the strongly connected components of G and G^{T} are the same, Lemma 22.14 implies that
$f(C) < f(C')$.   ∎

Corollary 22.15 provides the key to understanding why the strongly connected
components algorithm works. Let us examine what happens when we perform the
second depth-first search, which is on G^{T}. We start with the strongly connected
component C whose finishing time $f(C)$ is maximum. The search starts from
some vertex $x \in C$, and it visits all vertices in C. By Corollary 22.15, G^{T} contains
no edges from C to any other strongly connected component, and so the search
from x will not visit vertices in any other component. Thus, the tree rooted at x
contains exactly the vertices of C. Having completed visiting all vertices in C,
the search in line 3 selects as a root a vertex from some other strongly connected
component C' whose finishing time $f(C')$ is maximum over all components other
than C. Again, the search will visit all vertices in C', but by Corollary 22.15,
the only edges in G^{T} from C' to any other component must be to C, which we
have already visited. In general, when the depth-first search of G^{T} in line 3 visits
any strongly connected component, any edges out of that component must be to
components that the search already visited. Each depth-first tree, therefore, will be
exactly one strongly connected component. The following theorem formalizes this
argument.

Theorem 22.16
The STRONGLY-CONNECTED-COMPONENTS procedure correctly computes the
strongly connected components of the directed graph G provided as its input.

Proof   We argue by induction on the number of depth-first trees found in the
depth-first search of G^{T} in line 3 that the vertices of each tree form a strongly
connected component. The inductive hypothesis is that the first k trees produced
in line 3 are strongly connected components. The basis for the induction, when
$k = 0$, is trivial.

In the inductive step, we assume that each of the first k depth-first trees produced
in line 3 is a strongly connected component, and we consider the $(k + 1)$st tree
produced. Let the root of this tree be vertex u, and let u be in strongly connected
component C. Because of how we choose roots in the depth-first search in line 3,
$u.f = f(C) > f(C')$ for any strongly connected component C' other than C
that has yet to be visited. By the inductive hypothesis, at the time that the search
visits u, all other vertices of C are white. By the white-path theorem, therefore, all
other vertices of C are descendants of u in its depth-first tree. Moreover, by the
inductive hypothesis and by Corollary 22.15, any edges in G^{T} that leave C must be
to strongly connected components that have already been visited. Thus, no vertex

in any strongly connected component other than C will be a descendant of u during the depth-first search of G^T. Thus, the vertices of the depth-first tree in G^T that is rooted at u form exactly one strongly connected component, which completes the inductive step and the proof.   ∎

Here is another way to look at how the second depth-first search operates. Consider the component graph $(G^T)^{SCC}$ of G^T. If we map each strongly connected component visited in the second depth-first search to a vertex of $(G^T)^{SCC}$, the second depth-first search visits vertices of $(G^T)^{SCC}$ in the reverse of a topologically sorted order. If we reverse the edges of $(G^T)^{SCC}$, we get the graph $((G^T)^{SCC})^T$. Because $((G^T)^{SCC})^T = G^{SCC}$ (see Exercise 22.5-4), the second depth-first search visits the vertices of G^{SCC} in topologically sorted order.

Exercises

22.5-1
How can the number of strongly connected components of a graph change if a new edge is added?

22.5-2
Show how the procedure STRONGLY-CONNECTED-COMPONENTS works on the graph of Figure 22.6. Specifically, show the finishing times computed in line 1 and the forest produced in line 3. Assume that the loop of lines 5–7 of DFS considers vertices in alphabetical order and that the adjacency lists are in alphabetical order.

22.5-3
Professor Bacon claims that the algorithm for strongly connected components would be simpler if it used the original (instead of the transpose) graph in the second depth-first search and scanned the vertices in order of *increasing* finishing times. Does this simpler algorithm always produce correct results?

22.5-4
Prove that for any directed graph G, we have $((G^T)^{SCC})^T = G^{SCC}$. That is, the transpose of the component graph of G^T is the same as the component graph of G.

22.5-5
Give an $O(V + E)$-time algorithm to compute the component graph of a directed graph $G = (V, E)$. Make sure that there is at most one edge between two vertices in the component graph your algorithm produces.

22.5-6
Given a directed graph $G = (V, E)$, explain how to create another graph $G' = (V, E')$ such that (a) G' has the same strongly connected components as G, (b) G' has the same component graph as G, and (c) E' is as small as possible. Describe a fast algorithm to compute G'.

22.5-7
A directed graph $G = (V, E)$ is **semiconnected** if, for all pairs of vertices $u, v \in V$, we have $u \rightsquigarrow v$ or $v \rightsquigarrow u$. Give an efficient algorithm to determine whether or not G is semiconnected. Prove that your algorithm is correct, and analyze its running time.

Problems

22-1   Classifying edges by breadth-first search
A depth-first forest classifies the edges of a graph into tree, back, forward, and cross edges. A breadth-first tree can also be used to classify the edges reachable from the source of the search into the same four categories.

  a. Prove that in a breadth-first search of an undirected graph, the following properties hold:

    1. There are no back edges and no forward edges.

    2. For each tree edge (u, v), we have $v.d = u.d + 1$.

    3. For each cross edge (u, v), we have $v.d = u.d$ or $v.d = u.d + 1$.

  b. Prove that in a breadth-first search of a directed graph, the following properties hold:

    1. There are no forward edges.

    2. For each tree edge (u, v), we have $v.d = u.d + 1$.

    3. For each cross edge (u, v), we have $v.d \leq u.d + 1$.

    4. For each back edge (u, v), we have $0 \leq v.d \leq u.d$.

22-2   Articulation points, bridges, and biconnected components
Let $G = (V, E)$ be a connected, undirected graph. An **articulation point** of G is a vertex whose removal disconnects G. A **bridge** of G is an edge whose removal disconnects G. A **biconnected component** of G is a maximal set of edges such that any two edges in the set lie on a common simple cycle. Figure 22.10 illustrates

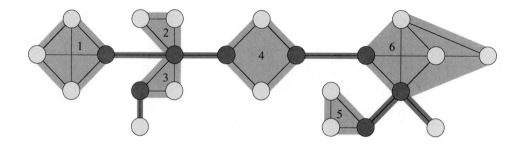

Figure 22.10   The articulation points, bridges, and biconnected components of a connected, undirected graph for use in Problem 22-2. The articulation points are the heavily shaded vertices, the bridges are the heavily shaded edges, and the biconnected components are the edges in the shaded regions, with a *bcc* numbering shown.

these definitions. We can determine articulation points, bridges, and biconnected components using depth-first search. Let $G_\pi = (V, E_\pi)$ be a depth-first tree of G.

a. Prove that the root of G_π is an articulation point of G if and only if it has at least two children in G_π.

b. Let v be a nonroot vertex of G_π. Prove that v is an articulation point of G if and only if v has a child s such that there is no back edge from s or any descendant of s to a proper ancestor of v.

c. Let

$$v.low = \min \begin{cases} v.d\,, \\ w.d : (u, w) \text{ is a back edge for some descendant } u \text{ of } v\,. \end{cases}$$

Show how to compute $v.low$ for all vertices $v \in V$ in $O(E)$ time.

d. Show how to compute all articulation points in $O(E)$ time.

e. Prove that an edge of G is a bridge if and only if it does not lie on any simple cycle of G.

f. Show how to compute all the bridges of G in $O(E)$ time.

g. Prove that the biconnected components of G partition the nonbridge edges of G.

h. Give an $O(E)$-time algorithm to label each edge e of G with a positive integer $e.bcc$ such that $e.bcc = e'.bcc$ if and only if e and e' are in the same biconnected component.

22-3   *Euler tour*

An **Euler tour** of a strongly connected, directed graph $G = (V, E)$ is a cycle that traverses each edge of G exactly once, although it may visit a vertex more than once.

a. Show that G has an Euler tour if and only if in-degree$(v) =$ out-degree(v) for each vertex $v \in V$.

b. Describe an $O(E)$-time algorithm to find an Euler tour of G if one exists. (*Hint:* Merge edge-disjoint cycles.)

22-4   *Reachability*

Let $G = (V, E)$ be a directed graph in which each vertex $u \in V$ is labeled with a unique integer $L(u)$ from the set $\{1, 2, \ldots, |V|\}$. For each vertex $u \in V$, let $R(u) = \{v \in V : u \rightsquigarrow v\}$ be the set of vertices that are reachable from u. Define $\min(u)$ to be the vertex in $R(u)$ whose label is minimum, i.e., $\min(u)$ is the vertex v such that $L(v) = \min\{L(w) : w \in R(u)\}$. Give an $O(V + E)$-time algorithm that computes $\min(u)$ for all vertices $u \in V$.

Chapter notes

Even [103] and Tarjan [330] are excellent references for graph algorithms.

Breadth-first search was discovered by Moore [260] in the context of finding paths through mazes. Lee [226] independently discovered the same algorithm in the context of routing wires on circuit boards.

Hopcroft and Tarjan [178] advocated the use of the adjacency-list representation over the adjacency-matrix representation for sparse graphs and were the first to recognize the algorithmic importance of depth-first search. Depth-first search has been widely used since the late 1950s, especially in artificial intelligence programs.

Tarjan [327] gave a linear-time algorithm for finding strongly connected components. The algorithm for strongly connected components in Section 22.5 is adapted from Aho, Hopcroft, and Ullman [6], who credit it to S. R. Kosaraju (unpublished) and M. Sharir [314]. Gabow [119] also developed an algorithm for strongly connected components that is based on contracting cycles and uses two stacks to make it run in linear time. Knuth [209] was the first to give a linear-time algorithm for topological sorting.

23 Minimum Spanning Trees

Electronic circuit designs often need to make the pins of several components electrically equivalent by wiring them together. To interconnect a set of n pins, we can use an arrangement of $n - 1$ wires, each connecting two pins. Of all such arrangements, the one that uses the least amount of wire is usually the most desirable.

We can model this wiring problem with a connected, undirected graph $G = (V, E)$, where V is the set of pins, E is the set of possible interconnections between pairs of pins, and for each edge $(u, v) \in E$, we have a weight $w(u, v)$ specifying the cost (amount of wire needed) to connect u and v. We then wish to find an acyclic subset $T \subseteq E$ that connects all of the vertices and whose total weight

$$w(T) = \sum_{(u,v) \in T} w(u, v)$$

is minimized. Since T is acyclic and connects all of the vertices, it must form a tree, which we call a *spanning tree* since it "spans" the graph G. We call the problem of determining the tree T the *minimum-spanning-tree problem*.[1] Figure 23.1 shows an example of a connected graph and a minimum spanning tree.

In this chapter, we shall examine two algorithms for solving the minimum-spanning-tree problem: Kruskal's algorithm and Prim's algorithm. We can easily make each of them run in time $O(E \lg V)$ using ordinary binary heaps. By using Fibonacci heaps, Prim's algorithm runs in time $O(E + V \lg V)$, which improves over the binary-heap implementation if $|V|$ is much smaller than $|E|$.

The two algorithms are greedy algorithms, as described in Chapter 16. Each step of a greedy algorithm must make one of several possible choices. The greedy strategy advocates making the choice that is best at the moment. Such a strategy does not generally guarantee that it will always find globally optimal solutions

---

[1] The phrase "minimum spanning tree" is a shortened form of the phrase "minimum-weight spanning tree." We are not, for example, minimizing the number of edges in T, since all spanning trees have exactly $|V| - 1$ edges by Theorem B.2.

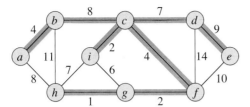

Figure 23.1   A minimum spanning tree for a connected graph. The weights on edges are shown, and the edges in a minimum spanning tree are shaded. The total weight of the tree shown is 37. This minimum spanning tree is not unique: removing the edge (b, c) and replacing it with the edge (a, h) yields another spanning tree with weight 37.

to problems. For the minimum-spanning-tree problem, however, we can prove that certain greedy strategies do yield a spanning tree with minimum weight. Although you can read this chapter independently of Chapter 16, the greedy methods presented here are a classic application of the theoretical notions introduced there.

Section 23.1 introduces a "generic" minimum-spanning-tree method that grows a spanning tree by adding one edge at a time. Section 23.2 gives two algorithms that implement the generic method. The first algorithm, due to Kruskal, is similar to the connected-components algorithm from Section 21.1. The second, due to Prim, resembles Dijkstra's shortest-paths algorithm (Section 24.3).

Because a tree is a type of graph, in order to be precise we must define a tree in terms of not just its edges, but its vertices as well. Although this chapter focuses on trees in terms of their edges, we shall operate with the understanding that the vertices of a tree T are those that some edge of T is incident on.

23.1   Growing a minimum spanning tree

Assume that we have a connected, undirected graph $G = (V, E)$ with a weight function $w : E \to \mathbb{R}$, and we wish to find a minimum spanning tree for G. The two algorithms we consider in this chapter use a greedy approach to the problem, although they differ in how they apply this approach.

This greedy strategy is captured by the following generic method, which grows the minimum spanning tree one edge at a time. The generic method manages a set of edges A, maintaining the following loop invariant:

Prior to each iteration, A is a subset of some minimum spanning tree.

At each step, we determine an edge (u, v) that we can add to A without violating this invariant, in the sense that $A \cup \{(u, v)\}$ is also a subset of a minimum spanning tree. We call such an edge a *safe edge* for A, since we can add it safely to A while maintaining the invariant.

GENERIC-MST(G, w)

```
1   A = ∅
2   while A does not form a spanning tree
3       find an edge (u, v) that is safe for A
4           A = A ∪ {(u, v)}
5   return A
```

We use the loop invariant as follows:

Initialization: After line 1, the set A trivially satisfies the loop invariant.

Maintenance: The loop in lines 2–4 maintains the invariant by adding only safe edges.

Termination: All edges added to A are in a minimum spanning tree, and so the set A returned in line 5 must be a minimum spanning tree.

The tricky part is, of course, finding a safe edge in line 3. One must exist, since when line 3 is executed, the invariant dictates that there is a spanning tree T such that $A \subseteq T$. Within the **while** loop body, A must be a proper subset of T, and therefore there must be an edge $(u, v) \in T$ such that $(u, v) \notin A$ and (u, v) is safe for A.

In the remainder of this section, we provide a rule (Theorem 23.1) for recognizing safe edges. The next section describes two algorithms that use this rule to find safe edges efficiently.

We first need some definitions. A *cut* $(S, V - S)$ of an undirected graph $G = (V, E)$ is a partition of V. Figure 23.2 illustrates this notion. We say that an edge $(u, v) \in E$ *crosses* the cut $(S, V - S)$ if one of its endpoints is in S and the other is in $V - S$. We say that a cut *respects* a set A of edges if no edge in A crosses the cut. An edge is a *light edge* crossing a cut if its weight is the minimum of any edge crossing the cut. Note that there can be more than one light edge crossing a cut in the case of ties. More generally, we say that an edge is a *light edge* satisfying a given property if its weight is the minimum of any edge satisfying the property.

Our rule for recognizing safe edges is given by the following theorem.

Theorem 23.1

Let $G = (V, E)$ be a connected, undirected graph with a real-valued weight function w defined on E. Let A be a subset of E that is included in some minimum spanning tree for G, let $(S, V - S)$ be any cut of G that respects A, and let (u, v) be a light edge crossing $(S, V - S)$. Then, edge (u, v) is safe for A.

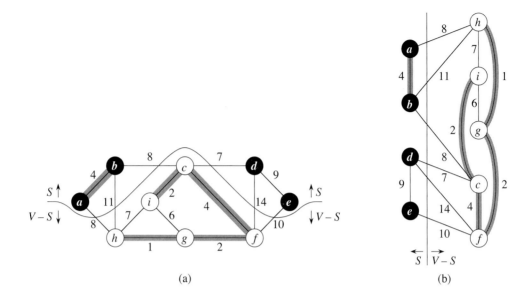

Figure 23.2 Two ways of viewing a cut $(S, V - S)$ of the graph from Figure 23.1. **(a)** Black vertices are in the set S, and white vertices are in $V - S$. The edges crossing the cut are those connecting white vertices with black vertices. The edge (d, c) is the unique light edge crossing the cut. A subset A of the edges is shaded; note that the cut $(S, V - S)$ respects A, since no edge of A crosses the cut. **(b)** The same graph with the vertices in the set S on the left and the vertices in the set $V - S$ on the right. An edge crosses the cut if it connects a vertex on the left with a vertex on the right.

Proof Let T be a minimum spanning tree that includes A, and assume that T does not contain the light edge (u, v), since if it does, we are done. We shall construct another minimum spanning tree T' that includes $A \cup \{(u, v)\}$ by using a cut-and-paste technique, thereby showing that (u, v) is a safe edge for A.

The edge (u, v) forms a cycle with the edges on the simple path p from u to v in T, as Figure 23.3 illustrates. Since u and v are on opposite sides of the cut $(S, V - S)$, at least one edge in T lies on the simple path p and also crosses the cut. Let (x, y) be any such edge. The edge (x, y) is not in A, because the cut respects A. Since (x, y) is on the unique simple path from u to v in T, removing (x, y) breaks T into two components. Adding (u, v) reconnects them to form a new spanning tree $T' = T - \{(x, y)\} \cup \{(u, v)\}$.

We next show that T' is a minimum spanning tree. Since (u, v) is a light edge crossing $(S, V - S)$ and (x, y) also crosses this cut, $w(u, v) \le w(x, y)$. Therefore,

$$
\begin{aligned}
w(T') &= w(T) - w(x, y) + w(u, v) \\
&\le w(T) .
\end{aligned}
$$

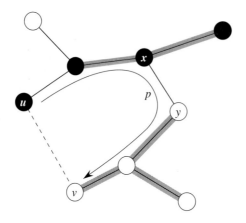

Figure 23.3   The proof of Theorem 23.1. Black vertices are in S, and white vertices are in $V - S$. The edges in the minimum spanning tree T are shown, but the edges in the graph G are not. The edges in A are shaded, and (u, v) is a light edge crossing the cut $(S, V - S)$. The edge (x, y) is an edge on the unique simple path p from u to v in T. To form a minimum spanning tree T' that contains (u, v), remove the edge (x, y) from T and add the edge (u, v).

But T is a minimum spanning tree, so that $w(T) \leq w(T')$; thus, T' must be a minimum spanning tree also.

It remains to show that (u, v) is actually a safe edge for A. We have $A \subseteq T'$, since $A \subseteq T$ and $(x, y) \notin A$; thus, $A \cup \{(u, v)\} \subseteq T'$. Consequently, since T' is a minimum spanning tree, (u, v) is safe for A.   ∎

Theorem 23.1 gives us a better understanding of the workings of the GENERIC-MST method on a connected graph $G = (V, E)$. As the method proceeds, the set A is always acyclic; otherwise, a minimum spanning tree including A would contain a cycle, which is a contradiction. At any point in the execution, the graph $G_A = (V, A)$ is a forest, and each of the connected components of G_A is a tree. (Some of the trees may contain just one vertex, as is the case, for example, when the method begins: A is empty and the forest contains $|V|$ trees, one for each vertex.) Moreover, any safe edge (u, v) for A connects distinct components of G_A, since $A \cup \{(u, v)\}$ must be acyclic.

The **while** loop in lines 2–4 of GENERIC-MST executes $|V| - 1$ times because it finds one of the $|V| - 1$ edges of a minimum spanning tree in each iteration. Initially, when $A = \emptyset$, there are $|V|$ trees in G_A, and each iteration reduces that number by 1. When the forest contains only a single tree, the method terminates.

The two algorithms in Section 23.2 use the following corollary to Theorem 23.1.

Corollary 23.2
Let $G = (V, E)$ be a connected, undirected graph with a real-valued weight function w defined on E. Let A be a subset of E that is included in some minimum spanning tree for G, and let $C = (V_C, E_C)$ be a connected component (tree) in the forest $G_A = (V, A)$. If (u, v) is a light edge connecting C to some other component in G_A, then (u, v) is safe for A.

Proof   The cut $(V_C, V - V_C)$ respects A, and (u, v) is a light edge for this cut. Therefore, (u, v) is safe for A.   ■

Exercises

23.1-1
Let (u, v) be a minimum-weight edge in a connected graph G. Show that (u, v) belongs to some minimum spanning tree of G.

23.1-2
Professor Sabatier conjectures the following converse of Theorem 23.1. Let $G = (V, E)$ be a connected, undirected graph with a real-valued weight function w defined on E. Let A be a subset of E that is included in some minimum spanning tree for G, let $(S, V - S)$ be any cut of G that respects A, and let (u, v) be a safe edge for A crossing $(S, V - S)$. Then, (u, v) is a light edge for the cut. Show that the professor's conjecture is incorrect by giving a counterexample.

23.1-3
Show that if an edge (u, v) is contained in some minimum spanning tree, then it is a light edge crossing some cut of the graph.

23.1-4
Give a simple example of a connected graph such that the set of edges $\{(u, v) :$ there exists a cut $(S, V - S)$ such that (u, v) is a light edge crossing $(S, V - S)\}$ does not form a minimum spanning tree.

23.1-5
Let e be a maximum-weight edge on some cycle of connected graph $G = (V, E)$. Prove that there is a minimum spanning tree of $G' = (V, E - \{e\})$ that is also a minimum spanning tree of G. That is, there is a minimum spanning tree of G that does not include e.

23.1-6
Show that a graph has a unique minimum spanning tree if, for every cut of the graph, there is a unique light edge crossing the cut. Show that the converse is not true by giving a counterexample.

23.1-7
Argue that if all edge weights of a graph are positive, then any subset of edges that connects all vertices and has minimum total weight must be a tree. Give an example to show that the same conclusion does not follow if we allow some weights to be nonpositive.

23.1-8
Let T be a minimum spanning tree of a graph G, and let L be the sorted list of the edge weights of T. Show that for any other minimum spanning tree T' of G, the list L is also the sorted list of edge weights of T'.

23.1-9
Let T be a minimum spanning tree of a graph $G = (V, E)$, and let V' be a subset of V. Let T' be the subgraph of T induced by V', and let G' be the subgraph of G induced by V'. Show that if T' is connected, then T' is a minimum spanning tree of G'.

23.1-10
Given a graph G and a minimum spanning tree T, suppose that we decrease the weight of one of the edges in T. Show that T is still a minimum spanning tree for G. More formally, let T be a minimum spanning tree for G with edge weights given by weight function w. Choose one edge $(x, y) \in T$ and a positive number k, and define the weight function w' by

$$w'(u, v) = \begin{cases} w(u, v) & \text{if } (u, v) \neq (x, y), \\ w(x, y) - k & \text{if } (u, v) = (x, y). \end{cases}$$

Show that T is a minimum spanning tree for G with edge weights given by w'.

23.1-11 ★
Given a graph G and a minimum spanning tree T, suppose that we decrease the weight of one of the edges not in T. Give an algorithm for finding the minimum spanning tree in the modified graph.

23.2   The algorithms of Kruskal and Prim

The two minimum-spanning-tree algorithms described in this section elaborate on the generic method. They each use a specific rule to determine a safe edge in line 3 of GENERIC-MST. In Kruskal's algorithm, the set A is a forest whose vertices are all those of the given graph. The safe edge added to A is always a least-weight edge in the graph that connects two distinct components. In Prim's algorithm, the set A forms a single tree. The safe edge added to A is always a least-weight edge connecting the tree to a vertex not in the tree.

Kruskal's algorithm

Kruskal's algorithm finds a safe edge to add to the growing forest by finding, of all the edges that connect any two trees in the forest, an edge (u, v) of least weight. Let C_1 and C_2 denote the two trees that are connected by (u, v). Since (u, v) must be a light edge connecting C_1 to some other tree, Corollary 23.2 implies that (u, v) is a safe edge for C_1. Kruskal's algorithm qualifies as a greedy algorithm because at each step it adds to the forest an edge of least possible weight.

Our implementation of Kruskal's algorithm is like the algorithm to compute connected components from Section 21.1. It uses a disjoint-set data structure to maintain several disjoint sets of elements. Each set contains the vertices in one tree of the current forest. The operation FIND-SET(u) returns a representative element from the set that contains u. Thus, we can determine whether two vertices u and v belong to the same tree by testing whether FIND-SET(u) equals FIND-SET(v). To combine trees, Kruskal's algorithm calls the UNION procedure.

MST-KRUSKAL(G, w)

```
1   A = ∅
2   for each vertex v ∈ G.V
3       MAKE-SET(v)
4   sort the edges of G.E into nondecreasing order by weight w
5   for each edge (u, v) ∈ G.E, taken in nondecreasing order by weight
6       if FIND-SET(u) ≠ FIND-SET(v)
7           A = A ∪ {(u, v)}
8           UNION(u, v)
9   return A
```

Figure 23.4 shows how Kruskal's algorithm works. Lines 1–3 initialize the set A to the empty set and create $|V|$ trees, one containing each vertex. The **for** loop in lines 5–8 examines edges in order of weight, from lowest to highest. The loop

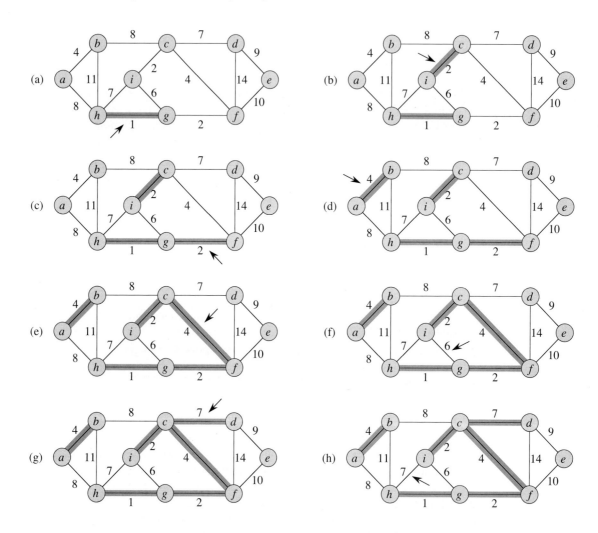

Figure 23.4 The execution of Kruskal's algorithm on the graph from Figure 23.1. Shaded edges belong to the forest A being grown. The algorithm considers each edge in sorted order by weight. An arrow points to the edge under consideration at each step of the algorithm. If the edge joins two distinct trees in the forest, it is added to the forest, thereby merging the two trees.

checks, for each edge (u, v), whether the endpoints u and v belong to the same tree. If they do, then the edge (u, v) cannot be added to the forest without creating a cycle, and the edge is discarded. Otherwise, the two vertices belong to different trees. In this case, line 7 adds the edge (u, v) to A, and line 8 merges the vertices in the two trees.

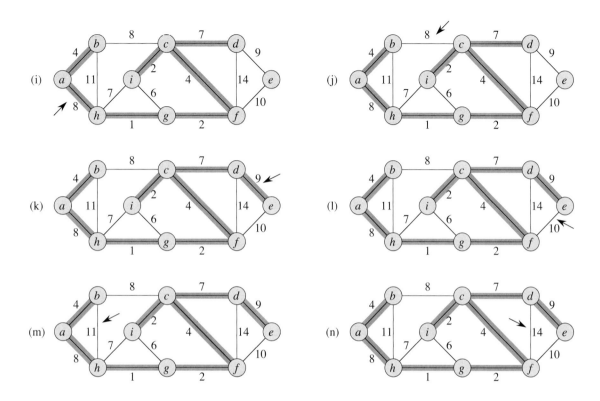

Figure 23.4, continued   Further steps in the execution of Kruskal's algorithm.

The running time of Kruskal's algorithm for a graph $G = (V, E)$ depends on how we implement the disjoint-set data structure. We assume that we use the disjoint-set-forest implementation of Section 21.3 with the union-by-rank and path-compression heuristics, since it is the asymptotically fastest implementation known. Initializing the set A in line 1 takes $O(1)$ time, and the time to sort the edges in line 4 is $O(E \lg E)$. (We will account for the cost of the $|V|$ MAKE-SET operations in the **for** loop of lines 2–3 in a moment.) The **for** loop of lines 5–8 performs $O(E)$ FIND-SET and UNION operations on the disjoint-set forest. Along with the $|V|$ MAKE-SET operations, these take a total of $O((V + E) \alpha(V))$ time, where α is the very slowly growing function defined in Section 21.4. Because we assume that G is connected, we have $|E| \geq |V| - 1$, and so the disjoint-set operations take $O(E\alpha(V))$ time. Moreover, since $\alpha(|V|) = O(\lg V) = O(\lg E)$, the total running time of Kruskal's algorithm is $O(E \lg E)$. Observing that $|E| < |V|^2$, we have $\lg |E| = O(\lg V)$, and so we can restate the running time of Kruskal's algorithm as $O(E \lg V)$.

Prim's algorithm

Like Kruskal's algorithm, Prim's algorithm is a special case of the generic minimum-spanning-tree method from Section 23.1. Prim's algorithm operates much like Dijkstra's algorithm for finding shortest paths in a graph, which we shall see in Section 24.3. Prim's algorithm has the property that the edges in the set A always form a single tree. As Figure 23.5 shows, the tree starts from an arbitrary root vertex r and grows until the tree spans all the vertices in V. Each step adds to the tree A a light edge that connects A to an isolated vertex—one on which no edge of A is incident. By Corollary 23.2, this rule adds only edges that are safe for A; therefore, when the algorithm terminates, the edges in A form a minimum spanning tree. This strategy qualifies as greedy since at each step it adds to the tree an edge that contributes the minimum amount possible to the tree's weight.

In order to implement Prim's algorithm efficiently, we need a fast way to select a new edge to add to the tree formed by the edges in A. In the pseudocode below, the connected graph G and the root r of the minimum spanning tree to be grown are inputs to the algorithm. During execution of the algorithm, all vertices that are *not* in the tree reside in a min-priority queue Q based on a *key* attribute. For each vertex v, the attribute $v.key$ is the minimum weight of any edge connecting v to a vertex in the tree; by convention, $v.key = \infty$ if there is no such edge. The attribute $v.\pi$ names the parent of v in the tree. The algorithm implicitly maintains the set A from GENERIC-MST as

$$A = \{(v, v.\pi) : v \in V - \{r\} - Q\} \ .$$

When the algorithm terminates, the min-priority queue Q is empty; the minimum spanning tree A for G is thus

$$A = \{(v, v.\pi) : v \in V - \{r\}\} \ .$$

MST-PRIM(G, w, r)

```
1   for each u ∈ G.V
2       u.key = ∞
3       u.π = NIL
4   r.key = 0
5   Q = G.V
6   while Q ≠ ∅
7       u = EXTRACT-MIN(Q)
8       for each v ∈ G.Adj[u]
9           if v ∈ Q and w(u, v) < v.key
10              v.π = u
11              v.key = w(u, v)
```

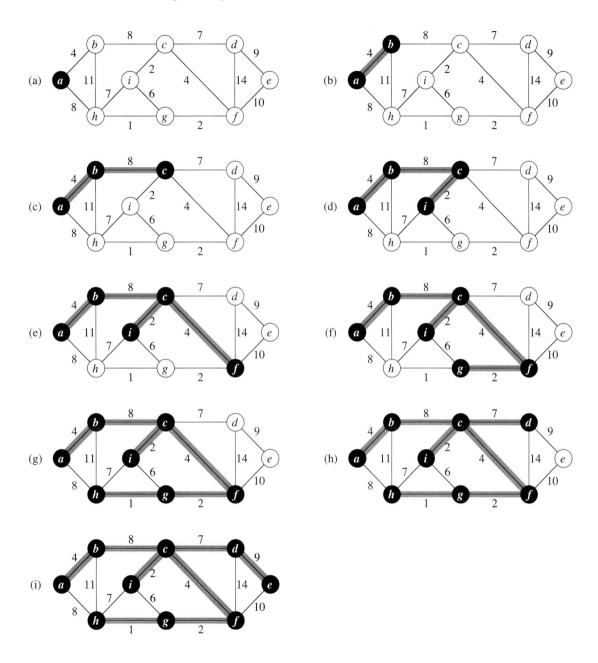

Figure 23.5   The execution of Prim's algorithm on the graph from Figure 23.1. The root vertex is a. Shaded edges are in the tree being grown, and black vertices are in the tree. At each step of the algorithm, the vertices in the tree determine a cut of the graph, and a light edge crossing the cut is added to the tree. In the second step, for example, the algorithm has a choice of adding either edge (b, c) or edge (a, h) to the tree since both are light edges crossing the cut.

Figure 23.5 shows how Prim's algorithm works. Lines 1–5 set the key of each vertex to ∞ (except for the root r, whose key is set to 0 so that it will be the first vertex processed), set the parent of each vertex to NIL, and initialize the min-priority queue Q to contain all the vertices. The algorithm maintains the following three-part loop invariant:

Prior to each iteration of the **while** loop of lines 6–11,

1. $A = \{(v, v.\pi) : v \in V - \{r\} - Q\}$.

2. The vertices already placed into the minimum spanning tree are those in $V - Q$.

3. For all vertices $v \in Q$, if $v.\pi \neq$ NIL, then $v.key < \infty$ and $v.key$ is the weight of a light edge $(v, v.\pi)$ connecting v to some vertex already placed into the minimum spanning tree.

Line 7 identifies a vertex $u \in Q$ incident on a light edge that crosses the cut $(V - Q, Q)$ (with the exception of the first iteration, in which $u = r$ due to line 4). Removing u from the set Q adds it to the set $V - Q$ of vertices in the tree, thus adding $(u, u.\pi)$ to A. The **for** loop of lines 8–11 updates the *key* and π attributes of every vertex v adjacent to u but not in the tree, thereby maintaining the third part of the loop invariant.

The running time of Prim's algorithm depends on how we implement the min-priority queue Q. If we implement Q as a binary min-heap (see Chapter 6), we can use the BUILD-MIN-HEAP procedure to perform lines 1–5 in $O(V)$ time. The body of the **while** loop executes $|V|$ times, and since each EXTRACT-MIN operation takes $O(\lg V)$ time, the total time for all calls to EXTRACT-MIN is $O(V \lg V)$. The **for** loop in lines 8–11 executes $O(E)$ times altogether, since the sum of the lengths of all adjacency lists is $2|E|$. Within the **for** loop, we can implement the test for membership in Q in line 9 in constant time by keeping a bit for each vertex that tells whether or not it is in Q, and updating the bit when the vertex is removed from Q. The assignment in line 11 involves an implicit DECREASE-KEY operation on the min-heap, which a binary min-heap supports in $O(\lg V)$ time. Thus, the total time for Prim's algorithm is $O(V \lg V + E \lg V) = O(E \lg V)$, which is asymptotically the same as for our implementation of Kruskal's algorithm.

We can improve the asymptotic running time of Prim's algorithm by using Fibonacci heaps. Chapter 19 shows that if a Fibonacci heap holds $|V|$ elements, an EXTRACT-MIN operation takes $O(\lg V)$ amortized time and a DECREASE-KEY operation (to implement line 11) takes $O(1)$ amortized time. Therefore, if we use a Fibonacci heap to implement the min-priority queue Q, the running time of Prim's algorithm improves to $O(E + V \lg V)$.

Exercises

23.2-1

Kruskal's algorithm can return different spanning trees for the same input graph G, depending on how it breaks ties when the edges are sorted into order. Show that for each minimum spanning tree T of G, there is a way to sort the edges of G in Kruskal's algorithm so that the algorithm returns T.

23.2-2

Suppose that we represent the graph $G = (V, E)$ as an adjacency matrix. Give a simple implementation of Prim's algorithm for this case that runs in $O(V^2)$ time.

23.2-3

For a sparse graph $G = (V, E)$, where $|E| = \Theta(V)$, is the implementation of Prim's algorithm with a Fibonacci heap asymptotically faster than the binary-heap implementation? What about for a dense graph, where $|E| = \Theta(V^2)$? How must the sizes $|E|$ and $|V|$ be related for the Fibonacci-heap implementation to be asymptotically faster than the binary-heap implementation?

23.2-4

Suppose that all edge weights in a graph are integers in the range from 1 to $|V|$. How fast can you make Kruskal's algorithm run? What if the edge weights are integers in the range from 1 to W for some constant W?

23.2-5

Suppose that all edge weights in a graph are integers in the range from 1 to $|V|$. How fast can you make Prim's algorithm run? What if the edge weights are integers in the range from 1 to W for some constant W?

23.2-6 ★

Suppose that the edge weights in a graph are uniformly distributed over the half-open interval $[0, 1)$. Which algorithm, Kruskal's or Prim's, can you make run faster?

23.2-7 ★

Suppose that a graph G has a minimum spanning tree already computed. How quickly can we update the minimum spanning tree if we add a new vertex and incident edges to G?

23.2-8

Professor Borden proposes a new divide-and-conquer algorithm for computing minimum spanning trees, which goes as follows. Given a graph $G = (V, E)$, partition the set V of vertices into two sets V_1 and V_2 such that $|V_1|$ and $|V_2|$ differ by at most 1. Let E_1 be the set of edges that are incident only on vertices in V_1, and let E_2 be the set of edges that are incident only on vertices in V_2. Recursively solve a minimum-spanning-tree problem on each of the two subgraphs $G_1 = (V_1, E_1)$ and $G_2 = (V_2, E_2)$. Finally, select the minimum-weight edge in E that crosses the cut (V_1, V_2), and use this edge to unite the resulting two minimum spanning trees into a single spanning tree.

Either argue that the algorithm correctly computes a minimum spanning tree of G, or provide an example for which the algorithm fails.

Problems

23-1   *Second-best minimum spanning tree*
Let $G = (V, E)$ be an undirected, connected graph whose weight function is $w : E \rightarrow \mathbb{R}$, and suppose that $|E| \geq |V|$ and all edge weights are distinct.

We define a second-best minimum spanning tree as follows. Let $\mathcal{T}$ be the set of all spanning trees of G, and let T' be a minimum spanning tree of G. Then a *second-best minimum spanning tree* is a spanning tree T such that $w(T) = \min_{T'' \in \mathcal{T} - \{T'\}} \{w(T'')\}$.

a. Show that the minimum spanning tree is unique, but that the second-best minimum spanning tree need not be unique.

b. Let T be the minimum spanning tree of G. Prove that G contains edges $(u, v) \in T$ and $(x, y) \notin T$ such that $T - \{(u, v)\} \cup \{(x, y)\}$ is a second-best minimum spanning tree of G.

c. Let T be a spanning tree of G and, for any two vertices $u, v \in V$, let $max[u, v]$ denote an edge of maximum weight on the unique simple path between u and v in T. Describe an $O(V^2)$-time algorithm that, given T, computes $max[u, v]$ for all $u, v \in V$.

d. Give an efficient algorithm to compute the second-best minimum spanning tree of G.

23-2   *Minimum spanning tree in sparse graphs*
For a very sparse connected graph $G = (V, E)$, we can further improve upon the $O(E + V \lg V)$ running time of Prim's algorithm with Fibonacci heaps by preprocessing G to decrease the number of vertices before running Prim's algorithm. In particular, we choose, for each vertex u, the minimum-weight edge (u, v) incident on u, and we put (u, v) into the minimum spanning tree under construction. We

then contract all chosen edges (see Section B.4). Rather than contracting these edges one at a time, we first identify sets of vertices that are united into the same new vertex. Then we create the graph that would have resulted from contracting these edges one at a time, but we do so by "renaming" edges according to the sets into which their endpoints were placed. Several edges from the original graph may be renamed the same as each other. In such a case, only one edge results, and its weight is the minimum of the weights of the corresponding original edges.

Initially, we set the minimum spanning tree T being constructed to be empty, and for each edge $(u, v) \in E$, we initialize the attributes $(u, v).orig = (u, v)$ and $(u, v).c = w(u, v)$. We use the *orig* attribute to reference the edge from the initial graph that is associated with an edge in the contracted graph. The c attribute holds the weight of an edge, and as edges are contracted, we update it according to the above scheme for choosing edge weights. The procedure MST-REDUCE takes inputs G and T, and it returns a contracted graph G' with updated attributes $orig'$ and c'. The procedure also accumulates edges of G into the minimum spanning tree T.

MST-REDUCE(G, T)

```
 1  for each v ∈ G.V
 2      v.mark = FALSE
 3      MAKE-SET(v)
 4  for each u ∈ G.V
 5      if u.mark == FALSE
 6          choose v ∈ G.Adj[u] such that (u, v).c is minimized
 7          UNION(u, v)
 8          T = T ∪ {(u, v).orig}
 9          u.mark = v.mark = TRUE
10  G'.V = {FIND-SET(v) : v ∈ G.V}
11  G'.E = ∅
12  for each (x, y) ∈ G.E
13      u = FIND-SET(x)
14      v = FIND-SET(y)
15      if u ≠ v
16          if (u, v) ∉ G'.E
17              G'.E = G'.E ∪ {(u, v)}
18              (u, v).orig' = (x, y).orig
19              (u, v).c' = (x, y).c
20          else if (x, y).c < (u, v).c'
21              (u, v).orig' = (x, y).orig
22              (u, v).c' = (x, y).c
23  construct adjacency lists G'.Adj for G'
24  return G' and T
```

a. Let T be the set of edges returned by MST-REDUCE, and let A be the minimum spanning tree of the graph G' formed by the call MST-PRIM(G', c', r), where c' is the weight attribute on the edges of $G'.E$ and r is any vertex in $G'.V$. Prove that $T \cup \{(x, y).orig' : (x, y) \in A\}$ is a minimum spanning tree of G.

b. Argue that $|G'.V| \le |V|/2$.

c. Show how to implement MST-REDUCE so that it runs in $O(E)$ time. (*Hint:* Use simple data structures.)

d. Suppose that we run k phases of MST-REDUCE, using the output G' produced by one phase as the input G to the next phase and accumulating edges in T. Argue that the overall running time of the k phases is $O(kE)$.

e. Suppose that after running k phases of MST-REDUCE, as in part (d), we run Prim's algorithm by calling MST-PRIM(G', c', r), where G', with weight attribute c', is returned by the last phase and r is any vertex in $G'.V$. Show how to pick k so that the overall running time is $O(E \lg \lg V)$. Argue that your choice of k minimizes the overall asymptotic running time.

f. For what values of $|E|$ (in terms of $|V|$) does Prim's algorithm with preprocessing asymptotically beat Prim's algorithm without preprocessing?

23-3   *Bottleneck spanning tree*

A ***bottleneck spanning tree*** T of an undirected graph G is a spanning tree of G whose largest edge weight is minimum over all spanning trees of G. We say that the value of the bottleneck spanning tree is the weight of the maximum-weight edge in T.

a. Argue that a minimum spanning tree is a bottleneck spanning tree.

Part (a) shows that finding a bottleneck spanning tree is no harder than finding a minimum spanning tree. In the remaining parts, we will show how to find a bottleneck spanning tree in linear time.

b. Give a linear-time algorithm that given a graph G and an integer b, determines whether the value of the bottleneck spanning tree is at most b.

c. Use your algorithm for part (b) as a subroutine in a linear-time algorithm for the bottleneck-spanning-tree problem. (*Hint:* You may want to use a subroutine that contracts sets of edges, as in the MST-REDUCE procedure described in Problem 23-2.)

23-4   *Alternative minimum-spanning-tree algorithms*

In this problem, we give pseudocode for three different algorithms. Each one takes a connected graph and a weight function as input and returns a set of edges T. For each algorithm, either prove that T is a minimum spanning tree or prove that T is not necessarily a minimum spanning tree. Also describe the most efficient implementation of each algorithm, whether or not it computes a minimum spanning tree.

a. MAYBE-MST-A(G, w)

```
1   sort the edges into nonincreasing order of edge weights w
2   T = E
3   for each edge e, taken in nonincreasing order by weight
4       if T − {e} is a connected graph
5           T = T − {e}
6   return T
```

b. MAYBE-MST-B(G, w)

```
1   T = ∅
2   for each edge e, taken in arbitrary order
3       if T ∪ {e} has no cycles
4           T = T ∪ {e}
5   return T
```

c. MAYBE-MST-C(G, w)

```
1   T = ∅
2   for each edge e, taken in arbitrary order
3       T = T ∪ {e}
4       if T has a cycle c
5           let e′ be a maximum-weight edge on c
6           T = T − {e′}
7   return T
```

Chapter notes

Tarjan [330] surveys the minimum-spanning-tree problem and provides excellent advanced material. Graham and Hell [151] compiled a history of the minimum-spanning-tree problem.

Tarjan attributes the first minimum-spanning-tree algorithm to a 1926 paper by O. Borůvka. Borůvka's algorithm consists of running $O(\lg V)$ iterations of the procedure MST-REDUCE described in Problem 23-2. Kruskal's algorithm was reported by Kruskal [222] in 1956. The algorithm commonly known as Prim's algorithm was indeed invented by Prim [285], but it was also invented earlier by V. Jarník in 1930.

The reason underlying why greedy algorithms are effective at finding minimum spanning trees is that the set of forests of a graph forms a graphic matroid. (See Section 16.4.)

When $|E| = \Omega(V \lg V)$, Prim's algorithm, implemented with Fibonacci heaps, runs in $O(E)$ time. For sparser graphs, using a combination of the ideas from Prim's algorithm, Kruskal's algorithm, and Borůvka's algorithm, together with advanced data structures, Fredman and Tarjan [114] give an algorithm that runs in $O(E \lg^* V)$ time. Gabow, Galil, Spencer, and Tarjan [120] improved this algorithm to run in $O(E \lg \lg^* V)$ time. Chazelle [60] gives an algorithm that runs in $O(E \, \hat{\alpha}(E, V))$ time, where $\hat{\alpha}(E, V)$ is the functional inverse of Ackermann's function. (See the chapter notes for Chapter 21 for a brief discussion of Ackermann's function and its inverse.) Unlike previous minimum-spanning-tree algorithms, Chazelle's algorithm does not follow the greedy method.

A related problem is ***spanning-tree verification***, in which we are given a graph $G = (V, E)$ and a tree $T \subseteq E$, and we wish to determine whether T is a minimum spanning tree of G. King [203] gives a linear-time algorithm to verify a spanning tree, building on earlier work of Komlós [215] and Dixon, Rauch, and Tarjan [90].

The above algorithms are all deterministic and fall into the comparison-based model described in Chapter 8. Karger, Klein, and Tarjan [195] give a randomized minimum-spanning-tree algorithm that runs in $O(V + E)$ expected time. This algorithm uses recursion in a manner similar to the linear-time selection algorithm in Section 9.3: a recursive call on an auxiliary problem identifies a subset of the edges E' that cannot be in any minimum spanning tree. Another recursive call on $E - E'$ then finds the minimum spanning tree. The algorithm also uses ideas from Borůvka's algorithm and King's algorithm for spanning-tree verification.

Fredman and Willard [116] showed how to find a minimum spanning tree in $O(V + E)$ time using a deterministic algorithm that is not comparison based. Their algorithm assumes that the data are b-bit integers and that the computer memory consists of addressable b-bit words.

24 Single-Source Shortest Paths

Professor Patrick wishes to find the shortest possible route from Phoenix to Indianapolis. Given a road map of the United States on which the distance between each pair of adjacent intersections is marked, how can she determine this shortest route?

One possible way would be to enumerate all the routes from Phoenix to Indianapolis, add up the distances on each route, and select the shortest. It is easy to see, however, that even disallowing routes that contain cycles, Professor Patrick would have to examine an enormous number of possibilities, most of which are simply not worth considering. For example, a route from Phoenix to Indianapolis that passes through Seattle is obviously a poor choice, because Seattle is several hundred miles out of the way.

In this chapter and in Chapter 25, we show how to solve such problems efficiently. In a **shortest-paths problem**, we are given a weighted, directed graph $G = (V, E)$, with weight function $w : E \to \mathbb{R}$ mapping edges to real-valued weights. The **weight** $w(p)$ of path $p = \langle v_0, v_1, \ldots, v_k \rangle$ is the sum of the weights of its constituent edges:

$$w(p) = \sum_{i=1}^{k} w(v_{i-1}, v_i) .$$

We define the **shortest-path weight** $\delta(u, v)$ from u to v by

$$\delta(u, v) = \begin{cases} \min\{w(p) : u \overset{p}{\rightsquigarrow} v\} & \text{if there is a path from } u \text{ to } v , \\ \infty & \text{otherwise .} \end{cases}$$

A **shortest path** from vertex u to vertex v is then defined as any path p with weight $w(p) = \delta(u, v)$.

In the Phoenix-to-Indianapolis example, we can model the road map as a graph: vertices represent intersections, edges represent road segments between intersections, and edge weights represent road distances. Our goal is to find a shortest path from a given intersection in Phoenix to a given intersection in Indianapolis.

Edge weights can represent metrics other than distances, such as time, cost, penalties, loss, or any other quantity that accumulates linearly along a path and that we would want to minimize.

The breadth-first-search algorithm from Section 22.2 is a shortest-paths algorithm that works on unweighted graphs, that is, graphs in which each edge has unit weight. Because many of the concepts from breadth-first search arise in the study of shortest paths in weighted graphs, you might want to review Section 22.2 before proceeding.

Variants

In this chapter, we shall focus on the ***single-source shortest-paths problem***: given a graph $G = (V, E)$, we want to find a shortest path from a given ***source*** vertex $s \in V$ to each vertex $v \in V$. The algorithm for the single-source problem can solve many other problems, including the following variants.

Single-destination shortest-paths problem: Find a shortest path to a given ***destination*** vertex t from each vertex v. By reversing the direction of each edge in the graph, we can reduce this problem to a single-source problem.

Single-pair shortest-path problem: Find a shortest path from u to v for given vertices u and v. If we solve the single-source problem with source vertex u, we solve this problem also. Moreover, all known algorithms for this problem have the same worst-case asymptotic running time as the best single-source algorithms.

All-pairs shortest-paths problem: Find a shortest path from u to v for every pair of vertices u and v. Although we can solve this problem by running a single-source algorithm once from each vertex, we usually can solve it faster. Additionally, its structure is interesting in its own right. Chapter 25 addresses the all-pairs problem in detail.

Optimal substructure of a shortest path

Shortest-paths algorithms typically rely on the property that a shortest path between two vertices contains other shortest paths within it. (The Edmonds-Karp maximum-flow algorithm in Chapter 26 also relies on this property.) Recall that optimal substructure is one of the key indicators that dynamic programming (Chapter 15) and the greedy method (Chapter 16) might apply. Dijkstra's algorithm, which we shall see in Section 24.3, is a greedy algorithm, and the Floyd-Warshall algorithm, which finds shortest paths between all pairs of vertices (see Section 25.2), is a dynamic-programming algorithm. The following lemma states the optimal-substructure property of shortest paths more precisely.

Lemma 24.1 (Subpaths of shortest paths are shortest paths)
Given a weighted, directed graph $G = (V, E)$ with weight function $w : E \to \mathbb{R}$,
let $p = \langle v_0, v_1, \ldots, v_k \rangle$ be a shortest path from vertex v_0 to vertex v_k and, for any
i and j such that $0 \le i \le j \le k$, let $p_{ij} = \langle v_i, v_{i+1}, \ldots, v_j \rangle$ be the subpath of p
from vertex v_i to vertex v_j. Then, p_{ij} is a shortest path from v_i to v_j.

Proof If we decompose path p into $v_0 \overset{p_{0i}}{\rightsquigarrow} v_i \overset{p_{ij}}{\rightsquigarrow} v_j \overset{p_{jk}}{\rightsquigarrow} v_k$, then we have that
$w(p) = w(p_{0i}) + w(p_{ij}) + w(p_{jk})$. Now, assume that there is a path p'_{ij} from v_i
to v_j with weight $w(p'_{ij}) < w(p_{ij})$. Then, $v_0 \overset{p_{0i}}{\rightsquigarrow} v_i \overset{p'_{ij}}{\rightsquigarrow} v_j \overset{p_{jk}}{\rightsquigarrow} v_k$ is a path from v_0
to v_k whose weight $w(p_{0i}) + w(p'_{ij}) + w(p_{jk})$ is less than $w(p)$, which contradicts
the assumption that p is a shortest path from v_0 to v_k.   ∎

Negative-weight edges

Some instances of the single-source shortest-paths problem may include edges
whose weights are negative. If the graph $G = (V, E)$ contains no negative-
weight cycles reachable from the source s, then for all $v \in V$, the shortest-path
weight $\delta(s, v)$ remains well defined, even if it has a negative value. If the graph
contains a negative-weight cycle reachable from s, however, shortest-path weights
are not well defined. No path from s to a vertex on the cycle can be a shortest path — we can always find a path with lower weight by following the proposed
"shortest" path and then traversing the negative-weight cycle. If there is a negative-
weight cycle on some path from s to v, we define $\delta(s, v) = -\infty$.

Figure 24.1 illustrates the effect of negative weights and negative-weight cycles on shortest-path weights. Because there is only one path from s to a (the
path $\langle s, a \rangle$), we have $\delta(s, a) = w(s, a) = 3$. Similarly, there is only one path
from s to b, and so $\delta(s, b) = w(s, a) + w(a, b) = 3 + (-4) = -1$. There are
infinitely many paths from s to c: $\langle s, c \rangle$, $\langle s, c, d, c \rangle$, $\langle s, c, d, c, d, c \rangle$, and so on.
Because the cycle $\langle c, d, c \rangle$ has weight $6 + (-3) = 3 > 0$, the shortest path from s
to c is $\langle s, c \rangle$, with weight $\delta(s, c) = w(s, c) = 5$. Similarly, the shortest path from s
to d is $\langle s, c, d \rangle$, with weight $\delta(s, d) = w(s, c) + w(c, d) = 11$. Analogously, there
are infinitely many paths from s to e: $\langle s, e \rangle$, $\langle s, e, f, e \rangle$, $\langle s, e, f, e, f, e \rangle$, and so
on. Because the cycle $\langle e, f, e \rangle$ has weight $3 + (-6) = -3 < 0$, however, there
is no shortest path from s to e. By traversing the negative-weight cycle $\langle e, f, e \rangle$
arbitrarily many times, we can find paths from s to e with arbitrarily large negative
weights, and so $\delta(s, e) = -\infty$. Similarly, $\delta(s, f) = -\infty$. Because g is reachable
from f, we can also find paths with arbitrarily large negative weights from s to g,
and so $\delta(s, g) = -\infty$. Vertices h, i, and j also form a negative-weight cycle. They
are not reachable from s, however, and so $\delta(s, h) = \delta(s, i) = \delta(s, j) = \infty$.

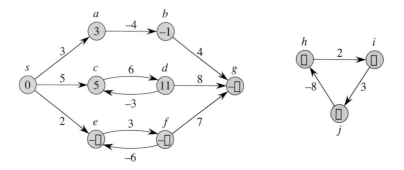

Figure 24.1   Negative edge weights in a directed graph. The shortest-path weight from source s appears within each vertex. Because vertices e and f form a negative-weight cycle reachable from s, they have shortest-path weights of $-\infty$. Because vertex g is reachable from a vertex whose shortest-path weight is $-\infty$, it, too, has a shortest-path weight of $-\infty$. Vertices such as h, i, and j are not reachable from s, and so their shortest-path weights are ∞, even though they lie on a negative-weight cycle.

Some shortest-paths algorithms, such as Dijkstra's algorithm, assume that all edge weights in the input graph are nonnegative, as in the road-map example. Others, such as the Bellman-Ford algorithm, allow negative-weight edges in the input graph and produce a correct answer as long as no negative-weight cycles are reachable from the source. Typically, if there is such a negative-weight cycle, the algorithm can detect and report its existence.

Cycles

Can a shortest path contain a cycle? As we have just seen, it cannot contain a negative-weight cycle. Nor can it contain a positive-weight cycle, since removing the cycle from the path produces a path with the same source and destination vertices and a lower path weight. That is, if $p = \langle v_0, v_1, \ldots, v_k \rangle$ is a path and $c = \langle v_i, v_{i+1}, \ldots, v_j \rangle$ is a positive-weight cycle on this path (so that $v_i = v_j$ and $w(c) > 0$), then the path $p' = \langle v_0, v_1, \ldots, v_i, v_{j+1}, v_{j+2}, \ldots, v_k \rangle$ has weight $w(p') = w(p) - w(c) < w(p)$, and so p cannot be a shortest path from v_0 to v_k.

That leaves only 0-weight cycles. We can remove a 0-weight cycle from any path to produce another path whose weight is the same. Thus, if there is a shortest path from a source vertex s to a destination vertex v that contains a 0-weight cycle, then there is another shortest path from s to v without this cycle. As long as a shortest path has 0-weight cycles, we can repeatedly remove these cycles from the path until we have a shortest path that is cycle-free. Therefore, without loss of generality we can assume that when we are finding shortest paths, they have no cycles, i.e., they are simple paths. Since any acyclic path in a graph $G = (V, E)$

contains at most $|V|$ distinct vertices, it also contains at most $|V| - 1$ edges. Thus, we can restrict our attention to shortest paths of at most $|V| - 1$ edges.

Representing shortest paths

We often wish to compute not only shortest-path weights, but the vertices on shortest paths as well. We represent shortest paths similarly to how we represented breadth-first trees in Section 22.2. Given a graph $G = (V, E)$, we maintain for each vertex $v \in V$ a **predecessor** $v.\pi$ that is either another vertex or NIL. The shortest-paths algorithms in this chapter set the π attributes so that the chain of predecessors originating at a vertex v runs backwards along a shortest path from s to v. Thus, given a vertex v for which $v.\pi \neq$ NIL, the procedure PRINT-PATH(G, s, v) from Section 22.2 will print a shortest path from s to v.

In the midst of executing a shortest-paths algorithm, however, the π values might not indicate shortest paths. As in breadth-first search, we shall be interested in the **predecessor subgraph** $G_\pi = (V_\pi, E_\pi)$ induced by the π values. Here again, we define the vertex set V_π to be the set of vertices of G with non-NIL predecessors, plus the source s:

$$V_\pi = \{v \in V : v.\pi \neq \text{NIL}\} \cup \{s\} \ .$$

The directed edge set E_π is the set of edges induced by the π values for vertices in V_π:

$$E_\pi = \{(v.\pi, v) \in E : v \in V_\pi - \{s\}\} \ .$$

We shall prove that the π values produced by the algorithms in this chapter have the property that at termination G_π is a "shortest-paths tree"—informally, a rooted tree containing a shortest path from the source s to every vertex that is reachable from s. A shortest-paths tree is like the breadth-first tree from Section 22.2, but it contains shortest paths from the source defined in terms of edge weights instead of numbers of edges. To be precise, let $G = (V, E)$ be a weighted, directed graph with weight function $w : E \rightarrow \mathbb{R}$, and assume that G contains no negative-weight cycles reachable from the source vertex $s \in V$, so that shortest paths are well defined. A **shortest-paths tree** rooted at s is a directed subgraph $G' = (V', E')$, where $V' \subseteq V$ and $E' \subseteq E$, such that

1. V' is the set of vertices reachable from s in G,

2. G' forms a rooted tree with root s, and

3. for all $v \in V'$, the unique simple path from s to v in G' is a shortest path from s to v in G.

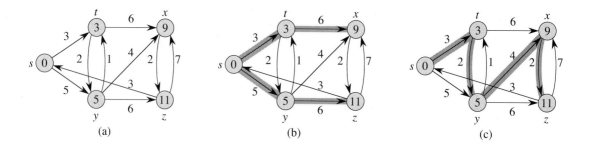

Figure 24.2   **(a)** A weighted, directed graph with shortest-path weights from source s. **(b)** The shaded edges form a shortest-paths tree rooted at the source s. **(c)** Another shortest-paths tree with the same root.

Shortest paths are not necessarily unique, and neither are shortest-paths trees. For example, Figure 24.2 shows a weighted, directed graph and two shortest-paths trees with the same root.

Relaxation

The algorithms in this chapter use the technique of ***relaxation***. For each vertex $v \in V$, we maintain an attribute $v.d$, which is an upper bound on the weight of a shortest path from source s to v. We call $v.d$ a ***shortest-path estimate***. We initialize the shortest-path estimates and predecessors by the following $\Theta(V)$-time procedure:

INITIALIZE-SINGLE-SOURCE(G, s)

1   **for** each vertex $v \in G.V$
2        $v.d = \infty$
3        $v.\pi = $ NIL
4   $s.d = 0$

After initialization, we have $v.\pi = $ NIL for all $v \in V$, $s.d = 0$, and $v.d = \infty$ for $v \in V - \{s\}$.

The process of ***relaxing*** an edge (u, v) consists of testing whether we can improve the shortest path to v found so far by going through u and, if so, updating $v.d$ and $v.\pi$. A relaxation step[1] may decrease the value of the shortest-path

---

[1] It may seem strange that the term "relaxation" is used for an operation that tightens an upper bound. The use of the term is historical. The outcome of a relaxation step can be viewed as a relaxation of the constraint $v.d \leq u.d + w(u, v)$, which, by the triangle inequality (Lemma 24.10), must be satisfied if $u.d = \delta(s, u)$ and $v.d = \delta(s, v)$. That is, if $v.d \leq u.d + w(u, v)$, there is no "pressure" to satisfy this constraint, so the constraint is "relaxed."

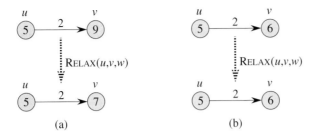

Figure 24.3 Relaxing an edge (u, v) with weight $w(u, v) = 2$. The shortest-path estimate of each vertex appears within the vertex. **(a)** Because $v.d > u.d + w(u, v)$ prior to relaxation, the value of $v.d$ decreases. **(b)** Here, $v.d \leq u.d + w(u, v)$ before relaxing the edge, and so the relaxation step leaves $v.d$ unchanged.

estimate $v.d$ and update v's predecessor attribute $v.\pi$. The following code performs a relaxation step on edge (u, v) in $O(1)$ time:

RELAX(u, v, w)

1   **if** $v.d > u.d + w(u, v)$
2       $v.d = u.d + w(u, v)$
3       $v.\pi = u$

Figure 24.3 shows two examples of relaxing an edge, one in which a shortest-path estimate decreases and one in which no estimate changes.

Each algorithm in this chapter calls INITIALIZE-SINGLE-SOURCE and then repeatedly relaxes edges. Moreover, relaxation is the only means by which shortest-path estimates and predecessors change. The algorithms in this chapter differ in how many times they relax each edge and the order in which they relax edges. Dijkstra's algorithm and the shortest-paths algorithm for directed acyclic graphs relax each edge exactly once. The Bellman-Ford algorithm relaxes each edge $|V| - 1$ times.

Properties of shortest paths and relaxation

To prove the algorithms in this chapter correct, we shall appeal to several properties of shortest paths and relaxation. We state these properties here, and Section 24.5 proves them formally. For your reference, each property stated here includes the appropriate lemma or corollary number from Section 24.5. The latter five of these properties, which refer to shortest-path estimates or the predecessor subgraph, implicitly assume that the graph is initialized with a call to INITIALIZE-SINGLE-SOURCE(G, s) and that the only way that shortest-path estimates and the predecessor subgraph change are by some sequence of relaxation steps.

Triangle inequality (Lemma 24.10)

   For any edge $(u, v) \in E$, we have $\delta(s, v) \leq \delta(s, u) + w(u, v)$.

Upper-bound property (Lemma 24.11)

   We always have $v.d \geq \delta(s, v)$ for all vertices $v \in V$, and once $v.d$ achieves the value $\delta(s, v)$, it never changes.

No-path property (Corollary 24.12)

   If there is no path from s to v, then we always have $v.d = \delta(s, v) = \infty$.

Convergence property (Lemma 24.14)

   If $s \leadsto u \to v$ is a shortest path in G for some $u, v \in V$, and if $u.d = \delta(s, u)$ at any time prior to relaxing edge (u, v), then $v.d = \delta(s, v)$ at all times afterward.

Path-relaxation property (Lemma 24.15)

   If $p = \langle v_0, v_1, \ldots, v_k \rangle$ is a shortest path from $s = v_0$ to v_k, and we relax the edges of p in the order $(v_0, v_1), (v_1, v_2), \ldots, (v_{k-1}, v_k)$, then $v_k.d = \delta(s, v_k)$. This property holds regardless of any other relaxation steps that occur, even if they are intermixed with relaxations of the edges of p.

Predecessor-subgraph property (Lemma 24.17)

   Once $v.d = \delta(s, v)$ for all $v \in V$, the predecessor subgraph is a shortest-paths tree rooted at s.

Chapter outline

Section 24.1 presents the Bellman-Ford algorithm, which solves the single-source shortest-paths problem in the general case in which edges can have negative weight. The Bellman-Ford algorithm is remarkably simple, and it has the further benefit of detecting whether a negative-weight cycle is reachable from the source. Section 24.2 gives a linear-time algorithm for computing shortest paths from a single source in a directed acyclic graph. Section 24.3 covers Dijkstra's algorithm, which has a lower running time than the Bellman-Ford algorithm but requires the edge weights to be nonnegative. Section 24.4 shows how we can use the Bellman-Ford algorithm to solve a special case of linear programming. Finally, Section 24.5 proves the properties of shortest paths and relaxation stated above.

   We require some conventions for doing arithmetic with infinities. We shall assume that for any real number $a \neq -\infty$, we have $a + \infty = \infty + a = \infty$. Also, to make our proofs hold in the presence of negative-weight cycles, we shall assume that for any real number $a \neq \infty$, we have $a + (-\infty) = (-\infty) + a = -\infty$.

   All algorithms in this chapter assume that the directed graph G is stored in the adjacency-list representation. Additionally, stored with each edge is its weight, so that as we traverse each adjacency list, we can determine the edge weights in $O(1)$ time per edge.

24.1 The Bellman-Ford algorithm

The ***Bellman-Ford algorithm*** solves the single-source shortest-paths problem in the general case in which edge weights may be negative. Given a weighted, directed graph $G = (V, E)$ with source s and weight function $w : E \rightarrow \mathbb{R}$, the Bellman-Ford algorithm returns a boolean value indicating whether or not there is a negative-weight cycle that is reachable from the source. If there is such a cycle, the algorithm indicates that no solution exists. If there is no such cycle, the algorithm produces the shortest paths and their weights.

The algorithm relaxes edges, progressively decreasing an estimate $v.d$ on the weight of a shortest path from the source s to each vertex $v \in V$ until it achieves the actual shortest-path weight $\delta(s, v)$. The algorithm returns TRUE if and only if the graph contains no negative-weight cycles that are reachable from the source.

BELLMAN-FORD(G, w, s)

```
1   INITIALIZE-SINGLE-SOURCE(G, s)
2   for i = 1 to |G.V| − 1
3       for each edge (u, v) ∈ G.E
4           RELAX(u, v, w)
5   for each edge (u, v) ∈ G.E
6       if v.d > u.d + w(u, v)
7           return FALSE
8   return TRUE
```

Figure 24.4 shows the execution of the Bellman-Ford algorithm on a graph with 5 vertices. After initializing the d and π values of all vertices in line 1, the algorithm makes $|V| - 1$ passes over the edges of the graph. Each pass is one iteration of the **for** loop of lines 2–4 and consists of relaxing each edge of the graph once. Figures 24.4(b)–(e) show the state of the algorithm after each of the four passes over the edges. After making $|V| - 1$ passes, lines 5–8 check for a negative-weight cycle and return the appropriate boolean value. (We'll see a little later why this check works.)

The Bellman-Ford algorithm runs in time $O(VE)$, since the initialization in line 1 takes $\Theta(V)$ time, each of the $|V| - 1$ passes over the edges in lines 2–4 takes $\Theta(E)$ time, and the **for** loop of lines 5–7 takes $O(E)$ time.

To prove the correctness of the Bellman-Ford algorithm, we start by showing that if there are no negative-weight cycles, the algorithm computes correct shortest-path weights for all vertices reachable from the source.

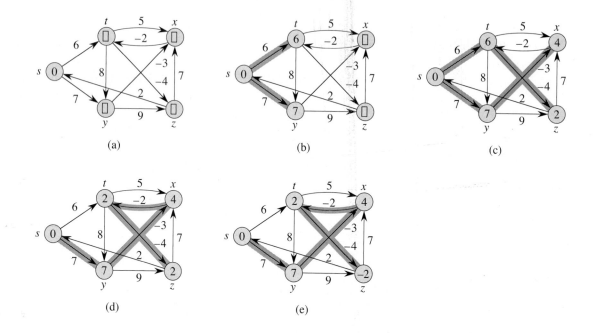

Figure 24.4 The execution of the Bellman-Ford algorithm. The source is vertex s. The d values appear within the vertices, and shaded edges indicate predecessor values: if edge (u, v) is shaded, then $v.\pi = u$. In this particular example, each pass relaxes the edges in the order $(t, x), (t, y), (t, z), (x, t), (y, x), (y, z), (z, x), (z, s), (s, t), (s, y)$. **(a)** The situation just before the first pass over the edges. **(b)–(e)** The situation after each successive pass over the edges. The d and π values in part (e) are the final values. The Bellman-Ford algorithm returns TRUE in this example.

Lemma 24.2

Let $G = (V, E)$ be a weighted, directed graph with source s and weight function $w : E \rightarrow \mathbb{R}$, and assume that G contains no negative-weight cycles that are reachable from s. Then, after the $|V| - 1$ iterations of the **for** loop of lines 2–4 of BELLMAN-FORD, we have $v.d = \delta(s, v)$ for all vertices v that are reachable from s.

Proof   We prove the lemma by appealing to the path-relaxation property. Consider any vertex v that is reachable from s, and let $p = \langle v_0, v_1, \ldots, v_k \rangle$, where $v_0 = s$ and $v_k = v$, be any shortest path from s to v. Because shortest paths are simple, p has at most $|V| - 1$ edges, and so $k \leq |V| - 1$. Each of the $|V| - 1$ iterations of the **for** loop of lines 2–4 relaxes all $|E|$ edges. Among the edges relaxed in the ith iteration, for $i = 1, 2, \ldots, k$, is (v_{i-1}, v_i). By the path-relaxation property, therefore, $v.d = v_k.d = \delta(s, v_k) = \delta(s, v)$.   ∎

Corollary 24.3

Let $G = (V, E)$ be a weighted, directed graph with source vertex s and weight function $w : E \rightarrow \mathbb{R}$. Then, for each vertex $v \in V$, there is a path from s to v if and only if BELLMAN-FORD terminates with $v.d < \infty$ when it is run on G.

Proof   The proof is left as Exercise 24.1-2. Note that this corollary allows G to have negative-weight cycles that are reachable from s, but that Lemma 24.2 does not.   ∎

Theorem 24.4 (Correctness of the Bellman-Ford algorithm)

Let BELLMAN-FORD be run on a weighted, directed graph $G = (V, E)$ with source s and weight function $w : E \rightarrow \mathbb{R}$. If G contains no negative-weight cycles that are reachable from s, then the algorithm returns TRUE, we have $v.d = \delta(s, v)$ for all vertices $v \in V$, and the predecessor subgraph G_π is a shortest-paths tree rooted at s. If G does contain a negative-weight cycle reachable from s, then the algorithm returns FALSE.

Proof   Suppose that graph G contains no negative-weight cycles that are reachable from the source s. We first prove the claim that at termination, $v.d = \delta(s, v)$ for all vertices $v \in V$. If vertex v is reachable from s, then Lemma 24.2 proves this claim. If v is not reachable from s, then the claim follows from the no-path property. Thus, the claim is proven. The predecessor-subgraph property, along with the claim, implies that G_π is a shortest-paths tree. Now we use the claim to show that BELLMAN-FORD returns TRUE. At termination, we have for all edges $(u, v) \in E$,

$$
\begin{aligned}
v.d &= \delta(s, v) \\
&\leq \delta(s, u) + w(u, v) \quad \text{(by the triangle inequality)} \\
&= u.d + w(u, v) \,,
\end{aligned}
$$

and so none of the tests in line 6 causes BELLMAN-FORD to return FALSE. Therefore, it returns TRUE.

Now, suppose that graph G contains a negative-weight cycle that is reachable from the source s; let this cycle be $c = \langle v_0, v_1, \ldots, v_k \rangle$, where $v_0 = v_k$. Then,

$$
\sum_{i=1}^{k} w(v_{i-1}, v_i) < 0 \,. \tag{24.1}
$$

Assume for the purpose of contradiction that the Bellman-Ford algorithm returns TRUE. Thus, $v_i.d \leq v_{i-1}.d + w(v_{i-1}, v_i)$ for $i = 1, 2, \ldots, k$. Summing the inequalities around cycle c gives us

$$\sum_{i=1}^{k} v_i.d \;\leq\; \sum_{i=1}^{k}(v_{i-1}.d + w(v_{i-1}, v_i))$$

$$= \sum_{i=1}^{k} v_{i-1}.d + \sum_{i=1}^{k} w(v_{i-1}, v_i) \,.$$

Since $v_0 = v_k$, each vertex in c appears exactly once in each of the summations $\sum_{i=1}^{k} v_i.d$ and $\sum_{i=1}^{k} v_{i-1}.d$, and so

$$\sum_{i=1}^{k} v_i.d = \sum_{i=1}^{k} v_{i-1}.d \,.$$

Moreover, by Corollary 24.3, $v_i.d$ is finite for $i = 1, 2, \ldots, k$. Thus,

$$0 \leq \sum_{i=1}^{k} w(v_{i-1}, v_i) \,,$$

which contradicts inequality (24.1). We conclude that the Bellman-Ford algorithm returns TRUE if graph G contains no negative-weight cycles reachable from the source, and FALSE otherwise. ■

Exercises

24.1-1
Run the Bellman-Ford algorithm on the directed graph of Figure 24.4, using vertex z as the source. In each pass, relax edges in the same order as in the figure, and show the d and π values after each pass. Now, change the weight of edge (z, x) to 4 and run the algorithm again, using s as the source.

24.1-2
Prove Corollary 24.3.

24.1-3
Given a weighted, directed graph $G = (V, E)$ with no negative-weight cycles, let m be the maximum over all vertices $v \in V$ of the minimum number of edges in a shortest path from the source s to v. (Here, the shortest path is by weight, not the number of edges.) Suggest a simple change to the Bellman-Ford algorithm that allows it to terminate in $m + 1$ passes, even if m is not known in advance.

24.1-4
Modify the Bellman-Ford algorithm so that it sets $v.d$ to $-\infty$ for all vertices v for which there is a negative-weight cycle on some path from the source to v.

24.1-5 ★

Let $G = (V, E)$ be a weighted, directed graph with weight function $w : E \rightarrow \mathbb{R}$. Give an $O(VE)$-time algorithm to find, for each vertex $v \in V$, the value $\delta^*(v) = \min_{u \in V} \{\delta(u, v)\}$.

24.1-6 ★

Suppose that a weighted, directed graph $G = (V, E)$ has a negative-weight cycle. Give an efficient algorithm to list the vertices of one such cycle. Prove that your algorithm is correct.

24.2   Single-source shortest paths in directed acyclic graphs

By relaxing the edges of a weighted dag (directed acyclic graph) $G = (V, E)$ according to a topological sort of its vertices, we can compute shortest paths from a single source in $\Theta(V + E)$ time. Shortest paths are always well defined in a dag, since even if there are negative-weight edges, no negative-weight cycles can exist.

The algorithm starts by topologically sorting the dag (see Section 22.4) to impose a linear ordering on the vertices. If the dag contains a path from vertex u to vertex v, then u precedes v in the topological sort. We make just one pass over the vertices in the topologically sorted order. As we process each vertex, we relax each edge that leaves the vertex.

DAG-SHORTEST-PATHS(G, w, s)

1 topologically sort the vertices of G
2 INITIALIZE-SINGLE-SOURCE(G, s)
3 **for** each vertex u, taken in topologically sorted order
4   **for** each vertex $v \in G.Adj[u]$
5   RELAX(u, v, w)

Figure 24.5 shows the execution of this algorithm.

The running time of this algorithm is easy to analyze. As shown in Section 22.4, the topological sort of line 1 takes $\Theta(V + E)$ time. The call of INITIALIZE-SINGLE-SOURCE in line 2 takes $\Theta(V)$ time. The **for** loop of lines 3–5 makes one iteration per vertex. Altogether, the **for** loop of lines 4–5 relaxes each edge exactly once. (We have used an aggregate analysis here.) Because each iteration of the inner **for** loop takes $\Theta(1)$ time, the total running time is $\Theta(V + E)$, which is linear in the size of an adjacency-list representation of the graph.

The following theorem shows that the DAG-SHORTEST-PATHS procedure correctly computes the shortest paths.

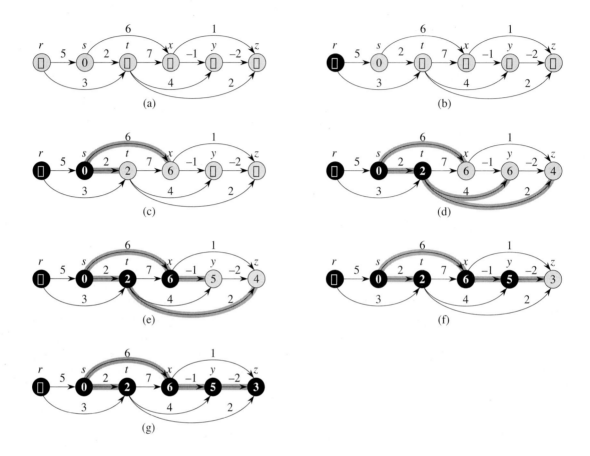

Figure 24.5 The execution of the algorithm for shortest paths in a directed acyclic graph. The vertices are topologically sorted from left to right. The source vertex is s. The d values appear within the vertices, and shaded edges indicate the π values. **(a)** The situation before the first iteration of the **for** loop of lines 3–5. **(b)–(g)** The situation after each iteration of the **for** loop of lines 3–5. The newly blackened vertex in each iteration was used as u in that iteration. The values shown in part (g) are the final values.

Theorem 24.5

If a weighted, directed graph $G = (V, E)$ has source vertex s and no cycles, then at the termination of the DAG-SHORTEST-PATHS procedure, $v.d = \delta(s, v)$ for all vertices $v \in V$, and the predecessor subgraph G_π is a shortest-paths tree.

Proof We first show that $v.d = \delta(s, v)$ for all vertices $v \in V$ at termination. If v is not reachable from s, then $v.d = \delta(s, v) = \infty$ by the no-path property. Now, suppose that v is reachable from s, so that there is a shortest path $p = \langle v_0, v_1, \ldots, v_k \rangle$, where $v_0 = s$ and $v_k = v$. Because we process the vertices in topologically sorted order, we relax the edges on p in the order $(v_0, v_1), (v_1, v_2), \ldots, (v_{k-1}, v_k)$. The path-relaxation property implies that $v_i.d = \delta(s, v_i)$ at termination for $i = 0, 1, \ldots, k$. Finally, by the predecessor-subgraph property, G_π is a shortest-paths tree.   ∎

An interesting application of this algorithm arises in determining critical paths in *PERT chart*[2] analysis. Edges represent jobs to be performed, and edge weights represent the times required to perform particular jobs. If edge (u, v) enters vertex v and edge (v, x) leaves v, then job (u, v) must be performed before job (v, x). A path through this dag represents a sequence of jobs that must be performed in a particular order. A *critical path* is a *longest* path through the dag, corresponding to the longest time to perform any sequence of jobs. Thus, the weight of a critical path provides a lower bound on the total time to perform all the jobs. We can find a critical path by either

* negating the edge weights and running DAG-SHORTEST-PATHS, or

* running DAG-SHORTEST-PATHS, with the modification that we replace "∞" by "−∞" in line 2 of INITIALIZE-SINGLE-SOURCE and ">" by "<" in the RELAX procedure.

Exercises

24.2-1
Run DAG-SHORTEST-PATHS on the directed graph of Figure 24.5, using vertex r as the source.

24.2-2
Suppose we change line 3 of DAG-SHORTEST-PATHS to read

3   **for** the first $|V| - 1$ vertices, taken in topologically sorted order

Show that the procedure would remain correct.

24.2-3
The PERT chart formulation given above is somewhat unnatural. In a more natural structure, vertices would represent jobs and edges would represent sequencing constraints; that is, edge (u, v) would indicate that job u must be performed before job v. We would then assign weights to vertices, not edges. Modify the DAG-SHORTEST-PATHS procedure so that it finds a longest path in a directed acyclic graph with weighted vertices in linear time.

---

[2]"PERT" is an acronym for "program evaluation and review technique."

24.2-4
Give an efficient algorithm to count the total number of paths in a directed acyclic graph. Analyze your algorithm.

24.3   Dijkstra's algorithm

Dijkstra's algorithm solves the single-source shortest-paths problem on a weighted, directed graph $G = (V, E)$ for the case in which all edge weights are nonnegative. In this section, therefore, we assume that $w(u, v) \geq 0$ for each edge $(u, v) \in E$. As we shall see, with a good implementation, the running time of Dijkstra's algorithm is lower than that of the Bellman-Ford algorithm.

Dijkstra's algorithm maintains a set S of vertices whose final shortest-path weights from the source s have already been determined. The algorithm repeatedly selects the vertex $u \in V - S$ with the minimum shortest-path estimate, adds u to S, and relaxes all edges leaving u. In the following implementation, we use a min-priority queue Q of vertices, keyed by their d values.

DIJKSTRA(G, w, s)

```
1  INITIALIZE-SINGLE-SOURCE(G, s)
2  S = Ø
3  Q = G.V
4  while Q ≠ Ø
5      u = EXTRACT-MIN(Q)
6      S = S ∪ {u}
7      for each vertex v ∈ G.Adj[u]
8          RELAX(u, v, w)
```

Dijkstra's algorithm relaxes edges as shown in Figure 24.6. Line 1 initializes the d and π values in the usual way, and line 2 initializes the set S to the empty set. The algorithm maintains the invariant that $Q = V - S$ at the start of each iteration of the **while** loop of lines 4–8. Line 3 initializes the min-priority queue Q to contain all the vertices in V; since $S = \emptyset$ at that time, the invariant is true after line 3. Each time through the **while** loop of lines 4–8, line 5 extracts a vertex u from $Q = V - S$ and line 6 adds it to set S, thereby maintaining the invariant. (The first time through this loop, $u = s$.) Vertex u, therefore, has the smallest shortest-path estimate of any vertex in $V - S$. Then, lines 7–8 relax each edge (u, v) leaving u, thus updating the estimate $v.d$ and the predecessor $v.\pi$ if we can improve the shortest path to v found so far by going through u. Observe that the algorithm never inserts vertices into Q after line 3 and that each vertex is extracted from Q

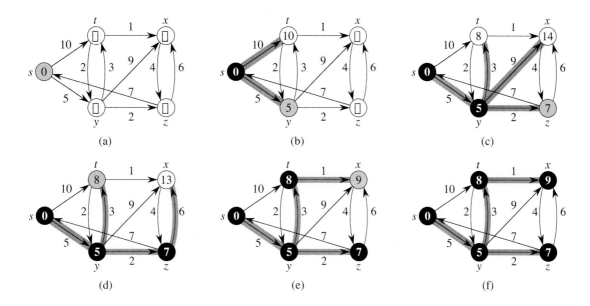

Figure 24.6 The execution of Dijkstra's algorithm. The source s is the leftmost vertex. The shortest-path estimates appear within the vertices, and shaded edges indicate predecessor values. Black vertices are in the set S, and white vertices are in the min-priority queue $Q = V - S$. **(a)** The situation just before the first iteration of the **while** loop of lines 4–8. The shaded vertex has the minimum d value and is chosen as vertex u in line 5. **(b)–(f)** The situation after each successive iteration of the **while** loop. The shaded vertex in each part is chosen as vertex u in line 5 of the next iteration. The d values and predecessors shown in part (f) are the final values.

and added to S exactly once, so that the **while** loop of lines 4–8 iterates exactly $|V|$ times.

Because Dijkstra's algorithm always chooses the "lightest" or "closest" vertex in $V - S$ to add to set S, we say that it uses a greedy strategy. Chapter 16 explains greedy strategies in detail, but you need not have read that chapter to understand Dijkstra's algorithm. Greedy strategies do not always yield optimal results in general, but as the following theorem and its corollary show, Dijkstra's algorithm does indeed compute shortest paths. The key is to show that each time it adds a vertex u to set S, we have $u.d = \delta(s, u)$.

Theorem 24.6 (Correctness of Dijkstra's algorithm)
Dijkstra's algorithm, run on a weighted, directed graph $G = (V, E)$ with non-negative weight function w and source s, terminates with $u.d = \delta(s, u)$ for all vertices $u \in V$.

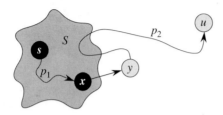

Figure 24.7   The proof of Theorem 24.6. Set S is nonempty just before vertex u is added to it. We decompose a shortest path p from source s to vertex u into $s \overset{p_1}{\leadsto} x \to y \overset{p_2}{\leadsto} u$, where y is the first vertex on the path that is not in S and $x \in S$ immediately precedes y. Vertices x and y are distinct, but we may have $s = x$ or $y = u$. Path p_2 may or may not reenter set S.

Proof   We use the following loop invariant:

> At the start of each iteration of the **while** loop of lines 4–8, $v.d = \delta(s, v)$ for each vertex $v \in S$.

It suffices to show for each vertex $u \in V$, we have $u.d = \delta(s, u)$ at the time when u is added to set S. Once we show that $u.d = \delta(s, u)$, we rely on the upper-bound property to show that the equality holds at all times thereafter.

Initialization: Initially, $S = \emptyset$, and so the invariant is trivially true.

Maintenance: We wish to show that in each iteration, $u.d = \delta(s, u)$ for the vertex added to set S. For the purpose of contradiction, let u be the first vertex for which $u.d \neq \delta(s, u)$ when it is added to set S. We shall focus our attention on the situation at the beginning of the iteration of the **while** loop in which u is added to S and derive the contradiction that $u.d = \delta(s, u)$ at that time by examining a shortest path from s to u. We must have $u \neq s$ because s is the first vertex added to set S and $s.d = \delta(s, s) = 0$ at that time. Because $u \neq s$, we also have that $S \neq \emptyset$ just before u is added to S. There must be some path from s to u, for otherwise $u.d = \delta(s, u) = \infty$ by the no-path property, which would violate our assumption that $u.d \neq \delta(s, u)$. Because there is at least one path, there is a shortest path p from s to u. Prior to adding u to S, path p connects a vertex in S, namely s, to a vertex in $V - S$, namely u. Let us consider the first vertex y along p such that $y \in V - S$, and let $x \in S$ be y's predecessor along p. Thus, as Figure 24.7 illustrates, we can decompose path p into $s \overset{p_1}{\leadsto} x \to y \overset{p_2}{\leadsto} u$. (Either of paths p_1 or p_2 may have no edges.)

We claim that $y.d = \delta(s, y)$ when u is added to S. To prove this claim, observe that $x \in S$. Then, because we chose u as the first vertex for which $u.d \neq \delta(s, u)$ when it is added to S, we had $x.d = \delta(s, x)$ when x was added to S. Edge (x, y) was relaxed at that time, and the claim follows from the convergence property.

We can now obtain a contradiction to prove that $u.d = \delta(s, u)$. Because y appears before u on a shortest path from s to u and all edge weights are nonnegative (notably those on path p_2), we have $\delta(s, y) \leq \delta(s, u)$, and thus

$$
\begin{aligned}
y.d &= \delta(s, y) \\
&\leq \delta(s, u) \\
&\leq u.d \quad \text{(by the upper-bound property)} \ .
\end{aligned}
\tag{24.2}
$$

But because both vertices u and y were in $V - S$ when u was chosen in line 5, we have $u.d \leq y.d$. Thus, the two inequalities in (24.2) are in fact equalities, giving

$$
y.d = \delta(s, y) = \delta(s, u) = u.d \ .
$$

Consequently, $u.d = \delta(s, u)$, which contradicts our choice of u. We conclude that $u.d = \delta(s, u)$ when u is added to S, and that this equality is maintained at all times thereafter.

Termination: At termination, $Q = \emptyset$ which, along with our earlier invariant that $Q = V - S$, implies that $S = V$. Thus, $u.d = \delta(s, u)$ for all vertices $u \in V$. ∎

Corollary 24.7

If we run Dijkstra's algorithm on a weighted, directed graph $G = (V, E)$ with nonnegative weight function w and source s, then at termination, the predecessor subgraph G_π is a shortest-paths tree rooted at s.

Proof   Immediate from Theorem 24.6 and the predecessor-subgraph property. ∎

Analysis

How fast is Dijkstra's algorithm? It maintains the min-priority queue Q by calling three priority-queue operations: INSERT (implicit in line 3), EXTRACT-MIN (line 5), and DECREASE-KEY (implicit in RELAX, which is called in line 8). The algorithm calls both INSERT and EXTRACT-MIN once per vertex. Because each vertex $u \in V$ is added to set S exactly once, each edge in the adjacency list $Adj[u]$ is examined in the **for** loop of lines 7–8 exactly once during the course of the algorithm. Since the total number of edges in all the adjacency lists is $|E|$, this **for** loop iterates a total of $|E|$ times, and thus the algorithm calls DECREASE-KEY at most $|E|$ times overall. (Observe once again that we are using aggregate analysis.)

The running time of Dijkstra's algorithm depends on how we implement the min-priority queue. Consider first the case in which we maintain the min-priority queue by taking advantage of the vertices being numbered 1 to $|V|$. We simply store $v.d$ in the vth entry of an array. Each INSERT and DECREASE-KEY operation takes $O(1)$ time, and each EXTRACT-MIN operation takes $O(V)$ time (since we have to search through the entire array), for a total time of $O(V^2 + E) = O(V^2)$.

If the graph is sufficiently sparse—in particular, $E = o(V^2/\lg V)$—we can improve the algorithm by implementing the min-priority queue with a binary min-heap. (As discussed in Section 6.5, the implementation should make sure that vertices and corresponding heap elements maintain handles to each other.) Each EXTRACT-MIN operation then takes time $O(\lg V)$. As before, there are $|V|$ such operations. The time to build the binary min-heap is $O(V)$. Each DECREASE-KEY operation takes time $O(\lg V)$, and there are still at most $|E|$ such operations. The total running time is therefore $O((V + E)\lg V)$, which is $O(E \lg V)$ if all vertices are reachable from the source. This running time improves upon the straightforward $O(V^2)$-time implementation if $E = o(V^2/\lg V)$.

We can in fact achieve a running time of $O(V \lg V + E)$ by implementing the min-priority queue with a Fibonacci heap (see Chapter 19). The amortized cost of each of the $|V|$ EXTRACT-MIN operations is $O(\lg V)$, and each DECREASE-KEY call, of which there are at most $|E|$, takes only $O(1)$ amortized time. Historically, the development of Fibonacci heaps was motivated by the observation that Dijkstra's algorithm typically makes many more DECREASE-KEY calls than EXTRACT-MIN calls, so that any method of reducing the amortized time of each DECREASE-KEY operation to $o(\lg V)$ without increasing the amortized time of EXTRACT-MIN would yield an asymptotically faster implementation than with binary heaps.

Dijkstra's algorithm resembles both breadth-first search (see Section 22.2) and Prim's algorithm for computing minimum spanning trees (see Section 23.2). It is like breadth-first search in that set S corresponds to the set of black vertices in a breadth-first search; just as vertices in S have their final shortest-path weights, so do black vertices in a breadth-first search have their correct breadth-first distances. Dijkstra's algorithm is like Prim's algorithm in that both algorithms use a min-priority queue to find the "lightest" vertex outside a given set (the set S in Dijkstra's algorithm and the tree being grown in Prim's algorithm), add this vertex into the set, and adjust the weights of the remaining vertices outside the set accordingly.

Exercises

24.3-1
Run Dijkstra's algorithm on the directed graph of Figure 24.2, first using vertex s as the source and then using vertex z as the source. In the style of Figure 24.6, show the d and π values and the vertices in set S after each iteration of the **while** loop.

24.3-2

Give a simple example of a directed graph with negative-weight edges for which Dijkstra's algorithm produces incorrect answers. Why doesn't the proof of Theorem 24.6 go through when negative-weight edges are allowed?

24.3-3

Suppose we change line 4 of Dijkstra's algorithm to the following.

4   **while** $|Q| > 1$

This change causes the **while** loop to execute $|V| - 1$ times instead of $|V|$ times. Is this proposed algorithm correct?

24.3-4

Professor Gaedel has written a program that he claims implements Dijkstra's algorithm. The program produces $v.d$ and $v.\pi$ for each vertex $v \in V$. Give an $O(V + E)$-time algorithm to check the output of the professor's program. It should determine whether the d and π attributes match those of some shortest-paths tree. You may assume that all edge weights are nonnegative.

24.3-5

Professor Newman thinks that he has worked out a simpler proof of correctness for Dijkstra's algorithm. He claims that Dijkstra's algorithm relaxes the edges of every shortest path in the graph in the order in which they appear on the path, and therefore the path-relaxation property applies to every vertex reachable from the source. Show that the professor is mistaken by constructing a directed graph for which Dijkstra's algorithm could relax the edges of a shortest path out of order.

24.3-6

We are given a directed graph $G = (V, E)$ on which each edge $(u, v) \in E$ has an associated value $r(u, v)$, which is a real number in the range $0 \leq r(u, v) \leq 1$ that represents the reliability of a communication channel from vertex u to vertex v. We interpret $r(u, v)$ as the probability that the channel from u to v will not fail, and we assume that these probabilities are independent. Give an efficient algorithm to find the most reliable path between two given vertices.

24.3-7

Let $G = (V, E)$ be a weighted, directed graph with positive weight function $w : E \rightarrow \{1, 2, \ldots, W\}$ for some positive integer W, and assume that no two vertices have the same shortest-path weights from source vertex s. Now suppose that we define an unweighted, directed graph $G' = (V \cup V', E')$ by replacing each edge $(u, v) \in E$ with $w(u, v)$ unit-weight edges in series. How many vertices does G' have? Now suppose that we run a breadth-first search on G'. Show that the order in which the breadth-first search of G' colors vertices in V black is the same as the order in which Dijkstra's algorithm extracts the vertices of V from the priority queue when it runs on G.

24.3-8

Let $G = (V, E)$ be a weighted, directed graph with nonnegative weight function $w : E \rightarrow \{0, 1, \ldots, W\}$ for some nonnegative integer W. Modify Dijkstra's algorithm to compute the shortest paths from a given source vertex s in $O(WV + E)$ time.

24.3-9

Modify your algorithm from Exercise 24.3-8 to run in $O((V + E)\lg W)$ time. (*Hint:* How many distinct shortest-path estimates can there be in $V - S$ at any point in time?)

24.3-10

Suppose that we are given a weighted, directed graph $G = (V, E)$ in which edges that leave the source vertex s may have negative weights, all other edge weights are nonnegative, and there are no negative-weight cycles. Argue that Dijkstra's algorithm correctly finds shortest paths from s in this graph.

24.4   Difference constraints and shortest paths

Chapter 29 studies the general linear-programming problem, in which we wish to optimize a linear function subject to a set of linear inequalities. In this section, we investigate a special case of linear programming that we reduce to finding shortest paths from a single source. We can then solve the single-source shortest-paths problem that results by running the Bellman-Ford algorithm, thereby also solving the linear-programming problem.

Linear programming

In the general ***linear-programming problem***, we are given an $m \times n$ matrix A, an m-vector b, and an n-vector c. We wish to find a vector x of n elements that maximizes the ***objective function*** $\sum_{i=1}^{n} c_i x_i$ subject to the m constraints given by $Ax \leq b$.

Although the simplex algorithm, which is the focus of Chapter 29, does not always run in time polynomial in the size of its input, there are other linear-programming algorithms that do run in polynomial time. We offer here two reasons to understand the setup of linear-programming problems. First, if we know that we can cast a given problem as a polynomial-sized linear-programming problem, then we immediately have a polynomial-time algorithm to solve the problem. Second, faster algorithms exist for many special cases of linear programming. For example, the single-pair shortest-path problem (Exercise 24.4-4) and the maximum-flow problem (Exercise 26.1-5) are special cases of linear programming.

Sometimes we don't really care about the objective function; we just wish to find any *feasible solution*, that is, any vector x that satisfies $Ax \leq b$, or to determine that no feasible solution exists. We shall focus on one such *feasibility problem*.

Systems of difference constraints

In a *system of difference constraints*, each row of the linear-programming matrix A contains one 1 and one -1, and all other entries of A are 0. Thus, the constraints given by $Ax \leq b$ are a set of m *difference constraints* involving n unknowns, in which each constraint is a simple linear inequality of the form

$$x_j - x_i \leq b_k ,$$

where $1 \leq i, j \leq n, i \neq j$, and $1 \leq k \leq m$.

For example, consider the problem of finding a 5-vector $x = (x_i)$ that satisfies

$$\begin{pmatrix} 1 & -1 & 0 & 0 & 0 \\ 1 & 0 & 0 & 0 & -1 \\ 0 & 1 & 0 & 0 & -1 \\ -1 & 0 & 1 & 0 & 0 \\ -1 & 0 & 0 & 1 & 0 \\ 0 & 0 & -1 & 1 & 0 \\ 0 & 0 & -1 & 0 & 1 \\ 0 & 0 & 0 & -1 & 1 \end{pmatrix} \begin{pmatrix} x_1 \\ x_2 \\ x_3 \\ x_4 \\ x_5 \end{pmatrix} \leq \begin{pmatrix} 0 \\ -1 \\ 1 \\ 5 \\ 4 \\ -1 \\ -3 \\ -3 \end{pmatrix} .$$

This problem is equivalent to finding values for the unknowns x_1, x_2, x_3, x_4, x_5, satisfying the following 8 difference constraints:

$$x_1 - x_2 \leq 0 , \tag{24.3}$$
$$x_1 - x_5 \leq -1 , \tag{24.4}$$
$$x_2 - x_5 \leq 1 , \tag{24.5}$$
$$x_3 - x_1 \leq 5 , \tag{24.6}$$
$$x_4 - x_1 \leq 4 , \tag{24.7}$$
$$x_4 - x_3 \leq -1 , \tag{24.8}$$
$$x_5 - x_3 \leq -3 , \tag{24.9}$$
$$x_5 - x_4 \leq -3 . \tag{24.10}$$

One solution to this problem is $x = (-5, -3, 0, -1, -4)$, which you can verify directly by checking each inequality. In fact, this problem has more than one solution. Another is $x' = (0, 2, 5, 4, 1)$. These two solutions are related: each component of x' is 5 larger than the corresponding component of x. This fact is not mere coincidence.

Lemma 24.8
Let $x = (x_1, x_2, \ldots, x_n)$ be a solution to a system $Ax \leq b$ of difference constraints, and let d be any constant. Then $x + d = (x_1 + d, x_2 + d, \ldots, x_n + d)$ is a solution to $Ax \leq b$ as well.

Proof   For each x_i and x_j, we have $(x_j + d) - (x_i + d) = x_j - x_i$. Thus, if x satisfies $Ax \leq b$, so does $x + d$.   ∎

Systems of difference constraints occur in many different applications. For example, the unknowns x_i may be times at which events are to occur. Each constraint states that at least a certain amount of time, or at most a certain amount of time, must elapse between two events. Perhaps the events are jobs to be performed during the assembly of a product. If we apply an adhesive that takes 2 hours to set at time x_1 and we have to wait until it sets to install a part at time x_2, then we have the constraint that $x_2 \geq x_1 + 2$ or, equivalently, that $x_1 - x_2 \leq -2$. Alternatively, we might require that the part be installed after the adhesive has been applied but no later than the time that the adhesive has set halfway. In this case, we get the pair of constraints $x_2 \geq x_1$ and $x_2 \leq x_1 + 1$ or, equivalently, $x_1 - x_2 \leq 0$ and $x_2 - x_1 \leq 1$.

Constraint graphs

We can interpret systems of difference constraints from a graph-theoretic point of view. In a system $Ax \leq b$ of difference constraints, we view the $m \times n$ linear-programming matrix A as the transpose of an incidence matrix (see Exercise 22.1-7) for a graph with n vertices and m edges. Each vertex v_i in the graph, for $i = 1, 2, \ldots, n$, corresponds to one of the n unknown variables x_i. Each directed edge in the graph corresponds to one of the m inequalities involving two unknowns.

More formally, given a system $Ax \leq b$ of difference constraints, the corresponding **constraint graph** is a weighted, directed graph $G = (V, E)$, where

$$V = \{v_0, v_1, \ldots, v_n\}$$

and

$$E = \{(v_i, v_j) : x_j - x_i \leq b_k \text{ is a constraint}\}$$
$$\cup \{(v_0, v_1), (v_0, v_2), (v_0, v_3), \ldots, (v_0, v_n)\} \ .$$

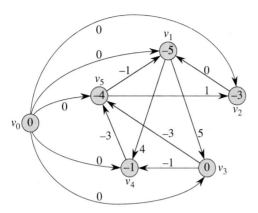

Figure 24.8 The constraint graph corresponding to the system (24.3)–(24.10) of difference constraints. The value of $\delta(v_0, v_i)$ appears in each vertex v_i. One feasible solution to the system is $x = (-5, -3, 0, -1, -4)$.

The constraint graph contains the additional vertex v_0, as we shall see shortly, to guarantee that the graph has some vertex which can reach all other vertices. Thus, the vertex set V consists of a vertex v_i for each unknown x_i, plus an additional vertex v_0. The edge set E contains an edge for each difference constraint, plus an edge (v_0, v_i) for each unknown x_i. If $x_j - x_i \leq b_k$ is a difference constraint, then the weight of edge (v_i, v_j) is $w(v_i, v_j) = b_k$. The weight of each edge leaving v_0 is 0. Figure 24.8 shows the constraint graph for the system (24.3)–(24.10) of difference constraints.

The following theorem shows that we can find a solution to a system of difference constraints by finding shortest-path weights in the corresponding constraint graph.

Theorem 24.9
Given a system $Ax \leq b$ of difference constraints, let $G = (V, E)$ be the corresponding constraint graph. If G contains no negative-weight cycles, then

$$x = (\delta(v_0, v_1), \delta(v_0, v_2), \delta(v_0, v_3), \ldots, \delta(v_0, v_n)) \tag{24.11}$$

is a feasible solution for the system. If G contains a negative-weight cycle, then there is no feasible solution for the system.

Proof We first show that if the constraint graph contains no negative-weight cycles, then equation (24.11) gives a feasible solution. Consider any edge $(v_i, v_j) \in E$. By the triangle inequality, $\delta(v_0, v_j) \leq \delta(v_0, v_i) + w(v_i, v_j)$ or, equivalently, $\delta(v_0, v_j) - \delta(v_0, v_i) \leq w(v_i, v_j)$. Thus, letting $x_i = \delta(v_0, v_i)$ and

$x_j = \delta(v_0, v_j)$ satisfies the difference constraint $x_j - x_i \le w(v_i, v_j)$ that corresponds to edge (v_i, v_j).

Now we show that if the constraint graph contains a negative-weight cycle, then the system of difference constraints has no feasible solution. Without loss of generality, let the negative-weight cycle be $c = \langle v_1, v_2, \ldots, v_k \rangle$, where $v_1 = v_k$. (The vertex v_0 cannot be on cycle c, because it has no entering edges.) Cycle c corresponds to the following difference constraints:

$$
\begin{aligned}
x_2 - x_1 &\le w(v_1, v_2)\,, \\
x_3 - x_2 &\le w(v_2, v_3)\,, \\
&\vdots \\
x_{k-1} - x_{k-2} &\le w(v_{k-2}, v_{k-1})\,, \\
x_k - x_{k-1} &\le w(v_{k-1}, v_k)\,.
\end{aligned}
$$

We will assume that x has a solution satisfying each of these k inequalities and then derive a contradiction. The solution must also satisfy the inequality that results when we sum the k inequalities together. If we sum the left-hand sides, each unknown x_i is added in once and subtracted out once (remember that $v_1 = v_k$ implies $x_1 = x_k$), so that the left-hand side of the sum is 0. The right-hand side sums to $w(c)$, and thus we obtain $0 \le w(c)$. But since c is a negative-weight cycle, $w(c) < 0$, and we obtain the contradiction that $0 \le w(c) < 0$.   ∎

Solving systems of difference constraints

Theorem 24.9 tells us that we can use the Bellman-Ford algorithm to solve a system of difference constraints. Because the constraint graph contains edges from the source vertex v_0 to all other vertices, any negative-weight cycle in the constraint graph is reachable from v_0. If the Bellman-Ford algorithm returns TRUE, then the shortest-path weights give a feasible solution to the system. In Figure 24.8, for example, the shortest-path weights provide the feasible solution $x = (-5, -3, 0, -1, -4)$, and by Lemma 24.8, $x = (d - 5, d - 3, d, d - 1, d - 4)$ is also a feasible solution for any constant d. If the Bellman-Ford algorithm returns FALSE, there is no feasible solution to the system of difference constraints.

A system of difference constraints with m constraints on n unknowns produces a graph with $n + 1$ vertices and $n + m$ edges. Thus, using the Bellman-Ford algorithm, we can solve the system in $O((n + 1)(n + m)) = O(n^2 + nm)$ time. Exercise 24.4-5 asks you to modify the algorithm to run in $O(nm)$ time, even if m is much less than n.

Exercises

24.4-1
Find a feasible solution or determine that no feasible solution exists for the following system of difference constraints:

$$
\begin{aligned}
x_1 - x_2 &\le 1, \\
x_1 - x_4 &\le -4, \\
x_2 - x_3 &\le 2, \\
x_2 - x_5 &\le 7, \\
x_2 - x_6 &\le 5, \\
x_3 - x_6 &\le 10, \\
x_4 - x_2 &\le 2, \\
x_5 - x_1 &\le -1, \\
x_5 - x_4 &\le 3, \\
x_6 - x_3 &\le -8.
\end{aligned}
$$

24.4-2
Find a feasible solution or determine that no feasible solution exists for the following system of difference constraints:

$$
\begin{aligned}
x_1 - x_2 &\le 4, \\
x_1 - x_5 &\le 5, \\
x_2 - x_4 &\le -6, \\
x_3 - x_2 &\le 1, \\
x_4 - x_1 &\le 3, \\
x_4 - x_3 &\le 5, \\
x_4 - x_5 &\le 10, \\
x_5 - x_3 &\le -4, \\
x_5 - x_4 &\le -8.
\end{aligned}
$$

24.4-3
Can any shortest-path weight from the new vertex v_0 in a constraint graph be positive? Explain.

24.4-4
Express the single-pair shortest-path problem as a linear program.

24.4-5

Show how to modify the Bellman-Ford algorithm slightly so that when we use it to solve a system of difference constraints with m inequalities on n unknowns, the running time is $O(nm)$.

24.4-6

Suppose that in addition to a system of difference constraints, we want to handle *equality constraints* of the form $x_i = x_j + b_k$. Show how to adapt the Bellman-Ford algorithm to solve this variety of constraint system.

24.4-7

Show how to solve a system of difference constraints by a Bellman-Ford-like algorithm that runs on a constraint graph without the extra vertex v_0.

24.4-8 ★

Let $Ax \leq b$ be a system of m difference constraints in n unknowns. Show that the Bellman-Ford algorithm, when run on the corresponding constraint graph, maximizes $\sum_{i=1}^{n} x_i$ subject to $Ax \leq b$ and $x_i \leq 0$ for all x_i.

24.4-9 ★

Show that the Bellman-Ford algorithm, when run on the constraint graph for a system $Ax \leq b$ of difference constraints, minimizes the quantity $(\max\{x_i\} - \min\{x_i\})$ subject to $Ax \leq b$. Explain how this fact might come in handy if the algorithm is used to schedule construction jobs.

24.4-10

Suppose that every row in the matrix A of a linear program $Ax \leq b$ corresponds to a difference constraint, a single-variable constraint of the form $x_i \leq b_k$, or a single-variable constraint of the form $-x_i \leq b_k$. Show how to adapt the Bellman-Ford algorithm to solve this variety of constraint system.

24.4-11

Give an efficient algorithm to solve a system $Ax \leq b$ of difference constraints when all of the elements of b are real-valued and all of the unknowns x_i must be integers.

24.4-12 ★

Give an efficient algorithm to solve a system $Ax \leq b$ of difference constraints when all of the elements of b are real-valued and a specified subset of some, but not necessarily all, of the unknowns x_i must be integers.

24.5   Proofs of shortest-paths properties

Throughout this chapter, our correctness arguments have relied on the triangle inequality, upper-bound property, no-path property, convergence property, path-relaxation property, and predecessor-subgraph property. We stated these properties without proof at the beginning of this chapter. In this section, we prove them.

The triangle inequality

In studying breadth-first search (Section 22.2), we proved as Lemma 22.1 a simple property of shortest distances in unweighted graphs. The triangle inequality generalizes the property to weighted graphs.

Lemma 24.10 (Triangle inequality)
Let $G = (V, E)$ be a weighted, directed graph with weight function $w : E \rightarrow \mathbb{R}$ and source vertex s. Then, for all edges $(u, v) \in E$, we have

$$\delta(s, v) \leq \delta(s, u) + w(u, v) \, .$$

Proof   Suppose that p is a shortest path from source s to vertex v. Then p has no more weight than any other path from s to v. Specifically, path p has no more weight than the particular path that takes a shortest path from source s to vertex u and then takes edge (u, v).

Exercise 24.5-3 asks you to handle the case in which there is no shortest path from s to v.   ∎

Effects of relaxation on shortest-path estimates

The next group of lemmas describes how shortest-path estimates are affected when we execute a sequence of relaxation steps on the edges of a weighted, directed graph that has been initialized by INITIALIZE-SINGLE-SOURCE.

Lemma 24.11 (Upper-bound property)
Let $G = (V, E)$ be a weighted, directed graph with weight function $w : E \rightarrow \mathbb{R}$. Let $s \in V$ be the source vertex, and let the graph be initialized by INITIALIZE-SINGLE-SOURCE(G, s). Then, $v.d \geq \delta(s, v)$ for all $v \in V$, and this invariant is maintained over any sequence of relaxation steps on the edges of G. Moreover, once $v.d$ achieves its lower bound $\delta(s, v)$, it never changes.

Proof   We prove the invariant $v.d \geq \delta(s, v)$ for all vertices $v \in V$ by induction over the number of relaxation steps.

For the basis, $v.d \geq \delta(s, v)$ is certainly true after initialization, since $v.d = \infty$ implies $v.d \geq \delta(s, v)$ for all $v \in V - \{s\}$, and since $s.d = 0 \geq \delta(s, s)$ (note that $\delta(s, s) = -\infty$ if s is on a negative-weight cycle and 0 otherwise).

For the inductive step, consider the relaxation of an edge (u, v). By the inductive hypothesis, $x.d \geq \delta(s, x)$ for all $x \in V$ prior to the relaxation. The only d value that may change is $v.d$. If it changes, we have

$$
\begin{aligned}
v.d \;&=\; u.d + w(u, v) \\
&\geq\; \delta(s, u) + w(u, v) \quad \text{(by the inductive hypothesis)} \\
&\geq\; \delta(s, v) \qquad\qquad\quad \text{(by the triangle inequality) ,}
\end{aligned}
$$

and so the invariant is maintained.

To see that the value of $v.d$ never changes once $v.d = \delta(s, v)$, note that having achieved its lower bound, $v.d$ cannot decrease because we have just shown that $v.d \geq \delta(s, v)$, and it cannot increase because relaxation steps do not increase d values. ∎

Corollary 24.12 (No-path property)
Suppose that in a weighted, directed graph $G = (V, E)$ with weight function $w : E \rightarrow \mathbb{R}$, no path connects a source vertex $s \in V$ to a given vertex $v \in V$. Then, after the graph is initialized by INITIALIZE-SINGLE-SOURCE(G, s), we have $v.d = \delta(s, v) = \infty$, and this equality is maintained as an invariant over any sequence of relaxation steps on the edges of G.

Proof   By the upper-bound property, we always have $\infty = \delta(s, v) \leq v.d$, and thus $v.d = \infty = \delta(s, v)$. ∎

Lemma 24.13
Let $G = (V, E)$ be a weighted, directed graph with weight function $w : E \rightarrow \mathbb{R}$, and let $(u, v) \in E$. Then, immediately after relaxing edge (u, v) by executing RELAX(u, v, w), we have $v.d \leq u.d + w(u, v)$.

Proof   If, just prior to relaxing edge (u, v), we have $v.d > u.d + w(u, v)$, then $v.d = u.d + w(u, v)$ afterward. If, instead, $v.d \leq u.d + w(u, v)$ just before the relaxation, then neither $u.d$ nor $v.d$ changes, and so $v.d \leq u.d + w(u, v)$ afterward. ∎

Lemma 24.14 (Convergence property)
Let $G = (V, E)$ be a weighted, directed graph with weight function $w : E \rightarrow \mathbb{R}$, let $s \in V$ be a source vertex, and let $s \rightsquigarrow u \rightarrow v$ be a shortest path in G for

some vertices $u, v \in V$. Suppose that G is initialized by INITIALIZE-SINGLE-SOURCE(G, s) and then a sequence of relaxation steps that includes the call RELAX(u, v, w) is executed on the edges of G. If $u.d = \delta(s, u)$ at any time prior to the call, then $v.d = \delta(s, v)$ at all times after the call.

Proof   By the upper-bound property, if $u.d = \delta(s, u)$ at some point prior to relaxing edge (u, v), then this equality holds thereafter. In particular, after relaxing edge (u, v), we have

$$
\begin{aligned}
v.d &\leq u.d + w(u, v) && \text{(by Lemma 24.13)} \\
&= \delta(s, u) + w(u, v) \\
&= \delta(s, v) && \text{(by Lemma 24.1) .}
\end{aligned}
$$

By the upper-bound property, $v.d \geq \delta(s, v)$, from which we conclude that $v.d = \delta(s, v)$, and this equality is maintained thereafter.   ∎

Lemma 24.15 (Path-relaxation property)

Let $G = (V, E)$ be a weighted, directed graph with weight function $w : E \to \mathbb{R}$, and let $s \in V$ be a source vertex. Consider any shortest path $p = \langle v_0, v_1, \ldots, v_k \rangle$ from $s = v_0$ to v_k. If G is initialized by INITIALIZE-SINGLE-SOURCE(G, s) and then a sequence of relaxation steps occurs that includes, in order, relaxing the edges $(v_0, v_1), (v_1, v_2), \ldots, (v_{k-1}, v_k)$, then $v_k.d = \delta(s, v_k)$ after these relaxations and at all times afterward. This property holds no matter what other edge relaxations occur, including relaxations that are intermixed with relaxations of the edges of p.

Proof   We show by induction that after the ith edge of path p is relaxed, we have $v_i.d = \delta(s, v_i)$. For the basis, $i = 0$, and before any edges of p have been relaxed, we have from the initialization that $v_0.d = s.d = 0 = \delta(s, s)$. By the upper-bound property, the value of $s.d$ never changes after initialization.

For the inductive step, we assume that $v_{i-1}.d = \delta(s, v_{i-1})$, and we examine what happens when we relax edge (v_{i-1}, v_i). By the convergence property, after relaxing this edge, we have $v_i.d = \delta(s, v_i)$, and this equality is maintained at all times thereafter.   ∎

Relaxation and shortest-paths trees

We now show that once a sequence of relaxations has caused the shortest-path estimates to converge to shortest-path weights, the predecessor subgraph G_π induced by the resulting π values is a shortest-paths tree for G. We start with the following lemma, which shows that the predecessor subgraph always forms a rooted tree whose root is the source.

Lemma 24.16

Let $G = (V, E)$ be a weighted, directed graph with weight function $w : E \rightarrow \mathbb{R}$, let $s \in V$ be a source vertex, and assume that G contains no negative-weight cycles that are reachable from s. Then, after the graph is initialized by INITIALIZE-SINGLE-SOURCE(G, s), the predecessor subgraph G_π forms a rooted tree with root s, and any sequence of relaxation steps on edges of G maintains this property as an invariant.

Proof   Initially, the only vertex in G_π is the source vertex, and the lemma is trivially true. Consider a predecessor subgraph G_π that arises after a sequence of relaxation steps. We shall first prove that G_π is acyclic. Suppose for the sake of contradiction that some relaxation step creates a cycle in the graph G_π. Let the cycle be $c = \langle v_0, v_1, \ldots, v_k \rangle$, where $v_k = v_0$. Then, $v_i.\pi = v_{i-1}$ for $i = 1, 2, \ldots, k$ and, without loss of generality, we can assume that relaxing edge (v_{k-1}, v_k) created the cycle in G_π.

We claim that all vertices on cycle c are reachable from the source s. Why? Each vertex on c has a non-NIL predecessor, and so each vertex on c was assigned a finite shortest-path estimate when it was assigned its non-NIL π value. By the upper-bound property, each vertex on cycle c has a finite shortest-path weight, which implies that it is reachable from s.

We shall examine the shortest-path estimates on c just prior to the call RELAX(v_{k-1}, v_k, w) and show that c is a negative-weight cycle, thereby contradicting the assumption that G contains no negative-weight cycles that are reachable from the source. Just before the call, we have $v_i.\pi = v_{i-1}$ for $i = 1, 2, \ldots, k - 1$. Thus, for $i = 1, 2, \ldots, k - 1$, the last update to $v_i.d$ was by the assignment $v_i.d = v_{i-1}.d + w(v_{i-1}, v_i)$. If $v_{i-1}.d$ changed since then, it decreased. Therefore, just before the call RELAX(v_{k-1}, v_k, w), we have

$$v_i.d \geq v_{i-1}.d + w(v_{i-1}, v_i) \qquad \text{for all } i = 1, 2, \ldots, k - 1 . \tag{24.12}$$

Because $v_k.\pi$ is changed by the call, immediately beforehand we also have the strict inequality

$$v_k.d > v_{k-1}.d + w(v_{k-1}, v_k) .$$

Summing this strict inequality with the $k - 1$ inequalities (24.12), we obtain the sum of the shortest-path estimates around cycle c:

$$\sum_{i=1}^{k} v_i.d > \sum_{i=1}^{k} (v_{i-1}.d + w(v_{i-1}, v_i))$$

$$= \sum_{i=1}^{k} v_{i-1}.d + \sum_{i=1}^{k} w(v_{i-1}, v_i) .$$

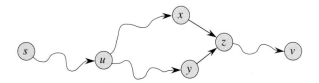

Figure 24.9   Showing that a simple path in G_π from source s to vertex v is unique. If there are two paths p_1 ($s \rightsquigarrow u \rightsquigarrow x \to z \rightsquigarrow v$) and p_2 ($s \rightsquigarrow u \rightsquigarrow y \to z \rightsquigarrow v$), where $x \neq y$, then $z.\pi = x$ and $z.\pi = y$, a contradiction.

But

$$\sum_{i=1}^{k} v_i.d = \sum_{i=1}^{k} v_{i-1}.d \, ,$$

since each vertex in the cycle c appears exactly once in each summation. This equality implies

$$0 > \sum_{i=1}^{k} w(v_{i-1}, v_i) \, .$$

Thus, the sum of weights around the cycle c is negative, which provides the desired contradiction.

We have now proven that G_π is a directed, acyclic graph. To show that it forms a rooted tree with root s, it suffices (see Exercise B.5-2) to prove that for each vertex $v \in V_\pi$, there is a unique simple path from s to v in G_π.

We first must show that a path from s exists for each vertex in V_π. The vertices in V_π are those with non-NIL π values, plus s. The idea here is to prove by induction that a path exists from s to all vertices in V_π. We leave the details as Exercise 24.5-6.

To complete the proof of the lemma, we must now show that for any vertex $v \in V_\pi$, the graph G_π contains at most one simple path from s to v. Suppose otherwise. That is, suppose that, as Figure 24.9 illustrates, G_π contains two simple paths from s to some vertex v: p_1, which we decompose into $s \rightsquigarrow u \rightsquigarrow x \to z \rightsquigarrow v$, and p_2, which we decompose into $s \rightsquigarrow u \rightsquigarrow y \to z \rightsquigarrow v$, where $x \neq y$ (though u could be s and z could be v). But then, $z.\pi = x$ and $z.\pi = y$, which implies the contradiction that $x = y$. We conclude that G_π contains a unique simple path from s to v, and thus G_π forms a rooted tree with root s.   ∎

We can now show that if, after we have performed a sequence of relaxation steps, all vertices have been assigned their true shortest-path weights, then the predecessor subgraph G_π is a shortest-paths tree.

Lemma 24.17 (Predecessor-subgraph property)
Let $G = (V, E)$ be a weighted, directed graph with weight function $w : E \to \mathbb{R}$, let $s \in V$ be a source vertex, and assume that G contains no negative-weight cycles that are reachable from s. Let us call INITIALIZE-SINGLE-SOURCE(G, s) and then execute any sequence of relaxation steps on edges of G that produces $v.d = \delta(s, v)$ for all $v \in V$. Then, the predecessor subgraph G_π is a shortest-paths tree rooted at s.

Proof We must prove that the three properties of shortest-paths trees given on page 647 hold for G_π. To show the first property, we must show that V_π is the set of vertices reachable from s. By definition, a shortest-path weight $\delta(s, v)$ is finite if and only if v is reachable from s, and thus the vertices that are reachable from s are exactly those with finite d values. But a vertex $v \in V - \{s\}$ has been assigned a finite value for $v.d$ if and only if $v.\pi \neq$ NIL. Thus, the vertices in V_π are exactly those reachable from s.

The second property follows directly from Lemma 24.16.

It remains, therefore, to prove the last property of shortest-paths trees: for each vertex $v \in V_\pi$, the unique simple path $s \overset{p}{\rightsquigarrow} v$ in G_π is a shortest path from s to v in G. Let $p = \langle v_0, v_1, \ldots, v_k \rangle$, where $v_0 = s$ and $v_k = v$. For $i = 1, 2, \ldots, k$, we have both $v_i.d = \delta(s, v_i)$ and $v_i.d \geq v_{i-1}.d + w(v_{i-1}, v_i)$, from which we conclude $w(v_{i-1}, v_i) \leq \delta(s, v_i) - \delta(s, v_{i-1})$. Summing the weights along path p yields

$$
\begin{aligned}
w(p) &= \sum_{i=1}^{k} w(v_{i-1}, v_i) \\
&\leq \sum_{i=1}^{k} (\delta(s, v_i) - \delta(s, v_{i-1})) \\
&= \delta(s, v_k) - \delta(s, v_0) \qquad \text{(because the sum telescopes)} \\
&= \delta(s, v_k) \qquad \text{(because } \delta(s, v_0) = \delta(s, s) = 0) \ .
\end{aligned}
$$

Thus, $w(p) \leq \delta(s, v_k)$. Since $\delta(s, v_k)$ is a lower bound on the weight of any path from s to v_k, we conclude that $w(p) = \delta(s, v_k)$, and thus p is a shortest path from s to $v = v_k$.   ∎

Exercises

24.5-1
Give two shortest-paths trees for the directed graph of Figure 24.2 (on page 648) other than the two shown.

24.5-2

Give an example of a weighted, directed graph $G = (V, E)$ with weight function $w : E \to \mathbb{R}$ and source vertex s such that G satisfies the following property: For every edge $(u, v) \in E$, there is a shortest-paths tree rooted at s that contains (u, v) and another shortest-paths tree rooted at s that does not contain (u, v).

24.5-3

Embellish the proof of Lemma 24.10 to handle cases in which shortest-path weights are ∞ or $-\infty$.

24.5-4

Let $G = (V, E)$ be a weighted, directed graph with source vertex s, and let G be initialized by INITIALIZE-SINGLE-SOURCE(G, s). Prove that if a sequence of relaxation steps sets $s.\pi$ to a non-NIL value, then G contains a negative-weight cycle.

24.5-5

Let $G = (V, E)$ be a weighted, directed graph with no negative-weight edges. Let $s \in V$ be the source vertex, and suppose that we allow $v.\pi$ to be the predecessor of v on *any* shortest path to v from source s if $v \in V - \{s\}$ is reachable from s, and NIL otherwise. Give an example of such a graph G and an assignment of π values that produces a cycle in G_π. (By Lemma 24.16, such an assignment cannot be produced by a sequence of relaxation steps.)

24.5-6

Let $G = (V, E)$ be a weighted, directed graph with weight function $w : E \to \mathbb{R}$ and no negative-weight cycles. Let $s \in V$ be the source vertex, and let G be initialized by INITIALIZE-SINGLE-SOURCE(G, s). Prove that for every vertex $v \in V_\pi$, there exists a path from s to v in G_π and that this property is maintained as an invariant over any sequence of relaxations.

24.5-7

Let $G = (V, E)$ be a weighted, directed graph that contains no negative-weight cycles. Let $s \in V$ be the source vertex, and let G be initialized by INITIALIZE-SINGLE-SOURCE(G, s). Prove that there exists a sequence of $|V| - 1$ relaxation steps that produces $v.d = \delta(s, v)$ for all $v \in V$.

24.5-8

Let G be an arbitrary weighted, directed graph with a negative-weight cycle reachable from the source vertex s. Show how to construct an infinite sequence of relaxations of the edges of G such that every relaxation causes a shortest-path estimate to change.

Problems

24-1   *Yen's improvement to Bellman-Ford*

Suppose that we order the edge relaxations in each pass of the Bellman-Ford algorithm as follows. Before the first pass, we assign an arbitrary linear order $v_1, v_2, \ldots, v_{|V|}$ to the vertices of the input graph $G = (V, E)$. Then, we partition the edge set E into $E_f \cup E_b$, where $E_f = \{(v_i, v_j) \in E : i < j\}$ and $E_b = \{(v_i, v_j) \in E : i > j\}$. (Assume that G contains no self-loops, so that every edge is in either E_f or E_b.) Define $G_f = (V, E_f)$ and $G_b = (V, E_b)$.

a. Prove that G_f is acyclic with topological sort $\langle v_1, v_2, \ldots, v_{|V|} \rangle$ and that G_b is acyclic with topological sort $\langle v_{|V|}, v_{|V|-1}, \ldots, v_1 \rangle$.

Suppose that we implement each pass of the Bellman-Ford algorithm in the following way. We visit each vertex in the order $v_1, v_2, \ldots, v_{|V|}$, relaxing edges of E_f that leave the vertex. We then visit each vertex in the order $v_{|V|}, v_{|V|-1}, \ldots, v_1$, relaxing edges of E_b that leave the vertex.

b. Prove that with this scheme, if G contains no negative-weight cycles that are reachable from the source vertex s, then after only $\lceil |V|/2 \rceil$ passes over the edges, $v.d = \delta(s, v)$ for all vertices $v \in V$.

c. Does this scheme improve the asymptotic running time of the Bellman-Ford algorithm?

24-2   *Nesting boxes*

A d-dimensional box with dimensions $(x_1, x_2, \ldots, x_d)$ **nests** within another box with dimensions $(y_1, y_2, \ldots, y_d)$ if there exists a permutation π on $\{1, 2, \ldots, d\}$ such that $x_{\pi(1)} < y_1, x_{\pi(2)} < y_2, \ldots, x_{\pi(d)} < y_d$.

a. Argue that the nesting relation is transitive.

b. Describe an efficient method to determine whether or not one d-dimensional box nests inside another.

c. Suppose that you are given a set of n d-dimensional boxes $\{B_1, B_2, \ldots, B_n\}$. Give an efficient algorithm to find the longest sequence $\langle B_{i_1}, B_{i_2}, \ldots, B_{i_k} \rangle$ of boxes such that B_{i_j} nests within $B_{i_{j+1}}$ for $j = 1, 2, \ldots, k - 1$. Express the running time of your algorithm in terms of n and d.

24-3 *Arbitrage*

Arbitrage is the use of discrepancies in currency exchange rates to transform one unit of a currency into more than one unit of the same currency. For example, suppose that 1 U.S. dollar buys 49 Indian rupees, 1 Indian rupee buys 2 Japanese yen, and 1 Japanese yen buys 0.0107 U.S. dollars. Then, by converting currencies, a trader can start with 1 U.S. dollar and buy $49 \times 2 \times 0.0107 = 1.0486$ U.S. dollars, thus turning a profit of 4.86 percent.

Suppose that we are given n currencies $c_1, c_2, \ldots, c_n$ and an $n \times n$ table R of exchange rates, such that one unit of currency c_i buys $R[i, j]$ units of currency c_j.

a. Give an efficient algorithm to determine whether or not there exists a sequence of currencies $\langle c_{i_1}, c_{i_2}, \ldots, c_{i_k} \rangle$ such that

$$R[i_1, i_2] \cdot R[i_2, i_3] \cdots R[i_{k-1}, i_k] \cdot R[i_k, i_1] > 1 .$$

Analyze the running time of your algorithm.

b. Give an efficient algorithm to print out such a sequence if one exists. Analyze the running time of your algorithm.

24-4 *Gabow's scaling algorithm for single-source shortest paths*

A *scaling* algorithm solves a problem by initially considering only the highest-order bit of each relevant input value (such as an edge weight). It then refines the initial solution by looking at the two highest-order bits. It progressively looks at more and more high-order bits, refining the solution each time, until it has examined all bits and computed the correct solution.

In this problem, we examine an algorithm for computing the shortest paths from a single source by scaling edge weights. We are given a directed graph $G = (V, E)$ with nonnegative integer edge weights w. Let $W = \max_{(u,v) \in E} \{w(u, v)\}$. Our goal is to develop an algorithm that runs in $O(E \lg W)$ time. We assume that all vertices are reachable from the source.

The algorithm uncovers the bits in the binary representation of the edge weights one at a time, from the most significant bit to the least significant bit. Specifically, let $k = \lceil \lg(W + 1) \rceil$ be the number of bits in the binary representation of W, and for $i = 1, 2, \ldots, k$, let $w_i(u, v) = \lfloor w(u, v)/2^{k-i} \rfloor$. That is, $w_i(u, v)$ is the "scaled-down" version of $w(u, v)$ given by the i most significant bits of $w(u, v)$. (Thus, $w_k(u, v) = w(u, v)$ for all $(u, v) \in E$.) For example, if $k = 5$ and $w(u, v) = 25$, which has the binary representation $\langle 11001 \rangle$, then $w_3(u, v) = \langle 110 \rangle = 6$. As another example with $k = 5$, if $w(u, v) = \langle 00100 \rangle = 4$, then $w_3(u, v) = \langle 001 \rangle = 1$. Let us define $\delta_i(u, v)$ as the shortest-path weight from vertex u to vertex v using weight function w_i. Thus, $\delta_k(u, v) = \delta(u, v)$ for all $u, v \in V$. For a given source vertex s, the scaling algorithm first computes the shortest-path weights $\delta_1(s, v)$ for all $v \in V$, then computes $\delta_2(s, v)$ for all $v \in V$, and so on, until it computes $\delta_k(s, v)$ for all $v \in V$. We assume throughout that $|E| \geq |V| - 1$, and we shall see that computing δ_i from δ_{i-1} takes $O(E)$ time, so that the entire algorithm takes $O(kE) = O(E \lg W)$ time.

a. Suppose that for all vertices $v \in V$, we have $\delta(s, v) \leq |E|$. Show that we can compute $\delta(s, v)$ for all $v \in V$ in $O(E)$ time.

b. Show that we can compute $\delta_1(s, v)$ for all $v \in V$ in $O(E)$ time.

Let us now focus on computing δ_i from δ_{i-1}.

c. Prove that for $i = 2, 3, \ldots, k$, we have either $w_i(u, v) = 2w_{i-1}(u, v)$ or $w_i(u, v) = 2w_{i-1}(u, v) + 1$. Then, prove that

$$2\delta_{i-1}(s, v) \leq \delta_i(s, v) \leq 2\delta_{i-1}(s, v) + |V| - 1$$

for all $v \in V$.

d. Define for $i = 2, 3, \ldots, k$ and all $(u, v) \in E$,

$$\hat{w}_i(u, v) = w_i(u, v) + 2\delta_{i-1}(s, u) - 2\delta_{i-1}(s, v).$$

Prove that for $i = 2, 3, \ldots, k$ and all $u, v \in V$, the "reweighted" value $\hat{w}_i(u, v)$ of edge (u, v) is a nonnegative integer.

e. Now, define $\hat{\delta}_i(s, v)$ as the shortest-path weight from s to v using the weight function $\hat{w}_i$. Prove that for $i = 2, 3, \ldots, k$ and all $v \in V$,

$$\delta_i(s, v) = \hat{\delta}_i(s, v) + 2\delta_{i-1}(s, v)$$

and that $\hat{\delta}_i(s, v) \leq |E|$.

f. Show how to compute $\delta_i(s, v)$ from $\delta_{i-1}(s, v)$ for all $v \in V$ in $O(E)$ time, and conclude that we can compute $\delta(s, v)$ for all $v \in V$ in $O(E \lg W)$ time.

24-5   *Karp's minimum mean-weight cycle algorithm*

Let $G = (V, E)$ be a directed graph with weight function $w : E \rightarrow \mathbb{R}$, and let $n = |V|$. We define the **mean weight** of a cycle $c = \langle e_1, e_2, \ldots, e_k \rangle$ of edges in E to be

$$\mu(c) = \frac{1}{k} \sum_{i=1}^{k} w(e_i).$$

Let $\mu^* = \min_c \mu(c)$, where c ranges over all directed cycles in G. We call a cycle c for which $\mu(c) = \mu^*$ a **minimum mean-weight cycle**. This problem investigates an efficient algorithm for computing μ^*.

Assume without loss of generality that every vertex $v \in V$ is reachable from a source vertex $s \in V$. Let $\delta(s, v)$ be the weight of a shortest path from s to v, and let $\delta_k(s, v)$ be the weight of a shortest path from s to v consisting of *exactly* k edges. If there is no path from s to v with exactly k edges, then $\delta_k(s, v) = \infty$.

a. Show that if $\mu^* = 0$, then G contains no negative-weight cycles and $\delta(s, v) = \min_{0 \le k \le n-1} \delta_k(s, v)$ for all vertices $v \in V$.

b. Show that if $\mu^* = 0$, then

$$\max_{0 \le k \le n-1} \frac{\delta_n(s, v) - \delta_k(s, v)}{n - k} \ge 0$$

for all vertices $v \in V$. (*Hint:* Use both properties from part (a).)

c. Let c be a 0-weight cycle, and let u and v be any two vertices on c. Suppose that $\mu^* = 0$ and that the weight of the simple path from u to v along the cycle is x. Prove that $\delta(s, v) = \delta(s, u) + x$. (*Hint:* The weight of the simple path from v to u along the cycle is $-x$.)

d. Show that if $\mu^* = 0$, then on each minimum mean-weight cycle there exists a vertex v such that

$$\max_{0 \le k \le n-1} \frac{\delta_n(s, v) - \delta_k(s, v)}{n - k} = 0 \;.$$

(*Hint:* Show how to extend a shortest path to any vertex on a minimum mean-weight cycle along the cycle to make a shortest path to the next vertex on the cycle.)

e. Show that if $\mu^* = 0$, then

$$\min_{v \in V} \max_{0 \le k \le n-1} \frac{\delta_n(s, v) - \delta_k(s, v)}{n - k} = 0 \;.$$

f. Show that if we add a constant t to the weight of each edge of G, then μ^* increases by t. Use this fact to show that

$$\mu^* = \min_{v \in V} \max_{0 \le k \le n-1} \frac{\delta_n(s, v) - \delta_k(s, v)}{n - k} \;.$$

g. Give an $O(VE)$-time algorithm to compute μ^*.

24-6   *Bitonic shortest paths*

A sequence is ***bitonic*** if it monotonically increases and then monotonically decreases, or if by a circular shift it monotonically increases and then monotonically decreases. For example the sequences $\langle 1, 4, 6, 8, 3, -2 \rangle$, $\langle 9, 2, -4, -10, -5 \rangle$, and $\langle 1, 2, 3, 4 \rangle$ are bitonic, but $\langle 1, 3, 12, 4, 2, 10 \rangle$ is not bitonic. (See Problem 15-3 for the bitonic euclidean traveling-salesman problem.)

Suppose that we are given a directed graph $G = (V, E)$ with weight function $w : E \to \mathbb{R}$, where all edge weights are unique, and we wish to find single-source shortest paths from a source vertex s. We are given one additional piece of information: for each vertex $v \in V$, the weights of the edges along any shortest path from s to v form a bitonic sequence.

Give the most efficient algorithm you can to solve this problem, and analyze its running time.

Chapter notes

Dijkstra's algorithm [88] appeared in 1959, but it contained no mention of a priority queue. The Bellman-Ford algorithm is based on separate algorithms by Bellman [38] and Ford [109]. Bellman describes the relation of shortest paths to difference constraints. Lawler [224] describes the linear-time algorithm for shortest paths in a dag, which he considers part of the folklore.

When edge weights are relatively small nonnegative integers, we have more efficient algorithms to solve the single-source shortest-paths problem. The sequence of values returned by the EXTRACT-MIN calls in Dijkstra's algorithm monotonically increases over time. As discussed in the chapter notes for Chapter 6, in this case several data structures can implement the various priority-queue operations more efficiently than a binary heap or a Fibonacci heap. Ahuja, Mehlhorn, Orlin, and Tarjan [8] give an algorithm that runs in $O(E + V \sqrt{\lg W})$ time on graphs with nonnegative edge weights, where W is the largest weight of any edge in the graph. The best bounds are by Thorup [337], who gives an algorithm that runs in $O(E \lg \lg V)$ time, and by Raman [291], who gives an algorithm that runs in $O\left(E + V \min \left\{(\lg V)^{1/3+\epsilon}, (\lg W)^{1/4+\epsilon}\right\}\right)$ time. These two algorithms use an amount of space that depends on the word size of the underlying machine. Although the amount of space used can be unbounded in the size of the input, it can be reduced to be linear in the size of the input using randomized hashing.

For undirected graphs with integer weights, Thorup [336] gives an $O(V + E)$-time algorithm for single-source shortest paths. In contrast to the algorithms mentioned in the previous paragraph, this algorithm is not an implementation of Dijkstra's algorithm, since the sequence of values returned by EXTRACT-MIN calls does not monotonically increase over time.

For graphs with negative edge weights, an algorithm due to Gabow and Tarjan [122] runs in $O(\sqrt{V}E\lg(VW))$ time, and one by Goldberg [137] runs in $O(\sqrt{V}E\lg W)$ time, where $W = \max_{(u,v)\in E}\{|w(u,v)|\}$.

Cherkassky, Goldberg, and Radzik [64] conducted extensive experiments comparing various shortest-path algorithms.

25   All-Pairs Shortest Paths

In this chapter, we consider the problem of finding shortest paths between all pairs of vertices in a graph. This problem might arise in making a table of distances between all pairs of cities for a road atlas. As in Chapter 24, we are given a weighted, directed graph $G = (V, E)$ with a weight function $w : E \rightarrow \mathbb{R}$ that maps edges to real-valued weights. We wish to find, for every pair of vertices $u, v \in V$, a shortest (least-weight) path from u to v, where the weight of a path is the sum of the weights of its constituent edges. We typically want the output in tabular form: the entry in u's row and v's column should be the weight of a shortest path from u to v.

We can solve an all-pairs shortest-paths problem by running a single-source shortest-paths algorithm $|V|$ times, once for each vertex as the source. If all edge weights are nonnegative, we can use Dijkstra's algorithm. If we use the linear-array implementation of the min-priority queue, the running time is $O(V^3 + VE) = O(V^3)$. The binary min-heap implementation of the min-priority queue yields a running time of $O(VE \lg V)$, which is an improvement if the graph is sparse. Alternatively, we can implement the min-priority queue with a Fibonacci heap, yielding a running time of $O(V^2 \lg V + VE)$.

If the graph has negative-weight edges, we cannot use Dijkstra's algorithm. Instead, we must run the slower Bellman-Ford algorithm once from each vertex. The resulting running time is $O(V^2 E)$, which on a dense graph is $O(V^4)$. In this chapter we shall see how to do better. We also investigate the relation of the all-pairs shortest-paths problem to matrix multiplication and study its algebraic structure.

Unlike the single-source algorithms, which assume an adjacency-list representation of the graph, most of the algorithms in this chapter use an adjacency-matrix representation. (Johnson's algorithm for sparse graphs, in Section 25.3, uses adjacency lists.) For convenience, we assume that the vertices are numbered $1, 2, \ldots, |V|$, so that the input is an $n \times n$ matrix W representing the edge weights of an n-vertex directed graph $G = (V, E)$. That is, $W = (w_{ij})$, where

$$w_{ij} = \begin{cases} 0 & \text{if } i = j\ , \\ \text{the weight of directed edge } (i, j) & \text{if } i \neq j \text{ and } (i, j) \in E\ , \\ \infty & \text{if } i \neq j \text{ and } (i, j) \notin E\ . \end{cases} \quad (25.1)$$

We allow negative-weight edges, but we assume for the time being that the input graph contains no negative-weight cycles.

The tabular output of the all-pairs shortest-paths algorithms presented in this chapter is an $n \times n$ matrix $D = (d_{ij})$, where entry d_{ij} contains the weight of a shortest path from vertex i to vertex j. That is, if we let $\delta(i, j)$ denote the shortest-path weight from vertex i to vertex j (as in Chapter 24), then $d_{ij} = \delta(i, j)$ at termination.

To solve the all-pairs shortest-paths problem on an input adjacency matrix, we need to compute not only the shortest-path weights but also a **predecessor matrix** $\Pi = (\pi_{ij})$, where π_{ij} is NIL if either $i = j$ or there is no path from i to j, and otherwise π_{ij} is the predecessor of j on some shortest path from i. Just as the predecessor subgraph G_π from Chapter 24 is a shortest-paths tree for a given source vertex, the subgraph induced by the ith row of the Π matrix should be a shortest-paths tree with root i. For each vertex $i \in V$, we define the **predecessor subgraph** of G for i as $G_{\pi,i} = (V_{\pi,i}, E_{\pi,i})$, where

$$V_{\pi,i} = \{j \in V : \pi_{ij} \neq \text{NIL}\} \cup \{i\}$$

and

$$E_{\pi,i} = \{(\pi_{ij}, j) : j \in V_{\pi,i} - \{i\}\}\ .$$

If $G_{\pi,i}$ is a shortest-paths tree, then the following procedure, which is a modified version of the PRINT-PATH procedure from Chapter 22, prints a shortest path from vertex i to vertex j.

PRINT-ALL-PAIRS-SHORTEST-PATH(Π, i, j)

1 **if** $i == j$
2   print i
3 **elseif** $\pi_{ij} ==$ NIL
4   print "no path from" i "to" j "exists"
5 **else** PRINT-ALL-PAIRS-SHORTEST-PATH(Π, i, π_{ij})
6   print j

In order to highlight the essential features of the all-pairs algorithms in this chapter, we won't cover the creation and properties of predecessor matrices as extensively as we dealt with predecessor subgraphs in Chapter 24. Some of the exercises cover the basics.

Chapter outline

Section 25.1 presents a dynamic-programming algorithm based on matrix multiplication to solve the all-pairs shortest-paths problem. Using the technique of "repeated squaring," we can achieve a running time of $\Theta(V^3 \lg V)$. Section 25.2 gives another dynamic-programming algorithm, the Floyd-Warshall algorithm, which runs in time $\Theta(V^3)$. Section 25.2 also covers the problem of finding the transitive closure of a directed graph, which is related to the all-pairs shortest-paths problem. Finally, Section 25.3 presents Johnson's algorithm, which solves the all-pairs shortest-paths problem in $O(V^2 \lg V + VE)$ time and is a good choice for large, sparse graphs.

Before proceeding, we need to establish some conventions for adjacency-matrix representations. First, we shall generally assume that the input graph $G = (V, E)$ has n vertices, so that $n = |V|$. Second, we shall use the convention of denoting matrices by uppercase letters, such as W, L, or D, and their individual elements by subscripted lowercase letters, such as w_{ij}, l_{ij}, or d_{ij}. Some matrices will have parenthesized superscripts, as in $L^{(m)} = \left(l_{ij}^{(m)}\right)$ or $D^{(m)} = \left(d_{ij}^{(m)}\right)$, to indicate iterates. Finally, for a given $n \times n$ matrix A, we shall assume that the value of n is stored in the attribute $A.rows$.

25.1   Shortest paths and matrix multiplication

This section presents a dynamic-programming algorithm for the all-pairs shortest-paths problem on a directed graph $G = (V, E)$. Each major loop of the dynamic program will invoke an operation that is very similar to matrix multiplication, so that the algorithm will look like repeated matrix multiplication. We shall start by developing a $\Theta(V^4)$-time algorithm for the all-pairs shortest-paths problem and then improve its running time to $\Theta(V^3 \lg V)$.

Before proceeding, let us briefly recap the steps given in Chapter 15 for developing a dynamic-programming algorithm.

1. Characterize the structure of an optimal solution.

2. Recursively define the value of an optimal solution.

3. Compute the value of an optimal solution in a bottom-up fashion.

We reserve the fourth step—constructing an optimal solution from computed information—for the exercises.

The structure of a shortest path

We start by characterizing the structure of an optimal solution. For the all-pairs shortest-paths problem on a graph $G = (V, E)$, we have proven (Lemma 24.1) that all subpaths of a shortest path are shortest paths. Suppose that we represent the graph by an adjacency matrix $W = (w_{ij})$. Consider a shortest path p from vertex i to vertex j, and suppose that p contains at most m edges. Assuming that there are no negative-weight cycles, m is finite. If $i = j$, then p has weight 0 and no edges. If vertices i and j are distinct, then we decompose path p into $i \overset{p'}{\leadsto} k \to j$, where path p' now contains at most $m - 1$ edges. By Lemma 24.1, p' is a shortest path from i to k, and so $\delta(i, j) = \delta(i, k) + w_{kj}$.

A recursive solution to the all-pairs shortest-paths problem

Now, let $l_{ij}^{(m)}$ be the minimum weight of any path from vertex i to vertex j that contains at most m edges. When $m = 0$, there is a shortest path from i to j with no edges if and only if $i = j$. Thus,

$$l_{ij}^{(0)} = \begin{cases} 0 & \text{if } i = j, \\ \infty & \text{if } i \neq j. \end{cases}$$

For $m \geq 1$, we compute $l_{ij}^{(m)}$ as the minimum of $l_{ij}^{(m-1)}$ (the weight of a shortest path from i to j consisting of at most $m - 1$ edges) and the minimum weight of any path from i to j consisting of at most m edges, obtained by looking at all possible predecessors k of j. Thus, we recursively define

$$l_{ij}^{(m)} = \min \left(l_{ij}^{(m-1)}, \min_{1 \leq k \leq n} \{ l_{ik}^{(m-1)} + w_{kj} \} \right)$$
$$= \min_{1 \leq k \leq n} \{ l_{ik}^{(m-1)} + w_{kj} \} . \tag{25.2}$$

The latter equality follows since $w_{jj} = 0$ for all j.

What are the actual shortest-path weights $\delta(i, j)$? If the graph contains no negative-weight cycles, then for every pair of vertices i and j for which $\delta(i, j) < \infty$, there is a shortest path from i to j that is simple and thus contains at most $n - 1$ edges. A path from vertex i to vertex j with more than $n - 1$ edges cannot have lower weight than a shortest path from i to j. The actual shortest-path weights are therefore given by

$$\delta(i, j) = l_{ij}^{(n-1)} = l_{ij}^{(n)} = l_{ij}^{(n+1)} = \cdots . \tag{25.3}$$

Computing the shortest-path weights bottom up

Taking as our input the matrix $W = (w_{ij})$, we now compute a series of matrices $L^{(1)}, L^{(2)}, \ldots, L^{(n-1)}$, where for $m = 1, 2, \ldots, n-1$, we have $L^{(m)} = \left(l_{ij}^{(m)}\right)$. The final matrix $L^{(n-1)}$ contains the actual shortest-path weights. Observe that $l_{ij}^{(1)} = w_{ij}$ for all vertices $i, j \in V$, and so $L^{(1)} = W$.

The heart of the algorithm is the following procedure, which, given matrices $L^{(m-1)}$ and W, returns the matrix $L^{(m)}$. That is, it extends the shortest paths computed so far by one more edge.

EXTEND-SHORTEST-PATHS(L, W)

```
1   n = L.rows
2   let L' = (l'_ij) be a new n × n matrix
3   for i = 1 to n
4       for j = 1 to n
5           l'_ij = ∞
6           for k = 1 to n
7               l'_ij = min(l'_ij, l_ik + w_kj)
8   return L'
```

The procedure computes a matrix $L' = (l'_{ij})$, which it returns at the end. It does so by computing equation (25.2) for all i and j, using L for $L^{(m-1)}$ and L' for $L^{(m)}$. (It is written without the superscripts to make its input and output matrices independent of m.) Its running time is $\Theta(n^3)$ due to the three nested **for** loops.

Now we can see the relation to matrix multiplication. Suppose we wish to compute the matrix product $C = A \cdot B$ of two $n \times n$ matrices A and B. Then, for $i, j = 1, 2, \ldots, n$, we compute

$$c_{ij} = \sum_{k=1}^{n} a_{ik} \cdot b_{kj} \,. \tag{25.4}$$

Observe that if we make the substitutions

$$
\begin{aligned}
l^{(m-1)} &\rightarrow a \,, \\
w &\rightarrow b \,, \\
l^{(m)} &\rightarrow c \,, \\
\min &\rightarrow + \,, \\
+ &\rightarrow \cdot
\end{aligned}
$$

in equation (25.2), we obtain equation (25.4). Thus, if we make these changes to EXTEND-SHORTEST-PATHS and also replace ∞ (the identity for min) by 0 (the identity for $+$), we obtain the same $\Theta(n^3)$-time procedure for multiplying square matrices that we saw in Section 4.2:

SQUARE-MATRIX-MULTIPLY(A, B)

```
1   n = A.rows
2   let C be a new n × n matrix
3   for i = 1 to n
4       for j = 1 to n
5           c_ij = 0
6           for k = 1 to n
7               c_ij = c_ij + a_ik · b_kj
8   return C
```

Returning to the all-pairs shortest-paths problem, we compute the shortest-path weights by extending shortest paths edge by edge. Letting $A \cdot B$ denote the matrix "product" returned by EXTEND-SHORTEST-PATHS(A, B), we compute the sequence of $n - 1$ matrices

$$
\begin{aligned}
L^{(1)} &= L^{(0)} \cdot W &= W \,, \\
L^{(2)} &= L^{(1)} \cdot W &= W^2 \,, \\
L^{(3)} &= L^{(2)} \cdot W &= W^3 \,, \\
&\qquad\vdots \\
L^{(n-1)} &= L^{(n-2)} \cdot W &= W^{n-1} \,.
\end{aligned}
$$

As we argued above, the matrix $L^{(n-1)} = W^{n-1}$ contains the shortest-path weights. The following procedure computes this sequence in $\Theta(n^4)$ time.

SLOW-ALL-PAIRS-SHORTEST-PATHS(W)

```
1   n = W.rows
2   L^(1) = W
3   for m = 2 to n − 1
4       let L^(m) be a new n × n matrix
5       L^(m) = EXTEND-SHORTEST-PATHS(L^(m−1), W)
6   return L^(n−1)
```

Figure 25.1 shows a graph and the matrices $L^{(m)}$ computed by the procedure SLOW-ALL-PAIRS-SHORTEST-PATHS.

Improving the running time

Our goal, however, is not to compute *all* the $L^{(m)}$ matrices: we are interested only in matrix $L^{(n-1)}$. Recall that in the absence of negative-weight cycles, equa-

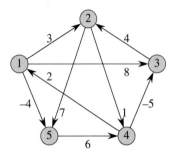

$$L^{(1)} = \begin{pmatrix} 0 & 3 & 8 & \infty & -4 \\ \infty & 0 & \infty & 1 & 7 \\ \infty & 4 & 0 & \infty & \infty \\ 2 & \infty & -5 & 0 & \infty \\ \infty & \infty & \infty & 6 & 0 \end{pmatrix} \qquad L^{(2)} = \begin{pmatrix} 0 & 3 & 8 & 2 & -4 \\ 3 & 0 & -4 & 1 & 7 \\ \infty & 4 & 0 & 5 & 11 \\ 2 & -1 & -5 & 0 & -2 \\ 8 & \infty & 1 & 6 & 0 \end{pmatrix}$$

$$L^{(3)} = \begin{pmatrix} 0 & 3 & -3 & 2 & -4 \\ 3 & 0 & -4 & 1 & -1 \\ 7 & 4 & 0 & 5 & 11 \\ 2 & -1 & -5 & 0 & -2 \\ 8 & 5 & 1 & 6 & 0 \end{pmatrix} \qquad L^{(4)} = \begin{pmatrix} 0 & 1 & -3 & 2 & -4 \\ 3 & 0 & -4 & 1 & -1 \\ 7 & 4 & 0 & 5 & 3 \\ 2 & -1 & -5 & 0 & -2 \\ 8 & 5 & 1 & 6 & 0 \end{pmatrix}$$

Figure 25.1   A directed graph and the sequence of matrices $L^{(m)}$ computed by SLOW-ALL-PAIRS-SHORTEST-PATHS. You might want to verify that $L^{(5)}$, defined as $L^{(4)} \cdot W$, equals $L^{(4)}$, and thus $L^{(m)} = L^{(4)}$ for all $m \geq 4$.

tion (25.3) implies $L^{(m)} = L^{(n-1)}$ for all integers $m \geq n - 1$. Just as traditional matrix multiplication is associative, so is matrix multiplication defined by the EXTEND-SHORTEST-PATHS procedure (see Exercise 25.1-4). Therefore, we can compute $L^{(n-1)}$ with only $\lceil \lg(n-1) \rceil$ matrix products by computing the sequence

$$
\begin{aligned}
L^{(1)} &= W, \\
L^{(2)} &= W^2 &= W \cdot W, \\
L^{(4)} &= W^4 &= W^2 \cdot W^2, \\
L^{(8)} &= W^8 &= W^4 \cdot W^4, \\
&\;\;\vdots \\
L^{(2^{\lceil \lg(n-1) \rceil})} &= W^{2^{\lceil \lg(n-1) \rceil}} &= W^{2^{\lceil \lg(n-1) \rceil -1}} \cdot W^{2^{\lceil \lg(n-1) \rceil -1}}.
\end{aligned}
$$

Since $2^{\lceil \lg(n-1) \rceil} \geq n - 1$, the final product $L^{(2^{\lceil \lg(n-1) \rceil})}$ is equal to $L^{(n-1)}$.

The following procedure computes the above sequence of matrices by using this technique of ***repeated squaring***.

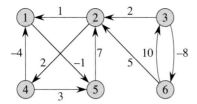

Figure 25.2 A weighted, directed graph for use in Exercises 25.1-1, 25.2-1, and 25.3-1.

FASTER-ALL-PAIRS-SHORTEST-PATHS(W)

```
1   n = W.rows
2   L⁽¹⁾ = W
3   m = 1
4   while m < n − 1
5       let L⁽²ᵐ⁾ be a new n × n matrix
6       L⁽²ᵐ⁾ = EXTEND-SHORTEST-PATHS(L⁽ᵐ⁾, L⁽ᵐ⁾)
7       m = 2m
8   return L⁽ᵐ⁾
```

In each iteration of the **while** loop of lines 4–7, we compute $L^{(2m)} = \left(L^{(m)}\right)^2$, starting with $m = 1$. At the end of each iteration, we double the value of m. The final iteration computes $L^{(n-1)}$ by actually computing $L^{(2m)}$ for some $n - 1 \le 2m < 2n - 2$. By equation (25.3), $L^{(2m)} = L^{(n-1)}$. The next time the test in line 4 is performed, m has been doubled, so now $m \ge n - 1$, the test fails, and the procedure returns the last matrix it computed.

Because each of the $\lceil \lg(n-1) \rceil$ matrix products takes $\Theta(n^3)$ time, FASTER-ALL-PAIRS-SHORTEST-PATHS runs in $\Theta(n^3 \lg n)$ time. Observe that the code is tight, containing no elaborate data structures, and the constant hidden in the Θ-notation is therefore small.

Exercises

25.1-1
Run SLOW-ALL-PAIRS-SHORTEST-PATHS on the weighted, directed graph of Figure 25.2, showing the matrices that result for each iteration of the loop. Then do the same for FASTER-ALL-PAIRS-SHORTEST-PATHS.

25.1-2
Why do we require that $w_{ii} = 0$ for all $1 \le i \le n$?

25.1-3

What does the matrix

$$
L^{(0)} = \begin{pmatrix}
0 & \infty & \infty & \cdots & \infty \\
\infty & 0 & \infty & \cdots & \infty \\
\infty & \infty & 0 & \cdots & \infty \\
\vdots & \vdots & \vdots & \ddots & \vdots \\
\infty & \infty & \infty & \cdots & 0
\end{pmatrix}
$$

used in the shortest-paths algorithms correspond to in regular matrix multiplication?

25.1-4

Show that matrix multiplication defined by EXTEND-SHORTEST-PATHS is associative.

25.1-5

Show how to express the single-source shortest-paths problem as a product of matrices and a vector. Describe how evaluating this product corresponds to a Bellman-Ford-like algorithm (see Section 24.1).

25.1-6

Suppose we also wish to compute the vertices on shortest paths in the algorithms of this section. Show how to compute the predecessor matrix Π from the completed matrix L of shortest-path weights in $O(n^3)$ time.

25.1-7

We can also compute the vertices on shortest paths as we compute the shortest-path weights. Define $\pi_{ij}^{(m)}$ as the predecessor of vertex j on any minimum-weight path from i to j that contains at most m edges. Modify the EXTEND-SHORTEST-PATHS and SLOW-ALL-PAIRS-SHORTEST-PATHS procedures to compute the matrices $\Pi^{(1)}, \Pi^{(2)}, \ldots, \Pi^{(n-1)}$ as the matrices $L^{(1)}, L^{(2)}, \ldots, L^{(n-1)}$ are computed.

25.1-8

The FASTER-ALL-PAIRS-SHORTEST-PATHS procedure, as written, requires us to store $\lceil \lg(n-1) \rceil$ matrices, each with n^2 elements, for a total space requirement of $\Theta(n^2 \lg n)$. Modify the procedure to require only $\Theta(n^2)$ space by using only two $n \times n$ matrices.

25.1-9

Modify FASTER-ALL-PAIRS-SHORTEST-PATHS so that it can determine whether the graph contains a negative-weight cycle.

25.1-10

Give an efficient algorithm to find the length (number of edges) of a minimum-length negative-weight cycle in a graph.

25.2 The Floyd-Warshall algorithm

In this section, we shall use a different dynamic-programming formulation to solve the all-pairs shortest-paths problem on a directed graph $G = (V, E)$. The resulting algorithm, known as the *Floyd-Warshall algorithm*, runs in $\Theta(V^3)$ time. As before, negative-weight edges may be present, but we assume that there are no negative-weight cycles. As in Section 25.1, we follow the dynamic-programming process to develop the algorithm. After studying the resulting algorithm, we present a similar method for finding the transitive closure of a directed graph.

The structure of a shortest path

In the Floyd-Warshall algorithm, we characterize the structure of a shortest path differently from how we characterized it in Section 25.1. The Floyd-Warshall algorithm considers the intermediate vertices of a shortest path, where an *intermediate* vertex of a simple path $p = \langle v_1, v_2, \ldots, v_l \rangle$ is any vertex of p other than v_1 or v_l, that is, any vertex in the set $\{v_2, v_3, \ldots, v_{l-1}\}$.

The Floyd-Warshall algorithm relies on the following observation. Under our assumption that the vertices of G are $V = \{1, 2, \ldots, n\}$, let us consider a subset $\{1, 2, \ldots, k\}$ of vertices for some k. For any pair of vertices $i, j \in V$, consider all paths from i to j whose intermediate vertices are all drawn from $\{1, 2, \ldots, k\}$, and let p be a minimum-weight path from among them. (Path p is simple.) The Floyd-Warshall algorithm exploits a relationship between path p and shortest paths from i to j with all intermediate vertices in the set $\{1, 2, \ldots, k - 1\}$. The relationship depends on whether or not k is an intermediate vertex of path p.

- If k is not an intermediate vertex of path p, then all intermediate vertices of path p are in the set $\{1, 2, \ldots, k - 1\}$. Thus, a shortest path from vertex i to vertex j with all intermediate vertices in the set $\{1, 2, \ldots, k - 1\}$ is also a shortest path from i to j with all intermediate vertices in the set $\{1, 2, \ldots, k\}$.

- If k is an intermediate vertex of path p, then we decompose p into $i \overset{p_1}{\rightsquigarrow} k \overset{p_2}{\rightsquigarrow} j$, as Figure 25.3 illustrates. By Lemma 24.1, p_1 is a shortest path from i to k with all intermediate vertices in the set $\{1, 2, \ldots, k\}$. In fact, we can make a slightly stronger statement. Because vertex k is not an intermediate vertex of path p_1, all intermediate vertices of p_1 are in the set $\{1, 2, \ldots, k - 1\}$. There-all intermediate vertices in $\{1, 2, \ldots, k-1\}$ all intermediate vertices in $\{1, 2, \ldots, k-1\}$

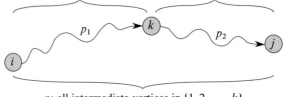

p: all intermediate vertices in $\{1, 2, \ldots, k\}$

Figure 25.3 Path p is a shortest path from vertex i to vertex j, and k is the highest-numbered intermediate vertex of p. Path p_1, the portion of path p from vertex i to vertex k, has all intermediate vertices in the set $\{1, 2, \ldots, k-1\}$. The same holds for path p_2 from vertex k to vertex j.

fore, p_1 is a shortest path from i to k with all intermediate vertices in the set $\{1, 2, \ldots, k-1\}$. Similarly, p_2 is a shortest path from vertex k to vertex j with all intermediate vertices in the set $\{1, 2, \ldots, k-1\}$.

A recursive solution to the all-pairs shortest-paths problem

Based on the above observations, we define a recursive formulation of shortest-path estimates that differs from the one in Section 25.1. Let $d_{ij}^{(k)}$ be the weight of a shortest path from vertex i to vertex j for which all intermediate vertices are in the set $\{1, 2, \ldots, k\}$. When $k = 0$, a path from vertex i to vertex j with no intermediate vertex numbered higher than 0 has no intermediate vertices at all. Such a path has at most one edge, and hence $d_{ij}^{(0)} = w_{ij}$. Following the above discussion, we define $d_{ij}^{(k)}$ recursively by

$$d_{ij}^{(k)} = \begin{cases} w_{ij} & \text{if } k = 0, \\ \min\left(d_{ij}^{(k-1)}, d_{ik}^{(k-1)} + d_{kj}^{(k-1)}\right) & \text{if } k \geq 1. \end{cases} \tag{25.5}$$

Because for any path, all intermediate vertices are in the set $\{1, 2, \ldots, n\}$, the matrix $D^{(n)} = \left(d_{ij}^{(n)}\right)$ gives the final answer: $d_{ij}^{(n)} = \delta(i, j)$ for all $i, j \in V$.

Computing the shortest-path weights bottom up

Based on recurrence (25.5), we can use the following bottom-up procedure to compute the values $d_{ij}^{(k)}$ in order of increasing values of k. Its input is an $n \times n$ matrix W defined as in equation (25.1). The procedure returns the matrix $D^{(n)}$ of shortest-path weights.

FLOYD-WARSHALL(W)

1   $n = W.rows$
2   $D^{(0)} = W$
3   **for** $k = 1$ **to** n
4   let $D^{(k)} = \left(d_{ij}^{(k)}\right)$ be a new $n \times n$ matrix
5   **for** $i = 1$ **to** n
6   **for** $j = 1$ **to** n
7               $d_{ij}^{(k)} = \min\left(d_{ij}^{(k-1)}, d_{ik}^{(k-1)} + d_{kj}^{(k-1)}\right)$
8   **return** $D^{(n)}$

Figure 25.4 shows the matrices $D^{(k)}$ computed by the Floyd-Warshall algorithm for the graph in Figure 25.1.

The running time of the Floyd-Warshall algorithm is determined by the triply nested **for** loops of lines 3–7. Because each execution of line 7 takes $O(1)$ time, the algorithm runs in time $\Theta(n^3)$. As in the final algorithm in Section 25.1, the code is tight, with no elaborate data structures, and so the constant hidden in the Θ-notation is small. Thus, the Floyd-Warshall algorithm is quite practical for even moderate-sized input graphs.

Constructing a shortest path

There are a variety of different methods for constructing shortest paths in the Floyd-Warshall algorithm. One way is to compute the matrix D of shortest-path weights and then construct the predecessor matrix Π from the D matrix. Exercise 25.1-6 asks you to implement this method so that it runs in $O(n^3)$ time. Given the predecessor matrix Π, the PRINT-ALL-PAIRS-SHORTEST-PATH procedure will print the vertices on a given shortest path.

Alternatively, we can compute the predecessor matrix Π while the algorithm computes the matrices $D^{(k)}$. Specifically, we compute a sequence of matrices $\Pi^{(0)}, \Pi^{(1)}, \ldots, \Pi^{(n)}$, where $\Pi = \Pi^{(n)}$ and we define $\pi_{ij}^{(k)}$ as the predecessor of vertex j on a shortest path from vertex i with all intermediate vertices in the set $\{1, 2, \ldots, k\}$.

We can give a recursive formulation of $\pi_{ij}^{(k)}$. When $k = 0$, a shortest path from i to j has no intermediate vertices at all. Thus,

$$\pi_{ij}^{(0)} = \begin{cases} \text{NIL} & \text{if } i = j \text{ or } w_{ij} = \infty\,, \\ i & \text{if } i \neq j \text{ and } w_{ij} < \infty\,. \end{cases} \tag{25.6}$$

For $k \geq 1$, if we take the path $i \rightsquigarrow k \rightsquigarrow j$, where $k \neq j$, then the predecessor of j we choose is the same as the predecessor of j we chose on a shortest path from k with all intermediate vertices in the set $\{1, 2, \ldots, k - 1\}$. Otherwise, we

$$
D^{(0)} = \begin{pmatrix} 0 & 3 & 8 & \infty & -4 \\ \infty & 0 & \infty & 1 & 7 \\ \infty & 4 & 0 & \infty & \infty \\ 2 & \infty & -5 & 0 & \infty \\ \infty & \infty & \infty & 6 & 0 \end{pmatrix} \qquad \Pi^{(0)} = \begin{pmatrix} \text{NIL} & 1 & 1 & \text{NIL} & 1 \\ \text{NIL} & \text{NIL} & \text{NIL} & 2 & 2 \\ \text{NIL} & 3 & \text{NIL} & \text{NIL} & \text{NIL} \\ 4 & \text{NIL} & 4 & \text{NIL} & \text{NIL} \\ \text{NIL} & \text{NIL} & \text{NIL} & 5 & \text{NIL} \end{pmatrix}
$$

$$
D^{(1)} = \begin{pmatrix} 0 & 3 & 8 & \infty & -4 \\ \infty & 0 & \infty & 1 & 7 \\ \infty & 4 & 0 & \infty & \infty \\ 2 & 5 & -5 & 0 & -2 \\ \infty & \infty & \infty & 6 & 0 \end{pmatrix} \qquad \Pi^{(1)} = \begin{pmatrix} \text{NIL} & 1 & 1 & \text{NIL} & 1 \\ \text{NIL} & \text{NIL} & \text{NIL} & 2 & 2 \\ \text{NIL} & 3 & \text{NIL} & \text{NIL} & \text{NIL} \\ 4 & 1 & 4 & \text{NIL} & 1 \\ \text{NIL} & \text{NIL} & \text{NIL} & 5 & \text{NIL} \end{pmatrix}
$$

$$
D^{(2)} = \begin{pmatrix} 0 & 3 & 8 & 4 & -4 \\ \infty & 0 & \infty & 1 & 7 \\ \infty & 4 & 0 & 5 & 11 \\ 2 & 5 & -5 & 0 & -2 \\ \infty & \infty & \infty & 6 & 0 \end{pmatrix} \qquad \Pi^{(2)} = \begin{pmatrix} \text{NIL} & 1 & 1 & 2 & 1 \\ \text{NIL} & \text{NIL} & \text{NIL} & 2 & 2 \\ \text{NIL} & 3 & \text{NIL} & 2 & 2 \\ 4 & 1 & 4 & \text{NIL} & 1 \\ \text{NIL} & \text{NIL} & \text{NIL} & 5 & \text{NIL} \end{pmatrix}
$$

$$
D^{(3)} = \begin{pmatrix} 0 & 3 & 8 & 4 & -4 \\ \infty & 0 & \infty & 1 & 7 \\ \infty & 4 & 0 & 5 & 11 \\ 2 & -1 & -5 & 0 & -2 \\ \infty & \infty & \infty & 6 & 0 \end{pmatrix} \qquad \Pi^{(3)} = \begin{pmatrix} \text{NIL} & 1 & 1 & 2 & 1 \\ \text{NIL} & \text{NIL} & \text{NIL} & 2 & 2 \\ \text{NIL} & 3 & \text{NIL} & 2 & 2 \\ 4 & 3 & 4 & \text{NIL} & 1 \\ \text{NIL} & \text{NIL} & \text{NIL} & 5 & \text{NIL} \end{pmatrix}
$$

$$
D^{(4)} = \begin{pmatrix} 0 & 3 & -1 & 4 & -4 \\ 3 & 0 & -4 & 1 & -1 \\ 7 & 4 & 0 & 5 & 3 \\ 2 & -1 & -5 & 0 & -2 \\ 8 & 5 & 1 & 6 & 0 \end{pmatrix} \qquad \Pi^{(4)} = \begin{pmatrix} \text{NIL} & 1 & 4 & 2 & 1 \\ 4 & \text{NIL} & 4 & 2 & 1 \\ 4 & 3 & \text{NIL} & 2 & 1 \\ 4 & 3 & 4 & \text{NIL} & 1 \\ 4 & 3 & 4 & 5 & \text{NIL} \end{pmatrix}
$$

$$
D^{(5)} = \begin{pmatrix} 0 & 1 & -3 & 2 & -4 \\ 3 & 0 & -4 & 1 & -1 \\ 7 & 4 & 0 & 5 & 3 \\ 2 & -1 & -5 & 0 & -2 \\ 8 & 5 & 1 & 6 & 0 \end{pmatrix} \qquad \Pi^{(5)} = \begin{pmatrix} \text{NIL} & 3 & 4 & 5 & 1 \\ 4 & \text{NIL} & 4 & 2 & 1 \\ 4 & 3 & \text{NIL} & 2 & 1 \\ 4 & 3 & 4 & \text{NIL} & 1 \\ 4 & 3 & 4 & 5 & \text{NIL} \end{pmatrix}
$$

Figure 25.4 The sequence of matrices $D^{(k)}$ and $\Pi^{(k)}$ computed by the Floyd-Warshall algorithm for the graph in Figure 25.1.

choose the same predecessor of j that we chose on a shortest path from i with all intermediate vertices in the set $\{1, 2, \ldots, k-1\}$. Formally, for $k \geq 1$,

$$
\pi_{ij}^{(k)} = \begin{cases} \pi_{ij}^{(k-1)} & \text{if } d_{ij}^{(k-1)} \leq d_{ik}^{(k-1)} + d_{kj}^{(k-1)} \, , \\ \pi_{kj}^{(k-1)} & \text{if } d_{ij}^{(k-1)} > d_{ik}^{(k-1)} + d_{kj}^{(k-1)} \, . \end{cases} \tag{25.7}
$$

We leave the incorporation of the $\Pi^{(k)}$ matrix computations into the FLOYD-WARSHALL procedure as Exercise 25.2-3. Figure 25.4 shows the sequence of $\Pi^{(k)}$ matrices that the resulting algorithm computes for the graph of Figure 25.1. The exercise also asks for the more difficult task of proving that the predecessor subgraph $G_{\pi,i}$ is a shortest-paths tree with root i. Exercise 25.2-7 asks for yet another way to reconstruct shortest paths.

Transitive closure of a directed graph

Given a directed graph $G = (V, E)$ with vertex set $V = \{1, 2, \ldots, n\}$, we might wish to determine whether G contains a path from i to j for all vertex pairs $i, j \in V$. We define the ***transitive closure*** of G as the graph $G^* = (V, E^*)$, where

$$
E^* = \{(i, j) : \text{there is a path from vertex } i \text{ to vertex } j \text{ in } G\} \, .
$$

One way to compute the transitive closure of a graph in $\Theta(n^3)$ time is to assign a weight of 1 to each edge of E and run the Floyd-Warshall algorithm. If there is a path from vertex i to vertex j, we get $d_{ij} < n$. Otherwise, we get $d_{ij} = \infty$.

There is another, similar way to compute the transitive closure of G in $\Theta(n^3)$ time that can save time and space in practice. This method substitutes the logical operations $\vee$ (logical OR) and $\wedge$ (logical AND) for the arithmetic operations min and $+$ in the Floyd-Warshall algorithm. For $i, j, k = 1, 2, \ldots, n$, we define $t_{ij}^{(k)}$ to be 1 if there exists a path in graph G from vertex i to vertex j with all intermediate vertices in the set $\{1, 2, \ldots, k\}$, and 0 otherwise. We construct the transitive closure $G^* = (V, E^*)$ by putting edge (i, j) into E^* if and only if $t_{ij}^{(n)} = 1$. A recursive definition of $t_{ij}^{(k)}$, analogous to recurrence (25.5), is

$$
t_{ij}^{(0)} = \begin{cases} 0 & \text{if } i \neq j \text{ and } (i, j) \notin E \, , \\ 1 & \text{if } i = j \text{ or } (i, j) \in E \, , \end{cases}
$$

and for $k \geq 1$,

$$
t_{ij}^{(k)} = t_{ij}^{(k-1)} \vee \left(t_{ik}^{(k-1)} \wedge t_{kj}^{(k-1)} \right) \, . \tag{25.8}
$$

As in the Floyd-Warshall algorithm, we compute the matrices $T^{(k)} = \left(t_{ij}^{(k)} \right)$ in order of increasing k.

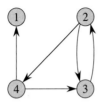

$$T^{(0)} = \begin{pmatrix} 1 & 0 & 0 & 0 \\ 0 & 1 & 1 & 1 \\ 0 & 1 & 1 & 0 \\ 1 & 0 & 1 & 1 \end{pmatrix} \quad T^{(1)} = \begin{pmatrix} 1 & 0 & 0 & 0 \\ 0 & 1 & 1 & 1 \\ 0 & 1 & 1 & 0 \\ 1 & 0 & 1 & 1 \end{pmatrix} \quad T^{(2)} = \begin{pmatrix} 1 & 0 & 0 & 0 \\ 0 & 1 & 1 & 1 \\ 0 & 1 & 1 & 1 \\ 1 & 0 & 1 & 1 \end{pmatrix}$$

$$T^{(3)} = \begin{pmatrix} 1 & 0 & 0 & 0 \\ 0 & 1 & 1 & 1 \\ 0 & 1 & 1 & 1 \\ 1 & 1 & 1 & 1 \end{pmatrix} \quad T^{(4)} = \begin{pmatrix} 1 & 0 & 0 & 0 \\ 1 & 1 & 1 & 1 \\ 1 & 1 & 1 & 1 \\ 1 & 1 & 1 & 1 \end{pmatrix}$$

Figure 25.5   A directed graph and the matrices $T^{(k)}$ computed by the transitive-closure algorithm.

TRANSITIVE-CLOSURE(G)

```
1   n = |G.V|
2   let T^(0) = (t_ij^(0)) be a new n × n matrix
3   for i = 1 to n
4       for j = 1 to n
5           if i == j or (i, j) ∈ G.E
6               t_ij^(0) = 1
7           else t_ij^(0) = 0
8   for k = 1 to n
9       let T^(k) = (t_ij^(k)) be a new n × n matrix
10      for i = 1 to n
11          for j = 1 to n
12              t_ij^(k) = t_ij^(k-1) ∨ (t_ik^(k-1) ∧ t_kj^(k-1))
13  return T^(n)
```

Figure 25.5 shows the matrices $T^{(k)}$ computed by the TRANSITIVE-CLOSURE procedure on a sample graph. The TRANSITIVE-CLOSURE procedure, like the Floyd-Warshall algorithm, runs in $\Theta(n^3)$ time. On some computers, though, logical operations on single-bit values execute faster than arithmetic operations on integer words of data. Moreover, because the direct transitive-closure algorithm uses only boolean values rather than integer values, its space requirement is less than the Floyd-Warshall algorithm's by a factor corresponding to the size of a word of computer storage.

Exercises

25.2-1
Run the Floyd-Warshall algorithm on the weighted, directed graph of Figure 25.2. Show the matrix $D^{(k)}$ that results for each iteration of the outer loop.

25.2-2
Show how to compute the transitive closure using the technique of Section 25.1.

25.2-3
Modify the FLOYD-WARSHALL procedure to compute the $\Pi^{(k)}$ matrices according to equations (25.6) and (25.7). Prove rigorously that for all $i \in V$, the predecessor subgraph $G_{\pi,i}$ is a shortest-paths tree with root i. (*Hint:* To show that $G_{\pi,i}$ is acyclic, first show that $\pi_{ij}^{(k)} = l$ implies $d_{ij}^{(k)} \geq d_{il}^{(k)} + w_{lj}$, according to the definition of $\pi_{ij}^{(k)}$. Then, adapt the proof of Lemma 24.16.)

25.2-4
As it appears above, the Floyd-Warshall algorithm requires $\Theta(n^3)$ space, since we compute $d_{ij}^{(k)}$ for $i, j, k = 1, 2, \ldots, n$. Show that the following procedure, which simply drops all the superscripts, is correct, and thus only $\Theta(n^2)$ space is required.

FLOYD-WARSHALL$'(W)$

```
1   n = W.rows
2   D = W
3   for k = 1 to n
4       for i = 1 to n
5           for j = 1 to n
6               d_ij = min (d_ij, d_ik + d_kj)
7   return D
```

25.2-5
Suppose that we modify the way in which equation (25.7) handles equality:

$$\pi_{ij}^{(k)} = \begin{cases} \pi_{ij}^{(k-1)} & \text{if } d_{ij}^{(k-1)} < d_{ik}^{(k-1)} + d_{kj}^{(k-1)}, \\ \pi_{kj}^{(k-1)} & \text{if } d_{ij}^{(k-1)} \geq d_{ik}^{(k-1)} + d_{kj}^{(k-1)}. \end{cases}$$

Is this alternative definition of the predecessor matrix Π correct?

25.2-6
How can we use the output of the Floyd-Warshall algorithm to detect the presence of a negative-weight cycle?

25.2-7
Another way to reconstruct shortest paths in the Floyd-Warshall algorithm uses values $\phi_{ij}^{(k)}$ for $i, j, k = 1, 2, \ldots, n$, where $\phi_{ij}^{(k)}$ is the highest-numbered intermediate vertex of a shortest path from i to j in which all intermediate vertices are in the set $\{1, 2, \ldots, k\}$. Give a recursive formulation for $\phi_{ij}^{(k)}$, modify the FLOYD-WARSHALL procedure to compute the $\phi_{ij}^{(k)}$ values, and rewrite the PRINT-ALL-PAIRS-SHORTEST-PATH procedure to take the matrix $\Phi = \left(\phi_{ij}^{(n)}\right)$ as an input. How is the matrix Φ like the s table in the matrix-chain multiplication problem of Section 15.2?

25.2-8
Give an $O(VE)$-time algorithm for computing the transitive closure of a directed graph $G = (V, E)$.

25.2-9
Suppose that we can compute the transitive closure of a directed acyclic graph in $f(|V|, |E|)$ time, where f is a monotonically increasing function of $|V|$ and $|E|$. Show that the time to compute the transitive closure $G^* = (V, E^*)$ of a general directed graph $G = (V, E)$ is then $f(|V|, |E|) + O(V + E^*)$.

25.3   Johnson's algorithm for sparse graphs

Johnson's algorithm finds shortest paths between all pairs in $O(V^2 \lg V + VE)$ time. For sparse graphs, it is asymptotically faster than either repeated squaring of matrices or the Floyd-Warshall algorithm. The algorithm either returns a matrix of shortest-path weights for all pairs of vertices or reports that the input graph contains a negative-weight cycle. Johnson's algorithm uses as subroutines both Dijkstra's algorithm and the Bellman-Ford algorithm, which Chapter 24 describes.

Johnson's algorithm uses the technique of ***reweighting***, which works as follows. If all edge weights w in a graph $G = (V, E)$ are nonnegative, we can find shortest paths between all pairs of vertices by running Dijkstra's algorithm once from each vertex; with the Fibonacci-heap min-priority queue, the running time of this all-pairs algorithm is $O(V^2 \lg V + VE)$. If G has negative-weight edges but no negative-weight cycles, we simply compute a new set of nonnegative edge weights that allows us to use the same method. The new set of edge weights $\hat{w}$ must satisfy two important properties:

1. For all pairs of vertices $u, v \in V$, a path p is a shortest path from u to v using weight function w if and only if p is also a shortest path from u to v using weight function $\hat{w}$.

2. For all edges (u, v), the new weight $\hat{w}(u, v)$ is nonnegative.

As we shall see in a moment, we can preprocess G to determine the new weight function $\hat{w}$ in $O(VE)$ time.

Preserving shortest paths by reweighting

The following lemma shows how easily we can reweight the edges to satisfy the first property above. We use δ to denote shortest-path weights derived from weight function w and $\hat{\delta}$ to denote shortest-path weights derived from weight function $\hat{w}$.

Lemma 25.1 (Reweighting does not change shortest paths)
Given a weighted, directed graph $G = (V, E)$ with weight function $w : E \to \mathbb{R}$, let $h : V \to \mathbb{R}$ be any function mapping vertices to real numbers. For each edge $(u, v) \in E$, define

$$\hat{w}(u, v) = w(u, v) + h(u) - h(v) . \tag{25.9}$$

Let $p = \langle v_0, v_1, \ldots, v_k \rangle$ be any path from vertex v_0 to vertex v_k. Then p is a shortest path from v_0 to v_k with weight function w if and only if it is a shortest path with weight function $\hat{w}$. That is, $w(p) = \delta(v_0, v_k)$ if and only if $\hat{w}(p) = \hat{\delta}(v_0, v_k)$. Furthermore, G has a negative-weight cycle using weight function w if and only if G has a negative-weight cycle using weight function $\hat{w}$.

Proof   We start by showing that

$$\hat{w}(p) = w(p) + h(v_0) - h(v_k) . \tag{25.10}$$

We have

$$
\begin{aligned}
\hat{w}(p) &= \sum_{i=1}^{k} \hat{w}(v_{i-1}, v_i) \\
&= \sum_{i=1}^{k} (w(v_{i-1}, v_i) + h(v_{i-1}) - h(v_i)) \\
&= \sum_{i=1}^{k} w(v_{i-1}, v_i) + h(v_0) - h(v_k) \quad \text{(because the sum telescopes)} \\
&= w(p) + h(v_0) - h(v_k) .
\end{aligned}
$$

Therefore, any path p from v_0 to v_k has $\hat{w}(p) = w(p) + h(v_0) - h(v_k)$. Because $h(v_0)$ and $h(v_k)$ do not depend on the path, if one path from v_0 to v_k is shorter than another using weight function w, then it is also shorter using $\hat{w}$. Thus, $w(p) = \delta(v_0, v_k)$ if and only if $\hat{w}(p) = \hat{\delta}(v_0, v_k)$.

Finally, we show that G has a negative-weight cycle using weight function w if and only if G has a negative-weight cycle using weight function $\hat{w}$. Consider any cycle $c = \langle v_0, v_1, \ldots, v_k \rangle$, where $v_0 = v_k$. By equation (25.10),

$$\begin{aligned} \hat{w}(c) &= w(c) + h(v_0) - h(v_k) \\ &= w(c), \end{aligned}$$

and thus c has negative weight using w if and only if it has negative weight using $\hat{w}$. ∎

Producing nonnegative weights by reweighting

Our next goal is to ensure that the second property holds: we want $\hat{w}(u, v)$ to be nonnegative for all edges $(u, v) \in E$. Given a weighted, directed graph $G = (V, E)$ with weight function $w : E \rightarrow \mathbb{R}$, we make a new graph $G' = (V', E')$, where $V' = V \cup \{s\}$ for some new vertex $s \notin V$ and $E' = E \cup \{(s, v) : v \in V\}$. We extend the weight function w so that $w(s, v) = 0$ for all $v \in V$. Note that because s has no edges that enter it, no shortest paths in G', other than those with source s, contain s. Moreover, G' has no negative-weight cycles if and only if G has no negative-weight cycles. Figure 25.6(a) shows the graph G' corresponding to the graph G of Figure 25.1.

Now suppose that G and G' have no negative-weight cycles. Let us define $h(v) = \delta(s, v)$ for all $v \in V'$. By the triangle inequality (Lemma 24.10), we have $h(v) \leq h(u) + w(u, v)$ for all edges $(u, v) \in E'$. Thus, if we define the new weights $\hat{w}$ by reweighting according to equation (25.9), we have $\hat{w}(u, v) = w(u, v) + h(u) - h(v) \geq 0$, and we have satisfied the second property. Figure 25.6(b) shows the graph G' from Figure 25.6(a) with reweighted edges.

Computing all-pairs shortest paths

Johnson's algorithm to compute all-pairs shortest paths uses the Bellman-Ford algorithm (Section 24.1) and Dijkstra's algorithm (Section 24.3) as subroutines. It assumes implicitly that the edges are stored in adjacency lists. The algorithm returns the usual $|V| \times |V|$ matrix $D = d_{ij}$, where $d_{ij} = \delta(i, j)$, or it reports that the input graph contains a negative-weight cycle. As is typical for an all-pairs shortest-paths algorithm, we assume that the vertices are numbered from 1 to $|V|$.

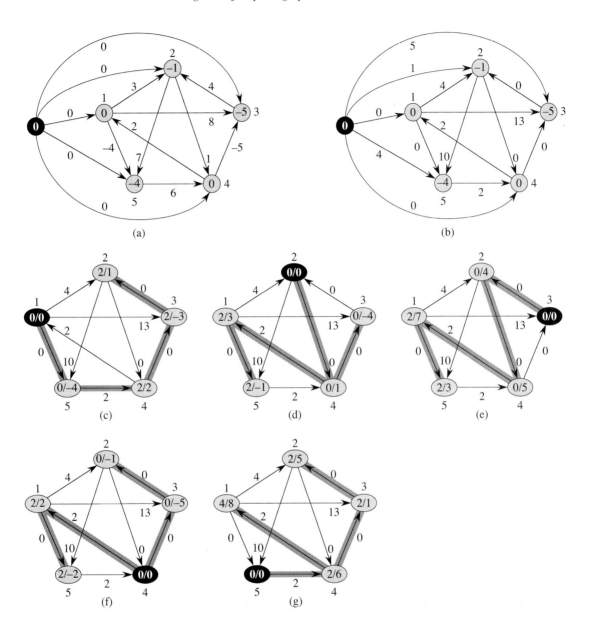

Figure 25.6 Johnson's all-pairs shortest-paths algorithm run on the graph of Figure 25.1. Vertex numbers appear outside the vertices. **(a)** The graph G' with the original weight function w. The new vertex s is black. Within each vertex v is $h(v) = \delta(s, v)$. **(b)** After reweighting each edge (u, v) with weight function $\hat{w}(u, v) = w(u, v) + h(u) - h(v)$. **(c)–(g)** The result of running Dijkstra's algorithm on each vertex of G using weight function $\hat{w}$. In each part, the source vertex u is black, and shaded edges are in the shortest-paths tree computed by the algorithm. Within each vertex v are the values $\hat{\delta}(u, v)$ and $\delta(u, v)$, separated by a slash. The value $d_{uv} = \delta(u, v)$ is equal to $\hat{\delta}(u, v) + h(v) - h(u)$.

JOHNSON(G, w)

```
 1   compute G', where G'.V = G.V ∪ {s},
            G'.E = G.E ∪ {(s, v) : v ∈ G.V}, and
            w(s, v) = 0 for all v ∈ G.V
 2   if BELLMAN-FORD(G', w, s) == FALSE
 3       print "the input graph contains a negative-weight cycle"
 4   else for each vertex v ∈ G'.V
 5           set h(v) to the value of δ(s, v)
                  computed by the Bellman-Ford algorithm
 6       for each edge (u, v) ∈ G'.E
 7           ŵ(u, v) = w(u, v) + h(u) − h(v)
 8       let D = (d_uv) be a new n × n matrix
 9       for each vertex u ∈ G.V
10           run DIJKSTRA(G, ŵ, u) to compute δ̂(u, v) for all v ∈ G.V
11           for each vertex v ∈ G.V
12               d_uv = δ̂(u, v) + h(v) − h(u)
13   return D
```

This code simply performs the actions we specified earlier. Line 1 produces G'. Line 2 runs the Bellman-Ford algorithm on G' with weight function w and source vertex s. If G', and hence G, contains a negative-weight cycle, line 3 reports the problem. Lines 4–12 assume that G' contains no negative-weight cycles. Lines 4–5 set $h(v)$ to the shortest-path weight $\delta(s, v)$ computed by the Bellman-Ford algorithm for all $v \in V'$. Lines 6–7 compute the new weights $\hat{w}$. For each pair of vertices $u, v \in V$, the **for** loop of lines 9–12 computes the shortest-path weight $\hat{\delta}(u, v)$ by calling Dijkstra's algorithm once from each vertex in V. Line 12 stores in matrix entry d_{uv} the correct shortest-path weight $\delta(u, v)$, calculated using equation (25.10). Finally, line 13 returns the completed D matrix. Figure 25.6 depicts the execution of Johnson's algorithm.

If we implement the min-priority queue in Dijkstra's algorithm by a Fibonacci heap, Johnson's algorithm runs in $O(V^2 \lg V + VE)$ time. The simpler binary min-heap implementation yields a running time of $O(VE \lg V)$, which is still asymptotically faster than the Floyd-Warshall algorithm if the graph is sparse.

Exercises

25.3-1
Use Johnson's algorithm to find the shortest paths between all pairs of vertices in the graph of Figure 25.2. Show the values of h and $\hat{w}$ computed by the algorithm.

25.3-2
What is the purpose of adding the new vertex s to V, yielding V'?

25.3-3
Suppose that $w(u, v) \geq 0$ for all edges $(u, v) \in E$. What is the relationship between the weight functions w and $\hat{w}$?

25.3-4
Professor Greenstreet claims that there is a simpler way to reweight edges than the method used in Johnson's algorithm. Letting $w^* = \min_{(u,v) \in E} \{w(u, v)\}$, just define $\hat{w}(u, v) = w(u, v) - w^*$ for all edges $(u, v) \in E$. What is wrong with the professor's method of reweighting?

25.3-5
Suppose that we run Johnson's algorithm on a directed graph G with weight function w. Show that if G contains a 0-weight cycle c, then $\hat{w}(u, v) = 0$ for every edge (u, v) in c.

25.3-6
Professor Michener claims that there is no need to create a new source vertex in line 1 of JOHNSON. He claims that instead we can just use $G' = G$ and let s be any vertex. Give an example of a weighted, directed graph G for which incorporating the professor's idea into JOHNSON causes incorrect answers. Then show that if G is strongly connected (every vertex is reachable from every other vertex), the results returned by JOHNSON with the professor's modification are correct.

Problems

25-1 *Transitive closure of a dynamic graph*
Suppose that we wish to maintain the transitive closure of a directed graph $G = (V, E)$ as we insert edges into E. That is, after each edge has been inserted, we want to update the transitive closure of the edges inserted so far. Assume that the graph G has no edges initially and that we represent the transitive closure as a boolean matrix.

a. Show how to update the transitive closure $G^* = (V, E^*)$ of a graph $G = (V, E)$ in $O(V^2)$ time when a new edge is added to G.

b. Give an example of a graph G and an edge e such that $\Omega(V^2)$ time is required to update the transitive closure after the insertion of e into G, no matter what algorithm is used.

c. Describe an efficient algorithm for updating the transitive closure as edges are inserted into the graph. For any sequence of n insertions, your algorithm should run in total time $\sum_{i=1}^{n} t_i = O(V^3)$, where t_i is the time to update the transitive closure upon inserting the ith edge. Prove that your algorithm attains this time bound.

25-2   *Shortest paths in ϵ-dense graphs*

A graph $G = (V, E)$ is *ϵ-dense* if $|E| = \Theta(V^{1+\epsilon})$ for some constant ϵ in the range $0 < \epsilon \leq 1$. By using d-ary min-heaps (see Problem 6-2) in shortest-paths algorithms on ϵ-dense graphs, we can match the running times of Fibonacci-heap-based algorithms without using as complicated a data structure.

a. What are the asymptotic running times for INSERT, EXTRACT-MIN, and DECREASE-KEY, as a function of d and the number n of elements in a d-ary min-heap? What are these running times if we choose $d = \Theta(n^\alpha)$ for some constant $0 < \alpha \leq 1$? Compare these running times to the amortized costs of these operations for a Fibonacci heap.

b. Show how to compute shortest paths from a single source on an ϵ-dense directed graph $G = (V, E)$ with no negative-weight edges in $O(E)$ time. (*Hint:* Pick d as a function of ϵ.)

c. Show how to solve the all-pairs shortest-paths problem on an ϵ-dense directed graph $G = (V, E)$ with no negative-weight edges in $O(VE)$ time.

d. Show how to solve the all-pairs shortest-paths problem in $O(VE)$ time on an ϵ-dense directed graph $G = (V, E)$ that may have negative-weight edges but has no negative-weight cycles.

Chapter notes

Lawler [224] has a good discussion of the all-pairs shortest-paths problem, although he does not analyze solutions for sparse graphs. He attributes the matrix-multiplication algorithm to the folklore. The Floyd-Warshall algorithm is due to Floyd [105], who based it on a theorem of Warshall [349] that describes how to compute the transitive closure of boolean matrices. Johnson's algorithm is taken from [192].

Several researchers have given improved algorithms for computing shortest paths via matrix multiplication. Fredman [111] shows how to solve the all-pairs shortest paths problem using $O(V^{5/2})$ comparisons between sums of edge weights and obtains an algorithm that runs in $O(V^3(\lg\lg V/\lg V)^{1/3})$ time, which is slightly better than the running time of the Floyd-Warshall algorithm. Han [159] reduced the running time to $O(V^3(\lg\lg V/\lg V)^{5/4})$. Another line of research demonstrates that we can apply algorithms for fast matrix multiplication (see the chapter notes for Chapter 4) to the all-pairs shortest paths problem. Let $O(n^\omega)$ be the running time of the fastest algorithm for multiplying $n \times n$ matrices; currently $\omega < 2.376$ [78]. Galil and Margalit [123, 124] and Seidel [308] designed algorithms that solve the all-pairs shortest paths problem in undirected, unweighted graphs in $(V^\omega p(V))$ time, where $p(n)$ denotes a particular function that is polylogarithmically bounded in n. In dense graphs, these algorithms are faster than the $O(VE)$ time needed to perform $|V|$ breadth-first searches. Several researchers have extended these results to give algorithms for solving the all-pairs shortest paths problem in undirected graphs in which the edge weights are integers in the range $\{1, 2, \ldots, W\}$. The asymptotically fastest such algorithm, by Shoshan and Zwick [316], runs in time $O(WV^\omega p(VW))$.

Karger, Koller, and Phillips [196] and independently McGeoch [247] have given a time bound that depends on E^*, the set of edges in E that participate in some shortest path. Given a graph with nonnegative edge weights, their algorithms run in $O(VE^* + V^2 \lg V)$ time and improve upon running Dijkstra's algorithm $|V|$ times when $|E^*| = o(E)$.

Baswana, Hariharan, and Sen [33] examined decremental algorithms for maintaining all-pairs shortest paths and transitive-closure information. Decremental algorithms allow a sequence of intermixed edge deletions and queries; by comparison, Problem 25-1, in which edges are inserted, asks for an incremental algorithm. The algorithms by Baswana, Hariharan, and Sen are randomized and, when a path exists, their transitive-closure algorithm can fail to report it with probability $1/n^c$ for an arbitrary $c > 0$. The query times are $O(1)$ with high probability. For transitive closure, the amortized time for each update is $O(V^{4/3} \lg^{1/3} V)$. For all-pairs shortest paths, the update times depend on the queries. For queries just giving the shortest-path weights, the amortized time per update is $O(V^3/E \lg^2 V)$. To report the actual shortest path, the amortized update time is $\min(O(V^{3/2}\sqrt{\lg V}), O(V^3/E \lg^2 V))$. Demetrescu and Italiano [84] showed how to handle update and query operations when edges are both inserted and deleted, as long as each given edge has a bounded range of possible values drawn from the real numbers.

Aho, Hopcroft, and Ullman [5] defined an algebraic structure known as a "closed semiring," which serves as a general framework for solving path problems in directed graphs. Both the Floyd-Warshall algorithm and the transitive-closure algorithm from Section 25.2 are instantiations of an all-pairs algorithm based on closed semirings. Maggs and Plotkin [240] showed how to find minimum spanning trees using a closed semiring.

26 Maximum Flow

Just as we can model a road map as a directed graph in order to find the shortest path from one point to another, we can also interpret a directed graph as a "flow network" and use it to answer questions about material flows. Imagine a material coursing through a system from a source, where the material is produced, to a sink, where it is consumed. The source produces the material at some steady rate, and the sink consumes the material at the same rate. The "flow" of the material at any point in the system is intuitively the rate at which the material moves. Flow networks can model many problems, including liquids flowing through pipes, parts through assembly lines, current through electrical networks, and information through communication networks.

We can think of each directed edge in a flow network as a conduit for the material. Each conduit has a stated capacity, given as a maximum rate at which the material can flow through the conduit, such as 200 gallons of liquid per hour through a pipe or 20 amperes of electrical current through a wire. Vertices are conduit junctions, and other than the source and sink, material flows through the vertices without collecting in them. In other words, the rate at which material enters a vertex must equal the rate at which it leaves the vertex. We call this property "flow conservation," and it is equivalent to Kirchhoff's current law when the material is electrical current.

In the maximum-flow problem, we wish to compute the greatest rate at which we can ship material from the source to the sink without violating any capacity constraints. It is one of the simplest problems concerning flow networks and, as we shall see in this chapter, this problem can be solved by efficient algorithms. Moreover, we can adapt the basic techniques used in maximum-flow algorithms to solve other network-flow problems.

This chapter presents two general methods for solving the maximum-flow problem. Section 26.1 formalizes the notions of flow networks and flows, formally defining the maximum-flow problem. Section 26.2 describes the classical method of Ford and Fulkerson for finding maximum flows. An application of this method, finding a maximum matching in an undirected bipartite graph, appears in Section 26.3. Section 26.4 presents the push-relabel method, which underlies many of the fastest algorithms for network-flow problems. Section 26.5 covers the "relabel-to-front" algorithm, a particular implementation of the push-relabel method that runs in time $O(V^3)$. Although this algorithm is not the fastest algorithm known, it illustrates some of the techniques used in the asymptotically fastest algorithms, and it is reasonably efficient in practice.

26.1   Flow networks

In this section, we give a graph-theoretic definition of flow networks, discuss their properties, and define the maximum-flow problem precisely. We also introduce some helpful notation.

Flow networks and flows

A *flow network* $G = (V, E)$ is a directed graph in which each edge $(u, v) \in E$ has a nonnegative *capacity* $c(u, v) \geq 0$. We further require that if E contains an edge (u, v), then there is no edge (v, u) in the reverse direction. (We shall see shortly how to work around this restriction.) If $(u, v) \notin E$, then for convenience we define $c(u, v) = 0$, and we disallow self-loops. We distinguish two vertices in a flow network: a *source* s and a *sink* t. For convenience, we assume that each vertex lies on some path from the source to the sink. That is, for each vertex $v \in V$, the flow network contains a path $s \rightsquigarrow v \rightsquigarrow t$. The graph is therefore connected and, since each vertex other than s has at least one entering edge, $|E| \geq |V| - 1$. Figure 26.1 shows an example of a flow network.

We are now ready to define flows more formally. Let $G = (V, E)$ be a flow network with a capacity function c. Let s be the source of the network, and let t be the sink. A *flow* in G is a real-valued function $f : V \times V \rightarrow \mathbb{R}$ that satisfies the following two properties:

Capacity constraint: For all $u, v \in V$, we require $0 \leq f(u, v) \leq c(u, v)$.

Flow conservation: For all $u \in V - \{s, t\}$, we require

$$\sum_{v \in V} f(v, u) = \sum_{v \in V} f(u, v) \, .$$

When $(u, v) \notin E$, there can be no flow from u to v, and $f(u, v) = 0$.

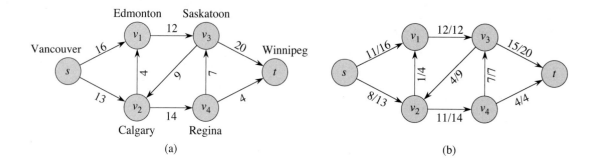

Figure 26.1   **(a)** A flow network $G = (V, E)$ for the Lucky Puck Company's trucking problem. The Vancouver factory is the source s, and the Winnipeg warehouse is the sink t. The company ships pucks through intermediate cities, but only $c(u, v)$ crates per day can go from city u to city v. Each edge is labeled with its capacity. **(b)** A flow f in G with value $|f| = 19$. Each edge (u, v) is labeled by $f(u, v)/c(u, v)$. The slash notation merely separates the flow and capacity; it does not indicate division.

We call the nonnegative quantity $f(u, v)$ the flow from vertex u to vertex v. The **value** $|f|$ of a flow f is defined as

$$|f| = \sum_{v \in V} f(s, v) - \sum_{v \in V} f(v, s) \,, \tag{26.1}$$

that is, the total flow out of the source minus the flow into the source. (Here, the $|\cdot|$ notation denotes flow value, not absolute value or cardinality.) Typically, a flow network will not have any edges into the source, and the flow into the source, given by the summation $\sum_{v \in V} f(v, s)$, will be 0. We include it, however, because when we introduce residual networks later in this chapter, the flow into the source will become significant. In the **maximum-flow problem**, we are given a flow network G with source s and sink t, and we wish to find a flow of maximum value.

Before seeing an example of a network-flow problem, let us briefly explore the definition of flow and the two flow properties. The capacity constraint simply says that the flow from one vertex to another must be nonnegative and must not exceed the given capacity. The flow-conservation property says that the total flow into a vertex other than the source or sink must equal the total flow out of that vertex — informally, "flow in equals flow out."

An example of flow

A flow network can model the trucking problem shown in Figure 26.1(a). The Lucky Puck Company has a factory (source s) in Vancouver that manufactures hockey pucks, and it has a warehouse (sink t) in Winnipeg that stocks them. Lucky

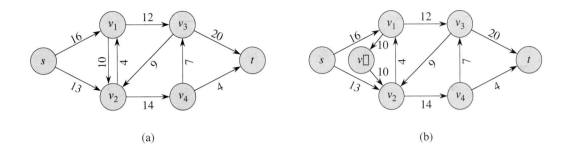

(a)   (b)

Figure 26.2   Converting a network with antiparallel edges to an equivalent one with no antiparallel edges. **(a)** A flow network containing both the edges (v_1, v_2) and (v_2, v_1). **(b)** An equivalent network with no antiparallel edges. We add the new vertex v', and we replace edge (v_1, v_2) by the pair of edges (v_1, v') and (v', v_2), both with the same capacity as (v_1, v_2).

Puck leases space on trucks from another firm to ship the pucks from the factory to the warehouse. Because the trucks travel over specified routes (edges) between cities (vertices) and have a limited capacity, Lucky Puck can ship at most $c(u, v)$ crates per day between each pair of cities u and v in Figure 26.1(a). Lucky Puck has no control over these routes and capacities, and so the company cannot alter the flow network shown in Figure 26.1(a). They need to determine the largest number p of crates per day that they can ship and then to produce this amount, since there is no point in producing more pucks than they can ship to their warehouse. Lucky Puck is not concerned with how long it takes for a given puck to get from the factory to the warehouse; they care only that p crates per day leave the factory and p crates per day arrive at the warehouse.

   We can model the "flow" of shipments with a flow in this network because the number of crates shipped per day from one city to another is subject to a capacity constraint. Additionally, the model must obey flow conservation, for in a steady state, the rate at which pucks enter an intermediate city must equal the rate at which they leave. Otherwise, crates would accumulate at intermediate cities.

Modeling problems with antiparallel edges

Suppose that the trucking firm offered Lucky Puck the opportunity to lease space for 10 crates in trucks going from Edmonton to Calgary. It would seem natural to add this opportunity to our example and form the network shown in Figure 26.2(a). This network suffers from one problem, however: it violates our original assumption that if an edge $(v_1, v_2) \in E$, then $(v_2, v_1) \notin E$. We call the two edges (v_1, v_2) and (v_2, v_1) ***antiparallel***. Thus, if we wish to model a flow problem with antiparallel edges, we must transform the network into an equivalent one containing no antiparallel edges. Figure 26.2(b) displays this equivalent network. We choose one of the two antiparallel edges, in this case (v_1, v_2), and split it by adding a new vertex v' and replacing edge (v_1, v_2) with the pair of edges (v_1, v') and (v', v_2). We also set the capacity of both new edges to the capacity of the original edge. The resulting network satisfies the property that if an edge is in the network, the reverse edge is not. Exercise 26.1-1 asks you to prove that the resulting network is equivalent to the original one.

Thus, we see that a real-world flow problem might be most naturally modeled by a network with antiparallel edges. It will be convenient to disallow antiparallel edges, however, and so we have a straightforward way to convert a network containing antiparallel edges into an equivalent one with no antiparallel edges.

Networks with multiple sources and sinks

A maximum-flow problem may have several sources and sinks, rather than just one of each. The Lucky Puck Company, for example, might actually have a set of m factories $\{s_1, s_2, \ldots, s_m\}$ and a set of n warehouses $\{t_1, t_2, \ldots, t_n\}$, as shown in Figure 26.3(a). Fortunately, this problem is no harder than ordinary maximum flow.

We can reduce the problem of determining a maximum flow in a network with multiple sources and multiple sinks to an ordinary maximum-flow problem. Figure 26.3(b) shows how to convert the network from (a) to an ordinary flow network with only a single source and a single sink. We add a **supersource** s and add a directed edge (s, s_i) with capacity $c(s, s_i) = \infty$ for each $i = 1, 2, \ldots, m$. We also create a new **supersink** t and add a directed edge (t_i, t) with capacity $c(t_i, t) = \infty$ for each $i = 1, 2, \ldots, n$. Intuitively, any flow in the network in (a) corresponds to a flow in the network in (b), and vice versa. The single source s simply provides as much flow as desired for the multiple sources s_i, and the single sink t likewise consumes as much flow as desired for the multiple sinks t_i. Exercise 26.1-2 asks you to prove formally that the two problems are equivalent.

Exercises

26.1-1
Show that splitting an edge in a flow network yields an equivalent network. More formally, suppose that flow network G contains edge (u, v), and we create a new flow network G' by creating a new vertex x and replacing (u, v) by new edges (u, x) and (x, v) with $c(u, x) = c(x, v) = c(u, v)$. Show that a maximum flow in G' has the same value as a maximum flow in G.

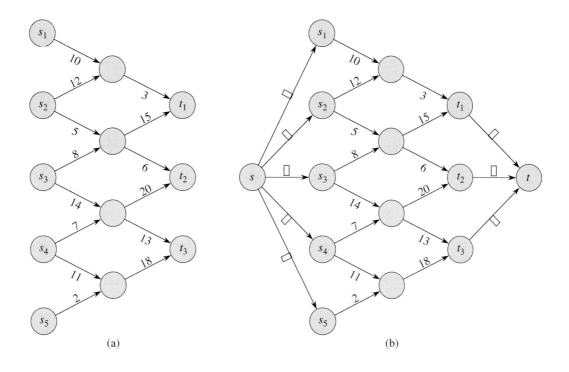

Figure 26.3   Converting a multiple-source, multiple-sink maximum-flow problem into a problem with a single source and a single sink. **(a)** A flow network with five sources $S = \{s_1, s_2, s_3, s_4, s_5\}$ and three sinks $T = \{t_1, t_2, t_3\}$. **(b)** An equivalent single-source, single-sink flow network. We add a supersource s and an edge with infinite capacity from s to each of the multiple sources. We also add a supersink t and an edge with infinite capacity from each of the multiple sinks to t.

26.1-2
Extend the flow properties and definitions to the multiple-source, multiple-sink problem. Show that any flow in a multiple-source, multiple-sink flow network corresponds to a flow of identical value in the single-source, single-sink network obtained by adding a supersource and a supersink, and vice versa.

26.1-3
Suppose that a flow network $G = (V, E)$ violates the assumption that the network contains a path $s \rightsquigarrow v \rightsquigarrow t$ for all vertices $v \in V$. Let u be a vertex for which there is no path $s \rightsquigarrow u \rightsquigarrow t$. Show that there must exist a maximum flow f in G such that $f(u, v) = f(v, u) = 0$ for all vertices $v \in V$.

26.1-4

Let f be a flow in a network, and let α be a real number. The **scalar flow product**, denoted αf, is a function from $V \times V$ to $\mathbb{R}$ defined by

$$(\alpha f)(u, v) = \alpha \cdot f(u, v) \, .$$

Prove that the flows in a network form a **convex set**. That is, show that if f_1 and f_2 are flows, then so is $\alpha f_1 + (1 - \alpha) f_2$ for all α in the range $0 \le \alpha \le 1$.

26.1-5

State the maximum-flow problem as a linear-programming problem.

26.1-6

Professor Adam has two children who, unfortunately, dislike each other. The problem is so severe that not only do they refuse to walk to school together, but in fact each one refuses to walk on any block that the other child has stepped on that day. The children have no problem with their paths crossing at a corner. Fortunately both the professor's house and the school are on corners, but beyond that he is not sure if it is going to be possible to send both of his children to the same school. The professor has a map of his town. Show how to formulate the problem of determining whether both his children can go to the same school as a maximum-flow problem.

26.1-7

Suppose that, in addition to edge capacities, a flow network has **vertex capacities**. That is each vertex v has a limit $l(v)$ on how much flow can pass through v. Show how to transform a flow network $G = (V, E)$ with vertex capacities into an equivalent flow network $G' = (V', E')$ without vertex capacities, such that a maximum flow in G' has the same value as a maximum flow in G. How many vertices and edges does G' have?

26.2   The Ford-Fulkerson method

This section presents the Ford-Fulkerson method for solving the maximum-flow problem. We call it a "method" rather than an "algorithm" because it encompasses several implementations with differing running times. The Ford-Fulkerson method depends on three important ideas that transcend the method and are relevant to many flow algorithms and problems: residual networks, augmenting paths, and cuts. These ideas are essential to the important max-flow min-cut theorem (Theorem 26.6), which characterizes the value of a maximum flow in terms of cuts of

the flow network. We end this section by presenting one specific implementation
of the Ford-Fulkerson method and analyzing its running time.

The Ford-Fulkerson method iteratively increases the value of the flow. We start
with $f(u, v) = 0$ for all $u, v \in V$, giving an initial flow of value 0. At each
iteration, we increase the flow value in G by finding an "augmenting path" in an
associated "residual network" G_f. Once we know the edges of an augmenting
path in G_f, we can easily identify specific edges in G for which we can change
the flow so that we increase the value of the flow. Although each iteration of the
Ford-Fulkerson method increases the value of the flow, we shall see that the flow
on any particular edge of G may increase or decrease; decreasing the flow on some
edges may be necessary in order to enable an algorithm to send more flow from the
source to the sink. We repeatedly augment the flow until the residual network has
no more augmenting paths. The max-flow min-cut theorem will show that upon
termination, this process yields a maximum flow.

FORD-FULKERSON-METHOD(G, s, t)

1   initialize flow f to 0
2   **while** there exists an augmenting path p in the residual network G_f
3   augment flow f along p
4   **return** f

In order to implement and analyze the Ford-Fulkerson method, we need to introduce several additional concepts.

Residual networks

Intuitively, given a flow network G and a flow f, the residual network G_f consists
of edges with capacities that represent how we can change the flow on edges of G.
An edge of the flow network can admit an amount of additional flow equal to the
edge's capacity minus the flow on that edge. If that value is positive, we place
that edge into G_f with a "residual capacity" of $c_f(u, v) = c(u, v) - f(u, v)$.
The only edges of G that are in G_f are those that can admit more flow; those
edges (u, v) whose flow equals their capacity have $c_f(u, v) = 0$, and they are not
in G_f.

The residual network G_f may also contain edges that are not in G, however.
As an algorithm manipulates the flow, with the goal of increasing the total flow, it
might need to decrease the flow on a particular edge. In order to represent a possible decrease of a positive flow $f(u, v)$ on an edge in G, we place an edge (v, u)
into G_f with residual capacity $c_f(v, u) = f(u, v)$—that is, an edge that can admit
flow in the opposite direction to (u, v), at most canceling out the flow on (u, v).
These reverse edges in the residual network allow an algorithm to send back flow

it has already sent along an edge. Sending flow back along an edge is equivalent to *decreasing* the flow on the edge, which is a necessary operation in many algorithms.

More formally, suppose that we have a flow network $G = (V, E)$ with source s and sink t. Let f be a flow in G, and consider a pair of vertices $u, v \in V$. We define the **residual capacity** $c_f(u, v)$ by

$$c_f(u, v) = \begin{cases} c(u, v) - f(u, v) & \text{if } (u, v) \in E , \\ f(v, u) & \text{if } (v, u) \in E , \\ 0 & \text{otherwise .} \end{cases} \qquad (26.2)$$

Because of our assumption that $(u, v) \in E$ implies $(v, u) \notin E$, exactly one case in equation (26.2) applies to each ordered pair of vertices.

As an example of equation (26.2), if $c(u, v) = 16$ and $f(u, v) = 11$, then we can increase $f(u, v)$ by up to $c_f(u, v) = 5$ units before we exceed the capacity constraint on edge (u, v). We also wish to allow an algorithm to return up to 11 units of flow from v to u, and hence $c_f(v, u) = 11$.

Given a flow network $G = (V, E)$ and a flow f, the **residual network** of G induced by f is $G_f = (V, E_f)$, where

$$E_f = \{(u, v) \in V \times V : c_f(u, v) > 0\} . \qquad (26.3)$$

That is, as promised above, each edge of the residual network, or **residual edge**, can admit a flow that is greater than 0. Figure 26.4(a) repeats the flow network G and flow f of Figure 26.1(b), and Figure 26.4(b) shows the corresponding residual network G_f. The edges in E_f are either edges in E or their reversals, and thus

$$|E_f| \leq 2 |E| .$$

Observe that the residual network G_f is similar to a flow network with capacities given by c_f. It does not satisfy our definition of a flow network because it may contain both an edge (u, v) and its reversal (v, u). Other than this difference, a residual network has the same properties as a flow network, and we can define a flow in the residual network as one that satisfies the definition of a flow, but with respect to capacities c_f in the network G_f.

A flow in a residual network provides a roadmap for adding flow to the original flow network. If f is a flow in G and f' is a flow in the corresponding residual network G_f, we define $f \uparrow f'$, the **augmentation** of flow f by f', to be a function from $V \times V$ to $\mathbb{R}$, defined by

$$(f \uparrow f')(u, v) = \begin{cases} f(u, v) + f'(u, v) - f'(v, u) & \text{if } (u, v) \in E , \\ 0 & \text{otherwise .} \end{cases} \qquad (26.4)$$

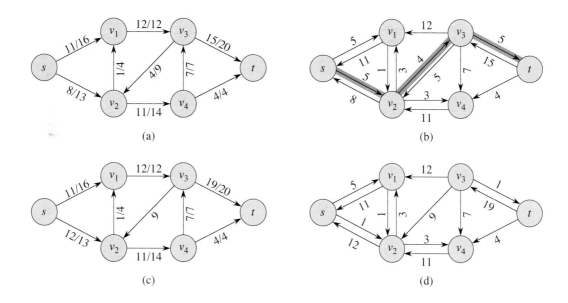

Figure 26.4 **(a)** The flow network G and flow f of Figure 26.1(b). **(b)** The residual network G_f with augmenting path p shaded; its residual capacity is $c_f(p) = c_f(v_2, v_3) = 4$. Edges with residual capacity equal to 0, such as (v_1, v_3), are not shown, a convention we follow in the remainder of this section. **(c)** The flow in G that results from augmenting along path p by its residual capacity 4. Edges carrying no flow, such as (v_3, v_2), are labeled only by their capacity, another convention we follow throughout. **(d)** The residual network induced by the flow in (c).

The intuition behind this definition follows the definition of the residual network. We increase the flow on (u, v) by $f'(u, v)$ but decrease it by $f'(v, u)$ because pushing flow on the reverse edge in the residual network signifies decreasing the flow in the original network. Pushing flow on the reverse edge in the residual network is also known as ***cancellation***. For example, if we send 5 crates of hockey pucks from u to v and send 2 crates from v to u, we could equivalently (from the perspective of the final result) just send 3 crates from u to v and none from v to u. Cancellation of this type is crucial for any maximum-flow algorithm.

Lemma 26.1
Let $G = (V, E)$ be a flow network with source s and sink t, and let f be a flow in G. Let G_f be the residual network of G induced by f, and let f' be a flow in G_f. Then the function $f \uparrow f'$ defined in equation (26.4) is a flow in G with value $|f \uparrow f'| = |f| + |f'|$.

Proof We first verify that $f \uparrow f'$ obeys the capacity constraint for each edge in E and flow conservation at each vertex in $V - \{s, t\}$.

For the capacity constraint, first observe that if $(u, v) \in E$, then $c_f(v, u) = f(u, v)$. Therefore, we have $f'(v, u) \le c_f(v, u) = f(u, v)$, and hence

$$
\begin{aligned}
(f \uparrow f')(u, v) &= f(u, v) + f'(u, v) - f'(v, u) \quad \text{(by equation (26.4))} \\
&\ge f(u, v) + f'(u, v) - f(u, v) \quad \text{(because } f'(v, u) \le f(u, v)) \\
&= f'(u, v) \\
&\ge 0 .
\end{aligned}
$$

In addition,

$$
\begin{aligned}
(f \uparrow f')&(u, v) \\
&= f(u, v) + f'(u, v) - f'(v, u) \quad \text{(by equation (26.4))} \\
&\le f(u, v) + f'(u, v) \qquad\qquad \text{(because flows are nonnegative)} \\
&\le f(u, v) + c_f(u, v) \qquad\qquad \text{(capacity constraint)} \\
&= f(u, v) + c(u, v) - f(u, v) \quad \text{(definition of } c_f) \\
&= c(u, v) .
\end{aligned}
$$

To show that flow conservation holds and that $|f \uparrow f'| = |f| + |f'|$, we first prove the claim that for all $u \in V$, we have

$$
\sum_{v \in V}(f \uparrow f')(u, v) - \sum_{v \in V}(f \uparrow f')(v, u)
$$

$$
= \sum_{v \in V} f(u, v) - \sum_{v \in V} f(v, u) + \sum_{v \in V} f'(u, v) - \sum_{v \in V} f'(v, u) . \quad (26.5)
$$

Because we disallow antiparallel edges in G (but not in G_f), we know that for each vertex u, there can be an edge (u, v) or (v, u) in G, but never both. For a fixed vertex u, let's define $V_1(u) = \{v : (u, v) \in E\}$ to be the set of vertices with edges from u, and $V_2(u) = \{v : (v, u) \in E\}$ to be the set of vertices with edges to u. We have $V_1(u) \cup V_2(u) \subseteq V$ and, because we disallow antiparallel edges, $V_1(u) \cap V_2(u) = \emptyset$. By the definition of flow augmentation in equation (26.4), only vertices in $V_1(u)$ can have positive $(f \uparrow f')(u, v)$, and only vertices in $V_2(u)$ can have positive $(f \uparrow f')(v, u)$. Starting from the left-hand side of equation (26.5), we use this fact and then reorder and group terms, giving

$$
\sum_{v \in V}(f \uparrow f')(u, v) - \sum_{v \in V}(f \uparrow f')(v, u)
$$

$$
= \sum_{v \in V_1(u)}(f \uparrow f')(u, v) - \sum_{v \in V_2(u)}(f \uparrow f')(v, u)
$$

$$
= \sum_{v \in V_1(u)}(f(u, v) + f'(u, v) - f'(v, u)) - \sum_{v \in V_2(u)}(f(v, u) + f'(v, u) - f'(u, v))
$$

$$= \sum_{v \in V_1(u)} f(u,v) + \sum_{v \in V_1(u)} f'(u,v) - \sum_{v \in V_1(u)} f'(v,u)$$

$$- \sum_{v \in V_2(u)} f(v,u) - \sum_{v \in V_2(u)} f'(v,u) + \sum_{v \in V_2(u)} f'(u,v)$$

$$= \sum_{v \in V_1(u)} f(u,v) - \sum_{v \in V_2(u)} f(v,u)$$

$$+ \sum_{v \in V_1(u)} f'(u,v) + \sum_{v \in V_2(u)} f'(u,v) - \sum_{v \in V_1(u)} f'(v,u) - \sum_{v \in V_2(u)} f'(v,u)$$

$$= \sum_{v \in V_1(u)} f(u,v) - \sum_{v \in V_2(u)} f(v,u) + \sum_{v \in V_1(u) \cup V_2(u)} f'(u,v) - \sum_{v \in V_1(u) \cup V_2(u)} f'(v,u) . \qquad (26.6)$$

In equation (26.6), we can extend all four summations to sum over V, since each additional term has value 0. (Exercise 26.2-1 asks you to prove this formally.) With all four summations over V, instead of just subsets of V, we get equation (26.5).

Now we are ready to prove flow conservation for $f \uparrow f'$ and that $|f \uparrow f'| = |f| + |f'|$. For the latter property, let $u = s$ in equation (26.5). Then, we have

$$|f \uparrow f'| = \sum_{v \in V} (f \uparrow f')(s,v) - \sum_{v \in V} (f \uparrow f')(v,s)$$

$$= \sum_{v \in V} f(s,v) - \sum_{v \in V} f(v,s) + \sum_{v \in V} f'(s,v) - \sum_{v \in V} f'(v,s)$$

$$= |f| + |f'| . \qquad (26.7)$$

For flow conservation, observe that for any vertex u that is neither s nor t, flow conservation for f and f' means that the right-hand side of equation (26.5) is 0, and thus $\sum_{v \in V} (f \uparrow f')(u,v) = \sum_{v \in V} (f \uparrow f')(v,u)$.   ∎

Augmenting paths

Given a flow network $G = (V, E)$ and a flow f, an ***augmenting path*** p is a simple path from s to t in the residual network G_f. By the definition of the residual network, we may increase the flow on an edge (u, v) of an augmenting path by up to $c_f(u, v)$ without violating the capacity constraint on whichever of (u, v) and (v, u) is in the original flow network G.

The shaded path in Figure 26.4(b) is an augmenting path. Treating the residual network G_f in the figure as a flow network, we can increase the flow through each edge of this path by up to 4 units without violating a capacity constraint, since the smallest residual capacity on this path is $c_f(v_2, v_3) = 4$. We call the maximum amount by which we can increase the flow on each edge in an augmenting path p the ***residual capacity*** of p, given by

$$c_f(p) = \min\{c_f(u, v) : (u, v) \text{ is on } p\} \; .$$

The following lemma, whose proof we leave as Exercise 26.2-7, makes the above argument more precise.

Lemma 26.2

Let $G = (V, E)$ be a flow network, let f be a flow in G, and let p be an augmenting path in G_f. Define a function $f_p : V \times V \to \mathbb{R}$ by

$$f_p(u, v) = \begin{cases} c_f(p) & \text{if } (u, v) \text{ is on } p \; , \\ 0 & \text{otherwise} \; . \end{cases} \qquad (26.8)$$

Then, f_p is a flow in G_f with value $|f_p| = c_f(p) > 0$.   ∎

The following corollary shows that if we augment f by f_p, we get another flow in G whose value is closer to the maximum. Figure 26.4(c) shows the result of augmenting the flow f from Figure 26.4(a) by the flow f_p in Figure 26.4(b), and Figure 26.4(d) shows the ensuing residual network.

Corollary 26.3

Let $G = (V, E)$ be a flow network, let f be a flow in G, and let p be an augmenting path in G_f. Let f_p be defined as in equation (26.8), and suppose that we augment f by f_p. Then the function $f \uparrow f_p$ is a flow in G with value $|f \uparrow f_p| = |f| + |f_p| > |f|$.

Proof   Immediate from Lemmas 26.1 and 26.2.   ∎

Cuts of flow networks

The Ford-Fulkerson method repeatedly augments the flow along augmenting paths until it has found a maximum flow. How do we know that when the algorithm terminates, we have actually found a maximum flow? The max-flow min-cut theorem, which we shall prove shortly, tells us that a flow is maximum if and only if its residual network contains no augmenting path. To prove this theorem, though, we must first explore the notion of a cut of a flow network.

A **cut** (S, T) of flow network $G = (V, E)$ is a partition of V into S and $T = V - S$ such that $s \in S$ and $t \in T$. (This definition is similar to the definition of "cut" that we used for minimum spanning trees in Chapter 23, except that here we are cutting a directed graph rather than an undirected graph, and we insist that $s \in S$ and $t \in T$.) If f is a flow, then the **net flow** $f(S, T)$ across the cut (S, T) is defined to be

$$f(S, T) = \sum_{u \in S} \sum_{v \in T} f(u, v) - \sum_{u \in S} \sum_{v \in T} f(v, u) \; . \qquad (26.9)$$

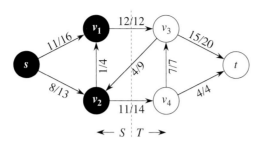

Figure 26.5 A cut (S, T) in the flow network of Figure 26.1(b), where $S = \{s, v_1, v_2\}$ and $T = \{v_3, v_4, t\}$. The vertices in S are black, and the vertices in T are white. The net flow across (S, T) is $f(S, T) = 19$, and the capacity is $c(S, T) = 26$.

The *capacity* of the cut (S, T) is

$$c(S, T) = \sum_{u \in S} \sum_{v \in T} c(u, v) . \tag{26.10}$$

A *minimum cut* of a network is a cut whose capacity is minimum over all cuts of the network.

The asymmetry between the definitions of flow and capacity of a cut is intentional and important. For capacity, we count only the capacities of edges going from S to T, ignoring edges in the reverse direction. For flow, we consider the flow going from S to T minus the flow going in the reverse direction from T to S. The reason for this difference will become clear later in this section.

Figure 26.5 shows the cut $(\{s, v_1, v_2\}, \{v_3, v_4, t\})$ in the flow network of Figure 26.1(b). The net flow across this cut is

$$
\begin{aligned}
f(v_1, v_3) + f(v_2, v_4) - f(v_3, v_2) &= 12 + 11 - 4 \\
&= 19 ,
\end{aligned}
$$

and the capacity of this cut is

$$
\begin{aligned}
c(v_1, v_3) + c(v_2, v_4) &= 12 + 14 \\
&= 26 .
\end{aligned}
$$

The following lemma shows that, for a given flow f, the net flow across any cut is the same, and it equals $|f|$, the value of the flow.

Lemma 26.4
Let f be a flow in a flow network G with source s and sink t, and let (S, T) be any cut of G. Then the net flow across (S, T) is $f(S, T) = |f|$.

Proof   We can rewrite the flow-conservation condition for any node $u \in V - \{s, t\}$ as

$$\sum_{v \in V} f(u, v) - \sum_{v \in V} f(v, u) = 0 . \tag{26.11}$$

Taking the definition of $|f|$ from equation (26.1) and adding the left-hand side of equation (26.11), which equals 0, summed over all vertices in $S - \{s\}$, gives

$$|f| = \sum_{v \in V} f(s, v) - \sum_{v \in V} f(v, s) + \sum_{u \in S - \{s\}} \left(\sum_{v \in V} f(u, v) - \sum_{v \in V} f(v, u) \right) .$$

Expanding the right-hand summation and regrouping terms yields

$$
\begin{aligned}
|f| &= \sum_{v \in V} f(s, v) - \sum_{v \in V} f(v, s) + \sum_{u \in S - \{s\}} \sum_{v \in V} f(u, v) - \sum_{u \in S - \{s\}} \sum_{v \in V} f(v, u) \\
&= \sum_{v \in V} \left(f(s, v) + \sum_{u \in S - \{s\}} f(u, v) \right) - \sum_{v \in V} \left(f(v, s) + \sum_{u \in S - \{s\}} f(v, u) \right) \\
&= \sum_{v \in V} \sum_{u \in S} f(u, v) - \sum_{v \in V} \sum_{u \in S} f(v, u) .
\end{aligned}
$$

Because $V = S \cup T$ and $S \cap T = \emptyset$, we can split each summation over V into summations over S and T to obtain

$$
\begin{aligned}
|f| &= \sum_{v \in S} \sum_{u \in S} f(u, v) + \sum_{v \in T} \sum_{u \in S} f(u, v) - \sum_{v \in S} \sum_{u \in S} f(v, u) - \sum_{v \in T} \sum_{u \in S} f(v, u) \\
&= \sum_{v \in T} \sum_{u \in S} f(u, v) - \sum_{v \in T} \sum_{u \in S} f(v, u) \\
&\quad + \left(\sum_{v \in S} \sum_{u \in S} f(u, v) - \sum_{v \in S} \sum_{u \in S} f(v, u) \right) .
\end{aligned}
$$

The two summations within the parentheses are actually the same, since for all vertices $x, y \in S$, the term $f(x, y)$ appears once in each summation. Hence, these summations cancel, and we have

$$
\begin{aligned}
|f| &= \sum_{u \in S} \sum_{v \in T} f(u, v) - \sum_{u \in S} \sum_{v \in T} f(v, u) \\
&= f(S, T) . \qquad \blacksquare
\end{aligned}
$$

A corollary to Lemma 26.4 shows how we can use cut capacities to bound the value of a flow.

Corollary 26.5
The value of any flow f in a flow network G is bounded from above by the capacity of any cut of G.

Proof   Let (S, T) be any cut of G and let f be any flow. By Lemma 26.4 and the capacity constraint,

$$
\begin{aligned}
|f| &= f(S, T) \\
&= \sum_{u \in S} \sum_{v \in T} f(u, v) - \sum_{u \in S} \sum_{v \in T} f(v, u) \\
&\leq \sum_{u \in S} \sum_{v \in T} f(u, v) \\
&\leq \sum_{u \in S} \sum_{v \in T} c(u, v) \\
&= c(S, T) \, .
\end{aligned}
$$
■

Corollary 26.5 yields the immediate consequence that the value of a maximum flow in a network is bounded from above by the capacity of a minimum cut of the network. The important max-flow min-cut theorem, which we now state and prove, says that the value of a maximum flow is in fact equal to the capacity of a minimum cut.

Theorem 26.6 (Max-flow min-cut theorem)
If f is a flow in a flow network $G = (V, E)$ with source s and sink t, then the following conditions are equivalent:

1. f is a maximum flow in G.
2. The residual network G_f contains no augmenting paths.
3. $|f| = c(S, T)$ for some cut (S, T) of G.

Proof   (1) $\Rightarrow$ (2): Suppose for the sake of contradiction that f is a maximum flow in G but that G_f has an augmenting path p. Then, by Corollary 26.3, the flow found by augmenting f by f_p, where f_p is given by equation (26.8), is a flow in G with value strictly greater than $|f|$, contradicting the assumption that f is a maximum flow.

(2) $\Rightarrow$ (3): Suppose that G_f has no augmenting path, that is, that G_f contains no path from s to t. Define

$$S = \{v \in V : \text{there exists a path from } s \text{ to } v \text{ in } G_f\}$$

and $T = V - S$. The partition (S, T) is a cut: we have $s \in S$ trivially and $t \notin S$ because there is no path from s to t in G_f. Now consider a pair of vertices

$u \in S$ and $v \in T$. If $(u, v) \in E$, we must have $f(u, v) = c(u, v)$, since otherwise $(u, v) \in E_f$, which would place v in set S. If $(v, u) \in E$, we must have $f(v, u) = 0$, because otherwise $c_f(u, v) = f(v, u)$ would be positive and we would have $(u, v) \in E_f$, which would place v in S. Of course, if neither (u, v) nor (v, u) is in E, then $f(u, v) = f(v, u) = 0$. We thus have

$$
\begin{aligned}
f(S, T) &= \sum_{u \in S} \sum_{v \in T} f(u, v) - \sum_{v \in T} \sum_{u \in S} f(v, u) \\
&= \sum_{u \in S} \sum_{v \in T} c(u, v) - \sum_{v \in T} \sum_{u \in S} 0 \\
&= c(S, T) .
\end{aligned}
$$

By Lemma 26.4, therefore, $|f| = f(S, T) = c(S, T)$.

(3) $\Rightarrow$ (1): By Corollary 26.5, $|f| \le c(S, T)$ for all cuts (S, T). The condition $|f| = c(S, T)$ thus implies that f is a maximum flow. ∎

The basic Ford-Fulkerson algorithm

In each iteration of the Ford-Fulkerson method, we find *some* augmenting path p and use p to modify the flow f. As Lemma 26.2 and Corollary 26.3 suggest, we replace f by $f \uparrow f_p$, obtaining a new flow whose value is $|f| + |f_p|$. The following implementation of the method computes the maximum flow in a flow network $G = (V, E)$ by updating the flow attribute $(u, v).f$ for each edge $(u, v) \in E$.[1] If $(u, v) \notin E$, we assume implicitly that $(u, v).f = 0$. We also assume that we are given the capacities $c(u, v)$ along with the flow network, and $c(u, v) = 0$ if $(u, v) \notin E$. We compute the residual capacity $c_f(u, v)$ in accordance with the formula (26.2). The expression $c_f(p)$ in the code is just a temporary variable that stores the residual capacity of the path p.

FORD-FULKERSON(G, s, t)

```
1   for each edge (u, v) ∈ G.E
2       (u, v).f = 0
3   while there exists a path p from s to t in the residual network G_f
4       c_f(p) = min {c_f(u, v) : (u, v) is in p}
5       for each edge (u, v) in p
6           if (u, v) ∈ G.E
7               (u, v).f = (u, v).f + c_f(p)
8           else (v, u).f = (v, u).f − c_f(p)
```

---

[1] Recall from Section 22.1 that we represent an attribute f for edge (u, v) with the same style of notation—$(u, v).f$—that we use for an attribute of any other object.

The FORD-FULKERSON algorithm simply expands on the FORD-FULKERSON-METHOD pseudocode given earlier. Figure 26.6 shows the result of each iteration in a sample run. Lines 1–2 initialize the flow f to 0. The **while** loop of lines 3–8 repeatedly finds an augmenting path p in G_f and augments flow f along p by the residual capacity $c_f(p)$. Each residual edge in path p is either an edge in the original network or the reversal of an edge in the original network. Lines 6–8 update the flow in each case appropriately, adding flow when the residual edge is an original edge and subtracting it otherwise. When no augmenting paths exist, the flow f is a maximum flow.

Analysis of Ford-Fulkerson

The running time of FORD-FULKERSON depends on how we find the augmenting path p in line 3. If we choose it poorly, the algorithm might not even terminate: the value of the flow will increase with successive augmentations, but it need not even converge to the maximum flow value.[2] If we find the augmenting path by using a breadth-first search (which we saw in Section 22.2), however, the algorithm runs in polynomial time. Before proving this result, we obtain a simple bound for the case in which we choose the augmenting path arbitrarily and all capacities are integers.

In practice, the maximum-flow problem often arises with integral capacities. If the capacities are rational numbers, we can apply an appropriate scaling transformation to make them all integral. If f^* denotes a maximum flow in the transformed network, then a straightforward implementation of FORD-FULKERSON executes the **while** loop of lines 3–8 at most $|f^*|$ times, since the flow value increases by at least one unit in each iteration.

We can perform the work done within the **while** loop efficiently if we implement the flow network $G = (V, E)$ with the right data structure and find an augmenting path by a linear-time algorithm. Let us assume that we keep a data structure corresponding to a directed graph $G' = (V, E')$, where $E' = \{(u, v) : (u, v) \in E \text{ or } (v, u) \in E\}$. Edges in the network G are also edges in G', and therefore we can easily maintain capacities and flows in this data structure. Given a flow f on G, the edges in the residual network G_f consist of all edges (u, v) of G' such that $c_f(u, v) > 0$, where c_f conforms to equation (26.2). The time to find a path in a residual network is therefore $O(V + E') = O(E)$ if we use either depth-first search or breadth-first search. Each iteration of the **while** loop thus takes $O(E)$ time, as does the initialization in lines 1–2, making the total running time of the FORD-FULKERSON algorithm $O(E \, |f^*|)$.

---

[2]The Ford-Fulkerson method might fail to terminate only if edge capacities are irrational numbers.

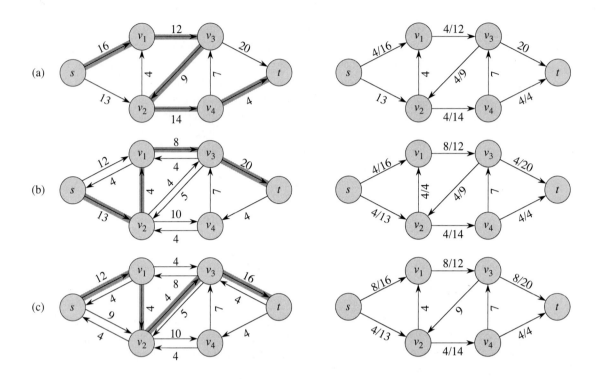

Figure 26.6 The execution of the basic Ford-Fulkerson algorithm. **(a)–(e)** Successive iterations of the **while** loop. The left side of each part shows the residual network G_f from line 3 with a shaded augmenting path p. The right side of each part shows the new flow f that results from augmenting f by f_p. The residual network in (a) is the input network G.

When the capacities are integral and the optimal flow value $|f^*|$ is small, the running time of the Ford-Fulkerson algorithm is good. Figure 26.7(a) shows an example of what can happen on a simple flow network for which $|f^*|$ is large. A maximum flow in this network has value 2,000,000: 1,000,000 units of flow traverse the path $s \rightarrow u \rightarrow t$, and another 1,000,000 units traverse the path $s \rightarrow v \rightarrow t$. If the first augmenting path found by FORD-FULKERSON is $s \rightarrow u \rightarrow v \rightarrow t$, shown in Figure 26.7(a), the flow has value 1 after the first iteration. The resulting residual network appears in Figure 26.7(b). If the second iteration finds the augmenting path $s \rightarrow v \rightarrow u \rightarrow t$, as shown in Figure 26.7(b), the flow then has value 2. Figure 26.7(c) shows the resulting residual network. We can continue, choosing the augmenting path $s \rightarrow u \rightarrow v \rightarrow t$ in the odd-numbered iterations and the augmenting path $s \rightarrow v \rightarrow u \rightarrow t$ in the even-numbered iterations. We would perform a total of 2,000,000 augmentations, increasing the flow value by only 1 unit in each.

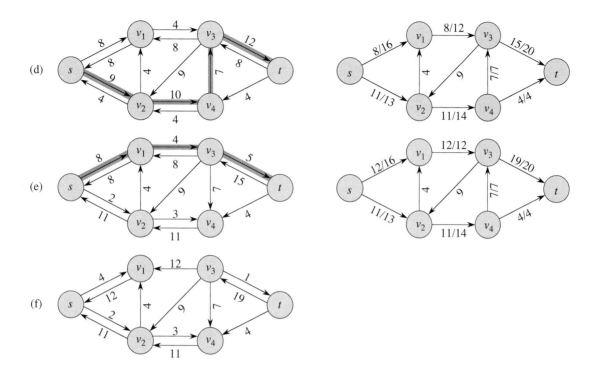

Figure 26.6, continued   **(f)** The residual network at the last **while** loop test. It has no augmenting paths, and the flow f shown in (e) is therefore a maximum flow. The value of the maximum flow found is 23.

The Edmonds-Karp algorithm

We can improve the bound on FORD-FULKERSON by finding the augmenting path p in line 3 with a breadth-first search. That is, we choose the augmenting path as a *shortest* path from s to t in the residual network, where each edge has unit distance (weight). We call the Ford-Fulkerson method so implemented the *Edmonds-Karp algorithm*. We now prove that the Edmonds-Karp algorithm runs in $O(VE^2)$ time.

The analysis depends on the distances to vertices in the residual network G_f. The following lemma uses the notation $\delta_f(u, v)$ for the shortest-path distance from u to v in G_f, where each edge has unit distance.

Lemma 26.7
If the Edmonds-Karp algorithm is run on a flow network $G = (V, E)$ with source s and sink t, then for all vertices $v \in V - \{s, t\}$, the shortest-path distance $\delta_f(s, v)$ in the residual network G_f increases monotonically with each flow augmentation.

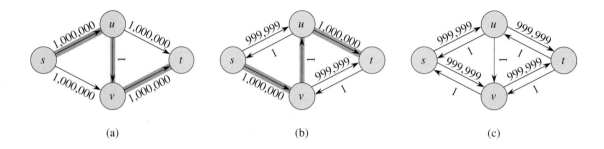

Figure 26.7 **(a)** A flow network for which FORD-FULKERSON can take $\Theta(E\,|f^*|)$ time, where f^* is a maximum flow, shown here with $|f^*| = 2{,}000{,}000$. The shaded path is an augmenting path with residual capacity 1. **(b)** The resulting residual network, with another augmenting path whose residual capacity is 1. **(c)** The resulting residual network.

Proof We will suppose that for some vertex $v \in V - \{s,t\}$, there is a flow augmentation that causes the shortest-path distance from s to v to decrease, and then we will derive a contradiction. Let f be the flow just before the first augmentation that decreases some shortest-path distance, and let f' be the flow just afterward. Let v be the vertex with the minimum $\delta_{f'}(s,v)$ whose distance was decreased by the augmentation, so that $\delta_{f'}(s,v) < \delta_f(s,v)$. Let $p = s \rightsquigarrow u \to v$ be a shortest path from s to v in $G_{f'}$, so that $(u,v) \in E_{f'}$ and

$$\delta_{f'}(s,u) = \delta_{f'}(s,v) - 1 .\tag{26.12}$$

Because of how we chose v, we know that the distance of vertex u from the source s did not decrease, i.e.,

$$\delta_{f'}(s,u) \geq \delta_f(s,u) .\tag{26.13}$$

We claim that $(u,v) \notin E_f$. Why? If we had $(u,v) \in E_f$, then we would also have

$$
\begin{aligned}
\delta_f(s,v) &\leq \delta_f(s,u) + 1 &&\text{(by Lemma 24.10, the triangle inequality)}\\
&\leq \delta_{f'}(s,u) + 1 &&\text{(by inequality (26.13))}\\
&= \delta_{f'}(s,v) &&\text{(by equation (26.12))} ,
\end{aligned}
$$

which contradicts our assumption that $\delta_{f'}(s,v) < \delta_f(s,v)$.

How can we have $(u,v) \notin E_f$ and $(u,v) \in E_{f'}$? The augmentation must have increased the flow from v to u. The Edmonds-Karp algorithm always augments flow along shortest paths, and therefore it augmented along a shortest path from s to u in G_f that has (v,u) as its last edge. Therefore,

$$
\begin{aligned}
\delta_f(s,v) &= \delta_f(s,u) - 1\\
&\leq \delta_{f'}(s,u) - 1 &&\text{(by inequality (26.13))}\\
&= \delta_{f'}(s,v) - 2 &&\text{(by equation (26.12))} ,
\end{aligned}
$$

which contradicts our assumption that $\delta_{f'}(s, v) < \delta_f(s, v)$. We conclude that our assumption that such a vertex v exists is incorrect.   ■

The next theorem bounds the number of iterations of the Edmonds-Karp algorithm.

Theorem 26.8
If the Edmonds-Karp algorithm is run on a flow network $G = (V, E)$ with source s and sink t, then the total number of flow augmentations performed by the algorithm is $O(VE)$.

Proof   We say that an edge (u, v) in a residual network G_f is **critical** on an augmenting path p if the residual capacity of p is the residual capacity of (u, v), that is, if $c_f(p) = c_f(u, v)$. After we have augmented flow along an augmenting path, any critical edge on the path disappears from the residual network. Moreover, at least one edge on any augmenting path must be critical. We will show that each of the $|E|$ edges can become critical at most $|V|/2$ times.

Let u and v be vertices in V that are connected by an edge in E. Since augmenting paths are shortest paths, when (u, v) is critical for the first time, we have

$$\delta_f(s, v) = \delta_f(s, u) + 1 \ .$$

Once the flow is augmented, the edge (u, v) disappears from the residual network. It cannot reappear later on another augmenting path until after the flow from u to v is decreased, which occurs only if (v, u) appears on an augmenting path. If f' is the flow in G when this event occurs, then we have

$$\delta_{f'}(s, u) = \delta_{f'}(s, v) + 1 \ .$$

Since $\delta_f(s, v) \leq \delta_{f'}(s, v)$ by Lemma 26.7, we have

$$
\begin{aligned}
\delta_{f'}(s, u) &= \delta_{f'}(s, v) + 1 \\
&\geq \delta_f(s, v) + 1 \\
&= \delta_f(s, u) + 2 \ .
\end{aligned}
$$

Consequently, from the time (u, v) becomes critical to the time when it next becomes critical, the distance of u from the source increases by at least 2. The distance of u from the source is initially at least 0. The intermediate vertices on a shortest path from s to u cannot contain s, u, or t (since (u, v) on an augmenting path implies that $u \neq t$). Therefore, until u becomes unreachable from the source, if ever, its distance is at most $|V| - 2$. Thus, after the first time that (u, v) becomes critical, it can become critical at most $(|V| - 2)/2 = |V|/2 - 1$ times more, for a total of at most $|V|/2$ times. Since there are $O(E)$ pairs of vertices that can have an edge between them in a residual network, the total number of critical edges during the entire execution of the Edmonds-Karp algorithm is $O(VE)$. Each augmenting path has at least one critical edge, and hence the theorem follows.   ∎

Because we can implement each iteration of FORD-FULKERSON in $O(E)$ time when we find the augmenting path by breadth-first search, the total running time of the Edmonds-Karp algorithm is $O(VE^2)$. We shall see that push-relabel algorithms can yield even better bounds. The algorithm of Section 26.4 gives a method for achieving an $O(V^2E)$ running time, which forms the basis for the $O(V^3)$-time algorithm of Section 26.5.

Exercises

26.2-1
Prove that the summations in equation (26.6) equal the summations in equation (26.5).

26.2-2
In Figure 26.1(b), what is the flow across the cut $(\{s, v_2, v_4\}, \{v_1, v_3, t\})$? What is the capacity of this cut?

26.2-3
Show the execution of the Edmonds-Karp algorithm on the flow network of Figure 26.1(a).

26.2-4
In the example of Figure 26.6, what is the minimum cut corresponding to the maximum flow shown? Of the augmenting paths appearing in the example, which one cancels flow?

26.2-5
Recall that the construction in Section 26.1 that converts a flow network with multiple sources and sinks into a single-source, single-sink network adds edges with infinite capacity. Prove that any flow in the resulting network has a finite value if the edges of the original network with multiple sources and sinks have finite capacity.

26.2-6
Suppose that each source s_i in a flow network with multiple sources and sinks produces exactly p_i units of flow, so that $\sum_{v \in V} f(s_i, v) = p_i$. Suppose also that each sink t_j consumes exactly q_j units, so that $\sum_{v \in V} f(v, t_j) = q_j$, where $\sum_i p_i = \sum_j q_j$. Show how to convert the problem of finding a flow f that obeys

these additional constraints into the problem of finding a maximum flow in a single-source, single-sink flow network.

26.2-7
Prove Lemma 26.2.

26.2-8
Suppose that we redefine the residual network to disallow edges into s. Argue that the procedure FORD-FULKERSON still correctly computes a maximum flow.

26.2-9
Suppose that both f and f' are flows in a network G and we compute flow $f \uparrow f'$. Does the augmented flow satisfy the flow conservation property? Does it satisfy the capacity constraint?

26.2-10
Show how to find a maximum flow in a network $G = (V, E)$ by a sequence of at most $|E|$ augmenting paths. (*Hint:* Determine the paths *after* finding the maximum flow.)

26.2-11
The **edge connectivity** of an undirected graph is the minimum number k of edges that must be removed to disconnect the graph. For example, the edge connectivity of a tree is 1, and the edge connectivity of a cyclic chain of vertices is 2. Show how to determine the edge connectivity of an undirected graph $G = (V, E)$ by running a maximum-flow algorithm on at most $|V|$ flow networks, each having $O(V)$ vertices and $O(E)$ edges.

26.2-12
Suppose that you are given a flow network G, and G has edges entering the source s. Let f be a flow in G with $|f| \geq 0$ and in which one of the edges (v, s) entering the source has $f(v, s) = 1$. Prove that there must exist another flow f' with $f'(v, s) = 0$ such that $|f| = |f'|$. Give an $O(E)$-time algorithm to compute f', given f, and assuming that all edge capacities are integers.

26.2-13
Suppose that you wish to find, among all minimum cuts in a flow network G with integral capacities, one that contains the smallest number of edges. Show how to modify the capacities of G to create a new flow network G' in which any minimum cut in G' is a minimum cut with the smallest number of edges in G.

26.3   Maximum bipartite matching

Some combinatorial problems can easily be cast as maximum-flow problems. The multiple-source, multiple-sink maximum-flow problem from Section 26.1 gave us one example. Some other combinatorial problems seem on the surface to have little to do with flow networks, but can in fact be reduced to maximum-flow problems. This section presents one such problem: finding a maximum matching in a bipartite graph. In order to solve this problem, we shall take advantage of an integrality property provided by the Ford-Fulkerson method. We shall also see how to use the Ford-Fulkerson method to solve the maximum-bipartite-matching problem on a graph $G = (V, E)$ in $O(VE)$ time.

The maximum-bipartite-matching problem

Given an undirected graph $G = (V, E)$, a **matching** is a subset of edges $M \subseteq E$ such that for all vertices $v \in V$, at most one edge of M is incident on v. We say that a vertex $v \in V$ is **matched** by the matching M if some edge in M is incident on v; otherwise, v is **unmatched**. A **maximum matching** is a matching of maximum cardinality, that is, a matching M such that for any matching M', we have $|M| \geq |M'|$. In this section, we shall restrict our attention to finding maximum matchings in bipartite graphs: graphs in which the vertex set can be partitioned into $V = L \cup R$, where L and R are disjoint and all edges in E go between L and R. We further assume that every vertex in V has at least one incident edge. Figure 26.8 illustrates the notion of a matching in a bipartite graph.

The problem of finding a maximum matching in a bipartite graph has many practical applications. As an example, we might consider matching a set L of machines with a set R of tasks to be performed simultaneously. We take the presence of edge (u, v) in E to mean that a particular machine $u \in L$ is capable of performing a particular task $v \in R$. A maximum matching provides work for as many machines as possible.

Finding a maximum bipartite matching

We can use the Ford-Fulkerson method to find a maximum matching in an undirected bipartite graph $G = (V, E)$ in time polynomial in $|V|$ and $|E|$. The trick is to construct a flow network in which flows correspond to matchings, as shown in Figure 26.8(c). We define the **corresponding flow network** $G' = (V', E')$ for the bipartite graph G as follows. We let the source s and sink t be new vertices not in V, and we let $V' = V \cup \{s, t\}$. If the vertex partition of G is $V = L \cup R$, the

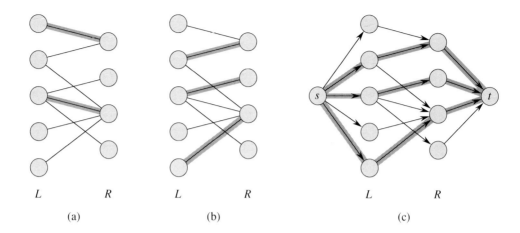

Figure 26.8   A bipartite graph $G = (V, E)$ with vertex partition $V = L \cup R$. **(a)** A matching with cardinality 2, indicated by shaded edges. **(b)** A maximum matching with cardinality 3. **(c)** The corresponding flow network G' with a maximum flow shown. Each edge has unit capacity. Shaded edges have a flow of 1, and all other edges carry no flow. The shaded edges from L to R correspond to those in the maximum matching from (b).

directed edges of G' are the edges of E, directed from L to R, along with $|V|$ new directed edges:

$$E' = \{(s, u) : u \in L\} \cup \{(u, v) : (u, v) \in E\} \cup \{(v, t) : v \in R\} \ .$$

To complete the construction, we assign unit capacity to each edge in E'. Since each vertex in V has at least one incident edge, $|E| \geq |V|/2$. Thus, $|E| \leq |E'| = |E| + |V| \leq 3|E|$, and so $|E'| = \Theta(E)$.

The following lemma shows that a matching in G corresponds directly to a flow in G's corresponding flow network G'. We say that a flow f on a flow network $G = (V, E)$ is ***integer-valued*** if $f(u, v)$ is an integer for all $(u, v) \in V \times V$.

Lemma 26.9
Let $G = (V, E)$ be a bipartite graph with vertex partition $V = L \cup R$, and let $G' = (V', E')$ be its corresponding flow network. If M is a matching in G, then there is an integer-valued flow f in G' with value $|f| = |M|$. Conversely, if f is an integer-valued flow in G', then there is a matching M in G with cardinality $|M| = |f|$.

Proof   We first show that a matching M in G corresponds to an integer-valued flow f in G'. Define f as follows. If $(u, v) \in M$, then $f(s, u) = f(u, v) = f(v, t) = 1$. For all other edges $(u, v) \in E'$, we define $f(u, v) = 0$. It is simple to verify that f satisfies the capacity constraint and flow conservation.

Intuitively, each edge $(u, v) \in M$ corresponds to one unit of flow in G' that traverses the path $s \rightarrow u \rightarrow v \rightarrow t$. Moreover, the paths induced by edges in M are vertex-disjoint, except for s and t. The net flow across cut $(L \cup \{s\}, R \cup \{t\})$ is equal to $|M|$; thus, by Lemma 26.4, the value of the flow is $|f| = |M|$.

To prove the converse, let f be an integer-valued flow in G', and let

$$M = \{(u, v) : u \in L, \ v \in R, \text{ and } f(u, v) > 0\} \ .$$

Each vertex $u \in L$ has only one entering edge, namely (s, u), and its capacity is 1. Thus, each $u \in L$ has at most one unit of flow entering it, and if one unit of flow does enter, by flow conservation, one unit of flow must leave. Furthermore, since f is integer-valued, for each $u \in L$, the one unit of flow can enter on at most one edge and can leave on at most one edge. Thus, one unit of flow enters u if and only if there is exactly one vertex $v \in R$ such that $f(u, v) = 1$, and at most one edge leaving each $u \in L$ carries positive flow. A symmetric argument applies to each $v \in R$. The set M is therefore a matching.

To see that $|M| = |f|$, observe that for every matched vertex $u \in L$, we have $f(s, u) = 1$, and for every edge $(u, v) \in E - M$, we have $f(u, v) = 0$. Consequently, $f(L \cup \{s\}, R \cup \{t\})$, the net flow across cut $(L \cup \{s\}, R \cup \{t\})$, is equal to $|M|$. Applying Lemma 26.4, we have that $|f| = f(L \cup \{s\}, R \cup \{t\}) = |M|$. ∎

Based on Lemma 26.9, we would like to conclude that a maximum matching in a bipartite graph G corresponds to a maximum flow in its corresponding flow network G', and we can therefore compute a maximum matching in G by running a maximum-flow algorithm on G'. The only hitch in this reasoning is that the maximum-flow algorithm might return a flow in G' for which some $f(u, v)$ is not an integer, even though the flow value $|f|$ must be an integer. The following theorem shows that if we use the Ford-Fulkerson method, this difficulty cannot arise.

Theorem 26.10 (Integrality theorem)
If the capacity function c takes on only integral values, then the maximum flow f produced by the Ford-Fulkerson method has the property that $|f|$ is an integer. Moreover, for all vertices u and v, the value of $f(u, v)$ is an integer.

Proof The proof is by induction on the number of iterations. We leave it as Exercise 26.3-2. ∎

We can now prove the following corollary to Lemma 26.9.

Corollary 26.11
The cardinality of a maximum matching M in a bipartite graph G equals the value of a maximum flow f in its corresponding flow network G'.

Proof We use the nomenclature from Lemma 26.9. Suppose that M is a maximum matching in G and that the corresponding flow f in G' is not maximum. Then there is a maximum flow f' in G' such that $|f'| > |f|$. Since the capacities in G' are integer-valued, by Theorem 26.10, we can assume that f' is integer-valued. Thus, f' corresponds to a matching M' in G with cardinality $|M'| = |f'| > |f| = |M|$, contradicting our assumption that M is a maximum matching. In a similar manner, we can show that if f is a maximum flow in G', its corresponding matching is a maximum matching on G. ∎

Thus, given a bipartite undirected graph G, we can find a maximum matching by creating the flow network G', running the Ford-Fulkerson method, and directly obtaining a maximum matching M from the integer-valued maximum flow f found. Since any matching in a bipartite graph has cardinality at most $\min(L, R) = O(V)$, the value of the maximum flow in G' is $O(V)$. We can therefore find a maximum matching in a bipartite graph in time $O(VE') = O(VE)$, since $|E'| = \Theta(E)$.

Exercises

26.3-1
Run the Ford-Fulkerson algorithm on the flow network in Figure 26.8(c) and show the residual network after each flow augmentation. Number the vertices in L top to bottom from 1 to 5 and in R top to bottom from 6 to 9. For each iteration, pick the augmenting path that is lexicographically smallest.

26.3-2
Prove Theorem 26.10.

26.3-3
Let $G = (V, E)$ be a bipartite graph with vertex partition $V = L \cup R$, and let G' be its corresponding flow network. Give a good upper bound on the length of any augmenting path found in G' during the execution of FORD-FULKERSON.

26.3-4 ★
A ***perfect matching*** is a matching in which every vertex is matched. Let $G = (V, E)$ be an undirected bipartite graph with vertex partition $V = L \cup R$, where $|L| = |R|$. For any $X \subseteq V$, define the ***neighborhood*** of X as

$$N(X) = \{y \in V : (x, y) \in E \text{ for some } x \in X\} ,$$

that is, the set of vertices adjacent to some member of X. Prove **Hall's theorem**: there exists a perfect matching in G if and only if $|A| \leq |N(A)|$ for every subset $A \subseteq L$.

26.3-5   ★

We say that a bipartite graph $G = (V, E)$, where $V = L \cup R$, is **d-regular** if every vertex $v \in V$ has degree exactly d. Every d-regular bipartite graph has $|L| = |R|$. Prove that every d-regular bipartite graph has a matching of cardinality $|L|$ by arguing that a minimum cut of the corresponding flow network has capacity $|L|$.

★ 26.4   Push-relabel algorithms

In this section, we present the "push-relabel" approach to computing maximum flows. To date, many of the asymptotically fastest maximum-flow algorithms are push-relabel algorithms, and the fastest actual implementations of maximum-flow algorithms are based on the push-relabel method. Push-relabel methods also efficiently solve other flow problems, such as the minimum-cost flow problem. This section introduces Goldberg's "generic" maximum-flow algorithm, which has a simple implementation that runs in $O(V^2E)$ time, thereby improving upon the $O(VE^2)$ bound of the Edmonds-Karp algorithm. Section 26.5 refines the generic algorithm to obtain another push-relabel algorithm that runs in $O(V^3)$ time.

Push-relabel algorithms work in a more localized manner than the Ford-Fulkerson method. Rather than examine the entire residual network to find an augmenting path, push-relabel algorithms work on one vertex at a time, looking only at the vertex's neighbors in the residual network. Furthermore, unlike the Ford-Fulkerson method, push-relabel algorithms do not maintain the flow-conservation property throughout their execution. They do, however, maintain a **preflow**, which is a function $f : V \times V \to \mathbb{R}$ that satisfies the capacity constraint and the following relaxation of flow conservation:

$$\sum_{v \in V} f(v, u) - \sum_{v \in V} f(u, v) \geq 0$$

for all vertices $u \in V - \{s\}$. That is, the flow into a vertex may exceed the flow out. We call the quantity

$$e(u) = \sum_{v \in V} f(v, u) - \sum_{v \in V} f(u, v) \qquad (26.14)$$

the **excess flow** into vertex u. The excess at a vertex is the amount by which the flow in exceeds the flow out. We say that a vertex $u \in V - \{s, t\}$ is **overflowing** if $e(u) > 0$.

We shall begin this section by describing the intuition behind the push-relabel method. We shall then investigate the two operations employed by the method: "pushing" preflow and "relabeling" a vertex. Finally, we shall present a generic push-relabel algorithm and analyze its correctness and running time.

Intuition

You can understand the intuition behind the push-relabel method in terms of fluid flows: we consider a flow network $G = (V, E)$ to be a system of interconnected pipes of given capacities. Applying this analogy to the Ford-Fulkerson method, we might say that each augmenting path in the network gives rise to an additional stream of fluid, with no branch points, flowing from the source to the sink. The Ford-Fulkerson method iteratively adds more streams of flow until no more can be added.

The generic push-relabel algorithm has a rather different intuition. As before, directed edges correspond to pipes. Vertices, which are pipe junctions, have two interesting properties. First, to accommodate excess flow, each vertex has an out-flow pipe leading to an arbitrarily large reservoir that can accumulate fluid. Second, each vertex, its reservoir, and all its pipe connections sit on a platform whose height increases as the algorithm progresses.

Vertex heights determine how flow is pushed: we push flow only downhill, that is, from a higher vertex to a lower vertex. The flow from a lower vertex to a higher vertex may be positive, but operations that push flow push it only downhill. We fix the height of the source at $|V|$ and the height of the sink at 0. All other vertex heights start at 0 and increase with time. The algorithm first sends as much flow as possible downhill from the source toward the sink. The amount it sends is exactly enough to fill each outgoing pipe from the source to capacity; that is, it sends the capacity of the cut $(s, V - \{s\})$. When flow first enters an intermediate vertex, it collects in the vertex's reservoir. From there, we eventually push it downhill.

We may eventually find that the only pipes that leave a vertex u and are not already saturated with flow connect to vertices that are on the same level as u or are uphill from u. In this case, to rid an overflowing vertex u of its excess flow, we must increase its height—an operation called "relabeling" vertex u. We increase its height to one unit more than the height of the lowest of its neighbors to which it has an unsaturated pipe. After a vertex is relabeled, therefore, it has at least one outgoing pipe through which we can push more flow.

Eventually, all the flow that can possibly get through to the sink has arrived there. No more can arrive, because the pipes obey the capacity constraints; the amount of flow across any cut is still limited by the capacity of the cut. To make the preflow a "legal" flow, the algorithm then sends the excess collected in the reservoirs of overflowing vertices back to the source by continuing to relabel vertices to above the fixed height $|V|$ of the source. As we shall see, once we have emptied all the reservoirs, the preflow is not only a "legal" flow, it is also a maximum flow.

The basic operations

From the preceding discussion, we see that a push-relabel algorithm performs two basic operations: pushing flow excess from a vertex to one of its neighbors and relabeling a vertex. The situations in which these operations apply depend on the heights of vertices, which we now define precisely.

Let $G = (V, E)$ be a flow network with source s and sink t, and let f be a preflow in G. A function $h : V \rightarrow \mathbb{N}$ is a ***height function***[3] if $h(s) = |V|$, $h(t) = 0$, and

$$h(u) \leq h(v) + 1$$

for every residual edge $(u, v) \in E_f$. We immediately obtain the following lemma.

Lemma 26.12
Let $G = (V, E)$ be a flow network, let f be a preflow in G, and let h be a height function on V. For any two vertices $u, v \in V$, if $h(u) > h(v) + 1$, then (u, v) is not an edge in the residual network.   ∎

The push operation
The basic operation PUSH(u, v) applies if u is an overflowing vertex, $c_f(u, v) > 0$, and $h(u) = h(v) + 1$. The pseudocode below updates the preflow f and the excess flows for u and v. It assumes that we can compute residual capacity $c_f(u, v)$ in constant time given c and f. We maintain the excess flow stored at a vertex u as the attribute $u.e$ and the height of u as the attribute $u.h$. The expression $\Delta_f(u, v)$ is a temporary variable that stores the amount of flow that we can push from u to v.

---

[3]In the literature, a height function is typically called a "distance function," and the height of a vertex is called a "distance label." We use the term "height" because it is more suggestive of the intuition behind the algorithm. We retain the use of the term "relabel" to refer to the operation that increases the height of a vertex. The height of a vertex is related to its distance from the sink t, as would be found in a breadth-first search of the transpose G^{T}.

PUSH(u, v)

1   **// Applies when**: u is overflowing, $c_f(u, v) > 0$, and $u.h = v.h + 1$.
2   **// Action**: Push $\Delta_f(u, v) = \min(u.e, c_f(u, v))$ units of flow from u to v.
3   $\Delta_f(u, v) = \min(u.e, c_f(u, v))$
4   **if** $(u, v) \in E$
5       $(u, v).f = (u, v).f + \Delta_f(u, v)$
6   **else** $(v, u).f = (v, u).f - \Delta_f(u, v)$
7   $u.e = u.e - \Delta_f(u, v)$
8   $v.e = v.e + \Delta_f(u, v)$

The code for PUSH operates as follows. Because vertex u has a positive excess $u.e$ and the residual capacity of (u, v) is positive, we can increase the flow from u to v by $\Delta_f(u, v) = \min(u.e, c_f(u, v))$ without causing $u.e$ to become negative or the capacity $c(u, v)$ to be exceeded. Line 3 computes the value $\Delta_f(u, v)$, and lines 4–6 update f. Line 5 increases the flow on edge (u, v), because we are pushing flow over a residual edge that is also an original edge. Line 6 decreases the flow on edge (v, u), because the residual edge is actually the reverse of an edge in the original network. Finally, lines 7–8 update the excess flows into vertices u and v. Thus, if f is a preflow before PUSH is called, it remains a preflow afterward.

Observe that nothing in the code for PUSH depends on the heights of u and v, yet we prohibit it from being invoked unless $u.h = v.h + 1$. Thus, we push excess flow downhill only by a height differential of 1. By Lemma 26.12, no residual edges exist between two vertices whose heights differ by more than 1, and thus, as long as the attribute h is indeed a height function, we would gain nothing by allowing flow to be pushed downhill by a height differential of more than 1.

We call the operation PUSH(u, v) a ***push*** from u to v. If a push operation applies to some edge (u, v) leaving a vertex u, we also say that the push operation applies to u. It is a ***saturating push*** if edge (u, v) in the residual network becomes ***saturated*** ($c_f(u, v) = 0$ afterward); otherwise, it is a ***nonsaturating push***. If an edge becomes saturated, it disappears from the residual network. A simple lemma characterizes one result of a nonsaturating push.

Lemma 26.13
After a nonsaturating push from u to v, the vertex u is no longer overflowing.

Proof   Since the push was nonsaturating, the amount of flow $\Delta_f(u, v)$ actually pushed must equal $u.e$ prior to the push. Since $u.e$ is reduced by this amount, it becomes 0 after the push.   ∎

The relabel operation

The basic operation RELABEL(u) applies if u is overflowing and if $u.h \leq v.h$ for all edges $(u, v) \in E_f$. In other words, we can relabel an overflowing vertex u if for every vertex v for which there is residual capacity from u to v, flow cannot be pushed from u to v because v is not downhill from u. (Recall that by definition, neither the source s nor the sink t can be overflowing, and so s and t are ineligible for relabeling.)

RELABEL(u)

1   **// Applies when:** u is overflowing and for all $v \in V$ such that $(u, v) \in E_f$,
          we have $u.h \leq v.h$.
2   **// Action:** Increase the height of u.
3    $u.h = 1 + \min\{v.h : (u, v) \in E_f\}$

When we call the operation RELABEL(u), we say that vertex u is ***relabeled***. Note that when u is relabeled, E_f must contain at least one edge that leaves u, so that the minimization in the code is over a nonempty set. This property follows from the assumption that u is overflowing, which in turn tells us that

$$u.e = \sum_{v \in V} f(v, u) - \sum_{v \in V} f(u, v) > 0 .$$

Since all flows are nonnegative, we must therefore have at least one vertex v such that $(v, u).f > 0$. But then, $c_f(u, v) > 0$, which implies that $(u, v) \in E_f$. The operation RELABEL(u) thus gives u the greatest height allowed by the constraints on height functions.

The generic algorithm

The generic push-relabel algorithm uses the following subroutine to create an initial preflow in the flow network.

INITIALIZE-PREFLOW(G, s)

1   **for** each vertex $v \in G.V$
2          $v.h = 0$
3          $v.e = 0$
4   **for** each edge $(u, v) \in G.E$
5          $(u, v).f = 0$
6    $s.h = |G.V|$
7   **for** each vertex $v \in s.Adj$
8          $(s, v).f = c(s, v)$
9          $v.e = c(s, v)$
10         $s.e = s.e - c(s, v)$

INITIALIZE-PREFLOW creates an initial preflow f defined by

$$(u, v).f = \begin{cases} c(u, v) & \text{if } u = s , \\ 0 & \text{otherwise} . \end{cases} \tag{26.15}$$

That is, we fill to capacity each edge leaving the source s, and all other edges carry no flow. For each vertex v adjacent to the source, we initially have $v.e = c(s, v)$, and we initialize $s.e$ to the negative of the sum of these capacities. The generic algorithm also begins with an initial height function h, given by

$$u.h = \begin{cases} |V| & \text{if } u = s , \\ 0 & \text{otherwise} . \end{cases} \tag{26.16}$$

Equation (26.16) defines a height function because the only edges (u, v) for which $u.h > v.h + 1$ are those for which $u = s$, and those edges are saturated, which means that they are not in the residual network.

Initialization, followed by a sequence of push and relabel operations, executed in no particular order, yields the GENERIC-PUSH-RELABEL algorithm:

GENERIC-PUSH-RELABEL(G)

1   INITIALIZE-PREFLOW(G, s)
2   **while** there exists an applicable push or relabel operation
3   select an applicable push or relabel operation and perform it

The following lemma tells us that as long as an overflowing vertex exists, at least one of the two basic operations applies.

Lemma 26.14 (An overflowing vertex can be either pushed or relabeled)
Let $G = (V, E)$ be a flow network with source s and sink t, let f be a preflow, and let h be any height function for f. If u is any overflowing vertex, then either a push or relabel operation applies to it.

Proof For any residual edge (u, v), we have $h(u) \leq h(v) + 1$ because h is a height function. If a push operation does not apply to an overflowing vertex u, then for all residual edges (u, v), we must have $h(u) < h(v) + 1$, which implies $h(u) \leq h(v)$. Thus, a relabel operation applies to u. ∎

Correctness of the push-relabel method

To show that the generic push-relabel algorithm solves the maximum-flow problem, we shall first prove that if it terminates, the preflow f is a maximum flow. We shall later prove that it terminates. We start with some observations about the height function h.

Lemma 26.15 (Vertex heights never decrease)

During the execution of the GENERIC-PUSH-RELABEL procedure on a flow network $G = (V, E)$, for each vertex $u \in V$, the height $u.h$ never decreases. Moreover, whenever a relabel operation is applied to a vertex u, its height $u.h$ increases by at least 1.

Proof   Because vertex heights change only during relabel operations, it suffices to prove the second statement of the lemma. If vertex u is about to be relabeled, then for all vertices v such that $(u, v) \in E_f$, we have $u.h \leq v.h$. Thus, $u.h < 1 + \min\{v.h : (u, v) \in E_f\}$, and so the operation must increase $u.h$.   ■

Lemma 26.16

Let $G = (V, E)$ be a flow network with source s and sink t. Then the execution of GENERIC-PUSH-RELABEL on G maintains the attribute h as a height function.

Proof   The proof is by induction on the number of basic operations performed. Initially, h is a height function, as we have already observed.

We claim that if h is a height function, then an operation RELABEL(u) leaves h a height function. If we look at a residual edge $(u, v) \in E_f$ that leaves u, then the operation RELABEL(u) ensures that $u.h \leq v.h + 1$ afterward. Now consider a residual edge (w, u) that enters u. By Lemma 26.15, $w.h \leq u.h + 1$ before the operation RELABEL(u) implies $w.h < u.h + 1$ afterward. Thus, the operation RELABEL(u) leaves h a height function.

Now, consider an operation PUSH(u, v). This operation may add the edge (v, u) to E_f, and it may remove (u, v) from E_f. In the former case, we have $v.h = u.h - 1 < u.h + 1$, and so h remains a height function. In the latter case, removing (u, v) from the residual network removes the corresponding constraint, and h again remains a height function.   ■

The following lemma gives an important property of height functions.

Lemma 26.17

Let $G = (V, E)$ be a flow network with source s and sink t, let f be a preflow in G, and let h be a height function on V. Then there is no path from the source s to the sink t in the residual network G_f.

Proof   Assume for the sake of contradiction that G_f contains a path p from s to t, where $p = \langle v_0, v_1, \ldots, v_k \rangle$, $v_0 = s$, and $v_k = t$. Without loss of generality, p is a simple path, and so $k < |V|$. For $i = 0, 1, \ldots, k - 1$, edge $(v_i, v_{i+1}) \in E_f$. Because h is a height function, $h(v_i) \leq h(v_{i+1}) + 1$ for $i = 0, 1, \ldots, k - 1$. Combining these inequalities over path p yields $h(s) \leq h(t) + k$. But because $h(t) = 0$, we have $h(s) \leq k < |V|$, which contradicts the requirement that $h(s) = |V|$ in a height function. ∎

We are now ready to show that if the generic push-relabel algorithm terminates, the preflow it computes is a maximum flow.

Theorem 26.18 (Correctness of the generic push-relabel algorithm)
If the algorithm GENERIC-PUSH-RELABEL terminates when run on a flow network $G = (V, E)$ with source s and sink t, then the preflow f it computes is a maximum flow for G.

Proof We use the following loop invariant:

> Each time the **while** loop test in line 2 in GENERIC-PUSH-RELABEL is executed, f is a preflow.

Initialization: INITIALIZE-PREFLOW makes f a preflow.

Maintenance: The only operations within the **while** loop of lines 2–3 are push and relabel. Relabel operations affect only height attributes and not the flow values; hence they do not affect whether f is a preflow. As argued on page 739, if f is a preflow prior to a push operation, it remains a preflow afterward.

Termination: At termination, each vertex in $V - \{s, t\}$ must have an excess of 0, because by Lemma 26.14 and the invariant that f is always a preflow, there are no overflowing vertices. Therefore, f is a flow. Lemma 26.16 shows that h is a height function at termination, and thus Lemma 26.17 tells us that there is no path from s to t in the residual network G_f. By the max-flow min-cut theorem (Theorem 26.6), therefore, f is a maximum flow. ∎

Analysis of the push-relabel method

To show that the generic push-relabel algorithm indeed terminates, we shall bound the number of operations it performs. We bound separately each of the three types of operations: relabels, saturating pushes, and nonsaturating pushes. With knowledge of these bounds, it is a straightforward problem to construct an algorithm that runs in $O(V^2 E)$ time. Before beginning the analysis, however, we prove an important lemma. Recall that we allow edges into the source in the residual network.

Lemma 26.19
Let $G = (V, E)$ be a flow network with source s and sink t, and let f be a preflow in G. Then, for any overflowing vertex x, there is a simple path from x to s in the residual network G_f.

Proof For an overflowing vertex x, let $U = \{v :$ there exists a simple path from x to v in $G_f\}$, and suppose for the sake of contradiction that $s \notin U$. Let $\overline{U} = V - U$.

We take the definition of excess from equation (26.14), sum over all vertices in U, and note that $V = U \cup \overline{U}$, to obtain

$$\sum_{u \in U} e(u)$$

$$= \sum_{u \in U} \left(\sum_{v \in V} f(v, u) - \sum_{v \in V} f(u, v) \right)$$

$$= \sum_{u \in U} \left(\left(\sum_{v \in U} f(v, u) + \sum_{v \in \overline{U}} f(v, u) \right) - \left(\sum_{v \in U} f(u, v) + \sum_{v \in \overline{U}} f(u, v) \right) \right)$$

$$= \sum_{u \in U} \sum_{v \in U} f(v, u) + \sum_{u \in U} \sum_{v \in \overline{U}} f(v, u) - \sum_{u \in U} \sum_{v \in U} f(u, v) - \sum_{u \in U} \sum_{v \in \overline{U}} f(u, v)$$

$$= \sum_{u \in U} \sum_{v \in \overline{U}} f(v, u) - \sum_{u \in U} \sum_{v \in \overline{U}} f(u, v) .$$

We know that the quantity $\sum_{u \in U} e(u)$ must be positive because $e(x) > 0$, $x \in U$, all vertices other than s have nonnegative excess, and, by assumption, $s \notin U$. Thus, we have

$$\sum_{u \in U} \sum_{v \in \overline{U}} f(v, u) - \sum_{u \in U} \sum_{v \in \overline{U}} f(u, v) > 0 . \qquad (26.17)$$

All edge flows are nonnegative, and so for equation (26.17) to hold, we must have $\sum_{u \in U} \sum_{v \in \overline{U}} f(v, u) > 0$. Hence, there must exist at least one pair of vertices $u' \in U$ and $v' \in \overline{U}$ with $f(v', u') > 0$. But, if $f(v', u') > 0$, there must be a residual edge (u', v'), which means that there is a simple path from x to v' (the path $x \rightsquigarrow u' \rightarrow v'$), thus contradicting the definition of U. $\blacksquare$

The next lemma bounds the heights of vertices, and its corollary bounds the number of relabel operations that are performed in total.

Lemma 26.20
Let $G = (V, E)$ be a flow network with source s and sink t. At any time during the execution of GENERIC-PUSH-RELABEL on G, we have $u.h \leq 2|V| - 1$ for all vertices $u \in V$.

Proof The heights of the source s and the sink t never change because these vertices are by definition not overflowing. Thus, we always have $s.h = |V|$ and $t.h = 0$, both of which are no greater than $2|V| - 1$.

Now consider any vertex $u \in V - \{s, t\}$. Initially, $u.h = 0 \leq 2|V| - 1$. We shall show that after each relabeling operation, we still have $u.h \leq 2|V| - 1$. When u is relabeled, it is overflowing, and Lemma 26.19 tells us that there is a simple path p from u to s in G_f. Let $p = \langle v_0, v_1, \ldots, v_k \rangle$, where $v_0 = u$, $v_k = s$, and $k \leq |V| - 1$ because p is simple. For $i = 0, 1, \ldots, k - 1$, we have $(v_i, v_{i+1}) \in E_f$, and therefore, by Lemma 26.16, $v_i.h \leq v_{i+1}.h + 1$. Expanding these inequalities over path p yields $u.h = v_0.h \leq v_k.h + k \leq s.h + (|V| - 1) = 2|V| - 1$. ∎

Corollary 26.21 (Bound on relabel operations)
Let $G = (V, E)$ be a flow network with source s and sink t. Then, during the execution of GENERIC-PUSH-RELABEL on G, the number of relabel operations is at most $2|V| - 1$ per vertex and at most $(2|V| - 1)(|V| - 2) < 2|V|^2$ overall.

Proof Only the $|V| - 2$ vertices in $V - \{s, t\}$ may be relabeled. Let $u \in V - \{s, t\}$. The operation RELABEL(u) increases $u.h$. The value of $u.h$ is initially 0 and by Lemma 26.20, it grows to at most $2|V| - 1$. Thus, each vertex $u \in V - \{s, t\}$ is relabeled at most $2|V| - 1$ times, and the total number of relabel operations performed is at most $(2|V| - 1)(|V| - 2) < 2|V|^2$. ∎

Lemma 26.20 also helps us to bound the number of saturating pushes.

Lemma 26.22 (Bound on saturating pushes)
During the execution of GENERIC-PUSH-RELABEL on any flow network $G = (V, E)$, the number of saturating pushes is less than $2|V||E|$.

Proof For any pair of vertices $u, v \in V$, we will count the saturating pushes from u to v and from v to u together, calling them the saturating pushes between u and v. If there are any such pushes, at least one of (u, v) and (v, u) is actually an edge in E. Now, suppose that a saturating push from u to v has occurred. At that time, $v.h = u.h - 1$. In order for another saturating push from u to v to occur later, the algorithm must first push flow from v to u, which cannot happen until $v.h = u.h + 1$. Since $u.h$ never decreases, in order for $v.h = u.h + 1$, the value of $v.h$ must increase by at least 2. Likewise, $u.h$ must increase by at least 2 between saturating pushes from v to u. Heights start at 0 and, by Lemma 26.20, never exceed $2|V| - 1$, which implies that the number of times any vertex can have its height increase by 2 is less than $|V|$. Since at least one of $u.h$ and $v.h$ must increase by 2 between any two saturating pushes between u and v, there are fewer than $2|V|$ saturating pushes between u and v. Multiplying by the number of edges gives a bound of less than $2|V||E|$ on the total number of saturating pushes. ∎

The following lemma bounds the number of nonsaturating pushes in the generic push-relabel algorithm.

Lemma 26.23 (Bound on nonsaturating pushes)

During the execution of GENERIC-PUSH-RELABEL on any flow network $G = (V, E)$, the number of nonsaturating pushes is less than $4|V|^2(|V| + |E|)$.

Proof Define a potential function $\Phi = \sum_{v:e(v)>0} v.h$. Initially, $\Phi = 0$, and the value of Φ may change after each relabeling, saturating push, and nonsaturating push. We will bound the amount that saturating pushes and relabelings can contribute to the increase of Φ. Then we will show that each nonsaturating push must decrease Φ by at least 1, and will use these bounds to derive an upper bound on the number of nonsaturating pushes.

Let us examine the two ways in which Φ might increase. First, relabeling a vertex u increases Φ by less than $2|V|$, since the set over which the sum is taken is the same and the relabeling cannot increase u's height by more than its maximum possible height, which, by Lemma 26.20, is at most $2|V| - 1$. Second, a saturating push from a vertex u to a vertex v increases Φ by less than $2|V|$, since no heights change and only vertex v, whose height is at most $2|V| - 1$, can possibly become overflowing.

Now we show that a nonsaturating push from u to v decreases Φ by at least 1. Why? Before the nonsaturating push, u was overflowing, and v may or may not have been overflowing. By Lemma 26.13, u is no longer overflowing after the push. In addition, unless v is the source, it may or may not be overflowing after the push. Therefore, the potential function Φ has decreased by exactly $u.h$, and it has increased by either 0 or $v.h$. Since $u.h - v.h = 1$, the net effect is that the potential function has decreased by at least 1.

Thus, during the course of the algorithm, the total amount of increase in Φ is due to relabelings and saturated pushes, and Corollary 26.21 and Lemma 26.22 constrain the increase to be less than $(2|V|)(2|V|^2) + (2|V|)(2|V||E|) = 4|V|^2(|V| + |E|)$. Since $\Phi \geq 0$, the total amount of decrease, and therefore the total number of nonsaturating pushes, is less than $4|V|^2(|V| + |E|)$. ∎

Having bounded the number of relabelings, saturating pushes, and nonsaturating pushes, we have set the stage for the following analysis of the GENERIC-PUSH-RELABEL procedure, and hence of any algorithm based on the push-relabel method.

Theorem 26.24

During the execution of GENERIC-PUSH-RELABEL on any flow network $G = (V, E)$, the number of basic operations is $O(V^2 E)$.

Proof Immediate from Corollary 26.21 and Lemmas 26.22 and 26.23. ∎

Thus, the algorithm terminates after $O(V^2E)$ operations. All that remains is to give an efficient method for implementing each operation and for choosing an appropriate operation to execute.

Corollary 26.25
There is an implementation of the generic push-relabel algorithm that runs in $O(V^2E)$ time on any flow network $G = (V, E)$.

Proof Exercise 26.4-2 asks you to show how to implement the generic algorithm with an overhead of $O(V)$ per relabel operation and $O(1)$ per push. It also asks you to design a data structure that allows you to pick an applicable operation in $O(1)$ time. The corollary then follows.   ■

Exercises

26.4-1
Prove that, after the procedure INITIALIZE-PREFLOW(G, s) terminates, we have $s.e \leq -|f^*|$, where f^* is a maximum flow for G.

26.4-2
Show how to implement the generic push-relabel algorithm using $O(V)$ time per relabel operation, $O(1)$ time per push, and $O(1)$ time to select an applicable operation, for a total time of $O(V^2E)$.

26.4-3
Prove that the generic push-relabel algorithm spends a total of only $O(VE)$ time in performing all the $O(V^2)$ relabel operations.

26.4-4
Suppose that we have found a maximum flow in a flow network $G = (V, E)$ using a push-relabel algorithm. Give a fast algorithm to find a minimum cut in G.

26.4-5
Give an efficient push-relabel algorithm to find a maximum matching in a bipartite graph. Analyze your algorithm.

26.4-6
Suppose that all edge capacities in a flow network $G = (V, E)$ are in the set $\{1, 2, \ldots, k\}$. Analyze the running time of the generic push-relabel algorithm in terms of $|V|$, $|E|$, and k. (*Hint:* How many times can each edge support a nonsaturating push before it becomes saturated?)

26.4-7
Show that we could change line 6 of INITIALIZE-PREFLOW to

6    $s.h = |G.V| - 2$

without affecting the correctness or asymptotic performance of the generic push-relabel algorithm.

26.4-8
Let $\delta_f(u, v)$ be the distance (number of edges) from u to v in the residual network G_f. Show that the GENERIC-PUSH-RELABEL procedure maintains the properties that $u.h < |V|$ implies $u.h \leq \delta_f(u, t)$ and that $u.h \geq |V|$ implies $u.h - |V| \leq \delta_f(u, s)$.

26.4-9 ★
As in the previous exercise, let $\delta_f(u, v)$ be the distance from u to v in the residual network G_f. Show how to modify the generic push-relabel algorithm to maintain the property that $u.h < |V|$ implies $u.h = \delta_f(u, t)$ and that $u.h \geq |V|$ implies $u.h - |V| = \delta_f(u, s)$. The total time that your implementation dedicates to maintaining this property should be $O(VE)$.

26.4-10
Show that the number of nonsaturating pushes executed by the GENERIC-PUSH-RELABEL procedure on a flow network $G = (V, E)$ is at most $4|V|^2|E|$ for $|V| \geq 4$.

★   **26.5   The relabel-to-front algorithm**

The push-relabel method allows us to apply the basic operations in any order at all. By choosing the order carefully and managing the network data structure efficiently, however, we can solve the maximum-flow problem faster than the $O(V^2E)$ bound given by Corollary 26.25. We shall now examine the relabel-to-front algorithm, a push-relabel algorithm whose running time is $O(V^3)$, which is asymptotically at least as good as $O(V^2E)$, and even better for dense networks.

The relabel-to-front algorithm maintains a list of the vertices in the network. Beginning at the front, the algorithm scans the list, repeatedly selecting an overflowing vertex u and then "discharging" it, that is, performing push and relabel operations until u no longer has a positive excess. Whenever we relabel a vertex, we move it to the front of the list (hence the name "relabel-to-front") and the algorithm begins its scan anew.

The correctness and analysis of the relabel-to-front algorithm depend on the notion of "admissible" edges: those edges in the residual network through which flow can be pushed. After proving some properties about the network of admissible edges, we shall investigate the discharge operation and then present and analyze the relabel-to-front algorithm itself.

Admissible edges and networks

If $G = (V, E)$ is a flow network with source s and sink t, f is a preflow in G, and h is a height function, then we say that (u, v) is an *admissible edge* if $c_f(u, v) > 0$ and $h(u) = h(v) + 1$. Otherwise, (u, v) is *inadmissible*. The *admissible network* is $G_{f,h} = (V, E_{f,h})$, where $E_{f,h}$ is the set of admissible edges.

The admissible network consists of those edges through which we can push flow. The following lemma shows that this network is a directed acyclic graph (dag).

Lemma 26.26 (The admissible network is acyclic)
If $G = (V, E)$ is a flow network, f is a preflow in G, and h is a height function on G, then the admissible network $G_{f,h} = (V, E_{f,h})$ is acyclic.

Proof   The proof is by contradiction. Suppose that $G_{f,h}$ contains a cycle $p = \langle v_0, v_1, \ldots, v_k \rangle$, where $v_0 = v_k$ and $k > 0$. Since each edge in p is admissible, we have $h(v_{i-1}) = h(v_i) + 1$ for $i = 1, 2, \ldots, k$. Summing around the cycle gives

$$\sum_{i=1}^{k} h(v_{i-1}) = \sum_{i=1}^{k} (h(v_i) + 1)$$

$$= \sum_{i=1}^{k} h(v_i) + k \ .$$

Because each vertex in cycle p appears once in each of the summations, we derive the contradiction that $0 = k$.   ∎

The next two lemmas show how push and relabel operations change the admissible network.

Lemma 26.27
Let $G = (V, E)$ be a flow network, let f be a preflow in G, and suppose that the attribute h is a height function. If a vertex u is overflowing and (u, v) is an admissible edge, then PUSH(u, v) applies. The operation does not create any new admissible edges, but it may cause (u, v) to become inadmissible.

Proof By the definition of an admissible edge, we can push flow from u to v. Since u is overflowing, the operation PUSH(u, v) applies. The only new residual edge that pushing flow from u to v can create is (v, u). Since $v.h = u.h - 1$, edge (v, u) cannot become admissible. If the operation is a saturating push, then $c_f(u, v) = 0$ afterward and (u, v) becomes inadmissible. ■

Lemma 26.28
Let $G = (V, E)$ be a flow network, let f be a preflow in G, and suppose that the attribute h is a height function. If a vertex u is overflowing and there are no admissible edges leaving u, then RELABEL(u) applies. After the relabel operation, there is at least one admissible edge leaving u, but there are no admissible edges entering u.

Proof If u is overflowing, then by Lemma 26.14, either a push or a relabel operation applies to it. If there are no admissible edges leaving u, then no flow can be pushed from u and so RELABEL(u) applies. After the relabel operation, $u.h = 1 + \min\{v.h : (u, v) \in E_f\}$. Thus, if v is a vertex that realizes the minimum in this set, the edge (u, v) becomes admissible. Hence, after the relabel, there is at least one admissible edge leaving u.

To show that no admissible edges enter u after a relabel operation, suppose that there is a vertex v such that (v, u) is admissible. Then, $v.h = u.h + 1$ after the relabel, and so $v.h > u.h + 1$ just before the relabel. But by Lemma 26.12, no residual edges exist between vertices whose heights differ by more than 1. Moreover, relabeling a vertex does not change the residual network. Thus, (v, u) is not in the residual network, and hence it cannot be in the admissible network. ■

Neighbor lists

Edges in the relabel-to-front algorithm are organized into "neighbor lists." Given a flow network $G = (V, E)$, the ***neighbor list*** $u.N$ for a vertex $u \in V$ is a singly linked list of the neighbors of u in G. Thus, vertex v appears in the list $u.N$ if $(u, v) \in E$ or $(v, u) \in E$. The neighbor list $u.N$ contains exactly those vertices v for which there may be a residual edge (u, v). The attribute $u.N.head$ points to the first vertex in $u.N$, and $v.next\text{-}neighbor$ points to the vertex following v in a neighbor list; this pointer is NIL if v is the last vertex in the neighbor list.

The relabel-to-front algorithm cycles through each neighbor list in an arbitrary order that is fixed throughout the execution of the algorithm. For each vertex u, the attribute $u.current$ points to the vertex currently under consideration in $u.N$. Initially, $u.current$ is set to $u.N.head$.

Discharging an overflowing vertex

An overflowing vertex u is **discharged** by pushing all of its excess flow through admissible edges to neighboring vertices, relabeling u as necessary to cause edges leaving u to become admissible. The pseudocode goes as follows.

DISCHARGE(u)

```
1   while u.e > 0
2       v = u.current
3       if v == NIL
4           RELABEL(u)
5           u.current = u.N.head
6       elseif c_f(u, v) > 0 and u.h == v.h + 1
7           PUSH(u, v)
8       else u.current = v.next-neighbor
```

Figure 26.9 steps through several iterations of the **while** loop of lines 1–8, which executes as long as vertex u has positive excess. Each iteration performs exactly one of three actions, depending on the current vertex v in the neighbor list $u.N$.

1. If v is NIL, then we have run off the end of $u.N$. Line 4 relabels vertex u, and then line 5 resets the current neighbor of u to be the first one in $u.N$. (Lemma 26.29 below states that the relabel operation applies in this situation.)

2. If v is non-NIL and (u, v) is an admissible edge (determined by the test in line 6), then line 7 pushes some (or possibly all) of u's excess to vertex v.

3. If v is non-NIL but (u, v) is inadmissible, then line 8 advances $u.current$ one position further in the neighbor list $u.N$.

Observe that if DISCHARGE is called on an overflowing vertex u, then the last action performed by DISCHARGE must be a push from u. Why? The procedure terminates only when $u.e$ becomes zero, and neither the relabel operation nor advancing the pointer $u.current$ affects the value of $u.e$.

We must be sure that when PUSH or RELABEL is called by DISCHARGE, the operation applies. The next lemma proves this fact.

Lemma 26.29
If DISCHARGE calls PUSH(u, v) in line 7, then a push operation applies to (u, v). If DISCHARGE calls RELABEL(u) in line 4, then a relabel operation applies to u.

Proof   The tests in lines 1 and 6 ensure that a push operation occurs only if the operation applies, which proves the first statement in the lemma.

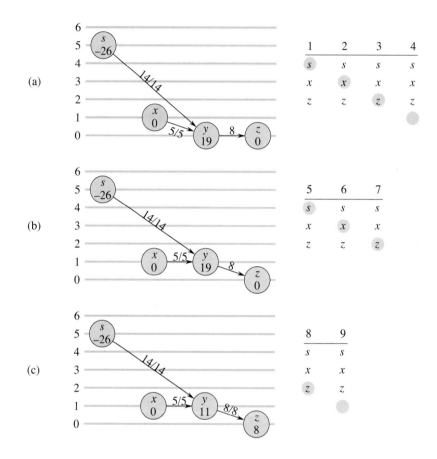

Figure 26.9 Discharging a vertex y. It takes 15 iterations of the **while** loop of DISCHARGE to push all the excess flow from y. Only the neighbors of y and edges of the flow network that enter or leave y are shown. In each part of the figure, the number inside each vertex is its excess at the beginning of the first iteration shown in the part, and each vertex is shown at its height throughout the part. The neighbor list $y.N$ at the beginning of each iteration appears on the right, with the iteration number on top. The shaded neighbor is $y.current$. **(a)** Initially, there are 19 units of excess to push from y, and $y.current = s$. Iterations 1, 2, and 3 just advance $y.current$, since there are no admissible edges leaving y. In iteration 4, $y.current =$ NIL (shown by the shading being below the neighbor list), and so y is relabeled and $y.current$ is reset to the head of the neighbor list. **(b)** After relabeling, vertex y has height 1. In iterations 5 and 6, edges (y, s) and (y, x) are found to be inadmissible, but iteration 7 pushes 8 units of excess flow from y to z. Because of the push, $y.current$ does not advance in this iteration. **(c)** Because the push in iteration 7 saturated edge (y, z), it is found inadmissible in iteration 8. In iteration 9, $y.current =$ NIL, and so vertex y is again relabeled and $y.current$ is reset.

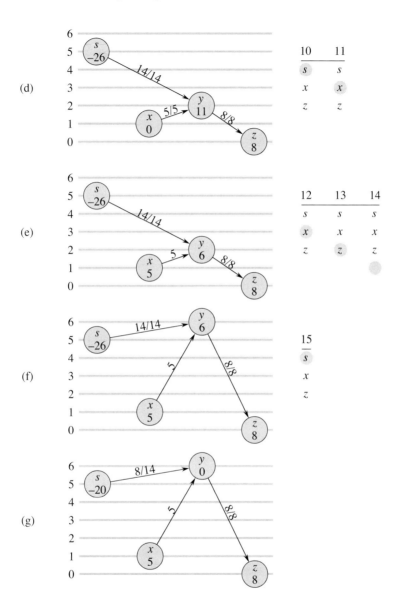

Figure 26.9, continued   **(d)** In iteration 10, (y, s) is inadmissible, but iteration 11 pushes 5 units of excess flow from y to x. **(e)** Because $y.current$ did not advance in iteration 11, iteration 12 finds (y, x) to be inadmissible. Iteration 13 finds (y, z) inadmissible, and iteration 14 relabels vertex y and resets $y.current$. **(f)** Iteration 15 pushes 6 units of excess flow from y to s. **(g)** Vertex y now has no excess flow, and DISCHARGE terminates. In this example, DISCHARGE both starts and finishes with the current pointer at the head of the neighbor list, but in general this need not be the case.

To prove the second statement, according to the test in line 1 and Lemma 26.28, we need only show that all edges leaving u are inadmissible. If a call to DISCHARGE(u) starts with the pointer $u.current$ at the head of u's neighbor list and finishes with it off the end of the list, then all of u's outgoing edges are inadmissible and a relabel operation applies. It is possible, however, that during a call to DISCHARGE(u), the pointer $u.current$ traverses only part of the list before the procedure returns. Calls to DISCHARGE on other vertices may then occur, but $u.current$ will continue moving through the list during the next call to DISCHARGE(u). We now consider what happens during a complete pass through the list, which begins at the head of $u.N$ and finishes with $u.current = $ NIL. Once $u.current$ reaches the end of the list, the procedure relabels u and begins a new pass. For the $u.current$ pointer to advance past a vertex $v \in u.N$ during a pass, the edge (u, v) must be deemed inadmissible by the test in line 6. Thus, by the time the pass completes, every edge leaving u has been determined to be inadmissible at some time during the pass. The key observation is that at the end of the pass, every edge leaving u is still inadmissible. Why? By Lemma 26.27, pushes cannot create any admissible edges, regardless of which vertex the flow is pushed from. Thus, any admissible edge must be created by a relabel operation. But the vertex u is not relabeled during the pass, and by Lemma 26.28, any other vertex v that is relabeled during the pass (resulting from a call of DISCHARGE(v)) has no entering admissible edges after relabeling. Thus, at the end of the pass, all edges leaving u remain inadmissible, which completes the proof. ∎

The relabel-to-front algorithm

In the relabel-to-front algorithm, we maintain a linked list L consisting of all vertices in $V - \{s, t\}$. A key property is that the vertices in L are topologically sorted according to the admissible network, as we shall see in the loop invariant that follows. (Recall from Lemma 26.26 that the admissible network is a dag.)

The pseudocode for the relabel-to-front algorithm assumes that the neighbor lists $u.N$ have already been created for each vertex u. It also assumes that $u.next$ points to the vertex that follows u in list L and that, as usual, $u.next = $ NIL if u is the last vertex in the list.

RELABEL-TO-FRONT(G, s, t)

```
 1  INITIALIZE-PREFLOW(G, s)
 2  L = G.V − {s, t}, in any order
 3  for each vertex u ∈ G.V − {s, t}
 4      u.current = u.N.head
 5  u = L.head
 6  while u ≠ NIL
 7      old-height = u.h
 8      DISCHARGE(u)
 9      if u.h > old-height
10          move u to the front of list L
11      u = u.next
```

The relabel-to-front algorithm works as follows. Line 1 initializes the preflow and heights to the same values as in the generic push-relabel algorithm. Line 2 initializes the list L to contain all potentially overflowing vertices, in any order. Lines 3–4 initialize the *current* pointer of each vertex u to the first vertex in u's neighbor list.

As Figure 26.10 illustrates, the **while** loop of lines 6–11 runs through the list L, discharging vertices. Line 5 makes it start with the first vertex in the list. Each time through the loop, line 8 discharges a vertex u. If u was relabeled by the DISCHARGE procedure, line 10 moves it to the front of list L. We can determine whether u was relabeled by comparing its height before the discharge operation, saved into the variable *old-height* in line 7, with its height afterward, in line 9. Line 11 makes the next iteration of the **while** loop use the vertex following u in list L. If line 10 moved u to the front of the list, the vertex used in the next iteration is the one following u in its new position in the list.

To show that RELABEL-TO-FRONT computes a maximum flow, we shall show that it is an implementation of the generic push-relabel algorithm. First, observe that it performs push and relabel operations only when they apply, since Lemma 26.29 guarantees that DISCHARGE performs them only when they apply. It remains to show that when RELABEL-TO-FRONT terminates, no basic operations apply. The remainder of the correctness argument relies on the following loop invariant:

> At each test in line 6 of RELABEL-TO-FRONT, list L is a topological sort of the vertices in the admissible network $G_{f,h} = (V, E_{f,h})$, and no vertex before u in the list has excess flow.

Initialization: Immediately after INITIALIZE-PREFLOW has been run, $s.h = |V|$ and $v.h = 0$ for all $v \in V - \{s\}$. Since $|V| \geq 2$ (because V contains at

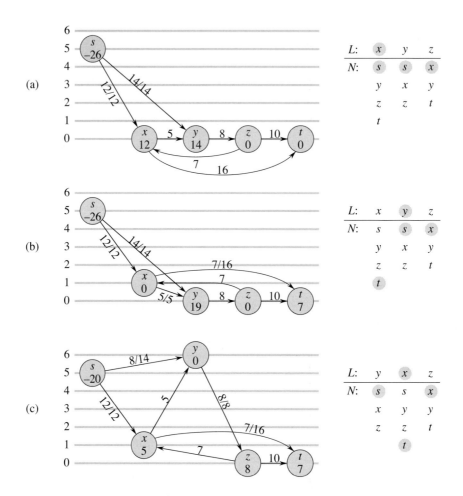

Figure 26.10 The action of RELABEL-TO-FRONT. **(a)** A flow network just before the first iteration of the **while** loop. Initially, 26 units of flow leave source s. On the right is shown the initial list $L = \langle x, y, z \rangle$, where initially $u = x$. Under each vertex in list L is its neighbor list, with the current neighbor shaded. Vertex x is discharged. It is relabeled to height 1, 5 units of excess flow are pushed to y, and the 7 remaining units of excess are pushed to the sink t. Because x is relabeled, it moves to the head of L, which in this case does not change the structure of L. **(b)** After x, the next vertex in L that is discharged is y. Figure 26.9 shows the detailed action of discharging y in this situation. Because y is relabeled, it is moved to the head of L. **(c)** Vertex x now follows y in L, and so it is again discharged, pushing all 5 units of excess flow to t. Because vertex x is not relabeled in this discharge operation, it remains in place in list L.

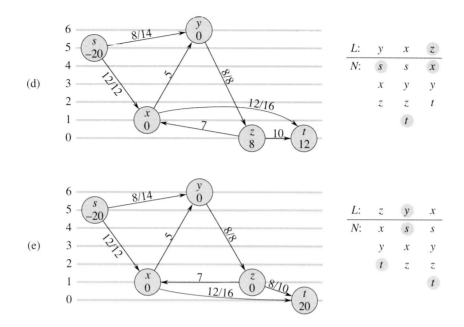

Figure 26.10, continued   **(d)** Since vertex z follows vertex x in L, it is discharged. It is relabeled to height 1 and all 8 units of excess flow are pushed to t. Because z is relabeled, it moves to the front of L. **(e)** Vertex y now follows vertex z in L and is therefore discharged. But because y has no excess, DISCHARGE immediately returns, and y remains in place in L. Vertex x is then discharged. Because it, too, has no excess, DISCHARGE again returns, and x remains in place in L. RELABEL-TO-FRONT has reached the end of list L and terminates. There are no overflowing vertices, and the preflow is a maximum flow.

least s and t), no edge can be admissible. Thus, $E_{f,h} = \emptyset$, and any ordering of $V - \{s, t\}$ is a topological sort of $G_{f,h}$.

Because u is initially the head of the list L, there are no vertices before it and so there are none before it with excess flow.

Maintenance: To see that each iteration of the **while** loop maintains the topological sort, we start by observing that the admissible network is changed only by push and relabel operations. By Lemma 26.27, push operations do not cause edges to become admissible. Thus, only relabel operations can create admissible edges. After a vertex u is relabeled, however, Lemma 26.28 states that there are no admissible edges entering u but there may be admissible edges leaving u. Thus, by moving u to the front of L, the algorithm ensures that any admissible edges leaving u satisfy the topological sort ordering.

To see that no vertex preceding u in L has excess flow, we denote the vertex that will be u in the next iteration by u'. The vertices that will precede u' in the next iteration include the current u (due to line 11) and either no other vertices (if u is relabeled) or the same vertices as before (if u is not relabeled). When u is discharged, it has no excess flow afterward. Thus, if u is relabeled during the discharge, no vertices preceding u' have excess flow. If u is not relabeled during the discharge, no vertices before it on the list acquired excess flow during this discharge, because L remained topologically sorted at all times during the discharge (as just pointed out, admissible edges are created only by relabeling, not pushing), and so each push operation causes excess flow to move only to vertices further down the list (or to s or t). Again, no vertices preceding u' have excess flow.

Termination: When the loop terminates, u is just past the end of L, and so the loop invariant ensures that the excess of every vertex is 0. Thus, no basic operations apply.

Analysis

We shall now show that RELABEL-TO-FRONT runs in $O(V^3)$ time on any flow network $G = (V, E)$. Since the algorithm is an implementation of the generic push-relabel algorithm, we shall take advantage of Corollary 26.21, which provides an $O(V)$ bound on the number of relabel operations executed per vertex and an $O(V^2)$ bound on the total number of relabel operations overall. In addition, Exercise 26.4-3 provides an $O(VE)$ bound on the total time spent performing relabel operations, and Lemma 26.22 provides an $O(VE)$ bound on the total number of saturating push operations.

Theorem 26.30
The running time of RELABEL-TO-FRONT on any flow network $G = (V, E)$ is $O(V^3)$.

Proof Let us consider a "phase" of the relabel-to-front algorithm to be the time between two consecutive relabel operations. There are $O(V^2)$ phases, since there are $O(V^2)$ relabel operations. Each phase consists of at most $|V|$ calls to DISCHARGE, which we can see as follows. If DISCHARGE does not perform a relabel operation, then the next call to DISCHARGE is further down the list L, and the length of L is less than $|V|$. If DISCHARGE does perform a relabel, the next call to DISCHARGE belongs to a different phase. Since each phase contains at most $|V|$ calls to DISCHARGE and there are $O(V^2)$ phases, the number of times DISCHARGE is called in line 8 of RELABEL-TO-FRONT is $O(V^3)$. Thus, the total work performed by the **while** loop in RELABEL-TO-FRONT, excluding the work performed within DISCHARGE, is at most $O(V^3)$.

We must now bound the work performed within DISCHARGE during the execution of the algorithm. Each iteration of the **while** loop within DISCHARGE performs one of three actions. We shall analyze the total amount of work involved in performing each of these actions.

We start with relabel operations (lines 4–5). Exercise 26.4-3 provides an $O(VE)$ time bound on all the $O(V^2)$ relabels that are performed.

Now, suppose that the action updates the $u.current$ pointer in line 8. This action occurs $O(\text{degree}(u))$ times each time a vertex u is relabeled, and $O(V \cdot \text{degree}(u))$ times overall for the vertex. For all vertices, therefore, the total amount of work done in advancing pointers in neighbor lists is $O(VE)$ by the handshaking lemma (Exercise B.4-1).

The third type of action performed by DISCHARGE is a push operation (line 7). We already know that the total number of saturating push operations is $O(VE)$. Observe that if a nonsaturating push is executed, DISCHARGE immediately returns, since the push reduces the excess to 0. Thus, there can be at most one nonsaturating push per call to DISCHARGE. As we have observed, DISCHARGE is called $O(V^3)$ times, and thus the total time spent performing nonsaturating pushes is $O(V^3)$.

The running time of RELABEL-TO-FRONT is therefore $O(V^3 + VE)$, which is $O(V^3)$.   ∎

Exercises

26.5-1
Illustrate the execution of RELABEL-TO-FRONT in the manner of Figure 26.10 for the flow network in Figure 26.1(a). Assume that the initial ordering of vertices in L is $\langle v_1, v_2, v_3, v_4 \rangle$ and that the neighbor lists are

$$
\begin{aligned}
v_1.N &= \langle s, v_2, v_3 \rangle , \\
v_2.N &= \langle s, v_1, v_3, v_4 \rangle , \\
v_3.N &= \langle v_1, v_2, v_4, t \rangle , \\
v_4.N &= \langle v_2, v_3, t \rangle .
\end{aligned}
$$

26.5-2   ★
We would like to implement a push-relabel algorithm in which we maintain a first-in, first-out queue of overflowing vertices. The algorithm repeatedly discharges the vertex at the head of the queue, and any vertices that were not overflowing before the discharge but are overflowing afterward are placed at the end of the queue. After the vertex at the head of the queue is discharged, it is removed. When the

queue is empty, the algorithm terminates. Show how to implement this algorithm to compute a maximum flow in $O(V^3)$ time.

26.5-3
Show that the generic algorithm still works if RELABEL updates $u.h$ by simply computing $u.h = u.h + 1$. How would this change affect the analysis of RELABEL-TO-FRONT?

26.5-4 ★
Show that if we always discharge a highest overflowing vertex, we can make the push-relabel method run in $O(V^3)$ time.

26.5-5
Suppose that at some point in the execution of a push-relabel algorithm, there exists an integer $0 < k \le |V| - 1$ for which no vertex has $v.h = k$. Show that all vertices with $v.h > k$ are on the source side of a minimum cut. If such a k exists, the **gap heuristic** updates every vertex $v \in V - \{s\}$ for which $v.h > k$, to set $v.h = \max(v.h, |V| + 1)$. Show that the resulting attribute h is a height function. (The gap heuristic is crucial in making implementations of the push-relabel method perform well in practice.)

Problems

26-1   Escape problem
An $n \times n$ **grid** is an undirected graph consisting of n rows and n columns of vertices, as shown in Figure 26.11. We denote the vertex in the ith row and the jth column by (i, j). All vertices in a grid have exactly four neighbors, except for the boundary vertices, which are the points (i, j) for which $i = 1$, $i = n$, $j = 1$, or $j = n$.

Given $m \le n^2$ starting points $(x_1, y_1), (x_2, y_2), \dots, (x_m, y_m)$ in the grid, the **escape problem** is to determine whether or not there are m vertex-disjoint paths from the starting points to any m different points on the boundary. For example, the grid in Figure 26.11(a) has an escape, but the grid in Figure 26.11(b) does not.

a. Consider a flow network in which vertices, as well as edges, have capacities. That is, the total positive flow entering any given vertex is subject to a capacity constraint. Show that determining the maximum flow in a network with edge and vertex capacities can be reduced to an ordinary maximum-flow problem on a flow network of comparable size.

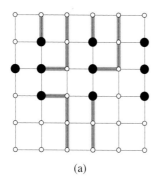 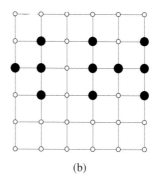

(a) (b)

Figure 26.11 Grids for the escape problem. Starting points are black, and other grid vertices are white. **(a)** A grid with an escape, shown by shaded paths. **(b)** A grid with no escape.

b. Describe an efficient algorithm to solve the escape problem, and analyze its running time.

26-2 *Minimum path cover*

A *path cover* of a directed graph $G = (V, E)$ is a set P of vertex-disjoint paths such that every vertex in V is included in exactly one path in P. Paths may start and end anywhere, and they may be of any length, including 0. A *minimum path cover* of G is a path cover containing the fewest possible paths.

a. Give an efficient algorithm to find a minimum path cover of a directed acyclic graph $G = (V, E)$. (*Hint:* Assuming that $V = \{1, 2, \dots, n\}$, construct the graph $G' = (V', E')$, where

$$V' = \{x_0, x_1, \dots, x_n\} \cup \{y_0, y_1, \dots, y_n\} ,$$
$$E' = \{(x_0, x_i) : i \in V\} \cup \{(y_i, y_0) : i \in V\} \cup \{(x_i, y_j) : (i, j) \in E\} ,$$

and run a maximum-flow algorithm.)

b. Does your algorithm work for directed graphs that contain cycles? Explain.

26-3 *Algorithmic consulting*

Professor Gore wants to open up an algorithmic consulting company. He has identified n important subareas of algorithms (roughly corresponding to different portions of this textbook), which he represents by the set $A = \{A_1, A_2, \dots, A_n\}$. In each subarea A_k, he can hire an expert in that area for c_k dollars. The consulting company has lined up a set $J = \{J_1, J_2, \dots, J_m\}$ of potential jobs. In order to perform job J_i, the company needs to have hired experts in a subset $R_i \subseteq A$ of subareas. Each expert can work on multiple jobs simultaneously. If the company chooses to accept job J_i, it must have hired experts in all subareas in R_i, and it will take in revenue of p_i dollars.

Professor Gore's job is to determine which subareas to hire experts in and which jobs to accept in order to maximize the net revenue, which is the total income from jobs accepted minus the total cost of employing the experts.

Consider the following flow network G. It contains a source vertex s, vertices $A_1, A_2, \ldots, A_n$, vertices $J_1, J_2, \ldots, J_m$, and a sink vertex t. For $k = 1, 2 \ldots, n$, the flow network contains an edge (s, A_k) with capacity $c(s, A_k) = c_k$, and for $i = 1, 2, \ldots, m$, the flow network contains an edge (J_i, t) with capacity $c(J_i, t) = p_i$. For $k = 1, 2, \ldots, n$ and $i = 1, 2, \ldots, m$, if $A_k \in R_i$, then G contains an edge (A_k, J_i) with capacity $c(A_k, J_i) = \infty$.

a. Show that if $J_i \in T$ for a finite-capacity cut (S, T) of G, then $A_k \in T$ for each $A_k \in R_i$.

b. Show how to determine the maximum net revenue from the capacity of a minimum cut of G and the given p_i values.

c. Give an efficient algorithm to determine which jobs to accept and which experts to hire. Analyze the running time of your algorithm in terms of m, n, and $r = \sum_{i=1}^{m} |R_i|$.

26-4   Updating maximum flow

Let $G = (V, E)$ be a flow network with source s, sink t, and integer capacities. Suppose that we are given a maximum flow in G.

a. Suppose that we increase the capacity of a single edge $(u, v) \in E$ by 1. Give an $O(V + E)$-time algorithm to update the maximum flow.

b. Suppose that we decrease the capacity of a single edge $(u, v) \in E$ by 1. Give an $O(V + E)$-time algorithm to update the maximum flow.

26-5   Maximum flow by scaling

Let $G = (V, E)$ be a flow network with source s, sink t, and an integer capacity $c(u, v)$ on each edge $(u, v) \in E$. Let $C = \max_{(u,v) \in E} c(u, v)$.

a. Argue that a minimum cut of G has capacity at most $C |E|$.

b. For a given number K, show how to find an augmenting path of capacity at least K in $O(E)$ time, if such a path exists.

We can use the following modification of FORD-FULKERSON-METHOD to compute a maximum flow in G:

MAX-FLOW-BY-SCALING(G, s, t)

1 $C = \max_{(u,v) \in E} c(u, v)$
2 initialize flow f to 0
3 $K = 2^{\lfloor \lg C \rfloor}$
4 **while** $K \geq 1$
5   **while** there exists an augmenting path p of capacity at least K
6   augment flow f along p
7      $K = K/2$
8 **return** f

c. Argue that MAX-FLOW-BY-SCALING returns a maximum flow.

d. Show that the capacity of a minimum cut of the residual network G_f is at most $2K |E|$ each time line 4 is executed.

e. Argue that the inner **while** loop of lines 5–6 executes $O(E)$ times for each value of K.

f. Conclude that MAX-FLOW-BY-SCALING can be implemented so that it runs in $O(E^2 \lg C)$ time.

26-6 The Hopcroft-Karp bipartite matching algorithm

In this problem, we describe a faster algorithm, due to Hopcroft and Karp, for finding a maximum matching in a bipartite graph. The algorithm runs in $O(\sqrt{V} E)$ time. Given an undirected, bipartite graph $G = (V, E)$, where $V = L \cup R$ and all edges have exactly one endpoint in L, let M be a matching in G. We say that a simple path P in G is an *augmenting path* with respect to M if it starts at an unmatched vertex in L, ends at an unmatched vertex in R, and its edges belong alternately to M and $E - M$. (This definition of an augmenting path is related to, but different from, an augmenting path in a flow network.) In this problem, we treat a path as a sequence of edges, rather than as a sequence of vertices. A shortest augmenting path with respect to a matching M is an augmenting path with a minimum number of edges.

Given two sets A and B, the *symmetric difference* $A \oplus B$ is defined as $(A - B) \cup (B - A)$, that is, the elements that are in exactly one of the two sets.

a. Show that if M is a matching and P is an augmenting path with respect to M, then the symmetric difference $M \oplus P$ is a matching and $|M \oplus P| = |M| + 1$. Show that if $P_1, P_2, \ldots, P_k$ are vertex-disjoint augmenting paths with respect to M, then the symmetric difference $M \oplus (P_1 \cup P_2 \cup \cdots \cup P_k)$ is a matching with cardinality $|M| + k$.

The general structure of our algorithm is the following:

HOPCROFT-KARP(G)

```
1  M = Ø
2  repeat
3      let 𝒫 = {P₁, P₂,..., Pₖ} be a maximal set of vertex-disjoint
              shortest augmenting paths with respect to M
4      M = M ⊕ (P₁ ∪ P₂ ∪ ⋯ ∪ Pₖ)
5  until 𝒫 == Ø
6  return M
```

The remainder of this problem asks you to analyze the number of iterations in the algorithm (that is, the number of iterations in the **repeat** loop) and to describe an implementation of line 3.

b. Given two matchings M and M^* in G, show that every vertex in the graph $G' = (V, M \oplus M^*)$ has degree at most 2. Conclude that G' is a disjoint union of simple paths or cycles. Argue that edges in each such simple path or cycle belong alternately to M or M^*. Prove that if $|M| \le |M^*|$, then $M \oplus M^*$ contains at least $|M^*| - |M|$ vertex-disjoint augmenting paths with respect to M.

Let l be the length of a shortest augmenting path with respect to a matching M, and let $P_1, P_2, \ldots, P_k$ be a maximal set of vertex-disjoint augmenting paths of length l with respect to M. Let $M' = M \oplus (P_1 \cup \cdots \cup P_k)$, and suppose that P is a shortest augmenting path with respect to M'.

c. Show that if P is vertex-disjoint from $P_1, P_2, \ldots, P_k$, then P has more than l edges.

d. Now suppose that P is not vertex-disjoint from $P_1, P_2, \ldots, P_k$. Let A be the set of edges $(M \oplus M') \oplus P$. Show that $A = (P_1 \cup P_2 \cup \cdots \cup P_k) \oplus P$ and that $|A| \ge (k + 1)l$. Conclude that P has more than l edges.

e. Prove that if a shortest augmenting path with respect to M has l edges, the size of the maximum matching is at most $|M| + |V|/(l + 1)$.

f. Show that the number of **repeat** loop iterations in the algorithm is at most $2\sqrt{|V|}$. (*Hint:* By how much can M grow after iteration number $\sqrt{|V|}$?)

g. Give an algorithm that runs in $O(E)$ time to find a maximal set of vertex-disjoint shortest augmenting paths $P_1, P_2, \ldots, P_k$ for a given matching M. Conclude that the total running time of HOPCROFT-KARP is $O(\sqrt{V}E)$.

Chapter notes

Ahuja, Magnanti, and Orlin [7], Even [103], Lawler [224], Papadimitriou and Steiglitz [271], and Tarjan [330] are good references for network flow and related algorithms. Goldberg, Tardos, and Tarjan [139] also provide a nice survey of algorithms for network-flow problems, and Schrijver [304] has written an interesting review of historical developments in the field of network flows.

The Ford-Fulkerson method is due to Ford and Fulkerson [109], who originated the formal study of many of the problems in the area of network flow, including the maximum-flow and bipartite-matching problems. Many early implementations of the Ford-Fulkerson method found augmenting paths using breadth-first search; Edmonds and Karp [102], and independently Dinic [89], proved that this strategy yields a polynomial-time algorithm. A related idea, that of using "blocking flows," was also first developed by Dinic [89]. Karzanov [202] first developed the idea of preflows. The push-relabel method is due to Goldberg [136] and Goldberg and Tarjan [140]. Goldberg and Tarjan gave an $O(V^3)$-time algorithm that uses a queue to maintain the set of overflowing vertices, as well as an algorithm that uses dynamic trees to achieve a running time of $O(VE \lg(V^2/E + 2))$. Several other researchers have developed push-relabel maximum-flow algorithms. Ahuja and Orlin [9] and Ahuja, Orlin, and Tarjan [10] gave algorithms that used scaling. Cheriyan and Maheshwari [62] proposed pushing flow from the overflowing vertex of maximum height. Cheriyan and Hagerup [61] suggested randomly permuting the neighbor lists, and several researchers [14, 204, 276] developed clever derandomizations of this idea, leading to a sequence of faster algorithms. The algorithm of King, Rao, and Tarjan [204] is the fastest such algorithm and runs in $O(VE \log_{E/(V \lg V)} V)$ time.

The asymptotically fastest algorithm to date for the maximum-flow problem, by Goldberg and Rao [138], runs in time $O(\min(V^{2/3}, E^{1/2})E \lg(V^2/E + 2) \lg C)$, where $C = \max_{(u,v) \in E} c(u, v)$. This algorithm does not use the push-relabel method but instead is based on finding blocking flows. All previous maximum-flow algorithms, including the ones in this chapter, use some notion of distance (the push-relabel algorithms use the analogous notion of height), with a length of 1 assigned implicitly to each edge. This new algorithm takes a different approach and assigns a length of 0 to high-capacity edges and a length of 1 to low-capacity edges. Informally, with respect to these lengths, shortest paths from the source to the sink tend to have high capacity, which means that fewer iterations need be performed.

In practice, push-relabel algorithms currently dominate augmenting-path or linear-programming based algorithms for the maximum-flow problem. A study by Cherkassky and Goldberg [63] underscores the importance of using two heuristics when implementing a push-relabel algorithm. The first heuristic is to periodically perform a breadth-first search of the residual network in order to obtain more accurate height values. The second heuristic is the gap heuristic, described in Exercise 26.5-5. Cherkassky and Goldberg conclude that the best choice of push-relabel variants is the one that chooses to discharge the overflowing vertex with the maximum height.

The best algorithm to date for maximum bipartite matching, discovered by Hopcroft and Karp [176], runs in $O(\sqrt{V}E)$ time and is described in Problem 26-6. The book by Lovász and Plummer [239] is an excellent reference on matching problems.

VII Selected Topics

Introduction

This part contains a selection of algorithmic topics that extend and complement earlier material in this book. Some chapters introduce new models of computation such as circuits or parallel computers. Others cover specialized domains such as computational geometry or number theory. The last two chapters discuss some of the known limitations to the design of efficient algorithms and introduce techniques for coping with those limitations.

Chapter 27 presents an algorithmic model for parallel computing based on dynamic multithreading. The chapter introduces the basics of the model, showing how to quantify parallelism in terms of the measures of work and span. It then investigates several interesting multithreaded algorithms, including algorithms for matrix multiplication and merge sorting.

Chapter 28 studies efficient algorithms for operating on matrices. It presents two general methods—LU decomposition and LUP decomposition—for solving linear equations by Gaussian elimination in $O(n^3)$ time. It also shows that matrix inversion and matrix multiplication can be performed equally fast. The chapter concludes by showing how to compute a least-squares approximate solution when a set of linear equations has no exact solution.

Chapter 29 studies linear programming, in which we wish to maximize or minimize an objective, given limited resources and competing constraints. Linear programming arises in a variety of practical application areas. This chapter covers how to formulate and solve linear programs. The solution method covered is the simplex algorithm, which is the oldest algorithm for linear programming. In contrast to many algorithms in this book, the simplex algorithm does not run in polynomial time in the worst case, but it is fairly efficient and widely used in practice.

Chapter 30 studies operations on polynomials and shows how to use a well-known signal-processing technique—the fast Fourier transform (FFT)—to multiply two degree-n polynomials in $O(n \lg n)$ time. It also investigates efficient implementations of the FFT, including a parallel circuit.

Chapter 31 presents number-theoretic algorithms. After reviewing elementary number theory, it presents Euclid's algorithm for computing greatest common divisors. Next, it studies algorithms for solving modular linear equations and for raising one number to a power modulo another number. Then, it explores an important application of number-theoretic algorithms: the RSA public-key cryptosystem. This cryptosystem can be used not only to encrypt messages so that an adversary cannot read them, but also to provide digital signatures. The chapter then presents the Miller-Rabin randomized primality test, with which we can find large primes efficiently—an essential requirement for the RSA system. Finally, the chapter covers Pollard's "rho" heuristic for factoring integers and discusses the state of the art of integer factorization.

Chapter 32 studies the problem of finding all occurrences of a given pattern string in a given text string, a problem that arises frequently in text-editing programs. After examining the naive approach, the chapter presents an elegant approach due to Rabin and Karp. Then, after showing an efficient solution based on finite automata, the chapter presents the Knuth-Morris-Pratt algorithm, which modifies the automaton-based algorithm to save space by cleverly preprocessing the pattern.

Chapter 33 considers a few problems in computational geometry. After discussing basic primitives of computational geometry, the chapter shows how to use a "sweeping" method to efficiently determine whether a set of line segments contains any intersections. Two clever algorithms for finding the convex hull of a set of points—Graham's scan and Jarvis's march—also illustrate the power of sweeping methods. The chapter closes with an efficient algorithm for finding the closest pair from among a given set of points in the plane.

Chapter 34 concerns NP-complete problems. Many interesting computational problems are NP-complete, but no polynomial-time algorithm is known for solving any of them. This chapter presents techniques for determining when a problem is NP-complete. Several classic problems are proved to be NP-complete: determining whether a graph has a hamiltonian cycle, determining whether a boolean formula is satisfiable, and determining whether a given set of numbers has a subset that adds up to a given target value. The chapter also proves that the famous traveling-salesman problem is NP-complete.

Chapter 35 shows how to find approximate solutions to NP-complete problems efficiently by using approximation algorithms. For some NP-complete problems, approximate solutions that are near optimal are quite easy to produce, but for others even the best approximation algorithms known work progressively more poorly as the problem size increases. Then, there are some problems for which we can invest increasing amounts of computation time in return for increasingly better approximate solutions. This chapter illustrates these possibilities with the vertex-cover problem (unweighted and weighted versions), an optimization version of 3-CNF satisfiability, the traveling-salesman problem, the set-covering problem, and the subset-sum problem.

27 Multithreaded Algorithms

The vast majority of algorithms in this book are *serial algorithms* suitable for running on a uniprocessor computer in which only one instruction executes at a time. In this chapter, we shall extend our algorithmic model to encompass *parallel algorithms*, which can run on a multiprocessor computer that permits multiple instructions to execute concurrently. In particular, we shall explore the elegant model of dynamic multithreaded algorithms, which are amenable to algorithmic design and analysis, as well as to efficient implementation in practice.

Parallel computers—computers with multiple processing units—have become increasingly common, and they span a wide range of prices and performance. Relatively inexpensive desktop and laptop *chip multiprocessors* contain a single *multicore* integrated-circuit chip that houses multiple processing "cores," each of which is a full-fledged processor that can access a common memory. At an intermediate price/performance point are clusters built from individual computers—often simple PC-class machines—with a dedicated network interconnecting them. The highest-priced machines are supercomputers, which often use a combination of custom architectures and custom networks to deliver the highest performance in terms of instructions executed per second.

Multiprocessor computers have been around, in one form or another, for decades. Although the computing community settled on the random-access machine model for serial computing early on in the history of computer science, no single model for parallel computing has gained as wide acceptance. A major reason is that vendors have not agreed on a single architectural model for parallel computers. For example, some parallel computers feature *shared memory*, where each processor can directly access any location of memory. Other parallel computers employ *distributed memory*, where each processor's memory is private, and an explicit message must be sent between processors in order for one processor to access the memory of another. With the advent of multicore technology, however, every new laptop and desktop machine is now a shared-memory parallel computer, and the trend appears to be toward shared-memory multiprocessing. Although time will tell, that is the approach we shall take in this chapter.

One common means of programming chip multiprocessors and other shared-memory parallel computers is by using *static threading*, which provides a software abstraction of "virtual processors," or *threads*, sharing a common memory. Each thread maintains an associated program counter and can execute code independently of the other threads. The operating system loads a thread onto a processor for execution and switches it out when another thread needs to run. Although the operating system allows programmers to create and destroy threads, these operations are comparatively slow. Thus, for most applications, threads persist for the duration of a computation, which is why we call them "static."

Unfortunately, programming a shared-memory parallel computer directly using static threads is difficult and error-prone. One reason is that dynamically partitioning the work among the threads so that each thread receives approximately the same load turns out to be a complicated undertaking. For any but the simplest of applications, the programmer must use complex communication protocols to implement a scheduler to load-balance the work. This state of affairs has led toward the creation of *concurrency platforms*, which provide a layer of software that coordinates, schedules, and manages the parallel-computing resources. Some concurrency platforms are built as runtime libraries, but others provide full-fledged parallel languages with compiler and runtime support.

Dynamic multithreaded programming

One important class of concurrency platform is *dynamic multithreading*, which is the model we shall adopt in this chapter. Dynamic multithreading allows programmers to specify parallelism in applications without worrying about communication protocols, load balancing, and other vagaries of static-thread programming. The concurrency platform contains a scheduler, which load-balances the computation automatically, thereby greatly simplifying the programmer's chore. Although the functionality of dynamic-multithreading environments is still evolving, almost all support two features: nested parallelism and parallel loops. Nested parallelism allows a subroutine to be "spawned," allowing the caller to proceed while the spawned subroutine is computing its result. A parallel loop is like an ordinary **for** loop, except that the iterations of the loop can execute concurrently.

These two features form the basis of the model for dynamic multithreading that we shall study in this chapter. A key aspect of this model is that the programmer needs to specify only the logical parallelism within a computation, and the threads within the underlying concurrency platform schedule and load-balance the computation among themselves. We shall investigate multithreaded algorithms written for this model, as well how the underlying concurrency platform can schedule computations efficiently.

Our model for dynamic multithreading offers several important advantages:

- It is a simple extension of our serial programming model. We can describe a multithreaded algorithm by adding to our pseudocode just four "concurrency" keywords: **parallel**, **spawn**, **sync**, and **new**. Moreover, if we delete these concurrency keywords from the multithreaded pseudocode, the resulting text is serial pseudocode for the same problem, which we call the "serialization" of the multithreaded algorithm.

- It provides a theoretically clean way to quantify parallelism based on the notions of "work" and "span."

- Many multithreaded algorithms involving nested parallelism follow naturally from the divide-and-conquer paradigm. Moreover, just as serial divide-and-conquer algorithms lend themselves to analysis by solving recurrences, so do multithreaded algorithms.

- The model is faithful to how parallel-computing practice is evolving. A growing number of concurrency platforms support one variant or another of dynamic multithreading, including Cilk [51, 118], Cilk++ [71], OpenMP [59], Task Parallel Library [230], and Threading Building Blocks [292].

Section 27.1 introduces the dynamic multithreading model and presents the metrics of work, span, and parallelism, which we shall use to analyze multithreaded algorithms. Section 27.2 investigates how to multiply matrices with multithreading, and Section 27.3 tackles the tougher problem of multithreading merge sort.

27.1   The basics of dynamic multithreading

We shall begin our exploration of dynamic multithreading using the example of computing Fibonacci numbers recursively. Recall that the Fibonacci numbers are defined by recurrence (3.22):

$$
\begin{aligned}
F_0 &= 0, \\
F_1 &= 1, \\
F_i &= F_{i-1} + F_{i-2} \qquad \text{for } i \geq 2.
\end{aligned}
$$

Here is a simple, recursive, serial algorithm to compute the nth Fibonacci number:

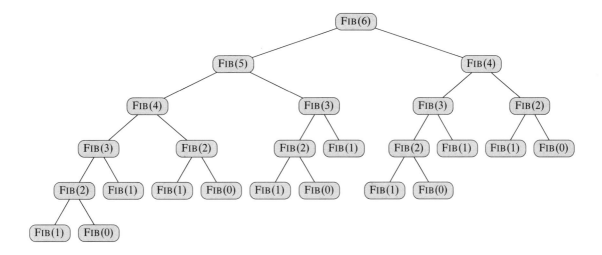

Figure 27.1 The tree of recursive procedure instances when computing FIB(6). Each instance of FIB with the same argument does the same work to produce the same result, providing an inefficient but interesting way to compute Fibonacci numbers.

FIB(n)

1   **if** $n \leq 1$
2   **return** n
3   **else** $x =$ FIB($n - 1$)
4       $y =$ FIB($n - 2$)
5   **return** $x + y$

You would not really want to compute large Fibonacci numbers this way, because this computation does much repeated work. Figure 27.1 shows the tree of recursive procedure instances that are created when computing F_6. For example, a call to FIB(6) recursively calls FIB(5) and then FIB(4). But, the call to FIB(5) also results in a call to FIB(4). Both instances of FIB(4) return the same result ($F_4 = 3$). Since the FIB procedure does not memoize, the second call to FIB(4) replicates the work that the first call performs.

Let $T(n)$ denote the running time of FIB(n). Since FIB(n) contains two recursive calls plus a constant amount of extra work, we obtain the recurrence

$$T(n) = T(n - 1) + T(n - 2) + \Theta(1) .$$

This recurrence has solution $T(n) = \Theta(F_n)$, which we can show using the substitution method. For an inductive hypothesis, assume that $T(n) \leq a F_n - b$, where $a > 1$ and $b > 0$ are constants. Substituting, we obtain

$$
\begin{aligned}
T(n) &\le (a F_{n-1} - b) + (a F_{n-2} - b) + \Theta(1) \\
&= a(F_{n-1} + F_{n-2}) - 2b + \Theta(1) \\
&= a F_n - b - (b - \Theta(1)) \\
&\le a F_n - b
\end{aligned}
$$

if we choose b large enough to dominate the constant in the $\Theta(1)$. We can then choose a large enough to satisfy the initial condition. The analytical bound

$$
T(n) = \Theta(\phi^n) , \tag{27.1}
$$

where $\phi = (1 + \sqrt{5})/2$ is the golden ratio, now follows from equation (3.25). Since F_n grows exponentially in n, this procedure is a particularly slow way to compute Fibonacci numbers. (See Problem 31-3 for much faster ways.)

Although the FIB procedure is a poor way to compute Fibonacci numbers, it makes a good example for illustrating key concepts in the analysis of multithreaded algorithms. Observe that within FIB(n), the two recursive calls in lines 3 and 4 to FIB($n-1$) and FIB($n-2$), respectively, are independent of each other: they could be called in either order, and the computation performed by one in no way affects the other. Therefore, the two recursive calls can run in parallel.

We augment our pseudocode to indicate parallelism by adding the ***concurrency keywords*** **spawn** and **sync**. Here is how we can rewrite the FIB procedure to use dynamic multithreading:

P-FIB(n)

1   **if** $n \le 1$
2   **return** n
3   **else** $x = $ **spawn** P-FIB($n - 1$)
4       $y = $ P-FIB($n - 2$)
5   **sync**
6   **return** $x + y$

Notice that if we delete the concurrency keywords **spawn** and **sync** from P-FIB, the resulting pseudocode text is identical to FIB (other than renaming the procedure in the header and in the two recursive calls). We define the ***serialization*** of a multithreaded algorithm to be the serial algorithm that results from deleting the multithreaded keywords: **spawn**, **sync**, and when we examine parallel loops, **parallel** and **new**. Indeed, our multithreaded pseudocode has the nice property that a serialization is always ordinary serial pseudocode to solve the same problem.

Nested parallelism occurs when the keyword **spawn** precedes a procedure call, as in line 3. The semantics of a spawn differs from an ordinary procedure call in that the procedure instance that executes the spawn—the ***parent***—may continue to execute in parallel with the spawned subroutine—its ***child***—instead of waiting for the child to complete, as would normally happen in a serial execution. In this case, while the spawned child is computing P-FIB$(n - 1)$, the parent may go on to compute P-FIB$(n - 2)$ in line 4 in parallel with the spawned child. Since the P-FIB procedure is recursive, these two subroutine calls themselves create nested parallelism, as do their children, thereby creating a potentially vast tree of subcomputations, all executing in parallel.

The keyword **spawn** does not say, however, that a procedure *must* execute concurrently with its spawned children, only that it *may*. The concurrency keywords express the *logical parallelism* of the computation, indicating which parts of the computation may proceed in parallel. At runtime, it is up to a *scheduler* to determine which subcomputations actually run concurrently by assigning them to available processors as the computation unfolds. We shall discuss the theory behind schedulers shortly.

A procedure cannot safely use the values returned by its spawned children until after it executes a **sync** statement, as in line 5. The keyword **sync** indicates that the procedure must wait as necessary for all its spawned children to complete before proceeding to the statement after the **sync**. In the P-FIB procedure, a **sync** is required before the **return** statement in line 6 to avoid the anomaly that would occur if x and y were summed before x was computed. In addition to explicit synchronization provided by the **sync** statement, every procedure executes a **sync** implicitly before it returns, thus ensuring that all its children terminate before it does.

A model for multithreaded execution

It helps to think of a *multithreaded computation*—the set of runtime instructions executed by a processor on behalf of a multithreaded program—as a directed acyclic graph $G = (V, E)$, called a *computation dag*. As an example, Figure 27.2 shows the computation dag that results from computing P-FIB(4). Conceptually, the vertices in V are instructions, and the edges in E represent dependencies between instructions, where $(u, v) \in E$ means that instruction u must execute before instruction v. For convenience, however, if a chain of instructions contains no parallel control (no **spawn**, **sync**, or **return** from a spawn—via either an explicit **return** statement or the return that happens implicitly upon reaching the end of a procedure), we may group them into a single *strand*, each of which represents one or more instructions. Instructions involving parallel control are not included in strands, but are represented in the structure of the dag. For example, if a strand has two successors, one of them must have been spawned, and a strand with multiple predecessors indicates the predecessors joined because of a **sync** statement. Thus, in the general case, the set V forms the set of strands, and the set E of directed edges represents dependencies between strands induced by parallel control.

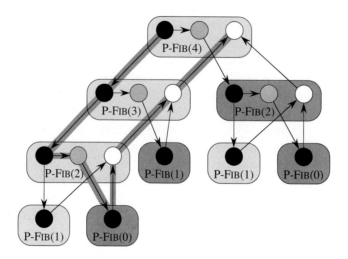

Figure 27.2 A directed acyclic graph representing the computation of P-Fib(4). Each circle represents one strand, with black circles representing either base cases or the part of the procedure (instance) up to the spawn of P-Fib($n - 1$) in line 3, shaded circles representing the part of the procedure that calls P-Fib($n - 2$) in line 4 up to the **sync** in line 5, where it suspends until the spawn of P-Fib($n - 1$) returns, and white circles representing the part of the procedure after the **sync** where it sums x and y up to the point where it returns the result. Each group of strands belonging to the same procedure is surrounded by a rounded rectangle, lightly shaded for spawned procedures and heavily shaded for called procedures. Spawn edges and call edges point downward, continuation edges point horizontally to the right, and return edges point upward. Assuming that each strand takes unit time, the work equals 17 time units, since there are 17 strands, and the span is 8 time units, since the critical path—shown with shaded edges—contains 8 strands.

If G has a directed path from strand u to strand v, we say that the two strands are *(logically) in series*. Otherwise, strands u and v are *(logically) in parallel*.

We can picture a multithreaded computation as a dag of strands embedded in a tree of procedure instances. For example, Figure 27.1 shows the tree of procedure instances for P-Fib(6) without the detailed structure showing strands. Figure 27.2 zooms in on a section of that tree, showing the strands that constitute each procedure. All directed edges connecting strands run either within a procedure or along undirected edges in the procedure tree.

We can classify the edges of a computation dag to indicate the kind of dependencies between the various strands. A *continuation edge* (u, u'), drawn horizontally in Figure 27.2, connects a strand u to its successor u' within the same procedure instance. When a strand u spawns a strand v, the dag contains a *spawn edge* (u, v), which points downward in the figure. *Call edges*, representing normal procedure calls, also point downward. Strand u spawning strand v differs from u calling v in that a spawn induces a horizontal continuation edge from u to the strand u' following u in its procedure, indicating that u' is free to execute at the same time as v, whereas a call induces no such edge. When a strand u returns to its calling procedure and x is the strand immediately following the next **sync** in the calling procedure, the computation dag contains *return edge* (u, x), which points upward. A computation starts with a single *initial strand*—the black vertex in the procedure labeled P-FIB(4) in Figure 27.2—and ends with a single *final strand*—the white vertex in the procedure labeled P-FIB(4).

We shall study the execution of multithreaded algorithms on an *ideal parallel computer*, which consists of a set of processors and a *sequentially consistent* shared memory. Sequential consistency means that the shared memory, which may in reality be performing many loads and stores from the processors at the same time, produces the same results as if at each step, exactly one instruction from one of the processors is executed. That is, the memory behaves as if the instructions were executed sequentially according to some global linear order that preserves the individual orders in which each processor issues its own instructions. For dynamic multithreaded computations, which are scheduled onto processors automatically by the concurrency platform, the shared memory behaves as if the multithreaded computation's instructions were interleaved to produce a linear order that preserves the partial order of the computation dag. Depending on scheduling, the ordering could differ from one run of the program to another, but the behavior of any execution can be understood by assuming that the instructions are executed in some linear order consistent with the computation dag.

In addition to making assumptions about semantics, the ideal-parallel-computer model makes some performance assumptions. Specifically, it assumes that each processor in the machine has equal computing power, and it ignores the cost of scheduling. Although this last assumption may sound optimistic, it turns out that for algorithms with sufficient "parallelism" (a term we shall define precisely in a moment), the overhead of scheduling is generally minimal in practice.

Performance measures

We can gauge the theoretical efficiency of a multithreaded algorithm by using two metrics: "work" and "span." The *work* of a multithreaded computation is the total time to execute the entire computation on one processor. In other words, the work is the sum of the times taken by each of the strands. For a computation dag in which each strand takes unit time, the work is just the number of vertices in the dag. The *span* is the longest time to execute the strands along any path in the dag. Again, for a dag in which each strand takes unit time, the span equals the number of vertices on a longest or *critical path* in the dag. (Recall from Section 24.2 that we can find a critical path in a dag $G = (V, E)$ in $\Theta(V + E)$ time.) For example, the computation dag of Figure 27.2 has 17 vertices in all and 8 vertices on its critical path, so that if each strand takes unit time, its work is 17 time units and its span is 8 time units.

The actual running time of a multithreaded computation depends not only on its work and its span, but also on how many processors are available and how the scheduler allocates strands to processors. To denote the running time of a multithreaded computation on P processors, we shall subscript by P. For example, we might denote the running time of an algorithm on P processors by T_P. The work is the running time on a single processor, or T_1. The span is the running time if we could run each strand on its own processor—in other words, if we had an unlimited number of processors—and so we denote the span by T_∞.

The work and span provide lower bounds on the running time T_P of a multi-threaded computation on P processors:

- In one step, an ideal parallel computer with P processors can do at most P units of work, and thus in T_P time, it can perform at most $P T_P$ work. Since the total work to do is T_1, we have $P T_P \geq T_1$. Dividing by P yields the **work law**:

$$T_P \geq T_1/P \ . \tag{27.2}$$

- A P-processor ideal parallel computer cannot run any faster than a machine with an unlimited number of processors. Looked at another way, a machine with an unlimited number of processors can emulate a P-processor machine by using just P of its processors. Thus, the **span law** follows:

$$T_P \geq T_\infty \ . \tag{27.3}$$

We define the **speedup** of a computation on P processors by the ratio T_1/T_P, which says how many times faster the computation is on P processors than on 1 processor. By the work law, we have $T_P \geq T_1/P$, which implies that $T_1/T_P \leq P$. Thus, the speedup on P processors can be at most P. When the speedup is linear in the number of processors, that is, when $T_1/T_P = \Theta(P)$, the computation exhibits **linear speedup**, and when $T_1/T_P = P$, we have **perfect linear speedup**.

The ratio T_1/T_∞ of the work to the span gives the **parallelism** of the multi-threaded computation. We can view the parallelism from three perspectives. As a ratio, the parallelism denotes the average amount of work that can be performed in parallel for each step along the critical path. As an upper bound, the parallelism gives the maximum possible speedup that can be achieved on any number of processors. Finally, and perhaps most important, the parallelism provides a limit on the possibility of attaining perfect linear speedup. Specifically, once the number of processors exceeds the parallelism, the computation cannot possibly achieve perfect linear speedup. To see this last point, suppose that $P > T_1/T_\infty$, in which case the span law implies that the speedup satisfies $T_1/T_P \leq T_1/T_\infty < P$. Moreover, if the number P of processors in the ideal parallel computer greatly exceeds the parallelism—that is, if $P \gg T_1/T_\infty$—then $T_1/T_P \ll P$, so that the speedup is much less than the number of processors. In other words, the more processors we use beyond the parallelism, the less perfect the speedup.

As an example, consider the computation P-FIB(4) in Figure 27.2, and assume that each strand takes unit time. Since the work is $T_1 = 17$ and the span is $T_\infty = 8$, the parallelism is $T_1/T_\infty = 17/8 = 2.125$. Consequently, achieving much more than double the speedup is impossible, no matter how many processors we employ to execute the computation. For larger input sizes, however, we shall see that P-FIB(n) exhibits substantial parallelism.

We define the *(parallel) slackness* of a multithreaded computation executed on an ideal parallel computer with P processors to be the ratio $(T_1/T_\infty)/P = T_1/(PT_\infty)$, which is the factor by which the parallelism of the computation exceeds the number of processors in the machine. Thus, if the slackness is less than 1, we cannot hope to achieve perfect linear speedup, because $T_1/(PT_\infty) < 1$ and the span law imply that the speedup on P processors satisfies $T_1/T_P \leq T_1/T_\infty < P$. Indeed, as the slackness decreases from 1 toward 0, the speedup of the computation diverges further and further from perfect linear speedup. If the slackness is greater than 1, however, the work per processor is the limiting constraint. As we shall see, as the slackness increases from 1, a good scheduler can achieve closer and closer to perfect linear speedup.

Scheduling

Good performance depends on more than just minimizing the work and span. The strands must also be scheduled efficiently onto the processors of the parallel machine. Our multithreaded programming model provides no way to specify which strands to execute on which processors. Instead, we rely on the concurrency platform's scheduler to map the dynamically unfolding computation to individual processors. In practice, the scheduler maps the strands to static threads, and the operating system schedules the threads on the processors themselves, but this extra level of indirection is unnecessary for our understanding of scheduling. We can just imagine that the concurrency platform's scheduler maps strands to processors directly.

A multithreaded scheduler must schedule the computation with no advance knowledge of when strands will be spawned or when they will complete—it must operate *on-line*. Moreover, a good scheduler operates in a distributed fashion, where the threads implementing the scheduler cooperate to load-balance the computation. Provably good on-line, distributed schedulers exist, but analyzing them is complicated.

Instead, to keep our analysis simple, we shall investigate an on-line **centralized** scheduler, which knows the global state of the computation at any given time. In particular, we shall analyze **greedy schedulers**, which assign as many strands to processors as possible in each time step. If at least P strands are ready to execute during a time step, we say that the step is a **complete step**, and a greedy scheduler assigns any P of the ready strands to processors. Otherwise, fewer than P strands are ready to execute, in which case we say that the step is an **incomplete step**, and the scheduler assigns each ready strand to its own processor.

From the work law, the best running time we can hope for on P processors is $T_P = T_1/P$, and from the span law the best we can hope for is $T_P = T_\infty$. The following theorem shows that greedy scheduling is provably good in that it achieves the sum of these two lower bounds as an upper bound.

Theorem 27.1
On an ideal parallel computer with P processors, a greedy scheduler executes a multithreaded computation with work T_1 and span T_∞ in time

$$T_P \leq T_1/P + T_\infty .\tag{27.4}$$

Proof   We start by considering the complete steps. In each complete step, the P processors together perform a total of P work. Suppose for the purpose of contradiction that the number of complete steps is strictly greater than $\lfloor T_1/P \rfloor$. Then, the total work of the complete steps is at least

$$
\begin{aligned}
P \cdot (\lfloor T_1/P \rfloor + 1) &= P \lfloor T_1/P \rfloor + P \\
&= T_1 - (T_1 \bmod P) + P \quad \text{(by equation (3.8))} \\
&> T_1 \quad\quad\quad\quad\quad\quad\quad\;\; \text{(by inequality (3.9))} .
\end{aligned}
$$

Thus, we obtain the contradiction that the P processors would perform more work than the computation requires, which allows us to conclude that the number of complete steps is at most $\lfloor T_1/P \rfloor$.

Now, consider an incomplete step. Let G be the dag representing the entire computation, and without loss of generality, assume that each strand takes unit time. (We can replace each longer strand by a chain of unit-time strands.) Let G' be the subgraph of G that has yet to be executed at the start of the incomplete step, and let G'' be the subgraph remaining to be executed after the incomplete step. A longest path in a dag must necessarily start at a vertex with in-degree 0. Since an incomplete step of a greedy scheduler executes all strands with in-degree 0 in G', the length of a longest path in G'' must be 1 less than the length of a longest path in G'. In other words, an incomplete step decreases the span of the unexecuted dag by 1. Hence, the number of incomplete steps is at most T_∞.

Since each step is either complete or incomplete, the theorem follows.   ■

The following corollary to Theorem 27.1 shows that a greedy scheduler always performs well.

Corollary 27.2
The running time T_P of any multithreaded computation scheduled by a greedy scheduler on an ideal parallel computer with P processors is within a factor of 2 of optimal.

Proof   Let T_P^* be the running time produced by an optimal scheduler on a machine with P processors, and let T_1 and T_∞ be the work and span of the computation, respectively. Since the work and span laws—inequalities (27.2) and (27.3)—give us $T_P^* \geq \max(T_1/P, T_\infty)$, Theorem 27.1 implies that

$$
\begin{aligned}
T_P &\leq & T_1/P + T_\infty \\
&\leq & 2 \cdot \max(T_1/P, T_\infty) \\
&\leq & 2T_P^* \, .
\end{aligned}
$$

■

The next corollary shows that, in fact, a greedy scheduler achieves near-perfect linear speedup on any multithreaded computation as the slackness grows.

Corollary 27.3
Let T_P be the running time of a multithreaded computation produced by a greedy scheduler on an ideal parallel computer with P processors, and let T_1 and T_∞ be the work and span of the computation, respectively. Then, if $P \ll T_1/T_\infty$, we have $T_P \approx T_1/P$, or equivalently, a speedup of approximately P.

Proof   If we suppose that $P \ll T_1/T_\infty$, then we also have $T_\infty \ll T_1/P$, and hence Theorem 27.1 gives us $T_P \leq T_1/P + T_\infty \approx T_1/P$. Since the work law (27.2) dictates that $T_P \geq T_1/P$, we conclude that $T_P \approx T_1/P$, or equivalently, that the speedup is $T_1/T_P \approx P$.

■

The $\ll$ symbol denotes "much less," but how much is "much less"? As a rule of thumb, a slackness of at least 10—that is, 10 times more parallelism than processors—generally suffices to achieve good speedup. Then, the span term in the greedy bound, inequality (27.4), is less than 10% of the work-per-processor term, which is good enough for most engineering situations. For example, if a computation runs on only 10 or 100 processors, it doesn't make sense to value parallelism of, say, 1,000,000 over parallelism of 10,000, even with the factor of 100 difference. As Problem 27-2 shows, sometimes by reducing extreme parallelism, we can obtain algorithms that are better with respect to other concerns and which still scale up well on reasonable numbers of processors.

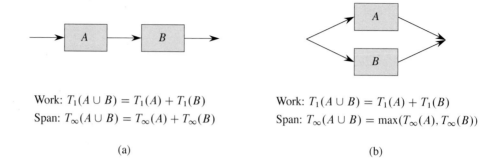

(a)   (b)

Figure 27.3 The work and span of composed subcomputations. **(a)** When two subcomputations are joined in series, the work of the composition is the sum of their work, and the span of the composition is the sum of their spans. **(b)** When two subcomputations are joined in parallel, the work of the composition remains the sum of their work, but the span of the composition is only the maximum of their spans.

Analyzing multithreaded algorithms

We now have all the tools we need to analyze multithreaded algorithms and provide good bounds on their running times on various numbers of processors. Analyzing the work is relatively straightforward, since it amounts to nothing more than analyzing the running time of an ordinary serial algorithm—namely, the serialization of the multithreaded algorithm—which you should already be familiar with, since that is what most of this textbook is about! Analyzing the span is more interesting, but generally no harder once you get the hang of it. We shall investigate the basic ideas using the P-FIB program.

Analyzing the work $T_1(n)$ of P-FIB(n) poses no hurdles, because we've already done it. The original FIB procedure is essentially the serialization of P-FIB, and hence $T_1(n) = T(n) = \Theta(\phi^n)$ from equation (27.1).

Figure 27.3 illustrates how to analyze the span. If two subcomputations are joined in series, their spans add to form the span of their composition, whereas if they are joined in parallel, the span of their composition is the maximum of the spans of the two subcomputations. For P-FIB(n), the spawned call to P-FIB$(n-1)$ in line 3 runs in parallel with the call to P-FIB$(n-2)$ in line 4. Hence, we can express the span of P-FIB(n) as the recurrence

$$
\begin{aligned}
T_\infty(n) &= \max(T_\infty(n-1), T_\infty(n-2)) + \Theta(1) \\
&= T_\infty(n-1) + \Theta(1) \,,
\end{aligned}
$$

which has solution $T_\infty(n) = \Theta(n)$.

The parallelism of P-FIB(n) is $T_1(n)/T_\infty(n) = \Theta(\phi^n/n)$, which grows dramatically as n gets large. Thus, on even the largest parallel computers, a modest value for n suffices to achieve near perfect linear speedup for P-FIB(n), because this procedure exhibits considerable parallel slackness.

Parallel loops

Many algorithms contain loops all of whose iterations can operate in parallel. As we shall see, we can parallelize such loops using the **spawn** and **sync** keywords, but it is much more convenient to specify directly that the iterations of such loops can run concurrently. Our pseudocode provides this functionality via the **parallel** concurrency keyword, which precedes the **for** keyword in a **for** loop statement.

As an example, consider the problem of multiplying an $n \times n$ matrix $A = (a_{ij})$ by an n-vector $x = (x_j)$. The resulting n-vector $y = (y_i)$ is given by the equation

$$y_i = \sum_{j=1}^{n} a_{ij} x_j \; ,$$

for $i = 1, 2, \ldots, n$. We can perform matrix-vector multiplication by computing all the entries of y in parallel as follows:

MAT-VEC(A, x)

```
1   n = A.rows
2   let y be a new vector of length n
3   parallel for i = 1 to n
4       y_i = 0
5   parallel for i = 1 to n
6       for new j = 1 to n
7           y_i = y_i + a_ij x_j
8   return y
```

In this code, the **parallel for** keywords in lines 3 and 5 indicate that the iterations of the respective loops may be run concurrently. The **new** keyword in line 6 indicates that a new variable j should be allocated for each iteration of i, rather than reusing the same variable, precluding different iterations of i from attempting to update the same variable j and causing a "race condition," which we shall examine in more detail starting on page 787.

A compiler can implement each **parallel for** loop as a divide-and-conquer subroutine using nested parallelism. For example, the **parallel for** loop in lines 5–7 can be implemented with the call MAT-VEC-MAIN-LOOP$(A, x, y, n, 1, n)$, where the compiler produces the auxiliary subroutine MAT-VEC-MAIN-LOOP as follows:

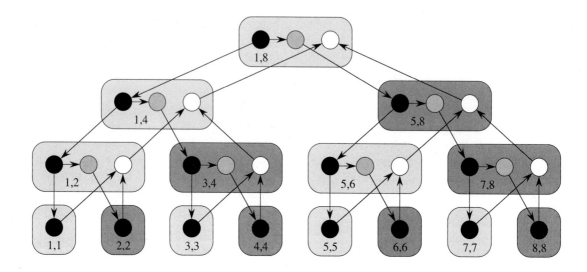

Figure 27.4   A dag representing the computation of MAT-VEC-MAIN-LOOP($A, x, y, 8, 1, 8$). The two numbers within each rounded rectangle give the values of the last two parameters (i and i' in the procedure header) in the invocation (spawn or call) of the procedure. The black circles represent strands corresponding to either the base case or the part of the procedure up to the spawn of MAT-VEC-MAIN-LOOP in line 5; the shaded circles represent strands corresponding to the part of the procedure that calls MAT-VEC-MAIN-LOOP in line 6 up to the **sync** in line 7, where it suspends until the spawned subroutine in line 5 returns; and the white circles represent strands corresponding to the (negligible) part of the procedure after the **sync** up to the point where it returns.

MAT-VEC-MAIN-LOOP(A, x, y, n, i, i')

```
1   if i == i'
2       for j = 1 to n
3           y_i = y_i + a_{ij}x_j
4   else mid = ⌊(i + i')/2⌋
5       spawn MAT-VEC-MAIN-LOOP(A, x, y, n, i, mid)
6       MAT-VEC-MAIN-LOOP(A, x, y, n, mid + 1, i')
7       sync
```

This code recursively spawns the first half of the iterations of the loop to execute in parallel with the second half of the iterations and then executes a **sync**, thereby creating a binary tree of execution where the leaves are individual loop iterations, as shown in Figure 27.4.

To calculate the work $T_1(n)$ of MAT-VEC on an $n \times n$ matrix, we simply compute the running time of its serialization, which we obtain by replacing the **parallel for** loops with ordinary **for** loops. Thus, we have $T_1(n) = \Theta(n^2)$, because the quadratic running time of the doubly nested loops in lines 5–7 dominates. This analysis seems to ignore the overhead for recursive spawning in implementing the parallel loops, however. In fact, the overhead of recursive spawning does increase the work of a parallel loop compared with that of its serialization, but not asymptotically. To see why, observe that since the tree of recursive procedure instances is a full binary tree, the number of internal nodes is 1 fewer than the number of leaves (see Exercise B.5-3). Each internal node performs constant work to divide the iteration range, and each leaf corresponds to an iteration of the loop, which takes at least constant time ($\Theta(n)$ time in this case). Thus, we can amortize the overhead of recursive spawning against the work of the iterations, contributing at most a constant factor to the overall work.

As a practical matter, dynamic-multithreading concurrency platforms sometimes ***coarsen*** the leaves of the recursion by executing several iterations in a single leaf, either automatically or under programmer control, thereby reducing the overhead of recursive spawning. This reduced overhead comes at the expense of also reducing the parallelism, however, but if the computation has sufficient parallel slackness, near-perfect linear speedup need not be sacrificed.

We must also account for the overhead of recursive spawning when analyzing the span of a parallel-loop construct. Since the depth of recursive calling is logarithmic in the number of iterations, for a parallel loop with n iterations in which the ith iteration has span $iter_\infty(i)$, the span is

$$T_\infty(n) = \Theta(\lg n) + \max_{1 \le i \le n} iter_\infty(i) \ .$$

For example, for MAT-VEC on an $n \times n$ matrix, the parallel initialization loop in lines 3–4 has span $\Theta(\lg n)$, because the recursive spawning dominates the constant-time work of each iteration. The span of the doubly nested loops in lines 5–7 is $\Theta(n)$, because each iteration of the outer **parallel for** loop contains n iterations of the inner (serial) **for** loop. The span of the remaining code in the procedure is constant, and thus the span is dominated by the doubly nested loops, yielding an overall span of $\Theta(n)$ for the whole procedure. Since the work is $\Theta(n^2)$, the parallelism is $\Theta(n^2)/\Theta(n) = \Theta(n)$. (Exercise 27.1-6 asks you to provide an implementation with even more parallelism.)

Race conditions

A multithreaded algorithm is ***deterministic*** if it always does the same thing on the same input, no matter how the instructions are scheduled on the multicore computer. It is ***nondeterministic*** if its behavior might vary from run to run. Often, a multithreaded algorithm that is intended to be deterministic fails to be, because it contains a "determinacy race."

Race conditions are the bane of concurrency. Famous race bugs include the Therac-25 radiation therapy machine, which killed three people and injured several others, and the North American Blackout of 2003, which left over 50 million people without power. These pernicious bugs are notoriously hard to find. You can run tests in the lab for days without a failure only to discover that your software sporadically crashes in the field.

A ***determinacy race*** occurs when two logically parallel instructions access the same memory location and at least one of the instructions performs a write. The following procedure illustrates a race condition:

RACE-EXAMPLE( )

```
1   x = 0
2   parallel for i = 1 to 2
3       x = x + 1
4   print x
```

After initializing x to 0 in line 1, RACE-EXAMPLE creates two parallel strands, each of which increments x in line 3. Although it might seem that RACE-EXAMPLE should always print the value 2 (its serialization certainly does), it could instead print the value 1. Let's see how this anomaly might occur.

When a processor increments x, the operation is not indivisible, but is composed of a sequence of instructions:

1. Read x from memory into one of the processor's registers.

2. Increment the value in the register.

3. Write the value in the register back into x in memory.

Figure 27.5(a) illustrates a computation dag representing the execution of RACE-EXAMPLE, with the strands broken down to individual instructions. Recall that since an ideal parallel computer supports sequential consistency, we can view the parallel execution of a multithreaded algorithm as an interleaving of instructions that respects the dependencies in the dag. Part (b) of the figure shows the values in an execution of the computation that elicits the anomaly. The value x is stored in memory, and r_1 and r_2 are processor registers. In step 1, one of the processors sets x to 0. In steps 2 and 3, processor 1 reads x from memory into its register r_1 and increments it, producing the value 1 in r_1. At that point, processor 2 comes into the picture, executing instructions 4–6. Processor 2 reads x from memory into register r_2; increments it, producing the value 1 in r_2; and then stores this value into x, setting x to 1. Now, processor 1 resumes with step 7, storing the value 1 in r_1 into x, which leaves the value of x unchanged. Therefore, step 8 prints the value 1, rather than 2, as the serialization would print.

We can see what has happened. If the effect of the parallel execution were that processor 1 executed all its instructions before processor 2, the value 2 would be

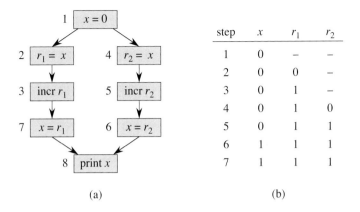

Figure 27.5 Illustration of the determinacy race in RACE-EXAMPLE. **(a)** A computation dag showing the dependencies among individual instructions. The processor registers are r_1 and r_2. Instructions unrelated to the race, such as the implementation of loop control, are omitted. **(b)** An execution sequence that elicits the bug, showing the values of x in memory and registers r_1 and r_2 for each step in the execution sequence.

printed. Conversely, if the effect were that processor 2 executed all its instructions before processor 1, the value 2 would still be printed. When the instructions of the two processors execute at the same time, however, it is possible, as in this example execution, that one of the updates to x is lost.

Of course, many executions do not elicit the bug. For example, if the execution order were $\langle 1, 2, 3, 7, 4, 5, 6, 8 \rangle$ or $\langle 1, 4, 5, 6, 2, 3, 7, 8 \rangle$, we would get the correct result. That's the problem with determinacy races. Generally, most orderings produce correct results—such as any in which the instructions on the left execute before the instructions on the right, or vice versa. But some orderings generate improper results when the instructions interleave. Consequently, races can be extremely hard to test for. You can run tests for days and never see the bug, only to experience a catastrophic system crash in the field when the outcome is critical.

Although we can cope with races in a variety of ways, including using mutual-exclusion locks and other methods of synchronization, for our purposes, we shall simply ensure that strands that operate in parallel are ***independent***: they have no determinacy races among them. Thus, in a **parallel for** construct, all the iterations should be independent. Sometimes that means using the **new** keyword to ensure that different iterations do not operate on the same variable, as in MAT-VEC. The **new** keyword allows the same variable name to be used in multiple iterations while referring to different memory locations, which renders accesses to the variable in the different iterations independent. Between a **spawn** and the corresponding **sync**, the code of the spawned child should be independent of the code of the parent, including code executed by additional spawned or called children. Note that arguments to a spawned child are evaluated in the parent before the actual spawn occurs, and thus the evaluation of arguments to a spawned subroutine is in series with any accesses to those arguments after the spawn.

As an example of how easy it is to generate code with races, here is a faulty implementation of multithreaded matrix-vector multiplication that achieves a span of $\Theta(\lg n)$ by parallelizing the inner **for** loop:

MAT-VEC-WRONG(A, x)

```
1   n = A.rows
2   let y be a new vector of length n
3   parallel for i = 1 to n
4       y_i = 0
5   parallel for i = 1 to n
6       parallel for new j = 1 to n
7           y_i = y_i + a_{ij} x_j
8   return y
```

This procedure is, unfortunately, incorrect due to races on updating y_i in line 7, which executes concurrently for all n values of j. Exercise 27.1-6 asks you to give a correct implementation with $\Theta(\lg n)$ span.

A multithreaded algorithm with races can sometimes be correct. As an example, two parallel threads might store the same value into a shared variable, and it wouldn't matter which stored the value first. Generally, however, we shall consider code with races to be illegal.

A chess lesson

We close this section with a true story that occurred during the development of the world-class multithreaded chess-playing program ★Socrates [80], although the timings below have been simplified for exposition. The program was prototyped on a 32-processor computer but was ultimately to run on a supercomputer with 512 processors. At one point, the developers incorporated an optimization into the program that reduced its running time on an important benchmark on the 32-processor machine from $T_{32} = 65$ seconds to $T'_{32} = 40$ seconds. Yet, the developers used the work and span performance measures to conclude that the optimized version, which was faster on 32 processors, would actually be slower than the original version on 512 processors. As a result, they abandoned the "optimization."

Here is their analysis. The original version of the program had work $T_1 = 2048$ seconds and span $T_\infty = 1$ second. If we treat inequality (27.4) as an equation, $T_P = T_1/P + T_\infty$, and use it as an approximation to the running time on P processors, we see that indeed $T_{32} = 2048/32 + 1 = 65$. With the optimization, the work became $T'_1 = 1024$ seconds and the span became $T'_\infty = 8$ seconds. Again using our approximation, we get $T'_{32} = 1024/32 + 8 = 40$.

The relative speeds of the two versions switch when we calculate the running times on 512 processors, however. In particular, we have $T_{512} = 2048/512+1 = 5$ seconds, and $T'_{512} = 1024/512 + 8 = 10$ seconds. The optimization that sped up the program on 32 processors would have made the program twice as slow on 512 processors! The optimized version's span of 8, which was not the dominant term in the running time on 32 processors, became the dominant term on 512 processors, nullifying the advantage from using more processors.

The moral of the story is that work and span can provide a better means of extrapolating performance than can measured running times.

Exercises

27.1-1
Suppose that we spawn P-FIB$(n - 2)$ in line 4 of P-FIB, rather than calling it as is done in the code. What is the impact on the asymptotic work, span, and parallelism?

27.1-2
Draw the computation dag that results from executing P-FIB(5). Assuming that each strand in the computation takes unit time, what are the work, span, and parallelism of the computation? Show how to schedule the dag on 3 processors using greedy scheduling by labeling each strand with the time step in which it is executed.

27.1-3
Prove that a greedy scheduler achieves the following time bound, which is slightly stronger than the bound proved in Theorem 27.1:

$$T_P \leq \frac{T_1 - T_\infty}{P} + T_\infty . \tag{27.5}$$

27.1-4
Construct a computation dag for which one execution of a greedy scheduler can take nearly twice the time of another execution of a greedy scheduler on the same number of processors. Describe how the two executions would proceed.

27.1-5
Professor Karan measures her deterministic multithreaded algorithm on 4, 10, and 64 processors of an ideal parallel computer using a greedy scheduler. She claims that the three runs yielded $T_4 = 80$ seconds, $T_{10} = 42$ seconds, and $T_{64} = 10$ seconds. Argue that the professor is either lying or incompetent. (*Hint:*

Use the work law (27.2), the span law (27.3), and inequality (27.5) from Exercise 27.1-3.)

27.1-6
Give a multithreaded algorithm to multiply an $n \times n$ matrix by an n-vector that achieves $\Theta(n^2 / \lg n)$ parallelism while maintaining $\Theta(n^2)$ work.

27.1-7
Consider the following multithreaded pseudocode for transposing an $n \times n$ matrix A in place:

P-Transpose(A)

```
1  n = A.rows
2  parallel for j = 2 to n
3      parallel for new i = 1 to j − 1
4          exchange a_ij with a_ji
```

Analyze the work, span, and parallelism of this algorithm.

27.1-8
Suppose that we replace the **parallel for** loop in line 3 of P-Transpose (see Exercise 27.1-7) with an ordinary **for** loop. Analyze the work, span, and parallelism of the resulting algorithm.

27.1-9
For how many processors do the two versions of the chess program run equally fast, assuming that $T_P = T_1/P + T_\infty$?

27.2   Multithreaded matrix multiplication

In this section, we examine how to multithread matrix multiplication, a problem whose serial running time we studied in Section 4.2. We'll look at multithreaded algorithms based on the standard triply nested loop, as well as divide-and-conquer algorithms.

Multithreaded matrix multiplication

The first algorithm we study is the straightforward algorithm based on parallelizing the loops in the procedure Square-Matrix-Multiply on page 75:

P-SQUARE-MATRIX-MULTIPLY(A, B)

1   $n = A.rows$
2   let C be a new $n \times n$ matrix
3   **parallel for** $i = 1$ to n
4   **parallel for new** $j = 1$ to n
5           $c_{ij} = 0$
6   **for new** $k = 1$ to n
7               $c_{ij} = c_{ij} + a_{ik} \cdot b_{kj}$
8   **return** C

To analyze this algorithm, observe that since the serialization of the algorithm is just SQUARE-MATRIX-MULTIPLY, the work is therefore simply $T_1(n) = \Theta(n^3)$, the same as the running time of SQUARE-MATRIX-MULTIPLY. The span is $T_\infty(n) = \Theta(n)$, because it follows a path down the tree of recursion for the **parallel for** loop starting in line 3, then down the tree of recursion for the **parallel for** loop starting in line 4, and then executes all n iterations of the ordinary **for** loop starting in line 6, resulting in a total span of $\Theta(\lg n) + \Theta(\lg n) + \Theta(n) = \Theta(n)$. Thus, the parallelism is $\Theta(n^3)/\Theta(n) = \Theta(n^2)$. Exercise 27.2-3 asks you to parallelize the inner loop to obtain a parallelism of $\Theta(n^3/\lg n)$, which you cannot do straightforwardly using **parallel for**, because you would create races.

A divide-and-conquer multithreaded algorithm for matrix multiplication

As we learned in Section 4.2, we can multiply $n \times n$ matrices serially in time $\Theta(n^{\lg 7}) = O(n^{2.81})$ using Strassen's divide-and-conquer strategy, which motivates us to look at multithreading such an algorithm. We begin, as we did in Section 4.2, with multithreading a simpler divide-and-conquer algorithm.

Recall from page 77 that the SQUARE-MATRIX-MULTIPLY-RECURSIVE procedure, which multiplies two $n \times n$ matrices A and B to produce the $n \times n$ matrix C, relies on partitioning each of the three matrices into four $n/2 \times n/2$ submatrices:

$$A = \begin{pmatrix} A_{11} & A_{12} \\ A_{21} & A_{22} \end{pmatrix}, \quad B = \begin{pmatrix} B_{11} & B_{12} \\ B_{21} & B_{22} \end{pmatrix}, \quad C = \begin{pmatrix} C_{11} & C_{12} \\ C_{21} & C_{22} \end{pmatrix}.$$

Then, we can write the matrix product as

$$\begin{pmatrix} C_{11} & C_{12} \\ C_{21} & C_{22} \end{pmatrix} = \begin{pmatrix} A_{11} & A_{12} \\ A_{21} & A_{22} \end{pmatrix} \begin{pmatrix} B_{11} & B_{12} \\ B_{21} & B_{22} \end{pmatrix}$$
$$= \begin{pmatrix} A_{11}B_{11} & A_{11}B_{12} \\ A_{21}B_{11} & A_{21}B_{12} \end{pmatrix} + \begin{pmatrix} A_{12}B_{21} & A_{12}B_{22} \\ A_{22}B_{21} & A_{22}B_{22} \end{pmatrix}. \tag{27.6}$$

Thus, to multiply two $n \times n$ matrices, we perform eight multiplications of $n/2 \times n/2$ matrices and one addition of $n \times n$ matrices. The following pseudocode implements this divide-and-conquer strategy using nested parallelism. Unlike the SQUARE-MATRIX-MULTIPLY-RECURSIVE procedure on which it is based, P-MATRIX-MULTIPLY-RECURSIVE takes the output matrix as a parameter to avoid allocating matrices unnecessarily.

P-MATRIX-MULTIPLY-RECURSIVE(C, A, B)

```
 1   n = A.rows
 2   if n == 1
 3       c₁₁ = a₁₁b₁₁
 4   else let T be a new n × n matrix
 5       partition A, B, C, and T into n/2 × n/2 submatrices
               A₁₁, A₁₂, A₂₁, A₂₂; B₁₁, B₁₂, B₂₁, B₂₂; C₁₁, C₁₂, C₂₁, C₂₂;
               and T₁₁, T₁₂, T₂₁, T₂₂; respectively
 6       spawn P-MATRIX-MULTIPLY-RECURSIVE(C₁₁, A₁₁, B₁₁)
 7       spawn P-MATRIX-MULTIPLY-RECURSIVE(C₁₂, A₁₁, B₁₂)
 8       spawn P-MATRIX-MULTIPLY-RECURSIVE(C₂₁, A₂₁, B₁₁)
 9       spawn P-MATRIX-MULTIPLY-RECURSIVE(C₂₂, A₂₁, B₁₂)
10       spawn P-MATRIX-MULTIPLY-RECURSIVE(T₁₁, A₁₂, B₂₁)
11       spawn P-MATRIX-MULTIPLY-RECURSIVE(T₁₂, A₁₂, B₂₂)
12       spawn P-MATRIX-MULTIPLY-RECURSIVE(T₂₁, A₂₂, B₂₁)
13       P-MATRIX-MULTIPLY-RECURSIVE(T₂₂, A₂₂, B₂₂)
14       sync
15       parallel for i = 1 to n
16           parallel for new j = 1 to n
17               cᵢⱼ = cᵢⱼ + tᵢⱼ
```

Line 3 handles the base case, where we are multiplying 1×1 matrices. We handle the recursive case in lines 4–17. We allocate a temporary matrix T in line 4, and line 5 partitions each of the matrices A, B, C, and T into $n/2 \times n/2$ submatrices. (As with SQUARE-MATRIX-MULTIPLY-RECURSIVE on page 77, we gloss over the minor issue of how to use index calculations to represent submatrix sections of a matrix.) The recursive call in line 6 sets the submatrix C_{11} to the submatrix product $A_{11}B_{11}$, so that C_{11} equals the first of the two terms that form its sum in equation (27.6). Similarly, lines 7–9 set C_{12}, C_{21}, and C_{22} to the first of the two terms that equal their sums in equation (27.6). Line 10 sets the submatrix T_{11} to the submatrix product $A_{12}B_{21}$, so that T_{11} equals the second of the two terms that form C_{11}'s sum. Lines 11–13 set T_{12}, T_{21}, and T_{22} to the second of the two terms that form the sums of C_{12}, C_{21}, and C_{22}, respectively. The first seven recursive calls are spawned, and the last one runs in the main strand. The **sync** statement in line 14 ensures that all the submatrix products in lines 6–13 have been computed, after which we add the products from T into C using the doubly nested **parallel for** loops in lines 15–17.

We first analyze the work $M_1(n)$ of the P-MATRIX-MULTIPLY-RECURSIVE procedure, echoing the serial running-time analysis of its progenitor SQUARE-MATRIX-MULTIPLY-RECURSIVE. In the recursive case, we partition in $\Theta(1)$ time, perform eight recursive multiplications of $n/2 \times n/2$ matrices, and finish up with the $\Theta(n^2)$ work from adding two $n \times n$ matrices. Thus, the recurrence for the work $M_1(n)$ is

$$
\begin{aligned}
M_1(n) &= 8M_1(n/2) + \Theta(n^2) \\
&= \Theta(n^3)
\end{aligned}
$$

by case 1 of the master theorem. In other words, the work of our multithreaded algorithm is asymptotically the same as the running time of the procedure SQUARE-MATRIX-MULTIPLY in Section 4.2, with its triply nested loops.

To determine the span $M_\infty(n)$ of P-MATRIX-MULTIPLY-RECURSIVE, we first observe that the span for partitioning is $\Theta(1)$, which is dominated by the $\Theta(\lg n)$ span of the doubly nested **parallel for** loops in lines 15–17. Because the eight parallel recursive calls all execute on matrices of the same size, the maximum span for any recursive call is just the span of any one. Hence, the recurrence for the span $M_\infty(n)$ of P-MATRIX-MULTIPLY-RECURSIVE is

$$
M_\infty(n) = M_\infty(n/2) + \Theta(\lg n) . \tag{27.7}
$$

This recurrence does not fall under any of the cases of the master theorem, but it does meet the condition of Exercise 4.6-2. By Exercise 4.6-2, therefore, the solution to recurrence (27.7) is $M_\infty(n) = \Theta(\lg^2 n)$.

Now that we know the work and span of P-MATRIX-MULTIPLY-RECURSIVE, we can compute its parallelism as $M_1(n)/M_\infty(n) = \Theta(n^3/\lg^2 n)$, which is very high.

Multithreading Strassen's method

To multithread Strassen's algorithm, we follow the same general outline as on page 79, only using nested parallelism:

1. Divide the input matrices A and B and output matrix C into $n/2 \times n/2$ submatrices, as in equation (27.6). This step takes $\Theta(1)$ work and span by index calculation.

2. Create 10 matrices $S_1, S_2, \ldots, S_{10}$, each of which is $n/2 \times n/2$ and is the sum or difference of two matrices created in step 1. We can create all 10 matrices with $\Theta(n^2)$ work and $\Theta(\lg n)$ span by using doubly nested **parallel for** loops.

3. Using the submatrices created in step 1 and the 10 matrices created in step 2, recursively spawn the computation of seven $n/2 \times n/2$ matrix products $P_1, P_2, \ldots, P_7$.

4. Compute the desired submatrices $C_{11}, C_{12}, C_{21}, C_{22}$ of the result matrix C by adding and subtracting various combinations of the P_i matrices, once again using doubly nested **parallel for** loops. We can compute all four submatrices with $\Theta(n^2)$ work and $\Theta(\lg n)$ span.

To analyze this algorithm, we first observe that since the serialization is the same as the original serial algorithm, the work is just the running time of the serialization, namely, $\Theta(n^{\lg 7})$. As for P-MATRIX-MULTIPLY-RECURSIVE, we can devise a recurrence for the span. In this case, seven recursive calls execute in parallel, but since they all operate on matrices of the same size, we obtain the same recurrence (27.7) as we did for P-MATRIX-MULTIPLY-RECURSIVE, which has solution $\Theta(\lg^2 n)$. Thus, the parallelism of multithreaded Strassen's method is $\Theta(n^{\lg 7}/\lg^2 n)$, which is high, though slightly less than the parallelism of P-MATRIX-MULTIPLY-RECURSIVE.

Exercises

27.2-1
Draw the computation dag for computing P-SQUARE-MATRIX-MULTIPLY on 2×2 matrices, labeling how the vertices in your diagram correspond to strands in the execution of the algorithm. Use the convention that spawn and call edges point downward, continuation edges point horizontally to the right, and return edges point upward. Assuming that each strand takes unit time, analyze the work, span, and parallelism of this computation.

27.2-2
Repeat Exercise 27.2-1 for P-MATRIX-MULTIPLY-RECURSIVE.

27.2-3
Give pseudocode for a multithreaded algorithm that multiplies two $n \times n$ matrices with work $\Theta(n^3)$ but span only $\Theta(\lg n)$. Analyze your algorithm.

27.2-4
Give pseudocode for an efficient multithreaded algorithm that multiplies a $p \times q$ matrix by a $q \times r$ matrix. Your algorithm should be highly parallel even if any of p, q, and r are 1. Analyze your algorithm.

27.2-5
Give pseudocode for an efficient multithreaded algorithm that transposes an $n \times n$ matrix in place by using divide-and-conquer and no **parallel for** loops to divide the matrix recursively into four $n/2 \times n/2$ submatrices. Analyze your algorithm.

27.2-6
Give pseudocode for an efficient multithreaded implementation of the Floyd-Warshall algorithm (see Section 25.2), which computes shortest paths between all pairs of vertices in an edge-weighted graph. Analyze your algorithm.

27.3 Multithreaded merge sort

We first saw serial merge sort in Section 2.3.1, and in Section 2.3.2 we analyzed its running time and showed it to be $\Theta(n \lg n)$. Because merge sort already uses the divide-and-conquer paradigm, it seems like a terrific candidate for multithreading using nested parallelism. We can easily modify the pseudocode so that the first recursive call is spawned:

MERGE-SORT$'(A, p, r)$

```
1  if p < r
2      q = ⌊(p + r)/2⌋
3      spawn MERGE-SORT'(A, p, q)
4      MERGE-SORT'(A, q + 1, r)
5      sync
6      MERGE(A, p, q, r)
```

Like its serial counterpart, MERGE-SORT$'$ sorts the subarray $A[p \mathinner{.\,.} r]$. After the two recursive subroutines in lines 3 and 4 have completed, which is ensured by the **sync** statement in line 5, MERGE-SORT$'$ calls the same MERGE procedure as on page 31.

Let us analyze MERGE-SORT$'$. To do so, we first need to analyze MERGE. Recall that its serial running time to merge n elements is $\Theta(n)$. Because MERGE is serial, both its work and its span are $\Theta(n)$. Thus, the following recurrence characterizes the work $MS'_1(n)$ of MERGE-SORT$'$ on n elements:

$$
\begin{aligned}
MS'_1(n) &= 2\, MS'_1(n/2) + \Theta(n) \\
&= \Theta(n \lg n)\,,
\end{aligned}
$$

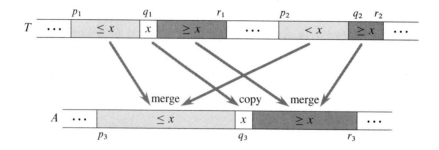

Figure 27.6 The idea behind the multithreaded merging of two sorted subarrays $T[p_1 .. r_1]$ and $T[p_2 .. r_2]$ into the subarray $A[p_3 .. r_3]$. Letting $x = T[q_1]$ be the median of $T[p_1 .. r_1]$ and q_2 be the place in $T[p_2 .. r_2]$ such that x would fall between $T[q_2 - 1]$ and $T[q_2]$, every element in subarrays $T[p_1 .. q_1 - 1]$ and $T[p_2 .. q_2 - 1]$ (lightly shaded) is less than or equal to x, and every element in the subarrays $T[q_1 + 1 .. r_1]$ and $T[q_2 + 1 .. r_2]$ (heavily shaded) is at least x. To merge, we compute the index q_3 where x belongs in $A[p_3 .. r_3]$, copy x into $A[q_3]$, and then recursively merge $T[p_1 .. q_1 - 1]$ with $T[p_2 .. q_2 - 1]$ into $A[p_3 .. q_3 - 1]$ and $T[q_1 + 1 .. r_1]$ with $T[q_2 + 1 .. r_2]$ into $A[q_3 + 1 .. r_3]$.

which is the same as the serial running time of merge sort. Since the two recursive calls of MERGE-SORT$'$ can run in parallel, the span MS'_∞ is given by the recurrence

$$
\begin{aligned}
MS'_\infty(n) &= MS'_\infty(n/2) + \Theta(n) \\
&= \Theta(n) .
\end{aligned}
$$

Thus, the parallelism of MERGE-SORT$'$ comes to $MS'_1(n)/MS'_\infty(n) = \Theta(\lg n)$, which is an unimpressive amount of parallelism. To sort 10 million elements, for example, it might achieve linear speedup on a few processors, but it would not scale up effectively to hundreds of processors.

You probably have already figured out where the parallelism bottleneck is in this multithreaded merge sort: the serial MERGE procedure. Although merging might initially seem to be inherently serial, we can, in fact, fashion a multithreaded version of it by using nested parallelism.

Our divide-and-conquer strategy for multithreaded merging, which is illustrated in Figure 27.6, operates on subarrays of an array T. Suppose that we are merging the two sorted subarrays $T[p_1 .. r_1]$ of length $n_1 = r_1 - p_1 + 1$ and $T[p_2 .. r_2]$ of length $n_2 = r_2 - p_2 + 1$ into another subarray $A[p_3 .. r_3]$, of length $n_3 = r_3 - p_3 + 1 = n_1 + n_2$. Without loss of generality, we make the simplifying assumption that $n_1 \geq n_2$.

We first find the middle element $x = T[q_1]$ of the subarray $T[p_1 .. r_1]$, where $q_1 = \lfloor (p_1 + r_1)/2 \rfloor$. Because the subarray is sorted, x is a median of $T[p_1 .. r_1]$: every element in $T[p_1 .. q_1 - 1]$ is no more than x, and every element in $T[q_1 + 1 .. r_1]$ is no less than x. We then use binary search to find the index q_2 in the subarray $T[p_2 .. r_2]$ so that the subarray would still be sorted if we inserted x between $T[q_2 - 1]$ and $T[q_2]$.

We next merge the original subarrays $T[p_1 .. r_1]$ and $T[p_2 .. r_2]$ into $A[p_3 .. r_3]$ as follows:

1. Set $q_3 = p_3 + (q_1 - p_1) + (q_2 - p_2)$.

2. Copy x into $A[q_3]$.

3. Recursively merge $T[p_1 .. q_1 - 1]$ with $T[p_2 .. q_2 - 1]$, and place the result into the subarray $A[p_3 .. q_3 - 1]$.

4. Recursively merge $T[q_1 + 1 .. r_1]$ with $T[q_2 .. r_2]$, and place the result into the subarray $A[q_3 + 1 .. r_3]$.

When we compute q_3, the quantity $q_1 - p_1$ is the number of elements in the subarray $T[p_1 .. q_1 - 1]$, and the quantity $q_2 - p_2$ is the number of elements in the subarray $T[p_2 .. q_2 - 1]$. Thus, their sum is the number of elements that end up before x in the subarray $A[p_3 .. r_3]$.

The base case occurs when $n_1 = n_2 = 0$, in which case we have no work to do to merge the two empty subarrays. Since we have assumed that the subarray $T[p_1 .. r_1]$ is at least as long as $T[p_2 .. r_2]$, that is, $n_1 \geq n_2$, we can check for the base case by just checking whether $n_1 = 0$. We must also ensure that the recursion properly handles the case when only one of the two subarrays is empty, which, by our assumption that $n_1 \geq n_2$, must be the subarray $T[p_2 .. r_2]$.

Now, let's put these ideas into pseudocode. We start with the binary search, which we express serially. The procedure BINARY-SEARCH(x, T, p, r) takes a key x and a subarray $T[p .. r]$, and it returns one of the following:

- If $T[p .. r]$ is empty ($r < p$), then it returns the index p.

- If $x \leq T[p]$, and hence less than or equal to all the elements of $T[p .. r]$, then it returns the index p.

- If $x > T[p]$, then it returns the largest index q in the range $p < q \leq r + 1$ such that $T[q - 1] < x$.

Here is the pseudocode:

BINARY-SEARCH(x, T, p, r)

```
1   low = p
2   high = max(p, r + 1)
3   while low < high
4       mid = ⌊(low + high)/2⌋
5       if x ≤ T[mid]
6           high = mid
7       else low = mid + 1
8   return high
```

The call BINARY-SEARCH(x, T, p, r) takes $\Theta(\lg n)$ serial time in the worst case, where $n = r - p + 1$ is the size of the subarray on which it runs. (See Exercise 2.3-5.) Since BINARY-SEARCH is a serial procedure, its worst-case work and span are both $\Theta(\lg n)$.

We are now prepared to write pseudocode for the multithreaded merging procedure itself. Like the MERGE procedure on page 31, the P-MERGE procedure assumes that the two subarrays to be merged lie within the same array. Unlike MERGE, however, P-MERGE does not assume that the two subarrays to be merged are adjacent within the array. (That is, P-MERGE does not require that $p_2 = r_1 + 1$.) Another difference between MERGE and P-MERGE is that P-MERGE takes as an argument an output subarray A into which the merged values should be stored. The call P-MERGE$(T, p_1, r_1, p_2, r_2, A, p_3)$ merges the sorted subarrays $T[p_1 .. r_1]$ and $T[p_2 .. r_2]$ into the subarray $A[p_3 .. r_3]$, where $r_3 = p_3 + (r_1 - p_1 + 1) + (r_2 - p_2 + 1) - 1 = p_3 + (r_1 - p_1) + (r_2 - p_2) + 1$ and is not provided as an input.

P-MERGE$(T, p_1, r_1, p_2, r_2, A, p_3)$

```
 1  n₁ = r₁ - p₁ + 1
 2  n₂ = r₂ - p₂ + 1
 3  if n₁ < n₂                    // ensure that n₁ ≥ n₂
 4      exchange p₁ with p₂
 5      exchange r₁ with r₂
 6      exchange n₁ with n₂
 7  if n₁ == 0                    // both empty?
 8      return
 9  else q₁ = ⌊(p₁ + r₁)/2⌋
10      q₂ = BINARY-SEARCH(T[q₁], T, p₂, r₂)
11      q₃ = p₃ + (q₁ - p₁) + (q₂ - p₂)
12      A[q₃] = T[q₁]
13      spawn P-MERGE(T, p₁, q₁ - 1, p₂, q₂ - 1, A, p₃)
14      P-MERGE(T, q₁ + 1, r₁, q₂, r₂, A, q₃ + 1)
15      sync
```

The P-MERGE procedure works as follows. Lines 1–2 compute the lengths n_1 and n_2 of the subarrays $T[p_1 .. r_1]$ and $T[p_2 .. r_2]$, respectively. Lines 3–6 enforce the assumption that $n_1 \geq n_2$. Line 7 tests for the base case, where the subarray $T[p_1 .. r_1]$ is empty (and hence so is $T[p_2 .. r_2]$), in which case we simply return. Lines 9–15 implement the divide-and-conquer strategy. Line 9 computes the midpoint of $T[p_1 .. r_1]$, and line 10 finds the point q_2 in $T[p_2 .. r_2]$ such that all elements in $T[p_2 .. q_2 - 1]$ are less than $T[q_1]$ (which corresponds to x) and all the elements in $T[q_2 .. r_2]$ are at least as large as $T[q_1]$. Line 11 computes the index q_3 of the element that divides the output subarray $A[p_3 \mathbin{..} r_3]$ into $A[p_3 \mathbin{..} q_3 - 1]$ and $A[q_3+1 \mathbin{..} r_3]$, and then line 12 copies $T[q_1]$ directly into $A[q_3]$.

Then, we recurse using nested parallelism. Line 13 spawns the first subproblem, while line 14 calls the second subproblem in parallel. The **sync** statement in line 15 ensures that the subproblems have completed before the procedure returns. (Since every procedure implicitly executes a **sync** before returning, we could have omitted the **sync** statement in line 15, but including it is good coding practice.) There is some cleverness in the coding to ensure that when the subarray $T[p_2 \mathbin{..} r_2]$ is empty, the code operates correctly. The way it works is that on each recursive call, a median element of $T[p_1 \mathbin{..} r_1]$ is placed into the output subarray, until $T[p_1 \mathbin{..} r_1]$ itself finally becomes empty, triggering the base case.

Analysis of multithreaded merging

We first derive a recurrence for the span $PM_\infty(n)$ of P-MERGE, where the two subarrays contain a total of $n = n_1 + n_2$ elements. Because the spawn in line 13 and the call in line 14 operate logically in parallel, we need examine only the costlier of the two calls. The key is to understand that in the worst case, the maximum number of elements in either of the recursive calls can be at most $3n/4$, which we see as follows. Because lines 3–6 ensure that $n_2 \le n_1$, it follows that $n_2 = 2n_2/2 \le (n_1 + n_2)/2 = n/2$. In the worst case, one of the two recursive calls merges $\lfloor n_1/2 \rfloor$ elements of $T[p_1 \mathbin{..} r_1]$ with all n_2 elements of $T[p_2 \mathbin{..} r_2]$, and hence the number of elements involved in the call is

$$
\begin{aligned}
\lfloor n_1/2 \rfloor + n_2 &\le n_1/2 + n_2/2 + n_2/2 \\
&= (n_1 + n_2)/2 + n_2/2 \\
&\le n/2 + n/4 \\
&= 3n/4 \ .
\end{aligned}
$$

Adding in the $\Theta(\lg n)$ cost of the call to BINARY-SEARCH in line 10, we obtain the following recurrence for the worst-case span:

$$PM_\infty(n) = PM_\infty(3n/4) + \Theta(\lg n) \ . \tag{27.8}$$

(For the base case, the span is $\Theta(1)$, since lines 1–8 execute in constant time.) This recurrence does not fall under any of the cases of the master theorem, but it meets the condition of Exercise 4.6-2. Therefore, the solution to recurrence (27.8) is $PM_\infty(n) = \Theta(\lg^2 n)$.

We now analyze the work $PM_1(n)$ of P-MERGE on n elements, which turns out to be $\Theta(n)$. Since each of the n elements must be copied from array T to array A, we have $PM_1(n) = \Omega(n)$. Thus, it remains only to show that $PM_1(n) = O(n)$.

We shall first derive a recurrence for the worst-case work. The binary search in line 10 costs $\Theta(\lg n)$ in the worst case, which dominates the other work outside of the recursive calls. For the recursive calls, observe that although the recursive calls in lines 13 and 14 might merge different numbers of elements, together the two recursive calls merge at most n elements (actually $n - 1$ elements, since $T[q_1]$ does not participate in either recursive call). Moreover, as we saw in analyzing the span, a recursive call operates on at most $3n/4$ elements. We therefore obtain the recurrence

$$PM_1(n) = PM_1(\alpha n) + PM_1((1 - \alpha)n) + O(\lg n) , \qquad (27.9)$$

where α lies in the range $1/4 \leq \alpha \leq 3/4$, and where we understand that the actual value of α may vary for each level of recursion.

We prove that recurrence (27.9) has solution $PM_1 = O(n)$ via the substitution method. Assume that $PM_1(n) \leq c_1 n - c_2 \lg n$ for some positive constants c_1 and c_2. Substituting gives us

$$
\begin{aligned}
PM_1(n) &\leq (c_1 \alpha n - c_2 \lg(\alpha n)) + (c_1(1 - \alpha)n - c_2 \lg((1 - \alpha)n)) + \Theta(\lg n) \\
&= c_1(\alpha + (1 - \alpha))n - c_2(\lg(\alpha n) + \lg((1 - \alpha)n)) + \Theta(\lg n) \\
&= c_1 n - c_2(\lg \alpha + \lg n + \lg(1 - \alpha) + \lg n) + \Theta(\lg n) \\
&= c_1 n - c_2 \lg n - (c_2(\lg n + \lg(\alpha(1 - \alpha))) - \Theta(\lg n)) \\
&\leq c_1 n - c_2 \lg n ,
\end{aligned}
$$

since we can choose c_2 large enough that $c_2(\lg n + \lg(\alpha(1 - \alpha)))$ dominates the $\Theta(\lg n)$ term. Furthermore, we can choose c_1 large enough to satisfy the base conditions of the recurrence. Since the work $PM_1(n)$ of P-MERGE is both $\Omega(n)$ and $O(n)$, we have $PM_1(n) = \Theta(n)$.

The parallelism of P-MERGE is $PM_1(n)/PM_\infty(n) = \Theta(n/\lg^2 n)$.

Multithreaded merge sort

Now that we have a nicely parallelized multithreaded merging procedure, we can incorporate it into a multithreaded merge sort. This version of merge sort is similar to the MERGE-SORT$'$ procedure we saw earlier, but unlike MERGE-SORT$'$, it takes as an argument an output subarray B, which will hold the sorted result. In particular, the call P-MERGE-SORT(A, p, r, B, s) sorts the elements in $A[p \mathinner{.\,.} r]$ and stores them in $B[s \mathinner{.\,.} s + r - p]$.

P-MERGE-SORT(A, p, r, B, s)

1 $n = r - p + 1$
2 **if** $n == 1$
3      $B[s] = A[p]$
4 **else** let $T[1 .. n]$ be a new array
5      $q = \lfloor (p + r)/2 \rfloor$
6      $q' = q - p + 1$
7   **spawn** P-MERGE-SORT$(A, p, q, T, 1)$
8   P-MERGE-SORT$(A, q + 1, r, T, q' + 1)$
9   **sync**
10   P-MERGE$(T, 1, q', q' + 1, n, B, s)$

After line 1 computes the number n of elements in the input subarray $A[p .. r]$, lines 2–3 handle the base case when the array has only 1 element. Lines 4–6 set up for the recursive spawn in line 7 and call in line 8, which operate in parallel. In particular, line 4 allocates a temporary array T with n elements to store the results of the recursive merge sorting. Line 5 calculates the index q of $A[p .. r]$ to divide the elements into the two subarrays $A[p .. q]$ and $A[q + 1 .. r]$ that will be sorted recursively, and line 6 goes on to compute the number q' of elements in the first subarray $A[p .. q]$, which line 8 uses to determine the starting index in T of where to store the sorted result of $A[q + 1 .. r]$. At that point, the spawn and recursive call are made, followed by the **sync** in line 9, which forces the procedure to wait until the spawned procedure is done. Finally, line 10 calls P-MERGE to merge the sorted subarrays, now in $T[1 .. q']$ and $T[q' + 1 .. n]$, into the output subarray $B[s .. s + r - p]$.

Analysis of multithreaded merge sort

We start by analyzing the work $PMS_1(n)$ of P-MERGE-SORT, which is considerably easier than analyzing the work of P-MERGE. Indeed, the work is given by the recurrence

$$
\begin{aligned}
PMS_1(n) &= 2 \, PMS_1(n/2) + PM_1(n) \\
&= 2 \, PMS_1(n/2) + \Theta(n) \, .
\end{aligned}
$$

This recurrence is the same as the recurrence (4.4) for ordinary MERGE-SORT from Section 2.3.1 and has solution $PMS_1(n) = \Theta(n \lg n)$ by case 2 of the master theorem.

We now derive and analyze a recurrence for the worst-case span $PMS_\infty(n)$. Because the two recursive calls to P-MERGE-SORT on lines 7 and 8 operate logically in parallel, we can ignore one of them, obtaining the recurrence

$$PMS_\infty(n) = PMS_\infty(n/2) + PM_\infty(n)$$
$$= PMS_\infty(n/2) + \Theta(\lg^2 n) . \tag{27.10}$$

As for recurrence (27.8), the master theorem does not apply to recurrence (27.10), but Exercise 4.6-2 does. The solution is $PMS_\infty(n) = \Theta(\lg^3 n)$, and so the span of P-MERGE-SORT is $\Theta(\lg^3 n)$.

Parallel merging gives P-MERGE-SORT a significant parallelism advantage over MERGE-SORT′. Recall that the parallelism of MERGE-SORT′, which calls the serial MERGE procedure, is only $\Theta(\lg n)$. For P-MERGE-SORT, the parallelism is

$$PMS_1(n)/PMS_\infty(n) = \Theta(n \lg n)/\Theta(\lg^3 n)$$
$$= \Theta(n/\lg^2 n) ,$$

which is much better both in theory and in practice. A good implementation in practice would sacrifice some parallelism by coarsening the base case in order to reduce the constants hidden by the asymptotic notation. The straightforward way to coarsen the base case is to switch to an ordinary serial sort, perhaps quicksort, when the size of the array is sufficiently small.

Exercises

27.3-1
Explain how to coarsen the base case of P-MERGE.

27.3-2
Instead of finding a median element in the larger subarray, as P-MERGE does, consider a variant that finds a median element of all the elements in the two sorted subarrays using the result of Exercise 9.3-8. Give pseudocode for an efficient multithreaded merging procedure that uses this median-finding procedure. Analyze your algorithm.

27.3-3
Give an efficient multithreaded algorithm for partitioning an array around a pivot, as is done by the PARTITION procedure on page 171. You need not partition the array in place. Make your algorithm as parallel as possible. Analyze your algorithm. (*Hint:* You may need an auxiliary array and may need to make more than one pass over the input elements.)

27.3-4
Give a multithreaded version of RECURSIVE-FFT on page 911. Make your implementation as parallel as possible. Analyze your algorithm.

27.3-5 ★

Give a multithreaded version of RANDOMIZED-SELECT on page 216. Make your implementation as parallel as possible. Analyze your algorithm. (*Hint:* Use the partitioning algorithm from Exercise 27.3-3.)

27.3-6 ★

Show how to multithread SELECT from Section 9.3. Make your implementation as parallel as possible. Analyze your algorithm.

Problems

27-1 *Implementing parallel loops using nested parallelism*

Consider the following multithreaded algorithm for performing pairwise addition on n-element arrays $A[1 . . n]$ and $B[1 . . n]$, storing the sums in $C[1 . . n]$:

SUM-ARRAYS(A, B, C)

1 **parallel for** $i = 1$ **to** $A.length$
2      $C[i] = A[i] + B[i]$

a. Rewrite the parallel loop in SUM-ARRAYS using nested parallelism (**spawn** and **sync**) in the manner of MAT-VEC-MAIN-LOOP. Analyze the parallelism of your implementation.

Consider the following alternative implementation of the parallel loop, which contains a value *grain-size* to be specified:

SUM-ARRAYS'(A, B, C)

1 $n = A.length$
2 *grain-size* = ?   **//** to be determined
3 $r = \lceil n/\textit{grain-size} \rceil$
4 **for** $k = 0$ **to** $r - 1$
5   **spawn** ADD-SUBARRAY($A, B, C, k \cdot \textit{grain-size} + 1$,
                              $\min((k + 1) \cdot \textit{grain-size}, n))$
6 **sync**

ADD-SUBARRAY(A, B, C, i, j)

1 **for** $k = i$ **to** j
2      $C[k] = A[k] + B[k]$

806 Chapter 27 Multithreaded Algorithms

b. Suppose that we set *grain-size* $= 1$. What is the parallelism of this implementation?

c. Give a formula for the span of SUM-ARRAYS′ in terms of n and *grain-size*. Derive the best value for *grain-size* to maximize parallelism.

27-2 Saving temporary space in matrix multiplication
The P-MATRIX-MULTIPLY-RECURSIVE procedure has the disadvantage that it must allocate a temporary matrix T of size $n \times n$, which can adversely affect the constants hidden by the Θ-notation. The P-MATRIX-MULTIPLY-RECURSIVE procedure does have high parallelism, however. For example, ignoring the constants in the Θ-notation, the parallelism for multiplying 1000×1000 matrices comes to approximately $1000^3/10^2 = 10^7$, since $\lg 1000 \approx 10$. Most parallel computers have far fewer than 10 million processors.

a. Describe a recursive multithreaded algorithm that eliminates the need for the temporary matrix T at the cost of increasing the span to $\Theta(n)$. (*Hint:* Compute $C = C + AB$ following the general strategy of P-MATRIX-MULTIPLY-RECURSIVE, but initialize C in parallel and insert a **sync** in a judiciously chosen location.)

b. Give and solve recurrences for the work and span of your implementation.

c. Analyze the parallelism of your implementation. Ignoring the constants in the Θ-notation, estimate the parallelism on 1000×1000 matrices. Compare with the parallelism of P-MATRIX-MULTIPLY-RECURSIVE.

27-3 Multithreaded matrix algorithms
a. Parallelize the LU-DECOMPOSITION procedure on page 821 by giving pseudocode for a multithreaded version of this algorithm. Make your implementation as parallel as possible, and analyze its work, span, and parallelism.

b. Do the same for LUP-DECOMPOSITION on page 824.

c. Do the same for LUP-SOLVE on page 817.

d. Do the same for a multithreaded algorithm based on equation (28.13) for inverting a symmetric positive-definite matrix.

27-4 Multithreading reductions and prefix computations

A $\otimes$-*reduction* of an array $x[1 .. n]$, where $\otimes$ is an associative operator, is the value

$$y = x[1] \otimes x[2] \otimes \cdots \otimes x[n] \, .$$

The following procedure computes the $\otimes$-reduction of a subarray $x[i .. j]$ serially.

REDUCE(x, i, j)

```
1   y = x[i]
2   for k = i + 1 to j
3       y = y ⊗ x[k]
4   return y
```

a. Use nested parallelism to implement a multithreaded algorithm P-REDUCE, which performs the same function with $\Theta(n)$ work and $\Theta(\lg n)$ span. Analyze your algorithm.

A related problem is that of computing a $\otimes$-*prefix computation*, sometimes called a $\otimes$-*scan*, on an array $x[1 .. n]$, where $\otimes$ is once again an associative operator. The $\otimes$-scan produces the array $y[1 .. n]$ given by

$$
\begin{aligned}
y[1] &= x[1] \, , \\
y[2] &= x[1] \otimes x[2] \, , \\
y[3] &= x[1] \otimes x[2] \otimes x[3] \, , \\
&\ \ \vdots \\
y[n] &= x[1] \otimes x[2] \otimes x[3] \otimes \cdots \otimes x[n] \, ,
\end{aligned}
$$

that is, all prefixes of the array x "summed" using the $\otimes$ operator. The following serial procedure SCAN performs a $\otimes$-prefix computation:

SCAN(x)

```
1   n = x.length
2   let y[1 .. n] be a new array
3   y[1] = x[1]
4   for i = 2 to n
5       y[i] = y[i − 1] ⊗ x[i]
6   return y
```

Unfortunately, multithreading SCAN is not straightforward. For example, changing the **for** loop to a **parallel for** loop would create races, since each iteration of the loop body depends on the previous iteration. The following procedure P-SCAN-1 performs the $\otimes$-prefix computation in parallel, albeit inefficiently:

P-SCAN-1(x)

1   $n = x.length$
2   let $y[1 .. n]$ be a new array
3   P-SCAN-1-AUX$(x, y, 1, n)$
4   **return** y

P-SCAN-1-AUX(x, y, i, j)

1   **parallel for** $l = i$ **to** j
2       $y[l] = $ P-REDUCE$(x, 1, l)$

b. Analyze the work, span, and parallelism of P-SCAN-1.

By using nested parallelism, we can obtain a more efficient $\otimes$-prefix computation:

P-SCAN-2(x)

1   $n = x.length$
2   let $y[1 .. n]$ be a new array
3   P-SCAN-2-AUX$(x, y, 1, n)$
4   **return** y

P-SCAN-2-AUX(x, y, i, j)

1   **if** $i == j$
2       $y[i] = x[i]$
3   **else** $k = \lfloor (i + j)/2 \rfloor$
4   **spawn** P-SCAN-2-AUX(x, y, i, k)
5   P-SCAN-2-AUX$(x, y, k + 1, j)$
6   **sync**
7   **parallel for** $l = k + 1$ **to** j
8           $y[l] = y[k] \otimes y[l]$

c. Argue that P-SCAN-2 is correct, and analyze its work, span, and parallelism.

We can improve on both P-SCAN-1 and P-SCAN-2 by performing the $\otimes$-prefix computation in two distinct passes over the data. On the first pass, we gather the terms for various contiguous subarrays of x into a temporary array t, and on the second pass we use the terms in t to compute the final result y. The following pseudocode implements this strategy, but certain expressions have been omitted:

P-SCAN-3(*x*)

1   *n* = *x.length*
2   let *y*[1 .. *n*] and *t*[1 .. *n*] be new arrays
3   *y*[1] = *x*[1]
4   **if** *n* > 1
5   P-SCAN-UP(*x*, *t*, 2, *n*)
6   P-SCAN-DOWN(*x*[1], *x*, *t*, *y*, 2, *n*)
7   **return** *y*

P-SCAN-UP(*x*, *t*, *i*, *j*)

1   **if** *i* == *j*
2   **return** *x*[*i*]
3   **else**
4   *k* = ⌊(*i* + *j*)/2⌋
5   *t*[*k*] = **spawn** P-SCAN-UP(*x*, *t*, *i*, *k*)
6   *right* = P-SCAN-UP(*x*, *t*, *k* + 1, *j*)
7   **sync**
8   **return** _____   **//** fill in the blank

P-SCAN-DOWN(*v*, *x*, *t*, *y*, *i*, *j*)

1   **if** *i* == *j*
2   *y*[*i*] = *v* ⊗ *x*[*i*]
3   **else**
4   *k* = ⌊(*i* + *j*)/2⌋
5   **spawn** P-SCAN-DOWN(_____, *x*, *t*, *y*, *i*, *k*)   **//** fill in the blank
6   P-SCAN-DOWN(_____, *x*, *t*, *y*, *k* + 1, *j*)   **//** fill in the blank
7   **sync**

d. Fill in the three missing expressions in line 8 of P-SCAN-UP and lines 5 and 6 of P-SCAN-DOWN. Argue that with expressions you supplied, P-SCAN-3 is correct. (*Hint:* Prove that the value *v* passed to P-SCAN-DOWN(*v*, *x*, *t*, *y*, *i*, *j*) satisfies *v* = *x*[1] ⊗ *x*[2] ⊗ ⋯ ⊗ *x*[*i* − 1].)

e. Analyze the work, span, and parallelism of P-SCAN-3.

27-5 *Multithreading a simple stencil calculation*

Computational science is replete with algorithms that require the entries of an array to be filled in with values that depend on the values of certain already computed neighboring entries, along with other information that does not change over the course of the computation. The pattern of neighboring entries does not change during the computation and is called a ***stencil***. For example, Section 15.4 presents a stencil algorithm to compute a longest common subsequence, where the value in entry $c[i, j]$ depends only on the values in $c[i-1, j]$, $c[i, j-1]$, and $c[i-1, j-1]$, as well as the elements x_i and y_j within the two sequences given as inputs. The input sequences are fixed, but the algorithm fills in the two-dimensional array c so that it computes entry $c[i, j]$ after computing all three entries $c[i-1, j]$, $c[i, j-1]$, and $c[i-1, j-1]$.

In this problem, we examine how to use nested parallelism to multithread a simple stencil calculation on an $n \times n$ array A in which, of the values in A, the value placed into entry $A[i, j]$ depends only on values in $A[i', j']$, where $i' \le i$ and $j' \le j$ (and of course, $i' \ne i$ or $j' \ne j$). In other words, the value in an entry depends only on values in entries that are above it and/or to its left, along with static information outside of the array. Furthermore, we assume throughout this problem that once we have filled in the entries upon which $A[i, j]$ depends, we can fill in $A[i, j]$ in $\Theta(1)$ time (as in the LCS-LENGTH procedure of Section 15.4).

We can partition the $n \times n$ array A into four $n/2 \times n/2$ subarrays as follows:

$$A = \begin{pmatrix} A_{11} & A_{12} \\ A_{21} & A_{22} \end{pmatrix}. \tag{27.11}$$

Observe now that we can fill in subarray A_{11} recursively, since it does not depend on the entries of the other three subarrays. Once A_{11} is complete, we can continue to fill in A_{12} and A_{21} recursively in parallel, because although they both depend on A_{11}, they do not depend on each other. Finally, we can fill in A_{22} recursively.

a. Give multithreaded pseudocode that performs this simple stencil calculation using a divide-and-conquer algorithm SIMPLE-STENCIL based on the decomposition (27.11) and the discussion above. (Don't worry about the details of the base case, which depends on the specific stencil.) Give and solve recurrences for the work and span of this algorithm in terms of n. What is the parallelism?

b. Modify your solution to part (a) to divide an $n \times n$ array into nine $n/3 \times n/3$ subarrays, again recursing with as much parallelism as possible. Analyze this algorithm. How much more or less parallelism does this algorithm have compared with the algorithm from part (a)?

c. Generalize your solutions to parts (a) and (b) as follows. Choose an integer $b \ge 2$. Divide an $n \times n$ array into b^2 subarrays, each of size $n/b \times n/b$, recursing with as much parallelism as possible. In terms of n and b, what are the work, span, and parallelism of your algorithm? Argue that, using this approach, the parallelism must be $o(n)$ for any choice of $b \ge 2$. (*Hint:* For this last argument, show that the exponent of n in the parallelism is strictly less than 1 for any choice of $b \ge 2$.)

d. Give pseudocode for a multithreaded algorithm for this simple stencil calculation that achieves $\Theta(n/\lg n)$ parallelism. Argue using notions of work and span that the problem, in fact, has $\Theta(n)$ inherent parallelism. As it turns out, the divide-and-conquer nature of our multithreaded pseudocode does not let us achieve this maximal parallelism.

27-6 *Randomized multithreaded algorithms*

Just as with ordinary serial algorithms, we sometimes want to implement randomized multithreaded algorithms. This problem explores how to adapt the various performance measures in order to handle the expected behavior of such algorithms. It also asks you to design and analyze a multithreaded algorithm for randomized quicksort.

a. Explain how to modify the work law (27.2), span law (27.3), and greedy scheduler bound (27.4) to work with expectations when T_P, T_1, and T_∞ are all random variables.

b. Consider a randomized multithreaded algorithm for which 1% of the time we have $T_1 = 10^4$ and $T_{10,000} = 1$, but for 99% of the time we have $T_1 = T_{10,000} = 10^9$. Argue that the *speedup* of a randomized multithreaded algorithm should be defined as $\mathrm{E}[T_1]/\mathrm{E}[T_P]$, rather than $\mathrm{E}[T_1/T_P]$.

c. Argue that the *parallelism* of a randomized multithreaded algorithm should be defined as the ratio $\mathrm{E}[T_1]/\mathrm{E}[T_\infty]$.

d. Multithread the RANDOMIZED-QUICKSORT algorithm on page 179 by using nested parallelism. (Do not parallelize RANDOMIZED-PARTITION.) Give the pseudocode for your P-RANDOMIZED-QUICKSORT algorithm.

e. Analyze your multithreaded algorithm for randomized quicksort. (*Hint:* Review the analysis of RANDOMIZED-SELECT on page 216.)

Chapter notes

Parallel computers, models for parallel computers, and algorithmic models for parallel programming have been around in various forms for years. Prior editions of this book included material on sorting networks and the PRAM (Parallel Random-Access Machine) model. The data-parallel model [48, 168] is another popular algorithmic programming model, which features operations on vectors and matrices as primitives.

Graham [149] and Brent [55] showed that there exist schedulers achieving the bound of Theorem 27.1. Eager, Zahorjan, and Lazowska [98] showed that any greedy scheduler achieves this bound and proposed the methodology of using work and span (although not by those names) to analyze parallel algorithms. Blelloch [47] developed an algorithmic programming model based on work and span (which he called the "depth" of the computation) for data-parallel programming. Blumofe and Leiserson [52] gave a distributed scheduling algorithm for dynamic multithreading based on randomized "work-stealing" and showed that it achieves the bound $E[T_P] \leq T_1/P + O(T_\infty)$. Arora, Blumofe, and Plaxton [19] and Blelloch, Gibbons, and Matias [49] also provided provably good algorithms for scheduling dynamic multithreaded computations.

The multithreaded pseudocode and programming model were heavily influenced by the Cilk [51, 118] project at MIT and the Cilk++ [71] extensions to C++ distributed by Cilk Arts, Inc. Many of the multithreaded algorithms in this chapter appeared in unpublished lecture notes by C. E. Leiserson and H. Prokop and have been implemented in Cilk or Cilk++. The multithreaded merge-sorting algorithm was inspired by an algorithm of Akl [12].

The notion of sequential consistency is due to Lamport [223].

28   Matrix Operations

Because operations on matrices lie at the heart of scientific computing, efficient algorithms for working with matrices have many practical applications. This chapter focuses on how to multiply matrices and solve sets of simultaneous linear equations. Appendix D reviews the basics of matrices.

Section 28.1 shows how to solve a set of linear equations using LUP decompositions. Then, Section 28.2 explores the close relationship between multiplying and inverting matrices. Finally, Section 28.3 discusses the important class of symmetric positive-definite matrices and shows how we can use them to find a least-squares solution to an overdetermined set of linear equations.

One important issue that arises in practice is *numerical stability*. Due to the limited precision of floating-point representations in actual computers, round-off errors in numerical computations may become amplified over the course of a computation, leading to incorrect results; we call such computations *numerically unstable*. Although we shall briefly consider numerical stability on occasion, we do not focus on it in this chapter. We refer you to the excellent book by Golub and Van Loan [144] for a thorough discussion of stability issues.

28.1   Solving systems of linear equations

Numerous applications need to solve sets of simultaneous linear equations. We can formulate a linear system as a matrix equation in which each matrix or vector element belongs to a field, typically the real numbers $\mathbb{R}$. This section discusses how to solve a system of linear equations using a method called LUP decomposition.

We start with a set of linear equations in n unknowns $x_1, x_2, \ldots, x_n$:

$$
\begin{aligned}
a_{11}x_1 + a_{12}x_2 + \cdots + a_{1n}x_n &= b_1 , \\
a_{21}x_1 + a_{22}x_2 + \cdots + a_{2n}x_n &= b_2 , \\
&\vdots \\
a_{n1}x_1 + a_{n2}x_2 + \cdots + a_{nn}x_n &= b_n .
\end{aligned}
\tag{28.1}
$$

A *solution* to the equations (28.1) is a set of values for $x_1, x_2, \ldots, x_n$ that satisfy all of the equations simultaneously. In this section, we treat only the case in which there are exactly n equations in n unknowns.

We can conveniently rewrite equations (28.1) as the matrix-vector equation

$$
\begin{pmatrix}
a_{11} & a_{12} & \cdots & a_{1n} \\
a_{21} & a_{22} & \cdots & a_{2n} \\
\vdots & \vdots & \ddots & \vdots \\
a_{n1} & a_{n2} & \cdots & a_{nn}
\end{pmatrix}
\begin{pmatrix}
x_1 \\ x_2 \\ \vdots \\ x_n
\end{pmatrix}
=
\begin{pmatrix}
b_1 \\ b_2 \\ \vdots \\ b_n
\end{pmatrix}
$$

or, equivalently, letting $A = (a_{ij})$, $x = (x_i)$, and $b = (b_i)$, as

$$
Ax = b .
\tag{28.2}
$$

If A is nonsingular, it possesses an inverse A^{-1}, and

$$
x = A^{-1}b
\tag{28.3}
$$

is the solution vector. We can prove that x is the unique solution to equation (28.2) as follows. If there are two solutions, x and x', then $Ax = Ax' = b$ and, letting I denote an identity matrix,

$$
\begin{aligned}
x &= Ix \\
&= (A^{-1}A)x \\
&= A^{-1}(Ax) \\
&= A^{-1}(Ax') \\
&= (A^{-1}A)x' \\
&= x' .
\end{aligned}
$$

In this section, we shall be concerned predominantly with the case in which A is nonsingular or, equivalently (by Theorem D.1), the rank of A is equal to the number n of unknowns. There are other possibilities, however, which merit a brief discussion. If the number of equations is less than the number n of unknowns — or, more generally, if the rank of A is less than n — then the system is *underdetermined*. An underdetermined system typically has infinitely many solutions, although it may have no solutions at all if the equations are inconsistent. If the number of equations exceeds the number n of unknowns, the system is *overdetermined*, and there may not exist any solutions. Section 28.3 addresses the important problem of finding good approximate solutions to overdetermined systems of linear equations.

Let us return to our problem of solving the system $Ax = b$ of n equations in n unknowns. We could compute A^{-1} and then, using equation (28.3), multiply b by A^{-1}, yielding $x = A^{-1}b$. This approach suffers in practice from numerical instability. Fortunately, another approach—LUP decomposition—is numerically stable and has the further advantage of being faster in practice.

Overview of LUP decomposition

The idea behind LUP decomposition is to find three $n \times n$ matrices L, U, and P such that

$$PA = LU ,$$ (28.4)

where

- L is a unit lower-triangular matrix,
- U is an upper-triangular matrix, and
- P is a permutation matrix.

We call matrices L, U, and P satisfying equation (28.4) an ***LUP decomposition*** of the matrix A. We shall show that every nonsingular matrix A possesses such a decomposition.

Computing an LUP decomposition for the matrix A has the advantage that we can more easily solve linear systems when they are triangular, as is the case for both matrices L and U. Once we have found an LUP decomposition for A, we can solve equation (28.2), $Ax = b$, by solving only triangular linear systems, as follows. Multiplying both sides of $Ax = b$ by P yields the equivalent equation $PAx = Pb$, which, by Exercise D.1-4, amounts to permuting the equations (28.1). Using our decomposition (28.4), we obtain

$$LUx = Pb .$$

We can now solve this equation by solving two triangular linear systems. Let us define $y = Ux$, where x is the desired solution vector. First, we solve the lower-triangular system

$$Ly = Pb$$ (28.5)

for the unknown vector y by a method called "forward substitution." Having solved for y, we then solve the upper-triangular system

$$Ux = y$$ (28.6)

for the unknown x by a method called "back substitution." Because the permutation matrix P is invertible (Exercise D.2-3), multiplying both sides of equation (28.4) by P^{-1} gives $P^{-1}PA = P^{-1}LU$, so that

$$A = P^{-1}LU \ . \tag{28.7}$$

Hence, the vector x is our solution to $Ax = b$:

$$
\begin{aligned}
Ax &= P^{-1}LUx & \text{(by equation (28.7))} \\
&= P^{-1}Ly & \text{(by equation (28.6))} \\
&= P^{-1}Pb & \text{(by equation (28.5))} \\
&= b \ .
\end{aligned}
$$

Our next step is to show how forward and back substitution work and then attack the problem of computing the LUP decomposition itself.

Forward and back substitution

Forward substitution can solve the lower-triangular system (28.5) in $\Theta(n^2)$ time, given L, P, and b. For convenience, we represent the permutation P compactly by an array $\pi[1 \mathinner{.\,.} n]$. For $i = 1, 2, \ldots, n$, the entry $\pi[i]$ indicates that $P_{i,\pi[i]} = 1$ and $P_{ij} = 0$ for $j \neq \pi[i]$. Thus, PA has $a_{\pi[i],j}$ in row i and column j, and Pb has $b_{\pi[i]}$ as its ith element. Since L is unit lower-triangular, we can rewrite equation (28.5) as

$$
\begin{aligned}
y_1 &&&&&= b_{\pi[1]} \ , \\
l_{21}y_1 &+& y_2 &&&= b_{\pi[2]} \ , \\
l_{31}y_1 &+& l_{32}y_2 &+& y_3 &= b_{\pi[3]} \ , \\
&&&\vdots \\
l_{n1}y_1 &+& l_{n2}y_2 &+& l_{n3}y_3 + \cdots + y_n &= b_{\pi[n]} \ .
\end{aligned}
$$

The first equation tells us that $y_1 = b_{\pi[1]}$. Knowing the value of y_1, we can substitute it into the second equation, yielding

$$y_2 = b_{\pi[2]} - l_{21}y_1 \ .$$

Now, we can substitute both y_1 and y_2 into the third equation, obtaining

$$y_3 = b_{\pi[3]} - (l_{31}y_1 + l_{32}y_2) \ .$$

In general, we substitute $y_1, y_2, \ldots, y_{i-1}$ "forward" into the ith equation to solve for y_i:

$$y_i = b_{\pi[i]} - \sum_{j=1}^{i-1} l_{ij} y_j \ .$$

Having solved for y, we solve for x in equation (28.6) using **back substitution**, which is similar to forward substitution. Here, we solve the nth equation first and work backward to the first equation. Like forward substitution, this process runs in $\Theta(n^2)$ time. Since U is upper-triangular, we can rewrite the system (28.6) as

$$
\begin{aligned}
u_{11}x_1 + u_{12}x_2 + \cdots + \quad u_{1,n-2}x_{n-2} + \quad u_{1,n-1}x_{n-1} + \quad u_{1n}x_n &= y_1 \ , \\
u_{22}x_2 + \cdots + \quad u_{2,n-2}x_{n-2} + \quad u_{2,n-1}x_{n-1} + \quad u_{2n}x_n &= y_2 \ , \\
&\vdots \\
u_{n-2,n-2}x_{n-2} + u_{n-2,n-1}x_{n-1} + u_{n-2,n}x_n &= y_{n-2} \ , \\
u_{n-1,n-1}x_{n-1} + u_{n-1,n}x_n &= y_{n-1} \ , \\
u_{n,n}x_n &= y_n \ .
\end{aligned}
$$

Thus, we can solve for $x_n, x_{n-1}, \ldots, x_1$ successively as follows:

$$
\begin{aligned}
x_n &= y_n/u_{n,n} \ , \\
x_{n-1} &= (y_{n-1} - u_{n-1,n}x_n)/u_{n-1,n-1} \ , \\
x_{n-2} &= (y_{n-2} - (u_{n-2,n-1}x_{n-1} + u_{n-2,n}x_n))/u_{n-2,n-2} \ , \\
&\vdots
\end{aligned}
$$

or, in general,

$$x_i = \left(y_i - \sum_{j=i+1}^{n} u_{ij}x_j \right) / u_{ii} \ .$$

Given P, L, U, and b, the procedure LUP-SOLVE solves for x by combining forward and back substitution. The pseudocode assumes that the dimension n appears in the attribute $L.rows$ and that the permutation matrix P is represented by the array π.

LUP-SOLVE(L, U, π, b)

```
1  n = L.rows
2  let x and y be new vectors of length n
3  for i = 1 to n
4      y_i = b_{π[i]} - Σ_{j=1}^{i-1} l_{ij} y_j
5  for i = n downto 1
6      x_i = (y_i - Σ_{j=i+1}^{n} u_{ij} x_j) / u_{ii}
7  return x
```

Procedure LUP-SOLVE solves for y using forward substitution in lines 3–4, and then it solves for x using backward substitution in lines 5–6. Since the summation within each of the **for** loops includes an implicit loop, the running time is $\Theta(n^2)$.

As an example of these methods, consider the system of linear equations defined by

$$\begin{pmatrix} 1 & 2 & 0 \\ 3 & 4 & 4 \\ 5 & 6 & 3 \end{pmatrix} x = \begin{pmatrix} 3 \\ 7 \\ 8 \end{pmatrix},$$

where

$$A = \begin{pmatrix} 1 & 2 & 0 \\ 3 & 4 & 4 \\ 5 & 6 & 3 \end{pmatrix},$$

$$b = \begin{pmatrix} 3 \\ 7 \\ 8 \end{pmatrix},$$

and we wish to solve for the unknown x. The LUP decomposition is

$$L = \begin{pmatrix} 1 & 0 & 0 \\ 0.2 & 1 & 0 \\ 0.6 & 0.5 & 1 \end{pmatrix},$$

$$U = \begin{pmatrix} 5 & 6 & 3 \\ 0 & 0.8 & -0.6 \\ 0 & 0 & 2.5 \end{pmatrix},$$

$$P = \begin{pmatrix} 0 & 0 & 1 \\ 1 & 0 & 0 \\ 0 & 1 & 0 \end{pmatrix}.$$

(You might want to verify that $PA = LU$.) Using forward substitution, we solve $Ly = Pb$ for y:

$$\begin{pmatrix} 1 & 0 & 0 \\ 0.2 & 1 & 0 \\ 0.6 & 0.5 & 1 \end{pmatrix} \begin{pmatrix} y_1 \\ y_2 \\ y_3 \end{pmatrix} = \begin{pmatrix} 8 \\ 3 \\ 7 \end{pmatrix},$$

obtaining

$$y = \begin{pmatrix} 8 \\ 1.4 \\ 1.5 \end{pmatrix}$$

by computing first y_1, then y_2, and finally y_3. Using back substitution, we solve $Ux = y$ for x:

$$\begin{pmatrix} 5 & 6 & 3 \\ 0 & 0.8 & -0.6 \\ 0 & 0 & 2.5 \end{pmatrix} \begin{pmatrix} x_1 \\ x_2 \\ x_3 \end{pmatrix} = \begin{pmatrix} 8 \\ 1.4 \\ 1.5 \end{pmatrix},$$

thereby obtaining the desired answer

$$x = \begin{pmatrix} -1.4 \\ 2.2 \\ 0.6 \end{pmatrix}$$

by computing first x_3, then x_2, and finally x_1.

Computing an LU decomposition

We have now shown that if we can create an LUP decomposition for a nonsingular matrix A, then forward and back substitution can solve the system $Ax = b$ of linear equations. Now we show how to efficiently compute an LUP decomposition for A. We start with the case in which A is an $n \times n$ nonsingular matrix and P is absent (or, equivalently, $P = I_n$). In this case, we factor $A = LU$. We call the two matrices L and U an **LU decomposition** of A.

We use a process known as **Gaussian elimination** to create an LU decomposition. We start by subtracting multiples of the first equation from the other equations in order to remove the first variable from those equations. Then, we subtract multiples of the second equation from the third and subsequent equations so that now the first and second variables are removed from them. We continue this process until the system that remains has an upper-triangular form—in fact, it is the matrix U. The matrix L is made up of the row multipliers that cause variables to be eliminated.

Our algorithm to implement this strategy is recursive. We wish to construct an LU decomposition for an $n \times n$ nonsingular matrix A. If $n = 1$, then we are done, since we can choose $L = I_1$ and $U = A$. For $n > 1$, we break A into four parts:

$$\begin{aligned} A &= \left(\begin{array}{c|ccc} a_{11} & a_{12} & \cdots & a_{1n} \\ \hline a_{21} & a_{22} & \cdots & a_{2n} \\ \vdots & \vdots & \ddots & \vdots \\ a_{n1} & a_{n2} & \cdots & a_{nn} \end{array} \right) \\ &= \begin{pmatrix} a_{11} & w^{\mathrm{T}} \\ v & A' \end{pmatrix}, \end{aligned}$$

where $v = (v_2, v_3, \ldots, v_n) = (a_{21}, a_{22}, \ldots, a_{n1})$ is a column $(n - 1)$-vector, $w^{\mathrm{T}} = (w_2, w_3, \ldots, w_n)^{\mathrm{T}} = (a_{12}, a_{13}, \ldots, a_{1n})^{\mathrm{T}}$ is a row $(n - 1)$-vector, and A' is an $(n - 1) \times (n - 1)$ matrix. Then, using matrix algebra (verify the equations by simply multiplying through), we can factor A as

$$
\begin{aligned}
A &= \begin{pmatrix} a_{11} & w^{\mathrm{T}} \\ v & A' \end{pmatrix} \\
&= \begin{pmatrix} 1 & 0 \\ v/a_{11} & I_{n-1} \end{pmatrix} \begin{pmatrix} a_{11} & w^{\mathrm{T}} \\ 0 & A' - vw^{\mathrm{T}}/a_{11} \end{pmatrix} .
\end{aligned}
\tag{28.8}
$$

The 0s in the first and second matrices of equation (28.8) are row and column $(n-1)$-vectors, respectively. The term vw^{T}/a_{11}, formed by taking the outer product of v and w and dividing each element of the result by a_{11}, is an $(n-1) \times (n-1)$ matrix, which conforms in size to the matrix A' from which it is subtracted. The resulting $(n-1) \times (n-1)$ matrix

$$
A' - vw^{\mathrm{T}}/a_{11}
\tag{28.9}
$$

is called the ***Schur complement*** of A with respect to a_{11}.

We claim that if A is nonsingular, then the Schur complement is nonsingular, too. Why? Suppose that the Schur complement, which is $(n-1) \times (n-1)$, is singular. Then by Theorem D.1, it has row rank strictly less than $n-1$. Because the bottom $n-1$ entries in the first column of the matrix

$$
\begin{pmatrix} a_{11} & w^{\mathrm{T}} \\ 0 & A' - vw^{\mathrm{T}}/a_{11} \end{pmatrix}
$$

are all 0, the bottom $n-1$ rows of this matrix must have row rank strictly less than $n-1$. The row rank of the entire matrix, therefore, is strictly less than n. Applying Exercise D.2-8 to equation (28.8), A has rank strictly less than n, and from Theorem D.1 we derive the contradiction that A is singular.

Because the Schur complement is nonsingular, we can now recursively find an LU decomposition for it. Let us say that

$$
A' - vw^{\mathrm{T}}/a_{11} = L'U' ,
$$

where L' is unit lower-triangular and U' is upper-triangular. Then, using matrix algebra, we have

$$
\begin{aligned}
A &= \begin{pmatrix} 1 & 0 \\ v/a_{11} & I_{n-1} \end{pmatrix} \begin{pmatrix} a_{11} & w^{\mathrm{T}} \\ 0 & A' - vw^{\mathrm{T}}/a_{11} \end{pmatrix} \\
&= \begin{pmatrix} 1 & 0 \\ v/a_{11} & I_{n-1} \end{pmatrix} \begin{pmatrix} a_{11} & w^{\mathrm{T}} \\ 0 & L'U' \end{pmatrix} \\
&= \begin{pmatrix} 1 & 0 \\ v/a_{11} & L' \end{pmatrix} \begin{pmatrix} a_{11} & w^{\mathrm{T}} \\ 0 & U' \end{pmatrix} \\
&= LU ,
\end{aligned}
$$

thereby providing our LU decomposition. (Note that because L' is unit lower-triangular, so is L, and because U' is upper-triangular, so is U.)

Of course, if $a_{11} = 0$, this method doesn't work, because it divides by 0. It also doesn't work if the upper leftmost entry of the Schur complement $A' - vw^T/a_{11}$ is 0, since we divide by it in the next step of the recursion. The elements by which we divide during LU decomposition are called ***pivots***, and they occupy the diagonal elements of the matrix U. The reason we include a permutation matrix P during LUP decomposition is that it allows us to avoid dividing by 0. When we use permutations to avoid division by 0 (or by small numbers, which would contribute to numerical instability), we are ***pivoting***.

An important class of matrices for which LU decomposition always works correctly is the class of symmetric positive-definite matrices. Such matrices require no pivoting, and thus we can employ the recursive strategy outlined above without fear of dividing by 0. We shall prove this result, as well as several others, in Section 28.3.

Our code for LU decomposition of a matrix A follows the recursive strategy, except that an iteration loop replaces the recursion. (This transformation is a standard optimization for a "tail-recursive" procedure—one whose last operation is a recursive call to itself. See Problem 7-4.) It assumes that the attribute $A.rows$ gives the dimension of A. We initialize the matrix U with 0s below the diagonal and matrix L with 1s on its diagonal and 0s above the diagonal. Each iteration works on a square submatrix, using its upper leftmost element as the pivot to compute the v and w vectors and the Schur complement, which becomes the square submatrix worked on by the next iteration.

LU-DECOMPOSITION(A)

```
 1   n = A.rows
 2   let L and U be new n × n matrices
 3   initialize U with 0s below the diagonal
 4   initialize L with 1s on the diagonal and 0s above the diagonal
 5   for k = 1 to n
 6       u_kk = a_kk
 7       for i = k + 1 to n
 8           l_ik = a_ik/a_kk        // a_ik holds v_i
 9           u_ki = a_ki             // a_ki holds w_i
10       for i = k + 1 to n
11           for j = k + 1 to n
12               a_ij = a_ij − l_ik u_kj
13   return L and U
```

The outer **for** loop beginning in line 5 iterates once for each recursive step. Within this loop, line 6 determines the pivot to be $u_{kk} = a_{kk}$. The **for** loop in lines 7–9 (which does not execute when $k = n$) uses the v and w vectors to update L and U.

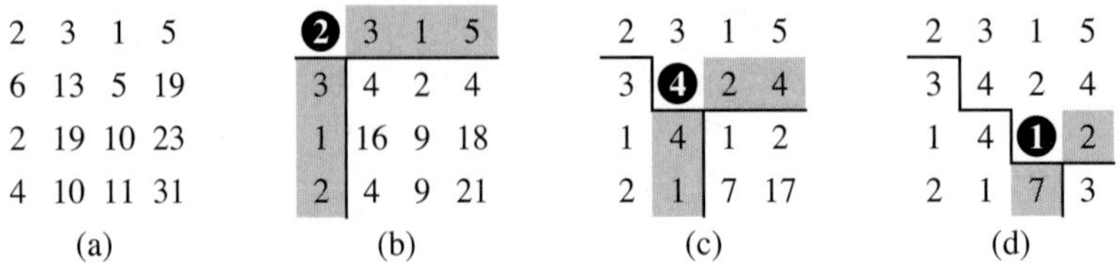

Figure 28.1 shows the matrices:

(a)
$$\begin{matrix} 2 & 3 & 1 & 5 \\ 6 & 13 & 5 & 19 \\ 2 & 19 & 10 & 23 \\ 4 & 10 & 11 & 31 \end{matrix}$$

(b)
$$\begin{matrix} 2 & 3 & 1 & 5 \\ 3 & 4 & 2 & 4 \\ 1 & 16 & 9 & 18 \\ 2 & 4 & 9 & 21 \end{matrix}$$

(c)
$$\begin{matrix} 2 & 3 & 1 & 5 \\ 3 & 4 & 2 & 4 \\ 1 & 4 & 1 & 2 \\ 2 & 1 & 7 & 17 \end{matrix}$$

(d)
$$\begin{matrix} 2 & 3 & 1 & 5 \\ 3 & 4 & 2 & 4 \\ 1 & 4 & 1 & 2 \\ 2 & 1 & 7 & 3 \end{matrix}$$

(e)
$$\begin{pmatrix} 2 & 3 & 1 & 5 \\ 6 & 13 & 5 & 19 \\ 2 & 19 & 10 & 23 \\ 4 & 10 & 11 & 31 \end{pmatrix} = \begin{pmatrix} 1 & 0 & 0 & 0 \\ 3 & 1 & 0 & 0 \\ 1 & 4 & 1 & 0 \\ 2 & 1 & 7 & 1 \end{pmatrix} \begin{pmatrix} 2 & 3 & 1 & 5 \\ 0 & 4 & 2 & 4 \\ 0 & 0 & 1 & 2 \\ 0 & 0 & 0 & 3 \end{pmatrix}$$
$$\quad\quad A \quad\quad\quad\quad\quad\quad L \quad\quad\quad\quad\quad\quad U$$

Figure 28.1 The operation of LU-DECOMPOSITION. **(a)** The matrix A. **(b)** The element $a_{11} = 2$ in the black circle is the pivot, the shaded column is v/a_{11}, and the shaded row is w^{T}. The elements of U computed thus far are above the horizontal line, and the elements of L are to the left of the vertical line. The Schur complement matrix $A' - vw^{\mathrm{T}}/a_{11}$ occupies the lower right. **(c)** We now operate on the Schur complement matrix produced from part (b). The element $a_{22} = 4$ in the black circle is the pivot, and the shaded column and row are v/a_{22} and w^{T} (in the partitioning of the Schur complement), respectively. Lines divide the matrix into the elements of U computed so far (above), the elements of L computed so far (left), and the new Schur complement (lower right). **(d)** After the next step, the matrix A is factored. (The element 3 in the new Schur complement becomes part of U when the recursion terminates.) **(e)** The factorization $A = LU$.

Line 8 determines the below-diagonal elements of L, storing v_i/a_{kk} in l_{ik}, and line 9 computes the above-diagonal elements of U, storing w_i in u_{ki}. Finally, lines 10–12 compute the elements of the Schur complement and store them back into the matrix A. (We don't need to divide by a_{kk} in line 12 because we already did so when we computed l_{ik} in line 8.) Because line 12 is triply nested, LU-DECOMPOSITION runs in time $\Theta(n^3)$.

Figure 28.1 illustrates the operation of LU-DECOMPOSITION. It shows a standard optimization of the procedure in which we store the significant elements of L and U in place in the matrix A. That is, we can set up a correspondence between each element a_{ij} and either l_{ij} (if $i > j$) or u_{ij} (if $i \leq j$) and update the matrix A so that it holds both L and U when the procedure terminates. To obtain the pseudocode for this optimization from the above pseudocode, just replace each reference to l or u by a; you can easily verify that this transformation preserves correctness.

Computing an LUP decomposition

Generally, in solving a system of linear equations $Ax = b$, we must pivot on off-diagonal elements of A to avoid dividing by 0. Dividing by 0 would, of course, be disastrous. But we also want to avoid dividing by a small value—even if A is nonsingular—because numerical instabilities can result. We therefore try to pivot on a large value.

The mathematics behind LUP decomposition is similar to that of LU decomposition. Recall that we are given an $n \times n$ nonsingular matrix A, and we wish to find a permutation matrix P, a unit lower-triangular matrix L, and an upper-triangular matrix U such that $PA = LU$. Before we partition the matrix A, as we did for LU decomposition, we move a nonzero element, say a_{k1}, from somewhere in the first column to the $(1, 1)$ position of the matrix. For numerical stability, we choose a_{k1} as the element in the first column with the greatest absolute value. (The first column cannot contain only 0s, for then A would be singular, because its determinant would be 0, by Theorems D.4 and D.5.) In order to preserve the set of equations, we exchange row 1 with row k, which is equivalent to multiplying A by a permutation matrix Q on the left (Exercise D.1-4). Thus, we can write QA as

$$QA = \begin{pmatrix} a_{k1} & w^{\mathrm{T}} \\ v & A' \end{pmatrix},$$

where $v = (a_{21}, a_{31}, \ldots, a_{n1})$, except that a_{11} replaces a_{k1}; $w^{\mathrm{T}} = (a_{k2}, a_{k3}, \ldots, a_{kn})^{\mathrm{T}}$; and A' is an $(n-1) \times (n-1)$ matrix. Since $a_{k1} \neq 0$, we can now perform much the same linear algebra as for LU decomposition, but now guaranteeing that we do not divide by 0:

$$\begin{aligned} QA &= \begin{pmatrix} a_{k1} & w^{\mathrm{T}} \\ v & A' \end{pmatrix} \\ &= \begin{pmatrix} 1 & 0 \\ v/a_{k1} & I_{n-1} \end{pmatrix} \begin{pmatrix} a_{k1} & w^{\mathrm{T}} \\ 0 & A' - vw^{\mathrm{T}}/a_{k1} \end{pmatrix}. \end{aligned}$$

As we saw for LU decomposition, if A is nonsingular, then the Schur complement $A' - vw^{\mathrm{T}}/a_{k1}$ is nonsingular, too. Therefore, we can recursively find an LUP decomposition for it, with unit lower-triangular matrix L', upper-triangular matrix U', and permutation matrix P', such that

$$P'(A' - vw^{\mathrm{T}}/a_{k1}) = L'U'.$$

Define

$$P = \begin{pmatrix} 1 & 0 \\ 0 & P' \end{pmatrix} Q,$$

which is a permutation matrix, since it is the product of two permutation matrices (Exercise D.1-4). We now have

$$
\begin{aligned}
PA &= \begin{pmatrix} 1 & 0 \\ 0 & P' \end{pmatrix} QA \\[4pt]
&= \begin{pmatrix} 1 & 0 \\ 0 & P' \end{pmatrix}\begin{pmatrix} 1 & 0 \\ v/a_{k1} & I_{n-1} \end{pmatrix}\begin{pmatrix} a_{k1} & w^{\mathrm{T}} \\ 0 & A' - vw^{\mathrm{T}}/a_{k1} \end{pmatrix} \\[4pt]
&= \begin{pmatrix} 1 & 0 \\ P'v/a_{k1} & P' \end{pmatrix}\begin{pmatrix} a_{k1} & w^{\mathrm{T}} \\ 0 & A' - vw^{\mathrm{T}}/a_{k1} \end{pmatrix} \\[4pt]
&= \begin{pmatrix} 1 & 0 \\ P'v/a_{k1} & I_{n-1} \end{pmatrix}\begin{pmatrix} a_{k1} & w^{\mathrm{T}} \\ 0 & P'(A' - vw^{\mathrm{T}}/a_{k1}) \end{pmatrix} \\[4pt]
&= \begin{pmatrix} 1 & 0 \\ P'v/a_{k1} & I_{n-1} \end{pmatrix}\begin{pmatrix} a_{k1} & w^{\mathrm{T}} \\ 0 & L'U' \end{pmatrix} \\[4pt]
&= \begin{pmatrix} 1 & 0 \\ P'v/a_{k1} & L' \end{pmatrix}\begin{pmatrix} a_{k1} & w^{\mathrm{T}} \\ 0 & U' \end{pmatrix} \\[4pt]
&= LU ,
\end{aligned}
$$

yielding the LUP decomposition. Because L' is unit lower-triangular, so is L, and because U' is upper-triangular, so is U.

Notice that in this derivation, unlike the one for LU decomposition, we must multiply both the column vector v/a_{k1} and the Schur complement $A' - vw^{\mathrm{T}}/a_{k1}$ by the permutation matrix P'. Here is the pseudocode for LUP decomposition:

LUP-DECOMPOSITION(A)

```
 1   n = A.rows
 2   let π[1 . . n] be a new array
 3   for i = 1 to n
 4        π[i] = i
 5   for k = 1 to n
 6        p = 0
 7        for i = k to n
 8             if |a_ik| > p
 9                  p = |a_ik|
10                  k' = i
11        if p == 0
12             error "singular matrix"
13        exchange π[k] with π[k']
14        for i = 1 to n
15             exchange a_ki with a_k'i
16        for i = k + 1 to n
17             a_ik = a_ik/a_kk
18             for j = k + 1 to n
19                  a_ij = a_ij − a_ik a_kj
```

Like LU-DECOMPOSITION, our LUP-DECOMPOSITION procedure replaces the recursion with an iteration loop. As an improvement over a direct implementation of the recursion, we dynamically maintain the permutation matrix P as an array π, where $\pi[i] = j$ means that the ith row of P contains a 1 in column j. We also implement the code to compute L and U "in place" in the matrix A. Thus, when the procedure terminates,

$$a_{ij} = \begin{cases} l_{ij} & \text{if } i > j \,, \\ u_{ij} & \text{if } i \le j \,. \end{cases}$$

Figure 28.2 illustrates how LUP-DECOMPOSITION factors a matrix. Lines 3–4 initialize the array π to represent the identity permutation. The outer **for** loop beginning in line 5 implements the recursion. Each time through the outer loop, lines 6–10 determine the element $a_{k'k}$ with largest absolute value of those in the current first column (column k) of the $(n - k + 1) \times (n - k + 1)$ matrix whose LUP decomposition we are finding. If all elements in the current first column are zero, lines 11–12 report that the matrix is singular. To pivot, we exchange $\pi[k']$ with $\pi[k]$ in line 13 and exchange the kth and k'th rows of A in lines 14–15, thereby making the pivot element a_{kk}. (The entire rows are swapped because in the derivation of the method above, not only is $A' - vw^{\mathrm{T}}/a_{k1}$ multiplied by P', but so is v/a_{k1}.) Finally, the Schur complement is computed by lines 16–19 in much the same way as it is computed by lines 7–12 of LU-DECOMPOSITION, except that here the operation is written to work in place.

Because of its triply nested loop structure, LUP-DECOMPOSITION has a running time of $\Theta(n^3)$, which is the same as that of LU-DECOMPOSITION. Thus, pivoting costs us at most a constant factor in time.

Exercises

28.1-1
Solve the equation

$$\begin{pmatrix} 1 & 0 & 0 \\ 4 & 1 & 0 \\ -6 & 5 & 1 \end{pmatrix} \begin{pmatrix} x_1 \\ x_2 \\ x_3 \end{pmatrix} = \begin{pmatrix} 3 \\ 14 \\ -7 \end{pmatrix}$$

by using forward substitution.

28.1-2
Find an LU decomposition of the matrix

$$\begin{pmatrix} 4 & -5 & 6 \\ 8 & -6 & 7 \\ 12 & -7 & 12 \end{pmatrix} .$$

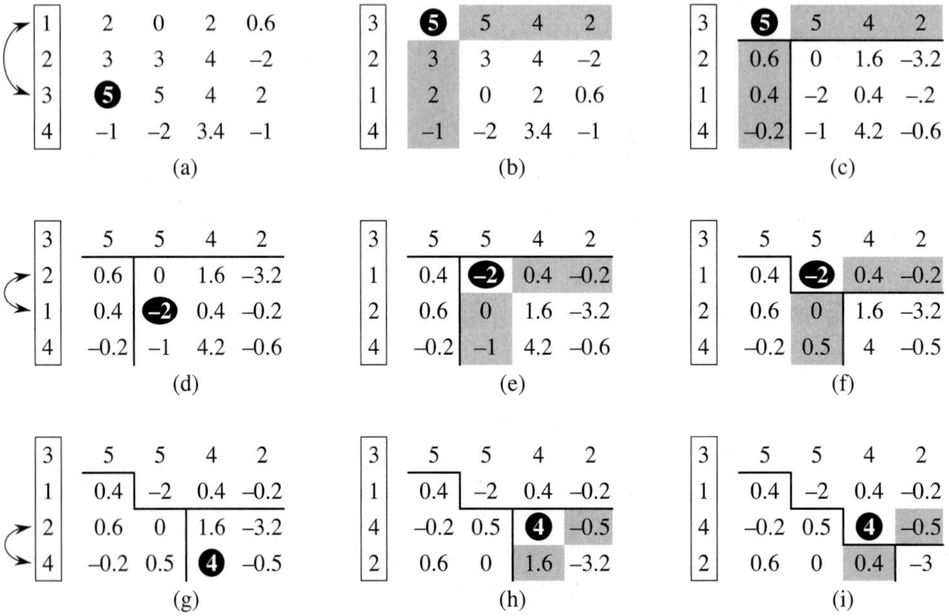

$$
\underbrace{\begin{pmatrix} 0 & 0 & 1 & 0 \\ 1 & 0 & 0 & 0 \\ 0 & 0 & 0 & 1 \\ 0 & 1 & 0 & 0 \end{pmatrix}}_{P}
\underbrace{\begin{pmatrix} 2 & 0 & 2 & 0.6 \\ 3 & 3 & 4 & -2 \\ 5 & 5 & 4 & 2 \\ -1 & -2 & 3.4 & -1 \end{pmatrix}}_{A}
=
\underbrace{\begin{pmatrix} 1 & 0 & 0 & 0 \\ 0.4 & 1 & 0 & 0 \\ -0.2 & 0.5 & 1 & 0 \\ 0.6 & 0 & 0.4 & 1 \end{pmatrix}}_{L}
\underbrace{\begin{pmatrix} 5 & 5 & 4 & 2 \\ 0 & -2 & 0.4 & -0.2 \\ 0 & 0 & 4 & -0.5 \\ 0 & 0 & 0 & -3 \end{pmatrix}}_{U}
$$

(j)

Figure 28.2 The operation of LUP-DECOMPOSITION. **(a)** The input matrix A with the identity permutation of the rows on the left. The first step of the algorithm determines that the element 5 in the black circle in the third row is the pivot for the first column. **(b)** Rows 1 and 3 are swapped and the permutation is updated. The shaded column and row represent v and w^{T}. **(c)** The vector v is replaced by $v/5$, and the lower right of the matrix is updated with the Schur complement. Lines divide the matrix into three regions: elements of U (above), elements of L (left), and elements of the Schur complement (lower right). **(d)–(f)** The second step. **(g)–(i)** The third step. No further changes occur on the fourth (final) step. **(j)** The LUP decomposition $PA = LU$.

28.1-3

Solve the equation

$$
\begin{pmatrix} 1 & 5 & 4 \\ 2 & 0 & 3 \\ 5 & 8 & 2 \end{pmatrix} \begin{pmatrix} x_1 \\ x_2 \\ x_3 \end{pmatrix} = \begin{pmatrix} 12 \\ 9 \\ 5 \end{pmatrix}
$$

by using an LUP decomposition.

28.1-4

Describe the LUP decomposition of a diagonal matrix.

28.1-5

Describe the LUP decomposition of a permutation matrix A, and prove that it is unique.

28.1-6

Show that for all $n \geq 1$, there exists a singular $n \times n$ matrix that has an LU decomposition.

28.1-7

In LU-DECOMPOSITION, is it necessary to perform the outermost **for** loop iteration when $k = n$? How about in LUP-DECOMPOSITION?

28.2 Inverting matrices

Although in practice we do not generally use matrix inverses to solve systems of linear equations, preferring instead to use more numerically stable techniques such as LUP decomposition, sometimes we need to compute a matrix inverse. In this section, we show how to use LUP decomposition to compute a matrix inverse. We also prove that matrix multiplication and computing the inverse of a matrix are equivalently hard problems, in that (subject to technical conditions) we can use an algorithm for one to solve the other in the same asymptotic running time. Thus, we can use Strassen's algorithm (see Section 4.2) for matrix multiplication to invert a matrix. Indeed, Strassen's original paper was motivated by the problem of showing that a set of a linear equations could be solved more quickly than by the usual method.

Computing a matrix inverse from an LUP decomposition

Suppose that we have an LUP decomposition of a matrix A in the form of three matrices L, U, and P such that $PA = LU$. Using LUP-SOLVE, we can solve an equation of the form $Ax = b$ in time $\Theta(n^2)$. Since the LUP decomposition depends on A but not b, we can run LUP-SOLVE on a second set of equations of the form $Ax = b'$ in additional time $\Theta(n^2)$. In general, once we have the LUP decomposition of A, we can solve, in time $\Theta(kn^2)$, k versions of the equation $Ax = b$ that differ only in b.

We can think of the equation

$$AX = I_n \, , \tag{28.10}$$

which defines the matrix X, the inverse of A, as a set of n distinct equations of the form $Ax = b$. To be precise, let X_i denote the ith column of X, and recall that the unit vector e_i is the ith column of I_n. We can then solve equation (28.10) for X by using the LUP decomposition for A to solve each equation

$$AX_i = e_i$$

separately for X_i. Once we have the LUP decomposition, we can compute each of the n columns X_i in time $\Theta(n^2)$, and so we can compute X from the LUP decomposition of A in time $\Theta(n^3)$. Since we can determine the LUP decomposition of A in time $\Theta(n^3)$, we can compute the inverse A^{-1} of a matrix A in time $\Theta(n^3)$.

Matrix multiplication and matrix inversion

We now show that the theoretical speedups obtained for matrix multiplication translate to speedups for matrix inversion. In fact, we prove something stronger: matrix inversion is equivalent to matrix multiplication, in the following sense. If $M(n)$ denotes the time to multiply two $n \times n$ matrices, then we can invert a nonsingular $n \times n$ matrix in time $O(M(n))$. Moreover, if $I(n)$ denotes the time to invert a nonsingular $n \times n$ matrix, then we can multiply two $n \times n$ matrices in time $O(I(n))$. We prove these results as two separate theorems.

Theorem 28.1 (Multiplication is no harder than inversion)
If we can invert an $n \times n$ matrix in time $I(n)$, where $I(n) = \Omega(n^2)$ and $I(n)$ satisfies the regularity condition $I(3n) = O(I(n))$, then we can multiply two $n \times n$ matrices in time $O(I(n))$.

Proof   Let A and B be $n \times n$ matrices whose matrix product C we wish to compute. We define the $3n \times 3n$ matrix D by

$$D = \begin{pmatrix} I_n & A & 0 \\ 0 & I_n & B \\ 0 & 0 & I_n \end{pmatrix}.$$

The inverse of D is

$$D^{-1} = \begin{pmatrix} I_n & -A & AB \\ 0 & I_n & -B \\ 0 & 0 & I_n \end{pmatrix},$$

and thus we can compute the product AB by taking the upper right $n \times n$ submatrix of D^{-1}.

We can construct matrix D in $\Theta(n^2)$ time, which is $O(I(n))$ because we assume that $I(n) = \Omega(n^2)$, and we can invert D in $O(I(3n)) = O(I(n))$ time, by the regularity condition on $I(n)$. We thus have $M(n) = O(I(n))$. ∎

Note that $I(n)$ satisfies the regularity condition whenever $I(n) = \Theta(n^c \lg^d n)$ for any constants $c > 0$ and $d \geq 0$.

The proof that matrix inversion is no harder than matrix multiplication relies on some properties of symmetric positive-definite matrices that we will prove in Section 28.3.

Theorem 28.2 (Inversion is no harder than multiplication)
Suppose we can multiply two $n \times n$ real matrices in time $M(n)$, where $M(n) = \Omega(n^2)$ and $M(n)$ satisfies the two regularity conditions $M(n + k) = O(M(n))$ for any k in the range $0 \leq k \leq n$ and $M(n/2) \leq cM(n)$ for some constant $c < 1/2$. Then we can compute the inverse of any real nonsingular $n \times n$ matrix in time $O(M(n))$.

Proof We prove the theorem here for real matrices. Exercise 28.2-6 asks you to generalize the proof for matrices whose entries are complex numbers.

We can assume that n is an exact power of 2, since we have

$$\begin{pmatrix} A & 0 \\ 0 & I_k \end{pmatrix}^{-1} = \begin{pmatrix} A^{-1} & 0 \\ 0 & I_k \end{pmatrix}$$

for any $k > 0$. Thus, by choosing k such that $n + k$ is a power of 2, we enlarge the matrix to a size that is the next power of 2 and obtain the desired answer A^{-1} from the answer to the enlarged problem. The first regularity condition on $M(n)$ ensures that this enlargement does not cause the running time to increase by more than a constant factor.

For the moment, let us assume that the $n \times n$ matrix A is symmetric and positive-definite. We partition each of A and its inverse A^{-1} into four $n/2 \times n/2$ submatrices:

$$A = \begin{pmatrix} B & C^{\mathrm{T}} \\ C & D \end{pmatrix} \quad \text{and} \quad A^{-1} = \begin{pmatrix} R & T \\ U & V \end{pmatrix}. \tag{28.11}$$

Then, if we let

$$S = D - CB^{-1}C^{\mathrm{T}} \tag{28.12}$$

be the Schur complement of A with respect to B (we shall see more about this form of Schur complement in Section 28.3), we have

$$A^{-1} = \begin{pmatrix} R & T \\ U & V \end{pmatrix} = \begin{pmatrix} B^{-1} + B^{-1}C^{\mathrm{T}}S^{-1}CB^{-1} & -B^{-1}C^{\mathrm{T}}S^{-1} \\ -S^{-1}CB^{-1} & S^{-1} \end{pmatrix}, \tag{28.13}$$

since $AA^{-1} = I_n$, as you can verify by performing the matrix multiplication. Because A is symmetric and positive-definite, Lemmas 28.4 and 28.5 in Section 28.3 imply that B and S are both symmetric and positive-definite. By Lemma 28.3 in Section 28.3, therefore, the inverses B^{-1} and S^{-1} exist, and by Exercise D.2-6, B^{-1} and S^{-1} are symmetric, so that $(B^{-1})^{\mathrm{T}} = B^{-1}$ and $(S^{-1})^{\mathrm{T}} = S^{-1}$. Therefore, we can compute the submatrices R, T, U, and V of A^{-1} as follows, where all matrices mentioned are $n/2 \times n/2$:

1. Form the submatrices B, C, C^{T}, and D of A.

2. Recursively compute the inverse B^{-1} of B.

3. Compute the matrix product $W = CB^{-1}$, and then compute its transpose W^{T}, which equals $B^{-1}C^{\mathrm{T}}$ (by Exercise D.1-2 and $(B^{-1})^{\mathrm{T}} = B^{-1}$).

4. Compute the matrix product $X = WC^{\mathrm{T}}$, which equals $CB^{-1}C^{\mathrm{T}}$, and then compute the matrix $S = D - X = D - CB^{-1}C^{\mathrm{T}}$.

5. Recursively compute the inverse S^{-1} of S, and set V to S^{-1}.

6. Compute the matrix product $Y = S^{-1}W$, which equals $S^{-1}CB^{-1}$, and then compute its transpose Y^{T}, which equals $B^{-1}C^{\mathrm{T}}S^{-1}$ (by Exercise D.1-2, $(B^{-1})^{\mathrm{T}} = B^{-1}$, and $(S^{-1})^{\mathrm{T}} = S^{-1}$). Set T to $-Y^{\mathrm{T}}$ and U to $-Y$.

7. Compute the matrix product $Z = W^{\mathrm{T}}Y$, which equals $B^{-1}C^{\mathrm{T}}S^{-1}CB^{-1}$, and set R to $B^{-1} + Z$.

Thus, we can invert an $n \times n$ symmetric positive-definite matrix by inverting two $n/2 \times n/2$ matrices in steps 2 and 5; performing four multiplications of $n/2 \times n/2$ matrices in steps 3, 4, 6, and 7; plus an additional cost of $O(n^2)$ for extracting submatrices from A, inserting submatrices into A^{-1}, and performing a constant number of additions, subtractions, and transposes on $n/2 \times n/2$ matrices. We get the recurrence

$$\begin{aligned} I(n) \ &\le \ 2I(n/2) + 4M(n/2) + O(n^2) \\ &= \ 2I(n/2) + \Theta(M(n)) \\ &= \ O(M(n)) \,. \end{aligned}$$

The second line holds because the second regularity condition in the statement of the theorem implies that $4M(n/2) < 2M(n)$ and because we assume that $M(n) = \Omega(n^2)$. The third line follows because the second regularity condition allows us to apply case 3 of the master theorem (Theorem 4.1).

It remains to prove that we can obtain the same asymptotic running time for matrix multiplication as for matrix inversion when A is invertible but not symmetric and positive-definite. The basic idea is that for any nonsingular matrix A, the matrix $A^{\mathrm{T}}A$ is symmetric (by Exercise D.1-2) and positive-definite (by Theorem D.6). The trick, then, is to reduce the problem of inverting A to the problem of inverting $A^{\mathrm{T}}A$.

The reduction is based on the observation that when A is an $n \times n$ nonsingular matrix, we have

$$A^{-1} = (A^{\mathrm{T}}A)^{-1}A^{\mathrm{T}} ,$$

since $((A^{\mathrm{T}}A)^{-1}A^{\mathrm{T}})A = (A^{\mathrm{T}}A)^{-1}(A^{\mathrm{T}}A) = I_n$ and a matrix inverse is unique. Therefore, we can compute A^{-1} by first multiplying A^{T} by A to obtain $A^{\mathrm{T}}A$, then inverting the symmetric positive-definite matrix $A^{\mathrm{T}}A$ using the above divide-and-conquer algorithm, and finally multiplying the result by A^{T}. Each of these three steps takes $O(M(n))$ time, and thus we can invert any nonsingular matrix with real entries in $O(M(n))$ time. ∎

The proof of Theorem 28.2 suggests a means of solving the equation $Ax = b$ by using LU decomposition without pivoting, so long as A is nonsingular. We multiply both sides of the equation by A^{T}, yielding $(A^{\mathrm{T}}A)x = A^{\mathrm{T}}b$. This transformation doesn't affect the solution x, since A^{T} is invertible, and so we can factor the symmetric positive-definite matrix $A^{\mathrm{T}}A$ by computing an LU decomposition. We then use forward and back substitution to solve for x with the right-hand side $A^{\mathrm{T}}b$. Although this method is theoretically correct, in practice the procedure LUP-DECOMPOSITION works much better. LUP decomposition requires fewer arithmetic operations by a constant factor, and it has somewhat better numerical properties.

Exercises

28.2-1

Let $M(n)$ be the time to multiply two $n \times n$ matrices, and let $S(n)$ denote the time required to square an $n \times n$ matrix. Show that multiplying and squaring matrices have essentially the same difficulty: an $M(n)$-time matrix-multiplication algorithm implies an $O(M(n))$-time squaring algorithm, and an $S(n)$-time squaring algorithm implies an $O(S(n))$-time matrix-multiplication algorithm.

28.2-2

Let $M(n)$ be the time to multiply two $n \times n$ matrices. Show that an $M(n)$-time matrix-multiplication algorithm implies an $O(M(n))$-time LUP-decomposition algorithm.

28.2-3

Let $M(n)$ be the time to multiply two $n \times n$ matrices, and let $D(n)$ denote the time required to find the determinant of an $n \times n$ matrix. Show that multiplying matrices and computing the determinant have essentially the same difficulty: an $M(n)$-time matrix-multiplication algorithm implies an $O(M(n))$-time determinant algorithm, and a $D(n)$-time determinant algorithm implies an $O(D(n))$-time matrix-multiplication algorithm.

28.2-4

Let $M(n)$ be the time to multiply two $n \times n$ boolean matrices, and let $T(n)$ be the time to find the transitive closure of an $n \times n$ boolean matrix. (See Section 25.2.) Show that an $M(n)$-time boolean matrix-multiplication algorithm implies an $O(M(n) \lg n)$-time transitive-closure algorithm, and a $T(n)$-time transitive-closure algorithm implies an $O(T(n))$-time boolean matrix-multiplication algorithm.

28.2-5

Does the matrix-inversion algorithm based on Theorem 28.2 work when matrix elements are drawn from the field of integers modulo 2? Explain.

28.2-6 ★

Generalize the matrix-inversion algorithm of Theorem 28.2 to handle matrices of complex numbers, and prove that your generalization works correctly. (*Hint:* Instead of the transpose of A, use the **conjugate transpose** A^*, which you obtain from the transpose of A by replacing every entry with its complex conjugate. Instead of symmetric matrices, consider **Hermitian** matrices, which are matrices A such that $A = A^*$.)

28.3   Symmetric positive-definite matrices and least-squares approximation

Symmetric positive-definite matrices have many interesting and desirable properties. For example, they are nonsingular, and we can perform LU decomposition on them without having to worry about dividing by 0. In this section, we shall prove several other important properties of symmetric positive-definite matrices and show an interesting application to curve fitting by a least-squares approximation.

The first property we prove is perhaps the most basic.

Lemma 28.3
Any positive-definite matrix is nonsingular.

Proof Suppose that a matrix A is singular. Then by Corollary D.3, there exists a nonzero vector x such that $Ax = 0$. Hence, $x^T A x = 0$, and A cannot be positive-definite. ∎

The proof that we can perform LU decomposition on a symmetric positive-definite matrix A without dividing by 0 is more involved. We begin by proving properties about certain submatrices of A. Define the kth ***leading submatrix*** of A to be the matrix A_k consisting of the intersection of the first k rows and first k columns of A.

Lemma 28.4
If A is a symmetric positive-definite matrix, then every leading submatrix of A is symmetric and positive-definite.

Proof That each leading submatrix A_k is symmetric is obvious. To prove that A_k is positive-definite, we assume that it is not and derive a contradiction. If A_k is not positive-definite, then there exists a k-vector $x_k \neq 0$ such that $x_k^T A_k x_k \leq 0$. Let A be $n \times n$, and

$$A = \begin{pmatrix} A_k & B^T \\ B & C \end{pmatrix} \qquad (28.14)$$

for submatrices B (which is $(n-k) \times k$) and C (which is $(n-k) \times (n-k)$). Define the n-vector $x = (x_k^T \quad 0)^T$, where $n - k$ 0s follow x_k. Then we have

$$\begin{aligned} x^T A x &= (x_k^T \quad 0)\begin{pmatrix} A_k & B^T \\ B & C \end{pmatrix}\begin{pmatrix} x_k \\ 0 \end{pmatrix} \\ &= (x_k^T \quad 0)\begin{pmatrix} A_k x_k \\ B x_k \end{pmatrix} \\ &= x_k^T A_k x_k \\ &\leq 0 , \end{aligned}$$

which contradicts A being positive-definite. ∎

We now turn to some essential properties of the Schur complement. Let A be a symmetric positive-definite matrix, and let A_k be a leading $k \times k$ submatrix of A. Partition A once again according to equation (28.14). We generalize equation (28.9) to define the ***Schur complement*** S of A with respect to A_k as

$$S = C - BA_k^{-1}B^{\mathrm{T}} . \tag{28.15}$$

(By Lemma 28.4, A_k is symmetric and positive-definite; therefore, A_k^{-1} exists by Lemma 28.3, and S is well defined.) Note that our earlier definition (28.9) of the Schur complement is consistent with equation (28.15), by letting $k = 1$.

The next lemma shows that the Schur-complement matrices of symmetric positive-definite matrices are themselves symmetric and positive-definite. We used this result in Theorem 28.2, and we need its corollary to prove the correctness of LU decomposition for symmetric positive-definite matrices.

Lemma 28.5 (Schur complement lemma)
If A is a symmetric positive-definite matrix and A_k is a leading $k \times k$ submatrix of A, then the Schur complement S of A with respect to A_k is symmetric and positive-definite.

Proof   Because A is symmetric, so is the submatrix C. By Exercise D.2-6, the product $BA_k^{-1}B^{\mathrm{T}}$ is symmetric, and by Exercise D.1-1, S is symmetric.

It remains to show that S is positive-definite. Consider the partition of A given in equation (28.14). For any nonzero vector x, we have $x^{\mathrm{T}}Ax > 0$ by the assumption that A is positive-definite. Let us break x into two subvectors y and z compatible with A_k and C, respectively. Because A_k^{-1} exists, we have

$$
\begin{aligned}
x^{\mathrm{T}}Ax &= (\, y^{\mathrm{T}} \quad z^{\mathrm{T}} \,) \begin{pmatrix} A_k & B^{\mathrm{T}} \\ B & C \end{pmatrix} \begin{pmatrix} y \\ z \end{pmatrix} \\
&= (\, y^{\mathrm{T}} \quad z^{\mathrm{T}} \,) \begin{pmatrix} A_k y + B^{\mathrm{T}} z \\ By + Cz \end{pmatrix} \\
&= y^{\mathrm{T}} A_k y + y^{\mathrm{T}} B^{\mathrm{T}} z + z^{\mathrm{T}} By + z^{\mathrm{T}} Cz \\
&= (y + A_k^{-1} B^{\mathrm{T}} z)^{\mathrm{T}} A_k (y + A_k^{-1} B^{\mathrm{T}} z) + z^{\mathrm{T}} (C - BA_k^{-1} B^{\mathrm{T}}) z , \tag{28.16}
\end{aligned}
$$

by matrix magic. (Verify by multiplying through.) This last equation amounts to "completing the square" of the quadratic form. (See Exercise 28.3-2.)

Since $x^{\mathrm{T}}Ax > 0$ holds for any nonzero x, let us pick any nonzero z and then choose $y = -A_k^{-1} B^{\mathrm{T}} z$, which causes the first term in equation (28.16) to vanish, leaving

$$z^{\mathrm{T}}(C - BA_k^{-1} B^{\mathrm{T}})z = z^{\mathrm{T}} Sz$$

as the value of the expression. For any $z \neq 0$, we therefore have $z^{\mathrm{T}} Sz = x^{\mathrm{T}}Ax > 0$, and thus S is positive-definite.   ∎

Corollary 28.6
LU decomposition of a symmetric positive-definite matrix never causes a division by 0.

Proof   Let A be a symmetric positive-definite matrix. We shall prove something stronger than the statement of the corollary: every pivot is strictly positive. The first pivot is a_{11}. Let e_1 be the first unit vector, from which we obtain $a_{11} = e_1^T A e_1 > 0$. Since the first step of LU decomposition produces the Schur complement of A with respect to $A_1 = (a_{11})$, Lemma 28.5 implies by induction that all pivots are positive.   ■

Least-squares approximation

One important application of symmetric positive-definite matrices arises in fitting curves to given sets of data points. Suppose that we are given a set of m data points

$$(x_1, y_1), (x_2, y_2), \ldots, (x_m, y_m) ,$$

where we know that the y_i are subject to measurement errors. We would like to determine a function $F(x)$ such that the approximation errors

$$\eta_i = F(x_i) - y_i \tag{28.17}$$

are small for $i = 1, 2, \ldots, m$. The form of the function F depends on the problem at hand. Here, we assume that it has the form of a linearly weighted sum,

$$F(x) = \sum_{j=1}^{n} c_j f_j(x) ,$$

where the number of summands n and the specific ***basis functions*** f_j are chosen based on knowledge of the problem at hand. A common choice is $f_j(x) = x^{j-1}$, which means that

$$F(x) = c_1 + c_2 x + c_3 x^2 + \cdots + c_n x^{n-1}$$

is a polynomial of degree $n - 1$ in x. Thus, given m data points $(x_1, y_1), (x_2, y_2), \ldots, (x_m, y_m)$, we wish to calculate n coefficients $c_1, c_2, \ldots, c_n$ that minimize the approximation errors $\eta_1, \eta_2, \ldots, \eta_m$.

By choosing $n = m$, we can calculate each y_i *exactly* in equation (28.17). Such a high-degree F "fits the noise" as well as the data, however, and generally gives poor results when used to predict y for previously unseen values of x. It is usually better to choose n significantly smaller than m and hope that by choosing the coefficients c_j well, we can obtain a function F that finds the significant patterns in the data points without paying undue attention to the noise. Some theoretical principles exist for choosing n, but they are beyond the scope of this text. In any case, once we choose a value of n that is less than m, we end up with an overdetermined set of equations whose solution we wish to approximate. We now show how to do so.

Let

$$
A = \begin{pmatrix}
f_1(x_1) & f_2(x_1) & \cdots & f_n(x_1) \\
f_1(x_2) & f_2(x_2) & \cdots & f_n(x_2) \\
\vdots & \vdots & \ddots & \vdots \\
f_1(x_m) & f_2(x_m) & \cdots & f_n(x_m)
\end{pmatrix}
$$

denote the matrix of values of the basis functions at the given points; that is, $a_{ij} = f_j(x_i)$. Let $c = (c_k)$ denote the desired n-vector of coefficients. Then,

$$
\begin{aligned}
Ac &= \begin{pmatrix}
f_1(x_1) & f_2(x_1) & \cdots & f_n(x_1) \\
f_1(x_2) & f_2(x_2) & \cdots & f_n(x_2) \\
\vdots & \vdots & \ddots & \vdots \\
f_1(x_m) & f_2(x_m) & \cdots & f_n(x_m)
\end{pmatrix}
\begin{pmatrix}
c_1 \\
c_2 \\
\vdots \\
c_n
\end{pmatrix} \\
&= \begin{pmatrix}
F(x_1) \\
F(x_2) \\
\vdots \\
F(x_m)
\end{pmatrix}
\end{aligned}
$$

is the m-vector of "predicted values" for y. Thus,

$$
\eta = Ac - y
$$

is the m-vector of **approximation errors**.

To minimize approximation errors, we choose to minimize the norm of the error vector η, which gives us a **least-squares solution**, since

$$
\|\eta\| = \left(\sum_{i=1}^{m} \eta_i^2 \right)^{1/2} .
$$

Because

$$
\|\eta\|^2 = \|Ac - y\|^2 = \sum_{i=1}^{m} \left(\sum_{j=1}^{n} a_{ij} c_j - y_i \right)^2 ,
$$

we can minimize $\|\eta\|$ by differentiating $\|\eta\|^2$ with respect to each c_k and then setting the result to 0:

$$\frac{d\,\|\eta\|^2}{dc_k} = \sum_{i=1}^{m} 2 \left(\sum_{j=1}^{n} a_{ij} c_j - y_i \right) a_{ik} = 0 \,. \tag{28.18}$$

The n equations (28.18) for $k = 1, 2, \ldots, n$ are equivalent to the single matrix equation

$$(Ac - y)^{\mathrm{T}} A = 0$$

or, equivalently (using Exercise D.1-2), to

$$A^{\mathrm{T}}(Ac - y) = 0 \,,$$

which implies

$$A^{\mathrm{T}} Ac = A^{\mathrm{T}} y \,. \tag{28.19}$$

In statistics, this is called the ***normal equation***. The matrix $A^{\mathrm{T}} A$ is symmetric by Exercise D.1-2, and if A has full column rank, then by Theorem D.6, $A^{\mathrm{T}} A$ is positive-definite as well. Hence, $(A^{\mathrm{T}} A)^{-1}$ exists, and the solution to equation (28.19) is

$$\begin{aligned} c &= \left((A^{\mathrm{T}} A)^{-1} A^{\mathrm{T}} \right) y \\ &= A^+ y \,, \end{aligned} \tag{28.20}$$

where the matrix $A^+ = \left((A^{\mathrm{T}} A)^{-1} A^{\mathrm{T}} \right)$ is the ***pseudoinverse*** of the matrix A. The pseudoinverse naturally generalizes the notion of a matrix inverse to the case in which A is not square. (Compare equation (28.20) as the approximate solution to $Ac = y$ with the solution $A^{-1}b$ as the exact solution to $Ax = b$.)

As an example of producing a least-squares fit, suppose that we have five data points

$$\begin{aligned} (x_1, y_1) &= (-1, 2) \,, \\ (x_2, y_2) &= (1, 1) \,, \\ (x_3, y_3) &= (2, 1) \,, \\ (x_4, y_4) &= (3, 0) \,, \\ (x_5, y_5) &= (5, 3) \,, \end{aligned}$$

shown as black dots in Figure 28.3. We wish to fit these points with a quadratic polynomial

$$F(x) = c_1 + c_2 x + c_3 x^2 \,.$$

We start with the matrix of basis-function values

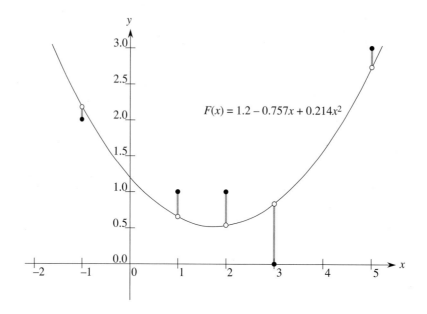

Figure 28.3   The least-squares fit of a quadratic polynomial to the set of five data points $\{(-1, 2), (1, 1), (2, 1), (3, 0), (5, 3)\}$. The black dots are the data points, and the white dots are their estimated values predicted by the polynomial $F(x) = 1.2 - 0.757x + 0.214x^2$, the quadratic polynomial that minimizes the sum of the squared errors. Each shaded line shows the error for one data point.

$$
A = \begin{pmatrix} 1 & x_1 & x_1^2 \\ 1 & x_2 & x_2^2 \\ 1 & x_3 & x_3^2 \\ 1 & x_4 & x_4^2 \\ 1 & x_5 & x_5^2 \end{pmatrix} = \begin{pmatrix} 1 & -1 & 1 \\ 1 & 1 & 1 \\ 1 & 2 & 4 \\ 1 & 3 & 9 \\ 1 & 5 & 25 \end{pmatrix},
$$

whose pseudoinverse is

$$
A^+ = \begin{pmatrix} 0.500 & 0.300 & 0.200 & 0.100 & -0.100 \\ -0.388 & 0.093 & 0.190 & 0.193 & -0.088 \\ 0.060 & -0.036 & -0.048 & -0.036 & 0.060 \end{pmatrix}.
$$

Multiplying y by A^+, we obtain the coefficient vector

$$
c = \begin{pmatrix} 1.200 \\ -0.757 \\ 0.214 \end{pmatrix},
$$

which corresponds to the quadratic polynomial

$$F(x) = 1.200 - 0.757x + 0.214x^2$$

as the closest-fitting quadratic to the given data, in a least-squares sense.

As a practical matter, we solve the normal equation (28.19) by multiplying y by A^{T} and then finding an LU decomposition of $A^{\mathrm{T}}A$. If A has full rank, the matrix $A^{\mathrm{T}}A$ is guaranteed to be nonsingular, because it is symmetric and positive-definite. (See Exercise D.1-2 and Theorem D.6.)

Exercises

28.3-1
Prove that every diagonal element of a symmetric positive-definite matrix is positive.

28.3-2
Let $A = \begin{pmatrix} a & b \\ b & c \end{pmatrix}$ be a 2×2 symmetric positive-definite matrix. Prove that its determinant $ac - b^2$ is positive by "completing the square" in a manner similar to that used in the proof of Lemma 28.5.

28.3-3
Prove that the maximum element in a symmetric positive-definite matrix lies on the diagonal.

28.3-4
Prove that the determinant of each leading submatrix of a symmetric positive-definite matrix is positive.

28.3-5
Let A_k denote the kth leading submatrix of a symmetric positive-definite matrix A. Prove that $\det(A_k)/\det(A_{k-1})$ is the kth pivot during LU decomposition, where, by convention, $\det(A_0) = 1$.

28.3-6
Find the function of the form

$$F(x) = c_1 + c_2 x \lg x + c_3 e^x$$

that is the best least-squares fit to the data points

$$(1, 1), (2, 1), (3, 3), (4, 8) \ .$$

28.3-7

Show that the pseudoinverse A^+ satisfies the following four equations:

$$
\begin{aligned}
AA^+A &= A, \\
A^+AA^+ &= A^+, \\
(AA^+)^\mathrm{T} &= AA^+, \\
(A^+A)^\mathrm{T} &= A^+A.
\end{aligned}
$$

Problems

28-1   Tridiagonal systems of linear equations

Consider the tridiagonal matrix

$$
A = \begin{pmatrix}
1 & -1 & 0 & 0 & 0 \\
-1 & 2 & -1 & 0 & 0 \\
0 & -1 & 2 & -1 & 0 \\
0 & 0 & -1 & 2 & -1 \\
0 & 0 & 0 & -1 & 2
\end{pmatrix}.
$$

a. Find an LU decomposition of A.

b. Solve the equation $Ax = \begin{pmatrix} 1 & 1 & 1 & 1 & 1 \end{pmatrix}^\mathrm{T}$ by using forward and back substitution.

c. Find the inverse of A.

d. Show how, for any $n \times n$ symmetric positive-definite, tridiagonal matrix A and any n-vector b, to solve the equation $Ax = b$ in $O(n)$ time by performing an LU decomposition. Argue that any method based on forming A^{-1} is asymptotically more expensive in the worst case.

e. Show how, for any $n \times n$ nonsingular, tridiagonal matrix A and any n-vector b, to solve the equation $Ax = b$ in $O(n)$ time by performing an LUP decomposition.

28-2   Splines

A practical method for interpolating a set of points with a curve is to use *cubic splines*. We are given a set $\{(x_i, y_i) : i = 0, 1, \ldots, n\}$ of $n + 1$ point-value pairs, where $x_0 < x_1 < \cdots < x_n$. We wish to fit a piecewise-cubic curve (spline) $f(x)$ to the points. That is, the curve $f(x)$ is made up of n cubic polynomials $f_i(x) = a_i + b_i x + c_i x^2 + d_i x^3$ for $i = 0, 1, \ldots, n - 1$, where if x falls in the range $x_i \leq x \leq x_{i+1}$, then the value of the curve is given by $f(x) = f_i(x - x_i)$. The points x_i at which the cubic polynomials are "pasted" together are called **knots**. For simplicity, we shall assume that $x_i = i$ for $i = 0, 1, \ldots, n$.

To ensure continuity of $f(x)$, we require that

$$f(x_i) \quad = \quad f_i(0) \quad = \quad y_i \, ,$$
$$f(x_{i+1}) \quad = \quad f_i(1) \quad = \quad y_{i+1}$$

for $i = 0, 1, \ldots, n - 1$. To ensure that $f(x)$ is sufficiently smooth, we also insist that the first derivative be continuous at each knot:

$$f'(x_{i+1}) = f_i'(1) = f_{i+1}'(0)$$

for $i = 0, 1, \ldots, n - 2$.

a. Suppose that for $i = 0, 1, \ldots, n$, we are given not only the point-value pairs $\{(x_i, y_i)\}$ but also the first derivatives $D_i = f'(x_i)$ at each knot. Express each coefficient a_i, b_i, c_i, and d_i in terms of the values y_i, y_{i+1}, D_i, and D_{i+1}. (Remember that $x_i = i$.) How quickly can we compute the $4n$ coefficients from the point-value pairs and first derivatives?

The question remains of how to choose the first derivatives of $f(x)$ at the knots. One method is to require the second derivatives to be continuous at the knots:

$$f''(x_{i+1}) = f_i''(1) = f_{i+1}''(0)$$

for $i = 0, 1, \ldots, n - 2$. At the first and last knots, we assume that $f''(x_0) = f_0''(0) = 0$ and $f''(x_n) = f_{n-1}''(1) = 0$; these assumptions make $f(x)$ a **natural** cubic spline.

b. Use the continuity constraints on the second derivative to show that for $i = 1, 2, \ldots, n - 1$,

$$D_{i-1} + 4D_i + D_{i+1} = 3(y_{i+1} - y_{i-1}) \, . \tag{28.21}$$

c. Show that

$$2D_0 + D_1 \quad = \quad 3(y_1 - y_0) \, , \tag{28.22}$$
$$D_{n-1} + 2D_n \quad = \quad 3(y_n - y_{n-1}) \, . \tag{28.23}$$

d. Rewrite equations (28.21)–(28.23) as a matrix equation involving the vector $D = \langle D_0, D_1, \ldots, D_n \rangle$ of unknowns. What attributes does the matrix in your equation have?

e. Argue that a natural cubic spline can interpolate a set of $n + 1$ point-value pairs in $O(n)$ time (see Problem 28-1).

f. Show how to determine a natural cubic spline that interpolates a set of $n + 1$ points (x_i, y_i) satisfying $x_0 < x_1 < \cdots < x_n$, even when x_i is not necessarily equal to i. What matrix equation must your method solve, and how quickly does your algorithm run?

Chapter notes

Many excellent texts describe numerical and scientific computation in much greater detail than we have room for here. The following are especially readable: George and Liu [132], Golub and Van Loan [144], Press, Teukolsky, Vetterling, and Flannery [283, 284], and Strang [323, 324].

Golub and Van Loan [144] discuss numerical stability. They show why $\det(A)$ is not necessarily a good indicator of the stability of a matrix A, proposing instead to use $\|A\|_\infty \|A^{-1}\|_\infty$, where $\|A\|_\infty = \max_{1 \le i \le n} \sum_{j=1}^{n} |a_{ij}|$. They also address the question of how to compute this value without actually computing A^{-1}.

Gaussian elimination, upon which the LU and LUP decompositions are based, was the first systematic method for solving linear systems of equations. It was also one of the earliest numerical algorithms. Although it was known earlier, its discovery is commonly attributed to C. F. Gauss (1777–1855). In his famous paper [325], Strassen showed that an $n \times n$ matrix can be inverted in $O(n^{\lg 7})$ time. Winograd [358] originally proved that matrix multiplication is no harder than matrix inversion, and the converse is due to Aho, Hopcroft, and Ullman [5].

Another important matrix decomposition is the ***singular value decomposition***, or ***SVD***. The SVD factors an $m \times n$ matrix A into $A = Q_1 \Sigma Q_2^{\mathrm{T}}$, where Σ is an $m \times n$ matrix with nonzero values only on the diagonal, Q_1 is $m \times m$ with mutually orthonormal columns, and Q_2 is $n \times n$, also with mutually orthonormal columns. Two vectors are ***orthonormal*** if their inner product is 0 and each vector has a norm of 1. The books by Strang [323, 324] and Golub and Van Loan [144] contain good treatments of the SVD.

Strang [324] has an excellent presentation of symmetric positive-definite matrices and of linear algebra in general.

29   Linear Programming

Many problems take the form of maximizing or minimizing an objective, given limited resources and competing constraints. If we can specify the objective as a linear function of certain variables, and if we can specify the constraints on resources as equalities or inequalities on those variables, then we have a *linear-programming problem*. Linear programs arise in a variety of practical applications. We begin by studying an application in electoral politics.

A political problem

Suppose that you are a politician trying to win an election. Your district has three different types of areas—urban, suburban, and rural. These areas have, respectively, 100,000, 200,000, and 50,000 registered voters. Although not all the registered voters actually go to the polls, you decide that to govern effectively, you would like at least half the registered voters in each of the three regions to vote for you. You are honorable and would never consider supporting policies in which you do not believe. You realize, however, that certain issues may be more effective in winning votes in certain places. Your primary issues are building more roads, gun control, farm subsidies, and a gasoline tax dedicated to improved public transit. According to your campaign staff's research, you can estimate how many votes you win or lose from each population segment by spending $1,000 on advertising on each issue. This information appears in the table of Figure 29.1. In this table, each entry indicates the number of thousands of either urban, suburban, or rural voters who would be won over by spending $1,000 on advertising in support of a particular issue. Negative entries denote votes that would be lost. Your task is to figure out the minimum amount of money that you need to spend in order to win 50,000 urban votes, 100,000 suburban votes, and 25,000 rural votes.

You could, by trial and error, devise a strategy that wins the required number of votes, but the strategy you come up with might not be the least expensive one. For example, you could devote $20,000 of advertising to building roads, $0 to gun control, $4,000 to farm subsidies, and $9,000 to a gasoline tax. In this case, you

policy	urban	suburban	rural
build roads	−2	5	3
gun control	8	2	−5
farm subsidies	0	0	10
gasoline tax	10	0	−2

Figure 29.1   The effects of policies on voters. Each entry describes the number of thousands of urban, suburban, or rural voters who could be won over by spending $1,000 on advertising support of a policy on a particular issue. Negative entries denote votes that would be lost.

would win $20(-2)+0(8)+4(0)+9(10) = 50$ thousand urban votes, $20(5)+0(2)+4(0)+9(0) = 100$ thousand suburban votes, and $20(3)+0(-5)+4(10)+9(-2) = 82$ thousand rural votes. You would win the exact number of votes desired in the urban and suburban areas and more than enough votes in the rural area. (In fact, in the rural area, you would receive more votes than there are voters.) In order to garner these votes, you would have paid for $20 + 0 + 4 + 9 = 33$ thousand dollars of advertising.

Naturally, you may wonder whether this strategy is the best possible. That is, could you achieve your goals while spending less on advertising? Additional trial and error might help you to answer this question, but wouldn't you rather have a systematic method for answering such questions? In order to develop one, we shall formulate this question mathematically. We introduce 4 variables:

- x_1 is the number of thousands of dollars spent on advertising on building roads,

- x_2 is the number of thousands of dollars spent on advertising on gun control,

- x_3 is the number of thousands of dollars spent on advertising on farm subsidies, and

- x_4 is the number of thousands of dollars spent on advertising on a gasoline tax.

We can write the requirement that we win at least 50,000 urban votes as

$$-2x_1 + 8x_2 + 0x_3 + 10x_4 \geq 50 . \tag{29.1}$$

Similarly, we can write the requirements that we win at least 100,000 suburban votes and 25,000 rural votes as

$$5x_1 + 2x_2 + 0x_3 + 0x_4 \geq 100 \tag{29.2}$$

and

$$3x_1 - 5x_2 + 10x_3 - 2x_4 \geq 25 . \tag{29.3}$$

Any setting of the variables x_1, x_2, x_3, x_4 that satisfies inequalities (29.1)–(29.3) yields a strategy that wins a sufficient number of each type of vote. In order to keep costs as small as possible, you would like to minimize the amount spent on advertising. That is, you want to minimize the expression

$$x_1 + x_2 + x_3 + x_4 . \tag{29.4}$$

Although negative advertising often occurs in political campaigns, there is no such thing as negative-cost advertising. Consequently, we require that

$$x_1 \geq 0, \; x_2 \geq 0, \; x_3 \geq 0, \; \text{and} \; x_4 \geq 0 . \tag{29.5}$$

Combining inequalities (29.1)–(29.3) and (29.5) with the objective of minimizing (29.4), we obtain what is known as a "linear program." We format this problem as

$$
\begin{array}{lrcrcrcrclr}
\text{minimize} & x_1 & + & x_2 & + & x_3 & + & x_4 & & & (29.6) \\
\text{subject to} & & & & & & & & & & \\
& -2x_1 & + & 8x_2 & + & 0x_3 & + & 10x_4 & \geq & 50 & (29.7) \\
& 5x_1 & + & 2x_2 & + & 0x_3 & + & 0x_4 & \geq & 100 & (29.8) \\
& 3x_1 & - & 5x_2 & + & 10x_3 & - & 2x_4 & \geq & 25 & (29.9) \\
& \multicolumn{7}{r}{x_1, x_2, x_3, x_4} & \geq & 0 \; . & (29.10)
\end{array}
$$

The solution of this linear program yields your optimal strategy.

General linear programs

In the general linear-programming problem, we wish to optimize a linear function subject to a set of linear inequalities. Given a set of real numbers $a_1, a_2, \ldots, a_n$ and a set of variables $x_1, x_2, \ldots, x_n$, we define a ***linear function*** f on those variables by

$$f(x_1, x_2, \ldots, x_n) = a_1 x_1 + a_2 x_2 + \cdots + a_n x_n = \sum_{j=1}^{n} a_j x_j .$$

If b is a real number and f is a linear function, then the equation

$$f(x_1, x_2, \ldots, x_n) = b$$

is a ***linear equality*** and the inequalities

$$f(x_1, x_2, \ldots, x_n) \leq b$$

and

$$f(x_1, x_2, \ldots, x_n) \geq b$$

are *linear inequalities*. We use the general term *linear constraints* to denote either linear equalities or linear inequalities. In linear programming, we do not allow strict inequalities. Formally, a *linear-programming problem* is the problem of either minimizing or maximizing a linear function subject to a finite set of linear constraints. If we are to minimize, then we call the linear program a *minimization linear program*, and if we are to maximize, then we call the linear program a *maximization linear program*.

The remainder of this chapter covers how to formulate and solve linear programs. Although several polynomial-time algorithms for linear programming have been developed, we will not study them in this chapter. Instead, we shall study the simplex algorithm, which is the oldest linear-programming algorithm. The simplex algorithm does not run in polynomial time in the worst case, but it is fairly efficient and widely used in practice.

An overview of linear programming

In order to describe properties of and algorithms for linear programs, we find it convenient to express them in canonical forms. We shall use two forms, *standard* and *slack*, in this chapter. We will define them precisely in Section 29.1. Informally, a linear program in standard form is the maximization of a linear function subject to linear *inequalities*, whereas a linear program in slack form is the maximization of a linear function subject to linear *equalities*. We shall typically use standard form for expressing linear programs, but we find it more convenient to use slack form when we describe the details of the simplex algorithm. For now, we restrict our attention to maximizing a linear function on n variables subject to a set of m linear inequalities.

Let us first consider the following linear program with two variables:

$$\text{maximize} \quad x_1 + x_2 \tag{29.11}$$

subject to

$$4x_1 - x_2 \leq 8 \tag{29.12}$$

$$2x_1 + x_2 \leq 10 \tag{29.13}$$

$$5x_1 - 2x_2 \geq -2 \tag{29.14}$$

$$x_1, x_2 \geq 0 . \tag{29.15}$$

We call any setting of the variables x_1 and x_2 that satisfies all the constraints (29.12)–(29.15) a *feasible solution* to the linear program. If we graph the constraints in the (x_1, x_2)-Cartesian coordinate system, as in Figure 29.2(a), we see

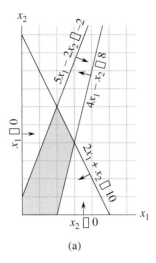
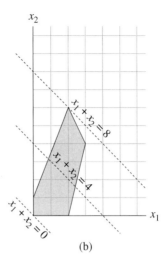

(a)   (b)

Figure 29.2 **(a)** The linear program given in (29.12)–(29.15). Each constraint is represented by a line and a direction. The intersection of the constraints, which is the feasible region, is shaded. **(b)** The dotted lines show, respectively, the points for which the objective value is 0, 4, and 8. The optimal solution to the linear program is $x_1 = 2$ and $x_2 = 6$ with objective value 8.

that the set of feasible solutions (shaded in the figure) forms a convex region[1] in the two-dimensional space. We call this convex region the *feasible region* and the function we wish to maximize the *objective function*. Conceptually, we could evaluate the objective function $x_1 + x_2$ at each point in the feasible region; we call the value of the objective function at a particular point the *objective value*. We could then identify a point that has the maximum objective value as an optimal solution. For this example (and for most linear programs), the feasible region contains an infinite number of points, and so we need to determine an efficient way to find a point that achieves the maximum objective value without explicitly evaluating the objective function at every point in the feasible region.

In two dimensions, we can optimize via a graphical procedure. The set of points for which $x_1 + x_2 = z$, for any z, is a line with a slope of -1. If we plot $x_1 + x_2 = 0$, we obtain the line with slope -1 through the origin, as in Figure 29.2(b). The intersection of this line and the feasible region is the set of feasible solutions that have an objective value of 0. In this case, that intersection of the line with the feasible region is the single point $(0, 0)$. More generally, for any z, the intersection

---

[1]An intuitive definition of a convex region is that it fulfills the requirement that for any two points in the region, all points on a line segment between them are also in the region.

of the line $x_1 + x_2 = z$ and the feasible region is the set of feasible solutions that have objective value z. Figure 29.2(b) shows the lines $x_1 + x_2 = 0$, $x_1 + x_2 = 4$, and $x_1 + x_2 = 8$. Because the feasible region in Figure 29.2 is bounded, there must be some maximum value z for which the intersection of the line $x_1 + x_2 = z$ and the feasible region is nonempty. Any point at which this occurs is an optimal solution to the linear program, which in this case is the point $x_1 = 2$ and $x_2 = 6$ with objective value 8.

It is no accident that an optimal solution to the linear program occurs at a vertex of the feasible region. The maximum value of z for which the line $x_1 + x_2 = z$ intersects the feasible region must be on the boundary of the feasible region, and thus the intersection of this line with the boundary of the feasible region is either a single vertex or a line segment. If the intersection is a single vertex, then there is just one optimal solution, and it is that vertex. If the intersection is a line segment, every point on that line segment must have the same objective value; in particular, both endpoints of the line segment are optimal solutions. Since each endpoint of a line segment is a vertex, there is an optimal solution at a vertex in this case as well.

Although we cannot easily graph linear programs with more than two variables, the same intuition holds. If we have three variables, then each constraint corresponds to a half-space in three-dimensional space. The intersection of these half-spaces forms the feasible region. The set of points for which the objective function obtains a given value z is now a plane (assuming no degenerate conditions). If all coefficients of the objective function are nonnegative, and if the origin is a feasible solution to the linear program, then as we move this plane away from the origin, in a direction normal to the objective function, we find points of increasing objective value. (If the origin is not feasible or if some coefficients in the objective function are negative, the intuitive picture becomes slightly more complicated.) As in two dimensions, because the feasible region is convex, the set of points that achieve the optimal objective value must include a vertex of the feasible region. Similarly, if we have n variables, each constraint defines a half-space in n-dimensional space. We call the feasible region formed by the intersection of these half-spaces a **simplex**. The objective function is now a hyperplane and, because of convexity, an optimal solution still occurs at a vertex of the simplex.

The **simplex algorithm** takes as input a linear program and returns an optimal solution. It starts at some vertex of the simplex and performs a sequence of iterations. In each iteration, it moves along an edge of the simplex from a current vertex to a neighboring vertex whose objective value is no smaller than that of the current vertex (and usually is larger.) The simplex algorithm terminates when it reaches a local maximum, which is a vertex from which all neighboring vertices have a smaller objective value. Because the feasible region is convex and the objective function is linear, this local optimum is actually a global optimum. In Section 29.4, we shall use a concept called "duality" to show that the solution returned by the simplex algorithm is indeed optimal.

Although the geometric view gives a good intuitive view of the operations of the simplex algorithm, we shall not refer to it explicitly when developing the details of the simplex algorithm in Section 29.3. Instead, we take an algebraic view. We first write the given linear program in slack form, which is a set of linear equalities. These linear equalities express some of the variables, called "basic variables," in terms of other variables, called "nonbasic variables." We move from one vertex to another by making a basic variable become nonbasic and making a nonbasic variable become basic. We call this operation a "pivot" and, viewed algebraically, it is nothing more than rewriting the linear program in an equivalent slack form.

The two-variable example described above was particularly simple. We shall need to address several more details in this chapter. These issues include identifying linear programs that have no solutions, linear programs that have no finite optimal solution, and linear programs for which the origin is not a feasible solution.

Applications of linear programming

Linear programming has a large number of applications. Any textbook on operations research is filled with examples of linear programming, and linear programming has become a standard tool taught to students in most business schools. The election scenario is one typical example. Two more examples of linear programming are the following:

- An airline wishes to schedule its flight crews. The Federal Aviation Administration imposes many constraints, such as limiting the number of consecutive hours that each crew member can work and insisting that a particular crew work only on one model of aircraft during each month. The airline wants to schedule crews on all of its flights using as few crew members as possible.

- An oil company wants to decide where to drill for oil. Siting a drill at a particular location has an associated cost and, based on geological surveys, an expected payoff of some number of barrels of oil. The company has a limited budget for locating new drills and wants to maximize the amount of oil it expects to find, given this budget.

With linear programs, we also model and solve graph and combinatorial problems, such as those appearing in this textbook. We have already seen a special case of linear programming used to solve systems of difference constraints in Section 24.4. In Section 29.2, we shall study how to formulate several graph and network-flow problems as linear programs. In Section 35.4, we shall use linear programming as a tool to find an approximate solution to another graph problem.

Algorithms for linear programming

This chapter studies the simplex algorithm. This algorithm, when implemented carefully, often solves general linear programs quickly in practice. With some carefully contrived inputs, however, the simplex algorithm can require exponential time. The first polynomial-time algorithm for linear programming was the ***ellipsoid algorithm***, which runs slowly in practice. A second class of polynomial-time algorithms are known as ***interior-point methods***. In contrast to the simplex algorithm, which moves along the exterior of the feasible region and maintains a feasible solution that is a vertex of the simplex at each iteration, these algorithms move through the interior of the feasible region. The intermediate solutions, while feasible, are not necessarily vertices of the simplex, but the final solution is a vertex. For large inputs, interior-point algorithms can run as fast as, and sometimes faster than, the simplex algorithm. The chapter notes point you to more information about these algorithms.

If we add to a linear program the additional requirement that all variables take on integer values, we have an ***integer linear program***. Exercise 34.5-3 asks you to show that just finding a feasible solution to this problem is NP-hard; since no polynomial-time algorithms are known for any NP-hard problems, there is no known polynomial-time algorithm for integer linear programming. In contrast, we can solve a general linear-programming problem in polynomial time.

In this chapter, if we have a linear program with variables $x = (x_1, x_2, \ldots, x_n)$ and wish to refer to a particular setting of the variables, we shall use the notation $\bar{x} = (\bar{x}_1, \bar{x}_2, \ldots, \bar{x}_n)$.

29.1   Standard and slack forms

This section describes two formats, standard form and slack form, that are useful when we specify and work with linear programs. In standard form, all the constraints are inequalities, whereas in slack form, all constraints are equalities (except for those that require the variables to be nonnegative).

Standard form

In ***standard form***, we are given n real numbers $c_1, c_2, \ldots, c_n$; m real numbers $b_1, b_2, \ldots, b_m$; and mn real numbers a_{ij} for $i = 1, 2, \ldots, m$ and $j = 1, 2, \ldots, n$. We wish to find n real numbers $x_1, x_2, \ldots, x_n$ that maximize $\quad \displaystyle\sum_{j=1}^{n} c_j x_j$ $\hfill$ (29.16)

subject to

$$\sum_{j=1}^{n} a_{ij} x_j \;\le\; b_i \quad \text{for } i = 1, 2, \ldots, m \hfill (29.17)$$

$$x_j \;\ge\; 0 \quad \text{for } j = 1, 2, \ldots, n \;. \hfill (29.18)$$

Generalizing the terminology we introduced for the two-variable linear program, we call expression (29.16) the *objective function* and the $n + m$ inequalities in lines (29.17) and (29.18) the *constraints*. The n constraints in line (29.18) are the *nonnegativity constraints*. An arbitrary linear program need not have nonnegativity constraints, but standard form requires them. Sometimes we find it convenient to express a linear program in a more compact form. If we create an $m \times n$ matrix $A = (a_{ij})$, an m-vector $b = (b_i)$, an n-vector $c = (c_j)$, and an n-vector $x = (x_j)$, then we can rewrite the linear program defined in (29.16)–(29.18) as

maximize $\quad c^{\mathrm{T}} x$ $\hfill$ (29.19)

subject to

$$Ax \;\le\; b \hfill (29.20)$$

$$x \;\ge\; 0 \;. \hfill (29.21)$$

In line (29.19), $c^{\mathrm{T}} x$ is the inner product of two vectors. In inequality (29.20), Ax is a matrix-vector product, and in inequality (29.21), $x \ge 0$ means that each entry of the vector x must be nonnegative. We see that we can specify a linear program in standard form by a tuple (A, b, c), and we shall adopt the convention that A, b, and c always have the dimensions given above.

We now introduce terminology to describe solutions to linear programs. We used some of this terminology in the earlier example of a two-variable linear program. We call a setting of the variables $\bar{x}$ that satisfies all the constraints a *feasible solution*, whereas a setting of the variables $\bar{x}$ that fails to satisfy at least one constraint is an *infeasible solution*. We say that a solution $\bar{x}$ has *objective value* $c^{\mathrm{T}}\bar{x}$. A feasible solution $\bar{x}$ whose objective value is maximum over all feasible solutions is an *optimal solution*, and we call its objective value $c^{\mathrm{T}}\bar{x}$ the *optimal objective value*. If a linear program has no feasible solutions, we say that the linear program is *infeasible*; otherwise it is *feasible*. If a linear program has some feasible solutions but does not have a finite optimal objective value, we say that the linear program is *unbounded*. Exercise 29.1-9 asks you to show that a linear program can have a finite optimal objective value even if the feasible region is not bounded.

Converting linear programs into standard form

It is always possible to convert a linear program, given as minimizing or maximizing a linear function subject to linear constraints, into standard form. A linear program might not be in standard form for any of four possible reasons:

1. The objective function might be a minimization rather than a maximization.

2. There might be variables without nonnegativity constraints.

3. There might be *equality constraints*, which have an equal sign rather than a less-than-or-equal-to sign.

4. There might be *inequality constraints*, but instead of having a less-than-or-equal-to sign, they have a greater-than-or-equal-to sign.

When converting one linear program L into another linear program L', we would like the property that an optimal solution to L' yields an optimal solution to L. To capture this idea, we say that two maximization linear programs L and L' are *equivalent* if for each feasible solution $\bar{x}$ to L with objective value z, there is a corresponding feasible solution $\bar{x}'$ to L' with objective value z, and for each feasible solution $\bar{x}'$ to L' with objective value z, there is a corresponding feasible solution $\bar{x}$ to L with objective value z. (This definition does not imply a one-to-one correspondence between feasible solutions.) A minimization linear program L and a maximization linear program L' are equivalent if for each feasible solution $\bar{x}$ to L with objective value z, there is a corresponding feasible solution $\bar{x}'$ to L' with objective value $-z$, and for each feasible solution $\bar{x}'$ to L' with objective value z, there is a corresponding feasible solution $\bar{x}$ to L with objective value $-z$.

We now show how to remove, one by one, each of the possible problems in the list above. After removing each one, we shall argue that the new linear program is equivalent to the old one.

To convert a minimization linear program L into an equivalent maximization linear program L', we simply negate the coefficients in the objective function. Since L and L' have identical sets of feasible solutions and, for any feasible solution, the objective value in L is the negative of the objective value in L', these two linear programs are equivalent. For example, if we have the linear program

$$\text{minimize} \quad -2x_1 + 3x_2$$

subject to

$$
\begin{aligned}
x_1 + x_2 &= 7 \\
x_1 - 2x_2 &\leq 4 \\
x_1 &\geq 0 \; ,
\end{aligned}
$$

and we negate the coefficients of the objective function, we obtain maximize $\quad 2x_1 \quad - \quad 3x_2$

subject to

$$
\begin{array}{rcrcl}
x_1 & + & x_2 & = & 7 \\
x_1 & - & 2x_2 & \le & 4 \\
x_1 & & & \ge & 0 \;.
\end{array}
$$

Next, we show how to convert a linear program in which some of the variables do not have nonnegativity constraints into one in which each variable has a non-negativity constraint. Suppose that some variable x_j does not have a nonnegativity constraint. Then, we replace each occurrence of x_j by $x_j' - x_j''$, and add the non-negativity constraints $x_j' \ge 0$ and $x_j'' \ge 0$. Thus, if the objective function has a term $c_j x_j$, we replace it by $c_j x_j' - c_j x_j''$, and if constraint i has a term $a_{ij} x_j$, we replace it by $a_{ij} x_j' - a_{ij} x_j''$. Any feasible solution $\hat{x}$ to the new linear program corresponds to a feasible solution $\bar{x}$ to the original linear program with $\bar{x}_j = \hat{x}_j' - \hat{x}_j''$ and with the same objective value. Also, any feasible solution $\bar{x}$ to the original linear program corresponds to a feasible solution $\hat{x}$ to the new linear program with $\hat{x}_j' = \bar{x}_j$ and $\hat{x}_j'' = 0$ if $\bar{x}_j \ge 0$, or with $\hat{x}_j'' = -\bar{x}_j$ and $\hat{x}_j' = 0$ if $\bar{x}_j < 0$. The two linear programs have the same objective value regardless of the sign of $\bar{x}_j$. Thus, the two linear programs are equivalent. We apply this conversion scheme to each variable that does not have a nonnegativity constraint to yield an equivalent linear program in which all variables have nonnegativity constraints.

Continuing the example, we want to ensure that each variable has a corresponding nonnegativity constraint. Variable x_1 has such a constraint, but variable x_2 does not. Therefore, we replace x_2 by two variables x_2' and x_2'', and we modify the linear program to obtain

maximize $\quad 2x_1 \quad - \quad 3x_2' \quad + \quad 3x_2''$

subject to

$$
\begin{array}{rcrcrcl}
x_1 & + & x_2' & - & x_2'' & = & 7 \\
x_1 & - & 2x_2' & + & 2x_2'' & \le & 4 \\
x_1, x_2', x_2'' & & & & & \ge & 0 \;.
\end{array} \tag{29.22}
$$

Next, we convert equality constraints into inequality constraints. Suppose that a linear program has an equality constraint $f(x_1, x_2, \dots, x_n) = b$. Since $x = y$ if and only if both $x \ge y$ and $x \le y$, we can replace this equality constraint by the pair of inequality constraints $f(x_1, x_2, \dots, x_n) \le b$ and $f(x_1, x_2, \dots, x_n) \ge b$. Repeating this conversion for each equality constraint yields a linear program in which all constraints are inequalities.

Finally, we can convert the greater-than-or-equal-to constraints to less-than-or-equal-to constraints by multiplying these constraints through by -1. That is, any inequality of the form

$$\sum_{j=1}^{n} a_{ij}x_j \geq b_i$$

is equivalent to

$$\sum_{j=1}^{n} -a_{ij}x_j \leq -b_i \ .$$

Thus, by replacing each coefficient a_{ij} by $-a_{ij}$ and each value b_i by $-b_i$, we obtain an equivalent less-than-or-equal-to constraint.

Finishing our example, we replace the equality in constraint (29.22) by two inequalities, obtaining

$$
\begin{array}{llllll}
\text{maximize} & 2x_1 & - & 3x_2' & + & 3x_2'' \\
\text{subject to} & & & & &
\end{array}
$$

$$
\begin{array}{rcrcrcl}
x_1 & + & x_2' & - & x_2'' & \leq & 7 \\
x_1 & + & x_2' & - & x_2'' & \geq & 7 \\
x_1 & - & 2x_2' & + & 2x_2'' & \leq & 4 \\
& & x_1, x_2', x_2'' & & & \geq & 0 \ .
\end{array} \tag{29.23}
$$

Finally, we negate constraint (29.23). For consistency in variable names, we rename x_2' to x_2 and x_2'' to x_3, obtaining the standard form

$$
\begin{array}{llllll}
\text{maximize} & 2x_1 & - & 3x_2 & + & 3x_3 \\
\text{subject to} & & & & &
\end{array} \tag{29.24}
$$

$$
\begin{array}{rcrcrcrl}
x_1 & + & x_2 & - & x_3 & \leq & 7 & \tag{29.25} \\
-x_1 & - & x_2 & + & x_3 & \leq & -7 & \tag{29.26} \\
x_1 & - & 2x_2 & + & 2x_3 & \leq & 4 & \tag{29.27} \\
& & x_1, x_2, x_3 & & & \geq & 0 \ . & \tag{29.28}
\end{array}
$$

Converting linear programs into slack form

To efficiently solve a linear program with the simplex algorithm, we prefer to express it in a form in which some of the constraints are equality constraints. More precisely, we shall convert it into a form in which the nonnegativity constraints are the only inequality constraints, and the remaining constraints are equalities. Let

$$\sum_{j=1}^{n} a_{ij}x_j \leq b_i \tag{29.29}$$

be an inequality constraint. We introduce a new variable s and rewrite inequality (29.29) as the two constraints

$$s = b_i - \sum_{j=1}^{n} a_{ij} x_j ,$$ (29.30)

$$s \geq 0 .$$ (29.31)

We call s a **slack variable** because it measures the **slack**, or difference, between the left-hand and right-hand sides of equation (29.29). (We shall soon see why we find it convenient to write the constraint with only the slack variable on the left-hand side.) Because inequality (29.29) is true if and only if both equation (29.30) and inequality (29.31) are true, we can convert each inequality constraint of a linear program in this way to obtain an equivalent linear program in which the only inequality constraints are the nonnegativity constraints. When converting from standard to slack form, we shall use x_{n+i} (instead of s) to denote the slack variable associated with the ith inequality. The ith constraint is therefore

$$x_{n+i} = b_i - \sum_{j=1}^{n} a_{ij} x_j ,$$ (29.32)

along with the nonnegativity constraint $x_{n+i} \geq 0$.

By converting each constraint of a linear program in standard form, we obtain a linear program in a different form. For example, for the linear program described in (29.24)–(29.28), we introduce slack variables x_4, x_5, and x_6, obtaining

maximize $\quad\quad\quad\quad\quad\quad 2x_1 \quad - \quad 3x_2 \quad + \quad 3x_3$ (29.33)

subject to

$$x_4 = 7 - x_1 - x_2 + x_3$$ (29.34)

$$x_5 = -7 + x_1 + x_2 - x_3$$ (29.35)

$$x_6 = 4 - x_1 + 2x_2 - 2x_3$$ (29.36)

$$x_1, x_2, x_3, x_4, x_5, x_6 \geq 0 .$$ (29.37)

In this linear program, all the constraints except for the nonnegativity constraints are equalities, and each variable is subject to a nonnegativity constraint. We write each equality constraint with one of the variables on the left-hand side of the equality and all others on the right-hand side. Furthermore, each equation has the same set of variables on the right-hand side, and these variables are also the only ones that appear in the objective function. We call the variables on the left-hand side of the equalities **basic variables** and those on the right-hand side **nonbasic variables**.

For linear programs that satisfy these conditions, we shall sometimes omit the words "maximize" and "subject to," as well as the explicit nonnegativity constraints. We shall also use the variable z to denote the value of the objective function. We call the resulting format *slack form*. If we write the linear program given in (29.33)–(29.37) in slack form, we obtain

$$z \quad = \qquad\qquad\quad 2x_1 \quad - \quad 3x_2 \quad + \quad 3x_3 \qquad\qquad (29.38)$$

$$x_4 \quad = \quad 7 \quad - \quad x_1 \quad - \quad x_2 \quad + \quad x_3 \qquad\qquad (29.39)$$

$$x_5 \quad = \quad -7 \quad + \quad x_1 \quad + \quad x_2 \quad - \quad x_3 \qquad\qquad (29.40)$$

$$x_6 \quad = \quad 4 \quad - \quad x_1 \quad + \quad 2x_2 \quad - \quad 2x_3 \; . \qquad\qquad (29.41)$$

As with standard form, we find it convenient to have a more concise notation for describing a slack form. As we shall see in Section 29.3, the sets of basic and nonbasic variables will change as the simplex algorithm runs. We use N to denote the set of indices of the nonbasic variables and B to denote the set of indices of the basic variables. We always have that $|N| = n$, $|B| = m$, and $N \cup B = \{1, 2, \ldots, n + m\}$. The equations are indexed by the entries of B, and the variables on the right-hand sides are indexed by the entries of N. As in standard form, we use b_i, c_j, and a_{ij} to denote constant terms and coefficients. We also use ν to denote an optional constant term in the objective function. (We shall see a little later that including the constant term in the objective function makes it easy to determine the value of the objective function.) Thus we can concisely define a slack form by a tuple (N, B, A, b, c, ν), denoting the slack form

$$z \quad = \quad \nu \quad + \quad \sum_{j \in N} c_j x_j \qquad\qquad (29.42)$$

$$x_i \quad = \quad b_i \quad - \quad \sum_{j \in N} a_{ij} x_j \quad \text{for } i \in B \, , \qquad\qquad (29.43)$$

in which all variables x are constrained to be nonnegative. Because we subtract the sum $\sum_{j \in N} a_{ij} x_j$ in (29.43), the values a_{ij} are actually the negatives of the coefficients as they "appear" in the slack form.

For example, in the slack form

$$z \quad = \quad 28 \quad - \quad \frac{x_3}{6} \quad - \quad \frac{x_5}{6} \quad - \quad \frac{2x_6}{3}$$

$$x_1 \quad = \quad 8 \quad + \quad \frac{x_3}{6} \quad + \quad \frac{x_5}{6} \quad - \quad \frac{x_6}{3}$$

$$x_2 \quad = \quad 4 \quad - \quad \frac{8x_3}{3} \quad - \quad \frac{2x_5}{3} \quad + \quad \frac{x_6}{3}$$

$$x_4 \quad = \quad 18 \quad - \quad \frac{x_3}{2} \quad + \quad \frac{x_5}{2} \, ,$$

we have $B = \{1, 2, 4\}$, $N = \{3, 5, 6\}$,

$$
A = \begin{pmatrix} a_{13} & a_{15} & a_{16} \\ a_{23} & a_{25} & a_{26} \\ a_{43} & a_{45} & a_{46} \end{pmatrix} = \begin{pmatrix} -1/6 & -1/6 & 1/3 \\ 8/3 & 2/3 & -1/3 \\ 1/2 & -1/2 & 0 \end{pmatrix},
$$

$$
b = \begin{pmatrix} b_1 \\ b_2 \\ b_4 \end{pmatrix} = \begin{pmatrix} 8 \\ 4 \\ 18 \end{pmatrix},
$$

$c = \begin{pmatrix} c_3 & c_5 & c_6 \end{pmatrix}^{\mathrm{T}} = \begin{pmatrix} -1/6 & -1/6 & -2/3 \end{pmatrix}^{\mathrm{T}}$, and $v = 28$. Note that the indices into A, b, and c are not necessarily sets of contiguous integers; they depend on the index sets B and N. As an example of the entries of A being the negatives of the coefficients as they appear in the slack form, observe that the equation for x_1 includes the term $x_3/6$, yet the coefficient a_{13} is actually $-1/6$ rather than $+1/6$.

Exercises

29.1-1
If we express the linear program in (29.24)–(29.28) in the compact notation of (29.19)–(29.21), what are n, m, A, b, and c?

29.1-2
Give three feasible solutions to the linear program in (29.24)–(29.28). What is the objective value of each one?

29.1-3
For the slack form in (29.38)–(29.41), what are N, B, A, b, c, and v?

29.1-4
Convert the following linear program into standard form:

$$
\begin{array}{llll}
\text{minimize} & 2x_1 & + & 7x_2 & + & x_3 \\
\text{subject to} & & & & & \\
& x_1 & & & - & x_3 & = & 7 \\
& 3x_1 & + & x_2 & & & \geq & 24 \\
& & & x_2 & & & \geq & 0 \\
& & & & & x_3 & \leq & 0 \;.
\end{array}
$$

29.1-5

Convert the following linear program into slack form:

maximize $2x_1 \qquad\qquad - \quad 6x_3$

subject to

$$
\begin{array}{rcrcrcrcl}
x_1 &+& x_2 &-& x_3 &\le& 7 \\
3x_1 &-& x_2 & & &\ge& 8 \\
-x_1 &+& 2x_2 &+& 2x_3 &\ge& 0 \\
\multicolumn{5}{c}{x_1, x_2, x_3} &\ge& 0 \ .
\end{array}
$$

What are the basic and nonbasic variables?

29.1-6

Show that the following linear program is infeasible:

maximize $3x_1 \quad - \quad 2x_2$

subject to

$$
\begin{array}{rcrcr}
x_1 &+& x_2 &\le& 2 \\
-2x_1 &-& 2x_2 &\le& -10 \\
\multicolumn{3}{c}{x_1, x_2} &\ge& 0 \ .
\end{array}
$$

29.1-7

Show that the following linear program is unbounded:

maximize $x_1 \quad - \quad x_2$

subject to

$$
\begin{array}{rcrcr}
-2x_1 &+& x_2 &\le& -1 \\
-x_1 &-& 2x_2 &\le& -2 \\
\multicolumn{3}{c}{x_1, x_2} &\ge& 0 \ .
\end{array}
$$

29.1-8

Suppose that we have a general linear program with n variables and m constraints, and suppose that we convert it into standard form. Give an upper bound on the number of variables and constraints in the resulting linear program.

29.1-9

Give an example of a linear program for which the feasible region is not bounded, but the optimal objective value is finite.

29.2   Formulating problems as linear programs

Although we shall focus on the simplex algorithm in this chapter, it is also important to be able to recognize when we can formulate a problem as a linear program. Once we cast a problem as a polynomial-sized linear program, we can solve it in polynomial time by the ellipsoid algorithm or interior-point methods. Several linear-programming software packages can solve problems efficiently, so that once the problem is in the form of a linear program, such a package can solve it.

We shall look at several concrete examples of linear-programming problems. We start with two problems that we have already studied: the single-source shortest-paths problem (see Chapter 24) and the maximum-flow problem (see Chapter 26). We then describe the minimum-cost-flow problem. Although the minimum-cost-flow problem has a polynomial-time algorithm that is not based on linear programming, we won't describe the algorithm. Finally, we describe the multicommodity-flow problem, for which the only known polynomial-time algorithm is based on linear programming.

When we solved graph problems in Part VI, we used attribute notation, such as $v.d$ and $(u, v).f$. Linear programs typically use subscripted variables rather than objects with attached attributes, however. Therefore, when we express variables in linear programs, we shall indicate vertices and edges through subscripts. For example, we denote the shortest-path weight for vertex v not by $v.d$ but by d_v. Similarly, we denote the flow from vertex u to vertex v not by $(u, v).f$ but by f_{uv}. For quantities that are given as inputs to problems, such as edge weights or capacities, we shall continue to use notations such as $w(u, v)$ and $c(u, v)$.

Shortest paths

We can formulate the single-source shortest-paths problem as a linear program. In this section, we shall focus on how to formulate the single-pair shortest-path problem, leaving the extension to the more general single-source shortest-paths problem as Exercise 29.2-3.

In the single-pair shortest-path problem, we are given a weighted, directed graph $G = (V, E)$, with weight function $w : E \to \mathbb{R}$ mapping edges to real-valued weights, a source vertex s, and destination vertex t. We wish to compute the value d_t, which is the weight of a shortest path from s to t. To express this problem as a linear program, we need to determine a set of variables and constraints that define when we have a shortest path from s to t. Fortunately, the Bellman-Ford algorithm does exactly this. When the Bellman-Ford algorithm terminates, it has computed, for each vertex v, a value d_v (using subscript notation here rather than attribute notation) such that for each edge $(u, v) \in E$, we have $d_v \leq d_u + w(u, v)$.

The source vertex initially receives a value $d_s = 0$, which never changes. Thus we obtain the following linear program to compute the shortest-path weight from s to t:

maximize d_t (29.44)

subject to

$$d_v \leq d_u + w(u,v) \quad \text{for each edge } (u,v) \in E , \tag{29.45}$$
$$d_s = 0 . \tag{29.46}$$

You might be surprised that this linear program maximizes an objective function when it is supposed to compute shortest paths. We do not want to minimize the objective function, since then setting $\bar{d}_v = 0$ for all $v \in V$ would yield an optimal solution to the linear program without solving the shortest-paths problem. We maximize because an optimal solution to the shortest-paths problem sets each $\bar{d}_v$ to $\min_{u:(u,v)\in E} \{\bar{d}_u + w(u,v)\}$, so that $\bar{d}_v$ is the largest value that is less than or equal to all of the values in the set $\{\bar{d}_u + w(u,v)\}$. We want to maximize d_v for all vertices v on a shortest path from s to t subject to these constraints on all vertices v, and maximizing d_t achieves this goal.

This linear program has $|V|$ variables d_v, one for each vertex $v \in V$. It also has $|E| + 1$ constraints: one for each edge, plus the additional constraint that the source vertex's shortest-path weight always has the value 0.

Maximum flow

Next, we express the maximum-flow problem as a linear program. Recall that we are given a directed graph $G = (V, E)$ in which each edge $(u, v) \in E$ has a nonnegative capacity $c(u, v) \geq 0$, and two distinguished vertices: a source s and a sink t. As defined in Section 26.1, a flow is a nonnegative real-valued function $f : V \times V \to \mathbb{R}$ that satisfies the capacity constraint and flow conservation. A maximum flow is a flow that satisfies these constraints and maximizes the flow value, which is the total flow coming out of the source minus the total flow into the source. A flow, therefore, satisfies linear constraints, and the value of a flow is a linear function. Recalling also that we assume that $c(u, v) = 0$ if $(u, v) \notin E$ and that there are no antiparallel edges, we can express the maximum-flow problem as a linear program:

maximize $\displaystyle\sum_{v \in V} f_{sv} - \sum_{v \in V} f_{vs}$ (29.47)

subject to

$$f_{uv} \leq c(u,v) \quad \text{for each } u, v \in V , \tag{29.48}$$
$$\sum_{v \in V} f_{vu} = \sum_{v \in V} f_{uv} \quad \text{for each } u \in V - \{s,t\} , \tag{29.49}$$
$$f_{uv} \geq 0 \quad \text{for each } u, v \in V . \tag{29.50}$$

This linear program has $|V|^2$ variables, corresponding to the flow between each pair of vertices, and it has $2|V|^2 + |V| - 2$ constraints.

It is usually more efficient to solve a smaller-sized linear program. The linear program in (29.47)–(29.50) has, for ease of notation, a flow and capacity of 0 for each pair of vertices u, v with $(u, v) \notin E$. It would be more efficient to rewrite the linear program so that it has $O(V + E)$ constraints. Exercise 29.2-5 asks you to do so.

Minimum-cost flow

In this section, we have used linear programming to solve problems for which we already knew efficient algorithms. In fact, an efficient algorithm designed specifically for a problem, such as Dijkstra's algorithm for the single-source shortest-paths problem, or the push-relabel method for maximum flow, will often be more efficient than linear programming, both in theory and in practice.

The real power of linear programming comes from the ability to solve new problems. Recall the problem faced by the politician in the beginning of this chapter. The problem of obtaining a sufficient number of votes, while not spending too much money, is not solved by any of the algorithms that we have studied in this book, yet we can solve it by linear programming. Books abound with such real-world problems that linear programming can solve. Linear programming is also particularly useful for solving variants of problems for which we may not already know of an efficient algorithm.

Consider, for example, the following generalization of the maximum-flow problem. Suppose that, in addition to a capacity $c(u, v)$ for each edge (u, v), we are given a real-valued cost $a(u, v)$. As in the maximum-flow problem, we assume that $c(u, v) = 0$ if $(u, v) \notin E$, and that there are no antiparallel edges. If we send f_{uv} units of flow over edge (u, v), we incur a cost of $a(u, v) f_{uv}$. We are also given a flow demand d. We wish to send d units of flow from s to t while minimizing the total cost $\sum_{(u,v) \in E} a(u, v) f_{uv}$ incurred by the flow. This problem is known as the ***minimum-cost-flow problem***.

Figure 29.3(a) shows an example of the minimum-cost-flow problem. We wish to send 4 units of flow from s to t while incurring the minimum total cost. Any particular legal flow, that is, a function f satisfying constraints (29.48)–(29.50), incurs a total cost of $\sum_{(u,v) \in E} a(u, v) f_{uv}$. We wish to find the particular 4-unit flow that minimizes this cost. Figure 29.3(b) shows an optimal solution, with total cost $\sum_{(u,v) \in E} a(u, v) f_{uv} = (2 \cdot 2) + (5 \cdot 2) + (3 \cdot 1) + (7 \cdot 1) + (1 \cdot 3) = 27$.

There are polynomial-time algorithms specifically designed for the minimum-cost-flow problem, but they are beyond the scope of this book. We can, however, express the minimum-cost-flow problem as a linear program. The linear program looks similar to the one for the maximum-flow problem with the additional con-

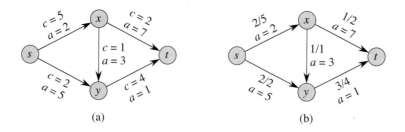

Figure 29.3 **(a)** An example of a minimum-cost-flow problem. We denote the capacities by c and the costs by a. Vertex s is the source and vertex t is the sink, and we wish to send 4 units of flow from s to t. **(b)** A solution to the minimum-cost flow problem in which 4 units of flow are sent from s to t. For each edge, the flow and capacity are written as flow/capacity.

straint that the value of the flow be exactly d units, and with the new objective function of minimizing the cost:

$$\text{minimize} \quad \sum_{(u,v)\in E} a(u,v) f_{uv} \tag{29.51}$$

$$
\begin{aligned}
\text{subject to} \\
f_{uv} &\leq c(u,v) && \text{for each } u,v \in V, \\
\sum_{v\in V} f_{vu} - \sum_{v\in V} f_{uv} &= 0 && \text{for each } u \in V - \{s,t\}, \\
\sum_{v\in V} f_{sv} - \sum_{v\in V} f_{vs} &= d, \\
f_{uv} &\geq 0 && \text{for each } u,v \in V. \tag{29.52}
\end{aligned}
$$

Multicommodity flow

As a final example, we consider another flow problem. Suppose that the Lucky Puck company from Section 26.1 decides to diversify its product line and ship not only hockey pucks, but also hockey sticks and hockey helmets. Each piece of equipment is manufactured in its own factory, has its own warehouse, and must be shipped, each day, from factory to warehouse. The sticks are manufactured in Vancouver and must be shipped to Saskatoon, and the helmets are manufactured in Edmonton and must be shipped to Regina. The capacity of the shipping network does not change, however, and the different items, or ***commodities***, must share the same network.

This example is an instance of a ***multicommodity-flow problem***. In this problem, we are again given a directed graph $G = (V, E)$ in which each edge $(u, v) \in E$ has a nonnegative capacity $c(u, v) \geq 0$. As in the maximum-flow problem, we implicitly assume that $c(u, v) = 0$ for $(u, v) \notin E$, and that the graph has no antiparallel edges. In addition, we are given k different commodities, $K_1, K_2, \ldots, K_k$, where we specify commodity i by the triple $K_i = (s_i, t_i, d_i)$. Here, vertex s_i is the source of commodity i, vertex t_i is the sink of commodity i, and d_i is the demand for commodity i, which is the desired flow value for the commodity from s_i to t_i. We define a flow for commodity i, denoted by f_i, (so that f_{iuv} is the flow of commodity i from vertex u to vertex v) to be a real-valued function that satisfies the flow-conservation and capacity constraints. We now define f_{uv}, the **aggregate flow**, to be the sum of the various commodity flows, so that $f_{uv} = \sum_{i=1}^{k} f_{iuv}$. The aggregate flow on edge (u, v) must be no more than the capacity of edge (u, v). We are not trying to minimize any objective function in this problem; we need only determine whether such a flow exists. Thus, we write a linear program with a "null" objective function:

minimize $\qquad\qquad\qquad 0$

subject to

$$\sum_{i=1}^{k} f_{iuv} \leq c(u, v) \quad \text{for each } u, v \in V ,$$

$$\sum_{v \in V} f_{iuv} - \sum_{v \in V} f_{ivu} = 0 \qquad \begin{array}{l}\text{for each } i = 1, 2, \ldots, k \text{ and} \\ \text{for each } u \in V - \{s_i, t_i\} ,\end{array}$$

$$\sum_{v \in V} f_{i, s_i, v} - \sum_{v \in V} f_{i, v, s_i} = d_i \qquad \text{for each } i = 1, 2, \ldots, k ,$$

$$f_{iuv} \geq 0 \qquad \begin{array}{l}\text{for each } u, v \in V \text{ and} \\ \text{for each } i = 1, 2, \ldots, k .\end{array}$$

The only known polynomial-time algorithm for this problem expresses it as a linear program and then solves it with a polynomial-time linear-programming algorithm.

Exercises

29.2-1
Put the single-pair shortest-path linear program from (29.44)–(29.46) into standard form.

29.2-2
Write out explicitly the linear program corresponding to finding the shortest path from node s to node y in Figure 24.2(a).

29.2-3
In the single-source shortest-paths problem, we want to find the shortest-path weights from a source vertex s to all vertices $v \in V$. Given a graph G, write a

linear program for which the solution has the property that d_v is the shortest-path weight from s to v for each vertex $v \in V$.

29.2-4
Write out explicitly the linear program corresponding to finding the maximum flow in Figure 26.1(a).

29.2-5
Rewrite the linear program for maximum flow (29.47)–(29.50) so that it uses only $O(V + E)$ constraints.

29.2-6
Write a linear program that, given a bipartite graph $G = (V, E)$, solves the maximum-bipartite-matching problem.

29.2-7
In the ***minimum-cost multicommodity-flow problem***, we are given directed graph $G = (V, E)$ in which each edge $(u, v) \in E$ has a nonnegative capacity $c(u, v) \geq 0$ and a cost $a(u, v)$. As in the multicommodity-flow problem, we are given k different commodities, $K_1, K_2, \ldots, K_k$, where we specify commodity i by the triple $K_i = (s_i, t_i, d_i)$. We define the flow f_i for commodity i and the aggregate flow f_{uv} on edge (u, v) as in the multicommodity-flow problem. A feasible flow is one in which the aggregate flow on each edge (u, v) is no more than the capacity of edge (u, v). The cost of a flow is $\sum_{u,v \in V} a(u, v) f_{uv}$, and the goal is to find the feasible flow of minimum cost. Express this problem as a linear program.

29.3   The simplex algorithm

The simplex algorithm is the classical method for solving linear programs. In contrast to most of the other algorithms in this book, its running time is not polynomial in the worst case. It does yield insight into linear programs, however, and is often remarkably fast in practice.

In addition to having a geometric interpretation, described earlier in this chapter, the simplex algorithm bears some similarity to Gaussian elimination, discussed in Section 28.1. Gaussian elimination begins with a system of linear equalities whose solution is unknown. In each iteration, we rewrite this system in an equivalent form that has some additional structure. After some number of iterations, we have rewritten the system so that the solution is simple to obtain. The simplex algorithm proceeds in a similar manner, and we can view it as Gaussian elimination for inequalities.

We now describe the main idea behind an iteration of the simplex algorithm. Associated with each iteration will be a "basic solution" that we can easily obtain from the slack form of the linear program: set each nonbasic variable to 0 and compute the values of the basic variables from the equality constraints. An iteration converts one slack form into an equivalent slack form. The objective value of the associated basic feasible solution will be no less than that at the previous iteration, and usually greater. To achieve this increase in the objective value, we choose a nonbasic variable such that if we were to increase that variable's value from 0, then the objective value would increase, too. The amount by which we can increase the variable is limited by the other constraints. In particular, we raise it until some basic variable becomes 0. We then rewrite the slack form, exchanging the roles of that basic variable and the chosen nonbasic variable. Although we have used a particular setting of the variables to guide the algorithm, and we shall use it in our proofs, the algorithm does not explicitly maintain this solution. It simply rewrites the linear program until an optimal solution becomes "obvious."

An example of the simplex algorithm

We begin with an extended example. Consider the following linear program in standard form:

$$\text{maximize} \quad 3x_1 + x_2 + 2x_3 \tag{29.53}$$

subject to

$$x_1 + x_2 + 3x_3 \le 30 \tag{29.54}$$

$$2x_1 + 2x_2 + 5x_3 \le 24 \tag{29.55}$$

$$4x_1 + x_2 + 2x_3 \le 36 \tag{29.56}$$

$$x_1, x_2, x_3 \ge 0 . \tag{29.57}$$

In order to use the simplex algorithm, we must convert the linear program into slack form; we saw how to do so in Section 29.1. In addition to being an algebraic manipulation, slack is a useful algorithmic concept. Recalling from Section 29.1 that each variable has a corresponding nonnegativity constraint, we say that an equality constraint is *tight* for a particular setting of its nonbasic variables if they cause the constraint's basic variable to become 0. Similarly, a setting of the nonbasic variables that would make a basic variable become negative *violates* that constraint. Thus, the slack variables explicitly maintain how far each constraint is from being tight, and so they help to determine how much we can increase values of nonbasic variables without violating any constraints.

Associating the slack variables x_4, x_5, and x_6 with inequalities (29.54)–(29.56), respectively, and putting the linear program into slack form, we obtain

$$z \quad = \qquad\qquad 3x_1 \quad + \quad x_2 \quad + \quad 2x_3 \tag{29.58}$$

$$x_4 \quad = \quad 30 \quad - \quad x_1 \quad - \quad x_2 \quad - \quad 3x_3 \tag{29.59}$$

$$x_5 \quad = \quad 24 \quad - \quad 2x_1 \quad - \quad 2x_2 \quad - \quad 5x_3 \tag{29.60}$$

$$x_6 \quad = \quad 36 \quad - \quad 4x_1 \quad - \quad x_2 \quad - \quad 2x_3 \ . \tag{29.61}$$

The system of constraints (29.59)–(29.61) has 3 equations and 6 variables. Any setting of the variables x_1, x_2, and x_3 defines values for x_4, x_5, and x_6; therefore, we have an infinite number of solutions to this system of equations. A solution is feasible if all of $x_1, x_2, \ldots, x_6$ are nonnegative, and there can be an infinite number of feasible solutions as well. The infinite number of possible solutions to a system such as this one will be useful in later proofs. We focus on the ***basic solution***: set all the (nonbasic) variables on the right-hand side to 0 and then compute the values of the (basic) variables on the left-hand side. In this example, the basic solution is $(\bar{x}_1, \bar{x}_2, \ldots, \bar{x}_6) = (0, 0, 0, 30, 24, 36)$ and it has objective value $z = (3 \cdot 0) + (1 \cdot 0) + (2 \cdot 0) = 0$. Observe that this basic solution sets $\bar{x}_i = b_i$ for each $i \in B$. An iteration of the simplex algorithm rewrites the set of equations and the objective function so as to put a different set of variables on the right-hand side. Thus, a different basic solution is associated with the rewritten problem. We emphasize that the rewrite does not in any way change the underlying linear-programming problem; the problem at one iteration has the identical set of feasible solutions as the problem at the previous iteration. The problem does, however, have a different basic solution than that of the previous iteration.

If a basic solution is also feasible, we call it a ***basic feasible solution***. As we run the simplex algorithm, the basic solution is almost always a basic feasible solution. We shall see in Section 29.5, however, that for the first few iterations of the simplex algorithm, the basic solution might not be feasible.

Our goal, in each iteration, is to reformulate the linear program so that the basic solution has a greater objective value. We select a nonbasic variable x_e whose coefficient in the objective function is positive, and we increase the value of x_e as much as possible without violating any of the constraints. The variable x_e becomes basic, and some other variable x_l becomes nonbasic. The values of other basic variables and of the objective function may also change.

To continue the example, let's think about increasing the value of x_1. As we increase x_1, the values of x_4, x_5, and x_6 all decrease. Because we have a nonnegativity constraint for each variable, we cannot allow any of them to become negative. If x_1 increases above 30, then x_4 becomes negative, and x_5 and x_6 become negative when x_1 increases above 12 and 9, respectively. The third constraint (29.61) is the tightest constraint, and it limits how much we can increase x_1. Therefore, we switch the roles of x_1 and x_6. We solve equation (29.61) for x_1 and obtain

$$x_1 = 9 - \frac{x_2}{4} - \frac{x_3}{2} - \frac{x_6}{4} \ . \tag{29.62}$$

To rewrite the other equations with x_6 on the right-hand side, we substitute for x_1 using equation (29.62). Doing so for equation (29.59), we obtain

$$
\begin{aligned}
x_4 &= 30 - x_1 - x_2 - 3x_3 \\
&= 30 - \left(9 - \frac{x_2}{4} - \frac{x_3}{2} - \frac{x_6}{4}\right) - x_2 - 3x_3 \\
&= 21 - \frac{3x_2}{4} - \frac{5x_3}{2} + \frac{x_6}{4} . && (29.63)
\end{aligned}
$$

Similarly, we combine equation (29.62) with constraint (29.60) and with objective function (29.58) to rewrite our linear program in the following form:

$$
z = 27 + \frac{x_2}{4} + \frac{x_3}{2} - \frac{3x_6}{4} \tag{29.64}
$$

$$
x_1 = 9 - \frac{x_2}{4} - \frac{x_3}{2} - \frac{x_6}{4} \tag{29.65}
$$

$$
x_4 = 21 - \frac{3x_2}{4} - \frac{5x_3}{2} + \frac{x_6}{4} \tag{29.66}
$$

$$
x_5 = 6 - \frac{3x_2}{2} - 4x_3 + \frac{x_6}{2} . \tag{29.67}
$$

We call this operation a **pivot**. As demonstrated above, a pivot chooses a nonbasic variable x_e, called the **entering variable**, and a basic variable x_l, called the **leaving variable**, and exchanges their roles.

The linear program described in equations (29.64)–(29.67) is equivalent to the linear program described in equations (29.58)–(29.61). We perform two operations in the simplex algorithm: rewrite equations so that variables move between the left-hand side and the right-hand side, and substitute one equation into another. The first operation trivially creates an equivalent problem, and the second, by elementary linear algebra, also creates an equivalent problem. (See Exercise 29.3-3.)

To demonstrate this equivalence, observe that our original basic solution $(0, 0, 0, 30, 24, 36)$ satisfies the new equations (29.65)–(29.67) and has objective value $27 + (1/4) \cdot 0 + (1/2) \cdot 0 - (3/4) \cdot 36 = 0$. The basic solution associated with the new linear program sets the nonbasic values to 0 and is $(9, 0, 0, 21, 6, 0)$, with objective value $z = 27$. Simple arithmetic verifies that this solution also satisfies equations (29.59)–(29.61) and, when plugged into objective function (29.58), has objective value $(3 \cdot 9) + (1 \cdot 0) + (2 \cdot 0) = 27$.

Continuing the example, we wish to find a new variable whose value we wish to increase. We do not want to increase x_6, since as its value increases, the objective value decreases. We can attempt to increase either x_2 or x_3; let us choose x_3. How far can we increase x_3 without violating any of the constraints? Constraint (29.65) limits it to 18, constraint (29.66) limits it to $42/5$, and constraint (29.67) limits it to $3/2$. The third constraint is again the tightest one, and therefore we rewrite the third constraint so that x_3 is on the left-hand side and x_5 is on the right-hand side. We then substitute this new equation, $x_3 = 3/2 - 3x_2/8 - x_5/4 + x_6/8$, into equations (29.64)–(29.66) and obtain the new, but equivalent, system

$$z = \frac{111}{4} + \frac{x_2}{16} - \frac{x_5}{8} - \frac{11x_6}{16} \tag{29.68}$$

$$x_1 = \frac{33}{4} - \frac{x_2}{16} + \frac{x_5}{8} - \frac{5x_6}{16} \tag{29.69}$$

$$x_3 = \frac{3}{2} - \frac{3x_2}{8} - \frac{x_5}{4} + \frac{x_6}{8} \tag{29.70}$$

$$x_4 = \frac{69}{4} + \frac{3x_2}{16} + \frac{5x_5}{8} - \frac{x_6}{16} . \tag{29.71}$$

This system has the associated basic solution $(33/4, 0, 3/2, 69/4, 0, 0)$, with objective value $111/4$. Now the only way to increase the objective value is to increase x_2. The three constraints give upper bounds of 132, 4, and ∞, respectively. (We get an upper bound of ∞ from constraint (29.71) because, as we increase x_2, the value of the basic variable x_4 increases also. This constraint, therefore, places no restriction on how much we can increase x_2.) We increase x_2 to 4, and it becomes nonbasic. Then we solve equation (29.70) for x_2 and substitute in the other equations to obtain

$$z = 28 - \frac{x_3}{6} - \frac{x_5}{6} - \frac{2x_6}{3} \tag{29.72}$$

$$x_1 = 8 + \frac{x_3}{6} + \frac{x_5}{6} - \frac{x_6}{3} \tag{29.73}$$

$$x_2 = 4 - \frac{8x_3}{3} - \frac{2x_5}{3} + \frac{x_6}{3} \tag{29.74}$$

$$x_4 = 18 - \frac{x_3}{2} + \frac{x_5}{2} . \tag{29.75}$$

At this point, all coefficients in the objective function are negative. As we shall see later in this chapter, this situation occurs only when we have rewritten the linear program so that the basic solution is an optimal solution. Thus, for this problem, the solution $(8, 4, 0, 18, 0, 0)$, with objective value 28, is optimal. We can now return to our original linear program given in (29.53)–(29.57). The only variables in the original linear program are x_1, x_2, and x_3, and so our solution is $x_1 = 8$, $x_2 = 4$, and $x_3 = 0$, with objective value $(3 \cdot 8) + (1 \cdot 4) + (2 \cdot 0) = 28$. Note that the values of the slack variables in the final solution measure how much slack remains in each inequality. Slack variable x_4 is 18, and in inequality (29.54), the left-hand side, with value $8 + 4 + 0 = 12$, is 18 less than the right-hand side of 30. Slack variables x_5 and x_6 are 0 and indeed, in inequalities (29.55) and (29.56), the left-hand and right-hand sides are equal. Observe also that even though the coefficients in the original slack form are integral, the coefficients in the other linear programs are not necessarily integral, and the intermediate solutions are not necessarily integral. Furthermore, the final solution to a linear program need not be integral; it is purely coincidental that this example has an integral solution.

Pivoting

We now formalize the procedure for pivoting. The procedure PIVOT takes as input a slack form, given by the tuple (N, B, A, b, c, v), the index l of the leaving variable x_l, and the index e of the entering variable x_e. It returns the tuple $(\widehat{N}, \widehat{B}, \widehat{A}, \widehat{b}, \widehat{c}, \widehat{v})$ describing the new slack form. (Recall again that the entries of the $m \times n$ matrices A and $\widehat{A}$ are actually the negatives of the coefficients that appear in the slack form.)

PIVOT(N, B, A, b, c, v, l, e)

```
 1   // Compute the coefficients of the equation for new basic variable xₑ.
 2   let  be a new m × n matrix
 3   b̂ₑ = bₗ/aₗₑ
 4   for each j ∈ N − {e}
 5        âₑⱼ = aₗⱼ/aₗₑ
 6   âₑₗ = 1/aₗₑ
 7   // Compute the coefficients of the remaining constraints.
 8   for each i ∈ B − {l}
 9        b̂ᵢ = bᵢ − aᵢₑb̂ₑ
10        for each j ∈ N − {e}
11             âᵢⱼ = aᵢⱼ − aᵢₑâₑⱼ
12        âᵢₗ = −aᵢₑâₑₗ
13   // Compute the objective function.
14   v̂ = v + cₑb̂ₑ
15   for each j ∈ N − {e}
16        ĉⱼ = cⱼ − cₑâₑⱼ
17   ĉₗ = −cₑâₑₗ
18   // Compute new sets of basic and nonbasic variables.
19   N̂ = N − {e} ∪ {l}
20   B̂ = B − {l} ∪ {e}
21   return (N̂, B̂, Â, b̂, ĉ, v̂)
```

PIVOT works as follows. Lines 3–6 compute the coefficients in the new equation for x_e by rewriting the equation that has x_l on the left-hand side to instead have x_e on the left-hand side. Lines 8–12 update the remaining equations by substituting the right-hand side of this new equation for each occurrence of x_e. Lines 14–17 do the same substitution for the objective function, and lines 19 and 20 update the sets of nonbasic and basic variables. Line 21 returns the new slack form. As given, if $a_{le} = 0$, PIVOT would cause an error by dividing by 0, but as we shall see in the proofs of Lemmas 29.2 and 29.12, we call PIVOT only when $a_{le} \neq 0$.

We now summarize the effect that PIVOT has on the values of the variables in the basic solution.

Lemma 29.1

Consider a call to $\text{PIVOT}(N, B, A, b, c, v, l, e)$ in which $a_{le} \neq 0$. Let the values returned from the call be $(\widehat{N}, \widehat{B}, \widehat{A}, \widehat{b}, \widehat{c}, \widehat{v})$, and let $\bar{x}$ denote the basic solution after the call. Then

1. $\bar{x}_j = 0$ for each $j \in \widehat{N}$.
2. $\bar{x}_e = b_l / a_{le}$.
3. $\bar{x}_i = b_i - a_{ie}\widehat{b}_e$ for each $i \in \widehat{B} - \{e\}$.

Proof   The first statement is true because the basic solution always sets all non-basic variables to 0. When we set each nonbasic variable to 0 in a constraint

$$x_i = \widehat{b}_i - \sum_{j \in \widehat{N}} \widehat{a}_{ij} x_j \ ,$$

we have that $\bar{x}_i = \widehat{b}_i$ for each $i \in \widehat{B}$. Since $e \in \widehat{B}$, line 3 of PIVOT gives

$$\bar{x}_e = \widehat{b}_e = b_l / a_{le} \ ,$$

which proves the second statement. Similarly, using line 9 for each $i \in \widehat{B} - \{e\}$, we have

$$\bar{x}_i = \widehat{b}_i = b_i - a_{ie}\widehat{b}_e \ ,$$

which proves the third statement.   ∎

The formal simplex algorithm

We are now ready to formalize the simplex algorithm, which we demonstrated by example. That example was a particularly nice one, and we could have had several other issues to address:

- How do we determine whether a linear program is feasible?
- What do we do if the linear program is feasible, but the initial basic solution is not feasible?
- How do we determine whether a linear program is unbounded?
- How do we choose the entering and leaving variables?

In Section 29.5, we shall show how to determine whether a problem is feasible, and if so, how to find a slack form in which the initial basic solution is feasible. Therefore, let us assume that we have a procedure INITIALIZE-SIMPLEX(A, b, c) that takes as input a linear program in standard form, that is, an $m \times n$ matrix $A = (a_{ij})$, an m-vector $b = (b_i)$, and an n-vector $c = (c_j)$. If the problem is infeasible, the procedure returns a message that the program is infeasible and then terminates. Otherwise, the procedure returns a slack form for which the initial basic solution is feasible.

The procedure SIMPLEX takes as input a linear program in standard form, as just described. It returns an n-vector $\bar{x} = (\bar{x}_j)$ that is an optimal solution to the linear program described in (29.19)–(29.21).

SIMPLEX(A, b, c)

```
 1   (N, B, A, b, c, v) = INITIALIZE-SIMPLEX(A, b, c)
 2   let Δ be a new vector of length m
 3   while some index j ∈ N has c_j > 0
 4       choose an index e ∈ N for which c_e > 0
 5       for each index i ∈ B
 6           if a_{ie} > 0
 7               Δ_i = b_i / a_{ie}
 8           else Δ_i = ∞
 9       choose an index l ∈ B that minimizes Δ_l
10       if Δ_l == ∞
11           return "unbounded"
12       else (N, B, A, b, c, v) = PIVOT(N, B, A, b, c, v, l, e)
13   for i = 1 to n
14       if i ∈ B
15           x̄_i = b_i
16       else x̄_i = 0
17   return (x̄_1, x̄_2, ..., x̄_n)
```

The SIMPLEX procedure works as follows. In line 1, it calls the procedure INITIALIZE-SIMPLEX(A, b, c), described above, which either determines that the linear program is infeasible or returns a slack form for which the basic solution is feasible. The **while** loop of lines 3–12 forms the main part of the algorithm. If all coefficients in the objective function are negative, then the **while** loop terminates. Otherwise, line 4 selects a variable x_e, whose coefficient in the objective function is positive, as the entering variable. Although we may choose any such variable as the entering variable, we assume that we use some prespecified deterministic rule. Next, lines 5–9 check each constraint and pick the one that most severely limits the amount by which we can increase x_e without violating any of the nonnegativity constraints; the basic variable associated with this constraint is x_l. Again, we are free to choose one of several variables as the leaving variable, but we assume that we use some prespecified deterministic rule. If none of the constraints limits the amount by which the entering variable can increase, the algorithm returns "unbounded" in line 11. Otherwise, line 12 exchanges the roles of the entering and leaving variables by calling PIVOT(N, B, A, b, c, v, l, e), as described above. Lines 13–16 compute a solution $\bar{x}_1, \bar{x}_2, \ldots, \bar{x}_n$ for the original linear-programming variables by setting all the nonbasic variables to 0 and each basic variable $\bar{x}_i$ to b_i, and line 17 returns these values.

To show that SIMPLEX is correct, we first show that if SIMPLEX has an initial feasible solution and eventually terminates, then it either returns a feasible solution or determines that the linear program is unbounded. Then, we show that SIMPLEX terminates. Finally, in Section 29.4 (Theorem 29.10) we show that the solution returned is optimal.

Lemma 29.2
Given a linear program (A, b, c), suppose that the call to INITIALIZE-SIMPLEX in line 1 of SIMPLEX returns a slack form for which the basic solution is feasible. Then if SIMPLEX returns a solution in line 17, that solution is a feasible solution to the linear program. If SIMPLEX returns "unbounded" in line 11, the linear program is unbounded.

Proof   We use the following three-part loop invariant:

At the start of each iteration of the **while** loop of lines 3–12,

1. the slack form is equivalent to the slack form returned by the call of INITIALIZE-SIMPLEX,
2. for each $i \in B$, we have $b_i \geq 0$, and
3. the basic solution associated with the slack form is feasible.

Initialization: The equivalence of the slack forms is trivial for the first iteration. We assume, in the statement of the lemma, that the call to INITIALIZE-SIMPLEX in line 1 of SIMPLEX returns a slack form for which the basic solution is feasible. Thus, the third part of the invariant is true. Because the basic solution is feasible, each basic variable x_i is nonnegative. Furthermore, since the basic solution sets each basic variable x_i to b_i, we have that $b_i \geq 0$ for all $i \in B$. Thus, the second part of the invariant holds.

Maintenance: We shall show that each iteration of the **while** loop maintains the loop invariant, assuming that the **return** statement in line 11 does not execute. We shall handle the case in which line 11 executes when we discuss termination.

An iteration of the **while** loop exchanges the role of a basic and a nonbasic variable by calling the PIVOT procedure. By Exercise 29.3-3, the slack form is equivalent to the one from the previous iteration which, by the loop invariant, is equivalent to the initial slack form.

We now demonstrate the second part of the loop invariant. We assume that at the start of each iteration of the **while** loop, $b_i \geq 0$ for each $i \in B$, and we shall show that these inequalities remain true after the call to PIVOT in line 12. Since the only changes to the variables b_i and the set B of basic variables occur in this assignment, it suffices to show that line 12 maintains this part of the invariant. We let b_i, a_{ij}, and B refer to values before the call of PIVOT, and $\hat{b}_i$ refer to values returned from PIVOT.

First, we observe that $\hat{b}_e \geq 0$ because $b_l \geq 0$ by the loop invariant, $a_{le} > 0$ by lines 6 and 9 of SIMPLEX, and $\hat{b}_e = b_l / a_{le}$ by line 3 of PIVOT.

For the remaining indices $i \in B - \{l\}$, we have that

$$
\begin{aligned}
\hat{b}_i &= b_i - a_{ie}\hat{b}_e && \text{(by line 9 of PIVOT)} \\
&= b_i - a_{ie}(b_l/a_{le}) && \text{(by line 3 of PIVOT) .}
\end{aligned}
\tag{29.76}
$$

We have two cases to consider, depending on whether $a_{ie} > 0$ or $a_{ie} \leq 0$. If $a_{ie} > 0$, then since we chose l such that

$$
b_l/a_{le} \leq b_i/a_{ie} \quad \text{for all } i \in B \, ,
\tag{29.77}
$$

we have

$$
\begin{aligned}
\hat{b}_i &= b_i - a_{ie}(b_l/a_{le}) && \text{(by equation (29.76))} \\
&\geq b_i - a_{ie}(b_i/a_{ie}) && \text{(by inequality (29.77))} \\
&= b_i - b_i \\
&= 0 \, ,
\end{aligned}
$$

and thus $\hat{b}_i \geq 0$. If $a_{ie} \leq 0$, then because a_{le}, b_i, and b_l are all nonnegative, equation (29.76) implies that $\hat{b}_i$ must be nonnegative, too.

We now argue that the basic solution is feasible, i.e., that all variables have nonnegative values. The nonbasic variables are set to 0 and thus are nonnegative. Each basic variable x_i is defined by the equation

$$
x_i = b_i - \sum_{j \in N} a_{ij} x_j \, .
$$

The basic solution sets $\bar{x}_i = b_i$. Using the second part of the loop invariant, we conclude that each basic variable $\bar{x}_i$ is nonnegative.

Termination: The **while** loop can terminate in one of two ways. If it terminates because of the condition in line 3, then the current basic solution is feasible and line 17 returns this solution. The other way it terminates is by returning "unbounded" in line 11. In this case, for each iteration of the **for** loop in lines 5–8, when line 6 is executed, we find that $a_{ie} \leq 0$. Consider the solution $\bar{x}$ defined as

$$
\bar{x}_i = \begin{cases} \infty & \text{if } i = e\,, \\ 0 & \text{if } i \in N - \{e\}\,, \\ b_i - \sum_{j \in N} a_{ij}\bar{x}_j & \text{if } i \in B\,. \end{cases}
$$

We now show that this solution is feasible, i.e., that all variables are nonnegative. The nonbasic variables other than $\bar{x}_e$ are 0, and $\bar{x}_e = \infty > 0$; thus all nonbasic variables are nonnegative. For each basic variable $\bar{x}_i$, we have

$$
\begin{aligned}
\bar{x}_i &= b_i - \sum_{j \in N} a_{ij}\bar{x}_j \\
&= b_i - a_{ie}\bar{x}_e\,.
\end{aligned}
$$

The loop invariant implies that $b_i \geq 0$, and we have $a_{ie} \leq 0$ and $\bar{x}_e = \infty > 0$. Thus, $\bar{x}_i \geq 0$.

Now we show that the objective value for the solution $\bar{x}$ is unbounded. From equation (29.42), the objective value is

$$
\begin{aligned}
z &= v + \sum_{j \in N} c_j \bar{x}_j \\
&= v + c_e \bar{x}_e\,.
\end{aligned}
$$

Since $c_e > 0$ (by line 4 of SIMPLEX) and $\bar{x}_e = \infty$, the objective value is ∞, and thus the linear program is unbounded. ∎

It remains to show that SIMPLEX terminates, and when it does terminate, the solution it returns is optimal. Section 29.4 will address optimality. We now discuss termination.

Termination

In the example given in the beginning of this section, each iteration of the simplex algorithm increased the objective value associated with the basic solution. As Exercise 29.3-2 asks you to show, no iteration of SIMPLEX can decrease the objective value associated with the basic solution. Unfortunately, it is possible that an iteration leaves the objective value unchanged. This phenomenon is called ***degeneracy***, and we shall now study it in greater detail.

The assignment in line 14 of PIVOT, $\hat{v} = v + c_e \hat{b}_e$, changes the objective value. Since SIMPLEX calls PIVOT only when $c_e > 0$, the only way for the objective value to remain unchanged (i.e., $\hat{v} = v$) is for $\hat{b}_e$ to be 0. This value is assigned as $\hat{b}_e = b_l/a_{le}$ in line 3 of PIVOT. Since we always call PIVOT with $a_{le} \neq 0$, we see that for $\hat{b}_e$ to equal 0, and hence the objective value to be unchanged, we must have $b_l = 0$.

Indeed, this situation can occur. Consider the linear program

$$
\begin{aligned}
z &= && x_1 &+& x_2 &+& x_3 \\
x_4 &= 8 &-& x_1 &-& x_2 \\
x_5 &= && && x_2 &-& x_3 \ .
\end{aligned}
$$

Suppose that we choose x_1 as the entering variable and x_4 as the leaving variable. After pivoting, we obtain

$$
\begin{aligned}
z &= 8 && &+& x_3 &-& x_4 \\
x_1 &= 8 &-& x_2 && &-& x_4 \\
x_5 &= && x_2 &-& x_3 \ .
\end{aligned}
$$

At this point, our only choice is to pivot with x_3 entering and x_5 leaving. Since $b_5 = 0$, the objective value of 8 remains unchanged after pivoting:

$$
\begin{aligned}
z &= 8 &+& x_2 &-& x_4 &-& x_5 \\
x_1 &= 8 &-& x_2 &-& x_4 \\
x_3 &= && x_2 && &-& x_5 \ .
\end{aligned}
$$

The objective value has not changed, but our slack form has. Fortunately, if we pivot again, with x_2 entering and x_1 leaving, the objective value increases (to 16), and the simplex algorithm can continue.

Degeneracy can prevent the simplex algorithm from terminating, because it can lead to a phenomenon known as ***cycling***: the slack forms at two different iterations of SIMPLEX are identical. Because of degeneracy, SIMPLEX could choose a sequence of pivot operations that leave the objective value unchanged but repeat a slack form within the sequence. Since SIMPLEX is a deterministic algorithm, if it cycles, then it will cycle through the same series of slack forms forever, never terminating.

Cycling is the only reason that SIMPLEX might not terminate. To show this fact, we must first develop some additional machinery.

At each iteration, SIMPLEX maintains A, b, c, and v in addition to the sets N and B. Although we need to explicitly maintain A, b, c, and v in order to implement the simplex algorithm efficiently, we can get by without maintaining them. In other words, the sets of basic and nonbasic variables suffice to uniquely determine the slack form. Before proving this fact, we prove a useful algebraic lemma.

Lemma 29.3

Let I be a set of indices. For each $j \in I$, let α_j and β_j be real numbers, and let x_j be a real-valued variable. Let γ be any real number. Suppose that for any settings of the x_j, we have

$$\sum_{j \in I} \alpha_j x_j = \gamma + \sum_{j \in I} \beta_j x_j \; . \tag{29.78}$$

Then $\alpha_j = \beta_j$ for each $j \in I$, and $\gamma = 0$.

Proof   Since equation (29.78) holds for any values of the x_j, we can use particular values to draw conclusions about α, β, and γ. If we let $x_j = 0$ for each $j \in I$, we conclude that $\gamma = 0$. Now pick an arbitrary index $j \in I$, and set $x_j = 1$ and $x_k = 0$ for all $k \neq j$. Then we must have $\alpha_j = \beta_j$. Since we picked j as any index in I, we conclude that $\alpha_j = \beta_j$ for each $j \in I$.   ∎

A particular linear program has many different slack forms; recall that each slack form has the same set of feasible and optimal solutions as the original linear program. We now show that the slack form of a linear program is uniquely determined by the set of basic variables. That is, given the set of basic variables, a unique slack form (unique set of coefficients and right-hand sides) is associated with those basic variables.

Lemma 29.4

Let (A, b, c) be a linear program in standard form. Given a set B of basic variables, the associated slack form is uniquely determined.

Proof   Assume for the purpose of contradiction that there are two different slack forms with the same set B of basic variables. The slack forms must also have identical sets $N = \{1, 2, \ldots, n + m\} - B$ of nonbasic variables. We write the first slack form as

$$z \;\; = \;\; v + \sum_{j \in N} c_j x_j \tag{29.79}$$

$$x_i \;\; = \;\; b_i - \sum_{j \in N} a_{ij} x_j \;\; \text{for } i \in B \; , \tag{29.80}$$

and the second as

$$z \;\; = \;\; v' + \sum_{j \in N} c'_j x_j \tag{29.81}$$

$$x_i \;\; = \;\; b'_i - \sum_{j \in N} a'_{ij} x_j \;\; \text{for } i \in B \; . \tag{29.82}$$

Consider the system of equations formed by subtracting each equation in line (29.82) from the corresponding equation in line (29.80). The resulting system is

$$0 = (b_i - b'_i) - \sum_{j \in N}(a_{ij} - a'_{ij})x_j \quad \text{for } i \in B$$

or, equivalently,

$$\sum_{j \in N} a_{ij}x_j = (b_i - b'_i) + \sum_{j \in N} a'_{ij}x_j \quad \text{for } i \in B \ .$$

Now, for each $i \in B$, apply Lemma 29.3 with $\alpha_j = a_{ij}, \beta_j = a'_{ij}, \gamma = b_i - b'_i$, and $I = N$. Since $\alpha_j = \beta_j$, we have that $a_{ij} = a'_{ij}$ for each $j \in N$, and since $\gamma = 0$, we have that $b_i = b'_i$. Thus, for the two slack forms, A and b are identical to A' and b'. Using a similar argument, Exercise 29.3-1 shows that it must also be the case that $c = c'$ and $v = v'$, and hence that the slack forms must be identical.   ∎

We can now show that cycling is the only possible reason that SIMPLEX might not terminate.

Lemma 29.5
If SIMPLEX fails to terminate in at most $\binom{n+m}{m}$ iterations, then it cycles.

Proof   By Lemma 29.4, the set B of basic variables uniquely determines a slack form. There are $n + m$ variables and $|B| = m$, and therefore, there are at most $\binom{n+m}{m}$ ways to choose B. Thus, there are only at most $\binom{n+m}{m}$ unique slack forms. Therefore, if SIMPLEX runs for more than $\binom{n+m}{m}$ iterations, it must cycle.   ∎

Cycling is theoretically possible, but extremely rare. We can prevent it by choosing the entering and leaving variables somewhat more carefully. One option is to perturb the input slightly so that it is impossible to have two solutions with the same objective value. Another option is to break ties by always choosing the variable with the smallest index, a strategy known as **Bland's rule**. We omit the proof that these strategies avoid cycling.

Lemma 29.6
If lines 4 and 9 of SIMPLEX always break ties by choosing the variable with the smallest index, then SIMPLEX must terminate.   ∎

We conclude this section with the following lemma.

Lemma 29.7

Assuming that INITIALIZE-SIMPLEX returns a slack form for which the basic solution is feasible, SIMPLEX either reports that a linear program is unbounded, or it terminates with a feasible solution in at most $\binom{n+m}{m}$ iterations.

Proof   Lemmas 29.2 and 29.6 show that if INITIALIZE-SIMPLEX returns a slack form for which the basic solution is feasible, SIMPLEX either reports that a linear program is unbounded, or it terminates with a feasible solution. By the contrapositive of Lemma 29.5, if SIMPLEX terminates with a feasible solution, then it terminates in at most $\binom{n+m}{m}$ iterations.   ∎

Exercises

29.3-1
Complete the proof of Lemma 29.4 by showing that it must be the case that $c = c'$ and $v = v'$.

29.3-2
Show that the call to PIVOT in line 12 of SIMPLEX never decreases the value of v.

29.3-3
Prove that the slack form given to the PIVOT procedure and the slack form that the procedure returns are equivalent.

29.3-4
Suppose we convert a linear program (A, b, c) in standard form to slack form. Show that the basic solution is feasible if and only if $b_i \geq 0$ for $i = 1, 2, \ldots, m$.

29.3-5
Solve the following linear program using SIMPLEX:

$$
\begin{array}{lrcrcl}
\text{maximize} & 18x_1 & + & 12.5x_2 & & \\
\text{subject to} & & & & & \\
& x_1 & + & x_2 & \leq & 20 \\
& x_1 & & & \leq & 12 \\
& & & x_2 & \leq & 16 \\
& & & x_1, x_2 & \geq & 0 \ .
\end{array}
$$

29.3-6
Solve the following linear program using SIMPLEX:

maximize $5x_1 - 3x_2$
subject to

$$
\begin{aligned}
x_1 - x_2 &\le 1 \\
2x_1 + x_2 &\le 2 \\
x_1, x_2 &\ge 0 .
\end{aligned}
$$

29.3-7
Solve the following linear program using SIMPLEX:

minimize $x_1 + x_2 + x_3$
subject to

$$
\begin{aligned}
2x_1 + 7.5x_2 + 3x_3 &\ge 10000 \\
20x_1 + 5x_2 + 10x_3 &\ge 30000 \\
x_1, x_2, x_3 &\ge 0 .
\end{aligned}
$$

29.3-8
In the proof of Lemma 29.5, we argued that there are at most $\binom{m+n}{n}$ ways to choose a set B of basic variables. Give an example of a linear program in which there are strictly fewer than $\binom{m+n}{n}$ ways to choose the set B.

29.4   Duality

We have proven that, under certain assumptions, SIMPLEX terminates. We have not yet shown that it actually finds an optimal solution to a linear program, however. In order to do so, we introduce a powerful concept called ***linear-programming duality***.

Duality enables us to prove that a solution is indeed optimal. We saw an example of duality in Chapter 26 with Theorem 26.6, the max-flow min-cut theorem. Suppose that, given an instance of a maximum-flow problem, we find a flow f with value $|f|$. How do we know whether f is a maximum flow? By the max-flow min-cut theorem, if we can find a cut whose value is also $|f|$, then we have verified that f is indeed a maximum flow. This relationship provides an example of duality: given a maximization problem, we define a related minimization problem such that the two problems have the same optimal objective values.

Given a linear program in which the objective is to maximize, we shall describe how to formulate a ***dual*** linear program in which the objective is to minimize and whose optimal value is identical to that of the original linear program. When referring to dual linear programs, we call the original linear program the ***primal***.

Given a primal linear program in standard form, as in (29.16)–(29.18), we define the dual linear program as

$$\text{minimize} \quad \sum_{i=1}^{m} b_i y_i \tag{29.83}$$

subject to

$$\sum_{i=1}^{m} a_{ij} y_i \geq c_j \quad \text{for } j = 1, 2, \ldots, n, \tag{29.84}$$

$$y_i \geq 0 \quad \text{for } i = 1, 2, \ldots, m. \tag{29.85}$$

To form the dual, we change the maximization to a minimization, exchange the roles of coefficients on the right-hand sides and the objective function, and replace each less-than-or-equal-to by a greater-than-or-equal-to. Each of the m constraints in the primal has an associated variable y_i in the dual, and each of the n constraints in the dual has an associated variable x_j in the primal. For example, consider the linear program given in (29.53)–(29.57). The dual of this linear program is

$$\text{minimize} \quad 30y_1 + 24y_2 + 36y_3 \tag{29.86}$$

subject to

$$
\begin{array}{rcrcrcl}
y_1 & + & 2y_2 & + & 4y_3 & \geq & 3 \\
y_1 & + & 2y_2 & + & y_3 & \geq & 1 \\
3y_1 & + & 5y_2 & + & 2y_3 & \geq & 2 \\
& & y_1, y_2, y_3 & & & \geq & 0 .
\end{array}
$$

$$\tag{29.87}$$
$$\tag{29.88}$$
$$\tag{29.89}$$
$$\tag{29.90}$$

We shall show in Theorem 29.10 that the optimal value of the dual linear program is always equal to the optimal value of the primal linear program. Furthermore, the simplex algorithm actually implicitly solves both the primal and the dual linear programs simultaneously, thereby providing a proof of optimality.

We begin by demonstrating ***weak duality***, which states that any feasible solution to the primal linear program has a value no greater than that of any feasible solution to the dual linear program.

Lemma 29.8 (Weak linear-programming duality)
Let $\bar{x}$ be any feasible solution to the primal linear program in (29.16)–(29.18) and let $\bar{y}$ be any feasible solution to the dual linear program in (29.83)–(29.85). Then, we have

$$\sum_{j=1}^{n} c_j \bar{x}_j \leq \sum_{i=1}^{m} b_i \bar{y}_i .$$

Proof   We have

$$\sum_{j=1}^{n} c_j \bar{x}_j \;\leq\; \sum_{j=1}^{n} \left(\sum_{i=1}^{m} a_{ij} \bar{y}_i \right) \bar{x}_j \quad \text{(by inequalities (29.84))}$$

$$= \sum_{i=1}^{m} \left(\sum_{j=1}^{n} a_{ij} \bar{x}_j \right) \bar{y}_i$$

$$\leq \sum_{i=1}^{m} b_i \bar{y}_i \qquad \text{(by inequalities (29.17))} \,. \qquad \blacksquare$$

Corollary 29.9
Let $\bar{x}$ be a feasible solution to a primal linear program (A, b, c), and let $\bar{y}$ be a feasible solution to the corresponding dual linear program. If

$$\sum_{j=1}^{n} c_j \bar{x}_j = \sum_{i=1}^{m} b_i \bar{y}_i \,,$$

then $\bar{x}$ and $\bar{y}$ are optimal solutions to the primal and dual linear programs, respectively.

Proof   By Lemma 29.8, the objective value of a feasible solution to the primal cannot exceed that of a feasible solution to the dual. The primal linear program is a maximization problem and the dual is a minimization problem. Thus, if feasible solutions $\bar{x}$ and $\bar{y}$ have the same objective value, neither can be improved. $\blacksquare$

Before proving that there always is a dual solution whose value is equal to that of an optimal primal solution, we describe how to find such a solution. When we ran the simplex algorithm on the linear program in (29.53)–(29.57), the final iteration yielded the slack form (29.72)–(29.75) with objective $z = 28 - x_3/6 - x_5/6 - 2x_6/3$, $B = \{1, 2, 4\}$, and $N = \{3, 5, 6\}$. As we shall show below, the basic solution associated with the final slack form is indeed an optimal solution to the linear program; an optimal solution to linear program (29.53)–(29.57) is therefore $(\bar{x}_1, \bar{x}_2, \bar{x}_3) = (8, 4, 0)$, with objective value $(3 \cdot 8) + (1 \cdot 4) + (2 \cdot 0) = 28$. As we also show below, we can read off an optimal dual solution: the negatives of the coefficients of the primal objective function are the values of the dual variables. More precisely, suppose that the last slack form of the primal is

$$z \;=\; v' + \sum_{j \in N} c'_j x_j$$

$$x_i \;=\; b'_i - \sum_{j \in N} a'_{ij} x_j \quad \text{for } i \in B \,.$$

Then, to produce an optimal dual solution, we set

$$\bar{y}_i = \begin{cases} -c'_{n+i} & \text{if } (n+i) \in N, \\ 0 & \text{otherwise} . \end{cases} \tag{29.91}$$

Thus, an optimal solution to the dual linear program defined in (29.86)–(29.90) is $\bar{y}_1 = 0$ (since $n+1 = 4 \in B$), $\bar{y}_2 = -c'_5 = 1/6$, and $\bar{y}_3 = -c'_6 = 2/3$. Evaluating the dual objective function (29.86), we obtain an objective value of $(30 \cdot 0) + (24 \cdot (1/6)) + (36 \cdot (2/3)) = 28$, which confirms that the objective value of the primal is indeed equal to the objective value of the dual. Combining these calculations with Lemma 29.8 yields a proof that the optimal objective value of the primal linear program is 28. We now show that this approach applies in general: we can find an optimal solution to the dual and simultaneously prove that a solution to the primal is optimal.

Theorem 29.10 (Linear-programming duality)
Suppose that SIMPLEX returns values $\bar{x} = (\bar{x}_1, \bar{x}_2, \ldots, \bar{x}_n)$ for the primal linear program (A, b, c). Let N and B denote the nonbasic and basic variables for the final slack form, let c' denote the coefficients in the final slack form, and let $\bar{y} = (\bar{y}_1, \bar{y}_2, \ldots, \bar{y}_m)$ be defined by equation (29.91). Then $\bar{x}$ is an optimal solution to the primal linear program, $\bar{y}$ is an optimal solution to the dual linear program, and

$$\sum_{j=1}^{n} c_j \bar{x}_j = \sum_{i=1}^{m} b_i \bar{y}_i . \tag{29.92}$$

Proof   By Corollary 29.9, if we can find feasible solutions $\bar{x}$ and $\bar{y}$ that satisfy equation (29.92), then $\bar{x}$ and $\bar{y}$ must be optimal primal and dual solutions. We shall now show that the solutions $\bar{x}$ and $\bar{y}$ described in the statement of the theorem satisfy equation (29.92).

Suppose that we run SIMPLEX on a primal linear program, as given in lines (29.16)–(29.18). The algorithm proceeds through a series of slack forms until it terminates with a final slack form with objective function

$$z = v' + \sum_{j \in N} c'_j x_j . \tag{29.93}$$

Since SIMPLEX terminated with a solution, by the condition in line 3 we know that

$$c'_j \leq 0 \quad \text{for all } j \in N . \tag{29.94}$$

If we define

$$c'_j = 0 \quad \text{for all } j \in B,\tag{29.95}$$

we can rewrite equation (29.93) as

$$
\begin{aligned}
z &= v' + \sum_{j \in N} c'_j x_j \\
&= v' + \sum_{j \in N} c'_j x_j + \sum_{j \in B} c'_j x_j \quad \text{(because } c'_j = 0 \text{ if } j \in B) \\
&= v' + \sum_{j=1}^{n+m} c'_j x_j \qquad\qquad \text{(because } N \cup B = \{1, 2, \dots, n+m\}). \tag{29.96}
\end{aligned}
$$

For the basic solution $\bar{x}$ associated with this final slack form, $\bar{x}_j = 0$ for all $j \in N$, and $z = v'$. Since all slack forms are equivalent, if we evaluate the original objective function on $\bar{x}$, we must obtain the same objective value:

$$
\begin{aligned}
\sum_{j=1}^{n} c_j \bar{x}_j &= v' + \sum_{j=1}^{n+m} c'_j \bar{x}_j \tag{29.97} \\
&= v' + \sum_{j \in N} c'_j \bar{x}_j + \sum_{j \in B} c'_j \bar{x}_j \\
&= v' + \sum_{j \in N} (c'_j \cdot 0) + \sum_{j \in B} (0 \cdot \bar{x}_j) \tag{29.98} \\
&= v' .
\end{aligned}
$$

We shall now show that $\bar{y}$, defined by equation (29.91), is feasible for the dual linear program and that its objective value $\sum_{i=1}^{m} b_i \bar{y}_i$ equals $\sum_{j=1}^{n} c_j \bar{x}_j$. Equation (29.97) says that the first and last slack forms, evaluated at $\bar{x}$, are equal. More generally, the equivalence of all slack forms implies that for *any* set of values $x = (x_1, x_2, \dots, x_n)$, we have

$$\sum_{j=1}^{n} c_j x_j = v' + \sum_{j=1}^{n+m} c'_j x_j .$$

Therefore, for any particular set of values $\bar{x} = (\bar{x}_1, \bar{x}_2, \dots, \bar{x}_n)$, we have

$$\sum_{j=1}^{n} c_j \bar{x}_j$$

$$= v' + \sum_{j=1}^{n+m} c'_j \bar{x}_j$$

$$= v' + \sum_{j=1}^{n} c'_j \bar{x}_j + \sum_{j=n+1}^{n+m} c'_j \bar{x}_j$$

$$= v' + \sum_{j=1}^{n} c'_j \bar{x}_j + \sum_{i=1}^{m} c'_{n+i} \bar{x}_{n+i}$$

$$= v' + \sum_{j=1}^{n} c'_j \bar{x}_j + \sum_{i=1}^{m} (-\bar{y}_i) \bar{x}_{n+i} \qquad \text{(by equations (29.91) and (29.95))}$$

$$= v' + \sum_{j=1}^{n} c'_j \bar{x}_j + \sum_{i=1}^{m} (-\bar{y}_i) \left(b_i - \sum_{j=1}^{n} a_{ij} \bar{x}_j \right) \qquad \text{(by equation (29.32))}$$

$$= v' + \sum_{j=1}^{n} c'_j \bar{x}_j - \sum_{i=1}^{m} b_i \bar{y}_i + \sum_{i=1}^{m} \sum_{j=1}^{n} (a_{ij} \bar{x}_j) \bar{y}_i$$

$$= v' + \sum_{j=1}^{n} c'_j \bar{x}_j - \sum_{i=1}^{m} b_i \bar{y}_i + \sum_{j=1}^{n} \sum_{i=1}^{m} (a_{ij} \bar{y}_i) \bar{x}_j$$

$$= \left(v' - \sum_{i=1}^{m} b_i \bar{y}_i \right) + \sum_{j=1}^{n} \left(c'_j + \sum_{i=1}^{m} a_{ij} \bar{y}_i \right) \bar{x}_j ,$$

so that

$$\sum_{j=1}^{n} c_j \bar{x}_j = \left(v' - \sum_{i=1}^{m} b_i \bar{y}_i \right) + \sum_{j=1}^{n} \left(c'_j + \sum_{i=1}^{m} a_{ij} \bar{y}_i \right) \bar{x}_j . \qquad (29.99)$$

Applying Lemma 29.3 to equation (29.99), we obtain

$$v' - \sum_{i=1}^{m} b_i \bar{y}_i = 0 , \qquad (29.100)$$

$$c'_j + \sum_{i=1}^{m} a_{ij} \bar{y}_i = c_j \quad \text{for } j = 1, 2, \ldots, n . \qquad (29.101)$$

By equation (29.100), we have that $\sum_{i=1}^{m} b_i \bar{y}_i = v'$, and hence the objective value of the dual $\left(\sum_{i=1}^{m} b_i \bar{y}_i \right)$ is equal to that of the primal (v'). It remains to show that the solution $\bar{y}$ is feasible for the dual problem. From inequalities (29.94) and equations (29.95), we have that $c'_j \leq 0$ for all $j = 1, 2, \ldots, n + m$. Hence, for any $j = 1, 2, \ldots, n$, equations (29.101) imply that

$$
\begin{aligned}
c_j &= c'_j + \sum_{i=1}^{m} a_{ij} \bar{y}_i \\
&\leq \sum_{i=1}^{m} a_{ij} \bar{y}_i \, ,
\end{aligned}
$$

which satisfies the constraints (29.84) of the dual. Finally, since $c'_j \leq 0$ for each $j \in N \cup B$, when we set $\bar{y}$ according to equation (29.91), we have that each $\bar{y}_i \geq 0$, and so the nonnegativity constraints are satisfied as well.   ■

We have shown that, given a feasible linear program, if INITIALIZE-SIMPLEX returns a feasible solution, and if SIMPLEX terminates without returning "unbounded," then the solution returned is indeed an optimal solution. We have also shown how to construct an optimal solution to the dual linear program.

Exercises

29.4-1
Formulate the dual of the linear program given in Exercise 29.3-5.

29.4-2
Suppose that we have a linear program that is not in standard form. We could produce the dual by first converting it to standard form, and then taking the dual. It would be more convenient, however, to be able to produce the dual directly. Explain how we can directly take the dual of an arbitrary linear program.

29.4-3
Write down the dual of the maximum-flow linear program, as given in lines (29.47)–(29.50) on page 860. Explain how to interpret this formulation as a minimum-cut problem.

29.4-4
Write down the dual of the minimum-cost-flow linear program, as given in lines (29.51)–(29.52) on page 862. Explain how to interpret this problem in terms of graphs and flows.

29.4-5
Show that the dual of the dual of a linear program is the primal linear program.

29.4-6

Which result from Chapter 26 can be interpreted as weak duality for the maximum-flow problem?

29.5   The initial basic feasible solution

In this section, we first describe how to test whether a linear program is feasible, and if it is, how to produce a slack form for which the basic solution is feasible. We conclude by proving the fundamental theorem of linear programming, which says that the SIMPLEX procedure always produces the correct result.

Finding an initial solution

In Section 29.3, we assumed that we had a procedure INITIALIZE-SIMPLEX that determines whether a linear program has any feasible solutions, and if it does, gives a slack form for which the basic solution is feasible. We describe this procedure here.

A linear program can be feasible, yet the initial basic solution might not be feasible. Consider, for example, the following linear program:

$$\text{maximize} \quad 2x_1 \; - \; x_2 \tag{29.102}$$

subject to

$$2x_1 \; - \; x_2 \; \leq \; 2 \tag{29.103}$$

$$x_1 \; - \; 5x_2 \; \leq \; -4 \tag{29.104}$$

$$x_1, x_2 \; \geq \; 0 \; . \tag{29.105}$$

If we were to convert this linear program to slack form, the basic solution would set $x_1 = 0$ and $x_2 = 0$. This solution violates constraint (29.104), and so it is not a feasible solution. Thus, INITIALIZE-SIMPLEX cannot just return the obvious slack form. In order to determine whether a linear program has any feasible solutions, we will formulate an ***auxiliary linear program***. For this auxiliary linear program, we can find (with a little work) a slack form for which the basic solution is feasible. Furthermore, the solution of this auxiliary linear program determines whether the initial linear program is feasible and if so, it provides a feasible solution with which we can initialize SIMPLEX.

Lemma 29.11

Let L be a linear program in standard form, given as in (29.16)–(29.18). Let x_0 be a new variable, and let L_{aux} be the following linear program with $n + 1$ variables:

maximize $\qquad\qquad -x_0$ $\hfill$ (29.106)

subject to

$$\sum_{j=1}^{n} a_{ij}x_j - x_0 \;\le\; b_i \quad \text{for } i = 1, 2, \ldots, m \,, \hfill (29.107)$$

$$x_j \;\ge\; 0 \quad \text{for } j = 0, 1, \ldots, n \,. \hfill (29.108)$$

Then L is feasible if and only if the optimal objective value of L_{aux} is 0.

Proof Suppose that L has a feasible solution $\bar{x} = (\bar{x}_1, \bar{x}_2, \ldots, \bar{x}_n)$. Then the solution $\bar{x}_0 = 0$ combined with $\bar{x}$ is a feasible solution to L_{aux} with objective value 0. Since $x_0 \ge 0$ is a constraint of L_{aux} and the objective function is to maximize $-x_0$, this solution must be optimal for L_{aux}.

Conversely, suppose that the optimal objective value of L_{aux} is 0. Then $\bar{x}_0 = 0$, and the remaining solution values of $\bar{x}$ satisfy the constraints of L. $\blacksquare$

We now describe our strategy to find an initial basic feasible solution for a linear program L in standard form:

INITIALIZE-SIMPLEX(A, b, c)

```
 1   let k be the index of the minimum b_i
 2   if b_k ≥ 0                           // is the initial basic solution feasible?
 3       return ({1, 2, ..., n}, {n + 1, n + 2, ..., n + m}, A, b, c, 0)
 4   form L_aux by adding -x_0 to the left-hand side of each constraint
             and setting the objective function to -x_0
 5   let (N, B, A, b, c, v) be the resulting slack form for L_aux
 6   l = n + k
 7   // L_aux has n + 1 nonbasic variables and m basic variables.
 8   (N, B, A, b, c, v) = PIVOT(N, B, A, b, c, v, l, 0)
 9   // The basic solution is now feasible for L_aux.
10   iterate the while loop of lines 3–12 of SIMPLEX until an optimal solution
             to L_aux is found
11   if the optimal solution to L_aux sets x̄_0 to 0
12       if x̄_0 is basic
13           perform one (degenerate) pivot to make it nonbasic
14       from the final slack form of L_aux, remove x_0 from the constraints and
               restore the original objective function of L, but replace each basic
               variable in this objective function by the right-hand side of its
               associated constraint
15       return the modified final slack form
16   else return "infeasible"
```

INITIALIZE-SIMPLEX works as follows. In lines 1–3, we implicitly test the basic solution to the initial slack form for L given by $N = \{1, 2, \ldots, n\}$, $B = \{n + 1, n + 2, \ldots, n + m\}$, $\bar{x}_i = b_i$ for all $i \in B$, and $\bar{x}_j = 0$ for all $j \in N$. (Creating the slack form requires no explicit effort, as the values of A, b, and c are the same in both slack and standard forms.) If line 2 finds this basic solution to be feasible—that is, $\bar{x}_i \geq 0$ for all $i \in N \cup B$—then line 3 returns the slack form. Otherwise, in line 4, we form the auxiliary linear program L_{aux} as in Lemma 29.11. Since the initial basic solution to L is not feasible, the initial basic solution to the slack form for L_{aux} cannot be feasible either. To find a basic feasible solution, we perform a single pivot operation. Line 6 selects $l = n + k$ as the index of the basic variable that will be the leaving variable in the upcoming pivot operation. Since the basic variables are $x_{n+1}, x_{n+2}, \ldots, x_{n+m}$, the leaving variable x_l will be the one with the most negative value. Line 8 performs that call of PIVOT, with x_0 entering and x_l leaving. We shall see shortly that the basic solution resulting from this call of PIVOT will be feasible. Now that we have a slack form for which the basic solution is feasible, we can, in line 10, repeatedly call PIVOT to fully solve the auxiliary linear program. As the test in line 11 demonstrates, if we find an optimal solution to L_{aux} with objective value 0, then in lines 12–14, we create a slack form for L for which the basic solution is feasible. To do so, we first, in lines 12–13, handle the degenerate case in which x_0 may still be basic with value $\bar{x}_0 = 0$. In this case, we perform a pivot step to remove x_0 from the basis, using any $e \in N$ such that $a_{0e} \neq 0$ as the entering variable. The new basic solution remains feasible; the degenerate pivot does not change the value of any variable. Next we delete all x_0 terms from the constraints and restore the original objective function for L. The original objective function may contain both basic and nonbasic variables. Therefore, in the objective function we replace each basic variable by the right-hand side of its associated constraint. Line 15 then returns this modified slack form. If, on the other hand, line 11 discovers that the original linear program L is infeasible, then line 16 returns this information.

We now demonstrate the operation of INITIALIZE-SIMPLEX on the linear program (29.102)–(29.105). This linear program is feasible if we can find nonnegative values for x_1 and x_2 that satisfy inequalities (29.103) and (29.104). Using Lemma 29.11, we formulate the auxiliary linear program

$$\text{maximize} \qquad\qquad -x_0 \qquad\qquad\qquad (29.109)$$

subject to

$$
\begin{aligned}
2x_1 &- x_2 &- x_0 &\leq 2 &\qquad (29.110)\\
x_1 &- 5x_2 &- x_0 &\leq -4 &\qquad (29.111)\\
&x_1, x_2, x_0 && \geq 0 \;.
\end{aligned}
$$

By Lemma 29.11, if the optimal objective value of this auxiliary linear program is 0, then the original linear program has a feasible solution. If the optimal objective value of this auxiliary linear program is negative, then the original linear program does not have a feasible solution.

We write this linear program in slack form, obtaining

$$
\begin{aligned}
z &= && && && && -\ x_0 \\
x_3 &= && 2 &&-\ 2x_1 &&+\ x_2 &&+\ x_0 \\
x_4 &= && -4 &&-\ x_1 &&+\ 5x_2 &&+\ x_0\ .
\end{aligned}
$$

We are not out of the woods yet, because the basic solution, which would set $x_4 = -4$, is not feasible for this auxiliary linear program. We can, however, with one call to PIVOT, convert this slack form into one in which the basic solution is feasible. As line 8 indicates, we choose x_0 to be the entering variable. In line 6, we choose as the leaving variable x_4, which is the basic variable whose value in the basic solution is most negative. After pivoting, we have the slack form

$$
\begin{aligned}
z &= -4 &&-\ x_1 &&+\ 5x_2 &&-\ x_4 \\
x_0 &= 4 &&+\ x_1 &&-\ 5x_2 &&+\ x_4 \\
x_3 &= 6 &&-\ x_1 &&-\ 4x_2 &&+\ x_4\ .
\end{aligned}
$$

The associated basic solution is $(\bar{x}_0, \bar{x}_1, \bar{x}_2, \bar{x}_3, \bar{x}_4) = (4, 0, 0, 6, 0)$, which is feasible. We now repeatedly call PIVOT until we obtain an optimal solution to L_{aux}. In this case, one call to PIVOT with x_2 entering and x_0 leaving yields

$$
\begin{aligned}
z &= && -\ x_0 \\
x_2 &= \frac{4}{5} &&-\ \frac{x_0}{5} &&+\ \frac{x_1}{5} &&+\ \frac{x_4}{5} \\
x_3 &= \frac{14}{5} &&+\ \frac{4x_0}{5} &&-\ \frac{9x_1}{5} &&+\ \frac{x_4}{5}\ .
\end{aligned}
$$

This slack form is the final solution to the auxiliary problem. Since this solution has $x_0 = 0$, we know that our initial problem was feasible. Furthermore, since $x_0 = 0$, we can just remove it from the set of constraints. We then restore the original objective function, with appropriate substitutions made to include only nonbasic variables. In our example, we get the objective function

$$
2x_1 - x_2 = 2x_1 - \left(\frac{4}{5} - \frac{x_0}{5} + \frac{x_1}{5} + \frac{x_4}{5} \right).
$$

Setting $x_0 = 0$ and simplifying, we get the objective function

$$
-\frac{4}{5} + \frac{9x_1}{5} - \frac{x_4}{5},
$$

and the slack form

$$z = -\frac{4}{5} + \frac{9x_1}{5} - \frac{x_4}{5}$$

$$x_2 = \frac{4}{5} + \frac{x_1}{5} + \frac{x_4}{5}$$

$$x_3 = \frac{14}{5} - \frac{9x_1}{5} + \frac{x_4}{5} .$$

This slack form has a feasible basic solution, and we can return it to procedure SIMPLEX.

We now formally show the correctness of INITIALIZE-SIMPLEX.

Lemma 29.12

If a linear program L has no feasible solution, then INITIALIZE-SIMPLEX returns "infeasible." Otherwise, it returns a valid slack form for which the basic solution is feasible.

Proof   First suppose that the linear program L has no feasible solution. Then by Lemma 29.11, the optimal objective value of L_{aux}, defined in (29.106)–(29.108), is nonzero, and by the nonnegativity constraint on x_0, the optimal objective value must be negative. Furthermore, this objective value must be finite, since setting $x_i = 0$, for $i = 1, 2, \ldots, n$, and $x_0 = |\min_{i=1}^{m} \{b_i\}|$ is feasible, and this solution has objective value $-|\min_{i=1}^{m} \{b_i\}|$. Therefore, line 10 of INITIALIZE-SIMPLEX finds a solution with a nonpositive objective value. Let $\bar{x}$ be the basic solution associated with the final slack form. We cannot have $\bar{x}_0 = 0$, because then L_{aux} would have objective value 0, which contradicts that the objective value is negative. Thus the test in line 11 results in line 16 returning "infeasible."

Suppose now that the linear program L does have a feasible solution. From Exercise 29.3-4, we know that if $b_i \geq 0$ for $i = 1, 2, \ldots, m$, then the basic solution associated with the initial slack form is feasible. In this case, lines 2–3 return the slack form associated with the input. (Converting the standard form to slack form is easy, since A, b, and c are the same in both.)

In the remainder of the proof, we handle the case in which the linear program is feasible but we do not return in line 3. We argue that in this case, lines 4–10 find a feasible solution to L_{aux} with objective value 0. First, by lines 1–2, we must have

$$b_k < 0 ,$$

and

$$b_k \leq b_i \quad \text{for each } i \in B . \tag{29.112}$$

In line 8, we perform one pivot operation in which the leaving variable x_l (recall that $l = n + k$, so that $b_l < 0$) is the left-hand side of the equation with minimum b_i, and the entering variable is x_0, the extra added variable. We now show that after this pivot, all entries of b are nonnegative, and hence the basic solution to L_{aux} is feasible. Letting $\bar{x}$ be the basic solution after the call to PIVOT, and letting $\hat{b}$ and $\hat{B}$ be values returned by PIVOT, Lemma 29.1 implies that

$$
\bar{x}_i = \begin{cases} b_i - a_{ie}\hat{b}_e & \text{if } i \in \hat{B} - \{e\}\,, \\ b_l/a_{le} & \text{if } i = e\,. \end{cases} \tag{29.113}
$$

The call to PIVOT in line 8 has $e = 0$. If we rewrite inequalities (29.107), to include coefficients a_{i0},

$$
\sum_{j=0}^{n} a_{ij}x_j \le b_i \quad \text{for } i = 1, 2, \ldots, m\,, \tag{29.114}
$$

then

$$
a_{i0} = a_{ie} = -1 \quad \text{for each } i \in B\,. \tag{29.115}
$$

(Note that a_{i0} is the coefficient of x_0 as it appears in inequalities (29.114), not the negation of the coefficient, because L_{aux} is in standard rather than slack form.) Since $l \in B$, we also have that $a_{le} = -1$. Thus, $b_l/a_{le} > 0$, and so $\bar{x}_e > 0$. For the remaining basic variables, we have

$$
\begin{aligned}
\bar{x}_i &= b_i - a_{ie}\hat{b}_e & \text{(by equation (29.113))} \\
&= b_i - a_{ie}(b_l/a_{le}) & \text{(by line 3 of PIVOT)} \\
&= b_i - b_l & \text{(by equation (29.115) and } a_{le} = -1) \\
&\ge 0 & \text{(by inequality (29.112))}\,,
\end{aligned}
$$

which implies that each basic variable is now nonnegative. Hence the basic solution after the call to PIVOT in line 8 is feasible. We next execute line 10, which solves L_{aux}. Since we have assumed that L has a feasible solution, Lemma 29.11 implies that L_{aux} has an optimal solution with objective value 0. Since all the slack forms are equivalent, the final basic solution to L_{aux} must have $\bar{x}_0 = 0$, and after removing x_0 from the linear program, we obtain a slack form that is feasible for L. Line 15 then returns this slack form.   ∎

Fundamental theorem of linear programming

We conclude this chapter by showing that the SIMPLEX procedure works. In particular, any linear program either is infeasible, is unbounded, or has an optimal solution with a finite objective value. In each case, SIMPLEX acts appropriately.

Theorem 29.13 (Fundamental theorem of linear programming)
Any linear program L, given in standard form, either

1. has an optimal solution with a finite objective value,

2. is infeasible, or

3. is unbounded.

If L is infeasible, SIMPLEX returns "infeasible." If L is unbounded, SIMPLEX returns "unbounded." Otherwise, SIMPLEX returns an optimal solution with a finite objective value.

Proof   By Lemma 29.12, if linear program L is infeasible, then SIMPLEX returns "infeasible." Now suppose that the linear program L is feasible. By Lemma 29.12, INITIALIZE-SIMPLEX returns a slack form for which the basic solution is feasible. By Lemma 29.7, therefore, SIMPLEX either returns "unbounded" or terminates with a feasible solution. If it terminates with a finite solution, then Theorem 29.10 tells us that this solution is optimal. On the other hand, if SIMPLEX returns "unbounded," Lemma 29.2 tells us the linear program L is indeed unbounded. Since SIMPLEX always terminates in one of these ways, the proof is complete.   ∎

Exercises

29.5-1
Give detailed pseudocode to implement lines 5 and 14 of INITIALIZE-SIMPLEX.

29.5-2
Show that when the main loop of SIMPLEX is run by INITIALIZE-SIMPLEX, it can never return "unbounded."

29.5-3
Suppose that we are given a linear program L in standard form, and suppose that for both L and the dual of L, the basic solutions associated with the initial slack forms are feasible. Show that the optimal objective value of L is 0.

29.5-4
Suppose that we allow strict inequalities in a linear program. Show that in this case, the fundamental theorem of linear programming does not hold.

29.5-5
Solve the following linear program using SIMPLEX:

$$\text{maximize} \quad x_1 \;+\; 3x_2$$

subject to

$$
\begin{array}{rcrcr}
x_1 & - & x_2 & \le & 8 \\
-x_1 & - & x_2 & \le & -3 \\
-x_1 & + & 4x_2 & \le & 2 \\
\multicolumn{3}{r}{x_1, x_2} & \ge & 0 \;.
\end{array}
$$

29.5-6
Solve the following linear program using SIMPLEX:

$$\text{maximize} \quad x_1 \;-\; 2x_2$$

subject to

$$
\begin{array}{rcrcr}
x_1 & + & 2x_2 & \le & 4 \\
-2x_1 & - & 6x_2 & \le & -12 \\
\multicolumn{3}{r}{x_2} & \le & 1 \\
\multicolumn{3}{r}{x_1, x_2} & \ge & 0 \;.
\end{array}
$$

29.5-7
Solve the following linear program using SIMPLEX:

$$\text{maximize} \quad x_1 \;+\; 3x_2$$

subject to

$$
\begin{array}{rcrcr}
-x_1 & + & x_2 & \le & -1 \\
-x_1 & - & x_2 & \le & -3 \\
-x_1 & + & 4x_2 & \le & 2 \\
\multicolumn{3}{r}{x_1, x_2} & \ge & 0 \;.
\end{array}
$$

29.5-8
Solve the linear program given in (29.6)–(29.10).

29.5-9
Consider the following 1-variable linear program, which we call P:

$$\text{maximize} \quad tx$$

subject to

$$
\begin{array}{rcl}
rx & \le & s \\
x & \ge & 0 \;,
\end{array}
$$

where r, s, and t are arbitrary real numbers. Let D be the dual of P.

State for which values of r, s, and t you can assert that

1. Both P and D have optimal solutions with finite objective values.
2. P is feasible, but D is infeasible.
3. D is feasible, but P is infeasible.
4. Neither P nor D is feasible.

Problems

29-1   *Linear-inequality feasibility*
Given a set of m linear inequalities on n variables $x_1, x_2, \ldots, x_n$, the *linear-inequality feasibility problem* asks whether there is a setting of the variables that simultaneously satisfies each of the inequalities.

a. Show that if we have an algorithm for linear programming, we can use it to solve a linear-inequality feasibility problem. The number of variables and constraints that you use in the linear-programming problem should be polynomial in n and m.

b. Show that if we have an algorithm for the linear-inequality feasibility problem, we can use it to solve a linear-programming problem. The number of variables and linear inequalities that you use in the linear-inequality feasibility problem should be polynomial in n and m, the number of variables and constraints in the linear program.

29-2   *Complementary slackness*
Complementary slackness describes a relationship between the values of primal variables and dual constraints and between the values of dual variables and primal constraints. Let $\bar{x}$ be a feasible solution to the primal linear program given in (29.16)–(29.18), and let $\bar{y}$ be a feasible solution to the dual linear program given in (29.83)–(29.85). Complementary slackness states that the following conditions are necessary and sufficient for $\bar{x}$ and $\bar{y}$ to be optimal:

$$\sum_{i=1}^{m} a_{ij}\bar{y}_i = c_j \text{ or } \bar{x}_j = 0 \quad \text{for } j = 1, 2, \ldots, n$$

and

$$\sum_{j=1}^{n} a_{ij}\bar{x}_j = b_i \text{ or } \bar{y}_i = 0 \quad \text{for } i = 1, 2, \ldots, m \text{ .}$$

a. Verify that complementary slackness holds for the linear program in lines (29.53)–(29.57).

b. Prove that complementary slackness holds for any primal linear program and its corresponding dual.

c. Prove that a feasible solution $\bar{x}$ to a primal linear program given in lines (29.16)–(29.18) is optimal if and only if there exist values $\bar{y} = (\bar{y}_1, \bar{y}_2, \ldots, \bar{y}_m)$ such that

1. $\bar{y}$ is a feasible solution to the dual linear program given in (29.83)–(29.85),
2. $\sum_{i=1}^{m} a_{ij} \bar{y}_i = c_j$ for all j such that $\bar{x}_j > 0$, and
3. $\bar{y}_i = 0$ for all i such that $\sum_{j=1}^{n} a_{ij} \bar{x}_j < b_i$.

29-3   *Integer linear programming*

An *integer linear-programming problem* is a linear-programming problem with the additional constraint that the variables x must take on integral values. Exercise 34.5-3 shows that just determining whether an integer linear program has a feasible solution is NP-hard, which means that there is no known polynomial-time algorithm for this problem.

a. Show that weak duality (Lemma 29.8) holds for an integer linear program.

b. Show that duality (Theorem 29.10) does not always hold for an integer linear program.

c. Given a primal linear program in standard form, let us define P to be the optimal objective value for the primal linear program, D to be the optimal objective value for its dual, IP to be the optimal objective value for the integer version of the primal (that is, the primal with the added constraint that the variables take on integer values), and ID to be the optimal objective value for the integer version of the dual. Assuming that both the primal integer program and the dual integer program are feasible and bounded, show that

$$IP \leq P = D \leq ID .$$

29-4   *Farkas's lemma*

Let A be an $m \times n$ matrix and c be an n-vector. Then Farkas's lemma states that exactly one of the systems

$$
\begin{aligned}
Ax &\leq 0 , \\
c^\mathrm{T} x &> 0
\end{aligned}
$$

and

$$
\begin{aligned}
A^\mathrm{T} y &= c , \\
y &\geq 0
\end{aligned}
$$

is solvable, where x is an n-vector and y is an m-vector. Prove Farkas's lemma.

29-5   *Minimum-cost circulation*

In this problem, we consider a variant of the minimum-cost-flow problem from Section 29.2 in which we are not given a demand, a source, or a sink. Instead, we are given, as before, a flow network and edge costs $a(u, v)$. A flow is feasible if it satisfies the capacity constraint on every edge and flow conservation at *every* vertex. The goal is to find, among all feasible flows, the one of minimum cost. We call this problem the ***minimum-cost-circulation problem.***

a. Formulate the minimum-cost-circulation problem as a linear program.

b. Suppose that for all edges $(u, v) \in E$, we have $a(u, v) > 0$. Characterize an optimal solution to the minimum-cost-circulation problem.

c. Formulate the maximum-flow problem as a minimum-cost-circulation problem linear program. That is given a maximum-flow problem instance $G = (V, E)$ with source s, sink t and edge capacities c, create a minimum-cost-circulation problem by giving a (possibly different) network $G' = (V', E')$ with edge capacities c' and edge costs a' such that you can discern a solution to the maximum-flow problem from a solution to the minimum-cost-circulation problem.

d. Formulate the single-source shortest-path problem as a minimum-cost-circulation problem linear program.

Chapter notes

This chapter only begins to study the wide field of linear programming. A number of books are devoted exclusively to linear programming, including those by Chvátal [69], Gass [130], Karloff [197], Schrijver [303], and Vanderbei [344]. Many other books give a good coverage of linear programming, including those by Papadimitriou and Steiglitz [271] and Ahuja, Magnanti, and Orlin [7]. The coverage in this chapter draws on the approach taken by Chvátal.

The simplex algorithm for linear programming was invented by G. Dantzig in 1947. Shortly after, researchers discovered how to formulate a number of problems in a variety of fields as linear programs and solve them with the simplex algorithm. As a result, applications of linear programming flourished, along with several algorithms. Variants of the simplex algorithm remain the most popular methods for solving linear-programming problems. This history appears in a number of places, including the notes in [69] and [197].

The ellipsoid algorithm was the first polynomial-time algorithm for linear programming and is due to L. G. Khachian in 1979; it was based on earlier work by N. Z. Shor, D. B. Judin, and A. S. Nemirovskii. Grötschel, Lovász, and Schrijver [154] describe how to use the ellipsoid algorithm to solve a variety of problems in combinatorial optimization. To date, the ellipsoid algorithm does not appear to be competitive with the simplex algorithm in practice.

Karmarkar's paper [198] includes a description of the first interior-point algorithm. Many subsequent researchers designed interior-point algorithms. Good surveys appear in the article of Goldfarb and Todd [141] and the book by Ye [361].

Analysis of the simplex algorithm remains an active area of research. V. Klee and G. J. Minty constructed an example on which the simplex algorithm runs through $2^n - 1$ iterations. The simplex algorithm usually performs very well in practice and many researchers have tried to give theoretical justification for this empirical observation. A line of research begun by K. H. Borgwardt, and carried on by many others, shows that under certain probabilistic assumptions on the input, the simplex algorithm converges in expected polynomial time. Spielman and Teng [322] made progress in this area, introducing the "smoothed analysis of algorithms" and applying it to the simplex algorithm.

The simplex algorithm is known to run efficiently in certain special cases. Particularly noteworthy is the network-simplex algorithm, which is the simplex algorithm, specialized to network-flow problems. For certain network problems, including the shortest-paths, maximum-flow, and minimum-cost-flow problems, variants of the network-simplex algorithm run in polynomial time. See, for example, the article by Orlin [268] and the citations therein.

30 Polynomials and the FFT

The straightforward method of adding two polynomials of degree n takes $\Theta(n)$ time, but the straightforward method of multiplying them takes $\Theta(n^2)$ time. In this chapter, we shall show how the fast Fourier transform, or FFT, can reduce the time to multiply polynomials to $\Theta(n \lg n)$.

The most common use for Fourier transforms, and hence the FFT, is in signal processing. A signal is given in the **time domain**: as a function mapping time to amplitude. Fourier analysis allows us to express the signal as a weighted sum of phase-shifted sinusoids of varying frequencies. The weights and phases associated with the frequencies characterize the signal in the **frequency domain**. Among the many everyday applications of FFT's are compression techniques used to encode digital video and audio information, including MP3 files. Several fine books delve into the rich area of signal processing; the chapter notes reference a few of them.

Polynomials

A **polynomial** in the variable x over an algebraic field F represents a function $A(x)$ as a formal sum:

$$A(x) = \sum_{j=0}^{n-1} a_j x^j \ .$$

We call the values $a_0, a_1, \ldots, a_{n-1}$ the **coefficients** of the polynomial. The coefficients are drawn from a field F, typically the set $\mathbb{C}$ of complex numbers. A polynomial $A(x)$ has **degree** k if its highest nonzero coefficient is a_k; we write that degree$(A) = k$. Any integer strictly greater than the degree of a polynomial is a **degree-bound** of that polynomial. Therefore, the degree of a polynomial of degree-bound n may be any integer between 0 and $n - 1$, inclusive.

We can define a variety of operations on polynomials. For **polynomial addition**, if $A(x)$ and $B(x)$ are polynomials of degree-bound n, their **sum** is a polynomial $C(x)$, also of degree-bound n, such that $C(x) = A(x) + B(x)$ for all x in the underlying field. That is, if

$$A(x) = \sum_{j=0}^{n-1} a_j x^j$$

and

$$B(x) = \sum_{j=0}^{n-1} b_j x^j \; ,$$

then

$$C(x) = \sum_{j=0}^{n-1} c_j x^j \; ,$$

where $c_j = a_j + b_j$ for $j = 0, 1, \ldots, n - 1$. For example, if we have the polynomials $A(x) = 6x^3 + 7x^2 - 10x + 9$ and $B(x) = -2x^3 + 4x - 5$, then $C(x) = 4x^3 + 7x^2 - 6x + 4$.

For ***polynomial multiplication***, if $A(x)$ and $B(x)$ are polynomials of degree-bound n, their ***product*** $C(x)$ is a polynomial of degree-bound $2n - 1$ such that $C(x) = A(x)B(x)$ for all x in the underlying field. You probably have multiplied polynomials before, by multiplying each term in $A(x)$ by each term in $B(x)$ and then combining terms with equal powers. For example, we can multiply $A(x) = 6x^3 + 7x^2 - 10x + 9$ and $B(x) = -2x^3 + 4x - 5$ as follows:

$$
\begin{array}{r}
6x^3 + 7x^2 - 10x + 9 \\
- 2x^3 \qquad\quad + 4x - 5 \\
\hline
- 30x^3 - 35x^2 + 50x - 45 \\
24x^4 + 28x^3 - 40x^2 + 36x \\
- 12x^6 - 14x^5 + 20x^4 - 18x^3 \\
\hline
- 12x^6 - 14x^5 + 44x^4 - 20x^3 - 75x^2 + 86x - 45
\end{array}
$$

Another way to express the product $C(x)$ is

$$C(x) = \sum_{j=0}^{2n-2} c_j x^j \; , \tag{30.1}$$

where

$$c_j = \sum_{k=0}^{j} a_k b_{j-k} \; . \tag{30.2}$$

Note that degree(C) = degree(A) + degree(B), implying that if A is a polynomial of degree-bound n_a and B is a polynomial of degree-bound n_b, then C is a polynomial of degree-bound $n_a + n_b - 1$. Since a polynomial of degree-bound k is also a polynomial of degree-bound $k + 1$, we will normally say that the product polynomial C is a polynomial of degree-bound $n_a + n_b$.

Chapter outline

Section 30.1 presents two ways to represent polynomials: the coefficient representation and the point-value representation. The straightforward method for multiplying polynomials—equations (30.1) and (30.2)—takes $\Theta(n^2)$ time when we represent polynomials in coefficient form, but only $\Theta(n)$ time when we represent them in point-value form. We can, however, multiply polynomials using the coefficient representation in only $\Theta(n \lg n)$ time by converting between the two representations. To see why this approach works, we must first study complex roots of unity, which we do in Section 30.2. Then, we use the FFT and its inverse, also described in Section 30.2, to perform the conversions. Section 30.3 shows how to implement the FFT quickly in both serial and parallel models.

This chapter uses complex numbers extensively, and within this chapter we use the symbol i exclusively to denote $\sqrt{-1}$.

30.1   Representing polynomials

The coefficient and point-value representations of polynomials are in a sense equivalent; that is, a polynomial in point-value form has a unique counterpart in coefficient form. In this section, we introduce the two representations and show how to combine them so that we can multiply two degree-bound n polynomials in $\Theta(n \lg n)$ time.

Coefficient representation

A **coefficient representation** of a polynomial $A(x) = \sum_{j=0}^{n-1} a_j x^j$ of degree-bound n is a vector of coefficients $a = (a_0, a_1, \ldots, a_{n-1})$. In matrix equations in this chapter, we shall generally treat vectors as column vectors.

The coefficient representation is convenient for certain operations on polynomials. For example, the operation of **evaluating** the polynomial $A(x)$ at a given point x_0 consists of computing the value of $A(x_0)$. We can evaluate a polynomial in $\Theta(n)$ time using **Horner's rule**:

$$A(x_0) = a_0 + x_0(a_1 + x_0(a_2 + \cdots + x_0(a_{n-2} + x_0(a_{n-1}))\cdots)) .$$

Similarly, adding two polynomials represented by the coefficient vectors $a = (a_0, a_1, \ldots, a_{n-1})$ and $b = (b_0, b_1, \ldots, b_{n-1})$ takes $\Theta(n)$ time: we just produce the coefficient vector $c = (c_0, c_1, \ldots, c_{n-1})$, where $c_j = a_j + b_j$ for $j = 0, 1, \ldots, n - 1$.

Now, consider multiplying two degree-bound n polynomials $A(x)$ and $B(x)$ represented in coefficient form. If we use the method described by equations (30.1) and (30.2), multiplying polynomials takes time $\Theta(n^2)$, since we must multiply each coefficient in the vector a by each coefficient in the vector b. The operation of multiplying polynomials in coefficient form seems to be considerably more difficult than that of evaluating a polynomial or adding two polynomials. The resulting coefficient vector c, given by equation (30.2), is also called the ***convolution*** of the input vectors a and b, denoted $c = a \otimes b$. Since multiplying polynomials and computing convolutions are fundamental computational problems of considerable practical importance, this chapter concentrates on efficient algorithms for them.

Point-value representation

A ***point-value representation*** of a polynomial $A(x)$ of degree-bound n is a set of n ***point-value pairs***

$$\{(x_0, y_0), (x_1, y_1), \ldots, (x_{n-1}, y_{n-1})\}$$

such that all of the x_k are distinct and

$$y_k = A(x_k) \tag{30.3}$$

for $k = 0, 1, \ldots, n - 1$. A polynomial has many different point-value representations, since we can use any set of n distinct points $x_0, x_1, \ldots, x_{n-1}$ as a basis for the representation.

Computing a point-value representation for a polynomial given in coefficient form is in principle straightforward, since all we have to do is select n distinct points $x_0, x_1, \ldots, x_{n-1}$ and then evaluate $A(x_k)$ for $k = 0, 1, \ldots, n - 1$. With Horner's method, evaluating a polynomial at n points takes time $\Theta(n^2)$. We shall see later that if we choose the points x_k cleverly, we can accelerate this computation to run in time $\Theta(n \lg n)$.

The inverse of evaluation—determining the coefficient form of a polynomial from a point-value representation—is ***interpolation***. The following theorem shows that interpolation is well defined when the desired interpolating polynomial must have a degree-bound equal to the given number of point-value pairs.

Theorem 30.1 (Uniqueness of an interpolating polynomial)
For any set $\{(x_0, y_0), (x_1, y_1), \ldots, (x_{n-1}, y_{n-1})\}$ of n point-value pairs such that all the x_k values are distinct, there is a unique polynomial $A(x)$ of degree-bound n such that $y_k = A(x_k)$ for $k = 0, 1, \ldots, n - 1$.

Proof   The proof relies on the existence of the inverse of a certain matrix. Equation (30.3) is equivalent to the matrix equation

$$
\begin{pmatrix}
1 & x_0 & x_0^2 & \cdots & x_0^{n-1} \\
1 & x_1 & x_1^2 & \cdots & x_1^{n-1} \\
\vdots & \vdots & \vdots & \ddots & \vdots \\
1 & x_{n-1} & x_{n-1}^2 & \cdots & x_{n-1}^{n-1}
\end{pmatrix}
\begin{pmatrix}
a_0 \\
a_1 \\
\vdots \\
a_{n-1}
\end{pmatrix}
=
\begin{pmatrix}
y_0 \\
y_1 \\
\vdots \\
y_{n-1}
\end{pmatrix}. \tag{30.4}
$$

The matrix on the left is denoted $V(x_0, x_1, \ldots, x_{n-1})$ and is known as a Vandermonde matrix. By Problem D-1, this matrix has determinant

$$
\prod_{0 \le j < k \le n-1} (x_k - x_j),
$$

and therefore, by Theorem D.5, it is invertible (that is, nonsingular) if the x_k are distinct. Thus, we can solve for the coefficients a_j uniquely given the point-value representation:

$$
a = V(x_0, x_1, \ldots, x_{n-1})^{-1} y .
$$ ∎

The proof of Theorem 30.1 describes an algorithm for interpolation based on solving the set (30.4) of linear equations. Using the LU decomposition algorithms of Chapter 28, we can solve these equations in time $O(n^3)$.

A faster algorithm for n-point interpolation is based on ***Lagrange's formula***:

$$
A(x) = \sum_{k=0}^{n-1} y_k \frac{\displaystyle\prod_{j \ne k}(x - x_j)}{\displaystyle\prod_{j \ne k}(x_k - x_j)} . \tag{30.5}
$$

You may wish to verify that the right-hand side of equation (30.5) is a polynomial of degree-bound n that satisfies $A(x_k) = y_k$ for all k. Exercise 30.1-5 asks you how to compute the coefficients of A using Lagrange's formula in time $\Theta(n^2)$.

Thus, n-point evaluation and interpolation are well-defined inverse operations that transform between the coefficient representation of a polynomial and a point-value representation.[1]   The algorithms described above for these problems take time $\Theta(n^2)$.

The point-value representation is quite convenient for many operations on polynomials. For addition, if $C(x) = A(x) + B(x)$, then $C(x_k) = A(x_k) + B(x_k)$ for any point x_k. More precisely, if we have a point-value representation for A,

---

[1] Interpolation is a notoriously tricky problem from the point of view of numerical stability. Although the approaches described here are mathematically correct, small differences in the inputs or round-off errors during computation can cause large differences in the result.

$$\{(x_0, y_0), (x_1, y_1), \ldots, (x_{n-1}, y_{n-1})\} \;,$$

and for B,

$$\{(x_0, y_0'), (x_1, y_1'), \ldots, (x_{n-1}, y_{n-1}')\}$$

(note that A and B are evaluated at the *same* n points), then a point-value representation for C is

$$\{(x_0, y_0 + y_0'), (x_1, y_1 + y_1'), \ldots, (x_{n-1}, y_{n-1} + y_{n-1}')\} \;.$$

Thus, the time to add two polynomials of degree-bound n in point-value form is $\Theta(n)$.

Similarly, the point-value representation is convenient for multiplying polynomials. If $C(x) = A(x)B(x)$, then $C(x_k) = A(x_k)B(x_k)$ for any point x_k, and we can pointwise multiply a point-value representation for A by a point-value representation for B to obtain a point-value representation for C. We must face the problem, however, that degree$(C) = $ degree$(A) + $ degree(B); if A and B are of degree-bound n, then C is of degree-bound $2n$. A standard point-value representation for A and B consists of n point-value pairs for each polynomial. When we multiply these together, we get n point-value pairs, but we need $2n$ pairs to interpolate a unique polynomial C of degree-bound $2n$. (See Exercise 30.1-4.) We must therefore begin with "extended" point-value representations for A and for B consisting of $2n$ point-value pairs each. Given an extended point-value representation for A,

$$\{(x_0, y_0), (x_1, y_1), \ldots, (x_{2n-1}, y_{2n-1})\} \;,$$

and a corresponding extended point-value representation for B,

$$\{(x_0, y_0'), (x_1, y_1'), \ldots, (x_{2n-1}, y_{2n-1}')\} \;,$$

then a point-value representation for C is

$$\{(x_0, y_0 y_0'), (x_1, y_1 y_1'), \ldots, (x_{2n-1}, y_{2n-1} y_{2n-1}')\} \;.$$

Given two input polynomials in extended point-value form, we see that the time to multiply them to obtain the point-value form of the result is $\Theta(n)$, much less than the time required to multiply polynomials in coefficient form.

Finally, we consider how to evaluate a polynomial given in point-value form at a new point. For this problem, we know of no simpler approach than converting the polynomial to coefficient form first, and then evaluating it at the new point.

Fast multiplication of polynomials in coefficient form

Can we use the linear-time multiplication method for polynomials in point-value form to expedite polynomial multiplication in coefficient form? The answer hinges

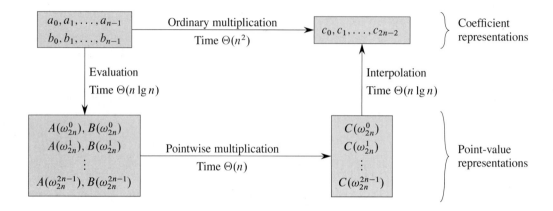

Figure 30.1 A graphical outline of an efficient polynomial-multiplication process. Representations on the top are in coefficient form, while those on the bottom are in point-value form. The arrows from left to right correspond to the multiplication operation. The ω_{2n} terms are complex $(2n)$th roots of unity.

on whether we can convert a polynomial quickly from coefficient form to point-value form (evaluate) and vice versa (interpolate).

We can use any points we want as evaluation points, but by choosing the evaluation points carefully, we can convert between representations in only $\Theta(n \lg n)$ time. As we shall see in Section 30.2, if we choose "complex roots of unity" as the evaluation points, we can produce a point-value representation by taking the discrete Fourier transform (or DFT) of a coefficient vector. We can perform the inverse operation, interpolation, by taking the "inverse DFT" of point-value pairs, yielding a coefficient vector. Section 30.2 will show how the FFT accomplishes the DFT and inverse DFT operations in $\Theta(n \lg n)$ time.

Figure 30.1 shows this strategy graphically. One minor detail concerns degree-bounds. The product of two polynomials of degree-bound n is a polynomial of degree-bound $2n$. Before evaluating the input polynomials A and B, therefore, we first double their degree-bounds to $2n$ by adding n high-order coefficients of 0. Because the vectors have $2n$ elements, we use "complex $(2n)$th roots of unity," which are denoted by the ω_{2n} terms in Figure 30.1.

Given the FFT, we have the following $\Theta(n \lg n)$-time procedure for multiplying two polynomials $A(x)$ and $B(x)$ of degree-bound n, where the input and output representations are in coefficient form. We assume that n is a power of 2; we can always meet this requirement by adding high-order zero coefficients.

1. *Double degree-bound:* Create coefficient representations of $A(x)$ and $B(x)$ as degree-bound $2n$ polynomials by adding n high-order zero coefficients to each.

2. *Evaluate:* Compute point-value representations of $A(x)$ and $B(x)$ of length $2n$ by applying the FFT of order $2n$ on each polynomial. These representations contain the values of the two polynomials at the $(2n)$th roots of unity.

3. *Pointwise multiply:* Compute a point-value representation for the polynomial $C(x) = A(x)B(x)$ by multiplying these values together pointwise. This representation contains the value of $C(x)$ at each $(2n)$th root of unity.

4. *Interpolate:* Create the coefficient representation of the polynomial $C(x)$ by applying the FFT on $2n$ point-value pairs to compute the inverse DFT.

Steps (1) and (3) take time $\Theta(n)$, and steps (2) and (4) take time $\Theta(n \lg n)$. Thus, once we show how to use the FFT, we will have proven the following.

Theorem 30.2
We can multiply two polynomials of degree-bound n in time $\Theta(n \lg n)$, with both the input and output representations in coefficient form.   ∎

Exercises

30.1-1
Multiply the polynomials $A(x) = 7x^3 - x^2 + x - 10$ and $B(x) = 8x^3 - 6x + 3$ using equations (30.1) and (30.2).

30.1-2
Another way to evaluate a polynomial $A(x)$ of degree-bound n at a given point x_0 is to divide $A(x)$ by the polynomial $(x - x_0)$, obtaining a quotient polynomial $q(x)$ of degree-bound $n - 1$ and a remainder r, such that

$$A(x) = q(x)(x - x_0) + r .$$

Clearly, $A(x_0) = r$. Show how to compute the remainder r and the coefficients of $q(x)$ in time $\Theta(n)$ from x_0 and the coefficients of A.

30.1-3
Derive a point-value representation for $A^{\text{rev}}(x) = \sum_{j=0}^{n-1} a_{n-1-j} x^j$ from a point-value representation for $A(x) = \sum_{j=0}^{n-1} a_j x^j$, assuming that none of the points is 0.

30.1-4
Prove that n distinct point-value pairs are necessary to uniquely specify a polynomial of degree-bound n, that is, if fewer than n distinct point-value pairs are given, they fail to specify a unique polynomial of degree-bound n. (*Hint:* Using Theorem 30.1, what can you say about a set of $n - 1$ point-value pairs to which you add one more arbitrarily chosen point-value pair?)

30.1-5

Show how to use equation (30.5) to interpolate in time $\Theta(n^2)$. (*Hint:* First compute the coefficient representation of the polynomial $\prod_j (x - x_j)$ and then divide by $(x - x_k)$ as necessary for the numerator of each term; see Exercise 30.1-2. You can compute each of the n denominators in time $O(n)$.)

30.1-6

Explain what is wrong with the "obvious" approach to polynomial division using a point-value representation, i.e., dividing the corresponding y values. Discuss separately the case in which the division comes out exactly and the case in which it doesn't.

30.1-7

Consider two sets A and B, each having n integers in the range from 0 to $10n$. We wish to compute the ***Cartesian sum*** of A and B, defined by

$$C = \{x + y : x \in A \text{ and } y \in B\} \ .$$

Note that the integers in C are in the range from 0 to $20n$. We want to find the elements of C and the number of times each element of C is realized as a sum of elements in A and B. Show how to solve the problem in $O(n \lg n)$ time. (*Hint:* Represent A and B as polynomials of degree at most $10n$.)

30.2   The DFT and FFT

In Section 30.1, we claimed that if we use complex roots of unity, we can evaluate and interpolate polynomials in $\Theta(n \lg n)$ time. In this section, we define complex roots of unity and study their properties, define the DFT, and then show how the FFT computes the DFT and its inverse in $\Theta(n \lg n)$ time.

Complex roots of unity

A ***complex nth root of unity*** is a complex number ω such that

$$\omega^n = 1 \ .$$

There are exactly n complex nth roots of unity: $e^{2\pi i k/n}$ for $k = 0, 1, \ldots, n - 1$. To interpret this formula, we use the definition of the exponential of a complex number:

$$e^{iu} = \cos(u) + i \sin(u) \ .$$

Figure 30.2 shows that the n complex roots of unity are equally spaced around the circle of unit radius centered at the origin of the complex plane. The value

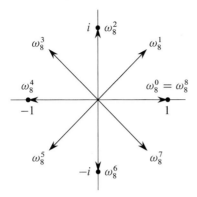

Figure 30.2   The values of $\omega_8^0, \omega_8^1, \ldots, \omega_8^7$ in the complex plane, where $\omega_8 = e^{2\pi i/8}$ is the principal 8th root of unity.

$$\omega_n = e^{2\pi i/n} \tag{30.6}$$

is the ***principal nth root of unity***;[2] all other complex nth roots of unity are powers of ω_n.

The n complex nth roots of unity,

$$\omega_n^0, \omega_n^1, \ldots, \omega_n^{n-1} \,,$$

form a group under multiplication (see Section 31.3). This group has the same structure as the additive group $(\mathbb{Z}_n, +)$ modulo n, since $\omega_n^n = \omega_n^0 = 1$ implies that $\omega_n^j \omega_n^k = \omega_n^{j+k} = \omega_n^{(j+k) \bmod n}$. Similarly, $\omega_n^{-1} = \omega_n^{n-1}$. The following lemmas furnish some essential properties of the complex nth roots of unity.

Lemma 30.3 (Cancellation lemma)
For any integers $n \geq 0$, $k \geq 0$, and $d > 0$,

$$\omega_{dn}^{dk} = \omega_n^k \,. \tag{30.7}$$

Proof   The lemma follows directly from equation (30.6), since

$$
\begin{aligned}
\omega_{dn}^{dk} &= \left(e^{2\pi i/dn}\right)^{dk} \\
&= \left(e^{2\pi i/n}\right)^{k} \\
&= \omega_n^k \,.
\end{aligned}
$$

■

---

[2]Many other authors define ω_n differently: $\omega_n = e^{-2\pi i/n}$. This alternative definition tends to be used for signal-processing applications. The underlying mathematics is substantially the same with either definition of ω_n.

Corollary 30.4
For any even integer $n > 0$,

$$\omega_n^{n/2} = \omega_2 = -1 \; .$$

Proof   The proof is left as Exercise 30.2-1.   ∎

Lemma 30.5 (Halving lemma)
If $n > 0$ is even, then the squares of the n complex nth roots of unity are the $n/2$ complex $(n/2)$th roots of unity.

Proof   By the cancellation lemma, we have $(\omega_n^k)^2 = \omega_{n/2}^k$, for any nonnegative integer k. Note that if we square all of the complex nth roots of unity, then we obtain each $(n/2)$th root of unity exactly twice, since

$$
\begin{aligned}
(\omega_n^{k+n/2})^2 &= \omega_n^{2k+n} \\
&= \omega_n^{2k} \omega_n^{n} \\
&= \omega_n^{2k} \\
&= (\omega_n^k)^2 \; .
\end{aligned}
$$

Thus, ω_n^k and $\omega_n^{k+n/2}$ have the same square. We could also have used Corollary 30.4 to prove this property, since $\omega_n^{n/2} = -1$ implies $\omega_n^{k+n/2} = -\omega_n^k$, and thus $(\omega_n^{k+n/2})^2 = (\omega_n^k)^2$.   ∎

As we shall see, the halving lemma is essential to our divide-and-conquer approach for converting between coefficient and point-value representations of polynomials, since it guarantees that the recursive subproblems are only half as large.

Lemma 30.6 (Summation lemma)
For any integer $n \geq 1$ and nonzero integer k not divisible by n,

$$\sum_{j=0}^{n-1} (\omega_n^k)^j = 0 \; .$$

Proof   Equation (A.5) applies to complex values as well as to reals, and so we have

$$\sum_{j=0}^{n-1} \left(\omega_n^k\right)^j = \frac{(\omega_n^k)^n - 1}{\omega_n^k - 1}$$

$$= \frac{(\omega_n^n)^k - 1}{\omega_n^k - 1}$$

$$= \frac{(1)^k - 1}{\omega_n^k - 1}$$

$$= 0 .$$

Because we require that k is not divisible by n, and because $\omega_n^k = 1$ only when k is divisible by n, we ensure that the denominator is not 0.   ∎

The DFT

Recall that we wish to evaluate a polynomial

$$A(x) = \sum_{j=0}^{n-1} a_j x^j$$

of degree-bound n at $\omega_n^0, \omega_n^1, \omega_n^2, \ldots, \omega_n^{n-1}$ (that is, at the n complex nth roots of unity).[3] We assume that A is given in coefficient form: $a = (a_0, a_1, \ldots, a_{n-1})$. Let us define the results y_k, for $k = 0, 1, \ldots, n-1$, by

$$y_k = A(\omega_n^k)$$

$$= \sum_{j=0}^{n-1} a_j \omega_n^{kj} . \tag{30.8}$$

The vector $y = (y_0, y_1, \ldots, y_{n-1})$ is the ***discrete Fourier transform (DFT)*** of the coefficient vector $a = (a_0, a_1, \ldots, a_{n-1})$. We also write $y = \text{DFT}_n(a)$.

The FFT

By using a method known as the ***fast Fourier transform (FFT)***, which takes advantage of the special properties of the complex roots of unity, we can compute $\text{DFT}_n(a)$ in time $\Theta(n \lg n)$, as opposed to the $\Theta(n^2)$ time of the straightforward method. We assume throughout that n is an exact power of 2. Although strategies

---

[3]The length n is actually what we referred to as $2n$ in Section 30.1, since we double the degree-bound of the given polynomials prior to evaluation. In the context of polynomial multiplication, therefore, we are actually working with complex $(2n)$th roots of unity.

for dealing with non-power-of-2 sizes are known, they are beyond the scope of this book.

The FFT method employs a divide-and-conquer strategy, using the even-indexed and odd-indexed coefficients of $A(x)$ separately to define the two new polynomials $A^{[0]}(x)$ and $A^{[1]}(x)$ of degree-bound $n/2$:

$$
\begin{aligned}
A^{[0]}(x) &= a_0 + a_2 x + a_4 x^2 + \cdots + a_{n-2} x^{n/2-1} , \\
A^{[1]}(x) &= a_1 + a_3 x + a_5 x^2 + \cdots + a_{n-1} x^{n/2-1} .
\end{aligned}
$$

Note that $A^{[0]}$ contains all the even-indexed coefficients of A (the binary representation of the index ends in 0) and $A^{[1]}$ contains all the odd-indexed coefficients (the binary representation of the index ends in 1). It follows that

$$
A(x) = A^{[0]}(x^2) + x A^{[1]}(x^2) , \tag{30.9}
$$

so that the problem of evaluating $A(x)$ at $\omega_n^0, \omega_n^1, \ldots, \omega_n^{n-1}$ reduces to

1. evaluating the degree-bound $n/2$ polynomials $A^{[0]}(x)$ and $A^{[1]}(x)$ at the points

    $$
    (\omega_n^0)^2, (\omega_n^1)^2, \ldots, (\omega_n^{n-1})^2 , \tag{30.10}
    $$

    and then

2. combining the results according to equation (30.9).

By the halving lemma, the list of values (30.10) consists not of n distinct values but only of the $n/2$ complex $(n/2)$th roots of unity, with each root occurring exactly twice. Therefore, we recursively evaluate the polynomials $A^{[0]}$ and $A^{[1]}$ of degree-bound $n/2$ at the $n/2$ complex $(n/2)$th roots of unity. These subproblems have exactly the same form as the original problem, but are half the size. We have now successfully divided an n-element DFT_n computation into two $n/2$-element $\mathrm{DFT}_{n/2}$ computations. This decomposition is the basis for the following recursive FFT algorithm, which computes the DFT of an n-element vector $a = (a_0, a_1, \ldots, a_{n-1})$, where n is a power of 2.

RECURSIVE-FFT(a)

```
 1  n = a.length                  // n is a power of 2
 2  if n == 1
 3       return a
 4  ω_n = e^{2πi/n}
 5  ω = 1
 6  a^{[0]} = (a_0, a_2, ..., a_{n-2})
 7  a^{[1]} = (a_1, a_3, ..., a_{n-1})
 8  y^{[0]} = RECURSIVE-FFT(a^{[0]})
 9  y^{[1]} = RECURSIVE-FFT(a^{[1]})
10  for k = 0 to n/2 - 1
11       y_k = y_k^{[0]} + ω y_k^{[1]}
12       y_{k+(n/2)} = y_k^{[0]} - ω y_k^{[1]}
13       ω = ω ω_n
14  return y                      // y is assumed to be a column vector
```

The RECURSIVE-FFT procedure works as follows. Lines 2–3 represent the basis of the recursion; the DFT of one element is the element itself, since in this case

$$
\begin{aligned}
y_0 &= a_0 \omega_1^0 \\
    &= a_0 \cdot 1 \\
    &= a_0 .
\end{aligned}
$$

Lines 6–7 define the coefficient vectors for the polynomials $A^{[0]}$ and $A^{[1]}$. Lines 4, 5, and 13 guarantee that ω is updated properly so that whenever lines 11–12 are executed, we have $\omega = \omega_n^k$. (Keeping a running value of ω from iteration to iteration saves time over computing ω_n^k from scratch each time through the **for** loop.) Lines 8–9 perform the recursive $\mathrm{DFT}_{n/2}$ computations, setting, for $k = 0, 1, \ldots, n/2 - 1$,

$$
\begin{aligned}
y_k^{[0]} &= A^{[0]}(\omega_{n/2}^k) , \\
y_k^{[1]} &= A^{[1]}(\omega_{n/2}^k) ,
\end{aligned}
$$

or, since $\omega_{n/2}^k = \omega_n^{2k}$ by the cancellation lemma,

$$
\begin{aligned}
y_k^{[0]} &= A^{[0]}(\omega_n^{2k}) , \\
y_k^{[1]} &= A^{[1]}(\omega_n^{2k}) .
\end{aligned}
$$

Lines 11–12 combine the results of the recursive $\text{DFT}_{n/2}$ calculations. For $y_0, y_1,$ $\ldots, y_{n/2-1}$, line 11 yields

$$
\begin{aligned}
y_k &= y_k^{[0]} + \omega_n^k y_k^{[1]} \\
&= A^{[0]}(\omega_n^{2k}) + \omega_n^k A^{[1]}(\omega_n^{2k}) \\
&= A(\omega_n^k) \qquad\qquad \text{(by equation (30.9))} .
\end{aligned}
$$

For $y_{n/2}, y_{n/2+1}, \ldots, y_{n-1}$, letting $k = 0, 1, \ldots, n/2 - 1$, line 12 yields

$$
\begin{aligned}
y_{k+(n/2)} &= y_k^{[0]} - \omega_n^k y_k^{[1]} \\
&= y_k^{[0]} + \omega_n^{k+(n/2)} y_k^{[1]} \qquad\qquad \text{(since } \omega_n^{k+(n/2)} = -\omega_n^k\text{)} \\
&= A^{[0]}(\omega_n^{2k}) + \omega_n^{k+(n/2)} A^{[1]}(\omega_n^{2k}) \\
&= A^{[0]}(\omega_n^{2k+n}) + \omega_n^{k+(n/2)} A^{[1]}(\omega_n^{2k+n}) \quad \text{(since } \omega_n^{2k+n} = \omega_n^{2k}\text{)} \\
&= A(\omega_n^{k+(n/2)}) \qquad\qquad \text{(by equation (30.9))} .
\end{aligned}
$$

Thus, the vector y returned by RECURSIVE-FFT is indeed the DFT of the input vector a.

Lines 11 and 12 multiply each value $y_k^{[1]}$ by ω_n^k, for $k = 0, 1, \ldots, n/2 - 1$. Line 11 adds this product to $y_k^{[0]}$, and line 12 subtracts it. Because we use each factor ω_n^k in both its positive and negative forms, we call the factors ω_n^k *twiddle factors*.

To determine the running time of procedure RECURSIVE-FFT, we note that exclusive of the recursive calls, each invocation takes time $\Theta(n)$, where n is the length of the input vector. The recurrence for the running time is therefore

$$
\begin{aligned}
T(n) &= 2T(n/2) + \Theta(n) \\
&= \Theta(n \lg n) .
\end{aligned}
$$

Thus, we can evaluate a polynomial of degree-bound n at the complex nth roots of unity in time $\Theta(n \lg n)$ using the fast Fourier transform.

Interpolation at the complex roots of unity

We now complete the polynomial multiplication scheme by showing how to interpolate the complex roots of unity by a polynomial, which enables us to convert from point-value form back to coefficient form. We interpolate by writing the DFT as a matrix equation and then looking at the form of the matrix inverse.

From equation (30.4), we can write the DFT as the matrix product $y = V_n a$, where V_n is a Vandermonde matrix containing the appropriate powers of ω_n:

$$
\begin{pmatrix} y_0 \\ y_1 \\ y_2 \\ y_3 \\ \vdots \\ y_{n-1} \end{pmatrix} = \begin{pmatrix} 1 & 1 & 1 & 1 & \cdots & 1 \\ 1 & \omega_n & \omega_n^2 & \omega_n^3 & \cdots & \omega_n^{n-1} \\ 1 & \omega_n^2 & \omega_n^4 & \omega_n^6 & \cdots & \omega_n^{2(n-1)} \\ 1 & \omega_n^3 & \omega_n^6 & \omega_n^9 & \cdots & \omega_n^{3(n-1)} \\ \vdots & \vdots & \vdots & \vdots & \ddots & \vdots \\ 1 & \omega_n^{n-1} & \omega_n^{2(n-1)} & \omega_n^{3(n-1)} & \cdots & \omega_n^{(n-1)(n-1)} \end{pmatrix} \begin{pmatrix} a_0 \\ a_1 \\ a_2 \\ a_3 \\ \vdots \\ a_{n-1} \end{pmatrix}.
$$

The (k, j) entry of V_n is ω_n^{kj}, for $j, k = 0, 1, \ldots, n-1$. The exponents of the entries of V_n form a multiplication table.

For the inverse operation, which we write as $a = \mathrm{DFT}_n^{-1}(y)$, we proceed by multiplying y by the matrix V_n^{-1}, the inverse of V_n.

Theorem 30.7
For $j, k = 0, 1, \ldots, n-1$, the (j, k) entry of V_n^{-1} is ω_n^{-kj}/n.

Proof We show that $V_n^{-1} V_n = I_n$, the $n \times n$ identity matrix. Consider the (j, j') entry of $V_n^{-1} V_n$:

$$
\begin{aligned}
[V_n^{-1} V_n]_{jj'} &= \sum_{k=0}^{n-1} (\omega_n^{-kj}/n)(\omega_n^{kj'}) \\
&= \sum_{k=0}^{n-1} \omega_n^{k(j'-j)}/n .
\end{aligned}
$$

This summation equals 1 if $j' = j$, and it is 0 otherwise by the summation lemma (Lemma 30.6). Note that we rely on $-(n-1) \le j' - j \le n-1$, so that $j' - j$ is not divisible by n, in order for the summation lemma to apply. ∎

Given the inverse matrix V_n^{-1}, we have that $\mathrm{DFT}_n^{-1}(y)$ is given by

$$
a_j = \frac{1}{n} \sum_{k=0}^{n-1} y_k \omega_n^{-kj} \tag{30.11}
$$

for $j = 0, 1, \ldots, n-1$. By comparing equations (30.8) and (30.11), we see that by modifying the FFT algorithm to switch the roles of a and y, replace ω_n by ω_n^{-1}, and divide each element of the result by n, we compute the inverse DFT (see Exercise 30.2-4). Thus, we can compute DFT_n^{-1} in $\Theta(n \lg n)$ time as well.

We see that, by using the FFT and the inverse FFT, we can transform a polynomial of degree-bound n back and forth between its coefficient representation and a point-value representation in time $\Theta(n \lg n)$. In the context of polynomial multiplication, we have shown the following.

Theorem 30.8 (Convolution theorem)
For any two vectors a and b of length n, where n is a power of 2,

$$a \otimes b = \mathrm{DFT}_{2n}^{-1}(\mathrm{DFT}_{2n}(a) \cdot \mathrm{DFT}_{2n}(b)),$$

where the vectors a and b are padded with 0s to length $2n$ and $\cdot$ denotes the componentwise product of two $2n$-element vectors. ∎

Exercises

30.2-1
Prove Corollary 30.4.

30.2-2
Compute the DFT of the vector $(0, 1, 2, 3)$.

30.2-3
Do Exercise 30.1-1 by using the $\Theta(n \lg n)$-time scheme.

30.2-4
Write pseudocode to compute DFT_n^{-1} in $\Theta(n \lg n)$ time.

30.2-5
Describe the generalization of the FFT procedure to the case in which n is a power of 3. Give a recurrence for the running time, and solve the recurrence.

30.2-6 ★
Suppose that instead of performing an n-element FFT over the field of complex numbers (where n is even), we use the ring $\mathbb{Z}_m$ of integers modulo m, where $m = 2^{tn/2} + 1$ and t is an arbitrary positive integer. Use $\omega = 2^t$ instead of ω_n as a principal nth root of unity, modulo m. Prove that the DFT and the inverse DFT are well defined in this system.

30.2-7
Given a list of values $z_0, z_1, \ldots, z_{n-1}$ (possibly with repetitions), show how to find the coefficients of a polynomial $P(x)$ of degree-bound $n + 1$ that has zeros only at $z_0, z_1, \ldots, z_{n-1}$ (possibly with repetitions). Your procedure should run in time $O(n \lg^2 n)$. (*Hint:* The polynomial $P(x)$ has a zero at z_j if and only if $P(x)$ is a multiple of $(x - z_j)$.)

30.2-8 ★
The ***chirp transform*** of a vector $a = (a_0, a_1, \ldots, a_{n-1})$ is the vector $y = (y_0, y_1, \ldots, y_{n-1})$, where $y_k = \sum_{j=0}^{n-1} a_j z^{kj}$ and z is any complex number. The

DFT is therefore a special case of the chirp transform, obtained by taking $z = \omega_n$. Show how to evaluate the chirp transform in time $O(n \lg n)$ for any complex number z. (*Hint:* Use the equation

$$y_k = z^{k^2/2} \sum_{j=0}^{n-1} \left(a_j z^{j^2/2} \right) \left(z^{-(k-j)^2/2} \right)$$

to view the chirp transform as a convolution.)

30.3 Efficient FFT implementations

Since the practical applications of the DFT, such as signal processing, demand the utmost speed, this section examines two efficient FFT implementations. First, we shall examine an iterative version of the FFT algorithm that runs in $\Theta(n \lg n)$ time but can have a lower constant hidden in the Θ-notation than the recursive version in Section 30.2. (Depending on the exact implementation, the recursive version may use the hardware cache more efficiently.) Then, we shall use the insights that led us to the iterative implementation to design an efficient parallel FFT circuit.

An iterative FFT implementation

We first note that the **for** loop of lines 10–13 of RECURSIVE-FFT involves computing the value $\omega_n^k \, y_k^{[1]}$ twice. In compiler terminology, we call such a value a *common subexpression*. We can change the loop to compute it only once, storing it in a temporary variable t.

> **for** $k = 0$ **to** $n/2 - 1$
> $\quad t = \omega \, y_k^{[1]}$
> $\quad y_k = y_k^{[0]} + t$
> $\quad y_{k+(n/2)} = y_k^{[0]} - t$
> $\quad \omega = \omega \, \omega_n$

The operation in this loop, multiplying the twiddle factor $\omega = \omega_n^k$ by $y_k^{[1]}$, storing the product into t, and adding and subtracting t from $y_k^{[0]}$, is known as a *butterfly operation* and is shown schematically in Figure 30.3.

We now show how to make the FFT algorithm iterative rather than recursive in structure. In Figure 30.4, we have arranged the input vectors to the recursive calls in an invocation of RECURSIVE-FFT in a tree structure, where the initial call is for $n = 8$. The tree has one node for each call of the procedure, labeled

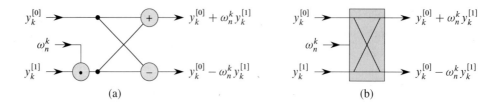

Figure 30.3 A butterfly operation. **(a)** The two input values enter from the left, the twiddle factor ω_n^k is multiplied by $y_k^{[1]}$, and the sum and difference are output on the right. **(b)** A simplified drawing of a butterfly operation. We will use this representation in a parallel FFT circuit.

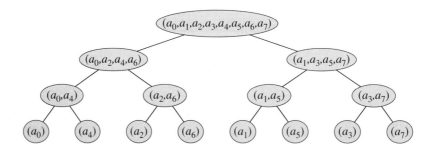

Figure 30.4 The tree of input vectors to the recursive calls of the RECURSIVE-FFT procedure. The initial invocation is for $n = 8$.

by the corresponding input vector. Each RECURSIVE-FFT invocation makes two recursive calls, unless it has received a 1-element vector. The first call appears in the left child, and the second call appears in the right child.

Looking at the tree, we observe that if we could arrange the elements of the initial vector a into the order in which they appear in the leaves, we could trace the execution of the RECURSIVE-FFT procedure, but bottom up instead of top down. First, we take the elements in pairs, compute the DFT of each pair using one butterfly operation, and replace the pair with its DFT. The vector then holds $n/2$ 2-element DFTs. Next, we take these $n/2$ DFTs in pairs and compute the DFT of the four vector elements they come from by executing two butterfly operations, replacing two 2-element DFTs with one 4-element DFT. The vector then holds $n/4$ 4-element DFTs. We continue in this manner until the vector holds two $(n/2)$-element DFTs, which we combine using $n/2$ butterfly operations into the final n-element DFT.

To turn this bottom-up approach into code, we use an array $A[0 \mathbin{.\,.} n-1]$ that initially holds the elements of the input vector a in the order in which they appear in the leaves of the tree of Figure 30.4. (We shall show later how to determine this order, which is known as a bit-reversal permutation.) Because we have to combine DFTs on each level of the tree, we introduce a variable s to count the levels, ranging from 1 (at the bottom, when we are combining pairs to form 2-element DFTs) to $\lg n$ (at the top, when we are combining two $(n/2)$-element DFTs to produce the final result). The algorithm therefore has the following structure:

```
1  for s = 1 to lg n
2      for k = 0 to n − 1 by 2ˢ
3          combine the two 2ˢ⁻¹-element DFTs in
                A[k .. k + 2ˢ⁻¹ − 1] and A[k + 2ˢ⁻¹ .. k + 2ˢ − 1]
                into one 2ˢ-element DFT in A[k .. k + 2ˢ − 1]
```

We can express the body of the loop (line 3) as more precise pseudocode. We copy the **for** loop from the RECURSIVE-FFT procedure, identifying $y^{[0]}$ with $A[k .. k + 2^{s-1} - 1]$ and $y^{[1]}$ with $A[k + 2^{s-1} .. k + 2^s - 1]$. The twiddle factor used in each butterfly operation depends on the value of s; it is a power of ω_m, where $m = 2^s$. (We introduce the variable m solely for the sake of readability.) We introduce another temporary variable u that allows us to perform the butterfly operation in place. When we replace line 3 of the overall structure by the loop body, we get the following pseudocode, which forms the basis of the parallel implementation we shall present later. The code first calls the auxiliary procedure BIT-REVERSE-COPY(a, A) to copy vector a into array A in the initial order in which we need the values.

ITERATIVE-FFT(a)

```
 1  BIT-REVERSE-COPY(a, A)
 2  n = a.length              // n is a power of 2
 3  for s = 1 to lg n
 4      m = 2ˢ
 5      ωₘ = e^{2πi/m}
 6      for k = 0 to n − 1 by m
 7          ω = 1
 8          for j = 0 to m/2 − 1
 9              t = ω A[k + j + m/2]
10              u = A[k + j]
11              A[k + j] = u + t
12              A[k + j + m/2] = u − t
13              ω = ω ωₘ
14  return A
```

How does BIT-REVERSE-COPY get the elements of the input vector a into the desired order in the array A? The order in which the leaves appear in Figure 30.4

is a ***bit-reversal permutation***. That is, if we let $\text{rev}(k)$ be the $\lg n$-bit integer formed by reversing the bits of the binary representation of k, then we want to place vector element a_k in array position $A[\text{rev}(k)]$. In Figure 30.4, for example, the leaves appear in the order $0, 4, 2, 6, 1, 5, 3, 7$; this sequence in binary is $000, 100, 010, 110, 001, 101, 011, 111$, and when we reverse the bits of each value we get the sequence $000, 001, 010, 011, 100, 101, 110, 111$. To see that we want a bit-reversal permutation in general, we note that at the top level of the tree, indices whose low-order bit is 0 go into the left subtree and indices whose low-order bit is 1 go into the right subtree. Stripping off the low-order bit at each level, we continue this process down the tree, until we get the order given by the bit-reversal permutation at the leaves.

Since we can easily compute the function $\text{rev}(k)$, the BIT-REVERSE-COPY procedure is simple:

BIT-REVERSE-COPY(a, A)

1   $n = a.length$
2   **for** $k = 0$ **to** $n - 1$
3       $A[\text{rev}(k)] = a_k$

The iterative FFT implementation runs in time $\Theta(n \lg n)$. The call to BIT-REVERSE-COPY(a, A) certainly runs in $O(n \lg n)$ time, since we iterate n times and can reverse an integer between 0 and $n - 1$, with $\lg n$ bits, in $O(\lg n)$ time. (In practice, because we usually know the initial value of n in advance, we would probably code a table mapping k to $\text{rev}(k)$, making BIT-REVERSE-COPY run in $\Theta(n)$ time with a low hidden constant. Alternatively, we could use the clever amortized reverse binary counter scheme described in Problem 17-1.) To complete the proof that ITERATIVE-FFT runs in time $\Theta(n \lg n)$, we show that $L(n)$, the number of times the body of the innermost loop (lines 8–13) executes, is $\Theta(n \lg n)$. The **for** loop of lines 6–13 iterates $n/m = n/2^s$ times for each value of s, and the innermost loop of lines 8–13 iterates $m/2 = 2^{s-1}$ times. Thus,

$$
\begin{aligned}
L(n) &= \sum_{s=1}^{\lg n} \frac{n}{2^s} \cdot 2^{s-1} \\
&= \sum_{s=1}^{\lg n} \frac{n}{2} \\
&= \Theta(n \lg n) .
\end{aligned}
$$

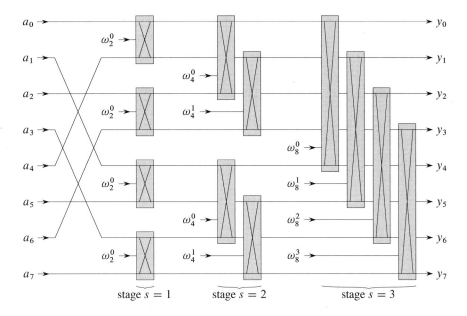

Figure 30.5   A circuit that computes the FFT in parallel, here shown on $n = 8$ inputs. Each butterfly operation takes as input the values on two wires, along with a twiddle factor, and it produces as outputs the values on two wires. The stages of butterflies are labeled to correspond to iterations of the outermost loop of the ITERATIVE-FFT procedure. Only the top and bottom wires passing through a butterfly interact with it; wires that pass through the middle of a butterfly do not affect that butterfly, nor are their values changed by that butterfly. For example, the top butterfly in stage 2 has nothing to do with wire 1 (the wire whose output is labeled y_1); its inputs and outputs are only on wires 0 and 2 (labeled y_0 and y_2, respectively). This circuit has depth $\Theta(\lg n)$ and performs $\Theta(n \lg n)$ butterfly operations altogether.

A parallel FFT circuit

We can exploit many of the properties that allowed us to implement an efficient iterative FFT algorithm to produce an efficient parallel algorithm for the FFT. We will express the parallel FFT algorithm as a circuit. Figure 30.5 shows a parallel FFT circuit, which computes the FFT on n inputs, for $n = 8$. The circuit begins with a bit-reverse permutation of the inputs, followed by $\lg n$ stages, each stage consisting of $n/2$ butterflies executed in parallel. The **depth** of the circuit—the maximum number of computational elements between any output and any input that can reach it—is therefore $\Theta(\lg n)$.

The leftmost part of the parallel FFT circuit performs the bit-reverse permutation, and the remainder mimics the iterative ITERATIVE-FFT procedure. Because each iteration of the outermost **for** loop performs $n/2$ independent butterfly operations, the circuit performs them in parallel. The value of s in each iteration within

ITERATIVE-FFT corresponds to a stage of butterflies shown in Figure 30.5. For $s = 1, 2, \ldots, \lg n$, stage s consists of $n/2^s$ groups of butterflies (corresponding to each value of k in ITERATIVE-FFT), with 2^{s-1} butterflies per group (corresponding to each value of j in ITERATIVE-FFT). The butterflies shown in Figure 30.5 correspond to the butterfly operations of the innermost loop (lines 9–12 of ITERATIVE-FFT). Note also that the twiddle factors used in the butterflies correspond to those used in ITERATIVE-FFT: in stage s, we use $\omega_m^0, \omega_m^1, \ldots, \omega_m^{m/2-1}$, where $m = 2^s$.

Exercises

30.3-1
Show how ITERATIVE-FFT computes the DFT of the input vector $(0, 2, 3, -1, 4, 5, 7, 9)$.

30.3-2
Show how to implement an FFT algorithm with the bit-reversal permutation occurring at the end, rather than at the beginning, of the computation. (*Hint:* Consider the inverse DFT.)

30.3-3
How many times does ITERATIVE-FFT compute twiddle factors in each stage? Rewrite ITERATIVE-FFT to compute twiddle factors only 2^{s-1} times in stage s.

30.3-4 ★
Suppose that the adders within the butterfly operations of the FFT circuit sometimes fail in such a manner that they always produce a zero output, independent of their inputs. Suppose that exactly one adder has failed, but that you don't know which one. Describe how you can identify the failed adder by supplying inputs to the overall FFT circuit and observing the outputs. How efficient is your method?

Problems

30-1 *Divide-and-conquer multiplication*

a. Show how to multiply two linear polynomials $ax + b$ and $cx + d$ using only three multiplications. (*Hint:* One of the multiplications is $(a + b) \cdot (c + d)$.)

b. Give two divide-and-conquer algorithms for multiplying two polynomials of degree-bound n in $\Theta(n^{\lg 3})$ time. The first algorithm should divide the input polynomial coefficients into a high half and a low half, and the second algorithm should divide them according to whether their index is odd or even.

c. Show how to multiply two n-bit integers in $O(n^{\lg 3})$ steps, where each step operates on at most a constant number of 1-bit values.

30-2 *Toeplitz matrices*

A ***Toeplitz matrix*** is an $n \times n$ matrix $A = (a_{ij})$ such that $a_{ij} = a_{i-1, j-1}$ for $i = 2, 3, \ldots, n$ and $j = 2, 3, \ldots, n$.

a. Is the sum of two Toeplitz matrices necessarily Toeplitz? What about the product?

b. Describe how to represent a Toeplitz matrix so that you can add two $n \times n$ Toeplitz matrices in $O(n)$ time.

c. Give an $O(n \lg n)$-time algorithm for multiplying an $n \times n$ Toeplitz matrix by a vector of length n. Use your representation from part (b).

d. Give an efficient algorithm for multiplying two $n \times n$ Toeplitz matrices. Analyze its running time.

30-3 *Multidimensional fast Fourier transform*

We can generalize the 1-dimensional discrete Fourier transform defined by equation (30.8) to d dimensions. The input is a d-dimensional array $A = (a_{j_1, j_2, \ldots, j_d})$ whose dimensions are $n_1, n_2, \ldots, n_d$, where $n_1 n_2 \cdots n_d = n$. We define the d-dimensional discrete Fourier transform by the equation

$$y_{k_1, k_2, \ldots, k_d} = \sum_{j_1 = 0}^{n_1 - 1} \sum_{j_2 = 0}^{n_2 - 1} \cdots \sum_{j_d = 0}^{n_d - 1} a_{j_1, j_2, \ldots, j_d} \omega_{n_1}^{j_1 k_1} \omega_{n_2}^{j_2 k_2} \cdots \omega_{n_d}^{j_d k_d}$$

for $0 \le k_1 < n_1, 0 \le k_2 < n_2, \ldots, 0 \le k_d < n_d$.

a. Show that we can compute a d-dimensional DFT by computing 1-dimensional DFTs on each dimension in turn. That is, we first compute n/n_1 separate 1-dimensional DFTs along dimension 1. Then, using the result of the DFTs along dimension 1 as the input, we compute n/n_2 separate 1-dimensional DFTs along dimension 2. Using this result as the input, we compute n/n_3 separate 1-dimensional DFTs along dimension 3, and so on, through dimension d.

b. Show that the ordering of dimensions does not matter, so that we can compute a d-dimensional DFT by computing the 1-dimensional DFTs in any order of the d dimensions.

c. Show that if we compute each 1-dimensional DFT by computing the fast Fourier transform, the total time to compute a d-dimensional DFT is $O(n \lg n)$, independent of d.

30-4   *Evaluating all derivatives of a polynomial at a point*

Given a polynomial $A(x)$ of degree-bound n, we define its tth derivative by

$$
A^{(t)}(x) = \begin{cases} A(x) & \text{if } t = 0, \\ \frac{d}{dx} A^{(t-1)}(x) & \text{if } 1 \le t \le n-1, \\ 0 & \text{if } t \ge n. \end{cases}
$$

From the coefficient representation $(a_0, a_1, \ldots, a_{n-1})$ of $A(x)$ and a given point x_0, we wish to determine $A^{(t)}(x_0)$ for $t = 0, 1, \ldots, n-1$.

a. Given coefficients $b_0, b_1, \ldots, b_{n-1}$ such that

$$
A(x) = \sum_{j=0}^{n-1} b_j (x - x_0)^j ,
$$

show how to compute $A^{(t)}(x_0)$, for $t = 0, 1, \ldots, n-1$, in $O(n)$ time.

b. Explain how to find $b_0, b_1, \ldots, b_{n-1}$ in $O(n \lg n)$ time, given $A(x_0 + \omega_n^k)$ for $k = 0, 1, \ldots, n-1$.

c. Prove that

$$
A(x_0 + \omega_n^k) = \sum_{r=0}^{n-1} \left(\frac{\omega_n^{kr}}{r!} \sum_{j=0}^{n-1} f(j) g(r-j) \right) ,
$$

where $f(j) = a_j \cdot j!$ and

$$
g(l) = \begin{cases} x_0^{-l}/(-l)! & \text{if } -(n-1) \le l \le 0, \\ 0 & \text{if } 1 \le l \le n-1. \end{cases}
$$

d. Explain how to evaluate $A(x_0 + \omega_n^k)$ for $k = 0, 1, \ldots, n-1$ in $O(n \lg n)$ time. Conclude that we can evaluate all nontrivial derivatives of $A(x)$ at x_0 in $O(n \lg n)$ time.

30-5 Polynomial evaluation at multiple points

We have seen how to evaluate a polynomial of degree-bound n at a single point in $O(n)$ time using Horner's rule. We have also discovered how to evaluate such a polynomial at all n complex roots of unity in $O(n \lg n)$ time using the FFT. We shall now show how to evaluate a polynomial of degree-bound n at n arbitrary points in $O(n \lg^2 n)$ time.

To do so, we shall assume that we can compute the polynomial remainder when one such polynomial is divided by another in $O(n \lg n)$ time, a result that we state without proof. For example, the remainder of $3x^3 + x^2 - 3x + 1$ when divided by $x^2 + x + 2$ is

$$(3x^3 + x^2 - 3x + 1) \bmod (x^2 + x + 2) = -7x + 5 .$$

Given the coefficient representation of a polynomial $A(x) = \sum_{k=0}^{n-1} a_k x^k$ and n points $x_0, x_1, \ldots, x_{n-1}$, we wish to compute the n values $A(x_0), A(x_1), \ldots, A(x_{n-1})$. For $0 \le i \le j \le n - 1$, define the polynomials $P_{ij}(x) = \prod_{k=i}^{j} (x - x_k)$ and $Q_{ij}(x) = A(x) \bmod P_{ij}(x)$. Note that $Q_{ij}(x)$ has degree at most $j - i$.

a. Prove that $A(x) \bmod (x - z) = A(z)$ for any point z.

b. Prove that $Q_{kk}(x) = A(x_k)$ and that $Q_{0,n-1}(x) = A(x)$.

c. Prove that for $i \le k \le j$, we have $Q_{ik}(x) = Q_{ij}(x) \bmod P_{ik}(x)$ and $Q_{kj}(x) = Q_{ij}(x) \bmod P_{kj}(x)$.

d. Give an $O(n \lg^2 n)$-time algorithm to evaluate $A(x_0), A(x_1), \ldots, A(x_{n-1})$.

30-6 FFT using modular arithmetic

As defined, the discrete Fourier transform requires us to compute with complex numbers, which can result in a loss of precision due to round-off errors. For some problems, the answer is known to contain only integers, and by using a variant of the FFT based on modular arithmetic, we can guarantee that the answer is calculated exactly. An example of such a problem is that of multiplying two polynomials with integer coefficients. Exercise 30.2-6 gives one approach, using a modulus of length $\Omega(n)$ bits to handle a DFT on n points. This problem gives another approach, which uses a modulus of the more reasonable length $O(\lg n)$; it requires that you understand the material of Chapter 31. Let n be a power of 2.

a. Suppose that we search for the smallest k such that $p = kn + 1$ is prime. Give a simple heuristic argument why we might expect k to be approximately $\ln n$. (The value of k might be much larger or smaller, but we can reasonably expect to examine $O(\lg n)$ candidate values of k on average.) How does the expected length of p compare to the length of n?

Let g be a generator of $\mathbb{Z}_p^*$, and let $w = g^k \bmod p$.

b. Argue that the DFT and the inverse DFT are well-defined inverse operations modulo p, where w is used as a principal nth root of unity.

c. Show how to make the FFT and its inverse work modulo p in time $O(n \lg n)$, where operations on words of $O(\lg n)$ bits take unit time. Assume that the algorithm is given p and w.

d. Compute the DFT modulo $p = 17$ of the vector $(0, 5, 3, 7, 7, 2, 1, 6)$. Note that $g = 3$ is a generator of $\mathbb{Z}_{17}^*$.

Chapter notes

Van Loan's book [343] provides an outstanding treatment of the fast Fourier transform. Press, Teukolsky, Vetterling, and Flannery [283, 284] have a good description of the fast Fourier transform and its applications. For an excellent introduction to signal processing, a popular FFT application area, see the texts by Oppenheim and Schafer [266] and Oppenheim and Willsky [267]. The Oppenheim and Schafer book also shows how to handle cases in which n is not an integer power of 2.

Fourier analysis is not limited to 1-dimensional data. It is widely used in image processing to analyze data in 2 or more dimensions. The books by Gonzalez and Woods [146] and Pratt [281] discuss multidimensional Fourier transforms and their use in image processing, and books by Tolimieri, An, and Lu [338] and Van Loan [343] discuss the mathematics of multidimensional fast Fourier transforms.

Cooley and Tukey [76] are widely credited with devising the FFT in the 1960s. The FFT had in fact been discovered many times previously, but its importance was not fully realized before the advent of modern digital computers. Although Press, Teukolsky, Vetterling, and Flannery attribute the origins of the method to Runge and König in 1924, an article by Heideman, Johnson, and Burrus [163] traces the history of the FFT as far back as C. F. Gauss in 1805.

Frigo and Johnson [117] developed a fast and flexible implementation of the FFT, called FFTW ("fastest Fourier transform in the West"). FFTW is designed for situations requiring multiple DFT computations on the same problem size. Before actually computing the DFTs, FFTW executes a "planner," which, by a series of trial runs, determines how best to decompose the FFT computation for the given problem size on the host machine. FFTW adapts to use the hardware cache efficiently, and once subproblems are small enough, FFTW solves them with optimized, straight-line code. Furthermore, FFTW has the unusual advantage of taking $\Theta(n \lg n)$ time for any problem size n, even when n is a large prime.

Although the standard Fourier transform assumes that the input represents points that are uniformly spaced in the time domain, other techniques can approximate the FFT on "nonequispaced" data. The article by Ware [348] provides an overview.

31   Number-Theoretic Algorithms

Number theory was once viewed as a beautiful but largely useless subject in pure mathematics. Today number-theoretic algorithms are used widely, due in large part to the invention of cryptographic schemes based on large prime numbers. These schemes are feasible because we can find large primes easily, and they are secure because we do not know how to factor the product of large primes (or solve related problems, such as computing discrete logarithms) efficiently. This chapter presents some of the number theory and related algorithms that underlie such applications.

Section 31.1 introduces basic concepts of number theory, such as divisibility, modular equivalence, and unique factorization. Section 31.2 studies one of the world's oldest algorithms: Euclid's algorithm for computing the greatest common divisor of two integers. Section 31.3 reviews concepts of modular arithmetic. Section 31.4 then studies the set of multiples of a given number a, modulo n, and shows how to find all solutions to the equation $ax \equiv b \pmod{n}$ by using Euclid's algorithm. The Chinese remainder theorem is presented in Section 31.5. Section 31.6 considers powers of a given number a, modulo n, and presents a repeated-squaring algorithm for efficiently computing $a^b \bmod n$, given a, b, and n. This operation is at the heart of efficient primality testing and of much modern cryptography. Section 31.7 then describes the RSA public-key cryptosystem. Section 31.8 examines a randomized primality test. We can use this test to find large primes efficiently, which we need to do in order to create keys for the RSA cryptosystem. Finally, Section 31.9 reviews a simple but effective heuristic for factoring small integers. It is a curious fact that factoring is one problem people may wish to be intractable, since the security of RSA depends on the difficulty of factoring large integers.

Size of inputs and cost of arithmetic computations

Because we shall be working with large integers, we need to adjust how we think about the size of an input and about the cost of elementary arithmetic operations.

In this chapter, a "large input" typically means an input containing "large integers" rather than an input containing "many integers" (as for sorting). Thus, we shall measure the size of an input in terms of the *number of bits* required to represent that input, not just the number of integers in the input. An algorithm with integer inputs $a_1, a_2, \ldots, a_k$ is a ***polynomial-time algorithm*** if it runs in time polynomial in $\lg a_1, \lg a_2, \ldots, \lg a_k$, that is, polynomial in the lengths of its binary-encoded inputs.

In most of this book, we have found it convenient to think of the elementary arithmetic operations (multiplications, divisions, or computing remainders) as primitive operations that take one unit of time. By counting the number of such arithmetic operations that an algorithm performs, we have a basis for making a reasonable estimate of the algorithm's actual running time on a computer. Elementary operations can be time-consuming, however, when their inputs are large. It thus becomes convenient to measure how many ***bit operations*** a number-theoretic algorithm requires. In this model, multiplying two β-bit integers by the ordinary method uses $\Theta(\beta^2)$ bit operations. Similarly, we can divide a β-bit integer by a shorter integer or take the remainder of a β-bit integer when divided by a shorter integer in time $\Theta(\beta^2)$ by simple algorithms. (See Exercise 31.1-12.) Faster methods are known. For example, a simple divide-and-conquer method for multiplying two β-bit integers has a running time of $\Theta(\beta^{\lg 3})$, and the fastest known method has a running time of $\Theta(\beta \lg \beta \lg \lg \beta)$. For practical purposes, however, the $\Theta(\beta^2)$ algorithm is often best, and we shall use this bound as a basis for our analyses.

We shall generally analyze algorithms in this chapter in terms of both the number of arithmetic operations and the number of bit operations they require.

31.1   Elementary number-theoretic notions

This section provides a brief review of notions from elementary number theory concerning the set $\mathbb{Z} = \{\ldots, -2, -1, 0, 1, 2, \ldots\}$ of integers and the set $\mathbb{N} = \{0, 1, 2, \ldots\}$ of natural numbers.

Divisibility and divisors

The notion of one integer being divisible by another is key to the theory of numbers. The notation $d \mid a$ (read "d ***divides*** a") means that $a = kd$ for some integer k. Every integer divides 0. If $a > 0$ and $d \mid a$, then $|d| \leq |a|$. If $d \mid a$, then we also say that a is a ***multiple*** of d. If d does not divide a, we write $d \nmid a$.

If $d \mid a$ and $d \geq 0$, we say that d is a ***divisor*** of a. Note that $d \mid a$ if and only if $-d \mid a$, so that no generality is lost by defining the divisors to be nonnegative, with the understanding that the negative of any divisor of a also divides a. A divisor of a nonzero integer a is at least 1 but not greater than $|a|$. For example, the divisors of 24 are 1, 2, 3, 4, 6, 8, 12, and 24.

Every positive integer a is divisible by the ***trivial divisors*** 1 and a. The nontrivial divisors of a are the ***factors*** of a. For example, the factors of 20 are 2, 4, 5, and 10.

Prime and composite numbers

An integer $a > 1$ whose only divisors are the trivial divisors 1 and a is a ***prime number*** or, more simply, a ***prime***. Primes have many special properties and play a critical role in number theory. The first 20 primes, in order, are

$$2, \; 3, \; 5, \; 7, \; 11, \; 13, \; 17, \; 19, \; 23, \; 29, \; 31, \; 37, \; 41, \; 43, \; 47, \; 53, \; 59, \; 61, \; 67, \; 71 \; .$$

Exercise 31.1-2 asks you to prove that there are infinitely many primes. An integer $a > 1$ that is not prime is a ***composite number*** or, more simply, a ***composite***. For example, 39 is composite because $3 \mid 39$. We call the integer 1 a ***unit***, and it is neither prime nor composite. Similarly, the integer 0 and all negative integers are neither prime nor composite.

The division theorem, remainders, and modular equivalence

Given an integer n, we can partition the integers into those that are multiples of n and those that are not multiples of n. Much number theory is based upon refining this partition by classifying the nonmultiples of n according to their remainders when divided by n. The following theorem provides the basis for this refinement. We omit the proof (but see, for example, Niven and Zuckerman [265]).

Theorem 31.1 (Division theorem)
For any integer a and any positive integer n, there exist unique integers q and r such that $0 \le r < n$ and $a = qn + r$. ∎

The value $q = \lfloor a/n \rfloor$ is the ***quotient*** of the division. The value $r = a \bmod n$ is the ***remainder*** (or ***residue***) of the division. We have that $n \mid a$ if and only if $a \bmod n = 0$.

We can partition the integers into n equivalence classes according to their remainders modulo n. The ***equivalence class modulo n*** containing an integer a is

$$[a]_n = \{a + kn : k \in \mathbb{Z}\} \; .$$

For example, $[3]_7 = \{\dots, -11, -4, 3, 10, 17, \dots\}$; we can also denote this set by $[-4]_7$ and $[10]_7$. Using the notation defined on page 54, we can say that writing $a \in [b]_n$ is the same as writing $a \equiv b \pmod{n}$. The set of all such equivalence classes is

$$\mathbb{Z}_n = \{[a]_n : 0 \le a \le n - 1\} . \tag{31.1}$$

When you see the definition

$$\mathbb{Z}_n = \{0, 1, \ldots, n - 1\} , \tag{31.2}$$

you should read it as equivalent to equation (31.1) with the understanding that 0 represents $[0]_n$, 1 represents $[1]_n$, and so on; each class is represented by its smallest nonnegative element. You should keep the underlying equivalence classes in mind, however. For example, if we refer to -1 as a member of $\mathbb{Z}_n$, we are really referring to $[n - 1]_n$, since $-1 \equiv n - 1 \pmod{n}$.

Common divisors and greatest common divisors

If d is a divisor of a and d is also a divisor of b, then d is a **common divisor** of a and b. For example, the divisors of 30 are 1, 2, 3, 5, 6, 10, 15, and 30, and so the common divisors of 24 and 30 are 1, 2, 3, and 6. Note that 1 is a common divisor of any two integers.

An important property of common divisors is that

$$d \mid a \text{ and } d \mid b \text{ implies } d \mid (a + b) \text{ and } d \mid (a - b) . \tag{31.3}$$

More generally, we have that

$$d \mid a \text{ and } d \mid b \text{ implies } d \mid (ax + by) \tag{31.4}$$

for any integers x and y. Also, if $a \mid b$, then either $|a| \le |b|$ or $b = 0$, which implies that

$$a \mid b \text{ and } b \mid a \text{ implies } a = \pm b . \tag{31.5}$$

The **greatest common divisor** of two integers a and b, not both zero, is the largest of the common divisors of a and b; we denote it by $\gcd(a, b)$. For example, $\gcd(24, 30) = 6$, $\gcd(5, 7) = 1$, and $\gcd(0, 9) = 9$. If a and b are both nonzero, then $\gcd(a, b)$ is an integer between 1 and $\min(|a|, |b|)$. We define $\gcd(0, 0)$ to be 0; this definition is necessary to make standard properties of the gcd function (such as equation (31.9) below) universally valid.

The following are elementary properties of the gcd function:

$$\gcd(a, b) \;=\; \gcd(b, a) , \tag{31.6}$$
$$\gcd(a, b) \;=\; \gcd(-a, b) , \tag{31.7}$$
$$\gcd(a, b) \;=\; \gcd(|a|, |b|) , \tag{31.8}$$
$$\gcd(a, 0) \;=\; |a| , \tag{31.9}$$
$$\gcd(a, ka) \;=\; |a| \qquad \text{for any } k \in \mathbb{Z} . \tag{31.10}$$

The following theorem provides an alternative and useful characterization of $\gcd(a, b)$.

Theorem 31.2

If a and b are any integers, not both zero, then $\gcd(a, b)$ is the smallest positive element of the set $\{ax + by : x, y \in \mathbb{Z}\}$ of linear combinations of a and b.

Proof Let s be the smallest positive such linear combination of a and b, and let $s = ax + by$ for some $x, y \in \mathbb{Z}$. Let $q = \lfloor a/s \rfloor$. Equation (3.8) then implies

$$
\begin{aligned}
a \bmod s &= a - qs \\
&= a - q(ax + by) \\
&= a(1 - qx) + b(-qy) ,
\end{aligned}
$$

and so $a \bmod s$ is a linear combination of a and b as well. But, since $0 \leq a \bmod s < s$, we have that $a \bmod s = 0$, because s is the smallest positive such linear combination. Therefore, we have that $s \mid a$ and, by analogous reasoning, $s \mid b$. Thus, s is a common divisor of a and b, and so $\gcd(a, b) \geq s$. Equation (31.4) implies that $\gcd(a, b) \mid s$, since $\gcd(a, b)$ divides both a and b and s is a linear combination of a and b. But $\gcd(a, b) \mid s$ and $s > 0$ imply that $\gcd(a, b) \leq s$. Combining $\gcd(a, b) \geq s$ and $\gcd(a, b) \leq s$ yields $\gcd(a, b) = s$. We conclude that s is the greatest common divisor of a and b. ∎

Corollary 31.3

For any integers a and b, if $d \mid a$ and $d \mid b$, then $d \mid \gcd(a, b)$.

Proof This corollary follows from equation (31.4), because $\gcd(a, b)$ is a linear combination of a and b by Theorem 31.2. ∎

Corollary 31.4

For all integers a and b and any nonnegative integer n,

$$\gcd(an, bn) = n \gcd(a, b) .$$

Proof If $n = 0$, the corollary is trivial. If $n > 0$, then $\gcd(an, bn)$ is the smallest positive element of the set $\{anx + bny : x, y \in \mathbb{Z}\}$, which is n times the smallest positive element of the set $\{ax + by : x, y \in \mathbb{Z}\}$. ∎

Corollary 31.5

For all positive integers n, a, and b, if $n \mid ab$ and $\gcd(a, n) = 1$, then $n \mid b$.

Proof We leave the proof as Exercise 31.1-5. ∎

Relatively prime integers

Two integers a and b are ***relatively prime*** if their only common divisor is 1, that is, if $\gcd(a, b) = 1$. For example, 8 and 15 are relatively prime, since the divisors of 8 are 1, 2, 4, and 8, and the divisors of 15 are 1, 3, 5, and 15. The following theorem states that if two integers are each relatively prime to an integer p, then their product is relatively prime to p.

Theorem 31.6
For any integers a, b, and p, if both $\gcd(a, p) = 1$ and $\gcd(b, p) = 1$, then $\gcd(ab, p) = 1$.

Proof It follows from Theorem 31.2 that there exist integers x, y, x', and y' such that

$$ax + py = 1,$$
$$bx' + py' = 1.$$

Multiplying these equations and rearranging, we have

$$ab(xx') + p(ybx' + y'ax + pyy') = 1.$$

Since 1 is thus a positive linear combination of ab and p, an appeal to Theorem 31.2 completes the proof. ∎

Integers $n_1, n_2, \ldots, n_k$ are ***pairwise relatively prime*** if, whenever $i \neq j$, we have $\gcd(n_i, n_j) = 1$.

Unique factorization

An elementary but important fact about divisibility by primes is the following.

Theorem 31.7
For all primes p and all integers a and b, if $p \mid ab$, then $p \mid a$ or $p \mid b$ (or both).

Proof Assume for the purpose of contradiction that $p \mid ab$, but that $p \nmid a$ and $p \nmid b$. Thus, $\gcd(a, p) = 1$ and $\gcd(b, p) = 1$, since the only divisors of p are 1 and p, and we assume that p divides neither a nor b. Theorem 31.6 then implies that $\gcd(ab, p) = 1$, contradicting our assumption that $p \mid ab$, since $p \mid ab$ implies $\gcd(ab, p) = p$. This contradiction completes the proof. ∎

A consequence of Theorem 31.7 is that we can uniquely factor any composite integer into a product of primes.

Theorem 31.8 (Unique factorization)
There is exactly one way to write any composite integer a as a product of the form

$$a = p_1^{e_1} p_2^{e_2} \cdots p_r^{e_r} ,$$

where the p_i are prime, $p_1 < p_2 < \cdots < p_r$, and the e_i are positive integers.

Proof   We leave the proof as Exercise 31.1-11.   ∎

As an example, the number 6000 is uniquely factored into primes as $2^4 \cdot 3 \cdot 5^3$.

Exercises

31.1-1
Prove that if $a > b > 0$ and $c = a + b$, then $c \bmod a = b$.

31.1-2
Prove that there are infinitely many primes. (*Hint:* Show that none of the primes $p_1, p_2, \ldots, p_k$ divide $(p_1 p_2 \cdots p_k) + 1$.)

31.1-3
Prove that if $a \mid b$ and $b \mid c$, then $a \mid c$.

31.1-4
Prove that if p is prime and $0 < k < p$, then $\gcd(k, p) = 1$.

31.1-5
Prove Corollary 31.5.

31.1-6
Prove that if p is prime and $0 < k < p$, then $p \mid \binom{p}{k}$. Conclude that for all integers a and b and all primes p,

$$(a + b)^p \equiv a^p + b^p \pmod{p} .$$

31.1-7
Prove that if a and b are any positive integers such that $a \mid b$, then

$$(x \bmod b) \bmod a = x \bmod a$$

for any x. Prove, under the same assumptions, that

$$x \equiv y \pmod{b} \text{ implies } x \equiv y \pmod{a}$$

for any integers x and y.

31.1-8

For any integer $k > 0$, an integer n is a **kth power** if there exists an integer a such that $a^k = n$. Furthermore, $n > 1$ is a **nontrivial power** if it is a kth power for some integer $k > 1$. Show how to determine whether a given β-bit integer n is a nontrivial power in time polynomial in β.

31.1-9

Prove equations (31.6)–(31.10).

31.1-10

Show that the gcd operator is associative. That is, prove that for all integers a, b, and c,

$$\gcd(a, \gcd(b, c)) = \gcd(\gcd(a, b), c) \, .$$

31.1-11 ★

Prove Theorem 31.8.

31.1-12

Give efficient algorithms for the operations of dividing a β-bit integer by a shorter integer and of taking the remainder of a β-bit integer when divided by a shorter integer. Your algorithms should run in time $\Theta(\beta^2)$.

31.1-13

Give an efficient algorithm to convert a given β-bit (binary) integer to a decimal representation. Argue that if multiplication or division of integers whose length is at most β takes time $M(\beta)$, then we can convert binary to decimal in time $\Theta(M(\beta) \lg \beta)$. (*Hint:* Use a divide-and-conquer approach, obtaining the top and bottom halves of the result with separate recursions.)

31.2   Greatest common divisor

In this section, we describe Euclid's algorithm for efficiently computing the greatest common divisor of two integers. When we analyze the running time, we shall see a surprising connection with the Fibonacci numbers, which yield a worst-case input for Euclid's algorithm.

We restrict ourselves in this section to nonnegative integers. This restriction is justified by equation (31.8), which states that $\gcd(a, b) = \gcd(|a|, |b|)$.

In principle, we can compute $\gcd(a, b)$ for positive integers a and b from the prime factorizations of a and b. Indeed, if

$$a = p_1^{e_1} p_2^{e_2} \cdots p_r^{e_r} , \tag{31.11}$$

$$b = p_1^{f_1} p_2^{f_2} \cdots p_r^{f_r} , \tag{31.12}$$

with zero exponents being used to make the set of primes $p_1, p_2, \ldots, p_r$ the same for both a and b, then, as Exercise 31.2-1 asks you to show,

$$\gcd(a, b) = p_1^{\min(e_1, f_1)} p_2^{\min(e_2, f_2)} \cdots p_r^{\min(e_r, f_r)} . \tag{31.13}$$

As we shall show in Section 31.9, however, the best algorithms to date for factoring do not run in polynomial time. Thus, this approach to computing greatest common divisors seems unlikely to yield an efficient algorithm.

Euclid's algorithm for computing greatest common divisors relies on the following theorem.

Theorem 31.9 (GCD recursion theorem)
For any nonnegative integer a and any positive integer b,

$$\gcd(a, b) = \gcd(b, a \bmod b) .$$

Proof   We shall show that $\gcd(a, b)$ and $\gcd(b, a \bmod b)$ divide each other, so that by equation (31.5) they must be equal (since they are both nonnegative).

We first show that $\gcd(a, b) \mid \gcd(b, a \bmod b)$. If we let $d = \gcd(a, b)$, then $d \mid a$ and $d \mid b$. By equation (3.8), $a \bmod b = a - qb$, where $q = \lfloor a/b \rfloor$. Since $a \bmod b$ is thus a linear combination of a and b, equation (31.4) implies that $d \mid (a \bmod b)$. Therefore, since $d \mid b$ and $d \mid (a \bmod b)$, Corollary 31.3 implies that $d \mid \gcd(b, a \bmod b)$ or, equivalently, that

$$\gcd(a, b) \mid \gcd(b, a \bmod b). \tag{31.14}$$

Showing that $\gcd(b, a \bmod b) \mid \gcd(a, b)$ is almost the same. If we now let $d = \gcd(b, a \bmod b)$, then $d \mid b$ and $d \mid (a \bmod b)$. Since $a = qb + (a \bmod b)$, where $q = \lfloor a/b \rfloor$, we have that a is a linear combination of b and $(a \bmod b)$. By equation (31.4), we conclude that $d \mid a$. Since $d \mid b$ and $d \mid a$, we have that $d \mid \gcd(a, b)$ by Corollary 31.3 or, equivalently, that

$$\gcd(b, a \bmod b) \mid \gcd(a, b). \tag{31.15}$$

Using equation (31.5) to combine equations (31.14) and (31.15) completes the proof.   ∎

Euclid's algorithm

The *Elements* of Euclid (circa 300 B.C.) describes the following gcd algorithm, although it may be of even earlier origin. We express Euclid's algorithm as a recursive program based directly on Theorem 31.9. The inputs a and b are arbitrary nonnegative integers.

EUCLID(a, b)

1 **if** $b == 0$
2   **return** a
3 **else return** EUCLID($b, a \bmod b$)

As an example of the running of EUCLID, consider the computation of $\gcd(30, 21)$:

$$
\begin{aligned}
\text{EUCLID}(30, 21) \; &= \; \text{EUCLID}(21, 9) \\
&= \; \text{EUCLID}(9, 3) \\
&= \; \text{EUCLID}(3, 0) \\
&= \; 3 \; .
\end{aligned}
$$

This computation calls EUCLID recursively three times.

The correctness of EUCLID follows from Theorem 31.9 and the property that if the algorithm returns a in line 2, then $b = 0$, so that equation (31.9) implies that $\gcd(a, b) = \gcd(a, 0) = a$. The algorithm cannot recurse indefinitely, since the second argument strictly decreases in each recursive call and is always nonnegative. Therefore, EUCLID always terminates with the correct answer.

The running time of Euclid's algorithm

We analyze the worst-case running time of EUCLID as a function of the size of a and b. We assume with no loss of generality that $a > b \geq 0$. To justify this assumption, observe that if $b > a \geq 0$, then EUCLID(a, b) immediately makes the recursive call EUCLID(b, a). That is, if the first argument is less than the second argument, EUCLID spends one recursive call swapping its arguments and then proceeds. Similarly, if $b = a > 0$, the procedure terminates after one recursive call, since $a \bmod b = 0$.

The overall running time of EUCLID is proportional to the number of recursive calls it makes. Our analysis makes use of the Fibonacci numbers F_k, defined by the recurrence (3.22).

Lemma 31.10
If $a > b \geq 1$ and the call EUCLID(a, b) performs $k \geq 1$ recursive calls, then $a \geq F_{k+2}$ and $b \geq F_{k+1}$.

Proof   The proof proceeds by induction on k. For the basis of the induction, let $k = 1$. Then, $b \geq 1 = F_2$, and since $a > b$, we must have $a \geq 2 = F_3$. Since $b > (a \bmod b)$, in each recursive call the first argument is strictly larger than the second; the assumption that $a > b$ therefore holds for each recursive call.

Assume inductively that the lemma holds if $k - 1$ recursive calls are made; we shall then prove that the lemma holds for k recursive calls. Since $k > 0$, we have $b > 0$, and $\text{EUCLID}(a, b)$ calls $\text{EUCLID}(b, a \bmod b)$ recursively, which in turn makes $k - 1$ recursive calls. The inductive hypothesis then implies that $b \geq F_{k+1}$ (thus proving part of the lemma), and $a \bmod b \geq F_k$. We have

$$
\begin{aligned}
b + (a \bmod b) &= b + (a - b \lfloor a/b \rfloor) \\
&\leq a,
\end{aligned}
$$

since $a > b > 0$ implies $\lfloor a/b \rfloor \geq 1$. Thus,

$$
\begin{aligned}
a &\geq b + (a \bmod b) \\
&\geq F_{k+1} + F_k \\
&= F_{k+2}.
\end{aligned}
$$
∎

The following theorem is an immediate corollary of this lemma.

Theorem 31.11 (Lamé's theorem)
For any integer $k \geq 1$, if $a > b \geq 1$ and $b < F_{k+1}$, then the call $\text{EUCLID}(a, b)$ makes fewer than k recursive calls. ∎

We can show that the upper bound of Theorem 31.11 is the best possible by showing that the call $\text{EUCLID}(F_{k+1}, F_k)$ makes exactly $k - 1$ recursive calls when $k \geq 2$. We use induction on k. For the base case, $k = 2$, and the call $\text{EUCLID}(F_3, F_2)$ makes exactly one recursive call, to $\text{EUCLID}(1, 0)$. (We have to start at $k = 2$, because when $k = 1$ we do not have $F_2 > F_1$.) For the inductive step, assume that $\text{EUCLID}(F_k, F_{k-1})$ makes exactly $k - 2$ recursive calls. For $k > 2$, we have $F_k > F_{k-1} > 0$ and $F_{k+1} = F_k + F_{k-1}$, and so by Exercise 31.1-1, we have $F_{k+1} \bmod F_k = F_{k-1}$. Thus, we have

$$
\begin{aligned}
\gcd(F_{k+1}, F_k) &= \gcd(F_k, F_{k+1} \bmod F_k) \\
&= \gcd(F_k, F_{k-1}).
\end{aligned}
$$

Therefore, the call $\text{EUCLID}(F_{k+1}, F_k)$ recurses one time more than the call $\text{EUCLID}(F_k, F_{k-1})$, or exactly $k - 1$ times, meeting the upper bound of Theorem 31.11.

Since F_k is approximately $\phi^k / \sqrt{5}$, where ϕ is the golden ratio $(1 + \sqrt{5})/2$ defined by equation (3.24), the number of recursive calls in EUCLID is $O(\lg b)$. (See

a	b	$\lfloor a/b \rfloor$	d	x	y
99	78	1	3	-11	14
78	21	3	3	3	-11
21	15	1	3	-2	3
15	6	2	3	1	-2
6	3	2	3	0	1
3	0	—	3	1	0

Figure 31.1 How EXTENDED-EUCLID computes $\gcd(99, 78)$. Each line shows one level of the recursion: the values of the inputs a and b, the computed value $\lfloor a/b \rfloor$, and the values d, x, and y returned. The triple (d, x, y) returned becomes the triple (d', x', y') used at the next higher level of recursion. The call EXTENDED-EUCLID(99, 78) returns $(3, -11, 14)$, so that $\gcd(99, 78) = 3 = 99 \cdot (-11) + 78 \cdot 14$.

Exercise 31.2-5 for a tighter bound.) Therefore, if we call EUCLID on two β-bit numbers, then it performs $O(\beta)$ arithmetic operations and $O(\beta^3)$ bit operations (assuming that multiplication and division of β-bit numbers take $O(\beta^2)$ bit operations). Problem 31-2 asks you to show an $O(\beta^2)$ bound on the number of bit operations.

The extended form of Euclid's algorithm

We now rewrite Euclid's algorithm to compute additional useful information. Specifically, we extend the algorithm to compute the integer coefficients x and y such that

$$d = \gcd(a, b) = ax + by \,. \tag{31.16}$$

Note that x and y may be zero or negative. We shall find these coefficients useful later for computing modular multiplicative inverses. The procedure EXTENDED-EUCLID takes as input a pair of nonnegative integers and returns a triple of the form (d, x, y) that satisfies equation (31.16).

EXTENDED-EUCLID(a, b)

```
1   if b == 0
2       return (a, 1, 0)
3   else (d', x', y') = EXTENDED-EUCLID(b, a mod b)
4       (d, x, y) = (d', y', x' - ⌊a/b⌋ y')
5       return (d, x, y)
```

Figure 31.1 illustrates how EXTENDED-EUCLID computes $\gcd(99, 78)$.

The EXTENDED-EUCLID procedure is a variation of the EUCLID procedure. Line 1 is equivalent to the test "$b == 0$" in line 1 of EUCLID. If $b = 0$, then

EXTENDED-EUCLID returns not only $d = a$ in line 2, but also the coefficients $x = 1$ and $y = 0$, so that $a = ax + by$. If $b \neq 0$, EXTENDED-EUCLID first computes (d', x', y') such that $d' = \gcd(b, a \bmod b)$ and

$$d' = bx' + (a \bmod b)y' \, . \tag{31.17}$$

As for EUCLID, we have in this case $d = \gcd(a, b) = d' = \gcd(b, a \bmod b)$. To obtain x and y such that $d = ax + by$, we start by rewriting equation (31.17) using the equation $d = d'$ and equation (3.8):

$$
\begin{aligned}
d &= bx' + (a - b\lfloor a/b \rfloor)y' \\
  &= ay' + b(x' - \lfloor a/b \rfloor y') \, .
\end{aligned}
$$

Thus, choosing $x = y'$ and $y = x' - \lfloor a/b \rfloor y'$ satisfies the equation $d = ax + by$, proving the correctness of EXTENDED-EUCLID.

Since the number of recursive calls made in EUCLID is equal to the number of recursive calls made in EXTENDED-EUCLID, the running times of EUCLID and EXTENDED-EUCLID are the same, to within a constant factor. That is, for $a > b > 0$, the number of recursive calls is $O(\lg b)$.

Exercises

31.2-1
Prove that equations (31.11) and (31.12) imply equation (31.13).

31.2-2
Compute the values (d, x, y) that the call EXTENDED-EUCLID $(899, 493)$ returns.

31.2-3
Prove that for all integers a, k, and n,

$$\gcd(a, n) = \gcd(a + kn, n) \, .$$

31.2-4
Rewrite EUCLID in an iterative form that uses only a constant amount of memory (that is, stores only a constant number of integer values).

31.2-5
If $a > b \geq 0$, show that the call EUCLID(a, b) makes at most $1 + \log_\phi b$ recursive calls. Improve this bound to $1 + \log_\phi(b/\gcd(a, b))$.

31.2-6
What does EXTENDED-EUCLID (F_{k+1}, F_k) return? Prove your answer correct.

31.2-7

Define the gcd function for more than two arguments by the recursive equation $\gcd(a_0, a_1, \ldots, a_n) = \gcd(a_0, \gcd(a_1, a_2, \ldots, a_n))$. Show that the gcd function returns the same answer independent of the order in which its arguments are specified. Also show how to find integers $x_0, x_1, \ldots, x_n$ such that $\gcd(a_0, a_1, \ldots, a_n) = a_0 x_0 + a_1 x_1 + \cdots + a_n x_n$. Show that the number of divisions performed by your algorithm is $O(n + \lg(\max\{a_0, a_1, \ldots, a_n\}))$.

31.2-8

Define $\operatorname{lcm}(a_1, a_2, \ldots, a_n)$ to be the **least common multiple** of the n integers $a_1, a_2, \ldots, a_n$, that is, the smallest nonnegative integer that is a multiple of each a_i. Show how to compute $\operatorname{lcm}(a_1, a_2, \ldots, a_n)$ efficiently using the (two-argument) gcd operation as a subroutine.

31.2-9

Prove that n_1, n_2, n_3, and n_4 are pairwise relatively prime if and only if

$$\gcd(n_1 n_2, n_3 n_4) = \gcd(n_1 n_3, n_2 n_4) = 1 .$$

More generally, show that $n_1, n_2, \ldots, n_k$ are pairwise relatively prime if and only if a set of $\lceil \lg k \rceil$ pairs of numbers derived from the n_i are relatively prime.

31.3 Modular arithmetic

Informally, we can think of modular arithmetic as arithmetic as usual over the integers, except that if we are working modulo n, then every result x is replaced by the element of $\{0, 1, \ldots, n-1\}$ that is equivalent to x, modulo n (that is, x is replaced by $x \bmod n$). This informal model suffices if we stick to the operations of addition, subtraction, and multiplication. A more formal model for modular arithmetic, which we now give, is best described within the framework of group theory.

Finite groups

A **group** $(S, \oplus)$ is a set S together with a binary operation $\oplus$ defined on S for which the following properties hold:

1. **Closure:** For all $a, b \in S$, we have $a \oplus b \in S$.

2. **Identity:** There exists an element $e \in S$, called the **identity** of the group, such that $e \oplus a = a \oplus e = a$ for all $a \in S$.

3. **Associativity:** For all $a, b, c \in S$, we have $(a \oplus b) \oplus c = a \oplus (b \oplus c)$.

4. **Inverses:** For each $a \in S$, there exists a unique element $b \in S$, called the *inverse* of a, such that $a \oplus b = b \oplus a = e$.

As an example, consider the familiar group $(\mathbb{Z}, +)$ of the integers $\mathbb{Z}$ under the operation of addition: 0 is the identity, and the inverse of a is $-a$. If a group $(S, \oplus)$ satisfies the *commutative law* $a \oplus b = b \oplus a$ for all $a, b \in S$, then it is an *abelian group*. If a group $(S, \oplus)$ satisfies $|S| < \infty$, then it is a *finite group*.

The groups defined by modular addition and multiplication

We can form two finite abelian groups by using addition and multiplication modulo n, where n is a positive integer. These groups are based on the equivalence classes of the integers modulo n, defined in Section 31.1.

To define a group on $\mathbb{Z}_n$, we need to have suitable binary operations, which we obtain by redefining the ordinary operations of addition and multiplication. We can easily define addition and multiplication operations for $\mathbb{Z}_n$, because the equivalence class of two integers uniquely determines the equivalence class of their sum or product. That is, if $a \equiv a' \pmod{n}$ and $b \equiv b' \pmod{n}$, then

$$a + b \equiv a' + b' \pmod{n},$$
$$ab \equiv a'b' \pmod{n}.$$

Thus, we define addition and multiplication modulo n, denoted $+_n$ and $\cdot_n$, by

$$
\begin{aligned}
[a]_n +_n [b]_n &= [a + b]_n, \\
[a]_n \cdot_n [b]_n &= [ab]_n.
\end{aligned}
\tag{31.18}
$$

(We can define subtraction similarly on $\mathbb{Z}_n$ by $[a]_n -_n [b]_n = [a - b]_n$, but division is more complicated, as we shall see.) These facts justify the common and convenient practice of using the smallest nonnegative element of each equivalence class as its representative when performing computations in $\mathbb{Z}_n$. We add, subtract, and multiply as usual on the representatives, but we replace each result x by the representative of its class, that is, by $x \bmod n$.

Using this definition of addition modulo n, we define the *additive group modulo n* as $(\mathbb{Z}_n, +_n)$. The size of the additive group modulo n is $|\mathbb{Z}_n| = n$. Figure 31.2(a) gives the operation table for the group $(\mathbb{Z}_6, +_6)$.

Theorem 31.12
The system $(\mathbb{Z}_n, +_n)$ is a finite abelian group.

Proof Equation (31.18) shows that $(\mathbb{Z}_n, +_n)$ is closed. Associativity and commutativity of $+_n$ follow from the associativity and commutativity of $+$:

$+_6$	0	1	2	3	4	5
0	0	1	2	3	4	5
1	1	2	3	4	5	0
2	2	3	4	5	0	1
3	3	4	5	0	1	2
4	4	5	0	1	2	3
5	5	0	1	2	3	4

$\cdot_{15}$	1	2	4	7	8	11	13	14
1	1	2	4	7	8	11	13	14
2	2	4	8	14	1	7	11	13
4	4	8	1	13	2	14	7	11
7	7	14	13	4	11	2	1	8
8	8	1	2	11	4	13	14	7
11	11	7	14	2	13	1	8	4
13	13	11	7	1	14	8	4	2
14	14	13	11	8	7	4	2	1

(a)   (b)

Figure 31.2 Two finite groups. Equivalence classes are denoted by their representative elements. **(a)** The group $(\mathbb{Z}_6, +_6)$. **(b)** The group $(\mathbb{Z}_{15}^*, \cdot_{15})$.

$$
\begin{aligned}
([a]_n +_n [b]_n) +_n [c]_n &= [a+b]_n +_n [c]_n \\
&= [(a+b)+c]_n \\
&= [a+(b+c)]_n \\
&= [a]_n +_n [b+c]_n \\
&= [a]_n +_n ([b]_n +_n [c]_n) \, ,
\end{aligned}
$$

$$
\begin{aligned}
[a]_n +_n [b]_n &= [a+b]_n \\
&= [b+a]_n \\
&= [b]_n +_n [a]_n \, .
\end{aligned}
$$

The identity element of $(\mathbb{Z}_n, +_n)$ is 0 (that is, $[0]_n$). The (additive) inverse of an element a (that is, of $[a]_n$) is the element $-a$ (that is, $[-a]_n$ or $[n-a]_n$), since $[a]_n +_n [-a]_n = [a-a]_n = [0]_n$.   ∎

Using the definition of multiplication modulo n, we define the ***multiplicative group modulo n*** as $(\mathbb{Z}_n^*, \cdot_n)$. The elements of this group are the set $\mathbb{Z}_n^*$ of elements in $\mathbb{Z}_n$ that are relatively prime to n, so that each one has a unique inverse, modulo n:

$$\mathbb{Z}_n^* = \{[a]_n \in \mathbb{Z}_n : \gcd(a, n) = 1\} \, .$$

To see that $\mathbb{Z}_n^*$ is well defined, note that for $0 \le a < n$, we have $a \equiv (a + kn)$ (mod n) for all integers k. By Exercise 31.2-3, therefore, $\gcd(a, n) = 1$ implies $\gcd(a + kn, n) = 1$ for all integers k. Since $[a]_n = \{a + kn : k \in \mathbb{Z}\}$, the set $\mathbb{Z}_n^*$ is well defined. An example of such a group is

$$\mathbb{Z}_{15}^* = \{1, 2, 4, 7, 8, 11, 13, 14\} \, ,$$

where the group operation is multiplication modulo 15. (Here we denote an element $[a]_{15}$ as a; for example, we denote $[7]_{15}$ as 7.) Figure 31.2(b) shows the group $(\mathbb{Z}_{15}^*, \cdot_{15})$. For example, $8 \cdot 11 \equiv 13 \pmod{15}$, working in $\mathbb{Z}_{15}^*$. The identity for this group is 1.

Theorem 31.13
The system $(\mathbb{Z}_n^*, \cdot_n)$ is a finite abelian group.

Proof   Theorem 31.6 implies that $(\mathbb{Z}_n^*, \cdot_n)$ is closed. Associativity and commutativity can be proved for $\cdot_n$ as they were for $+_n$ in the proof of Theorem 31.12. The identity element is $[1]_n$. To show the existence of inverses, let a be an element of $\mathbb{Z}_n^*$ and let (d, x, y) be returned by EXTENDED-EUCLID(a, n). Then, $d = 1$, since $a \in \mathbb{Z}_n^*$, and

$$ax + ny = 1 \tag{31.19}$$

or, equivalently,

$$ax \equiv 1 \pmod{n} .$$

Thus, $[x]_n$ is a multiplicative inverse of $[a]_n$, modulo n. Furthermore, we claim that $[x]_n \in \mathbb{Z}_n^*$. To see why, equation (31.19) demonstrates that the smallest positive linear combination of x and n must be 1. Therefore, Theorem 31.2 implies that $\gcd(x, n) = 1$. We defer the proof that inverses are uniquely defined until Corollary 31.26.   ■

As an example of computing multiplicative inverses, suppose that $a = 5$ and $n = 11$. Then EXTENDED-EUCLID(a, n) returns $(d, x, y) = (1, -2, 1)$, so that $1 = 5 \cdot (-2) + 11 \cdot 1$. Thus, $[-2]_{11}$ (i.e., $[9]_{11}$) is the multiplicative inverse of $[5]_{11}$.

When working with the groups $(\mathbb{Z}_n, +_n)$ and $(\mathbb{Z}_n^*, \cdot_n)$ in the remainder of this chapter, we follow the convenient practice of denoting equivalence classes by their representative elements and denoting the operations $+_n$ and $\cdot_n$ by the usual arithmetic notations $+$ and $\cdot$ (or juxtaposition, so that $ab = a \cdot b$) respectively. Also, equivalences modulo n may also be interpreted as equations in $\mathbb{Z}_n$. For example, the following two statements are equivalent:

$$ax \equiv b \pmod{n} ,$$
$$[a]_n \cdot_n [x]_n = [b]_n .$$

As a further convenience, we sometimes refer to a group $(S, \oplus)$ merely as S when the operation $\oplus$ is understood from context. We may thus refer to the groups $(\mathbb{Z}_n, +_n)$ and $(\mathbb{Z}_n^*, \cdot_n)$ as $\mathbb{Z}_n$ and $\mathbb{Z}_n^*$, respectively.

We denote the (multiplicative) inverse of an element a by $(a^{-1} \bmod n)$. Division in $\mathbb{Z}_n^*$ is defined by the equation $a/b \equiv ab^{-1} \pmod{n}$. For example, in $\mathbb{Z}_{15}^*$

we have that $7^{-1} \equiv 13 \pmod{15}$, since $7 \cdot 13 = 91 \equiv 1 \pmod{15}$, so that $4/7 \equiv 4 \cdot 13 \equiv 7 \pmod{15}$.

The size of $\mathbb{Z}_n^*$ is denoted $\phi(n)$. This function, known as **Euler's phi function**, satisfies the equation

$$\phi(n) = n \prod_{p : p \text{ is prime and } p \mid n} \left(1 - \frac{1}{p}\right), \tag{31.20}$$

so that p runs over all the primes dividing n (including n itself, if n is prime). We shall not prove this formula here. Intuitively, we begin with a list of the n remainders $\{0, 1, \ldots, n-1\}$ and then, for each prime p that divides n, cross out every multiple of p in the list. For example, since the prime divisors of 45 are 3 and 5,

$$\begin{aligned} \phi(45) &= 45 \left(1 - \frac{1}{3}\right)\left(1 - \frac{1}{5}\right) \\ &= 45 \left(\frac{2}{3}\right)\left(\frac{4}{5}\right) \\ &= 24 . \end{aligned}$$

If p is prime, then $\mathbb{Z}_p^* = \{1, 2, \ldots, p-1\}$, and

$$\begin{aligned} \phi(p) &= p\left(1 - \frac{1}{p}\right) \\ &= p - 1 . \end{aligned} \tag{31.21}$$

If n is composite, then $\phi(n) < n - 1$, although it can be shown that

$$\phi(n) > \frac{n}{e^\gamma \ln\ln n + \frac{3}{\ln\ln n}} \tag{31.22}$$

for $n \geq 3$, where $\gamma = 0.5772156649\ldots$ is **Euler's constant**. A somewhat simpler (but looser) lower bound for $n > 5$ is

$$\phi(n) > \frac{n}{6 \ln\ln n} . \tag{31.23}$$

The lower bound (31.22) is essentially the best possible, since

$$\liminf_{n \to \infty} \frac{\phi(n)}{n / \ln\ln n} = e^{-\gamma} . \tag{31.24}$$

Subgroups

If $(S, \oplus)$ is a group, $S' \subseteq S$, and $(S', \oplus)$ is also a group, then $(S', \oplus)$ is a **subgroup** of $(S, \oplus)$. For example, the even integers form a subgroup of the integers under the operation of addition. The following theorem provides a useful tool for recognizing subgroups.

Theorem 31.14 (A nonempty closed subset of a finite group is a subgroup)
If $(S, \oplus)$ is a finite group and S' is any nonempty subset of S such that $a \oplus b \in S'$ for all $a, b \in S'$, then $(S', \oplus)$ is a subgroup of $(S, \oplus)$.

Proof   We leave the proof as Exercise 31.3-3.   ∎

For example, the set $\{0, 2, 4, 6\}$ forms a subgroup of $\mathbb{Z}_8$, since it is nonempty and closed under the operation $+$ (that is, it is closed under $+_8$).

The following theorem provides an extremely useful constraint on the size of a subgroup; we omit the proof.

Theorem 31.15 (Lagrange's theorem)
If $(S, \oplus)$ is a finite group and $(S', \oplus)$ is a subgroup of $(S, \oplus)$, then $|S'|$ is a divisor of $|S|$.   ∎

A subgroup S' of a group S is a **proper** subgroup if $S' \neq S$. We shall use the following corollary in our analysis in Section 31.8 of the Miller-Rabin primality test procedure.

Corollary 31.16
If S' is a proper subgroup of a finite group S, then $|S'| \leq |S|/2$.   ∎

Subgroups generated by an element

Theorem 31.14 gives us an easy way to produce a subgroup of a finite group $(S, \oplus)$: choose an element a and take all elements that can be generated from a using the group operation. Specifically, define $a^{(k)}$ for $k \geq 1$ by

$$a^{(k)} = \bigoplus_{i=1}^{k} a = \underbrace{a \oplus a \oplus \cdots \oplus a}_{k} \, .$$

For example, if we take $a = 2$ in the group $\mathbb{Z}_6$, the sequence $a^{(1)}, a^{(2)}, a^{(3)}, \ldots$ is

$$2, 4, 0, 2, 4, 0, 2, 4, 0, \ldots \, .$$

In the group $\mathbb{Z}_n$, we have $a^{(k)} = ka \bmod n$, and in the group $\mathbb{Z}_n^*$, we have $a^{(k)} = a^k \bmod n$. We define the **subgroup generated by a**, denoted $\langle a \rangle$ or $(\langle a \rangle, \oplus)$, by

$$\langle a \rangle = \{a^{(k)} : k \geq 1\} \, .$$

We say that a **generates** the subgroup $\langle a \rangle$ or that a is a **generator** of $\langle a \rangle$. Since S is finite, $\langle a \rangle$ is a finite subset of S, possibly including all of S. Since the associativity of $\oplus$ implies

$$a^{(i)} \oplus a^{(j)} = a^{(i+j)} \ ,$$

$\langle a \rangle$ is closed and therefore, by Theorem 31.14, $\langle a \rangle$ is a subgroup of S. For example, in $\mathbb{Z}_6$, we have

$$
\begin{aligned}
\langle 0 \rangle &= \{0\} \ , \\
\langle 1 \rangle &= \{0, 1, 2, 3, 4, 5\} \ , \\
\langle 2 \rangle &= \{0, 2, 4\} \ .
\end{aligned}
$$

Similarly, in $\mathbb{Z}_7^*$, we have

$$
\begin{aligned}
\langle 1 \rangle &= \{1\} \ , \\
\langle 2 \rangle &= \{1, 2, 4\} \ , \\
\langle 3 \rangle &= \{1, 2, 3, 4, 5, 6\} \ .
\end{aligned}
$$

The **order** of a (in the group S), denoted $\mathrm{ord}(a)$, is defined as the smallest positive integer t such that $a^{(t)} = e$.

Theorem 31.17
For any finite group $(S, \oplus)$ and any $a \in S$, the order of a is equal to the size of the subgroup it generates, or $\mathrm{ord}(a) = |\langle a \rangle|$.

Proof   Let $t = \mathrm{ord}(a)$. Since $a^{(t)} = e$ and $a^{(t+k)} = a^{(t)} \oplus a^{(k)} = a^{(k)}$ for $k \geq 1$, if $i > t$, then $a^{(i)} = a^{(j)}$ for some $j < i$. Thus, as we generate elements by a, we see no new elements after $a^{(t)}$. Thus, $\langle a \rangle = \{a^{(1)}, a^{(2)}, \ldots, a^{(t)}\}$, and so $|\langle a \rangle| \leq t$. To show that $|\langle a \rangle| \geq t$, we show that each element of the sequence $a^{(1)}, a^{(2)}, \ldots, a^{(t)}$ is distinct. Suppose for the purpose of contradiction that $a^{(i)} = a^{(j)}$ for some i and j satisfying $1 \leq i < j \leq t$. Then, $a^{(i+k)} = a^{(j+k)}$ for $k \geq 0$. But this equality implies that $a^{(i+(t-j))} = a^{(j+(t-j))} = e$, a contradiction, since $i + (t - j) < t$ but t is the least positive value such that $a^{(t)} = e$. Therefore, each element of the sequence $a^{(1)}, a^{(2)}, \ldots, a^{(t)}$ is distinct, and $|\langle a \rangle| \geq t$. We conclude that $\mathrm{ord}(a) = |\langle a \rangle|$.   ■

Corollary 31.18
The sequence $a^{(1)}, a^{(2)}, \ldots$ is periodic with period $t = \mathrm{ord}(a)$; that is, $a^{(i)} = a^{(j)}$ if and only if $i \equiv j \pmod{t}$.   ■

Consistent with the above corollary, we define $a^{(0)}$ as e and $a^{(i)}$ as $a^{(i \bmod t)}$, where $t = \mathrm{ord}(a)$, for all integers i.

Corollary 31.19
If $(S, \oplus)$ is a finite group with identity e, then for all $a \in S$,

$$a^{(|S|)} = e \ .$$

Proof Lagrange's theorem (Theorem 31.15) implies that $\text{ord}(a) \mid |S|$, and so $|S| \equiv 0 \pmod{t}$, where $t = \text{ord}(a)$. Therefore, $a^{(|S|)} = a^{(0)} = e$. ∎

Exercises

31.3-1
Draw the group operation tables for the groups $(\mathbb{Z}_4, +_4)$ and $(\mathbb{Z}_5^*, \cdot_5)$. Show that these groups are isomorphic by exhibiting a one-to-one correspondence α between their elements such that $a + b \equiv c \pmod{4}$ if and only if $\alpha(a) \cdot \alpha(b) \equiv \alpha(c) \pmod{5}$.

31.3-2
List all subgroups of $\mathbb{Z}_9$ and of $\mathbb{Z}_{13}^*$.

31.3-3
Prove Theorem 31.14.

31.3-4
Show that if p is prime and e is a positive integer, then

$$\phi(p^e) = p^{e-1}(p-1) .$$

31.3-5
Show that for any integer $n > 1$ and for any $a \in \mathbb{Z}_n^*$, the function $f_a : \mathbb{Z}_n^* \to \mathbb{Z}_n^*$ defined by $f_a(x) = ax \bmod n$ is a permutation of $\mathbb{Z}_n^*$.

31.4   Solving modular linear equations

We now consider the problem of finding solutions to the equation

$$ax \equiv b \pmod{n} , \tag{31.25}$$

where $a > 0$ and $n > 0$. This problem has several applications; for example, we shall use it as part of the procedure for finding keys in the RSA public-key cryptosystem in Section 31.7. We assume that a, b, and n are given, and we wish to find all values of x, modulo n, that satisfy equation (31.25). The equation may have zero, one, or more than one such solution.

Let $\langle a \rangle$ denote the subgroup of $\mathbb{Z}_n$ generated by a. Since $\langle a \rangle = \{a^{(x)} : x > 0\} = \{ax \bmod n : x > 0\}$, equation (31.25) has a solution if and only if $[b] \in \langle a \rangle$. Lagrange's theorem (Theorem 31.15) tells us that $|\langle a \rangle|$ must be a divisor of n. The following theorem gives us a precise characterization of $\langle a \rangle$.

Theorem 31.20
For any positive integers a and n, if $d = \gcd(a, n)$, then

$$\langle a \rangle = \langle d \rangle = \{0, d, 2d, \ldots, ((n/d) - 1)d\} \tag{31.26}$$

in $\mathbb{Z}_n$, and thus

$$|\langle a \rangle| = n/d .$$

Proof We begin by showing that $d \in \langle a \rangle$. Recall that EXTENDED-EUCLID(a, n) produces integers x' and y' such that $ax' + ny' = d$. Thus, $ax' \equiv d \pmod{n}$, so that $d \in \langle a \rangle$. In other words, d is a multiple of a in $\mathbb{Z}_n$.

Since $d \in \langle a \rangle$, it follows that every multiple of d belongs to $\langle a \rangle$, because any multiple of a multiple of a is itself a multiple of a. Thus, $\langle a \rangle$ contains every element in $\{0, d, 2d, \ldots, ((n/d) - 1)d\}$. That is, $\langle d \rangle \subseteq \langle a \rangle$.

We now show that $\langle a \rangle \subseteq \langle d \rangle$. If $m \in \langle a \rangle$, then $m = ax \bmod n$ for some integer x, and so $m = ax + ny$ for some integer y. However, $d \mid a$ and $d \mid n$, and so $d \mid m$ by equation (31.4). Therefore, $m \in \langle d \rangle$.

Combining these results, we have that $\langle a \rangle = \langle d \rangle$. To see that $|\langle a \rangle| = n/d$, observe that there are exactly n/d multiples of d between 0 and $n - 1$, inclusive. ∎

Corollary 31.21
The equation $ax \equiv b \pmod{n}$ is solvable for the unknown x if and only if $d \mid b$, where $d = \gcd(a, n)$.

Proof The equation $ax \equiv b \pmod{n}$ is solvable if and only if $[b] \in \langle a \rangle$, which is the same as saying

$$(b \bmod n) \in \{0, d, 2d, \ldots, ((n/d) - 1)d\} ,$$

by Theorem 31.20. If $0 \le b < n$, then $b \in \langle a \rangle$ if and only if $d \mid b$, since the members of $\langle a \rangle$ are precisely the multiples of d. If $b < 0$ or $b \ge n$, the corollary then follows from the observation that $d \mid b$ if and only if $d \mid (b \bmod n)$, since b and $b \bmod n$ differ by a multiple of n, which is itself a multiple of d. ∎

Corollary 31.22
The equation $ax \equiv b \pmod{n}$ either has d distinct solutions modulo n, where $d = \gcd(a, n)$, or it has no solutions.

Proof If $ax \equiv b \pmod{n}$ has a solution, then $b \in \langle a \rangle$. By Theorem 31.17, $\text{ord}(a) = |\langle a \rangle|$, and so Corollary 31.18 and Theorem 31.20 imply that the sequence $ai \bmod n$, for $i = 0, 1, \ldots$, is periodic with period $|\langle a \rangle| = n/d$. If $b \in \langle a \rangle$, then b appears exactly d times in the sequence $ai \bmod n$, for $i = 0, 1, \ldots, n - 1$, since the length-(n/d) block of values $\langle a \rangle$ repeats exactly d times as i increases from 0 to $n-1$. The indices x of the d positions for which $ax \bmod n = b$ are the solutions of the equation $ax \equiv b \pmod{n}$. ∎

Theorem 31.23
Let $d = \gcd(a, n)$, and suppose that $d = ax' + ny'$ for some integers x' and y' (for example, as computed by EXTENDED-EUCLID). If $d \mid b$, then the equation $ax \equiv b \pmod{n}$ has as one of its solutions the value x_0, where

$$x_0 = x'(b/d) \bmod n .$$

Proof We have

$$
\begin{aligned}
ax_0 &\equiv ax'(b/d) \pmod{n} \\
&\equiv d(b/d) \pmod{n} \quad (\text{because } ax' \equiv d \pmod{n}) \\
&\equiv b \pmod{n},
\end{aligned}
$$

and thus x_0 is a solution to $ax \equiv b \pmod{n}$. ∎

Theorem 31.24
Suppose that the equation $ax \equiv b \pmod{n}$ is solvable (that is, $d \mid b$, where $d = \gcd(a, n)$) and that x_0 is any solution to this equation. Then, this equation has exactly d distinct solutions, modulo n, given by $x_i = x_0 + i(n/d)$ for $i = 0, 1, \ldots, d-1$.

Proof Because $n/d > 0$ and $0 \le i(n/d) < n$ for $i = 0, 1, \ldots, d-1$, the values $x_0, x_1, \ldots, x_{d-1}$ are all distinct, modulo n. Since x_0 is a solution of $ax \equiv b \pmod{n}$, we have $ax_0 \bmod n \equiv b \pmod{n}$. Thus, for $i = 0, 1, \ldots, d-1$, we have

$$
\begin{aligned}
ax_i \bmod n &= a(x_0 + in/d) \bmod n \\
&= (ax_0 + ain/d) \bmod n \\
&= ax_0 \bmod n \quad (\text{because } d \mid a \text{ implies that } ain/d \text{ is a multiple of } n) \\
&\equiv b \pmod{n},
\end{aligned}
$$

and hence $ax_i \equiv b \pmod{n}$, making x_i a solution, too. By Corollary 31.22, the equation $ax \equiv b \pmod{n}$ has exactly d solutions, so that $x_0, x_1, \ldots, x_{d-1}$ must be all of them. ∎

We have now developed the mathematics needed to solve the equation $ax \equiv b \pmod{n}$; the following algorithm prints all solutions to this equation. The inputs a and n are arbitrary positive integers, and b is an arbitrary integer.

MODULAR-LINEAR-EQUATION-SOLVER(a, b, n)

1   $(d, x', y') = $ EXTENDED-EUCLID(a, n)
2   **if** $d \mid b$
3      $x_0 = x'(b/d) \bmod n$
4   **for** $i = 0$ **to** $d - 1$
5   print $(x_0 + i(n/d)) \bmod n$
6   **else** print "no solutions"

As an example of the operation of this procedure, consider the equation $14x \equiv 30 \pmod{100}$ (here, $a = 14$, $b = 30$, and $n = 100$). Calling EXTENDED-EUCLID in line 1, we obtain $(d, x', y') = (2, -7, 1)$. Since $2 \mid 30$, lines 3–5 execute. Line 3 computes $x_0 = (-7)(15) \bmod 100 = 95$. The loop on lines 4–5 prints the two solutions 95 and 45.

The procedure MODULAR-LINEAR-EQUATION-SOLVER works as follows. Line 1 computes $d = \gcd(a, n)$, along with two values x' and y' such that $d = ax' + ny'$, demonstrating that x' is a solution to the equation $ax' \equiv d \pmod{n}$. If d does not divide b, then the equation $ax \equiv b \pmod{n}$ has no solution, by Corollary 31.21. Line 2 checks to see whether $d \mid b$; if not, line 6 reports that there are no solutions. Otherwise, line 3 computes a solution x_0 to $ax \equiv b \pmod{n}$, in accordance with Theorem 31.23. Given one solution, Theorem 31.24 states that adding multiples of (n/d), modulo n, yields the other $d - 1$ solutions. The **for** loop of lines 4–5 prints out all d solutions, beginning with x_0 and spaced n/d apart, modulo n.

MODULAR-LINEAR-EQUATION-SOLVER performs $O(\lg n + \gcd(a, n))$ arithmetic operations, since EXTENDED-EUCLID performs $O(\lg n)$ arithmetic operations, and each iteration of the **for** loop of lines 4–5 performs a constant number of arithmetic operations.

The following corollaries of Theorem 31.24 give specializations of particular interest.

Corollary 31.25
For any $n > 1$, if $\gcd(a, n) = 1$, then the equation $ax \equiv b \pmod{n}$ has a unique solution, modulo n.   ■

If $b = 1$, a common case of considerable interest, the x we are looking for is a *multiplicative inverse* of a, modulo n.

Corollary 31.26
For any $n > 1$, if $\gcd(a, n) = 1$, then the equation $ax \equiv 1 \pmod{n}$ has a unique solution, modulo n. Otherwise, it has no solution.   ■

Thanks to Corollary 31.26, we can use the notation $a^{-1} \bmod n$ to refer to *the* multiplicative inverse of a, modulo n, when a and n are relatively prime. If $\gcd(a, n) = 1$, then the unique solution to the equation $ax \equiv 1 \pmod{n}$ is the integer x returned by EXTENDED-EUCLID, since the equation

$$\gcd(a, n) = 1 = ax + ny$$

implies $ax \equiv 1 \pmod{n}$. Thus, we can compute $a^{-1} \bmod n$ efficiently using EXTENDED-EUCLID.

Exercises

31.4-1
Find all solutions to the equation $35x \equiv 10 \pmod{50}$.

31.4-2
Prove that the equation $ax \equiv ay \pmod{n}$ implies $x \equiv y \pmod{n}$ whenever $\gcd(a, n) = 1$. Show that the condition $\gcd(a, n) = 1$ is necessary by supplying a counterexample with $\gcd(a, n) > 1$.

31.4-3
Consider the following change to line 3 of the procedure MODULAR-LINEAR-EQUATION-SOLVER:

3    $x_0 = x'(b/d) \bmod (n/d)$

Will this work? Explain why or why not.

31.4-4 ★
Let p be prime and $f(x) \equiv f_0 + f_1 x + \cdots + f_t x^t \pmod{p}$ be a polynomial of degree t, with coefficients f_i drawn from $\mathbb{Z}_p$. We say that $a \in \mathbb{Z}_p$ is a ***zero*** of f if $f(a) \equiv 0 \pmod{p}$. Prove that if a is a zero of f, then $f(x) \equiv (x - a)g(x) \pmod{p}$ for some polynomial $g(x)$ of degree $t - 1$. Prove by induction on t that if p is prime, then a polynomial $f(x)$ of degree t can have at most t distinct zeros modulo p.

31.5   The Chinese remainder theorem

Around A.D. 100, the Chinese mathematician Sun-Tsŭ solved the problem of finding those integers x that leave remainders 2, 3, and 2 when divided by 3, 5, and 7 respectively. One such solution is $x = 23$; all solutions are of the form $23 + 105k$

for arbitrary integers k. The "Chinese remainder theorem" provides a correspondence between a system of equations modulo a set of pairwise relatively prime moduli (for example, 3, 5, and 7) and an equation modulo their product (for example, 105).

The Chinese remainder theorem has two major applications. Let the integer n be factored as $n = n_1 n_2 \cdots n_k$, where the factors n_i are pairwise relatively prime. First, the Chinese remainder theorem is a descriptive "structure theorem" that describes the structure of $\mathbb{Z}_n$ as identical to that of the Cartesian product $\mathbb{Z}_{n_1} \times \mathbb{Z}_{n_2} \times \cdots \times \mathbb{Z}_{n_k}$ with componentwise addition and multiplication modulo n_i in the ith component. Second, this description helps us to design efficient algorithms, since working in each of the systems $\mathbb{Z}_{n_i}$ can be more efficient (in terms of bit operations) than working modulo n.

Theorem 31.27 (Chinese remainder theorem)
Let $n = n_1 n_2 \cdots n_k$, where the n_i are pairwise relatively prime. Consider the correspondence

$$a \leftrightarrow (a_1, a_2, \ldots, a_k),\tag{31.27}$$

where $a \in \mathbb{Z}_n$, $a_i \in \mathbb{Z}_{n_i}$, and

$$a_i = a \bmod n_i$$

for $i = 1, 2, \ldots, k$. Then, mapping (31.27) is a one-to-one correspondence (bijection) between $\mathbb{Z}_n$ and the Cartesian product $\mathbb{Z}_{n_1} \times \mathbb{Z}_{n_2} \times \cdots \times \mathbb{Z}_{n_k}$. Operations performed on the elements of $\mathbb{Z}_n$ can be equivalently performed on the corresponding k-tuples by performing the operations independently in each coordinate position in the appropriate system. That is, if

$$\begin{aligned} a &\leftrightarrow (a_1, a_2, \ldots, a_k),\\ b &\leftrightarrow (b_1, b_2, \ldots, b_k),\end{aligned}$$

then

$$(a + b) \bmod n \leftrightarrow ((a_1 + b_1) \bmod n_1, \ldots, (a_k + b_k) \bmod n_k),\tag{31.28}$$
$$(a - b) \bmod n \leftrightarrow ((a_1 - b_1) \bmod n_1, \ldots, (a_k - b_k) \bmod n_k),\tag{31.29}$$
$$(ab) \bmod n \leftrightarrow (a_1 b_1 \bmod n_1, \ldots, a_k b_k \bmod n_k).\tag{31.30}$$

Proof Transforming between the two representations is fairly straightforward. Going from a to $(a_1, a_2, \ldots, a_k)$ is quite easy and requires only k "mod" operations.

Computing a from inputs $(a_1, a_2, \ldots, a_k)$ is a bit more complicated. We begin by defining $m_i = n/n_i$ for $i = 1, 2, \ldots, k$; thus m_i is the product of all of the n_j's other than n_i: $m_i = n_1 n_2 \cdots n_{i-1} n_{i+1} \cdots n_k$. We next define

$$c_i = m_i(m_i^{-1} \bmod n_i) \tag{31.31}$$

for $i = 1, 2, \ldots, k$. Equation (31.31) is always well defined: since m_i and n_i are relatively prime (by Theorem 31.6), Corollary 31.26 guarantees that $m_i^{-1} \bmod n_i$ exists. Finally, we can compute a as a function of $a_1, a_2, \ldots, a_k$ as follows:

$$a \equiv (a_1c_1 + a_2c_2 + \cdots + a_kc_k) \pmod{n} . \tag{31.32}$$

We now show that equation (31.32) ensures that $a \equiv a_i \pmod{n_i}$ for $i = 1, 2, \ldots, k$. Note that if $j \neq i$, then $m_j \equiv 0 \pmod{n_i}$, which implies that $c_j \equiv m_j \equiv 0 \pmod{n_i}$. Note also that $c_i \equiv 1 \pmod{n_i}$, from equation (31.31). We thus have the appealing and useful correspondence

$$c_i \leftrightarrow (0, 0, \ldots, 0, 1, 0, \ldots, 0) ,$$

a vector that has 0s everywhere except in the ith coordinate, where it has a 1; the c_i thus form a "basis" for the representation, in a certain sense. For each i, therefore, we have

$$
\begin{aligned}
a &\equiv a_i c_i &\pmod{n_i} \\
&\equiv a_i m_i (m_i^{-1} \bmod n_i) &\pmod{n_i} \\
&\equiv a_i &\pmod{n_i} ,
\end{aligned}
$$

which is what we wished to show: our method of computing a from the a_i's produces a result a that satisfies the constraints $a \equiv a_i \pmod{n_i}$ for $i = 1, 2, \ldots, k$. The correspondence is one-to-one, since we can transform in both directions. Finally, equations (31.28)–(31.30) follow directly from Exercise 31.1-7, since $x \bmod n_i = (x \bmod n) \bmod n_i$ for any x and $i = 1, 2, \ldots, k$. ∎

We shall use the following corollaries later in this chapter.

Corollary 31.28
If $n_1, n_2, \ldots, n_k$ are pairwise relatively prime and $n = n_1 n_2 \cdots n_k$, then for any integers $a_1, a_2, \ldots, a_k$, the set of simultaneous equations

$$x \equiv a_i \pmod{n_i} ,$$

for $i = 1, 2, \ldots, k$, has a unique solution modulo n for the unknown x. ∎

Corollary 31.29
If $n_1, n_2, \ldots, n_k$ are pairwise relatively prime and $n = n_1 n_2 \cdots n_k$, then for all integers x and a,

$$x \equiv a \pmod{n_i}$$

for $i = 1, 2, \ldots, k$ if and only if

$$x \equiv a \pmod{n} . \qquad\blacksquare$$

	0	1	2	3	4	5	6	7	8	9	10	11	12
0	0	40	15	55	30	5	45	20	60	35	10	50	25
1	26	1	41	16	56	31	6	46	21	61	36	11	51
2	52	27	2	42	17	57	32	7	47	22	62	37	12
3	13	53	28	3	43	18	58	33	8	48	23	63	38
4	39	14	54	29	4	44	19	59	34	9	49	24	64

Figure 31.3 An illustration of the Chinese remainder theorem for $n_1 = 5$ and $n_2 = 13$. For this example, $c_1 = 26$ and $c_2 = 40$. In row i, column j is shown the value of a, modulo 65, such that $a \bmod 5 = i$ and $a \bmod 13 = j$. Note that row 0, column 0 contains a 0. Similarly, row 4, column 12 contains a 64 (equivalent to -1). Since $c_1 = 26$, moving down a row increases a by 26. Similarly, $c_2 = 40$ means that moving right by a column increases a by 40. Increasing a by 1 corresponds to moving diagonally downward and to the right, wrapping around from the bottom to the top and from the right to the left.

As an example of the application of the Chinese remainder theorem, suppose we are given the two equations

$$a \equiv 2 \pmod 5,$$
$$a \equiv 3 \pmod{13},$$

so that $a_1 = 2$, $n_1 = m_2 = 5$, $a_2 = 3$, and $n_2 = m_1 = 13$, and we wish to compute $a \bmod 65$, since $n = n_1 n_2 = 65$. Because $13^{-1} \equiv 2 \pmod 5$ and $5^{-1} \equiv 8 \pmod{13}$, we have

$$c_1 = 13(2 \bmod 5) = 26,$$
$$c_2 = 5(8 \bmod 13) = 40,$$

and

$$
\begin{aligned}
a &\equiv 2 \cdot 26 + 3 \cdot 40 && \pmod{65} \\
  &\equiv 52 + 120 && \pmod{65} \\
  &\equiv 42 && \pmod{65}.
\end{aligned}
$$

See Figure 31.3 for an illustration of the Chinese remainder theorem, modulo 65.

Thus, we can work modulo n by working modulo n directly or by working in the transformed representation using separate modulo n_i computations, as convenient. The computations are entirely equivalent.

Exercises

31.5-1
Find all solutions to the equations $x \equiv 4 \pmod 5$ and $x \equiv 5 \pmod{11}$.

31.5-2
Find all integers x that leave remainders $1, 2, 3$ when divided by $9, 8, 7$ respectively.

31.5-3
Argue that, under the definitions of Theorem 31.27, if $\gcd(a, n) = 1$, then

$$(a^{-1} \bmod n) \leftrightarrow ((a_1^{-1} \bmod n_1), (a_2^{-1} \bmod n_2), \ldots, (a_k^{-1} \bmod n_k)) .$$

31.5-4
Under the definitions of Theorem 31.27, prove that for any polynomial f, the number of roots of the equation $f(x) \equiv 0 \pmod{n}$ equals the product of the number of roots of each of the equations $f(x) \equiv 0 \pmod{n_1}$, $f(x) \equiv 0 \pmod{n_2}$, $\ldots$, $f(x) \equiv 0 \pmod{n_k}$.

31.6   Powers of an element

Just as we often consider the multiples of a given element a, modulo n, we consider the sequence of powers of a, modulo n, where $a \in \mathbb{Z}_n^*$:

$$a^0, a^1, a^2, a^3, \ldots, \tag{31.33}$$

modulo n. Indexing from 0, the 0th value in this sequence is $a^0 \bmod n = 1$, and the ith value is $a^i \bmod n$. For example, the powers of 3 modulo 7 are

i	0	1	2	3	4	5	6	7	8	9	10	11	$\cdots$
$3^i \bmod 7$	1	3	2	6	4	5	1	3	2	6	4	5	$\cdots$

whereas the powers of 2 modulo 7 are

i	0	1	2	3	4	5	6	7	8	9	10	11	$\cdots$
$2^i \bmod 7$	1	2	4	1	2	4	1	2	4	1	2	4	$\cdots$

In this section, let $\langle a \rangle$ denote the subgroup of $\mathbb{Z}_n^*$ generated by a by repeated multiplication, and let $\text{ord}_n(a)$ (the "order of a, modulo n") denote the order of a in $\mathbb{Z}_n^*$. For example, $\langle 2 \rangle = \{1, 2, 4\}$ in $\mathbb{Z}_7^*$, and $\text{ord}_7(2) = 3$. Using the definition of the Euler phi function $\phi(n)$ as the size of $\mathbb{Z}_n^*$ (see Section 31.3), we now translate Corollary 31.19 into the notation of $\mathbb{Z}_n^*$ to obtain Euler's theorem and specialize it to $\mathbb{Z}_p^*$, where p is prime, to obtain Fermat's theorem.

Theorem 31.30 (Euler's theorem)
For any integer $n > 1$,

$$a^{\phi(n)} \equiv 1 \pmod{n} \text{ for all } a \in \mathbb{Z}_n^* .$$

∎

Theorem 31.31 (Fermat's theorem)
If p is prime, then

$$a^{p-1} \equiv 1 \pmod{p} \text{ for all } a \in \mathbb{Z}_p^* \,.$$

Proof By equation (31.21), $\phi(p) = p - 1$ if p is prime. ∎

Fermat's theorem applies to every element in $\mathbb{Z}_p$ except 0, since $0 \notin \mathbb{Z}_p^*$. For all $a \in \mathbb{Z}_p$, however, we have $a^p \equiv a \pmod{p}$ if p is prime.

If $\mathrm{ord}_n(g) = |\mathbb{Z}_n^*|$, then every element in $\mathbb{Z}_n^*$ is a power of g, modulo n, and g is a ***primitive root*** or a ***generator*** of $\mathbb{Z}_n^*$. For example, 3 is a primitive root, modulo 7, but 2 is not a primitive root, modulo 7. If $\mathbb{Z}_n^*$ possesses a primitive root, the group $\mathbb{Z}_n^*$ is ***cyclic***. We omit the proof of the following theorem, which is proven by Niven and Zuckerman [265].

Theorem 31.32
The values of $n > 1$ for which $\mathbb{Z}_n^*$ is cyclic are 2, 4, p^e, and $2p^e$, for all primes $p > 2$ and all positive integers e. ∎

If g is a primitive root of $\mathbb{Z}_n^*$ and a is any element of $\mathbb{Z}_n^*$, then there exists a z such that $g^z \equiv a \pmod{n}$. This z is a ***discrete logarithm*** or an ***index*** of a, modulo n, to the base g; we denote this value as $\mathrm{ind}_{n,g}(a)$.

Theorem 31.33 (Discrete logarithm theorem)
If g is a primitive root of $\mathbb{Z}_n^*$, then the equation $g^x \equiv g^y \pmod{n}$ holds if and only if the equation $x \equiv y \pmod{\phi(n)}$ holds.

Proof Suppose first that $x \equiv y \pmod{\phi(n)}$. Then, $x = y + k\phi(n)$ for some integer k. Therefore,

$$
\begin{aligned}
g^x &\equiv g^{y+k\phi(n)} &&\pmod{n} \\
&\equiv g^y \cdot (g^{\phi(n)})^k &&\pmod{n} \\
&\equiv g^y \cdot 1^k &&\pmod{n} &&\text{(by Euler's theorem)} \\
&\equiv g^y &&\pmod{n} \,.
\end{aligned}
$$

Conversely, suppose that $g^x \equiv g^y \pmod{n}$. Because the sequence of powers of g generates every element of $\langle g \rangle$ and $|\langle g \rangle| = \phi(n)$, Corollary 31.18 implies that the sequence of powers of g is periodic with period $\phi(n)$. Therefore, if $g^x \equiv g^y \pmod{n}$, then we must have $x \equiv y \pmod{\phi(n)}$. ∎

We now turn our attention to the square roots of 1, modulo a prime power. The following theorem will be useful in our development of a primality-testing algorithm in Section 31.8.

Theorem 31.34

If p is an odd prime and $e \geq 1$, then the equation

$$x^2 \equiv 1 \pmod{p^e} \tag{31.34}$$

has only two solutions, namely $x = 1$ and $x = -1$.

Proof   Equation (31.34) is equivalent to

$$p^e \mid (x - 1)(x + 1) \, .$$

Since $p > 2$, we can have $p \mid (x - 1)$ or $p \mid (x + 1)$, but not both. (Otherwise, by property (31.3), p would also divide their difference $(x + 1) - (x - 1) = 2$.) If $p \nmid (x - 1)$, then $\gcd(p^e, x - 1) = 1$, and by Corollary 31.5, we would have $p^e \mid (x + 1)$. That is, $x \equiv -1 \pmod{p^e}$. Symmetrically, if $p \nmid (x + 1)$, then $\gcd(p^e, x + 1) = 1$, and Corollary 31.5 implies that $p^e \mid (x - 1)$, so that $x \equiv 1 \pmod{p^e}$. Therefore, either $x \equiv -1 \pmod{p^e}$ or $x \equiv 1 \pmod{p^e}$.   ∎

A number x is a ***nontrivial square root of 1, modulo n***, if it satisfies the equation $x^2 \equiv 1 \pmod{n}$ but x is equivalent to neither of the two "trivial" square roots: 1 or -1, modulo n. For example, 6 is a nontrivial square root of 1, modulo 35. We shall use the following corollary to Theorem 31.34 in the correctness proof in Section 31.8 for the Miller-Rabin primality-testing procedure.

Corollary 31.35

If there exists a nontrivial square root of 1, modulo n, then n is composite.

Proof   By the contrapositive of Theorem 31.34, if there exists a nontrivial square root of 1, modulo n, then n cannot be an odd prime or a power of an odd prime. If $x^2 \equiv 1 \pmod{2}$, then $x \equiv 1 \pmod{2}$, and so all square roots of 1, modulo 2, are trivial. Thus, n cannot be prime. Finally, we must have $n > 1$ for a nontrivial square root of 1 to exist. Therefore, n must be composite.   ∎

Raising to powers with repeated squaring

A frequently occurring operation in number-theoretic computations is raising one number to a power modulo another number, also known as ***modular exponentiation***. More precisely, we would like an efficient way to compute $a^b \bmod n$, where a and b are nonnegative integers and n is a positive integer. Modular exponentiation is an essential operation in many primality-testing routines and in the RSA public-key cryptosystem. The method of ***repeated squaring*** solves this problem efficiently using the binary representation of b.

Let $\langle b_k, b_{k-1}, \ldots, b_1, b_0 \rangle$ be the binary representation of b. (That is, the binary representation is $k + 1$ bits long, b_k is the most significant bit, and b_0 is the least

i	9	8	7	6	5	4	3	2	1	0
b_i	1	0	0	0	1	1	0	0	0	0
c	1	2	4	8	17	35	70	140	280	560
d	7	49	157	526	160	241	298	166	67	1

Figure 31.4 The results of MODULAR-EXPONENTIATION when computing a^b (mod n), where $a = 7, b = 560 = \langle 1000110000 \rangle$, and $n = 561$. The values are shown after each execution of the **for** loop. The final result is 1.

significant bit.) The following procedure computes a^c mod n as c is increased by doublings and incrementations from 0 to b.

MODULAR-EXPONENTIATION(a, b, n)

```
1   c = 0
2   d = 1
3   let ⟨b_k, b_{k−1}, . . . , b_0⟩ be the binary representation of b
4   for i = k downto 0
5       c = 2c
6       d = (d · d) mod n
7       if b_i == 1
8           c = c + 1
9           d = (d · a) mod n
10  return d
```

The essential use of squaring in line 6 of each iteration explains the name "repeated squaring." As an example, for $a = 7$, $b = 560$, and $n = 561$, the algorithm computes the sequence of values modulo 561 shown in Figure 31.4; the sequence of exponents used appears in the row of the table labeled by c.

The variable c is not really needed by the algorithm but is included for the following two-part loop invariant:

Just prior to each iteration of the **for** loop of lines 4–9,

1. The value of c is the same as the prefix $\langle b_k, b_{k−1}, \ldots, b_{i+1} \rangle$ of the binary representation of b, and

2. $d = a^c$ mod n.

We use this loop invariant as follows:

Initialization: Initially, $i = k$, so that the prefix $\langle b_k, b_{k−1}, \ldots, b_{i+1} \rangle$ is empty, which corresponds to $c = 0$. Moreover, $d = 1 = a^0$ mod n.

Maintenance: Let c' and d' denote the values of c and d at the end of an iteration of the **for** loop, and thus the values prior to the next iteration. Each iteration updates $c' = 2c$ (if $b_i = 0$) or $c' = 2c + 1$ (if $b_i = 1$), so that c will be correct prior to the next iteration. If $b_i = 0$, then $d' = d^2 \bmod n = (a^c)^2 \bmod n = a^{2c} \bmod n = a^{c'} \bmod n$. If $b_i = 1$, then $d' = d^2 a \bmod n = (a^c)^2 a \bmod n = a^{2c+1} \bmod n = a^{c'} \bmod n$. In either case, $d = a^c \bmod n$ prior to the next iteration.

Termination: At termination, $i = -1$. Thus, $c = b$, since c has the value of the prefix $\langle b_k, b_{k-1}, \dots, b_0 \rangle$ of b's binary representation. Hence $d = a^c \bmod n = a^b \bmod n$.

If the inputs a, b, and n are β-bit numbers, then the total number of arithmetic operations required is $O(\beta)$ and the total number of bit operations required is $O(\beta^3)$.

Exercises

31.6-1
Draw a table showing the order of every element in $\mathbb{Z}_{11}^*$. Pick the smallest primitive root g and compute a table giving $\mathrm{ind}_{11,g}(x)$ for all $x \in \mathbb{Z}_{11}^*$.

31.6-2
Give a modular exponentiation algorithm that examines the bits of b from right to left instead of left to right.

31.6-3
Assuming that you know $\phi(n)$, explain how to compute $a^{-1} \bmod n$ for any $a \in \mathbb{Z}_n^*$ using the procedure MODULAR-EXPONENTIATION.

31.7   The RSA public-key cryptosystem

With a public-key cryptosystem, we can encrypt messages sent between two communicating parties so that an eavesdropper who overhears the encrypted messages will not be able to decode them. A public-key cryptosystem also enables a party to append an unforgeable "digital signature" to the end of an electronic message. Such a signature is the electronic version of a handwritten signature on a paper document. It can be easily checked by anyone, forged by no one, yet loses its validity if any bit of the message is altered. It therefore provides authentication of both the identity of the signer and the contents of the signed message. It is the perfect tool for electronically signed business contracts, electronic checks, electronic purchase orders, and other electronic communications that parties wish to authenticate.

The RSA public-key cryptosystem relies on the dramatic difference between the ease of finding large prime numbers and the difficulty of factoring the product of two large prime numbers. Section 31.8 describes an efficient procedure for finding large prime numbers, and Section 31.9 discusses the problem of factoring large integers.

Public-key cryptosystems

In a public-key cryptosystem, each participant has both a ***public key*** and a ***secret key***. Each key is a piece of information. For example, in the RSA cryptosystem, each key consists of a pair of integers. The participants "Alice" and "Bob" are traditionally used in cryptography examples; we denote their public and secret keys as P_A, S_A for Alice and P_B, S_B for Bob.

Each participant creates his or her own public and secret keys. Secret keys are kept secret, but public keys can be revealed to anyone or even published. In fact, it is often convenient to assume that everyone's public key is available in a public directory, so that any participant can easily obtain the public key of any other participant.

The public and secret keys specify functions that can be applied to any message. Let $\mathcal{D}$ denote the set of permissible messages. For example, $\mathcal{D}$ might be the set of all finite-length bit sequences. In the simplest, and original, formulation of public-key cryptography, we require that the public and secret keys specify one-to-one functions from $\mathcal{D}$ to itself. We denote the function corresponding to Alice's public key P_A by $P_A()$ and the function corresponding to her secret key S_A by $S_A()$. The functions $P_A()$ and $S_A()$ are thus permutations of $\mathcal{D}$. We assume that the functions $P_A()$ and $S_A()$ are efficiently computable given the corresponding key P_A or S_A.

The public and secret keys for any participant are a "matched pair" in that they specify functions that are inverses of each other. That is,

$$M = S_A(P_A(M)) , \tag{31.35}$$
$$M = P_A(S_A(M)) \tag{31.36}$$

for any message $M \in \mathcal{D}$. Transforming M with the two keys P_A and S_A successively, in either order, yields the message M back.

In a public-key cryptosystem, we require that no one but Alice be able to compute the function $S_A()$ in any practical amount of time. This assumption is crucial to keeping encrypted mail sent to Alice private and to knowing that Alice's digital signatures are authentic. Alice must keep S_A secret; if she does not, she loses her uniqueness and the cryptosystem cannot provide her with unique capabilities. The assumption that only Alice can compute $S_A()$ must hold even though everyone

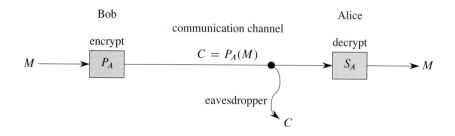

Figure 31.5 Encryption in a public key system. Bob encrypts the message M using Alice's public key P_A and transmits the resulting ciphertext $C = P_A(M)$ over a communication channel to Alice. An eavesdropper who captures the transmitted ciphertext gains no information about M. Alice receives C and decrypts it using her secret key to obtain the original message $M = S_A(C)$.

knows P_A and can compute $P_A()$, the inverse function to $S_A()$, efficiently. In order to design a workable public-key cryptosystem, we must figure out how to create a system in which we can reveal a transformation $P_A()$ without thereby revealing how to compute the corresponding inverse transformation $S_A()$. This task appears formidable, but we shall see how to accomplish it.

In a public-key cryptosystem, encryption works as shown in Figure 31.5. Suppose Bob wishes to send Alice a message M encrypted so that it will look like unintelligible gibberish to an eavesdropper. The scenario for sending the message goes as follows.

- Bob obtains Alice's public key P_A (from a public directory or directly from Alice).

- Bob computes the ***ciphertext*** $C = P_A(M)$ corresponding to the message M and sends C to Alice.

- When Alice receives the ciphertext C, she applies her secret key S_A to retrieve the original message: $S_A(C) = S_A(P_A(M)) = M$.

Because $S_A()$ and $P_A()$ are inverse functions, Alice can compute M from C. Because only Alice is able to compute $S_A()$, Alice is the only one who can compute M from C. Because Bob encrypts M using $P_A()$, only Alice can understand the transmitted message.

We can just as easily implement digital signatures within our formulation of a public-key cryptosystem. (There are other ways of approaching the problem of constructing digital signatures, but we shall not go into them here.) Suppose now that Alice wishes to send Bob a digitally signed response M'. Figure 31.6 shows how the digital-signature scenario proceeds.

- Alice computes her ***digital signature*** σ for the message M' using her secret key S_A and the equation $\sigma = S_A(M')$.

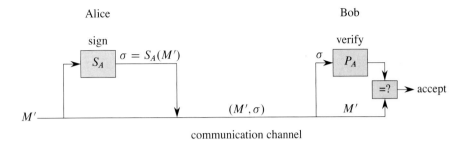

Figure 31.6   Digital signatures in a public-key system. Alice signs the message M' by appending her digital signature $\sigma = S_A(M')$ to it. She transmits the message/signature pair (M', σ) to Bob, who verifies it by checking the equation $M' = P_A(\sigma)$. If the equation holds, he accepts (M', σ) as a message that Alice has signed.

- Alice sends the message/signature pair (M', σ) to Bob.

- When Bob receives (M', σ), he can verify that it originated from Alice by using Alice's public key to verify the equation $M' = P_A(\sigma)$. (Presumably, M' contains Alice's name, so Bob knows whose public key to use.) If the equation holds, then Bob concludes that the message M' was actually signed by Alice. If the equation fails to hold, Bob concludes either that the message M' or the digital signature σ was corrupted by transmission errors or that the pair (M', σ) is an attempted forgery.

Because a digital signature provides both authentication of the signer's identity and authentication of the contents of the signed message, it is analogous to a handwritten signature at the end of a written document.

A digital signature must be verifiable by anyone who has access to the signer's public key. A signed message can be verified by one party and then passed on to other parties who can also verify the signature. For example, the message might be an electronic check from Alice to Bob. After Bob verifies Alice's signature on the check, he can give the check to his bank, who can then also verify the signature and effect the appropriate funds transfer.

A signed message is not necessarily encrypted; the message can be "in the clear" and not protected from disclosure. By composing the above protocols for encryption and for signatures, we can create messages that are both signed and encrypted. The signer first appends his or her digital signature to the message and then encrypts the resulting message/signature pair with the public key of the intended recipient. The recipient decrypts the received message with his or her secret key to obtain both the original message and its digital signature. The recipient can then verify the signature using the public key of the signer. The corresponding combined process using paper-based systems would be to sign the paper document and then seal the document inside a paper envelope that is opened only by the intended recipient.

The RSA cryptosystem

In the **RSA public-key cryptosystem**, a participant creates his or her public and secret keys with the following procedure:

1. Select at random two large prime numbers p and q such that $p \neq q$. The primes p and q might be, say, 1024 bits each.

2. Compute $n = pq$.

3. Select a small odd integer e that is relatively prime to $\phi(n)$, which, by equation (31.20), equals $(p - 1)(q - 1)$.

4. Compute d as the multiplicative inverse of e, modulo $\phi(n)$. (Corollary 31.26 guarantees that d exists and is uniquely defined. We can use the technique of Section 31.4 to compute d, given e and $\phi(n)$.)

5. Publish the pair $P = (e, n)$ as the participant's **RSA public key**.

6. Keep secret the pair $S = (d, n)$ as the participant's **RSA secret key**.

For this scheme, the domain $\mathcal{D}$ is the set $\mathbb{Z}_n$. To transform a message M associated with a public key $P = (e, n)$, compute

$$P(M) = M^e \bmod n . \tag{31.37}$$

To transform a ciphertext C associated with a secret key $S = (d, n)$, compute

$$S(C) = C^d \bmod n . \tag{31.38}$$

These equations apply to both encryption and signatures. To create a signature, the signer applies his or her secret key to the message to be signed, rather than to a ciphertext. To verify a signature, the public key of the signer is applied to it, rather than to a message to be encrypted.

We can implement the public-key and secret-key operations using the procedure MODULAR-EXPONENTIATION described in Section 31.6. To analyze the running time of these operations, assume that the public key (e, n) and secret key (d, n) satisfy $\lg e = O(1)$, $\lg d \leq \beta$, and $\lg n \leq \beta$. Then, applying a public key requires $O(1)$ modular multiplications and uses $O(\beta^2)$ bit operations. Applying a secret key requires $O(\beta)$ modular multiplications, using $O(\beta^3)$ bit operations.

Theorem 31.36 (Correctness of RSA)
The RSA equations (31.37) and (31.38) define inverse transformations of $\mathbb{Z}_n$ satisfying equations (31.35) and (31.36).

Proof From equations (31.37) and (31.38), we have that for any $M \in \mathbb{Z}_n$,

$$P(S(M)) = S(P(M)) = M^{ed} \pmod{n} .$$

Since e and d are multiplicative inverses modulo $\phi(n) = (p-1)(q-1)$,

$$ed = 1 + k(p-1)(q-1)$$

for some integer k. But then, if $M \not\equiv 0 \pmod{p}$, we have

$$
\begin{aligned}
M^{ed} &\equiv M(M^{p-1})^{k(q-1)} && \pmod{p} \\
&\equiv M((M \bmod p)^{p-1})^{k(q-1)} && \pmod{p} \\
&\equiv M(1)^{k(q-1)} && \pmod{p} && \text{(by Theorem 31.31)} \\
&\equiv M && \pmod{p} .
\end{aligned}
$$

Also, $M^{ed} \equiv M \pmod{p}$ if $M \equiv 0 \pmod{p}$. Thus,

$$M^{ed} \equiv M \pmod{p}$$

for all M. Similarly,

$$M^{ed} \equiv M \pmod{q}$$

for all M. Thus, by Corollary 31.29 to the Chinese remainder theorem,

$$M^{ed} \equiv M \pmod{n}$$

for all M.   ∎

The security of the RSA cryptosystem rests in large part on the difficulty of factoring large integers. If an adversary can factor the modulus n in a public key, then the adversary can derive the secret key from the public key, using the knowledge of the factors p and q in the same way that the creator of the public key used them. Therefore, if factoring large integers is easy, then breaking the RSA cryptosystem is easy. The converse statement, that if factoring large integers is hard, then breaking RSA is hard, is unproven. After two decades of research, however, no easier method has been found to break the RSA public-key cryptosystem than to factor the modulus n. And as we shall see in Section 31.9, factoring large integers is surprisingly difficult. By randomly selecting and multiplying together two 1024-bit primes, we can create a public key that cannot be "broken" in any feasible amount of time with current technology. In the absence of a fundamental breakthrough in the design of number-theoretic algorithms, and when implemented with care following recommended standards, the RSA cryptosystem is capable of providing a high degree of security in applications.

In order to achieve security with the RSA cryptosystem, however, we should use integers that are quite long—hundreds or even more than one thousand bits long—to resist possible advances in the art of factoring. At the time of this writing (2009), RSA moduli were commonly in the range of 768 to 2048 bits. To create moduli of such sizes, we must be able to find large primes efficiently. Section 31.8 addresses this problem.

For efficiency, RSA is often used in a "hybrid" or "key-management" mode with fast non-public-key cryptosystems. With such a system, the encryption and decryption keys are identical. If Alice wishes to send a long message M to Bob privately, she selects a random key K for the fast non-public-key cryptosystem and encrypts M using K, obtaining ciphertext C. Here, C is as long as M, but K is quite short. Then, she encrypts K using Bob's public RSA key. Since K is short, computing $P_B(K)$ is fast (much faster than computing $P_B(M)$). She then transmits $(C, P_B(K))$ to Bob, who decrypts $P_B(K)$ to obtain K and then uses K to decrypt C, obtaining M.

We can use a similar hybrid approach to make digital signatures efficiently. This approach combines RSA with a public ***collision-resistant hash function*** h—a function that is easy to compute but for which it is computationally infeasible to find two messages M and M' such that $h(M) = h(M')$. The value $h(M)$ is a short (say, 256-bit) "fingerprint" of the message M. If Alice wishes to sign a message M, she first applies h to M to obtain the fingerprint $h(M)$, which she then encrypts with her secret key. She sends $(M, S_A(h(M)))$ to Bob as her signed version of M. Bob can verify the signature by computing $h(M)$ and verifying that P_A applied to $S_A(h(M))$ as received equals $h(M)$. Because no one can create two messages with the same fingerprint, it is computationally infeasible to alter a signed message and preserve the validity of the signature.

Finally, we note that the use of ***certificates*** makes distributing public keys much easier. For example, assume there is a "trusted authority" T whose public key is known by everyone. Alice can obtain from T a signed message (her certificate) stating that "Alice's public key is P_A." This certificate is "self-authenticating" since everyone knows P_T. Alice can include her certificate with her signed messages, so that the recipient has Alice's public key immediately available in order to verify her signature. Because her key was signed by T, the recipient knows that Alice's key is really Alice's.

Exercises

31.7-1
Consider an RSA key set with $p = 11$, $q = 29$, $n = 319$, and $e = 3$. What value of d should be used in the secret key? What is the encryption of the message $M = 100$?

31.7-2

Prove that if Alice's public exponent e is 3 and an adversary obtains Alice's secret exponent d, where $0 < d < \phi(n)$, then the adversary can factor Alice's modulus n in time polynomial in the number of bits in n. (Although you are not asked to prove it, you may be interested to know that this result remains true even if the condition $e = 3$ is removed. See Miller [255].)

31.7-3 ★

Prove that RSA is multiplicative in the sense that

$$P_A(M_1)P_A(M_2) \equiv P_A(M_1 M_2) \pmod{n}.$$

Use this fact to prove that if an adversary had a procedure that could efficiently decrypt 1 percent of messages from $\mathbb{Z}_n$ encrypted with P_A, then he could employ a probabilistic algorithm to decrypt every message encrypted with P_A with high probability.

★ 31.8 Primality testing

In this section, we consider the problem of finding large primes. We begin with a discussion of the density of primes, proceed to examine a plausible, but incomplete, approach to primality testing, and then present an effective randomized primality test due to Miller and Rabin.

The density of prime numbers

For many applications, such as cryptography, we need to find large "random" primes. Fortunately, large primes are not too rare, so that it is feasible to test random integers of the appropriate size until we find a prime. The ***prime distribution function*** $\pi(n)$ specifies the number of primes that are less than or equal to n. For example, $\pi(10) = 4$, since there are 4 prime numbers less than or equal to 10, namely, 2, 3, 5, and 7. The prime number theorem gives a useful approximation to $\pi(n)$.

Theorem 31.37 (Prime number theorem)
$$\lim_{n \to \infty} \frac{\pi(n)}{n / \ln n} = 1.$$ ■

The approximation $n / \ln n$ gives reasonably accurate estimates of $\pi(n)$ even for small n. For example, it is off by less than 6% at $n = 10^9$, where $\pi(n) =$

50,847,534 and $n/\ln n \approx 48{,}254{,}942$. (To a number theorist, 10^9 is a small number.)

We can view the process of randomly selecting an integer n and determining whether it is prime as a Bernoulli trial (see Section C.4). By the prime number theorem, the probability of a success—that is, the probability that n is prime—is approximately $1/\ln n$. The geometric distribution tells us how many trials we need to obtain a success, and by equation (C.32), the expected number of trials is approximately $\ln n$. Thus, we would expect to examine approximately $\ln n$ integers chosen randomly near n in order to find a prime that is of the same length as n. For example, we expect that finding a 1024-bit prime would require testing approximately $\ln 2^{1024} \approx 710$ randomly chosen 1024-bit numbers for primality. (Of course, we can cut this figure in half by choosing only odd integers.)

In the remainder of this section, we consider the problem of determining whether or not a large odd integer n is prime. For notational convenience, we assume that n has the prime factorization

$$n = p_1^{e_1} p_2^{e_2} \cdots p_r^{e_r} \, , \tag{31.39}$$

where $r \geq 1$, $p_1, p_2, \ldots, p_r$ are the prime factors of n, and $e_1, e_2, \ldots, e_r$ are positive integers. The integer n is prime if and only if $r = 1$ and $e_1 = 1$.

One simple approach to the problem of testing for primality is ***trial division***. We try dividing n by each integer $2, 3, \ldots, \lfloor \sqrt{n} \rfloor$. (Again, we may skip even integers greater than 2.) It is easy to see that n is prime if and only if none of the trial divisors divides n. Assuming that each trial division takes constant time, the worst-case running time is $\Theta(\sqrt{n})$, which is exponential in the length of n. (Recall that if n is encoded in binary using β bits, then $\beta = \lceil \lg(n + 1) \rceil$, and so $\sqrt{n} = \Theta(2^{\beta/2})$.) Thus, trial division works well only if n is very small or happens to have a small prime factor. When it works, trial division has the advantage that it not only determines whether n is prime or composite, but also determines one of n's prime factors if n is composite.

In this section, we are interested only in finding out whether a given number n is prime; if n is composite, we are not concerned with finding its prime factorization. As we shall see in Section 31.9, computing the prime factorization of a number is computationally expensive. It is perhaps surprising that it is much easier to tell whether or not a given number is prime than it is to determine the prime factorization of the number if it is not prime.

Pseudoprimality testing

We now consider a method for primality testing that "almost works" and in fact is good enough for many practical applications. Later on, we shall present a refinement of this method that removes the small defect. Let $\mathbb{Z}_n^+$ denote the nonzero elements of $\mathbb{Z}_n$:

$$\mathbb{Z}_n^+ = \{1, 2, \ldots, n-1\} \ .$$

If n is prime, then $\mathbb{Z}_n^+ = \mathbb{Z}_n^*$.

We say that n is a ***base-a pseudoprime*** if n is composite and

$$a^{n-1} \equiv 1 \pmod{n} \ . \tag{31.40}$$

Fermat's theorem (Theorem 31.31) implies that if n is prime, then n satisfies equation (31.40) for every a in $\mathbb{Z}_n^+$. Thus, if we can find any $a \in \mathbb{Z}_n^+$ such that n does *not* satisfy equation (31.40), then n is certainly composite. Surprisingly, the converse *almost* holds, so that this criterion forms an almost perfect test for primality. We test to see whether n satisfies equation (31.40) for $a = 2$. If not, we declare n to be composite by returning COMPOSITE. Otherwise, we return PRIME, guessing that n is prime (when, in fact, all we know is that n is either prime or a base-2 pseudoprime).

The following procedure pretends in this manner to be checking the primality of n. It uses the procedure MODULAR-EXPONENTIATION from Section 31.6. We assume that the input n is an odd integer greater than 2.

PSEUDOPRIME(n)

1 **if** MODULAR-EXPONENTIATION$(2, n-1, n) \not\equiv 1 \pmod{n}$
2   **return** COMPOSITE   // definitely
3 **else return** PRIME   // we hope!

This procedure can make errors, but only of one type. That is, if it says that n is composite, then it is always correct. If it says that n is prime, however, then it makes an error only if n is a base-2 pseudoprime.

How often does this procedure err? Surprisingly rarely. There are only 22 values of n less than 10,000 for which it errs; the first four such values are 341, 561, 645, and 1105. We won't prove it, but the probability that this program makes an error on a randomly chosen β-bit number goes to zero as $\beta \to \infty$. Using more precise estimates due to Pomerance [279] of the number of base-2 pseudoprimes of a given size, we may estimate that a randomly chosen 512-bit number that is called prime by the above procedure has less than one chance in 10^{20} of being a base-2 pseudoprime, and a randomly chosen 1024-bit number that is called prime has less than one chance in 10^{41} of being a base-2 pseudoprime. So if you are merely trying to find a large prime for some application, for all practical purposes you almost never go wrong by choosing large numbers at random until one of them causes PSEUDOPRIME to return PRIME. But when the numbers being tested for primality are not randomly chosen, we need a better approach for testing primality.

As we shall see, a little more cleverness, and some randomization, will yield a primality-testing routine that works well on all inputs.

Unfortunately, we cannot entirely eliminate all the errors by simply checking equation (31.40) for a second base number, say $a = 3$, because there exist composite integers n, known as ***Carmichael numbers***, that satisfy equation (31.40) for *all* $a \in \mathbb{Z}_n^*$. (We note that equation (31.40) does fail when $\gcd(a, n) > 1$—that is, when $a \notin \mathbb{Z}_n^*$—but hoping to demonstrate that n is composite by finding such an a can be difficult if n has only large prime factors.) The first three Carmichael numbers are 561, 1105, and 1729. Carmichael numbers are extremely rare; there are, for example, only 255 of them less than 100,000,000. Exercise 31.8-2 helps explain why they are so rare.

We next show how to improve our primality test so that it won't be fooled by Carmichael numbers.

The Miller-Rabin randomized primality test

The Miller-Rabin primality test overcomes the problems of the simple test PSEU-DOPRIME with two modifications:

- It tries several randomly chosen base values a instead of just one base value.

- While computing each modular exponentiation, it looks for a nontrivial square root of 1, modulo n, during the final set of squarings. If it finds one, it stops and returns COMPOSITE. Corollary 31.35 from Section 31.6 justifies detecting composites in this manner.

The pseudocode for the Miller-Rabin primality test follows. The input $n > 2$ is the odd number to be tested for primality, and s is the number of randomly chosen base values from $\mathbb{Z}_n^+$ to be tried. The code uses the random-number generator RANDOM described on page 117: RANDOM$(1, n - 1)$ returns a randomly chosen integer a satisfying $1 \leq a \leq n-1$. The code uses an auxiliary procedure WITNESS such that WITNESS(a, n) is TRUE if and only if a is a "witness" to the composite-ness of n—that is, if it is possible using a to prove (in a manner that we shall see) that n is composite. The test WITNESS(a, n) is an extension of, but more effective than, the test

$$a^{n-1} \not\equiv 1 \pmod{n}$$

that formed the basis (using $a = 2$) for PSEUDOPRIME. We first present and justify the construction of WITNESS, and then we shall show how we use it in the Miller-Rabin primality test. Let $n - 1 = 2^t u$ where $t \geq 1$ and u is odd; i.e., the binary representation of $n - 1$ is the binary representation of the odd integer u followed by exactly t zeros. Therefore, $a^{n-1} \equiv (a^u)^{2^t} \pmod{n}$, so that we can compute $a^{n-1} \bmod n$ by first computing $a^u \bmod n$ and then squaring the result t times successively.

WITNESS(a, n)

```
1  let t and u be such that t ≥ 1, u is odd, and n − 1 = 2^t u
2  x_0 = MODULAR-EXPONENTIATION(a, u, n)
3  for i = 1 to t
4      x_i = x_{i-1}^2 mod n
5      if x_i == 1 and x_{i-1} ≠ 1 and x_{i-1} ≠ n − 1
6          return TRUE
7  if x_t ≠ 1
8      return TRUE
9  return FALSE
```

This pseudocode for WITNESS computes $a^{n-1} \bmod n$ by first computing the value $x_0 = a^u \bmod n$ in line 2 and then squaring the result t times in a row in the **for** loop of lines 3–6. By induction on i, the sequence $x_0, x_1, \ldots, x_t$ of values computed satisfies the equation $x_i \equiv a^{2^i u} \pmod{n}$ for $i = 0, 1, \ldots, t$, so that in particular $x_t \equiv a^{n-1} \pmod{n}$. After line 4 performs a squaring step, however, the loop may terminate early if lines 5–6 detect that a nontrivial square root of 1 has just been discovered. (We shall explain these tests shortly.) If so, the algorithm stops and returns TRUE. Lines 7–8 return TRUE if the value computed for $x_t \equiv a^{n-1} \pmod{n}$ is not equal to 1, just as the PSEUDOPRIME procedure returns COMPOSITE in this case. Line 9 returns FALSE if we haven't returned TRUE in lines 6 or 8.

We now argue that if WITNESS(a, n) returns TRUE, then we can construct a proof that n is composite using a as a witness.

If WITNESS returns TRUE from line 8, then it has discovered that $x_t = a^{n-1} \bmod n \neq 1$. If n is prime, however, we have by Fermat's theorem (Theorem 31.31) that $a^{n-1} \equiv 1 \pmod{n}$ for all $a \in \mathbb{Z}_n^+$. Therefore, n cannot be prime, and the equation $a^{n-1} \bmod n \neq 1$ proves this fact.

If WITNESS returns TRUE from line 6, then it has discovered that x_{i-1} is a nontrivial square root of 1, modulo n, since we have that $x_{i-1} \not\equiv \pm 1 \pmod{n}$ yet $x_i \equiv x_{i-1}^2 \equiv 1 \pmod{n}$. Corollary 31.35 states that only if n is composite can there exist a nontrivial square root of 1 modulo n, so that demonstrating that x_{i-1} is a nontrivial square root of 1 modulo n proves that n is composite.

This completes our proof of the correctness of WITNESS. If we find that the call WITNESS(a, n) returns TRUE, then n is surely composite, and the witness a, along with the reason that the procedure returns TRUE (did it return from line 6 or from line 8?), provides a proof that n is composite.

At this point, we briefly present an alternative description of the behavior of WITNESS as a function of the sequence $X = \langle x_0, x_1, \ldots, x_t \rangle$, which we shall find useful later on, when we analyze the efficiency of the Miller-Rabin primality test. Note that if $x_i = 1$ for some $0 \le i < t$, WITNESS might not compute the rest of the sequence. If it were to do so, however, each value $x_{i+1}, x_{i+2}, \ldots, x_t$ would be 1, and we consider these positions in the sequence X as being all 1s. We have four cases:

1. $X = \langle \ldots, d \rangle$, where $d \ne 1$: the sequence X does not end in 1. Return TRUE in line 8; a is a witness to the compositeness of n (by Fermat's Theorem).

2. $X = \langle 1, 1, \ldots, 1 \rangle$: the sequence X is all 1s. Return FALSE; a is not a witness to the compositeness of n.

3. $X = \langle \ldots, -1, 1, \ldots, 1 \rangle$: the sequence X ends in 1, and the last non-1 is equal to -1. Return FALSE; a is not a witness to the compositeness of n.

4. $X = \langle \ldots, d, 1, \ldots, 1 \rangle$, where $d \ne \pm 1$: the sequence X ends in 1, but the last non-1 is not -1. Return TRUE in line 6; a is a witness to the compositeness of n, since d is a nontrivial square root of 1.

We now examine the Miller-Rabin primality test based on the use of WITNESS. Again, we assume that n is an odd integer greater than 2.

MILLER-RABIN(n, s)

```
1  for j = 1 to s
2      a = RANDOM(1, n − 1)
3      if WITNESS(a, n)
4          return COMPOSITE        // definitely
5  return PRIME                    // almost surely
```

The procedure MILLER-RABIN is a probabilistic search for a proof that n is composite. The main loop (beginning on line 1) picks up to s random values of a from $\mathbb{Z}_n^+$ (line 2). If one of the a's picked is a witness to the compositeness of n, then MILLER-RABIN returns COMPOSITE on line 4. Such a result is always correct, by the correctness of WITNESS. If MILLER-RABIN finds no witness in s trials, then the procedure assumes that this is because no witnesses exist, and therefore it assumes that n is prime. We shall see that this result is likely to be correct if s is large enough, but that there is still a tiny chance that the procedure may be unlucky in its choice of a's and that witnesses do exist even though none has been found.

To illustrate the operation of MILLER-RABIN, let n be the Carmichael number 561, so that $n - 1 = 560 = 2^4 \cdot 35$, $t = 4$, and $u = 35$. If the procedure chooses $a = 7$ as a base, Figure 31.4 in Section 31.6 shows that WITNESS computes $x_0 \equiv a^{35} \equiv 241 \pmod{561}$ and thus computes the sequence

$X = \langle 241, 298, 166, 67, 1 \rangle$. Thus, WITNESS discovers a nontrivial square root of 1 in the last squaring step, since $a^{280} \equiv 67 \pmod{n}$ and $a^{560} \equiv 1 \pmod{n}$. Therefore, $a = 7$ is a witness to the compositeness of n, WITNESS$(7, n)$ returns TRUE, and MILLER-RABIN returns COMPOSITE.

If n is a β-bit number, MILLER-RABIN requires $O(s\beta)$ arithmetic operations and $O(s\beta^3)$ bit operations, since it requires asymptotically no more work than s modular exponentiations.

Error rate of the Miller-Rabin primality test

If MILLER-RABIN returns PRIME, then there is a very slim chance that it has made an error. Unlike PSEUDOPRIME, however, the chance of error does not depend on n; there are no bad inputs for this procedure. Rather, it depends on the size of s and the "luck of the draw" in choosing base values a. Moreover, since each test is more stringent than a simple check of equation (31.40), we can expect on general principles that the error rate should be small for randomly chosen integers n. The following theorem presents a more precise argument.

Theorem 31.38
If n is an odd composite number, then the number of witnesses to the compositeness of n is at least $(n - 1)/2$.

Proof The proof shows that the number of nonwitnesses is at most $(n - 1)/2$, which implies the theorem.

We start by claiming that any nonwitness must be a member of $\mathbb{Z}_n^*$. Why? Consider any nonwitness a. It must satisfy $a^{n-1} \equiv 1 \pmod{n}$ or, equivalently, $a \cdot a^{n-2} \equiv 1 \pmod{n}$. Thus, the equation $ax \equiv 1 \pmod{n}$ has a solution, namely a^{n-2}. By Corollary 31.21, $\gcd(a, n) \mid 1$, which in turn implies that $\gcd(a, n) = 1$. Therefore, a is a member of $\mathbb{Z}_n^*$; all nonwitnesses belong to $\mathbb{Z}_n^*$.

To complete the proof, we show that not only are all nonwitnesses contained in $\mathbb{Z}_n^*$, they are all contained in a proper subgroup B of $\mathbb{Z}_n^*$ (recall that we say B is a *proper* subgroup of $\mathbb{Z}_n^*$ when B is subgroup of $\mathbb{Z}_n^*$ but B is not equal to $\mathbb{Z}_n^*$). By Corollary 31.16, we then have $|B| \leq |\mathbb{Z}_n^*|/2$. Since $|\mathbb{Z}_n^*| \leq n - 1$, we obtain $|B| \leq (n - 1)/2$. Therefore, the number of nonwitnesses is at most $(n - 1)/2$, so that the number of witnesses must be at least $(n - 1)/2$.

We now show how to find a proper subgroup B of $\mathbb{Z}_n^*$ containing all of the nonwitnesses. We break the proof into two cases.

Case 1: There exists an $x \in \mathbb{Z}_n^*$ such that

$$x^{n-1} \not\equiv 1 \pmod{n}.$$

In other words, n is not a Carmichael number. Because, as we noted earlier, Carmichael numbers are extremely rare, case 1 is the main case that arises "in practice" (e.g., when n has been chosen randomly and is being tested for primality).

Let $B = \{b \in \mathbb{Z}_n^* : b^{n-1} \equiv 1 \pmod{n}\}$. Clearly, B is nonempty, since $1 \in B$. Since B is closed under multiplication modulo n, we have that B is a subgroup of $\mathbb{Z}_n^*$ by Theorem 31.14. Note that every nonwitness belongs to B, since a nonwitness a satisfies $a^{n-1} \equiv 1 \pmod{n}$. Since $x \in \mathbb{Z}_n^* - B$, we have that B is a proper subgroup of $\mathbb{Z}_n^*$.

Case 2: For all $x \in \mathbb{Z}_n^*$,

$$x^{n-1} \equiv 1 \pmod{n} . \tag{31.41}$$

In other words, n is a Carmichael number. This case is extremely rare in practice. However, the Miller-Rabin test (unlike a pseudo-primality test) can efficiently determine that Carmichael numbers are composite, as we now show.

In this case, n cannot be a prime power. To see why, let us suppose to the contrary that $n = p^e$, where p is a prime and $e > 1$. We derive a contradiction as follows. Since we assume that n is odd, p must also be odd. Theorem 31.32 implies that $\mathbb{Z}_n^*$ is a cyclic group: it contains a generator g such that $\mathrm{ord}_n(g) = |\mathbb{Z}_n^*| = \phi(n) = p^e(1 - 1/p) = (p-1)p^{e-1}$. (The formula for $\phi(n)$ comes from equation (31.20).) By equation (31.41), we have $g^{n-1} \equiv 1 \pmod{n}$. Then the discrete logarithm theorem (Theorem 31.33, taking $y = 0$) implies that $n - 1 \equiv 0 \pmod{\phi(n)}$, or

$$(p-1)p^{e-1} \mid p^e - 1 .$$

This is a contradiction for $e > 1$, since $(p-1)p^{e-1}$ is divisible by the prime p but $p^e - 1$ is not. Thus, n is not a prime power.

Since the odd composite number n is not a prime power, we decompose it into a product $n_1 n_2$, where n_1 and n_2 are odd numbers greater than 1 that are relatively prime to each other. (There may be several ways to decompose n, and it does not matter which one we choose. For example, if $n = p_1^{e_1} p_2^{e_2} \cdots p_r^{e_r}$, then we can choose $n_1 = p_1^{e_1}$ and $n_2 = p_2^{e_2} p_3^{e_3} \cdots p_r^{e_r}$.)

Recall that we define t and u so that $n - 1 = 2^t u$, where $t \geq 1$ and u is odd, and that for an input a, the procedure WITNESS computes the sequence

$$X = \langle a^u, a^{2u}, a^{2^2 u}, \ldots, a^{2^t u} \rangle$$

(all computations are performed modulo n).

Let us call a pair (v, j) of integers *acceptable* if $v \in \mathbb{Z}_n^*$, $j \in \{0, 1, \ldots, t\}$, and

$$v^{2^j u} \equiv -1 \pmod{n} .$$

Acceptable pairs certainly exist since u is odd; we can choose $v = n - 1$ and $j = 0$, so that $(n - 1, 0)$ is an acceptable pair. Now pick the largest possible j such that there exists an acceptable pair (v, j), and fix v so that (v, j) is an acceptable pair. Let

$$B = \{x \in \mathbb{Z}_n^* : x^{2^j u} \equiv \pm 1 \pmod{n}\} \,.$$

Since B is closed under multiplication modulo n, it is a subgroup of $\mathbb{Z}_n^*$. By Theorem 31.15, therefore, $|B|$ divides $|\mathbb{Z}_n^*|$. Every nonwitness must be a member of B, since the sequence X produced by a nonwitness must either be all 1s or else contain a -1 no later than the jth position, by the maximality of j. (If (a, j') is acceptable, where a is a nonwitness, we must have $j' \leq j$ by how we chose j.)

We now use the existence of v to demonstrate that there exists a $w \in \mathbb{Z}_n^* - B$, and hence that B is a proper subgroup of $\mathbb{Z}_n^*$. Since $v^{2^j u} \equiv -1 \pmod{n}$, we have $v^{2^j u} \equiv -1 \pmod{n_1}$ by Corollary 31.29 to the Chinese remainder theorem. By Corollary 31.28, there exists a w simultaneously satisfying the equations

$$w \equiv v \pmod{n_1} \,,$$
$$w \equiv 1 \pmod{n_2} \,.$$

Therefore,

$$w^{2^j u} \equiv -1 \pmod{n_1} \,,$$
$$w^{2^j u} \equiv 1 \pmod{n_2} \,.$$

By Corollary 31.29, $w^{2^j u} \not\equiv 1 \pmod{n_1}$ implies $w^{2^j u} \not\equiv 1 \pmod{n}$, and $w^{2^j u} \not\equiv -1 \pmod{n_2}$ implies $w^{2^j u} \not\equiv -1 \pmod{n}$. Hence, we conclude that $w^{2^j u} \not\equiv \pm 1 \pmod{n}$, and so $w \notin B$.

It remains to show that $w \in \mathbb{Z}_n^*$, which we do by first working separately modulo n_1 and modulo n_2. Working modulo n_1, we observe that since $v \in \mathbb{Z}_n^*$, we have that $\gcd(v, n) = 1$, and so also $\gcd(v, n_1) = 1$; if v does not have any common divisors with n, then it certainly does not have any common divisors with n_1. Since $w \equiv v \pmod{n_1}$, we see that $\gcd(w, n_1) = 1$. Working modulo n_2, we observe that $w \equiv 1 \pmod{n_2}$ implies $\gcd(w, n_2) = 1$. To combine these results, we use Theorem 31.6, which implies that $\gcd(w, n_1 n_2) = \gcd(w, n) = 1$. That is, $w \in \mathbb{Z}_n^*$.

Therefore $w \in \mathbb{Z}_n^* - B$, and we finish case 2 with the conclusion that B is a proper subgroup of $\mathbb{Z}_n^*$.

In either case, we see that the number of witnesses to the compositeness of n is at least $(n - 1)/2$. ∎

Theorem 31.39
For any odd integer $n > 2$ and positive integer s, the probability that MILLER-RABIN(n, s) errs is at most 2^{-s}.

Proof   Using Theorem 31.38, we see that if n is composite, then each execution of the **for** loop of lines 1–4 has a probability of at least $1/2$ of discovering a witness x to the compositeness of n. MILLER-RABIN makes an error only if it is so unlucky as to miss discovering a witness to the compositeness of n on each of the s iterations of the main loop. The probability of such a sequence of misses is at most 2^{-s}. ∎

If n is prime, MILLER-RABIN always reports PRIME, and if n is composite, the chance that MILLER-RABIN reports PRIME is at most 2^{-s}.

When applying MILLER-RABIN to a large randomly chosen integer n, however, we need to consider as well the prior probability that n is prime, in order to correctly interpret MILLER-RABIN's result. Suppose that we fix a bit length β and choose at random an integer n of length β bits to be tested for primality. Let A denote the event that n is prime. By the prime number theorem (Theorem 31.37), the probability that n is prime is approximately

$$\Pr\{A\} \approx 1/\ln n$$
$$\approx 1.443/\beta .$$

Now let B denote the event that MILLER-RABIN returns PRIME. We have that $\Pr\{\overline{B} \mid A\} = 0$ (or equivalently, that $\Pr\{B \mid A\} = 1$) and $\Pr\{B \mid \overline{A}\} \leq 2^{-s}$ (or equivalently, that $\Pr\{\overline{B} \mid \overline{A}\} > 1 - 2^{-s}$).

But what is $\Pr\{A \mid B\}$, the probability that n is prime, given that MILLER-RABIN has returned PRIME? By the alternate form of Bayes's theorem (equation (C.18)) we have

$$\Pr\{A \mid B\} = \frac{\Pr\{A\}\Pr\{B \mid A\}}{\Pr\{A\}\Pr\{B \mid A\} + \Pr\{\overline{A}\}\Pr\{B \mid \overline{A}\}}$$
$$\approx \frac{1}{1 + 2^{-s}(\ln n - 1)} .$$

This probability does not exceed $1/2$ until s exceeds $\lg(\ln n - 1)$. Intuitively, that many initial trials are needed just for the confidence derived from failing to find a witness to the compositeness of n to overcome the prior bias in favor of n being composite. For a number with $\beta = 1024$ bits, this initial testing requires about

$$\lg(\ln n - 1) \approx \lg(\beta/1.443)$$
$$\approx 9$$

trials. In any case, choosing $s = 50$ should suffice for almost any imaginable application.

In fact, the situation is much better. If we are trying to find large primes by applying MILLER-RABIN to large randomly chosen odd integers, then choosing a small value of s (say 3) is very unlikely to lead to erroneous results, though we won't prove it here. The reason is that for a randomly chosen odd composite integer n, the expected number of nonwitnesses to the compositeness of n is likely to be very much smaller than $(n-1)/2$.

If the integer n is not chosen randomly, however, the best that can be proven is that the number of nonwitnesses is at most $(n-1)/4$, using an improved version of Theorem 31.38. Furthermore, there do exist integers n for which the number of nonwitnesses is $(n-1)/4$.

Exercises

31.8-1
Prove that if an odd integer $n > 1$ is not a prime or a prime power, then there exists a nontrivial square root of 1 modulo n.

31.8-2 ★
It is possible to strengthen Euler's theorem slightly to the form

$$a^{\lambda(n)} \equiv 1 \pmod{n} \text{ for all } a \in \mathbb{Z}_n^*,$$

where $n = p_1^{e_1} \cdots p_r^{e_r}$ and $\lambda(n)$ is defined by

$$\lambda(n) = \text{lcm}(\phi(p_1^{e_1}), \ldots, \phi(p_r^{e_r})). \tag{31.42}$$

Prove that $\lambda(n) \mid \phi(n)$. A composite number n is a Carmichael number if $\lambda(n) \mid n-1$. The smallest Carmichael number is $561 = 3 \cdot 11 \cdot 17$; here, $\lambda(n) = \text{lcm}(2, 10, 16) = 80$, which divides 560. Prove that Carmichael numbers must be both "square-free" (not divisible by the square of any prime) and the product of at least three primes. (For this reason, they are not very common.)

31.8-3
Prove that if x is a nontrivial square root of 1, modulo n, then $\gcd(x - 1, n)$ and $\gcd(x + 1, n)$ are both nontrivial divisors of n.

★ 31.9 Integer factorization

Suppose we have an integer n that we wish to ***factor***, that is, to decompose into a product of primes. The primality test of the preceding section may tell us that n is composite, but it does not tell us the prime factors of n. Factoring a large integer n seems to be much more difficult than simply determining whether n is prime or composite. Even with today's supercomputers and the best algorithms to date, we cannot feasibly factor an arbitrary 1024-bit number.

Pollard's rho heuristic

Trial division by all integers up to R is guaranteed to factor completely any number up to R^2. For the same amount of work, the following procedure, POLLARD-RHO, factors any number up to R^4 (unless we are unlucky). Since the procedure is only a heuristic, neither its running time nor its success is guaranteed, although the procedure is highly effective in practice. Another advantage of the POLLARD-RHO procedure is that it uses only a constant number of memory locations. (If you wanted to, you could easily implement POLLARD-RHO on a programmable pocket calculator to find factors of small numbers.)

POLLARD-RHO(n)

```
1  i = 1
2  x₁ = RANDOM(0, n − 1)
3  y = x₁
4  k = 2
5  while TRUE
6      i = i + 1
7      xᵢ = (x²ᵢ₋₁ − 1) mod n
8      d = gcd(y − xᵢ, n)
9      if d ≠ 1 and d ≠ n
10         print d
11     if i == k
12         y = xᵢ
13         k = 2k
```

The procedure works as follows. Lines 1–2 initialize i to 1 and x_1 to a randomly chosen value in $\mathbb{Z}_n$. The **while** loop beginning on line 5 iterates forever, searching for factors of n. During each iteration of the **while** loop, line 7 uses the recurrence

$$x_i = (x_{i-1}^2 - 1) \bmod n \tag{31.43}$$

to produce the next value of x_i in the infinite sequence

$$x_1, x_2, x_3, x_4, \ldots, \tag{31.44}$$

with line 6 correspondingly incrementing i. The pseudocode is written using subscripted variables x_i for clarity, but the program works the same if all of the subscripts are dropped, since only the most recent value of x_i needs to be maintained. With this modification, the procedure uses only a constant number of memory locations.

Every so often, the program saves the most recently generated x_i value in the variable y. Specifically, the values that are saved are the ones whose subscripts are powers of 2:

$x_1, x_2, x_4, x_8, x_{16}, \ldots$.

Line 3 saves the value x_1, and line 12 saves x_k whenever i is equal to k. The variable k is initialized to 2 in line 4, and line 13 doubles it whenever line 12 updates y. Therefore, k follows the sequence $2, 4, 8, 16 \ldots$ and always gives the subscript of the next value x_k to be saved in y.

Lines 8–10 try to find a factor of n, using the saved value of y and the current value of x_i. Specifically, line 8 computes the greatest common divisor $d = \gcd(y - x_i, n)$. If line 9 finds d to be a nontrivial divisor of n, then line 10 prints d.

This procedure for finding a factor may seem somewhat mysterious at first. Note, however, that POLLARD-RHO never prints an incorrect answer; any number it prints is a nontrivial divisor of n. POLLARD-RHO might not print anything at all, though; it comes with no guarantee that it will print any divisors. We shall see, however, that we have good reason to expect POLLARD-RHO to print a factor p of n after $\Theta(\sqrt{p})$ iterations of the **while** loop. Thus, if n is composite, we can expect this procedure to discover enough divisors to factor n completely after approximately $n^{1/4}$ updates, since every prime factor p of n except possibly the largest one is less than $\sqrt{n}$.

We begin our analysis of how this procedure behaves by studying how long it takes a random sequence modulo n to repeat a value. Since $\mathbb{Z}_n$ is finite, and since each value in the sequence (31.44) depends only on the previous value, the sequence (31.44) eventually repeats itself. Once we reach an x_i such that $x_i = x_j$ for some $j < i$, we are in a cycle, since $x_{i+1} = x_{j+1}$, $x_{i+2} = x_{j+2}$, and so on. The reason for the name "rho heuristic" is that, as Figure 31.7 shows, we can draw the sequence $x_1, x_2, \ldots, x_{j-1}$ as the "tail" of the rho and the cycle $x_j, x_{j+1}, \ldots, x_i$ as the "body" of the rho.

Let us consider the question of how long it takes for the sequence of x_i to repeat. This information is not exactly what we need, but we shall see later how to modify the argument. For the purpose of this estimation, let us assume that the function

$$f_n(x) = (x^2 - 1) \bmod n$$

behaves like a "random" function. Of course, it is not really random, but this assumption yields results consistent with the observed behavior of POLLARD-RHO. We can then consider each x_i to have been independently drawn from $\mathbb{Z}_n$ according to a uniform distribution on $\mathbb{Z}_n$. By the birthday-paradox analysis of Section 5.4.1, we expect $\Theta(\sqrt{n})$ steps to be taken before the sequence cycles.

Now for the required modification. Let p be a nontrivial factor of n such that $\gcd(p, n/p) = 1$. For example, if n has the factorization $n = p_1^{e_1} p_2^{e_2} \cdots p_r^{e_r}$, then we may take p to be $p_1^{e_1}$. (If $e_1 = 1$, then p is just the smallest prime factor of n, a good example to keep in mind.)

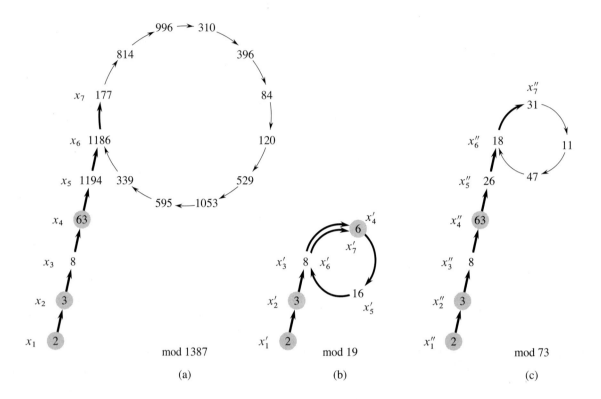

Figure 31.7 Pollard's rho heuristic. **(a)** The values produced by the recurrence $x_{i+1} = (x_i^2 - 1) \bmod 1387$, starting with $x_1 = 2$. The prime factorization of 1387 is $19 \cdot 73$. The heavy arrows indicate the iteration steps that are executed before the factor 19 is discovered. The light arrows point to unreached values in the iteration, to illustrate the "rho" shape. The shaded values are the y values stored by POLLARD-RHO. The factor 19 is discovered upon reaching $x_7 = 177$, when $\gcd(63 - 177, 1387) = 19$ is computed. The first x value that would be repeated is 1186, but the factor 19 is discovered before this value is repeated. **(b)** The values produced by the same recurrence, modulo 19. Every value x_i given in part (a) is equivalent, modulo 19, to the value x_i' shown here. For example, both $x_4 = 63$ and $x_7 = 177$ are equivalent to 6, modulo 19. **(c)** The values produced by the same recurrence, modulo 73. Every value x_i given in part (a) is equivalent, modulo 73, to the value x_i'' shown here. By the Chinese remainder theorem, each node in part (a) corresponds to a pair of nodes, one from part (b) and one from part (c).

The sequence $\langle x_i \rangle$ induces a corresponding sequence $\langle x_i' \rangle$ modulo p, where

$$x_i' = x_i \bmod p$$

for all i.

Furthermore, because f_n is defined using only arithmetic operations (squaring and subtraction) modulo n, we can compute x_{i+1}' from x_i'; the "modulo p" view of the sequence is a smaller version of what is happening modulo n:

$$
\begin{aligned}
x'_{i+1} &= x_{i+1} \bmod p \\
&= f_n(x_i) \bmod p \\
&= ((x_i^2 - 1) \bmod n) \bmod p \\
&= (x_i^2 - 1) \bmod p \qquad\qquad \text{(by Exercise 31.1-7)} \\
&= ((x_i \bmod p)^2 - 1) \bmod p \\
&= ((x'_i)^2 - 1) \bmod p \\
&= f_p(x'_i) \, .
\end{aligned}
$$

Thus, although we are not explicitly computing the sequence $\langle x'_i \rangle$, this sequence is well defined and obeys the same recurrence as the sequence $\langle x_i \rangle$.

Reasoning as before, we find that the expected number of steps before the sequence $\langle x'_i \rangle$ repeats is $\Theta(\sqrt{p})$. If p is small compared to n, the sequence $\langle x'_i \rangle$ might repeat much more quickly than the sequence $\langle x_i \rangle$. Indeed, as parts (b) and (c) of Figure 31.7 show, the $\langle x'_i \rangle$ sequence repeats as soon as two elements of the sequence $\langle x_i \rangle$ are merely equivalent modulo p, rather than equivalent modulo n.

Let t denote the index of the first repeated value in the $\langle x'_i \rangle$ sequence, and let $u > 0$ denote the length of the cycle that has been thereby produced. That is, t and $u > 0$ are the smallest values such that $x'_{t+i} = x'_{t+u+i}$ for all $i \geq 0$. By the above arguments, the expected values of t and u are both $\Theta(\sqrt{p})$. Note that if $x'_{t+i} = x'_{t+u+i}$, then $p \mid (x_{t+u+i} - x_{t+i})$. Thus, $\gcd(x_{t+u+i} - x_{t+i}, n) > 1$.

Therefore, once POLLARD-RHO has saved as y any value x_k such that $k \geq t$, then $y \bmod p$ is always on the cycle modulo p. (If a new value is saved as y, that value is also on the cycle modulo p.) Eventually, k is set to a value that is greater than u, and the procedure then makes an entire loop around the cycle modulo p without changing the value of y. The procedure then discovers a factor of n when x_i "runs into" the previously stored value of y, modulo p, that is, when $x_i \equiv y \pmod{p}$.

Presumably, the factor found is the factor p, although it may occasionally happen that a multiple of p is discovered. Since the expected values of both t and u are $\Theta(\sqrt{p})$, the expected number of steps required to produce the factor p is $\Theta(\sqrt{p})$.

This algorithm might not perform quite as expected, for two reasons. First, the heuristic analysis of the running time is not rigorous, and it is possible that the cycle of values, modulo p, could be much larger than $\sqrt{p}$. In this case, the algorithm performs correctly but much more slowly than desired. In practice, this issue seems to be moot. Second, the divisors of n produced by this algorithm might always be one of the trivial divisors 1 or n. For example, suppose that $n = pq$, where p and q are prime. It can happen that the values of t and u for p are identical with the values of t and u for q, and thus the factor p is always revealed in the same gcd operation that reveals the factor q. Since both factors are revealed at the same time, the trivial divisor $pq = n$ is revealed, which is useless. Again, this problem seems to be insignificant in practice. If necessary, we can restart the heuristic with a different recurrence of the form $x_{i+1} = (x_i^2 - c) \bmod n$. (We should avoid the values $c = 0$ and $c = 2$ for reasons we will not go into here, but other values are fine.)

Of course, this analysis is heuristic and not rigorous, since the recurrence is not really "random." Nonetheless, the procedure performs well in practice, and it seems to be as efficient as this heuristic analysis indicates. It is the method of choice for finding small prime factors of a large number. To factor a β-bit composite number n completely, we only need to find all prime factors less than $\lfloor n^{1/2} \rfloor$, and so we expect POLLARD-RHO to require at most $n^{1/4} = 2^{\beta/4}$ arithmetic operations and at most $n^{1/4}\beta^2 = 2^{\beta/4}\beta^2$ bit operations. POLLARD-RHO's ability to find a small factor p of n with an expected number $\Theta(\sqrt{p})$ of arithmetic operations is often its most appealing feature.

Exercises

31.9-1
Referring to the execution history shown in Figure 31.7(a), when does POLLARD-RHO print the factor 73 of 1387?

31.9-2
Suppose that we are given a function $f : \mathbb{Z}_n \to \mathbb{Z}_n$ and an initial value $x_0 \in \mathbb{Z}_n$. Define $x_i = f(x_{i-1})$ for $i = 1, 2, \ldots$. Let t and $u > 0$ be the smallest values such that $x_{t+i} = x_{t+u+i}$ for $i = 0, 1, \ldots$. In the terminology of Pollard's rho algorithm, t is the length of the tail and u is the length of the cycle of the rho. Give an efficient algorithm to determine t and u exactly, and analyze its running time.

31.9-3
How many steps would you expect POLLARD-RHO to require to discover a factor of the form p^e, where p is prime and $e > 1$?

31.9-4 ★
One disadvantage of POLLARD-RHO as written is that it requires one gcd computation for each step of the recurrence. Instead, we could batch the gcd computations by accumulating the product of several x_i values in a row and then using this product instead of x_i in the gcd computation. Describe carefully how you would implement this idea, why it works, and what batch size you would pick as the most effective when working on a β-bit number n.

Problems

31-1 *Binary gcd algorithm*

Most computers can perform the operations of subtraction, testing the parity (odd or even) of a binary integer, and halving more quickly than computing remainders. This problem investigates the ***binary gcd algorithm***, which avoids the remainder computations used in Euclid's algorithm.

a. Prove that if a and b are both even, then $\gcd(a, b) = 2 \cdot \gcd(a/2, b/2)$.

b. Prove that if a is odd and b is even, then $\gcd(a, b) = \gcd(a, b/2)$.

c. Prove that if a and b are both odd, then $\gcd(a, b) = \gcd((a - b)/2, b)$.

d. Design an efficient binary gcd algorithm for input integers a and b, where $a \geq b$, that runs in $O(\lg a)$ time. Assume that each subtraction, parity test, and halving takes unit time.

31-2 *Analysis of bit operations in Euclid's algorithm*

a. Consider the ordinary "paper and pencil" algorithm for long division: dividing a by b, which yields a quotient q and remainder r. Show that this method requires $O((1 + \lg q) \lg b)$ bit operations.

b. Define $\mu(a, b) = (1 + \lg a)(1 + \lg b)$. Show that the number of bit operations performed by EUCLID in reducing the problem of computing $\gcd(a, b)$ to that of computing $\gcd(b, a \bmod b)$ is at most $c(\mu(a, b) - \mu(b, a \bmod b))$ for some sufficiently large constant $c > 0$.

c. Show that EUCLID(a, b) requires $O(\mu(a, b))$ bit operations in general and $O(\beta^2)$ bit operations when applied to two β-bit inputs.

31-3 *Three algorithms for Fibonacci numbers*

This problem compares the efficiency of three methods for computing the nth Fibonacci number F_n, given n. Assume that the cost of adding, subtracting, or multiplying two numbers is $O(1)$, independent of the size of the numbers.

a. Show that the running time of the straightforward recursive method for computing F_n based on recurrence (3.22) is exponential in n. (See, for example, the FIB procedure on page 775.)

b. Show how to compute F_n in $O(n)$ time using memoization.

c. Show how to compute F_n in $O(\lg n)$ time using only integer addition and multiplication. (*Hint:* Consider the matrix

$$\begin{pmatrix} 0 & 1 \\ 1 & 1 \end{pmatrix}$$

and its powers.)

d. Assume now that adding two β-bit numbers takes $\Theta(\beta)$ time and that multiplying two β-bit numbers takes $\Theta(\beta^2)$ time. What is the running time of these three methods under this more reasonable cost measure for the elementary arithmetic operations?

31-4   *Quadratic residues*

Let p be an odd prime. A number $a \in Z_p^*$ is a *quadratic residue* if the equation $x^2 = a \pmod{p}$ has a solution for the unknown x.

a. Show that there are exactly $(p-1)/2$ quadratic residues, modulo p.

b. If p is prime, we define the *Legendre symbol* $\left(\frac{a}{p}\right)$, for $a \in \mathbb{Z}_p^*$, to be 1 if a is a quadratic residue modulo p and -1 otherwise. Prove that if $a \in \mathbb{Z}_p^*$, then

$$\left(\frac{a}{p}\right) \equiv a^{(p-1)/2} \pmod{p} .$$

Give an efficient algorithm that determines whether a given number a is a quadratic residue modulo p. Analyze the efficiency of your algorithm.

c. Prove that if p is a prime of the form $4k+3$ and a is a quadratic residue in $\mathbb{Z}_p^*$, then $a^{k+1} \bmod p$ is a square root of a, modulo p. How much time is required to find the square root of a quadratic residue a modulo p?

d. Describe an efficient randomized algorithm for finding a nonquadratic residue, modulo an arbitrary prime p, that is, a member of $\mathbb{Z}_p^*$ that is not a quadratic residue. How many arithmetic operations does your algorithm require on average?

Chapter notes

Niven and Zuckerman [265] provide an excellent introduction to elementary number theory. Knuth [210] contains a good discussion of algorithms for finding the greatest common divisor, as well as other basic number-theoretic algorithms. Bach [30] and Riesel [295] provide more recent surveys of computational number theory. Dixon [91] gives an overview of factorization and primality testing. The conference proceedings edited by Pomerance [280] contains several excellent survey articles. More recently, Bach and Shallit [31] have provided an exceptional overview of the basics of computational number theory.

Knuth [210] discusses the origin of Euclid's algorithm. It appears in Book 7, Propositions 1 and 2, of the Greek mathematician Euclid's *Elements*, which was written around 300 B.C. Euclid's description may have been derived from an algorithm due to Eudoxus around 375 B.C. Euclid's algorithm may hold the honor of being the oldest nontrivial algorithm; it is rivaled only by an algorithm for multiplication known to the ancient Egyptians. Shallit [312] chronicles the history of the analysis of Euclid's algorithm.

Knuth attributes a special case of the Chinese remainder theorem (Theorem 31.27) to the Chinese mathematician Sun-Tsŭ, who lived sometime between 200 B.C. and A.D. 200—the date is quite uncertain. The same special case was given by the Greek mathematician Nichomachus around A.D. 100. It was generalized by Chhin Chiu-Shao in 1247. The Chinese remainder theorem was finally stated and proved in its full generality by L. Euler in 1734.

The randomized primality-testing algorithm presented here is due to Miller [255] and Rabin [289]; it is the fastest randomized primality-testing algorithm known, to within constant factors. The proof of Theorem 31.39 is a slight adaptation of one suggested by Bach [29]. A proof of a stronger result for MILLER-RABIN was given by Monier [258, 259]. For many years primality-testing was the classic example of a problem where randomization appeared to be necessary to obtain an efficient (polynomial-time) algorithm. In 2002, however, Agrawal, Kayal, and Saxema [4] surprised everyone with their deterministic polynomial-time primality-testing algorithm. Until then, the fastest deterministic primality testing algorithm known, due to Cohen and Lenstra [73], ran in time $(\lg n)^{O(\lg \lg \lg n)}$ on input n, which is just slightly superpolynomial. Nonetheless, for practical purposes randomized primality-testing algorithms remain more efficient and are preferred.

The problem of finding large "random" primes is nicely discussed in an article by Beauchemin, Brassard, Crépeau, Goutier, and Pomerance [36].

The concept of a public-key cryptosystem is due to Diffie and Hellman [87]. The RSA cryptosystem was proposed in 1977 by Rivest, Shamir, and Adleman [296]. Since then, the field of cryptography has blossomed. Our understanding of the RSA cryptosystem has deepened, and modern implementations use significant refinements of the basic techniques presented here. In addition, many new techniques have been developed for proving cryptosystems to be secure. For example, Goldwasser and Micali [142] show that randomization can be an effective tool in the design of secure public-key encryption schemes. For signature schemes,

Goldwasser, Micali, and Rivest [143] present a digital-signature scheme for which every conceivable type of forgery is provably as difficult as factoring. Menezes, van Oorschot, and Vanstone [254] provide an overview of applied cryptography.

The rho heuristic for integer factorization was invented by Pollard [277]. The version presented here is a variant proposed by Brent [56].

The best algorithms for factoring large numbers have a running time that grows roughly exponentially with the cube root of the length of the number n to be factored. The general number-field sieve factoring algorithm (as developed by Buhler, Lenstra, and Pomerance [57] as an extension of the ideas in the number-field sieve factoring algorithm by Pollard [278] and Lenstra et al. [232] and refined by Coppersmith [77] and others) is perhaps the most efficient such algorithm in general for large inputs. Although it is difficult to give a rigorous analysis of this algorithm, under reasonable assumptions we can derive a running-time estimate of $L(1/3, n)^{1.902+o(1)}$, where $L(\alpha, n) = e^{(\ln n)^{\alpha} (\ln \ln n)^{1-\alpha}}$.

The elliptic-curve method due to Lenstra [233] may be more effective for some inputs than the number-field sieve method, since, like Pollard's rho method, it can find a small prime factor p quite quickly. With this method, the time to find p is estimated to be $L(1/2, p)^{\sqrt{2}+o(1)}$.

32 String Matching

Text-editing programs frequently need to find all occurrences of a pattern in the text. Typically, the text is a document being edited, and the pattern searched for is a particular word supplied by the user. Efficient algorithms for this problem—called "string matching"—can greatly aid the responsiveness of the text-editing program. Among their many other applications, string-matching algorithms search for particular patterns in DNA sequences. Internet search engines also use them to find Web pages relevant to queries.

We formalize the string-matching problem as follows. We assume that the text is an array $T[1 .. n]$ of length n and that the pattern is an array $P[1 .. m]$ of length $m \leq n$. We further assume that the elements of P and T are characters drawn from a finite alphabet Σ. For example, we may have $\Sigma = \{0, 1\}$ or $\Sigma = \{a, b, \ldots, z\}$. The character arrays P and T are often called *strings* of characters.

Referring to Figure 32.1, we say that pattern P *occurs with shift s* in text T (or, equivalently, that pattern P *occurs beginning at position s + 1* in text T) if $0 \leq s \leq n - m$ and $T[s + 1 .. s + m] = P[1 .. m]$ (that is, if $T[s + j] = P[j]$, for $1 \leq j \leq m$). If P occurs with shift s in T, then we call s a *valid shift*; otherwise, we call s an *invalid shift*. The *string-matching problem* is the problem of finding all valid shifts with which a given pattern P occurs in a given text T.

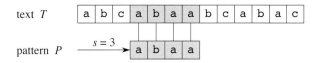

Figure 32.1 An example of the string-matching problem, where we want to find all occurrences of the pattern $P = $ abaa in the text $T = $ abcabaabcabac. The pattern occurs only once in the text, at shift $s = 3$, which we call a valid shift. A vertical line connects each character of the pattern to its matching character in the text, and all matched characters are shaded.

Algorithm	Preprocessing time	Matching time
Naive	0	$O((n - m + 1)m)$
Rabin-Karp	$\Theta(m)$	$O((n - m + 1)m)$
Finite automaton	$O(m\,|\Sigma|)$	$\Theta(n)$
Knuth-Morris-Pratt	$\Theta(m)$	$\Theta(n)$

Figure 32.2   The string-matching algorithms in this chapter and their preprocessing and matching times.

Except for the naive brute-force algorithm, which we review in Section 32.1, each string-matching algorithm in this chapter performs some preprocessing based on the pattern and then finds all valid shifts; we call this latter phase "matching." Figure 32.2 shows the preprocessing and matching times for each of the algorithms in this chapter. The total running time of each algorithm is the sum of the preprocessing and matching times. Section 32.2 presents an interesting string-matching algorithm, due to Rabin and Karp. Although the $\Theta((n - m + 1)m)$ worst-case running time of this algorithm is no better than that of the naive method, it works much better on average and in practice. It also generalizes nicely to other pattern-matching problems. Section 32.3 then describes a string-matching algorithm that begins by constructing a finite automaton specifically designed to search for occurrences of the given pattern P in a text. This algorithm takes $O(m\,|\Sigma|)$ preprocessing time, but only $\Theta(n)$ matching time. Section 32.4 presents the similar, but much cleverer, Knuth-Morris-Pratt (or KMP) algorithm; it has the same $\Theta(n)$ matching time, and it reduces the preprocessing time to only $\Theta(m)$.

Notation and terminology

We denote by Σ^* (read "sigma-star") the set of all finite-length strings formed using characters from the alphabet Σ. In this chapter, we consider only finite-length strings. The zero-length *empty string*, denoted ε, also belongs to Σ^*. The length of a string x is denoted $|x|$. The *concatenation* of two strings x and y, denoted xy, has length $|x| + |y|$ and consists of the characters from x followed by the characters from y.

We say that a string w is a *prefix* of a string x, denoted $w \sqsubset x$, if $x = wy$ for some string $y \in \Sigma^*$. Note that if $w \sqsubset x$, then $|w| \leq |x|$. Similarly, we say that a string w is a *suffix* of a string x, denoted $w \sqsupset x$, if $x = yw$ for some $y \in \Sigma^*$. As with a prefix, $w \sqsupset x$ implies $|w| \leq |x|$. For example, we have $\text{ab} \sqsubset \text{abcca}$ and $\text{cca} \sqsupset \text{abcca}$. The empty string ε is both a suffix and a prefix of every string. For any strings x and y and any character a, we have $x \sqsupset y$ if and only if $xa \sqsupset ya$.

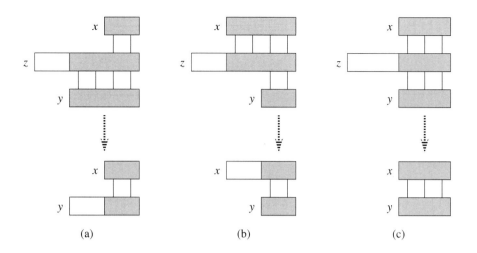

Figure 32.3 A graphical proof of Lemma 32.1. We suppose that $x \sqsupset z$ and $y \sqsupset z$. The three parts of the figure illustrate the three cases of the lemma. Vertical lines connect matching regions (shown shaded) of the strings. **(a)** If $|x| \leq |y|$, then $x \sqsupset y$. **(b)** If $|x| \geq |y|$, then $y \sqsupset x$. **(c)** If $|x| = |y|$, then $x = y$.

Also note that $\sqsubset$ and $\sqsupset$ are transitive relations. The following lemma will be useful later.

Lemma 32.1 (Overlapping-suffix lemma)
Suppose that x, y, and z are strings such that $x \sqsupset z$ and $y \sqsupset z$. If $|x| \leq |y|$, then $x \sqsupset y$. If $|x| \geq |y|$, then $y \sqsupset x$. If $|x| = |y|$, then $x = y$.

Proof   See Figure 32.3 for a graphical proof.   ∎

For brevity of notation, we denote the k-character prefix $P[1 . . k]$ of the pattern $P[1 . . m]$ by P_k. Thus, $P_0 = \varepsilon$ and $P_m = P = P[1 . . m]$. Similarly, we denote the k-character prefix of the text T by T_k. Using this notation, we can state the string-matching problem as that of finding all shifts s in the range $0 \leq s \leq n - m$ such that $P \sqsupset T_{s+m}$.

In our pseudocode, we allow two equal-length strings to be compared for equality as a primitive operation. If the strings are compared from left to right and the comparison stops when a mismatch is discovered, we assume that the time taken by such a test is a linear function of the number of matching characters discovered. To be precise, the test "$x == y$" is assumed to take time $\Theta(t + 1)$, where t is the length of the longest string z such that $z \sqsubset x$ and $z \sqsubset y$. (We write $\Theta(t + 1)$ rather than $\Theta(t)$ to handle the case in which $t = 0$; the first characters compared do not match, but it takes a positive amount of time to perform this comparison.)

32.1   The naive string-matching algorithm

The naive algorithm finds all valid shifts using a loop that checks the condition $P[1..m] = T[s + 1..s + m]$ for each of the $n - m + 1$ possible values of s.

NAIVE-STRING-MATCHER(T, P)

```
1   n = T.length
2   m = P.length
3   for s = 0 to n − m
4       if P[1..m] == T[s + 1..s + m]
5           print "Pattern occurs with shift" s
```

Figure 32.4 portrays the naive string-matching procedure as sliding a "template" containing the pattern over the text, noting for which shifts all of the characters on the template equal the corresponding characters in the text. The **for** loop of lines 3–5 considers each possible shift explicitly. The test in line 4 determines whether the current shift is valid; this test implicitly loops to check corresponding character positions until all positions match successfully or a mismatch is found. Line 5 prints out each valid shift s.

Procedure NAIVE-STRING-MATCHER takes time $O((n - m + 1)m)$, and this bound is tight in the worst case. For example, consider the text string a^n (a string of n a's) and the pattern a^m. For each of the $n - m + 1$ possible values of the shift s, the implicit loop on line 4 to compare corresponding characters must execute m times to validate the shift. The worst-case running time is thus $\Theta((n - m + 1)m)$, which is $\Theta(n^2)$ if $m = \lfloor n/2 \rfloor$. Because it requires no preprocessing, NAIVE-STRING-MATCHER's running time equals its matching time.

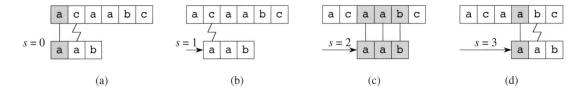

Figure 32.4 The operation of the naive string matcher for the pattern $P = \mathtt{aab}$ and the text $T = \mathtt{acaabc}$. We can imagine the pattern P as a template that we slide next to the text. **(a)–(d)** The four successive alignments tried by the naive string matcher. In each part, vertical lines connect corresponding regions found to match (shown shaded), and a jagged line connects the first mismatched character found, if any. The algorithm finds one occurrence of the pattern, at shift $s = 2$, shown in part (c).

As we shall see, NAIVE-STRING-MATCHER is not an optimal procedure for this problem. Indeed, in this chapter we shall see that the Knuth-Morris-Pratt algorithm is much better in the worst case. The naive string-matcher is inefficient because it entirely ignores information gained about the text for one value of s when it considers other values of s. Such information can be quite valuable, however. For example, if $P = \text{aaab}$ and we find that $s = 0$ is valid, then none of the shifts 1, 2, or 3 are valid, since $T[4] = \text{b}$. In the following sections, we examine several ways to make effective use of this sort of information.

Exercises

32.1-1
Show the comparisons the naive string matcher makes for the pattern $P = \text{0001}$ in the text $T = \text{000010001010001}$.

32.1-2
Suppose that all characters in the pattern P are different. Show how to accelerate NAIVE-STRING-MATCHER to run in time $O(n)$ on an n-character text T.

32.1-3
Suppose that pattern P and text T are *randomly* chosen strings of length m and n, respectively, from the d-ary alphabet $\Sigma_d = \{0, 1, \ldots, d - 1\}$, where $d \geq 2$. Show that the *expected* number of character-to-character comparisons made by the implicit loop in line 4 of the naive algorithm is

$$(n - m + 1)\frac{1 - d^{-m}}{1 - d^{-1}} \leq 2(n - m + 1)$$

over all executions of this loop. (Assume that the naive algorithm stops comparing characters for a given shift once it finds a mismatch or matches the entire pattern.) Thus, for randomly chosen strings, the naive algorithm is quite efficient.

32.1-4
Suppose we allow the pattern P to contain occurrences of a ***gap character*** $\diamond$ that can match an *arbitrary* string of characters (even one of zero length). For example, the pattern $\text{ab}\diamond\text{ba}\diamond\text{c}$ occurs in the text cabccbacbacab as

c ab cc ba cba c ab
  ab $\diamond$ ba $\diamond$ c

and as

c ab ccbac ba   c ab .
  ab $\diamond$ ba $\diamond$ c

Note that the gap character may occur an arbitrary number of times in the pattern but not at all in the text. Give a polynomial-time algorithm to determine whether such a pattern P occurs in a given text T, and analyze the running time of your algorithm.

32.2   The Rabin-Karp algorithm

Rabin and Karp proposed a string-matching algorithm that performs well in practice and that also generalizes to other algorithms for related problems, such as two-dimensional pattern matching. The Rabin-Karp algorithm uses $\Theta(m)$ preprocessing time, and its worst-case running time is $\Theta((n-m+1)m)$. Based on certain assumptions, however, its average-case running time is better.

This algorithm makes use of elementary number-theoretic notions such as the equivalence of two numbers modulo a third number. You might want to refer to Section 31.1 for the relevant definitions.

For expository purposes, let us assume that $\Sigma = \{0, 1, 2, \ldots, 9\}$, so that each character is a decimal digit. (In the general case, we can assume that each character is a digit in radix-d notation, where $d = |\Sigma|$.) We can then view a string of k consecutive characters as representing a length-k decimal number. The character string 31415 thus corresponds to the decimal number 31,415. Because we interpret the input characters as both graphical symbols and digits, we find it convenient in this section to denote them as we would digits, in our standard text font.

Given a pattern $P[1 \mathbin{.\,.} m]$, let p denote its corresponding decimal value. In a similar manner, given a text $T[1 \mathbin{.\,.} n]$, let t_s denote the decimal value of the length-m substring $T[s + 1 \mathbin{.\,.} s + m]$, for $s = 0, 1, \ldots, n - m$. Certainly, $t_s = p$ if and only if $T[s + 1 \mathbin{.\,.} s + m] = P[1 \mathbin{.\,.} m]$; thus, s is a valid shift if and only if $t_s = p$. If we could compute p in time $\Theta(m)$ and all the t_s values in a total of $\Theta(n - m + 1)$ time,[1] then we could determine all valid shifts s in time $\Theta(m) + \Theta(n - m + 1) = \Theta(n)$ by comparing p with each of the t_s values. (For the moment, let's not worry about the possibility that p and the t_s values might be very large numbers.)

We can compute p in time $\Theta(m)$ using Horner's rule (see Section 30.1):

$$p = P[m] + 10\,(P[m-1] + 10(P[m-2] + \cdots + 10(P[2] + 10P[1])\cdots))\,.$$

Similarly, we can compute t_0 from $T[1 \mathbin{.\,.} m]$ in time $\Theta(m)$.

---

[1] We write $\Theta(n - m + 1)$ instead of $\Theta(n - m)$ because s takes on $n - m + 1$ different values. The "+1" is significant in an asymptotic sense because when $m = n$, computing the lone t_s value takes $\Theta(1)$ time, not $\Theta(0)$ time.

To compute the remaining values $t_1, t_2, \ldots, t_{n-m}$ in time $\Theta(n - m)$, we observe that we can compute t_{s+1} from t_s in constant time, since

$$t_{s+1} = 10(t_s - 10^{m-1} T[s + 1]) + T[s + m + 1] . \tag{32.1}$$

Subtracting $10^{m-1} T[s + 1]$ removes the high-order digit from t_s, multiplying the result by 10 shifts the number left by one digit position, and adding $T[s + m + 1]$ brings in the appropriate low-order digit. For example, if $m = 5$ and $t_s = 31415$, then we wish to remove the high-order digit $T[s + 1] = 3$ and bring in the new low-order digit (suppose it is $T[s + 5 + 1] = 2$) to obtain

$$\begin{aligned} t_{s+1} &= 10(31415 - 10000 \cdot 3) + 2 \\ &= 14152 . \end{aligned}$$

If we precompute the constant 10^{m-1} (which we can do in time $O(\lg m)$ using the techniques of Section 31.6, although for this application a straightforward $O(m)$-time method suffices), then each execution of equation (32.1) takes a constant number of arithmetic operations. Thus, we can compute p in time $\Theta(m)$, and we can compute all of $t_0, t_1, \ldots, t_{n-m}$ in time $\Theta(n - m + 1)$. Therefore, we can find all occurrences of the pattern $P[1 .. m]$ in the text $T[1 .. n]$ with $\Theta(m)$ preprocessing time and $\Theta(n - m + 1)$ matching time.

Until now, we have intentionally overlooked one problem: p and t_s may be too large to work with conveniently. If P contains m characters, then we cannot reasonably assume that each arithmetic operation on p (which is m digits long) takes "constant time." Fortunately, we can solve this problem easily, as Figure 32.5 shows: compute p and the t_s values modulo a suitable modulus q. We can compute p modulo q in $\Theta(m)$ time and all the t_s values modulo q in $\Theta(n - m + 1)$ time. If we choose the modulus q as a prime such that $10q$ just fits within one computer word, then we can perform all the necessary computations with single-precision arithmetic. In general, with a d-ary alphabet $\{0, 1, \ldots, d - 1\}$, we choose q so that dq fits within a computer word and adjust the recurrence equation (32.1) to work modulo q, so that it becomes

$$t_{s+1} = (d(t_s - T[s + 1]h) + T[s + m + 1]) \bmod q , \tag{32.2}$$

where $h \equiv d^{m-1} \pmod{q}$ is the value of the digit "1" in the high-order position of an m-digit text window.

The solution of working modulo q is not perfect, however: $t_s \equiv p \pmod{q}$ does not imply that $t_s = p$. On the other hand, if $t_s \not\equiv p \pmod{q}$, then we definitely have that $t_s \neq p$, so that shift s is invalid. We can thus use the test $t_s \equiv p \pmod{q}$ as a fast heuristic test to rule out invalid shifts s. Any shift s for which $t_s \equiv p \pmod{q}$ must be tested further to see whether s is really valid or we just have a *spurious hit*. This additional test explicitly checks the condition

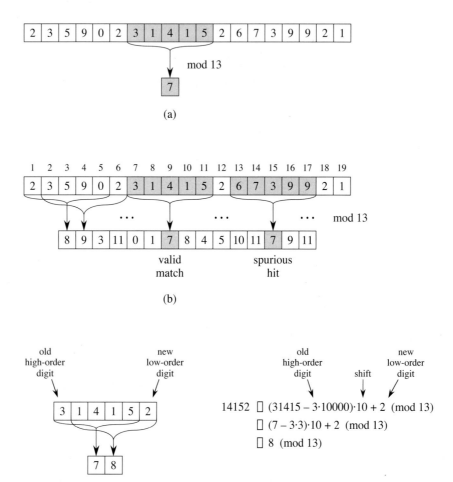

Figure 32.5 The Rabin-Karp algorithm. Each character is a decimal digit, and we compute values modulo 13. **(a)** A text string. A window of length 5 is shown shaded. The numerical value of the shaded number, computed modulo 13, yields the value 7. **(b)** The same text string with values computed modulo 13 for each possible position of a length-5 window. Assuming the pattern $P = 31415$, we look for windows whose value modulo 13 is 7, since $31415 \equiv 7 \pmod{13}$. The algorithm finds two such windows, shown shaded in the figure. The first, beginning at text position 7, is indeed an occurrence of the pattern, while the second, beginning at text position 13, is a spurious hit. **(c)** How to compute the value for a window in constant time, given the value for the previous window. The first window has value 31415. Dropping the high-order digit 3, shifting left (multiplying by 10), and then adding in the low-order digit 2 gives us the new value 14152. Because all computations are performed modulo 13, the value for the first window is 7, and the value for the new window is 8.

$P[1..m] = T[s + 1..s + m]$. If q is large enough, then we hope that spurious hits occur infrequently enough that the cost of the extra checking is low.

The following procedure makes these ideas precise. The inputs to the procedure are the text T, the pattern P, the radix d to use (which is typically taken to be $|\Sigma|$), and the prime q to use.

RABIN-KARP-MATCHER(T, P, d, q)

```
 1   n = T.length
 2   m = P.length
 3   h = d^{m-1} mod q
 4   p = 0
 5   t_0 = 0
 6   for i = 1 to m                    // preprocessing
 7        p = (dp + P[i]) mod q
 8        t_0 = (dt_0 + T[i]) mod q
 9   for s = 0 to n - m                // matching
10        if p == t_s
11             if P[1..m] == T[s + 1..s + m]
12                  print "Pattern occurs with shift" s
13        if s < n - m
14             t_{s+1} = (d(t_s - T[s + 1]h) + T[s + m + 1]) mod q
```

The procedure RABIN-KARP-MATCHER works as follows. All characters are interpreted as radix-d digits. The subscripts on t are provided only for clarity; the program works correctly if all the subscripts are dropped. Line 3 initializes h to the value of the high-order digit position of an m-digit window. Lines 4–8 compute p as the value of $P[1..m] \bmod q$ and t_0 as the value of $T[1..m] \bmod q$. The **for** loop of lines 9–14 iterates through all possible shifts s, maintaining the following invariant:

Whenever line 10 is executed, $t_s = T[s + 1..s + m] \bmod q$.

If $p = t_s$ in line 10 (a "hit"), then line 11 checks to see whether $P[1..m] = T[s + 1..s + m]$ in order to rule out the possibility of a spurious hit. Line 12 prints out any valid shifts that are found. If $s < n - m$ (checked in line 13), then the **for** loop will execute at least one more time, and so line 14 first executes to ensure that the loop invariant holds when we get back to line 10. Line 14 computes the value of $t_{s+1} \bmod q$ from the value of $t_s \bmod q$ in constant time using equation (32.2) directly.

RABIN-KARP-MATCHER takes $\Theta(m)$ preprocessing time, and its matching time is $\Theta((n - m + 1)m)$ in the worst case, since (like the naive string-matching algorithm) the Rabin-Karp algorithm explicitly verifies every valid shift. If $P = \texttt{a}^m$

and $T = \text{a}^n$, then verifying takes time $\Theta((n-m+1)m)$, since each of the $n-m+1$ possible shifts is valid.

In many applications, we expect few valid shifts—perhaps some constant c of them. In such applications, the expected matching time of the algorithm is only $O((n - m + 1) + cm) = O(n + m)$, plus the time required to process spurious hits. We can base a heuristic analysis on the assumption that reducing values modulo q acts like a random mapping from Σ^* to $\mathbb{Z}_q$. (See the discussion on the use of division for hashing in Section 11.3.1. It is difficult to formalize and prove such an assumption, although one viable approach is to assume that q is chosen randomly from integers of the appropriate size. We shall not pursue this formalization here.) We can then expect that the number of spurious hits is $O(n/q)$, since we can estimate the chance that an arbitrary t_s will be equivalent to p, modulo q, as $1/q$. Since there are $O(n)$ positions at which the test of line 10 fails and we spend $O(m)$ time for each hit, the expected matching time taken by the Rabin-Karp algorithm is

$$O(n) + O(m(v + n/q)) \, ,$$

where v is the number of valid shifts. This running time is $O(n)$ if $v = O(1)$ and we choose $q \geq m$. That is, if the expected number of valid shifts is small ($O(1)$) and we choose the prime q to be larger than the length of the pattern, then we can expect the Rabin-Karp procedure to use only $O(n + m)$ matching time. Since $m \leq n$, this expected matching time is $O(n)$.

Exercises

32.2-1
Working modulo $q = 11$, how many spurious hits does the Rabin-Karp matcher encounter in the text $T = 3141592653589793$ when looking for the pattern $P = 26$?

32.2-2
How would you extend the Rabin-Karp method to the problem of searching a text string for an occurrence of any one of a given set of k patterns? Start by assuming that all k patterns have the same length. Then generalize your solution to allow the patterns to have different lengths.

32.2-3
Show how to extend the Rabin-Karp method to handle the problem of looking for a given $m \times m$ pattern in an $n \times n$ array of characters. (The pattern may be shifted vertically and horizontally, but it may not be rotated.)

32.2-4

Alice has a copy of a long n-bit file $A = \langle a_{n-1}, a_{n-2}, \ldots, a_0 \rangle$, and Bob similarly has an n-bit file $B = \langle b_{n-1}, b_{n-2}, \ldots, b_0 \rangle$. Alice and Bob wish to know if their files are identical. To avoid transmitting all of A or B, they use the following fast probabilistic check. Together, they select a prime $q > 1000n$ and randomly select an integer x from $\{0, 1, \ldots, q - 1\}$. Then, Alice evaluates

$$A(x) = \left(\sum_{i=0}^{n-1} a_i x^i \right) \bmod q$$

and Bob similarly evaluates $B(x)$. Prove that if $A \neq B$, there is at most one chance in 1000 that $A(x) = B(x)$, whereas if the two files are the same, $A(x)$ is necessarily the same as $B(x)$. (*Hint:* See Exercise 31.4-4.)

32.3 String matching with finite automata

Many string-matching algorithms build a finite automaton—a simple machine for processing information—that scans the text string T for all occurrences of the pattern P. This section presents a method for building such an automaton. These string-matching automata are very efficient: they examine each text character *exactly once*, taking constant time per text character. The matching time used—after preprocessing the pattern to build the automaton—is therefore $\Theta(n)$. The time to build the automaton, however, can be large if Σ is large. Section 32.4 describes a clever way around this problem.

We begin this section with the definition of a finite automaton. We then examine a special string-matching automaton and show how to use it to find occurrences of a pattern in a text. Finally, we shall show how to construct the string-matching automaton for a given input pattern.

Finite automata

A *finite automaton* M, illustrated in Figure 32.6, is a 5-tuple $(Q, q_0, A, \Sigma, \delta)$, where

- Q is a finite set of *states*,
- $q_0 \in Q$ is the *start state*,
- $A \subseteq Q$ is a distinguished set of *accepting states*,
- Σ is a finite *input alphabet*,
- δ is a function from $Q \times \Sigma$ into Q, called the *transition function* of M.

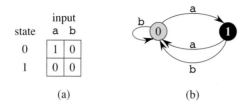

	input	
state	a	b
0	1	0
1	0	0

(a)   (b)

Figure 32.6 A simple two-state finite automaton with state set $Q = \{0, 1\}$, start state $q_0 = 0$, and input alphabet $\Sigma = \{a, b\}$. **(a)** A tabular representation of the transition function δ. **(b)** An equivalent state-transition diagram. State 1, shown blackened, is the only accepting state. Directed edges represent transitions. For example, the edge from state 1 to state 0 labeled b indicates that $\delta(1, b) = 0$. This automaton accepts those strings that end in an odd number of a's. More precisely, it accepts a string x if and only if $x = yz$, where $y = \varepsilon$ or y ends with a b, and $z = a^k$, where k is odd. For example, on input abaaa, including the start state, this automaton enters the sequence of states $\langle 0, 1, 0, 1, 0, 1 \rangle$, and so it accepts this input. For input abbaa, it enters the sequence of states $\langle 0, 1, 0, 0, 1, 0 \rangle$, and so it rejects this input.

The finite automaton begins in state q_0 and reads the characters of its input string one at a time. If the automaton is in state q and reads input character a, it moves ("makes a transition") from state q to state $\delta(q, a)$. Whenever its current state q is a member of A, the machine M has **accepted** the string read so far. An input that is not accepted is **rejected**.

A finite automaton M induces a function ϕ, called the **final-state function**, from Σ^* to Q such that $\phi(w)$ is the state M ends up in after scanning the string w. Thus, M accepts a string w if and only if $\phi(w) \in A$. We define the function ϕ recursively, using the transition function:

$$\phi(\varepsilon) = q_0 \,,$$
$$\phi(wa) = \delta(\phi(w), a) \quad \text{for } w \in \Sigma^*, a \in \Sigma \,.$$

String-matching automata

For a given pattern P, we construct a string-matching automaton in a preprocessing step before using it to search the text string. Figure 32.7 illustrates the automaton for the pattern $P = $ ababaca. From now on, we shall assume that P is a given fixed pattern string; for brevity, we shall not indicate the dependence upon P in our notation.

In order to specify the string-matching automaton corresponding to a given pattern $P[1 \,..\, m]$, we first define an auxiliary function σ, called the **suffix function** corresponding to P. The function σ maps Σ^* to $\{0, 1, \ldots, m\}$ such that $\sigma(x)$ is the length of the longest prefix of P that is also a suffix of x:

$$\sigma(x) = \max \{k : P_k \sqsupset x\} \,. \tag{32.3}$$

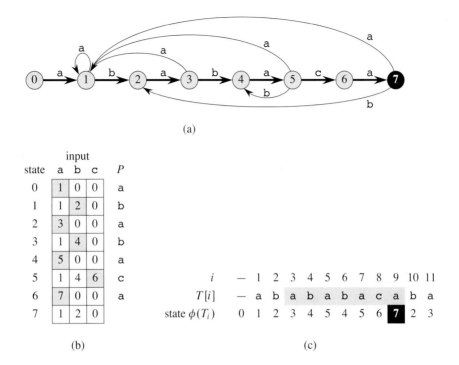

(a)

	input			
state	a	b	c	*P*
0	1	0	0	a
1	1	2	0	b
2	3	0	0	a
3	1	4	0	b
4	5	0	0	a
5	1	4	6	c
6	7	0	0	a
7	1	2	0	

(b)

i	—	1	2	3	4	5	6	7	8	9	10	11
T[*i*]	—	a	b	a	b	a	b	a	c	a	b	a
state $\phi(T_i)$	0	1	2	3	4	5	4	5	6	7	2	3

(c)

Figure 32.7 (a) A state-transition diagram for the string-matching automaton that accepts all strings ending in the string ababaca. State 0 is the start state, and state 7 (shown blackened) is the only accepting state. The transition function δ is defined by equation (32.4), and a directed edge from state *i* to state *j* labeled *a* represents $\delta(i, a) = j$. The right-going edges forming the "spine" of the automaton, shown heavy in the figure, correspond to successful matches between pattern and input characters. Except for the edges from state 7 to states 1 and 2, the left-going edges correspond to mismatches. Some edges corresponding to mismatches are omitted; by convention, if a state *i* has no outgoing edge labeled *a* for some $a \in \Sigma$, then $\delta(i, a) = 0$. (b) The corresponding transition function δ, and the pattern string $P = $ ababaca. The entries corresponding to successful matches between pattern and input characters are shown shaded. (c) The operation of the automaton on the text $T = $ abababacaba. Under each text character $T[i]$ appears the state $\phi(T_i)$ that the automaton is in after processing the prefix T_i. The automaton finds one occurrence of the pattern, ending in position 9.

The suffix function σ is well defined since the empty string $P_0 = \varepsilon$ is a suffix of every string. As examples, for the pattern $P = $ ab, we have $\sigma(\varepsilon) = 0$, $\sigma(\text{ccaca}) = 1$, and $\sigma(\text{ccab}) = 2$. For a pattern P of length m, we have $\sigma(x) = m$ if and only if $P \sqsupset x$. From the definition of the suffix function, $x \sqsupset y$ implies $\sigma(x) \leq \sigma(y)$.

We define the string-matching automaton that corresponds to a given pattern $P[1..m]$ as follows:

- The state set Q is $\{0, 1, \ldots, m\}$. The start state q_0 is state 0, and state m is the only accepting state.

- The transition function δ is defined by the following equation, for any state q and character a:

$$\delta(q, a) = \sigma(P_q a) . \tag{32.4}$$

We define $\delta(q, a) = \sigma(P_q a)$ because we want to keep track of the longest prefix of the pattern P that has matched the text string T so far. We consider the most recently read characters of T. In order for a substring of T—let's say the substring ending at $T[i]$—to match some prefix P_j of P, this prefix P_j must be a suffix of T_i. Suppose that $q = \phi(T_i)$, so that after reading T_i, the automaton is in state q. We design the transition function δ so that this state number, q, tells us the length of the longest prefix of P that matches a suffix of T_i. That is, in state q, $P_q \sqsupset T_i$ and $q = \sigma(T_i)$. (Whenever $q = m$, all m characters of P match a suffix of T_i, and so we have found a match.) Thus, since $\phi(T_i)$ and $\sigma(T_i)$ both equal q, we shall see (in Theorem 32.4, below) that the automaton maintains the following invariant:

$$\phi(T_i) = \sigma(T_i) . \tag{32.5}$$

If the automaton is in state q and reads the next character $T[i + 1] = a$, then we want the transition to lead to the state corresponding to the longest prefix of P that is a suffix of $T_i a$, and that state is $\sigma(T_i a)$. Because P_q is the longest prefix of P that is a suffix of T_i, the longest prefix of P that is a suffix of $T_i a$ is not only $\sigma(T_i a)$, but also $\sigma(P_q a)$. (Lemma 32.3, on page 1000, proves that $\sigma(T_i a) = \sigma(P_q a)$.) Thus, when the automaton is in state q, we want the transition function on character a to take the automaton to state $\sigma(P_q a)$.

There are two cases to consider. In the first case, $a = P[q + 1]$, so that the character a continues to match the pattern; in this case, because $\delta(q, a) = q+1$, the transition continues to go along the "spine" of the automaton (the heavy edges in Figure 32.7). In the second case, $a \neq P[q+1]$, so that a does not continue to match the pattern. Here, we must find a smaller prefix of P that is also a suffix of T_i. Because the preprocessing step matches the pattern against itself when creating the string-matching automaton, the transition function quickly identifies the longest such smaller prefix of P.

Let's look at an example. The string-matching automaton of Figure 32.7 has $\delta(5, \mathrm{c}) = 6$, illustrating the first case, in which the match continues. To illustrate the second case, observe that the automaton of Figure 32.7 has $\delta(5, \mathrm{b}) = 4$. We make this transition because if the automaton reads a b in state $q = 5$, then $P_q\mathrm{b} -$ ababab, and the longest prefix of P that is also a suffix of ababab is $P_4 =$ abab.

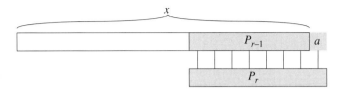

Figure 32.8 An illustration for the proof of Lemma 32.2. The figure shows that $r \leq \sigma(x) + 1$, where $r = \sigma(xa)$.

To clarify the operation of a string-matching automaton, we now give a simple, efficient program for simulating the behavior of such an automaton (represented by its transition function δ) in finding occurrences of a pattern P of length m in an input text $T[1 \mathinner{.\,.} n]$. As for any string-matching automaton for a pattern of length m, the state set Q is $\{0, 1, \ldots, m\}$, the start state is 0, and the only accepting state is state m.

FINITE-AUTOMATON-MATCHER(T, δ, m)

```
1   n = T.length
2   q = 0
3   for i = 1 to n
4       q = δ(q, T[i])
5       if q == m
6           print "Pattern occurs with shift" i − m
```

From the simple loop structure of FINITE-AUTOMATON-MATCHER, we can easily see that its matching time on a text string of length n is $\Theta(n)$. This matching time, however, does not include the preprocessing time required to compute the transition function δ. We address this problem later, after first proving that the procedure FINITE-AUTOMATON-MATCHER operates correctly.

Consider how the automaton operates on an input text $T[1 \mathinner{.\,.} n]$. We shall prove that the automaton is in state $\sigma(T_i)$ after scanning character $T[i]$. Since $\sigma(T_i) = m$ if and only if $P \sqsupset T_i$, the machine is in the accepting state m if and only if it has just scanned the pattern P. To prove this result, we make use of the following two lemmas about the suffix function σ.

Lemma 32.2 (Suffix-function inequality)
For any string x and character a, we have $\sigma(xa) \leq \sigma(x) + 1$.

Proof   Referring to Figure 32.8, let $r = \sigma(xa)$. If $r = 0$, then the conclusion $\sigma(xa) = r \leq \sigma(x) + 1$ is trivially satisfied, by the nonnegativity of $\sigma(x)$. Now assume that $r > 0$. Then, $P_r \sqsupset xa$, by the definition of σ. Thus, $P_{r-1} \sqsupset x$, by

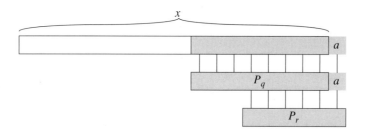

Figure 32.9   An illustration for the proof of Lemma 32.3. The figure shows that $r = \sigma(P_q a)$, where $q = \sigma(x)$ and $r = \sigma(xa)$.

dropping the a from the end of P_r and from the end of xa. Therefore, $r - 1 \leq \sigma(x)$, since $\sigma(x)$ is the largest k such that $P_k \sqsupset x$, and thus $\sigma(xa) = r \leq \sigma(x) + 1$.   ∎

Lemma 32.3 (Suffix-function recursion lemma)
For any string x and character a, if $q = \sigma(x)$, then $\sigma(xa) = \sigma(P_q a)$.

Proof   From the definition of σ, we have $P_q \sqsupset x$. As Figure 32.9 shows, we also have $P_q a \sqsupset xa$. If we let $r = \sigma(xa)$, then $P_r \sqsupset xa$ and, by Lemma 32.2, $r \leq q + 1$. Thus, we have $|P_r| = r \leq q + 1 = |P_q a|$. Since $P_q a \sqsupset xa$, $P_r \sqsupset xa$, and $|P_r| \leq |P_q a|$, Lemma 32.1 implies that $P_r \sqsupset P_q a$. Therefore, $r \leq \sigma(P_q a)$, that is, $\sigma(xa) \leq \sigma(P_q a)$. But we also have $\sigma(P_q a) \leq \sigma(xa)$, since $P_q a \sqsupset xa$. Thus, $\sigma(xa) = \sigma(P_q a)$.   ∎

We are now ready to prove our main theorem characterizing the behavior of a string-matching automaton on a given input text. As noted above, this theorem shows that the automaton is merely keeping track, at each step, of the longest prefix of the pattern that is a suffix of what has been read so far. In other words, the automaton maintains the invariant (32.5).

Theorem 32.4
If ϕ is the final-state function of a string-matching automaton for a given pattern P and $T[1 \mathinner{..} n]$ is an input text for the automaton, then

$$\phi(T_i) = \sigma(T_i)$$

for $i = 0, 1, \ldots, n$.

Proof   The proof is by induction on i. For $i = 0$, the theorem is trivially true, since $T_0 = \varepsilon$. Thus, $\phi(T_0) = 0 = \sigma(T_0)$.

Now, we assume that $\phi(T_i) = \sigma(T_i)$ and prove that $\phi(T_{i+1}) = \sigma(T_{i+1})$. Let q denote $\phi(T_i)$, and let a denote $T[i+1]$. Then,

$$
\begin{aligned}
\phi(T_{i+1}) &= \phi(T_i a) && \text{(by the definitions of } T_{i+1} \text{ and } a) \\
&= \delta(\phi(T_i), a) && \text{(by the definition of } \phi) \\
&= \delta(q, a) && \text{(by the definition of } q) \\
&= \sigma(P_q a) && \text{(by the definition (32.4) of } \delta) \\
&= \sigma(T_i a) && \text{(by Lemma 32.3 and induction)} \\
&= \sigma(T_{i+1}) && \text{(by the definition of } T_{i+1}) \ .
\end{aligned}
$$
■

By Theorem 32.4, if the machine enters state q on line 4, then q is the largest value such that $P_q \sqsupset T_i$. Thus, we have $q = m$ on line 5 if and only if the machine has just scanned an occurrence of the pattern P. We conclude that FINITE-AUTOMATON-MATCHER operates correctly.

Computing the transition function

The following procedure computes the transition function δ from a given pattern $P[1 \mathinner{\ldotp\ldotp} m]$.

COMPUTE-TRANSITION-FUNCTION(P, Σ)

```
1   m = P.length
2   for q = 0 to m
3       for each character a ∈ Σ
4           k = min(m + 1, q + 2)
5           repeat
6               k = k − 1
7           until P_k ⊐ P_q a
8           δ(q, a) = k
9   return δ
```

This procedure computes $\delta(q, a)$ in a straightforward manner according to its definition in equation (32.4). The nested loops beginning on lines 2 and 3 consider all states q and all characters a, and lines 4–8 set $\delta(q, a)$ to be the largest k such that $P_k \sqsupset P_q a$. The code starts with the largest conceivable value of k, which is $\min(m, q + 1)$. It then decreases k until $P_k \sqsupset P_q a$, which must eventually occur, since $P_0 = \varepsilon$ is a suffix of every string.

The running time of COMPUTE-TRANSITION-FUNCTION is $O(m^3 |\Sigma|)$, because the outer loops contribute a factor of $m |\Sigma|$, the inner **repeat** loop can run at most $m + 1$ times, and the test $P_k \sqsupset P_q a$ on line 7 can require comparing up to m characters. Much faster procedures exist; by utilizing some cleverly computed information about the pattern P (see Exercise 32.4-8), we can improve the time required to compute δ from P to $O(m\,|\Sigma|)$. With this improved procedure for computing δ, we can find all occurrences of a length-m pattern in a length-n text over an alphabet Σ with $O(m\,|\Sigma|)$ preprocessing time and $\Theta(n)$ matching time.

Exercises

32.3-1
Construct the string-matching automaton for the pattern $P = $ aabab and illustrate its operation on the text string $T = $ aaababaabaababaab.

32.3-2
Draw a state-transition diagram for a string-matching automaton for the pattern ababbabbababbababbabb over the alphabet $\Sigma = \{$a, b$\}$.

32.3-3
We call a pattern P ***nonoverlappable*** if $P_k \sqsupset P_q$ implies $k = 0$ or $k = q$. Describe the state-transition diagram of the string-matching automaton for a nonoverlappable pattern.

32.3-4 $\star$
Given two patterns P and P', describe how to construct a finite automaton that determines all occurrences of *either* pattern. Try to minimize the number of states in your automaton.

32.3-5
Given a pattern P containing gap characters (see Exercise 32.1-4), show how to build a finite automaton that can find an occurrence of P in a text T in $O(n)$ matching time, where $n = |T|$.

$\star$ **32.4   The Knuth-Morris-Pratt algorithm**

We now present a linear-time string-matching algorithm due to Knuth, Morris, and Pratt. This algorithm avoids computing the transition function δ altogether, and its matching time is $\Theta(n)$ using just an auxiliary function π, which we precompute from the pattern in time $\Theta(m)$ and store in an array $\pi[1 \mathinner{.\,.} m]$. The array π allows us to compute the transition function δ efficiently (in an amortized sense) "on the fly" as needed. Loosely speaking, for any state $q = 0, 1, \ldots, m$ and any character

$a \in \Sigma$, the value $\pi[q]$ contains the information we need to compute $\delta(q, a)$ but that does not depend on a. Since the array π has only m entries, whereas δ has $\Theta(m \, |\Sigma|)$ entries, we save a factor of $|\Sigma|$ in the preprocessing time by computing π rather than δ.

The prefix function for a pattern

The prefix function π for a pattern encapsulates knowledge about how the pattern matches against shifts of itself. We can take advantage of this information to avoid testing useless shifts in the naive pattern-matching algorithm and to avoid precomputing the full transition function δ for a string-matching automaton.

Consider the operation of the naive string matcher. Figure 32.10(a) shows a particular shift s of a template containing the pattern $P = \mathtt{ababaca}$ against a text T. For this example, $q = 5$ of the characters have matched successfully, but the 6th pattern character fails to match the corresponding text character. The information that q characters have matched successfully determines the corresponding text characters. Knowing these q text characters allows us to determine immediately that certain shifts are invalid. In the example of the figure, the shift $s + 1$ is necessarily invalid, since the first pattern character ($\mathtt{a}$) would be aligned with a text character that we know does not match the first pattern character, but does match the second pattern character ($\mathtt{b}$). The shift $s' = s + 2$ shown in part (b) of the figure, however, aligns the first three pattern characters with three text characters that must necessarily match. In general, it is useful to know the answer to the following question:

> Given that pattern characters $P[1 \mathinner{.\,.} q]$ match text characters $T[s+1 \mathinner{.\,.} s+q]$, what is the least shift $s' > s$ such that for some $k < q$,
>
> $$P[1 \mathinner{.\,.} k] = T[s' + 1 \mathinner{.\,.} s' + k] \, , \tag{32.6}$$
>
> where $s' + k = s + q$?

In other words, knowing that $P_q \sqsupset T_{s+q}$, we want the longest proper prefix P_k of P_q that is also a suffix of T_{s+q}. (Since $s' + k = s + q$, if we are given s and q, then finding the smallest shift s' is tantamount to finding the longest prefix length k.) We add the difference $q - k$ in the lengths of these prefixes of P to the shift s to arrive at our new shift s', so that $s' = s + (q - k)$. In the best case, $k = 0$, so that $s' = s + q$, and we immediately rule out shifts $s + 1, s + 2, \ldots, s + q - 1$. In any case, at the new shift s' we don't need to compare the first k characters of P with the corresponding characters of T, since equation (32.6) guarantees that they match.

We can precompute the necessary information by comparing the pattern against itself, as Figure 32.10(c) demonstrates. Since $T[s' + 1 \mathinner{.\,.} s' + k]$ is part of the

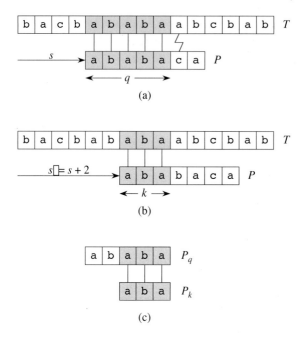

Figure 32.10   The prefix function π. **(a)** The pattern $P = \texttt{ababaca}$ aligns with a text T so that the first $q = 5$ characters match. Matching characters, shown shaded, are connected by vertical lines. **(b)** Using only our knowledge of the 5 matched characters, we can deduce that a shift of $s + 1$ is invalid, but that a shift of $s' = s+2$ is consistent with everything we know about the text and therefore is potentially valid. **(c)** We can precompute useful information for such deductions by comparing the pattern with itself. Here, we see that the longest prefix of P that is also a proper suffix of P_5 is P_3. We represent this precomputed information in the array π, so that $\pi[5] = 3$. Given that q characters have matched successfully at shift s, the next potentially valid shift is at $s' = s + (q - \pi[q])$ as shown in part (b).

known portion of the text, it is a suffix of the string P_q. Therefore, we can interpret equation (32.6) as asking for the greatest $k < q$ such that $P_k \sqsupset P_q$. Then, the new shift $s' = s + (q - k)$ is the next potentially valid shift. We will find it convenient to store, for each value of q, the number k of matching characters at the new shift s', rather than storing, say, $s' - s$.

We formalize the information that we precompute as follows. Given a pattern $P[1 \mathbin{.\,.} m]$, the ***prefix function*** for the pattern P is the function $\pi : \{1, 2, \ldots, m\} \to \{0, 1, \ldots, m - 1\}$ such that

$$\pi[q] = \max \{k : k < q \text{ and } P_k \sqsupset P_q\} \ .$$

That is, $\pi[q]$ is the length of the longest prefix of P that is a proper suffix of P_q. Figure 32.11(a) gives the complete prefix function π for the pattern $\texttt{ababaca}$.

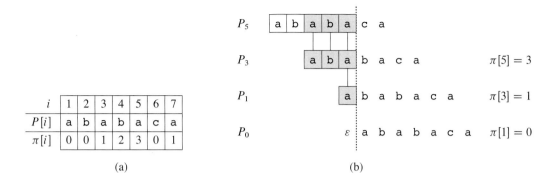

i	1	2	3	4	5	6	7
$P[i]$	a	b	a	b	a	c	a
$\pi[i]$	0	0	1	2	3	0	1

(a)

(b)

Figure 32.11   An illustration of Lemma 32.5 for the pattern $P = $ ababaca and $q = 5$. **(a)** The π function for the given pattern. Since $\pi[5] = 3$, $\pi[3] = 1$, and $\pi[1] = 0$, by iterating π we obtain $\pi^*[5] = \{3, 1, 0\}$. **(b)** We slide the template containing the pattern P to the right and note when some prefix P_k of P matches up with some proper suffix of P_5; we get matches when $k = 3$, 1, and 0. In the figure, the first row gives P, and the dotted vertical line is drawn just after P_5. Successive rows show all the shifts of P that cause some prefix P_k of P to match some suffix of P_5. Successfully matched characters are shown shaded. Vertical lines connect aligned matching characters. Thus, $\{k : k < 5 \text{ and } P_k \sqsupset P_5\} = \{3, 1, 0\}$. Lemma 32.5 claims that $\pi^*[q] = \{k : k < q \text{ and } P_k \sqsupset P_q\}$ for all q.

The pseudocode below gives the Knuth-Morris-Pratt matching algorithm as the procedure KMP-MATCHER. For the most part, the procedure follows from FINITE-AUTOMATON-MATCHER, as we shall see. KMP-MATCHER calls the auxiliary procedure COMPUTE-PREFIX-FUNCTION to compute π.

KMP-MATCHER(T, P)

```
 1  n = T.length
 2  m = P.length
 3  π = COMPUTE-PREFIX-FUNCTION(P)
 4  q = 0                          // number of characters matched
 5  for i = 1 to n                 // scan the text from left to right
 6      while q > 0 and P[q + 1] ≠ T[i]
 7          q = π[q]               // next character does not match
 8      if P[q + 1] == T[i]
 9          q = q + 1              // next character matches
10      if q == m                  // is all of P matched?
11          print "Pattern occurs with shift" i − m
12          q = π[q]               // look for the next match
```

COMPUTE-PREFIX-FUNCTION(P)

```
 1   m = P.length
 2   let π[1..m] be a new array
 3   π[1] = 0
 4   k = 0
 5   for q = 2 to m
 6       while k > 0 and P[k + 1] ≠ P[q]
 7           k = π[k]
 8       if P[k + 1] == P[q]
 9           k = k + 1
10       π[q] = k
11   return π
```

These two procedures have much in common, because both match a string against the pattern P: KMP-MATCHER matches the text T against P, and COMPUTE-PREFIX-FUNCTION matches P against itself.

We begin with an analysis of the running times of these procedures. Proving these procedures correct will be more complicated.

Running-time analysis

The running time of COMPUTE-PREFIX-FUNCTION is $\Theta(m)$, which we show by using the aggregate method of amortized analysis (see Section 17.1). The only tricky part is showing that the **while** loop of lines 6–7 executes $O(m)$ times altogether. We shall show that it makes at most $m - 1$ iterations. We start by making some observations about k. First, line 4 starts k at 0, and the only way that k increases is by the increment operation in line 9, which executes at most once per iteration of the **for** loop of lines 5–10. Thus, the total increase in k is at most $m - 1$. Second, since $k < q$ upon entering the **for** loop and each iteration of the loop increments q, we always have $k < q$. Therefore, the assignments in lines 3 and 10 ensure that $\pi[q] < q$ for all $q = 1, 2, \ldots, m$, which means that each iteration of the **while** loop decreases k. Third, k never becomes negative. Putting these facts together, we see that the total decrease in k from the **while** loop is bounded from above by the total increase in k over all iterations of the **for** loop, which is $m - 1$. Thus, the **while** loop iterates at most $m - 1$ times in all, and COMPUTE-PREFIX-FUNCTION runs in time $\Theta(m)$.

Exercise 32.4-4 asks you to show, by a similar aggregate analysis, that the matching time of KMP-MATCHER is $\Theta(n)$.

Compared with FINITE-AUTOMATON-MATCHER, by using π rather than δ, we have reduced the time for preprocessing the pattern from $O(m|\Sigma|)$ to $\Theta(m)$, while keeping the actual matching time bounded by $\Theta(n)$.

Correctness of the prefix-function computation

We shall see a little later that the prefix function π helps us simulate the transition function δ in a string-matching automaton. But first, we need to prove that the procedure COMPUTE-PREFIX-FUNCTION does indeed compute the prefix function correctly. In order to do so, we will need to find all prefixes P_k that are proper suffixes of a given prefix P_q. The value of $\pi[q]$ gives us the longest such prefix, but the following lemma, illustrated in Figure 32.11, shows that by iterating the prefix function π, we can indeed enumerate all the prefixes P_k that are proper suffixes of P_q. Let

$$\pi^*[q] = \{\pi[q], \pi^{(2)}[q], \pi^{(3)}[q], \ldots, \pi^{(t)}[q]\},$$

where $\pi^{(i)}[q]$ is defined in terms of functional iteration, so that $\pi^{(0)}[q] = q$ and $\pi^{(i)}[q] = \pi[\pi^{(i-1)}[q]]$ for $i \geq 1$, and where the sequence in $\pi^*[q]$ stops upon reaching $\pi^{(t)}[q] = 0$.

Lemma 32.5 (Prefix-function iteration lemma)
Let P be a pattern of length m with prefix function π. Then, for $q = 1, 2, \ldots, m$, we have $\pi^*[q] = \{k : k < q \text{ and } P_k \sqsupset P_q\}$.

Proof We first prove that $\pi^*[q] \subseteq \{k : k < q \text{ and } P_k \sqsupset P_q\}$ or, equivalently,

$$i \in \pi^*[q] \text{ implies } P_i \sqsupset P_q. \tag{32.7}$$

If $i \in \pi^*[q]$, then $i = \pi^{(u)}[q]$ for some $u > 0$. We prove equation (32.7) by induction on u. For $u = 1$, we have $i = \pi[q]$, and the claim follows since $i < q$ and $P_{\pi[q]} \sqsupset P_q$ by the definition of π. Using the relations $\pi[i] < i$ and $P_{\pi[i]} \sqsupset P_i$ and the transitivity of $<$ and $\sqsupset$ establishes the claim for all i in $\pi^*[q]$. Therefore, $\pi^*[q] \subseteq \{k : k < q \text{ and } P_k \sqsupset P_q\}$.

We now prove that $\{k : k < q \text{ and } P_k \sqsupset P_q\} \subseteq \pi^*[q]$ by contradiction. Suppose to the contrary that the set $\{k : k < q \text{ and } P_k \sqsupset P_q\} - \pi^*[q]$ is nonempty, and let j be the largest number in the set. Because $\pi[q]$ is the largest value in $\{k : k < q \text{ and } P_k \sqsupset P_q\}$ and $\pi[q] \in \pi^*[q]$, we must have $j < \pi[q]$, and so we let j' denote the smallest integer in $\pi^*[q]$ that is greater than j. (We can choose $j' = \pi[q]$ if no other number in $\pi^*[q]$ is greater than j.) We have $P_j \sqsupset P_q$ because $j \in \{k : k < q \text{ and } P_k \sqsupset P_q\}$, and from $j' \in \pi^*[q]$ and equation (32.7), we have $P_{j'} \sqsupset P_q$. Thus, $P_j \sqsupset P_{j'}$ by Lemma 32.1, and j is the largest value less than j' with this property. Therefore, we must have $\pi[j'] = j$ and, since $j' \in \pi^*[q]$, we must have $j \in \pi^*[q]$ as well. This contradiction proves the lemma. ∎

The algorithm COMPUTE-PREFIX-FUNCTION computes $\pi[q]$, in order, for $q = 1, 2, \ldots, m$. Setting $\pi[1]$ to 0 in line 3 of COMPUTE-PREFIX-FUNCTION is certainly correct, since $\pi[q] < q$ for all q. We shall use the following lemma and its corollary to prove that COMPUTE-PREFIX-FUNCTION computes $\pi[q]$ correctly for $q > 1$.

Lemma 32.6

Let P be a pattern of length m, and let π be the prefix function for P. For $q = 1, 2, \ldots, m$, if $\pi[q] > 0$, then $\pi[q] - 1 \in \pi^*[q - 1]$.

Proof Let $r = \pi[q] > 0$, so that $r < q$ and $P_r \sqsupset P_q$; thus, $r - 1 < q - 1$ and $P_{r-1} \sqsupset P_{q-1}$ (by dropping the last character from P_r and P_q, which we can do because $r > 0$). By Lemma 32.5, therefore, $r - 1 \in \pi^*[q - 1]$. Thus, we have $\pi[q] - 1 = r - 1 \in \pi^*[q - 1]$. ∎

For $q = 2, 3, \ldots, m$, define the subset $E_{q-1} \subseteq \pi^*[q - 1]$ by

$$
\begin{aligned}
E_{q-1} &= \{k \in \pi^*[q - 1] : P[k + 1] = P[q]\} \\
&= \{k : k < q - 1 \text{ and } P_k \sqsupset P_{q-1} \text{ and } P[k + 1] = P[q]\} \text{ (by Lemma 32.5)} \\
&= \{k : k < q - 1 \text{ and } P_{k+1} \sqsupset P_q\} .
\end{aligned}
$$

The set E_{q-1} consists of the values $k < q - 1$ for which $P_k \sqsupset P_{q-1}$ and for which, because $P[k + 1] = P[q]$, we have $P_{k+1} \sqsupset P_q$. Thus, E_{q-1} consists of those values $k \in \pi^*[q - 1]$ such that we can extend P_k to P_{k+1} and get a proper suffix of P_q.

Corollary 32.7

Let P be a pattern of length m, and let π be the prefix function for P. For $q = 2, 3, \ldots, m$,

$$
\pi[q] = \begin{cases} 0 & \text{if } E_{q-1} = \emptyset , \\ 1 + \max\{k \in E_{q-1}\} & \text{if } E_{q-1} \neq \emptyset . \end{cases}
$$

Proof If E_{q-1} is empty, there is no $k \in \pi^*[q - 1]$ (including $k = 0$) for which we can extend P_k to P_{k+1} and get a proper suffix of P_q. Therefore $\pi[q] = 0$.

If E_{q-1} is nonempty, then for each $k \in E_{q-1}$ we have $k + 1 < q$ and $P_{k+1} \sqsupset P_q$. Therefore, from the definition of $\pi[q]$, we have

$$
\pi[q] \geq 1 + \max\{k \in E_{q-1}\} . \tag{32.8}
$$

Note that $\pi[q] > 0$. Let $r = \pi[q] - 1$, so that $r + 1 = \pi[q]$ and therefore $P_{r+1} \sqsupset P_q$. Since $r + 1 > 0$, we have $P[r + 1] = P[q]$. Furthermore, by Lemma 32.6, we have $r \in \pi^*[q - 1]$. Therefore, $r \in E_{q-1}$, and so $r \leq \max\{k \in E_{q-1}\}$ or, equivalently,

$$
\pi[q] \leq 1 + \max\{k \in E_{q-1}\} . \tag{32.9}
$$

Combining equations (32.8) and (32.9) completes the proof. ∎

We now finish the proof that COMPUTE-PREFIX-FUNCTION computes π correctly. In the procedure COMPUTE-PREFIX-FUNCTION, at the start of each iteration of the **for** loop of lines 5–10, we have that $k = \pi[q - 1]$. This condition is enforced by lines 3 and 4 when the loop is first entered, and it remains true in each successive iteration because of line 10. Lines 6–9 adjust k so that it becomes the correct value of $\pi[q]$. The **while** loop of lines 6–7 searches through all values $k \in \pi^*[q - 1]$ until it finds a value of k for which $P[k + 1] = P[q]$; at that point, k is the largest value in the set E_{q-1}, so that, by Corollary 32.7, we can set $\pi[q]$ to $k + 1$. If the **while** loop cannot find a $k \in \pi^*[q - 1]$ such that $P[k + 1] = P[q]$, then k equals 0 at line 8. If $P[1] = P[q]$, then we should set both k and $\pi[q]$ to 1; otherwise we should leave k alone and set $\pi[q]$ to 0. Lines 8–10 set k and $\pi[q]$ correctly in either case. This completes our proof of the correctness of COMPUTE-PREFIX-FUNCTION.

Correctness of the Knuth-Morris-Pratt algorithm

We can think of the procedure KMP-MATCHER as a reimplemented version of the procedure FINITE-AUTOMATON-MATCHER, but using the prefix function π to compute state transitions. Specifically, we shall prove that in the ith iteration of the **for** loops of both KMP-MATCHER and FINITE-AUTOMATON-MATCHER, the state q has the same value when we test for equality with m (at line 10 in KMP-MATCHER and at line 5 in FINITE-AUTOMATON-MATCHER). Once we have argued that KMP-MATCHER simulates the behavior of FINITE-AUTOMATON-MATCHER, the correctness of KMP-MATCHER follows from the correctness of FINITE-AUTOMATON-MATCHER (though we shall see a little later why line 12 in KMP-MATCHER is necessary).

Before we formally prove that KMP-MATCHER correctly simulates FINITE-AUTOMATON-MATCHER, let's take a moment to understand how the prefix function π replaces the δ transition function. Recall that when a string-matching automaton is in state q and it scans a character $a = T[i]$, it moves to a new state $\delta(q, a)$. If $a = P[q + 1]$, so that a continues to match the pattern, then $\delta(q, a) = q + 1$. Otherwise, $a \neq P[q + 1]$, so that a does not continue to match the pattern, and $0 \leq \delta(q, a) \leq q$. In the first case, when a continues to match, KMP-MATCHER moves to state $q + 1$ without referring to the π function: the **while** loop test in line 6 comes up false the first time, the test in line 8 comes up true, and line 9 increments q.

The π function comes into play when the character a does not continue to match the pattern, so that the new state $\delta(q, a)$ is either q or to the left of q along the spine of the automaton. The **while** loop of lines 6–7 in KMP-MATCHER iterates through the states in $\pi^*[q]$, stopping either when it arrives in a state, say q', such that a matches $P[q' + 1]$ or q' has gone all the way down to 0. If a matches $P[q' + 1]$, then line 9 sets the new state to $q' + 1$, which should equal $\delta(q, a)$ for the simulation to work correctly. In other words, the new state $\delta(q, a)$ should be either state 0 or one greater than some state in $\pi^*[q]$.

Let's look at the example in Figures 32.7 and 32.11, which are for the pattern $P = \texttt{ababaca}$. Suppose that the automaton is in state $q = 5$; the states in $\pi^*[5]$ are, in descending order, 3, 1, and 0. If the next character scanned is $\texttt{c}$, then we can easily see that the automaton moves to state $\delta(5, \texttt{c}) = 6$ in both FINITE-AUTOMATON-MATCHER and KMP-MATCHER. Now suppose that the next character scanned is instead $\texttt{b}$, so that the automaton should move to state $\delta(5, \texttt{b}) = 4$. The **while** loop in KMP-MATCHER exits having executed line 7 once, and it arrives in state $q' = \pi[5] = 3$. Since $P[q' + 1] = P[4] = \texttt{b}$, the test in line 8 comes up true, and KMP-MATCHER moves to the new state $q' + 1 = 4 = \delta(5, \texttt{b})$. Finally, suppose that the next character scanned is instead $\texttt{a}$, so that the automaton should move to state $\delta(5, \texttt{a}) = 1$. The first three times that the test in line 6 executes, the test comes up true. The first time, we find that $P[6] = \texttt{c} \neq \texttt{a}$, and KMP-MATCHER moves to state $\pi[5] = 3$ (the first state in $\pi^*[5]$). The second time, we find that $P[4] = \texttt{b} \neq \texttt{a}$ and move to state $\pi[3] = 1$ (the second state in $\pi^*[5]$). The third time, we find that $P[2] = \texttt{b} \neq \texttt{a}$ and move to state $\pi[1] = 0$ (the last state in $\pi^*[5]$). The **while** loop exits once it arrives in state $q' = 0$. Now, line 8 finds that $P[q' + 1] = P[1] = \texttt{a}$, and line 9 moves the automaton to the new state $q' + 1 = 1 = \delta(5, \texttt{a})$.

Thus, our intuition is that KMP-MATCHER iterates through the states in $\pi^*[q]$ in decreasing order, stopping at some state q' and then possibly moving to state $q' + 1$. Although that might seem like a lot of work just to simulate computing $\delta(q, a)$, bear in mind that asymptotically, KMP-MATCHER is no slower than FINITE-AUTOMATON-MATCHER.

We are now ready to formally prove the correctness of the Knuth-Morris-Pratt algorithm. By Theorem 32.4, we have that $q = \sigma(T_i)$ after each time we execute line 4 of FINITE-AUTOMATON-MATCHER. Therefore, it suffices to show that the same property holds with regard to the **for** loop in KMP-MATCHER. The proof proceeds by induction on the number of loop iterations. Initially, both procedures set q to 0 as they enter their respective **for** loops for the first time. Consider iteration i of the **for** loop in KMP-MATCHER, and let q' be state at the start of this loop iteration. By the inductive hypothesis, we have $q' = \sigma(T_{i-1})$. We need to show that $q = \sigma(T_i)$ at line 10. (Again, we shall handle line 12 separately.)

When we consider the character $T[i]$, the longest prefix of P that is a suffix of T_i is either $P_{q'+1}$ (if $P[q' + 1] = T[i]$) or some prefix (not necessarily proper, and possibly empty) of $P_{q'}$. We consider separately the three cases in which $\sigma(T_i) = 0$, $\sigma(T_i) = q' + 1$, and $0 < \sigma(T_i) \leq q'$.

- If $\sigma(T_i) = 0$, then $P_0 = \varepsilon$ is the only prefix of P that is a suffix of T_i. The **while** loop of lines 6–7 iterates through the values in $\pi^*[q']$, but although $P_q \sqsupset T_{i-1}$ for every $q \in \pi^*[q']$, the loop never finds a q such that $P[q+1] = T[i]$. The loop terminates when q reaches 0, and of course line 9 does not execute. Therefore, $q = 0$ at line 10, so that $q = \sigma(T_i)$.

- If $\sigma(T_i) = q' + 1$, then $P[q' + 1] = T[i]$, and the **while** loop test in line 6 fails the first time through. Line 9 executes, incrementing q so that afterward we have $q = q' + 1 = \sigma(T_i)$.

- If $0 < \sigma(T_i) \le q'$, then the **while** loop of lines 6–7 iterates at least once, checking in decreasing order each value $q \in \pi^*[q']$ until it stops at some $q < q'$. Thus, P_q is the longest prefix of $P_{q'}$ for which $P[q+1] = T[i]$, so that when the **while** loop terminates, $q + 1 = \sigma(P_{q'}T[i])$. Since $q' = \sigma(T_{i-1})$, Lemma 32.3 implies that $\sigma(T_{i-1}T[i]) = \sigma(P_{q'}T[i])$. Thus, we have

$$
\begin{aligned}
q + 1 &= \sigma(P_{q'}T[i]) \\
&= \sigma(T_{i-1}T[i]) \\
&= \sigma(T_i)
\end{aligned}
$$

when the **while** loop terminates. After line 9 increments q, we have $q = \sigma(T_i)$.

Line 12 is necessary in KMP-MATCHER, because otherwise, we might reference $P[m + 1]$ on line 6 after finding an occurrence of P. (The argument that $q = \sigma(T_{i-1})$ upon the next execution of line 6 remains valid by the hint given in Exercise 32.4-8: $\delta(m, a) = \delta(\pi[m], a)$ or, equivalently, $\sigma(Pa) = \sigma(P_{\pi[m]}a)$ for any $a \in \Sigma$.) The remaining argument for the correctness of the Knuth-Morris-Pratt algorithm follows from the correctness of FINITE-AUTOMATON-MATCHER, since we have shown that KMP-MATCHER simulates the behavior of FINITE-AUTOMATON-MATCHER.

Exercises

32.4-1
Compute the prefix function π for the pattern `ababbabbabbababbabb`.

32.4-2
Give an upper bound on the size of $\pi^*[q]$ as a function of q. Give an example to show that your bound is tight.

32.4-3
Explain how to determine the occurrences of pattern P in the text T by examining the π function for the string PT (the string of length $m+n$ that is the concatenation of P and T).

32.4-4
Use an aggregate analysis to show that the running time of KMP-MATCHER is $\Theta(n)$.

32.4-5
Use a potential function to show that the running time of KMP-MATCHER is $\Theta(n)$.

32.4-6
Show how to improve KMP-MATCHER by replacing the occurrence of π in line 7 (but not line 12) by π', where π' is defined recursively for $q = 1, 2, \ldots, m - 1$ by the equation

$$
\pi'[q] = \begin{cases} 0 & \text{if } \pi[q] = 0 , \\ \pi'[\pi[q]] & \text{if } \pi[q] \neq 0 \text{ and } P[\pi[q] + 1] = P[q + 1] , \\ \pi[q] & \text{if } \pi[q] \neq 0 \text{ and } P[\pi[q] + 1] \neq P[q + 1] . \end{cases}
$$

Explain why the modified algorithm is correct, and explain in what sense this change constitutes an improvement.

32.4-7
Give a linear-time algorithm to determine whether a text T is a cyclic rotation of another string T'. For example, `arc` and `car` are cyclic rotations of each other.

32.4-8 ★
Give an $O(m\,|\Sigma|)$-time algorithm for computing the transition function δ for the string-matching automaton corresponding to a given pattern P. (*Hint:* Prove that $\delta(q, a) = \delta(\pi[q], a)$ if $q = m$ or $P[q + 1] \neq a$.)

Problems

32-1   *String matching based on repetition factors*
Let y^i denote the concatenation of string y with itself i times. For example, $(ab)^3 = ababab$. We say that a string $x \in \Sigma^*$ has ***repetition factor*** r if $x = y^r$ for some string $y \in \Sigma^*$ and some $r > 0$. Let $\rho(x)$ denote the largest r such that x has repetition factor r.

a. Give an efficient algorithm that takes as input a pattern $P[1 \mathinner{.\,.} m]$ and computes the value $\rho(P_i)$ for $i = 1, 2, \ldots, m$. What is the running time of your algorithm?

b. For any pattern $P[1 \mathinner{.\,.} m]$, let $\rho^*(P)$ be defined as $\max_{1 \le i \le m} \rho(P_i)$. Prove that if the pattern P is chosen randomly from the set of all binary strings of length m, then the expected value of $\rho^*(P)$ is $O(1)$.

c. Argue that the following string-matching algorithm correctly finds all occurrences of pattern P in a text $T[1 \mathinner{.\,.} n]$ in time $O(\rho^*(P)n + m)$:

REPETITION-MATCHER(P, T)

```
 1  m = P.length
 2  n = T.length
 3  k = 1 + ρ*(P)
 4  q = 0
 5  s = 0
 6  while s ≤ n − m
 7      if T[s + q + 1] == P[q + 1]
 8          q = q + 1
 9          if q == m
10              print "Pattern occurs with shift" s
11      if q == m or T[s + q + 1] ≠ P[q + 1]
12          s = s + max(1, ⌈q/k⌉)
13          q = 0
```

This algorithm is due to Galil and Seiferas. By extending these ideas greatly, they obtained a linear-time string-matching algorithm that uses only $O(1)$ storage beyond what is required for P and T.

Chapter notes

The relation of string matching to the theory of finite automata is discussed by Aho, Hopcroft, and Ullman [5]. The Knuth-Morris-Pratt algorithm [214] was invented independently by Knuth and Pratt and by Morris; they published their work jointly. Reingold, Urban, and Gries [294] give an alternative treatment of the Knuth-Morris-Pratt algorithm. The Rabin-Karp algorithm was proposed by Karp and Rabin [201]. Galil and Seiferas [126] give an interesting deterministic linear-time string-matching algorithm that uses only $O(1)$ space beyond that required to store the pattern and text.

33   Computational Geometry

Computational geometry is the branch of computer science that studies algorithms for solving geometric problems. In modern engineering and mathematics, computational geometry has applications in such diverse fields as computer graphics, robotics, VLSI design, computer-aided design, molecular modeling, metallurgy, manufacturing, textile layout, forestry, and statistics. The input to a computational-geometry problem is typically a description of a set of geometric objects, such as a set of points, a set of line segments, or the vertices of a polygon in counterclockwise order. The output is often a response to a query about the objects, such as whether any of the lines intersect, or perhaps a new geometric object, such as the convex hull (smallest enclosing convex polygon) of the set of points.

In this chapter, we look at a few computational-geometry algorithms in two dimensions, that is, in the plane. We represent each input object by a set of points $\{p_1, p_2, p_3, \ldots\}$, where each $p_i = (x_i, y_i)$ and $x_i, y_i \in \mathbb{R}$. For example, we represent an n-vertex polygon P by a sequence $\langle p_0, p_1, p_2, \ldots, p_{n-1} \rangle$ of its vertices in order of their appearance on the boundary of P. Computational geometry can also apply to three dimensions, and even higher-dimensional spaces, but such problems and their solutions can be very difficult to visualize. Even in two dimensions, however, we can see a good sample of computational-geometry techniques.

Section 33.1 shows how to answer basic questions about line segments efficiently and accurately: whether one segment is clockwise or counterclockwise from another that shares an endpoint, which way we turn when traversing two adjoining line segments, and whether two line segments intersect. Section 33.2 presents a technique called "sweeping" that we use to develop an $O(n \lg n)$-time algorithm for determining whether a set of n line segments contains any intersections. Section 33.3 gives two "rotational-sweep" algorithms that compute the convex hull (smallest enclosing convex polygon) of a set of n points: Graham's scan, which runs in time $O(n \lg n)$, and Jarvis's march, which takes $O(nh)$ time, where h is the number of vertices of the convex hull. Finally, Section 33.4 gives an $O(n \lg n)$-time divide-and-conquer algorithm for finding the closest pair of points in a set of n points in the plane.

33.1   Line-segment properties

Several of the computational-geometry algorithms in this chapter require answers to questions about the properties of line segments. A ***convex combination*** of two distinct points $p_1 = (x_1, y_1)$ and $p_2 = (x_2, y_2)$ is any point $p_3 = (x_3, y_3)$ such that for some α in the range $0 \le \alpha \le 1$, we have $x_3 = \alpha x_1 + (1 - \alpha) x_2$ and $y_3 = \alpha y_1 + (1 - \alpha) y_2$. We also write that $p_3 = \alpha p_1 + (1 - \alpha) p_2$. Intuitively, p_3 is any point that is on the line passing through p_1 and p_2 and is on or between p_1 and p_2 on the line. Given two distinct points p_1 and p_2, the ***line segment*** $\overline{p_1 p_2}$ is the set of convex combinations of p_1 and p_2. We call p_1 and p_2 the ***endpoints*** of segment $\overline{p_1 p_2}$. Sometimes the ordering of p_1 and p_2 matters, and we speak of the ***directed segment*** $\overrightarrow{p_1 p_2}$. If p_1 is the ***origin*** $(0, 0)$, then we can treat the directed segment $\overrightarrow{p_1 p_2}$ as the ***vector*** p_2.

In this section, we shall explore the following questions:

1. Given two directed segments $\overrightarrow{p_0 p_1}$ and $\overrightarrow{p_0 p_2}$, is $\overrightarrow{p_0 p_1}$ clockwise from $\overrightarrow{p_0 p_2}$ with respect to their common endpoint p_0?

2. Given two line segments $\overline{p_0 p_1}$ and $\overline{p_1 p_2}$, if we traverse $\overline{p_0 p_1}$ and then $\overline{p_1 p_2}$, do we make a left turn at point p_1?

3. Do line segments $\overline{p_1 p_2}$ and $\overline{p_3 p_4}$ intersect?

There are no restrictions on the given points.

We can answer each question in $O(1)$ time, which should come as no surprise since the input size of each question is $O(1)$. Moreover, our methods use only additions, subtractions, multiplications, and comparisons. We need neither division nor trigonometric functions, both of which can be computationally expensive and prone to problems with round-off error. For example, the "straightforward" method of determining whether two segments intersect—compute the line equation of the form $y = mx + b$ for each segment (m is the slope and b is the y-intercept), find the point of intersection of the lines, and check whether this point is on both segments—uses division to find the point of intersection. When the segments are nearly parallel, this method is very sensitive to the precision of the division operation on real computers. The method in this section, which avoids division, is much more accurate.

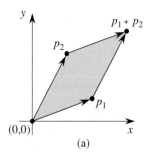
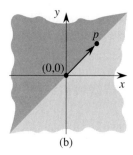

(a)   (b)

Figure 33.1 **(a)** The cross product of vectors p_1 and p_2 is the signed area of the parallelogram. **(b)** The lightly shaded region contains vectors that are clockwise from p. The darkly shaded region contains vectors that are counterclockwise from p.

Cross products

Computing cross products lies at the heart of our line-segment methods. Consider vectors p_1 and p_2, shown in Figure 33.1(a). We can interpret the **cross product** $p_1 \times p_2$ as the signed area of the parallelogram formed by the points $(0, 0)$, p_1, p_2, and $p_1 + p_2 = (x_1 + x_2, y_1 + y_2)$. An equivalent, but more useful, definition gives the cross product as the determinant of a matrix:[1]

$$
\begin{aligned}
p_1 \times p_2 &= \det \begin{pmatrix} x_1 & x_2 \\ y_1 & y_2 \end{pmatrix} \\
&= x_1 y_2 - x_2 y_1 \\
&= -p_2 \times p_1 \ .
\end{aligned}
$$

If $p_1 \times p_2$ is positive, then p_1 is clockwise from p_2 with respect to the origin $(0, 0)$; if this cross product is negative, then p_1 is counterclockwise from p_2. (See Exercise 33.1-1.) Figure 33.1(b) shows the clockwise and counterclockwise regions relative to a vector p. A boundary condition arises if the cross product is 0; in this case, the vectors are **colinear**, pointing in either the same or opposite directions.

  To determine whether a directed segment $\overrightarrow{p_0 p_1}$ is closer to a directed segment $\overrightarrow{p_0 p_2}$ in a clockwise direction or in a counterclockwise direction with respect to their common endpoint p_0, we simply translate to use p_0 as the origin. That is, we let $p_1 - p_0$ denote the vector $p_1' = (x_1', y_1')$, where $x_1' = x_1 - x_0$ and $y_1' = y_1 - y_0$, and we define $p_2 - p_0$ similarly. We then compute the cross product

---

[1]Actually, the cross product is a three-dimensional concept. It is a vector that is perpendicular to both p_1 and p_2 according to the "right-hand rule" and whose magnitude is $|x_1 y_2 - x_2 y_1|$. In this chapter, however, we find it convenient to treat the cross product simply as the value $x_1 y_2 - x_2 y_1$.

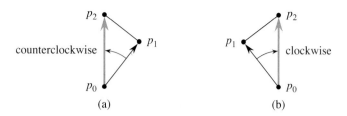

Figure 33.2 Using the cross product to determine how consecutive line segments $\overline{p_0 p_1}$ and $\overline{p_1 p_2}$ turn at point p_1. We check whether the directed segment $\overrightarrow{p_0 p_2}$ is clockwise or counterclockwise relative to the directed segment $\overrightarrow{p_0 p_1}$. **(a)** If counterclockwise, the points make a left turn. **(b)** If clockwise, they make a right turn.

$$(p_1 - p_0) \times (p_2 - p_0) = (x_1 - x_0)(y_2 - y_0) - (x_2 - x_0)(y_1 - y_0) \, .$$

If this cross product is positive, then $\overrightarrow{p_0 p_1}$ is clockwise from $\overrightarrow{p_0 p_2}$; if negative, it is counterclockwise.

Determining whether consecutive segments turn left or right

Our next question is whether two consecutive line segments $\overline{p_0 p_1}$ and $\overline{p_1 p_2}$ turn left or right at point p_1. Equivalently, we want a method to determine which way a given angle $\angle p_0 p_1 p_2$ turns. Cross products allow us to answer this question without computing the angle. As Figure 33.2 shows, we simply check whether directed segment $\overrightarrow{p_0 p_2}$ is clockwise or counterclockwise relative to directed segment $\overrightarrow{p_0 p_1}$. To do so, we compute the cross product $(p_2 - p_0) \times (p_1 - p_0)$. If the sign of this cross product is negative, then $\overrightarrow{p_0 p_2}$ is counterclockwise with respect to $\overrightarrow{p_0 p_1}$, and thus we make a left turn at p_1. A positive cross product indicates a clockwise orientation and a right turn. A cross product of 0 means that points p_0, p_1, and p_2 are colinear.

Determining whether two line segments intersect

To determine whether two line segments intersect, we check whether each segment straddles the line containing the other. A segment $\overline{p_1 p_2}$ **straddles** a line if point p_1 lies on one side of the line and point p_2 lies on the other side. A boundary case arises if p_1 or p_2 lies directly on the line. Two line segments intersect if and only if either (or both) of the following conditions holds:

1. Each segment straddles the line containing the other.

2. An endpoint of one segment lies on the other segment. (This condition comes from the boundary case.)

The following procedures implement this idea. SEGMENTS-INTERSECT returns TRUE if segments $\overline{p_1 p_2}$ and $\overline{p_3 p_4}$ intersect and FALSE if they do not. It calls the subroutines DIRECTION, which computes relative orientations using the cross-product method above, and ON-SEGMENT, which determines whether a point known to be colinear with a segment lies on that segment.

SEGMENTS-INTERSECT(p_1, p_2, p_3, p_4)

```
 1   d₁ = DIRECTION(p₃, p₄, p₁)
 2   d₂ = DIRECTION(p₃, p₄, p₂)
 3   d₃ = DIRECTION(p₁, p₂, p₃)
 4   d₄ = DIRECTION(p₁, p₂, p₄)
 5   if ((d₁ > 0 and d₂ < 0) or (d₁ < 0 and d₂ > 0)) and
              ((d₃ > 0 and d₄ < 0) or (d₃ < 0 and d₄ > 0))
 6        return TRUE
 7   elseif d₁ == 0 and ON-SEGMENT(p₃, p₄, p₁)
 8        return TRUE
 9   elseif d₂ == 0 and ON-SEGMENT(p₃, p₄, p₂)
10        return TRUE
11   elseif d₃ == 0 and ON-SEGMENT(p₁, p₂, p₃)
12        return TRUE
13   elseif d₄ == 0 and ON-SEGMENT(p₁, p₂, p₄)
14        return TRUE
15   else return FALSE
```

DIRECTION(p_i, p_j, p_k)

```
 1   return (p_k − p_i) × (p_j − p_i)
```

ON-SEGMENT(p_i, p_j, p_k)

```
 1   if min(x_i, x_j) ≤ x_k ≤ max(x_i, x_j) and min(y_i, y_j) ≤ y_k ≤ max(y_i, y_j)
 2        return TRUE
 3   else return FALSE
```

SEGMENTS-INTERSECT works as follows. Lines 1–4 compute the relative orientation d_i of each endpoint p_i with respect to the other segment. If all the relative orientations are nonzero, then we can easily determine whether segments $\overline{p_1 p_2}$ and $\overline{p_3 p_4}$ intersect, as follows. Segment $\overline{p_1 p_2}$ straddles the line containing segment $\overline{p_3 p_4}$ if directed segments $\overrightarrow{p_3 p_1}$ and $\overrightarrow{p_3 p_2}$ have opposite orientations relative to $\overrightarrow{p_3 p_4}$. In this case, the signs of d_1 and d_2 differ. Similarly, $\overline{p_3 p_4}$ straddles the line containing $\overline{p_1 p_2}$ if the signs of d_3 and d_4 differ. If the test of line 5 is true, then the segments straddle each other, and SEGMENTS-INTERSECT returns TRUE. Figure 33.3(a) shows this case. Otherwise, the segments do not straddle

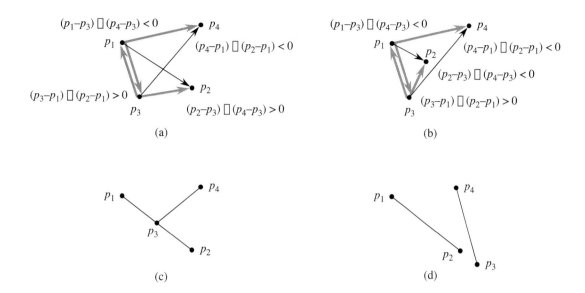

Figure 33.3 Cases in the procedure SEGMENTS-INTERSECT. **(a)** The segments $\overline{p_1 p_2}$ and $\overline{p_3 p_4}$ straddle each other's lines. Because $\overline{p_3 p_4}$ straddles the line containing $\overline{p_1 p_2}$, the signs of the cross products $(p_3 - p_1) \times (p_2 - p_1)$ and $(p_4 - p_1) \times (p_2 - p_1)$ differ. Because $\overline{p_1 p_2}$ straddles the line containing $\overline{p_3 p_4}$, the signs of the cross products $(p_1 - p_3) \times (p_4 - p_3)$ and $(p_2 - p_3) \times (p_4 - p_3)$ differ. **(b)** Segment $\overline{p_3 p_4}$ straddles the line containing $\overline{p_1 p_2}$, but $\overline{p_1 p_2}$ does not straddle the line containing $\overline{p_3 p_4}$. The signs of the cross products $(p_1 - p_3) \times (p_4 - p_3)$ and $(p_2 - p_3) \times (p_4 - p_3)$ are the same. **(c)** Point p_3 is colinear with $\overline{p_1 p_2}$ and is between p_1 and p_2. **(d)** Point p_3 is colinear with $\overline{p_1 p_2}$, but it is not between p_1 and p_2. The segments do not intersect.

each other's lines, although a boundary case may apply. If all the relative orientations are nonzero, no boundary case applies. All the tests against 0 in lines 7–13 then fail, and SEGMENTS-INTERSECT returns FALSE in line 15. Figure 33.3(b) shows this case.

A boundary case occurs if any relative orientation d_k is 0. Here, we know that p_k is colinear with the other segment. It is directly on the other segment if and only if it is between the endpoints of the other segment. The procedure ON-SEGMENT returns whether p_k is between the endpoints of segment $\overline{p_i p_j}$, which will be the other segment when called in lines 7–13; the procedure assumes that p_k is colinear with segment $\overline{p_i p_j}$. Figures 33.3(c) and (d) show cases with colinear points. In Figure 33.3(c), p_3 is on $\overline{p_1 p_2}$, and so SEGMENTS-INTERSECT returns TRUE in line 12. No endpoints are on other segments in Figure 33.3(d), and so SEGMENTS-INTERSECT returns FALSE in line 15.

Other applications of cross products

Later sections of this chapter introduce additional uses for cross products. In Section 33.3, we shall need to sort a set of points according to their polar angles with respect to a given origin. As Exercise 33.1-3 asks you to show, we can use cross products to perform the comparisons in the sorting procedure. In Section 33.2, we shall use red-black trees to maintain the vertical ordering of a set of line segments. Rather than keeping explicit key values which we compare to each other in the red-black tree code, we shall compute a cross-product to determine which of two segments that intersect a given vertical line is above the other.

Exercises

33.1-1
Prove that if $p_1 \times p_2$ is positive, then vector p_1 is clockwise from vector p_2 with respect to the origin $(0, 0)$ and that if this cross product is negative, then p_1 is counterclockwise from p_2.

33.1-2
Professor van Pelt proposes that only the x-dimension needs to be tested in line 1 of ON-SEGMENT. Show why the professor is wrong.

33.1-3
The ***polar angle*** of a point p_1 with respect to an origin point p_0 is the angle of the vector $p_1 - p_0$ in the usual polar coordinate system. For example, the polar angle of $(3, 5)$ with respect to $(2, 4)$ is the angle of the vector $(1, 1)$, which is 45 degrees or $\pi/4$ radians. The polar angle of $(3, 3)$ with respect to $(2, 4)$ is the angle of the vector $(1, -1)$, which is 315 degrees or $7\pi/4$ radians. Write pseudocode to sort a sequence $\langle p_1, p_2, \ldots, p_n \rangle$ of n points according to their polar angles with respect to a given origin point p_0. Your procedure should take $O(n \lg n)$ time and use cross products to compare angles.

33.1-4
Show how to determine in $O(n^2 \lg n)$ time whether any three points in a set of n points are colinear.

33.1-5
A ***polygon*** is a piecewise-linear, closed curve in the plane. That is, it is a curve ending on itself that is formed by a sequence of straight-line segments, called the ***sides*** of the polygon. A point joining two consecutive sides is a ***vertex*** of the polygon. If the polygon is ***simple***, as we shall generally assume, it does not cross itself. The set of points in the plane enclosed by a simple polygon forms the ***interior*** of

the polygon, the set of points on the polygon itself forms its ***boundary***, and the set of points surrounding the polygon forms its ***exterior***. A simple polygon is ***convex*** if, given any two points on its boundary or in its interior, all points on the line segment drawn between them are contained in the polygon's boundary or interior. A vertex of a convex polygon cannot be expressed as a convex combination of any two distinct points on the boundary or in the interior of the polygon.

Professor Amundsen proposes the following method to determine whether a sequence $\langle p_0, p_1, \ldots, p_{n-1} \rangle$ of n points forms the consecutive vertices of a convex polygon. Output "yes" if the set $\{ \angle p_i p_{i+1} p_{i+2} : i = 0, 1, \ldots, n-1 \}$, where subscript addition is performed modulo n, does not contain both left turns and right turns; otherwise, output "no." Show that although this method runs in linear time, it does not always produce the correct answer. Modify the professor's method so that it always produces the correct answer in linear time.

33.1-6

Given a point $p_0 = (x_0, y_0)$, the ***right horizontal ray*** from p_0 is the set of points $\{ p_i = (x_i, y_i) : x_i \geq x_0 \text{ and } y_i = y_0 \}$, that is, it is the set of points due right of p_0 along with p_0 itself. Show how to determine whether a given right horizontal ray from p_0 intersects a line segment $\overline{p_1 p_2}$ in $O(1)$ time by reducing the problem to that of determining whether two line segments intersect.

33.1-7

One way to determine whether a point p_0 is in the interior of a simple, but not necessarily convex, polygon P is to look at any ray from p_0 and check that the ray intersects the boundary of P an odd number of times but that p_0 itself is not on the boundary of P. Show how to compute in $\Theta(n)$ time whether a point p_0 is in the interior of an n-vertex polygon P. (*Hint:* Use Exercise 33.1-6. Make sure your algorithm is correct when the ray intersects the polygon boundary at a vertex and when the ray overlaps a side of the polygon.)

33.1-8

Show how to compute the area of an n-vertex simple, but not necessarily convex, polygon in $\Theta(n)$ time. (See Exercise 33.1-5 for definitions pertaining to polygons.)

33.2 Determining whether any pair of segments intersects

This section presents an algorithm for determining whether any two line segments in a set of segments intersect. The algorithm uses a technique known as "sweeping," which is common to many computational-geometry algorithms. Moreover, as the exercises at the end of this section show, this algorithm, or simple variations of it, can help solve other computational-geometry problems.

The algorithm runs in $O(n \lg n)$ time, where n is the number of segments we are given. It determines only whether or not any intersection exists; it does not print all the intersections. (By Exercise 33.2-1, it takes $\Omega(n^2)$ time in the worst case to find *all* the intersections in a set of n line segments.)

In *sweeping*, an imaginary vertical *sweep line* passes through the given set of geometric objects, usually from left to right. We treat the spatial dimension that the sweep line moves across, in this case the x-dimension, as a dimension of time. Sweeping provides a method for ordering geometric objects, usually by placing them into a dynamic data structure, and for taking advantage of relationships among them. The line-segment-intersection algorithm in this section considers all the line-segment endpoints in left-to-right order and checks for an intersection each time it encounters an endpoint.

To describe and prove correct our algorithm for determining whether any two of n line segments intersect, we shall make two simplifying assumptions. First, we assume that no input segment is vertical. Second, we assume that no three input segments intersect at a single point. Exercises 33.2-8 and 33.2-9 ask you to show that the algorithm is robust enough that it needs only a slight modification to work even when these assumptions do not hold. Indeed, removing such simplifying assumptions and dealing with boundary conditions often present the most difficult challenges when programming computational-geometry algorithms and proving their correctness.

Ordering segments

Because we assume that there are no vertical segments, we know that any input segment intersecting a given vertical sweep line intersects it at a single point. Thus, we can order the segments that intersect a vertical sweep line according to the y-coordinates of the points of intersection.

To be more precise, consider two segments s_1 and s_2. We say that these segments are *comparable* at x if the vertical sweep line with x-coordinate x intersects both of them. We say that s_1 is *above* s_2 at x, written $s_1 \succeq_x s_2$, if s_1 and s_2 are comparable at x and the intersection of s_1 with the sweep line at x is higher than the intersection of s_2 with the same sweep line, or if s_1 and s_2 intersect at the sweep line. In Figure 33.4(a), for example, we have the relationships $a \succeq_r c$, $a \succeq_t b$, $b \succeq_t c$, $a \succeq_t c$, and $b \succeq_u c$. Segment d is not comparable with any other segment.

For any given x, the relation "$\succeq_x$" is a total preorder (see Section B.2) for all segments that intersect the sweep line at x. That is, the relation is transitive, and if segments s_1 and s_2 each intersect the sweep line at x, then either $s_1 \succeq_x s_2$ or $s_2 \succeq_x s_1$, or both (if s_1 and s_2 intersect at the sweep line). (The relation $\succeq_x$ is

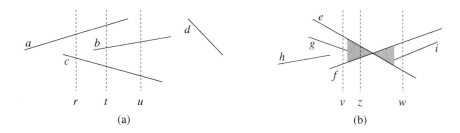

Figure 33.4 The ordering among line segments at various vertical sweep lines. **(a)** We have $a \succeq_r c$, $a \succeq_t b$, $b \succeq_t c$, $a \succeq_t c$, and $b \succeq_u c$. Segment d is comparable with no other segment shown. **(b)** When segments e and f intersect, they reverse their orders: we have $e \succeq_v f$ but $f \succeq_w e$. Any sweep line (such as z) that passes through the shaded region has e and f consecutive in the ordering given by the relation $\succeq_z$.

also reflexive, but neither symmetric nor antisymmetric.) The total preorder may differ for differing values of x, however, as segments enter and leave the ordering. A segment enters the ordering when its left endpoint is encountered by the sweep, and it leaves the ordering when its right endpoint is encountered.

What happens when the sweep line passes through the intersection of two segments? As Figure 33.4(b) shows, the segments reverse their positions in the total preorder. Sweep lines v and w are to the left and right, respectively, of the point of intersection of segments e and f, and we have $e \succeq_v f$ and $f \succeq_w e$. Note that because we assume that no three segments intersect at the same point, there must be some vertical sweep line x for which intersecting segments e and f are *consecutive* in the total preorder $\succeq_x$. Any sweep line that passes through the shaded region of Figure 33.4(b), such as z, has e and f consecutive in its total preorder.

Moving the sweep line

Sweeping algorithms typically manage two sets of data:

1. The ***sweep-line status*** gives the relationships among the objects that the sweep line intersects.

2. The ***event-point schedule*** is a sequence of points, called ***event points***, which we order from left to right according to their x-coordinates. As the sweep progresses from left to right, whenever the sweep line reaches the x-coordinate of an event point, the sweep halts, processes the event point, and then resumes. Changes to the sweep-line status occur only at event points.

For some algorithms (the algorithm asked for in Exercise 33.2-7, for example), the event-point schedule develops dynamically as the algorithm progresses. The algorithm at hand, however, determines all the event points before the sweep, based solely on simple properties of the input data. In particular, each segment endpoint is an event point. We sort the segment endpoints by increasing x-coordinate and proceed from left to right. (If two or more endpoints are ***covertical***, i.e., they have the same x-coordinate, we break the tie by putting all the covertical left endpoints before the covertical right endpoints. Within a set of covertical left endpoints, we put those with lower y-coordinates first, and we do the same within a set of covertical right endpoints.) When we encounter a segment's left endpoint, we insert the segment into the sweep-line status, and we delete the segment from the sweep-line status upon encountering its right endpoint. Whenever two segments first become consecutive in the total preorder, we check whether they intersect.

The sweep-line status is a total preorder T, for which we require the following operations:

- INSERT(T, s): insert segment s into T.

- DELETE(T, s): delete segment s from T.

- ABOVE(T, s): return the segment immediately above segment s in T.

- BELOW(T, s): return the segment immediately below segment s in T.

It is possible for segments s_1 and s_2 to be mutually above each other in the total preorder T; this situation can occur if s_1 and s_2 intersect at the sweep line whose total preorder is given by T. In this case, the two segments may appear in either order in T.

If the input contains n segments, we can perform each of the operations INSERT, DELETE, ABOVE, and BELOW in $O(\lg n)$ time using red-black trees. Recall that the red-black-tree operations in Chapter 13 involve comparing keys. We can replace the key comparisons by comparisons that use cross products to determine the relative ordering of two segments (see Exercise 33.2-2).

Segment-intersection pseudocode

The following algorithm takes as input a set S of n line segments, returning the boolean value TRUE if any pair of segments in S intersects, and FALSE otherwise. A red-black tree maintains the total preorder T.

ANY-SEGMENTS-INTERSECT(S)

```
 1  T = Ø
 2  sort the endpoints of the segments in S from left to right,
          breaking ties by putting left endpoints before right endpoints
          and breaking further ties by putting points with lower
          y-coordinates first
 3  for each point p in the sorted list of endpoints
 4      if p is the left endpoint of a segment s
 5          INSERT(T, s)
 6          if (ABOVE(T, s) exists and intersects s)
                or (BELOW(T, s) exists and intersects s)
 7              return TRUE
 8      if p is the right endpoint of a segment s
 9          if both ABOVE(T, s) and BELOW(T, s) exist
                and ABOVE(T, s) intersects BELOW(T, s)
10              return TRUE
11          DELETE(T, s)
12  return FALSE
```

Figure 33.5 illustrates how the algorithm works. Line 1 initializes the total preorder to be empty. Line 2 determines the event-point schedule by sorting the $2n$ segment endpoints from left to right, breaking ties as described above. One way to perform line 2 is by lexicographically sorting the endpoints on (x, e, y), where x and y are the usual coordinates, $e = 0$ for a left endpoint, and $e = 1$ for a right endpoint.

Each iteration of the **for** loop of lines 3–11 processes one event point p. If p is the left endpoint of a segment s, line 5 adds s to the total preorder, and lines 6–7 return TRUE if s intersects either of the segments it is consecutive with in the total preorder defined by the sweep line passing through p. (A boundary condition occurs if p lies on another segment s'. In this case, we require only that s and s' be placed consecutively into T.) If p is the right endpoint of a segment s, then we need to delete s from the total preorder. But first, lines 9–10 return TRUE if there is an intersection between the segments surrounding s in the total preorder defined by the sweep line passing through p. If these segments do not intersect, line 11 deletes segment s from the total preorder. If the segments surrounding segment s intersect, they would have become consecutive after deleting s had the **return** statement in line 10 not prevented line 11 from executing. The correctness argument, which follows, will make it clear why it suffices to check the segments surrounding s. Finally, if we never find any intersections after having processed all $2n$ event points, line 12 returns FALSE.

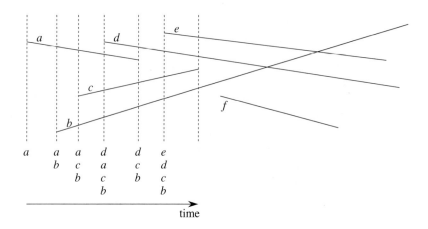

Figure 33.5   The execution of ANY-SEGMENTS-INTERSECT. Each dashed line is the sweep line at an event point. Except for the rightmost sweep line, the ordering of segment names below each sweep line corresponds to the total preorder T at the end of the **for** loop processing the corresponding event point. The rightmost sweep line occurs when processing the right endpoint of segment c; because segments d and b surround c and intersect each other, the procedure returns TRUE.

Correctness

To show that ANY-SEGMENTS-INTERSECT is correct, we will prove that the call ANY-SEGMENTS-INTERSECT(S) returns TRUE if and only if there is an intersection among the segments in S.

It is easy to see that ANY-SEGMENTS-INTERSECT returns TRUE (on lines 7 and 10) only if it finds an intersection between two of the input segments. Hence, if it returns TRUE, there is an intersection.

We also need to show the converse: that if there is an intersection, then ANY-SEGMENTS-INTERSECT returns TRUE. Let us suppose that there is at least one intersection. Let p be the leftmost intersection point, breaking ties by choosing the point with the lowest y-coordinate, and let a and b be the segments that intersect at p. Since no intersections occur to the left of p, the order given by T is correct at all points to the left of p. Because no three segments intersect at the same point, a and b become consecutive in the total preorder at some sweep line z.[2] Moreover, z is to the left of p or goes through p. Some segment endpoint q on sweep line z

---

[2]If we allow three segments to intersect at the same point, there may be an intervening segment c that intersects both a and b at point p. That is, we may have $a \succeq_w c$ and $c \succeq_w b$ for all sweep lines w to the left of p for which $a \succeq_w b$. Exercise 33.2-8 asks you to show that ANY-SEGMENTS-INTERSECT is correct even if three segments do intersect at the same point.

is the event point at which a and b become consecutive in the total preorder. If p is on sweep line z, then $q = p$. If p is not on sweep line z, then q is to the left of p. In either case, the order given by T is correct just before encountering q. (Here is where we use the lexicographic order in which the algorithm processes event points. Because p is the lowest of the leftmost intersection points, even if p is on sweep line z and some other intersection point p' is on z, event point $q = p$ is processed before the other intersection p' can interfere with the total preorder T. Moreover, even if p is the left endpoint of one segment, say a, and the right endpoint of the other segment, say b, because left endpoint events occur before right endpoint events, segment b is in T upon first encountering segment a.) Either event point q is processed by ANY-SEGMENTS-INTERSECT or it is not processed.

If q is processed by ANY-SEGMENTS-INTERSECT, only two possible actions may occur:

1. Either a or b is inserted into T, and the other segment is above or below it in the total preorder. Lines 4–7 detect this case.

2. Segments a and b are already in T, and a segment between them in the total preorder is deleted, making a and b become consecutive. Lines 8–11 detect this case.

In either case, we find the intersection p and ANY-SEGMENTS-INTERSECT returns TRUE.

If event point q is not processed by ANY-SEGMENTS-INTERSECT, the procedure must have returned before processing all event points. This situation could have occurred only if ANY-SEGMENTS-INTERSECT had already found an intersection and returned TRUE.

Thus, if there is an intersection, ANY-SEGMENTS-INTERSECT returns TRUE. As we have already seen, if ANY-SEGMENTS-INTERSECT returns TRUE, there is an intersection. Therefore, ANY-SEGMENTS-INTERSECT always returns a correct answer.

Running time

If set S contains n segments, then ANY-SEGMENTS-INTERSECT runs in time $O(n \lg n)$. Line 1 takes $O(1)$ time. Line 2 takes $O(n \lg n)$ time, using merge sort or heapsort. The **for** loop of lines 3–11 iterates at most once per event point, and so with $2n$ event points, the loop iterates at most $2n$ times. Each iteration takes $O(\lg n)$ time, since each red-black-tree operation takes $O(\lg n)$ time and, using the method of Section 33.1, each intersection test takes $O(1)$ time. The total time is thus $O(n \lg n)$.

Exercises

33.2-1
Show that a set of n line segments may contain $\Theta(n^2)$ intersections.

33.2-2
Given two segments a and b that are comparable at x, show how to determine in $O(1)$ time which of $a \succeq_x b$ or $b \succeq_x a$ holds. Assume that neither segment is vertical. (*Hint:* If a and b do not intersect, you can just use cross products. If a and b intersect—which you can of course determine using only cross products—you can still use only addition, subtraction, and multiplication, avoiding division. Of course, in the application of the $\succeq_x$ relation used here, if a and b intersect, we can just stop and declare that we have found an intersection.)

33.2-3
Professor Mason suggests that we modify ANY-SEGMENTS-INTERSECT so that instead of returning upon finding an intersection, it prints the segments that intersect and continues on to the next iteration of the **for** loop. The professor calls the resulting procedure PRINT-INTERSECTING-SEGMENTS and claims that it prints all intersections, from left to right, as they occur in the set of line segments. Professor Dixon disagrees, claiming that Professor Mason's idea is incorrect. Which professor is right? Will PRINT-INTERSECTING-SEGMENTS always find the leftmost intersection first? Will it always find all the intersections?

33.2-4
Give an $O(n \lg n)$-time algorithm to determine whether an n-vertex polygon is simple.

33.2-5
Give an $O(n \lg n)$-time algorithm to determine whether two simple polygons with a total of n vertices intersect.

33.2-6
A **disk** consists of a circle plus its interior and is represented by its center point and radius. Two disks intersect if they have any point in common. Give an $O(n \lg n)$-time algorithm to determine whether any two disks in a set of n intersect.

33.2-7
Given a set of n line segments containing a total of k intersections, show how to output all k intersections in $O((n + k) \lg n)$ time.

33.2-8
Argue that ANY-SEGMENTS-INTERSECT works correctly even if three or more segments intersect at the same point.

33.2-9
Show that ANY-SEGMENTS-INTERSECT works correctly in the presence of vertical segments if we treat the bottom endpoint of a vertical segment as if it were a left endpoint and the top endpoint as if it were a right endpoint. How does your answer to Exercise 33.2-2 change if we allow vertical segments?

33.3   Finding the convex hull

The ***convex hull*** of a set Q of points, denoted by $CH(Q)$, is the smallest convex polygon P for which each point in Q is either on the boundary of P or in its interior. (See Exercise 33.1-5 for a precise definition of a convex polygon.) We implicitly assume that all points in the set Q are unique and that Q contains at least three points which are not colinear. Intuitively, we can think of each point in Q as being a nail sticking out from a board. The convex hull is then the shape formed by a tight rubber band that surrounds all the nails. Figure 33.6 shows a set of points and its convex hull.

In this section, we shall present two algorithms that compute the convex hull of a set of n points. Both algorithms output the vertices of the convex hull in counterclockwise order. The first, known as Graham's scan, runs in $O(n \lg n)$ time. The second, called Jarvis's march, runs in $O(nh)$ time, where h is the number of vertices of the convex hull. As Figure 33.6 illustrates, every vertex of $CH(Q)$ is a

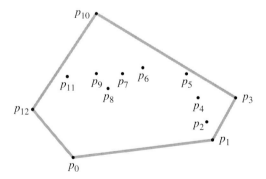

Figure 33.6   A set of points $Q = \{p_0, p_1, \ldots, p_{12}\}$ with its convex hull $CH(Q)$ in gray.

point in Q. Both algorithms exploit this property, deciding which vertices in Q to keep as vertices of the convex hull and which vertices in Q to reject.

We can compute convex hulls in $O(n \lg n)$ time by any one of several methods. Both Graham's scan and Jarvis's march use a technique called "rotational sweep," processing vertices in the order of the polar angles they form with a reference vertex. Other methods include the following:

- In the ***incremental method***, we first sort the points from left to right, yielding a sequence $\langle p_1, p_2, \ldots, p_n \rangle$. At the ith stage, we update the convex hull of the $i - 1$ leftmost points, $\text{CH}(\{p_1, p_2, \ldots, p_{i-1}\})$, according to the ith point from the left, thus forming $\text{CH}(\{p_1, p_2, \ldots, p_i\})$. Exercise 33.3-6 asks you how to implement this method to take a total of $O(n \lg n)$ time.

- In the ***divide-and-conquer method***, we divide the set of n points in $\Theta(n)$ time into two subsets, one containing the leftmost $\lceil n/2 \rceil$ points and one containing the rightmost $\lfloor n/2 \rfloor$ points, recursively compute the convex hulls of the subsets, and then, by means of a clever method, combine the hulls in $O(n)$ time. The running time is described by the familiar recurrence $T(n) = 2T(n/2) + O(n)$, and so the divide-and-conquer method runs in $O(n \lg n)$ time.

- The ***prune-and-search method*** is similar to the worst-case linear-time median algorithm of Section 9.3. With this method, we find the upper portion (or "upper chain") of the convex hull by repeatedly throwing out a constant fraction of the remaining points until only the upper chain of the convex hull remains. We then do the same for the lower chain. This method is asymptotically the fastest: if the convex hull contains h vertices, it runs in only $O(n \lg h)$ time.

Computing the convex hull of a set of points is an interesting problem in its own right. Moreover, algorithms for some other computational-geometry problems start by computing a convex hull. Consider, for example, the two-dimensional ***farthest-pair problem***: we are given a set of n points in the plane and wish to find the two points whose distance from each other is maximum. As Exercise 33.3-3 asks you to prove, these two points must be vertices of the convex hull. Although we won't prove it here, we can find the farthest pair of vertices of an n-vertex convex polygon in $O(n)$ time. Thus, by computing the convex hull of the n input points in $O(n \lg n)$ time and then finding the farthest pair of the resulting convex-polygon vertices, we can find the farthest pair of points in any set of n points in $O(n \lg n)$ time.

Graham's scan

Graham's scan solves the convex-hull problem by maintaining a stack S of candidate points. It pushes each point of the input set Q onto the stack one time, and it eventually pops from the stack each point that is not a vertex of CH(Q). When the algorithm terminates, stack S contains exactly the vertices of CH(Q), in counterclockwise order of their appearance on the boundary.

The procedure GRAHAM-SCAN takes as input a set Q of points, where $|Q| \geq 3$. It calls the functions TOP(S), which returns the point on top of stack S without changing S, and NEXT-TO-TOP(S), which returns the point one entry below the top of stack S without changing S. As we shall prove in a moment, the stack S returned by GRAHAM-SCAN contains, from bottom to top, exactly the vertices of CH(Q) in counterclockwise order.

GRAHAM-SCAN(Q)

```
 1  let p₀ be the point in Q with the minimum y-coordinate,
        or the leftmost such point in case of a tie
 2  let ⟨p₁, p₂, ..., pₘ⟩ be the remaining points in Q,
        sorted by polar angle in counterclockwise order around p₀
        (if more than one point has the same angle, remove all but
        the one that is farthest from p₀)
 3  if m < 2
 4      return "convex hull is empty"
 5  else let S be an empty stack
 6      PUSH(S, p₀)
 7      PUSH(S, p₁)
 8      PUSH(S, p₂)
 9      for i = 3 to m
10          while the angle formed by points NEXT-TO-TOP(S), TOP(S),
                    and pᵢ makes a nonleft turn
11              POP(S)
12          PUSH(S, pᵢ)
13      return S
```

Figure 33.7 illustrates the progress of GRAHAM-SCAN. Line 1 chooses point p_0 as the point with the lowest y-coordinate, picking the leftmost such point in case of a tie. Since there is no point in Q that is below p_0 and any other points with the same y-coordinate are to its right, p_0 must be a vertex of CH(Q). Line 2 sorts the remaining points of Q by polar angle relative to p_0, using the same method—comparing cross products—as in Exercise 33.1-3. If two or more points have the same polar angle relative to p_0, all but the farthest such point are convex combinations of p_0 and the farthest point, and so we remove them entirely from consideration. We let m denote the number of points other than p_0 that remain. The polar angle, measured in radians, of each point in Q relative to p_0 is in the half-open interval $[0, \pi)$. Since the points are sorted according to polar angles, they are sorted in counterclockwise order relative to p_0. We designate this sorted

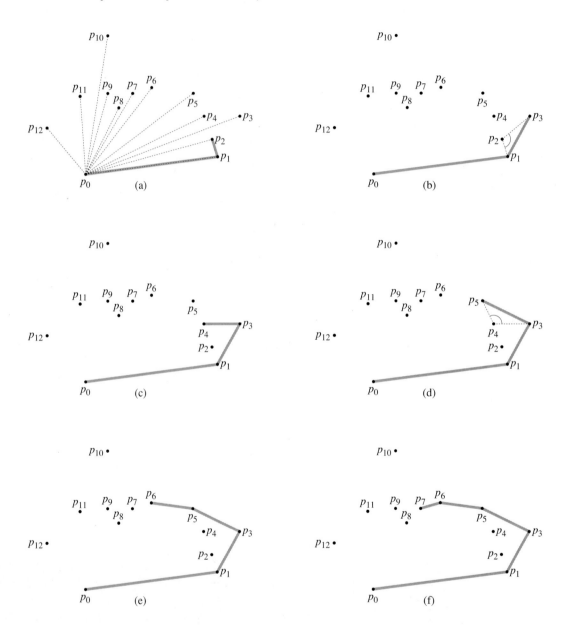

Figure 33.7 The execution of GRAHAM-SCAN on the set Q of Figure 33.6. The current convex hull contained in stack S is shown in gray at each step. **(a)** The sequence $\langle p_1, p_2, \ldots, p_{12} \rangle$ of points numbered in order of increasing polar angle relative to p_0, and the initial stack S containing p_0, p_1, and p_2. **(b)–(k)** Stack S after each iteration of the **for** loop of lines 9–12. Dashed lines show nonleft turns, which cause points to be popped from the stack. In part (h), for example, the right turn at angle $\angle p_7 p_8 p_9$ causes p_8 to be popped, and then the right turn at angle $\angle p_6 p_7 p_9$ causes p_7 to be popped.

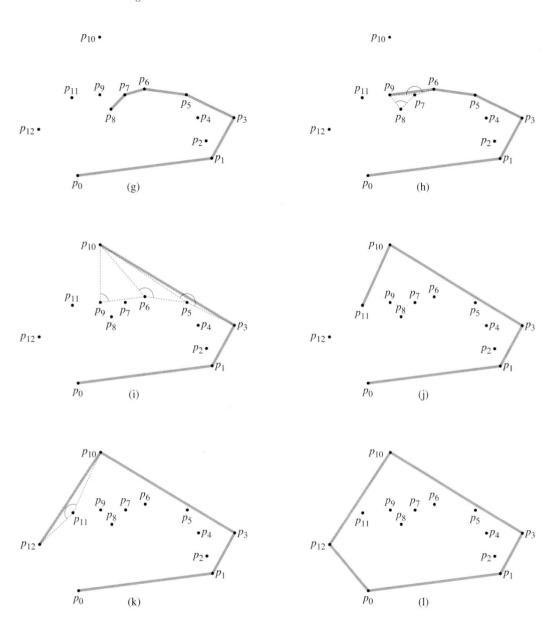

Figure 33.7, continued   **(l)** The convex hull returned by the procedure, which matches that of Figure 33.6.

sequence of points by $\langle p_1, p_2, \ldots, p_m \rangle$. Note that points p_1 and p_m are vertices of CH(Q) (see Exercise 33.3-1). Figure 33.7(a) shows the points of Figure 33.6 sequentially numbered in order of increasing polar angle relative to p_0.

The remainder of the procedure uses the stack S. Lines 5–8 initialize the stack to contain, from bottom to top, the first three points p_0, p_1, and p_2. Figure 33.7(a) shows the initial stack S. The **for** loop of lines 9–12 iterates once for each point in the subsequence $\langle p_3, p_4, \ldots, p_m \rangle$. We shall see that after processing point p_i, stack S contains, from bottom to top, the vertices of CH($\{p_0, p_1, \ldots, p_i\}$) in counterclockwise order. The **while** loop of lines 10–11 removes points from the stack if we find them not to be vertices of the convex hull. When we traverse the convex hull counterclockwise, we should make a left turn at each vertex. Thus, each time the **while** loop finds a vertex at which we make a nonleft turn, we pop the vertex from the stack. (By checking for a nonleft turn, rather than just a right turn, this test precludes the possibility of a straight angle at a vertex of the resulting convex hull. We want no straight angles, since no vertex of a convex polygon may be a convex combination of other vertices of the polygon.) After we pop all vertices that have nonleft turns when heading toward point p_i, we push p_i onto the stack. Figures 33.7(b)–(k) show the state of the stack S after each iteration of the **for** loop. Finally, GRAHAM-SCAN returns the stack S in line 13. Figure 33.7(l) shows the corresponding convex hull.

The following theorem formally proves the correctness of GRAHAM-SCAN.

Theorem 33.1 (Correctness of Graham's scan)
If GRAHAM-SCAN executes on a set Q of points, where $|Q| \geq 3$, then at termination, the stack S consists of, from bottom to top, exactly the vertices of CH(Q) in counterclockwise order.

Proof   After line 2, we have the sequence of points $\langle p_1, p_2, \ldots, p_m \rangle$. Let us define, for $i = 2, 3, \ldots, m$, the subset of points $Q_i = \{p_0, p_1, \ldots, p_i\}$. The points in $Q - Q_m$ are those that were removed because they had the same polar angle relative to p_0 as some point in Q_m; these points are not in CH(Q), and so CH(Q_m) = CH(Q). Thus, it suffices to show that when GRAHAM-SCAN terminates, the stack S consists of the vertices of CH(Q_m) in counterclockwise order, when listed from bottom to top. Note that just as p_0, p_1, and p_m are vertices of CH(Q), the points p_0, p_1, and p_i are all vertices of CH(Q_i).

The proof uses the following loop invariant:

> At the start of each iteration of the **for** loop of lines 9–12, stack S consists of, from bottom to top, exactly the vertices of CH(Q_{i-1}) in counterclockwise order.

Initialization: The invariant holds the first time we execute line 9, since at that time, stack S consists of exactly the vertices of $Q_2 = Q_{i-1}$, and this set of three

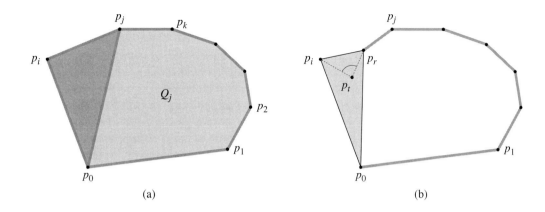

Figure 33.8   The proof of correctness of GRAHAM-SCAN. **(a)** Because p_i's polar angle relative to p_0 is greater than p_j's polar angle, and because the angle $\angle p_k p_j p_i$ makes a left turn, adding p_i to CH(Q_j) gives exactly the vertices of CH($Q_j \cup \{p_i\}$). **(b)** If the angle $\angle p_r p_t p_i$ makes a nonleft turn, then p_t is either in the interior of the triangle formed by p_0, p_r, and p_i or on a side of the triangle, which means that it cannot be a vertex of CH(Q_i).

vertices forms its own convex hull. Moreover, they appear in counterclockwise order from bottom to top.

Maintenance: Entering an iteration of the **for** loop, the top point on stack S is p_{i-1}, which was pushed at the end of the previous iteration (or before the first iteration, when $i = 3$). Let p_j be the top point on S after executing the while loop of lines 10–11 but before line 12 pushes p_i, and let p_k be the point just below p_j on S. At the moment that p_j is the top point on S and we have not yet pushed p_i, stack S contains exactly the same points it contained after iteration j of the **for** loop. By the loop invariant, therefore, S contains exactly the vertices of CH(Q_j) at that moment, and they appear in counterclockwise order from bottom to top.

Let us continue to focus on this moment just before pushing p_i. We know that p_i's polar angle relative to p_0 is greater than p_j's polar angle and that the angle $\angle p_k p_j p_i$ makes a left turn (otherwise we would have popped p_j). Therefore, because S contains exactly the vertices of CH(Q_j), we see from Figure 33.8(a) that once we push p_i, stack S will contain exactly the vertices of CH($Q_j \cup \{p_i\}$), still in counterclockwise order from bottom to top.

We now show that CH($Q_j \cup \{p_i\}$) is the same set of points as CH(Q_i). Consider any point p_t that was popped during iteration i of the **for** loop, and let p_r be the point just below p_t on stack S at the time p_t was popped (p_r might be p_j). The angle $\angle p_r p_t p_i$ makes a nonleft turn, and the polar angle of p_t relative to p_0 is greater than the polar angle of p_r. As Figure 33.8(b) shows, p_t must be either in the interior of the triangle formed by p_0, p_r, and p_i or on a side of this triangle (but it is not a vertex of the triangle). Clearly, since p_t is within a triangle formed by three other points of Q_i, it cannot be a vertex of $CH(Q_i)$. Since p_t is not a vertex of $CH(Q_i)$, we have that

$$CH(Q_i - \{p_t\}) = CH(Q_i) \ . \tag{33.1}$$

Let P_i be the set of points that were popped during iteration i of the **for** loop. Since the equality (33.1) applies for all points in P_i, we can apply it repeatedly to show that $CH(Q_i - P_i) = CH(Q_i)$. But $Q_i - P_i = Q_j \cup \{p_i\}$, and so we conclude that $CH(Q_j \cup \{p_i\}) = CH(Q_i - P_i) = CH(Q_i)$.

We have shown that once we push p_i, stack S contains exactly the vertices of $CH(Q_i)$ in counterclockwise order from bottom to top. Incrementing i will then cause the loop invariant to hold for the next iteration.

Termination: When the loop terminates, we have $i = m + 1$, and so the loop invariant implies that stack S consists of exactly the vertices of $CH(Q_m)$, which is $CH(Q)$, in counterclockwise order from bottom to top. This completes the proof. ∎

We now show that the running time of GRAHAM-SCAN is $O(n \lg n)$, where $n = |Q|$. Line 1 takes $\Theta(n)$ time. Line 2 takes $O(n \lg n)$ time, using merge sort or heapsort to sort the polar angles and the cross-product method of Section 33.1 to compare angles. (We can remove all but the farthest point with the same polar angle in total of $O(n)$ time over all n points.) Lines 5–8 take $O(1)$ time. Because $m \leq n - 1$, the **for** loop of lines 9–12 executes at most $n - 3$ times. Since PUSH takes $O(1)$ time, each iteration takes $O(1)$ time exclusive of the time spent in the **while** loop of lines 10–11, and thus overall the **for** loop takes $O(n)$ time exclusive of the nested **while** loop.

We use aggregate analysis to show that the **while** loop takes $O(n)$ time overall. For $i = 0, 1, \ldots, m$, we push each point p_i onto stack S exactly once. As in the analysis of the MULTIPOP procedure of Section 17.1, we observe that we can pop at most the number of items that we push. At least three points—p_0, p_1, and p_m—are never popped from the stack, so that in fact at most $m - 2$ POP operations are performed in total. Each iteration of the **while** loop performs one POP, and so there are at most $m - 2$ iterations of the **while** loop altogether. Since the test in line 10 takes $O(1)$ time, each call of POP takes $O(1)$ time, and $m \leq n - 1$, the total time taken by the **while** loop is $O(n)$. Thus, the running time of GRAHAM-SCAN is $O(n \lg n)$.

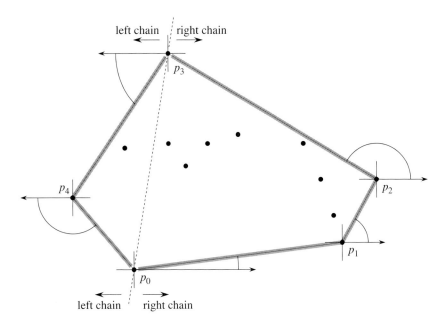

Figure 33.9   The operation of Jarvis's march. We choose the first vertex as the lowest point p_0. The next vertex, p_1, has the smallest polar angle of any point with respect to p_0. Then, p_2 has the smallest polar angle with respect to p_1. The right chain goes as high as the highest point p_3. Then, we construct the left chain by finding smallest polar angles with respect to the negative x-axis.

Jarvis's march

Jarvis's march computes the convex hull of a set Q of points by a technique known as ***package wrapping*** (or ***gift wrapping***). The algorithm runs in time $O(nh)$, where h is the number of vertices of $CH(Q)$. When h is $o(\lg n)$, Jarvis's march is asymptotically faster than Graham's scan.

Intuitively, Jarvis's march simulates wrapping a taut piece of paper around the set Q. We start by taping the end of the paper to the lowest point in the set, that is, to the same point p_0 with which we start Graham's scan. We know that this point must be a vertex of the convex hull. We pull the paper to the right to make it taut, and then we pull it higher until it touches a point. This point must also be a vertex of the convex hull. Keeping the paper taut, we continue in this way around the set of vertices until we come back to our original point p_0.

More formally, Jarvis's march builds a sequence $H = \langle p_0, p_1, \ldots, p_{h-1} \rangle$ of the vertices of $CH(Q)$. We start with p_0. As Figure 33.9 shows, the next vertex p_1 in the convex hull has the smallest polar angle with respect to p_0. (In case of ties, we choose the point farthest from p_0.) Similarly, p_2 has the smallest polar angle with respect to p_1, and so on. When we reach the highest vertex, say p_k (breaking ties by choosing the farthest such vertex), we have constructed, as Figure 33.9 shows, the ***right chain*** of CH(Q). To construct the ***left chain***, we start at p_k and choose p_{k+1} as the point with the smallest polar angle with respect to p_k, but *from the negative x-axis*. We continue on, forming the left chain by taking polar angles from the negative x-axis, until we come back to our original vertex p_0.

We could implement Jarvis's march in one conceptual sweep around the convex hull, that is, without separately constructing the right and left chains. Such implementations typically keep track of the angle of the last convex-hull side chosen and require the sequence of angles of hull sides to be strictly increasing (in the range of 0 to 2π radians). The advantage of constructing separate chains is that we need not explicitly compute angles; the techniques of Section 33.1 suffice to compare angles.

If implemented properly, Jarvis's march has a running time of $O(nh)$. For each of the h vertices of CH(Q), we find the vertex with the minimum polar angle. Each comparison between polar angles takes $O(1)$ time, using the techniques of Section 33.1. As Section 9.1 shows, we can compute the minimum of n values in $O(n)$ time if each comparison takes $O(1)$ time. Thus, Jarvis's march takes $O(nh)$ time.

Exercises

33.3-1
Prove that in the procedure GRAHAM-SCAN, points p_1 and p_m must be vertices of CH(Q).

33.3-2
Consider a model of computation that supports addition, comparison, and multiplication and for which there is a lower bound of $\Omega(n \lg n)$ to sort n numbers. Prove that $\Omega(n \lg n)$ is a lower bound for computing, in order, the vertices of the convex hull of a set of n points in such a model.

33.3-3
Given a set of points Q, prove that the pair of points farthest from each other must be vertices of CH(Q).

33.3-4
For a given polygon P and a point q on its boundary, the ***shadow*** of q is the set of points r such that the segment $\overline{qr}$ is entirely on the boundary or in the interior of P. As Figure 33.10 illustrates, a polygon P is ***star-shaped*** if there exists a point p in the interior of P that is in the shadow of every point on the boundary of P. The set of all such points p is called the ***kernel*** of P. Given an n-vertex,

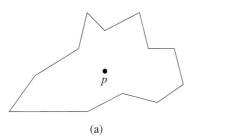 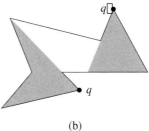

(a)   (b)

Figure 33.10 The definition of a star-shaped polygon, for use in Exercise 33.3-4. **(a)** A star-shaped polygon. The segment from point p to any point q on the boundary intersects the boundary only at q. **(b)** A non-star-shaped polygon. The shaded region on the left is the shadow of q, and the shaded region on the right is the shadow of q'. Since these regions are disjoint, the kernel is empty.

star-shaped polygon P specified by its vertices in counterclockwise order, show how to compute CH(P) in $O(n)$ time.

33.3-5
In the ***on-line convex-hull problem***, we are given the set Q of n points one point at a time. After receiving each point, we compute the convex hull of the points seen so far. Obviously, we could run Graham's scan once for each point, with a total running time of $O(n^2 \lg n)$. Show how to solve the on-line convex-hull problem in a total of $O(n^2)$ time.

33.3-6 ★
Show how to implement the incremental method for computing the convex hull of n points so that it runs in $O(n \lg n)$ time.

33.4 Finding the closest pair of points

We now consider the problem of finding the closest pair of points in a set Q of $n \geq 2$ points. "Closest" refers to the usual euclidean distance: the distance between points $p_1 = (x_1, y_1)$ and $p_2 = (x_2, y_2)$ is $\sqrt{(x_1 - x_2)^2 + (y_1 - y_2)^2}$. Two points in set Q may be coincident, in which case the distance between them is zero. This problem has applications in, for example, traffic-control systems. A system for controlling air or sea traffic might need to identify the two closest vehicles in order to detect potential collisions.

A brute-force closest-pair algorithm simply looks at all the $\binom{n}{2} = \Theta(n^2)$ pairs of points. In this section, we shall describe a divide-and-conquer algorithm for this problem, whose running time is described by the familiar recurrence $T(n) = 2T(n/2) + O(n)$. Thus, this algorithm uses only $O(n \lg n)$ time.

The divide-and-conquer algorithm

Each recursive invocation of the algorithm takes as input a subset $P \subseteq Q$ and arrays X and Y, each of which contains all the points of the input subset P. The points in array X are sorted so that their x-coordinates are monotonically increasing. Similarly, array Y is sorted by monotonically increasing y-coordinate. Note that in order to attain the $O(n \lg n)$ time bound, we cannot afford to sort in each recursive call; if we did, the recurrence for the running time would be $T(n) = 2T(n/2) + O(n \lg n)$, whose solution is $T(n) = O(n \lg^2 n)$. (Use the version of the master method given in Exercise 4.6-2.) We shall see a little later how to use "presorting" to maintain this sorted property without actually sorting in each recursive call.

A given recursive invocation with inputs P, X, and Y first checks whether $|P| \leq 3$. If so, the invocation simply performs the brute-force method described above: try all $\binom{|P|}{2}$ pairs of points and return the closest pair. If $|P| > 3$, the recursive invocation carries out the divide-and-conquer paradigm as follows.

Divide: Find a vertical line l that bisects the point set P into two sets P_L and P_R such that $|P_L| = \lceil |P|/2 \rceil$, $|P_R| = \lfloor |P|/2 \rfloor$, all points in P_L are on or to the left of line l, and all points in P_R are on or to the right of l. Divide the array X into arrays X_L and X_R, which contain the points of P_L and P_R respectively, sorted by monotonically increasing x-coordinate. Similarly, divide the array Y into arrays Y_L and Y_R, which contain the points of P_L and P_R respectively, sorted by monotonically increasing y-coordinate.

Conquer: Having divided P into P_L and P_R, make two recursive calls, one to find the closest pair of points in P_L and the other to find the closest pair of points in P_R. The inputs to the first call are the subset P_L and arrays X_L and Y_L; the second call receives the inputs P_R, X_R, and Y_R. Let the closest-pair distances returned for P_L and P_R be δ_L and δ_R, respectively, and let $\delta = \min(\delta_L, \delta_R)$.

Combine: The closest pair is either the pair with distance δ found by one of the recursive calls, or it is a pair of points with one point in P_L and the other in P_R. The algorithm determines whether there is a pair with one point in P_L and the other point in P_R and whose distance is less than δ. Observe that if a pair of points has distance less than δ, both points of the pair must be within δ units of line l. Thus, as Figure 33.11(a) shows, they both must reside in the 2δ-wide vertical strip centered at line l. To find such a pair, if one exists, we do the following:

1. Create an array Y', which is the array Y with all points not in the 2δ-wide vertical strip removed. The array Y' is sorted by y-coordinate, just as Y is.

2. For each point p in the array Y', try to find points in Y' that are within δ units of p. As we shall see shortly, only the 7 points in Y' that follow p need be considered. Compute the distance from p to each of these 7 points, and keep track of the closest-pair distance δ' found over all pairs of points in Y'.

3. If $\delta' < \delta$, then the vertical strip does indeed contain a closer pair than the recursive calls found. Return this pair and its distance δ'. Otherwise, return the closest pair and its distance δ found by the recursive calls.

The above description omits some implementation details that are necessary to achieve the $O(n \lg n)$ running time. After proving the correctness of the algorithm, we shall show how to implement the algorithm to achieve the desired time bound.

Correctness

The correctness of this closest-pair algorithm is obvious, except for two aspects. First, by bottoming out the recursion when $|P| \leq 3$, we ensure that we never try to solve a subproblem consisting of only one point. The second aspect is that we need only check the 7 points following each point p in array Y'; we shall now prove this property.

Suppose that at some level of the recursion, the closest pair of points is $p_L \in P_L$ and $p_R \in P_R$. Thus, the distance δ' between p_L and p_R is strictly less than δ. Point p_L must be on or to the left of line l and less than δ units away. Similarly, p_R is on or to the right of l and less than δ units away. Moreover, p_L and p_R are within δ units of each other vertically. Thus, as Figure 33.11(a) shows, p_L and p_R are within a $\delta \times 2\delta$ rectangle centered at line l. (There may be other points within this rectangle as well.)

We next show that at most 8 points of P can reside within this $\delta \times 2\delta$ rectangle. Consider the $\delta \times \delta$ square forming the left half of this rectangle. Since all points within P_L are at least δ units apart, at most 4 points can reside within this square; Figure 33.11(b) shows how. Similarly, at most 4 points in P_R can reside within the $\delta \times \delta$ square forming the right half of the rectangle. Thus, at most 8 points of P can reside within the $\delta \times 2\delta$ rectangle. (Note that since points on line l may be in either P_L or P_R, there may be up to 4 points on l. This limit is achieved if there are two pairs of coincident points such that each pair consists of one point from P_L and one point from P_R, one pair is at the intersection of l and the top of the rectangle, and the other pair is where l intersects the bottom of the rectangle.)

Having shown that at most 8 points of P can reside within the rectangle, we can easily see why we need to check only the 7 points following each point in the array Y'. Still assuming that the closest pair is p_L and p_R, let us assume without

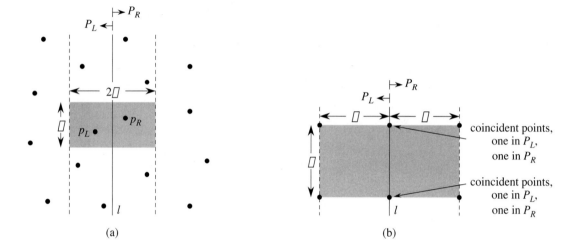

Figure 33.11   Key concepts in the proof that the closest-pair algorithm needs to check only 7 points following each point in the array Y'. **(a)** If $p_L \in P_L$ and $p_R \in P_R$ are less than δ units apart, they must reside within a $\delta \times 2\delta$ rectangle centered at line l. **(b)** How 4 points that are pairwise at least δ units apart can all reside within a $\delta \times \delta$ square. On the left are 4 points in P_L, and on the right are 4 points in P_R. The $\delta \times 2\delta$ rectangle can contain 8 points if the points shown on line l are actually pairs of coincident points with one point in P_L and one in P_R.

loss of generality that p_L precedes p_R in array Y'. Then, even if p_L occurs as early as possible in Y' and p_R occurs as late as possible, p_R is in one of the 7 positions following p_L. Thus, we have shown the correctness of the closest-pair algorithm.

Implementation and running time

As we have noted, our goal is to have the recurrence for the running time be $T(n) = 2T(n/2) + O(n)$, where $T(n)$ is the running time for a set of n points. The main difficulty comes from ensuring that the arrays X_L, X_R, Y_L, and Y_R, which are passed to recursive calls, are sorted by the proper coordinate and also that the array Y' is sorted by y-coordinate. (Note that if the array X that is received by a recursive call is already sorted, then we can easily divide set P into P_L and P_R in linear time.)

The key observation is that in each call, we wish to form a sorted subset of a sorted array. For example, a particular invocation receives the subset P and the array Y, sorted by y-coordinate. Having partitioned P into P_L and P_R, it needs to form the arrays Y_L and Y_R, which are sorted by y-coordinate, in linear time. We can view the method as the opposite of the MERGE procedure from merge sort in

Section 2.3.1: we are splitting a sorted array into two sorted arrays. The following pseudocode gives the idea.

```
1   let Y_L[1 .. Y.length] and Y_R[1 .. Y.length] be new arrays
2   Y_L.length = Y_R.length = 0
3   for i = 1 to Y.length
4       if Y[i] ∈ P_L
5           Y_L.length = Y_L.length + 1
6           Y_L[Y_L.length] = Y[i]
7       else Y_R.length = Y_R.length + 1
8           Y_R[Y_R.length] = Y[i]
```

We simply examine the points in array Y in order. If a point $Y[i]$ is in P_L, we append it to the end of array Y_L; otherwise, we append it to the end of array Y_R. Similar pseudocode works for forming arrays X_L, X_R, and Y'.

The only remaining question is how to get the points sorted in the first place. We **presort** them; that is, we sort them once and for all *before* the first recursive call. We pass these sorted arrays into the first recursive call, and from there we whittle them down through the recursive calls as necessary. Presorting adds an additional $O(n \lg n)$ term to the running time, but now each step of the recursion takes linear time exclusive of the recursive calls. Thus, if we let $T(n)$ be the running time of each recursive step and $T'(n)$ be the running time of the entire algorithm, we get $T'(n) = T(n) + O(n \lg n)$ and

$$T(n) = \begin{cases} 2T(n/2) + O(n) & \text{if } n > 3 , \\ O(1) & \text{if } n \le 3 . \end{cases}$$

Thus, $T(n) = O(n \lg n)$ and $T'(n) = O(n \lg n)$.

Exercises

33.4-1
Professor Williams comes up with a scheme that allows the closest-pair algorithm to check only 5 points following each point in array Y'. The idea is always to place points on line l into set P_L. Then, there cannot be pairs of coincident points on line l with one point in P_L and one in P_R. Thus, at most 6 points can reside in the $\delta \times 2\delta$ rectangle. What is the flaw in the professor's scheme?

33.4-2
Show that it actually suffices to check only the points in the 5 array positions following each point in the array Y'.

33.4-3

We can define the distance between two points in ways other than euclidean. In the plane, the L_m-*distance* between points p_1 and p_2 is given by the expression $(|x_1 - x_2|^m + |y_1 - y_2|^m)^{1/m}$. Euclidean distance, therefore, is L_2-distance. Modify the closest-pair algorithm to use the L_1-distance, which is also known as the **Manhattan distance**.

33.4-4

Given two points p_1 and p_2 in the plane, the L_∞-distance between them is given by $\max(|x_1 - x_2|, |y_1 - y_2|)$. Modify the closest-pair algorithm to use the L_∞-distance.

33.4-5

Suppose that $\Omega(n)$ of the points given to the closest-pair algorithm are covertical. Show how to determine the sets P_L and P_R and how to determine whether each point of Y is in P_L or P_R so that the running time for the closest-pair algorithm remains $O(n \lg n)$.

33.4-6

Suggest a change to the closest-pair algorithm that avoids presorting the Y array but leaves the running time as $O(n \lg n)$. (*Hint:* Merge sorted arrays Y_L and Y_R to form the sorted array Y.)

Problems

33-1   Convex layers

Given a set Q of points in the plane, we define the **convex layers** of Q inductively. The first convex layer of Q consists of those points in Q that are vertices of $CH(Q)$. For $i > 1$, define Q_i to consist of the points of Q with all points in convex layers $1, 2, \ldots, i - 1$ removed. Then, the ith convex layer of Q is $CH(Q_i)$ if $Q_i \neq \emptyset$ and is undefined otherwise.

a. Give an $O(n^2)$-time algorithm to find the convex layers of a set of n points.

b. Prove that $\Omega(n \lg n)$ time is required to compute the convex layers of a set of n points with any model of computation that requires $\Omega(n \lg n)$ time to sort n real numbers.

33-2 *Maximal layers*

Let Q be a set of n points in the plane. We say that point (x, y) ***dominates*** point (x', y') if $x \geq x'$ and $y \geq y'$. A point in Q that is dominated by no other points in Q is said to be ***maximal***. Note that Q may contain many maximal points, which can be organized into ***maximal layers*** as follows. The first maximal layer L_1 is the set of maximal points of Q. For $i > 1$, the ith maximal layer L_i is the set of maximal points in $Q - \bigcup_{j=1}^{i-1} L_j$.

Suppose that Q has k nonempty maximal layers, and let y_i be the y-coordinate of the leftmost point in L_i for $i = 1, 2, \ldots, k$. For now, assume that no two points in Q have the same x- or y-coordinate.

a. Show that $y_1 > y_2 > \cdots > y_k$.

Consider a point (x, y) that is to the left of any point in Q and for which y is distinct from the y-coordinate of any point in Q. Let $Q' = Q \cup \{(x, y)\}$.

b. Let j be the minimum index such that $y_j < y$, unless $y < y_k$, in which case we let $j = k + 1$. Show that the maximal layers of Q' are as follows:

- If $j \leq k$, then the maximal layers of Q' are the same as the maximal layers of Q, except that L_j also includes (x, y) as its new leftmost point.
- If $j = k + 1$, then the first k maximal layers of Q' are the same as for Q, but in addition, Q' has a nonempty $(k + 1)$st maximal layer: $L_{k+1} = \{(x, y)\}$.

c. Describe an $O(n \lg n)$-time algorithm to compute the maximal layers of a set Q of n points. (*Hint:* Move a sweep line from right to left.)

d. Do any difficulties arise if we now allow input points to have the same x- or y-coordinate? Suggest a way to resolve such problems.

33-3 *Ghostbusters and ghosts*

A group of n Ghostbusters is battling n ghosts. Each Ghostbuster carries a proton pack, which shoots a stream at a ghost, eradicating it. A stream goes in a straight line and terminates when it hits the ghost. The Ghostbusters decide upon the following strategy. They will pair off with the ghosts, forming n Ghostbuster-ghost pairs, and then simultaneously each Ghostbuster will shoot a stream at his chosen ghost. As we all know, it is *very* dangerous to let streams cross, and so the Ghostbusters must choose pairings for which no streams will cross.

Assume that the position of each Ghostbuster and each ghost is a fixed point in the plane and that no three positions are colinear.

a. Argue that there exists a line passing through one Ghostbuster and one ghost such that the number of Ghostbusters on one side of the line equals the number of ghosts on the same side. Describe how to find such a line in $O(n \lg n)$ time.

b. Give an $O(n^2 \lg n)$-time algorithm to pair Ghostbusters with ghosts in such a way that no streams cross.

33-4 *Picking up sticks*

Professor Charon has a set of n sticks, which are piled up in some configuration. Each stick is specified by its endpoints, and each endpoint is an ordered triple giving its (x, y, z) coordinates. No stick is vertical. He wishes to pick up all the sticks, one at a time, subject to the condition that he may pick up a stick only if there is no other stick on top of it.

a. Give a procedure that takes two sticks a and b and reports whether a is above, below, or unrelated to b.

b. Describe an efficient algorithm that determines whether it is possible to pick up all the sticks, and if so, provides a legal order in which to pick them up.

33-5 *Sparse-hulled distributions*

Consider the problem of computing the convex hull of a set of points in the plane that have been drawn according to some known random distribution. Sometimes, the number of points, or size, of the convex hull of n points drawn from such a distribution has expectation $O(n^{1-\epsilon})$ for some constant $\epsilon > 0$. We call such a distribution *sparse-hulled*. Sparse-hulled distributions include the following:

- Points drawn uniformly from a unit-radius disk. The convex hull has expected size $\Theta(n^{1/3})$.

- Points drawn uniformly from the interior of a convex polygon with k sides, for any constant k. The convex hull has expected size $\Theta(\lg n)$.

- Points drawn according to a two-dimensional normal distribution. The convex hull has expected size $\Theta(\sqrt{\lg n})$.

a. Given two convex polygons with n_1 and n_2 vertices respectively, show how to compute the convex hull of all $n_1 + n_2$ points in $O(n_1 + n_2)$ time. (The polygons may overlap.)

b. Show how to compute the convex hull of a set of n points drawn independently according to a sparse-hulled distribution in $O(n)$ average-case time. (*Hint:* Recursively find the convex hulls of the first $n/2$ points and the second $n/2$ points, and then combine the results.)

Chapter notes

This chapter barely scratches the surface of computational-geometry algorithms and techniques. Books on computational geometry include those by Preparata and Shamos [282], Edelsbrunner [99], and O'Rourke [269].

Although geometry has been studied since antiquity, the development of algorithms for geometric problems is relatively new. Preparata and Shamos note that the earliest notion of the complexity of a problem was given by E. Lemoine in 1902. He was studying euclidean constructions—those using a compass and a ruler—and devised a set of five primitives: placing one leg of the compass on a given point, placing one leg of the compass on a given line, drawing a circle, passing the ruler's edge through a given point, and drawing a line. Lemoine was interested in the number of primitives needed to effect a given construction; he called this amount the "simplicity" of the construction.

The algorithm of Section 33.2, which determines whether any segments intersect, is due to Shamos and Hoey [313].

The original version of Graham's scan is given by Graham [150]. The package-wrapping algorithm is due to Jarvis [189]. Using a decision-tree model of computation, Yao [359] proved a worst-case lower bound of $\Omega(n \lg n)$ for the running time of any convex-hull algorithm. When the number of vertices h of the convex hull is taken into account, the prune-and-search algorithm of Kirkpatrick and Seidel [206], which takes $O(n \lg h)$ time, is asymptotically optimal.

The $O(n \lg n)$-time divide-and-conquer algorithm for finding the closest pair of points is by Shamos and appears in Preparata and Shamos [282]. Preparata and Shamos also show that the algorithm is asymptotically optimal in a decision-tree model.

34 NP-Completeness

Almost all the algorithms we have studied thus far have been ***polynomial-time al-gorithms***: on inputs of size n, their worst-case running time is $O(n^k)$ for some constant k. You might wonder whether *all* problems can be solved in polynomial time. The answer is no. For example, there are problems, such as Turing's famous "Halting Problem," that cannot be solved by any computer, no matter how much time we allow. There are also problems that can be solved, but not in time $O(n^k)$ for any constant k. Generally, we think of problems that are solvable by polynomial-time algorithms as being tractable, or easy, and problems that require superpolynomial time as being intractable, or hard.

The subject of this chapter, however, is an interesting class of problems, called the "NP-complete" problems, whose status is unknown. No polynomial-time algorithm has yet been discovered for an NP-complete problem, nor has anyone yet been able to prove that no polynomial-time algorithm can exist for any one of them. This so-called P ≠ NP question has been one of the deepest, most perplexing open research problems in theoretical computer science since it was first posed in 1971.

Several NP-complete problems are particularly tantalizing because they seem on the surface to be similar to problems that we know how to solve in polynomial time. In each of the following pairs of problems, one is solvable in polynomial time and the other is NP-complete, but the difference between problems appears to be slight:

Shortest vs. longest simple paths: In Chapter 24, we saw that even with negative edge weights, we can find *shortest* paths from a single source in a directed graph $G = (V, E)$ in $O(VE)$ time. Finding a *longest* simple path between two vertices is difficult, however. Merely determining whether a graph contains a simple path with at least a given number of edges is NP-complete.

Euler tour vs. hamiltonian cycle: An ***Euler tour*** of a strongly connected, directed graph $G = (V, E)$ is a cycle that traverses each *edge* of G exactly once, although it is allowed to visit each vertex more than once. By Problem 22-3, we can determine whether a graph has an Euler tour in only $O(E)$ time and, in fact, we can find the edges of the Euler tour in $O(E)$ time. A ***hamiltonian cycle*** of a directed graph $G = (V, E)$ is a simple cycle that contains each *vertex* in V. Determining whether a directed graph has a hamiltonian cycle is NP-complete. (Later in this chapter, we shall prove that determining whether an *undirected* graph has a hamiltonian cycle is NP-complete.)

2-CNF satisfiability vs. 3-CNF satisfiability: A boolean formula contains variables whose values are 0 or 1; boolean connectives such as $\wedge$ (AND), $\vee$ (OR), and $\neg$ (NOT); and parentheses. A boolean formula is ***satisfiable*** if there exists some assignment of the values 0 and 1 to its variables that causes it to evaluate to 1. We shall define terms more formally later in this chapter, but informally, a boolean formula is in ***k-conjunctive normal form***, or k-CNF, if it is the AND of clauses of ORs of exactly k variables or their negations. For example, the boolean formula $(x_1 \vee \neg x_2) \wedge (\neg x_1 \vee x_3) \wedge (\neg x_2 \vee \neg x_3)$ is in 2-CNF. (It has the satisfying assignment $x_1 = 1, x_2 = 0, x_3 = 1$.) Although we can determine in polynomial time whether a 2-CNF formula is satisfiable, we shall see later in this chapter that determining whether a 3-CNF formula is satisfiable is NP-complete.

NP-completeness and the classes P and NP

Throughout this chapter, we shall refer to three classes of problems: P, NP, and NPC, the latter class being the NP-complete problems. We describe them informally here, and we shall define them more formally later on.

The class P consists of those problems that are solvable in polynomial time. More specifically, they are problems that can be solved in time $O(n^k)$ for some constant k, where n is the size of the input to the problem. Most of the problems examined in previous chapters are in P.

The class NP consists of those problems that are "verifiable" in polynomial time. What do we mean by a problem being verifiable? If we were somehow given a "certificate" of a solution, then we could verify that the certificate is correct in time polynomial in the size of the input to the problem. For example, in the hamiltonian-cycle problem, given a directed graph $G = (V, E)$, a certificate would be a sequence $\langle v_1, v_2, v_3, \ldots, v_{|V|} \rangle$ of $|V|$ vertices. We could easily check in polynomial time that $(v_i, v_{i+1}) \in E$ for $i = 1, 2, 3, \ldots, |V| - 1$ and that $(v_{|V|}, v_1) \in E$ as well. As another example, for 3-CNF satisfiability, a certificate would be an assignment of values to variables. We could check in polynomial time that this assignment satisfies the boolean formula.

Any problem in P is also in NP, since if a problem is in P then we can solve it in polynomial time without even being supplied a certificate. We shall formalize this notion later in this chapter, but for now we can believe that $P \subseteq NP$. The open question is whether or not P is a proper subset of NP.

Informally, a problem is in the class NPC—and we refer to it as being ***NP-complete***—if it is in NP and is as "hard" as any problem in NP. We shall formally define what it means to be as hard as any problem in NP later in this chapter. In the meantime, we will state without proof that if *any* NP-complete problem can be solved in polynomial time, then *every* problem in NP has a polynomial-time algorithm. Most theoretical computer scientists believe that the NP-complete problems are intractable, since given the wide range of NP-complete problems that have been studied to date—without anyone having discovered a polynomial-time solution to any of them—it would be truly astounding if all of them could be solved in polynomial time. Yet, given the effort devoted thus far to proving that NP-complete problems are intractable—without a conclusive outcome—we cannot rule out the possibility that the NP-complete problems are in fact solvable in polynomial time.

To become a good algorithm designer, you must understand the rudiments of the theory of NP-completeness. If you can establish a problem as NP-complete, you provide good evidence for its intractability. As an engineer, you would then do better to spend your time developing an approximation algorithm (see Chapter 35) or solving a tractable special case, rather than searching for a fast algorithm that solves the problem exactly. Moreover, many natural and interesting problems that on the surface seem no harder than sorting, graph searching, or network flow are in fact NP-complete. Therefore, you should become familiar with this remarkable class of problems.

Overview of showing problems to be NP-complete

The techniques we use to show that a particular problem is NP-complete differ fundamentally from the techniques used throughout most of this book to design and analyze algorithms. When we demonstrate that a problem is NP-complete, we are making a statement about how hard it is (or at least how hard we think it is), rather than about how easy it is. We are not trying to prove the existence of an efficient algorithm, but instead that no efficient algorithm is likely to exist. In this way, NP-completeness proofs bear some similarity to the proof in Section 8.1 of an $\Omega(n \lg n)$-time lower bound for any comparison sort algorithm; the specific techniques used for showing NP-completeness differ from the decision-tree method used in Section 8.1, however.

We rely on three key concepts in showing a problem to be NP-complete:

Decision problems vs. optimization problems

Many problems of interest are ***optimization problems***, in which each feasible (i.e., "legal") solution has an associated value, and we wish to find a feasible solution with the best value. For example, in a problem that we call SHORTEST-PATH, we are given an undirected graph G and vertices u and v, and we wish to find a path from u to v that uses the fewest edges. In other words, SHORTEST-PATH is the single-pair shortest-path problem in an unweighted, undirected graph. NP-completeness applies directly not to optimization problems, however, but to ***decision problems***, in which the answer is simply "yes" or "no" (or, more formally, "1" or "0").

Although NP-complete problems are confined to the realm of decision problems, we can take advantage of a convenient relationship between optimization problems and decision problems. We usually can cast a given optimization problem as a related decision problem by imposing a bound on the value to be optimized. For example, a decision problem related to SHORTEST-PATH is PATH: given an undirected graph G, vertices u and v, and an integer k, does a path exist from u to v consisting of at most k edges?

The relationship between an optimization problem and its related decision problem works in our favor when we try to show that the optimization problem is "hard." That is because the decision problem is in a sense "easier," or at least "no harder." As a specific example, we can solve PATH by solving SHORTEST-PATH and then comparing the number of edges in the shortest path found to the value of the decision-problem parameter k. In other words, if an optimization problem is easy, its related decision problem is easy as well. Stated in a way that has more relevance to NP-completeness, if we can provide evidence that a decision problem is hard, we also provide evidence that its related optimization problem is hard. Thus, even though it restricts attention to decision problems, the theory of NP-completeness often has implications for optimization problems as well.

Reductions

The above notion of showing that one problem is no harder or no easier than another applies even when both problems are decision problems. We take advantage of this idea in almost every NP-completeness proof, as follows. Let us consider a decision problem A, which we would like to solve in polynomial time. We call the input to a particular problem an ***instance*** of that problem; for example, in PATH, an instance would be a particular graph G, particular vertices u and v of G, and a particular integer k. Now suppose that we already know how to solve a different decision problem B in polynomial time. Finally, suppose that we have a procedure that transforms any instance α of A into some instance β of B with the following characteristics:

- The transformation takes polynomial time.

- The answers are the same. That is, the answer for α is "yes" if and only if the answer for β is also "yes."

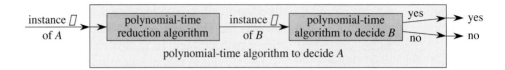

Figure 34.1 How to use a polynomial-time reduction algorithm to solve a decision problem A in polynomial time, given a polynomial-time decision algorithm for another problem B. In polynomial time, we transform an instance α of A into an instance β of B, we solve B in polynomial time, and we use the answer for β as the answer for α.

We call such a procedure a polynomial-time *reduction algorithm* and, as Figure 34.1 shows, it provides us a way to solve problem A in polynomial time:

1. Given an instance α of problem A, use a polynomial-time reduction algorithm to transform it to an instance β of problem B.

2. Run the polynomial-time decision algorithm for B on the instance β.

3. Use the answer for β as the answer for α.

As long as each of these steps takes polynomial time, all three together do also, and so we have a way to decide on α in polynomial time. In other words, by "reducing" solving problem A to solving problem B, we use the "easiness" of B to prove the "easiness" of A.

Recalling that NP-completeness is about showing how hard a problem is rather than how easy it is, we use polynomial-time reductions in the opposite way to show that a problem is NP-complete. Let us take the idea a step further, and show how we could use polynomial-time reductions to show that no polynomial-time algorithm can exist for a particular problem B. Suppose we have a decision problem A for which we already know that no polynomial-time algorithm can exist. (Let us not concern ourselves for now with how to find such a problem A.) Suppose further that we have a polynomial-time reduction transforming instances of A to instances of B. Now we can use a simple proof by contradiction to show that no polynomial-time algorithm can exist for B. Suppose otherwise; i.e., suppose that B has a polynomial-time algorithm. Then, using the method shown in Figure 34.1, we would have a way to solve problem A in polynomial time, which contradicts our assumption that there is no polynomial-time algorithm for A.

For NP-completeness, we cannot assume that there is absolutely no polynomial-time algorithm for problem A. The proof methodology is similar, however, in that we prove that problem B is NP-complete on the assumption that problem A is also NP-complete.

A first NP-complete problem

Because the technique of reduction relies on having a problem already known to be NP-complete in order to prove a different problem NP-complete, we need a "first" NP-complete problem. The problem we shall use is the circuit-satisfiability problem, in which we are given a boolean combinational circuit composed of AND, OR, and NOT gates, and we wish to know whether there exists some set of boolean inputs to this circuit that causes its output to be 1. We shall prove that this first problem is NP-complete in Section 34.3.

Chapter outline

This chapter studies the aspects of NP-completeness that bear most directly on the analysis of algorithms. In Section 34.1, we formalize our notion of "problem" and define the complexity class P of polynomial-time solvable decision problems. We also see how these notions fit into the framework of formal-language theory. Section 34.2 defines the class NP of decision problems whose solutions are verifiable in polynomial time. It also formally poses the P ≠ NP question.

Section 34.3 shows we can relate problems via polynomial-time "reductions." It defines NP-completeness and sketches a proof that one problem, called "circuit satisfiability," is NP-complete. Having found one NP-complete problem, we show in Section 34.4 how to prove other problems to be NP-complete much more simply by the methodology of reductions. We illustrate this methodology by showing that two formula-satisfiability problems are NP-complete. With additional reductions, we show in Section 34.5 a variety of other problems to be NP-complete.

34.1 Polynomial time

We begin our study of NP-completeness by formalizing our notion of polynomial-time solvable problems. We generally regard these problems as tractable, but for philosophical, not mathematical, reasons. We can offer three supporting arguments.

First, although we may reasonably regard a problem that requires time $\Theta(n^{100})$ to be intractable, very few practical problems require time on the order of such a high-degree polynomial. The polynomial-time computable problems encountered in practice typically require much less time. Experience has shown that once the first polynomial-time algorithm for a problem has been discovered, more efficient algorithms often follow. Even if the current best algorithm for a problem has a running time of $\Theta(n^{100})$, an algorithm with a much better running time will likely soon be discovered.

Second, for many reasonable models of computation, a problem that can be solved in polynomial time in one model can be solved in polynomial time in another. For example, the class of problems solvable in polynomial time by the serial random-access machine used throughout most of this book is the same as the class of problems solvable in polynomial time on abstract Turing machines.[1] It is also the same as the class of problems solvable in polynomial time on a parallel computer when the number of processors grows polynomially with the input size.

Third, the class of polynomial-time solvable problems has nice closure properties, since polynomials are closed under addition, multiplication, and composition. For example, if the output of one polynomial-time algorithm is fed into the input of another, the composite algorithm is polynomial. Exercise 34.1-5 asks you to show that if an algorithm makes a constant number of calls to polynomial-time subroutines and performs an additional amount of work that also takes polynomial time, then the running time of the composite algorithm is polynomial.

Abstract problems

To understand the class of polynomial-time solvable problems, we must first have a formal notion of what a "problem" is. We define an *abstract problem* Q to be a binary relation on a set I of problem *instances* and a set S of problem *solutions*. For example, an instance for SHORTEST-PATH is a triple consisting of a graph and two vertices. A solution is a sequence of vertices in the graph, with perhaps the empty sequence denoting that no path exists. The problem SHORTEST-PATH itself is the relation that associates each instance of a graph and two vertices with a shortest path in the graph that connects the two vertices. Since shortest paths are not necessarily unique, a given problem instance may have more than one solution.

This formulation of an abstract problem is more general than we need for our purposes. As we saw above, the theory of NP-completeness restricts attention to *decision problems*: those having a yes/no solution. In this case, we can view an abstract decision problem as a function that maps the instance set I to the solution set $\{0, 1\}$. For example, a decision problem related to SHORTEST-PATH is the problem PATH that we saw earlier. If $i = \langle G, u, v, k \rangle$ is an instance of the decision problem PATH, then PATH$(i) = 1$ (yes) if a shortest path from u to v has at most k edges, and PATH$(i) = 0$ (no) otherwise. Many abstract problems are not decision problems, but rather *optimization problems*, which require some value to be minimized or maximized. As we saw above, however, we can usually recast an optimization problem as a decision problem that is no harder.

---

[1] See Hopcroft and Ullman [180] or Lewis and Papadimitriou [236] for a thorough treatment of the Turing-machine model.

Encodings

In order for a computer program to solve an abstract problem, we must represent problem instances in a way that the program understands. An ***encoding*** of a set S of abstract objects is a mapping e from S to the set of binary strings.[2] For example, we are all familiar with encoding the natural numbers $\mathbb{N} = \{0, 1, 2, 3, 4, \ldots\}$ as the strings $\{0, 1, 10, 11, 100, \ldots\}$. Using this encoding, $e(17) = 10001$. If you have looked at computer representations of keyboard characters, you probably have seen the ASCII code, where, for example, the encoding of A is 1000001. We can encode a compound object as a binary string by combining the representations of its constituent parts. Polygons, graphs, functions, ordered pairs, programs—all can be encoded as binary strings.

Thus, a computer algorithm that "solves" some abstract decision problem actually takes an encoding of a problem instance as input. We call a problem whose instance set is the set of binary strings a ***concrete problem***. We say that an algorithm ***solves*** a concrete problem in time $O(T(n))$ if, when it is provided a problem instance i of length $n = |i|$, the algorithm can produce the solution in $O(T(n))$ time.[3] A concrete problem is ***polynomial-time solvable***, therefore, if there exists an algorithm to solve it in time $O(n^k)$ for some constant k.

We can now formally define the ***complexity class* P** as the set of concrete decision problems that are polynomial-time solvable.

We can use encodings to map abstract problems to concrete problems. Given an abstract decision problem Q mapping an instance set I to $\{0, 1\}$, an encoding $e : I \rightarrow \{0, 1\}^*$ can induce a related concrete decision problem, which we denote by $e(Q)$.[4] If the solution to an abstract-problem instance $i \in I$ is $Q(i) \in \{0, 1\}$, then the solution to the concrete-problem instance $e(i) \in \{0, 1\}^*$ is also $Q(i)$. As a technicality, some binary strings might represent no meaningful abstract-problem instance. For convenience, we shall assume that any such string maps arbitrarily to 0. Thus, the concrete problem produces the same solutions as the abstract problem on binary-string instances that represent the encodings of abstract-problem instances.

We would like to extend the definition of polynomial-time solvability from concrete problems to abstract problems by using encodings as the bridge, but we would

---

[2]The codomain of e need not be *binary* strings; any set of strings over a finite alphabet having at least 2 symbols will do.

[3]We assume that the algorithm's output is separate from its input. Because it takes at least one time step to produce each bit of the output and the algorithm takes $O(T(n))$ time steps, the size of the output is $O(T(n))$.

[4]We denote by $\{0, 1\}^*$ the set of all strings composed of symbols from the set $\{0, 1\}$.

like the definition to be independent of any particular encoding. That is, the efficiency of solving a problem should not depend on how the problem is encoded. Unfortunately, it depends quite heavily on the encoding. For example, suppose that an integer k is to be provided as the sole input to an algorithm, and suppose that the running time of the algorithm is $\Theta(k)$. If the integer k is provided in **unary**—a string of k 1s—then the running time of the algorithm is $O(n)$ on length-n inputs, which is polynomial time. If we use the more natural binary representation of the integer k, however, then the input length is $n = \lfloor \lg k \rfloor + 1$. In this case, the running time of the algorithm is $\Theta(k) = \Theta(2^n)$, which is exponential in the size of the input. Thus, depending on the encoding, the algorithm runs in either polynomial or superpolynomial time.

How we encode an abstract problem matters quite a bit to how we understand polynomial time. We cannot really talk about solving an abstract problem without first specifying an encoding. Nevertheless, in practice, if we rule out "expensive" encodings such as unary ones, the actual encoding of a problem makes little difference to whether the problem can be solved in polynomial time. For example, representing integers in base 3 instead of binary has no effect on whether a problem is solvable in polynomial time, since we can convert an integer represented in base 3 to an integer represented in base 2 in polynomial time.

We say that a function $f : \{0, 1\}^* \to \{0, 1\}^*$ is **polynomial-time computable** if there exists a polynomial-time algorithm A that, given any input $x \in \{0, 1\}^*$, produces as output $f(x)$. For some set I of problem instances, we say that two encodings e_1 and e_2 are **polynomially related** if there exist two polynomial-time computable functions f_{12} and f_{21} such that for any $i \in I$, we have $f_{12}(e_1(i)) = e_2(i)$ and $f_{21}(e_2(i)) = e_1(i)$.[5] That is, a polynomial-time algorithm can compute the encoding $e_2(i)$ from the encoding $e_1(i)$, and vice versa. If two encodings e_1 and e_2 of an abstract problem are polynomially related, whether the problem is polynomial-time solvable or not is independent of which encoding we use, as the following lemma shows.

Lemma 34.1
Let Q be an abstract decision problem on an instance set I, and let e_1 and e_2 be polynomially related encodings on I. Then, $e_1(Q) \in P$ if and only if $e_2(Q) \in P$.

---

[5]Technically, we also require the functions f_{12} and f_{21} to "map noninstances to noninstances." A **noninstance** of an encoding e is a string $x \in \{0, 1\}^*$ such that there is no instance i for which $e(i) = x$. We require that $f_{12}(x) = y$ for every noninstance x of encoding e_1, where y is some noninstance of e_2, and that $f_{21}(x') = y'$ for every noninstance x' of e_2, where y' is some noninstance of e_1.

Proof We need only prove the forward direction, since the backward direction is symmetric. Suppose, therefore, that $e_1(Q)$ can be solved in time $O(n^k)$ for some constant k. Further, suppose that for any problem instance i, the encoding $e_1(i)$ can be computed from the encoding $e_2(i)$ in time $O(n^c)$ for some constant c, where $n = |e_2(i)|$. To solve problem $e_2(Q)$, on input $e_2(i)$, we first compute $e_1(i)$ and then run the algorithm for $e_1(Q)$ on $e_1(i)$. How long does this take? Converting encodings takes time $O(n^c)$, and therefore $|e_1(i)| = O(n^c)$, since the output of a serial computer cannot be longer than its running time. Solving the problem on $e_1(i)$ takes time $O(|e_1(i)|^k) = O(n^{ck})$, which is polynomial since both c and k are constants. ∎

Thus, whether an abstract problem has its instances encoded in binary or base 3 does not affect its "complexity," that is, whether it is polynomial-time solvable or not; but if instances are encoded in unary, its complexity may change. In order to be able to converse in an encoding-independent fashion, we shall generally assume that problem instances are encoded in any reasonable, concise fashion, unless we specifically say otherwise. To be precise, we shall assume that the encoding of an integer is polynomially related to its binary representation, and that the encoding of a finite set is polynomially related to its encoding as a list of its elements, enclosed in braces and separated by commas. (ASCII is one such encoding scheme.) With such a "standard" encoding in hand, we can derive reasonable encodings of other mathematical objects, such as tuples, graphs, and formulas. To denote the standard encoding of an object, we shall enclose the object in angle braces. Thus, $\langle G \rangle$ denotes the standard encoding of a graph G.

As long as we implicitly use an encoding that is polynomially related to this standard encoding, we can talk directly about abstract problems without reference to any particular encoding, knowing that the choice of encoding has no effect on whether the abstract problem is polynomial-time solvable. Henceforth, we shall generally assume that all problem instances are binary strings encoded using the standard encoding, unless we explicitly specify the contrary. We shall also typically neglect the distinction between abstract and concrete problems. You should watch out for problems that arise in practice, however, in which a standard encoding is not obvious and the encoding does make a difference.

A formal-language framework

By focusing on decision problems, we can take advantage of the machinery of formal-language theory. Let's review some definitions from that theory. An ***alphabet*** Σ is a finite set of symbols. A ***language*** L over Σ is any set of strings made up of symbols from Σ. For example, if $\Sigma = \{0, 1\}$, the set $L = \{10, 11, 101, 111, 1011, 1101, 10001, \ldots\}$ is the language of binary representations of prime numbers. We denote the ***empty string*** by ε, the ***empty language*** by $\emptyset$, and the language of all strings over Σ by Σ^*. For example, if $\Sigma = \{0, 1\}$, then $\Sigma^* = \{\varepsilon, 0, 1, 00, 01, 10, 11, 000, \ldots\}$ is the set of all binary strings. Every language L over Σ is a subset of Σ^*.

We can perform a variety of operations on languages. Set-theoretic operations, such as ***union*** and ***intersection***, follow directly from the set-theoretic definitions. We define the ***complement*** of L by $\overline{L} = \Sigma^* - L$. The ***concatenation*** $L_1 L_2$ of two languages L_1 and L_2 is the language

$$L = \{x_1 x_2 : x_1 \in L_1 \text{ and } x_2 \in L_2\} \ .$$

The ***closure*** or ***Kleene star*** of a language L is the language

$$L^* = \{\varepsilon\} \cup L \cup L^2 \cup L^3 \cup \cdots \ ,$$

where L^k is the language obtained by concatenating L to itself k times.

From the point of view of language theory, the set of instances for any decision problem Q is simply the set Σ^*, where $\Sigma = \{0, 1\}$. Since Q is entirely characterized by those problem instances that produce a 1 (yes) answer, we can view Q as a language L over $\Sigma = \{0, 1\}$, where

$$L = \{x \in \Sigma^* : Q(x) = 1\} \ .$$

For example, the decision problem PATH has the corresponding language

$$\begin{aligned}
\text{PATH} = \{\langle G, u, v, k \rangle : \ & G = (V, E) \text{ is an undirected graph,} \\
& u, v \in V, \\
& k \geq 0 \text{ is an integer, and} \\
& \text{there exists a path from } u \text{ to } v \text{ in } G \\
& \text{consisting of at most } k \text{ edges} \} \ .
\end{aligned}$$

(Where convenient, we shall sometimes use the same name—PATH in this case— to refer to both a decision problem and its corresponding language.)

The formal-language framework allows us to express concisely the relation between decision problems and algorithms that solve them. We say that an algorithm A ***accepts*** a string $x \in \{0, 1\}^*$ if, given input x, the algorithm's output $A(x)$ is 1. The language ***accepted*** by an algorithm A is the set of strings $L = \{x \in \{0, 1\}^* : A(x) = 1\}$, that is, the set of strings that the algorithm accepts. An algorithm A ***rejects*** a string x if $A(x) = 0$.

Even if language L is accepted by an algorithm A, the algorithm will not necessarily reject a string $x \notin L$ provided as input to it. For example, the algorithm may loop forever. A language L is ***decided*** by an algorithm A if every binary string in L is accepted by A and every binary string not in L is rejected by A. A language L is ***accepted in polynomial time*** by an algorithm A if it is accepted by A and if in addition there exists a constant k such that for any length-n string $x \in L$,

algorithm A accepts x in time $O(n^k)$. A language L is ***decided in polynomial
time*** by an algorithm A if there exists a constant k such that for any length-n string
$x \in \{0, 1\}^*$, the algorithm correctly decides whether $x \in L$ in time $O(n^k)$. Thus,
to accept a language, an algorithm need only produce an answer when provided a
string in L, but to decide a language, it must correctly accept or reject every string
in $\{0, 1\}^*$.

As an example, the language PATH can be accepted in polynomial time. One
polynomial-time accepting algorithm verifies that G encodes an undirected graph,
verifies that u and v are vertices in G, uses breadth-first search to compute a shortest path from u to v in G, and then compares the number of edges on the shortest
path obtained with k. If G encodes an undirected graph and the path found from u
to v has at most k edges, the algorithm outputs 1 and halts. Otherwise, the algorithm runs forever. This algorithm does not decide PATH, however, since it does
not explicitly output 0 for instances in which a shortest path has more than k edges.
A decision algorithm for PATH must explicitly reject binary strings that do not belong to PATH. For a decision problem such as PATH, such a decision algorithm is
easy to design: instead of running forever when there is not a path from u to v with
at most k edges, it outputs 0 and halts. (It must also output 0 and halt if the input
encoding is faulty.) For other problems, such as Turing's Halting Problem, there
exists an accepting algorithm, but no decision algorithm exists.

We can informally define a ***complexity class*** as a set of languages, membership
in which is determined by a ***complexity measure***, such as running time, of an
algorithm that determines whether a given string x belongs to language L. The
actual definition of a complexity class is somewhat more technical.[6]

Using this language-theoretic framework, we can provide an alternative definition of the complexity class P:

$$P = \{L \subseteq \{0, 1\}^* : \text{there exists an algorithm } A \text{ that decides } L$$
$$\text{in polynomial time}\} \, .$$

In fact, P is also the class of languages that can be accepted in polynomial time.

Theorem 34.2
$P = \{L : L \text{ is accepted by a polynomial-time algorithm}\} \, .$

Proof Because the class of languages decided by polynomial-time algorithms is
a subset of the class of languages accepted by polynomial-time algorithms, we
need only show that if L is accepted by a polynomial-time algorithm, it is decided by a polynomial-time algorithm. Let L be the language accepted by some

---

[6]For more on complexity classes, see the seminal paper by Hartmanis and Stearns [162].

polynomial-time algorithm A. We shall use a classic "simulation" argument to construct another polynomial-time algorithm A' that decides L. Because A accepts L in time $O(n^k)$ for some constant k, there also exists a constant c such that A accepts L in at most cn^k steps. For any input string x, the algorithm A' simulates cn^k steps of A. After simulating cn^k steps, algorithm A' inspects the behavior of A. If A has accepted x, then A' accepts x by outputting a 1. If A has not accepted x, then A' rejects x by outputting a 0. The overhead of A' simulating A does not increase the running time by more than a polynomial factor, and thus A' is a polynomial-time algorithm that decides L.   ∎

Note that the proof of Theorem 34.2 is nonconstructive. For a given language $L \in P$, we may not actually know a bound on the running time for the algorithm A that accepts L. Nevertheless, we know that such a bound exists, and therefore, that an algorithm A' exists that can check the bound, even though we may not be able to find the algorithm A' easily.

Exercises

34.1-1
Define the optimization problem LONGEST-PATH-LENGTH as the relation that associates each instance of an undirected graph and two vertices with the number of edges in a longest simple path between the two vertices. Define the decision problem LONGEST-PATH $= \{\langle G, u, v, k \rangle : G = (V, E)$ is an undirected graph, $u, v \in V$, $k \geq 0$ is an integer, and there exists a simple path from u to v in G consisting of at least k edges$\}$. Show that the optimization problem LONGEST-PATH-LENGTH can be solved in polynomial time if and only if LONGEST-PATH $\in P$.

34.1-2
Give a formal definition for the problem of finding the longest simple cycle in an undirected graph. Give a related decision problem. Give the language corresponding to the decision problem.

34.1-3
Give a formal encoding of directed graphs as binary strings using an adjacency-matrix representation. Do the same using an adjacency-list representation. Argue that the two representations are polynomially related.

34.1-4
Is the dynamic-programming algorithm for the 0-1 knapsack problem that is asked for in Exercise 16.2-2 a polynomial-time algorithm? Explain your answer.

34.1-5
Show that if an algorithm makes at most a constant number of calls to polynomial-time subroutines and performs an additional amount of work that also takes polynomial time, then it runs in polynomial time. Also show that a polynomial number of calls to polynomial-time subroutines may result in an exponential-time algorithm.

34.1-6
Show that the class P, viewed as a set of languages, is closed under union, intersection, concatenation, complement, and Kleene star. That is, if $L_1, L_2 \in P$, then $L_1 \cup L_2 \in P$, $L_1 \cap L_2 \in P$, $L_1 L_2 \in P$, $\overline{L_1} \in P$, and $L_1^* \in P$.

34.2 Polynomial-time verification

We now look at algorithms that verify membership in languages. For example, suppose that for a given instance $\langle G, u, v, k \rangle$ of the decision problem PATH, we are also given a path p from u to v. We can easily check whether p is a path in G and whether the length of p is at most k, and if so, we can view p as a "certificate" that the instance indeed belongs to PATH. For the decision problem PATH, this certificate doesn't seem to buy us much. After all, PATH belongs to P—in fact, we can solve PATH in linear time—and so verifying membership from a given certificate takes as long as solving the problem from scratch. We shall now examine a problem for which we know of no polynomial-time decision algorithm and yet, given a certificate, verification is easy.

Hamiltonian cycles

The problem of finding a hamiltonian cycle in an undirected graph has been studied for over a hundred years. Formally, a ***hamiltonian cycle*** of an undirected graph $G = (V, E)$ is a simple cycle that contains each vertex in V. A graph that contains a hamiltonian cycle is said to be ***hamiltonian***; otherwise, it is ***nonhamiltonian***. The name honors W. R. Hamilton, who described a mathematical game on the dodecahedron (Figure 34.2(a)) in which one player sticks five pins in any five consecutive vertices and the other player must complete the path to form a cycle

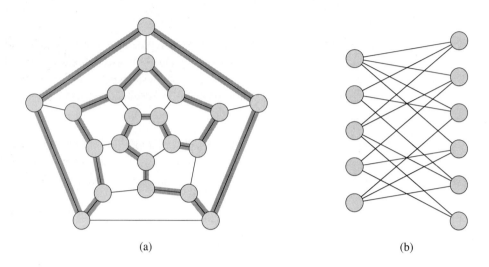

Figure 34.2 **(a)** A graph representing the vertices, edges, and faces of a dodecahedron, with a hamiltonian cycle shown by shaded edges. **(b)** A bipartite graph with an odd number of vertices. Any such graph is nonhamiltonian.

containing all the vertices.[7] The dodecahedron is hamiltonian, and Figure 34.2(a) shows one hamiltonian cycle. Not all graphs are hamiltonian, however. For example, Figure 34.2(b) shows a bipartite graph with an odd number of vertices. Exercise 34.2-2 asks you to show that all such graphs are nonhamiltonian.

We can define the ***hamiltonian-cycle problem***, "Does a graph G have a hamiltonian cycle?" as a formal language:

HAM-CYCLE = $\{\langle G \rangle : G$ is a hamiltonian graph$\}$.

How might an algorithm decide the language HAM-CYCLE? Given a problem instance $\langle G \rangle$, one possible decision algorithm lists all permutations of the vertices of G and then checks each permutation to see if it is a hamiltonian cycle. What is the running time of this algorithm? If we use the "reasonable" encoding of a graph as its adjacency matrix, the number m of vertices in the graph is $\Omega(\sqrt{n})$, where $n = |\langle G \rangle|$ is the length of the encoding of G. There are $m!$ possible permutations

---

[7]In a letter dated 17 October 1856 to his friend John T. Graves, Hamilton [157, p. 624] wrote, "I have found that some young persons have been much amused by trying a new mathematical game which the Icosion furnishes, one person sticking five pins in any five consecutive points ... and the other player then aiming to insert, which by the theory in this letter can always be done, fifteen other pins, in cyclical succession, so as to cover all the other points, and to end in immediate proximity to the pin wherewith his antagonist had begun."

of the vertices, and therefore the running time is $\Omega(m!) = \Omega(\sqrt{n}\,!) = \Omega(2^{\sqrt{n}})$, which is not $O(n^k)$ for any constant k. Thus, this naive algorithm does not run in polynomial time. In fact, the hamiltonian-cycle problem is NP-complete, as we shall prove in Section 34.5.

Verification algorithms

Consider a slightly easier problem. Suppose that a friend tells you that a given graph G is hamiltonian, and then offers to prove it by giving you the vertices in order along the hamiltonian cycle. It would certainly be easy enough to verify the proof: simply verify that the provided cycle is hamiltonian by checking whether it is a permutation of the vertices of V and whether each of the consecutive edges along the cycle actually exists in the graph. You could certainly implement this verification algorithm to run in $O(n^2)$ time, where n is the length of the encoding of G. Thus, a proof that a hamiltonian cycle exists in a graph can be verified in polynomial time.

We define a ***verification algorithm*** as being a two-argument algorithm A, where one argument is an ordinary input string x and the other is a binary string y called a ***certificate***. A two-argument algorithm A ***verifies*** an input string x if there exists a certificate y such that $A(x, y) = 1$. The ***language verified*** by a verification algorithm A is

$$L = \{x \in \{0, 1\}^* : \text{there exists } y \in \{0, 1\}^* \text{ such that } A(x, y) = 1\} \; .$$

Intuitively, an algorithm A verifies a language L if for any string $x \in L$, there exists a certificate y that A can use to prove that $x \in L$. Moreover, for any string $x \notin L$, there must be no certificate proving that $x \in L$. For example, in the hamiltonian-cycle problem, the certificate is the list of vertices in some hamiltonian cycle. If a graph is hamiltonian, the hamiltonian cycle itself offers enough information to verify this fact. Conversely, if a graph is not hamiltonian, there can be no list of vertices that fools the verification algorithm into believing that the graph is hamiltonian, since the verification algorithm carefully checks the proposed "cycle" to be sure.

The complexity class NP

The ***complexity class* NP** is the class of languages that can be verified by a polynomial-time algorithm.[8] More precisely, a language L belongs to NP if and only if there exist a two-input polynomial-time algorithm A and a constant c such that

$$L = \{x \in \{0, 1\}^* : \text{there exists a certificate } y \text{ with } |y| = O(|x|^c) \\ \text{such that } A(x, y) = 1\} \, .$$

We say that algorithm A ***verifies*** language L ***in polynomial time***.

From our earlier discussion on the hamiltonian-cycle problem, we now see that HAM-CYCLE $\in$ NP. (It is always nice to know that an important set is nonempty.) Moreover, if $L \in$ P, then $L \in$ NP, since if there is a polynomial-time algorithm to decide L, the algorithm can be easily converted to a two-argument verification algorithm that simply ignores any certificate and accepts exactly those input strings it determines to be in L. Thus, P $\subseteq$ NP.

It is unknown whether P $=$ NP, but most researchers believe that P and NP are not the same class. Intuitively, the class P consists of problems that can be solved quickly. The class NP consists of problems for which a solution can be verified quickly. You may have learned from experience that it is often more difficult to solve a problem from scratch than to verify a clearly presented solution, especially when working under time constraints. Theoretical computer scientists generally believe that this analogy extends to the classes P and NP, and thus that NP includes languages that are not in P.

There is more compelling, though not conclusive, evidence that P $\neq$ NP—the existence of languages that are "NP-complete." We shall study this class in Section 34.3.

Many other fundamental questions beyond the P $\neq$ NP question remain unresolved. Figure 34.3 shows some possible scenarios. Despite much work by many researchers, no one even knows whether the class NP is closed under complement. That is, does $L \in$ NP imply $\overline{L} \in$ NP? We can define the ***complexity class* co-NP** as the set of languages L such that $\overline{L} \in$ NP. We can restate the question of whether NP is closed under complement as whether NP $=$ co-NP. Since P is closed under complement (Exercise 34.1-6), it follows from Exercise 34.2-9 that P $\subseteq$ NP $\cap$ co-NP. Once again, however, no one knows whether P $=$ NP $\cap$ co-NP or whether there is some language in NP $\cap$ co-NP $-$ P.

---

[8]The name "NP" stands for "nondeterministic polynomial time." The class NP was originally studied in the context of nondeterminism, but this book uses the somewhat simpler yet equivalent notion of verification. Hopcroft and Ullman [180] give a good presentation of NP-completeness in terms of nondeterministic models of computation.

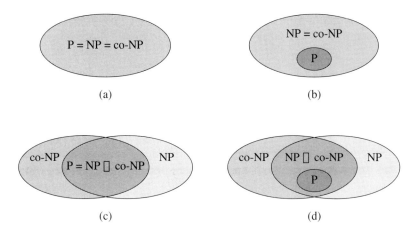

Figure 34.3 Four possibilities for relationships among complexity classes. In each diagram, one region enclosing another indicates a proper-subset relation. **(a)** P = NP = co-NP. Most researchers regard this possibility as the most unlikely. **(b)** If NP is closed under complement, then NP = co-NP, but it need not be the case that P = NP. **(c)** P = NP∩co-NP, but NP is not closed under complement. **(d)** NP ≠ co-NP and P ≠ NP ∩ co-NP. Most researchers regard this possibility as the most likely.

Thus, our understanding of the precise relationship between P and NP is woefully incomplete. Nevertheless, even though we might not be able to prove that a particular problem is intractable, if we can prove that it is NP-complete, then we have gained valuable information about it.

Exercises

34.2-1
Consider the language GRAPH-ISOMORPHISM = $\{\langle G_1, G_2 \rangle : G_1$ and G_2 are isomorphic graphs$\}$. Prove that GRAPH-ISOMORPHISM ∈ NP by describing a polynomial-time algorithm to verify the language.

34.2-2
Prove that if G is an undirected bipartite graph with an odd number of vertices, then G is nonhamiltonian.

34.2-3
Show that if HAM-CYCLE ∈ P, then the problem of listing the vertices of a hamiltonian cycle, in order, is polynomial-time solvable.

34.2-4

Prove that the class NP of languages is closed under union, intersection, concatenation, and Kleene star. Discuss the closure of NP under complement.

34.2-5

Show that any language in NP can be decided by an algorithm running in time $2^{O(n^k)}$ for some constant k.

34.2-6

A ***hamiltonian path*** in a graph is a simple path that visits every vertex exactly once. Show that the language HAM-PATH $= \{\langle G, u, v \rangle :$ there is a hamiltonian path from u to v in graph $G\}$ belongs to NP.

34.2-7

Show that the hamiltonian-path problem from Exercise 34.2-6 can be solved in polynomial time on directed acyclic graphs. Give an efficient algorithm for the problem.

34.2-8

Let ϕ be a boolean formula constructed from the boolean input variables $x_1, x_2,$ $\ldots, x_k$, negations ($\neg$), ANDs ($\wedge$), ORs ($\vee$), and parentheses. The formula ϕ is a ***tautology*** if it evaluates to 1 for every assignment of 1 and 0 to the input variables. Define TAUTOLOGY as the language of boolean formulas that are tautologies. Show that TAUTOLOGY $\in$ co-NP.

34.2-9

Prove that P $\subseteq$ co-NP.

34.2-10

Prove that if NP $\neq$ co-NP, then P $\neq$ NP.

34.2-11

Let G be a connected, undirected graph with at least 3 vertices, and let G^3 be the graph obtained by connecting all pairs of vertices that are connected by a path in G of length at most 3. Prove that G^3 is hamiltonian. (*Hint:* Construct a spanning tree for G, and use an inductive argument.)

34.3   NP-completeness and reducibility

Perhaps the most compelling reason why theoretical computer scientists believe that P ≠ NP comes from the existence of the class of "NP-complete" problems. This class has the intriguing property that if *any* NP-complete problem can be solved in polynomial time, then *every* problem in NP has a polynomial-time solution, that is, P = NP. Despite years of study, though, no polynomial-time algorithm has ever been discovered for any NP-complete problem.

The language HAM-CYCLE is one NP-complete problem. If we could decide HAM-CYCLE in polynomial time, then we could solve every problem in NP in polynomial time. In fact, if NP − P should turn out to be nonempty, we could say with certainty that HAM-CYCLE ∈ NP − P.

The NP-complete languages are, in a sense, the "hardest" languages in NP. In this section, we shall show how to compare the relative "hardness" of languages using a precise notion called "polynomial-time reducibility." Then we formally define the NP-complete languages, and we finish by sketching a proof that one such language, called CIRCUIT-SAT, is NP-complete. In Sections 34.4 and 34.5, we shall use the notion of reducibility to show that many other problems are NP-complete.

Reducibility

Intuitively, a problem Q can be reduced to another problem Q' if any instance of Q can be "easily rephrased" as an instance of Q', the solution to which provides a solution to the instance of Q. For example, the problem of solving linear equations in an indeterminate x reduces to the problem of solving quadratic equations. Given a linear-equation instance $ax + b = 0$ (with solution $x = -b/a$), we transform it to the quadratic equation $ax^2 + bx + 0 = 0$, whose solutions are $x = 0$ and $x = -b/a$, thereby providing a solution to $ax + b = 0$. Thus, if a problem Q reduces to another problem Q', then Q is, in a sense, "no harder to solve" than Q'.

Returning to our formal-language framework for decision problems, we say that a language L_1 is **polynomial-time reducible** to a language L_2, written $L_1 \leq_P L_2$, if there exists a polynomial-time computable function $f : \{0, 1\}^* \rightarrow \{0, 1\}^*$ such that for all $x \in \{0, 1\}^*$,

$$x \in L_1 \text{ if and only if } f(x) \in L_2 . \tag{34.1}$$

We call the function f the **reduction function**, and a polynomial-time algorithm F that computes f is a **reduction algorithm**.

Figure 34.4 illustrates the idea of a polynomial-time reduction from a language L_1 to another language L_2. Each language is a subset of $\{0, 1\}^*$. The reduction function f provides a polynomial-time mapping such that if $x \in L_1$,

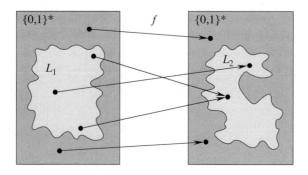

Figure 34.4   An illustration of a polynomial-time reduction from a language L_1 to a language L_2 via a reduction function f. For any input $x \in \{0, 1\}^*$, the question of whether $x \in L_1$ has the same answer as the question of whether $f(x) \in L_2$.

then $f(x) \in L_2$. Moreover, if $x \notin L_1$, then $f(x) \notin L_2$. Thus, the reduction function maps any instance x of the decision problem represented by the language L_1 to an instance $f(x)$ of the problem represented by L_2. Providing an answer to whether $f(x) \in L_2$ directly provides the answer to whether $x \in L_1$.

Polynomial-time reductions give us a powerful tool for proving that various languages belong to P.

Lemma 34.3

If $L_1, L_2 \subseteq \{0, 1\}^*$ are languages such that $L_1 \leq_P L_2$, then $L_2 \in$ P implies $L_1 \in$ P.

Proof   Let A_2 be a polynomial-time algorithm that decides L_2, and let F be a polynomial-time reduction algorithm that computes the reduction function f. We shall construct a polynomial-time algorithm A_1 that decides L_1.

Figure 34.5 illustrates how we construct A_1. For a given input $x \in \{0, 1\}^*$, algorithm A_1 uses F to transform x into $f(x)$, and then it uses A_2 to test whether $f(x) \in L_2$. Algorithm A_1 takes the output from algorithm A_2 and produces that answer as its own output.

The correctness of A_1 follows from condition (34.1). The algorithm runs in polynomial time, since both F and A_2 run in polynomial time (see Exercise 34.1-5). ∎

NP-completeness

Polynomial-time reductions provide a formal means for showing that one problem is at least as hard as another, to within a polynomial-time factor. That is, if $L_1 \leq_P L_2$, then L_1 is not more than a polynomial factor harder than L_2, which is

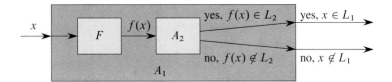

Figure 34.5 The proof of Lemma 34.3. The algorithm F is a reduction algorithm that computes the reduction function f from L_1 to L_2 in polynomial time, and A_2 is a polynomial-time algorithm that decides L_2. Algorithm A_1 decides whether $x \in L_1$ by using F to transform any input x into $f(x)$ and then using A_2 to decide whether $f(x) \in L_2$.

why the "less than or equal to" notation for reduction is mnemonic. We can now define the set of NP-complete languages, which are the hardest problems in NP.

A language $L \subseteq \{0, 1\}^*$ is **NP-complete** if

1. $L \in$ NP, and

2. $L' \leq_P L$ for every $L' \in$ NP.

If a language L satisfies property 2, but not necessarily property 1, we say that L is **NP-hard**. We also define NPC to be the class of NP-complete languages.

As the following theorem shows, NP-completeness is at the crux of deciding whether P is in fact equal to NP.

Theorem 34.4
If any NP-complete problem is polynomial-time solvable, then P $=$ NP. Equivalently, if any problem in NP is not polynomial-time solvable, then no NP-complete problem is polynomial-time solvable.

Proof Suppose that $L \in$ P and also that $L \in$ NPC. For any $L' \in$ NP, we have $L' \leq_P L$ by property 2 of the definition of NP-completeness. Thus, by Lemma 34.3, we also have that $L' \in$ P, which proves the first statement of the theorem.

To prove the second statement, note that it is the contrapositive of the first statement. ∎

It is for this reason that research into the P $\neq$ NP question centers around the NP-complete problems. Most theoretical computer scientists believe that P $\neq$ NP, which leads to the relationships among P, NP, and NPC shown in Figure 34.6. But, for all we know, someone may yet come up with a polynomial-time algorithm for an NP-complete problem, thus proving that P $=$ NP. Nevertheless, since no polynomial-time algorithm for any NP-complete problem has yet been discov-

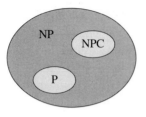

Figure 34.6 How most theoretical computer scientists view the relationships among P, NP, and NPC. Both P and NPC are wholly contained within NP, and P ∩ NPC = ∅.

ered, a proof that a problem is NP-complete provides excellent evidence that it is intractable.

Circuit satisfiability

We have defined the notion of an NP-complete problem, but up to this point, we have not actually proved that any problem is NP-complete. Once we prove that at least one problem is NP-complete, we can use polynomial-time reducibility as a tool to prove other problems to be NP-complete. Thus, we now focus on demonstrating the existence of an NP-complete problem: the circuit-satisfiability problem.

Unfortunately, the formal proof that the circuit-satisfiability problem is NP-complete requires technical detail beyond the scope of this text. Instead, we shall informally describe a proof that relies on a basic understanding of boolean combinational circuits.

Boolean combinational circuits are built from boolean combinational elements that are interconnected by wires. A *boolean combinational element* is any circuit element that has a constant number of boolean inputs and outputs and that performs a well-defined function. Boolean values are drawn from the set $\{0, 1\}$, where 0 represents FALSE and 1 represents TRUE.

The boolean combinational elements that we use in the circuit-satisfiability problem compute simple boolean functions, and they are known as *logic gates*. Figure 34.7 shows the three basic logic gates that we use in the circuit-satisfiability problem: the *NOT gate* (or *inverter*), the *AND gate*, and the *OR gate*. The NOT gate takes a single binary *input* x, whose value is either 0 or 1, and produces a binary *output* z whose value is opposite that of the input value. Each of the other two gates takes two binary inputs x and y and produces a single binary output z.

We can describe the operation of each gate, and of any boolean combinational element, by a *truth table*, shown under each gate in Figure 34.7. A truth table gives the outputs of the combinational element for each possible setting of the inputs. For

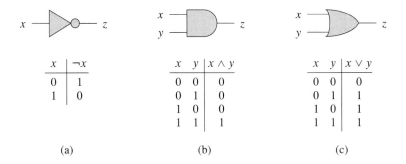

Figure 34.7 Three basic logic gates, with binary inputs and outputs. Under each gate is the truth table that describes the gate's operation. (**a**) The NOT gate. (**b**) The AND gate. (**c**) The OR gate.

example, the truth table for the OR gate tells us that when the inputs are $x = 0$ and $y = 1$, the output value is $z = 1$. We use the symbols $\neg$ to denote the NOT function, $\wedge$ to denote the AND function, and $\vee$ to denote the OR function. Thus, for example, $0 \vee 1 = 1$.

We can generalize AND and OR gates to take more than two inputs. An AND gate's output is 1 if all of its inputs are 1, and its output is 0 otherwise. An OR gate's output is 1 if any of its inputs are 1, and its output is 0 otherwise.

A **boolean combinational circuit** consists of one or more boolean combinational elements interconnected by **wires**. A wire can connect the output of one element to the input of another, thereby providing the output value of the first element as an input value of the second. Figure 34.8 shows two similar boolean combinational circuits, differing in only one gate. Part (a) of the figure also shows the values on the individual wires, given the input $\langle x_1 = 1, x_2 = 1, x_3 = 0 \rangle$. Although a single wire may have no more than one combinational-element output connected to it, it can feed several element inputs. The number of element inputs fed by a wire is called the **fan-out** of the wire. If no element output is connected to a wire, the wire is a **circuit input**, accepting input values from an external source. If no element input is connected to a wire, the wire is a **circuit output**, providing the results of the circuit's computation to the outside world. (An internal wire can also fan out to a circuit output.) For the purpose of defining the circuit-satisfiability problem, we limit the number of circuit outputs to 1, though in actual hardware design, a boolean combinational circuit may have multiple outputs.

Boolean combinational circuits contain no cycles. In other words, suppose we create a directed graph $G = (V, E)$ with one vertex for each combinational element and with k directed edges for each wire whose fan-out is k; the graph contains a directed edge (u, v) if a wire connects the output of element u to an input of element v. Then G must be acyclic.

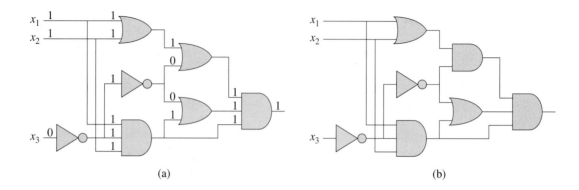

Figure 34.8 Two instances of the circuit-satisfiability problem. **(a)** The assignment $\langle x_1 = 1,$ $x_2 = 1, x_3 = 0 \rangle$ to the inputs of this circuit causes the output of the circuit to be 1. The circuit is therefore satisfiable. **(b)** No assignment to the inputs of this circuit can cause the output of the circuit to be 1. The circuit is therefore unsatisfiable.

A ***truth assignment*** for a boolean combinational circuit is a set of boolean input values. We say that a one-output boolean combinational circuit is ***satisfiable*** if it has a ***satisfying assignment***: a truth assignment that causes the output of the circuit to be 1. For example, the circuit in Figure 34.8(a) has the satisfying assignment $\langle x_1 = 1, x_2 = 1, x_3 = 0 \rangle$, and so it is satisfiable. As Exercise 34.3-1 asks you to show, no assignment of values to x_1, x_2, and x_3 causes the circuit in Figure 34.8(b) to produce a 1 output; it always produces 0, and so it is unsatisfiable.

The ***circuit-satisfiability problem*** is, "Given a boolean combinational circuit composed of AND, OR, and NOT gates, is it satisfiable?" In order to pose this question formally, however, we must agree on a standard encoding for circuits. The ***size*** of a boolean combinational circuit is the number of boolean combinational elements plus the number of wires in the circuit. We could devise a graphlike encoding that maps any given circuit C into a binary string $\langle C \rangle$ whose length is polynomial in the size of the circuit itself. As a formal language, we can therefore define

CIRCUIT-SAT $= \{\langle C \rangle : C$ is a satisfiable boolean combinational circuit$\}$.

The circuit-satisfiability problem arises in the area of computer-aided hardware optimization. If a subcircuit always produces 0, that subcircuit is unnecessary; the designer can replace it by a simpler subcircuit that omits all logic gates and provides the constant 0 value as its output. You can see why we would like to have a polynomial-time algorithm for this problem.

Given a circuit C, we might attempt to determine whether it is satisfiable by simply checking all possible assignments to the inputs. Unfortunately, if the circuit has k inputs, then we would have to check up to 2^k possible assignments. When the size of C is polynomial in k, checking each one takes $\Omega(2^k)$ time, which is superpolynomial in the size of the circuit.[9] In fact, as we have claimed, there is strong evidence that no polynomial-time algorithm exists that solves the circuit-satisfiability problem because circuit satisfiability is NP-complete. We break the proof of this fact into two parts, based on the two parts of the definition of NP-completeness.

Lemma 34.5
The circuit-satisfiability problem belongs to the class NP.

Proof   We shall provide a two-input, polynomial-time algorithm A that can verify CIRCUIT-SAT. One of the inputs to A is (a standard encoding of) a boolean combinational circuit C. The other input is a certificate corresponding to an assignment of boolean values to the wires in C. (See Exercise 34.3-4 for a smaller certificate.)

We construct the algorithm A as follows. For each logic gate in the circuit, it checks that the value provided by the certificate on the output wire is correctly computed as a function of the values on the input wires. Then, if the output of the entire circuit is 1, the algorithm outputs 1, since the values assigned to the inputs of C provide a satisfying assignment. Otherwise, A outputs 0.

Whenever a satisfiable circuit C is input to algorithm A, there exists a certificate whose length is polynomial in the size of C and that causes A to output a 1. Whenever an unsatisfiable circuit is input, no certificate can fool A into believing that the circuit is satisfiable. Algorithm A runs in polynomial time: with a good implementation, linear time suffices. Thus, we can verify CIRCUIT-SAT in polynomial time, and CIRCUIT-SAT $\in$ NP.   ■

The second part of proving that CIRCUIT-SAT is NP-complete is to show that the language is NP-hard. That is, we must show that every language in NP is polynomial-time reducible to CIRCUIT-SAT. The actual proof of this fact is full of technical intricacies, and so we shall settle for a sketch of the proof based on some understanding of the workings of computer hardware.

A computer program is stored in the computer memory as a sequence of instructions. A typical instruction encodes an operation to be performed, addresses of operands in memory, and an address where the result is to be stored. A special memory location, called the ***program counter***, keeps track of which instruc-

---

[9]On the other hand, if the size of the circuit C is $\Theta(2^k)$, then an algorithm whose running time is $O(2^k)$ has a running time that is polynomial in the circuit size. Even if P $\neq$ NP, this situation would not contradict the NP-completeness of the problem; the existence of a polynomial-time algorithm for a special case does not imply that there is a polynomial-time algorithm for all cases.

tion is to be executed next. The program counter automatically increments upon fetching each instruction, thereby causing the computer to execute instructions sequentially. The execution of an instruction can cause a value to be written to the program counter, however, which alters the normal sequential execution and allows the computer to loop and perform conditional branches.

At any point during the execution of a program, the computer's memory holds the entire state of the computation. (We take the memory to include the program itself, the program counter, working storage, and any of the various bits of state that a computer maintains for bookkeeping.) We call any particular state of computer memory a *configuration*. We can view the execution of an instruction as mapping one configuration to another. The computer hardware that accomplishes this mapping can be implemented as a boolean combinational circuit, which we denote by M in the proof of the following lemma.

Lemma 34.6
The circuit-satisfiability problem is NP-hard.

Proof   Let L be any language in NP. We shall describe a polynomial-time algorithm F computing a reduction function f that maps every binary string x to a circuit $C = f(x)$ such that $x \in L$ if and only if $C \in$ CIRCUIT-SAT.

Since $L \in$ NP, there must exist an algorithm A that verifies L in polynomial time. The algorithm F that we shall construct uses the two-input algorithm A to compute the reduction function f.

Let $T(n)$ denote the worst-case running time of algorithm A on length-n input strings, and let $k \geq 1$ be a constant such that $T(n) = O(n^k)$ and the length of the certificate is $O(n^k)$. (The running time of A is actually a polynomial in the total input size, which includes both an input string and a certificate, but since the length of the certificate is polynomial in the length n of the input string, the running time is polynomial in n.)

The basic idea of the proof is to represent the computation of A as a sequence of configurations. As Figure 34.9 illustrates, we can break each configuration into parts consisting of the program for A, the program counter and auxiliary machine state, the input x, the certificate y, and working storage. The combinational circuit M, which implements the computer hardware, maps each configuration c_i to the next configuration c_{i+1}, starting from the initial configuration c_0. Algorithm A writes its output—0 or 1—to some designated location by the time it finishes executing, and if we assume that thereafter A halts, the value never changes. Thus, if the algorithm runs for at most $T(n)$ steps, the output appears as one of the bits in $c_{T(n)}$.

The reduction algorithm F constructs a single combinational circuit that computes all configurations produced by a given initial configuration. The idea is to

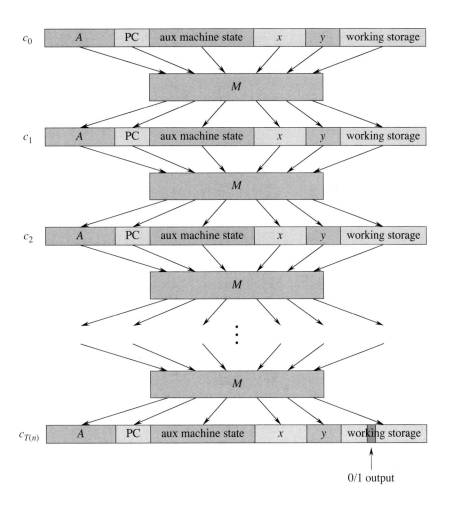

0/1 output

Figure 34.9   The sequence of configurations produced by an algorithm A running on an input x and certificate y. Each configuration represents the state of the computer for one step of the computation and, besides A, x, and y, includes the program counter (PC), auxiliary machine state, and working storage. Except for the certificate y, the initial configuration c_0 is constant. A boolean combinational circuit M maps each configuration to the next configuration. The output is a distinguished bit in the working storage.

paste together $T(n)$ copies of the circuit M. The output of the ith circuit, which produces configuration c_i, feeds directly into the input of the $(i+1)$st circuit. Thus, the configurations, rather than being stored in the computer's memory, simply reside as values on the wires connecting copies of M.

Recall what the polynomial-time reduction algorithm F must do. Given an input x, it must compute a circuit $C = f(x)$ that is satisfiable if and only if there exists a certificate y such that $A(x, y) = 1$. When F obtains an input x, it first computes $n = |x|$ and constructs a combinational circuit C' consisting of $T(n)$ copies of M. The input to C' is an initial configuration corresponding to a computation on $A(x, y)$, and the output is the configuration $c_{T(n)}$.

Algorithm F modifies circuit C' slightly to construct the circuit $C = f(x)$. First, it wires the inputs to C' corresponding to the program for A, the initial program counter, the input x, and the initial state of memory directly to these known values. Thus, the only remaining inputs to the circuit correspond to the certificate y. Second, it ignores all outputs from C', except for the one bit of $c_{T(n)}$ corresponding to the output of A. This circuit C, so constructed, computes $C(y) = A(x, y)$ for any input y of length $O(n^k)$. The reduction algorithm F, when provided an input string x, computes such a circuit C and outputs it.

We need to prove two properties. First, we must show that F correctly computes a reduction function f. That is, we must show that C is satisfiable if and only if there exists a certificate y such that $A(x, y) = 1$. Second, we must show that F runs in polynomial time.

To show that F correctly computes a reduction function, let us suppose that there exists a certificate y of length $O(n^k)$ such that $A(x, y) = 1$. Then, if we apply the bits of y to the inputs of C, the output of C is $C(y) = A(x, y) = 1$. Thus, if a certificate exists, then C is satisfiable. For the other direction, suppose that C is satisfiable. Hence, there exists an input y to C such that $C(y) = 1$, from which we conclude that $A(x, y) = 1$. Thus, F correctly computes a reduction function.

To complete the proof sketch, we need only show that F runs in time polynomial in $n = |x|$. The first observation we make is that the number of bits required to represent a configuration is polynomial in n. The program for A itself has constant size, independent of the length of its input x. The length of the input x is n, and the length of the certificate y is $O(n^k)$. Since the algorithm runs for at most $O(n^k)$ steps, the amount of working storage required by A is polynomial in n as well. (We assume that this memory is contiguous; Exercise 34.3-5 asks you to extend the argument to the situation in which the locations accessed by A are scattered across a much larger region of memory and the particular pattern of scattering can differ for each input x.)

The combinational circuit M implementing the computer hardware has size polynomial in the length of a configuration, which is $O(n^k)$; hence, the size of M is polynomial in n. (Most of this circuitry implements the logic of the memory system.) The circuit C consists of at most $t = O(n^k)$ copies of M, and hence it has size polynomial in n. The reduction algorithm F can construct C from x in polynomial time, since each step of the construction takes polynomial time. ∎

The language CIRCUIT-SAT is therefore at least as hard as any language in NP, and since it belongs to NP, it is NP-complete.

Theorem 34.7
The circuit-satisfiability problem is NP-complete.

Proof Immediate from Lemmas 34.5 and 34.6 and from the definition of NP-completeness. ∎

Exercises

34.3-1
Verify that the circuit in Figure 34.8(b) is unsatisfiable.

34.3-2
Show that the $\leq_P$ relation is a transitive relation on languages. That is, show that if $L_1 \leq_P L_2$ and $L_2 \leq_P L_3$, then $L_1 \leq_P L_3$.

34.3-3
Prove that $L \leq_P \overline{L}$ if and only if $\overline{L} \leq_P L$.

34.3-4
Show that we could have used a satisfying assignment as a certificate in an alternative proof of Lemma 34.5. Which certificate makes for an easier proof?

34.3-5
The proof of Lemma 34.6 assumes that the working storage for algorithm A occupies a contiguous region of polynomial size. Where in the proof do we exploit this assumption? Argue that this assumption does not involve any loss of generality.

34.3-6
A language L is **complete** for a language class C with respect to polynomial-time reductions if $L \in C$ and $L' \leq_P L$ for all $L' \in C$. Show that $\emptyset$ and $\{0, 1\}^*$ are the only languages in P that are not complete for P with respect to polynomial-time reductions.

34.3-7

Show that, with respect to polynomial-time reductions (see Exercise 34.3-6), L is complete for NP if and only if $\bar{L}$ is complete for co-NP.

34.3-8

The reduction algorithm F in the proof of Lemma 34.6 constructs the circuit $C = f(x)$ based on knowledge of x, A, and k. Professor Sartre observes that the string x is input to F, but only the existence of A, k, and the constant factor implicit in the $O(n^k)$ running time is known to F (since the language L belongs to NP), not their actual values. Thus, the professor concludes that F can't possibly construct the circuit C and that the language CIRCUIT-SAT is not necessarily NP-hard. Explain the flaw in the professor's reasoning.

34.4   NP-completeness proofs

We proved that the circuit-satisfiability problem is NP-complete by a direct proof that $L \leq_P$ CIRCUIT-SAT for every language $L \in$ NP. In this section, we shall show how to prove that languages are NP-complete without directly reducing *every* language in NP to the given language. We shall illustrate this methodology by proving that various formula-satisfiability problems are NP-complete. Section 34.5 provides many more examples of the methodology.

The following lemma is the basis of our method for showing that a language is NP-complete.

Lemma 34.8

If L is a language such that $L' \leq_P L$ for some $L' \in$ NPC, then L is NP-hard. If, in addition, $L \in$ NP, then $L \in$ NPC.

Proof   Since L' is NP-complete, for all $L'' \in$ NP, we have $L'' \leq_P L'$. By supposition, $L' \leq_P L$, and thus by transitivity (Exercise 34.3-2), we have $L'' \leq_P L$, which shows that L is NP-hard. If $L \in$ NP, we also have $L \in$ NPC.   ∎

In other words, by reducing a known NP-complete language L' to L, we implicitly reduce every language in NP to L. Thus, Lemma 34.8 gives us a method for proving that a language L is NP-complete:

1. Prove $L \in$ NP.

2. Select a known NP-complete language L'.

3. Describe an algorithm that computes a function f mapping every instance $x \in \{0, 1\}^*$ of L' to an instance $f(x)$ of L.

4. Prove that the function f satisfies $x \in L'$ if and only if $f(x) \in L$ for all $x \in \{0, 1\}^*$.

5. Prove that the algorithm computing f runs in polynomial time.

(Steps 2–5 show that L is NP-hard.) This methodology of reducing from a single known NP-complete language is far simpler than the more complicated process of showing directly how to reduce from every language in NP. Proving CIRCUIT-SAT $\in$ NPC has given us a "foot in the door." Because we know that the circuit-satisfiability problem is NP-complete, we now can prove much more easily that other problems are NP-complete. Moreover, as we develop a catalog of known NP-complete problems, we will have more and more choices for languages from which to reduce.

Formula satisfiability

We illustrate the reduction methodology by giving an NP-completeness proof for the problem of determining whether a boolean formula, not a circuit, is satisfiable. This problem has the historical honor of being the first problem ever shown to be NP-complete.

We formulate the *(formula) satisfiability* problem in terms of the language SAT as follows. An instance of SAT is a boolean formula ϕ composed of

1. n boolean variables: $x_1, x_2, \ldots, x_n$;

2. m boolean connectives: any boolean function with one or two inputs and one output, such as $\wedge$ (AND), $\vee$ (OR), $\neg$ (NOT), $\rightarrow$ (implication), $\leftrightarrow$ (if and only if); and

3. parentheses. (Without loss of generality, we assume that there are no redundant parentheses, i.e., a formula contains at most one pair of parentheses per boolean connective.)

We can easily encode a boolean formula ϕ in a length that is polynomial in $n + m$. As in boolean combinational circuits, a *truth assignment* for a boolean formula ϕ is a set of values for the variables of ϕ, and a *satisfying assignment* is a truth assignment that causes it to evaluate to 1. A formula with a satisfying assignment is a *satisfiable* formula. The satisfiability problem asks whether a given boolean formula is satisfiable; in formal-language terms,

SAT $= \{\langle \phi \rangle : \phi$ is a satisfiable boolean formula$\}$.

As an example, the formula

$$\phi = ((x_1 \rightarrow x_2) \vee \neg((\neg x_1 \leftrightarrow x_3) \vee x_4)) \wedge \neg x_2$$

has the satisfying assignment $\langle x_1 = 0, x_2 = 0, x_3 = 1, x_4 = 1 \rangle$, since

$$
\begin{aligned}
\phi \; &= \; ((0 \rightarrow 0) \vee \neg((\neg 0 \leftrightarrow 1) \vee 1)) \wedge \neg 0 \\
&= \; (1 \vee \neg(1 \vee 1)) \wedge 1 \\
&= \; (1 \vee 0) \wedge 1 \\
&= \; 1 \, ,
\end{aligned}
\tag{34.2}
$$

and thus this formula ϕ belongs to SAT.

The naive algorithm to determine whether an arbitrary boolean formula is satisfiable does not run in polynomial time. A formula with n variables has 2^n possible assignments. If the length of $\langle \phi \rangle$ is polynomial in n, then checking every assignment requires $\Omega(2^n)$ time, which is superpolynomial in the length of $\langle \phi \rangle$. As the following theorem shows, a polynomial-time algorithm is unlikely to exist.

Theorem 34.9
Satisfiability of boolean formulas is NP-complete.

Proof   We start by arguing that SAT $\in$ NP. Then we prove that SAT is NP-hard by showing that CIRCUIT-SAT $\leq_P$ SAT; by Lemma 34.8, this will prove the theorem.

To show that SAT belongs to NP, we show that a certificate consisting of a satisfying assignment for an input formula ϕ can be verified in polynomial time. The verifying algorithm simply replaces each variable in the formula with its corresponding value and then evaluates the expression, much as we did in equation (34.2) above. This task is easy to do in polynomial time. If the expression evaluates to 1, then the algorithm has verified that the formula is satisfiable. Thus, SAT is in NP.

To prove that SAT is NP-hard, we show that CIRCUIT-SAT $\leq_P$ SAT. In other words, we need to show how to reduce any instance of circuit satisfiability to an instance of formula satisfiability in polynomial time. We can use induction to express any boolean combinational circuit as a boolean formula. We simply look at the gate that produces the circuit output and inductively express each of the gate's inputs as formulas. We then obtain the formula for the circuit by writing an expression that applies the gate's function to its inputs' formulas.

Unfortunately, this straightforward method does not amount to a polynomial-time reduction. As Exercise 34.4-1 asks you to show, shared subformulas—which arise from gates whose output wires have fan-out of 2 or more—can cause the size of the generated formula to grow exponentially. Thus, the reduction algorithm must be somewhat more clever.

Figure 34.10 illustrates how we overcome this problem, using as an example the circuit from Figure 34.8(a). For each wire x_i in the circuit C, the formula ϕ

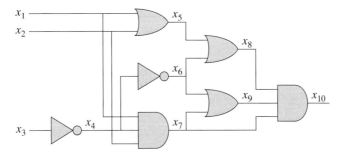

Figure 34.10 Reducing circuit satisfiability to formula satisfiability. The formula produced by the reduction algorithm has a variable for each wire in the circuit.

has a variable x_i. We can now express how each gate operates as a small formula involving the variables of its incident wires. For example, the operation of the output AND gate is $x_{10} \leftrightarrow (x_7 \wedge x_8 \wedge x_9)$. We call each of these small formulas a *clause*.

The formula ϕ produced by the reduction algorithm is the AND of the circuit-output variable with the conjunction of clauses describing the operation of each gate. For the circuit in the figure, the formula is

$$\begin{aligned}
\phi = \; & x_{10} \wedge (x_4 \leftrightarrow \neg x_3) \\
& \wedge (x_5 \leftrightarrow (x_1 \vee x_2)) \\
& \wedge (x_6 \leftrightarrow \neg x_4) \\
& \wedge (x_7 \leftrightarrow (x_1 \wedge x_2 \wedge x_4)) \\
& \wedge (x_8 \leftrightarrow (x_5 \vee x_6)) \\
& \wedge (x_9 \leftrightarrow (x_6 \vee x_7)) \\
& \wedge (x_{10} \leftrightarrow (x_7 \wedge x_8 \wedge x_9)) \;.
\end{aligned}$$

Given a circuit C, it is straightforward to produce such a formula ϕ in polynomial time.

Why is the circuit C satisfiable exactly when the formula ϕ is satisfiable? If C has a satisfying assignment, then each wire of the circuit has a well-defined value, and the output of the circuit is 1. Therefore, when we assign wire values to variables in ϕ, each clause of ϕ evaluates to 1, and thus the conjunction of all evaluates to 1. Conversely, if some assignment causes ϕ to evaluate to 1, the circuit C is satisfiable by an analogous argument. Thus, we have shown that CIRCUIT-SAT $\leq_{\mathrm{P}}$ SAT, which completes the proof. ∎

3-CNF satisfiability

We can prove many problems NP-complete by reducing from formula satisfiability. The reduction algorithm must handle any input formula, though, and this requirement can lead to a huge number of cases that we must consider. We often prefer to reduce from a restricted language of boolean formulas, so that we need to consider fewer cases. Of course, we must not restrict the language so much that it becomes polynomial-time solvable. One convenient language is 3-CNF satisfiability, or 3-CNF-SAT.

We define 3-CNF satisfiability using the following terms. A *literal* in a boolean formula is an occurrence of a variable or its negation. A boolean formula is in *conjunctive normal form*, or *CNF*, if it is expressed as an AND of *clauses*, each of which is the OR of one or more literals. A boolean formula is in *3-conjunctive normal form*, or *3-CNF*, if each clause has exactly three distinct literals.

For example, the boolean formula

$$(x_1 \lor \neg x_1 \lor \neg x_2) \land (x_3 \lor x_2 \lor x_4) \land (\neg x_1 \lor \neg x_3 \lor \neg x_4)$$

is in 3-CNF. The first of its three clauses is $(x_1 \lor \neg x_1 \lor \neg x_2)$, which contains the three literals x_1, $\neg x_1$, and $\neg x_2$.

In 3-CNF-SAT, we are asked whether a given boolean formula ϕ in 3-CNF is satisfiable. The following theorem shows that a polynomial-time algorithm that can determine the satisfiability of boolean formulas is unlikely to exist, even when they are expressed in this simple normal form.

Theorem 34.10

Satisfiability of boolean formulas in 3-conjunctive normal form is NP-complete.

Proof   The argument we used in the proof of Theorem 34.9 to show that SAT $\in$ NP applies equally well here to show that 3-CNF-SAT $\in$ NP. By Lemma 34.8, therefore, we need only show that SAT $\leq_P$ 3-CNF-SAT.

We break the reduction algorithm into three basic steps. Each step progressively transforms the input formula ϕ closer to the desired 3-conjunctive normal form.

The first step is similar to the one used to prove CIRCUIT-SAT $\leq_P$ SAT in Theorem 34.9. First, we construct a binary "parse" tree for the input formula ϕ, with literals as leaves and connectives as internal nodes. Figure 34.11 shows such a parse tree for the formula

$$\phi = ((x_1 \rightarrow x_2) \lor \neg((\neg x_1 \leftrightarrow x_3) \lor x_4)) \land \neg x_2 . \tag{34.3}$$

Should the input formula contain a clause such as the OR of several literals, we use associativity to parenthesize the expression fully so that every internal node in the resulting tree has 1 or 2 children. We can now think of the binary parse tree as a circuit for computing the function.

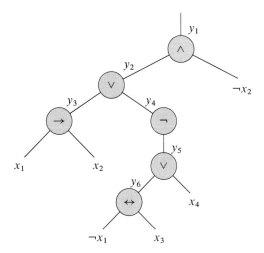

Figure 34.11   The tree corresponding to the formula $\phi = ((x_1 \rightarrow x_2) \vee \neg((\neg x_1 \leftrightarrow x_3) \vee x_4)) \wedge \neg x_2$.

Mimicking the reduction in the proof of Theorem 34.9, we introduce a variable y_i for the output of each internal node. Then, we rewrite the original formula ϕ as the AND of the root variable and a conjunction of clauses describing the operation of each node. For the formula (34.3), the resulting expression is

$$
\begin{aligned}
\phi' = \; & y_1 \wedge (y_1 \leftrightarrow (y_2 \wedge \neg x_2)) \\
& \wedge (y_2 \leftrightarrow (y_3 \vee y_4)) \\
& \wedge (y_3 \leftrightarrow (x_1 \rightarrow x_2)) \\
& \wedge (y_4 \leftrightarrow \neg y_5) \\
& \wedge (y_5 \leftrightarrow (y_6 \vee x_4)) \\
& \wedge (y_6 \leftrightarrow (\neg x_1 \leftrightarrow x_3)) \;.
\end{aligned}
$$

Observe that the formula ϕ' thus obtained is a conjunction of clauses ϕ'_i, each of which has at most 3 literals. The only requirement that we might fail to meet is that each clause has to be an OR of 3 literals.

The second step of the reduction converts each clause ϕ'_i into conjunctive normal form. We construct a truth table for ϕ'_i by evaluating all possible assignments to its variables. Each row of the truth table consists of a possible assignment of the variables of the clause, together with the value of the clause under that assignment. Using the truth-table entries that evaluate to 0, we build a formula in ***disjunctive normal form*** (or ***DNF***)—an OR of ANDs—that is equivalent to $\neg \phi'_i$. We then negate this formula and convert it into a CNF formula ϕ''_i by using ***DeMorgan's***

y_1	y_2	x_2	$(y_1 \leftrightarrow (y_2 \wedge \neg x_2))$
1	1	1	0
1	1	0	1
1	0	1	0
1	0	0	0
0	1	1	1
0	1	0	0
0	0	1	1
0	0	0	1

Figure 34.12   The truth table for the clause $(y_1 \leftrightarrow (y_2 \wedge \neg x_2))$.

laws for propositional logic,

$$\neg(a \wedge b) \;=\; \neg a \vee \neg b \,,$$
$$\neg(a \vee b) \;=\; \neg a \wedge \neg b \,,$$

to complement all literals, change ORs into ANDs, and change ANDs into ORs.

In our example, we convert the clause $\phi_1' = (y_1 \leftrightarrow (y_2 \wedge \neg x_2))$ into CNF as follows. The truth table for ϕ_1' appears in Figure 34.12. The DNF formula equivalent to $\neg\phi_1'$ is

$$(y_1 \wedge y_2 \wedge x_2) \vee (y_1 \wedge \neg y_2 \wedge x_2) \vee (y_1 \wedge \neg y_2 \wedge \neg x_2) \vee (\neg y_1 \wedge y_2 \wedge \neg x_2) \,.$$

Negating and applying DeMorgan's laws, we get the CNF formula

$$\begin{aligned}
\phi_1'' \;=\; & (\neg y_1 \vee \neg y_2 \vee \neg x_2) \wedge (\neg y_1 \vee y_2 \vee \neg x_2) \\
& \wedge (\neg y_1 \vee y_2 \vee x_2) \wedge (y_1 \vee \neg y_2 \vee x_2) \,,
\end{aligned}$$

which is equivalent to the original clause ϕ_1'.

At this point, we have converted each clause ϕ_i' of the formula ϕ' into a CNF formula ϕ_i'', and thus ϕ' is equivalent to the CNF formula ϕ'' consisting of the conjunction of the ϕ_i''. Moreover, each clause of ϕ'' has at most 3 literals.

The third and final step of the reduction further transforms the formula so that each clause has *exactly* 3 distinct literals. We construct the final 3-CNF formula ϕ''' from the clauses of the CNF formula ϕ''. The formula ϕ''' also uses two auxiliary variables that we shall call p and q. For each clause C_i of ϕ'', we include the following clauses in ϕ''':

- If C_i has 3 distinct literals, then simply include C_i as a clause of ϕ'''.

- If C_i has 2 distinct literals, that is, if $C_i = (l_1 \vee l_2)$, where l_1 and l_2 are literals, then include $(l_1 \vee l_2 \vee p) \wedge (l_1 \vee l_2 \vee \neg p)$ as clauses of ϕ'''. The literals p and $\neg p$ merely fulfill the syntactic requirement that each clause of ϕ''' has exactly 3 distinct literals. Whether $p = 0$ or $p = 1$, one of the clauses is equivalent to $l_1 \vee l_2$, and the other evaluates to 1, which is the identity for AND.

- If C_i has just 1 distinct literal l, then include $(l \vee p \vee q) \wedge (l \vee p \vee \neg q) \wedge (l \vee \neg p \vee q) \wedge (l \vee \neg p \vee \neg q)$ as clauses of ϕ'''. Regardless of the values of p and q, one of the four clauses is equivalent to l, and the other 3 evaluate to 1.

We can see that the 3-CNF formula ϕ''' is satisfiable if and only if ϕ is satisfiable by inspecting each of the three steps. Like the reduction from CIRCUIT-SAT to SAT, the construction of ϕ' from ϕ in the first step preserves satisfiability. The second step produces a CNF formula ϕ'' that is algebraically equivalent to ϕ'. The third step produces a 3-CNF formula ϕ''' that is effectively equivalent to ϕ'', since any assignment to the variables p and q produces a formula that is algebraically equivalent to ϕ''.

We must also show that the reduction can be computed in polynomial time. Constructing ϕ' from ϕ introduces at most 1 variable and 1 clause per connective in ϕ. Constructing ϕ'' from ϕ' can introduce at most 8 clauses into ϕ'' for each clause from ϕ', since each clause of ϕ' has at most 3 variables, and the truth table for each clause has at most $2^3 = 8$ rows. The construction of ϕ''' from ϕ'' introduces at most 4 clauses into ϕ''' for each clause of ϕ''. Thus, the size of the resulting formula ϕ''' is polynomial in the length of the original formula. Each of the constructions can easily be accomplished in polynomial time. ∎

Exercises

34.4-1
Consider the straightforward (nonpolynomial-time) reduction in the proof of Theorem 34.9. Describe a circuit of size n that, when converted to a formula by this method, yields a formula whose size is exponential in n.

34.4-2
Show the 3-CNF formula that results when we use the method of Theorem 34.10 on the formula (34.3).

34.4-3
Professor Jagger proposes to show that SAT $\leq_P$ 3-CNF-SAT by using only the truth-table technique in the proof of Theorem 34.10, and not the other steps. That is, the professor proposes to take the boolean formula ϕ, form a truth table for its variables, derive from the truth table a formula in 3-DNF that is equivalent to $\neg\phi$, and then negate and apply DeMorgan's laws to produce a 3-CNF formula equivalent to ϕ. Show that this strategy does not yield a polynomial-time reduction.

34.4-4

Show that the problem of determining whether a boolean formula is a tautology is complete for co-NP. (*Hint:* See Exercise 34.3-7.)

34.4-5

Show that the problem of determining the satisfiability of boolean formulas in disjunctive normal form is polynomial-time solvable.

34.4-6

Suppose that someone gives you a polynomial-time algorithm to decide formula satisfiability. Describe how to use this algorithm to find satisfying assignments in polynomial time.

34.4-7

Let 2-CNF-SAT be the set of satisfiable boolean formulas in CNF with exactly 2 literals per clause. Show that 2-CNF-SAT $\in$ P. Make your algorithm as efficient as possible. (*Hint:* Observe that $x \lor y$ is equivalent to $\neg x \rightarrow y$. Reduce 2-CNF-SAT to an efficiently solvable problem on a directed graph.)

34.5 NP-complete problems

NP-complete problems arise in diverse domains: boolean logic, graphs, arithmetic, network design, sets and partitions, storage and retrieval, sequencing and scheduling, mathematical programming, algebra and number theory, games and puzzles, automata and language theory, program optimization, biology, chemistry, physics, and more. In this section, we shall use the reduction methodology to provide NP-completeness proofs for a variety of problems drawn from graph theory and set partitioning.

Figure 34.13 outlines the structure of the NP-completeness proofs in this section and Section 34.4. We prove each language in the figure to be NP-complete by reduction from the language that points to it. At the root is CIRCUIT-SAT, which we proved NP-complete in Theorem 34.7.

34.5.1 The clique problem

A *clique* in an undirected graph $G = (V, E)$ is a subset $V' \subseteq V$ of vertices, each pair of which is connected by an edge in E. In other words, a clique is a complete subgraph of G. The *size* of a clique is the number of vertices it contains. The *clique problem* is the optimization problem of finding a clique of maximum size in

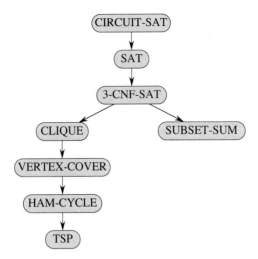

Figure 34.13 The structure of NP-completeness proofs in Sections 34.4 and 34.5. All proofs ultimately follow by reduction from the NP-completeness of CIRCUIT-SAT.

a graph. As a decision problem, we ask simply whether a clique of a given size k exists in the graph. The formal definition is

$$\text{CLIQUE} = \{\langle G, k\rangle : G \text{ is a graph containing a clique of size } k\} \ .$$

A naive algorithm for determining whether a graph $G = (V, E)$ with $|V|$ vertices has a clique of size k is to list all k-subsets of V, and check each one to see whether it forms a clique. The running time of this algorithm is $\Omega(k^2\binom{|V|}{k})$, which is polynomial if k is a constant. In general, however, k could be near $|V|/2$, in which case the algorithm runs in superpolynomial time. Indeed, an efficient algorithm for the clique problem is unlikely to exist.

Theorem 34.11
The clique problem is NP-complete.

Proof To show that CLIQUE $\in$ NP, for a given graph $G = (V, E)$, we use the set $V' \subseteq V$ of vertices in the clique as a certificate for G. We can check whether V' is a clique in polynomial time by checking whether, for each pair $u, v \in V'$, the edge (u, v) belongs to E.

We next prove that 3-CNF-SAT $\le_P$ CLIQUE, which shows that the clique problem is NP-hard. You might be surprised that we should be able to prove such a result, since on the surface logical formulas seem to have little to do with graphs.

The reduction algorithm begins with an instance of 3-CNF-SAT. Let $\phi = C_1 \wedge C_2 \wedge \cdots \wedge C_k$ be a boolean formula in 3-CNF with k clauses. For $r =$

$$C_1 = x_1 \vee \neg x_2 \vee \neg x_3$$

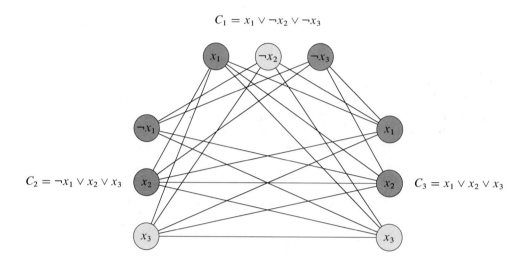

Figure 34.14   The graph G derived from the 3-CNF formula $\phi = C_1 \wedge C_2 \wedge C_3$, where $C_1 = (x_1 \vee \neg x_2 \vee \neg x_3)$, $C_2 = (\neg x_1 \vee x_2 \vee x_3)$, and $C_3 = (x_1 \vee x_2 \vee x_3)$, in reducing 3-CNF-SAT to CLIQUE. A satisfying assignment of the formula has $x_2 = 0$, $x_3 = 1$, and x_1 either 0 or 1. This assignment satisfies C_1 with $\neg x_2$, and it satisfies C_2 and C_3 with x_3, corresponding to the clique with lightly shaded vertices.

$1, 2, \ldots, k$, each clause C_r has exactly three distinct literals l_1^r, l_2^r, and l_3^r. We shall construct a graph G such that ϕ is satisfiable if and only if G has a clique of size k.

We construct the graph $G = (V, E)$ as follows. For each clause $C_r = (l_1^r \vee l_2^r \vee l_3^r)$ in ϕ, we place a triple of vertices v_1^r, v_2^r, and v_3^r into V. We put an edge between two vertices v_i^r and v_j^s if both of the following hold:

- v_i^r and v_j^s are in different triples, that is, $r \neq s$, and

- their corresponding literals are **consistent**, that is, l_i^r is not the negation of l_j^s.

We can easily build this graph from ϕ in polynomial time. As an example of this construction, if we have

$$\phi = (x_1 \vee \neg x_2 \vee \neg x_3) \wedge (\neg x_1 \vee x_2 \vee x_3) \wedge (x_1 \vee x_2 \vee x_3) \,,$$

then G is the graph shown in Figure 34.14.

We must show that this transformation of ϕ into G is a reduction. First, suppose that ϕ has a satisfying assignment. Then each clause C_r contains at least one literal l_i^r that is assigned 1, and each such literal corresponds to a vertex v_i^r. Picking one such "true" literal from each clause yields a set V' of k vertices. We claim that V' is a clique. For any two vertices $v_i^r, v_j^s \in V'$, where $r \neq s$, both corresponding literals l_i^r and l_j^s map to 1 by the given satisfying assignment, and thus the literals cannot be complements. Thus, by the construction of G, the edge (v_i^r, v_j^s) belongs to E.

Conversely, suppose that G has a clique V' of size k. No edges in G connect vertices in the same triple, and so V' contains exactly one vertex per triple. We can assign 1 to each literal l_i^r such that $v_i^r \in V'$ without fear of assigning 1 to both a literal and its complement, since G contains no edges between inconsistent literals. Each clause is satisfied, and so ϕ is satisfied. (Any variables that do not correspond to a vertex in the clique may be set arbitrarily.) ∎

In the example of Figure 34.14, a satisfying assignment of ϕ has $x_2 = 0$ and $x_3 = 1$. A corresponding clique of size $k = 3$ consists of the vertices corresponding to $\neg x_2$ from the first clause, x_3 from the second clause, and x_3 from the third clause. Because the clique contains no vertices corresponding to either x_1 or $\neg x_1$, we can set x_1 to either 0 or 1 in this satisfying assignment.

Observe that in the proof of Theorem 34.11, we reduced an arbitrary instance of 3-CNF-SAT to an instance of CLIQUE with a particular structure. You might think that we have shown only that CLIQUE is NP-hard in graphs in which the vertices are restricted to occur in triples and in which there are no edges between vertices in the same triple. Indeed, we have shown that CLIQUE is NP-hard only in this restricted case, but this proof suffices to show that CLIQUE is NP-hard in general graphs. Why? If we had a polynomial-time algorithm that solved CLIQUE on general graphs, it would also solve CLIQUE on restricted graphs.

The opposite approach—reducing instances of 3-CNF-SAT with a special structure to general instances of CLIQUE—would not have sufficed, however. Why not? Perhaps the instances of 3-CNF-SAT that we chose to reduce from were "easy," and so we would not have reduced an NP-hard problem to CLIQUE.

Observe also that the reduction used the instance of 3-CNF-SAT, but not the solution. We would have erred if the polynomial-time reduction had relied on knowing whether the formula ϕ is satisfiable, since we do not know how to decide whether ϕ is satisfiable in polynomial time.

34.5.2 The vertex-cover problem

A ***vertex cover*** of an undirected graph $G = (V, E)$ is a subset $V' \subseteq V$ such that if $(u, v) \in E$, then $u \in V'$ or $v \in V'$ (or both). That is, each vertex "covers" its incident edges, and a vertex cover for G is a set of vertices that covers all the edges in E. The ***size*** of a vertex cover is the number of vertices in it. For example, the graph in Figure 34.15(b) has a vertex cover $\{w, z\}$ of size 2.

The ***vertex-cover problem*** is to find a vertex cover of minimum size in a given graph. Restating this optimization problem as a decision problem, we wish to

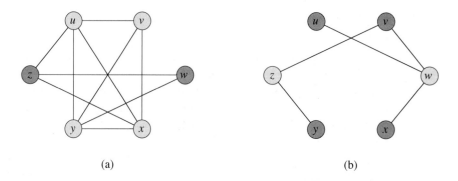

(a)   (b)

Figure 34.15   Reducing CLIQUE to VERTEX-COVER. **(a)** An undirected graph $G = (V, E)$ with clique $V' = \{u, v, x, y\}$. **(b)** The graph $\overline{G}$ produced by the reduction algorithm that has vertex cover $V - V' = \{w, z\}$.

determine whether a graph has a vertex cover of a given size k. As a language, we define

VERTEX-COVER $= \{\langle G, k \rangle$: graph G has a vertex cover of size $k\}$.

The following theorem shows that this problem is NP-complete.

Theorem 34.12
The vertex-cover problem is NP-complete.

Proof   We first show that VERTEX-COVER $\in$ NP. Suppose we are given a graph $G = (V, E)$ and an integer k. The certificate we choose is the vertex cover $V' \subseteq V$ itself. The verification algorithm affirms that $|V'| = k$, and then it checks, for each edge $(u, v) \in E$, that $u \in V'$ or $v \in V'$. We can easily verify the certificate in polynomial time.

We prove that the vertex-cover problem is NP-hard by showing that CLIQUE $\leq_P$ VERTEX-COVER. This reduction relies on the notion of the "complement" of a graph. Given an undirected graph $G = (V, E)$, we define the ***complement*** of G as $\overline{G} = (V, \overline{E})$, where $\overline{E} = \{(u, v) : u, v \in V, u \neq v, \text{ and } (u, v) \notin E\}$. In other words, $\overline{G}$ is the graph containing exactly those edges that are not in G. Figure 34.15 shows a graph and its complement and illustrates the reduction from CLIQUE to VERTEX-COVER.

The reduction algorithm takes as input an instance $\langle G, k \rangle$ of the clique problem. It computes the complement $\overline{G}$, which we can easily do in polynomial time. The output of the reduction algorithm is the instance $\langle \overline{G}, |V| - k \rangle$ of the vertex-cover problem. To complete the proof, we show that this transformation is indeed a reduction: the graph G has a clique of size k if and only if the graph $\overline{G}$ has a vertex cover of size $|V| - k$.

Suppose that G has a clique $V' \subseteq V$ with $|V'| = k$. We claim that $V - V'$ is a vertex cover in $\overline{G}$. Let (u, v) be any edge in $\overline{E}$. Then, $(u, v) \notin E$, which implies that at least one of u or v does not belong to V', since every pair of vertices in V' is connected by an edge of E. Equivalently, at least one of u or v is in $V - V'$, which means that edge (u, v) is covered by $V - V'$. Since (u, v) was chosen arbitrarily from $\overline{E}$, every edge of $\overline{E}$ is covered by a vertex in $V - V'$. Hence, the set $V - V'$, which has size $|V| - k$, forms a vertex cover for $\overline{G}$.

Conversely, suppose that $\overline{G}$ has a vertex cover $V' \subseteq V$, where $|V'| = |V| - k$. Then, for all $u, v \in V$, if $(u, v) \in \overline{E}$, then $u \in V'$ or $v \in V'$ or both. The contrapositive of this implication is that for all $u, v \in V$, if $u \notin V'$ and $v \notin V'$, then $(u, v) \in E$. In other words, $V - V'$ is a clique, and it has size $|V| - |V'| = k$. ∎

Since VERTEX-COVER is NP-complete, we don't expect to find a polynomial-time algorithm for finding a minimum-size vertex cover. Section 35.1 presents a polynomial-time "approximation algorithm," however, which produces "approximate" solutions for the vertex-cover problem. The size of a vertex cover produced by the algorithm is at most twice the minimum size of a vertex cover.

Thus, we shouldn't give up hope just because a problem is NP-complete. We may be able to design a polynomial-time approximation algorithm that obtains near-optimal solutions, even though finding an optimal solution is NP-complete. Chapter 35 gives several approximation algorithms for NP-complete problems.

34.5.3 The hamiltonian-cycle problem

We now return to the hamiltonian-cycle problem defined in Section 34.2.

Theorem 34.13
The hamiltonian cycle problem is NP-complete.

Proof We first show that HAM-CYCLE belongs to NP. Given a graph $G = (V, E)$, our certificate is the sequence of $|V|$ vertices that makes up the hamiltonian cycle. The verification algorithm checks that this sequence contains each vertex in V exactly once and that with the first vertex repeated at the end, it forms a cycle in G. That is, it checks that there is an edge between each pair of consecutive vertices and between the first and last vertices. We can verify the certificate in polynomial time.

We now prove that VERTEX-COVER $\leq_P$ HAM-CYCLE, which shows that HAM-CYCLE is NP-complete. Given an undirected graph $G = (V, E)$ and an

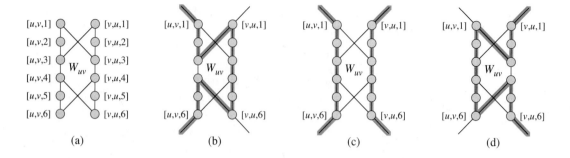

Figure 34.16   The widget used in reducing the vertex-cover problem to the hamiltonian-cycle problem. An edge (u, v) of graph G corresponds to widget W_{uv} in the graph G' created in the reduction. **(a)** The widget, with individual vertices labeled. **(b)–(d)** The shaded paths are the only possible ones through the widget that include all vertices, assuming that the only connections from the widget to the remainder of G' are through vertices $[u, v, 1]$, $[u, v, 6]$, $[v, u, 1]$, and $[v, u, 6]$.

integer k, we construct an undirected graph $G' = (V', E')$ that has a hamiltonian cycle if and only if G has a vertex cover of size k.

Our construction uses a ***widget***, which is a piece of a graph that enforces certain properties. Figure 34.16(a) shows the widget we use. For each edge $(u, v) \in E$, the graph G' that we construct will contain one copy of this widget, which we denote by W_{uv}. We denote each vertex in W_{uv} by $[u, v, i]$ or $[v, u, i]$, where $1 \leq i \leq 6$, so that each widget W_{uv} contains 12 vertices. Widget W_{uv} also contains the 14 edges shown in Figure 34.16(a).

Along with the internal structure of the widget, we enforce the properties we want by limiting the connections between the widget and the remainder of the graph G' that we construct. In particular, only vertices $[u, v, 1]$, $[u, v, 6]$, $[v, u, 1]$, and $[v, u, 6]$ will have edges incident from outside W_{uv}. Any hamiltonian cycle of G' must traverse the edges of W_{uv} in one of the three ways shown in Figures 34.16(b)–(d). If the cycle enters through vertex $[u, v, 1]$, it must exit through vertex $[u, v, 6]$, and it either visits all 12 of the widget's vertices (Figure 34.16(b)) or the six vertices $[u, v, 1]$ through $[u, v, 6]$ (Figure 34.16(c)). In the latter case, the cycle will have to reenter the widget to visit vertices $[v, u, 1]$ through $[v, u, 6]$. Similarly, if the cycle enters through vertex $[v, u, 1]$, it must exit through vertex $[v, u, 6]$, and it either visits all 12 of the widget's vertices (Figure 34.16(d)) or the six vertices $[v, u, 1]$ through $[v, u, 6]$ (Figure 34.16(c)). No other paths through the widget that visit all 12 vertices are possible. In particular, it is impossible to construct two vertex-disjoint paths, one of which connects $[u, v, 1]$ to $[v, u, 6]$ and the other of which connects $[v, u, 1]$ to $[u, v, 6]$, such that the union of the two paths contains all of the widget's vertices.

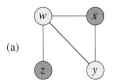

(a)

(b)

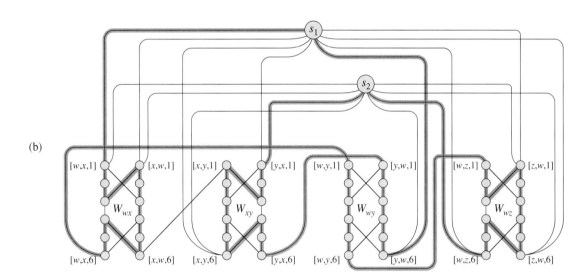

Figure 34.17   Reducing an instance of the vertex-cover problem to an instance of the hamiltonian-cycle problem. **(a)** An undirected graph G with a vertex cover of size 2, consisting of the lightly shaded vertices w and y. **(b)** The undirected graph G' produced by the reduction, with the hamiltonian cycle corresponding to the vertex cover shaded. The vertex cover $\{w, y\}$ corresponds to edges $(s_1, [w, x, 1])$ and $(s_2, [y, x, 1])$ appearing in the hamiltonian cycle.

The only other vertices in V' other than those of widgets are ***selector vertices*** $s_1, s_2, \ldots, s_k$. We use edges incident on selector vertices in G' to select the k vertices of the cover in G.

In addition to the edges in widgets, E' contains two other types of edges, which Figure 34.17 shows. First, for each vertex $u \in V$, we add edges to join pairs of widgets in order to form a path containing all widgets corresponding to edges incident on u in G. We arbitrarily order the vertices adjacent to each vertex $u \in V$ as $u^{(1)}, u^{(2)}, \ldots, u^{(\mathrm{degree}(u))}$, where $\mathrm{degree}(u)$ is the number of vertices adjacent to u. We create a path in G' through all the widgets corresponding to edges incident on u by adding to E' the edges $\{([u, u^{(i)}, 6], [u, u^{(i+1)}, 1]) : 1 \leq i \leq \mathrm{degree}(u) - 1\}$. In Figure 34.17, for example, we order the vertices adjacent to w as x, y, z, and so graph G' in part (b) of the figure includes the edges

$([w, x, 6], [w, y, 1])$ and $([w, y, 6], [w, z, 1])$. For each vertex $u \in V$, these edges in G' fill in a path containing all widgets corresponding to edges incident on u in G.

The intuition behind these edges is that if we choose a vertex $u \in V$ in the vertex cover of G, we can construct a path from $[u, u^{(1)}, 1]$ to $[u, u^{(\text{degree}(u))}, 6]$ in G' that "covers" all widgets corresponding to edges incident on u. That is, for each of these widgets, say $W_{u,u^{(i)}}$, the path either includes all 12 vertices (if u is in the vertex cover but $u^{(i)}$ is not) or just the six vertices $[u, u^{(i)}, 1], [u, u^{(i)}, 2], \ldots, [u, u^{(i)}, 6]$ (if both u and $u^{(i)}$ are in the vertex cover).

The final type of edge in E' joins the first vertex $[u, u^{(1)}, 1]$ and the last vertex $[u, u^{(\text{degree}(u))}, 6]$ of each of these paths to each of the selector vertices. That is, we include the edges

$$\{(s_j, [u, u^{(1)}, 1]) : u \in V \text{ and } 1 \leq j \leq k\}$$
$$\cup \{(s_j, [u, u^{(\text{degree}(u))}, 6]) : u \in V \text{ and } 1 \leq j \leq k\}.$$

Next, we show that the size of G' is polynomial in the size of G, and hence we can construct G' in time polynomial in the size of G. The vertices of G' are those in the widgets, plus the selector vertices. With 12 vertices per widget, plus $k \leq |V|$ selector vertices, we have a total of

$$
\begin{aligned}
|V'| &= 12 |E| + k \\
&\leq 12 |E| + |V|
\end{aligned}
$$

vertices. The edges of G' are those in the widgets, those that go between widgets, and those connecting selector vertices to widgets. Each widget contains 14 edges, totaling $14 |E|$ in all widgets. For each vertex $u \in V$, graph G' has $\text{degree}(u) - 1$ edges going between widgets, so that summed over all vertices in V,

$$\sum_{u \in V} (\text{degree}(u) - 1) = 2 |E| - |V|$$

edges go between widgets. Finally, G' has two edges for each pair consisting of a selector vertex and a vertex of V, totaling $2k |V|$ such edges. The total number of edges of G' is therefore

$$
\begin{aligned}
|E'| &= (14 |E|) + (2 |E| - |V|) + (2k |V|) \\
&= 16 |E| + (2k - 1) |V| \\
&\leq 16 |E| + (2 |V| - 1) |V| .
\end{aligned}
$$

Now we show that the transformation from graph G to G' is a reduction. That is, we must show that G has a vertex cover of size k if and only if G' has a hamiltonian cycle.

Suppose that $G = (V, E)$ has a vertex cover $V^* \subseteq V$ of size k. Let $V^* = \{u_1, u_2, \ldots, u_k\}$. As Figure 34.17 shows, we form a hamiltonian cycle in G' by including the following edges[10] for each vertex $u_j \in V^*$. Include edges $\{([u_j, u_j^{(i)}, 6], [u_j, u_j^{(i+1)}, 1]) : 1 \le i \le \mathrm{degree}(u_j) - 1\}$, which connect all widgets corresponding to edges incident on u_j. We also include the edges within these widgets as Figures 34.16(b)–(d) show, depending on whether the edge is covered by one or two vertices in V^*. The hamiltonian cycle also includes the edges

$$\{(s_j, [u_j, u_j^{(1)}, 1]) : 1 \le j \le k\}$$
$$\cup \{(s_{j+1}, [u_j, u_j^{(\mathrm{degree}(u_j))}, 6]) : 1 \le j \le k - 1\}$$
$$\cup \{(s_1, [u_k, u_k^{(\mathrm{degree}(u_k))}, 6])\} \,.$$

By inspecting Figure 34.17, you can verify that these edges form a cycle. The cycle starts at s_1, visits all widgets corresponding to edges incident on u_1, then visits s_2, visits all widgets corresponding to edges incident on u_2, and so on, until it returns to s_1. The cycle visits each widget either once or twice, depending on whether one or two vertices of V^* cover its corresponding edge. Because V^* is a vertex cover for G, each edge in E is incident on some vertex in V^*, and so the cycle visits each vertex in each widget of G'. Because the cycle also visits every selector vertex, it is hamiltonian.

Conversely, suppose that $G' = (V', E')$ has a hamiltonian cycle $C \subseteq E'$. We claim that the set

$$V^* = \{u \in V : (s_j, [u, u^{(1)}, 1]) \in C \text{ for some } 1 \le j \le k\} \tag{34.4}$$

is a vertex cover for G. To see why, partition C into maximal paths that start at some selector vertex s_i, traverse an edge $(s_i, [u, u^{(1)}, 1])$ for some $u \in V$, and end at a selector vertex s_j without passing through any other selector vertex. Let us call each such path a "cover path." From how G' is constructed, each cover path must start at some s_i, take the edge $(s_i, [u, u^{(1)}, 1])$ for some vertex $u \in V$, pass through all the widgets corresponding to edges in E incident on u, and then end at some selector vertex s_j. We refer to this cover path as p_u, and by equation (34.4), we put u into V^*. Each widget visited by p_u must be W_{uv} or W_{vu} for some $v \in V$. For each widget visited by p_u, its vertices are visited by either one or two cover paths. If they are visited by one cover path, then edge $(u, v) \in E$ is covered in G by vertex u. If two cover paths visit the widget, then the other cover path must be p_v, which implies that $v \in V^*$, and edge $(u, v) \in E$ is covered by both u and v.

---

[10]Technically, we define a cycle in terms of vertices rather than edges (see Section B.4). In the interest of clarity, we abuse notation here and define the hamiltonian cycle in terms of edges.

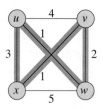

Figure 34.18   An instance of the traveling-salesman problem. Shaded edges represent a minimum-cost tour, with cost 7.

Because each vertex in each widget is visited by some cover path, we see that each edge in E is covered by some vertex in V^*.   ∎

34.5.4   The traveling-salesman problem

In the ***traveling-salesman problem***, which is closely related to the hamiltonian-cycle problem, a salesman must visit n cities. Modeling the problem as a complete graph with n vertices, we can say that the salesman wishes to make a ***tour***, or hamiltonian cycle, visiting each city exactly once and finishing at the city he starts from. The salesman incurs a nonnegative integer cost $c(i, j)$ to travel from city i to city j, and the salesman wishes to make the tour whose total cost is minimum, where the total cost is the sum of the individual costs along the edges of the tour. For example, in Figure 34.18, a minimum-cost tour is $\langle u, w, v, x, u \rangle$, with cost 7. The formal language for the corresponding decision problem is

$$\text{TSP} = \{\langle G, c, k \rangle : G = (V, E) \text{ is a complete graph,}$$
$$c \text{ is a function from } V \times V \to \mathbb{N},$$
$$k \in \mathbb{N}, \text{ and}$$
$$G \text{ has a traveling-salesman tour with cost at most } k\} .$$

The following theorem shows that a fast algorithm for the traveling-salesman problem is unlikely to exist.

Theorem 34.14
The traveling-salesman problem is NP-complete.

Proof   We first show that TSP belongs to NP. Given an instance of the problem, we use as a certificate the sequence of n vertices in the tour. The verification algorithm checks that this sequence contains each vertex exactly once, sums up the edge costs, and checks whether the sum is at most k. This process can certainly be done in polynomial time.

To prove that TSP is NP-hard, we show that HAM-CYCLE $\leq_P$ TSP. Let $G = (V, E)$ be an instance of HAM-CYCLE. We construct an instance of TSP as follows. We form the complete graph $G' = (V, E')$, where $E' = \{(i, j) : i, j \in V$ and $i \neq j\}$, and we define the cost function c by

$$c(i, j) = \begin{cases} 0 & \text{if } (i, j) \in E, \\ 1 & \text{if } (i, j) \notin E. \end{cases}$$

(Note that because G is undirected, it has no self-loops, and so $c(v, v) = 1$ for all vertices $v \in V$.) The instance of TSP is then $\langle G', c, 0 \rangle$, which we can easily create in polynomial time.

We now show that graph G has a hamiltonian cycle if and only if graph G' has a tour of cost at most 0. Suppose that graph G has a hamiltonian cycle h. Each edge in h belongs to E and thus has cost 0 in G'. Thus, h is a tour in G' with cost 0. Conversely, suppose that graph G' has a tour h' of cost at most 0. Since the costs of the edges in E' are 0 and 1, the cost of tour h' is exactly 0 and each edge on the tour must have cost 0. Therefore, h' contains only edges in E. We conclude that h' is a hamiltonian cycle in graph G. ∎

34.5.5 The subset-sum problem

We next consider an arithmetic NP-complete problem. In the *subset-sum problem*, we are given a finite set S of positive integers and an integer *target* $t > 0$. We ask whether there exists a subset $S' \subseteq S$ whose elements sum to t. For example, if $S = \{1, 2, 7, 14, 49, 98, 343, 686, 2409, 2793, 16808, 17206, 117705, 117993\}$ and $t = 138457$, then the subset $S' = \{1, 2, 7, 98, 343, 686, 2409, 17206, 117705\}$ is a solution.

As usual, we define the problem as a language:

SUBSET-SUM $= \{\langle S, t \rangle : $ there exists a subset $S' \subseteq S$ such that $t = \sum_{s \in S'} s\}$.

As with any arithmetic problem, it is important to recall that our standard encoding assumes that the input integers are coded in binary. With this assumption in mind, we can show that the subset-sum problem is unlikely to have a fast algorithm.

Theorem 34.15
The subset-sum problem is NP-complete.

Proof To show that SUBSET-SUM is in NP, for an instance $\langle S, t \rangle$ of the problem, we let the subset S' be the certificate. A verification algorithm can check whether $t = \sum_{s \in S'} s$ in polynomial time.

We now show that 3-CNF-SAT $\leq_P$ SUBSET-SUM. Given a 3-CNF formula ϕ over variables $x_1, x_2, \ldots, x_n$ with clauses $C_1, C_2, \ldots, C_k$, each containing exactly three distinct literals, the reduction algorithm constructs an instance $\langle S, t \rangle$ of the subset-sum problem such that ϕ is satisfiable if and only if there exists a subset of S whose sum is exactly t. Without loss of generality, we make two simplifying assumptions about the formula ϕ. First, no clause contains both a variable and its negation, for such a clause is automatically satisfied by any assignment of values to the variables. Second, each variable appears in at least one clause, because it does not matter what value is assigned to a variable that appears in no clauses.

The reduction creates two numbers in set S for each variable x_i and two numbers in S for each clause C_j. We shall create numbers in base 10, where each number contains $n+k$ digits and each digit corresponds to either one variable or one clause. Base 10 (and other bases, as we shall see) has the property we need of preventing carries from lower digits to higher digits.

As Figure 34.19 shows, we construct set S and target t as follows. We label each digit position by either a variable or a clause. The least significant k digits are labeled by the clauses, and the most significant n digits are labeled by variables.

- The target t has a 1 in each digit labeled by a variable and a 4 in each digit labeled by a clause.

- For each variable x_i, set S contains two integers v_i and v_i'. Each of v_i and v_i' has a 1 in the digit labeled by x_i and 0s in the other variable digits. If literal x_i appears in clause C_j, then the digit labeled by C_j in v_i contains a 1. If literal $\neg x_i$ appears in clause C_j, then the digit labeled by C_j in v_i' contains a 1. All other digits labeled by clauses in v_i and v_i' are 0.

  All v_i and v_i' values in set S are unique. Why? For $l \neq i$, no v_l or v_l' values can equal v_i and v_i' in the most significant n digits. Furthermore, by our simplifying assumptions above, no v_i and v_i' can be equal in all k least significant digits. If v_i and v_i' were equal, then x_i and $\neg x_i$ would have to appear in exactly the same set of clauses. But we assume that no clause contains both x_i and $\neg x_i$ and that either x_i or $\neg x_i$ appears in some clause, and so there must be some clause C_j for which v_i and v_i' differ.

- For each clause C_j, set S contains two integers s_j and s_j'. Each of s_j and s_j' has 0s in all digits other than the one labeled by C_j. For s_j, there is a 1 in the C_j digit, and s_j' has a 2 in this digit. These integers are "slack variables," which we use to get each clause-labeled digit position to add to the target value of 4.

  Simple inspection of Figure 34.19 demonstrates that all s_j and s_j' values in S are unique in set S.

Note that the greatest sum of digits in any one digit position is 6, which occurs in the digits labeled by clauses (three 1s from the v_i and v_i' values, plus 1 and 2 from

		x_1	x_2	x_3	C_1	C_2	C_3	C_4
v_1	=	1	0	0	1	0	0	1
v_1'	=	1	0	0	0	1	1	0
v_2	=	0	1	0	0	0	0	1
v_2'	=	0	1	0	1	1	1	0
v_3	=	0	0	1	0	0	1	1
v_3'	=	0	0	1	1	1	0	0
s_1	=	0	0	0	1	0	0	0
s_1'	=	0	0	0	2	0	0	0
s_2	=	0	0	0	0	1	0	0
s_2'	=	0	0	0	0	2	0	0
s_3	=	0	0	0	0	0	1	0
s_3'	=	0	0	0	0	0	2	0
s_4	=	0	0	0	0	0	0	1
s_4'	=	0	0	0	0	0	0	2
t	=	1	1	1	4	4	4	4

Figure 34.19 The reduction of 3-CNF-SAT to SUBSET-SUM. The formula in 3-CNF is $\phi = C_1 \wedge C_2 \wedge C_3 \wedge C_4$, where $C_1 = (x_1 \vee \neg x_2 \vee \neg x_3)$, $C_2 = (\neg x_1 \vee \neg x_2 \vee \neg x_3)$, $C_3 = (\neg x_1 \vee \neg x_2 \vee x_3)$, and $C_4 = (x_1 \vee x_2 \vee x_3)$. A satisfying assignment of ϕ is $\langle x_1 = 0, x_2 = 0, x_3 = 1 \rangle$. The set S produced by the reduction consists of the base-10 numbers shown; reading from top to bottom, $S = \{1001001, 1000110, 100001, 101110, 10011, 11100, 1000, 2000, 100, 200, 10, 20, 1, 2\}$. The target t is 1114444. The subset $S' \subseteq S$ is lightly shaded, and it contains v_1', v_2', and v_3, corresponding to the satisfying assignment. It also contains slack variables s_1, s_1', s_2', s_3, s_4, and s_4' to achieve the target value of 4 in the digits labeled by C_1 through C_4.

the s_j and s_j' values). Interpreting these numbers in base 10, therefore, no carries can occur from lower digits to higher digits.[11]

We can perform the reduction in polynomial time. The set S contains $2n + 2k$ values, each of which has $n + k$ digits, and the time to produce each digit is polynomial in $n + k$. The target t has $n + k$ digits, and the reduction produces each in constant time.

We now show that the 3-CNF formula ϕ is satisfiable if and only if there exists a subset $S' \subseteq S$ whose sum is t. First, suppose that ϕ has a satisfying assignment. For $i = 1, 2, \ldots, n$, if $x_i = 1$ in this assignment, then include v_i in S'. Otherwise, include v_i'. In other words, we include in S' exactly the v_i and v_i' values that cor-

---

[11] In fact, any base b, where $b \geq 7$, would work. The instance at the beginning of this subsection is the set S and target t in Figure 34.19 interpreted in base 7, with S listed in sorted order.

respond to literals with the value 1 in the satisfying assignment. Having included either v_i or v_i', but not both, for all i, and having put 0 in the digits labeled by variables in all s_j and s_j', we see that for each variable-labeled digit, the sum of the values of S' must be 1, which matches those digits of the target t. Because each clause is satisfied, the clause contains some literal with the value 1. Therefore, each digit labeled by a clause has at least one 1 contributed to its sum by a v_i or v_i' value in S'. In fact, 1, 2, or 3 literals may be 1 in each clause, and so each clause-labeled digit has a sum of 1, 2, or 3 from the v_i and v_i' values in S'. In Figure 34.19 for example, literals $\neg x_1$, $\neg x_2$, and x_3 have the value 1 in a satisfying assignment. Each of clauses C_1 and C_4 contains exactly one of these literals, and so together v_1', v_2', and v_3 contribute 1 to the sum in the digits for C_1 and C_4. Clause C_2 contains two of these literals, and v_1', v_2', and v_3 contribute 2 to the sum in the digit for C_2. Clause C_3 contains all three of these literals, and v_1', v_2', and v_3 contribute 3 to the sum in the digit for C_3. We achieve the target of 4 in each digit labeled by clause C_j by including in S' the appropriate nonempty subset of slack variables $\{s_j, s_j'\}$. In Figure 34.19, S' includes s_1, s_1', s_2', s_3, s_4, and s_4'. Since we have matched the target in all digits of the sum, and no carries can occur, the values of S' sum to t.

Now, suppose that there is a subset $S' \subseteq S$ that sums to t. The subset S' must include exactly one of v_i and v_i' for each $i = 1, 2, \ldots, n$, for otherwise the digits labeled by variables would not sum to 1. If $v_i \in S'$, we set $x_i = 1$. Otherwise, $v_i' \in S'$, and we set $x_i = 0$. We claim that every clause C_j, for $j = 1, 2, \ldots, k$, is satisfied by this assignment. To prove this claim, note that to achieve a sum of 4 in the digit labeled by C_j, the subset S' must include at least one v_i or v_i' value that has a 1 in the digit labeled by C_j, since the contributions of the slack variables s_j and s_j' together sum to at most 3. If S' includes a v_i that has a 1 in C_j's position, then the literal x_i appears in clause C_j. Since we have set $x_i = 1$ when $v_i \in S'$, clause C_j is satisfied. If S' includes a v_i' that has a 1 in that position, then the literal $\neg x_i$ appears in C_j. Since we have set $x_i = 0$ when $v_i' \in S'$, clause C_j is again satisfied. Thus, all clauses of ϕ are satisfied, which completes the proof. ∎

Exercises

34.5-1
The **subgraph-isomorphism problem** takes two undirected graphs G_1 and G_2, and it asks whether G_1 is isomorphic to a subgraph of G_2. Show that the subgraph-isomorphism problem is NP-complete.

34.5-2
Given an integer $m \times n$ matrix A and an integer m-vector b, the **0-1 integer-programming problem** asks whether there exists an integer n-vector x with ele-

ments in the set $\{0, 1\}$ such that $Ax \le b$. Prove that 0-1 integer programming is NP-complete. (*Hint:* Reduce from 3-CNF-SAT.)

34.5-3

The *integer linear-programming problem* is like the 0-1 integer-programming problem given in Exercise 34.5-2, except that the values of the vector x may be any integers rather than just 0 or 1. Assuming that the 0-1 integer-programming problem is NP-hard, show that the integer linear-programming problem is NP-complete.

34.5-4

Show how to solve the subset-sum problem in polynomial time if the target value t is expressed in unary.

34.5-5

The *set-partition problem* takes as input a set S of numbers. The question is whether the numbers can be partitioned into two sets A and $\overline{A} = S - A$ such that $\sum_{x \in A} x = \sum_{x \in \overline{A}} x$. Show that the set-partition problem is NP-complete.

34.5-6

Show that the hamiltonian-path problem is NP-complete.

34.5-7

The *longest-simple-cycle problem* is the problem of determining a simple cycle (no repeated vertices) of maximum length in a graph. Formulate a related decision problem, and show that the decision problem is NP-complete.

34.5-8

In the *half 3-CNF satisfiability* problem, we are given a 3-CNF formula ϕ with n variables and m clauses, where m is even. We wish to determine whether there exists a truth assignment to the variables of ϕ such that exactly half the clauses evaluate to 0 and exactly half the clauses evaluate to 1. Prove that the half 3-CNF satisfiability problem is NP-complete.

Problems

34-1 *Independent set*

An *independent set* of a graph $G = (V, E)$ is a subset $V' \subseteq V$ of vertices such that each edge in E is incident on at most one vertex in V'. The *independent-set problem* is to find a maximum-size independent set in G.

a. Formulate a related decision problem for the independent-set problem, and prove that it is NP-complete. (*Hint:* Reduce from the clique problem.)

b. Suppose that you are given a "black-box" subroutine to solve the decision problem you defined in part (a). Give an algorithm to find an independent set of maximum size. The running time of your algorithm should be polynomial in $|V|$ and $|E|$, counting queries to the black box as a single step.

Although the independent-set decision problem is NP-complete, certain special cases are polynomial-time solvable.

c. Give an efficient algorithm to solve the independent-set problem when each vertex in G has degree 2. Analyze the running time, and prove that your algorithm works correctly.

d. Give an efficient algorithm to solve the independent-set problem when G is bipartite. Analyze the running time, and prove that your algorithm works correctly. (*Hint:* Use the results of Section 26.3.)

34-2   *Bonnie and Clyde*

Bonnie and Clyde have just robbed a bank. They have a bag of money and want to divide it up. For each of the following scenarios, either give a polynomial-time algorithm, or prove that the problem is NP-complete. The input in each case is a list of the n items in the bag, along with the value of each.

a. The bag contains n coins, but only 2 different denominations: some coins are worth x dollars, and some are worth y dollars. Bonnie and Clyde wish to divide the money exactly evenly.

b. The bag contains n coins, with an arbitrary number of different denominations, but each denomination is a nonnegative integer power of 2, i.e., the possible denominations are 1 dollar, 2 dollars, 4 dollars, etc. Bonnie and Clyde wish to divide the money exactly evenly.

c. The bag contains n checks, which are, in an amazing coincidence, made out to "Bonnie or Clyde." They wish to divide the checks so that they each get the exact same amount of money.

d. The bag contains n checks as in part (c), but this time Bonnie and Clyde are willing to accept a split in which the difference is no larger than 100 dollars.

34-3   *Graph coloring*

Mapmakers try to use as few colors as possible when coloring countries on a map, as long as no two countries that share a border have the same color. We can model this problem with an undirected graph $G = (V, E)$ in which each vertex represents a country and vertices whose respective countries share a border are adjacent. Then, a **k-coloring** is a function $c : V \rightarrow \{1, 2, \ldots, k\}$ such that $c(u) \neq c(v)$ for every edge $(u, v) \in E$. In other words, the numbers $1, 2, \ldots, k$ represent the k colors, and adjacent vertices must have different colors. The **graph-coloring problem** is to determine the minimum number of colors needed to color a given graph.

a. Give an efficient algorithm to determine a 2-coloring of a graph, if one exists.

b. Cast the graph-coloring problem as a decision problem. Show that your decision problem is solvable in polynomial time if and only if the graph-coloring problem is solvable in polynomial time.

c. Let the language 3-COLOR be the set of graphs that can be 3-colored. Show that if 3-COLOR is NP-complete, then your decision problem from part (b) is NP-complete.

To prove that 3-COLOR is NP-complete, we use a reduction from 3-CNF-SAT. Given a formula ϕ of m clauses on n variables $x_1, x_2, \ldots, x_n$, we construct a graph $G = (V, E)$ as follows. The set V consists of a vertex for each variable, a vertex for the negation of each variable, 5 vertices for each clause, and 3 special vertices: TRUE, FALSE, and RED. The edges of the graph are of two types: "literal" edges that are independent of the clauses and "clause" edges that depend on the clauses. The literal edges form a triangle on the special vertices and also form a triangle on x_i, $\neg x_i$, and RED for $i = 1, 2, \ldots, n$.

d. Argue that in any 3-coloring c of a graph containing the literal edges, exactly one of a variable and its negation is colored $c(\text{TRUE})$ and the other is colored $c(\text{FALSE})$. Argue that for any truth assignment for ϕ, there exists a 3-coloring of the graph containing just the literal edges.

The widget shown in Figure 34.20 helps to enforce the condition corresponding to a clause $(x \lor y \lor z)$. Each clause requires a unique copy of the 5 vertices that are heavily shaded in the figure; they connect as shown to the literals of the clause and the special vertex TRUE.

e. Argue that if each of x, y, and z is colored $c(\text{TRUE})$ or $c(\text{FALSE})$, then the widget is 3-colorable if and only if at least one of x, y, or z is colored $c(\text{TRUE})$.

f. Complete the proof that 3-COLOR is NP-complete.

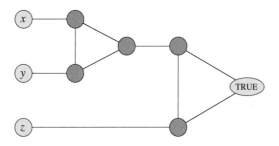

Figure 34.20 The widget corresponding to a clause $(x \lor y \lor z)$, used in Problem 34-3.

34-4 Scheduling with profits and deadlines

Suppose that we have one machine and a set of n tasks $a_1, a_2, \ldots, a_n$, each of which requires time on the machine. Each task a_j requires t_j time units on the machine (its processing time), yields a profit of p_j, and has a deadline d_j. The machine can process only one task at a time, and task a_j must run without interruption for t_j consecutive time units. If we complete task a_j by its deadline d_j, we receive a profit p_j, but if we complete it after its deadline, we receive no profit. As an optimization problem, we are given the processing times, profits, and deadlines for a set of n tasks, and we wish to find a schedule that completes all the tasks and returns the greatest amount of profit. The processing times, profits, and deadlines are all nonnegative numbers.

a. State this problem as a decision problem.

b. Show that the decision problem is NP-complete.

c. Give a polynomial-time algorithm for the decision problem, assuming that all processing times are integers from 1 to n. (*Hint:* Use dynamic programming.)

d. Give a polynomial-time algorithm for the optimization problem, assuming that all processing times are integers from 1 to n.

Chapter notes

The book by Garey and Johnson [129] provides a wonderful guide to NP-completeness, discussing the theory at length and providing a catalogue of many problems that were known to be NP-complete in 1979. The proof of Theorem 34.13 is adapted from their book, and the list of NP-complete problem domains at the beginning of Section 34.5 is drawn from their table of contents. Johnson wrote a series of 23 columns in the *Journal of Algorithms* between 1981 and 1992 reporting new developments in NP-completeness. Hopcroft, Motwani, and Ullman [177], Lewis and Papadimitriou [236], Papadimitriou [270], and Sipser [317] have good treatments of NP-completeness in the context of complexity theory. NP-completeness and several reductions also appear in books by Aho, Hopcroft, and Ullman [5]; Dasgupta, Papadimitriou, and Vazirani [82]; Johnsonbaugh and Schaefer [193]; and Kleinberg and Tardos [208].

The class P was introduced in 1964 by Cobham [72] and, independently, in 1965 by Edmonds [100], who also introduced the class NP and conjectured that $P \neq NP$. The notion of NP-completeness was proposed in 1971 by Cook [75], who gave the first NP-completeness proofs for formula satisfiability and 3-CNF satisfiability. Levin [234] independently discovered the notion, giving an NP-completeness proof for a tiling problem. Karp [199] introduced the methodology of reductions in 1972 and demonstrated the rich variety of NP-complete problems. Karp's paper included the original NP-completeness proofs of the clique, vertex-cover, and hamiltonian-cycle problems. Since then, thousands of problems have been proven to be NP-complete by many researchers. In a talk at a meeting celebrating Karp's 60th birthday in 1995, Papadimitriou remarked, "about 6000 papers each year have the term 'NP-complete' on their title, abstract, or list of keywords. This is more than each of the terms 'compiler,' 'database,' 'expert,' 'neural network,' or 'operating system.' "

Recent work in complexity theory has shed light on the complexity of computing approximate solutions. This work gives a new definition of NP using "probabilistically checkable proofs." This new definition implies that for problems such as clique, vertex cover, the traveling-salesman problem with the triangle inequality, and many others, computing good approximate solutions is NP-hard and hence no easier than computing optimal solutions. An introduction to this area can be found in Arora's thesis [20]; a chapter by Arora and Lund in Hochbaum [172]; a survey article by Arora [21]; a book edited by Mayr, Prömel, and Steger [246]; and a survey article by Johnson [191].

35 Approximation Algorithms

Many problems of practical significance are NP-complete, yet they are too important to abandon merely because we don't know how to find an optimal solution in polynomial time. Even if a problem is NP-complete, there may be hope. We have at least three ways to get around NP-completeness. First, if the actual inputs are small, an algorithm with exponential running time may be perfectly satisfactory. Second, we may be able to isolate important special cases that we can solve in polynomial time. Third, we might come up with approaches to find *near-optimal* solutions in polynomial time (either in the worst case or the expected case). In practice, near-optimality is often good enough. We call an algorithm that returns near-optimal solutions an ***approximation algorithm***. This chapter presents polynomial-time approximation algorithms for several NP-complete problems.

Performance ratios for approximation algorithms

Suppose that we are working on an optimization problem in which each potential solution has a positive cost, and we wish to find a near-optimal solution. Depending on the problem, we may define an optimal solution as one with maximum possible cost or one with minimum possible cost; that is, the problem may be either a maximization or a minimization problem.

We say that an algorithm for a problem has an ***approximation ratio*** of $\rho(n)$ if, for any input of size n, the cost C of the solution produced by the algorithm is within a factor of $\rho(n)$ of the cost C^* of an optimal solution:

$$\max \left(\frac{C}{C^*}, \frac{C^*}{C} \right) \leq \rho(n) . \tag{35.1}$$

If an algorithm achieves an approximation ratio of $\rho(n)$, we call it a ***$\rho(n)$-approximation algorithm***. The definitions of the approximation ratio and of a $\rho(n)$-approximation algorithm apply to both minimization and maximization problems. For a maximization problem, $0 < C \leq C^*$, and the ratio C^*/C gives the factor by which the cost of an optimal solution is larger than the cost of the approximate solution. Similarly, for a minimization problem, $0 < C^* \leq C$, and the ratio C/C^* gives the factor by which the cost of the approximate solution is larger than the cost of an optimal solution. Because we assume that all solutions have positive cost, these ratios are always well defined. The approximation ratio of an approximation algorithm is never less than 1, since $C/C^* \leq 1$ implies $C^*/C \geq 1$. Therefore, a 1-approximation algorithm[1] produces an optimal solution, and an approximation algorithm with a large approximation ratio may return a solution that is much worse than optimal.

For many problems, we have polynomial-time approximation algorithms with small constant approximation ratios, although for other problems, the best known polynomial-time approximation algorithms have approximation ratios that grow as functions of the input size n. An example of such a problem is the set-cover problem presented in Section 35.3.

Some NP-complete problems allow polynomial-time approximation algorithms that can achieve increasingly better approximation ratios by using more and more computation time. That is, we can trade computation time for the quality of the approximation. An example is the subset-sum problem studied in Section 35.5. This situation is important enough to deserve a name of its own.

An ***approximation scheme*** for an optimization problem is an approximation algorithm that takes as input not only an instance of the problem, but also a value $\epsilon > 0$ such that for any fixed ϵ, the scheme is a $(1 + \epsilon)$-approximation algorithm. We say that an approximation scheme is a ***polynomial-time approximation scheme*** if for any fixed $\epsilon > 0$, the scheme runs in time polynomial in the size n of its input instance.

The running time of a polynomial-time approximation scheme can increase very rapidly as ϵ decreases. For example, the running time of a polynomial-time approximation scheme might be $O(n^{2/\epsilon})$. Ideally, if ϵ decreases by a constant factor, the running time to achieve the desired approximation should not increase by more than a constant factor (though not necessarily the same constant factor by which ϵ decreased).

We say that an approximation scheme is a ***fully polynomial-time approximation scheme*** if it is an approximation scheme and its running time is polynomial in both $1/\epsilon$ and the size n of the input instance. For example, the scheme might have a running time of $O((1/\epsilon)^2 n^3)$. With such a scheme, any constant-factor decrease in ϵ comes with a corresponding constant-factor increase in the running time.

---

[1] When the approximation ratio is independent of n, we use the terms "approximation ratio of ρ" and "ρ-approximation algorithm," indicating no dependence on n.

Chapter outline

The first four sections of this chapter present some examples of polynomial-time approximation algorithms for NP-complete problems, and the fifth section presents a fully polynomial-time approximation scheme. Section 35.1 begins with a study of the vertex-cover problem, an NP-complete minimization problem that has an approximation algorithm with an approximation ratio of 2. Section 35.2 presents an approximation algorithm with an approximation ratio of 2 for the case of the traveling-salesman problem in which the cost function satisfies the triangle inequality. It also shows that without the triangle inequality, for any constant $\rho \geq 1$, a ρ-approximation algorithm cannot exist unless P $=$ NP. In Section 35.3, we show how to use a greedy method as an effective approximation algorithm for the set-covering problem, obtaining a covering whose cost is at worst a logarithmic factor larger than the optimal cost. Section 35.4 presents two more approximation algorithms. First we study the optimization version of 3-CNF satisfiability and give a simple randomized algorithm that produces a solution with an expected approximation ratio of 8/7. Then we examine a weighted variant of the vertex-cover problem and show how to use linear programming to develop a 2-approximation algorithm. Finally, Section 35.5 presents a fully polynomial-time approximation scheme for the subset-sum problem.

35.1   The vertex-cover problem

Section 34.5.2 defined the vertex-cover problem and proved it NP-complete. Recall that a ***vertex cover*** of an undirected graph $G = (V, E)$ is a subset $V' \subseteq V$ such that if (u, v) is an edge of G, then either $u \in V'$ or $v \in V'$ (or both). The size of a vertex cover is the number of vertices in it.

The ***vertex-cover problem*** is to find a vertex cover of minimum size in a given undirected graph. We call such a vertex cover an ***optimal vertex cover***. This problem is the optimization version of an NP-complete decision problem.

Even though we don't know how to find an optimal vertex cover in a graph G in polynomial time, we can efficiently find a vertex cover that is near-optimal. The following approximation algorithm takes as input an undirected graph G and returns a vertex cover whose size is guaranteed to be no more than twice the size of an optimal vertex cover.

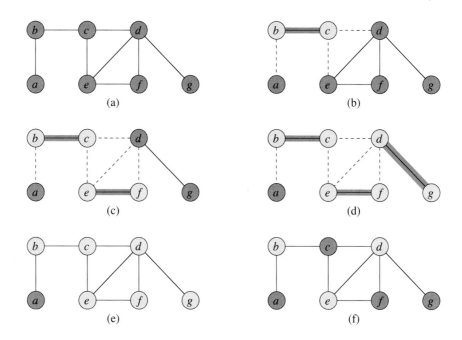

Figure 35.1   The operation of APPROX-VERTEX-COVER. **(a)** The input graph G, which has 7 vertices and 8 edges. **(b)** The edge (b, c), shown heavy, is the first edge chosen by APPROX-VERTEX-COVER. Vertices b and c, shown lightly shaded, are added to the set C containing the vertex cover being created. Edges (a, b), (c, e), and (c, d), shown dashed, are removed since they are now covered by some vertex in C. **(c)** Edge (e, f) is chosen; vertices e and f are added to C. **(d)** Edge (d, g) is chosen; vertices d and g are added to C. **(e)** The set C, which is the vertex cover produced by APPROX-VERTEX-COVER, contains the six vertices b, c, d, e, f, g. **(f)** The optimal vertex cover for this problem contains only three vertices: b, d, and e.

APPROX-VERTEX-COVER (G)

1   $C = \emptyset$
2   $E' = G.E$
3   **while** $E' \neq \emptyset$
4   let (u, v) be an arbitrary edge of E'
5        $C = C \cup \{u, v\}$
6   remove from E' every edge incident on either u or v
7   **return** C

Figure 35.1 illustrates how APPROX-VERTEX-COVER operates on an example graph. The variable C contains the vertex cover being constructed. Line 1 initializes C to the empty set. Line 2 sets E' to be a copy of the edge set $G.E$ of the graph. The loop of lines 3–6 repeatedly picks an edge (u, v) from E', adds its endpoints u and v to C, and deletes all edges in E' that are covered by either u or v. Finally, line 7 returns the vertex cover C. The running time of this algorithm is $O(V + E)$, using adjacency lists to represent E'.

Theorem 35.1
APPROX-VERTEX-COVER is a polynomial-time 2-approximation algorithm.

Proof   We have already shown that APPROX-VERTEX-COVER runs in polynomial time.

The set C of vertices that is returned by APPROX-VERTEX-COVER is a vertex cover, since the algorithm loops until every edge in $G.E$ has been covered by some vertex in C.

To see that APPROX-VERTEX-COVER returns a vertex cover that is at most twice the size of an optimal cover, let A denote the set of edges that line 4 of APPROX-VERTEX-COVER picked. In order to cover the edges in A, any vertex cover—in particular, an optimal cover C^*—must include at least one endpoint of each edge in A. No two edges in A share an endpoint, since once an edge is picked in line 4, all other edges that are incident on its endpoints are deleted from E' in line 6. Thus, no two edges in A are covered by the same vertex from C^*, and we have the lower bound

$$|C^*| \geq |A| \tag{35.2}$$

on the size of an optimal vertex cover. Each execution of line 4 picks an edge for which neither of its endpoints is already in C, yielding an upper bound (an exact upper bound, in fact) on the size of the vertex cover returned:

$$|C| = 2|A| \ . \tag{35.3}$$

Combining equations (35.2) and (35.3), we obtain

$$\begin{aligned} |C| &= 2|A| \\ &\leq 2|C^*| \ , \end{aligned}$$

thereby proving the theorem.   ∎

Let us reflect on this proof. At first, you might wonder how we can possibly prove that the size of the vertex cover returned by APPROX-VERTEX-COVER is at most twice the size of an optimal vertex cover, when we do not even know the size of an optimal vertex cover. Instead of requiring that we know the exact size of an optimal vertex cover, we rely on a lower bound on the size. As Exercise 35.1-2 asks you to show, the set A of edges that line 4 of APPROX-VERTEX-COVER selects is actually a maximal matching in the graph G. (A *maximal matching* is a matching that is not a proper subset of any other matching.) The size of a maximal matching is, as we argued in the proof of Theorem 35.1, a lower bound on the size of an optimal vertex cover. The algorithm returns a vertex cover whose size is at most twice the size of the maximal matching A. By relating the size of the solution returned to the lower bound, we obtain our approximation ratio. We will use this methodology in later sections as well.

Exercises

35.1-1
Give an example of a graph for which APPROX-VERTEX-COVER always yields a suboptimal solution.

35.1-2
Prove that the set of edges picked in line 4 of APPROX-VERTEX-COVER forms a maximal matching in the graph G.

35.1-3   ★
Professor Bündchen proposes the following heuristic to solve the vertex-cover problem. Repeatedly select a vertex of highest degree, and remove all of its incident edges. Give an example to show that the professor's heuristic does not have an approximation ratio of 2. (*Hint:* Try a bipartite graph with vertices of uniform degree on the left and vertices of varying degree on the right.)

35.1-4
Give an efficient greedy algorithm that finds an optimal vertex cover for a tree in linear time.

35.1-5
From the proof of Theorem 34.12, we know that the vertex-cover problem and the NP-complete clique problem are complementary in the sense that an optimal vertex cover is the complement of a maximum-size clique in the complement graph. Does this relationship imply that there is a polynomial-time approximation algorithm with a constant approximation ratio for the clique problem? Justify your answer.

35.2   The traveling-salesman problem

In the traveling-salesman problem introduced in Section 34.5.4, we are given a complete undirected graph $G = (V, E)$ that has a nonnegative integer cost $c(u, v)$ associated with each edge $(u, v) \in E$, and we must find a hamiltonian cycle (a tour) of G with minimum cost. As an extension of our notation, let $c(A)$ denote the total cost of the edges in the subset $A \subseteq E$:

$$c(A) = \sum_{(u,v) \in A} c(u,v) \,.$$

In many practical situations, the least costly way to go from a place u to a place w is to go directly, with no intermediate steps. Put another way, cutting out an intermediate stop never increases the cost. We formalize this notion by saying that the cost function c satisfies the ***triangle inequality*** if, for all vertices $u, v, w \in V$,

$$c(u, w) \le c(u, v) + c(v, w) \,.$$

The triangle inequality seems as though it should naturally hold, and it is automatically satisfied in several applications. For example, if the vertices of the graph are points in the plane and the cost of traveling between two vertices is the ordinary euclidean distance between them, then the triangle inequality is satisfied. Furthermore, many cost functions other than euclidean distance satisfy the triangle inequality.

As Exercise 35.2-2 shows, the traveling-salesman problem is NP-complete even if we require that the cost function satisfy the triangle inequality. Thus, we should not expect to find a polynomial-time algorithm for solving this problem exactly. Instead, we look for good approximation algorithms.

In Section 35.2.1, we examine a 2-approximation algorithm for the traveling-salesman problem with the triangle inequality. In Section 35.2.2, we show that without the triangle inequality, a polynomial-time approximation algorithm with a constant approximation ratio does not exist unless $P = NP$.

35.2.1   The traveling-salesman problem with the triangle inequality

Applying the methodology of the previous section, we shall first compute a structure—a minimum spanning tree—whose weight gives a lower bound on the length of an optimal traveling-salesman tour. We shall then use the minimum spanning tree to create a tour whose cost is no more than twice that of the minimum spanning tree's weight, as long as the cost function satisfies the triangle inequality. The following algorithm implements this approach, calling the minimum-spanning-tree algorithm MST-PRIM from Section 23.2 as a subroutine. The parameter G is a complete undirected graph, and the cost function c satisfies the triangle inequality.

APPROX-TSP-TOUR(G, c)

1   select a vertex $r \in G.V$ to be a "root" vertex
2   compute a minimum spanning tree T for G from root r
      using MST-PRIM(G, c, r)
3   let H be a list of vertices, ordered according to when they are first visited
      in a preorder tree walk of T
4   **return** the hamiltonian cycle H

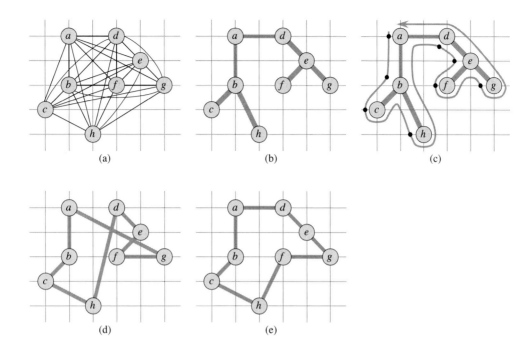

Figure 35.2 The operation of APPROX-TSP-TOUR. **(a)** A complete undirected graph. Vertices lie on intersections of integer grid lines. For example, f is one unit to the right and two units up from h. The cost function between two points is the ordinary euclidean distance. **(b)** A minimum spanning tree T of the complete graph, as computed by MST-PRIM. Vertex a is the root vertex. Only edges in the minimum spanning tree are shown. The vertices happen to be labeled in such a way that they are added to the main tree by MST-PRIM in alphabetical order. **(c)** A walk of T, starting at a. A full walk of the tree visits the vertices in the order $a, b, c, b, h, b, a, d, e, f, e, g, e, d, a$. A preorder walk of T lists a vertex just when it is first encountered, as indicated by the dot next to each vertex, yielding the ordering a, b, c, h, d, e, f, g. **(d)** A tour obtained by visiting the vertices in the order given by the preorder walk, which is the tour H returned by APPROX-TSP-TOUR. Its total cost is approximately 19.074. **(e)** An optimal tour H^* for the original complete graph. Its total cost is approximately 14.715.

Recall from Section 12.1 that a preorder tree walk recursively visits every vertex in the tree, listing a vertex when it is first encountered, before visiting any of its children.

Figure 35.2 illustrates the operation of APPROX-TSP-TOUR. Part (a) of the figure shows a complete undirected graph, and part (b) shows the minimum spanning tree T grown from root vertex a by MST-PRIM. Part (c) shows how a preorder walk of T visits the vertices, and part (d) displays the corresponding tour, which is the tour returned by APPROX-TSP-TOUR. Part (e) displays an optimal tour, which is about 23% shorter.

By Exercise 23.2-2, even with a simple implementation of MST-PRIM, the running time of APPROX-TSP-TOUR is $\Theta(V^2)$. We now show that if the cost function for an instance of the traveling-salesman problem satisfies the triangle inequality, then APPROX-TSP-TOUR returns a tour whose cost is not more than twice the cost of an optimal tour.

Theorem 35.2
APPROX-TSP-TOUR is a polynomial-time 2-approximation algorithm for the traveling-salesman problem with the triangle inequality.

Proof   We have already seen that APPROX-TSP-TOUR runs in polynomial time.

Let H^* denote an optimal tour for the given set of vertices. We obtain a spanning tree by deleting any edge from a tour, and each edge cost is nonnegative. Therefore, the weight of the minimum spanning tree T computed in line 2 of APPROX-TSP-TOUR provides a lower bound on the cost of an optimal tour:

$$c(T) \leq c(H^*) . \tag{35.4}$$

A *full walk* of T lists the vertices when they are first visited and also whenever they are returned to after a visit to a subtree. Let us call this full walk W. The full walk of our example gives the order

$$a, b, c, b, h, b, a, d, e, f, e, g, e, d, a .$$

Since the full walk traverses every edge of T exactly twice, we have (extending our definition of the cost c in the natural manner to handle multisets of edges)

$$c(W) = 2c(T) . \tag{35.5}$$

Inequality (35.4) and equation (35.5) imply that

$$c(W) \leq 2c(H^*) , \tag{35.6}$$

and so the cost of W is within a factor of 2 of the cost of an optimal tour.

Unfortunately, the full walk W is generally not a tour, since it visits some vertices more than once. By the triangle inequality, however, we can delete a visit to any vertex from W and the cost does not increase. (If we delete a vertex v from W between visits to u and w, the resulting ordering specifies going directly from u to w.) By repeatedly applying this operation, we can remove from W all but the first visit to each vertex. In our example, this leaves the ordering

$$a, b, c, h, d, e, f, g .$$

This ordering is the same as that obtained by a preorder walk of the tree T. Let H be the cycle corresponding to this preorder walk. It is a hamiltonian cycle, since every vertex is visited exactly once, and in fact it is the cycle computed by APPROX-TSP-TOUR. Since H is obtained by deleting vertices from the full walk W, we have

$$c(H) \leq c(W) . \tag{35.7}$$

Combining inequalities (35.6) and (35.7) gives $c(H) \leq 2c(H^*)$, which completes the proof.   ∎

In spite of the nice approximation ratio provided by Theorem 35.2, APPROX-TSP-TOUR is usually not the best practical choice for this problem. There are other approximation algorithms that typically perform much better in practice. (See the references at the end of this chapter.)

35.2.2   The general traveling-salesman problem

If we drop the assumption that the cost function c satisfies the triangle inequality, then we cannot find good approximate tours in polynomial time unless P = NP.

Theorem 35.3
If P $\neq$ NP, then for any constant $\rho \geq 1$, there is no polynomial-time approximation algorithm with approximation ratio ρ for the general traveling-salesman problem.

Proof   The proof is by contradiction. Suppose to the contrary that for some number $\rho \geq 1$, there is a polynomial-time approximation algorithm A with approximation ratio ρ. Without loss of generality, we assume that ρ is an integer, by rounding it up if necessary. We shall then show how to use A to solve instances of the hamiltonian-cycle problem (defined in Section 34.2) in polynomial time. Since Theorem 34.13 tells us that the hamiltonian-cycle problem is NP-complete, Theorem 34.4 implies that if we can solve it in polynomial time, then P = NP.

Let $G = (V, E)$ be an instance of the hamiltonian-cycle problem. We wish to determine efficiently whether G contains a hamiltonian cycle by making use of the hypothesized approximation algorithm A. We turn G into an instance of the traveling-salesman problem as follows. Let $G' = (V, E')$ be the complete graph on V; that is,

$$E' = \{(u, v) : u, v \in V \text{ and } u \neq v\} .$$

Assign an integer cost to each edge in E' as follows:

$$c(u, v) = \begin{cases} 1 & \text{if } (u, v) \in E , \\ \rho |V| + 1 & \text{otherwise} . \end{cases}$$

We can create representations of G' and c from a representation of G in time polynomial in $|V|$ and $|E|$.

Now, consider the traveling-salesman problem (G', c). If the original graph G has a hamiltonian cycle H, then the cost function c assigns to each edge of H a cost of 1, and so (G', c) contains a tour of cost $|V|$. On the other hand, if G does not contain a hamiltonian cycle, then any tour of G' must use some edge not in E. But any tour that uses an edge not in E has a cost of at least

$$
\begin{aligned}
(\rho|V| + 1) + (|V| - 1) &= \rho|V| + |V| \\
&> \rho|V| \ .
\end{aligned}
$$

Because edges not in G are so costly, there is a gap of at least $\rho|V|$ between the cost of a tour that is a hamiltonian cycle in G (cost $|V|$) and the cost of any other tour (cost at least $\rho|V| + |V|$). Therefore, the cost of a tour that is not a hamiltonian cycle in G is at least a factor of $\rho + 1$ greater than the cost of a tour that is a hamiltonian cycle in G.

Now, suppose that we apply the approximation algorithm A to the traveling-salesman problem (G', c). Because A is guaranteed to return a tour of cost no more than ρ times the cost of an optimal tour, if G contains a hamiltonian cycle, then A must return it. If G has no hamiltonian cycle, then A returns a tour of cost more than $\rho|V|$. Therefore, we can use A to solve the hamiltonian-cycle problem in polynomial time. ∎

The proof of Theorem 35.3 serves as an example of a general technique for proving that we cannot approximate a problem very well. Suppose that given an NP-hard problem X, we can produce in polynomial time a minimization problem Y such that "yes" instances of X correspond to instances of Y with value at most k (for some k), but that "no" instances of X correspond to instances of Y with value greater than ρk. Then, we have shown that, unless $P = NP$, there is no polynomial-time ρ-approximation algorithm for problem Y.

Exercises

35.2-1
Suppose that a complete undirected graph $G = (V, E)$ with at least 3 vertices has a cost function c that satisfies the triangle inequality. Prove that $c(u, v) \geq 0$ for all $u, v \in V$.

35.2-2
Show how in polynomial time we can transform one instance of the traveling-salesman problem into another instance whose cost function satisfies the triangle inequality. The two instances must have the same set of optimal tours. Explain why such a polynomial-time transformation does not contradict Theorem 35.3, assuming that $P \neq NP$.

35.2-3

Consider the following ***closest-point heuristic*** for building an approximate traveling-salesman tour whose cost function satisfies the triangle inequality. Begin with a trivial cycle consisting of a single arbitrarily chosen vertex. At each step, identify the vertex u that is not on the cycle but whose distance to any vertex on the cycle is minimum. Suppose that the vertex on the cycle that is nearest u is vertex v. Extend the cycle to include u by inserting u just after v. Repeat until all vertices are on the cycle. Prove that this heuristic returns a tour whose total cost is not more than twice the cost of an optimal tour.

35.2-4

In the ***bottleneck traveling-salesman problem***, we wish to find the hamiltonian cycle that minimizes the cost of the most costly edge in the cycle. Assuming that the cost function satisfies the triangle inequality, show that there exists a polynomial-time approximation algorithm with approximation ratio 3 for this problem. (*Hint:* Show recursively that we can visit all the nodes in a bottleneck spanning tree, as discussed in Problem 23-3, exactly once by taking a full walk of the tree and skipping nodes, but without skipping more than two consecutive intermediate nodes. Show that the costliest edge in a bottleneck spanning tree has a cost that is at most the cost of the costliest edge in a bottleneck hamiltonian cycle.)

35.2-5

Suppose that the vertices for an instance of the traveling-salesman problem are points in the plane and that the cost $c(u, v)$ is the euclidean distance between points u and v. Show that an optimal tour never crosses itself.

35.3 The set-covering problem

The set-covering problem is an optimization problem that models many problems that require resources to be allocated. Its corresponding decision problem generalizes the NP-complete vertex-cover problem and is therefore also NP-hard. The approximation algorithm developed to handle the vertex-cover problem doesn't apply here, however, and so we need to try other approaches. We shall examine a simple greedy heuristic with a logarithmic approximation ratio. That is, as the size of the instance gets larger, the size of the approximate solution may grow, relative to the size of an optimal solution. Because the logarithm function grows rather slowly, however, this approximation algorithm may nonetheless give useful results.

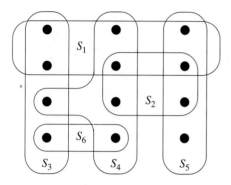

Figure 35.3 An instance $(X, \mathcal{F})$ of the set-covering problem, where X consists of the 12 black points and $\mathcal{F} = \{S_1, S_2, S_3, S_4, S_5, S_6\}$. A minimum-size set cover is $\mathcal{C} = \{S_3, S_4, S_5\}$, with size 3. The greedy algorithm produces a cover of size 4 by selecting either the sets S_1, S_4, S_5, and S_3 or the sets S_1, S_4, S_5, and S_6, in order.

An instance $(X, \mathcal{F})$ of the ***set-covering problem*** consists of a finite set X and a family $\mathcal{F}$ of subsets of X, such that every element of X belongs to at least one subset in $\mathcal{F}$:

$$X = \bigcup_{S \in \mathcal{F}} S .$$

We say that a subset $S \in \mathcal{F}$ ***covers*** its elements. The problem is to find a minimum-size subset $\mathcal{C} \subseteq \mathcal{F}$ whose members cover all of X:

$$X = \bigcup_{S \in \mathcal{C}} S . \tag{35.8}$$

We say that any $\mathcal{C}$ satisfying equation (35.8) ***covers*** X. Figure 35.3 illustrates the set-covering problem. The size of $\mathcal{C}$ is the number of sets it contains, rather than the number of individual elements in these sets, since every subset $\mathcal{C}$ that covers X must contain all $|X|$ individual elements. In Figure 35.3, the minimum set cover has size 3.

The set-covering problem abstracts many commonly arising combinatorial problems. As a simple example, suppose that X represents a set of skills that are needed to solve a problem and that we have a given set of people available to work on the problem. We wish to form a committee, containing as few people as possible, such that for every requisite skill in X, at least one member of the committee has that skill. In the decision version of the set-covering problem, we ask whether a covering exists with size at most k, where k is an additional parameter specified in the problem instance. The decision version of the problem is NP-complete, as Exercise 35.3-2 asks you to show.

A greedy approximation algorithm

The greedy method works by picking, at each stage, the set S that covers the greatest number of remaining elements that are uncovered.

GREEDY-SET-COVER($X, \mathcal{F}$)

```
1  U = X
2  𝒞 = ∅
3  while U ≠ ∅
4      select an S ∈ ℱ that maximizes |S ∩ U|
5      U = U − S
6      𝒞 = 𝒞 ∪ {S}
7  return 𝒞
```

In the example of Figure 35.3, GREEDY-SET-COVER adds to $\mathcal{C}$, in order, the sets S_1, S_4, and S_5, followed by either S_3 or S_6.

The algorithm works as follows. The set U contains, at each stage, the set of remaining uncovered elements. The set $\mathcal{C}$ contains the cover being constructed. Line 4 is the greedy decision-making step, choosing a subset S that covers as many uncovered elements as possible (breaking ties arbitrarily). After S is selected, line 5 removes its elements from U, and line 6 places S into $\mathcal{C}$. When the algorithm terminates, the set $\mathcal{C}$ contains a subfamily of $\mathcal{F}$ that covers X.

We can easily implement GREEDY-SET-COVER to run in time polynomial in $|X|$ and $|\mathcal{F}|$. Since the number of iterations of the loop on lines 3–6 is bounded from above by $\min(|X|, |\mathcal{F}|)$, and we can implement the loop body to run in time $O(|X||\mathcal{F}|)$, a simple implementation runs in time $O(|X||\mathcal{F}|\min(|X|, |\mathcal{F}|))$. Exercise 35.3-3 asks for a linear-time algorithm.

Analysis

We now show that the greedy algorithm returns a set cover that is not too much larger than an optimal set cover. For convenience, in this chapter we denote the dth harmonic number $H_d = \sum_{i=1}^{d} 1/i$ (see Section A.1) by $H(d)$. As a boundary condition, we define $H(0) = 0$.

Theorem 35.4
GREEDY-SET-COVER is a polynomial-time $\rho(n)$-approximation algorithm, where

$$\rho(n) = H(\max\{|S| : S \in \mathcal{F}\}) \, .$$

Proof   We have already shown that GREEDY-SET-COVER runs in polynomial time.

To show that GREEDY-SET-COVER is a $\rho(n)$-approximation algorithm, we assign a cost of 1 to each set selected by the algorithm, distribute this cost over the elements covered for the first time, and then use these costs to derive the desired relationship between the size of an optimal set cover $\mathcal{C}^*$ and the size of the set cover $\mathcal{C}$ returned by the algorithm. Let S_i denote the ith subset selected by GREEDY-SET-COVER; the algorithm incurs a cost of 1 when it adds S_i to $\mathcal{C}$. We spread this cost of selecting S_i evenly among the elements covered for the first time by S_i. Let c_x denote the cost allocated to element x, for each $x \in X$. Each element is assigned a cost only once, when it is covered for the first time. If x is covered for the first time by S_i, then

$$c_x = \frac{1}{|S_i - (S_1 \cup S_2 \cup \cdots \cup S_{i-1})|} \, .$$

Each step of the algorithm assigns 1 unit of cost, and so

$$|\mathcal{C}| = \sum_{x \in X} c_x \, . \tag{35.9}$$

Each element $x \in X$ is in at least one set in the optimal cover $\mathcal{C}^*$, and so we have

$$\sum_{S \in \mathcal{C}^*} \sum_{x \in S} c_x \geq \sum_{x \in X} c_x \, . \tag{35.10}$$

Combining equation (35.9) and inequality (35.10), we have that

$$|\mathcal{C}| \leq \sum_{S \in \mathcal{C}^*} \sum_{x \in S} c_x \, . \tag{35.11}$$

The remainder of the proof rests on the following key inequality, which we shall prove shortly. For any set S belonging to the family $\mathcal{F}$,

$$\sum_{x \in S} c_x \leq H(|S|) \, . \tag{35.12}$$

From inequalities (35.11) and (35.12), it follows that

$$\begin{aligned} |\mathcal{C}| &\leq \sum_{S \in \mathcal{C}^*} H(|S|) \\ &\leq |\mathcal{C}^*| \cdot H(\max\{|S| : S \in \mathcal{F}\}) \, , \end{aligned}$$

thus proving the theorem.

All that remains is to prove inequality (35.12). Consider any set $S \in \mathcal{F}$ and any $i = 1, 2, \ldots, |\mathcal{C}|$, and let

$$u_i = |S - (S_1 \cup S_2 \cup \cdots \cup S_i)|$$

be the number of elements in S that remain uncovered after the algorithm has selected sets $S_1, S_2, \ldots, S_i$. We define $u_0 = |S|$ to be the number of elements of S, which are all initially uncovered. Let k be the least index such that $u_k = 0$, so that every element in S is covered by at least one of the sets $S_1, S_2, \ldots, S_k$ and some element in S is uncovered by $S_1 \cup S_2 \cup \cdots \cup S_{k-1}$. Then, $u_{i-1} \geq u_i$, and $u_{i-1} - u_i$ elements of S are covered for the first time by S_i, for $i = 1, 2, \ldots, k$. Thus,

$$\sum_{x \in S} c_x = \sum_{i=1}^{k} (u_{i-1} - u_i) \cdot \frac{1}{|S_i - (S_1 \cup S_2 \cup \cdots \cup S_{i-1})|} \, .$$

Observe that

$$\begin{aligned} |S_i - (S_1 \cup S_2 \cup \cdots \cup S_{i-1})| &\geq |S - (S_1 \cup S_2 \cup \cdots \cup S_{i-1})| \\ &= u_{i-1} \, , \end{aligned}$$

because the greedy choice of S_i guarantees that S cannot cover more new elements than S_i does (otherwise, the algorithm would have chosen S instead of S_i). Consequently, we obtain

$$\sum_{x \in S} c_x \leq \sum_{i=1}^{k} (u_{i-1} - u_i) \cdot \frac{1}{u_{i-1}} \, .$$

We now bound this quantity as follows:

$$\begin{aligned} \sum_{x \in S} c_x &\leq \sum_{i=1}^{k} (u_{i-1} - u_i) \cdot \frac{1}{u_{i-1}} \\ &= \sum_{i=1}^{k} \sum_{j=u_i+1}^{u_{i-1}} \frac{1}{u_{i-1}} \\ &\leq \sum_{i=1}^{k} \sum_{j=u_i+1}^{u_{i-1}} \frac{1}{j} \qquad \text{(because } j \leq u_{i-1}) \\ &= \sum_{i=1}^{k} \left(\sum_{j=1}^{u_{i-1}} \frac{1}{j} - \sum_{j=1}^{u_i} \frac{1}{j} \right) \\ &= \sum_{i=1}^{k} (H(u_{i-1}) - H(u_i)) \\ &= H(u_0) - H(u_k) \qquad \text{(because the sum telescopes)} \\ &= H(u_0) - H(0) \\ &= H(u_0) \qquad \text{(because } H(0) = 0) \\ &= H(|S|) \, , \end{aligned}$$

which completes the proof of inequality (35.12).   ■

Corollary 35.5
GREEDY-SET-COVER is a polynomial-time $(\ln |X| + 1)$-approximation algorithm.

Proof   Use inequality (A.14) and Theorem 35.4.   ∎

In some applications, $\max \{|S| : S \in \mathcal{F}\}$ is a small constant, and so the solution returned by GREEDY-SET-COVER is at most a small constant times larger than optimal. One such application occurs when this heuristic finds an approximate vertex cover for a graph whose vertices have degree at most 3. In this case, the solution found by GREEDY-SET-COVER is not more than $H(3) = 11/6$ times as large as an optimal solution, a performance guarantee that is slightly better than that of APPROX-VERTEX-COVER.

Exercises

35.3-1
Consider each of the following words as a set of letters: {`arid, dash, drain, heard, lost, nose, shun, slate, snare, thread`}. Show which set cover GREEDY-SET-COVER produces when we break ties in favor of the word that appears first in the dictionary.

35.3-2
Show that the decision version of the set-covering problem is NP-complete by reducing it from the vertex-cover problem.

35.3-3
Show how to implement GREEDY-SET-COVER in such a way that it runs in time

$$O\left(\sum_{S \in \mathcal{F}} |S|\right).$$

35.3-4
Show that the following weaker form of Theorem 35.4 is trivially true:

$$|\mathcal{C}| \le |\mathcal{C}^*| \max \{|S| : S \in \mathcal{F}\} .$$

35.3-5
GREEDY-SET-COVER can return a number of different solutions, depending on how we break ties in line 4. Give a procedure BAD-SET-COVER-INSTANCE(n) that returns an n-element instance of the set-covering problem for which, depending on how we break ties in line 4, GREEDY-SET-COVER can return a number of different solutions that is exponential in n.

35.4 Randomization and linear programming

In this section, we study two useful techniques for designing approximation algorithms: randomization and linear programming. We shall give a simple randomized algorithm for an optimization version of 3-CNF satisfiability, and then we shall use linear programming to help design an approximation algorithm for a weighted version of the vertex-cover problem. This section only scratches the surface of these two powerful techniques. The chapter notes give references for further study of these areas.

A randomized approximation algorithm for MAX-3-CNF satisfiability

Just as some randomized algorithms compute exact solutions, some randomized algorithms compute approximate solutions. We say that a randomized algorithm for a problem has an **approximation ratio** of $\rho(n)$ if, for any input of size n, the *expected* cost C of the solution produced by the randomized algorithm is within a factor of $\rho(n)$ of the cost C^* of an optimal solution:

$$\max \left(\frac{C}{C^*}, \frac{C^*}{C} \right) \leq \rho(n) \, . \tag{35.13}$$

We call a randomized algorithm that achieves an approximation ratio of $\rho(n)$ a **randomized $\rho(n)$-approximation algorithm.** In other words, a randomized approximation algorithm is like a deterministic approximation algorithm, except that the approximation ratio is for an expected cost.

A particular instance of 3-CNF satisfiability, as defined in Section 34.4, may or may not be satisfiable. In order to be satisfiable, there must exist an assignment of the variables so that every clause evaluates to 1. If an instance is not satisfiable, we may want to compute how "close" to satisfiable it is, that is, we may wish to find an assignment of the variables that satisfies as many clauses as possible. We call the resulting maximization problem **MAX-3-CNF satisfiability.** The input to MAX-3-CNF satisfiability is the same as for 3-CNF satisfiability, and the goal is to return an assignment of the variables that maximizes the number of clauses evaluating to 1. We now show that randomly setting each variable to 1 with probability $1/2$ and to 0 with probability $1/2$ yields a randomized 8/7-approximation algorithm. According to the definition of 3-CNF satisfiability from Section 34.4, we require each clause to consist of exactly three distinct literals. We further assume that no clause contains both a variable and its negation. (Exercise 35.4-1 asks you to remove this last assumption.)

Theorem 35.6

Given an instance of MAX-3-CNF satisfiability with n variables $x_1, x_2, \ldots, x_n$ and m clauses, the randomized algorithm that independently sets each variable to 1 with probability $1/2$ and to 0 with probability $1/2$ is a randomized $8/7$-approximation algorithm.

Proof   Suppose that we have independently set each variable to 1 with probability $1/2$ and to 0 with probability $1/2$. For $i = 1, 2, \ldots, m$, we define the indicator random variable

$$Y_i = I\{\text{clause } i \text{ is satisfied}\},$$

so that $Y_i = 1$ as long as we have set at least one of the literals in the ith clause to 1. Since no literal appears more than once in the same clause, and since we have assumed that no variable and its negation appear in the same clause, the settings of the three literals in each clause are independent. A clause is not satisfied only if all three of its literals are set to 0, and so $\Pr\{\text{clause } i \text{ is not satisfied}\} = (1/2)^3 = 1/8$. Thus, we have $\Pr\{\text{clause } i \text{ is satisfied}\} = 1 - 1/8 = 7/8$, and by Lemma 5.1, we have $E[Y_i] = 7/8$. Let Y be the number of satisfied clauses overall, so that $Y = Y_1 + Y_2 + \cdots + Y_m$. Then, we have

$$
\begin{aligned}
E[Y] &= E\left[\sum_{i=1}^{m} Y_i\right] \\
&= \sum_{i=1}^{m} E[Y_i] \qquad \text{(by linearity of expectation)} \\
&= \sum_{i=1}^{m} 7/8 \\
&= 7m/8 .
\end{aligned}
$$

Clearly, m is an upper bound on the number of satisfied clauses, and hence the approximation ratio is at most $m/(7m/8) = 8/7$.   ∎

Approximating weighted vertex cover using linear programming

In the ***minimum-weight vertex-cover problem***, we are given an undirected graph $G = (V, E)$ in which each vertex $v \in V$ has an associated positive weight $w(v)$. For any vertex cover $V' \subseteq V$, we define the weight of the vertex cover $w(V') = \sum_{v \in V'} w(v)$. The goal is to find a vertex cover of minimum weight.

We cannot apply the algorithm used for unweighted vertex cover, nor can we use a random solution; both methods may return solutions that are far from optimal. We shall, however, compute a lower bound on the weight of the minimum-weight vertex cover, by using a linear program. We shall then "round" this solution and use it to obtain a vertex cover.

Suppose that we associate a variable $x(v)$ with each vertex $v \in V$, and let us require that $x(v)$ equals either 0 or 1 for each $v \in V$. We put v into the vertex cover if and only if $x(v) = 1$. Then, we can write the constraint that for any edge (u, v), at least one of u and v must be in the vertex cover as $x(u) + x(v) \geq 1$. This view gives rise to the following **0-1 integer program** for finding a minimum-weight vertex cover:

$$\text{minimize} \quad \sum_{v \in V} w(v)\, x(v) \tag{35.14}$$

subject to

$$x(u) + x(v) \geq 1 \qquad \text{for each } (u, v) \in E \tag{35.15}$$
$$x(v) \in \{0, 1\} \quad \text{for each } v \in V . \tag{35.16}$$

In the special case in which all the weights $w(v)$ are equal to 1, this formulation is the optimization version of the NP-hard vertex-cover problem. Suppose, however, that we remove the constraint that $x(v) \in \{0, 1\}$ and replace it by $0 \leq x(v) \leq 1$. We then obtain the following linear program, which is known as the **linear-programming relaxation**:

$$\text{minimize} \quad \sum_{v \in V} w(v)\, x(v) \tag{35.17}$$

subject to

$$x(u) + x(v) \geq 1 \quad \text{for each } (u, v) \in E \tag{35.18}$$
$$x(v) \leq 1 \quad \text{for each } v \in V \tag{35.19}$$
$$x(v) \geq 0 \quad \text{for each } v \in V . \tag{35.20}$$

Any feasible solution to the 0-1 integer program in lines (35.14)–(35.16) is also a feasible solution to the linear program in lines (35.17)–(35.20). Therefore, the value of an optimal solution to the linear program gives a lower bound on the value of an optimal solution to the 0-1 integer program, and hence a lower bound on the optimal weight in the minimum-weight vertex-cover problem.

The following procedure uses the solution to the linear-programming relaxation to construct an approximate solution to the minimum-weight vertex-cover problem:

APPROX-MIN-WEIGHT-VC(G, w)

1   $C = \emptyset$
2   compute $\bar{x}$, an optimal solution to the linear program in lines (35.17)–(35.20)
3   **for** each $v \in V$
4   **if** $\bar{x}(v) \geq 1/2$
5         $C = C \cup \{v\}$
6   **return** C

The APPROX-MIN-WEIGHT-VC procedure works as follows. Line 1 initial-izes the vertex cover to be empty. Line 2 formulates the linear program in lines (35.17)–(35.20) and then solves this linear program. An optimal solution gives each vertex v an associated value $\bar{x}(v)$, where $0 \leq \bar{x}(v) \leq 1$. We use this value to guide the choice of which vertices to add to the vertex cover C in lines 3–5. If $\bar{x}(v) \geq 1/2$, we add v to C; otherwise we do not. In effect, we are "rounding" each fractional variable in the solution to the linear program to 0 or 1 in order to obtain a solution to the 0-1 integer program in lines (35.14)–(35.16). Finally, line 6 returns the vertex cover C.

Theorem 35.7
Algorithm APPROX-MIN-WEIGHT-VC is a polynomial-time 2-approximation al-gorithm for the minimum-weight vertex-cover problem.

Proof   Because there is a polynomial-time algorithm to solve the linear program in line 2, and because the **for** loop of lines 3–5 runs in polynomial time, APPROX-MIN-WEIGHT-VC is a polynomial-time algorithm.

Now we show that APPROX-MIN-WEIGHT-VC is a 2-approximation algo-rithm. Let C^* be an optimal solution to the minimum-weight vertex-cover prob-lem, and let z^* be the value of an optimal solution to the linear program in lines (35.17)–(35.20). Since an optimal vertex cover is a feasible solution to the linear program, z^* must be a lower bound on $w(C^*)$, that is,

$$z^* \leq w(C^*) . \tag{35.21}$$

Next, we claim that by rounding the fractional values of the variables $\bar{x}(v)$, we produce a set C that is a vertex cover and satisfies $w(C) \leq 2z^*$. To see that C is a vertex cover, consider any edge $(u, v) \in E$. By constraint (35.18), we know that $x(u) + x(v) \geq 1$, which implies that at least one of $\bar{x}(u)$ and $\bar{x}(v)$ is at least $1/2$. Therefore, at least one of u and v is included in the vertex cover, and so every edge is covered.

Now, we consider the weight of the cover. We have

$$z^* = \sum_{v \in V} w(v)\, \bar{x}(v)$$

$$\geq \sum_{v \in V : \bar{x}(v) \geq 1/2} w(v)\, \bar{x}(v)$$

$$\geq \sum_{v \in V : \bar{x}(v) \geq 1/2} w(v) \cdot \frac{1}{2}$$

$$= \sum_{v \in C} w(v) \cdot \frac{1}{2}$$

$$= \frac{1}{2} \sum_{v \in C} w(v)$$

$$= \frac{1}{2} w(C) \,. \tag{35.22}$$

Combining inequalities (35.21) and (35.22) gives

$$w(C) \leq 2z^* \leq 2w(C^*) \,,$$

and hence APPROX-MIN-WEIGHT-VC is a 2-approximation algorithm.   ■

Exercises

35.4-1
Show that even if we allow a clause to contain both a variable and its negation, randomly setting each variable to 1 with probability $1/2$ and to 0 with probability $1/2$ still yields a randomized 8/7-approximation algorithm.

35.4-2
The ***MAX-CNF satisfiability problem*** is like the MAX-3-CNF satisfiability problem, except that it does not restrict each clause to have exactly 3 literals. Give a randomized 2-approximation algorithm for the MAX-CNF satisfiability problem.

35.4-3
In the MAX-CUT problem, we are given an unweighted undirected graph $G = (V, E)$. We define a cut $(S, V - S)$ as in Chapter 23 and the ***weight*** of a cut as the number of edges crossing the cut. The goal is to find a cut of maximum weight. Suppose that for each vertex v, we randomly and independently place v in S with probability $1/2$ and in $V - S$ with probability $1/2$. Show that this algorithm is a randomized 2-approximation algorithm.

35.4-4

Show that the constraints in line (35.19) are redundant in the sense that if we remove them from the linear program in lines (35.17)–(35.20), any optimal solution to the resulting linear program must satisfy $x(v) \leq 1$ for each $v \in V$.

35.5 The subset-sum problem

Recall from Section 34.5.5 that an instance of the subset-sum problem is a pair (S, t), where S is a set $\{x_1, x_2, \ldots, x_n\}$ of positive integers and t is a positive integer. This decision problem asks whether there exists a subset of S that adds up exactly to the target value t. As we saw in Section 34.5.5, this problem is NP-complete.

The optimization problem associated with this decision problem arises in practical applications. In the optimization problem, we wish to find a subset of $\{x_1, x_2, \ldots, x_n\}$ whose sum is as large as possible but not larger than t. For example, we may have a truck that can carry no more than t pounds, and n different boxes to ship, the ith of which weighs x_i pounds. We wish to fill the truck with as heavy a load as possible without exceeding the given weight limit.

In this section, we present an exponential-time algorithm that computes the optimal value for this optimization problem, and then we show how to modify the algorithm so that it becomes a fully polynomial-time approximation scheme. (Recall that a fully polynomial-time approximation scheme has a running time that is polynomial in $1/\epsilon$ as well as in the size of the input.)

An exponential-time exact algorithm

Suppose that we computed, for each subset S' of S, the sum of the elements in S', and then we selected, among the subsets whose sum does not exceed t, the one whose sum was closest to t. Clearly this algorithm would return the optimal solution, but it could take exponential time. To implement this algorithm, we could use an iterative procedure that, in iteration i, computes the sums of all subsets of $\{x_1, x_2, \ldots, x_i\}$, using as a starting point the sums of all subsets of $\{x_1, x_2, \ldots, x_{i-1}\}$. In doing so, we would realize that once a particular subset S' had a sum exceeding t, there would be no reason to maintain it, since no superset of S' could be the optimal solution. We now give an implementation of this strategy.

The procedure EXACT-SUBSET-SUM takes an input set $S = \{x_1, x_2, \ldots, x_n\}$ and a target value t; we'll see its pseudocode in a moment. This procedure iteratively computes L_i, the list of sums of all subsets of $\{x_1, \ldots, x_i\}$ that do not exceed t, and then it returns the maximum value in L_n.

If L is a list of positive integers and x is another positive integer, then we let $L + x$ denote the list of integers derived from L by increasing each element of L by x. For example, if $L = \langle 1, 2, 3, 5, 9 \rangle$, then $L + 2 = \langle 3, 4, 5, 7, 11 \rangle$. We also use this notation for sets, so that

$$S + x = \{s + x : s \in S\} \ .$$

We also use an auxiliary procedure MERGE-LISTS(L, L'), which returns the sorted list that is the merge of its two sorted input lists L and L' with duplicate values removed. Like the MERGE procedure we used in merge sort (Section 2.3.1), MERGE-LISTS runs in time $O(|L| + |L'|)$. We omit the pseudocode for MERGE-LISTS.

EXACT-SUBSET-SUM(S, t)

```
1   n = |S|
2   L₀ = ⟨0⟩
3   for i = 1 to n
4       Lᵢ = MERGE-LISTS(Lᵢ₋₁, Lᵢ₋₁ + xᵢ)
5           remove from Lᵢ every element that is greater than t
6   return the largest element in Lₙ
```

To see how EXACT-SUBSET-SUM works, let P_i denote the set of all values obtained by selecting a (possibly empty) subset of $\{x_1, x_2, \ldots, x_i\}$ and summing its members. For example, if $S = \{1, 4, 5\}$, then

$$P_1 = \{0, 1\} \ ,$$
$$P_2 = \{0, 1, 4, 5\} \ ,$$
$$P_3 = \{0, 1, 4, 5, 6, 9, 10\} \ .$$

Given the identity

$$P_i = P_{i-1} \cup (P_{i-1} + x_i) \ , \tag{35.23}$$

we can prove by induction on i (see Exercise 35.5-1) that the list L_i is a sorted list containing every element of P_i whose value is not more than t. Since the length of L_i can be as much as 2^i, EXACT-SUBSET-SUM is an exponential-time algorithm in general, although it is a polynomial-time algorithm in the special cases in which t is polynomial in $|S|$ or all the numbers in S are bounded by a polynomial in $|S|$.

A fully polynomial-time approximation scheme

We can derive a fully polynomial-time approximation scheme for the subset-sum problem by "trimming" each list L_i after it is created. The idea behind trimming is that if two values in L are close to each other, then since we want just an approximate solution, we do not need to maintain both of them explicitly. More precisely, we use a trimming parameter δ such that $0 < \delta < 1$. When we **trim** a list L by δ, we remove as many elements from L as possible, in such a way that if L' is the result of trimming L, then for every element y that was removed from L, there is an element z still in L' that approximates y, that is,

$$\frac{y}{1+\delta} \le z \le y . \tag{35.24}$$

We can think of such a z as "representing" y in the new list L'. Each removed element y is represented by a remaining element z satisfying inequality (35.24). For example, if $\delta = 0.1$ and

$$L = \langle 10, 11, 12, 15, 20, 21, 22, 23, 24, 29 \rangle ,$$

then we can trim L to obtain

$$L' = \langle 10, 12, 15, 20, 23, 29 \rangle ,$$

where the deleted value 11 is represented by 10, the deleted values 21 and 22 are represented by 20, and the deleted value 24 is represented by 23. Because every element of the trimmed version of the list is also an element of the original version of the list, trimming can dramatically decrease the number of elements kept while keeping a close (and slightly smaller) representative value in the list for each deleted element.

The following procedure trims list $L = \langle y_1, y_2, \ldots, y_m \rangle$ in time $\Theta(m)$, given L and δ, and assuming that L is sorted into monotonically increasing order. The output of the procedure is a trimmed, sorted list.

$\text{TRIM}(L, \delta)$

```
1   let m be the length of L
2   L' = ⟨y₁⟩
3   last = y₁
4   for i = 2 to m
5       if yᵢ > last · (1 + δ)        // yᵢ ≥ last because L is sorted
6           append yᵢ onto the end of L'
7           last = yᵢ
8   return L'
```

The procedure scans the elements of L in monotonically increasing order. A number is appended onto the returned list L' only if it is the first element of L or if it cannot be represented by the most recent number placed into L'.

Given the procedure TRIM, we can construct our approximation scheme as follows. This procedure takes as input a set $S = \{x_1, x_2, \ldots, x_n\}$ of n integers (in arbitrary order), a target integer t, and an "approximation parameter" ϵ, where

$$0 < \epsilon < 1 . \tag{35.25}$$

It returns a value z whose value is within a $1 + \epsilon$ factor of the optimal solution.

APPROX-SUBSET-SUM(S, t, ϵ)

```
1   n = |S|
2   L₀ = ⟨0⟩
3   for i = 1 to n
4       Lᵢ = MERGE-LISTS(Lᵢ₋₁, Lᵢ₋₁ + xᵢ)
5       Lᵢ = TRIM(Lᵢ, ε/2n)
6       remove from Lᵢ every element that is greater than t
7   let z* be the largest value in Lₙ
8   return z*
```

Line 2 initializes the list L_0 to be the list containing just the element 0. The **for** loop in lines 3–6 computes L_i as a sorted list containing a suitably trimmed version of the set P_i, with all elements larger than t removed. Since we create L_i from L_{i-1}, we must ensure that the repeated trimming doesn't introduce too much compounded inaccuracy. In a moment, we shall see that APPROX-SUBSET-SUM returns a correct approximation if one exists.

As an example, suppose we have the instance

$$S = \langle 104, 102, 201, 101 \rangle$$

with $t = 308$ and $\epsilon = 0.40$. The trimming parameter δ is $\epsilon/8 = 0.05$. APPROX-SUBSET-SUM computes the following values on the indicated lines:

line 2: L_0 = $\langle 0 \rangle$,

line 4: L_1 = $\langle 0, 104 \rangle$,
line 5: L_1 = $\langle 0, 104 \rangle$,
line 6: L_1 = $\langle 0, 104 \rangle$,

line 4: L_2 = $\langle 0, 102, 104, 206 \rangle$,
line 5: L_2 = $\langle 0, 102, 206 \rangle$,
line 6: L_2 = $\langle 0, 102, 206 \rangle$,

line 4: L_3 = $\langle 0, 102, 201, 206, 303, 407 \rangle$,
line 5: L_3 = $\langle 0, 102, 201, 303, 407 \rangle$,
line 6: L_3 = $\langle 0, 102, 201, 303 \rangle$,

line 4: L_4 = $\langle 0, 101, 102, 201, 203, 302, 303, 404 \rangle$,
line 5: L_4 = $\langle 0, 101, 201, 302, 404 \rangle$,
line 6: L_4 = $\langle 0, 101, 201, 302 \rangle$.

The algorithm returns $z^* = 302$ as its answer, which is well within $\epsilon = 40\%$ of the optimal answer $307 = 104 + 102 + 101$; in fact, it is within 2%.

Theorem 35.8
APPROX-SUBSET-SUM is a fully polynomial-time approximation scheme for the subset-sum problem.

Proof   The operations of trimming L_i in line 5 and removing from L_i every element that is greater than t maintain the property that every element of L_i is also a member of P_i. Therefore, the value z^* returned in line 8 is indeed the sum of some subset of S. Let $y^* \in P_n$ denote an optimal solution to the subset-sum problem. Then, from line 6, we know that $z^* \le y^*$. By inequality (35.1), we need to show that $y^*/z^* \le 1 + \epsilon$. We must also show that the running time of this algorithm is polynomial in both $1/\epsilon$ and the size of the input.

As Exercise 35.5-2 asks you to show, for every element y in P_i that is at most t, there exists an element $z \in L_i$ such that

$$\frac{y}{(1 + \epsilon/2n)^i} \le z \le y . \tag{35.26}$$

Inequality (35.26) must hold for $y^* \in P_n$, and therefore there exists an element $z \in L_n$ such that

$$\frac{y^*}{(1 + \epsilon/2n)^n} \le z \le y^* ,$$

and thus

$$\frac{y^*}{z} \le \left(1 + \frac{\epsilon}{2n}\right)^n . \tag{35.27}$$

Since there exists an element $z \in L_n$ fulfilling inequality (35.27), the inequality must hold for z^*, which is the largest value in L_n; that is,

$$\frac{y^*}{z^*} \le \left(1 + \frac{\epsilon}{2n}\right)^n . \tag{35.28}$$

Now, we show that $y^*/z^* \le 1 + \epsilon$. We do so by showing that $(1 + \epsilon/2n)^n \le 1 + \epsilon$. By equation (3.14), we have $\lim_{n \to \infty}(1 + \epsilon/2n)^n = e^{\epsilon/2}$. Exercise 35.5-3 asks you to show that

$$\frac{d}{dn}\left(1 + \frac{\epsilon}{2n}\right)^n > 0 . \tag{35.29}$$

Therefore, the function $(1 + \epsilon/2n)^n$ increases with n as it approaches its limit of $e^{\epsilon/2}$, and we have

$$\left(1 + \frac{\epsilon}{2n}\right)^n \ \leq \ e^{\epsilon/2}$$

$$\leq \ 1 + \epsilon/2 + (\epsilon/2)^2 \quad \text{(by inequality (3.13))}$$

$$\leq \ 1 + \epsilon \qquad\qquad\quad \text{(by inequality (35.25))} . \qquad\qquad (35.30)$$

Combining inequalities (35.28) and (35.30) completes the analysis of the approximation ratio.

To show that APPROX-SUBSET-SUM is a fully polynomial-time approximation scheme, we derive a bound on the length of L_i. After trimming, successive elements z and z' of L_i must have the relationship $z'/z > 1+\epsilon/2n$. That is, they must differ by a factor of at least $1 + \epsilon/2n$. Each list, therefore, contains the value 0, possibly the value 1, and up to $\lfloor \log_{1+\epsilon/2n} t \rfloor$ additional values. The number of elements in each list L_i is at most

$$\log_{1+\epsilon/2n} t + 2 \ = \ \frac{\ln t}{\ln(1 + \epsilon/2n)} + 2$$

$$\leq \ \frac{2n(1 + \epsilon/2n)\ln t}{\epsilon} + 2 \quad \text{(by inequality (3.17))}$$

$$< \ \frac{3n \ln t}{\epsilon} + 2 \qquad\qquad\quad \text{(by inequality (35.25))} .$$

This bound is polynomial in the size of the input—which is the number of bits $\lg t$ needed to represent t plus the number of bits needed to represent the set S, which is in turn polynomial in n—and in $1/\epsilon$. Since the running time of APPROX-SUBSET-SUM is polynomial in the lengths of the L_i, we conclude that APPROX-SUBSET-SUM is a fully polynomial-time approximation scheme.   ∎

Exercises

35.5-1
Prove equation (35.23). Then show that after executing line 5 of EXACT-SUBSET-SUM, L_i is a sorted list containing every element of P_i whose value is not more than t.

35.5-2
Using induction on i, prove inequality (35.26).

35.5-3
Prove inequality (35.29).

35.5-4
How would you modify the approximation scheme presented in this section to find a good approximation to the smallest value not less than t that is a sum of some subset of the given input list?

35.5-5
Modify the APPROX-SUBSET-SUM procedure to also return the subset of S that sums to the value z^*.

Problems

35-1   *Bin packing*
Suppose that we are given a set of n objects, where the size s_i of the ith object satisfies $0 < s_i < 1$. We wish to pack all the objects into the minimum number of unit-size bins. Each bin can hold any subset of the objects whose total size does not exceed 1.

a. Prove that the problem of determining the minimum number of bins required is NP-hard. (*Hint:* Reduce from the subset-sum problem.)

The ***first-fit*** heuristic takes each object in turn and places it into the first bin that can accommodate it. Let $S = \sum_{i=1}^{n} s_i$.

b. Argue that the optimal number of bins required is at least $\lceil S \rceil$.

c. Argue that the first-fit heuristic leaves at most one bin less than half full.

d. Prove that the number of bins used by the first-fit heuristic is never more than $\lceil 2S \rceil$.

e. Prove an approximation ratio of 2 for the first-fit heuristic.

f. Give an efficient implementation of the first-fit heuristic, and analyze its running time.

35-2   *Approximating the size of a maximum clique*
Let $G = (V, E)$ be an undirected graph. For any $k \geq 1$, define $G^{(k)}$ to be the undirected graph $(V^{(k)}, E^{(k)})$, where $V^{(k)}$ is the set of all ordered k-tuples of vertices from V and $E^{(k)}$ is defined so that $(v_1, v_2, \ldots, v_k)$ is adjacent to $(w_1, w_2, \ldots, w_k)$ if and only if for $i = 1, 2, \ldots, k$, either vertex v_i is adjacent to w_i in G, or else $v_i = w_i$.

a. Prove that the size of the maximum clique in $G^{(k)}$ is equal to the kth power of the size of the maximum clique in G.

b. Argue that if there is an approximation algorithm that has a constant approximation ratio for finding a maximum-size clique, then there is a polynomial-time approximation scheme for the problem.

35-3 Weighted set-covering problem

Suppose that we generalize the set-covering problem so that each set S_i in the family $\mathcal{F}$ has an associated weight w_i and the weight of a cover $\mathcal{C}$ is $\sum_{S_i \in \mathcal{C}} w_i$. We wish to determine a minimum-weight cover. (Section 35.3 handles the case in which $w_i = 1$ for all i.)

Show how to generalize the greedy set-covering heuristic in a natural manner to provide an approximate solution for any instance of the weighted set-covering problem. Show that your heuristic has an approximation ratio of $H(d)$, where d is the maximum size of any set S_i.

35-4 Maximum matching

Recall that for an undirected graph G, a matching is a set of edges such that no two edges in the set are incident on the same vertex. In Section 26.3, we saw how to find a maximum matching in a bipartite graph. In this problem, we will look at matchings in undirected graphs in general (i.e., the graphs are not required to be bipartite).

a. A *maximal matching* is a matching that is not a proper subset of any other matching. Show that a maximal matching need not be a maximum matching by exhibiting an undirected graph G and a maximal matching M in G that is not a maximum matching. (*Hint:* You can find such a graph with only four vertices.)

b. Consider an undirected graph $G = (V, E)$. Give an $O(E)$-time greedy algorithm to find a maximal matching in G.

In this problem, we shall concentrate on a polynomial-time approximation algorithm for maximum matching. Whereas the fastest known algorithm for maximum matching takes superlinear (but polynomial) time, the approximation algorithm here will run in linear time. You will show that the linear-time greedy algorithm for maximal matching in part (b) is a 2-approximation algorithm for maximum matching.

c. Show that the size of a maximum matching in G is a lower bound on the size of any vertex cover for G.

d. Consider a maximal matching M in $G = (V, E)$. Let

$$T = \{v \in V : \text{some edge in } M \text{ is incident on } v\} \ .$$

What can you say about the subgraph of G induced by the vertices of G that are not in T?

e. Conclude from part (d) that $2\,|M|$ is the size of a vertex cover for G.

f. Using parts (c) and (e), prove that the greedy algorithm in part (b) is a 2-approximation algorithm for maximum matching.

35-5   *Parallel machine scheduling*

In the ***parallel-machine-scheduling problem***, we are given n jobs, $J_1, J_2, \ldots, J_n$, where each job J_k has an associated nonnegative processing time of p_k. We are also given m identical machines, $M_1, M_2, \ldots, M_m$. Any job can run on any machine. A ***schedule*** specifies, for each job J_k, the machine on which it runs and the time period during which it runs. Each job J_k must run on some machine M_i for p_k consecutive time units, and during that time period no other job may run on M_i. Let C_k denote the ***completion time*** of job J_k, that is, the time at which job J_k completes processing. Given a schedule, we define $C_{\max} = \max_{1 \le j \le n} C_j$ to be the ***makespan*** of the schedule. The goal is to find a schedule whose makespan is minimum.

For example, suppose that we have two machines M_1 and M_2 and that we have four jobs J_1, J_2, J_3, J_4, with $p_1 = 2$, $p_2 = 12$, $p_3 = 4$, and $p_4 = 5$. Then one possible schedule runs, on machine M_1, job J_1 followed by job J_2, and on machine M_2, it runs job J_4 followed by job J_3. For this schedule, $C_1 = 2$, $C_2 = 14$, $C_3 = 9$, $C_4 = 5$, and $C_{\max} = 14$. An optimal schedule runs J_2 on machine M_1, and it runs jobs J_1, J_3, and J_4 on machine M_2. For this schedule, $C_1 = 2$, $C_2 = 12$, $C_3 = 6$, $C_4 = 11$, and $C_{\max} = 12$.

Given a parallel-machine-scheduling problem, we let $C_{\max}^*$ denote the makespan of an optimal schedule.

a. Show that the optimal makespan is at least as large as the greatest processing time, that is,

$$C_{\max}^* \ge \max_{1 \le k \le n} p_k \ .$$

b. Show that the optimal makespan is at least as large as the average machine load, that is,

$$C_{\max}^* \ge \frac{1}{m} \sum_{1 \le k \le n} p_k \ .$$

Suppose that we use the following greedy algorithm for parallel machine scheduling: whenever a machine is idle, schedule any job that has not yet been scheduled.

c. Write pseudocode to implement this greedy algorithm. What is the running time of your algorithm?

d. For the schedule returned by the greedy algorithm, show that

$$
C_{\max} \leq \frac{1}{m} \sum_{1 \leq k \leq n} p_k + \max_{1 \leq k \leq n} p_k \;.
$$

Conclude that this algorithm is a polynomial-time 2-approximation algorithm.

35-6 *Approximating a maximum spanning tree*

Let $G = (V, E)$ be an undirected graph with distinct edge weights $w(u, v)$ on each edge $(u, v) \in E$. For each vertex $v \in V$, let $\max(v) = \text{argmax}_{(u,v) \in E} \{w(u, v)\}$ be the maximum-weight edge incident on that vertex. Let $S_G = \{\max(v) : v \in V\}$ be the set of maximum-weight edges incident on each vertex, and let T_G be the maximum-weight spanning tree of G, that is, the spanning tree of maximum total weight. For any subset of edges $E' \subseteq E$, define $w(E') = \sum_{(u,v) \in E'} w(u, v)$.

a. Give an example of a graph with at least 4 vertices for which $S_G = T_G$.

b. Give an example of a graph with at least 4 vertices for which $S_G \neq T_G$.

c. Prove that $S_G \subseteq T_G$ for any graph G.

d. Prove that $w(S_G) \geq w(T_G)/2$ for any graph G.

e. Give an $O(V + E)$-time algorithm to compute a 2-approximation to the maximum spanning tree.

35-7 *An approximation algorithm for the 0-1 knapsack problem*

Recall the knapsack problem from Section 16.2. There are n items, where the ith item is worth v_i dollars and weighs w_i pounds. We are also given a knapsack that can hold at most W pounds. Here, we add the further assumptions that each weight w_i is at most W and that the items are indexed in monotonically decreasing order of their values: $v_1 \geq v_2 \geq \cdots \geq v_n$.

In the 0-1 knapsack problem, we wish to find a subset of the items whose total weight is at most W and whose total value is maximum. The fractional knapsack problem is like the 0-1 knapsack problem, except that we are allowed to take a fraction of each item, rather than being restricted to taking either all or none of each item. If we take a fraction x_i of item i, where $0 \le x_i \le 1$, we contribute $x_i w_i$ to the weight of the knapsack and receive value $x_i v_i$. Our goal is to develop a polynomial-time 2-approximation algorithm for the 0-1 knapsack problem.

In order to design a polynomial-time algorithm, we consider restricted instances of the 0-1 knapsack problem. Given an instance I of the knapsack problem, we form restricted instances I_j, for $j = 1, 2, \ldots, n$, by removing items $1, 2, \ldots, j-1$ and requiring the solution to include item j (all of item j in both the fractional and 0-1 knapsack problems). No items are removed in instance I_1. For instance I_j, let P_j denote an optimal solution to the 0-1 problem and Q_j denote an optimal solution to the fractional problem.

a. Argue that an optimal solution to instance I of the 0-1 knapsack problem is one of $\{P_1, P_2, \ldots, P_n\}$.

b. Prove that we can find an optimal solution Q_j to the fractional problem for instance I_j by including item j and then using the greedy algorithm in which at each step, we take as much as possible of the unchosen item in the set $\{j+1, j+2, \ldots, n\}$ with maximum value per pound v_i/w_i.

c. Prove that we can always construct an optimal solution Q_j to the fractional problem for instance I_j that includes at most one item fractionally. That is, for all items except possibly one, we either include all of the item or none of the item in the knapsack.

d. Given an optimal solution Q_j to the fractional problem for instance I_j, form solution R_j from Q_j by deleting any fractional items from Q_j. Let $v(S)$ denote the total value of items taken in a solution S. Prove that $v(R_j) \ge v(Q_j)/2 \ge v(P_j)/2$.

e. Give a polynomial-time algorithm that returns a maximum-value solution from the set $\{R_1, R_2, \ldots, R_n\}$, and prove that your algorithm is a polynomial-time 2-approximation algorithm for the 0-1 knapsack problem.

Chapter notes

Although methods that do not necessarily compute exact solutions have been known for thousands of years (for example, methods to approximate the value of π), the notion of an approximation algorithm is much more recent. Hochbaum [172] credits Garey, Graham, and Ullman [128] and Johnson [190] with formalizing the concept of a polynomial-time approximation algorithm. The first such algorithm is often credited to Graham [149].

Since this early work, thousands of approximation algorithms have been designed for a wide range of problems, and there is a wealth of literature on this field. Recent texts by Ausiello et al. [26], Hochbaum [172], and Vazirani [345] deal exclusively with approximation algorithms, as do surveys by Shmoys [315] and Klein and Young [207]. Several other texts, such as Garey and Johnson [129] and Papadimitriou and Steiglitz [271], have significant coverage of approximation algorithms as well. Lawler, Lenstra, Rinnooy Kan, and Shmoys [225] provide an extensive treatment of approximation algorithms for the traveling-salesman problem.

Papadimitriou and Steiglitz attribute the algorithm APPROX-VERTEX-COVER to F. Gavril and M. Yannakakis. The vertex-cover problem has been studied extensively (Hochbaum [172] lists 16 different approximation algorithms for this problem), but all the approximation ratios are at least $2 - o(1)$.

The algorithm APPROX-TSP-TOUR appears in a paper by Rosenkrantz, Stearns, and Lewis [298]. Christofides improved on this algorithm and gave a $3/2$-approximation algorithm for the traveling-salesman problem with the triangle inequality. Arora [22] and Mitchell [257] have shown that if the points are in the euclidean plane, there is a polynomial-time approximation scheme. Theorem 35.3 is due to Sahni and Gonzalez [301].

The analysis of the greedy heuristic for the set-covering problem is modeled after the proof published by Chvátal [68] of a more general result; the basic result as presented here is due to Johnson [190] and Lovász [238].

The algorithm APPROX-SUBSET-SUM and its analysis are loosely modeled after related approximation algorithms for the knapsack and subset-sum problems by Ibarra and Kim [187].

Problem 35-7 is a combinatorial version of a more general result on approximating knapsack-type integer programs by Bienstock and McClosky [45].

The randomized algorithm for MAX-3-CNF satisfiability is implicit in the work of Johnson [190]. The weighted vertex-cover algorithm is by Hochbaum [171]. Section 35.4 only touches on the power of randomization and linear programming in the design of approximation algorithms. A combination of these two ideas yields a technique called "randomized rounding," which formulates a problem as an integer linear program, solves the linear-programming relaxation, and interprets the variables in the solution as probabilities. These probabilities then help guide the solution of the original problem. This technique was first used by Raghavan and Thompson [290], and it has had many subsequent uses. (See Motwani, Naor, and Raghavan [261] for a survey.) Several other notable recent ideas in the field of approximation algorithms include the primal-dual method (see Goemans and Williamson [135] for a survey), finding sparse cuts for use in divide-and-conquer algorithms [229], and the use of semidefinite programming [134].

As mentioned in the chapter notes for Chapter 34, recent results in probabilistically checkable proofs have led to lower bounds on the approximability of many problems, including several in this chapter. In addition to the references there, the chapter by Arora and Lund [23] contains a good description of the relationship between probabilistically checkable proofs and the hardness of approximating various problems.

VIII Appendix: Mathematical Background

Introduction

When we analyze algorithms, we often need to draw upon a body of mathematical tools. Some of these tools are as simple as high-school algebra, but others may be new to you. In Part I, we saw how to manipulate asymptotic notations and solve recurrences. This appendix comprises a compendium of several other concepts and methods we use to analyze algorithms. As noted in the introduction to Part I, you may have seen much of the material in this appendix before having read this book (although the specific notational conventions we use might occasionally differ from those you have seen elsewhere). Hence, you should treat this appendix as reference material. As in the rest of this book, however, we have included exercises and problems, in order for you to improve your skills in these areas.

Appendix A offers methods for evaluating and bounding summations, which occur frequently in the analysis of algorithms. Many of the formulas here appear in any calculus text, but you will find it convenient to have these methods compiled in one place.

Appendix B contains basic definitions and notations for sets, relations, functions, graphs, and trees. It also gives some basic properties of these mathematical objects.

Appendix C begins with elementary principles of counting: permutations, combinations, and the like. The remainder contains definitions and properties of basic probability. Most of the algorithms in this book require no probability for their analysis, and thus you can easily omit the latter sections of the chapter on a first reading, even without skimming them. Later, when you encounter a probabilistic analysis that you want to understand better, you will find Appendix C well organized for reference purposes.

Appendix D defines matrices, their operations, and some of their basic properties. You have probably seen most of this material already if you have taken a course in linear algebra, but you might find it helpful to have one place to look for our notation and definitions.

A Summations

When an algorithm contains an iterative control construct such as a **while** or **for** loop, we can express its running time as the sum of the times spent on each execution of the body of the loop. For example, we found in Section 2.2 that the jth iteration of insertion sort took time proportional to j in the worst case. By adding up the time spent on each iteration, we obtained the summation (or series)

$$\sum_{j=2}^{n} j \; .$$

When we evaluated this summation, we attained a bound of $\Theta(n^2)$ on the worst-case running time of the algorithm. This example illustrates why you should know how to manipulate and bound summations.

Section A.1 lists several basic formulas involving summations. Section A.2 offers useful techniques for bounding summations. We present the formulas in Section A.1 without proof, though proofs for some of them appear in Section A.2 to illustrate the methods of that section. You can find most of the other proofs in any calculus text.

A.1 Summation formulas and properties

Given a sequence $a_1, a_2, \ldots, a_n$ of numbers, where n is a nonnegative integer, we can write the finite sum $a_1 + a_2 + \cdots + a_n$ as

$$\sum_{k=1}^{n} a_k \; .$$

If $n = 0$, the value of the summation is defined to be 0. The value of a finite series is always well defined, and we can add its terms in any order.

Given an infinite sequence $a_1, a_2, \ldots$ of numbers, we can write the infinite sum $a_1 + a_2 + \cdots$ as

$$\sum_{k=1}^{\infty} a_k \ ,$$

which we interpret to mean

$$\lim_{n \to \infty} \sum_{k=1}^{n} a_k \ .$$

If the limit does not exist, the series **diverges**; otherwise, it **converges**. The terms of a convergent series cannot always be added in any order. We can, however, rearrange the terms of an **absolutely convergent series**, that is, a series $\sum_{k=1}^{\infty} a_k$ for which the series $\sum_{k=1}^{\infty} |a_k|$ also converges.

Linearity

For any real number c and any finite sequences $a_1, a_2, \ldots, a_n$ and $b_1, b_2, \ldots, b_n$,

$$\sum_{k=1}^{n} (ca_k + b_k) = c \sum_{k=1}^{n} a_k + \sum_{k=1}^{n} b_k \ .$$

The linearity property also applies to infinite convergent series.

We can exploit the linearity property to manipulate summations incorporating asymptotic notation. For example,

$$\sum_{k=1}^{n} \Theta(f(k)) = \Theta \left(\sum_{k=1}^{n} f(k) \right) .$$

In this equation, the Θ-notation on the left-hand side applies to the variable k, but on the right-hand side, it applies to n. We can also apply such manipulations to infinite convergent series.

Arithmetic series

The summation

$$\sum_{k=1}^{n} k = 1 + 2 + \cdots + n \ ,$$

is an **arithmetic series** and has the value

$$\sum_{k=1}^{n} k \quad = \quad \frac{1}{2} n(n+1) \tag{A.1}$$

$$\quad = \quad \Theta(n^2) \ . \tag{A.2}$$

Sums of squares and cubes

We have the following summations of squares and cubes:

$$\sum_{k=0}^{n} k^2 = \frac{n(n+1)(2n+1)}{6} , \qquad (A.3)$$

$$\sum_{k=0}^{n} k^3 = \frac{n^2(n+1)^2}{4} . \qquad (A.4)$$

Geometric series

For real $x \neq 1$, the summation

$$\sum_{k=0}^{n} x^k = 1 + x + x^2 + \cdots + x^n$$

is a **geometric** or **exponential series** and has the value

$$\sum_{k=0}^{n} x^k = \frac{x^{n+1} - 1}{x - 1} . \qquad (A.5)$$

When the summation is infinite and $|x| < 1$, we have the infinite decreasing geometric series

$$\sum_{k=0}^{\infty} x^k = \frac{1}{1 - x} . \qquad (A.6)$$

Because we assume that $0^0 = 1$, these formulas apply even when $x = 0$.

Harmonic series

For positive integers n, the nth **harmonic number** is

$$
\begin{aligned}
H_n &= 1 + \frac{1}{2} + \frac{1}{3} + \frac{1}{4} + \cdots + \frac{1}{n} \\
&= \sum_{k=1}^{n} \frac{1}{k} \\
&= \ln n + O(1) .
\end{aligned}
\qquad (A.7)
$$

(We shall prove a related bound in Section A.2.)

Integrating and differentiating series

By integrating or differentiating the formulas above, additional formulas arise. For example, by differentiating both sides of the infinite geometric series (A.6) and multiplying by x, we get

$$\sum_{k=0}^{\infty} k x^k = \frac{x}{(1-x)^2} \tag{A.8}$$

for $|x| < 1$.

Telescoping series

For any sequence $a_0, a_1, \ldots, a_n$,

$$\sum_{k=1}^{n} (a_k - a_{k-1}) = a_n - a_0 , \tag{A.9}$$

since each of the terms $a_1, a_2, \ldots, a_{n-1}$ is added in exactly once and subtracted out exactly once. We say that the sum **telescopes**. Similarly,

$$\sum_{k=0}^{n-1} (a_k - a_{k+1}) = a_0 - a_n .$$

As an example of a telescoping sum, consider the series

$$\sum_{k=1}^{n-1} \frac{1}{k(k+1)} .$$

Since we can rewrite each term as

$$\frac{1}{k(k+1)} = \frac{1}{k} - \frac{1}{k+1} ,$$

we get

$$\begin{aligned}
\sum_{k=1}^{n-1} \frac{1}{k(k+1)} &= \sum_{k=1}^{n-1} \left(\frac{1}{k} - \frac{1}{k+1} \right) \\
&= 1 - \frac{1}{n} .
\end{aligned}$$

Products

We can write the finite product $a_1 a_2 \cdots a_n$ as

$$\prod_{k=1}^{n} a_k .$$

If $n = 0$, the value of the product is defined to be 1. We can convert a formula with a product to a formula with a summation by using the identity

$$\lg \left(\prod_{k=1}^{n} a_k \right) = \sum_{k=1}^{n} \lg a_k .$$

Exercises

A.1-1
Find a simple formula for $\sum_{k=1}^{n}(2k-1)$.

A.1-2 ★
Show that $\sum_{k=1}^{n}1/(2k-1) = \ln(\sqrt{n}) + O(1)$ by manipulating the harmonic series.

A.1-3
Show that $\sum_{k=0}^{\infty}k^2 x^k = x(1+x)/(1-x)^3$ for $|x| < 1$.

A.1-4 ★
Show that $\sum_{k=0}^{\infty}(k-1)/2^k = 0$.

A.1-5 ★
Evaluate the sum $\sum_{k=1}^{\infty}(2k+1)x^{2k}$ for $|x| < 1$.

A.1-6
Prove that $\sum_{k=1}^{n}O(f_k(i)) = O\left(\sum_{k=1}^{n}f_k(i)\right)$ by using the linearity property of summations.

A.1-7
Evaluate the product $\prod_{k=1}^{n}2 \cdot 4^k$.

A.1-8 ★
Evaluate the product $\prod_{k=2}^{n}(1-1/k^2)$.

A.2   Bounding summations

We have many techniques at our disposal for bounding the summations that describe the running times of algorithms. Here are some of the most frequently used methods.

Mathematical induction

The most basic way to evaluate a series is to use mathematical induction. As an example, let us prove that the arithmetic series $\sum_{k=1}^{n}k$ evaluates to $\frac{1}{2}n(n+1)$. We can easily verify this assertion for $n = 1$. We make the inductive assumption that it holds for n, and we prove that it holds for $n + 1$. We have

$$\sum_{k=1}^{n+1} k = \sum_{k=1}^{n} k + (n + 1)$$

$$= \frac{1}{2}n(n + 1) + (n + 1)$$

$$= \frac{1}{2}(n + 1)(n + 2) .$$

You don't always need to guess the exact value of a summation in order to use mathematical induction. Instead, you can use induction to prove a bound on a summation. As an example, let us prove that the geometric series $\sum_{k=0}^{n} 3^k$ is $O(3^n)$. More specifically, let us prove that $\sum_{k=0}^{n} 3^k \leq c3^n$ for some constant c. For the initial condition $n = 0$, we have $\sum_{k=0}^{0} 3^k = 1 \leq c \cdot 1$ as long as $c \geq 1$. Assuming that the bound holds for n, let us prove that it holds for $n + 1$. We have

$$\sum_{k=0}^{n+1} 3^k = \sum_{k=0}^{n} 3^k + 3^{n+1}$$

$$\leq c3^n + 3^{n+1} \qquad \text{(by the inductive hypothesis)}$$

$$= \left(\frac{1}{3} + \frac{1}{c}\right) c3^{n+1}$$

$$\leq c3^{n+1}$$

as long as $(1/3 + 1/c) \leq 1$ or, equivalently, $c \geq 3/2$. Thus, $\sum_{k=0}^{n} 3^k = O(3^n)$, as we wished to show.

We have to be careful when we use asymptotic notation to prove bounds by induction. Consider the following fallacious proof that $\sum_{k=1}^{n} k = O(n)$. Certainly, $\sum_{k=1}^{1} k = O(1)$. Assuming that the bound holds for n, we now prove it for $n + 1$:

$$\sum_{k=1}^{n+1} k = \sum_{k=1}^{n} k + (n + 1)$$

$$= O(n) + (n + 1) \qquad \Longleftarrow wrong!!$$

$$= O(n + 1) .$$

The bug in the argument is that the "constant" hidden by the "big-oh" grows with n and thus is not constant. We have not shown that the same constant works for *all* n.

Bounding the terms

We can sometimes obtain a good upper bound on a series by bounding each term of the series, and it often suffices to use the largest term to bound the others. For example, a quick upper bound on the arithmetic series (A.1) is

$$\sum_{k=1}^{n} k \le \sum_{k=1}^{n} n$$
$$= n^2 .$$

In general, for a series $\sum_{k=1}^{n} a_k$, if we let $a_{\max} = \max_{1 \le k \le n} a_k$, then

$$\sum_{k=1}^{n} a_k \le n \cdot a_{\max} .$$

The technique of bounding each term in a series by the largest term is a weak method when the series can in fact be bounded by a geometric series. Given the series $\sum_{k=0}^{n} a_k$, suppose that $a_{k+1}/a_k \le r$ for all $k \ge 0$, where $0 < r < 1$ is a constant. We can bound the sum by an infinite decreasing geometric series, since $a_k \le a_0 r^k$, and thus

$$\sum_{k=0}^{n} a_k \le \sum_{k=0}^{\infty} a_0 r^k$$
$$= a_0 \sum_{k=0}^{\infty} r^k$$
$$= a_0 \frac{1}{1-r} .$$

We can apply this method to bound the summation $\sum_{k=1}^{\infty} (k/3^k)$. In order to start the summation at $k = 0$, we rewrite it as $\sum_{k=0}^{\infty} ((k+1)/3^{k+1})$. The first term ($a_0$) is $1/3$, and the ratio (r) of consecutive terms is

$$\frac{(k+2)/3^{k+2}}{(k+1)/3^{k+1}} = \frac{1}{3} \cdot \frac{k+2}{k+1}$$
$$\le \frac{2}{3}$$

for all $k \ge 0$. Thus, we have

$$\sum_{k=1}^{\infty} \frac{k}{3^k} = \sum_{k=0}^{\infty} \frac{k+1}{3^{k+1}}$$
$$\le \frac{1}{3} \cdot \frac{1}{1 - 2/3}$$
$$= 1 .$$

A common bug in applying this method is to show that the ratio of consecutive terms is less than 1 and then to assume that the summation is bounded by a geometric series. An example is the infinite harmonic series, which diverges since

$$\sum_{k=1}^{\infty} \frac{1}{k} = \lim_{n \to \infty} \sum_{k=1}^{n} \frac{1}{k}$$

$$= \lim_{n \to \infty} \Theta(\lg n)$$

$$= \infty .$$

The ratio of the $(k+1)$st and kth terms in this series is $k/(k+1) < 1$, but the series is not bounded by a decreasing geometric series. To bound a series by a geometric series, we must show that there is an $r < 1$, which is a *constant*, such that the ratio of all pairs of consecutive terms never exceeds r. In the harmonic series, no such r exists because the ratio becomes arbitrarily close to 1.

Splitting summations

One way to obtain bounds on a difficult summation is to express the series as the sum of two or more series by partitioning the range of the index and then to bound each of the resulting series. For example, suppose we try to find a lower bound on the arithmetic series $\sum_{k=1}^{n} k$, which we have already seen has an upper bound of n^2. We might attempt to bound each term in the summation by the smallest term, but since that term is 1, we get a lower bound of n for the summation—far off from our upper bound of n^2.

We can obtain a better lower bound by first splitting the summation. Assume for convenience that n is even. We have

$$\sum_{k=1}^{n} k = \sum_{k=1}^{n/2} k + \sum_{k=n/2+1}^{n} k$$

$$\geq \sum_{k=1}^{n/2} 0 + \sum_{k=n/2+1}^{n} (n/2)$$

$$= (n/2)^2$$

$$= \Omega(n^2) ,$$

which is an asymptotically tight bound, since $\sum_{k=1}^{n} k = O(n^2)$.

For a summation arising from the analysis of an algorithm, we can often split the summation and ignore a constant number of the initial terms. Generally, this technique applies when each term a_k in a summation $\sum_{k=0}^{n} a_k$ is independent of n.

Then for any constant $k_0 > 0$, we can write

$$\sum_{k=0}^{n} a_k = \sum_{k=0}^{k_0-1} a_k + \sum_{k=k_0}^{n} a_k$$

$$= \Theta(1) + \sum_{k=k_0}^{n} a_k ,$$

since the initial terms of the summation are all constant and there are a constant number of them. We can then use other methods to bound $\sum_{k=k_0}^{n} a_k$. This technique applies to infinite summations as well. For example, to find an asymptotic upper bound on

$$\sum_{k=0}^{\infty} \frac{k^2}{2^k} ,$$

we observe that the ratio of consecutive terms is

$$\frac{(k+1)^2 / 2^{k+1}}{k^2 / 2^k} = \frac{(k+1)^2}{2k^2}$$

$$\leq \frac{8}{9}$$

if $k \geq 3$. Thus, the summation can be split into

$$\sum_{k=0}^{\infty} \frac{k^2}{2^k} = \sum_{k=0}^{2} \frac{k^2}{2^k} + \sum_{k=3}^{\infty} \frac{k^2}{2^k}$$

$$\leq \sum_{k=0}^{2} \frac{k^2}{2^k} + \frac{9}{8} \sum_{k=0}^{\infty} \left(\frac{8}{9}\right)^k$$

$$= O(1) ,$$

since the first summation has a constant number of terms and the second summation is a decreasing geometric series.

The technique of splitting summations can help us determine asymptotic bounds in much more difficult situations. For example, we can obtain a bound of $O(\lg n)$ on the harmonic series (A.7):

$$H_n = \sum_{k=1}^{n} \frac{1}{k} .$$

We do so by splitting the range 1 to n into $\lfloor \lg n \rfloor + 1$ pieces and upper-bounding the contribution of each piece by 1. For $i = 0, 1, \ldots, \lfloor \lg n \rfloor$, the ith piece consists of the terms starting at $1/2^i$ and going up to but not including $1/2^{i+1}$. The last piece might contain terms not in the original harmonic series, and thus we have

$$\sum_{k=1}^{n} \frac{1}{k} \leq \sum_{i=0}^{\lfloor \lg n \rfloor} \sum_{j=0}^{2^i-1} \frac{1}{2^i + j}$$

$$\leq \sum_{i=0}^{\lfloor \lg n \rfloor} \sum_{j=0}^{2^i-1} \frac{1}{2^i}$$

$$= \sum_{i=0}^{\lfloor \lg n \rfloor} 1$$

$$\leq \lg n + 1 . \tag{A.10}$$

Approximation by integrals

When a summation has the form $\sum_{k=m}^{n} f(k)$, where $f(k)$ is a monotonically increasing function, we can approximate it by integrals:

$$\int_{m-1}^{n} f(x)\,dx \leq \sum_{k=m}^{n} f(k) \leq \int_{m}^{n+1} f(x)\,dx . \tag{A.11}$$

Figure A.1 justifies this approximation. The summation is represented as the area of the rectangles in the figure, and the integral is the shaded region under the curve. When $f(k)$ is a monotonically decreasing function, we can use a similar method to provide the bounds

$$\int_{m}^{n+1} f(x)\,dx \leq \sum_{k=m}^{n} f(k) \leq \int_{m-1}^{n} f(x)\,dx . \tag{A.12}$$

The integral approximation (A.12) gives a tight estimate for the nth harmonic number. For a lower bound, we obtain

$$\sum_{k=1}^{n} \frac{1}{k} \geq \int_{1}^{n+1} \frac{dx}{x}$$

$$= \ln(n+1) . \tag{A.13}$$

For the upper bound, we derive the inequality

$$\sum_{k=2}^{n} \frac{1}{k} \leq \int_{1}^{n} \frac{dx}{x}$$

$$= \ln n ,$$

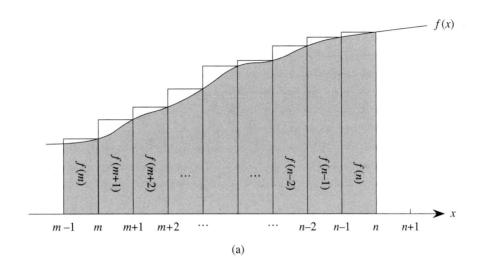

(a)

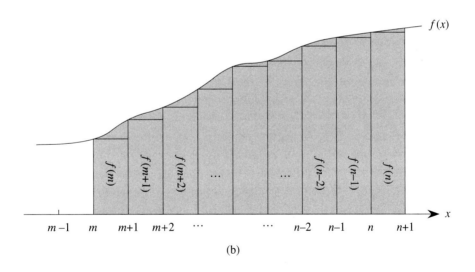

(b)

Figure A.1 Approximation of $\sum_{k=m}^{n} f(k)$ by integrals. The area of each rectangle is shown within the rectangle, and the total rectangle area represents the value of the summation. The integral is represented by the shaded area under the curve. By comparing areas in **(a)**, we get $\int_{m-1}^{n} f(x)\,dx \leq \sum_{k=m}^{n} f(k)$, and then by shifting the rectangles one unit to the right, we get $\sum_{k=m}^{n} f(k) \leq \int_{m}^{n+1} f(x)\,dx$ in **(b)**.

which yields the bound

$$\sum_{k=1}^{n} \frac{1}{k} \leq \ln n + 1 .$$ (A.14)

Exercises

A.2-1
Show that $\sum_{k=1}^{n} 1/k^2$ is bounded above by a constant.

A.2-2
Find an asymptotic upper bound on the summation

$$\sum_{k=0}^{\lfloor \lg n \rfloor} \lceil n/2^k \rceil .$$

A.2-3
Show that the nth harmonic number is $\Omega(\lg n)$ by splitting the summation.

A.2-4
Approximate $\sum_{k=1}^{n} k^3$ with an integral.

A.2-5
Why didn't we use the integral approximation (A.12) directly on $\sum_{k=1}^{n} 1/k$ to obtain an upper bound on the nth harmonic number?

Problems

A-1 *Bounding summations*
Give asymptotically tight bounds on the following summations. Assume that $r \geq 0$ and $s \geq 0$ are constants.

a. $\displaystyle\sum_{k=1}^{n} k^r .$

b. $\displaystyle\sum_{k=1}^{n} \lg^s k .$

$$c. \quad \sum_{k=1}^{n} k^r \lg^s k.$$

Appendix notes

Knuth [209] provides an excellent reference for the material presented here. You can find basic properties of series in any good calculus book, such as Apostol [18] or Thomas et al. [334].

B   Sets, Etc.

Many chapters of this book touch on the elements of discrete mathematics. This appendix reviews more completely the notations, definitions, and elementary properties of sets, relations, functions, graphs, and trees. If you are already well versed in this material, you can probably just skim this chapter.

B.1   Sets

A *set* is a collection of distinguishable objects, called its *members* or *elements*. If an object x is a member of a set S, we write $x \in S$ (read "x is a member of S" or, more briefly, "x is in S"). If x is not a member of S, we write $x \notin S$. We can describe a set by explicitly listing its members as a list inside braces. For example, we can define a set S to contain precisely the numbers 1, 2, and 3 by writing $S = \{1, 2, 3\}$. Since 2 is a member of the set S, we can write $2 \in S$, and since 4 is not a member, we have $4 \notin S$. A set cannot contain the same object more than once,[1] and its elements are not ordered. Two sets A and B are *equal*, written $A = B$, if they contain the same elements. For example, $\{1, 2, 3, 1\} = \{1, 2, 3\} = \{3, 2, 1\}$.

We adopt special notations for frequently encountered sets:

- $\emptyset$ denotes the *empty set*, that is, the set containing no members.

- $\mathbb{Z}$ denotes the set of *integers*, that is, the set $\{\ldots, -2, -1, 0, 1, 2, \ldots\}$.

- $\mathbb{R}$ denotes the set of *real numbers*.

- $\mathbb{N}$ denotes the set of *natural numbers*, that is, the set $\{0, 1, 2, \ldots\}$.[2]

---

[1] A variation of a set, which can contain the same object more than once, is called a *multiset*.

[2] Some authors start the natural numbers with 1 instead of 0. The modern trend seems to be to start with 0.

If all the elements of a set A are contained in a set B, that is, if $x \in A$ implies $x \in B$, then we write $A \subseteq B$ and say that A is a **subset** of B. A set A is a **proper subset** of B, written $A \subset B$, if $A \subseteq B$ but $A \neq B$. (Some authors use the symbol "$\subset$" to denote the ordinary subset relation, rather than the proper-subset relation.) For any set A, we have $A \subseteq A$. For two sets A and B, we have $A = B$ if and only if $A \subseteq B$ and $B \subseteq A$. For any three sets A, B, and C, if $A \subseteq B$ and $B \subseteq C$, then $A \subseteq C$. For any set A, we have $\emptyset \subseteq A$.

We sometimes define sets in terms of other sets. Given a set A, we can define a set $B \subseteq A$ by stating a property that distinguishes the elements of B. For example, we can define the set of even integers by $\{x : x \in \mathbb{Z} \text{ and } x/2 \text{ is an integer}\}$. The colon in this notation is read "such that." (Some authors use a vertical bar in place of the colon.)

Given two sets A and B, we can also define new sets by applying **set operations**:

- The **intersection** of sets A and B is the set

$$A \cap B = \{x : x \in A \text{ and } x \in B\} \ .$$

- The **union** of sets A and B is the set

$$A \cup B = \{x : x \in A \text{ or } x \in B\} \ .$$

- The **difference** between two sets A and B is the set

$$A - B = \{x : x \in A \text{ and } x \notin B\} \ .$$

Set operations obey the following laws:

Empty set laws:

$$A \cap \emptyset = \emptyset \ ,$$
$$A \cup \emptyset = A \ .$$

Idempotency laws:

$$A \cap A = A \ ,$$
$$A \cup A = A \ .$$

Commutative laws:

$$A \cap B = B \cap A \ ,$$
$$A \cup B = B \cup A \ .$$

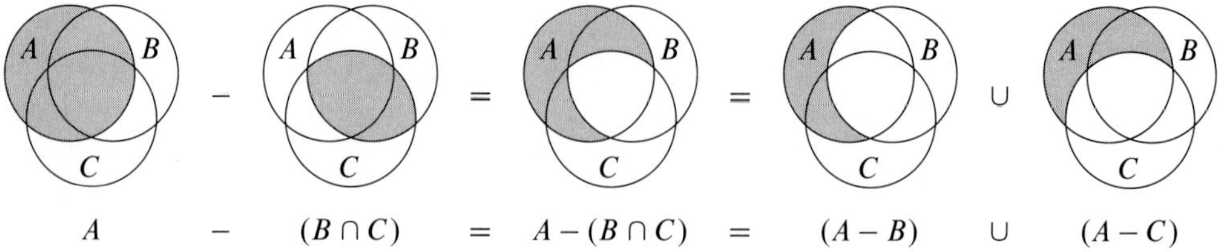

$$A \quad - \quad (B \cap C) \quad = \quad A - (B \cap C) \quad = \quad (A - B) \quad \cup \quad (A - C)$$

Figure B.1   A Venn diagram illustrating the first of DeMorgan's laws (B.2). Each of the sets A, B, and C is represented as a circle.

Associative laws:

$$A \cap (B \cap C) = (A \cap B) \cap C,$$
$$A \cup (B \cup C) = (A \cup B) \cup C.$$

Distributive laws:

$$A \cap (B \cup C) = (A \cap B) \cup (A \cap C),$$
$$A \cup (B \cap C) = (A \cup B) \cap (A \cup C). \tag{B.1}$$

Absorption laws:

$$A \cap (A \cup B) = A,$$
$$A \cup (A \cap B) = A.$$

DeMorgan's laws:

$$A - (B \cap C) = (A - B) \cup (A - C),$$
$$A - (B \cup C) = (A - B) \cap (A - C). \tag{B.2}$$

Figure B.1 illustrates the first of DeMorgan's laws, using a ***Venn diagram***: a graphical picture in which sets are represented as regions of the plane.

Often, all the sets under consideration are subsets of some larger set U called the ***universe***. For example, if we are considering various sets made up only of integers, the set $\mathbb{Z}$ of integers is an appropriate universe. Given a universe U, we define the ***complement*** of a set A as $\overline{A} = U - A = \{x : x \in U \text{ and } x \notin A\}$. For any set $A \subseteq U$, we have the following laws:

$$\overline{\overline{A}} = A,$$
$$A \cap \overline{A} = \emptyset,$$
$$A \cup \overline{A} = U.$$

We can rewrite DeMorgan's laws (B.2) with set complements. For any two sets $B, C \subseteq U$, we have

$$\overline{B \cap C} = \overline{B} \cup \overline{C},$$
$$\overline{B \cup C} = \overline{B} \cap \overline{C}.$$

Two sets A and B are **disjoint** if they have no elements in common, that is, if $A \cap B = \emptyset$. A collection $\mathcal{S} = \{S_i\}$ of nonempty sets forms a **partition** of a set S if

- the sets are **pairwise disjoint**, that is, $S_i, S_j \in \mathcal{S}$ and $i \neq j$ imply $S_i \cap S_j = \emptyset$, and

- their union is S, that is,

$$S = \bigcup_{S_i \in \mathcal{S}} S_i .$$

In other words, $\mathcal{S}$ forms a partition of S if each element of S appears in exactly one $S_i \in \mathcal{S}$.

The number of elements in a set is the **cardinality** (or **size**) of the set, denoted $|S|$. Two sets have the same cardinality if their elements can be put into a one-to-one correspondence. The cardinality of the empty set is $|\emptyset| = 0$. If the cardinality of a set is a natural number, we say the set is **finite**; otherwise, it is **infinite**. An infinite set that can be put into a one-to-one correspondence with the natural numbers $\mathbb{N}$ is **countably infinite**; otherwise, it is **uncountable**. For example, the integers $\mathbb{Z}$ are countable, but the reals $\mathbb{R}$ are uncountable.

For any two finite sets A and B, we have the identity

$$|A \cup B| = |A| + |B| - |A \cap B| , \tag{B.3}$$

from which we can conclude that

$$|A \cup B| \leq |A| + |B| .$$

If A and B are disjoint, then $|A \cap B| = 0$ and thus $|A \cup B| = |A| + |B|$. If $A \subseteq B$, then $|A| \leq |B|$.

A finite set of n elements is sometimes called an **n-set**. A 1-set is called a **singleton**. A subset of k elements of a set is sometimes called a **k-subset**.

We denote the set of all subsets of a set S, including the empty set and S itself, by 2^S; we call 2^S the **power set** of S. For example, $2^{\{a,b\}} = \{\emptyset, \{a\}, \{b\}, \{a, b\}\}$. The power set of a finite set S has cardinality $2^{|S|}$ (see Exercise B.1-5).

We sometimes care about setlike structures in which the elements are ordered. An **ordered pair** of two elements a and b is denoted (a, b) and is defined formally as the set $(a, b) = \{a, \{a, b\}\}$. Thus, the ordered pair (a, b) is *not* the same as the ordered pair (b, a).

The ***Cartesian product*** of two sets A and B, denoted $A \times B$, is the set of all ordered pairs such that the first element of the pair is an element of A and the second is an element of B. More formally,

$$A \times B = \{(a, b) : a \in A \text{ and } b \in B\} \ .$$

For example, $\{a, b\} \times \{a, b, c\} = \{(a, a), (a, b), (a, c), (b, a), (b, b), (b, c)\}$. When A and B are finite sets, the cardinality of their Cartesian product is

$$|A \times B| = |A| \cdot |B| \ . \tag{B.4}$$

The Cartesian product of n sets $A_1, A_2, \ldots, A_n$ is the set of ***n-tuples***

$$A_1 \times A_2 \times \cdots \times A_n = \{(a_1, a_2, \ldots, a_n) : a_i \in A_i \text{ for } i = 1, 2, \ldots, n\} \ ,$$

whose cardinality is

$$|A_1 \times A_2 \times \cdots \times A_n| = |A_1| \cdot |A_2| \cdots |A_n|$$

if all sets are finite. We denote an n-fold Cartesian product over a single set A by the set

$$A^n = A \times A \times \cdots \times A \ ,$$

whose cardinality is $|A^n| = |A|^n$ if A is finite. We can also view an n-tuple as a finite sequence of length n (see page 1166).

Exercises

B.1-1
Draw Venn diagrams that illustrate the first of the distributive laws (B.1).

B.1-2
Prove the generalization of DeMorgan's laws to any finite collection of sets:

$$\overline{A_1 \cap A_2 \cap \cdots \cap A_n} = \overline{A_1} \cup \overline{A_2} \cup \cdots \cup \overline{A_n} \ ,$$
$$\overline{A_1 \cup A_2 \cup \cdots \cup A_n} = \overline{A_1} \cap \overline{A_2} \cap \cdots \cap \overline{A_n} \ .$$

B.1-3 ★
Prove the generalization of equation (B.3), which is called the ***principle of inclusion and exclusion***:

$$|A_1 \cup A_2 \cup \cdots \cup A_n| =$$

$$|A_1| + |A_2| + \cdots + |A_n|$$

$$- |A_1 \cap A_2| - |A_1 \cap A_3| - \cdots \qquad \text{(all pairs)}$$

$$+ |A_1 \cap A_2 \cap A_3| + \cdots \qquad \text{(all triples)}$$

$$\vdots$$

$$+ (-1)^{n-1} |A_1 \cap A_2 \cap \cdots \cap A_n| \ .$$

B.1-4
Show that the set of odd natural numbers is countable.

B.1-5
Show that for any finite set S, the power set 2^S has $2^{|S|}$ elements (that is, there are $2^{|S|}$ distinct subsets of S).

B.1-6
Give an inductive definition for an n-tuple by extending the set-theoretic definition for an ordered pair.

B.2 Relations

A ***binary relation*** R on two sets A and B is a subset of the Cartesian product $A \times B$. If $(a, b) \in R$, we sometimes write $a \, R \, b$. When we say that R is a binary relation on a set A, we mean that R is a subset of $A \times A$. For example, the "less than" relation on the natural numbers is the set $\{(a, b) : a, b \in \mathbb{N} \text{ and } a < b\}$. An n-ary relation on sets $A_1, A_2, \ldots, A_n$ is a subset of $A_1 \times A_2 \times \cdots \times A_n$.

A binary relation $R \subseteq A \times A$ is ***reflexive*** if

$$a \, R \, a$$

for all $a \in A$. For example, "$=$" and "$\leq$" are reflexive relations on $\mathbb{N}$, but "$<$" is not. The relation R is ***symmetric*** if

$$a \, R \, b \text{ implies } b \, R \, a$$

for all $a, b \in A$. For example, "$=$" is symmetric, but "$<$" and "$\leq$" are not. The relation R is ***transitive*** if

$$a \, R \, b \text{ and } b \, R \, c \text{ imply } a \, R \, c$$

for all $a, b, c \in A$. For example, the relations "$<$," "$\leq$," and "$=$" are transitive, but the relation $R = \{(a, b) : a, b \in \mathbb{N} \text{ and } a = b - 1\}$ is not, since $3 \mathrel{R} 4$ and $4 \mathrel{R} 5$ do not imply $3 \mathrel{R} 5$.

A relation that is reflexive, symmetric, and transitive is an ***equivalence relation***. For example, "$=$" is an equivalence relation on the natural numbers, but "$<$" is not. If R is an equivalence relation on a set A, then for $a \in A$, the ***equivalence class*** of a is the set $[a] = \{b \in A : a \mathrel{R} b\}$, that is, the set of all elements equivalent to a. For example, if we define $R = \{(a, b) : a, b \in \mathbb{N} \text{ and } a + b \text{ is an even number}\}$, then R is an equivalence relation, since $a + a$ is even (reflexive), $a + b$ is even implies $b + a$ is even (symmetric), and $a + b$ is even and $b + c$ is even imply $a + c$ is even (transitive). The equivalence class of 4 is $[4] = \{0, 2, 4, 6, \ldots\}$, and the equivalence class of 3 is $[3] = \{1, 3, 5, 7, \ldots\}$. A basic theorem of equivalence classes is the following.

Theorem B.1 (An equivalence relation is the same as a partition)
The equivalence classes of any equivalence relation R on a set A form a partition of A, and any partition of A determines an equivalence relation on A for which the sets in the partition are the equivalence classes.

Proof   For the first part of the proof, we must show that the equivalence classes of R are nonempty, pairwise-disjoint sets whose union is A. Because R is reflexive, $a \in [a]$, and so the equivalence classes are nonempty; moreover, since every element $a \in A$ belongs to the equivalence class $[a]$, the union of the equivalence classes is A. It remains to show that the equivalence classes are pairwise disjoint, that is, if two equivalence classes $[a]$ and $[b]$ have an element c in common, then they are in fact the same set. Suppose that $a \mathrel{R} c$ and $b \mathrel{R} c$. By symmetry, $c \mathrel{R} b$, and by transitivity, $a \mathrel{R} b$. Thus, for any arbitrary element $x \in [a]$, we have $x \mathrel{R} a$ and, by transitivity, $x \mathrel{R} b$, and thus $[a] \subseteq [b]$. Similarly, $[b] \subseteq [a]$, and thus $[a] = [b]$.

For the second part of the proof, let $\mathcal{A} = \{A_i\}$ be a partition of A, and define $R = \{(a, b) : \text{there exists } i \text{ such that } a \in A_i \text{ and } b \in A_i\}$. We claim that R is an equivalence relation on A. Reflexivity holds, since $a \in A_i$ implies $a \mathrel{R} a$. Symmetry holds, because if $a \mathrel{R} b$, then a and b are in the same set A_i, and hence $b \mathrel{R} a$. If $a \mathrel{R} b$ and $b \mathrel{R} c$, then all three elements are in the same set A_i, and thus $a \mathrel{R} c$ and transitivity holds. To see that the sets in the partition are the equivalence classes of R, observe that if $a \in A_i$, then $x \in [a]$ implies $x \in A_i$, and $x \in A_i$ implies $x \in [a]$.   ■

A binary relation R on a set A is ***antisymmetric*** if

$a \mathrel{R} b$ and $b \mathrel{R} a$ imply $a = b$.

For example, the "$\leq$" relation on the natural numbers is antisymmetric, since $a \leq b$ and $b \leq a$ imply $a = b$. A relation that is reflexive, antisymmetric, and transitive is a **partial order**, and we call a set on which a partial order is defined a **partially ordered set**. For example, the relation "is a descendant of" is a partial order on the set of all people (if we view individuals as being their own descendants).

In a partially ordered set A, there may be no single "maximum" element a such that $b \ R \ a$ for all $b \in A$. Instead, the set may contain several **maximal** elements a such that for no $b \in A$, where $b \neq a$, is it the case that $a \ R \ b$. For example, a collection of different-sized boxes may contain several maximal boxes that don't fit inside any other box, yet it has no single "maximum" box into which any other box will fit.[3]

A relation R on a set A is a **total relation** if for all $a, b \in A$, we have $a \ R \ b$ or $b \ R \ a$ (or both), that is, if every pairing of elements of A is related by R. A partial order that is also a total relation is a **total order** or **linear order**. For example, the relation "$\leq$" is a total order on the natural numbers, but the "is a descendant of" relation is not a total order on the set of all people, since there are individuals neither of whom is descended from the other. A total relation that is transitive, but not necessarily either symmetric or antisymmetric, is a **total preorder**.

Exercises

B.2-1
Prove that the subset relation "$\subseteq$" on all subsets of $\mathbb{Z}$ is a partial order but not a total order.

B.2-2
Show that for any positive integer n, the relation "equivalent modulo n" is an equivalence relation on the integers. (We say that $a \equiv b \pmod{n}$ if there exists an integer q such that $a - b = qn$.) Into what equivalence classes does this relation partition the integers?

B.2-3
Give examples of relations that are

a. reflexive and symmetric but not transitive,

b. reflexive and transitive but not symmetric,

c. symmetric and transitive but not reflexive.

---

[3]To be precise, in order for the "fit inside" relation to be a partial order, we need to view a box as fitting inside itself.

B.2-4

Let S be a finite set, and let R be an equivalence relation on $S \times S$. Show that if in addition R is antisymmetric, then the equivalence classes of S with respect to R are singletons.

B.2-5

Professor Narcissus claims that if a relation R is symmetric and transitive, then it is also reflexive. He offers the following proof. By symmetry, $a \mathrel{R} b$ implies $b \mathrel{R} a$. Transitivity, therefore, implies $a \mathrel{R} a$. Is the professor correct?

B.3   Functions

Given two sets A and B, a **function** f is a binary relation on A and B such that for all $a \in A$, there exists precisely one $b \in B$ such that $(a, b) \in f$. The set A is called the **domain** of f, and the set B is called the **codomain** of f. We sometimes write $f : A \to B$; and if $(a, b) \in f$, we write $b = f(a)$, since b is uniquely determined by the choice of a.

Intuitively, the function f assigns an element of B to each element of A. No element of A is assigned two different elements of B, but the same element of B can be assigned to two different elements of A. For example, the binary relation

$$f = \{(a, b) : a, b \in \mathbb{N} \text{ and } b = a \bmod 2\}$$

is a function $f : \mathbb{N} \to \{0, 1\}$, since for each natural number a, there is exactly one value b in $\{0, 1\}$ such that $b = a \bmod 2$. For this example, $0 = f(0)$, $1 = f(1)$, $0 = f(2)$, etc. In contrast, the binary relation

$$g = \{(a, b) : a, b \in \mathbb{N} \text{ and } a + b \text{ is even}\}$$

is not a function, since $(1, 3)$ and $(1, 5)$ are both in g, and thus for the choice $a = 1$, there is not precisely one b such that $(a, b) \in g$.

Given a function $f : A \to B$, if $b = f(a)$, we say that a is the **argument** of f and that b is the **value** of f at a. We can define a function by stating its value for every element of its domain. For example, we might define $f(n) = 2n$ for $n \in \mathbb{N}$, which means $f = \{(n, 2n) : n \in \mathbb{N}\}$. Two functions f and g are **equal** if they have the same domain and codomain and if, for all a in the domain, $f(a) = g(a)$.

A **finite sequence** of length n is a function f whose domain is the set of n integers $\{0, 1, \ldots, n-1\}$. We often denote a finite sequence by listing its values: $\langle f(0), f(1), \ldots, f(n-1) \rangle$. An **infinite sequence** is a function whose domain is the set $\mathbb{N}$ of natural numbers. For example, the Fibonacci sequence, defined by recurrence (3.22), is the infinite sequence $\langle 0, 1, 1, 2, 3, 5, 8, 13, 21, \ldots \rangle$.

When the domain of a function f is a Cartesian product, we often omit the extra parentheses surrounding the argument of f. For example, if we had a function $f : A_1 \times A_2 \times \cdots \times A_n \to B$, we would write $b = f(a_1, a_2, \ldots, a_n)$ instead of $b = f((a_1, a_2, \ldots, a_n))$. We also call each a_i an **argument** to the function f, though technically the (single) argument to f is the n-tuple $(a_1, a_2, \ldots, a_n)$.

If $f : A \to B$ is a function and $b = f(a)$, then we sometimes say that b is the **image** of a under f. The image of a set $A' \subseteq A$ under f is defined by

$$f(A') = \{b \in B : b = f(a) \text{ for some } a \in A'\} \;.$$

The **range** of f is the image of its domain, that is, $f(A)$. For example, the range of the function $f : \mathbb{N} \to \mathbb{N}$ defined by $f(n) = 2n$ is $f(\mathbb{N}) = \{m : m = 2n$ for some $n \in \mathbb{N}\}$, in other words, the set of nonnegative even integers.

A function is a **surjection** if its range is its codomain. For example, the function $f(n) = \lfloor n/2 \rfloor$ is a surjective function from $\mathbb{N}$ to $\mathbb{N}$, since every element in $\mathbb{N}$ appears as the value of f for some argument. In contrast, the function $f(n) = 2n$ is not a surjective function from $\mathbb{N}$ to $\mathbb{N}$, since no argument to f can produce 3 as a value. The function $f(n) = 2n$ is, however, a surjective function from the natural numbers to the even numbers. A surjection $f : A \to B$ is sometimes described as mapping A **onto** B. When we say that f is onto, we mean that it is surjective.

A function $f : A \to B$ is an **injection** if distinct arguments to f produce distinct values, that is, if $a \neq a'$ implies $f(a) \neq f(a')$. For example, the function $f(n) = 2n$ is an injective function from $\mathbb{N}$ to $\mathbb{N}$, since each even number b is the image under f of at most one element of the domain, namely $b/2$. The function $f(n) = \lfloor n/2 \rfloor$ is not injective, since the value 1 is produced by two arguments: 2 and 3. An injection is sometimes called a **one-to-one** function.

A function $f : A \to B$ is a **bijection** if it is injective and surjective. For example, the function $f(n) = (-1)^n \lceil n/2 \rceil$ is a bijection from $\mathbb{N}$ to $\mathbb{Z}$:

$$
\begin{aligned}
0 &\to 0 \;, \\
1 &\to -1 \;, \\
2 &\to 1 \;, \\
3 &\to -2 \;, \\
4 &\to 2 \;, \\
&\;\;\vdots
\end{aligned}
$$

The function is injective, since no element of $\mathbb{Z}$ is the image of more than one element of $\mathbb{N}$. It is surjective, since every element of $\mathbb{Z}$ appears as the image of some element of $\mathbb{N}$. Hence, the function is bijective. A bijection is sometimes called a **one-to-one correspondence**, since it pairs elements in the domain and codomain. A bijection from a set A to itself is sometimes called a **permutation**.

When a function f is bijective, we define its **inverse** f^{-1} as

$$f^{-1}(b) = a \text{ if and only if } f(a) = b \;.$$

For example, the inverse of the function $f(n) = (-1)^n \lceil n/2 \rceil$ is

$$
f^{-1}(m) = \begin{cases} 2m & \text{if } m \geq 0, \\ -2m - 1 & \text{if } m < 0. \end{cases}
$$

Exercises

B.3-1
Let A and B be finite sets, and let $f : A \to B$ be a function. Show that

a. if f is injective, then $|A| \leq |B|$;

b. if f is surjective, then $|A| \geq |B|$.

B.3-2
Is the function $f(x) = x + 1$ bijective when the domain and the codomain are $\mathbb{N}$? Is it bijective when the domain and the codomain are $\mathbb{Z}$?

B.3-3
Give a natural definition for the inverse of a binary relation such that if a relation is in fact a bijective function, its relational inverse is its functional inverse.

B.3-4 ★
Give a bijection from $\mathbb{Z}$ to $\mathbb{Z} \times \mathbb{Z}$.

B.4   Graphs

This section presents two kinds of graphs: directed and undirected. Certain definitions in the literature differ from those given here, but for the most part, the differences are slight. Section 22.1 shows how we can represent graphs in computer memory.

A **directed graph** (or **digraph**) G is a pair (V, E), where V is a finite set and E is a binary relation on V. The set V is called the **vertex set** of G, and its elements are called **vertices** (singular: **vertex**). The set E is called the **edge set** of G, and its elements are called **edges**. Figure B.2(a) is a pictorial representation of a directed graph on the vertex set $\{1, 2, 3, 4, 5, 6\}$. Vertices are represented by circles in the figure, and edges are represented by arrows. Note that **self-loops**—edges from a vertex to itself—are possible.

In an **undirected graph** $G = (V, E)$, the edge set E consists of *unordered* pairs of vertices, rather than ordered pairs. That is, an edge is a set $\{u, v\}$, where

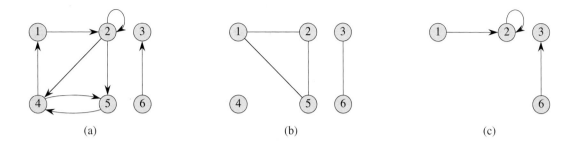

Figure B.2   Directed and undirected graphs. **(a)** A directed graph $G = (V, E)$, where $V = \{1, 2, 3, 4, 5, 6\}$ and $E = \{(1, 2), (2, 2), (2, 4), (2, 5), (4, 1), (4, 5), (5, 4), (6, 3)\}$. The edge $(2, 2)$ is a self-loop. **(b)** An undirected graph $G = (V, E)$, where $V = \{1, 2, 3, 4, 5, 6\}$ and $E = \{(1, 2), (1, 5), (2, 5), (3, 6)\}$. The vertex 4 is isolated. **(c)** The subgraph of the graph in part (a) induced by the vertex set $\{1, 2, 3, 6\}$.

$u, v \in V$ and $u \neq v$. By convention, we use the notation (u, v) for an edge, rather than the set notation $\{u, v\}$, and we consider (u, v) and (v, u) to be the same edge. In an undirected graph, self-loops are forbidden, and so every edge consists of two distinct vertices. Figure B.2(b) is a pictorial representation of an undirected graph on the vertex set $\{1, 2, 3, 4, 5, 6\}$.

Many definitions for directed and undirected graphs are the same, although certain terms have slightly different meanings in the two contexts. If (u, v) is an edge in a directed graph $G = (V, E)$, we say that (u, v) is ***incident from*** or ***leaves*** vertex u and is ***incident to*** or ***enters*** vertex v. For example, the edges leaving vertex 2 in Figure B.2(a) are $(2, 2)$, $(2, 4)$, and $(2, 5)$. The edges entering vertex 2 are $(1, 2)$ and $(2, 2)$. If (u, v) is an edge in an undirected graph $G = (V, E)$, we say that (u, v) is ***incident on*** vertices u and v. In Figure B.2(b), the edges incident on vertex 2 are $(1, 2)$ and $(2, 5)$.

If (u, v) is an edge in a graph $G = (V, E)$, we say that vertex v is ***adjacent*** to vertex u. When the graph is undirected, the adjacency relation is symmetric. When the graph is directed, the adjacency relation is not necessarily symmetric. If v is adjacent to u in a directed graph, we sometimes write $u \rightarrow v$. In parts (a) and (b) of Figure B.2, vertex 2 is adjacent to vertex 1, since the edge $(1, 2)$ belongs to both graphs. Vertex 1 is *not* adjacent to vertex 2 in Figure B.2(a), since the edge $(2, 1)$ does not belong to the graph.

The ***degree*** of a vertex in an undirected graph is the number of edges incident on it. For example, vertex 2 in Figure B.2(b) has degree 2. A vertex whose degree is 0, such as vertex 4 in Figure B.2(b), is ***isolated***. In a directed graph, the ***out-degree*** of a vertex is the number of edges leaving it, and the ***in-degree*** of a vertex is the number of edges entering it. The ***degree*** of a vertex in a directed graph is its in-degree plus its out-degree. Vertex 2 in Figure B.2(a) has in-degree 2, out-degree 3, and degree 5.

A ***path*** of ***length*** k from a vertex u to a vertex u' in a graph $G = (V, E)$ is a sequence $\langle v_0, v_1, v_2, \ldots, v_k \rangle$ of vertices such that $u = v_0$, $u' = v_k$, and $(v_{i-1}, v_i) \in E$ for $i = 1, 2, \ldots, k$. The length of the path is the number of edges in the path. The path ***contains*** the vertices $v_0, v_1, \ldots, v_k$ and the edges $(v_0, v_1), (v_1, v_2), \ldots, (v_{k-1}, v_k)$. (There is always a 0-length path from u to u.) If there is a path p from u to u', we say that u' is ***reachable*** from u via p, which we sometimes write as $u \overset{p}{\rightsquigarrow} u'$ if G is directed. A path is ***simple*** [4]if all vertices in the path are distinct. In Figure B.2(a), the path $\langle 1, 2, 5, 4 \rangle$ is a simple path of length 3. The path $\langle 2, 5, 4, 5 \rangle$ is not simple.

A ***subpath*** of path $p = \langle v_0, v_1, \ldots, v_k \rangle$ is a contiguous subsequence of its vertices. That is, for any $0 \le i \le j \le k$, the subsequence of vertices $\langle v_i, v_{i+1}, \ldots, v_j \rangle$ is a subpath of p.

In a directed graph, a path $\langle v_0, v_1, \ldots, v_k \rangle$ forms a ***cycle*** if $v_0 = v_k$ and the path contains at least one edge. The cycle is ***simple*** if, in addition, $v_1, v_2, \ldots, v_k$ are distinct. A self-loop is a cycle of length 1. Two paths $\langle v_0, v_1, v_2, \ldots, v_{k-1}, v_0 \rangle$ and $\langle v'_0, v'_1, v'_2, \ldots, v'_{k-1}, v'_0 \rangle$ form the same cycle if there exists an integer j such that $v'_i = v_{(i+j) \bmod k}$ for $i = 0, 1, \ldots, k-1$. In Figure B.2(a), the path $\langle 1, 2, 4, 1 \rangle$ forms the same cycle as the paths $\langle 2, 4, 1, 2 \rangle$ and $\langle 4, 1, 2, 4 \rangle$. This cycle is simple, but the cycle $\langle 1, 2, 4, 5, 4, 1 \rangle$ is not. The cycle $\langle 2, 2 \rangle$ formed by the edge $(2, 2)$ is a self-loop. A directed graph with no self-loops is ***simple***. In an undirected graph, a path $\langle v_0, v_1, \ldots, v_k \rangle$ forms a ***cycle*** if $k > 0$, $v_0 = v_k$, and all edges on the path are distinct; the cycle is ***simple*** if $v_1, v_2, \ldots, v_k$ are distinct. For example, in Figure B.2(b), the path $\langle 1, 2, 5, 1 \rangle$ is a simple cycle. A graph with no simple cycles is ***acyclic***.

An undirected graph is ***connected*** if every vertex is reachable from all other vertices. The ***connected components*** of an undirected graph are the equivalence classes of vertices under the "is reachable from" relation. The graph in Figure B.2(b) has three connected components: $\{1, 2, 5\}$, $\{3, 6\}$, and $\{4\}$. Every vertex in $\{1, 2, 5\}$ is reachable from every other vertex in $\{1, 2, 5\}$. An undirected graph is connected if it has exactly one connected component. The edges of a connected component are those that are incident on only the vertices of the component; in other words, edge (u, v) is an edge of a connected component only if both u and v are vertices of the component.

---

[4]Some authors refer to what we call a path as a "walk" and to what we call a simple path as just a "path." We use the terms "path" and "simple path" throughout this book in a manner consistent with their definitions.

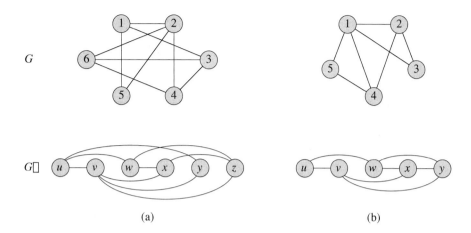

G

G'

(a)   (b)

Figure B.3 **(a)** A pair of isomorphic graphs. The vertices of the top graph are mapped to the vertices of the bottom graph by $f(1) = u$, $f(2) = v$, $f(3) = w$, $f(4) = x$, $f(5) = y$, $f(6) = z$. **(b)** Two graphs that are not isomorphic, since the top graph has a vertex of degree 4 and the bottom graph does not.

A directed graph is ***strongly connected*** if every two vertices are reachable from each other. The ***strongly connected components*** of a directed graph are the equivalence classes of vertices under the "are mutually reachable" relation. A directed graph is strongly connected if it has only one strongly connected component. The graph in Figure B.2(a) has three strongly connected components: $\{1, 2, 4, 5\}$, $\{3\}$, and $\{6\}$. All pairs of vertices in $\{1, 2, 4, 5\}$ are mutually reachable. The vertices $\{3, 6\}$ do not form a strongly connected component, since vertex 6 cannot be reached from vertex 3.

Two graphs $G = (V, E)$ and $G' = (V', E')$ are ***isomorphic*** if there exists a bijection $f : V \to V'$ such that $(u, v) \in E$ if and only if $(f(u), f(v)) \in E'$. In other words, we can relabel the vertices of G to be vertices of G', maintaining the corresponding edges in G and G'. Figure B.3(a) shows a pair of isomorphic graphs G and G' with respective vertex sets $V = \{1, 2, 3, 4, 5, 6\}$ and $V' = \{u, v, w, x, y, z\}$. The mapping from V to V' given by $f(1) = u$, $f(2) = v$, $f(3) = w$, $f(4) = x$, $f(5) = y$, $f(6) = z$ provides the required bijective function. The graphs in Figure B.3(b) are not isomorphic. Although both graphs have 5 vertices and 7 edges, the top graph has a vertex of degree 4 and the bottom graph does not.

We say that a graph $G' = (V', E')$ is a ***subgraph*** of $G = (V, E)$ if $V' \subseteq V$ and $E' \subseteq E$. Given a set $V' \subseteq V$, the subgraph of G ***induced*** by V' is the graph $G' = (V', E')$, where

$$E' = \{(u, v) \in E : u, v \in V'\} \ .$$

The subgraph induced by the vertex set $\{1, 2, 3, 6\}$ in Figure B.2(a) appears in Figure B.2(c) and has the edge set $\{(1, 2), (2, 2), (6, 3)\}$.

Given an undirected graph $G = (V, E)$, the ***directed version*** of G is the directed graph $G' = (V, E')$, where $(u, v) \in E'$ if and only if $(u, v) \in E$. That is, we replace each undirected edge (u, v) in G by the two directed edges (u, v) and (v, u) in the directed version. Given a directed graph $G = (V, E)$, the ***undirected version*** of G is the undirected graph $G' = (V, E')$, where $(u, v) \in E'$ if and only if $u \neq v$ and E contains at least one of the edges (u, v) and (v, u). That is, the undirected version contains the edges of G "with their directions removed" and with self-loops eliminated. (Since (u, v) and (v, u) are the same edge in an undirected graph, the undirected version of a directed graph contains it only once, even if the directed graph contains both edges (u, v) and (v, u).) In a directed graph $G = (V, E)$, a ***neighbor*** of a vertex u is any vertex that is adjacent to u in the undirected version of G. That is, v is a neighbor of u if $u \neq v$ and either $(u, v) \in E$ or $(v, u) \in E$. In an undirected graph, u and v are neighbors if they are adjacent.

Several kinds of graphs have special names. A ***complete graph*** is an undirected graph in which every pair of vertices is adjacent. A ***bipartite graph*** is an undirected graph $G = (V, E)$ in which V can be partitioned into two sets V_1 and V_2 such that $(u, v) \in E$ implies either $u \in V_1$ and $v \in V_2$ or $u \in V_2$ and $v \in V_1$. That is, all edges go between the two sets V_1 and V_2. An acyclic, undirected graph is a ***forest***, and a connected, acyclic, undirected graph is a ***(free) tree*** (see Section B.5). We often take the first letters of "directed acyclic graph" and call such a graph a ***dag***.

There are two variants of graphs that you may occasionally encounter. A ***multigraph*** is like an undirected graph, but it can have both multiple edges between vertices and self-loops. A ***hypergraph*** is like an undirected graph, but each ***hyperedge***, rather than connecting two vertices, connects an arbitrary subset of vertices. Many algorithms written for ordinary directed and undirected graphs can be adapted to run on these graphlike structures.

The ***contraction*** of an undirected graph $G = (V, E)$ by an edge $e = (u, v)$ is a graph $G' = (V', E')$, where $V' = V - \{u, v\} \cup \{x\}$ and x is a new vertex. The set of edges E' is formed from E by deleting the edge (u, v) and, for each vertex w adjacent to u or v, deleting whichever of (u, w) and (v, w) is in E and adding the new edge (x, w). In effect, u and v are "contracted" into a single vertex.

Exercises

B.4-1
Attendees of a faculty party shake hands to greet each other, and each professor remembers how many times he or she shook hands. At the end of the party, the department head adds up the number of times that each professor shook hands.

Show that the result is even by proving the **handshaking lemma**: if $G = (V, E)$ is an undirected graph, then

$$\sum_{v \in V} \text{degree}(v) = 2|E| .$$

B.4-2
Show that if a directed or undirected graph contains a path between two vertices u and v, then it contains a simple path between u and v. Show that if a directed graph contains a cycle, then it contains a simple cycle.

B.4-3
Show that any connected, undirected graph $G = (V, E)$ satisfies $|E| \geq |V| - 1$.

B.4-4
Verify that in an undirected graph, the "is reachable from" relation is an equivalence relation on the vertices of the graph. Which of the three properties of an equivalence relation hold in general for the "is reachable from" relation on the vertices of a directed graph?

B.4-5
What is the undirected version of the directed graph in Figure B.2(a)? What is the directed version of the undirected graph in Figure B.2(b)?

B.4-6 ★
Show that we can represent a hypergraph by a bipartite graph if we let incidence in the hypergraph correspond to adjacency in the bipartite graph. (*Hint:* Let one set of vertices in the bipartite graph correspond to vertices of the hypergraph, and let the other set of vertices of the bipartite graph correspond to hyperedges.)

B.5 Trees

As with graphs, there are many related, but slightly different, notions of trees. This section presents definitions and mathematical properties of several kinds of trees. Sections 10.4 and 22.1 describe how we can represent trees in computer memory.

B.5.1 Free trees

As defined in Section B.4, a *free tree* is a connected, acyclic, undirected graph. We often omit the adjective "free" when we say that a graph is a tree. If an undirected graph is acyclic but possibly disconnected, it is a *forest*. Many algorithms that work

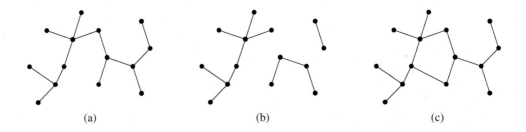

Figure B.4 **(a)** A free tree. **(b)** A forest. **(c)** A graph that contains a cycle and is therefore neither a tree nor a forest.

for trees also work for forests. Figure B.4(a) shows a free tree, and Figure B.4(b) shows a forest. The forest in Figure B.4(b) is not a tree because it is not connected. The graph in Figure B.4(c) is connected but neither a tree nor a forest, because it contains a cycle.

The following theorem captures many important facts about free trees.

Theorem B.2 (Properties of free trees)
Let $G = (V, E)$ be an undirected graph. The following statements are equivalent.

1. G is a free tree.

2. Any two vertices in G are connected by a unique simple path.

3. G is connected, but if any edge is removed from E, the resulting graph is disconnected.

4. G is connected, and $|E| = |V| - 1$.

5. G is acyclic, and $|E| = |V| - 1$.

6. G is acyclic, but if any edge is added to E, the resulting graph contains a cycle.

Proof $(1) \Rightarrow (2)$: Since a tree is connected, any two vertices in G are connected by at least one simple path. Suppose, for the sake of contradiction, that vertices u and v are connected by two distinct simple paths p_1 and p_2, as shown in Figure B.5. Let w be the vertex at which the paths first diverge; that is, w is the first vertex on both p_1 and p_2 whose successor on p_1 is x and whose successor on p_2 is y, where $x \neq y$. Let z be the first vertex at which the paths reconverge; that is, z is the first vertex following w on p_1 that is also on p_2. Let p' be the subpath of p_1 from w through x to z, and let p'' be the subpath of p_2 from w through y to z. Paths p' and p'' share no vertices except their endpoints. Thus, the path obtained by concatenating p' and the reverse of p'' is a cycle, which contradicts our assumption

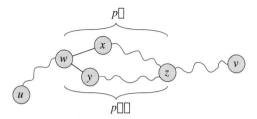

Figure B.5   A step in the proof of Theorem B.2: if (1) G is a free tree, then (2) any two vertices in G are connected by a unique simple path. Assume for the sake of contradiction that vertices u and v are connected by two distinct simple paths p_1 and p_2. These paths first diverge at vertex w, and they first reconverge at vertex z. The path p' concatenated with the reverse of the path p'' forms a cycle, which yields the contradiction.

that G is a tree. Thus, if G is a tree, there can be at most one simple path between two vertices.

(2) $\Rightarrow$ (3): If any two vertices in G are connected by a unique simple path, then G is connected. Let (u, v) be any edge in E. This edge is a path from u to v, and so it must be the unique path from u to v. If we remove (u, v) from G, there is no path from u to v, and hence its removal disconnects G.

(3) $\Rightarrow$ (4): By assumption, the graph G is connected, and by Exercise B.4-3, we have $|E| \geq |V| - 1$. We shall prove $|E| \leq |V| - 1$ by induction. A connected graph with $n = 1$ or $n = 2$ vertices has $n - 1$ edges. Suppose that G has $n \geq 3$ vertices and that all graphs satisfying (3) with fewer than n vertices also satisfy $|E| \leq |V| - 1$. Removing an arbitrary edge from G separates the graph into $k \geq 2$ connected components (actually $k = 2$). Each component satisfies (3), or else G would not satisfy (3). If we view each connected component V_i, with edge set E_i, as its own free tree, then because each component has fewer than $|V|$ vertices, by the inductive hypothesis we have $|E_i| \leq |V_i| - 1$. Thus, the number of edges in all components combined is at most $|V| - k \leq |V| - 2$. Adding in the removed edge yields $|E| \leq |V| - 1$.

(4) $\Rightarrow$ (5): Suppose that G is connected and that $|E| = |V| - 1$. We must show that G is acyclic. Suppose that G has a cycle containing k vertices $v_1, v_2, \ldots, v_k$, and without loss of generality assume that this cycle is simple. Let $G_k = (V_k, E_k)$ be the subgraph of G consisting of the cycle. Note that $|V_k| = |E_k| = k$. If $k < |V|$, there must be a vertex $v_{k+1} \in V - V_k$ that is adjacent to some vertex $v_i \in V_k$, since G is connected. Define $G_{k+1} = (V_{k+1}, E_{k+1})$ to be the subgraph of G with $V_{k+1} = V_k \cup \{v_{k+1}\}$ and $E_{k+1} = E_k \cup \{(v_i, v_{k+1})\}$. Note that $|V_{k+1}| = |E_{k+1}| = k + 1$. If $k + 1 < |V|$, we can continue, defining G_{k+2} in the same manner, and so forth, until we obtain $G_n = (V_n, E_n)$, where $n = |V|$,

$V_n = V$, and $|E_n| = |V_n| = |V|$. Since G_n is a subgraph of G, we have $E_n \subseteq E$, and hence $|E| \geq |V|$, which contradicts the assumption that $|E| = |V| - 1$. Thus, G is acyclic.

(5) $\Rightarrow$ (6): Suppose that G is acyclic and that $|E| = |V| - 1$. Let k be the number of connected components of G. Each connected component is a free tree by definition, and since (1) implies (5), the sum of all edges in all connected components of G is $|V| - k$. Consequently, we must have $k = 1$, and G is in fact a tree. Since (1) implies (2), any two vertices in G are connected by a unique simple path. Thus, adding any edge to G creates a cycle.

(6) $\Rightarrow$ (1): Suppose that G is acyclic but that adding any edge to E creates a cycle. We must show that G is connected. Let u and v be arbitrary vertices in G. If u and v are not already adjacent, adding the edge (u, v) creates a cycle in which all edges but (u, v) belong to G. Thus, the cycle minus edge (u, v) must contain a path from u to v, and since u and v were chosen arbitrarily, G is connected. ∎

B.5.2   Rooted and ordered trees

A ***rooted tree*** is a free tree in which one of the vertices is distinguished from the others. We call the distinguished vertex the ***root*** of the tree. We often refer to a vertex of a rooted tree as a ***node***[5] of the tree. Figure B.6(a) shows a rooted tree on a set of 12 nodes with root 7.

Consider a node x in a rooted tree T with root r. We call any node y on the unique simple path from r to x an ***ancestor*** of x. If y is an ancestor of x, then x is a ***descendant*** of y. (Every node is both an ancestor and a descendant of itself.) If y is an ancestor of x and $x \neq y$, then y is a ***proper ancestor*** of x and x is a ***proper descendant*** of y. The ***subtree rooted at x*** is the tree induced by descendants of x, rooted at x. For example, the subtree rooted at node 8 in Figure B.6(a) contains nodes 8, 6, 5, and 9.

If the last edge on the simple path from the root r of a tree T to a node x is (y, x), then y is the ***parent*** of x, and x is a ***child*** of y. The root is the only node in T with no parent. If two nodes have the same parent, they are ***siblings***. A node with no children is a ***leaf*** or ***external node***. A nonleaf node is an ***internal node***.

---

[5]The term "node" is often used in the graph theory literature as a synonym for "vertex." We reserve the term "node" to mean a vertex of a rooted tree.

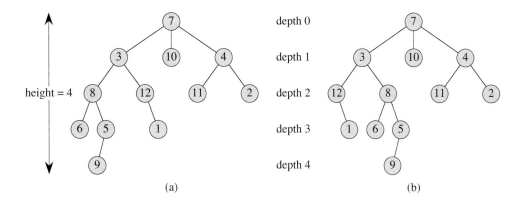

Figure B.6   Rooted and ordered trees. **(a)** A rooted tree with height 4. The tree is drawn in a standard way: the root (node 7) is at the top, its children (nodes with depth 1) are beneath it, their children (nodes with depth 2) are beneath them, and so forth. If the tree is ordered, the relative left-to-right order of the children of a node matters; otherwise it doesn't. **(b)** Another rooted tree. As a rooted tree, it is identical to the tree in (a), but as an ordered tree it is different, since the children of node 3 appear in a different order.

The number of children of a node x in a rooted tree T equals the **degree** of x.[6] The length of the simple path from the root r to a node x is the **depth** of x in T. A **level** of a tree consists of all nodes at the same depth. The **height** of a node in a tree is the number of edges on the longest simple downward path from the node to a leaf, and the height of a tree is the height of its root. The height of a tree is also equal to the largest depth of any node in the tree.

An **ordered tree** is a rooted tree in which the children of each node are ordered. That is, if a node has k children, then there is a first child, a second child, ..., and a kth child. The two trees in Figure B.6 are different when considered to be ordered trees, but the same when considered to be just rooted trees.

B.5.3   Binary and positional trees

We define binary trees recursively. A **binary tree** T is a structure defined on a finite set of nodes that either

- contains no nodes, or

---

[6]Notice that the degree of a node depends on whether we consider T to be a rooted tree or a free tree. The degree of a vertex in a free tree is, as in any undirected graph, the number of adjacent vertices. In a rooted tree, however, the degree is the number of children—the parent of a node does not count toward its degree.

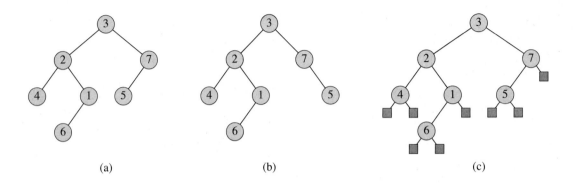

       (a)   (b)   (c)

Figure B.7 Binary trees. **(a)** A binary tree drawn in a standard way. The left child of a node is drawn beneath the node and to the left. The right child is drawn beneath and to the right. **(b)** A binary tree different from the one in (a). In (a), the left child of node 7 is 5 and the right child is absent. In (b), the left child of node 7 is absent and the right child is 5. As ordered trees, these trees are the same, but as binary trees, they are distinct. **(c)** The binary tree in (a) represented by the internal nodes of a full binary tree: an ordered tree in which each internal node has degree 2. The leaves in the tree are shown as squares.

-    is composed of three disjoint sets of nodes: a ***root*** node, a binary tree called its ***left subtree***, and a binary tree called its ***right subtree***.

The binary tree that contains no nodes is called the ***empty tree*** or ***null tree***, sometimes denoted NIL. If the left subtree is nonempty, its root is called the ***left child*** of the root of the entire tree. Likewise, the root of a nonnull right subtree is the ***right child*** of the root of the entire tree. If a subtree is the null tree NIL, we say that the child is ***absent*** or ***missing***. Figure B.7(a) shows a binary tree.

A binary tree is not simply an ordered tree in which each node has degree at most 2. For example, in a binary tree, if a node has just one child, the position of the child—whether it is the ***left child*** or the ***right child***—matters. In an ordered tree, there is no distinguishing a sole child as being either left or right. Figure B.7(b) shows a binary tree that differs from the tree in Figure B.7(a) because of the position of one node. Considered as ordered trees, however, the two trees are identical.

We can represent the positioning information in a binary tree by the internal nodes of an ordered tree, as shown in Figure B.7(c). The idea is to replace each missing child in the binary tree with a node having no children. These leaf nodes are drawn as squares in the figure. The tree that results is a ***full binary tree***: each node is either a leaf or has degree exactly 2. There are no degree-1 nodes. Consequently, the order of the children of a node preserves the position information.

We can extend the positioning information that distinguishes binary trees from ordered trees to trees with more than 2 children per node. In a ***positional tree***, the

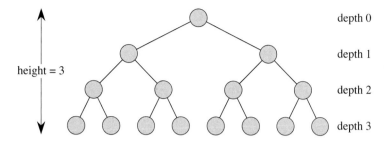

Figure B.8   A complete binary tree of height 3 with 8 leaves and 7 internal nodes.

children of a node are labeled with distinct positive integers. The ith child of a node is **absent** if no child is labeled with integer i. A **k-ary** tree is a positional tree in which for every node, all children with labels greater than k are missing. Thus, a binary tree is a k-ary tree with $k = 2$.

A **complete k-ary tree** is a k-ary tree in which all leaves have the same depth and all internal nodes have degree k. Figure B.8 shows a complete binary tree of height 3. How many leaves does a complete k-ary tree of height h have? The root has k children at depth 1, each of which has k children at depth 2, etc. Thus, the number of leaves at depth h is k^h. Consequently, the height of a complete k-ary tree with n leaves is $\log_k n$. The number of internal nodes of a complete k-ary tree of height h is

$$1 + k + k^2 + \cdots + k^{h-1} = \sum_{i=0}^{h-1} k^i$$
$$= \frac{k^h - 1}{k - 1}$$

by equation (A.5). Thus, a complete binary tree has $2^h - 1$ internal nodes.

Exercises

B.5-1
Draw all the free trees composed of the three vertices x, y, and z. Draw all the rooted trees with nodes x, y, and z with x as the root. Draw all the ordered trees with nodes x, y, and z with x as the root. Draw all the binary trees with nodes x, y, and z with x as the root.

B.5-2

Let $G = (V, E)$ be a directed acyclic graph in which there is a vertex $v_0 \in V$ such that there exists a unique path from v_0 to every vertex $v \in V$. Prove that the undirected version of G forms a tree.

B.5-3

Show by induction that the number of degree-2 nodes in any nonempty binary tree is 1 fewer than the number of leaves. Conclude that the number of internal nodes in a full binary tree is 1 fewer than the number of leaves.

B.5-4

Use induction to show that a nonempty binary tree with n nodes has height at least $\lfloor \lg n \rfloor$.

B.5-5 ★

The *internal path length* of a full binary tree is the sum, taken over all internal nodes of the tree, of the depth of each node. Likewise, the *external path length* is the sum, taken over all leaves of the tree, of the depth of each leaf. Consider a full binary tree with n internal nodes, internal path length i, and external path length e. Prove that $e = i + 2n$.

B.5-6 ★

Let us associate a "weight" $w(x) = 2^{-d}$ with each leaf x of depth d in a binary tree T, and let L be the set of leaves of T. Prove that $\sum_{x \in L} w(x) \leq 1$. (This is known as the *Kraft inequality*.)

B.5-7 ★

Show that if $L \geq 2$, then every binary tree with L leaves contains a subtree having between $L/3$ and $2L/3$ leaves, inclusive.

Problems

B-1 *Graph coloring*

Given an undirected graph $G = (V, E)$, a *k-coloring* of G is a function $c : V \to \{0, 1, \ldots, k - 1\}$ such that $c(u) \neq c(v)$ for every edge $(u, v) \in E$. In other words, the numbers $0, 1, \ldots, k - 1$ represent the k colors, and adjacent vertices must have different colors.

a. Show that any tree is 2-colorable.

b. Show that the following are equivalent:

1. G is bipartite.
2. G is 2-colorable.
3. G has no cycles of odd length.

c. Let d be the maximum degree of any vertex in a graph G. Prove that we can color G with $d + 1$ colors.

d. Show that if G has $O(|V|)$ edges, then we can color G with $O(\sqrt{|V|})$ colors.

B-2 *Friendly graphs*

Reword each of the following statements as a theorem about undirected graphs, and then prove it. Assume that friendship is symmetric but not reflexive.

a. Any group of at least two people contains at least two people with the same number of friends in the group.

b. Every group of six people contains either at least three mutual friends or at least three mutual strangers.

c. Any group of people can be partitioned into two subgroups such that at least half the friends of each person belong to the subgroup of which that person is *not* a member.

d. If everyone in a group is the friend of at least half the people in the group, then the group can be seated around a table in such a way that everyone is seated between two friends.

B-3 *Bisecting trees*

Many divide-and-conquer algorithms that operate on graphs require that the graph be bisected into two nearly equal-sized subgraphs, which are induced by a partition of the vertices. This problem investigates bisections of trees formed by removing a small number of edges. We require that whenever two vertices end up in the same subtree after removing edges, then they must be in the same partition.

a. Show that we can partition the vertices of any n-vertex binary tree into two sets A and B, such that $|A| \le 3n/4$ and $|B| \le 3n/4$, by removing a single edge.

b. Show that the constant $3/4$ in part (a) is optimal in the worst case by giving an example of a simple binary tree whose most evenly balanced partition upon removal of a single edge has $|A| = 3n/4$.

c. Show that by removing at most $O(\lg n)$ edges, we can partition the vertices of any n-vertex binary tree into two sets A and B such that $|A| = \lfloor n/2 \rfloor$ and $|B| = \lceil n/2 \rceil$.

Appendix notes

G. Boole pioneered the development of symbolic logic, and he introduced many of the basic set notations in a book published in 1854. Modern set theory was created by G. Cantor during the period 1874–1895. Cantor focused primarily on sets of infinite cardinality. The term "function" is attributed to G. W. Leibniz, who used it to refer to several kinds of mathematical formulas. His limited definition has been generalized many times. Graph theory originated in 1736, when L. Euler proved that it was impossible to cross each of the seven bridges in the city of Königsberg exactly once and return to the starting point.

The book by Harary [160] provides a useful compendium of many definitions and results from graph theory.

C   Counting and Probability

This appendix reviews elementary combinatorics and probability theory. If you have a good background in these areas, you may want to skim the beginning of this appendix lightly and concentrate on the later sections. Most of this book's chapters do not require probability, but for some chapters it is essential.

Section C.1 reviews elementary results in counting theory, including standard formulas for counting permutations and combinations. The axioms of probability and basic facts concerning probability distributions form Section C.2. Random variables are introduced in Section C.3, along with the properties of expectation and variance. Section C.4 investigates the geometric and binomial distributions that arise from studying Bernoulli trials. The study of the binomial distribution continues in Section C.5, an advanced discussion of the "tails" of the distribution.

C.1   Counting

Counting theory tries to answer the question "How many?" without actually enumerating all the choices. For example, we might ask, "How many different n-bit numbers are there?" or "How many orderings of n distinct elements are there?" In this section, we review the elements of counting theory. Since some of the material assumes a basic understanding of sets, you might wish to start by reviewing the material in Section B.1.

Rules of sum and product

We can sometimes express a set of items that we wish to count as a union of disjoint sets or as a Cartesian product of sets.

The ***rule of sum*** says that the number of ways to choose one element from one of two *disjoint* sets is the sum of the cardinalities of the sets. That is, if A and B are two finite sets with no members in common, then $|A \cup B| = |A| + |B|$, which follows from equation (B.3). For example, each position on a car's license plate is a letter or a digit. The number of possibilities for each position is therefore $26 + 10 = 36$, since there are 26 choices if it is a letter and 10 choices if it is a digit.

The *rule of product* says that the number of ways to choose an ordered pair is the number of ways to choose the first element times the number of ways to choose the second element. That is, if A and B are two finite sets, then $|A \times B| = |A| \cdot |B|$, which is simply equation (B.4). For example, if an ice-cream parlor offers 28 flavors of ice cream and 4 toppings, the number of possible sundaes with one scoop of ice cream and one topping is $28 \cdot 4 = 112$.

Strings

A *string* over a finite set S is a sequence of elements of S. For example, there are 8 binary strings of length 3:

$$000, 001, 010, 011, 100, 101, 110, 111 .$$

We sometimes call a string of length k a *k-string*. A *substring* s' of a string s is an ordered sequence of consecutive elements of s. A *k-substring* of a string is a substring of length k. For example, 010 is a 3-substring of 01101001 (the 3-substring that begins in position 4), but 111 is not a substring of 01101001.

We can view a k-string over a set S as an element of the Cartesian product S^k of k-tuples; thus, there are $|S|^k$ strings of length k. For example, the number of binary k-strings is 2^k. Intuitively, to construct a k-string over an n-set, we have n ways to pick the first element; for each of these choices, we have n ways to pick the second element; and so forth k times. This construction leads to the k-fold product $n \cdot n \cdots n = n^k$ as the number of k-strings.

Permutations

A *permutation* of a finite set S is an ordered sequence of all the elements of S, with each element appearing exactly once. For example, if $S = \{a, b, c\}$, then S has 6 permutations:

$$abc, acb, bac, bca, cab, cba .$$

There are $n!$ permutations of a set of n elements, since we can choose the first element of the sequence in n ways, the second in $n - 1$ ways, the third in $n - 2$ ways, and so on.

A *k-permutation* of S is an ordered sequence of k elements of S, with no element appearing more than once in the sequence. (Thus, an ordinary permutation is an n-permutation of an n-set.) The twelve 2-permutations of the set $\{a, b, c, d\}$ are

$ab, ac, ad, ba, bc, bd, ca, cb, cd, da, db, dc$.

The number of k-permutations of an n-set is

$$n(n-1)(n-2) \cdots (n-k+1) = \frac{n!}{(n-k)!} \, , \tag{C.1}$$

since we have n ways to choose the first element, $n-1$ ways to choose the second element, and so on, until we have selected k elements, the last being a selection from the remaining $n-k+1$ elements.

Combinations

A **k-combination** of an n-set S is simply a k-subset of S. For example, the 4-set $\{a, b, c, d\}$ has six 2-combinations:

ab, ac, ad, bc, bd, cd .

(Here we use the shorthand of denoting the 2-subset $\{a, b\}$ by ab, and so on.) We can construct a k-combination of an n-set by choosing k distinct (different) elements from the n-set. The order in which we select the elements does not matter.

We can express the number of k-combinations of an n-set in terms of the number of k-permutations of an n-set. Every k-combination has exactly $k!$ permutations of its elements, each of which is a distinct k-permutation of the n-set. Thus, the number of k-combinations of an n-set is the number of k-permutations divided by $k!$; from equation (C.1), this quantity is

$$\frac{n!}{k! \, (n-k)!} \, . \tag{C.2}$$

For $k = 0$, this formula tells us that the number of ways to choose 0 elements from an n-set is 1 (not 0), since $0! = 1$.

Binomial coefficients

The notation $\binom{n}{k}$ (read "n choose k") denotes the number of k-combinations of an n-set. From equation (C.2), we have

$$\binom{n}{k} = \frac{n!}{k! \, (n-k)!} \, .$$

This formula is symmetric in k and $n-k$:

$$\binom{n}{k} = \binom{n}{n-k} \, . \tag{C.3}$$

These numbers are also known as ***binomial coefficients***, due to their appearance in the ***binomial expansion***:

$$(x + y)^n = \sum_{k=0}^{n} \binom{n}{k} x^k y^{n-k} . \tag{C.4}$$

A special case of the binomial expansion occurs when $x = y = 1$:

$$2^n = \sum_{k=0}^{n} \binom{n}{k} .$$

This formula corresponds to counting the 2^n binary n-strings by the number of 1s they contain: $\binom{n}{k}$ binary n-strings contain exactly k 1s, since we have $\binom{n}{k}$ ways to choose k out of the n positions in which to place the 1s.

Many identities involve binomial coefficients. The exercises at the end of this section give you the opportunity to prove a few.

Binomial bounds

We sometimes need to bound the size of a binomial coefficient. For $1 \leq k \leq n$, we have the lower bound

$$\binom{n}{k} = \frac{n(n-1) \cdots (n-k+1)}{k(k-1) \cdots 1}$$

$$= \left(\frac{n}{k}\right) \left(\frac{n-1}{k-1}\right) \cdots \left(\frac{n-k+1}{1}\right)$$

$$\geq \left(\frac{n}{k}\right)^k .$$

Taking advantage of the inequality $k! \geq (k/e)^k$ derived from Stirling's approximation (3.18), we obtain the upper bounds

$$\binom{n}{k} = \frac{n(n-1) \cdots (n-k+1)}{k(k-1) \cdots 1}$$

$$\leq \frac{n^k}{k!}$$

$$\leq \left(\frac{en}{k}\right)^k . \tag{C.5}$$

For all integers k such that $0 \leq k \leq n$, we can use induction (see Exercise C.1-12) to prove the bound

$$\binom{n}{k} \le \frac{n^n}{k^k(n-k)^{n-k}} , \tag{C.6}$$

where for convenience we assume that $0^0 = 1$. For $k = \lambda n$, where $0 \le \lambda \le 1$, we can rewrite this bound as

$$\begin{aligned}
\binom{n}{\lambda n} &\le \frac{n^n}{(\lambda n)^{\lambda n}((1-\lambda)n)^{(1-\lambda)n}} \\
&= \left(\left(\frac{1}{\lambda} \right)^{\lambda} \left(\frac{1}{1-\lambda} \right)^{1-\lambda} \right)^n \\
&= 2^{n\,H(\lambda)} ,
\end{aligned}$$

where

$$H(\lambda) = -\lambda \lg \lambda - (1-\lambda) \lg(1-\lambda) \tag{C.7}$$

is the *(binary) entropy function* and where, for convenience, we assume that $0 \lg 0 = 0$, so that $H(0) = H(1) = 0$.

Exercises

C.1-1
How many k-substrings does an n-string have? (Consider identical k-substrings at different positions to be different.) How many substrings does an n-string have in total?

C.1-2
An n-input, m-output *boolean function* is a function from $\{\text{TRUE}, \text{FALSE}\}^n$ to $\{\text{TRUE}, \text{FALSE}\}^m$. How many n-input, 1-output boolean functions are there? How many n-input, m-output boolean functions are there?

C.1-3
In how many ways can n professors sit around a circular conference table? Consider two seatings to be the same if one can be rotated to form the other.

C.1-4
In how many ways can we choose three distinct numbers from the set $\{1, 2, \ldots, 99\}$ so that their sum is even?

C.1-5
Prove the identity

$$\binom{n}{k} = \frac{n}{k}\binom{n-1}{k-1} \tag{C.8}$$

for $0 < k \le n$.

C.1-6
Prove the identity

$$\binom{n}{k} = \frac{n}{n-k}\binom{n-1}{k}$$

for $0 \le k < n$.

C.1-7
To choose k objects from n, you can make one of the objects distinguished and consider whether the distinguished object is chosen. Use this approach to prove that

$$\binom{n}{k} = \binom{n-1}{k} + \binom{n-1}{k-1}.$$

C.1-8
Using the result of Exercise C.1-7, make a table for $n = 0, 1, \ldots, 6$ and $0 \le k \le n$ of the binomial coefficients $\binom{n}{k}$ with $\binom{0}{0}$ at the top, $\binom{1}{0}$ and $\binom{1}{1}$ on the next line, and so forth. Such a table of binomial coefficients is called ***Pascal's triangle***.

C.1-9
Prove that

$$\sum_{i=1}^{n} i = \binom{n+1}{2}.$$

C.1-10
Show that for any integers $n \ge 0$ and $0 \le k \le n$, the expression $\binom{n}{k}$ achieves its maximum value when $k = \lfloor n/2 \rfloor$ or $k = \lceil n/2 \rceil$.

C.1-11 ★
Argue that for any integers $n \ge 0$, $j \ge 0$, $k \ge 0$, and $j + k \le n$,

$$\binom{n}{j+k} \le \binom{n}{j}\binom{n-j}{k}. \tag{C.9}$$

Provide both an algebraic proof and an argument based on a method for choosing $j + k$ items out of n. Give an example in which equality does not hold.

C.1-12 ★

Use induction on all integers k such that $0 \leq k \leq n/2$ to prove inequality (C.6), and use equation (C.3) to extend it to all integers k such that $0 \leq k \leq n$.

C.1-13 ★

Use Stirling's approximation to prove that

$$\binom{2n}{n} = \frac{2^{2n}}{\sqrt{\pi n}}(1 + O(1/n)) . \tag{C.10}$$

C.1-14 ★

By differentiating the entropy function $H(\lambda)$, show that it achieves its maximum value at $\lambda = 1/2$. What is $H(1/2)$?

C.1-15 ★

Show that for any integer $n \geq 0$,

$$\sum_{k=0}^{n} \binom{n}{k} k = n2^{n-1} . \tag{C.11}$$

C.2   Probability

Probability is an essential tool for the design and analysis of probabilistic and randomized algorithms. This section reviews basic probability theory.

We define probability in terms of a ***sample space*** S, which is a set whose elements are called ***elementary events***. We can think of each elementary event as a possible outcome of an experiment. For the experiment of flipping two distinguishable coins, with each individual flip resulting in a head (H) or a tail (T), we can view the sample space as consisting of the set of all possible 2-strings over $\{H, T\}$:

$$S = \{HH, HT, TH, TT\} .$$

An *event* is a subset[1] of the sample space S. For example, in the experiment of flipping two coins, the event of obtaining one head and one tail is $\{\text{HT}, \text{TH}\}$. The event S is called the *certain event*, and the event $\emptyset$ is called the *null event*. We say that two events A and B are *mutually exclusive* if $A \cap B = \emptyset$. We sometimes treat an elementary event $s \in S$ as the event $\{s\}$. By definition, all elementary events are mutually exclusive.

Axioms of probability

A *probability distribution* $\Pr\{\}$ on a sample space S is a mapping from events of S to real numbers satisfying the following *probability axioms*:

1. $\Pr\{A\} \geq 0$ for any event A.

2. $\Pr\{S\} = 1$.

3. $\Pr\{A \cup B\} = \Pr\{A\} + \Pr\{B\}$ for any two mutually exclusive events A and B. More generally, for any (finite or countably infinite) sequence of events $A_1, A_2, \ldots$ that are pairwise mutually exclusive,

$$\Pr\left\{\bigcup_i A_i\right\} = \sum_i \Pr\{A_i\} \ .$$

We call $\Pr\{A\}$ the *probability* of the event A. We note here that axiom 2 is a normalization requirement: there is really nothing fundamental about choosing 1 as the probability of the certain event, except that it is natural and convenient.

Several results follow immediately from these axioms and basic set theory (see Section B.1). The null event $\emptyset$ has probability $\Pr\{\emptyset\} = 0$. If $A \subseteq B$, then $\Pr\{A\} \leq \Pr\{B\}$. Using $\overline{A}$ to denote the event $S - A$ (the *complement* of A), we have $\Pr\{\overline{A}\} = 1 - \Pr\{A\}$. For any two events A and B,

$$\Pr\{A \cup B\} = \Pr\{A\} + \Pr\{B\} - \Pr\{A \cap B\} \tag{C.12}$$
$$\leq \Pr\{A\} + \Pr\{B\} \ . \tag{C.13}$$

---

[1]For a general probability distribution, there may be some subsets of the sample space S that are not considered to be events. This situation usually arises when the sample space is uncountably infinite. The main requirement for what subsets are events is that the set of events of a sample space be closed under the operations of taking the complement of an event, forming the union of a finite or countable number of events, and taking the intersection of a finite or countable number of events. Most of the probability distributions we shall see are over finite or countable sample spaces, and we shall generally consider all subsets of a sample space to be events. A notable exception is the continuous uniform probability distribution, which we shall see shortly.

In our coin-flipping example, suppose that each of the four elementary events has probability $1/4$. Then the probability of getting at least one head is

$$\Pr\{\text{HH}, \text{HT}, \text{TH}\} = \Pr\{\text{HH}\} + \Pr\{\text{HT}\} + \Pr\{\text{TH}\}$$
$$= 3/4 .$$

Alternatively, since the probability of getting strictly less than one head is $\Pr\{\text{TT}\} = 1/4$, the probability of getting at least one head is $1 - 1/4 = 3/4$.

Discrete probability distributions

A probability distribution is **discrete** if it is defined over a finite or countably infinite sample space. Let S be the sample space. Then for any event A,

$$\Pr\{A\} = \sum_{s \in A} \Pr\{s\} ,$$

since elementary events, specifically those in A, are mutually exclusive. If S is finite and every elementary event $s \in S$ has probability

$$\Pr\{s\} = 1/|S| ,$$

then we have the **uniform probability distribution** on S. In such a case the experiment is often described as "picking an element of S at random."

As an example, consider the process of flipping a **fair coin**, one for which the probability of obtaining a head is the same as the probability of obtaining a tail, that is, $1/2$. If we flip the coin n times, we have the uniform probability distribution defined on the sample space $S = \{\text{H}, \text{T}\}^n$, a set of size 2^n. We can represent each elementary event in S as a string of length n over $\{\text{H}, \text{T}\}$, each string occurring with probability $1/2^n$. The event

$$A = \{\text{exactly } k \text{ heads and exactly } n - k \text{ tails occur}\}$$

is a subset of S of size $|A| = \binom{n}{k}$, since $\binom{n}{k}$ strings of length n over $\{\text{H}, \text{T}\}$ contain exactly k H's. The probability of event A is thus $\Pr\{A\} = \binom{n}{k}/2^n$.

Continuous uniform probability distribution

The continuous uniform probability distribution is an example of a probability distribution in which not all subsets of the sample space are considered to be events. The continuous uniform probability distribution is defined over a closed interval $[a, b]$ of the reals, where $a < b$. Our intuition is that each point in the interval $[a, b]$ should be "equally likely." There are an uncountable number of points, however, so if we give all points the same finite, positive probability, we cannot simultaneously satisfy axioms 2 and 3. For this reason, we would like to associate a probability only with *some* of the subsets of S, in such a way that the axioms are satisfied for these events.

For any closed interval $[c, d]$, where $a \leq c \leq d \leq b$, the **continuous uniform probability distribution** defines the probability of the event $[c, d]$ to be

$$\Pr\{[c, d]\} = \frac{d - c}{b - a} .$$

Note that for any point $x = [x, x]$, the probability of x is 0. If we remove the endpoints of an interval $[c, d]$, we obtain the open interval (c, d). Since $[c, d] = [c, c] \cup (c, d) \cup [d, d]$, axiom 3 gives us $\Pr\{[c, d]\} = \Pr\{(c, d)\}$. Generally, the set of events for the continuous uniform probability distribution contains any subset of the sample space $[a, b]$ that can be obtained by a finite or countable union of open and closed intervals, as well as certain more complicated sets.

Conditional probability and independence

Sometimes we have some prior partial knowledge about the outcome of an experiment. For example, suppose that a friend has flipped two fair coins and has told you that at least one of the coins showed a head. What is the probability that both coins are heads? The information given eliminates the possibility of two tails. The three remaining elementary events are equally likely, so we infer that each occurs with probability $1/3$. Since only one of these elementary events shows two heads, the answer to our question is $1/3$.

Conditional probability formalizes the notion of having prior partial knowledge of the outcome of an experiment. The **conditional probability** of an event A given that another event B occurs is defined to be

$$\Pr\{A \mid B\} = \frac{\Pr\{A \cap B\}}{\Pr\{B\}} \qquad\qquad (C.14)$$

whenever $\Pr\{B\} \neq 0$. (We read "$\Pr\{A \mid B\}$" as "the probability of A given B.") Intuitively, since we are given that event B occurs, the event that A also occurs is $A \cap B$. That is, $A \cap B$ is the set of outcomes in which both A and B occur. Because the outcome is one of the elementary events in B, we normalize the probabilities of all the elementary events in B by dividing them by $\Pr\{B\}$, so that they sum to 1. The conditional probability of A given B is, therefore, the ratio of the probability of event $A \cap B$ to the probability of event B. In the example above, A is the event that both coins are heads, and B is the event that at least one coin is a head. Thus, $\Pr\{A \mid B\} = (1/4)/(3/4) = 1/3$.

Two events are **independent** if

$$\Pr\{A \cap B\} = \Pr\{A\} \Pr\{B\} , \qquad\qquad (C.15)$$

which is equivalent, if $\Pr\{B\} \neq 0$, to the condition

$\Pr\{A \mid B\} = \Pr\{A\}$.

For example, suppose that we flip two fair coins and that the outcomes are independent. Then the probability of two heads is $(1/2)(1/2) = 1/4$. Now suppose that one event is that the first coin comes up heads and the other event is that the coins come up differently. Each of these events occurs with probability $1/2$, and the probability that both events occur is $1/4$; thus, according to the definition of independence, the events are independent—even though you might think that both events depend on the first coin. Finally, suppose that the coins are welded together so that they both fall heads or both fall tails and that the two possibilities are equally likely. Then the probability that each coin comes up heads is $1/2$, but the probability that they both come up heads is $1/2 \neq (1/2)(1/2)$. Consequently, the event that one comes up heads and the event that the other comes up heads are not independent.

A collection $A_1, A_2, \ldots, A_n$ of events is said to be *pairwise independent* if

$$\Pr\{A_i \cap A_j\} = \Pr\{A_i\}\Pr\{A_j\}$$

for all $1 \leq i < j \leq n$. We say that the events of the collection are *(mutually) independent* if every k-subset $A_{i_1}, A_{i_2}, \ldots, A_{i_k}$ of the collection, where $2 \leq k \leq n$ and $1 \leq i_1 < i_2 < \cdots < i_k \leq n$, satisfies

$$\Pr\{A_{i_1} \cap A_{i_2} \cap \cdots \cap A_{i_k}\} = \Pr\{A_{i_1}\}\Pr\{A_{i_2}\} \cdots \Pr\{A_{i_k}\} .$$

For example, suppose we flip two fair coins. Let A_1 be the event that the first coin is heads, let A_2 be the event that the second coin is heads, and let A_3 be the event that the two coins are different. We have

$$
\begin{aligned}
\Pr\{A_1\} &= 1/2 , \\
\Pr\{A_2\} &= 1/2 , \\
\Pr\{A_3\} &= 1/2 , \\
\Pr\{A_1 \cap A_2\} &= 1/4 , \\
\Pr\{A_1 \cap A_3\} &= 1/4 , \\
\Pr\{A_2 \cap A_3\} &= 1/4 , \\
\Pr\{A_1 \cap A_2 \cap A_3\} &= 0 .
\end{aligned}
$$

Since for $1 \leq i < j \leq 3$, we have $\Pr\{A_i \cap A_j\} = \Pr\{A_i\}\Pr\{A_j\} = 1/4$, the events A_1, A_2, and A_3 are pairwise independent. The events are not mutually independent, however, because $\Pr\{A_1 \cap A_2 \cap A_3\} = 0$ and $\Pr\{A_1\}\Pr\{A_2\}\Pr\{A_3\} = 1/8 \neq 0$.

Bayes's theorem

From the definition of conditional probability (C.14) and the commutative law $A \cap B = B \cap A$, it follows that for two events A and B, each with nonzero probability,

$$
\begin{aligned}
\Pr\{A \cap B\} &= \Pr\{B\}\Pr\{A \mid B\} & \text{(C.16)}\\
&= \Pr\{A\}\Pr\{B \mid A\} \ .
\end{aligned}
$$

Solving for $\Pr\{A \mid B\}$, we obtain

$$
\Pr\{A \mid B\} = \frac{\Pr\{A\}\Pr\{B \mid A\}}{\Pr\{B\}} , \tag{C.17}
$$

which is known as **Bayes's theorem**. The denominator $\Pr\{B\}$ is a normalizing constant, which we can reformulate as follows. Since $B = (B \cap A) \cup (B \cap \overline{A})$, and since $B \cap A$ and $B \cap \overline{A}$ are mutually exclusive events,

$$
\begin{aligned}
\Pr\{B\} &= \Pr\{B \cap A\} + \Pr\{B \cap \overline{A}\}\\
&= \Pr\{A\}\Pr\{B \mid A\} + \Pr\{\overline{A}\}\Pr\{B \mid \overline{A}\} \ .
\end{aligned}
$$

Substituting into equation (C.17), we obtain an equivalent form of Bayes's theorem:

$$
\Pr\{A \mid B\} = \frac{\Pr\{A\}\Pr\{B \mid A\}}{\Pr\{A\}\Pr\{B \mid A\} + \Pr\{\overline{A}\}\Pr\{B \mid \overline{A}\}} . \tag{C.18}
$$

Bayes's theorem can simplify the computing of conditional probabilities. For example, suppose that we have a fair coin and a biased coin that always comes up heads. We run an experiment consisting of three independent events: we choose one of the two coins at random, we flip that coin once, and then we flip it again. Suppose that the coin we have chosen comes up heads both times. What is the probability that it is biased?

We solve this problem using Bayes's theorem. Let A be the event that we choose the biased coin, and let B be the event that the chosen coin comes up heads both times. We wish to determine $\Pr\{A \mid B\}$. We have $\Pr\{A\} = 1/2$, $\Pr\{B \mid A\} = 1$, $\Pr\{\overline{A}\} = 1/2$, and $\Pr\{B \mid \overline{A}\} = 1/4$; hence,

$$
\begin{aligned}
\Pr\{A \mid B\} &= \frac{(1/2) \cdot 1}{(1/2) \cdot 1 + (1/2) \cdot (1/4)}\\
&= 4/5 \ .
\end{aligned}
$$

Exercises

C.2-1

Professor Rosencrantz flips a fair coin once. Professor Guildenstern flips a fair coin twice. What is the probability that Professor Rosencrantz obtains more heads than Professor Guildenstern?

C.2-2

Prove **Boole's inequality**: For any finite or countably infinite sequence of events $A_1, A_2, \ldots$,

$$\Pr\{A_1 \cup A_2 \cup \cdots\} \le \Pr\{A_1\} + \Pr\{A_2\} + \cdots . \tag{C.19}$$

C.2-3

Suppose we shuffle a deck of 10 cards, each bearing a distinct number from 1 to 10, to mix the cards thoroughly. We then remove three cards, one at a time, from the deck. What is the probability that we select the three cards in sorted (increasing) order?

C.2-4

Prove that

$$\Pr\{A \mid B\} + \Pr\{\overline{A} \mid B\} = 1 .$$

C.2-5

Prove that for any collection of events $A_1, A_2, \ldots, A_n$,

$$\Pr\{A_1 \cap A_2 \cap \cdots \cap A_n\} = \Pr\{A_1\} \cdot \Pr\{A_2 \mid A_1\} \cdot \Pr\{A_3 \mid A_1 \cap A_2\} \cdots$$
$$\Pr\{A_n \mid A_1 \cap A_2 \cap \cdots \cap A_{n-1}\} .$$

C.2-6 ★

Describe a procedure that takes as input two integers a and b such that $0 < a < b$ and, using fair coin flips, produces as output heads with probability a/b and tails with probability $(b - a)/b$. Give a bound on the expected number of coin flips, which should be $O(1)$. (*Hint:* Represent a/b in binary.)

C.2-7 ★

Show how to construct a set of n events that are pairwise independent but such that no subset of $k > 2$ of them is mutually independent.

C.2-8 ★

Two events A and B are **conditionally independent**, given C, if

$$\Pr\{A \cap B \mid C\} = \Pr\{A \mid C\} \cdot \Pr\{B \mid C\} .$$

Give a simple but nontrivial example of two events that are not independent but are conditionally independent given a third event.

C.2-9 ★

You are a contestant in a game show in which a prize is hidden behind one of three curtains. You will win the prize if you select the correct curtain. After you have picked one curtain but before the curtain is lifted, the emcee lifts one of the other curtains, knowing that it will reveal an empty stage, and asks if you would like to switch from your current selection to the remaining curtain. How would your chances change if you switch? (This question is the celebrated ***Monty Hall problem***, named after a game-show host who often presented contestants with just this dilemma.)

C.2-10 ★

A prison warden has randomly picked one prisoner among three to go free. The other two will be executed. The guard knows which one will go free but is forbidden to give any prisoner information regarding his status. Let us call the prisoners X, Y, and Z. Prisoner X asks the guard privately which of Y or Z will be executed, arguing that since he already knows that at least one of them must die, the guard won't be revealing any information about his own status. The guard tells X that Y is to be executed. Prisoner X feels happier now, since he figures that either he or prisoner Z will go free, which means that his probability of going free is now $1/2$. Is he right, or are his chances still $1/3$? Explain.

C.3   Discrete random variables

A *(discrete) random variable* X is a function from a finite or countably infinite sample space S to the real numbers. It associates a real number with each possible outcome of an experiment, which allows us to work with the probability distribution induced on the resulting set of numbers. Random variables can also be defined for uncountably infinite sample spaces, but they raise technical issues that are unnecessary to address for our purposes. Henceforth, we shall assume that random variables are discrete.

For a random variable X and a real number x, we define the event $X = x$ to be $\{s \in S : X(s) = x\}$; thus,

$$\Pr\{X = x\} = \sum_{s \in S : X(s) = x} \Pr\{s\} \ .$$

The function

$$f(x) = \Pr\{X = x\}$$

is the ***probability density function*** of the random variable X. From the probability axioms, $\Pr\{X = x\} \geq 0$ and $\sum_x \Pr\{X = x\} = 1$.

As an example, consider the experiment of rolling a pair of ordinary, 6-sided dice. There are 36 possible elementary events in the sample space. We assume that the probability distribution is uniform, so that each elementary event $s \in S$ is equally likely: $\Pr\{s\} = 1/36$. Define the random variable X to be the *maximum* of the two values showing on the dice. We have $\Pr\{X = 3\} = 5/36$, since X assigns a value of 3 to 5 of the 36 possible elementary events, namely, $(1,3)$, $(2,3)$, $(3,3)$, $(3,2)$, and $(3,1)$.

We often define several random variables on the same sample space. If X and Y are random variables, the function

$$f(x, y) = \Pr\{X = x \text{ and } Y = y\}$$

is the ***joint probability density function*** of X and Y. For a fixed value y,

$$\Pr\{Y = y\} = \sum_x \Pr\{X = x \text{ and } Y = y\} \ ,$$

and similarly, for a fixed value x,

$$\Pr\{X = x\} = \sum_y \Pr\{X = x \text{ and } Y = y\} \ .$$

Using the definition (C.14) of conditional probability, we have

$$\Pr\{X = x \mid Y = y\} = \frac{\Pr\{X = x \text{ and } Y = y\}}{\Pr\{Y = y\}} \ .$$

We define two random variables X and Y to be ***independent*** if for all x and y, the events $X = x$ and $Y = y$ are independent or, equivalently, if for all x and y, we have $\Pr\{X = x \text{ and } Y = y\} = \Pr\{X = x\}\Pr\{Y = y\}$.

Given a set of random variables defined over the same sample space, we can define new random variables as sums, products, or other functions of the original variables.

Expected value of a random variable

The simplest and most useful summary of the distribution of a random variable is the "average" of the values it takes on. The ***expected value*** (or, synonymously, ***expectation*** or ***mean***) of a discrete random variable X is

$$\mathrm{E}[X] = \sum_x x \cdot \Pr\{X = x\} \ , \tag{C.20}$$

which is well defined if the sum is finite or converges absolutely. Sometimes the expectation of X is denoted by μ_X or, when the random variable is apparent from context, simply by μ.

Consider a game in which you flip two fair coins. You earn \$3 for each head but lose \$2 for each tail. The expected value of the random variable X representing your earnings is

$$
\begin{aligned}
\mathrm{E}\,[X] &= 6 \cdot \Pr\{2 \text{ H's}\} + 1 \cdot \Pr\{1 \text{ H}, 1 \text{ T}\} - 4 \cdot \Pr\{2 \text{ T's}\} \\
&= 6(1/4) + 1(1/2) - 4(1/4) \\
&= 1 .
\end{aligned}
$$

The expectation of the sum of two random variables is the sum of their expectations, that is,

$$
\mathrm{E}\,[X + Y] = \mathrm{E}\,[X] + \mathrm{E}\,[Y] , \tag{C.21}
$$

whenever $\mathrm{E}\,[X]$ and $\mathrm{E}\,[Y]$ are defined. We call this property ***linearity of expectation***, and it holds even if X and Y are not independent. It also extends to finite and absolutely convergent summations of expectations. Linearity of expectation is the key property that enables us to perform probabilistic analyses by using indicator random variables (see Section 5.2).

If X is any random variable, any function $g(x)$ defines a new random variable $g(X)$. If the expectation of $g(X)$ is defined, then

$$
\mathrm{E}\,[g(X)] = \sum_x g(x) \cdot \Pr\{X = x\} .
$$

Letting $g(x) = ax$, we have for any constant a,

$$
\mathrm{E}\,[aX] = a\mathrm{E}\,[X] . \tag{C.22}
$$

Consequently, expectations are linear: for any two random variables X and Y and any constant a,

$$
\mathrm{E}\,[aX + Y] = a\mathrm{E}\,[X] + \mathrm{E}\,[Y] . \tag{C.23}
$$

When two random variables X and Y are independent and each has a defined expectation,

$$
\begin{aligned}
\mathrm{E}\,[XY] &= \sum_x \sum_y xy \cdot \Pr\{X = x \text{ and } Y = y\} \\
&= \sum_x \sum_y xy \cdot \Pr\{X = x\} \Pr\{Y = y\} \\
&= \left(\sum_x x \cdot \Pr\{X = x\} \right) \left(\sum_y y \cdot \Pr\{Y = y\} \right) \\
&= \mathrm{E}\,[X]\mathrm{E}\,[Y] .
\end{aligned}
$$

In general, when n random variables $X_1, X_2, \ldots, X_n$ are mutually independent,

$$
\mathrm{E}\,[X_1 X_2 \cdots X_n] = \mathrm{E}\,[X_1]\mathrm{E}\,[X_2] \cdots \mathrm{E}\,[X_n] . \tag{C.24}
$$

When a random variable X takes on values from the set of natural numbers $\mathbb{N} = \{0, 1, 2, \ldots\}$, we have a nice formula for its expectation:

$$
\begin{aligned}
\mathrm{E}[X] &= \sum_{i=0}^{\infty} i \cdot \Pr\{X = i\} \\
&= \sum_{i=0}^{\infty} i (\Pr\{X \geq i\} - \Pr\{X \geq i + 1\}) \\
&= \sum_{i=1}^{\infty} \Pr\{X \geq i\} \; ,
\end{aligned}
\tag{C.25}
$$

since each term $\Pr\{X \geq i\}$ is added in i times and subtracted out $i - 1$ times (except $\Pr\{X \geq 0\}$, which is added in 0 times and not subtracted out at all).

When we apply a convex function $f(x)$ to a random variable X, *Jensen's inequality* gives us

$$
\mathrm{E}[f(X)] \geq f(\mathrm{E}[X]) \; ,
\tag{C.26}
$$

provided that the expectations exist and are finite. (A function $f(x)$ is **convex** if for all x and y and for all $0 \leq \lambda \leq 1$, we have $f(\lambda x + (1 - \lambda)y) \leq \lambda f(x) + (1 - \lambda) f(y)$.)

Variance and standard deviation

The expected value of a random variable does not tell us how "spread out" the variable's values are. For example, if we have random variables X and Y for which $\Pr\{X = 1/4\} = \Pr\{X = 3/4\} = 1/2$ and $\Pr\{Y = 0\} = \Pr\{Y = 1\} = 1/2$, then both $\mathrm{E}[X]$ and $\mathrm{E}[Y]$ are $1/2$, yet the actual values taken on by Y are farther from the mean than the actual values taken on by X.

The notion of variance mathematically expresses how far from the mean a random variable's values are likely to be. The **variance** of a random variable X with mean $\mathrm{E}[X]$ is

$$
\begin{aligned}
\mathrm{Var}[X] &= \mathrm{E}\left[(X - \mathrm{E}[X])^2\right] \\
&= \mathrm{E}\left[X^2 - 2X\mathrm{E}[X] + \mathrm{E}^2[X]\right] \\
&= \mathrm{E}\left[X^2\right] - 2\mathrm{E}[X\mathrm{E}[X]] + \mathrm{E}^2[X] \\
&= \mathrm{E}\left[X^2\right] - 2\mathrm{E}^2[X] + \mathrm{E}^2[X] \\
&= \mathrm{E}\left[X^2\right] - \mathrm{E}^2[X] \; .
\end{aligned}
\tag{C.27}
$$

To justify the equality $\mathrm{E}[\mathrm{E}^2[X]] = \mathrm{E}^2[X]$, note that because $\mathrm{E}[X]$ is a real number and not a random variable, so is $\mathrm{E}^2[X]$. The equality $\mathrm{E}[X\mathrm{E}[X]] = \mathrm{E}^2[X]$

follows from equation (C.22), with $a = \mathrm{E}[X]$. Rewriting equation (C.27) yields an expression for the expectation of the square of a random variable:

$$\mathrm{E}[X^2] = \mathrm{Var}[X] + \mathrm{E}^2[X] \ . \tag{C.28}$$

The variance of a random variable X and the variance of aX are related (see Exercise C.3-10):

$$\mathrm{Var}[aX] = a^2 \mathrm{Var}[X] \ .$$

When X and Y are independent random variables,

$$\mathrm{Var}[X + Y] = \mathrm{Var}[X] + \mathrm{Var}[Y] \ .$$

In general, if n random variables $X_1, X_2, \ldots, X_n$ are pairwise independent, then

$$\mathrm{Var}\left[\sum_{i=1}^{n} X_i\right] = \sum_{i=1}^{n} \mathrm{Var}[X_i] \ . \tag{C.29}$$

The **standard deviation** of a random variable X is the nonnegative square root of the variance of X. The standard deviation of a random variable X is sometimes denoted σ_X or simply σ when the random variable X is understood from context. With this notation, the variance of X is denoted σ^2.

Exercises

C.3-1
Suppose we roll two ordinary, 6-sided dice. What is the expectation of the sum of the two values showing? What is the expectation of the maximum of the two values showing?

C.3-2
An array $A[1 .. n]$ contains n distinct numbers that are randomly ordered, with each permutation of the n numbers being equally likely. What is the expectation of the index of the maximum element in the array? What is the expectation of the index of the minimum element in the array?

C.3-3
A carnival game consists of three dice in a cage. A player can bet a dollar on any of the numbers 1 through 6. The cage is shaken, and the payoff is as follows. If the player's number doesn't appear on any of the dice, he loses his dollar. Otherwise, if his number appears on exactly k of the three dice, for $k = 1, 2, 3$, he keeps his dollar and wins k more dollars. What is his expected gain from playing the carnival game once?

C.3-4

Argue that if X and Y are nonnegative random variables, then

$$E[\max(X, Y)] \leq E[X] + E[Y] .$$

C.3-5 ★

Let X and Y be independent random variables. Prove that $f(X)$ and $g(Y)$ are independent for any choice of functions f and g.

C.3-6 ★

Let X be a nonnegative random variable, and suppose that $E[X]$ is well defined. Prove **Markov's inequality**:

$$\Pr\{X \geq t\} \leq E[X]/t \tag{C.30}$$

for all $t > 0$.

C.3-7 ★

Let S be a sample space, and let X and X' be random variables such that $X(s) \geq X'(s)$ for all $s \in S$. Prove that for any real constant t,

$$\Pr\{X \geq t\} \geq \Pr\{X' \geq t\} .$$

C.3-8

Which is larger: the expectation of the square of a random variable, or the square of its expectation?

C.3-9

Show that for any random variable X that takes on only the values 0 and 1, we have $\text{Var}[X] = E[X] E[1 - X]$.

C.3-10

Prove that $\text{Var}[aX] = a^2 \text{Var}[X]$ from the definition (C.27) of variance.

C.4   The geometric and binomial distributions

We can think of a coin flip as an instance of a **Bernoulli trial**, which is an experiment with only two possible outcomes: **success**, which occurs with probability p, and **failure**, which occurs with probability $q = 1 - p$. When we speak of **Bernoulli trials** collectively, we mean that the trials are mutually independent and, unless we specifically say otherwise, that each has the same probability p for success. Two

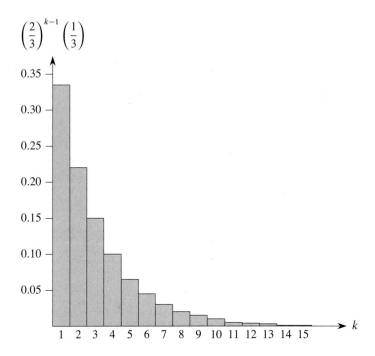

Figure C.1   A geometric distribution with probability $p = 1/3$ of success and a probability $q = 1 - p$ of failure. The expectation of the distribution is $1/p = 3$.

important distributions arise from Bernoulli trials: the geometric distribution and the binomial distribution.

The geometric distribution

Suppose we have a sequence of Bernoulli trials, each with a probability p of success and a probability $q = 1 - p$ of failure. How many trials occur before we obtain a success? Let us define the random variable X be the number of trials needed to obtain a success. Then X has values in the range $\{1, 2, \ldots\}$, and for $k \geq 1$,

$$\Pr\{X = k\} = q^{k-1}p , \tag{C.31}$$

since we have $k - 1$ failures before the one success. A probability distribution satisfying equation (C.31) is said to be a ***geometric distribution***. Figure C.1 illustrates such a distribution.

Assuming that $q < 1$, we can calculate the expectation of a geometric distribution using identity (A.8):

$$
\begin{aligned}
\mathrm{E}\left[X\right] &= \sum_{k=1}^{\infty} k q^{k-1} p \\
&= \frac{p}{q} \sum_{k=0}^{\infty} k q^{k} \\
&= \frac{p}{q} \cdot \frac{q}{(1-q)^2} \\
&= \frac{p}{q} \cdot \frac{q}{p^2} \\
&= 1/p .
\end{aligned}
\tag{C.32}
$$

Thus, on average, it takes $1/p$ trials before we obtain a success, an intuitive result. The variance, which can be calculated similarly, but using Exercise A.1-3, is

$$
\mathrm{Var}\left[X\right] = q/p^2 .
\tag{C.33}
$$

As an example, suppose we repeatedly roll two dice until we obtain either a seven or an eleven. Of the 36 possible outcomes, 6 yield a seven and 2 yield an eleven. Thus, the probability of success is $p = 8/36 = 2/9$, and we must roll $1/p = 9/2 = 4.5$ times on average to obtain a seven or eleven.

The binomial distribution

How many successes occur during n Bernoulli trials, where a success occurs with probability p and a failure with probability $q = 1 - p$? Define the random variable X to be the number of successes in n trials. Then X has values in the range $\{0, 1, \ldots, n\}$, and for $k = 0, 1, \ldots, n$,

$$
\Pr\{X = k\} = \binom{n}{k} p^k q^{n-k} ,
\tag{C.34}
$$

since there are $\binom{n}{k}$ ways to pick which k of the n trials are successes, and the probability that each occurs is $p^k q^{n-k}$. A probability distribution satisfying equation (C.34) is said to be a ***binomial distribution***. For convenience, we define the family of binomial distributions using the notation

$$
b(k; n, p) = \binom{n}{k} p^k (1 - p)^{n-k} .
\tag{C.35}
$$

Figure C.2 illustrates a binomial distribution. The name "binomial" comes from the right-hand side of equation (C.34) being the kth term of the expansion of $(p + q)^n$. Consequently, since $p + q = 1$,

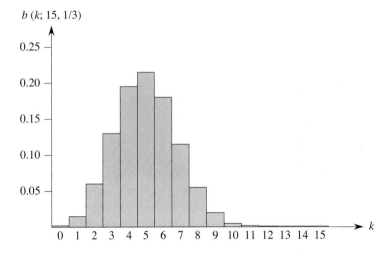

Figure C.2   The binomial distribution $b(k; 15, 1/3)$ resulting from $n = 15$ Bernoulli trials, each with probability $p = 1/3$ of success. The expectation of the distribution is $np = 5$.

$$\sum_{k=0}^{n} b(k; n, p) = 1 \,, \tag{C.36}$$

as axiom 2 of the probability axioms requires.

We can compute the expectation of a random variable having a binomial distribution from equations (C.8) and (C.36). Let X be a random variable that follows the binomial distribution $b(k; n, p)$, and let $q = 1 - p$. By the definition of expectation, we have

$$\begin{aligned}
E[X] &= \sum_{k=0}^{n} k \cdot \Pr\{X = k\} \\
&= \sum_{k=0}^{n} k \cdot b(k; n, p) \\
&= \sum_{k=1}^{n} k \binom{n}{k} p^k q^{n-k} \\
&= np \sum_{k=1}^{n} \binom{n-1}{k-1} p^{k-1} q^{n-k} \quad \text{(by equation (C.8))} \\
&= np \sum_{k=0}^{n-1} \binom{n-1}{k} p^k q^{(n-1)-k}
\end{aligned}$$

$$= np \sum_{k=0}^{n-1} b(k; n-1, p)$$

$$= np \qquad \text{(by equation (C.36))} . \qquad (C.37)$$

By using the linearity of expectation, we can obtain the same result with substantially less algebra. Let X_i be the random variable describing the number of successes in the ith trial. Then $E[X_i] = p \cdot 1 + q \cdot 0 = p$, and by linearity of expectation (equation (C.21)), the expected number of successes for n trials is

$$E[X] = E\left[\sum_{i=1}^{n} X_i\right]$$

$$= \sum_{i=1}^{n} E[X_i]$$

$$= \sum_{i=1}^{n} p$$

$$= np . \qquad (C.38)$$

We can use the same approach to calculate the variance of the distribution. Using equation (C.27), we have $\text{Var}[X_i] = E[X_i^2] - E^2[X_i]$. Since X_i only takes on the values 0 and 1, we have $X_i^2 = X_i$, which implies $E[X_i^2] = E[X_i] = p$. Hence,

$$\text{Var}[X_i] = p - p^2 = p(1 - p) = pq . \qquad (C.39)$$

To compute the variance of X, we take advantage of the independence of the n trials; thus, by equation (C.29),

$$\text{Var}[X] = \text{Var}\left[\sum_{i=1}^{n} X_i\right]$$

$$= \sum_{i=1}^{n} \text{Var}[X_i]$$

$$= \sum_{i=1}^{n} pq$$

$$= npq . \qquad (C.40)$$

As Figure C.2 shows, the binomial distribution $b(k; n, p)$ increases with k until it reaches the mean np, and then it decreases. We can prove that the distribution always behaves in this manner by looking at the ratio of successive terms:

$$\frac{b(k;n,p)}{b(k-1;n,p)} = \frac{\binom{n}{k}p^k q^{n-k}}{\binom{n}{k-1}p^{k-1}q^{n-k+1}}$$

$$= \frac{n!(k-1)!(n-k+1)!p}{k!(n-k)!n!q}$$

$$= \frac{(n-k+1)p}{kq} \tag{C.41}$$

$$= 1 + \frac{(n+1)p-k}{kq} .$$

This ratio is greater than 1 precisely when $(n+1)p - k$ is positive. Consequently, $b(k;n,p) > b(k-1;n,p)$ for $k < (n+1)p$ (the distribution increases), and $b(k;n,p) < b(k-1;n,p)$ for $k > (n+1)p$ (the distribution decreases). If $k = (n+1)p$ is an integer, then $b(k;n,p) = b(k-1;n,p)$, and so the distribution then has two maxima: at $k = (n+1)p$ and at $k-1 = (n+1)p-1 = np - q$. Otherwise, it attains a maximum at the unique integer k that lies in the range $np - q < k < (n+1)p$.

The following lemma provides an upper bound on the binomial distribution.

Lemma C.1
Let $n \geq 0$, let $0 < p < 1$, let $q = 1 - p$, and let $0 \leq k \leq n$. Then

$$b(k;n,p) \leq \left(\frac{np}{k}\right)^k \left(\frac{nq}{n-k}\right)^{n-k} .$$

Proof   Using equation (C.6), we have

$$b(k;n,p) = \binom{n}{k}p^k q^{n-k}$$

$$\leq \left(\frac{n}{k}\right)^k \left(\frac{n}{n-k}\right)^{n-k} p^k q^{n-k}$$

$$= \left(\frac{np}{k}\right)^k \left(\frac{nq}{n-k}\right)^{n-k} . \qquad \blacksquare$$

Exercises

C.4-1
Verify axiom 2 of the probability axioms for the geometric distribution.

C.4-2
How many times on average must we flip 6 fair coins before we obtain 3 heads and 3 tails?

C.4-3
Show that $b(k;n,p) = b(n-k;n,q)$, where $q = 1 - p$.

C.4-4
Show that value of the maximum of the binomial distribution $b(k;n,p)$ is approximately $1/\sqrt{2\pi npq}$, where $q = 1 - p$.

C.4-5 ★
Show that the probability of no successes in n Bernoulli trials, each with probability $p = 1/n$, is approximately $1/e$. Show that the probability of exactly one success is also approximately $1/e$.

C.4-6 ★
Professor Rosencrantz flips a fair coin n times, and so does Professor Guildenstern. Show that the probability that they get the same number of heads is $\binom{2n}{n}/4^n$. (*Hint:* For Professor Rosencrantz, call a head a success; for Professor Guildenstern, call a tail a success.) Use your argument to verify the identity

$$\sum_{k=0}^{n} \binom{n}{k}^2 = \binom{2n}{n}.$$

C.4-7 ★
Show that for $0 \le k \le n$,

$$b(k;n,1/2) \le 2^{n\,H(k/n)-n},$$

where $H(x)$ is the entropy function (C.7).

C.4-8 ★
Consider n Bernoulli trials, where for $i = 1,2,\ldots,n$, the ith trial has probability p_i of success, and let X be the random variable denoting the total number of successes. Let $p \ge p_i$ for all $i = 1,2,\ldots,n$. Prove that for $1 \le k \le n$,

$$\Pr\{X < k\} \ge \sum_{i=0}^{k-1} b(i;n,p).$$

C.4-9 ★
Let X be the random variable for the total number of successes in a set A of n Bernoulli trials, where the ith trial has a probability p_i of success, and let X' be the random variable for the total number of successes in a second set A' of n Bernoulli trials, where the ith trial has a probability $p'_i \ge p_i$ of success. Prove that for $0 \le k \le n$,

$$\Pr\{X' \geq k\} \geq \Pr\{X \geq k\} \;.$$

(*Hint:* Show how to obtain the Bernoulli trials in A' by an experiment involving the trials of A, and use the result of Exercise C.3-7.)

★ C.5   The tails of the binomial distribution

The probability of having at least, or at most, k successes in n Bernoulli trials, each with probability p of success, is often of more interest than the probability of having exactly k successes. In this section, we investigate the **tails** of the binomial distribution: the two regions of the distribution $b(k;n, p)$ that are far from the mean np. We shall prove several important bounds on (the sum of all terms in) a tail.

We first provide a bound on the right tail of the distribution $b(k;n, p)$. We can determine bounds on the left tail by inverting the roles of successes and failures.

Theorem C.2
Consider a sequence of n Bernoulli trials, where success occurs with probability p. Let X be the random variable denoting the total number of successes. Then for $0 \leq k \leq n$, the probability of at least k successes is

$$\Pr\{X \geq k\} \;=\; \sum_{i=k}^{n} b(i;n, p)$$

$$\leq \; \binom{n}{k} p^k \;.$$

Proof   For $S \subseteq \{1, 2, \ldots, n\}$, we let A_S denote the event that the ith trial is a success for every $i \in S$. Clearly $\Pr\{A_S\} = p^k$ if $|S| = k$. We have

$$
\begin{aligned}
\Pr\{X \geq k\} \;&=\; \Pr\{\text{there exists } S \subseteq \{1, 2, \ldots, n\} : |S| = k \text{ and } A_S\} \\
&=\; \Pr\left\{ \bigcup_{S \subseteq \{1,2,\ldots,n\}:|S|=k} A_S \right\} \\
&\leq\; \sum_{S \subseteq \{1,2,\ldots,n\}:|S|=k} \Pr\{A_S\} \qquad \text{(by inequality (C.19))} \\
&=\; \binom{n}{k} p^k \;.
\end{aligned}
$$

∎

The following corollary restates the theorem for the left tail of the binomial distribution. In general, we shall leave it to you to adapt the proofs from one tail to the other.

Corollary C.3

Consider a sequence of n Bernoulli trials, where success occurs with probability p. If X is the random variable denoting the total number of successes, then for $0 \le k \le n$, the probability of at most k successes is

$$\Pr\{X \le k\} = \sum_{i=0}^{k} b(i; n, p)$$

$$\le \binom{n}{n-k}(1-p)^{n-k}$$

$$= \binom{n}{k}(1-p)^{n-k} . \qquad \blacksquare$$

Our next bound concerns the left tail of the binomial distribution. Its corollary shows that, far from the mean, the left tail diminishes exponentially.

Theorem C.4

Consider a sequence of n Bernoulli trials, where success occurs with probability p and failure with probability $q = 1 - p$. Let X be the random variable denoting the total number of successes. Then for $0 < k < np$, the probability of fewer than k successes is

$$\Pr\{X < k\} = \sum_{i=0}^{k-1} b(i; n, p)$$

$$< \frac{kq}{np - k} b(k; n, p) .$$

Proof We bound the series $\sum_{i=0}^{k-1} b(i; n, p)$ by a geometric series using the technique from Section A.2, page 1151. For $i = 1, 2, \ldots, k$, we have from equation (C.41),

$$\frac{b(i-1; n, p)}{b(i; n, p)} = \frac{iq}{(n - i + 1)p}$$

$$< \frac{iq}{(n - i)p}$$

$$\le \frac{kq}{(n - k)p} .$$

If we let

$$
\begin{aligned}
x &= \frac{kq}{(n-k)p} \\
&< \frac{kq}{(n-np)p} \\
&= \frac{kq}{nqp} \\
&= \frac{k}{np} \\
&< 1,
\end{aligned}
$$

it follows that

$$b(i-1;n,p) < x\,b(i;n,p)$$

for $0 < i \le k$. Iteratively applying this inequality $k - i$ times, we obtain

$$b(i;n,p) < x^{k-i}\,b(k;n,p)$$

for $0 \le i < k$, and hence

$$
\begin{aligned}
\sum_{i=0}^{k-1} b(i;n,p) &< \sum_{i=0}^{k-1} x^{k-i} b(k;n,p) \\
&< b(k;n,p) \sum_{i=1}^{\infty} x^i \\
&= \frac{x}{1-x} b(k;n,p) \\
&= \frac{kq}{np-k} b(k;n,p) .
\end{aligned}
$$

■

Corollary C.5

Consider a sequence of n Bernoulli trials, where success occurs with probability p and failure with probability $q = 1 - p$. Then for $0 < k \le np/2$, the probability of fewer than k successes is less than one half of the probability of fewer than $k + 1$ successes.

Proof   Because $k \le np/2$, we have

$$
\frac{kq}{np-k} \le \frac{(np/2)q}{np-(np/2)}
$$

$$= \frac{(np/2)q}{np/2}$$
$$\leq 1 ,$$
$$(C.42)$$

since $q \leq 1$. Letting X be the random variable denoting the number of successes, Theorem C.4 and inequality (C.42) imply that the probability of fewer than k successes is

$$\Pr\{X < k\} = \sum_{i=0}^{k-1} b(i;n, p) < b(k;n, p) .$$

Thus we have

$$\frac{\Pr\{X < k\}}{\Pr\{X < k + 1\}} = \frac{\sum_{i=0}^{k-1} b(i;n, p)}{\sum_{i=0}^{k} b(i;n, p)}$$

$$= \frac{\sum_{i=0}^{k-1} b(i;n, p)}{\sum_{i=0}^{k-1} b(i;n, p) + b(k;n, p)}$$

$$< 1/2 ,$$

since $\sum_{i=0}^{k-1} b(i;n, p) < b(k;n, p)$. ∎

Bounds on the right tail follow similarly. Exercise C.5-2 asks you to prove them.

Corollary C.6
Consider a sequence of n Bernoulli trials, where success occurs with probability p. Let X be the random variable denoting the total number of successes. Then for $np < k < n$, the probability of more than k successes is

$$\Pr\{X > k\} = \sum_{i=k+1}^{n} b(i;n, p)$$

$$< \frac{(n - k)p}{k - np} b(k;n, p) . \qquad ∎$$

Corollary C.7
Consider a sequence of n Bernoulli trials, where success occurs with probability p and failure with probability $q = 1 - p$. Then for $(np + n)/2 < k < n$, the probability of more than k successes is less than one half of the probability of more than $k - 1$ successes. ∎

The next theorem considers n Bernoulli trials, each with a probability p_i of success, for $i = 1, 2, \ldots, n$. As the subsequent corollary shows, we can use the theorem to provide a bound on the right tail of the binomial distribution by setting $p_i = p$ for each trial.

Theorem C.8

Consider a sequence of n Bernoulli trials, where in the ith trial, for $i = 1, 2, \ldots, n$, success occurs with probability p_i and failure occurs with probability $q_i = 1 - p_i$. Let X be the random variable describing the total number of successes, and let $\mu = \mathrm{E}[X]$. Then for $r > \mu$,

$$\Pr\{X - \mu \geq r\} \leq \left(\frac{\mu e}{r}\right)^r .$$

Proof Since for any $\alpha > 0$, the function $e^{\alpha x}$ is strictly increasing in x,

$$\Pr\{X - \mu \geq r\} = \Pr\{e^{\alpha(X-\mu)} \geq e^{\alpha r}\} , \tag{C.43}$$

where we will determine α later. Using Markov's inequality (C.30), we obtain

$$\Pr\{e^{\alpha(X-\mu)} \geq e^{\alpha r}\} \leq \mathrm{E}\left[e^{\alpha(X-\mu)}\right] e^{-\alpha r} . \tag{C.44}$$

The bulk of the proof consists of bounding $\mathrm{E}\left[e^{\alpha(X-\mu)}\right]$ and substituting a suitable value for α in inequality (C.44). First, we evaluate $\mathrm{E}\left[e^{\alpha(X-\mu)}\right]$. Using the technique of indicator random variables (see Section 5.2), let $X_i = \mathrm{I}\{$the ith Bernoulli trial is a success$\}$ for $i = 1, 2, \ldots, n$; that is, X_i is the random variable that is 1 if the ith Bernoulli trial is a success and 0 if it is a failure. Thus,

$$X = \sum_{i=1}^{n} X_i ,$$

and by linearity of expectation,

$$\mu = \mathrm{E}[X] = \mathrm{E}\left[\sum_{i=1}^{n} X_i\right] = \sum_{i=1}^{n} \mathrm{E}[X_i] = \sum_{i=1}^{n} p_i ,$$

which implies

$$X - \mu = \sum_{i=1}^{n} (X_i - p_i) .$$

To evaluate $\mathrm{E}\left[e^{\alpha(X-\mu)}\right]$, we substitute for $X - \mu$, obtaining

$$
\begin{aligned}
\mathrm{E}\left[e^{\alpha(X-\mu)}\right] &= \mathrm{E}\left[e^{\alpha \sum_{i=1}^{n}(X_i - p_i)}\right] \\
&= \mathrm{E}\left[\prod_{i=1}^{n} e^{\alpha(X_i - p_i)}\right] \\
&= \prod_{i=1}^{n} \mathrm{E}\left[e^{\alpha(X_i - p_i)}\right] ,
\end{aligned}
$$

which follows from (C.24), since the mutual independence of the random variables X_i implies the mutual independence of the random variables $e^{\alpha(X_i - p_i)}$ (see Exercise C.3-5). By the definition of expectation,

$$
\begin{aligned}
\mathrm{E}\left[e^{\alpha(X_i - p_i)}\right] &= e^{\alpha(1 - p_i)} p_i + e^{\alpha(0 - p_i)} q_i \\
&= p_i e^{\alpha q_i} + q_i e^{-\alpha p_i} \\
&\le p_i e^{\alpha} + 1 \\
&\le \exp(p_i e^{\alpha}) \,,
\end{aligned}
\tag{C.45}
$$

where $\exp(x)$ denotes the exponential function: $\exp(x) = e^x$. (Inequality (C.45) follows from the inequalities $\alpha > 0$, $q_i \le 1$, $e^{\alpha q_i} \le e^{\alpha}$, and $e^{-\alpha p_i} \le 1$, and the last line follows from inequality (3.12).) Consequently,

$$
\begin{aligned}
\mathrm{E}\left[e^{\alpha(X - \mu)}\right] &= \prod_{i=1}^{n} \mathrm{E}\left[e^{\alpha(X_i - p_i)}\right] \\
&\le \prod_{i=1}^{n} \exp(p_i e^{\alpha}) \\
&= \exp\left(\sum_{i=1}^{n} p_i e^{\alpha}\right) \\
&= \exp(\mu e^{\alpha}) \,,
\end{aligned}
\tag{C.46}
$$

since $\mu = \sum_{i=1}^{n} p_i$. Therefore, from equation (C.43) and inequalities (C.44) and (C.46), it follows that

$$
\Pr\{X - \mu \ge r\} \le \exp(\mu e^{\alpha} - \alpha r) \,.
\tag{C.47}
$$

Choosing $\alpha = \ln(r/\mu)$ (see Exercise C.5-7), we obtain

$$
\begin{aligned}
\Pr\{X - \mu \ge r\} &\le \exp(\mu e^{\ln(r/\mu)} - r \ln(r/\mu)) \\
&= \exp(r - r \ln(r/\mu)) \\
&= \frac{e^r}{(r/\mu)^r} \\
&= \left(\frac{\mu e}{r}\right)^r \,.
\end{aligned}
$$

■

When applied to Bernoulli trials in which each trial has the same probability of success, Theorem C.8 yields the following corollary bounding the right tail of a binomial distribution.

Corollary C.9

Consider a sequence of n Bernoulli trials, where in each trial success occurs with probability p and failure occurs with probability $q = 1 - p$. Then for $r > np$,

$$\Pr\{X - np \geq r\} = \sum_{k=\lceil np+r \rceil}^{n} b(k;n,p)$$

$$\leq \left(\frac{npe}{r}\right)^{r}.$$

Proof   By equation (C.37), we have $\mu = \mathrm{E}\,[X] = np$.   ■

Exercises

C.5-1   ★
Which is less likely: obtaining no heads when you flip a fair coin n times, or obtaining fewer than n heads when you flip the coin $4n$ times?

C.5-2   ★
Prove Corollaries C.6 and C.7.

C.5-3   ★
Show that

$$\sum_{i=0}^{k-1}\binom{n}{i}a^{i} < (a+1)^{n}\,\frac{k}{na-k(a+1)}\,b(k;n,a/(a+1))$$

for all $a > 0$ and all k such that $0 < k < na/(a+1)$.

C.5-4   ★
Prove that if $0 < k < np$, where $0 < p < 1$ and $q = 1 - p$, then

$$\sum_{i=0}^{k-1}p^{i}q^{n-i} < \frac{kq}{np-k}\left(\frac{np}{k}\right)^{k}\left(\frac{nq}{n-k}\right)^{n-k}.$$

C.5-5   ★
Use Theorem C.8 to show that

$$\Pr\{\mu - X \geq r\} \leq \left(\frac{(n-\mu)e}{r}\right)^{r}$$

for $r > n - \mu$. Similarly, use Corollary C.9 to show that

$$\Pr\{np - X \geq r\} \leq \left(\frac{nqe}{r}\right)^{r}$$

for $r > n - np$.

C.5-6 ★

Consider a sequence of n Bernoulli trials, where in the ith trial, for $i = 1, 2, \ldots, n$, success occurs with probability p_i and failure occurs with probability $q_i = 1 - p_i$. Let X be the random variable describing the total number of successes, and let $\mu = \mathrm{E}[X]$. Show that for $r \geq 0$,

$$\Pr\{X - \mu \geq r\} \leq e^{-r^2/2n} .$$

(*Hint:* Prove that $p_i e^{\alpha q_i} + q_i e^{-\alpha p_i} \leq e^{\alpha^2/2}$. Then follow the outline of the proof of Theorem C.8, using this inequality in place of inequality (C.45).)

C.5-7 ★

Show that choosing $\alpha = \ln(r/\mu)$ minimizes the right-hand side of inequality (C.47).

Problems

C-1 Balls and bins

In this problem, we investigate the effect of various assumptions on the number of ways of placing n balls into b distinct bins.

a. Suppose that the n balls are distinct and that their order within a bin does not matter. Argue that the number of ways of placing the balls in the bins is b^n.

b. Suppose that the balls are distinct and that the balls in each bin are ordered. Prove that there are exactly $(b + n - 1)!/(b - 1)!$ ways to place the balls in the bins. (*Hint:* Consider the number of ways of arranging n distinct balls and $b - 1$ indistinguishable sticks in a row.)

c. Suppose that the balls are identical, and hence their order within a bin does not matter. Show that the number of ways of placing the balls in the bins is $\binom{b+n-1}{n}$. (*Hint:* Of the arrangements in part (b), how many are repeated if the balls are made identical?)

d. Suppose that the balls are identical and that no bin may contain more than one ball, so that $n \leq b$. Show that the number of ways of placing the balls is $\binom{b}{n}$.

e. Suppose that the balls are identical and that no bin may be left empty. Assuming that $n \geq b$, show that the number of ways of placing the balls is $\binom{n-1}{b-1}$.

Appendix notes

The first general methods for solving probability problems were discussed in a famous correspondence between B. Pascal and P. de Fermat, which began in 1654, and in a book by C. Huygens in 1657. Rigorous probability theory began with the work of J. Bernoulli in 1713 and A. De Moivre in 1730. Further developments of the theory were provided by P.-S. Laplace, S.-D. Poisson, and C. F. Gauss.

Sums of random variables were originally studied by P. L. Chebyshev and A. A. Markov. A. N. Kolmogorov axiomatized probability theory in 1933. Chernoff [66] and Hoeffding [173] provided bounds on the tails of distributions. Seminal work in random combinatorial structures was done by P. Erdős.

Knuth [209] and Liu [237] are good references for elementary combinatorics and counting. Standard textbooks such as Billingsley [46], Chung [67], Drake [95], Feller [104], and Rozanov [300] offer comprehensive introductions to probability.

D Matrices

Matrices arise in numerous applications, including, but by no means limited to, scientific computing. If you have seen matrices before, much of the material in this appendix will be familiar to you, but some of it might be new. Section D.1 covers basic matrix definitions and operations, and Section D.2 presents some basic matrix properties.

D.1 Matrices and matrix operations

In this section, we review some basic concepts of matrix theory and some fundamental properties of matrices.

Matrices and vectors

A *matrix* is a rectangular array of numbers. For example,

$$A = \begin{pmatrix} a_{11} & a_{12} & a_{13} \\ a_{21} & a_{22} & a_{23} \end{pmatrix}$$
$$= \begin{pmatrix} 1 & 2 & 3 \\ 4 & 5 & 6 \end{pmatrix} \tag{D.1}$$

is a 2×3 matrix $A = (a_{ij})$, where for $i = 1, 2$ and $j = 1, 2, 3$, we denote the element of the matrix in row i and column j by a_{ij}. We use uppercase letters to denote matrices and corresponding subscripted lowercase letters to denote their elements. We denote the set of all $m \times n$ matrices with real-valued entries by $\mathbb{R}^{m \times n}$ and, in general, the set of $m \times n$ matrices with entries drawn from a set S by $S^{m \times n}$.

The *transpose* of a matrix A is the matrix A^{T} obtained by exchanging the rows and columns of A. For the matrix A of equation (D.1),

$$A^\mathrm{T} = \begin{pmatrix} 1 & 4 \\ 2 & 5 \\ 3 & 6 \end{pmatrix}.$$

A *vector* is a one-dimensional array of numbers. For example,

$$x = \begin{pmatrix} 2 \\ 3 \\ 5 \end{pmatrix}$$

is a vector of size 3. We sometimes call a vector of length n an *n-vector*. We use lowercase letters to denote vectors, and we denote the ith element of a size-n vector x by x_i, for $i = 1, 2, \ldots, n$. We take the standard form of a vector to be as a *column vector* equivalent to an $n \times 1$ matrix; the corresponding *row vector* is obtained by taking the transpose:

$$x^\mathrm{T} = (\, 2 \quad 3 \quad 5 \,).$$

The *unit vector* e_i is the vector whose ith element is 1 and all of whose other elements are 0. Usually, the size of a unit vector is clear from the context.

A *zero matrix* is a matrix all of whose entries are 0. Such a matrix is often denoted 0, since the ambiguity between the number 0 and a matrix of 0s is usually easily resolved from context. If a matrix of 0s is intended, then the size of the matrix also needs to be derived from the context.

Square matrices

Square $n \times n$ matrices arise frequently. Several special cases of square matrices are of particular interest:

1. A *diagonal matrix* has $a_{ij} = 0$ whenever $i \neq j$. Because all of the off-diagonal elements are zero, we can specify the matrix by listing the elements along the diagonal:

$$\mathrm{diag}(a_{11}, a_{22}, \ldots, a_{nn}) = \begin{pmatrix} a_{11} & 0 & \cdots & 0 \\ 0 & a_{22} & \cdots & 0 \\ \vdots & \vdots & \ddots & \vdots \\ 0 & 0 & \cdots & a_{nn} \end{pmatrix}.$$

2. The $n \times n$ *identity matrix* I_n is a diagonal matrix with 1s along the diagonal:

$$\begin{aligned} I_n &= \mathrm{diag}(1, 1, \ldots, 1) \\ &= \begin{pmatrix} 1 & 0 & \cdots & 0 \\ 0 & 1 & \cdots & 0 \\ \vdots & \vdots & \ddots & \vdots \\ 0 & 0 & \cdots & 1 \end{pmatrix}. \end{aligned}$$

When I appears without a subscript, we derive its size from the context. The ith column of an identity matrix is the unit vector e_i.

3. A ***tridiagonal matrix*** T is one for which $t_{ij} = 0$ if $|i - j| > 1$. Nonzero entries appear only on the main diagonal, immediately above the main diagonal ($t_{i,i+1}$ for $i = 1, 2, \ldots, n - 1$), or immediately below the main diagonal ($t_{i+1,i}$ for $i = 1, 2, \ldots, n - 1$):

$$T = \begin{pmatrix} t_{11} & t_{12} & 0 & 0 & \cdots & 0 & 0 & 0 \\ t_{21} & t_{22} & t_{23} & 0 & \cdots & 0 & 0 & 0 \\ 0 & t_{32} & t_{33} & t_{34} & \cdots & 0 & 0 & 0 \\ \vdots & \vdots & \vdots & \vdots & \ddots & \vdots & \vdots & \vdots \\ 0 & 0 & 0 & 0 & \cdots & t_{n-2,n-2} & t_{n-2,n-1} & 0 \\ 0 & 0 & 0 & 0 & \cdots & t_{n-1,n-2} & t_{n-1,n-1} & t_{n-1,n} \\ 0 & 0 & 0 & 0 & \cdots & 0 & t_{n,n-1} & t_{nn} \end{pmatrix} .$$

4. An ***upper-triangular matrix*** U is one for which $u_{ij} = 0$ if $i > j$. All entries below the diagonal are zero:

$$U = \begin{pmatrix} u_{11} & u_{12} & \cdots & u_{1n} \\ 0 & u_{22} & \cdots & u_{2n} \\ \vdots & \vdots & \ddots & \vdots \\ 0 & 0 & \cdots & u_{nn} \end{pmatrix} .$$

An upper-triangular matrix is ***unit upper-triangular*** if it has all 1s along the diagonal.

5. A ***lower-triangular matrix*** L is one for which $l_{ij} = 0$ if $i < j$. All entries above the diagonal are zero:

$$L = \begin{pmatrix} l_{11} & 0 & \cdots & 0 \\ l_{21} & l_{22} & \cdots & 0 \\ \vdots & \vdots & \ddots & \vdots \\ l_{n1} & l_{n2} & \cdots & l_{nn} \end{pmatrix} .$$

A lower-triangular matrix is ***unit lower-triangular*** if it has all 1s along the diagonal.

6. A **permutation matrix** P has exactly one 1 in each row or column, and 0s elsewhere. An example of a permutation matrix is

$$P = \begin{pmatrix} 0 & 1 & 0 & 0 & 0 \\ 0 & 0 & 0 & 1 & 0 \\ 1 & 0 & 0 & 0 & 0 \\ 0 & 0 & 0 & 0 & 1 \\ 0 & 0 & 1 & 0 & 0 \end{pmatrix}.$$

Such a matrix is called a permutation matrix because multiplying a vector x by a permutation matrix has the effect of permuting (rearranging) the elements of x. Exercise D.1-4 explores additional properties of permutation matrices.

7. A **symmetric matrix** A satisfies the condition $A = A^{\mathrm{T}}$. For example,

$$\begin{pmatrix} 1 & 2 & 3 \\ 2 & 6 & 4 \\ 3 & 4 & 5 \end{pmatrix}$$

is a symmetric matrix.

Basic matrix operations

The elements of a matrix or vector are numbers from a number system, such as the real numbers, the complex numbers, or integers modulo a prime. The number system defines how to add and multiply numbers. We can extend these definitions to encompass addition and multiplication of matrices.

We define **matrix addition** as follows. If $A = (a_{ij})$ and $B = (b_{ij})$ are $m \times n$ matrices, then their matrix sum $C = (c_{ij}) = A + B$ is the $m \times n$ matrix defined by

$$c_{ij} = a_{ij} + b_{ij}$$

for $i = 1, 2, \ldots, m$ and $j = 1, 2, \ldots, n$. That is, matrix addition is performed componentwise. A zero matrix is the identity for matrix addition:

$$A + 0 = A = 0 + A .$$

If λ is a number and $A = (a_{ij})$ is a matrix, then $\lambda A = (\lambda a_{ij})$ is the **scalar multiple** of A obtained by multiplying each of its elements by λ. As a special case, we define the **negative** of a matrix $A = (a_{ij})$ to be $-1 \cdot A = -A$, so that the ijth entry of $-A$ is $-a_{ij}$. Thus,

$$A + (-A) = 0 = (-A) + A .$$

We use the negative of a matrix to define ***matrix subtraction***: $A - B = A + (-B)$.

We define ***matrix multiplication*** as follows. We start with two matrices A and B that are ***compatible*** in the sense that the number of columns of A equals the number of rows of B. (In general, an expression containing a matrix product AB is always assumed to imply that matrices A and B are compatible.) If $A = (a_{ik})$ is an $m \times n$ matrix and $B = (b_{kj})$ is an $n \times p$ matrix, then their matrix product $C = AB$ is the $m \times p$ matrix $C = (c_{ij})$, where

$$c_{ij} = \sum_{k=1}^{n} a_{ik} b_{kj} \tag{D.2}$$

for $i = 1, 2, \ldots, m$ and $j = 1, 2, \ldots, p$. The procedure SQUARE-MATRIX-MULTIPLY in Section 4.2 implements matrix multiplication in the straightforward manner based on equation (D.2), assuming that the matrices are square: $m = n = p$. To multiply $n \times n$ matrices, SQUARE-MATRIX-MULTIPLY performs n^3 multiplications and $n^2(n-1)$ additions, and so its running time is $\Theta(n^3)$.

Matrices have many (but not all) of the algebraic properties typical of numbers. Identity matrices are identities for matrix multiplication:

$$I_m A = A I_n = A$$

for any $m \times n$ matrix A. Multiplying by a zero matrix gives a zero matrix:

$$A\,0 = 0\,.$$

Matrix multiplication is associative:

$$A(BC) = (AB)C$$

for compatible matrices A, B, and C. Matrix multiplication distributes over addition:

$$
\begin{aligned}
A(B + C) &= AB + AC\,, \\
(B + C)D &= BD + CD\,.
\end{aligned}
$$

For $n > 1$, multiplication of $n \times n$ matrices is not commutative. For example, if $A = \begin{pmatrix} 0 & 1 \\ 0 & 0 \end{pmatrix}$ and $B = \begin{pmatrix} 0 & 0 \\ 1 & 0 \end{pmatrix}$, then

$$AB = \begin{pmatrix} 1 & 0 \\ 0 & 0 \end{pmatrix}$$

and

$$BA = \begin{pmatrix} 0 & 0 \\ 0 & 1 \end{pmatrix}\,.$$

We define matrix-vector products or vector-vector products as if the vector were the equivalent $n \times 1$ matrix (or a $1 \times n$ matrix, in the case of a row vector). Thus, if A is an $m \times n$ matrix and x is an n-vector, then Ax is an m-vector. If x and y are n-vectors, then

$$x^{\mathrm{T}} y = \sum_{i=1}^{n} x_i y_i$$

is a number (actually a 1×1 matrix) called the **inner product** of x and y. The matrix $x y^{\mathrm{T}}$ is an $n \times n$ matrix Z called the **outer product** of x and y, with $z_{ij} = x_i y_j$. The **(euclidean) norm** $\|x\|$ of an n-vector x is defined by

$$\begin{aligned}
\|x\| &= (x_1^2 + x_2^2 + \cdots + x_n^2)^{1/2} \\
&= (x^{\mathrm{T}} x)^{1/2} .
\end{aligned}$$

Thus, the norm of x is its length in n-dimensional euclidean space.

Exercises

D.1-1
Show that if A and B are symmetric $n \times n$ matrices, then so are $A + B$ and $A - B$.

D.1-2
Prove that $(AB)^{\mathrm{T}} = B^{\mathrm{T}} A^{\mathrm{T}}$ and that $A^{\mathrm{T}} A$ is always a symmetric matrix.

D.1-3
Prove that the product of two lower-triangular matrices is lower-triangular.

D.1-4
Prove that if P is an $n \times n$ permutation matrix and A is an $n \times n$ matrix, then the matrix product PA is A with its rows permuted, and the matrix product AP is A with its columns permuted. Prove that the product of two permutation matrices is a permutation matrix.

D.2   Basic matrix properties

In this section, we define some basic properties pertaining to matrices: inverses, linear dependence and independence, rank, and determinants. We also define the class of positive-definite matrices.

Matrix inverses, ranks, and determinants

We define the *inverse* of an $n \times n$ matrix A to be the $n \times n$ matrix, denoted A^{-1} (if it exists), such that $AA^{-1} = I_n = A^{-1}A$. For example,

$$\begin{pmatrix} 1 & 1 \\ 1 & 0 \end{pmatrix}^{-1} = \begin{pmatrix} 0 & 1 \\ 1 & -1 \end{pmatrix} .$$

Many nonzero $n \times n$ matrices do not have inverses. A matrix without an inverse is called *noninvertible*, or *singular*. An example of a nonzero singular matrix is

$$\begin{pmatrix} 1 & 0 \\ 1 & 0 \end{pmatrix} .$$

If a matrix has an inverse, it is called *invertible*, or *nonsingular*. Matrix inverses, when they exist, are unique. (See Exercise D.2-1.) If A and B are nonsingular $n \times n$ matrices, then

$$(BA)^{-1} = A^{-1}B^{-1} .$$

The inverse operation commutes with the transpose operation:

$$(A^{-1})^{\mathrm{T}} = (A^{\mathrm{T}})^{-1} .$$

The vectors $x_1, x_2, \ldots, x_n$ are *linearly dependent* if there exist coefficients $c_1, c_2, \ldots, c_n$, not all of which are zero, such that $c_1 x_1 + c_2 x_2 + \cdots + c_n x_n = 0$. The row vectors $x_1 = (1 \quad 2 \quad 3)$, $x_2 = (2 \quad 6 \quad 4)$, and $x_3 = (4 \quad 11 \quad 9)$ are linearly dependent, for example, since $2x_1 + 3x_2 - 2x_3 = 0$. If vectors are not linearly dependent, they are *linearly independent*. For example, the columns of an identity matrix are linearly independent.

The *column rank* of a nonzero $m \times n$ matrix A is the size of the largest set of linearly independent columns of A. Similarly, the *row rank* of A is the size of the largest set of linearly independent rows of A. A fundamental property of any matrix A is that its row rank always equals its column rank, so that we can simply refer to the *rank* of A. The rank of an $m \times n$ matrix is an integer between 0 and $\min(m, n)$, inclusive. (The rank of a zero matrix is 0, and the rank of an $n \times n$ identity matrix is n.) An alternate, but equivalent and often more useful, definition is that the rank of a nonzero $m \times n$ matrix A is the smallest number r such that there exist matrices B and C of respective sizes $m \times r$ and $r \times n$ such that

$$A = BC .$$

A square $n \times n$ matrix has *full rank* if its rank is n. An $m \times n$ matrix has *full column rank* if its rank is n. The following theorem gives a fundamental property of ranks.

Theorem D.1
A square matrix has full rank if and only if it is nonsingular.   ∎

A ***null vector*** for a matrix A is a nonzero vector x such that $Ax = 0$. The following theorem (whose proof is left as Exercise D.2-7) and its corollary relate the notions of column rank and singularity to null vectors.

Theorem D.2
A matrix A has full column rank if and only if it does not have a null vector.   ∎

Corollary D.3
A square matrix A is singular if and only if it has a null vector.   ∎

The ijth ***minor*** of an $n \times n$ matrix A, for $n > 1$, is the $(n-1) \times (n-1)$ matrix $A_{[ij]}$ obtained by deleting the ith row and jth column of A. We define the ***determinant*** of an $n \times n$ matrix A recursively in terms of its minors by

$$\det(A) = \begin{cases} a_{11} & \text{if } n = 1, \\ \displaystyle\sum_{j=1}^{n} (-1)^{1+j} a_{1j} \det(A_{[1j]}) & \text{if } n > 1. \end{cases}$$

The term $(-1)^{i+j} \det(A_{[ij]})$ is known as the ***cofactor*** of the element a_{ij}.

The following theorems, whose proofs are omitted here, express fundamental properties of the determinant.

Theorem D.4 (Determinant properties)
The determinant of a square matrix A has the following properties:

- If any row or any column of A is zero, then $\det(A) = 0$.

- The determinant of A is multiplied by λ if the entries of any one row (or any one column) of A are all multiplied by λ.

- The determinant of A is unchanged if the entries in one row (respectively, column) are added to those in another row (respectively, column).

- The determinant of A equals the determinant of A^{T}.

- The determinant of A is multiplied by -1 if any two rows (or any two columns) are exchanged.

Also, for any square matrices A and B, we have $\det(AB) = \det(A) \det(B)$.   ∎

Theorem D.5
An $n \times n$ matrix A is singular if and only if $\det(A) = 0$. ∎

Positive-definite matrices

Positive-definite matrices play an important role in many applications. An $n \times n$ matrix A is ***positive-definite*** if $x^{\mathrm{T}} A x > 0$ for all n-vectors $x \neq 0$. For example, the identity matrix is positive-definite, since for any nonzero vector $x = (\, x_1 \quad x_2 \quad \cdots \quad x_n \,)^{\mathrm{T}}$,

$$
\begin{aligned}
x^{\mathrm{T}} I_n x \;&=\; x^{\mathrm{T}} x \\
&=\; \sum_{i=1}^{n} x_i^2 \\
&>\; 0 \,.
\end{aligned}
$$

Matrices that arise in applications are often positive-definite due to the following theorem.

Theorem D.6
For any matrix A with full column rank, the matrix $A^{\mathrm{T}} A$ is positive-definite.

Proof We must show that $x^{\mathrm{T}}(A^{\mathrm{T}} A) x > 0$ for any nonzero vector x. For any vector x,

$$
\begin{aligned}
x^{\mathrm{T}}(A^{\mathrm{T}} A) x \;&=\; (Ax)^{\mathrm{T}}(Ax) \quad \text{(by Exercise D.1-2)} \\
&=\; \|Ax\|^2 \,.
\end{aligned}
$$

Note that $\|Ax\|^2$ is just the sum of the squares of the elements of the vector Ax. Therefore, $\|Ax\|^2 \geq 0$. If $\|Ax\|^2 = 0$, every element of Ax is 0, which is to say $Ax = 0$. Since A has full column rank, $Ax = 0$ implies $x = 0$, by Theorem D.2. Hence, $A^{\mathrm{T}} A$ is positive-definite. ∎

Section 28.3 explores other properties of positive-definite matrices.

Exercises

D.2-1
Prove that matrix inverses are unique, that is, if B and C are inverses of A, then $B = C$.

D.2-2
Prove that the determinant of a lower-triangular or upper-triangular matrix is equal to the product of its diagonal elements. Prove that the inverse of a lower-triangular matrix, if it exists, is lower-triangular.

D.2-3
Prove that if P is a permutation matrix, then P is invertible, its inverse is P^T, and P^T is a permutation matrix.

D.2-4
Let A and B be $n \times n$ matrices such that $AB = I$. Prove that if A' is obtained from A by adding row j into row i, where $i \neq j$, then subtracting column i from column j of B yields the inverse B' of A'.

D.2-5
Let A be a nonsingular $n \times n$ matrix with complex entries. Show that every entry of A^{-1} is real if and only if every entry of A is real.

D.2-6
Show that if A is a nonsingular, symmetric, $n \times n$ matrix, then A^{-1} is symmetric. Show that if B is an arbitrary $m \times n$ matrix, then the $m \times m$ matrix given by the product BAB^T is symmetric.

D.2-7
Prove Theorem D.2. That is, show that a matrix A has full column rank if and only if $Ax = 0$ implies $x = 0$. (*Hint:* Express the linear dependence of one column on the others as a matrix-vector equation.)

D.2-8
Prove that for any two compatible matrices A and B,

$$\text{rank}(AB) \leq \min(\text{rank}(A), \text{rank}(B)),$$

where equality holds if either A or B is a nonsingular square matrix. (*Hint:* Use the alternate definition of the rank of a matrix.)

Problems

D-1   *Vandermonde matrix*
Given numbers $x_0, x_1, \ldots, x_{n-1}$, prove that the determinant of the ***Vandermonde matrix***

$$V(x_0, x_1, \ldots, x_{n-1}) = \begin{pmatrix} 1 & x_0 & x_0^2 & \cdots & x_0^{n-1} \\ 1 & x_1 & x_1^2 & \cdots & x_1^{n-1} \\ \vdots & \vdots & \vdots & \ddots & \vdots \\ 1 & x_{n-1} & x_{n-1}^2 & \cdots & x_{n-1}^{n-1} \end{pmatrix}$$

is

$$\det(V(x_0, x_1, \ldots, x_{n-1})) = \prod_{0 \le j < k \le n-1} (x_k - x_j) \, .$$

(*Hint:* Multiply column i by $-x_0$ and add it to column $i + 1$ for $i = n - 1$, $n - 2, \ldots, 1$, and then use induction.)

D-2   *Permutations defined by matrix-vector multiplication over GF(2)*

One class of permutations of the integers in the set $S_n = \{0, 1, 2, \ldots, 2^n - 1\}$ is defined by matrix multiplication over $GF(2)$. For each integer x in S_n, we view its binary representation as an n-bit vector

$$\begin{pmatrix} x_0 \\ x_1 \\ x_2 \\ \vdots \\ x_{n-1} \end{pmatrix},$$

where $x = \sum_{i=0}^{n-1} x_i 2^i$. If A is an $n \times n$ matrix in which each entry is either 0 or 1, then we can define a permutation mapping each value x in S_n to the number whose binary representation is the matrix-vector product Ax. Here, we perform all arithmetic over $GF(2)$: all values are either 0 or 1, and with one exception the usual rules of addition and multiplication apply. The exception is that $1 + 1 = 0$. You can think of arithmetic over $GF(2)$ as being just like regular integer arithmetic, except that you use only the least significant bit.

As an example, for $S_2 = \{0, 1, 2, 3\}$, the matrix

$$A = \begin{pmatrix} 1 & 0 \\ 1 & 1 \end{pmatrix}$$

defines the following permutation π_A: $\pi_A(0) = 0$, $\pi_A(1) = 3$, $\pi_A(2) = 2$, $\pi_A(3) = 1$. To see why $\pi_A(3) = 1$, observe that, working in $GF(2)$,

$$\begin{aligned} \pi_A(3) &= \begin{pmatrix} 1 & 0 \\ 1 & 1 \end{pmatrix} \begin{pmatrix} 1 \\ 1 \end{pmatrix} \\ &= \begin{pmatrix} 1 \cdot 1 + 0 \cdot 1 \\ 1 \cdot 1 + 1 \cdot 1 \end{pmatrix} \\ &= \begin{pmatrix} 1 \\ 0 \end{pmatrix}, \end{aligned}$$

which is the binary representation of 1.

For the remainder of this problem, we work over $GF(2)$, and all matrix and vector entries are 0 or 1. We define the rank of a 0-1 matrix (a matrix for which each entry is either 0 or 1) over $GF(2)$ the same as for a regular matrix, but with all arithmetic that determines linear independence performed over $GF(2)$. We define the ***range*** of an $n \times n$ 0-1 matrix A by

$$R(A) = \{y : y = Ax \text{ for some } x \in S_n\} ,$$

so that $R(A)$ is the set of numbers in S_n that we can produce by multiplying each value x in S_n by A.

a. If r is the rank of matrix A, prove that $|R(A)| = 2^r$. Conclude that A defines a permutation on S_n only if A has full rank.

For a given $n \times n$ matrix A and a given value $y \in R(A)$, we define the ***preimage*** of y by

$$P(A, y) = \{x : Ax = y\} ,$$

so that $P(A, y)$ is the set of values in S_n that map to y when multiplied by A.

b. If r is the rank of $n \times n$ matrix A and $y \in R(A)$, prove that $|P(A, y)| = 2^{n-r}$.

Let $0 \leq m \leq n$, and suppose we partition the set S_n into blocks of consecutive numbers, where the ith block consists of the 2^m numbers $i2^m, i2^m + 1$, $i2^m + 2, \ldots, (i + 1)2^m - 1$. For any subset $S \subseteq S_n$, define $B(S, m)$ to be the set of size-2^m blocks of S_n containing some element of S. As an example, when $n = 3$, $m = 1$, and $S = \{1, 4, 5\}$, then $B(S, m)$ consists of blocks 0 (since 1 is in the 0th block) and 2 (since both 4 and 5 are in block 2).

c. Let r be the rank of the lower left $(n - m) \times m$ submatrix of A, that is, the matrix formed by taking the intersection of the bottom $n - m$ rows and the leftmost m columns of A. Let S be any size-2^m block of S_n, and let $S' = \{y : y = Ax \text{ for some } x \in S\}$. Prove that $|B(S', m)| = 2^r$ and that for each block in $B(S', m)$, exactly 2^{m-r} numbers in S map to that block.

Because multiplying the zero vector by any matrix yields a zero vector, the set of permutations of S_n defined by multiplying by $n \times n$ 0-1 matrices with full rank over $GF(2)$ cannot include all permutations of S_n. Let us extend the class of permutations defined by matrix-vector multiplication to include an additive term, so that $x \in S_n$ maps to $Ax + c$, where c is an n-bit vector and addition is performed over $GF(2)$. For example, when

$$A = \begin{pmatrix} 1 & 0 \\ 1 & 1 \end{pmatrix}$$

and

$$c = \begin{pmatrix} 0 \\ 1 \end{pmatrix},$$

we get the following permutation $\pi_{A,c}$: $\pi_{A,c}(0) = 2$, $\pi_{A,c}(1) = 1$, $\pi_{A,c}(2) = 0$, $\pi_{A,c}(3) = 3$. We call any permutation that maps $x \in S_n$ to $Ax + c$, for some $n \times n$ 0-1 matrix A with full rank and some n-bit vector c, a **linear permutation**.

d. Use a counting argument to show that the number of linear permutations of S_n is much less than the number of permutations of S_n.

e. Give an example of a value of n and a permutation of S_n that cannot be achieved by any linear permutation. (*Hint:* For a given permutation, think about how multiplying a matrix by a unit vector relates to the columns of the matrix.)

Appendix notes

Linear-algebra textbooks provide plenty of background information on matrices. The books by Strang [323, 324] are particularly good.

Bibliography

[1] Milton Abramowitz and Irene A. Stegun, editors. *Handbook of Mathematical Functions*. Dover, 1965.

[2] G. M. Adel'son-Vel'skiĭ and E. M. Landis. An algorithm for the organization of information. *Soviet Mathematics Doklady*, 3(5):1259–1263, 1962.

[3] Alok Aggarwal and Jeffrey Scott Vitter. The input/output complexity of sorting and related problems. *Communications of the ACM*, 31(9):1116–1127, 1988.

[4] Manindra Agrawal, Neeraj Kayal, and Nitin Saxena. PRIMES is in P. *Annals of Mathematics*, 160(2):781–793, 2004.

[5] Alfred V. Aho, John E. Hopcroft, and Jeffrey D. Ullman. *The Design and Analysis of Computer Algorithms*. Addison-Wesley, 1974.

[6] Alfred V. Aho, John E. Hopcroft, and Jeffrey D. Ullman. *Data Structures and Algorithms*. Addison-Wesley, 1983.

[7] Ravindra K. Ahuja, Thomas L. Magnanti, and James B. Orlin. *Network Flows: Theory, Algorithms, and Applications*. Prentice Hall, 1993.

[8] Ravindra K. Ahuja, Kurt Mehlhorn, James B. Orlin, and Robert E. Tarjan. Faster algorithms for the shortest path problem. *Journal of the ACM*, 37(2):213–223, 1990.

[9] Ravindra K. Ahuja and James B. Orlin. A fast and simple algorithm for the maximum flow problem. *Operations Research*, 37(5):748–759, 1989.

[10] Ravindra K. Ahuja, James B. Orlin, and Robert E. Tarjan. Improved time bounds for the maximum flow problem. *SIAM Journal on Computing*, 18(5):939–954, 1989.

[11] Miklós Ajtai, Nimrod Megiddo, and Orli Waarts. Improved algorithms and analysis for secretary problems and generalizations. In *Proceedings of the 36th Annual Symposium on Foundations of Computer Science*, pages 473–482, 1995.

[12] Selim G. Akl. *The Design and Analysis of Parallel Algorithms*. Prentice Hall, 1989.

[13] Mohamad Akra and Louay Bazzi. On the solution of linear recurrence equations. *Computational Optimization and Applications*, 10(2):195–210, 1998.

[14] Noga Alon. Generating pseudo-random permutations and maximum flow algorithms. *Information Processing Letters*, 35:201–204, 1990.

[15] Arne Andersson. Balanced search trees made simple. In *Proceedings of the Third Workshop on Algorithms and Data Structures*, volume 709 of *Lecture Notes in Computer Science*, pages 60–71. Springer, 1993.

[16] Arne Andersson. Faster deterministic sorting and searching in linear space. In *Proceedings of the 37th Annual Symposium on Foundations of Computer Science*, pages 135–141, 1996.

[17] Arne Andersson, Torben Hagerup, Stefan Nilsson, and Rajeev Raman. Sorting in linear time? *Journal of Computer and System Sciences*, 57:74–93, 1998.

[18] Tom M. Apostol. *Calculus*, volume 1. Blaisdell Publishing Company, second edition, 1967.

[19] Nimar S. Arora, Robert D. Blumofe, and C. Greg Plaxton. Thread scheduling for multiprogrammed multiprocessors. In *Proceedings of the 10th Annual ACM Symposium on Parallel Algorithms and Architectures*, pages 119–129, 1998.

[20] Sanjeev Arora. *Probabilistic checking of proofs and the hardness of approximation problems*. PhD thesis, University of California, Berkeley, 1994.

[21] Sanjeev Arora. The approximability of NP-hard problems. In *Proceedings of the 30th Annual ACM Symposium on Theory of Computing*, pages 337–348, 1998.

[22] Sanjeev Arora. Polynomial time approximation schemes for euclidean traveling salesman and other geometric problems. *Journal of the ACM*, 45(5):753–782, 1998.

[23] Sanjeev Arora and Carsten Lund. Hardness of approximations. In Dorit S. Hochbaum, editor, *Approximation Algorithms for NP-Hard Problems*, pages 399–446. PWS Publishing Company, 1997.

[24] Javed A. Aslam. A simple bound on the expected height of a randomly built binary search tree. Technical Report TR2001-387, Dartmouth College Department of Computer Science, 2001.

[25] Mikhail J. Atallah, editor. *Algorithms and Theory of Computation Handbook*. CRC Press, 1999.

[26] G. Ausiello, P. Crescenzi, G. Gambosi, V. Kann, A. Marchetti-Spaccamela, and M. Protasi. *Complexity and Approximation: Combinatorial Optimization Problems and Their Approximability Properties*. Springer, 1999.

[27] Shai Avidan and Ariel Shamir. Seam carving for content-aware image resizing. *ACM Transactions on Graphics*, 26(3), article 10, 2007.

[28] Sara Baase and Allen Van Gelder. *Computer Algorithms: Introduction to Design and Analysis*. Addison-Wesley, third edition, 2000.

[29] Eric Bach. Private communication, 1989.

[30] Eric Bach. Number-theoretic algorithms. In *Annual Review of Computer Science*, volume 4, pages 119–172. Annual Reviews, Inc., 1990.

[31] Eric Bach and Jeffrey Shallit. *Algorithmic Number Theory—Volume I: Efficient Algorithms*. The MIT Press, 1996.

[32] David H. Bailey, King Lee, and Horst D. Simon. Using Strassen's algorithm to accelerate the solution of linear systems. *The Journal of Supercomputing*, 4(4):357–371, 1990.

[33] Surender Baswana, Ramesh Hariharan, and Sandeep Sen. Improved decremental algorithms for maintaining transitive closure and all-pairs shortest paths. *Journal of Algorithms*, 62(2):74–92, 2007.

[34] R. Bayer. Symmetric binary B-trees: Data structure and maintenance algorithms. *Acta Informatica*, 1(4):290–306, 1972.

[35] R. Bayer and E. M. McCreight. Organization and maintenance of large ordered indexes. *Acta Informatica*, 1(3):173–189, 1972.

[36] Pierre Beauchemin, Gilles Brassard, Claude Crépeau, Claude Goutier, and Carl Pomerance. The generation of random numbers that are probably prime. *Journal of Cryptology*, 1(1):53–64, 1988.

[37] Richard Bellman. *Dynamic Programming*. Princeton University Press, 1957.

[38] Richard Bellman. On a routing problem. *Quarterly of Applied Mathematics*, 16(1):87–90, 1958.

[39] Michael Ben-Or. Lower bounds for algebraic computation trees. In *Proceedings of the Fifteenth Annual ACM Symposium on Theory of Computing*, pages 80–86, 1983.

[40] Michael A. Bender, Erik D. Demaine, and Martin Farach-Colton. Cache-oblivious B-trees. In *Proceedings of the 41st Annual Symposium on Foundations of Computer Science*, pages 399–409, 2000.

[41] Samuel W. Bent and John W. John. Finding the median requires $2n$ comparisons. In *Proceedings of the Seventeenth Annual ACM Symposium on Theory of Computing*, pages 213–216, 1985.

[42] Jon L. Bentley. *Writing Efficient Programs*. Prentice Hall, 1982.

[43] Jon L. Bentley. *Programming Pearls*. Addison-Wesley, 1986.

[44] Jon L. Bentley, Dorothea Haken, and James B. Saxe. A general method for solving divide-and-conquer recurrences. *SIGACT News*, 12(3):36–44, 1980.

[45] Daniel Bienstock and Benjamin McClosky. Tightening simplex mixed-integer sets with guaranteed bounds. *Optimization Online*, July 2008.

[46] Patrick Billingsley. *Probability and Measure*. John Wiley & Sons, second edition, 1986.

[47] Guy E. Blelloch. *Scan Primitives and Parallel Vector Models*. PhD thesis, Department of Electrical Engineering and Computer Science, MIT, 1989. Available as MIT Laboratory for Computer Science Technical Report MIT/LCS/TR-463.

[48] Guy E. Blelloch. Programming parallel algorithms. *Communications of the ACM*, 39(3):85–97, 1996.

[49] Guy E. Blelloch, Phillip B. Gibbons, and Yossi Matias. Provably efficient scheduling for languages with fine-grained parallelism. In *Proceedings of the 7th Annual ACM Symposium on Parallel Algorithms and Architectures*, pages 1–12, 1995.

[50] Manuel Blum, Robert W. Floyd, Vaughan Pratt, Ronald L. Rivest, and Robert E. Tarjan. Time bounds for selection. *Journal of Computer and System Sciences*, 7(4):448–461, 1973.

[51] Robert D. Blumofe, Christopher F. Joerg, Bradley C. Kuszmaul, Charles E. Leiserson, Keith H. Randall, and Yuli Zhou. Cilk: An efficient multithreaded runtime system. *Journal of Parallel and Distributed Computing*, 37(1):55–69, 1996.

[52] Robert D. Blumofe and Charles E. Leiserson. Scheduling multithreaded computations by work stealing. *Journal of the ACM*, 46(5):720–748, 1999.

[53] Béla Bollobás. *Random Graphs*. Academic Press, 1985.

[54] Gilles Brassard and Paul Bratley. *Fundamentals of Algorithmics*. Prentice Hall, 1996.

[55] Richard P. Brent. The parallel evaluation of general arithmetic expressions. *Journal of the ACM*, 21(2):201–206, 1974.

[56] Richard P. Brent. An improved Monte Carlo factorization algorithm. *BIT*, 20(2):176–184, 1980.

[57] J. P. Buhler, H. W. Lenstra, Jr., and Carl Pomerance. Factoring integers with the number field sieve. In A. K. Lenstra and H. W. Lenstra, Jr., editors, *The Development of the Number Field Sieve*, volume 1554 of *Lecture Notes in Mathematics*, pages 50–94. Springer, 1993.

[58] J. Lawrence Carter and Mark N. Wegman. Universal classes of hash functions. *Journal of Computer and System Sciences*, 18(2):143–154, 1979.

[59] Barbara Chapman, Gabriele Jost, and Ruud van der Pas. *Using OpenMP: Portable Shared Memory Parallel Programming*. The MIT Press, 2007.

[60] Bernard Chazelle. A minimum spanning tree algorithm with inverse-Ackermann type complexity. *Journal of the ACM*, 47(6):1028–1047, 2000.

[61] Joseph Cheriyan and Torben Hagerup. A randomized maximum-flow algorithm. *SIAM Journal on Computing*, 24(2):203–226, 1995.

[62] Joseph Cheriyan and S. N. Maheshwari. Analysis of preflow push algorithms for maximum network flow. *SIAM Journal on Computing*, 18(6):1057–1086, 1989.

[63] Boris V. Cherkassky and Andrew V. Goldberg. On implementing the push-relabel method for the maximum flow problem. *Algorithmica*, 19(4):390–410, 1997.

[64] Boris V. Cherkassky, Andrew V. Goldberg, and Tomasz Radzik. Shortest paths algorithms: Theory and experimental evaluation. *Mathematical Programming*, 73(2):129–174, 1996.

[65] Boris V. Cherkassky, Andrew V. Goldberg, and Craig Silverstein. Buckets, heaps, lists and monotone priority queues. *SIAM Journal on Computing*, 28(4):1326–1346, 1999.

[66] H. Chernoff. A measure of asymptotic efficiency for tests of a hypothesis based on the sum of observations. *Annals of Mathematical Statistics*, 23(4):493–507, 1952.

[67] Kai Lai Chung. *Elementary Probability Theory with Stochastic Processes*. Springer, 1974.

[68] V. Chvátal. A greedy heuristic for the set-covering problem. *Mathematics of Operations Research*, 4(3):233–235, 1979.

[69] V. Chvátal. *Linear Programming*. W. H. Freeman and Company, 1983.

[70] V. Chvátal, D. A. Klarner, and D. E. Knuth. Selected combinatorial research problems. Technical Report STAN-CS-72-292, Computer Science Department, Stanford University, 1972.

[71] Cilk Arts, Inc., Burlington, Massachusetts. *Cilk++ Programmer's Guide*, 2008. Available at http://www.cilk.com/archive/docs/cilk1guide.

[72] Alan Cobham. The intrinsic computational difficulty of functions. In *Proceedings of the 1964 Congress for Logic, Methodology, and the Philosophy of Science*, pages 24–30. North-Holland, 1964.

[73] H. Cohen and H. W. Lenstra, Jr. Primality testing and Jacobi sums. *Mathematics of Computation*, 42(165):297–330, 1984.

[74] Douglas Comer. The ubiquitous B-tree. *ACM Computing Surveys*, 11(2):121–137, 1979.

[75] Stephen Cook. The complexity of theorem proving procedures. In *Proceedings of the Third Annual ACM Symposium on Theory of Computing*, pages 151–158, 1971.

[76] James W. Cooley and John W. Tukey. An algorithm for the machine calculation of complex Fourier series. *Mathematics of Computation*, 19(90):297–301, 1965.

[77] Don Coppersmith. Modifications to the number field sieve. *Journal of Cryptology*, 6(3):169–180, 1993.

[78] Don Coppersmith and Shmuel Winograd. Matrix multiplication via arithmetic progression. *Journal of Symbolic Computation*, 9(3):251–280, 1990.

[79] Thomas H. Cormen, Thomas Sundquist, and Leonard F. Wisniewski. Asymptotically tight bounds for performing BMMC permutations on parallel disk systems. *SIAM Journal on Computing*, 28(1):105–136, 1998.

[80] Don Dailey and Charles E. Leiserson. Using Cilk to write multiprocessor chess programs. In H. J. van den Herik and B. Monien, editors, *Advances in Computer Games*, volume 9, pages 25–52. University of Maastricht, Netherlands, 2001.

[81] Paolo D'Alberto and Alexandru Nicolau. Adaptive Strassen's matrix multiplication. In *Proceedings of the 21st Annual International Conference on Supercomputing*, pages 284–292, June 2007.

[82] Sanjoy Dasgupta, Christos Papadimitriou, and Umesh Vazirani. *Algorithms*. McGraw-Hill, 2008.

[83] Roman Dementiev, Lutz Kettner, Jens Mehnert, and Peter Sanders. Engineering a sorted list data structure for 32 bit keys. In *Proceedings of the Sixth Workshop on Algorithm Engineering and Experiments and the First Workshop on Analytic Algorithmics and Combinatorics*, pages 142–151, January 2004.

[84] Camil Demetrescu and Giuseppe F. Italiano. Fully dynamic all pairs shortest paths with real edge weights. *Journal of Computer and System Sciences*, 72(5):813–837, 2006.

[85] Eric V. Denardo and Bennett L. Fox. Shortest-route methods: 1. Reaching, pruning, and buckets. *Operations Research*, 27(1):161–186, 1979.

[86] Martin Dietzfelbinger, Anna Karlin, Kurt Mehlhorn, Friedhelm Meyer auf der Heide, Hans Rohnert, and Robert E. Tarjan. Dynamic perfect hashing: Upper and lower bounds. *SIAM Journal on Computing*, 23(4):738–761, 1994.

[87] Whitfield Diffie and Martin E. Hellman. New directions in cryptography. *IEEE Transactions on Information Theory*, IT-22(6):644–654, 1976.

[88] E. W. Dijkstra. A note on two problems in connexion with graphs. *Numerische Mathematik*, 1(1):269–271, 1959.

[89] E. A. Dinic. Algorithm for solution of a problem of maximum flow in a network with power estimation. *Soviet Mathematics Doklady*, 11(5):1277–1280, 1970.

[90] Brandon Dixon, Monika Rauch, and Robert E. Tarjan. Verification and sensitivity analysis of minimum spanning trees in linear time. *SIAM Journal on Computing*, 21(6):1184–1192, 1992.

[91] John D. Dixon. Factorization and primality tests. *The American Mathematical Monthly*, 91(6):333–352, 1984.

[92] Dorit Dor, Johan Håstad, Staffan Ulfberg, and Uri Zwick. On lower bounds for selecting the median. *SIAM Journal on Discrete Mathematics*, 14(3):299–311, 2001.

[93] Dorit Dor and Uri Zwick. Selecting the median. *SIAM Journal on Computing*, 28(5):1722–1758, 1999.

[94] Dorit Dor and Uri Zwick. Median selection requires $(2 + \epsilon)n$ comparisons. *SIAM Journal on Discrete Mathematics*, 14(3):312–325, 2001.

[95] Alvin W. Drake. *Fundamentals of Applied Probability Theory*. McGraw-Hill, 1967.

[96] James R. Driscoll, Harold N. Gabow, Ruth Shrairman, and Robert E. Tarjan. Relaxed heaps: An alternative to Fibonacci heaps with applications to parallel computation. *Communications of the ACM*, 31(11):1343–1354, 1988.

[97] James R. Driscoll, Neil Sarnak, Daniel D. Sleator, and Robert E. Tarjan. Making data structures persistent. *Journal of Computer and System Sciences*, 38(1):86–124, 1989.

[98] Derek L. Eager, John Zahorjan, and Edward D. Lazowska. Speedup versus efficiency in parallel systems. *IEEE Transactions on Computers*, 38(3):408–423, 1989.

[99] Herbert Edelsbrunner. *Algorithms in Combinatorial Geometry*, volume 10 of *EATCS Monographs on Theoretical Computer Science*. Springer, 1987.

[100] Jack Edmonds. Paths, trees, and flowers. *Canadian Journal of Mathematics*, 17:449–467, 1965.

[101] Jack Edmonds. Matroids and the greedy algorithm. *Mathematical Programming*, 1(1):127–136, 1971.

[102] Jack Edmonds and Richard M. Karp. Theoretical improvements in the algorithmic efficiency for network flow problems. *Journal of the ACM*, 19(2):248–264, 1972.

[103] Shimon Even. *Graph Algorithms*. Computer Science Press, 1979.

[104] William Feller. *An Introduction to Probability Theory and Its Applications*. John Wiley & Sons, third edition, 1968.

[105] Robert W. Floyd. Algorithm 97 (SHORTEST PATH). *Communications of the ACM*, 5(6):345, 1962.

[106] Robert W. Floyd. Algorithm 245 (TREESORT). *Communications of the ACM*, 7(12):701, 1964.

[107] Robert W. Floyd. Permuting information in idealized two-level storage. In Raymond E. Miller and James W. Thatcher, editors, *Complexity of Computer Computations*, pages 105–109. Plenum Press, 1972.

[108] Robert W. Floyd and Ronald L. Rivest. Expected time bounds for selection. *Communications of the ACM*, 18(3):165–172, 1975.

[109] Lestor R. Ford, Jr. and D. R. Fulkerson. *Flows in Networks*. Princeton University Press, 1962.

[110] Lestor R. Ford, Jr. and Selmer M. Johnson. A tournament problem. *The American Mathematical Monthly*, 66(5):387–389, 1959.

[111] Michael L. Fredman. New bounds on the complexity of the shortest path problem. *SIAM Journal on Computing*, 5(1):83–89, 1976.

[112] Michael L. Fredman, János Komlós, and Endre Szemerédi. Storing a sparse table with $O(1)$ worst case access time. *Journal of the ACM*, 31(3):538–544, 1984.

[113] Michael L. Fredman and Michael E. Saks. The cell probe complexity of dynamic data structures. In *Proceedings of the Twenty First Annual ACM Symposium on Theory of Computing*, pages 345–354, 1989.

[114] Michael L. Fredman and Robert E. Tarjan. Fibonacci heaps and their uses in improved network optimization algorithms. *Journal of the ACM*, 34(3):596–615, 1987.

[115] Michael L. Fredman and Dan E. Willard. Surpassing the information theoretic bound with fusion trees. *Journal of Computer and System Sciences*, 47(3):424–436, 1993.

[116] Michael L. Fredman and Dan E. Willard. Trans-dichotomous algorithms for minimum spanning trees and shortest paths. *Journal of Computer and System Sciences*, 48(3):533–551, 1994.

[117] Matteo Frigo and Steven G. Johnson. The design and implementation of FFTW3. *Proceedings of the IEEE*, 93(2):216–231, 2005.

[118] Matteo Frigo, Charles E. Leiserson, and Keith H. Randall. The implementation of the Cilk-5 multithreaded language. In *Proceedings of the 1998 ACM SIGPLAN Conference on Programming Language Design and Implementation*, pages 212–223, 1998.

[119] Harold N. Gabow. Path-based depth-first search for strong and biconnected components. *Information Processing Letters*, 74(3–4):107–114, 2000.

[120] Harold N. Gabow, Z. Galil, T. Spencer, and Robert E. Tarjan. Efficient algorithms for finding minimum spanning trees in undirected and directed graphs. *Combinatorica*, 6(2):109–122, 1986.

[121] Harold N. Gabow and Robert E. Tarjan. A linear-time algorithm for a special case of disjoint set union. *Journal of Computer and System Sciences*, 30(2):209–221, 1985.

[122] Harold N. Gabow and Robert E. Tarjan. Faster scaling algorithms for network problems. *SIAM Journal on Computing*, 18(5):1013–1036, 1989.

[123] Zvi Galil and Oded Margalit. All pairs shortest distances for graphs with small integer length edges. *Information and Computation*, 134(2):103–139, 1997.

[124] Zvi Galil and Oded Margalit. All pairs shortest paths for graphs with small integer length edges. *Journal of Computer and System Sciences*, 54(2):243–254, 1997.

[125] Zvi Galil and Kunsoo Park. Dynamic programming with convexity, concavity and sparsity. *Theoretical Computer Science*, 92(1):49–76, 1992.

[126] Zvi Galil and Joel Seiferas. Time-space-optimal string matching. *Journal of Computer and System Sciences*, 26(3):280–294, 1983.

[127] Igal Galperin and Ronald L. Rivest. Scapegoat trees. In *Proceedings of the 4th ACM-SIAM Symposium on Discrete Algorithms*, pages 165–174, 1993.

[128] Michael R. Garey, R. L. Graham, and J. D. Ullman. Worst-case analyis of memory allocation algorithms. In *Proceedings of the Fourth Annual ACM Symposium on Theory of Computing*, pages 143–150, 1972.

[129] Michael R. Garey and David S. Johnson. *Computers and Intractability: A Guide to the Theory of NP-Completeness*. W. H. Freeman, 1979.

[130] Saul Gass. *Linear Programming: Methods and Applications*. International Thomson Publishing, fourth edition, 1975.

[131] Fănică Gavril. Algorithms for minimum coloring, maximum clique, minimum covering by cliques, and maximum independent set of a chordal graph. *SIAM Journal on Computing*, 1(2):180–187, 1972.

[132] Alan George and Joseph W-H Liu. *Computer Solution of Large Sparse Positive Definite Systems*. Prentice Hall, 1981.

[133] E. N. Gilbert and E. F. Moore. Variable-length binary encodings. *Bell System Technical Journal*, 38(4):933–967, 1959.

[134] Michel X. Goemans and David P. Williamson. Improved approximation algorithms for maximum cut and satisfiability problems using semidefinite programming. *Journal of the ACM*, 42(6):1115–1145, 1995.

[135] Michel X. Goemans and David P. Williamson. The primal-dual method for approximation algorithms and its application to network design problems. In Dorit S. Hochbaum, editor, *Approximation Algorithms for NP-Hard Problems*, pages 144–191. PWS Publishing Company, 1997.

[136] Andrew V. Goldberg. *Efficient Graph Algorithms for Sequential and Parallel Computers*. PhD thesis, Department of Electrical Engineering and Computer Science, MIT, 1987.

[137] Andrew V. Goldberg. Scaling algorithms for the shortest paths problem. *SIAM Journal on Computing*, 24(3):494–504, 1995.

[138] Andrew V. Goldberg and Satish Rao. Beyond the flow decomposition barrier. *Journal of the ACM*, 45(5):783–797, 1998.

[139] Andrew V. Goldberg, Éva Tardos, and Robert E. Tarjan. Network flow algorithms. In Bernhard Korte, László Lovász, Hans Jürgen Prömel, and Alexander Schrijver, editors, *Paths, Flows, and VLSI-Layout*, pages 101–164. Springer, 1990.

[140] Andrew V. Goldberg and Robert E. Tarjan. A new approach to the maximum flow problem. *Journal of the ACM*, 35(4):921–940, 1988.

[141] D. Goldfarb and M. J. Todd. Linear programming. In G. L. Nemhauser, A. H. G. Rinnooy-Kan, and M. J. Todd, editors, *Handbook in Operations Research and Management Science, Vol. 1, Optimization*, pages 73–170. Elsevier Science Publishers, 1989.

[142] Shafi Goldwasser and Silvio Micali. Probabilistic encryption. *Journal of Computer and System Sciences*, 28(2):270–299, 1984.

[143] Shafi Goldwasser, Silvio Micali, and Ronald L. Rivest. A digital signature scheme secure against adaptive chosen-message attacks. *SIAM Journal on Computing*, 17(2):281–308, 1988.

[144] Gene H. Golub and Charles F. Van Loan. *Matrix Computations*. The Johns Hopkins University Press, third edition, 1996.

[145] G. H. Gonnet. *Handbook of Algorithms and Data Structures*. Addison-Wesley, 1984.

[146] Rafael C. Gonzalez and Richard E. Woods. *Digital Image Processing*. Addison-Wesley, 1992.

[147] Michael T. Goodrich and Roberto Tamassia. *Data Structures and Algorithms in Java*. John Wiley & Sons, 1998.

[148] Michael T. Goodrich and Roberto Tamassia. *Algorithm Design: Foundations, Analysis, and Internet Examples*. John Wiley & Sons, 2001.

[149] Ronald L. Graham. Bounds for certain multiprocessor anomalies. *Bell System Technical Journal*, 45(9):1563–1581, 1966.

[150] Ronald L. Graham. An efficient algorithm for determining the convex hull of a finite planar set. *Information Processing Letters*, 1(4):132–133, 1972.

[151] Ronald L. Graham and Pavol Hell. On the history of the minimum spanning tree problem. *Annals of the History of Computing*, 7(1):43–57, 1985.

[152] Ronald L. Graham, Donald E. Knuth, and Oren Patashnik. *Concrete Mathematics*. Addison-Wesley, second edition, 1994.

[153] David Gries. *The Science of Programming*. Springer, 1981.

[154] M. Grötschel, László Lovász, and Alexander Schrijver. *Geometric Algorithms and Combinatorial Optimization*. Springer, 1988.

[155] Leo J. Guibas and Robert Sedgewick. A dichromatic framework for balanced trees. In *Proceedings of the 19th Annual Symposium on Foundations of Computer Science*, pages 8–21, 1978.

[156] Dan Gusfield. *Algorithms on Strings, Trees, and Sequences: Computer Science and Computational Biology*. Cambridge University Press, 1997.

[157] H. Halberstam and R. E. Ingram, editors. *The Mathematical Papers of Sir William Rowan Hamilton*, volume III (Algebra). Cambridge University Press, 1967.

[158] Yijie Han. Improved fast integer sorting in linear space. In *Proceedings of the 12th ACM-SIAM Symposium on Discrete Algorithms*, pages 793–796, 2001.

[159] Yijie Han. An $O(n^3(\log\log n/\log n)^{5/4})$ time algorithm for all pairs shortest path. *Algorithmica*, 51(4):428–434, 2008.

[160] Frank Harary. *Graph Theory*. Addison-Wesley, 1969.

[161] Gregory C. Harfst and Edward M. Reingold. A potential-based amortized analysis of the union-find data structure. *SIGACT News*, 31(3):86–95, 2000.

[162] J. Hartmanis and R. E. Stearns. On the computational complexity of algorithms. *Transactions of the American Mathematical Society*, 117:285–306, May 1965.

[163] Michael T. Heideman, Don H. Johnson, and C. Sidney Burrus. Gauss and the history of the Fast Fourier Transform. *IEEE ASSP Magazine*, 1(4):14–21, 1984.

[164] Monika R. Henzinger and Valerie King. Fully dynamic biconnectivity and transitive closure. In *Proceedings of the 36th Annual Symposium on Foundations of Computer Science*, pages 664–672, 1995.

[165] Monika R. Henzinger and Valerie King. Randomized fully dynamic graph algorithms with polylogarithmic time per operation. *Journal of the ACM*, 46(4):502–516, 1999.

[166] Monika R. Henzinger, Satish Rao, and Harold N. Gabow. Computing vertex connectivity: New bounds from old techniques. *Journal of Algorithms*, 34(2):222–250, 2000.

[167] Nicholas J. Higham. Exploiting fast matrix multiplication within the level 3 BLAS. *ACM Transactions on Mathematical Software*, 16(4):352–368, 1990.

[168] W. Daniel Hillis and Jr. Guy L. Steele. Data parallel algorithms. *Communications of the ACM*, 29(12):1170–1183, 1986.

[169] C. A. R. Hoare. Algorithm 63 (PARTITION) and algorithm 65 (FIND). *Communications of the ACM*, 4(7):321–322, 1961.

[170] C. A. R. Hoare. Quicksort. *The Computer Journal*, 5(1):10–15, 1962.

[171] Dorit S. Hochbaum. Efficient bounds for the stable set, vertex cover and set packing problems. *Discrete Applied Mathematics*, 6(3):243–254, 1983.

[172] Dorit S. Hochbaum, editor. *Approximation Algorithms for NP-Hard Problems*. PWS Publishing Company, 1997.

[173] W. Hoeffding. On the distribution of the number of successes in independent trials. *Annals of Mathematical Statistics*, 27(3):713–721, 1956.

[174] Micha Hofri. *Probabilistic Analysis of Algorithms*. Springer, 1987.

[175] Micha Hofri. *Analysis of Algorithms*. Oxford University Press, 1995.

[176] John E. Hopcroft and Richard M. Karp. An $n^{5/2}$ algorithm for maximum matchings in bipartite graphs. *SIAM Journal on Computing*, 2(4):225–231, 1973.

[177] John E. Hopcroft, Rajeev Motwani, and Jeffrey D. Ullman. *Introduction to Automata Theory, Languages, and Computation*. Addison Wesley, third edition, 2006.

[178] John E. Hopcroft and Robert E. Tarjan. Efficient algorithms for graph manipulation. *Communications of the ACM*, 16(6):372–378, 1973.

[179] John E. Hopcroft and Jeffrey D. Ullman. Set merging algorithms. *SIAM Journal on Computing*, 2(4):294–303, 1973.

[180] John E. Hopcroft and Jeffrey D. Ullman. *Introduction to Automata Theory, Languages, and Computation*. Addison-Wesley, 1979.

[181] Ellis Horowitz, Sartaj Sahni, and Sanguthevar Rajasekaran. *Computer Algorithms*. Computer Science Press, 1998.

[182] T. C. Hu and M. T. Shing. Computation of matrix chain products. Part I. *SIAM Journal on Computing*, 11(2):362–373, 1982.

[183] T. C. Hu and M. T. Shing. Computation of matrix chain products. Part II. *SIAM Journal on Computing*, 13(2):228–251, 1984.

[184] T. C. Hu and A. C. Tucker. Optimal computer search trees and variable-length alphabetic codes. *SIAM Journal on Applied Mathematics*, 21(4):514–532, 1971.

[185] David A. Huffman. A method for the construction of minimum-redundancy codes. *Proceedings of the IRE*, 40(9):1098–1101, 1952.

[186] Steven Huss-Lederman, Elaine M. Jacobson, Jeremy R. Johnson, Anna Tsao, and Thomas Turnbull. Implementation of Strassen's algorithm for matrix multiplication. In *Proceedings of the 1996 ACM/IEEE Conference on Supercomputing*, article 32, 1996.

[187] Oscar H. Ibarra and Chul E. Kim. Fast approximation algorithms for the knapsack and sum of subset problems. *Journal of the ACM*, 22(4):463–468, 1975.

[188] E. J. Isaac and R. C. Singleton. Sorting by address calculation. *Journal of the ACM*, 3(3):169–174, 1956.

[189] R. A. Jarvis. On the identification of the convex hull of a finite set of points in the plane. *Information Processing Letters*, 2(1):18–21, 1973.

[190] David S. Johnson. Approximation algorithms for combinatorial problems. *Journal of Computer and System Sciences*, 9(3):256–278, 1974.

[191] David S. Johnson. The NP-completeness column: An ongoing guide—The tale of the second prover. *Journal of Algorithms*, 13(3):502–524, 1992.

[192] Donald B. Johnson. Efficient algorithms for shortest paths in sparse networks. *Journal of the ACM*, 24(1):1–13, 1977.

[193] Richard Johnsonbaugh and Marcus Schaefer. *Algorithms*. Pearson Prentice Hall, 2004.

[194] A. Karatsuba and Yu. Ofman. Multiplication of multidigit numbers on automata. *Soviet Physics—Doklady*, 7(7):595–596, 1963. Translation of an article in *Doklady Akademii Nauk SSSR*, 145(2), 1962.

[195] David R. Karger, Philip N. Klein, and Robert E. Tarjan. A randomized linear-time algorithm to find minimum spanning trees. *Journal of the ACM*, 42(2):321–328, 1995.

[196] David R. Karger, Daphne Koller, and Steven J. Phillips. Finding the hidden path: Time bounds for all-pairs shortest paths. *SIAM Journal on Computing*, 22(6):1199–1217, 1993.

[197] Howard Karloff. *Linear Programming*. Birkhäuser, 1991.

[198] N. Karmarkar. A new polynomial-time algorithm for linear programming. *Combinatorica*, 4(4):373–395, 1984.

[199] Richard M. Karp. Reducibility among combinatorial problems. In Raymond E. Miller and James W. Thatcher, editors, *Complexity of Computer Computations*, pages 85–103. Plenum Press, 1972.

[200] Richard M. Karp. An introduction to randomized algorithms. *Discrete Applied Mathematics*, 34(1–3):165–201, 1991.

[201] Richard M. Karp and Michael O. Rabin. Efficient randomized pattern-matching algorithms. *IBM Journal of Research and Development*, 31(2):249–260, 1987.

[202] A. V. Karzanov. Determining the maximal flow in a network by the method of preflows. *Soviet Mathematics Doklady*, 15(2):434–437, 1974.

[203] Valerie King. A simpler minimum spanning tree verification algorithm. *Algorithmica*, 18(2):263–270, 1997.

[204] Valerie King, Satish Rao, and Robert E. Tarjan. A faster deterministic maximum flow algorithm. *Journal of Algorithms*, 17(3):447–474, 1994.

[205] Jeffrey H. Kingston. *Algorithms and Data Structures: Design, Correctness, Analysis*. Addison-Wesley, second edition, 1997.

[206] D. G. Kirkpatrick and R. Seidel. The ultimate planar convex hull algorithm? *SIAM Journal on Computing*, 15(2):287–299, 1986.

[207] Philip N. Klein and Neal E. Young. Approximation algorithms for NP-hard optimization problems. In *CRC Handbook on Algorithms*, pages 34-1–34-19. CRC Press, 1999.

[208] Jon Kleinberg and Éva Tardos. *Algorithm Design*. Addison-Wesley, 2006.

[209] Donald E. Knuth. *Fundamental Algorithms*, volume 1 of *The Art of Computer Programming*. Addison-Wesley, 1968. Third edition, 1997.

[210] Donald E. Knuth. *Seminumerical Algorithms*, volume 2 of *The Art of Computer Programming*. Addison-Wesley, 1969. Third edition, 1997.

[211] Donald E. Knuth. *Sorting and Searching*, volume 3 of *The Art of Computer Programming*. Addison-Wesley, 1973. Second edition, 1998.

[212] Donald E. Knuth. Optimum binary search trees. *Acta Informatica*, 1(1):14–25, 1971.

[213] Donald E. Knuth. Big omicron and big omega and big theta. *SIGACT News*, 8(2):18–23, 1976.

[214] Donald E. Knuth, James H. Morris, Jr., and Vaughan R. Pratt. Fast pattern matching in strings. *SIAM Journal on Computing*, 6(2):323–350, 1977.

[215] J. Komlós. Linear verification for spanning trees. *Combinatorica*, 5(1):57–65, 1985.

[216] Bernhard Korte and László Lovász. Mathematical structures underlying greedy algorithms. In F. Gecseg, editor, *Fundamentals of Computation Theory*, volume 117 of *Lecture Notes in Computer Science*, pages 205–209. Springer, 1981.

[217] Bernhard Korte and László Lovász. Structural properties of greedoids. *Combinatorica*, 3(3–4):359–374, 1983.

[218] Bernhard Korte and László Lovász. Greedoids—A structural framework for the greedy algorithm. In W. Pulleybank, editor, *Progress in Combinatorial Optimization*, pages 221–243. Academic Press, 1984.

[219] Bernhard Korte and László Lovász. Greedoids and linear objective functions. *SIAM Journal on Algebraic and Discrete Methods*, 5(2):229–238, 1984.

[220] Dexter C. Kozen. *The Design and Analysis of Algorithms*. Springer, 1992.

[221] David W. Krumme, George Cybenko, and K. N. Venkataraman. Gossiping in minimal time. *SIAM Journal on Computing*, 21(1):111–139, 1992.

[222] Joseph B. Kruskal, Jr. On the shortest spanning subtree of a graph and the traveling salesman problem. *Proceedings of the American Mathematical Society*, 7(1):48–50, 1956.

[223] Leslie Lamport. How to make a multiprocessor computer that correctly executes multiprocess programs. *IEEE Transactions on Computers*, C-28(9):690–691, 1979.

[224] Eugene L. Lawler. *Combinatorial Optimization: Networks and Matroids*. Holt, Rinehart, and Winston, 1976.

[225] Eugene L. Lawler, J. K. Lenstra, A. H. G. Rinnooy Kan, and D. B. Shmoys, editors. *The Traveling Salesman Problem*. John Wiley & Sons, 1985.

[226] C. Y. Lee. An algorithm for path connection and its applications. *IRE Transactions on Electronic Computers*, EC-10(3):346–365, 1961.

[227] Tom Leighton. Tight bounds on the complexity of parallel sorting. *IEEE Transactions on Computers*, C-34(4):344–354, 1985.

[228] Tom Leighton. Notes on better master theorems for divide-and-conquer recurrences. Class notes. Available at http://citeseer.ist.psu.edu/252350.html, October 1996.

[229] Tom Leighton and Satish Rao. Multicommodity max-flow min-cut theorems and their use in designing approximation algorithms. *Journal of the ACM*, 46(6):787–832, 1999.

[230] Daan Leijen and Judd Hall. Optimize managed code for multi-core machines. *MSDN Magazine*, October 2007.

[231] Debra A. Lelewer and Daniel S. Hirschberg. Data compression. *ACM Computing Surveys*, 19(3):261–296, 1987.

[232] A. K. Lenstra, H. W. Lenstra, Jr., M. S. Manasse, and J. M. Pollard. The number field sieve. In A. K. Lenstra and H. W. Lenstra, Jr., editors, *The Development of the Number Field Sieve*, volume 1554 of *Lecture Notes in Mathematics*, pages 11–42. Springer, 1993.

[233] H. W. Lenstra, Jr. Factoring integers with elliptic curves. *Annals of Mathematics*, 126(3):649–673, 1987.

[234] L. A. Levin. Universal sorting problems. *Problemy Peredachi Informatsii*, 9(3):265–266, 1973. In Russian.

[235] Anany Levitin. *Introduction to the Design & Analysis of Algorithms*. Addison-Wesley, 2007.

[236] Harry R. Lewis and Christos H. Papadimitriou. *Elements of the Theory of Computation*. Prentice Hall, second edition, 1998.

[237] C. L. Liu. *Introduction to Combinatorial Mathematics*. McGraw-Hill, 1968.

[238] László Lovász. On the ratio of optimal integral and fractional covers. *Discrete Mathematics*, 13(4):383–390, 1975.

[239] László Lovász and Michael D. Plummer. *Matching Theory*, volume 121 of *Annals of Discrete Mathematics*. North Holland, 1986.

[240] Bruce M. Maggs and Serge A. Plotkin. Minimum-cost spanning tree as a path-finding problem. *Information Processing Letters*, 26(6):291–293, 1988.

[241] Michael Main. *Data Structures and Other Objects Using Java*. Addison-Wesley, 1999.

[242] Udi Manber. *Introduction to Algorithms: A Creative Approach*. Addison-Wesley, 1989.

[243] Conrado Martínez and Salvador Roura. Randomized binary search trees. *Journal of the ACM*, 45(2):288–323, 1998.

[244] William J. Masek and Michael S. Paterson. A faster algorithm computing string edit distances. *Journal of Computer and System Sciences*, 20(1):18–31, 1980.

[245] H. A. Maurer, Th. Ottmann, and H.-W. Six. Implementing dictionaries using binary trees of very small height. *Information Processing Letters*, 5(1):11–14, 1976.

[246] Ernst W. Mayr, Hans Jürgen Prömel, and Angelika Steger, editors. *Lectures on Proof Verification and Approximation Algorithms*, volume 1367 of *Lecture Notes in Computer Science*. Springer, 1998.

[247] C. C. McGeoch. All pairs shortest paths and the essential subgraph. *Algorithmica*, 13(5):426–441, 1995.

[248] M. D. McIlroy. A killer adversary for quicksort. *Software—Practice and Experience*, 29(4):341–344, 1999.

[249] Kurt Mehlhorn. *Sorting and Searching*, volume 1 of *Data Structures and Algorithms*. Springer, 1984.

[250] Kurt Mehlhorn. *Graph Algorithms and NP-Completeness*, volume 2 of *Data Structures and Algorithms*. Springer, 1984.

[251] Kurt Mehlhorn. *Multidimensional Searching and Computational Geometry*, volume 3 of *Data Structures and Algorithms*. Springer, 1984.

[252] Kurt Mehlhorn and Stefan Näher. Bounded ordered dictionaries in $O(\log \log N)$ time and $O(n)$ space. *Information Processing Letters*, 35(4):183–189, 1990.

[253] Kurt Mehlhorn and Stefan Näher. *LEDA: A Platform for Combinatorial and Geometric Computing*. Cambridge University Press, 1999.

[254] Alfred J. Menezes, Paul C. van Oorschot, and Scott A. Vanstone. *Handbook of Applied Cryptography*. CRC Press, 1997.

[255] Gary L. Miller. Riemann's hypothesis and tests for primality. *Journal of Computer and System Sciences*, 13(3):300–317, 1976.

[256] John C. Mitchell. *Foundations for Programming Languages*. The MIT Press, 1996.

[257] Joseph S. B. Mitchell. Guillotine subdivisions approximate polygonal subdivisions: A simple polynomial-time approximation scheme for geometric TSP, k-MST, and related problems. *SIAM Journal on Computing*, 28(4):1298–1309, 1999.

[258] Louis Monier. *Algorithmes de Factorisation D'Entiers*. PhD thesis, L'Université Paris-Sud, 1980.

[259] Louis Monier. Evaluation and comparison of two efficient probabilistic primality testing algorithms. *Theoretical Computer Science*, 12(1):97–108, 1980.

[260] Edward F. Moore. The shortest path through a maze. In *Proceedings of the International Symposium on the Theory of Switching*, pages 285–292. Harvard University Press, 1959.

[261] Rajeev Motwani, Joseph (Seffi) Naor, and Prabhakar Raghavan. Randomized approximation algorithms in combinatorial optimization. In Dorit Hochbaum, editor, *Approximation Algorithms for NP-Hard Problems*, chapter 11, pages 447–481. PWS Publishing Company, 1997.

[262] Rajeev Motwani and Prabhakar Raghavan. *Randomized Algorithms*. Cambridge University Press, 1995.

[263] J. I. Munro and V. Raman. Fast stable in-place sorting with $O(n)$ data moves. *Algorithmica*, 16(2):151–160, 1996.

[264] J. Nievergelt and E. M. Reingold. Binary search trees of bounded balance. *SIAM Journal on Computing*, 2(1):33–43, 1973.

[265] Ivan Niven and Herbert S. Zuckerman. *An Introduction to the Theory of Numbers*. John Wiley & Sons, fourth edition, 1980.

[266] Alan V. Oppenheim and Ronald W. Schafer, with John R. Buck. *Discrete-Time Signal Processing*. Prentice Hall, second edition, 1998.

[267] Alan V. Oppenheim and Alan S. Willsky, with S. Hamid Nawab. *Signals and Systems*. Prentice Hall, second edition, 1997.

[268] James B. Orlin. A polynomial time primal network simplex algorithm for minimum cost flows. *Mathematical Programming*, 78(1):109–129, 1997.

[269] Joseph O'Rourke. *Computational Geometry in C*. Cambridge University Press, second edition, 1998.

[270] Christos H. Papadimitriou. *Computational Complexity*. Addison-Wesley, 1994.

[271] Christos H. Papadimitriou and Kenneth Steiglitz. *Combinatorial Optimization: Algorithms and Complexity*. Prentice Hall, 1982.

[272] Michael S. Paterson. Progress in selection. In *Proceedings of the Fifth Scandinavian Workshop on Algorithm Theory*, pages 368–379, 1996.

[273] Mihai Pătrașcu and Mikkel Thorup. Time-space trade-offs for predecessor search. In *Proceedings of the 38th Annual ACM Symposium on Theory of Computing*, pages 232–240, 2006.

[274] Mihai Pătrașcu and Mikkel Thorup. Randomization does not help searching predecessors. In *Proceedings of the 18th ACM-SIAM Symposium on Discrete Algorithms*, pages 555–564, 2007.

[275] Pavel A. Pevzner. *Computational Molecular Biology: An Algorithmic Approach*. The MIT Press, 2000.

[276] Steven Phillips and Jeffery Westbrook. Online load balancing and network flow. In *Proceedings of the 25th Annual ACM Symposium on Theory of Computing*, pages 402–411, 1993.

[277] J. M. Pollard. A Monte Carlo method for factorization. *BIT*, 15(3):331–334, 1975.

[278] J. M. Pollard. Factoring with cubic integers. In A. K. Lenstra and H. W. Lenstra, Jr., editors, *The Development of the Number Field Sieve*, volume 1554 of *Lecture Notes in Mathematics*, pages 4–10. Springer, 1993.

[279] Carl Pomerance. On the distribution of pseudoprimes. *Mathematics of Computation*, 37(156):587–593, 1981.

[280] Carl Pomerance, editor. *Proceedings of the AMS Symposia in Applied Mathematics: Computational Number Theory and Cryptography*. American Mathematical Society, 1990.

[281] William K. Pratt. *Digital Image Processing*. John Wiley & Sons, fourth edition, 2007.

[282] Franco P. Preparata and Michael Ian Shamos. *Computational Geometry: An Introduction*. Springer, 1985.

[283] William H. Press, Saul A. Teukolsky, William T. Vetterling, and Brian P. Flannery. *Numerical Recipes in C++: The Art of Scientific Computing*. Cambridge University Press, second edition, 2002.

[284] William H. Press, Saul A. Teukolsky, William T. Vetterling, and Brian P. Flannery. *Numerical Recipes: The Art of Scientific Computing*. Cambridge University Press, third edition, 2007.

[285] R. C. Prim. Shortest connection networks and some generalizations. *Bell System Technical Journal*, 36(6):1389–1401, 1957.

[286] William Pugh. Skip lists: A probabilistic alternative to balanced trees. *Communications of the ACM*, 33(6):668–676, 1990.

[287] Paul W. Purdom, Jr. and Cynthia A. Brown. *The Analysis of Algorithms*. Holt, Rinehart, and Winston, 1985.

[288] Michael O. Rabin. Probabilistic algorithms. In J. F. Traub, editor, *Algorithms and Complexity: New Directions and Recent Results*, pages 21–39. Academic Press, 1976.

[289] Michael O. Rabin. Probabilistic algorithm for testing primality. *Journal of Number Theory*, 12(1):128–138, 1980.

[290] P. Raghavan and C. D. Thompson. Randomized rounding: A technique for provably good algorithms and algorithmic proofs. *Combinatorica*, 7(4):365–374, 1987.

[291] Rajeev Raman. Recent results on the single-source shortest paths problem. *SIGACT News*, 28(2):81–87, 1997.

[292] James Reinders. *Intel Threading Building Blocks: Outfitting C++ for Multi-core Processor Parallelism*. O'Reilly Media, Inc., 2007.

[293] Edward M. Reingold, Jürg Nievergelt, and Narsingh Deo. *Combinatorial Algorithms: Theory and Practice*. Prentice Hall, 1977.

[294] Edward M. Reingold, Kenneth J. Urban, and David Gries. K-M-P string matching revisited. *Information Processing Letters*, 64(5):217–223, 1997.

[295] Hans Riesel. *Prime Numbers and Computer Methods for Factorization*, volume 126 of *Progress in Mathematics*. Birkhäuser, second edition, 1994.

[296] Ronald L. Rivest, Adi Shamir, and Leonard M. Adleman. A method for obtaining digital signatures and public-key cryptosystems. *Communications of the ACM*, 21(2):120–126, 1978. See also U.S. Patent 4,405,829.

[297] Herbert Robbins. A remark on Stirling's formula. *American Mathematical Monthly*, 62(1):26–29, 1955.

[298] D. J. Rosenkrantz, R. E. Stearns, and P. M. Lewis. An analysis of several heuristics for the traveling salesman problem. *SIAM Journal on Computing*, 6(3):563–581, 1977.

[299] Salvador Roura. An improved master theorem for divide-and-conquer recurrences. In *Proceedings of Automata, Languages and Programming, 24th International Colloquium, ICALP'97*, volume 1256 of *Lecture Notes in Computer Science*, pages 449–459. Springer, 1997.

[300] Y. A. Rozanov. *Probability Theory: A Concise Course*. Dover, 1969.

[301] S. Sahni and T. Gonzalez. P-complete approximation problems. *Journal of the ACM*, 23(3):555–565, 1976.

[302] A. Schönhage, M. Paterson, and N. Pippenger. Finding the median. *Journal of Computer and System Sciences*, 13(2):184–199, 1976.

[303] Alexander Schrijver. *Theory of Linear and Integer Programming*. John Wiley & Sons, 1986.

[304] Alexander Schrijver. Paths and flows—A historical survey. *CWI Quarterly*, 6(3):169–183, 1993.

[305] Robert Sedgewick. Implementing quicksort programs. *Communications of the ACM*, 21(10):847–857, 1978.

[306] Robert Sedgewick. *Algorithms*. Addison-Wesley, second edition, 1988.

[307] Robert Sedgewick and Philippe Flajolet. *An Introduction to the Analysis of Algorithms*. Addison-Wesley, 1996.

[308] Raimund Seidel. On the all-pairs-shortest-path problem in unweighted undirected graphs. *Journal of Computer and System Sciences*, 51(3):400–403, 1995.

[309] Raimund Seidel and C. R. Aragon. Randomized search trees. *Algorithmica*, 16(4–5):464–497, 1996.

[310] João Setubal and João Meidanis. *Introduction to Computational Molecular Biology*. PWS Publishing Company, 1997.

[311] Clifford A. Shaffer. *A Practical Introduction to Data Structures and Algorithm Analysis*. Prentice Hall, second edition, 2001.

[312] Jeffrey Shallit. Origins of the analysis of the Euclidean algorithm. *Historia Mathematica*, 21(4):401–419, 1994.

[313] Michael I. Shamos and Dan Hoey. Geometric intersection problems. In *Proceedings of the 17th Annual Symposium on Foundations of Computer Science*, pages 208–215, 1976.

[314] M. Sharir. A strong-connectivity algorithm and its applications in data flow analysis. *Computers and Mathematics with Applications*, 7(1):67–72, 1981.

[315] David B. Shmoys. Computing near-optimal solutions to combinatorial optimization problems. In William Cook, László Lovász, and Paul Seymour, editors, *Combinatorial Optimization*, volume 20 of *DIMACS Series in Discrete Mathematics and Theoretical Computer Science*. American Mathematical Society, 1995.

[316] Avi Shoshan and Uri Zwick. All pairs shortest paths in undirected graphs with integer weights. In *Proceedings of the 40th Annual Symposium on Foundations of Computer Science*, pages 605–614, 1999.

[317] Michael Sipser. *Introduction to the Theory of Computation*. Thomson Course Technology, second edition, 2006.

[318] Steven S. Skiena. *The Algorithm Design Manual*. Springer, second edition, 1998.

[319] Daniel D. Sleator and Robert E. Tarjan. A data structure for dynamic trees. *Journal of Computer and System Sciences*, 26(3):362–391, 1983.

[320] Daniel D. Sleator and Robert E. Tarjan. Self-adjusting binary search trees. *Journal of the ACM*, 32(3):652–686, 1985.

[321] Joel Spencer. *Ten Lectures on the Probabilistic Method*, volume 64 of *CBMS-NSF Regional Conference Series in Applied Mathematics*. Society for Industrial and Applied Mathematics, 1993.

[322] Daniel A. Spielman and Shang-Hua Teng. Smoothed analysis of algorithms: Why the simplex algorithm usually takes polynomial time. *Journal of the ACM*, 51(3):385–463, 2004.

[323] Gilbert Strang. *Introduction to Applied Mathematics*. Wellesley-Cambridge Press, 1986.

[324] Gilbert Strang. *Linear Algebra and Its Applications*. Thomson Brooks/Cole, fourth edition, 2006.

[325] Volker Strassen. Gaussian elimination is not optimal. *Numerische Mathematik*, 14(3):354–356, 1969.

[326] T. G. Szymanski. A special case of the maximal common subsequence problem. Technical Report TR-170, Computer Science Laboratory, Princeton University, 1975.

[327] Robert E. Tarjan. Depth first search and linear graph algorithms. *SIAM Journal on Computing*, 1(2):146–160, 1972.

[328] Robert E. Tarjan. Efficiency of a good but not linear set union algorithm. *Journal of the ACM*, 22(2):215–225, 1975.

[329] Robert E. Tarjan. A class of algorithms which require nonlinear time to maintain disjoint sets. *Journal of Computer and System Sciences*, 18(2):110–127, 1979.

[330] Robert E. Tarjan. *Data Structures and Network Algorithms*. Society for Industrial and Applied Mathematics, 1983.

[331] Robert E. Tarjan. Amortized computational complexity. *SIAM Journal on Algebraic and Discrete Methods*, 6(2):306–318, 1985.

[332] Robert E. Tarjan. Class notes: Disjoint set union. COS 423, Princeton University, 1999.

[333] Robert E. Tarjan and Jan van Leeuwen. Worst-case analysis of set union algorithms. *Journal of the ACM*, 31(2):245–281, 1984.

[334] George B. Thomas, Jr., Maurice D. Weir, Joel Hass, and Frank R. Giordano. *Thomas' Calculus*. Addison-Wesley, eleventh edition, 2005.

[335] Mikkel Thorup. Faster deterministic sorting and priority queues in linear space. In *Proceedings of the 9th ACM-SIAM Symposium on Discrete Algorithms*, pages 550–555, 1998.

[336] Mikkel Thorup. Undirected single-source shortest paths with positive integer weights in linear time. *Journal of the ACM*, 46(3):362–394, 1999.

[337] Mikkel Thorup. On RAM priority queues. *SIAM Journal on Computing*, 30(1):86–109, 2000.

[338] Richard Tolimieri, Myoung An, and Chao Lu. *Mathematics of Multidimensional Fourier Transform Algorithms*. Springer, second edition, 1997.

[339] P. van Emde Boas. Preserving order in a forest in less than logarithmic time. In *Proceedings of the 16th Annual Symposium on Foundations of Computer Science*, pages 75–84, 1975.

[340] P. van Emde Boas. Preserving order in a forest in less than logarithmic time and linear space. *Information Processing Letters*, 6(3):80–82, 1977.

[341] P. van Emde Boas, R. Kaas, and E. Zijlstra. Design and implementation of an efficient priority queue. *Mathematical Systems Theory*, 10(1):99–127, 1976.

[342] Jan van Leeuwen, editor. *Handbook of Theoretical Computer Science, Volume A: Algorithms and Complexity*. Elsevier Science Publishers and the MIT Press, 1990.

[343] Charles Van Loan. *Computational Frameworks for the Fast Fourier Transform*. Society for Industrial and Applied Mathematics, 1992.

[344] Robert J. Vanderbei. *Linear Programming: Foundations and Extensions*. Kluwer Academic Publishers, 1996.

[345] Vijay V. Vazirani. *Approximation Algorithms*. Springer, 2001.

[346] Rakesh M. Verma. General techniques for analyzing recursive algorithms with applications. *SIAM Journal on Computing*, 26(2):568–581, 1997.

[347] Hao Wang and Bill Lin. Pipelined van Emde Boas tree: Algorithms, analysis, and applications. In *26th IEEE International Conference on Computer Communications*, pages 2471–2475, 2007.

[348] Antony F. Ware. Fast approximate Fourier transforms for irregularly spaced data. *SIAM Review*, 40(4):838–856, 1998.

[349] Stephen Warshall. A theorem on boolean matrices. *Journal of the ACM*, 9(1):11–12, 1962.

[350] Michael S. Waterman. *Introduction to Computational Biology, Maps, Sequences and Genomes*. Chapman & Hall, 1995.

[351] Mark Allen Weiss. *Data Structures and Problem Solving Using C++*. Addison-Wesley, second edition, 2000.

[352] Mark Allen Weiss. *Data Structures and Problem Solving Using Java*. Addison-Wesley, third edition, 2006.

[353] Mark Allen Weiss. *Data Structures and Algorithm Analysis in C++*. Addison-Wesley, third edition, 2007.

[354] Mark Allen Weiss. *Data Structures and Algorithm Analysis in Java*. Addison-Wesley, second edition, 2007.

[355] Hassler Whitney. On the abstract properties of linear dependence. *American Journal of Mathematics*, 57(3):509–533, 1935.

[356] Herbert S. Wilf. *Algorithms and Complexity*. A K Peters, second edition, 2002.

[357] J. W. J. Williams. Algorithm 232 (HEAPSORT). *Communications of the ACM*, 7(6):347–348, 1964.

[358] Shmuel Winograd. On the algebraic complexity of functions. In *Actes du Congrès International des Mathématiciens*, volume 3, pages 283–288, 1970.

[359] Andrew C.-C. Yao. A lower bound to finding convex hulls. *Journal of the ACM*, 28(4):780–787, 1981.

[360] Chee Yap. A real elementary approach to the master recurrence and generalizations. Unpublished manuscript. Available at http://cs.nyu.edu/yap/papers/, July 2008.

[361] Yinyu Ye. *Interior Point Algorithms: Theory and Analysis*. John Wiley & Sons, 1997.

[362] Daniel Zwillinger, editor. *CRC Standard Mathematical Tables and Formulae*. Chapman & Hall/CRC Press, 31st edition, 2003.

Index

This index uses the following conventions. Numbers are alphabetized as if spelled out; for example, "2-3-4 tree" is indexed as if it were "two-three-four tree." When an entry refers to a place other than the main text, the page number is followed by a tag: ex. for exercise, pr. for problem, fig. for figure, and n. for footnote. A tagged page number often indicates the first page of an exercise or problem, which is not necessarily the page on which the reference actually appears.